Philipsburg
EASTON
Whitehall
Township
Lowhill
Weisenburg
BETHLEHEM
NORTHAMPTON
Maccorgy
Salisbury
Maxetawny
Long Swamp
Upper Milford
Upper Saucon
Springfield
Nockamixon
Richland
Tenecum
Hereford
Manor of Ruscomb
Lower Milford
Upper Hanover
Bedminster
Oley
Rockhill
Colebrook Dale
Exeter
BUCKS
Plumstead
Buckingham
Amity
Douglass
Hilltown
Warwick
Franconia
Hatfield
New Britain
COUN
Wrightstown
Union
Schuylkill R.
Coventry
Bebber
Montgomery
Northampton
Worcester
Horsham
Warminster
Vincent
East Nantmel
PHILADELPHIA
Pikeland
Charlestown
Upper Merion
Plymouth
Whitemarsh
Dublin
Abington
HESTER
Springtown
Uehland
Trududfrin
COUNTY
Lower Merion
Cheltenham
Oxford
Bristol
East Calm
Whiteland
Radnor
Blockley
Northern Liberties
Goshen
Willistown
Newtown
Haverford
COUNTY
East Bradford
Westtown
Marple
Edgemont
Birmingham
Thornbury
Middletown
Springfield
DERBY
Kingsess
Concord
Chester
Ridley
Gloucester
Kennet
Bethel
Upper Chichester
Lower Chichester
Haddonfield
Woodberry
PART OF
NEW CASTLE
WILMINGTON
DELAWARE RIVER
NEWCASTLE
COUNTY

10

June 1–September 30, 1778

Paul H. Smith, Editor

Gerard W. Gawalt, Rosemary Fry Plakas, Eugene R. Sheridan
Associate Editors

LIBRARY OF CONGRESS WASHINGTON 1983

This volume is printed on permanent/durable paper.

Library of Congress Cataloging in Publication Data
(Revised for volume 10)
Main entry under title:

Letters of delegates to Congress, 1774–1789.

Includes bibliographical references and indexes.
Supt. of Docs. no.: LC 1.34:10
1. United States. Continental Congress—History—Sources—Collected works. I. Smith, Paul Hubert, 1931– .
JK1033.L47 973.3'12 76-2592
ISBN 0-8444-0177-3 (set)
ISBN 0-8444-0434-9 (v. 10)

For sale by the Superintendent of Documents, U.S. Government Printing Office
Washington, D.C. 20402

Editorial Method and Apparatus

In its treatment of documents this edition of delegate letters strives to achieve a middle ground between facsimile reproduction and thorough modernization. The original spelling and grammar are allowed to stand except where editorial changes or insertions are required to make the text intelligible. For example, when a badly misspelled word is misleading, the correct spelling is inserted in roman type in brackets after the word. Moreover, words omitted through oversight have been supplied at appropriate places in italic type in brackets. Obvious slips of the pen and inadvertent repetitions are usually silently corrected. Capitalization and punctuation have been standardized according to certain conventions. Each sentence begins with a capital letter, as do all proper and geographic names as well as days of the week and months of the year. Doubtful cases have been resolved in favor of modern usage; otherwise the usage of the original texts has been followed. Generally, abbreviations, contractions, and monetary signs are preserved as they appear in manuscript except when they are ambiguous or misleading. On the other hand, the thorn and the tilde are consistenly expanded. "Ye" always appears as "The," for instance, and "rec̃vd" as "received." Likewise, "pr." and tailed *p*'s are always expanded to "per," "pre," or "pro," as the case demands. Finally, superscript letters are always lowered to the line.

Gaps in the text are indicated by ellipses in brackets for missing words and by blank spaces in brackets for missing numbers. Conjectural readings are supplied in roman type in brackets, and editorial insertions in italic type in brackets. Material canceled in manuscript but restored to the printed text is included in italic type in angle brackets ("square parentheses"). Marginalia in letters are treated as postscripts if not obviously keyed to the body of the document, and postscripts which appear without explicit designation are supplied with a *P.S.* in brackets. Documents are arranged chronologically, with more than one document of the same date arranged alphabetically according to writer. Documents dated only by the month or by the year are placed at the end of the respective month or year. Place-and-date lines always appear on the same line with the salutation regardless of their position in the manuscript.

A descriptive note at the foot of each entry provides abbreviations indicating the nature and location of the document when it was copied for this project, except for privately owned manuscripts whose ownership is explained. The descriptive note also contains information on the document's authorship if explanation is necessary, and endorsements or addresses are quoted when they contain more than routine information. Other editorial practices employed in this work are explained in the sections on editorial apparatus which follow.

TEXTUAL DEVICES

The following devices will be used in this work to clarify the text.

[. . .], [. . . .]	One or two words missing and not conjecturable.
[. . .][1], [. . . .][1]	More than two words missing; subjoined footnote estimates amount of material missing.
[ ]	Number or part of a number missing or illegible.
[ ][1]	Blank space in manuscript; explanation in subjoined footnote.
[roman]	Conjectural reading for missing or illegible matter; question mark inserted if reading is doubtful.
[*italic*]	Editorial insertion in the text.
⟨*italic*⟩	Matter crossed out in manuscript but restored.

DESCRIPTIVE SYMBOLS

The following symbols are used in this work to describe the kinds of documents drawn upon. When more than one symbol is used in the descriptive note, the first to appear is that from which the main text is taken.

RC	recipient's copy
FC	file copy
LB	letterbook copy
MS	manuscript
Tr	transcript (used to designate not only contemporary and later handwritten copies of manuscripts, but also printed documents)

LOCATION SYMBOLS

The following symbols, denoting institutions holding the manuscripts printed in the present volume, are taken from *Symbols of American Libraries,* 12th ed. (Washington: Library of Congress, 1980).

CSmH	Henry E. Huntington Library, San Marino, Calif.
Ct	Connecticut State Library, Hartford

CtHi	Connecticut Historical Society, Hartford
CtNhHi	New Haven Colony Historical Society, New Haven, Conn.
CtY	Yale University, New Haven, Conn.
DLC	Library of Congress
DLC(ESR)	Library of Congress, Early State Records Collection
DNA	National Archives and Records Service
M–Ar	Massachusetts Archives, Boston
MDaAr	Danvers Historical Society, Danvers, Mass.
MH–H	Harvard University, Houghton Library, Cambridge, Mass.
MHi	Massachusetts Historical Society, Boston
MWA	American Antiquarian Society, Worcester, Mass.
MdAA	Maryland Hall of Records, Annapolis
MdHi	Maryland Historical Society, Baltimore
MeHi	Maine Historical Society, Portland
NCooHi	New York State Historical Association, Cooperstown
NHi	New-York Historical Society, New York
NN	New York Public Library, New York
NNC	Columbia University, New York
NRom	Jervis Library Association, Rome, N.Y.
NbO	Omaha Public Library, Omaha, Neb.
Nc–Ar	North Carolina State Department of Archives and History, Raleigh
NcD	Duke University, Durham, N.C.
NcU	University of North Carolina, Chapel Hill
Nh–Ar	New Hampshire Division of Archives and Records Management, Concord
NhHi	New Hampshire Historical Society, Concord
Nj	New Jersey State Library, Trenton
NjMoHP	Morristown National Historical Park, Morristown, N.J.
NjP	Princeton University, Princeton, N.J.
OClWHi	Western Reserve Historical Society, Cleveland, Ohio
PHC	Haverford College, Haverford, Pa.
PHarH	Pennsylvania Historical and Museum Commission, Harrisburg
PHi	Historical Society of Pennsylvania, Philadelphia
PPAmP	American Philosophical Society, Philadelphia
PPL	Library Company of Philadelphia
PPRF	Rosenbach Foundation, Philadelphia
R–Ar	Rhode Island State Archives, Providence
RHi	Rhode Island Historical Society, Providence
RNHi	Newport Historical Society, Newport, R.I.
ScC	Charleston Library Society, Charleston, S.C.

ScHi	South Carolina Historical Society, Charleston, S.C.
ViHi	Virginia Historical Society, Richmond
ViU	University of Virginia, Charlottesville
ViW	College of William and Mary, Williamsburg, Va.

ABBREVIATIONS AND SHORT TITLES

Adams, *Diary* (Butterfield)
Adams, John. *Diary and Autobiography of John Adams.* Edited by Lyman H. Butterfield et al. 4 vols. Cambridge: Harvard University Press, Belknap Press, 1961.

Adams, *Family Correspondence* (Butterfield)
Butterfield, Lyman H., et al., eds. *Adams Family Correspondence.* Cambridge: Harvard University Press, Belknap Press, 1963–.

Adams, *Writings* (Cushing)
Adams, Samuel. *The Writings of Samuel Adams.* Edited by Harry A. Cushing. 4 vols. Boston: G.P. Putnam's Sons, 1904–8.

Bartlett, *Papers* (Mevers)
Bartlett, Josiah. *The Papers of Josiah Bartlett.* Edited by Frank C. Mevers. Hanover, N.H.: Published for the New Hampshire Historical Society by the University Press of New England, 1979.

Beaumarchais, *Correspondance* (Morton and Spinelli)
Beaumarchais, Pierre Augustin Caron de. *Correspondance [de] Beaumarchais.* Edited by Brian N. Morton and Donald C. Spinelli. Paris: A.G. Nizet, 1969–.

Bio. Dir. Cong.
U.S. Congress. *Biographical Directory of the American Congress, 1774–1971.* Washington: U.S. Government Printing Office, 1971.

Burnett, *Letters*
Burnett, Edmund C., ed. *Letters of Members of the Continental Congress.* 8 vols. Washington: Carnegie Institution of Washington, 1921–36.

Clinton, *Papers* (Hastings)
Clinton, George. *Public Papers of George Clinton, First Governor of New York, 1777–1795, 1801–1804.* Edited by Hugh Hastings and J. A. Holden. 10 vols. New York and Albany: Wynkoop Hallenbeck Crawford Co. et al., 1899–1914.

DAB
Dictionary of American Biography. Edited by Allen Johnson and Dumas Malone.

Davies, *Documents of the American Revolution*
Davies, Kenneth Gordon, ed. *Documents of the American Revolution, 1770–1783.* 21 vols. Dublin: Irish University Press, 1972–81.

Evans, *Am. Bibliography*
Evans, Charles. *American Bibliography.* 12 vols. Chicago: Privately printed, 1903–34.

Franklin, *Writings* (Smyth)
Franklin, Benjamin. *The Writings of Benjamin Franklin.* Edited by Albert Smyth. 10 vols. New York: Macmillan Co., 1905–7.

Gérard, *Dispatches* (Baisnée and Meng)
Baisnée, Jules A., and Meng, John J., trans., "Philadelphia and the Revolution: French Diplomacy in the United States, 1778–1779." *Records of the American Catholic Historical Society of Philadelphia* 56–59 (1945–48): passim.

Greene, *Papers* (Showman)
Greene, Nathanael. *The Papers of General Nathanael Greene.* Edited by Richard K. Showman et al. Chapel Hill: Published for the Rhode Island Historical Society by the University of North Carolina Press, 1976–.

Heitman, *Historical Register*
Heitman, Francis Bernard. *Historical Register of Officers of the Continental Army during the War of the Revolution, April, 1775 to December, 1783.* Washington [Baltimore]: Press of Nichols, Killam & Maffit, 1893.

Henry, *Patrick Henry*
Henry, William Wirt. *Patrick Henry: Life, Correspondence and Speeches.* 3 vols. New York: Charles Scribner's Sons, 1891.

Jay, *Papers* (Morris)
Jay, John. *John Jay; The Making of a Revolutionary: Unpublished Papers, 1745–1780.* Edited by Richard B. Morris et al. New York: Harper & Row, 1975.

Jefferson, *Papers* (Boyd)
Jefferson, Thomas. *The Papers of Thomas Jefferson.* Edited by Julian P. Boyd et al. Princeton: Princeton University Press, 1950–.

JCC
U.S. Continental Congress. *Journals of the Continental Congress, 1774–1789.* 34 vols. Edited by Worthington C. Ford et al. Washington: Library of Congress, 1904–37.

"Lafayette-Laurens Letters," *SCHGM*
"Letters from the Marquis de Lafayette to Honorable Henry Laurens, 1777–1780." *South Carolina Historical and Genealogical Magazine* 7–9 (1906–08): passim.

Lafayette, *Papers* (Idzerda)
Idzerda, Stanley J. et al., eds. *Lafayette in the Age of the American Revolution: Selected Letters and Papers, 1776–1790.* Ithaca: Cornell University Press, 1977–.

Lee, *Letters* (Ballagh)
Lee, Richard Henry. *The Letters of Richard Henry Lee.* Edited by James C. Ballagh. 2 vols. New York: Macmillan Co., 1911–14.

Livingston, *Papers* (Prince)
Livingston, William. *The Papers of William Livingston.* Edited by

Carl E. Prince et al. Trenton: New Jersey Historical Commission, 1979–.

Md. Archives

Archives of Maryland. Edited by William H. Browne et al. Baltimore: Maryland Historical Society, 1883–.

Meng, *Gérard Despatches*

Gérard, Conrad Alexandre. *Despatches and Instructions of Conrad Alexandre Gérard*. Edited by John J. Meng. Baltimore: Johns Hopkins Press, 1939.

Morgan, *Naval Documents*

Morgan, William James, et al., eds. *Naval Documents of the American Revolution*. Washington: Department of the Navy, 1964–.

N.C. State Records

North Carolina. *The State Records of North Carolina*. Edited by Walter Clark. Vols. 11–26. Winston and Goldsboro, N.C.: N.I. and J.C. Stewart et al., 1895–1914.

N.H. State Papers

New Hampshire. *Provincial and State Papers*. 40 vols. Concord, 1867–1943.

NYHS Collections

Collections of the New-York Historical Society

Pa. Archives

Pennsylvania Archives. 9 series, 119 vols. in 120. Philadelphia: J. Severns & Co., 1852–56; Harrisburg: State printer, 1874–1935.

Pa. Council Minutes

Pennsylvania. *Minutes of the Supreme Executive Council of Pennsylvania, from Its Organization to the Revolution*. 6 vols. [*Colonial Records of Pennsylvania*, vols. 11–16]. Harrisburg: Theo. Fenn & Co., 1852–53.

Parliamentary History

The Parlimentary History of England, from the Earliest Period to the Year 1803. 36 vols. London: T.C. Hansard, 1806–20.

Paullin, *Marine Committee Letters*

Paullin, Charles O., ed. *Out-Letters of Continental Marine Committee and Board of Admiralty, 1776–1780*. 2 vols. New York: Printed for the Naval History Society by the De Vinne Press, 1914.

PCC

Papers of the Continental Congress. National Archives and Records Service. Washington, D.C.

PMHB

Pennsylvania Magazine of History and Biography.

PRO

Public Record Office. London

Roche, *Joseph Reed*
Roche, John F. *Joseph Reed: A Moderate in the American Revolution.* New York: Columbia University Press, 1957.

Rodney, *Letters* (Ryden)
Rodney, Caesar. *Letters to and from Caesar Rodney, 1756–1786.* Edited by George H. Ryden. Philadelphia: University of Pennsylvania Press, 1933.

Shipton, *Harvard Graduates*
Shipton, Clifford K. *Biographical Sketches of Those Who Attended Harvard College.* Sibley's Harvard Graduates. Boston: Massachusetts Historical Society, 1873–.

Simms, *Laurens Army Correspondence*
Laurens, John. *The Army Correspondence of Colonel John Laurens in the Years 1777–78.* Edited by William Gilmore Simms. New York: n.p., 1867.

Sullivan, *Letters* (Hammond)
Sullivan, John. *Letters and Papers of Major-General John Sullivan.* Edited by Otis G. Hammond. 3 vols. Collections of the New Hampshire Historical Society, vols. 13–15. Concord: New Hampshire Historical Society, 1930–39.

Trumbull, *Papers* (MHS Colls.)
Trumbull, Jonathan, Sr. *The Trumbull Papers.* 4 vols. Massachusetts Historical Society Collections, 5th ser., vols. 9–10; 7th ser., vols. 2–3. Boston: Massachusetts Historical Society, 1885–1902.

Warren-Adams Letters
Warren-Adams Letters, Being Chiefly a Correspondence among John Adams, Samuel Adams, and James Warren. 2 vols. Massachusetts Historical Society Collections, vols. 72–73. Boston: Massachusetts Historical Society, 1917–25.

Washington, *Writings* (Fitzpatrick)
Washington, George. *The Writings of George Washington.* Edited by John C. Fitzpatrick. 39 vols. Washington: Government Printing Office, 1931–44.

Wharton, *Diplomatic Correspondence*
Wharton, Francis, ed. *The Revolutionary Diplomatic Correspondence of the United States.* 6 vols. Washington: Government Printing Office, 1889.

Acknowledgments

To the Library of Congress, the Congress of the United States, and the Ford Foundation this edition owes its existence. It is fitting, therefore, that we take this opportunity to acknowledge the foresight of the Library's administration in planning a timely and comprehensive observance of the American Revolution Bicentennial, of the Congress in funding a Bicentennial Office in the Library, and of the Ford Foundation in making a generous grant in support of this project as a scholarly contribution to the celebration of the Bicentennial era. It is with the most profound gratitude that the editors acknowledge their appreciation to all those who bore responsibility for the decisions that made possible these contributions. Our appreciation is also extended to the innumerable persons who have contributed to enriching the holdings of the Library of Congress to make it the premier institution for conducting research on the American Revolution.

The photocopies of the more than twenty-one thousand documents that have been collected for this project have been assembled through the cooperation of several hundred institutions and private individuals devoted to preserving the documentary record upon which the history and traditions of the American people rest, and it is to their work that a documentary publication of this nature should ultimately be dedicated. Unfortunately, the many individual contributors to this collecting effort cannot be adequately recognized, but for permission to print documents appearing in the present volume we are especially grateful to the following institutions: the American Antiquarian Society, American Philosophical Society, Archives du ministère des affaires étrangères (Paris), Archives nationales (Paris), Charleston Library Society, Columbia University, Connecticut Historical Society, Connecticut State Library, Danvers Historical Society, Duke University, Harvard University, Haverford College, Henry E. Huntington Library, Jervis Library Association, Maine Historical Society, Maryland Hall of Records, Maryland Historical Society, Massachusetts Archives Division, Massachusetts Historical Society, Morristown National Historical Park, National Archives and Records Service, New Hampshire Division of Archives and Records Management, New Hampshire Historical Society, New Haven Colony Historical Society, New Jersey State Library, Newport Historical Society, New-York Historical Society, New York Public Library, New York State Historical Association, North Carolina State Department of Archives and History, University of North Carolina, Omaha Public Library, Pennsylvania Historical and Museum Commission, Historical Society of Pennsylvania, Library Company of Philadelphia, Princeton University, Public Record Office (London), Rhode Island Historical Society, Rhode Island State Archives, Rosenbach Foundation, South Carolina Historical Society, Virginia Historical Society, University of Virginia, Western Reserve Historical Society, College of William and Mary, and Yale University. And in addition we express our thanks and appreciation to the following persons: Mr. Sol Feinstone, Mr. John F. Reed, Mrs. Lawrence M. C. Smith, Mr. Robert J. Sudderth, Jr., and Mr. and Mrs. Rodney M. Wilson.

This work has benefited not only from Edmund C. Burnett's pathfinding 8-volume edition of *Letters of Members of the Continental Congress* but also from the generous cooperation of the editors of several other documentary publications with a common focus on the revolutionary era. From them the Library has borrowed heavily and to them it owes a debt it can never adequately acknowledge. It is a pleasure to give special thanks to the editors of the papers of John Adams, Benjamin Franklin, Thomas Jefferson, Henry Laurens, James Madison, and George Washington. Finally, we owe thanks to the historians who have served on the Advisory Committee on the Library's American Revolution Bicentennial Program, and especially to Mr. Julian P. Boyd, Mr. Lyman H. Butterfield, and Mr. Merrill Jensen, who generously acted as an advisory committee for the *Letters* project.

Paul H. Smith
Historical Publications Office
Manuscript Division

Chronology of Congress

June 1–September 30, 1778

June 1	Debates instructions for the American commissioners in Europe.
June 4	Recommends suspension of state price regulations; directs Washington to "proceed in arranging" the army.
June 6	Rejects peace proposals submitted by Lord Howe and Sir Henry Clinton.
June 8	Embargoes provisions (effective June 10–November 15, 1778).
June 11	Receives notice of the arrival of the Carlisle peace commission at Philadelphia; orders expedition against Fort Detroit; orders quartermaster department inquiry.
June 13	Receives letter from the Carlisle peace commission.
June 17	Adopts reply to the Carlisle peace commission; orders halt to personal "correspondence with the enemy."
June 20	Receives notice of the British evacuation of Philadelphia; resolves to emit additional $5 million in Continental currency.
June 22–25	Debates proposed state amendments to the Articles of Confederation.
June 25	Orders reinforcements for Rhode Island.
June 26	Orders Articles of Confederation to be engrossed for signing.
June 27	Adjourns from York, "to Thursday next, to meet at the State House in Philadelphia."
July 2–6	Convenes in Philadelphia, but adjourns "from day to day" for lack of a quorum.
July 7	Achieves quorum; thanks Washington for "gaining the important victory of Monmouth."
July 9	Corrects engrossed Articles of Confederation and begins the signing; directs committee of arrangement to repair to headquarters.
July 11	Receives news of the arrival in Delaware Bay of the French fleet carrying Conrad Alexandre

	Gérard and Silas Deane; directs Washington to prepare for a joint Franco-American offensive.
July 14	Appoints committee to arrange public reception for the French minister Gérard.
July 18	Rejects renewed overtures from the Carlisle peace commission.
July 20	Endorses Ebenezer Hazard's plan to collect "various state papers relative to the origin and progress of the several European settlements in North America."
July 23	Orders inventory of goods left in Philadelphia at the time of the British evacuation; receives Jean Holker's commissions as French marine agent and consul in Philadelphia.
July 25	Defers attack on Fort Detroit; adopts measures for Pennsylvania and New York frontier defense.
July 30	Emits additional $5 million in Continental currency.
July 31	Appoints committee to "superintend an entertainment" for the French minister.
August 1	Consigns tobacco for payment of Beaumarchais' contract claims.
August 3	Investigates commissaries Benjamin Flower and Cornelius Sweers for fraud.
August 6	Holds formal audience with French minister Gérard.
August 7	Debates proposal to discipline board of war members for disregarding an order of Congress.
August 10	Postpones proposal to exchange former New Jersey governor William Franklin for Delaware president John McKinly.
August 11	Adopts declaration denouncing peace commissioner George Johnstone for attempted bribery of American leaders.
August 13	Curtails issuance of passes for travel to British-occupied New York; orders Silas Deane to attend Congress.
August 15	Orders Silas Deane to prepare an oral report on his mission to France; adopts resolution for maintaining the secrecy of correspondence of the committee for foreign affairs.
August 17	Hears Silas Deane's testimony; receives resignation of Maj. Gen. Thomas Mifflin.

August 20	Refers report on the inspector general's department to Washington; rejects motion to exchange William Franklin for John McKinly.
August 21	Orders printing of the proceedings of Gen. Charles Lee's court-martial; hears Silas Deane conclude "the general account" of his mission to France.
August 24	Orders the release of commissary Benjamin Flowers and the prosecution of deputy commissary Cornelius Sweers.
August 28	Receives news of failure of the Franco-American attack on Newport.
August 31	Adopts measures to improve recruitment of the Continental Army.
September 1	Refers passport application of British secret agent John Temple to the state of Pennsylvania.
September 2	Recommends granting exemptions to the provisions embargo.
September 3	Resolves to permit recruitment of German mercenary deserters; postpones expedition planned against Seneca Indians.
September 5	Ignores appeal of secret British agent Dr. John Berkenhout for release from Pennsylvania jail; emits additional $5 million in continental currency.
September 9	Votes thanks to Gen. John Sullivan for the conduct of his forces at Rhode Island; orders Rhode Island expedition inquiry.
September 11	Authorizes dispersal of Gen. John Burgoyne's Convention Army for its more convenient subsistence; urges Maryland to curb evasions of the embargo.
September 14	Appoints Benjamin Franklin minister plenipotentiary to France; approves exchange of William Franklin for John McKinly.
September 19	Reads committee of finance report; orders finance report printed.
September 22	Orders examination of William Carmichael on the activities of Silas Deane in France.
September 25	Appeals to Virginia and North Carolina to aid South Carolina and Georgia; appoints Benjamin Lincoln to command the southern department.

September 26	Reorganizes the offices of the treasury; emits an additional $10 million in Continental currency.
September 28	Conducts examination of William Carmichael.
September 30	Conducts examination of William Carmichael; reassigns Casimir Pulaski's legion.

List of Delegates to Congress

This section lists both the dates on which delegates were elected to terms falling within the period covered by this volume and the inclusive dates of their attendance. The former are generally ascertainable from contemporary state records, but the latter are often elusive bits of information derived from the journals of Congress or extrapolated from references contained in the delegates' correspondence, and in such cases the "facts" are inevitably conjectural. It is not possible to determine interruptions in the attendance of many delegates, and no attempt has been made to record interruptions in service caused by illness or brief trips home, especially of delegates from New Jersey, Delaware, Maryland, and Pennsylvania living within easy access of Congress. For occasional references to such periods of intermittent service as survive in the correspondence and notes of various delegates, see the index under individual delegates. Until fuller information is provided in a consolidated summary of delegate attendance in the final volume of this series, the reader is advised to consult Burnett, *Letters,* 3:li–lxii, for additional information on conjectural dates of attendance. Brief biographical sketches of all the delegates are available in the *Biographical Directory of the American Congress, 1774–1971,* and fuller sketches of more than half of the delegates can be found in the *Dictionary of American Biography*.

CONNECTICUT

Andrew Adams
Elected: October 11, 1777
Attended: July 9 to September 30, 1778

Eliphalet Dyer
Elected: October 11, 1777
Did not attend June to September 1778

Oliver Ellsworth
Elected: October 11, 1777
Did not attend June to September 1778

Titus Hosmer
Elected: October 11, 1777
Attended June 23 to Steptember 10, 1778

Samuel Huntington
Elected: October 11, 1777
Attended: June 1 to July 9, 1778
Roger Sherman
Elected: October 11, 1777
Attended: June 1 to September 30, 1778 (on mission with Committee of Arrangement, ca. August 18 to October 1, 1778)
Oliver Wolcott
Elected: October 11, 1777
Attended: June 1 to July 9, 1778

DELAWARE

Thomas McKean
Elected: December 17, 1777
Attended: June 1 to July 7?; August 15 to September 14, 1778
Caesar Rodney
Elected: December 17, 1777
Did not attend in 1778
Nicholas Van Dyke
Elected: December 17, 1777
Attended: September 2–16? 1778

GEORGIA

Joseph Clay
Elected: February 26, 1778
Did not attend Congress
Lyman Hall
Elected: February 26, 1778
Did not attend in 1778
Edward Langworthy
Elected: February 26, 1778
Attended: June 1–27; August 15 to September 30, 1778
Edward Telfair
Elected: February 26, 1778
Attended: July 13 to Steptember 30, 1778
George Walton
Elected: February 26, 1778
Did not attend in 1778
John Walton
Elected: February 26, 1778
Attended: July 23 to August 4?; August 31? to September 30, 1778
Joseph Wood
Elected: February 26, 1778
Did not attend June to September 1778

MARYLAND

Charles Carroll of Carrollton
Elected: December 5, 1777
Attended: June 1–27, 1778
Samuel Chase
Elected: December 5, 1777
Attended: July 2? to September 30, 1778
James Forbes
Elected: December 22, 1777
Attended: July 13 to September 30, 1778
John Henry
Elected: December 22, 1777
Attended: August 29 to September 30, 1778
George Plater
Elected: December 5, 1777
Attended: June 1–27; July 22 to September 22? 1778
Thomas Stone
Elected: December 5, 1777
Attended: September 25–30, 1778

MASSACHUSETTS

Samuel Adams
Elected: December 4, 1777
Attended: June 1 to September 30, 1778
Francis Dana
Elected: December 4, 1777
Attended: June 1 to August 11, 1778
Elbridge Gerry
Elected: December 4, 1777
Attended: June 1 to September 30, 1778
John Hancock
Elected: December 4, 1777
Attended: June 19 to July 9, 1778
Samuel Holten
Elected: February 20, 1778
Attended: June 20 to September 30, 1778
James Lovell
Elected: December 4, 1777
Attended: June 1 to September 30, 1778
Robert Treat Paine
Elected: December 4, 1777
Did not attend in 1778

NEW HAMPSHIRE

Josiah Bartlett
Elected: March 14, August 14, 1778
Attended: June 1 to September 30, 1778
George Frost
Elected: August 18, 1778
Did not attend June to September 1778
Ebenezer Thompson
Elected: August 14, 1778
Declined
Timothy Walker
Elected: August 14, 1778
Declined
John Wentworth
Elected: March 14, August 18, 1778
Attended: June 1–27? 1778
William Whipple
Elected: August 18, 1778
Did not attend June to September 1778

NEW JERSEY

Elias Boudinot
Elected: November 20, 1777
Attended: July 6–August 20, 1778
Abraham Clark
Elected: November 20, 1777
Did not attend June to September 1778
Jonathan Elmer
Elected: November 20, 1777
Attended: June 1 to July 25; August 18 to September 2; September 16–17? 1778
Nathaniel Scudder
Elected: November 20, 1777
Attended: June 19 to July 7; July 24 to August 31, 1778
John Witherspoon
Elected: November 20, 1777
Attended: June 1 to July 30; August 7–17?; August 27 to September 4?; September 15–26? 1778

NEW YORK

James Duane
Elected: October 3, 1777
Did not attend June to September 1778

William Duer
Elected: October 3, 1777
Attended: June 1 to September 30, 1778
Francis Lewis
Elected: October 3, 1777
Attended: June 11–27; July 31 to September 30, 1778 (on Marine Committee business to North Carolina, ca. May–June, 1778)
Philip Livingston
Elected: October 3, 1777
Did not attend in June 1778; died June 12
Gouverneur Morris
Elected October 3, 1777
Attended: June 1 to September 30, 1778
Philip Schuyler
Elected: March 25, 1778
Did not attend in 1778

NORTH CAROLINA

Thomas Burke
Elected: August 12, 1778
Did not attend June to September 1778
Cornelius Harnett
Elected: April 25, 1778
Attended: August 10 to September 30, 1778
Whitmell Hill
Elected: August 12, 1778
Did not attend June to September 1778
Abner Nash
Elected: April 25, 1778
Declined
John Penn
Elected: April 25, 1778
Attended: July 16 to September 30, 1778
John Williams
Elected: April 28, 1778
Attended: August 4 to September 30, 1778

PENNSYLVANIA

William Clingan
Elected: December 10, 1777
Attended: June 16?–27; September 14?–30, 1778
Benjamin Franklin
Elected: December 10, 1777
Did not attend in 1778

Robert Morris
Elected: December 10, 1777
Attended: July 9 to August 15?; August 25? to September 30, 1778

Joseph Reed
Elected: December 10, 1777
Attended: July 15 to September 30, 1778 (on mission with Committee of Arrangement, ca. June 10–28; August 18 to September 14)

Daniel Roberdeau
Elected: December 10, 1777
Attended: June 1–27; August 7–11?; August 18? to September 30, 1778

James Smith
Elected: December 10, 1777
Attended: June 23–27?; August 11 to September 9?; September 22–30, 1778

Jonathan Bayard Smith
Elected: December 10, 1777
Attended: June 16 to July 11? 1778

RHODE ISLAND

John Collins
Elected: May 6, 1778
Attended: June 20–26?; July 24–29? 1778

William Ellery
Elected: May 6, 1778
Attended: June 1 to July 9, 1778

Stephen Hopkins
Elected: May 6, 1778
Did not attend in 1778

Henry Marchant
Elected: May 6, 1778
Attended: June 8 to September 30, 1778

SOUTH CAROLINA

William Henry Drayton
Elected: January 21, 1778
Attended: June 1 to September 30, 1778

Thomas Heyward
Elected: January 22, 1778
Attended: June 6 to August 20, 1778

Richard Hutson
Elected: January 22, 1778
Attended: June 1–27? 1778

Henry Laurens
Elected: January 21, 1778
Attended: June 1 to September 30, 1778
John Mathews
Elected: January 22, 1778
Attended: June 1 to August 15; August 26? to September 30, 1778

VIRGINIA

Thomas Adams
Elected: December 9, 1777; May 29, 1778
Attended: June 1 to August 28, 1778
John Banister
Elected: November 19, 1777; May 29, 1778
Attended: June 1 to September 24, 1778 (on mission with Committee of Arrangement, ca. August 18 to September 21, 1778)
Cyrus Griffin
Elected: May 29, 1778
Attended: August 19 to September 30, 1778
John Harvie
Elected: May 22, 1777; May 29, 1778
Attended: July 13 to September 30, 1778
Francis Lightfoot Lee
Elected: May 22, 1777; May 29, 1778
Did not attend June to September 1778
Richard Henry Lee
Elected: January 23; May 29, 1778
Attended: June 1 to September 30, 1778
Meriwether Smith
Elected: May 29, 1778
Attended: September 28–30, 1778

Illustrations

Map of Pennsylvania endpapers

Lancaster and York, Pennsylvania, where Congress convened when the British moved into Philadelphia in September 1777 and continued to meet through June 1778, are visible on this southeast quarter of a map of Pennsylvania by Robert Sayer and John Bennett, "exhibiting not only the improved parts of that Province, but also its extensive frontiers: Laid down from actual surveys and chiefly from the late map of W. Scull published in 1770; and humbly inscribed to the Honourable Thomas Penn and Richard Penn, Esquires, true and absolute proprietaries & Governors of the Province of Pennsylvania and the territories thereunto belonging" (London, 1775).

Geography and Map Division, Library of Congress.

Philip Livingston 108

The fifth son of Philip, the second lord of Livingston Manor, Livingston was born in Albany into one of the largest and most influential families in America. Active in the prerevolutionary movement in New York, he was elected to the Continental Congress in 1774, which he attended with considerable regularity the next four years. His experience as a New York merchant made him a valuable member of the Secret Committee and its successor, the Committee of Commerce. And he was often engaged in the work of the Marine Committee and of ad hoc committees appointed to manage commissary and supply problems. Although he was a signer of the Declaration of Independence, he had gone home in April 1776, returning only in early July and thus playing a minor role in the final movement for independence. Some historians assumed that he did not participate in the final debate on the declaration because his name does not appear on a July 2 New York delegate letter signed by five of his colleagues. But since John Witherspoon reported from Philadelphia on July 3 that he had just conversed with Livingston, the evidence on this point is ambiguous. In 1777 Livingston left Philadelphia a month before the British drove Congress to York in September, and he did not rejoin his colleagues until early May 1778. Within a few days he became ill, and he died at York on June 12 at the age of 62, whereupon Congress resolved that the delegates would "continue in mourning for the space of one month." He was buried there the same evening.

Attributed to Abraham Delanoy. Courtesy of the Taconic State Park Commission, Staatsburg, New York.

William Henry Drayton 117

A wealthy, English-educated, South Carolina, lawyer-planter, Drayton was appointed to the province's royal council in 1771 and only slowly emerged as a leader of the American Revolution. Not until his dismissal from the council for his 1774 publication of *A Letter of Freeman of South Carolina to the Deputies of North-America* attacking the royal prerogative did he become a popular figure in his native province. He was subsequently elected to several of the revolutionary bodies that assumed political control of South Carolina and in 1776 became the first chief justice of the state. Disqualified from a seat in the state assembly because of his judicial post, Drayton was nevertheless elected to Congress early in 1778, and he assumed his seat in March while that body was still at York. He was a signer of the Articles of Confederation, an ardent supporter of the French alliance, and the author of a number of published attacks on the British commissioners who arrived in America in June 1778 to disseminate the North Ministry's new peace proposals. An able and energetic delegate, Drayton was also a frequent critic of his colleague President Henry Laurens, and consequently the two dominant members of the South Carolina delegation often worked at cross purposes. Communication between the two men remained so strained that when Drayton contracted typhus the following year, Laurens remained unaware of the condition of his colleague for nearly three weeks. Drayton died of that illness in September 1779 at the age of 37. Although the personal papers Drayton had with him in Philadelphia were destroyed upon his death, he was saved from obscurity in part because of the efforts of his son John, who in 1821 published a collection of documents related to his father's career under the title *Memoirs of the American Revolution*.

From Pierre Eugène Du Simitière, *Portraits des Généraux, Ministres, et Magistrats que se sont rendu célèbres dans la revolution des treize Etats-Unis de l'Amérique de Septentrional* (Paris, 1781).

Gouverneur Morris 203

Morris was born at the manor of Morrisania, N.Y., the son of Lewis Morris, second lord of the manor, and Sarah Gouverneur. Although he was a conservative member of the landed aristocracy of Westchester County, he plunged into radical politics once war began at Lexington and was elected to the principal congresses and conventions that directed the revolutionary movement in New York during 1775–76. When only 24 years old, he had a hand in framing New York's new constitution, with his close associates John Jay and

Robert R. Livingston, and the following year he was elected to represent the state in Congress. Despite his youth, Morris was one of the most dynamic of the delegates, and because of his abilities and remarkably facile pen, he quickly became one of the workhorses of Congress. While he served, he drafted more important congressional papers than any other delegate, and he was the author of Congress' 1778 "Address to the Inhabitants of the United States" and 1779 *Observations on the American Revolution.*

As a member of the committee at camp during the winter of 1778, he acquired detailed knowledge of numerous problems related to the army's distress and developed great admiration for Washington. He was from the outset an ardent nationalist, readily becoming embroiled in controversies involving the assertion of Continental over state authority, and he was one of the most outspoken of delegates in denunciation of the Carlisle commissioners when they attempted to launch the North Ministry's new peace offensive. An innovator and proponent of vigorous action, he developed a number of proposals for sweeping administrative reform and urged the creation of efficient executive departments.

Although Morris left Congress in 1779, never to return to elective office, his influence in American public life continued. He made Pennsylvania his home and there emerged as one of the country's financial experts. He was appointed assistant to Robert Morris when the latter was named to the newly created post of Superintendent of Finance in 1781. In 1787 he was elected a member of the Pennsylvania delegation to the Constitutional Convention, and he is probably best remembered for his work in putting the new federal constitution into its final literary form as chairman of the convention's committee of style. Named minister to France by Washington in 1792, he observed the revolutionary reign of terror in Paris at firsthand, but he was recalled from his post in 1794 at the request of the French in retaliation for America's opposition to Citizen Genet. Morris virtually ended his public career with his departure from France. He returned eventually to Morrisiana where he died in 1816.

Engraving by James B. Longacre after a painting by Thomas Sully.

Charles Lee 228

When the Continental Army was created in the summer of 1775, Lee was probably the most highly regarded professional military man in the colonies. He had served with distinction in the British army during the French and Indian War, attaining the rank of lieutenant colonel, but after being placed on half pay at the war's end he became something of a soldier of fortune, serving for a time with

Polish forces in eastern Europe before migrating to America and taking up land in Virginia in 1773. His reputation landed him an appointment in June 1775 as major general, second in command of the Continental Army, and during the first year of fighting his performance in the field equaled the expectations of his supporters. But during the fateful 1776 New York campaign, he became a critic of Washington's leadership and subsequently suffered the humiliation of being captured by surprise in December. He had only recently been exchanged when the British evacuated Philadelphia in June 1778. Because of his rank he was given the honor of leading the attack on the British army withdrawing across New Jersey even though he had voiced opposition to the plan that had been agreed upon. The result was a fiasco at the battle of Monmouth on June 28, 1778, that ended Lee's career as a successful soldier. Retreating without warning almost as the fighting began, Lee was criticized for failure to engage the enemy and angrily relieved on the spot by Washington, who rallied the Americans in the face of superior force and achieved a battlefield stalemate. Directing an insulting letter to Washington, who refused to apologize for his treatment of him at Monmouth, Lee demanded an inquiry for which a court-martial was appointed in July. The military tribunal found him guilty of disobedience, misbehavior, and disrespect, for which he received the sentence of a twelve-month suspension from the army. Lee, however, took his case to Congress, to the public prints, and to the duelling field. After many delays, Congress finally sustained the verdict of the court-martial on December 5, 1778. On the eve of Lee's return to duty the following December, Congress narrowly rejected a motion to dismiss him from the army, but the move nevertheless had the effect of provoking the general, widely regarded as an eccentric, to an intemperate protest. The following month Congress accordingly dismissed him, ending Lee's colorful and controversial career less than two years before his death at age 51.

Mezzotint by Thomlinson, 1775. Prints and Photographs Division, Library of Congress. No likeness of Lee drawn from life is known.

College Hall 269

When Congress concluded its final session at York on Saturday June 27, Secretary Thomson recorded in the journals, "Adjourned to Thursday next, to meet at the State House in Philadelphia." But "Thursday next" came and went before enough delegates assembled in Philadelphia to convene a quorum on July 7, and several additional days elapsed before Congress could reoccupy its former quarters in the Pennsylvania State House. In the meantime, "the Congress meets in College Hall," Josiah Bartlett explained on July 13, "as the State House was left by the enemy in a most filthy and sordid situation, as were many of the public and private buildings in the City." Although it is not known precisely how long Congress continued to meet in "College Hall," which was built for the Philadelphia Academy in 1740 on Fourth Street between Arch and Market, it is clear from the comments of Bartlett and President Henry Laurens that the structure served briefly as the site of the continent's highest legislative body. Pictured here is a sketch of a "Restored Group of Old Buildings," as they are believed to have been located when they formed the core of the original University of Pennsylvania. The central Hall is flanked by the mansion of the first provost and by Franklin House on the left, and by a dormitory added in 1762 on the right.

From the Independence National Historical Park Collection, National Park Service, Department of the Interior, Philadelphia, Pa.

The elaborate public reception held for Gérard, France's first minister to the United States, on August 6, 1778, symbolized the high expectations with which Congress regarded the Franco-American alliance. Planning the reception occupied much of the delegates' time for nearly a month after they learned on July 11 that the French fleet carrying Gérard had entered Delaware Bay. Ignoring a long tradition of distrust of an inveterate enemy, the delegates nearly unanimously endeavored to make the most of the alliance. Despite early disappointments experienced when the French navy failed to carry out projected attacks against British forces at both New York and Newport in the summer of 1778, confidence in the French forces and in the king's minister in Philadelphia remained strong. Gérard brought to his new post the experience of a long diplomatic career extending back to a post as secretary to the French legation at the court of the Elector Palatine in 1753. Nevertheless, he eventually undermined his usefulness to the French government by becoming involved in congressional politics, particularly in becoming too closely allied to Silas Deane in his controversy with the partisans of Arthur Lee and in failing to cultivate delegates from regions of America most deeply distrustful of France. Gérard did gain a well-deserved reputation as an able spokesman for French interests, leading even such a francophobe as Samuel Adams to concede that "he is determined to merit the Character of his own Court, of a vigilant and faithful Minister." Because of ill health and mounting frustration over his increasing involvement in the partisan maneuvers of delegates deemed friendly to French interests, Gérard returned to France in October 1779. Although he was sometimes misinformed about the motives and proceedings of Congress, his detailed dispatches to Paris often provide some of the most useful testimony available on the delegates' activities in and out of Congress.

Painting by Charles Willson Peale, 1779. Independence National Historical Park Collection.

George Johnstone's Declaration 425

A member of Parliament and former governor of British West Florida, Johnstone was the most visible and disruptive member of the peace commission appointed to present the North Ministry's conciliatory proposals of February 1778, which were conceived in part to forestall consummation of the Franco-American alliance. Selected as a replacement for Richard Jackson, an acknowledged expert on American affairs, Johnstone joined a commission consisting of the young and inexperienced earl of Carlisle, William Eden, and the Howe brothers—Admiral Lord Richard and General Sir William. Although the Howe brothers had extensive American experience, as commanders respectively of his majesty's naval and military forces in North America, Johnstone was the only commissioner with significant civil experience and a circle of American friends to draw upon in this enterprise.

Arriving after the announcement of the signing of the Franco-American treaties and on the eve of the British evacuation of Philadelphia, the commissioners were doomed to failure from the start. Their maladroit dealings with members of Congress and other American leaders, exemplified by Johnstone's effort to bribe Joseph Reed, ensured them a hostile reception. And by August 11, when Congress publicly denounced Johnstone's overtures to Reed and others, the commissioners had virtually exhausted the options open to them. In an effort to resuscitate the commission's work, Johnstone announced his resignation in the August 26 statement reproduced here, leaving to two secret agents, John Temple and Dr. John Berkenhout, whatever hope remained to salvage the ministry's peace plans. Although Carlisle made another effort on October 3 to circumvent official opposition by proclaiming Britain's "benevolent overtures" directly to the "free Inhabitants of the said Colonies, of every Rank and Denomination," the gesture had no visible effect and the commissioners returned to London in December empty-handed.

Peter Force Collection, Manuscript Division, Library of Congress.

Finance Report, September 19, 1778 665

Long troubled by the deterioration of the country's finances, Congress on August 27 appointed a committee consisting of Elbridge Gerry, Richard Henry Lee, Gouverneur Morris, Robert Morris, and John Witherspoon "to consider of the state of the money and finances of the United States." The committee submitted this report, drafted by Gouverneur Morris, on September 19, which was then printed for the use of the delegates as the several points contained in it were taken up in debate during succeeding weeks. Although many of Morris' proposals received little serious attention, and the report was amended and resubmitted to a second committee on October 13, the document offers insights into a number of fiscal issues considered by the delegates at this time. Blanks in the printed document were filled in during the ensuing debates, and many of its features survived in the various finance resolutions eventually adopted on December 31, 1778, and January 2, 1779.

Papers of the Continental Congress, National Archives and Records Service.

LETTERS OF DELEGATES TO CONGRESS

10

June 1–
September 30, 1778

Samuel Adams to James Warren

My dear sir, York Town June 1 1778

I wrote to you a few Days ago by Mr Brailsford, since which I have receivd your Favors of the 10th & 13th of May.[1] The Arts you mention as being practiced by the Tories in Boston, to prejudice the People against our new Connection, are similar to those which I find on reading a late Philada Paper, are practiced there. The Danger of Popery is particularly held up by the Partizans of that King, who would wish to drain Ireland of its Catholicks to carry on his bloody Purposes in America. I do not wonder that a certain Gentleman, though of the Character you have describd, should joyn in such an objection. He may think it will give him Popularity among a particular Class of Men, & serve *one* Purpose which I beleive he has constantly in View; but I am satisfied that such a Suggestion will have a different Effect.[2]

I have receivd several Letters from my Friend Dr Lee since my Arrival here. Those by the Way of Boston are Duplicates, and contain Nothing of Importance more than what we receivd by Mr Dean. I wish you would revive in the House of Representatives the Proposition which was made last Winter relating to that Gentleman. I have an additional Reason inclining me to urge this Matter, which I will communicate to you at another Time, and which I am very sure you will approve of. At present I beleive you are satisfied that it is both Policy & Justice that it should be done.[3]

Congress has been pleasd to put me on the Marine Committee.[4] I mention this to you, in hopes that I shall have the Pleasure of receiving your Letters the oftener on that Account, & particularly on the Subject of the Navy, which I will use my utmost Endeavors to build up. The Committee have orderd a Letter to your Board by this Post.[5] Capt Burk is to have the Command of the Resistance which may be a Step to further Promotion hereafter.[6] The French Gentleman[7] who was *fed with Promises* at Boston and afterwards substantially releivd by you is highly esteemd by this Committee, and will be rewarded & employed & Capt Peck is not unnoticed. The new Frigate at Salisbury, though before christned by another Name, has that of the *Alliance* given to her by the Committee.

This Letter I intended to have finishd & forwarded by the Post, this Morning (June 2), but was prevented. Capt Barry who is to take the Command of the Raughley will deliver it to you. I am apprehensive for our Friend Mr. J. A.[8] who if I mistake not had saild 7 Weeks when the last Vessel left Nantz. The Bearer is in Haste.

Adieu

RC (MHi). In Adams' hand, though not signed.

1 Warren's May 10 and 13 letters to Adams are in *Warren-Adams Letters,* 2:9–10.

2 Adams is referring to John Hancock, who, according to Warren, had failed to attend a reception for French officers. Warren also accused the "Tories" of using "the danger of Popery" to instill "prejudices into the minds of the people against our Connections with France." Ibid., 2:9.

3 Adams was seeking a grant of land from the Massachusetts government for Arthur Lee, but not until after Lee's 1780 return to America did the Massachusetts General Court grant him 600 acres of Maine land as compensation for his services as Massachusetts agent in England before the war. Shipton, *Harvard Graduates,* 18:257; and *Warren-Adams Letters,* 2:25, 168.

4 Adams was appointed to the Marine Committee on May 27, 1778. *JCC,* 11:537.

5 See Marine Committee to the Eastern Navy Board, May 30, 1778.

6 For the appointment of Capt. William Burke, see Marine Committee to John Bradford, April 28, 1778.

7 Pierre Landais.

8 John Adams.

Josiah Bartlett to Mary Bartlett

My Dear, York Town June first 1778

I send this inclosed in a letter to Colo Langdon of Portsmouth. Hope it will find you & the family well as it leaves me. I have wrote & sent 3 letters before this Just to let you know I am well.[1] I have heard nothing from you since I left home nor Do I Expect to, till next week. I want much to hear from you all, but especially from Rhoda. Last week it was very cold here for the time of year, and a frost was Expected: if it was as much Colder with you as you are further north, I fear great hurt has been Done by the frost in New Hampshire.

The lottery finished last week, and by a list of the prizes of 500 Dollars & above published in the paper I find we have not Drawn any of the great prizes; whither we have Drawn any of the Smaller prizes I shall Know in a few Days. This place appears to be more healthy than Philadela But find great Difficulty to procure good accomodations. I put up at present at a German House. Mr. Wentworth has arrived, has had the small pox favorable. Charles Chace is well.

Yours &c, Josiah Bartlett

RC (NhHi).

1 Bartlett's May 17 letter to his wife has not been found, but for those of May 21 and 26, see Bartlett to Mary Bartlett, May 21, 1778, note 3.

Josiah Bartlett to John Langdon

My Dear Sir, York Town June 1st 1778.

Before you receive this, I suppose you will have rec'd the Order of Congress for going on with your ship, which is to be changed to a two decker and to carry 56 guns—viz 28 of 24 lbs & 28 of 18 lbs.[1]

Mr Wentworth was innoculated at Fishkill, rode to Reading where he remained a week, is now here and attended Congress the day before yesterday.

As to news I have nothing material to write you. The substance of the treaty with France you know. The Ship which arrived from Spain only brought a duplicate of that Treaty. Spain will not accede to the treaty till the arrival of her West India fleet, unless drove to it by England. It is then expected she will act as openly as France. Our Ambassadors inform us Spain and Portugal have settled their disputes & Portugal has acceded to the family compact. The extract of a letter in the enclosed paper dated February 28th 1778 is from Mr Lee one of our Commissioners.[2]

The common opinion in the army is that the enemy are about to leave Philadelphia, while some suspect it to be only a political manoeuvre to draw our army into a disadvantageous situation and to attack them. The Tories are stealing out of the City and taking the Oaths to the State. We have no further account of the famous British Commissioners who are to restore peace to America. I believe before this time they are satisfied they will effect nothing unless they enlarge the powers given by their late act of Parliament. One of our Ambassadors tells us the British Ministry publicly gave out that they have sent half a million of guineas to pave the way to a reconciliation and that Lord North informed Count Maurepas that he was sure of a majority of Congress. To such vile shifts are they drove to prevent foreign powers from assisting or acknowledging us; but all will be in vain. Give my best regards to General Whipple and remember me to all friends. I shall hope to hear from you as often as convenient.

I am your friend and most obt servant, Josiah Bartlett

Tr (DLC).

[1] Congress had approved these revised plans for the frigate being built at Portsmouth on May 29. *JCC*, 11:555. See also Marine Committee to Langdon, May 30; and William Ellery to William Whipple, May 31, 1778.

[2] Arthur Lee's February 28 letter to the Committee for Foreign Affairs is in Wharton, *Diplomatic Correspondence*, 2:509–10.

Charles Carroll of Carrollton to Charles Carroll, Sr.

Dear Papa, 1778 June 1st

I wrote to you yesterday by Mr. Henry; Who was to have set off this day for Annapolis but has been detained by the rain. It gives me pleasure to hear Molly continues to grow better. A letter of the 28th past from Gen. Washington was read this morning in Congress. The General is of opinion the Enemy will leave Pha. soon, but notwithstanding all the appearances of an approaching departure, there is one circumstance agt. it; they are fortifying their redoubts.

Inclosed you have a letter which I lately recd. from Fitzgerald. Wishing you all perfect health I remain, Yr. affectionate Son,

Ch. Carroll of Carrollton

RC (MdHi).

Committee of Congress Report

[June 1, 1778][1]

The joint Committee to whom was referred the motion respecting foreign Treaties have agreed upon the following Report.

Resolved that the Commissioners of these United States at the Courts of Versailles, Vienna & Berlin, be directed to confer with the Ambassadors or Envoys at the above Courts respectively, from those of Portugal,*[2] Russia [St. Petersburg],[3] Sweeden,* Denmark,* and the States General of Holland,* upon the Inclination that these latter States may entertain of receiving in a friendly manner Commissioners from the United States of America,* assuring the sd. Ambassadors or Envoys of the desire of this Congress to enter into the most friendly commercial Engagements with their respective Courts.* And in Case the sd. Commissioners shall find the sd. Courts or any of them inclined to enter into such friendly commercial Engagements, that then, for the Purpose of concluding such Treaties, the Commissioners [appointed to represent the United States of No. America] at the Court of Madrid shall repair to the Court of Lisbon[4] and one of the [Commissioners appointed to represent these States] at the Court of Versailles, as shall be agreed by them, shall repair if necessary to the Hague,* & Copenhagen, and the Commissioners at the Courts of Vienna & Berlin shall repair to St. Petersburgh & Stockholm.

That for these Purposes Commissions be sent blank to the Commissioners at the Court of France, to be filled up as Occasion may require.

That the Commissioners be directed to correspond with each

other, and, previous to any overtures of the Court of Petersburgh, the Commissioners at the Court of Versailles be directed to consult with that Court upon the propriety of making such Overtures; and govern themselves accordingly.

That whatever Treaties may be entered into in consequence of these Instructions shall be in Terms of the most perfect equality & Reciprocity, and no way repugnant to the Treaty of Paris of the 6th of February last.

MS (ScHi). Written by James Lovell and annotated by Henry Laurens.

1 This report is undoubtedly the work of the "joint committee" created on June 1 by the addition of William Henry Drayton, William Duer, and James Smith to the Committee for Foreign Affairs. This committee was appointed to report on "the instructions to the commissioners in Europe," and it brought in this report during the afternoon of the same day. The issue was debated that day and again on June 2, but without a final result. The questions of expanded diplomatic relations, commercial treaties, and the appointment of new commissioners had been before Congress since mid-April and continued to be a major area of disagreement in Congress throughout 1778. See *JCC*, 10:372, 411, 414, 11:473, 505, 546–47, 559, 563. See also Henry Laurens to John Rutledge, June 3; and James Lovell to Benjamin Franklin, June 20, 1778.

2 The asterisks here and below indicate points in the document where Henry Laurens wrote above the line either "Agd" or "Ay," apparently to indicate that agreement had been reached on these passages during debate in Congress on the committee report.

3 Words in brackets here and below were inserted between the lines of Lovell's draft committee report by Laurens.

4 At this point in the MS Henry Laurens placed an "A" above the line to which he keyed the following note he penned at the bottom of this document: "if necessary, otherwise to conclude a Treaty with the Court of Lisbon, at Madrid or elsewhere as the case may require with any person properly authorized for that purpose by the Court of Lisbon. Ag."

Henry Laurens to John Houstoun

Honorable Sir, 1st June 1778

I had the honor of writing to you on the 14th Ulto.[1] by Messenger Sharp & of presenting to Congress on the 25th your Honor's dispatches of the 20th March which had reached me the preceeding Evening. These were referred to a select Committee, upon whose Report the Inclosed Act of Congress of the 29th is founded, to which I beg leave to refer as containing all the Commands I have received.[2]

The Enemy within the circumjacent lines of Philadelphia have for a fortnight past shewn strong marks of a design to evacuate that City, the embarkation of their Cannon & Baggage, their Horses & forage & the flight of many hundreds called Tories who flock into our Camp & into Lancaster & York in order to make their peace are evidences of such an intention, nevertheless I have doubts, & will not beleive Mr. Clinton going, until he shall be fairly gone. If he can get rid of all the Citizens he will have fewer mouths to consume provision now become very scarce within his narrow confines. Philadelphia will become a complete Garrison subject altogether to Articles of War & his general Orders. There will be less danger from spies & fewer critics upon his general conduct—& if further, he can so far amuse us as to retard intended reinforcements for Valley forge until he shall be Strengthened by such as he himself expects. The debarkation of Cannon & Baggage will be an easy work & he will applaud himself upon the success of his Stratagem. I am happy in finding General Washington acts as if he had also his doubts, although in the last Letter received from him he writes—

"The Enemy are Still (28th May) in Philadelphia but the intelligence from thence is so clear & so Strong, it is as certain as any event can be, that is contingent, that they mean to abandon it. Against the various measures they are pursuing which point to an evacuation I can learn but of a Single circumstance opposed. They are working at their Redoubts with great industry, but this fact tho' certainly true cannot be of Sufficient weight to raise a doubt upon the subject & must be considered as merely calculated to deceive us & mask their designs, we cannot by the most diligent searches discover whether their movement will be by Land or Sea."

In this State of uncertainty the General has detached General Maxwell with a large detachment to join General Dickinson in Jersey with orders to annoy the Enemy if a March through that State Shall be attempted, & has called in General Smallwood from Wilmington & I am well assured the utmost vigilance is observed in Camp. Twenty Six days have passed over Since General Howe or General Clinton or both have propagated the Report of the intended evacuation. If the object requiring their removal is important, they have certainly lingered away time in a manner apparently inconsistent with an important demand, but I will not be further troublesome with conjectures—a few days more will produce demonstration. The bustle & shew in New York is nearly similer to this in Philadelphia. There they have about 2060 British, 1250 Hessians & 2893 American Levies, & 100 Anspachers—this account may be relied on—& tis thought they mean to ascend North River by Land or Sea. If these from Philadelphia should join, the whole will be Strong, but I hope not too Strong to be Burgoyned. I should observe the computed number in Philadelphia is 8 to 9 Thousand greatly diminished lately by death & Desertion. The papers which you will receive Sir within this inclosure will convey some intelligence, the Letter from the Reverend Mr. Kirkland[3] gives a pleasing prospect of peace with the Six Nations, we are endeavoring to cultivate their present disposition into friendship by every proper means.

I have the honor to be &ca.

LB (DNA: PCC, item 13).

1 See Laurens to Rawlins Lowndes, May 14, 1778, note 2.

2 In his March 20 letter to Laurens, John Houstoun, the governor of Georgia, complained that Gen. Robert Howe, the commander of the southern military department, had shown a lack of respect for state authority by refusing to accede to a request by the Georgia Assembly that he undertake an expedition against East Florida and asked Congress to pass an act "expressive of the Subordinate Relation in which the Military stand to the Civil." PCC, item 73, fols. 181–85. In order to substantiate his allegation against Howe, Houstoun also sent Laurens substantial supporting evidence consisting of minutes of the assembly and letters of Howe for the period January–February 1778. Ibid., fols. 141–79. Congress referred all this material to the Committee at Camp, which had been involved almost from the beginning of the year in reforming the Continental Army, and on May 29 it approved a report by the committee which stated that Continental commanders—though "amenable to the laws of the State in which they reside in common with other citizens"—still had the final say in conducting military operations, that Howe had been duly respectful to Georgia state authorities, and that measures were being considered to relieve the state. See *JCC*, 11:530, 553–54.

This day Laurens also transmitted Congress' May 29 resolves on this issue to Gen. Robert Howe under cover of the following note. "I have barely a moment for inclosing an Act of Congress of the 29th Ulto. for declaring the sense of Congress that all Military Officers & Soldiers ought to be amenable to the Laws of the State & on your particular conduct in the State of Georgia.

"I will if possible in a seperate Letter give you the Current News—here I can only add repeated assurances of being with great Regard &ca." PCC, item 13, 1:349.

3 On May 26 Congress had read and referred to the Board of War a May 4 letter from Rev. Samuel Kirkland to Gen. Philip Schuyler that contained a message to Schuyler from some Senecas describing recent dealings of the Iroquois confederation with British Indian agent Col. John Butler. See PCC, item 153, 3:326–28; and *JCC*, 11:536. Kirkland was a Congregational minister from Connecticut who served as a missionary to the Iroquois and also acted as an unofficial Indian agent for Congress. See these *Letters*, 1:592n.

Henry Laurens to Rawlins Lowndes

Dear Sir, 1st June 1778.

My last to your Excellency of the 14th Ulto.[1] went by Messenger Sharp.

The Committee to whom Your Excellency's Letters of the 13th & 18th April had been referred having made their Report to Congress the inclosed Act of the 29th Ulto. was thereupon produced to which I beg leave to refer.[2]

Congress are truly sensible of the necessity of marking a limit to the Military in every State, be this as it may, from the tenor of a Resolve in an Act which I am to transmit to Georgia[3] there appears to me an opening for disputes between the Executive of a State & the officer commanding the Troops in such State. Even in cases where the Salvation of the State may be at hazard, a capricious, or a sensible Officer, according to my interpretation may under sanction of this Resolve withdraw every Troop from a State whenever he shall judge it proper to do so, notwithstanding a former instruction.[4] At best it will encourage dispute. Being restrained within my now Sphere of Duty when this was offered I could do no more than intimate in private my now feelings to one of my Colleagues & to the Member who had framed the Act.[5]

As these Gentlemen received no impressions from my remarks, I therefore doubt the force of them. Nevertheless as I cannot divest my mind of its original Ideas on the subject, I take the liberty of Submitting my opinion to your Excellency.

The Resolve is general, concerns the whole Union & may particularly affect the State of South Carolina. I shall therefore subjoin a Copy for the information of your Excellency & the Executive of the State.

"Resolved, (29th May 1778) that all Military Officers & Soldiers in the service of the United States are & of right ought to be amenable to the Laws of the State in which they reside in common with other Citizens, but as to the propriety of undertaking distant expeditions or enterprizes or other Military operations & the mode of conducting them the General or Commanding Officer must finally judge & determine at his peril."

A Commanding Officer as a little reflexion will shew, may shield himself in almost every Case by unanimity of voices in a Council of War & by means which have sometimes been practiced & which may again be adopted.

Under this Resolution I conceive every Garrison may be Stripped, if not of all, of the best Men by a Commander of Troops whenever he shall determine the propriety of a distant expedition. The want of access to a Military Chest may be some Check, but if there be danger in the power adventitious Checks I humbly apprehend cannot Safely be relied on for preventing the exercise.

I acknowledge I have not time at this Instant for examining & comparing the former Resolve alluded to above*—as I remember the General or Commander cannot March out of our State more than ⅓d of the Troops without order of Congress or consent of the president. If this be all he can do now, why this new & general Resolve Your Excellency will judge & you will be pleased to receive this from me as a private & pardon me for making it the vehicle of the public Act first mentioned.

I shall do my self the honor of writing again by Capt Cochran such intelligence as the time affords but must at present conclude, which I beg leave to do with repeated assurances of being with great Regard & Respect, &ca.

LB (ScHi).

1 Although Laurens' last official letter to South Carolina president Lowndes was dated May 14, he had also written to him privately on May 17, 1778.

[2] For the various resolves pertaining to South Carolina passed by Congress on May 29, see *JCC*, 11:551–53. Discussions of the provenance of these resolves can be found in the editorial notes to Laurens' May 14 and 17 letters to Lowndes and in his May 18, 1778, letter to William Moultrie. Laurens also enclosed a copy of one of these resolves—requesting an account of Continental stores in South Carolina—with a brief covering letter he wrote this day to Abraham Livingston, Continental agent in Charleston. PCC, item 13, 1:349.

[3] See Laurens to John Houstoun, this date, note 2.

[4] Laurens inserted an asterisk at this point to key his reference to "the former Resolve" in the next-to-last paragraph of this letter. The "former Instruction" mentioned by Laurens was a June 18, 1776, resolve whereby Congress decreed that not more than one-third of the Continental troops raised in South Carolina could be removed from there "without the express order of Congress or the consent of the president of that colony." *JCC*, 5:462–63.

[5] Francis Dana was the author of the May 25 resolve affirming the primacy of Continental commanders over state officials in the conduct of military operations that Laurens is discussing here. See *JCC*, 11:554n.1.

Henry Laurens to William Moultrie

Dear General, 1st June 1778

I beg leave to refer to my last under the 18th May by Messenger Sharp.

The Committee to whom were referred the Letters from President Lowndes & your Self having made their Report Congress thereupon formed an Act on the 29th Inst. a Copy of which you will receive within the present Inclosure for your information and government.[1]

General Clinton makes great shew of an intention to evacuate the City of Philadelphia & for aught I know he may be Sincere, but he has been so very long about the business, as to Strengthen the jealousies which I had entertained from his earliest pretence. If there be an absolute necessity for his going to New York, any part of the West Indies, Ireland or England, his dilatoriness is inconsistent with the necessity.

If he can so far alarm all the Tory Citizens as to get rid of them either by sending them to England & by suffering Thousands to fly to Camp & into different parts of this State he will have fewer mouths to feed, the whole City will become a Garrison governed by articles of War & his general orders—he will be less exposed to danger from Spies, & less harrassed by Complaints & applications from Cits, in plain Coats & broad Hats. If he can by all his parade of departure, prevail upon us to believe him so far as to relax our endeavours to reinforce Valley forge until the reinforcements which he expects shall arrive, his Stratagem will have succeeded. 'Tis certain that within a few days past he has been hard at work on the Redoubts—no manifest proof of a design to quit them. All therefore is conjecture—it is most consistent with Safety to believe he is attempting to deceive & to act accordingly. If he goes, he will at least give us

Credit for good Generalship, for he is informed of every Step we take. If he stay's he will find no encouragement to attempt us by Surprise.

I have the honor to be

LB (DNA: PCC, item 13). Addressed: "Brigdr. General Moultrie, Charles Town."

1 For further information on General Moultrie's dispute with Pres. Rawlins Lowndes of South Carolina over the accountability of a Continental deputy paymaster to state authority, see *JCC,* 11:552–53; and Laurens to Lowndes, May 17, and to Moultrie, May 18, 1778.

Robert Morris to Lux & Bowley

Gentn. Manheim June 1st. 1778

Please to deliver to the order of Jona Potts Esqr Dy Director General of the Contl Hospitals Two Hogsheads marked VMC [*&*] EC, No. 25 & 26 Contg Salt Petre and which were Imported in the Schooner Rambler, Capt Jona Buffington, from Martinico, being Shipped by Wm Bingham Eqr to your address subject to my orders,[1] & your complyance will much oblige, sirs, Your Obedt hble servant,

Robt Morris.

RC (Mrs. Lawrence M.C. Smith, Germantown, Pa., 1976). Addressed: "To Messrs. Lux & Bowley, Merchts., Baltimore."

1 Another document related to Morris' activities in procuring medicines for the Continental service at this time is in the William A. Smith Collection, NN. It consists of an "Invoice of Medicines Sold Doctr. Wm Shippen for use of the States of America," dated April 5, 1778, on the verso of which Morris penned the following receipt dated Manheim, June 1, 1778. "Then Received of Jona Potts Esqr. Dy Director Genl. his draft of this date on Jos. Shippen junr Esqr. Secy & paymaster of the Genl Hospital for Twenty thousand four hundred & twenty four Dollars which when pd. is in full of the within bill of Medicines Recd by order & for Acct of Messrs. Lux & Bowley of Baltimore, Robt. Morris."

Oliver Wolcott to Laura Wolcott

My Dear, York Town lt June 1778

I believe my last Letter to you was by Brown, since which nothing Material has occurred. The Enemy are Undoubtedly preparing to leave Philedelphia and probably will do so within a Week. Whether G Britain will yeild the American Contest or rather than do so will engage in a War with France is yet unknown. If she has not already She must immediately take a decided Part in this Affair.

I find that I shall not Return home so soon as I expected when I wrote some of my last Letters. Mr. Ellsworth has lately wrote Me a Letter that in case Mr. Adams shall not come forward he will do so by the latter End of this Month. I trust that it will not be long before that I am releived.

By the Enclosed Paper you will find that None of us have made our Fortunes in the Lottery. I will take an early Oppertunity to know the Real Fate of the Tickets of which I have the Numbers.

This Letter goes by the common Post but I hope it may come to your Hand. My best Regards to my Family and Friends. Yours affectionately,

Oliver Wolcott

P.S. I was just Sealing my Letter before I tho't to Acquaint you that I have been fully informed that the Affair which was apprehended might have essentially affected my Election, had no Effect.[1] From the Circumstance of my almost forgetting to mention it, you will justly Inferr it that my own Apprehensions were such as not to have the least Influence upon my Mind, which I assure you was truly the Case.

RC (CtHi).

[1] See Wolcott to Laura Wolcott, May 17, 1778, note 2.

Elbridge Gerry to John Avery

Sir

York Town June 2d 1778

A few Days ago I received by the Hand of the Secretary, an order of the Hone. Council of Massachusetts Bay relative to an Account of General Arnold's, and having examined the Files of the Treasury, find that it is transmitted to the Commissioners of Accounts in the northern Department. To accomplish the Design of the order, I have transmitted it to the Commissioners & desired them to "forward to You a Copy of the Account" without Delay.[1] You'll please to communicate this with my respectful Compliments to the honorable Board & beleive me to be with much Esteem sir your hum sert,

E Gerry

FC (MHi).

[1] At the bottom of this sheet of paper, Gerry drafted the following undated letter to the commissioners of accounts in the northern department: "Inclosed is an Order wch I have recd from the Council of Massa Bay, relative to an Account exhibited to the State by General Arnold; I find on examining the Files of the Treasury that the Account was deliverd to Mr. Milligan for the use of the Commissioners of the northern Department, & shall be glad to have a Copy of it without Delay transmitted to John Avery Esqr. Deputy Secry of the State at Boston."

Henry Laurens to Rawlins Lowndes

Dear Sir, 2d June [1778]

I beg leave to refer your Excellency to a Letter which I had the honor of writing yesterday dispatched by Capt. Cochran this Morning & to the Sundry Copies of Papers of intelligence which will accompany this.

Notwithstanding all appearances, I will not trust General Clinton. I beleive he is going somewhere, I would watch him everywhere, one of the Strongest marks of his determination to go & to go by Sea too, was shipping his light Horse. These were all relanded & shod the 31st May, possibly to morrow we shall hear they are all unshod & on Ship board again.

Your Excellency will see what it is Said by General Gates[1] & will by comparing Notes be more competent to judge of designs by all this apparent bustle—the present is an important moment, every succeeding second promises accounts of some great event. Is it impossible, that immediately after the retiring of General Clinton the arrival of Commissioners may be announced? Whatever shall happen shall be communicated with all possible dispatch to your Excellency by, Sir, Your Excellys. most obdt. Servt.[2]

LB (ScHi).

1 This day Congress read a May 21 letter from Gen. Horatio Gates to Washington, in which he reported that the British were apparently preparing to evacuate Forts Washington and Independence in New York, as well as a May 25 letter from Gates to Gov. Jonathan Trumbull of Connecticut, in which he conjectured that the British army in Philadelphia might join with British forces from New York City and launch an attack on either upstate New York or one of the New England states. See PCC, item 154, 1:340–42, 350–51; and *JCC*, 11:560.

2 Laurens also wrote the following brief letter to President Lowndes on June 3: "His Excellency President Lowndes is requested to cause Copies of the Inclosed Establishment of the Army of the United States of North America to be published in the Several Gazettes in Charles Town [*and*] to transmit to [two] of the Inclosed to Major General Howe, two to Brigadier General Moultrie." PCC, item 13, 1:351. For the May 27, May 29, and June 2 resolves on the Continental Army referred to by Laurens, see *JCC*, 11:538–43, 554–55, 560–61.

James Lovell to William Whipple

Sir,[1] June 2d 1778.

I send you the only list of prizes which has been published. The remainder must be in a pamphlet as it would require 5 Gazettes complete to give out the whole. The managers are directed to make the publication immediately.[2] If the printers will not take the trouble of printing the list off in small portions till all is finished to oblige their customers the Loan and Post Offices must allow people to examine gratis at their several offices where Lists should be deposited.

It is impossible to give you any thing determinate as to the motions of the Enemy. The last information of the General to us, made it appear very doubtful whether the enemy would go off by land or water. Every circumstance spoke the latter, except that a great number of boats were preparing at Staten Island. It is to day reported that the horses are again landed to be shod. I do not give this as certain, for there are a set of most infamous liars practising upon the public daily.

My warmest regards to your dearest friends. J.L.

Tr (DLC). Captioned by the transcriber: "James Lovell to (John Langdon)?"

1 Although the transcriber suggested that John Langdon was the recipient of this letter, it seems probable that it was actually directed to William Whipple. Lovell had long maintained a regular correspondence with Whipple, and the subject of his first paragraph, the Continental lottery, was a topic that is frequently found in their correspondence.

2 For Congress' June 3 resolve ordering the dissemination of pamphlets containing the results of the recent drawing "in the first class of the lottery of the United States," see *JCC,* 11:564.

Robert Morris to John Brown

Dear Sir Manheim June 2d 1778

I received your favour of the 29th enclosing Doctr Craigies draft on Doctr Potts & have got an order on the paymaster of the Hospital for the Money. Mr. Mease paid your draft to Robt Gray & I thank You for sending the Money to Mr Hudson to pay Carter Braxtons draft on me, as well as for paying Colo. Banister part of his demand, be pleased to pay him the remainders, & also Mrs. Duncan for the balance due on the bills. I hope you have received the Money for Colo. Griffins draft & herein you will find John Bradfords bill dated Boston 13th May last on the Commercial Committee for 4000 Dollars in favour of Cap Patrick Brown with his blank endorsation, please to receive this Money & place it to my Credit. I expect to see you before long unless I go down to Philadelphia & am Dr sir, Your Obedt Hble servt. Robt Morris

June 4th. I have now recd your letter of yesterday & herein send all the papers that are here relative to the Cargoes shipped by Messrs. Gardoqui & Sons. I wish I cou'd tell Mr Hill any fixed course of Exchange but there is no such thing at present. I wou'd not give more than 300 per Cent now if that. Please to cause the letters sent herewith to be delivered. I hope to set out for Philada. in the morning & am Dr sir, Yours &c, RM.

RC (NjP).

Samuel Adams to Baron Steuben

Sir, York Town June 3d 1778

I very gratefully acknowledge the Receipt of your Favor of the 28th of May by Mr Ternant, as well as another which was deliverd to me in Boston. It affords me great Satisfaction to find that Congress, sensible of your Merit, have put it in your Power to do eminent Service to our Country in the Army, and that your Services are so acceptable there.[1] This is the Fulfillment of my earnest Wishes when I had the Pleasure of conversing with you in Boston. May Heaven prosper you. Mr. Ternants Haste prevents my adding more than that I am with very cordial Esteem, Your affectionate very humble servt, Saml Adams

RC (NN). Addressed by Elbridge Gerry: "Major General Baron de Steuben, at Head Quarters, Valley Forge, favd. per Monsr. Ternant."

1 Steuben had been appointed a major general and inspector general of the Continental Army on May 5, 1778. *JCC*, 11:465.

Samuel Huntington to Benjamin Huntington

Sir[1] York Town 3rd June 1778

Through the Smiles of Divine providence public affairs Seem to have taken a Surprising turn in favour of these United States.

It Seems almost beyond a doubt from repeated Accounts the Enemy are about to leave Philadelphia. We expect every hour to hear the City is evacuated, but their rout or destination is unknown. The Tories are in great distress, Some in despair are taking passage to fly their Incensed Country, others coming out of the City & taking the Oaths to the Government here.

We yesterday receivd advice by a Vessel arrivd at Baltimore in Sixteen days from Martinico that war was declared between France and England, but this I give you as Ship news that wants Confermation; however this may be, it is certain the favourable Sentiments of France, Spain & Other European powers with regard to these United States have Involved our Enemies in the greatest perplexity & Confusion.

The State of our Currency Seems now the greatest difficulty with us & requires Immediate attention, tho, the Credit of Continental Bills is rising in these parts, Congress Seem to be Of Opinion that Regulating the prices of Articles by Law will be of no advantage in the present Situation of our affairs. I expect a Resolution will pass this day recommending the suspension of Such Act where it is passd and Some other measures be adopted as a more Suitable & raddical Cure of the Evil.[2]

I hope Soon to be relieved by the arrival of Some one of the Delegates to take my Seat, my health requires Some relaxation from so close confinement & Fatigue in business. I am with Esteem, your humble Servt, Samll Huntington

RC (NRom).

[1] Benjamin Huntington (1736–1800), a Norwich, Conn., attorney who had represented Connecticut at the New England Convention on price regulation in January 1778, was currently speaker of the Connecticut House of Representatives. Although Benjamin did not become involved in national politics as early as his second cousin Samuel, he served as a delegate to Congress in 1780, 1782–83, and 1788, and represented Connecticut in the first federal Congress. He subsequently served as judge of the superior court of Connecticut from 1793 to 1798. Franklin B. Dexter, *Biographical Sketches of the Graduates of Yale College,* 6 vols. (New York: Henry Holt and Co, 1885–1919), 2:696–98.

[2] On June 4 Congress approved the report of a committee, to which Samuel Huntington had been appointed on the third, which recommended to the states that laws regulating prices be repealed or suspended. See *JCC,* 11:563, 569–70; and Henry Laurens to William Livingston, June 5, 1778, note 2. See also Henry Laurens to the States, June 10, 1778, note 1.

Henry Laurens to John Lewis Gervais

Dear Sir, 3d June 1778

My last to you was the 18th May by Messenger Sharp, Since which I have received none of your favors.

The Extreme quantity of business in public duty which Commands my constant attention deprives me of that pleasure which I should receive in holding a long conversation with you. I must submit at present to the necessity of referring you to papers which will be inclosed with this for intelligence to His Excellency the president & to Mr. Wells.

Communicate as much as possible & immediately to Mr. Williamson & Mr. Galphin especially the Indian Talks which will afford these friends much Satisfaction.[1]

I have assisted the Chief Justice with materials & means in part & he has sketched a long Letter for general information.[2] I shall very soon write to them, to Mr. Kershaw, Mr Warley, Mr. Zahn & to my Dear friend Mr. Manigault. I intreat you present me in the most affectionate & respectful terms to him & to Mrs. Manigault, I hope he will forgive my too long Silence. My Love, Compliments & kind salutations wherever due. I say nothing on my own affairs what can I say to the purpose. You will continue to write to me all that is needful—& now my respectful Compliments & best wishes to Mrs. Gervais & the Children concludes the present trouble from My Dear Sir Your very affectionate friend & Servant

LB (ScHi).

1 This day Congress read Gen. Philip Schuyler's May 11 talk with the Oneidas and the Tuscaroras in which he informed them of the alliance between France and the United States. See PCC, item 153, 3:317–21; and *JCC*, 11:563. George Galphin was Continental Indian agent in South Carolina and Andrew Williamson was a South Carolina frontiersman and militia colonel. James H. O'Donnell, III, *Southern Indians in the American Revolution* (Knoxville: University of Tennessee Press, 1973), pp. 20–25.

2 This "long Letter" by Chief Justice William Henry Drayton has not been found, nor have any similar Drayton letters mentioned by Laurens in his subsequent correspondence with various South Carolinians.

Henry Laurens to John Rutledge

Dear Sir, 3d June 1778

I had the honor of writing to you on the 4th Ulto by Messenger Cross.[1] Every day since has been prolific of intelligence but the great event which has occupied almost every one's conversation & expectation is not yet come. The Enemy, in all the bustle of preparation for evacuating Philadelphia, remained in possession the 1st Inst.

Within the present Inclosure you will find papers which will lay before you much of the Intelligence which I allude to, & from better hands. I trust Sir, you will collect from better hands such articles as are omitted in these. The Chief Justice, who has more time, is very Diligent in preparing a circular Letter full of matter, you will undoubtedly have the perusal of one of the Copies.

We have before us in Congress a plan for extending Commissioners & friendly commercial Treaties at the Courts of Lisbon, Hague, Stockholm, Copenhagen & St. Petersburgh.[2] Two whole days the subject has been upon the Anvil & very laboriously hammered. I have had the presumption to wish myself on the floor once or twice, from an opinion that even the little commercial knowledge I am possessed of might have struck light. There is not a Merchant present, & not a Book in Town to assist a Speculatist, but there's another obstacle to dispatch in this point, which as a silent spectator & auditor I can see pretty clearly & half understand—a plurality of Officers partly established & further aimed at. One of the Ministers at Versailles[3] who is Minister at Madrid, is tendered as the proper person to treat with Lisbon. The Minister intended, if practicable, for Berlin & Vienna[4] it is proposed should negotiate with the Northern

Courts; hence those minds, disposed to assign a Minister to a Court & no more, are embarrassed. Here a kind of delicacy, mark'd in my plain vocabulary, "false," restrains them from Speaking out, hitherto therefore the contest has been confined to advanced guards & now & then upon the flanks. If it became me, I should be very apt to carry arguments home by the shortest in-offensive course—in my present situation, however important the point, I do not see my duty in interposition either within or out of Doors. The Subject which has cost already two very precious days, will probably be postponed the third & possibly a very necessary measure too long delayed because some of us are not inclined to conduct it properly.

Captn. Landais a skilful Sea Officer has prevailed upon us to reduce in Stile the 74 Gun Ship which had been intended at Portsmouth. His plan which we have adopted, is to lay Decks only; to Mount on the lower 28 24 & on the upper 28 18-pounders. The building will be much less expensive—the Vessel sail faster—& be of equal force with 450 instead of 600 Men & now the workmen who had been taken off will be ordered to proceed.[5]

I am thinking very seriously of an enterprize against the place where you & I Sir once sent John Burnet, we may if the British Troops should withdraw & not pay Charles Town too serious a visit obtain proper Officers & Men for beginning the operation the 1st November, the most proper Month in the twelve.[6]

The Remark which I made on our Treaty of 6th Febry. respecting Bahama & the latent views of Spain, were not a little exploded here,[7] but since we have been told, that Court is desirous of repossessing Pensacola,[8] which might have been predicted without pretension to much depth in politics. Gentlemen begin to reflect our feelings however are generally porportioned to the distance from danger. New England's jealousies are excited by the proximity of Canada. Carolina sees the destruction of her Commerce, from Bahama & Florida in the hands of an Enemy, I say nothing of Georgia because she is not represented.

I have the honour to be &ca.

P.S. Major General Conway is just come to town in order to explain his meaning in a Letter of April, which Congress in his opinion had mistaken, and immediately notified him that his Resignation was accepted.[9] If he fails of success in that point he intimates to me his hopes of a Recommendatory Certificate of his behaviour—whether this alternative will be listned to, is doubtful. Gentlemen feel keen resentment for the unprovoked gross affronts which he offered in January last to our worthy Commander in Chief; besides, he has been strongly charged with malconduct in other respects which it seems incumbent on him to answer, before he can expect general countenance in Congress.

P.M. The forepart of this day devoted to Selling the Bear's Skin,[10] it might have diverted you Sir, to have heard the variety of sentiments delivered in each extreme upon this momentous Subject. The wrangling of two honest Lawyers who both mean the same thing is no novelty, but the manners of two Chief Justices[11] in conducting their debates were curious enough, & if other people were right they were both wrong. People are anxious to know how we shall dispose of the goods, Wares & Merchandize which we shall find in the City. Some seemingly Wise, some very foolish & many premature propositions must be expected in a three hours discussion of this nature. A new Report may reconcile all opinions to mine, *delivered only here,* & which for aught I know may be ranged in the second Class—"take especial care to guard against removal of any article after the Enemy shall have withdrawn. When the City is actually in your possession dispose of the Men & remaining property consistently with Justice, good Policy, & the Laws of the State."[12]

LB (ScHi).

1 Laurens' last extant letter to former South Carolina president John Rutledge was actually written on May 19, 1778.

2 See Committee of Congress Report, June 1, 1778.

3 Laurens inserted an asterisk at this point in the text to key the following note at the bottom of the page: "A L"—that is, Arthur Lee.

4 Laurens inserted an "x" at this point in the text to key the following note at the bottom of the page: "W L"—that is, William Lee.

5 See *JCC,* 11:555.

6 Laurens may be referring to an expedition against St. Augustine, although Congress had just sustained Gen. Robert Howe's refusal to participate in an attack on East Florida proposed by the government of Georgia. See Laurens to John Houstoun, June 1, 1778, note 2. On November 2, 1778, Congress did authorize Gen. Benjamin Lincoln, Howe's successor as commander of the southern military department, to undertake an expedition against East Florida, but the British invasion of Georgia the following month thwarted the plan. *JCC,* 12:1091, 1116–21.

7 See Laurens to Rutledge, May 4, 1778.

8 Arthur Lee had reported this intelligence about Spanish intentions in his February 10, 1778, letter to the Committee for Foreign Affairs, which according to the endorsement was received on May 18. See Wharton, *Diplomatic Correspondence,* 2:491–92; and PCC, item 83, fols. 127–34.

9 For a discussion of Congress' acceptance of Gen. Thomas Conway's resignation, see Laurens to Washington, April 28, 1778, note 3.

10 Laurens' allusion to the old adage "catch the bear before you sell his skin" was stimulated by the delegates' debate this day of a committee report on the purchase of "cloathing and other Articles" for the Continental Army that might be left behind after the British evacuated Philadelphia. *JCC,* 11:564–65. This report was prompted by Washington's request for guidance on the subject in his May 31–June 1 letter to Laurens. Washington, *Writings* (Fitzpatrick), 11:498–500.

11 William Henry Drayton and Thomas McKean.

12 The resolves on this issue that Congress approved on June 4 did not precisely correspond with Laurens' suggestions. See *JCC,* 11:571.

Robert Morris to Jonathan Potts

Dear Sir
Manheim June 3d. 1778

Since you left this I have received a letter [. . .] from Carter Braxton Esqr of Virginia telling me, that as all the British Ships of War have left Chesapeak Bay he had thoughts of sending the Nine Packages of Medicines under his care by Water to Mr. Jonathan Hudson at Baltimore, which I mention that you may write Mr Hudson what to do with them shou'd they come there, however as I gave Doctr Shippen an order on Mr Braxton for them long since, I shou'd think that order will stop their coming by Water if he sent it forward, but you can give directions both ways & one or other will take effect.

I am Sir, Your Obed hble servt. Robt Morris

RC (DLC). Addressed: "Jona. Potts Esqr, Depy Director Genl of the Hospitals, York Town."

Henry Laurens to Baron Steuben

Sir,
York-Town, June 4th 1778

I had the honor of your Letter of 27th May by the hands of Mr. Ternant on Sunday last, which I laid before Congress, and had appointed an hour for waiting on that Gentleman, to the Board of War, but some other circumstances engaged his time.[1] It is a very extraordinary thing for me to be a whole hour from this Table unless I am in Congress, and I was the more concerned at the disappointment, because I had intended to have introduced Mr Ternant to several of the Delegates, but indeed we are in such a place, and fare so meanly, as to render it painful to have Gentlemen introduced, because it is not in our power to shew that respect which we would wish to do to Strangers.

Mr. Ternant addressed himself to the Board of War, but as his departure was more sudden than I had expected, and no report concerning him having been yet sent to Congress, I am ignorant of his proceedings there, I have often heard of Mr Ternants merit, and shall be happy on that account, as well as from my respect for you Sir, to render him any service in my power, which I must candidly inform you is as limited and circumscribed as that of any other Member of Congress. I have the honor to be with very sincere esteem &c. yours &c. Henry Laurens

Tr (MH–H).

[1] A transcript of Steuben's May 27 letter to Laurens, in which he announced that he was sending Jean Baptiste Ternant to York to receive "several Instruc-

tions" from the Board of War pertaining to the inspector general's department and recommended him to Congress' "peculiar Consideration," is in the Laurens Papers, ScHi. Ternant, who was serving under Steuben as sub-inspector of infantry without rank, was commissioned a lieutenant colonel in the Continental Army on September 25, 1778, and ordered to serve as "inspector to the troops" in South Carolina and Georgia. *JCC,* 12:952.

Henry Laurens to George Washington

Sir. York Town 4th June 1778.

Since my last under the 31st May, I have had the honor of presenting Your Excellency's sundry favours of the 21st, 28th, 28th & 31st Ulto. & 1st Inst.[1] These are dispersed in the hands of Committees and at present I have only to forward to Your Excellency, the undermentioned Papers.

1. Establishment of the American Army by Acts of Congress of the 28th [27th] & 29 May & 1st [2d] June—about 200 Copies in two Bundles.[2] Your Excellency will be pleased to make the necessary distribution in the Army at Valley forge.

2. about 500 Copies of the Oath of Abjuration &c.[3] If Your Excellency shall find it necessary to call for more of these, be pleased to give me an early intimation, in order to set the press to work.

Copies of the Establishment of the Army, I mean to transmit to morrow to General Gates, General Sullivan & General Heath, & have already sent a few to the President of South Carolina, to General Howe & General Moultrie. I have requested the president to order Copies in both Gazettes at Charles Town & I presume all the Printers in the several states will adopt them to fill up a part of their respective Publications. If any further step shall appear to be necessary I request Your Excellency will be pleased to direct me. I intend to morrow to send Copies to Maryland, Virginia & North Carolina & in due course to each of the United States, these, tho' in the line of my Duty may appear to be works of supererogation, since Your Excellency as Commander in Chief will I presume give them all the circulation that is necessary, & also that a Mode must still be adopted for carrying the arrangement into Execution. In the mean time these will serve at least for general information, & being without special direction from Congress I have done what appears to be inoffensive.

I have the honour to be, With the highest Esteem & Respect, Sir, Your Excellency's Most obedient & humble servant,

Henry Laurens,
President of Congress

5th. Inclosed your Excellency will find an Act of Congress of yesterday for carrying the Establishment of the Army into Execution.[4]

Your Excellency's favor of the 2d is come to hand & presented.[5]

RC (DLC).

[1] These letters are in PCC, item 152, 6:43, 47–48, 51, 55–57, and Washington, *Writings* (Fitzpatrick), 11:429–30, 471–72, 498–500. The letter of the "1st Inst." was actually a postscript to Washington's May 31 letter.

[2] For these resolves, see *JCC*, 11:538–43, 554–55, 560–61. For the John Dunlap broadside (Evans, *Am. Bibliography*, no. 16126) in which they were printed, see illustration, these *Letters*, 9:762. For a discussion of their provenance, see ibid, p. 695n.2.

[3] For the oath of allegiance that Congress decided on February 3, 1778, to require of "every officer who holds or shall hereafter hold a commission or office from Congress," see *JCC*, 10:114–15.

[4] See *JCC*, 11:570.

[5] Washington's June 2 letter to Laurens is in PCC, item 152, 6:59–60, and Washington, *Writings* (Fitzpatrick), 12:8–9.

Daniel Roberdeau to George Washington

Sir, York June 4th, 1778

I am ever loath to intrude on your Excellency, as I well know the great embarrassments attending your important sphere do not admit of any unnecessary or fruitless Correspondence, but I am as sensible of your attention to the most minute Circumstance which has a tendancy to promote the common Cause, therefore permit me to inform your Excellency that the want of Smelters of lead is the only remora now in the way of supplying your Army in the most speedy & ample manner with that necessary Article, now transported from distant parts of the Continent, from a vein of Ore in this State, within nine miles of the navigation of a branch of Juniata. A large quantity of Ore is at the pits mouth, a mill for stamping constructed, & a Furnace will be finished, I expect within ten days from this time, but Artificers of the above Class are so scarce in this young Country, that having tryed to obtain them by advertising and from Deserters from the Brittish Army, I am at length constrained reluctantly to trouble you on the Subject.

Colonel Scammell hints an expedient of sending into Philada, to bring out such, with a promise of a handsome reward. I would most cheerfully give such reward, but know not how to set about so hazardous an enterprize. My own mind has suggested the probability of such Characters being in your own Army, and whether they, only three wanted, can serve their Country equally in the capacity of Soldiers. One Edward Harris a Sergeant of the 15th Virginia Regiment has been mentioned to me as a man of sobriety, integrity and ingenuity in analyzing Metals, but does not profess to be compitent to the Business on a large scale, he has been spoke to in my behalf by Major Clark, and is willing to be enlarged on furlow to make a tryal. I will not trouble your Excellency by enlarging on these hints. Major Clark will proffer Encouragements if you should think proper, to issue your orders for obtaining these useful Artificers, without whom the prospect however flattering of a great internal resource of lead must fail.[1] To prevent the Evacuation of the frontier of Bedford County and for the general defence against Indian incursions I have built with Logs at the Mine in Sinking Spring Valley at the foot of Tushes Mountain, a Fort, Cabbin fashion, 50 yds. square with a Bastion at each Corner. The Fort consists of 48 Cabbins about twelve feet square exclusive of the Bastions. I left Major Robt. Clugage a discreet Officer in Command with about seventy men chiefly Militia, with a few Continental Troops raised to serve until the 1st Decr. next. I most sincerely congratulate your Excellency on the happy prospect of publick Affairs and am with unfeigned regard, Your Excellencys most obedient & very huml. Ser,

Daniel Roberdeau

RC (DLC).

[1] Washington's June 15 response, reporting that Sergeant Harris had been directed to join Roberdeau and that an inquiry was being conducted to locate two other experienced smelters, is in Washington, *Writings* (Fitzpatrick), 12:65–66. For additional information on Roberdeau's activities in developing a lead mine in western Pennsylvania, see Roberdeau to George Bryan, May 30, 1778, note; and Darwin H. Stapleton, "General Daniel Roberdeau and the Lead Mine Expedition, 1778–1779," *Pennsylvania History* 38 (October 1971): 361–71.

Samuel Huntington to Jabez Huntington

Sir York Town 5th June 1778

As I have no Important Intelligence to Communicate more than is contained in my Letter to the Governor, & what you will otherways obtain, I do my self the pleasure to give you the following Annecdote.

It Seems a Cowardly Tory of large Landed Estate in York County had fled to the enemy in Philadelphia the winter past, & when he discovered the movements of the enemy shiping their Stores, baggage &c of late; Indicating their departure he applied to their General to know what He should do, the General replied he was busy & sent him to an under Officer. The Tory with anxiety asked the Officer what he should do as he perceived they were going away. The officer told him He must do as they did when in difficulty make the best shift he could. The Tory Still dissatisfied told him all this was come upon him for being loyal & faithfull to the King & queried what shall I do, I expected protection. The officer replied go seek a passage on board some vessel &c. The Tory with vehement anxiety queried but what the Devil shall I do with my Estate, The Officer replied, Damn you! why did you not Stay at home & fight to defend it with your Country & so dismissd his applicant.

Thus the Story goes; said to be reported by one who heard the Conversation, but I forbear to mention the Tories name at present.

I am Sir with Esteem, your humble servant,

Saml Huntington

RC (CSmH).

Henry Laurens to Nathanael Greene

Dear Sir, 5th June 1778

Yesterday I presented your favor of the 1st Inst. to Congress, thence it was committed to the Board of War & not yet Reported upon,[1] I have therefore no Commands from the House & you will be so good as to receive this as private which I mean to convey you the Sentiments of Gentlemen who are your friends. I know you must be anxious for an answer, this is the best I can at present return. The moment Congress shall have determined on the Subject of your application you shall be properly informed.

I have the honour to be

LB (DNA: PCC, item 13).

[1] Quartermaster General Nathanael Greene's June 1 letter to Laurens—in which he requested a set of the regulations pertaining to his department and asked if he was authorized to supply Continental officers at public expense with valises and portmanteaus to store the excess baggage they had been ordered by Washington to leave behind at Valley Forge or to replace horses and riding equipment lost in the line of duty—is in PCC, item 192, fols. 5–7; and Greene, *Papers* (Showman), 2:420–22.

Henry Laurens to the Marquis de Lafayette

Dear Sir, 5th June 1778[1]

I have before me Your Excellency's favor of the 1st[2] which reached me late last Night & at the Same time one for General Conway which I delivered to him.

Your Excellency put rather a hard task on me by desiring me Speak to Congress on behalf of General Conway after referring to Your Excellency's Sentiments of that Gentleman; nevertheless I had determined in the most proper & becoming manner to have presented the Marquis delafayette's message in his favor, had not the General himself put it out of my power.

General Conway called on me this Morning & after some time spent in a manner which appeared to me very extraordinary he expressed his "Surprize that I had delivered to Congress his Letter of 22d April intimating his desire to resign his Commission"—said he "had intended it a private confidential Letter, that he had also written to the president of the Board of War & expected I would have conferred with him upon the Subject, instead of doing so, I had *made* a private Letter public."[3] All this & much more of the same specie, were expressed in manner & terms altogether dissonant from the General's former soft mode of address. I had thought that I had learned to be surprized at nothing, but in this instance I discovered my mistake, I was *greatly* surprized at the weakness & wickedness of the attempt.

I replied to the General, "if I have erred it has been unwittingly, Your Letter appeared to me to have been intended for Congress, I never had the honor of a private Correspondence with General Conway, it would have been improper in me to have conferred with the President of the Board of War, if a conference had been expected why had not the president called upon me. You injure me exceedingly by the imputation of exposing in public what was intended to be private. I feel my self satisfied that this behaviour is unprovoked & unmeritted, but General, the Letter is at hand, let us appeal to that. I have really forgot the Contents."

I then sent to the Secretary's Office for the Letter, the perusal of it Heightned my surprize. I shall take the Liberty of enclosing an exact Copy in order that you may judge Sir whether it had been designed to be private. The General has delivered me a Memorial directed to Congress,[4] I intimated that with his memorial, "I should deliver also his Letter of the 18th [22d] April & take the sense of Congress whether it was private or public, that if it should appear I had acted improperly, I would make every becoming concession."

Accordingly I appealed to Congress, I could do no less under so gross a charge. The House were astonished & condescended to offer a Resolution in my favour, which I declined with thanks, adding "that their opinion was satisfactory to me without further trouble—the Letter would always Speak for itself." The General's Memorial was ordered to lie on the Table, & although I am sure there were Gentlemen present who had been disposed to speak in the General's favor, yet there was not a dissenting Voice.[5]

Your Excellency as a Man of honor & feeling I am persuaded will be surprized too at this very extraordinary circumstance, but how much more when you are told that on the 18th May the General wrote to Congress & apologized for the former Letter by saying he was an Irishman & therefore hoped proper allowances would be made for his mode of expression, which had not been intended to give offence, or words to this effect for I have not the Letter before me.[6]

The Letter in question of 22d April is undubitably public.

On the 18th May the General acknowledges it to be so by apologizing for its tenor.

On the 4th June he modestly avers *upon his honor* that it was intended to be private & in the face of the Letter maintains that position.

Sir I am happy in a mind capable of forgiving the greatest injuries & incapable of Malice. I would now rather do General Conway a favor than requite his injustice but I desire never again to converse or correspond with him.[7]

I request Your Excellency will be so obliging to shew this to Colonel John Laurens & also the inclosed Letter.[8] I have taken up so much of your Excellency's time & have also so many other Letters to write as renders it necessary for me to conclude.

I shall have the honor of writing again in a day or two. Mean time I continue with the highest regard & Esteem.

LB (ScHi).

[1] Laurens may have drafted this letter on June 4, the day Congress tabled the memorial from Gen. Thomas Conway discussed in it, although he may have begun writing just after midnight the morning of the fifth. In either event, in his June 5 letter to his son John, Laurens referred to "my Letter of yesterday to the Marquis."

[2] Lafayette's June 1 letter to Laurens, urging him to assist General Conway in his quest for "some kind of certificate from Congress," is in Lafayette, *Papers* (Idzerda), 2:64–65.

[3] See also Laurens to Washington, April 28, 1778, note 3.

[4] Conway's June 4 memorial, in which he unconvincingly argued that Congress had misconstrued his April 22 letter to Laurens as an offer to resign from the army, is in PCC, item 41, 2:51–53.

[5] See *JCC*, 11:567.

[6] Conway's May 18 letter to Congress, which was read and tabled on May 26, is in PCC, item 159, fols. 477–79.

[7] That Laurens was not the only delegate who was hostile to Conway's claims is evident from the general's own account of the reception he encountered at York at this time. "I never had a sufficient idea of Cabals," Conway explained in a letter to Horatio Gates on June 7, "untill I reach'd this place. My reception you may imagine was not a warm one. I must except Mr Sam Adams, Coll. Richard Henry Lee and a few others who are attached to you but who can not oppose the torrent. Before my arrival General Mifflin had joined general Washington's army Where he Commands a Division. One Mr Carroll from Maryland upon whose friendshipp I Depended is one of the hottest of the Cabal. He told me a few Days agoe almost Literally, that any Body that Displea'd or did not admire the Commander in chief ought not to be Kept in the army. Mr Carroll might be a good papist, but I am sure the Sentiments he expresses are neither roman nor catholick. I expect to Depart from this Court in a very few Days." Gates Papers, NHi.

[8] The "inclosed Letter" was a copy of the April 22 letter from Conway to Laurens that had prompted Congress to accept the general's resignation. See Laurens to John Laurens, June 5, 1778.

Henry Laurens to John Laurens

My Dear son, York Town 5th June 1778

I wrote you a few hasty lines this Morning, immediately after which I had occasion to wish that a little dash of hypocrisy had been thrown into my frame. In came General Conway with a Letter in his hand & in an obsequious address, different from that of yesterday, asked me if I were sending Letters to Camp. I decently replied in the affirmative, desiring him to put his Letter upon the Table, it should be forwarded with other dispatches immediately. So far duty in Office demanded good manners on my part. He then asked in a low & soft tone "did not the Marquis delafayette Mr President write you in my behalf" & was proceeding to further conversation, I felt the injury he had attempted, & instantly replied, I have really forgot General Conway & I must beg Sir you will excuse me.[1]

I had informed him yesterday Morning so very explicitly that the Marquis had writ to me & he had extorted from me repetitions of the same so very often, I judged it necessary to intimate that my memory was as defective as his own, & by begging him to excuse me, I meant, from all future conversation or correspondence. If this honest & frank proceedure is censurable then I have cause to wish for a little dash of hypocrisy, but upon a fair estimate of my past life & a review of a multitude of extraordinary circumstances which have chequered it, I find a Balance largely in favor of honesty & therefore I cast out the wish.

You will have seen my Letter of yesterday to the Marquis & General Conway's of the 22d April. A Copy of this shall be inclosed & also Copy of his Letter of the 18th May—lay these together & tell me if I could notwithstanding my general maxim resist against surprize at the audacity of a Man who should in rude language in my own House charge me in presence of one of my Secretaries with having made a confidential private Letter, public, to his prejudice—& repeating the same in a Memorial to Congress, charging me with the Memorial in order that I might exhibit & Read my own Indictment.[2] You will observe in this Letter of the 18th May he acknowledges the Receipt of mine the in which he had been informed that his former Letter of 18th [22d] April had been presented to Congress &c.[3] Can there be a stronger instance of effrontry than appears in his conduct by trumping up a pretence on the 4th June that his Letter was private, confidential & not intended for public view. Congress happened at the reading of his Memorial to be very full; every Member seemed struck with amazement & although there were several Gentlemen who I am sure would otherwise have pressed warmly for some kind of handsome dismission to him, there was not a dissenting voice to the Order for dismissing his Memorial without consideration. I'll trouble you no longer about this compound of weakness & impudence.

You will oblige me by transmitting if you can procure the Philadelphia account of the late Military excursion, particulars of General Grant &c.

I am still of opinion that there is stratagem in Mr. Clinton's proceeding, possibly he may be preparing for withdrawing his Troops upon the arrival of the expected Commissioners, from an opinion that we shall persist in our late Resolution.[4] Consider 'tis above a Month since he or his predecessor propagated the account of their intended removal, the object which required it, if any must be of importance—have his motives been consonant, certainly not. I therefore smile at the various opinions which I hear solemnly delivered, for the disposal of effects in the City & view them equally shrewd with his who sold the Bear Skin.[5] You must have another Ceremony, before he moves, for Exchange of Prisoners, he will find it very expensive to remove them by Water & very troublesome & hazardous to take them a Land March through New Jersey where he must expect to be harrassed. In a word, 'tis impossible to trace minutely his designs—don't trust false fires—watch his motions & [*be*] double guarded.

My Dear Son, I pray God to bless you. Henry Laurens

[*P.S.*] Inclosed you will find a Dominica Gazette containing a Letter from Lancaster &c. When you have done with it I beg you will return it.

Jacob Shubrick & Will Cattle, both Officers in the Carolina Regiments dead.

Dick Shubrick died a few Months ago.

RC (MHi: William Gilmore Simms Collection deposit, 1973).

1 See Laurens to Lafayette, this date.

2 See ibid., note 4.

3 Thomas Conway's May 18 letter to Laurens, in which he acknowledged receipt of the president's May 7 letter informing him of Congress' acceptance of his offer to resign from the army, is in PCC, item 159, fols. 477–79.

4 Laurens is referring to Congress' April 22, 1778, resolve not to enter into any negotiations with British peace commissioners unless they first agreed either to withdraw all British military and naval forces from the United States or recognize American independence. *JCC*, 10:374–80.

5 See Laurens to John Rutledge, June 3, 1778, note 10.

Henry Laurens to William Livingston

Sir, 5th June 1778.

I had the honor of writing to Your Excellency the 25th Ulto. by Doctr. Scudder, & since that time of presenting to Congress your Excellency's favors of the 20th & 26th of the same Month.[1]

At present I have only in charge to transmit the inclosed Act of Congress of yesterday recommending a suspension or Repeal of Acts of Assembly for regulating prices of Goods in all the States where such Acts have been passed.[2] I have the honor to be

[*P.S.*] Aside—late in the Evening.

I am just now honored by Addresses from Lord Howe & Sir H. Clinton of which when matured your Excellency shall be further informed.[3]

LB (DNA: PCC, item 13).

1 In his May 20 and 26 letters to Laurens, Governor Livingston acknowledged receipt of Congress' May 6 resolves on the French alliance, May 8 address to the people of the United States, and May 11 proclamation on neutral rights and requested more "Commissions, Bonds & Instructions for Captains of Privateers." See PCC, item 67, fols. 367, 371; and *JCC*, 11:468–71, 474–81, 486. For Laurens' response to Livingston's request, see Laurens to Livingston, July 17, 1778.

2 See *JCC*, 11:569–70. Congress passed this "Act" after reading Commissary Geneial Jeremiah Wadsworth's May 27 letter to Laurens as well as his May 26 able to obtain beef for the army because of a state law which had set the price of memorial to the Connecticut Assembly in which he complained that he was unbeef too low. PCC, item 78, 23:499–503. See also James Lovell to Samuel Adams, April 18, 1778, note 11.

3 See William Henry Drayton's Draft Letter to Lord Howe, June 6, 1779.

Henry Laurens to Jonathan Trumbull, Sr.

Sir 5th June [1778]

I had the honor of the 3d Inst. of presenting your Excellency's favour of 28th Ulto. to Congress with the correspondence of Mr. Tryon inclosed.[1]

Congress were well pleased with your Excellency's Reply & have ordered it to be printed.

Within the present Inclosure your Excellency will receive an Act of Congress of yesterday recommending to the Several States to suspend or repeal Laws passed for regulating prices of Commodities.[2]

I have the honor to be

LB (DNA: PCC, item 13).

1 Governor Trumbull's May 28 letter to Laurens is in PCC, item 66, fol. 394. Enclosed with it were copies of a May 21 letter from Gov. William Tryon to Trumbull, in which the Connecticut governor was asked to distribute copies of

three parliamentary acts of reconciliation, and Trumbull's May 25 reply, in which the British official's request was emphatically denied. Ibid., fol. 398. For a discussion of an earlier exchange of correspondence between Trumbull and Tryon on the same issue, see Connecticut Delegates to Trumbull, May 18, 1778, note 3.

2 Laurens also transmitted a copy of this act with a brief covering letter he wrote this day to Commissary General Jeremiah Wadsworth, who was then in Connecticut trying to purchase beef for the army. John F. Reed Collection, King of Prussia, Pa.; and PCC, item 13, 1:352.

Henry Laurens to George Washington

Sir. York Town 5 June 1778.

I had the honor of writing to Your Excellency under yesterdays date with a P.S. of this Morning by Saxton.

A Report on Your Excellency's Letter of the 1st Inst. relative to measures necessary to be taken in Philadelphia in case the Enemy shall abandon that City had been considered in part yesterday & I had entertained hopes the whole would have been determined this Morning, but other business having interfered & occasioned delay I judge it necessary to transmit the inclosed Resolve, which, if it is ever to have operation, I apprehend cannot reach Your Excellency too soon.[1]

I have the honor to be, With the highest Esteem & Respect, Sir, Your Excellency's Most Obedient servant,

Henry Laurens, President of Congress

[*P.S.*] Your Excellency's favor of the 4th together with divers dispatches from Sr. H. Clinton & Lord Howe &c. came to hand late this Evening now 10 oClock, shall be laid before Congress to morrow.[2]

RC (DLC).

1 See *JCC*, 11:571; and Laurens to John Rutledge, June 3, 1778, note 10.

2 See William Henry Drayton's Draft Letter to Lord Howe, June 6, 1778.

Thomas McKean to William A. Atlee

Dear Sir,[1] York-Town. June 5th. 1778.

Upon receipt of your favour of the 26th Ulto. I applied to some of the members of the Board of war respecting the Instructions they had given to General Pulaski for inlisting Prisoners of war, and was told they had given such, and had wrote to you about it; this made me think it unnecessary to write to you, but upon examining the Acts of Congress on this head I found the Board were wrong, and that no prisoners of war can be inlisted in that Legion, or in any other Corps. Congress decided accordingly yesterday, of which you will be informed by the President.[2] Tho' we have a surplus of privates of the Enemy at present after exchanging our own, yet they have Citizens and may make more prisoners; besides from my knowledge of the human heart I am convinced that if these prisoners of war were to come to a close & hot engagement with the enemy, the fear of the latter in case of their being made prisoners would induce them to seek safety in flight.

Your favour of yesterday is come to hand, and my opinion, respecting the propriety of admitting the persons proclaimed traitors by Council, is as follows. The Proclamation amounts to no more than a charge of treason, the not surrendering by the day prescribed is full conviction, and the Act of Assembly pronounces the judgment (if I may use the phraze) or attaints the party.[3] Now if the Evidence amounts to no more than common fame, or public notoriety, that the party named in the proclamation had left his usual place of abode and gone into the city of Philadelphia, without some proof of an Overt-Act, such as bearing arms, or annexing his person to the troops of the Enemy as a pioneer, labourer or soldier, or furnishing them with provisions, or intelligence &c and he surrenders himself within the time limited in the proclamation, I should think he ought to be bailed. The Justices of the Supream Court, in Term-time, or any one of them, in the vacation, have a discretionary power to bail in all cases whatsoever, even for murder or treason; but the *general* rule is, if it stands indifferent or doubtful in the opinion of the Judge, whether the party is innocent or guilty, he ought to be bailed; if the evidence of guilt preponderates it should be done with caution; if it is clear the party should be committed and no Bail taken, unless for the cause of sickness, or an infectious disease prevailing & spreading in the Goal &c. Agreeable to this opinion I have admitted James Bracken of this county (whose name is inserted in one of the proclamations) to Bail, and shall in all other cases conduct accordingly; but I am not satisfied that a Justice of the peace can take bail in these cases, I think he must either send the party to a Judge of the Supreme court for examination or commit him.

After a sufficient time has elapsed for discriminating, the Sta[te may?] no doubt grant a general Pardon, excepting your cruel fellows & some men of property, whose estates really ought to be confiscated, tho' their lives are spared. Parricides should at least give some evidence of repentance before they are forgiven, and they deserve the punishment of suspence at any rate. The application and interest that will be made by the relatives & friends of the culprits for mercy will create respect to the Rulers, and their granting it on every reasonable occasion will reconcile & endear men to the

Government: besides Pardoning is a God-like power, and a God-like virtue.

I am, dear Sir, with my best respects to Mrs. Atlee, Your most obedient humble servant, Tho M:Kean

RC (DLC). Addressed: "The Honoble William Augustus Atlee Esquire At Lancaster."

[1] William A. Atlee (1735–93), a prominent leader of the revolutionary movement in Lancaster, Pa., during 1774–76, had been a deputy commissary of prisoners since his appointment by Elias Boudinot in August 1777. By virtue of his appointment as assistant judge of the Pennsylvania Supreme Court in April 1777, he was also a judicial colleague of Chief Justice McKean. *Pa. Archives*, 2d ser. 3:687.

[2] The Board of War also instructed Deputy Commissary of Prisoners Atlee on this issue this day. "Your letter to Congress of the 2d instant," Col. Timothy Pickering wrote, "has been referred to the board, with the sense of Congress intimated at the same time, that prisoners of war should not be inlisted into *any* corps in the service of the United States. The licence given Genl. Pulaski to inlist prisoners, is to be considered as recalled. The licence was founded on a supposed intention of Congress to permit the inlistment of prisoners into that particular corps. Prisoners were in fact included in the resolve (as originally drawn up) as well as deserters; and tho' the former were finally struck out; yet the information given to the board led them to the determination mentioned in their former letter to you on the subject." Peter Force Collection, DLC.

For a discussion of this issue, see Henry Laurens to Atlee, May 29, 1778, note 2.

[3] The Pennsylvania Council's May 8 proclamation is in *Pa. Council Minutes*, 11:483–85.

Oliver Wolcott to Laura Wolcott

My Dear, York Town 5 June 1778

My last to you was of the 1st instant which you probably will receive from the Post Office Hartford. Nothing Material has occurred since then. We do not hear that the Enemy have left Philadelpa, but they undoubtedly will do so in a Very few Days if they have not already done it. The most of their Ships it is said are gone down to N Castle. A most dreadfull Anxiety excercises the Philadelphian Torys. The capital ones go off with the Enemy. Others less guilty determin to trust to the Clemency of their Country. Steps are taken to Obviate some Mischief which might be apprehended upon the first Evacuation of the City—so that I hope the Disorders which might be otherwise expected, will be prevented. It is supposed the Enemy will in the first Instance go to N York—from thence it is not improbable Many will go to the West Indies. Indeed I should not think it Very Strange if the whole should leave the Continent in a short Time, for if G Britain enters into a War with France the Forces which she has here will be wanted to Defend her own Dominions. If she shall chuse to Avoid this War and shall admit our Independence, which I rather expect, her Troops will be unnecessary here. My own Opinion is that G Britain will not continue a Land War in this Country—and I am perswaded that the proud Spirit of that Nation is more humbled than it ever has been since it had an Existence. This great Variation in the Circumstances of our Affairs "is the Lord's Doings" and it is truly Wonderfull. May We ascribe it, to that Great Cause which produces all the Good which We Experience.

I imagine that Congress will Return to Philadelphia within a forthnight or three Weeks as it is Very desirable to regain the Ground which has been lost. Altho for myself were I to continue in this Country during the summer I should much preferr being here than to be in the City.

I have heard Nothing from you since Brown came down. I hope that a mercifull Providence takes care of you and the Family. I trust it will not be long before I shall see you. You will know sooner than I shall when it will be—as it will depend upon my being releived.

I mentioned in my former Letter that I had been informed precisely of the Events of the last Election, by which it seems my Freind was greatly mistaken. Had it indeed been otherwise I should not have suffered but a Slight uneasiness.

Oliver will attend to the objects of Peace. The War will have but a Very Short Duration in my Opinion. The Tickets of which I took the Numbers are all drawn, Blank, so that We must Venture again. I Wish as you have Opportunity that you would let me hear from you. By a Letter from Mr. Elsworth I suppose it is probable that he will not be here sooner than by the End of the present Month.

A Recommendation of Congress goes by this Express to our assembly to suspend or Repeal the Regulating Act. My Love to my Children and Freinds. By the Blessing of God I do and have injoyed more Health than ever I did before on this Service. I am, Yours most affectionately, Oliver Wolcott

RC (CtHi).

William Henry Drayton's Draft Letter to Lord Howe

My Lord [June 6, 1778][1]

I have had the honor to lay your ⟨*Lordships*⟩ letter of the with the Acts of the British Parliament enclosed before Congress: and I am instructed to acquaint your Lordship that they have already expressed their sentiments upon[2] those Acts in a publication of the 22nd of April last.[3]

Your Lordship may be assured, that when the King of Great Britain shall be seriously disposed to put an end to the unprovoked & cruel war ⟨*that has been*⟩ waged against these United States, Congress will readily attend to such terms of Peace, as may consist with the Honor of Independent Nations, the Interest of their Constituents, & the sacred regard they mean to pay to Treaties. I have the honor to be, My Lord &c.

MS (ScHi). In the hand of William Henry Drayton and amended by Henry Laurens. Endorsed by Laurens: "Draught to Ld Howe & Sir H. Clinton 6 June 1778." This is one of a number of congressional documents among Laurens' private papers that he failed to lodge with Secretary Thomson for inclusion in the PCC.

1 William Henry Drayton drafted this letter for President Laurens' signature in response to a May 27 letter from Lord Howe and a June 3 letter from Sir Henry Clinton—two members of the Carlisle peace commission. Both had forwarded to Congress two acts of Parliament embodying Lord North's latest peace proposals and a third repealing the Massachusetts Government Act of 1774. Howe's letter is in PCC, item 78, 11:299; Clinton's is in the Peter Force Collection, DLC. These letters and papers were transmitted to Congress by Washington with his June 4 letter to Laurens, which is in PCC, item 152, 6:63, and Washington, *Writings* (Fitzpatrick), 12:18. Washington also sent Congress letters addressed to him by Howe dated May 27 and by Clinton, dated May 30 and June 3, all notifying him of the same three acts of Parliament. See PCC, item 152, 6:67, 71, 75.

Congress read Howe's and Clinton's letters to Laurens this day and referred them to a committee made up of Drayton, Richard Henry Lee, Gouverneur Morris, John Witherspoon, and Samuel Adams, who were instructed to "retire into the next room and prepare an answer to Lord Howe and General Clinton's letters." After both Drayton and Lee had composed draft replies to Lord Howe, Congress this day approved Drayton's more moderate letter for transmittal to Howe under President Laurens' signature and directed that "a similar letter be sent to General Clinton." See *JCC,* 11:572–74; and Richard Henry Lee's Draft Letter to Lord Howe, this date. Laurens then sent a slightly modified version of Drayton's draft to Howe and Clinton. It is interesting to note that Laurens dated the RC's of his letters to Howe and Clinton "6th May" instead of "6th June 1778," although both letters are dated correctly in Laurens' presidential letterbook. See the copy Laurens made this date of his letter to Howe in the Washington Papers, DLC; the RC of his letter to Clinton in P.R.O. 30/55, 11:106; and PCC item 13, 1:355–56. Finally, it is also noteworthy that at least one delegate considered even Drayton's moderate draft letter to Howe and Clinton too harsh. See Charles Carroll of Carrollton to Charles Carroll, Sr., June 7, 1778.

For further information on the work of the Carlisle commission, see Weldon A. Brown, *Empire or Independence: A Study in the Failure of Reconciliation, 1774–1783* (Baton Rouge: Louisiana State University Press, 1941), chaps. 9–10; Alan S. Brown, "William Eden and the American Revolution" (Ph.D. diss., University of Michigan, 1953), chap. 5; and Alan S. Brown, "The British Peace Offer of 1778: A Study in Ministerial Confusion," *Papers of the Michigan Academy of Science, Arts and Letters* 40 (1955): 249–60.

2 At this point in Drayton's draft Laurens added the words "bills not essentially different from."

3 For Congress' earlier response to Lord North's conciliatory proposals when rumors of them reached America in April, see *JCC,* 10:374–80.

Henry Laurens to George Washington

Sir York Town 6th May [*i.e.* June] 1778.

Referring to my Letter of yesterday's date forwarded by the hands of Messenger Davis, I proceed to inform Your Excellency that having laid before Congress the Letters from Lord Viscount Howe & Sir H Clinton I have received instructions from the House to return the necessary replies.

Accordingly, Your Excellency will find within this Inclosure a Packet directed to His Lordship & another to Sir Henry which Your Excellency will be pleased to send forward.

I requested permission of Congress to transmit to Your Excellency Copies of these Addresses, which Your Excellency will find inclosed in one draught admitting the proper variations of Title.

I have the honor to be, With the most perfect Regard & Respect, Sir, Your Excellency's Obedient & most humble servant,

Henry Laurens,
President of Congress.

RC (DLC).

Richard Henry Lee's Draft Letter to Lord Howe

My Lord [June 6, 1778][1]

The unprovoked and cruel war that has been waged against these States, renders every idea inadmissible, that proposes a return to the domination of that Power which by its own Acts of devastation and slaughter, has forced a separation. The Acts of the British Parliament lately transmitted by your Lordship having this domination principally in view require no further comment. But the good people of N.A. my Lord not insensible of what belongs to humanity, can forgive their enemies, and wish to stop the effusion of human blood. When therefore the king of G.B. shall be seriously disposed to peace, Congress will readily attend to such terms as may consist with the honor of Independent nations, with the interest of their Constituents, and with the sacred regard they mean to pay to Treaties.

By order of Congress
⟨*H. Laurens*⟩

MS (ViU). In the hand of Richard Henry Lee.

1 Richard Henry Lee wrote this intended letter to Lord Howe as a member of the committee appointed this day to formulate a response to recently received letters from Howe and Sir Henry Clinton forwarding three conciliatory acts of Par-

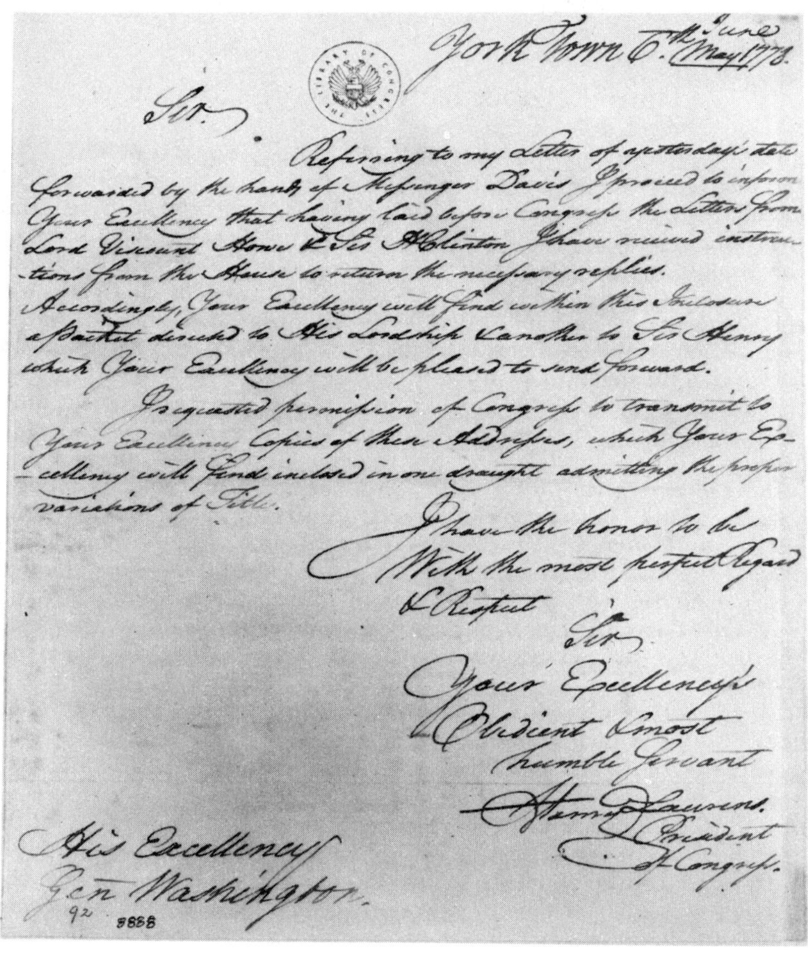

York Town 6th June ~~May~~ 1778.

Sir

Referring to my Letter of yesterday's date forwarded by the hands of Messenger Davis I proceed to inform Your Excellency that having laid before Congress the Letters from Lord Viscount Howe & Sir H Clinton I have received instructions from the House to return the necessary replies.

Accordingly, Your Excellency will find within this Inclosure a Packet directed to His Lordship & another to Sir Henry which Your Excellency will be pleased to send forward.

I requested permission of Congress to transmit to Your Excellency Copies of these Addresses, which Your Excellency will find inclosed in one draught admitting the proper variations of Title.

I have the honor to be
With the most perfect Regard
& Respect
Sir
Your Excellency's
Obedient & most
humble Servant
Henry Laurens.
President
of Congress.

His Excellency
Gen Washington.

President Laurens' June 6, 1778, letter to General Washington, enclosing Congress' response to Lord Howe and Gen. Henry Clinton liament to Congress. Since the delegates approved a more moderate reply to Howe drawn up by William Henry Drayton, one of Lee's colleagues on this committee, it is possible that Lee's draft was never presented to Congress for consideration. See *JCC,* 11:572–74.

Daniel Roberdeau to George Bryan

Sir, York June 6th. 1778

The Delegates of this State are honored with the commands of Council respecting a supply of money for paying of Clothing; and the State of the Frontiers, these together with the petition of some of the Inhabitant of Northumberland were duely laid before Congress, *and without a word of debate,* refered, the former to the Treasury, the latter to the board of War, with an order to confer with the Gentlemen who were Bearers of the Petition. I expect a favorable Issue to this Business on Monday.[1]

Two Letters one from Lord Howe, the other from Genl. Clinton to *Congress* with the three Acts of Parliament, which are the Subjects of publick speculation, were under consideration this day, and a short answer given to the Letters.[2] A copy is prohibited, as indellicate until the Letters get to hand, in substance it refers to the resolves of Congress on two Bills circulated substantially the same as two of the above, that when the King shall be *seriously* disposed to peace, Congress will be ready to put an End to the cruel unprovoked war waged against America, on Terms honorable to our Nation, for the Interest of our Constituents and with a sacred regard to Treaties.

My Accot. exhibited to the Assembly when last in Lancaster refers to a debit of which I was not then possessed paid Capt. Piper who guarded Wm. Todd to Lancaster for his Expences, which is now before me in a proper entry £6.11.3. If that Sum could be added, and the whole remitted by you on the order in the hands of Mrs. Smith, it would be of great service as my late engagement in the Lead works has proved a moth to my circulating Cash and oblige me make free with a friend in borrowing. I hope to congratulate you soon on regaining our Capital, some step will be taken by Congress for securing property until a deliberate discrimination can be made, in which a due regard to the prerogatives of the State will be attended to.[3] I am with respectful salutation to Council, Sir, Yr. most obt. & very huml. Servt. Daniel Roberdeau

RC (PHi). Addressed: "The Honorable George Bryan Esquire, Vice President of the State of Pennsilvania. Lancaster."

1 Two letters of June 5 from the Pennsylvania Council to the state's delegates were laid before Congress this day, but only the message concerning Pennsylvania's frontiers survives. For the letter "respecting a supply of money" referred

to the Board of Treasury, see *JCC,* 11:574; and Auditor General John Gibson's June 10 reply to Bryan in *Pa. Archives,* 1st ser. 6:591–92. The letter pertaining to Northumberland County's defense is in PCC, item 69, fols. 529–30, and was printed under the date June 4, 1778, in *Pa. Archives,* 1st ser. 6:577. The June 1 petition of the Northumberland inhabitants is in PCC, item 42, 6:190–92, and was endorsed by Secretary Thomson: "referred to the board of war. The board to confer with the person who brot. this Memorial." For the Board of War's and Congress' response to the council's plea for assistance in protecting the state's frontier inhabitants, see ibid., pp. 586–87; and *JCC,* 11:576–77.

[2] See *JCC,* 11:572–75.

[3] Congress' June 4 resolution on the anticipated evacuation of Philadelphia was apparently copied and forwarded by Roberdeau to Bryan. It was printed in *Pa. Archives* under the date June 5, 1778, with the following note appended. "Dr Sir, I write at a publick Table, much embarrassed, to hand you the above Copy of a Resolution of Congress. I am, very respectfully, Dr Sir, yr most obt hum. Servt. Dan'l Roberdeau. P.S. My design is that you may cast about & be in readiness to appoint proper persons." *Pa. Archives,* 1st ser. 6:578–79.

Daniel Roberdeau to Timothy Matlack

Sir,

York June 6th 1778

If your orders are positive for returning the Books borrowed they must be complied with, but if otherwise they will be retained, as they will be useful in a very little time in determining a point on the same subject they were called for,[1] therefore I shall wait your answer as these books cannot be procured, as I know, any where else at present. My Sisters acknowledge your polite notice and hope with me to congratulate you shortly on regaining our Capital. I am respectfully, Sir, Yr. most obt. huml. Sert.

Daniel Roberdeau

P.S. If possible let Books remain, of which care shall be taken.

Desire Mr. Foulke to buy me a few quires of good paper.

RC (PHi). Addressed: "Timothy Matlack, Esquire, Lancaster." Endorsed: "Reced 11 June 1778, TM."

[1] Perhaps a reference to the books that were the subject of Elbridge Gerry's letter to Thomas Wharton of November 8, 1777, in these *Letters,* 8:242.

Josiah Bartlett to Mary Bartlett

My Dear

York Town June 7th 1778

Last Wednesday the 3d Instant I Recd yours of the 16th of May, am very glad to hear you are well & that Rhoda is rather better. I am in good health as is Charles Chace, Mr Wentworth & his man. We have procured Lodgings at a German House about a Quarter of a mile from the Court house where the Congress Sets, his name is

Andrus Hoffman. Their manner of Cooking their victuals is very Different from the English Manner, tho they Do what they can to accomodate us. They understand but little English, Just Enough to be understood.

I have wrote to you Several times the last Dated the first Instant some of which I hope you have Recd before now.

Yesterday Congress Receivd letters from Lord Howe & Genl. Clinton informing us that they were two of the Commissioners appointed by Parliament to Settle the Dispute with America. But as it appears by the act of Parliament which they sent us they are not authorised to acknowledge our Independance I Suspect a peace will not soon take place tho I believe that the fighting Business is chiefly over. I have wrote major Philbrick more fully about it.[1]

I informed my Children in my last that they had not Drawn any of the large prizes in the lottery. I cannot now tell them whither they have Drawn any of the smaller prizes for I have not been able to get a Sight of the list but make no doubt I shall be able to do it in my next.

I hope you & my family are Still in health & that affairs go on well.

Remember me to Mr Thurston, Dr Gale, Mr Thayer, Capt Calef & all friends.

I am yours &c, Josiah Bartlett

RC (NhHi).

1 Not found.

Charles Carroll of Carrollton to Charles Carroll, Sr.

Dr. Papa, 7th June 1778.

I think I acknowledged the receipt of your letter of the 27th past in my past letter. I imagine the vines, by the dying of the old wood, must have suffered principally from the wetness of the winter, and of the month of April & if So, this mischief must have been encreased by the flatness of the beds in which they are planted. The failure of apples in the home Orchard must proceed from the nature of the Soil, and its exposition; the soil is stiff, cold, & livery.

Friday evening the Congress received letters from Ld. Howe, & Sir H. Clinton inclosing 3 acts of Parliat. two of them comformable to the drafts of bills, which you have seen, & the 3d An Act for repealing the Act for altering the Charter of the Massachusets Bay. Inclosed you have copies of the above letters;[1] they were directed to Henry Laurens Esqr. *President of Congress*. By the Acts it appears that 5 Commissioners are to be appointed to treat under the powers within the Acts; and from the Letters of Ld Howe & Clinton you will observe that Ld Howe is one of the Commissioners, but that Sir

H. Clinton is not, from which circumstance I conclude that Sir Henry's command is to be but temporary, and that some person of distinction is coming out to be commander in chief, probably Lord Amherst.[2] Altho' it is mentioned by Ld. Howe, or Clinton that these Acts were just recd., we know the vessel which brought them, has been arrived upwards of 3 weeks. The answer of Congress, which was sent off yesterday is short, and to this effect.

The President in the name of Congress acknowleges the receipt of their letters & the Acts of Parliat. and refers them to the Resolves of Congress of the 22d April upon the bills (from which the Acts do not materially differ) for the sense of Congress upon the acts. He then informs them, that when the King of G B shall be seriously disposed to peace and to put an end to the unprovoked & cruel war which he has waged against us, we shall chearfully consent to put a stop to its calamities by concluding a peace with his B. Majesty, on terms consistent with our Independance, the interest of our constituents, and the sacred regard due to our treaties. I could have wished the words "*seriously disposed,*" "*unprovoked*" & "*cruel war*" had not been thrust into this, otherwise unexceptionable, letter. Ld. Howe's & Clinton's letters are polite, they seem to have cautiously avoided any terms which might give offence; in this particular I wish we had imitated their example.

It is certain most of the Enemy's shipping have fallen down the river below Newcastle; it is equally certain that they have embarked their sick, wounded, heavy baggage & artillery, great quantities of military stores & merchandize, yet notwithstanding all these appearances, it is my own opinion, that the Enemy will not abandon Pha. till the fall, or till they are constrained to leave it by the superiority of our arms. If they should not acknowledge our Independance, they will take the field with their army light and unencumbered, and endeavour to try the fortune of a battle. I do not think they will acknowlege our Independance before next winter, unless the King of Prussia, and other powers of Germany should have followed the example of France. If the British Marine should not be greatly superior to that of France & Spain, it is my opinion the British court will acknowlege our Independance, & thus avoid a war with France & Spain in conjunction with us, which would probably end in the entire expulsion of the British from this Continent. Our General thinks the Enemy intend to march thro' Jersey to South Amboy. They have got and it seems are getting many boats there with an intent as it is conjectured to pass their army over from thence to Staten Island. A few more weeks, or perhaps, days will ease us of the anxiety of all conjectures on this account.

Gen. Schuyler writes to Governor Morris, a Delegate from New York, that he is informed the northern Indians are disposed to quit the British interest & to embrace ours. If So, this will put a stop the cruelties the middle Indians are committing on the frontiers of this State. But to restrain their ravages we shall not depend on that event: a force is preparing to march agt. them to carry the war into their country.

Monday morning 8th June

A 52 Gun Ship is arrived from France at Hampton in Virga. assigned by Mons. de Beaumarchais to his Agent here Mr. Francy; She has brought a most valuable cargo, the prime cost of which in France Mr. Francy assured me was a million of Livres.[3] Her cargo consists of a great variety of articles, amongst others 8 thousand suits of regimentals.

Mr. Francy informs me that he has letters from France of the 29th March acquainting him that the King of Prussia had marched 60 thousand men into Bavaria, that they had taken possession of 3 towns & a fort from which they drove the Austrian garrisons, that the Emperor had ordered 60 [*thousand*] men to the support of his troops already in Bavaria. That war was declared between Russia & the Porte; that the French had detained all the English vessels in their ports in consequence of a refusal from the court of London to deliver up an American vessel taken by an English privateer on the coast of France, and which had been demanded by the Court of Versailles.

I wish the war between the Prussians & Austrians may not take off the attention of the French from their marine & approaching war with England.

P.M. 8 o'clock

I recd. yours of the 4th instant by the post this morning. If you petition the Assembly for a repeal of the tender Law, I hope you will avoid all indecent & waste expressions in it. You may urge very forcible reasons in decent & moderate language. You ask me whether I think the continental bills will be redeemed according to their tenor? If peace should be concluded in a year from this I make no doubt, our debts will be paid off. Consider what Sums will be collected by taxes, from the amount of our own; consider the growing population of this country, the variety of its products, its fitness for navigation & commerce, and the freedom of our different governments, and then I believe you will no longer doubt the Public faith. Too many are interested in the debt not to pay it off; it will be the work of time, and perhaps a part of our paper currency may circulate in Europe; if so, the remainder will rise to par in a year or two after peace. It gives me the greatest Satisfaction to hear you continue to enjoy yr. health. I am, yr. affectionate Son,

Ch. Carroll of Carrollton

P.S. I beg you will send Sam up so as to be here by the 20th instant;

send by him a £100 in large bills chiefly; every thing here is inconceivably dear; altho' I have kept no horses here my allowance will hardly make me whole; indeed I believe it will not. Sam must bring with him 3 horses. Chase I expect will be up by that time, & I shall write to him by this post to come that I may return.

RC (MdHi).

1 Carroll enclosed letters from Lord Howe to Washington, May 27; from Henry Clinton to Washington, May 30 and June 3; and from Washington to Clinton, May 30, and to President Laurens, June 4, 1778. See Carroll Papers, MdHi; and William Henry Drayton's Draft Letter to Lord Howe, June 6, 1778, note 1.

2 Carroll's conjectures on this point were in error, for Sir Henry Clinton was indeed one of the peace commissioners and he retained his command until 1782.

3 For Congress' response to the arrival of *Le Fier Roderique* carrying a large shipment from Beaumarchais, see Committee of Congress Report, June 10, 1778.

Henry Laurens to John Laurens

My Dear son, York Town 7th June 1778.

I wrote to you the 5th & the same Evening late your favor of the 4th came to hand. Casting my Eye on my Copy Book just now I was startled at the dates prefixed there to Cöpies of Letters which I writ yesterday to the Commander in Chief, to Lord Howe & to Sir Henry Clinton all, May, instead of June. If the originals have carried the same blunder, I shall be much ashamed. 'Tis impossible to develop the secret from my Copyists memory because admitting the first error to have been mine, if his senses had been awake he would have pointed to the error immediately. If the Letter to the General is misdated I shall conclude both the others are. You asked me some time ago why I did not employ a Secretary, I'll tell you I don't know where to get a good one—& I can't bear any other. James[1] can Copy extremely well when he is attentive, but his constitution is not the strongest, he sometimes flags & some times nods. I do not wonder at it—but I do, how I hold it out. I have a sort of Secretary, a genteel decent Young Man but I get very little from him,[2] he has been spoiled in another office & has acquired habits which are to me very disagreeable. Congress meet twice a day, the consequence of which is delay of business there and intolerable confinement to the President.

The Idea of the Enemy's intended abandonment of Philadelphia, pervades every mind, & I am very certain our Cause suffers greatly from the general belief of an event being at hand, which we ought to think depends wholly on our own exertions & to act accordingly. Thirteen days have elapsed since the Enemy's draught of three days provision & Canteens filled with Rum—Women & children embarked, Hospital utensils & Boxes of Arms shiped, notice given to the Police & honest Mr. Coombes's intelligence. I should think none but women & Children will rely upon any thing they [say] or trust to any thing they do—yet there is such confidence in their flimsey assurances. I was going on to write you a long Letter but an opportunity instantly presenting & being anxious to acquaint his Excellency the General with a recent act of humanity on the part the Enemy in the moment of treating with us I shall confine myself to the following extract from General Sullivan's Letter 26 May, just received.[3] The Chief Justice regrets we had not this intelligence before the Letters to Lord Howe & General Clinton were sent.

"I beg leave to inform Congress that on the Night of the 24 Inst about 600 British & Hessian Troops at R Id embarked on board two Ships of War, two Tenders & about 30 flat bottoms, passed up the River & landed before day between Warren & Papasquash point, at daylight marched in two bodies for Warren & the head of Kukemull River where were about 70 flat bottom boats & one of the State Gallies, they burned all the Boats, 12 escaped & set fire to the Galley, this was afterward extinguished with much hurt to the Gally—then set fire to the meeting house at Warren & to seven dwelling Houses & retreated toward Bristol where the Ships had fallen down with the flat Bottoms to receive them. They burned in Bristol 22 Houses among which was Govr Bradford's in their Tour every species of Cruelty was displayed, 20 of the Inhabitants were taken & carried off—almost every House was plundered without distinction between friend & foes. Some Women who had been long noted as their faithful friends were compelled by the Bayonet to stand while they were robbed of their Buckles, Rings, handkerchiefs &c &c. I received intelligence of the Landing about 8 oClock, the Country was immedy. alarmed, the Troops put in motion & lest an attempt might be intended upon this place or the Western Shore some part of the Militia were called in to guard them. The rest were Marched toward the Enemy, all the Massachusetts ordered to meet & oppose them, they assembled with great alacrity & marched with much expedition. Colo. Barton ordered to Muster what force he could on the Road to assist Colo. Crary's Regiment stationed at Bristol & had [*got*] into the Enemy's Rear. The Colo. with Crary's Regiment & such force as he had collected in all near 200, attacked their Retreat & I believe did them much injury—the Gallant Colonel dangerously wounded in the action. I arrived on the ground ½ past 11 oClock. The Troops from this place & a large body of Militia were about 2 Miles in the Rear, many of them had marched near 20 Miles in less than four hours. When I arrived the Enemys Rear had embarked & gone near an hour. I know nothing of their loss—we had 2 or 3 killed, several wounded & 5 taken."

The Chief Justice charges me not to conclude without presenting his Compliments. Adieu, H L

[*P.S.*] If the General has not received the above it will be proper to communicate it. I am very full of bodily pain but supported by Spirits which are not worn out. You will receive 4 Letters inclosed—3 I believe from Harry,[4] he writes a fine hand.[5] I am almost determined upon sending for him.

A third attempt has been made to finish the destruction of Charles Town by fire.

Mr. Gervais's Compliments 8th May.

RC (MHi: William Gilmore Simms Collection deposit, 1973).

1 James Custer.

2 Moses Young.

3 The full text of Gen. John Sullivan's May 26 letter to Laurens is in PCC, item 160, fols. 125–26.

4 Henry Laurens, Jr. (1763–1821), Laurens' youngest surviving son, was being educated in England. David D. Wallace, *The Life of Henry Laurens* (New York: G.P. Putnam's Sons, 1915), pp. 182, 188, 365n.3.

5 Laurens noted in his private letter book that he also sent John "1 Packet containing a Letter from Madame Le Marchioness to Monsr. Le Marquis delafayette, 1 Packet containing 4 Letters for Baron Stüben [*and*] 1 small French Letter to Baron deKalb." Laurens Papers, ScHi.

Samuel Adams to Samuel P. Savage

My dear sir, York Town June 8 1778

I had the Pleasure of receiving a Letter from you while I was on my late Journey to this Place, which I do not recollect to have answerd.

Last Saturday President Laurens recd a Letter from Ld Howe & another from Genl Clinton each inclosing Copy of an Act of the British Parliamt conformable to the Bills which have already been publishd. An Answer was returned to his Lordship & the General in which they are informd that "When the British King shall be *seriously* disposd to put an End to the unprovokd and cruel War waged against these united States, Congress will be ready to attend to such Terms of Peace as shall be consistent with the Honor of independent Nations, the Interest of their Constituents and the sacred Regard which they mean to show to Treaties."[1]

Will you permit me to recommend to your Circle Mr. Doree the Bearer of this Letter. He is a French Gentleman and is mentiond to me by my Friends in this Town as very deserving of Notice.

Be so kind as to call on my dear Mrs A and let her know that I am in health & have not Leisure to write to her at present.

My Regards to Mrs Savage, Mr Scollay & his Family &c &c. Adieu my dear Sir, S A

RC (MHi).

1 See William Henry Drayton's Draft Letter to Lord Howe, June 6, 1778.

Henry Laurens to George Washington

Dear sir, York Town 8th June 1778

My Colleague Mr. Drayton having shewn me about a fortnight ago the draught of a Report which he had prepared, stating charges against the General Officers who lately abandoned Tyconderoga & flattering me with assurances that he would soon offer it to Congress I delayed replying to Your Excellency's favor of the 29th Ulto.[1] hoping for ground to intimate that, that business was ready to be dispatched to Your Excellency for the further necessary order. But to my great mortification it continues to be procrastinated, some of the Gentlemen of the Committee it seems are or have been desirous of new lights; in a word Sir, I am quite in opinion with those Gentlemen who say "the not proceeding in this matter is cruel & oppressive"—although I am as well convinced, the delay has not been calculated or intended to distress the parties affected—it has arisen from a vapid desultory habit, which if I am not mistaken, I have seen, squander Millions & endanger States. I speak with warmth & I believe with equal truth. On my Country's account as well as from a feeling for the Culprit Officers I am really ashamed of our conduct respecting the particular affair in question—however as I can always take a decent freedom with my Colleague, who is really a diligent Man, I will not let him pass a day unreminded of the necessity for bringing forward his report. I sent off a Messenger to day with a Letter to Lancaster[2] at his request for collecting somewhat relative to the business & I think he hinted that when that ingredient should be obtained the Report would be complete.[3]

Frequent Items have been given in Public of the disagreements of our Commissioners—this day a private perusal of Papers treating on that subject gave me much pain.

I fear an investigation upon the arrival of Mr. Deane who is every hour expected will spread the trouble wide. I have suppressed all that has been written to me & have sealed my Lips except to Your Excellency & one other Gentleman. I know all the Gentlemen yonder, some of them very intimately, know their tempers & habits & think I can mark out causes, but I can only deplore their impolitic & I was going to say School Boy jarrings & dread the consequences of a heated & injudicious discussion on this side.

9th. Late last Night Your Excellency's public Letter of the 7th was brought to me.[4] I shall lay it before Congress at 10 oClock. Lord Abingdon's protest does honor to Mr Morris of N. York,[5] the merit of our Resolves of 22d April is fairly to be ascribed to him.[6]

I have lately much regretted that I had it not in my power to transmit to Your Excellency some of the English Papers which we had received & which indeed came originally into my own hands but judged it my Duty to present them to the House, where they were so, & so suddenly, dispersed as to deprive me of the reading even one of them, yet I dare not say, I'll take better care another time, my own duty will be to do, as I have done.

In order to save time I have sent to the Secretary's Office a Young Man to Copy the Resolves of Congress required by Your Excellency, & which will be found here inclosed.[7]

I am with the most sincere Regard & Esteem, Sir, Your Excellency's much obliged & most obedient servant,

Henry Laurens

[*P.S.*] Your Excellency will do me the honor to accept this as private.

RC (DLC).

1 In a brief postscript to his May 29 letter to Laurens, Washington had expressed the wish that Congress "would lay the charge, and order tryal" of the officers involved in the loss of Ticonderoga and Mount Independence during the summer of 1777. Washington, *Writings* (Fitzpatrick), 11:476. For discussions of the dilatory congressional investigation of this case, which had begun the previous August, see John Hancock to Arthur St. Clair and Philip Schuyler, August 5, 1777, note; Committee of Congress to Washington, February 7, note; and Laurens to Washington, April 4, 1778, note 2.

2 Not found.

3 William Henry Drayton's report specifying charges against Gens. Arthur St. Clair and Philip Schuyler in connection with the loss of Ticonderoga and Mount Independence was ordered to be sent to Washington on June 20. *JCC,* 11:593–603. The committee on whose behalf Drayton wrote this report had been appointed on April 29, 1778. *JCC,* 10:403.

4 Washington's June 7 letter to Laurens is in PCC, item 152, 6:83–84, and Washington, *Writings* (Fitzpatrick), 12:27–28.

5 For the earl of Abingdon's March 9, 1778, protest in the House of Lords against Lord North's conciliatory bills, which argued that they did not go far enough in redressing basic American grievances, see *Parliamentary History,* 19:867–70. For the use Americans had previously made of Abingdon's pro-American views, see John Henry to Thomas Johnson, February 17, 1778, note 2.

6 Gouverneur Morris was the author of Congress' initial response to Lord North's February 1778 conciliatory proposals. See *JCC,* 10:374–80; and Morris to John Jay, May 3, 1778.

7 For the May 19, 1778, resolve on pay and rations for Continental officers, of which Washington had requested a copy, see *JCC,* 11:512.

James Lovell to John Adams

Dear Sir

June 8th. 1778

I fear I omitted to send the Resolve of May 5th with 3 past Packets. I shall be vexed if it does not reach you with the Ratifications as, on the Timing of it depends much of its Propriety.[1] I was strangely betrayed by its having been dated the 4th in a mistaken alteration, when A.B.C. were sent Eastward.

By Letters yesterday from Mr. Beaumarchais I find Mr. Deane is probably on this Continent so that we may know the exact State of our Account wth. Mr. Hortales.[2] The present Cargo in the fier Roderique is to be sold outright for Cash or Produce, Congress having the first Offer it belongs to Mr. Beaumarchais not to Hortales &c. I hope there is no mystery in this, for I really approve of the Thing. I am glad it does not belong to the Continent: but I wish to know whether any of those Vessels lately *taken* belong to Mr. B and whether this would not have belonged to H had it been *lost*. This may be an amusing Speculation for you.

Mr. D's Recall I find is attributed very much to Plots of A L.[3] You know this to be unjust, and that Facts are as in my Letter to Dr. Franklin.[4]

All things speak the Enemy's departure from Philada. Intending to pass across the Jersies to Staten Island they found the Militia to a Man ready to waylay them and that some Continentals were detached. They have therefore given an Air of Peace to their Motions, and asking for an immediate Exchange of Prisoners "because they are going away," they are levelling their Works, as we repeatedly hear tho the cautious Genl. has not yet told us the latter part but he was surprized that they "still" remained on the 1st. They meant however to celebrate the 4th there—the birthday of the foolish King.

Mr. S A[5] has come forward, and Things go on very well here except that we want many Lessons on Finance. Give them to us—with a little Practicability, if you please, wrought into your nicest Systems.

Affectionately, J L

[*P.S.*] Let Mr. A.L. see the inclosed.

RC (MHi). Endorsed by Adams: "Mr. Lovell, June 8 1778, ans. Sept. 25, 1778."

1 For further information on Congress' May 5 directive to the commissioners "to use their best endeavours to procure the abolition" of the 11th and 12th articles of the Franco-American treaty of amity and commerce dealing with the duty-free status of molasses imported from the French West Indies to America and all American merchandise exported to those islands, see Committee for Foreign Affairs to the Commissioners at Paris, May 14, 1778, note 2.

This day Lovell also wrote the following note to Samuel and Robert Purviance at Baltimore requesting them to forward copies of this resolve and this letter to Adams: "I must intreat you to forward the enclosed to France, either directly, or by the Islands, giving critical instructions to keep them from falling into the hands of the Enemy. They are of great importance, and were unluckily omitted in three packets which are gone." PCC, item 79, fol. 233.

2 For further information on Congress' action on the accounts of Caron de Beaumarchais, see Committee of Congress Report, June 10, 1778.

3 That is, Silas Deane and Arthur Lee.

4 In his May 15 letter to Dr. Franklin, Lovell had explained that Deane was recalled because of congressional anger over excessive commissions issued to foreign officers, but that he was now needed to explain his transactions with Caron de Beaumarchais. Although Lovell thus shifted the responsibility for Deane's recall from Arthur Lee to himself and other dissatisfied members of Congress, the

quarrel between the supporters of Deane and those of Arthur and William Lee had only begun to rumble through Congress. The serious nature of this coming storm can be seen in a letter written this day in Virginia by Benjamin Harrison, a former member of Congress, to Robert Morris, who with Harrison was a partisan supporter and business associate of Deane's. Concerning the Lee brothers, Harrison wrote: "You, who know them not, can form but an imperfect idea of those on that side of the water by what you have seen on this, they being much more designing, vindictive, and overbearing. Perhaps you may think this impossible, but be assured it is a fact, and that they are no more fit for the characters they bear than any man that can be thought on; however they are fixed, and I suppose America must suffer them for a season longer, as the cabal is at present too powerful to afford us the least prospect of their removal." Wharton, *Diplomatic Correspondence,* 2:607–8.

5 That is, Samuel Adams.

Maryland Delegates to Thomas Johnson

Sir, 8th June 1778 York

Your letter of the 2d instant was put into our hands this morning by Col. Smith, and referred to the board of war.[1] We sincerely wish the State of our cloathing at or near the army may be Such as to Suffer that Board to give the order in the extent you desire. Col. Smith will receive their answer tomorrow. We hope, and have the strongest reason to believe, our army will never again be exposed to the same inconveniences & distress they have hitherto suffered from the want of cloathing. We understand 8 or ten thousand suits are in the 50 gun Ship lately arrived in Virginia, and still larger supplies have arrived at the Eastward.

By all accounts from Camp & Philadelphia the Enemy appear to be on the eve of evacuating that city: it is conjectured they will march thro' the Jersies to South Amboy, where it is said a number of boats are in readiness to carry them over to Staten Island.

War between Prussia & Austria respecting the division of the late Elector of Bavaria's territories by the latest accounts from Europe is much to be apprehended: and Mr. Francy informed us that war was certainly declared between Russia & the Porte.

The French court had detained all English vessels in their ports in a consequence of a refusal by the Court of London to deliver up an American vessel captured on the coast of France by an English Privateer.

We inclose you copies of letters from Ld. Howe's & Sir Henry Clinton's letters to Gen. Washington & to Congress and our answer.[2] These may be printed if you think proper, and we beg the favor of you to lay them before the Assembly. We are with great respect, Your Excellency's Most obedt. hunble Servants,

Ch. Carroll of Carrollton

Geo. Plater

RC (MdAA). Written by Carroll and signed by Carroll and Plater.

1 For the Maryland Council's June 2 letter to its delegates requesting clothing for the state's troops, see *Md. Archives,* 21:120–21; PCC, item 70, fols. 255–58; and *JCC,* 11:578.

2 These are copies of the same letters that Carroll sent to his father the preceding day. See Charles Carroll of Carrollton to Charles Carroll, Sr., June 7, 1778, note 1.

Rhode Island Delegates to William Greene

Sir, Pensylvania York Town June 8th, 1778

Mr. Marchant arrived at this Town the sixth Instant.[1] The Situation of Mr. Ellery's Family necessitates his Return in a few Days. Confederation, it is expected, will soon be taken up;[2] and if Congress should determine that, immediately upon the Completion of that Business, no State can be represented without two Members, the State we have the Honor to represent may not have that Share in the Common Counsells of the States, which Our Interests and Circumstances require. Solicitous this may not be the Case we hope One of Our Colleagues will soon give his attendance. We lament the Waste and Destruction made upon Our State by that more than Savage Barbarity peculiar to Britons; But we are utterly at a Loss to account for that cruel Desertion of Our Sister States, which has thus laid Our State *bare* to the Insults and Ravages of Our Enemies. This is a Subject we feel most pungently, and shall not fail to endeavour to excite in Congress a common Feeling with us, that if possible some Steps may be taken for our Relief.

It is expected the Enemy will very soon leave Philadelphia, but for what Quarters is uncertain. We hope the New-England States will hold Themselves in watchful Readiness. The Enemy ought to be expected in every Quarter, that so let them come where they will, They may meet with a proper Reception. A large Ship from France of Upwards fifty Guns is arrived to the Southward, with large Supplies for Our Army. We inclose Your Excellency the last York Paper, and Are most respectfully, Your Excellency's most obedient and humble Servts. William Ellery

Hy. Marchant

RC (R–Ar). Written by Marchant and signed by Marchant and Ellery.

1 According to the journals, Marchant took his seat in Congress on Monday, June 8. *JCC,* 11:575.

2 Congress finally resumed consideration of the Articles of Confederation on June 20. *JCC,* 11:625, 628.

Henry Laurens to Richard Caswell

Sir. York Town 9th June 1778.

I had the honour of addressing Your Excellency the 26th Ulto. & since of presenting to Congress your Excellency's favour of 6th Inst. being the 2d of this date.[1]

Within the present Inclosure will be found the following Acts of Congress.

1—27th May for an Establishment of the American Army.[2]

2—28th for reforming the North Carolina Battalions.[3]

3—4th June for suspending or repealing Acts of Assembly for regulating prices—this I believe Sir does not apply to North Carolina.[4]

4—6th June for extending subsistence Money to Officers of Militia.[5]

5—8th June for laying a General Embargo on Provisions.[6]

To these & to the enclosed P. S.[7] & more particularly to a seperate Circular[8] which I shall deliver with this to Capt. Blount I beg leave to refer.

Capt Blount has long been detained by the Treasury but the Multiplicity of business there I presume has rendered an earlier dispatch impracticable.[9]

I am with very great Esteem & Respect, Sir, Your Excellency's most obedient servant, Henry Laurens,
President of Congress.

RC (DLC).

1 Governor Caswell's second May 6 letter to Laurens, recommending chevalier de Cambray "to the notice and protection of the Honorable Congress," was read by the delegates on June 4. See *JCC*, 11:567; and *N.C. State Records*, 13:123. Nine days later Congress decided to make Cambray—a French artillery and engineering officer who had arrived in North Carolina in February 1778 and had since been involved in constructing coastal fortifications for the state—a member of the "corps of engineers commanded by Brigadier du Portail, with the rank and pay of a lieutenant colonel." *JCC*, 11:604–5. Congress had read another May 6 letter from Caswell on May 25. *JCC*, 11:530.

2 See *JCC*, 11:539–43.

3 These resolves were actually passed on May 29. *JCC*, 11:550–51. See also Laurens to Caswell, May 26, 1778, note.

4 See *JCC*, 11:569–70; and Laurens to William Livingston, June 5, 1778, note 2.

5 See *JCC*, 11:560–61, 573.

6 For an explanation of the passage of this embargo, see Laurens to the States, June 10, 1778.

Laurens also transmitted copies of the resolves of May 27 and June 4, 6, and 8 listed here with brief covering letters he wrote this day to Govs. Thomas Johnson of Maryland, Patrick Henry of Virginia, and John Houstoun of Georgia. See PCC, item 13, 1:360–63; and Red Books, MdAA. In addition Laurens sent Henry a June 4 resolve "for appointing Commissioners for holding a Treaty with Indians at Fort Pitt on the 23d July." See *JCC*, 11:568.

7 See Laurens to Caswell, June 11, 1778.

8 See Laurens to the States, June 10, 1778.

[9] Capt. Reading Blount was in York to take custody of the $100,000 that Congress had agreed on May 29 to pay North Carolina to cover the cost of filling her Continental quota. *JCC*, 11:550–51.

Henry Laurens to George Clinton

Sir 9 June [1778]

I had the honor of addressing Your Excellency on the 23d Ulto. by Barkly.

The present will be accompanied by the undermentioned Acts of Congress.

1. Of 27th May—for an Establishment of the American Army.

2. Of 6 June—for extending to officers of Militia subsistence Money in lieu of extra Rations.

3. 8 June—Laying a general Embargo on certain Articles of provision[1]—this measure appears to be so absolutely necessary as leaves no doubt but that each State whence exportation might otherwise be made will immediately adopt and strictly observe the Act. Had this bar been laid to furnishing the enemy with provision twelve months ago, St. Augustine would probably have been abandoned, the West Indies driven to great necessity, and possibly our invaders from the Continent.

I shall add a printed paper containing Lord Abingdon's Speech and protest in the British House of Lords[2] which does honor to Mr Morris of New York—to him may be fairly ascribed the merit of the Act of Congress 22nd April.[3]

I am with the highest Esteem &c.

LB (DNA: PCC, item 13).

[1] Laurens also transmitted copies of these three "Acts" with brief covering letters he wrote this day to Govs. William Livingston of New Jersey and Jonathan Trumbull, Sr., of Connecticut. PCC, item 13, 1:358–60.

[2] Laurens inserted an "xx" at this point in the text to key the following note he wrote at the end of the LB of this letter: "words omitted, introducing the Act of Congress of the 22d April on the British Conciliatory Bills."

[3] The equivalent sentence in Laurens' letter of this date to Governor Trumbull states: "I shall add a printed paper which will shew Your Excellency that the opinions of Congress on the pretended conciliatory Acts of Parliament are not confined to this side of the Atlantic." PCC, item 13, 1:359.

Henry Laurens to William Greene

Sir. York Town 9th June 1778

I had the honour of presenting to Congress your notification of being appointed to the Government of the State of Rhode Island & Providence Plantations,[1] permit me Sir, to congratulate with you on this testimony of the Esteem of Your fellow Citizens & to wish you a happy administration.

Within the present Inclosure will be found the undermentioned Acts of Congress.

1 . . . 27th May for Establishment of the American Army.

2 . . . 4 June for suspending or repealing Acts of Assembly for regulating prices of goods.

3 . . . 6 June for allowing subsistence in lieu of Rations to the Militia.

4 . . . 8 June for laying a general Embargo on certain articles of Provision,[2] the absolute necessity for this measure is so extremely apparent as leaves no room to doubt of its being carried into immediate execution & strictly observed.

I have the honor to be, With very great Respect, Sir, Your Excellencys Obedient humble servant, Henry Laurens,
President of Congress

RC (R–Ar). Addressed: "His Excellency William Green Esquire, Governor of Rhode Island & Providence Plantations."

1 See *JCC*, 11:537.

2 Laurens also transmitted copies of these four "Acts" this day to the Massachusetts Council, and to Vice President George Bryan of Pennsylvania he sent three of the four. See PCC, item 13, 1:357–58; and Revolutionary Letters, M–Ar. At the same time, he also sent Massachusetts a May 30 resolve on the maintenance of the Convention Army, and instead of the June 4 resolve on price regulation he forwarded to Pennsylvania a June 4 resolve on an Indian conference at Fort Pitt and a June 8 resolve on the defense of Northumberland County. See *JCC*, 11:556, 568, 576–77.

Henry Laurens to John Laurens

My Dear Son very early 9th June [1778]

Late last night your favor of the 7th obliged me very much, write on & make me as well acquainted with movements of all kinds as you can.

Inclosed you will find the Resolution required.[1] My duty to the Marquis. I have delivered his Letters to Mr. Cambray, Mr. Lee &ca—will do as far as in my power all he desires & commands & will have the honor of paying my respects to him to morrow.

I dont much like my old friends interviews with an old acquaintance[2] whom he had so lately seen. I wish I could see you for half an hour. I pray God protect you.

LB (ScHi).

1 Although John Laurens' June 7 letter has not been found, it should be noted that in his June 9 letter to his father he asked for Congress' May 21 resolves on negotiations for a prisoner exchange between Generals Howe and Washington. See *JCC*, 11:520–21; and Simms, *Laurens Army Correspondence*, pp. 178–81.

[2] Laurens is referring respectively to Lafayette and Thomas Conway. See Laurens to Lafayette, June 5, 1778.

Henry Laurens to Rawlins Lowndes

Sir, 9th June 1778

On the 3d Inst. by the hands of Captn. Cochran I transmitted to your Excellency several Copies of an Establishment of the American Army & requested your Excellency to make a distribution of some of those papers to Major General Howe & Brigadier Moultrie.[1] Orders are given by Congress for carrying this Act into execution at Valley forge,[2] the Commander in Chief may from thence extend it to all the distant posts, unless I am wrong in my opinion that a farther order of Congress will be necessary for that purpose.

Please to receive Sir, with the present Inclosure the undermentioned Acts of Congress, together with Copy of a circular Letter which will be dated the 10th written by order of Congress.

The Acts

1. of 4th June recommending a suspension or repeal of Acts of Assembly for regulating prices—this I believe will not apply to So. Carolina.

2. 6th June, for extending subsistence Money to all officers of Militia &ca. in lieu of extra Rations.

3. 8th June, for a general Embargo on provisions for a limitted time.

I have the honor to be &ca.

LB (DNA: PCC, item 13).

[1] See Laurens to Lowndes, June 2, 1778, note 2.

[2] See *JCC*, 11:570.

Henry Laurens to Casimir Pulaski

Dear General, 9th June 1778

Inclosed I have the honor of transmitting a Letter which I lately received for you from France.

I likewise inclose a Petition lately preferred by John Griffith to Congress in which he Sets forth cruel treatment which he received from some of the Officers of your Legion at Lancaster.[1] This man will wait on you in two or three days. I have given him assurances of obtaining ample redress through your Love of Justice & determination to preserve good order in the Corps, especially in the article of Money which was taken from him.

Permit me to add, Sir, that the affray at Stokes's has given much umbrage. If the Officers of the Legion indulge themselves in such irregular sallies as these which have been complained of, the Corps will soon fall into disrepute, I am confident Sir you will take the necessary measures for laying them under proper restraints for the future.

Your Letter of the 1st Inst. I had the honour of presenting to Congress the 4th when it was committed to the Board of War for consideration.[2]

I am with great regard

LB (ScHi).

[1] John Griffith's petition is not in PCC, and his case is not mentioned in the journals. For a discussion of some other problems that Pulaski's independent corps was creating for Congress at this time, see Laurens to William Atlee, May 29, 1778, note 2.

[2] Pulaski's letter to Laurens, which is dated "Baltimore the 1st May" but which according to Secretary Charles Thomson's endorsement "shd be June," is in PCC, item 164, fols. 9–10. In this letter Pulaski asked Congress to grant commissions to a number of officers he had appointed to serve in his corps, requested additional funds to cover the cost of raising this unit, and insisted that Congress insert in his commission the date he entered Continental service. No report by the Board of War on Pulaski's letter has been found.

Henry Laurens to Meshech Weare

Honorable Sir. York Town 9th June 1778

On the 27th May by Messenger Brailsford I transmitted you an Act of Congress Recommending an exemption from Militia service [*for*] Deserters & Prisoners from the British Army & Navy.[1] I still remain without any of your favors & althogether ignorant whether any of my Letters & the Acts of Congress which accompanied them for upwards of seven Months past have reached your hands.

The Present is intended to forward an Act of Congress of the 8th Inst laying a General Embargo on the exportation of divers articles of Provision from these states for a limited term. The reasons which preface the Act are so cogent as leaves no room to doubt that each State will carry the Act into immediate effect.

I remain with great Respect, Sir, Your obedient humble servant

Henry Laurens, President of Congress.

[*P.S.*] You will likewise receive herewith two other Acts of Congress. 1 of the 27 May for an establishment of the Army,

1 of 2d Inst for subsistence Money in lieu of Rations to the Militia,[2] & another of the 4th recommending a suspension or Repeal of Acts of Assembly for regulating prices.

RC (Nh-Ar).

1 See Laurens to Jonathan Trumbull, Sr., May 27, 1778, note 3.
2 This resolve was actually approved on June 6. *JCC,* 11:573.

James Lovell to Horatio Gates

Dear General York Town June 9th. 1778

Here we are still the Sport of Lyars. One Day we are told the Enemy are filling their Ditches and preparing to leave Philada., en Ami; in the next we are informed of new Works & fresh arrived Troops. For my own Part, I think they will aim to give us a Drubbing on one Quarter or another. We have therefore laid an Embargo on all Provisions both with a View to our own Supply and the Enemy's Distress;[1] and we shall urge the States to instant Exertions for the compleat Number of Levies.[2]

I did not expect Johnston wd. have come over with the Commissioners. I think he will return with a Load of Chagrin. However, we have told Lord Howe that when the King of Gr. Br. is seriously disposed to put an End to this unprovoked & cruel War we will readily negotiate Peace on Terms consistent with the Honour of Independent States, the Interest of our Constituents and the Faith of Alliances. This answer must be under Consideration of the Commissioners Carlisle, Johnstone & Eden now here in America.

I have seen a *Bulletin particulaire* in which you are said to have made Advances towards Peace by your Letter, which is therein published, to Ld. Thanet. And tho' Mr. Bingham mentions the French are allarmed; yet the Hand Bill does you the Credit to say that you have eased the Pride of England by making the *first* Overture, but you have wisely done it sans comprometttre Les Colonies.[3]

I supsect you will get a Letter from Johnstone or Earle Thanet thro' him.

I wish you may get some hearty Lads from the Eastward if it is only to make an handsome Feu dejoye upon a Peace. Little will be lost in such a Case: But much is to be gained, if War is the View of Britain.

You must not think me negligent as to using a Pen, tho' your Favour has lain long by me unacknowledged, for I assure you, I have almost continually been writing since I had the Pleasure of seeing you. This kind of Apology I have made lest your next Favour should have something of "Asperity" mixt with it. I wish you may be properly purblind to the Peccadillos of your Friends till this one Campaign more is over. And then we will settle who is jealous, fretfull, misled, waspish &c. and we will be sure not to condemn ourselves but as Swift says about Hell we will conclude upon Paris or Rome and think ourselves happy that all's well at Home.

I wish you and yours Health & every Happiness, being your affectionate, humble Servant,

James Lovell

RC (NHi).

[1] On June 8, Congress had ordered an embargo on provisions, to be in effect from June 10 to November 15, 1778, unless Congress revoked it sooner. *JCC*, 11:578.

[2] Congress approved the draft of a circular letter on state levies on June 10. *JCC*, 11:583.

[3] Gates' undated letter to the earl of Thanet, appealing to Britain to recognize American independence, was printed in the April 29, 1778, issue of the *Pennsylvania Evening Post*, which also contained a report of the duke of Richmond's unsuccessful effort to have the House of Lords take this proposal into consideration.

Thomas McKean to Nathanael Greene

Sir,

York-Town June 9th. 1778.

I just now received your favour of the 3d instant, and am not a little surprized that the Sheriff of Northampton county should have permitted Colo. Robert L. Hooper, after he was arrested by virtue of my Precept, to wait upon you until he had appeared before me.[1]

You say, Sir, "Colo. Hooper waited upon me to communicate his situation, & to know if the circumstances of the army would admit of his absence, but as the army is just upon the wing, and part of it will in all probability march through his district, I could not without great necessity *consent* to his being absent, as there is *no other person* that can give the necessary aid upon this occasion."

I do not think, Sir, that the absence, sickness or even death of Mr. Hooper could be attended with such a consequence, that *no other person* could be found who could give the necessary aid upon this occasion; but what attracts my attention most is your observation, that *you* cannot without great necessity *consent to his being absent*. As to that, Sir, I shall not ask *your consent*, nor that of any person in or out of the army, whether my Precept shall be obeyed or not in Pennsylvania.

The warrant for the arresting Mr. Hooper being special, no other magistrate can take cognizance thereof but myself. The mode you propose of giving bail cannot be adopted for many reasons.

I should be very sorry to find, that the execution of criminal law should impede the operations of the army in any instance, but should be more so to find the latter impede the former.

I am, Sir, with great respect, Your most obedient humble servant,

M:K.

FC (PHi).

[1] Gen. Nathanael Greene's June 3 letter to McKean, which had been directed to the latter in his capacity as chief justice of the Pennsylvania Supreme Court,

was an attempt to deflect the court away from Robert L. Hooper, Jr., a deputy quartermaster general who had been in trouble with the state of Pennsylvania since mid-1777. According to Greene, "Colo Robert L. Hooper of North Hampton County, one of my Deputies in the QMG's department informs me, he has lately been served with a warrant from under Your hand, charging him with having libeled the Magistrates of this State in a Letter to Gouverneur Morris Esqr. and directing the Sheriff to bring him before you at York Town." McKean Papers, PHi.

State officials Jonathan Dickinson Sergeant and John Arndt had accused Hooper of misusing government funds and property, refusing to take the state oath of allegiance, and encouraging other residents of Northampton County to refuse to subscribe to the oath, but the charges went unsubstantiated because of Hooper's intimidation of the two men. Hooper had written to Gouverneur Morris in the aftermath of a violent episode in which Hooper had severely beaten one of his accusers, Attorney General Sergeant, and threatened the other, Justice of the Peace Arndt, both of whom were also members of the Pennsylvania Council of Safety. As President Thomas Wharton complained to McKean on February 15, 1778: "An incident at Reading some days past disturbs me. Mr. Sergeant being there, as Attorney General at the Quarter Sessions, was assaulted and beaten by Robert Lettis Hooper, Esquire, on account of some information the former gave in the late Council of Safety of this State." Wharton continued: "It happened that Mr. Sergeant left Town without finishing this affidavit. Another, drawn for Mr. Arndt, of Northampton, was left in the same state. When Mr. Arndt was traveling homewards he was threatened & insulted by Hooper, & threats were also liberally made openly by him, against Mr. Sergeant. I was told that if he went to the Decemr Court in Easton he would be threshed. This however, did not happen. That Mr. Hooper by these menaces intended to prevent Evidence being collected I will not say, but that they had such a tendency is obvious." *Pa. Archives,* 1st ser. 6:266–67.

Relations between state and Continental officials were exacerbated after Hooper wrote an intemperate letter to Gouverneur Morris, whom Hooper believed would be sympathetic to him because of an ongoing conflict between Morris and the Pennsylvania authorities over the state price control law. Morris apparently showed the letter at army headquarters, where he was serving as a member of the Committee at Camp. When Joseph Reed, a staunch Pennsylvania supporter and also a member of the Committee at Camp, saw the letter, he probably reported Hooper's written attack on the state council to McKean, who then issued a writ for Hooper's arrest.

Despite McKean's desire to have him tried, Hooper was probably not brought to trial. Hooper, however, did write the following apology on August 31, 1778, to Pennsylvania Vice President George Byran. "I cannot deny to you, honourable Sir, that I have a very great contempt for Mr. Sarjent and Mr. Arndt, as private Gentlemen. They have made several attempts to ruin my reputation as an Officer in the service of the States, and have induced the honourable Council to exhibit charges against me which Mr. Sarjent & Mr. Arndt could not support. This drew me into a personal Quarrell with them, but on my honour, Sir, I don't recollect, that at the time of these disputes I ever reflected on Council, but it is true, that very soon after a dispute which happened between Mr. Sarjent and me, and whilest I was warm with resentment against him, I wrote a Letter to the Hon'ble Governeur Morris, the particular Expressions in which Letter I don't well remember, but believe, from information, that they were generally ungentlemanly and indeasent. I hope, Sir, you will believe, and that the honourable Council will believe, that I have long had a great personal regard for the late worthy President and you, and that I have ever had reason to esteem those Gentlemen in Council with whom I have the honour to be acquainted as worthy Citizens and that I am sorry to find that the expressions in that Letter may be construed to extend to you or them. I hope you will believe that they were not my deliberate sentiments, and that I am incapable of treating so respectable a Body with the least disrespect.

"I should not have taken the liberty to trouble your honour with this Letter if you was a stranger to my general character, which I am happy to say is the reverse of what has been represented to Council—permitt me then to request you will be pleased to assure Council that I never meant to reflect on their honour's honourable body. It is extremely disagreeable to me to know that they think I have, and as (since I entered into a parole agreement with Mr. Arndt, in June, 1777,) I have assisted the Magistrates in executing the laws of the State. I mean to continue so to do, and hope by a steady, firm and just behaviour to all men to take off the prejudices conceived against my General conduct as a Citizen & an officer in the service of the United States, and finally to merit the esteem of Council." *Pa. Archives,* 2nd ser. 3:236–37.

When Joseph Reed later became President of Pennsylvania, he renewed his attack on Hooper in a lengthy April 15, 1779, memorial to Congress which led to subsequent efforts to court-martial him. In December 1779 a committee of Congress recommended charges against Hooper, but he apparently escaped a judicial test of his public actions when his position as deputy quartermaster general was abolished in a July 15, 1780, reorganization of the army commissary system.

See *JCC,* 12:1245–46, 13:453–54; John M. Coleman, *Thomas McKean, Forgotten Leader of the Revolution* (Rockaway, N.J.: American Faculty Press, 1975), pp. 225–26; Robert L. Brunhouse, *The Counter-Revolution in Pennsylvania, 1776–1790* (Harrisburg: Pennsylvania Historical Commission, 1942), pp. 47–49; Max M. Mintz, *Gouverneur Morris and the American Revolution* (Norman: University of Oklahoma Press, 1970), pp. 95–96; Charles Henry Hart, "Colonel Robert Lettis Hooper," *PMHB* 36 (January 1912): 60–91; Greene, *Papers* (Showman), 2:331n.2, 424–25, 429–30; Daniel Roberdeau to Thomas Wharton, January 16, note 2 and February 17, 1778, note 2; Henry Laurens' Notes of Debates, March 26, note 1; and Gouverneur Morris to Joseph Reed, April 9, 1779.

Thomas McKean to Sarah McKean

My dear Sally, York-Town. June 9th. 1778.

Your favour of the 6th instant I received by Sam and am glad to hear you are well. As I expect to hear from the President of the Delaware State every day, & expect some money from thence; and as the boys are not equipped for their journey, I have thought it best to stay here a few days longer. When you are ready and the boys put in order for school, you will be so good as to send Sam immediately for me. It will be as convenient for us to go by the place where the boys are to stay, in our way to Newcastle county, as any rout we could take.

I have tried to get you a maid, but in vain; I offered 20/ a week, but the Jades won't leave Town. Do get one for the time we shall stay in Paxton, let the price be what it may. In a very few days I expect Philada. will be evacuated by the Enemy, and on that event I must push there, and take a house, while rents are low.

Lord Howe & General Clinton have at last found out the way of writing to Congress. We had a letter from each, directed to *Henry*

Laurens Esquire President of Congress at York-Town, on Saturday morning; they let Congress know that they have it in command from His Majesty to lay their Acts of Parliament before *Congress,* and to communicate them to the *Commander in chief of their Armies* &c. Congress referred them to their determination on the 22d of April last, and let them know whenever their King is seriously disposed to put an end to the present unprovoked & cruel war, Congress will be ready to conclude a peace upon terms honorable to *Independant* Nations, and beneficial for their Constituents &c. As the answer will probably be received to day in Philadelphia I do not think they will stay three days longer.

You have by Sam

1 Paper pins	£ 0.15.0
2 doz shirt buttons @ 3/9	0. 7.6
5 skenes of white thread @ 2/6	0.12.6
8 & ½ yards striped hollands @ 30/	12.15.0
	£14.10.0

No good Bohea tea at present, but shall get some soon. Coffee at Baltimore for 7/ and 6/6 a pound. There is a French ship, of 52 guns and 450 men, arrived in Virginia, with a cargo which cost one hundred & thirty five thousand pounds sterling on board. All is landed safe at Williamsburg, and many other arrivals to the Eastward.

Give my love to the children, kiss Sall for me; I suppose she will walk and talk by the time I get home. Remember me to Miss Nelly Reed & Sammy Sterrett. Adieu. Your most affectionate,

Tho M:Kean

RC (PHi).

Gouverneur Morris to George Washington

Dear Genl. York Town 9th June 1778

I have sent to your Address three Bundles containing the several Materials collected by the Committee for arrang. the army.[1] This Business being now put under your Care I trust you will be enabled speedily to put your Army in the Situation you wish excepting always the Deficiency of Numbers which is upon the whole well enough since thereby it happens that less of the Resources of the Country are consumed and this is certainly a War of Resources. The Opinion of Congress relative to Phila. you have doubtless ere this received.[2] Mine did not arise from any Pleasure I take in the Distresses of my Fellow Creatures, still less from that horrid Love of Proscriptions which however dictated certainly disgraces human

Nature. Simply I wished that our Enemies should be mulcted before they were received into our Bosom and that we might thereby possess ourselves of the Sinews of War.[3] Should there be still other Desiderata as to the Army which indeed I well know there are pray let me hear of them in a Letter to which I shall call the attention of the House who have now entangled themselves in such an Infinity of Matter that some Management is really necessary to lead them to the most serious and important Objects. The Committee had written to Govr. Clinton for his Assistance in Arranging the Regts not with you.[4] So much as I received in Answer to that Application you will find among the Bundles.[5] Whatever may come to Hand regarding Gansevoort's Regt. I shall do myself the Honor to transmit immediately. I am called away.

Should Mrs. Washington be still in Camp which I confess is rather unlikely pray present my Respects to her.

I have the Honor to be Dr General, Yours sincerely,

Gouvr Morris

RC (DLC).

1 See *JCC*, 11:570.

2 See *JCC*, 11:571.

3 See Morris to Washington, May 27, 1778.

4 See Committee at Camp to George Clinton, March 16, 1778.

5 See Governor Clinton's May 14 letter to Morris in Clinton, *Papers* (Hastings), 3:308–10.

Joseph Reed to Nathanael Greene

Dr. General Mr Henrys, June 9, 1778

By a Resolve of Congress the General, Mr. Dana & myself are appointed a Committee to arrange the Army & I have postponed my Return Home in Consequence. I suppose you will have some Direction to quarter us, but as you are pretty thick at Moore Hall I will relieve you from the Incumbrance of self & Servant for the present by remaining at Mr. Henry's. But in this Case I must beg you to send over some Oats or other Grain for my Horses as we are very destitute.[1] Your Compliance will oblige, Dr. Sir, Your Affect. & Obed, Hbble Serv, Jos. Reed

RC (NHi).

1 On June 13 Reed wrote the following brief letter, from "Major Henry's," to commissary general of forage Clement Biddle on the same subject. "As I am detained here by being a Member of the Committee of Arrangement I must beg you would send by my servant some Grain for my Horses none being to be obtained on this Side the Schuykill. I wrote a day or two ago to Genl. Green on this Head not recollecting that I should have applied to you—but none being then in Camp I had only his Promise to supply me as soon as it arrived." American Manuscripts, MH–H.

Joseph Reed to Esther Reed

My dear Hetty Mr. Henry's June 9. 1778

I got down here the Day after I left you & found a Number of Philadelphians hovering round the Camp in sure & certain Hope of soon entering the City—in which they have been much disappointed. There appeared on Friday every Reason to believe the Town would be evacuated in a few Hours, but that Evening the Commissioners arrivd, viz. Ld. Carlisle, Govr. Johnston & Mr. Eden—when an immediate Stop was put to all farther Embarkation, a great deal of Baggage was brought back & some Goods relanded. In short Appearances are now as much for their Stay as they were against it last Week. There has been no formal Annunciation as yet of the Arrival of the Commissioners but it is expected hourly. Most of those who have been mischievously active against us are going with them, but many of the Country Refugees have come out to sue for Grace & among them my Friend Lusely. Even Mr Galloway has made an Attempt for Favour, but Genl. Clinton would not permit him to go on with it, so that he is now going off with them, if they should go. On Saturday under the Protection of a Flag I went down as low as Vandering's to see what Mrs. Yard had done but found nothing. Jacob Baker has gone in to day & I have sent a Message by him to her. Mr. Pettit does not seem so well recovered as I had expected, his Hands are very much broke out, he sets out for York Town tomorrow both as a Journey of Health & Business. The Army strengthens very fast & both Officers & Men make a much more reputable Appearance than they did formerly. There is the utmost Appearance of Harmony & that all Faction & Opposition of every kind has ceased. Mrs. Washington & the other Ladies except Mrs. Knox have left Camp. The Commissioners say positively that there is no French War & I am inclined to believe it. Many Persons are very sanguine that the Enemy must evacuate Philadelphia after having sent their Baggage &c. off but I doubt that Event is not so near as they wish but when the Operations of War will be & how soon the Campaign will open I am much at a Loss to determine. This Morning the current Opinion is that they will do what they should have done last Year, go up the North River & cut off our Communication with the New England States, but I do not see how they can leave this Army behind them with any Reputation, or what Success in that Quarter could ballance the Discredit of leaving Philada. & giving up the middle States. I came over from Camp on Sunday Evening with the full Intention of setting out early in the Morning for Fleming Town, when I received a Message from the General that I was appointed one of a Committee to arrange the Army with him & that the other Gentleman might be hourly expected. The next Morning I received a Copy of the Resolve & as it is a Business of much Importance & admitting of no

Delay I concluded to stay rather than have it wait for me. I do not know how long it may take us but I should think it cannot exceed a Week—when I shall immediately return to you. By that Time some certain Judgment may be formed of the Enemy's Intentions of leaving Town on which my Journy to York Town will depend. I could wish to hear from my dear Hetty in the mean Time in which Case you will direct to me under Cover to Mr. Cox & Mr. Pettit in their publick Characters, so that it will be opened if they should happen to be absent.

I have given you all the News & would have sent you a Lancaster Paper if I had one—tho I do not recollect that there is any Thing of Consequence in it.

I am with Love to the Children & your Mamma, my dear Girls, ever faithful & affectionate, J Reed

[*P.S.*] You will find in some part of the Desk in your Room some Papers wrappd in a News Paper, viz. the Establishment of the Army & others relating to the same Subject. I should be glad you would forward them by some safe Oppy—if none presents soon let them be sent to Mr. Furman to be forwarded with all Expedition.

June 11 1778. I wrote the above & waited for an Oppy. to forward it which I have not met with. The other Gentleman is not yet arrived so that I am idling away my Time here. The Commissioners have formally announced their Arrival in a Letter directed to the General with all his Titles. The Congress too have all their Titles. Sr. Harry Clinton requested a safe Conduct for Dr. Ferguson Secretary to the Commission to go to Congress which has been refused. Nothing new from Philada. since I wrote the above. I am my dear Hetty's Affect.

J Reed

RC (NHi).

Committee of Congress Report on *Le Fier Roderique*

[June 10, 1778][1]

Your Committee to whom were referred the Letter from Caron de Beau Marchais to the Committee of Commerce dated at Paris the twenty third of March last and the Letter from Chevallie to Congress dated at Hampton the 28th of May last beg Leave to report.

That having considered the said Letters it is their Opinion that the Mistery in which the Transactions of the House of Roderigo Hortalez & Co. hath been hitherto involved cannot be fully cleared up at present and that it would be more prudent to wait the Arrival of Mr. Deane or at least of Mr. Carmichael who being more acquainted with those Affairs may throw Light upon them useful to Congress or those whom they may employ to investigate it. Your Committee are the more inclined to this from the Consideration

1. That the Continent being (upon every Principle) already much indebted to Monsr. Beau Marchais should the present Cargoe appear to be the Property of these States a proper Deduction from his Account may hereafter be made. &

2. That the Contracts entered into with his Agent Monsr. Franci will be amply sufficient for that Purpose should the Debt of these States not be so great as is above supposed.[2]

Wherefore your Committee are of Opinion that without entering into an Inquiry where there is not sufficient Evidence to attain to any fixed Conclusion it will be proper to consider the Cargoe of the Ship *Le Fier Roderique* as the Property of the said Monsr. Beau Marchais. And to purchase from his Agents such Articles as may be necessary for the Use of these States.

In order to determine what Price may be given for such Articles your Committee beg Leave to observe that the Returns of the said Cargoe being to be made in Tobacco it will be necessary to estimate the same accordingly. That the Average Price of this Article formerly was about four Dollars per Ct. and at present about twelve, being three times the former Price. That if upon £100 Stg. in Commodities £100 be allowed for Charges, Freight, Insurance or Risque and Profit then calculating Dollars as high as five Shillings Sterling will be 800 Dollars which formerly would have purchased 20,000 lbs of Tobacco and that Tobacco will now sell for 2,400 Dollars Wherefore there should be allowed from this State 2,400 Dollars for every £100 Stg. of Commodities. On the other Hand if he be allowed £300 Stg. per Ct. on the outward and the same on the homeward bound Voyage amounting to 900 Stg. or 20,000 Livres being the Price of 10,000 lbs of Tobacco in France then Tobacco being here estimated at 12 DD the same would amount to 1200 Dollars on every £100 Stg. But further as it is the Interest of these States to state the Price of Tobacco low it may be proper to contract for it to be delivered at the Rate of 10 Dollars per Ct. in which Case the amount according to the above Calculations would be 1000 and 2000 DD per £100 Stg. Wherefore taking a Medium of 1500 may on the whole appear proper to limit the Price not to exceed the Rate 1500 D. or £450 Virginia Currency per 100 Stg. to be paid in Tobacco at a Price not less than 10 Dollars or £5 of the same Currency.

Your Committee further observe that in order to avoid all Competition between Purchasers it will be proper that as the Governour of Virginia is in Treaty for the Cargoe to apply to him to purchase for the united States such of the Articles as may be necessary for them under the Restrictions above mentioned.

And your Committee beg Leave further to observe that the said Monsr. Beau Marchais having by his Agent offered to Congress a Contract in the Alternative either to pay in France for the Goods he shall transmit with all Costs and Charges, Freight, Insurance, Interest, Commissions &ca. or that he shall transmit the same at his Risque to be paid for in America at the current Price. And Congress having chosen the former have thereby in the Opinion of your Committee exposed themselves to great Fraud and also to the Loss of the Goods which will not probably be transported with such Care when at the Risque of these united States as when on the Account of the Individual shipping them. Besides as it is probable that Goods will become much plentier by an open Commerce with France they will probably come much cheaper purchased here than in Europe. Wherefore they conceive it would be proper to alter the Contract with Monsr. Franci if he shall incline thereto. All the above disagreed.[3]

The Committee &c Report the following Resolutions[4]

Whereas by the Letter[5] of Monsr. Beaumarchais it appears that[6] the Cargoe of the Ship *Le Fier Rodrique* is to be offered to Congress to be by them purchased or such Part thereof as they may think proper in Preference of all others: And whereas his Excellency Patrick Henry Esq Governor of Virginia is in treaty therefor with Monsr. Chevallie the Consignee of the said Cargoe[7] Resolved that Govr. Henry be requested to purchase [for] the united States the Articles contained in the List hereto annexed being part of the Cargo of the French Ship Lefier Roderique[8] as cheap as he can not exceeding the Price following towit £450 Virginia Money for every £100 Stg. to be paid in Tobacco at ten Dollars per Ct. And that a Letter be written to his Excellency explaining the Principles of such Limitation. Agd.[9]

Resolved that the Commercial Committee be directed to confer with Monsr. Franci and if he shall incline thereto to alter the Cont[rac]t made with him on the Part of Monsr. Beau Marchais and these S[tates] so far as to adopt the Offer of the said Monsr. Beaumarchais to transport the Articles oft ordered by Congress to the Continent at his own Risque to be paid for here at the Price of such Articles when they shall arrive.

List of Articles

Boulets ronde de divers Calibres 33, 24, 16, 12, 8.	Leaden Bullets of different Sizes
Bas de Soie assortie de Laine aussi assortis	Mens Silk and Woollen Stockings

Burreta de Laine	Woollen Caps.
Boucles	The different Kinds of Buckles
Boutons Pour Habits complets de Msr les Officiers & Pour Habillement des Soldats	Uniform Buttons for Officers and Soldiers
Boutons de Manches	Sleeve Buttons
Cadix [. . .] pour doublures d'Habits uniformes Rouge	Red Cadiz for the Lining of Uniforms
Chemise Garnies Fines et commune	Coarse and fine Shirts
Couvertes de Laine Fines et communes	Woollen Blankets
Chapeaux communes pour Soldats	Soldiers Hats
Draps Fins pour Habits d'Officers Ditto communs pour Soldats Do Legers pour Soldats	Clothes fine for Officers Ditto coarse for soldiers & light Do for Soldiers
Ecritoire de Cuivre	Brass Ink Stands
Flanelles de Laine Blanche	White Flannell
Fil assorti	Sewing Thread
Guetres pour Soldats en Toiles	Linnen spatterdashes for Soldiers
Habits uniformes complets pour soldats	Soldiers Cloathing ready made.
Mouchoire de Soie de chollet & Facon de Beam	An assortment of Handkerchiefs
Poudre de Guerre	Gun Powder
Poignets de Chemise	Wristbands for shirts
Pierre a Fusils Pistolets &c	Flints
Sergettes pour Doublures habits d'officiers Ecarlatte, Bleu Ciel, Vertes, Brune et a la Piece aussi pour [. . .] blanche	Serget of different Colors viz Scarlett, sky blue, Brown & White for Linings

MS (DNA: RG 76, Beaumarchais Claims File). In the hand of Gouverneur Morris, with amendments by Henry Laurens. President Laurens undoubtedly made his amendments when this report was considered by Congress on June 10.

1 On June 8 Congress had appointed a committee consisting of Gouverneur Morris, John Banister, and Francis Dana to consider a March 23 letter to the Committee of Commerce from "Messrs. Beaumarchais & Co." and a May 28 letter from a certain "Mr. Chevallie," the supercargo of Beamarchais' ship *Le Fier Roderique*. Although neither of these letters is in PCC, a March 23 letter from Beaumarchais to Congress, describing his commercial dealings with Arthur Lee and Silas Deane, is in Beaumarchais, *Correspondance* (Morton and Spinelli),

4:91–94. The report Morris drafted on behalf of the committee was taken up in Congress on June 10, at which time the delegates approved a considerably abbreviated version of it, which merely requested Gov. Patrick Henry of Virginia to purchase certain parts of the cargo of *Le Fier Roderique* at a price proposed by Morris in his report. See *JCC,* 11:576, 584. It seems virtually certain that Congress rejected or postponed consideration of the rest of Morris' report because of a reluctance to become further entangled at this time in the vexing question of whether it was obligated to pay for the military supplies Beaumarchais had shipped to the United States.

2 See *JCC,* 10:316–18.

3 Last four words added by Laurens.

4 Laurens added these words in place of Morris' original statement: "Your Committee on the whole Matter submit the following Resolutions."

5 Laurens inserted the last two words in place of "the Orders."

6 Last three words added by Laurens.

7 Laurens wrote "PPd [postponed]" between the lines above "Cargoe."

8 Last eleven words added by Laurens.

9 Word written by Laurens. See also Laurens to Patrick Henry, June 13, 1778.

Henry Laurens to the States

Sir 10 June 1778[1]

Authentic intelligence received by Congress from many quarters leave it no longer doubtful in what manner the Enemy mean to conduct their plan of Conciliation. Under delusive appearances of pacific Acts and Peace-making Commissioners, already their Military Reinforcements begin to arrive, and already they have commenced the Campaign in many places with Acts of cruelty and devastation.

Indian irruptions and burning houses, in the moment of dispersing propositions for Peace, evince the insidious designs of the Enemy and demonstrate the necessity of wisdom in Council; of strength and vigour in the field. The former may be employed to distress the Enemy greatly, by withholding from them the provisions of America, and the latter by quickly collecting powerful Armies to take advantage of their present weakness.[2]

The present moment unimproved may be productive of most pernicious consequences, and the public safety demands strong and united efforts.

Experience hath shewn that the Marine force of our Enemies enables them to secure, for the support of their Armies, almost the whole of our exported provisions, and therefore Congress, impressed with the necessity of preventing the supplies derived to our foes from this source, and desirous of supplying the Armies of the United States, have, upon mature deliberation, laid an Embargo on provisions of all kinds, and they earnestly request the vigorous exercise of the powers of your State to carry into effectual execution this most necessary measure.

The urgent necessity for the provisions with which your State is to furnish the Army, induces Congress to press upon you, Sir, immediate and constant attention to this important business, and the present absence of the Enemy's ships from the Bay of Chesapeak may be improved by seizing the opportunity of water conveyance to the Head of Elk.[3]

LB (DNA: PCC, item 13). Endorsed: "Circular to the several States in Union including Delaware all forw[ar]d[e]d." It is significant that this letter appears in Laurens' presidential letterbook immediately after his June 14 letter to John Sullivan, for which see note 3 below.

1 This letter is based upon a draft that reflects the work of two committees of Congress. The first, which was appointed on June 3 to consider a May 27 letter from Commissary General Jeremiah Wadsworth dealing with his difficulties in procuring beef, submitted reports calling for the suspension or repeal of state laws regulating prices and for the imposition of a six-month embargo on provisions that were approved by Congress on June 4 and 8 respectively. See *JCC*, 11:563, 569–70, 572, 578–79; and Laurens to William Livingston, June 5, 1778, note 2. Although Congress resolved on the eighth that "it be earnestly recommended to the respective states, to take the most effective measures for carrying . . . [the embargo] into immediate execution," the task of embodying this recommendation in a circular letter to the states fell to another committee, which was appointed the following day to consider a June 3 letter from Gen. Horatio Gates, recently reappointed to the northern military department. It was this second committee that drafted the present circular letter, which won congressional approval this day, and that addressed itself not only to Gates' concerns but also to the first committee's call for an embargo. See *JCC*, 11:579, 582–84; and PCC, item 154, 1:374–406.

2 At this point in the LB, Laurens inexplicably omitted a paragraph which, upon instruction from Congress, he was supposed to send to every state except North Carolina, South Carolina, and Georgia: "In duty, therefore, to their constituents, Congress earnestly call upon you, sir, and your State, to adopt the most effectual and vigorous measures for speedily reinforcing the continental army with your quota of troops." *JCC*, 11:583.

An examination of some of the RC's of this letter reveals that Laurens was inconsistent in carrying out this order. For example, he left this paragraph out of the letter he sent to Pres. Caesar Rodney of Delaware but put it in the one he sent to Gov. Richard Caswell of North Carolina. See American Manuscripts, MH-H; and *N.C. State Records*, 13:156–58. This paragraph also does not appear in the copy of this letter in Laurens' private letterbook. Laurens Papers, ScHi.

3 Although Laurens was instructed to include the foregoing paragraph only in the letters he sent to the governors of Maryland, Virginia, and North Carolina, he inadvertently left it out of his letter to North Carolina, an oversight he corrected on June 14 when he wrote a brief covering letter to Governor Caswell enclosing a copy of the omitted paragraph. PCC, item 13, 1:367. As the document note makes clear, the marginal note that Laurens wrote next to this paragraph in his presidential letterbook—"this Paragraph to the Governors of Maryland, Virginia & North Carolina"—could not have been written before June 14.

Marine Committee to the Commissioners at Paris

Marine Committee, York in Penna.
Honorable Gentn June 10th 1778.

There is wanted for A fifty Six Gun Ship now building at Portsmouth in the State of New Hampshire, Twenty eight 24 pounders Cannon & Twenty eight 18 Pounders which we request you will order to be shipped for that Port or the Port of Boston by the first Opportunity. Should the Continental Frigates Boston and Providence be in France when this gets to hand they may take in those Cannon and in that case you will please to ship an equal number of each Size sufficient to Ballast Said Frigates, as we shall have occasion for more than will be wanted for the 56 Gun ship. We request your attention to this business and are Honorable Gentn, with great respect, Your very Obedt servants,[1]

Richard Henry Lee. C. M.

RC (PPAmP). In the hand of John Brown and signed by Chairman Lee. Endorsed by John Adams: "Letter Marine Comtee. June 10, 1778. for 28. 24—Pounders and 28. 18s."

[1] The Marine Committee Letter Book contains the following postscript: "P.S. We request you will order our ships of war to sail in company as it is the practice of the enemy so to do." Paullin, *Marine Committee Letters*, 1:255–56.

John Wentworth to John Langdon

Dear Sir, York Town Penna. June 10. 1778.

I should have done myself the honor to have informed you of our arrival and of some other matters before this, but my worthy colleague on closing a letter a few days since acquainted me that he addressed it to you—and had given you such information respecting the ship and other affairs as he thought necessary.[1] I therefore hoped to be excused if I delayed writing for a short space. I trust the alteration in the vessel can by no means disconcert any plan of your's. How far it may benefit, or injure the public, I am incapable of judging.

The enemy at Philadelphia for three weeks past have been doing and undoing—one day extremely busy in fortifying and the next in demolishing—in short their manoeuvres are so various as to render it utterly impossible to guess what measures they mean finally to pursue. From every circumstance however their intention to evacuate the City is beyond doubt; how long that step may be retarded by the late arrival of Commissioners from England is altogether uncertain. The Commissioners have directed their General to apply to General Washington to obtain a passport for a Dr Ferguson, Secretary to their King's Commission, to wait on Congress. General Washington has submitted the matter, which is not yet determined upon.[2]

I hardly think Congress will have the *honor* of seeing those gentlemen Commissioners very soon, unless they comply with measures which from the present conduct of the enemy we have little reason to expect. They have come out for the pretended purpose of settling the dispute to the mutual advantage of both parties and their army have very lately commenced another campaign with marks of cruelty peculiar to themselves. The barbarities committed on the defenceless inhabitants of the frontiers of this State and of Virginia by the savage Tories and a few of the British troops are almost incredible; means are now devising to put a stop to such tragical proceedings.

I do not recollect any thing further worth communicating, but as any matters of that kind shall turn up you will doubtless have them from one or the other of us.

I pursued my plan relative to the small pox and had the disorder very favorable.

We had an agreeable journey enough for the times, though we were considerably hardshipped in passing through Connecticut being often pushed to find provender for our horses or entertainment for ourselves—occasioned partly by the multiplicity of travellers, but principally by the *wisdom* of partial regulations, that State you know having come fully into the mode of restricting prices. Before that happened I imagine a traveller must have met with most excellent fare; for we could scarcely ride a mile without reaching the *sign of a sign*. So powerful were the operations of the Act that nothing but the posts were left standing. I am too well acquainted with your generosity to attempt an apology for troubling you with the letter to Mrs Wentworth[3] and should she forward to your hands a letter for me, I must presume on your kindness so much further as to desire you to cover it in a line.

I am Sir, with great esteem your much obliged and obt very hble servt,

John Wentworth Jr

Tr (DLC).

1 See Josiah Bartlett to John Langdon, June 1, 1778.

2 For further information on the arrival of the British peace commissioners, see Joseph Reed to Esther Reed, June 9, 1778. Belatedly learning that the British army was preparing to evacuate Philadelphia, the commissioners hastily tried to communicate with Congress by using their secretary, Dr. Adam Ferguson, as a messenger. But General Washington refused to grant Ferguson a passport to York and sent the commissioners' request to Congress, which on June 17 approved Washington's handling of Ferguson's passport application, although the commissioners' dispatches had already reached Congress under a flag of truce on June 13. See Committee of Congress Proposed Report, June 11, 1778; and Weldon Brown, *Empire or Independence: A Study in the Failure of Reconciliation* (Baton Rouge: Louisiana State University Press, 1941), pp. 260–65.

3 Not found.

Charles Carroll of Carrollton to Charles Carroll, Sr.

Dr Papa,

11th June 1778

Mr. Stevenson going to Baltimore gives me an opportunity of informing you of the arrival of the British Commissioners Ld. Carlile, Governor Johnstone & Wm. Eden. They have demanded of Gen. Washington a pass for their Secretary a Mr Ferguson to come to Congress. The General refused the request untill the pleasure was known whether they would receive the Secretary. A committee of Congress is appointed to report on this matter. I believe Congress will not receive any message or officer from the Commissioners unless they withdraw their troops or acknowlege our Independance, at least I think they can not pursue a different conduct without being inconsistent.

You have Ld. Abington's protest inclosed. My love to Molly & Mrs. Darnall & the little ones. I am, yr affectionate Son,

Ch. Carroll of Carrollton

RC (MdHi).

Committee of Congress Proposed Report

[June 11, 1778]

The Committee to whom was referred General Washingtons letter of the 9th instant with its inclosure, beg leave to report as their opinion that Mr. President do transmit the following answer to the Generals letter.[1]

Sir,

York the 11th of June 1778

Your letter of the 9th instant with its inclosure from Sr. Henry Clinton notifying the arrival of Commissioners from Great Britain and desiring a passport for Doctor Ferguson has been laid before Congress. I am instructed to inform you that it is the direction of Congress you should acquaint Sr. Henry Clinton, that in letters of the sixth of this month to himself and Lord Howe, Congress have expressed their sentiments of the only admissible principles upon which they can attend to propositions for peace. If the Commissioners from the King of Great Britain, who best know their own powers, shall upon due consideration of them, be satisfied that they are adequate to the purpose of making peace upon the principles contained in the said letters, and thereupon request a Passport for Doctor Ferguson, you are at liberty to grant it.

I have the honor to be &c.

MS (ScHi). In the hand of Richard Henry Lee.

1 Washington's June 9 letter to Henry Laurens, and the copies he enclosed of Sir Henry Clinton's request for a passport for Adam Ferguson (to transmit a letter from the Carlisle peace commissioners to Congress) and of Washington's reply to Clinton (refusing the passport and explaining that the request was being referred to Congress), are in PCC, item 152, 6:87–93, and Washington, *Writings* (Fitzpatrick), 12:38–39. On June 11 Congress referred these letters to a committee composed of Samuel Adams, Richard Henry Lee, and Henry Marchant. The committee submitted a report on the 12th, which was then considered and postponed, and Congress had resumed debating this issue on the 13th when Washington's express arrived with a packet from the Carlisle commissioners that had been sent by Dr. Ferguson to Washington's headquarters. *JCC,* 11:585, 593, 605–6.

It is probable that this proposed report was the one read in Congress on June 12. Writing to William Heath and to Philip Schuyler on the morning of the 12th, Henry Laurens predicted that the decision on a passport for Ferguson would involve a demand to know his intended business, which was not explicitly required in this proposed report. But Laurens' comments do suggest that the question of granting a passport to Ferguson had not been decided without debate. And the fact that this report and Lee's proposed resolution on Dr. Ferguson are located among the Henry Laurens papers further supports the conjecture that both proposals were considered in Congress on the 12th. However, comments by Josiah Bartlett and by Samuel Adams on the 13th suggest that Congress was about to refuse a passport and order Washington to transmit the commissioners' letter by his own express when an express arrived at midday June 13 with the commissioner's packet, thus making the passport question moot. Nevertheless, once the proper response to the peace commissioners' letter had been determined, Congress on June 17 unanimously approved the conduct of Washington in refusing a passport to Dr. Ferguson. See *JCC,* 11:616; letters of June 12 from Josiah Bartlett to Nathaniel Folsom, and from Henry Laurens to William Heath, and to Philip Schuyler; Richard Henry Lee's Proposed Resolution, June 12; and Samuel Adams to James Warren, June 13, 1778. For a discussion of Congress' response to the British peace commissioners, see Samuel Adams to James Warren, June 13, 1778, note 3.

Francis Dana to George Washington

Dear Sir York June 11th 1778

I had the honor last evening of your favor of the 9th inst. requesting me to repair to camp to assist in the business of arranging the army as soon as possible.[1] Although I am impressed with the necessity of that business being finished without delay, yet I cannot in duty to the State I represent quit Congress till the Confederation is ratified, which I hope will be done in a few days. In the mean time the arrangement may go on as Genl. Reed[2] will doubtless be at hand to assist you. He has paid a particular attention to the battalions of this State; those of Maryland, on account of their distance from your camp, the committee cou'd make no enquiry about, those also may be arranged without any assistance from me, and indeed I know nothing about either of them. Those to which I paid a particular attention were the battalions of New Hampshire, Massachusetts,

Rhode Island, Jersey and Virginia; the last of which may be settled by conferring with the General Officers of that line, whose recommendation we followed. I will get the necessary papers from Mr. Morris and forward them to you. With the hope of taking some labour from off your hands, I should have been happy to have given my immediate attendance in camp. I trust by the time you, with the assistance of Genl. Reed, may have gone through the battalions of this State, Maryland and Virginia, to have the pleasure of affording you in this business all the assistance in my power.

I am Dr. Sir, with much respect & esteem, your most obedt. & obliged hble Servant, Fra Dana

[*P.S.*] Should Mrs. Washington be with you, you will be pleased to make my most respectful complements acceptable to her.

RC (DLC).

1 On June 4 Congress had appointed Dana to the committee on arrangement of the army, and on June 9, after receiving a copy of this resolve, Washington had written to Dana urging him to come to camp "as soon as possible." See *JCC*, 11:570; and Washington, *Writings* (Fitzpatrick), 12:38.

2 Joseph Reed, who was already at army headquarters, had also been appointed to the committee on arrangement of the army. See *JCC*, 11:570; and Reed to Esther Reed, June 9, 1778.

Henry Laurens to Richard Caswell

P.S. private. 11th June 1778

Your Excellency will find inclosed several Copies of Lord Abingdon's Speech & Protest in the British House of Lords upon the Acts of Parliament for Removing all doubts concerning Taxation &c. These as I endeavor to do all Papers proper for public information, I shall disperse as extensively as possible.

I shall add Copies of a late correspondence between Lord Howe, Sir H. Clinton, General Washington & Congress.

Last Night late I received a Letter from General Washington. Sir H. Clinton had requested a Passport for Doct Ferguson Secretary to the Commissioners to attend Congress. General Washington demur'd until he should inform Congress—this will be subject of our consideration at 10 oClock.

Doctor Ferguson was tutor to Lord Chesterfield at Geneva, where a Young Gentleman with whom I correspond in Camp knew him intimately—he says "the Doctor is known in the litterary World & whose profound knowledge makes him very respectable."[1]

"Preparations for abandoning the City still continue, the Enemy pretend 'tis impossible for them to continue there much longer, they are not to March through the Jerseys but on the Jersy side down the

Delaware & embark at some convenient place." Very serious, pretty trifling—when they are gone, I will beleive them. I shall not be surprized if they March down & in one Weeks time return with all their Ships & a reinforcement—several Transports with 800 Troops are arrived at New York & more are daily expected. HL.

RC (Nc–Ar). This is a special postscript Laurens added to the text of the June 10 circular letter to the states that was sent to Governor Caswell.

1 In this and the following paragraph Laurens is quoting from a June 9 letter written by his son John. Simms, *Laurens Army Correspondence*, pp. 181–83.

Henry Laurens to John Laurens

My Dear Son, 11th June 1778

I thank you much for your favor of the 9th.[1] Your Sentiments are great & as I think they are just, these intelligences help me forward.

Congress will send an answer & I trust, a proper answer to Sir Henry Clinton's application for a passport for your old acquaintance Doctor Ferguson.

If you were here in this Room I could entertain you five minutes with description of an excellent attempt in favor of pivot which was not only ousted but brought on a proposition which, as a Man of honor he must have wished for, as a Man of politeness he must have wished for it, because all the World wished for it.[2]

Your antagonists I find have not yet turned their backs, the more motions they make the more I suspect them. When they shall be fairly gone I will sing te deum, but 'till then my duty & my Interest dictate infidelity & command me to be watchful.

The long continuance of repeated accounts marking their intended embarkation has injured our Cause more than you are aware of. Adieu.

LB (ScHi).

1 See Simms, *Laurens Army Correspondence*, pp. 181–83.

2 Laurens is alluding to the call for an investigation of former quartermaster general Thomas Mifflin that Congress approved this day. *JCC*, 11:591–92. In previous correspondence with his son, Laurens had used the term *pivot* to designate Mifflin's role in the so-called Conway Cabal. That John Laurens understood the use of it in the present letter as a reference to Mifflin is indicated by this statement in his June 14 reply: "The inquiry into the conduct of the late quarter masters, must give pleasure to every man who wishes to see the betrayers of public trusts brought to condign punishment." See Simms, *Laurens Army Correspondence*, p. 185; and Laurens to John Laurens, January 8, 1778, note 6.

Henry Laurens to George Washington

Sir,

York Town 11th June 1778.

Late last Night I was honored with Your Excellency's favor of the 9th accompanied by Sir Henry Clinton's application for a passport for Doctor Ferguson & Your Excellency's reply—these I presented to Congress this Morning, & 'tis probable I shall receive from the House the necessary Commands to morrow. In the mean time I am ordered to transmit to Your Excellency an Act of Congress of the present date, directing an enquiry to be made into the conduct of the late Quarter Master general & other Officers in that department, which will be found within the present Inclosure.[1]

I have the honor to be, With the greatest Esteem & Respect, Sir, Your Excellency's Most obedient servant,

Henry Laurens, President of Congress.

RC (DLC).

[1] The original motion on this issue offered in Congress this day called upon Washington to investigate the conduct of former quartermaster general Thomas Mifflin and his subordinates and provided that "if it shall appear that the extraordinary deficiencies thereof, and the consequent distresses of the army, were chargeable to the misconduct of the said quarter master general or any of the said officers that a court martial be forthwith held on the delinquents." Congress rejected the motion in this form by a vote of seven states to three with one divided, but then approved a slightly amended version of it, omitting the word *forthwith,* without a roll call vote. See *JCC,* 11:591–92.

Congress' call for this inquiry nevertheless produced meager results, for Washington was too busy to conduct the investigation called for, and Congress refused to accede to Mifflin's request that it conduct one of its own. Consequently, Mifflin resigned from the army in August 1778 and began a newspaper campaign designed to force Congress to set up a special committee of inquiry. Although Mifflin's appeals to public opinion eventually led Congress on January 23, 1779, to renew its request to Washington to investigate the former quartermaster general, Washington demurred on the grounds that Mifflin was no longer a member of the army, and there the matter ended. For an account of this episode which concludes that Mifflin was guilty of no irregularities during his two terms as quartermaster general, from August 1775 to June 1776 and from September 1776 to November 1777, see Kenneth R. Rossman, *Thomas Mifflin and the Politics of the American Revolution* (Chapel Hill: University of North Carolina Press, 1952), chap. 12.

Joseph Reed to Esther Reed

Qr. Master Generals Office
June 11, 1778, 2 oClock

My dear Hetty

Upon coming over to Head Quarters this Morning I found two large Packets from England containing a very long Letter from your Brother,[1] one from Govr. Johnston[2] & several for you & your Mamma, the latter I now forward as I would do his to me but I have just received it & am anxious to forward yours to you which I do by Express. I have also some News Papers, Letters, Papers &c. all in the same Style of Penitence & Hope that we may again unite & be a happy People. Denny goes very far in his Letter. I have perused it but once & it is so long that I cannot read it again without detaining the Messenger which I do not care to do. But I beg you not to be so taken with what I send you as to forget to look for the Papers mentioned in my other Letter. I do not know when I shall be able to see you as my Colleague is not come but I will forward you all the News Papers & Papers as soon as I have perused them. I have one Peice of bad News. Johnny is alive it is true but behaves much amiss. He is idling his Time in France in very low Company instead of going to England as I expected & I fear spending me a great deal of Money. I shall write my dear Girl every few Days & oftner if any Thing occurs worth Notice. You will do the same by me as I have mentioned in my other Letter. I am my Dear Hettys very affect. J Reed

RC (NHi).

1 Dennis De Berdt (ca. 1742–1817), London merchant and the last colonial agent of the New Jersey Assembly. See Roche, *Joseph Reed*, pp. 18–29; and these *Letters*, 4:489n.2.

2 For the letters of De Berdt and former West Florida governor George Johnstone, see Reed's letters to Johnstone, June 13, note 1, and to De Berdt, July 19, 1778, note 1.

Josiah Bartlett to Nathaniel Folsom

Dear Sir York Town June 12th 1778

I arrived here the 21st ulto, & was obliged to put up at Stake's Tavern for several Days before I Could procure other Lodgings, I now put up at one Hoffmans on the west Side of the Bridge quite at the west end of the Town at a German House, where I am obliged to be a German in most Respects. We have been in hopes ever Since we arrived here that we should soon get back to Philadelphia, But the accounts from thence are so various & Contradictory and the arrival of the Brittish Commisrs at that place makes the Enemys Design of Removal Somewhat Problematical. If they mean to Evacuate the place, I Expect it will soon be Effected, as Genl Washington has Removed our army towards the City. The latter End of May Genl Clinton & Lord Howe Sent the late famous acts of the Brittish Parliament to G. Washington and Requested leave to Send out a person to him, which He Refused & informed them that if what they had to Communicate to him was what came under the military Department, He Desired it might be Sent him in writing, but if it was of any other nature their applications ought to be made to Congress; the Begining of this month they sent the same acts in a letter Signed by Ld Howe & G Clinton Directed to the President of Congress Signifying their being authentick Copies & saying they wished they might have the Desired Effect, the Congress Directed the President to inform them that when the King of England was seriously inclined to put an end to the cruel and unprovoked war he had waged against the United States they would readily concur in all proper measures Consistent with the Rights of Independant Nations, The Interest of their Constituents & the sacred Regard they owed to Treaties. The 9th Instant Genl Clinton sent a letter to G Washington informing him of the arrival of the Earl of Carlisle, Mr Eden & Governor Johnstone the Commisrs and Requesting him to grant passports to Dr. Ferguson their Secretary to repair the next morning with letters to Congress; G. Washington refused the passports till he Recd the order of Congress on that matter, the Congress have not yet Determined on it. I believe he will not be permitted to come to Congress But G Washington ordered to Receive the letters at the line & send them to us. A French Ship of 50 Guns is arrived at Virginia with Cloathing &c &c.

The Congress have not yet Ratified the Confederation, two or 3 of the States not having signified their assent, I Expect it will not be long before it will be Confirmed. The Indians & some Tories have committed Depradations on the western parts of this State & Virginia, measure are taking to Chastize them I hope Effectually.[1] Give my sincere regards to the Council of Safety & accept the Same your self from him who is your sincere friend and Humble Servant,

Josiah Bartlett

RC (PHi).

1 On June 11 Congress had voted to send an expedition of 3,000 men against the British outpost at Detroit "and to compel to terms of peace such of the Indian nations now in arms against these states as lie on, or contiguous to, the route betwixt Fort Pitt and Detroit." See *JCC,* 11:587–90; and Henry Laurens to Horatio Gates, June 12, 1778, note 3.

Henry Laurens to Benjamin Farrar

Sir 12 June [1778]

Had it been in my power your Messenger should have begun his return within an hour of his arrival but it has occasioned me some messages and applications to get him away even so early as the present.

I put both the letters which you favoured me with into the hands of Colonel Pickering at present first at the Board of War, said every thing I could in favor of the good intentions of Colo. Gaillard, yourself and Mr Torquand and obtained from him a promise of writing in such terms to General Hand as will take off all Embargo upon you,[1] I know he has written by the bearer and am persuaded has fulfilled his promise to me.

I wish you all prosperity and continued friendship for these states & Remain Sir &c.

LB (ScHi). Addressed: "Benjamin Farrar Esqr. Red Stone."

1 For information on Farrar's efforts to move from South Carolina to West Florida with his family, see these *Letters,* 9:235.

Henry Laurens to Horatio Gates

Sir York Town 12 June 1778

I have lately had the honor of presenting to Congress your several favors of the 27th May Committed to the Board of War[1] & 3d Inst committed to a special Committee but have not received any particular Commands.[2] I believe the Board of War have written on the former, I can detain the Messengers no longer.

With this Sir, you will receive several Copies of the intended Establishment of the Army & of an Act for extending subsistence Money to Officers of Militia, to which I add Copies of Lord Abingdon's Speech & protest & to morrow I will forward the late correspondence between Lord Howe & Sir H Clinton with Congress through General Washington.

I have the honor to be, With very sincere regard & Esteem, Sir, Your obedient & Most humble servant,

Henry Laurens, President of Congress

[*P.S.*] Congress yesterday Voted 932,743⅓ Dollars for carrying the Indian War into their own Country—the Commanding Officer & I beleive Officers to be appointed by Major General Gates.[3]

RC (NHi).

1 General Gates' May 27 letter to Laurens, which was referred to the Board of

War on June 2, dealt with the state of supplies in the northern department, and the need for Congress to give some sign of favor to Thomas Conway, and the appointment of William Malcom as deputy adjutant general in place of Robert Troup. See PCC, item 154, 1:332–34; and *JCC,* 11:560.

[2] For one step Congress had already taken in response to Gates' June 3 letter to Laurens, see Laurens to the States, June 10, 1778, note 1.

[3] See the report on countering "the cruelties lately exercised by the savages on the frontiers of New York, Pensylvania and Virginia" in *JCC,* 11:587–91. For accounts of the provenance of this report, see Laurens' letters to Philip Schuyler, April 8, note 1; to David Espy and Others, May 17, note; and to Philip Schuyler, May 28, 1778, note 1. Laurens' description of this report is not entirely accurate. Although the report called for expeditions to be mounted against the British garrison at Detroit and the Senecas in northern New York, Gates was only to be in charge of the latter. Neither of these expeditions was carried out in 1778.

Henry Laurens to William Heath

Dear sir,

York Town 12 June 1778

Since my last of the 26th Ulto. (Public) I have not been honoured with any of your favors nor have I at present any Commands from Congress. The Treasury I hope have replenished the public Chest in your department, & advised of the arrival of the Money which General Burgoyne was so good as to leave for us.

Inclosed with this will be found Copies of the intended Establishment of the Army & of News Papers containing Lord Abindon's Speech & Protest upon the mis-called Conciliatory Acts of Parliament.

The Commissioners at Philadelphia are anxious to send a Messenger & Message to Congress if I guess right at opinions. The decision this Morning will be to demand an explanation of the business, as a preliminary.

The Enemy still pretend to be moving from Philadelphia; when they shall be fairly gone, I shall beleive them.

I am with great Regard, Sir, Your obedient & humble servant,

Henry Laurens, Private

[*P.S.*] 932,743⅓ Dollars Voted yesterday for carrying the Indian War into their own Country.

RC (MHi).

Henry Laurens to Rawlins Lowndes

Dr sir

12 June [1778]

I beg leave to refer your Excellency to my Letters by Capt. Cochran under the 1st and 2d Inst. and also to my Public Addresses by this conveyance under the 9 and 10 Inst. This is devoted to accompany News Papers printed and M. S. and certain Scraps below. My application to business for a few days past has been extremely intense, I dare not detain the present Messenger an hour, from these considerations I rely upon your Excellency's indulgence—and I must also rely upon the Chief Justice for giving to the Public in So. Carolina the present current interresting intelligence more copiously than my time and avocations will allow me to attempt.

We have advice from Mr. Bingham Esquire agent at Martinico that many, I think he says, all American Prisoners had been discharged from confinement in the English Islands—many of them had arrived at Martinico. If I were to measure the humanity of the English Governments by the practices of British Commanders and Officers here, the conclusion would infallibly be, that scarcity of provision had produced this extraordinary mark of Clemency.

The Indians Northward and Westward have taken their Lesson from the Savages at Philadelphia, New-York & R Island. In the very Act of negociating for Peace they are burning, murdering and Scalping. Congress yesterday voted 932,743⅓ Dollars for raising about 3000 men for carrying the war into the Indian Country—the proper Officers in the Northern department to be appointed by General Gates. General McIntosh will command at Fort Pitt and against Detroit if we proceed.

An Enquiry is ordered by Congress into the conduct of Major General Mifflin and the Officers in his late department of Quarter Master General. There was a violent opposition of near four hours. 'Tis amazing to me, who am persuaded as a Man of honor, the General must wish for an investigation in order to satisfy the public who at present clamor exceedingly upon the subjects of neglect, mis-application, peculation &c. An enquiry will remove every groundless imputation.

The last authentic advices from Philada. are of the 9th Current.

The Enemy continued their preparations for removal, at that time they pretended they were to cross Delaware, march down the Eastern shore and embark at some convenient place below, now to me this appears Childish. Why hazard the crossing a river, the fatigue of a long march in the heat of Summer, the desertions which will infallibly happen, when all might be avoided by an easy and safe embarkation at the City and march in one tide 60—and if favoured by wind 160 miles—yet people swallow this and tenfold more gross propositions. Indulging a belief of their intention to leave us wholly has much injured our recruiting service.

I have the honor to be

LB (ScHi).

1 See Laurens to Washington, June 11, 1778, note.

Henry Laurens to Philip Schuyler

Sir

12 June [1778]

In consequence of your favors of the 17 and 29 May which I have lately had the honor of presenting to Congress, I expect to receive commands to be transmitted to you tomorrow.[1]

At present I must request you, Sir, to accept this as private, and with it a few Copies of Lord Abingdon's Speech upon the pretendedly conciliatory Acts of Parliament—the intended Establishment of the Army &c.

The Commissioners at Philada. are anxious to send Doctor Ferguson their Secretary with a message to Congress. If I guess right at opinions the answer will be a demand or somewhat like one, to know his intended business.

I moved Congress yesterday to call for the report on the Tyconderoga affair, it will be made this morning.[2]

I Am &c.

LB (DNA: PCC, item 13).

[1] General Schuyler's May 17 letter to Laurens, in which he announced that he had informed the Iroquois of the French alliance, and his May 29 letter, in which he relayed intelligence about Seneca hostility to the United States and discussed the possibility of another invasion of Canada, are in PCC, item 153, 3:314–15, 330–33.

[2] On this day Congress read a report by William Henry Drayton specifying charges against Schuyler and Arthur St. Clair for their role in the loss of Ticonderoga and Mount Independence during the summer of 1777, and eight days later ordered Washington to convene a court-martial to determine the validity of the allegations. See *JCC*, 11:593–603, 628. See also Laurens to Washington, June 8, 1778, note 1.

Richard Henry Lee's Proposed Resolution

[June 12? 1778][1]

Resolved that as the enemy are daily practising insidious and delusive arts to impose upon the good people of these States, that whenever a Passport shall be granted for Dr. Ferguson to come to Congress, he be attended by an escort of Light Horse under the command of an Officer of politeness, discernment, and zeal, by whose vigilance improper communications may be prevented.[2]

MS (ScHi). In the hand of Richard Henry Lee.

[1] Lee probably offered this proposed resolution on June 12 while Congress was considering whether to grant Dr. Adam Ferguson a passport to transmit a letter from the Carlisle peace commissioners to Congress. Lee may have written this resolve on June 11 when he was drafting a proposed report for the committee appointed that day to consider this issue, and it could have been considered in

Congress as late as the morning of June 13, but it seems likely that the resolve was penned during the debate on the 12th.

2 On the verso of the scrap of paper on which Lee drafted this resolve are two notes written by Henry Laurens and Charles Thomson. Their content and appearance suggest that the president and secretary of Congress exchanged these notes while debate on the passport request was in progress on June 12. At the top of the document Laurens penned the query: "If Doctr. Ferguson comes here will it not follow that some conference will be had & what is the conclusion?"

To which Thomson replied: "I suppose he will bring a letter sealed and if sealed he should be confined to his room & an answer to the letter sent by him or by a special messenger of Congress but no conference ought or can with propriety be held with him.

"Tho from curiosity I fancy conferences will be held with him by the members possibly not to any great purpose on our side."

Francis Lewis to John Langdon

Dear Sir York Town 12 June 1778

Don Juan d Miralles a Spanish Gentleman of fortune who lately arrived at Chs. Town So. Carolina from the Havanna, had at Chs. Town procured a ship laden with near 1200 Casks of Rice to be purchased for him and sent for Cadiz.[1]

Don Miralles is now in this Town & yesterday receiv'd a letter from his Agent at Chs. Town advisg that his ship was taken by a British ship of War, retaken by a privateer belonging to one of the Eastern States on this Continent. The ship is called the Nuestra Senora Del Carmen, Don Francisco Pruna Masr., sail'd from Cha. Town 27th March last, she had a Spanish Register, and cleared as from the Havanna directly for Cadiz, for a covering, in case she was examined by a British armed Vessell.

As it is probable this Vessell may be brought into some of the Eastern Ports, if within your district, I must desire you would enter a claim in behalf of said Don Juan D Miralles to both Vessell & Cargo, geting the salvage adjusted agreeable to the resolves of Congress. The expences shall be thankfully repaid you by, Sir, your very Huml Servt, Fra. Lewis

RC (PHi). Endorsed: "Given to me by Mrs Elwyn daughter of Governor Langdon . . . R Gilmore, 1829."

1 Don Juan de Miralles, a Cuban landowner fluent in English and French, was an agent of the Spanish government who had been appointed in December 1777 by Diego José Navarro, the governor general of Cuba, and directed to proceed to the seat of Congress in the guise of a merchant so that he could there gather intelligence on "the present state of the war, the principal advantages gained by each party and the respective forces, the inclination of both or either to continue the war or to abandon it, and any design prejudicial to Spain and her American possessions which they may attempt." Navarro's December 17, 1777, instructions to Miralles are in Papeles Procedentes de Cuba, Legajo 1290, Archivo General de

Indias, Seville. It should be noted that Navarro launched Miralles' mission on instructions from José de Gálvez, the minister of the Indies in Madrid. See Gálvez to Navarro, August 26, 1777, ibid. For a detailed account of Miralles' career as a Spanish agent in York and Philadelphia, see Herminio Portell-Vilá, *Los "Otros Extranjeros" en La Revolucion Norteamericana* (Miami, Fla.: Ediciones Universal, 1978), pp. 57–92.

It is worth noting that Miralles was already acquainted with a few members of Congress before his arrival in York on June 9, though only two of them are mentioned by name in his correspondence with his superiors. The first was John Mathews, with whom Miralles had become acquainted during his stay in Charleston, S.C., from January to April; and the second was Francis Lewis, whom he had met in Edenton, N.C., in May while Lewis was transacting business for the Marine Committee in that state.

Miralles' subsequent reports to Navarro and Gálvez contain considerable information for the study of Congress and the relations of delegates with foreign agents. In his May 13, 1778, letter to Navarro, for example, written from Edenton, N.C., where he arrived on May 10, Miralles explained his introduction to Lewis as follows. "The very day I arrived in this city I had an opportunity to speak to the Honourable Francis Lewis, one of the members of Congress who is commissioned by it to make certain contracts having to do with supplying the American Army. He has been very courteous to me and has introduced me to the leading citizens of the city [Edenton] . . . and he has offered to accompany me to the site of the Congress, where he is going to take his seat. I have become acquainted with more than six members of the Congress and I hope they will make possible my friendship with all the others, which will make my life in the provinces more pleasant."

And he recounted another meeting with Lewis in his May 16 dispatch to Navarro. "As soon as notice of the treaty [of alliance with France] was received in this city [Edenton] the Municipal Council planned a great banquet for all citizens on the following day, which was yesterday. To it were invited the Frenchmen most conspicuous here, employees of the merchant ships of their nation come to trade here. I was invited also and they seated me on the right hand of the master of ceremonies, the Honourable Francis Lewis. It is impossible to exaggerate the universal pleasure which this news has given the inhabitants of this city, who hope that our Court will join in the treaty. After dinner there followed thirteen toasts, each one followed by thirteen cannon shots. The sixth was for the health of Louis XVI, the Most Christian King of France, and the seventh for our Catholic Monarch Sire, Don Carlos III. It did not escape notice that they had placed in the middle those worthy sovereigns with whom they should have begun."

Writing from Baltimore on June 6 to José de Gálvez, Miralles also explained an interesting conversation he had had, while passing through Williamsburg, with Gov. Patrick Henry, "who overwhelmed me with the most courteous expressions." "They all hope for war between Spain and England," Miralles reported, "and I believe that news of it would cause as much pleasure as did the alliance of France with these united provinces.

"The Governor told me of having received on the 26th of last month a report that a party of men from Virginia authorized by him and another party of Americans sent by the Congress had gone down the Ohio river to the Mississippi and had captured the settlements and forts which the English had in Nachitoches and in the Illinois and had seized a 20-gun ship and other ships loaded with indigo worth 4,000 pounds sterling. Governor Henry suggested to me the ease with which the province of Mississippi or Movila, and Panzacola, which France and Spain ceded to England, could be captured by sending the Americans who are in Nachitoches and others as well if it seemed necessary down to join the garrison of Nueva Orleans, whose Governor could command the expedition. He said that the province of San Augustin de la Florida could be taken by part of the troops of the provinces of South Carolina and Georgia near Florida. He gave me this plan, written by his own hand, dated the 20th of last month and signed with his two initials, P.H., and told me that he would propose it to the Congress directly. I think that his plan is easy to carry out. . . ."

Miralles' letters from Edenton and Baltimore to Navarro and Gálvez are in Papeles Procedentes de Cuba, Legajo 1281. For his first report to Navarro after reaching York on June 9, see Henry Laurens to Patrick Henry, June 27, 1778, note 4. Quotations from Miralles' correspondence quoted in this work have been taken from translations provided by Aileen Moore Topping, who has recently completed collecting the voluminous reports from America of Miralles and Francisco Rendon, who succeeded the former upon his death in Philadelphia in 1780.

Oliver Wolcott to Laura Wolcott

My Dear, York Town 12 June 1778

I Wrote to you about a Week ago by Skinner, informing of you that I was then well, a Favour which is still continued to me. I wish much to hear from you or rathar to Return home to my Family which I hope I may soon do. It is said that Mr. Hosmere is probably on his way, if so I suppose Mr. Elsworth or Adams is with him. Brown I suppose will be here in a few days by whom I hope to hear from you.

The Schollars I see by the Hartford Paper are called upon to attend at N Haven. I imagine this Measure is an impracticable one. While Things are in their present Situation in our State I cannot believe that the Students can be Subsisted at N Haven. But you will either Send Oliver there or not as you shall judge expedient.

Whatever has lately occurred here has been communicated in my Letter to Mr. Reeve.[1] The Enemy will endeavour if possible to divide the Americans, but I believe that it will not be in their Power. Congress are united and firm not to enter into any kind of Negotiation but upon the acknowledged Principles of our Independence. This is an interesting Period. But I beleive that the same Merciful Providence which has hitherto saved us will bring the present Controversy to a happy issue. My Love to my Children and Freinds. Your's Affectionately, Oliver Wolcott

RC (CtHi).

[1] Wolcott's letter to Tapping Reeve has not been found.

Samuel Adams to James Warren

My dear sir, York Town June 13 1778

Since my last I have seen a List of the new Councillors & Representatives of our State. I am sorry to find that your Name is not in the List. I presume you declind the Choice, which I still very much disapprove of, for Reasons you have before heard me mention.[1]

By the inclosd News Paper you will see that the Scene begins to open. You may depend upon it that Congress will not attend to my Propositions until Independence is acknowledgd. The Day before yesterday, we were informd by a Letter from General Washington that Sr. H. Clinton had requested a Passport for Dr Ferguson Secretary to the British Kings Commissioners who was chargd with a Letter from them to Congress; and that he had acquainted Sr Henry that he could not grant the Request till he should receive the Directions of Congress. In the Midst of a Debate on the Report of a Committee on this Subject,[2] the Letters were brought in, having been receivd by our General & forwarded.[3] This Mode of Conveyance suited the Inclination of the House, they being, as I thought, at that Juncture ready to assent to a Proposition approving of the Generals Conduct in refusing to grant a Passport to the *Messenger*, and expressing themselves content that he should receive the Message & send it by a Messenger of his own. The Contents of the Letter, as far as they were read, appeard extraordinary indeed & showd plainly that their Design was to draw us back to a Subjection to their King. Some Expressions in the Letter gave particular Disgust to all the Members. The House adjournd till Monday when I think I may assure you the subject will be treated with becoming Spirit and Propriety.

I wish you would speak to some leading Member in the House of Representatives relating to the Resolution which was offerd concerning Dr. Lee. I have a Reason which strongly influences me to wish that such a Resolution may now pass. Justice & Policy as well as Gratitude require it. There are a few bad Men, one of whom you are not unacquainted with, who, so far from desiring that Respect should be shown to that patriotick & highly deserving Gentleman would rejoyce to see him disgrac'd.

My friendly Regards to your good Lady and all Friends. Adieu.

RC (MHi). In Adams' hand, though not signed.

[1] In a May 31 letter to Adams, which Adams obviously had not yet received, Warren suggested that John Hancock's "party" was responsible for keeping him out of the state government. "It may not satisfy you to carry it to the Account only of the versatility and Caprice of Mankind. They have had their Effects, but they would not do alone. Envy and the Ambition of some people has aided them, and the policy or rather what you will call the Cunning of a party here, who have set up an Idol they are determined to worship with or without reason has had the greatest. They have even made use of the Tories to prevent my being Chose by my Town, who made their Appearance on this Occasion for the first Time for seven Years. The partiality of you and the rest of my friends has made me an object of great Importance with this party, and every thing is done to get me out of sight. In short the plan is to Sacrifise you and me to the Shrine of

their Idol, I hope for the sake of the Character and Interest of our Country they wont Succeed against you." *Warren-Adams Letters,* 2:13–14.

Significantly, John Pickering, a political ally of John Hancock, replaced Warren as speaker of the Massachusetts House of Representatives when the general court assembled. William Fowler, *The Baron of Beacon Hill. A Biography of John Hancock* (Boston: Houghton Mifflin Co., 1980), p. 229.

2 See Committee of Congress Proposed Report, June 11, 1778, note.

3 Under the cover of his June 11 letter to President Laurens, Washington had enclosed a packet of letters and documents from the earl of Carlisle, William Eden and George Johnstone, the three British peace commissioners who had arrived in Philadelphia on June 6. These included a June 9 letter to Congress from the three commissioners describing the terms on which they hoped to negotiate a reconciliation and asking for a meeting with Congress "either collectively or by deputation"; a copy of their commission from the king; and texts of the three conciliatory acts recently passed by Parliament. See Washington, *Writings* (Fitzpatrick), 12:46; and Davies, *Documents of the American Revolution,* 15:135–37. The RC of the commissioners' June 9 letter is in the Peter Force Collection, DLC, as are a number of other original documents pertaining to their mission.

At first Congress was uncertain how to respond to the British overture. President Laurens began reading the commissioners' letter to the delegates on the same day it was received, but when he came to an insulting reference to the French alliance—"the insidious interposition of a power which has from the first settlement of these colonies been actuated with enmity to us both"—he was interrupted by Gouverneur Morris, who moved that no further action be taken on the letter "because of the offensive language against his most Christian majesty." After extended debate on this motion, however, Congress rejected it on June 16 and proceeded to read the letter from the commissioners as well as their royal commission and the three acts of Parliament. It then appointed a committee consisting of Samuel Adams, William Henry Drayton, Richard Henry Lee, Gouverneur Morris, and John Witherspoon to consider these documents. Lee and Witherspoon both produced draft replies to the commissioners, but the one Congress approved on June 17 for transmission as a presidential letter was the work of Morris and reiterated Congress' position that peace negotiations were impossible unless the British agreed to recognize American independence or withdrew their army and navy from the United States. See *JCC,* 11:605–6, 608–11, 614–15; Lee's and Witherspoon's Draft Letters to the Carlisle Commissioners, June 16; Laurens to the Carlisle Commissioners, June 17; and Gouverneur Morris to John Jay, June 23, 1778.

Drayton and Morris also replied unofficially to the commissioners in lengthy pseudonymous letters that originally appeared in the June 20 issue of the *Pennsylvania Gazette* and that are printed in this volume under the dates June 17 and June 20 respectively.

Henry Laurens to Horatio Gates

Sir York Town 13th June 1778

I had the honor of writing to you Yesterday by Messenger Boldon.

Within the present Inclosure you will receive an Act of Congress for repelling hostilities of the unfriendly Indians by carrying the War into their Towns & granting for that purpose 932,743⅓ Dollars.

The News Paper Inclosed will shew you a late correspondence between Philadelphia & Congress.[1]

Congress will some time to day determine on a proper answer to Sir H. Clinton's late attempt to obtain a Passport for Doctor Ferguson Secretary to the Commissioners to attend them at York Town without previously announcing the subject of his errand.*

I have the honor to be, With great Regard & Esteem, Sir, Your obedient & Most humble servant,

Henry Laurens, President of Congress

[*P.S.*] This Messenger[2] having been long detained stands in need of Money. I have supplyed him with Sixty Dollars, please to inform the proper Officer.

*While Congress were this Morning in debate on this subject a large Packet from Head Quarters was ushered into the House & delivered to me. I suggested that this, holding up the Packet, might prove an attempt to mend the whole, & so it happened. Doctor Ferguson had proceeded with a Flag to Radnor but finding he could not obtain a Passport left his dispatches which were under a superb direction & triple Seals, the device of the latter, a fond Mother embracing returning Children, both, no doubt, projected for the occasion—here honour & duty bid me stop. Congress having heard me read two Pages of the Commissioners address gave me direction to seal up the whole & adjourned to Monday Morning.

I have a confidence in Congress that their future determination on this important subject will give the People satisfaction & do themselves honor on both sides the Atlantic.

Governor Johnson is liberal in addresses to particular persons, under his single signature, among others he has honoured me with a Letter much too polite to be sincere—he has sent me Letters from my old & best freinds in London all tending to the same point to wheedle us into resubjection, but if I do not misinterpret the intimations of one, a Man of as good sense as any in G Britain, & high in Esteem with the first Men on both sides at Court, these same Commissioners now are, or very soon will be, possessed of such Powers as will be acceptable at the Court House of York Town. You will be pleased Sir to receive this P.S. as the private respects of Your obliged & obedient servant, Henry Laurens

[*P.S.*] Lord Carlisle & Comp the Commissioners, adventured the 10th Inst under an escort of Light Troops to take an airing as far as German Town. I am in hopes if they repeat this frolic, which is certainly calculated for shewing themselves to the people, they will be introduced to an audience under an Escort of our own.

RC (NHi).

1 This day's issue of the *Pennsylvania Gazette* contained Laurens' recent correspondence with Lord Howe and Sir Henry Clinton on the subject of the Carlisle

peace commission, for which see William Henry Drayton's Draft Letter to Lord Howe, June 6, 1778, note 1.

2 Identified by Laurens in the presidential letterbook copy of this letter as "Simon Crugier," the messenger who apparently was also to carry Laurens' June 14 letter to Gen. John Sullivan. PCC, item 13, 1:366, 368.

Henry Laurens to Patrick Henry

Sir 13th June [1778]

I had the honor of writing to you the 9th by Barry.[1] In the Act for laying an Embargo then transmitted, there should have been an addition of a clause which I apprehend was omitted, and therefore I trouble Your Excellency with a Copy inclosed and beg leave to refer to it.[2]

Your Excellency will also find inclosed two other Acts of Congress viz.

10th June Requesting Your Excellency to purchase under a limitation certain articles for the use of these United States from on board the French ship Le feir Roderique.[3]

And I am ordered to intimate to Your Excellency to take the opinion of persons properly skilled, respecting the prime cost and a comparative quality of the Goods, particularly that of shoes.

11th June for raising troops to repel the hostilities of Indians by carrying the War into their Countries and for granting 932,743⅓ Dollars for that purpose.[4]

I have the honor to be &c.

LB (DNA: PCC, item 13).

1 See Laurens to Richard Caswell, June 9, 1778, note 6.

2 Laurens also enclosed a text of the omitted clause of the June 8 embargo resolve with a brief covering letter he wrote this day to Gov. Thomas Johnson of Maryland. Red Books, MdAA. The clause Laurens sent to Henry and Johnson has not been identified. See *JCC*, 11:578–79.

3 Governor Henry's July 4 response to Laurens on the subject of this congressional request is in Henry, *Patrick Henry*, 3:178–79.

4 Congress agreed to postpone this expedition on July 25 after reading Governor Henry's pessimistic assessment of it in his July 8 reply to Laurens' letter. See Laurens to David Espy and Others, May 17, 1778, note.

Henry Laurens to John Laurens

My Dear Son 13 June [1778]

I thank you for your very sensible Letter of the 11th which came with the General's dispatches at past 1 o'clock just as Congress were about to adjourn.[1] How came those important papers to travel so very tardily?

Congress I think determined properly to reflect a little, and I have no doubt but that on Monday their Resolutions will be equally proper.

I must in the course of duty send a special Messenger to His Excellency the General tomorrow Morning, by him I shall write again, probably he will be with you before this. This is chiefly intended to recommend to your Civilities Mons. Du Cambray and Captain Cottineau, both these Gentlemen I believe have Letters of introduction to General Washington.

If a certain Gentleman[2] should again venture to Germantown I wish he may be personally introduced at your Head Quarters by an Escort of *our* Light Horse. He relies much upon the Letters which he has brought to private persons, many of which will not be so frankly and openly transmitted as those to you and me. I have no doubt of his circulating such by means of a few people now in Philada. among whom in my private opinion Mr. Thos. Willing is the most *dangerous*. There is a connection from that Quarter which I hold to be *dangerous* because not enough suspected. I Am &c.[3]

LB (ScHi).

1 John Laurens' June 11 letter to his father is in Simms, *Laurens Army Correspondence*, pp. 183–85.

2 George Johnstone.

3 This day Laurens also wrote a brief letter to Col. Leonard Marbury of Georgia, acknowledging "the favor of your Letter of the 7th Inst. together with Sundry dispatches from Georgia which have been presented to Congress." Laurens Papers, ScHi. Marbury's letter has not been found, but for a list of the documents from Georgia that he transmitted to Congress, see *JCC*, 11:622, which indicates that they were not presented to Congress until June 19. See also Laurens to John Houstoun, June 22, 1778.

James Lovell to Abigail Adams

June 13th. 1778 York Town

Amiable tho unjust Portia! doubly unjust!—to yourself, and to me. Must I only write to you in the Language of Gazettes, enumerating, on the Part of Britain, Acts of Deceit, Insolence and Cruelty; or, on the part of America, Instances of Patience under repeated Losses, Fortitude under uncommon Hardships, and Humanity under the grossest Provocations to Revenge? Must I suppress Opinion, Sentiment and just Encomium upon the Gracefullness of a lovely suffering Wife or Mother? It seems I must or be taxed as a Flatterer. Immured for many Months in a Prison, and, upon escape from thence, confined in a narrow Circle, with He-Creatures, drudging, plodding Politicians, for an equally tedious Period of Time, I did not suspect that my Pen could now run in such a Stile of social Intercourse as to provoke a delicate Judge among the Polishers of the Manners of our Race to call me Adulator. After having called you unjust, I will not set so light by my Decission as to venture to make, *to you,* any Remarks upon the remaining Parts of your Letter now before me, whether original or quoted. I will content myself, as I have done for a Month back, with *secret* Admiration.

Mr. Thaxter sending a Course of printed Papers,[1] it becomes unnecessary for me at this Time to try my Hand at paragraph Writing. But I cannot omit to say that I hardly conceive it possible that your Information of the Capture of the Boston can be good, as neither the Fishkill nor Pokipsie Gazettes mention it; and their Publishers are more in the Way than you to know what is the News in the City of New York. I do not mention this to cheat you with false Hope; for, be assured, I think you qualified to hear bad News. And I will prove that this is not Flattery; for I will give you whatever comes to my Knowledge in Regard to my worthy Friend, your dearest, be it good or bad. And I will continue to esteem you for many good Qualities, though you make your Slips now and then by calling Names and misconstruing the honest Sentiments of Your sincere humble Servant,

James Lovell

RC (MHi). Adams, *Family Correspondence* (Butterfield), 3:43–44.

1 In his June 13 letter to Abigail, which is in the Adams Papers, MHi, John Thaxter inclosed copies of some Pennsylvania newspapers, probably including a copy of the *Pennsylvania Gazette* of June 13 containing documents relative to the Carlisle commission.

Massachusetts Delegates to Massachusetts Council

Sir

York Town June 13th. 1778.

The Intelligence which Congress has very lately received of the Enemies repeated Depredations in the State of Rhode Island & Providence Plantations gave Occasion to the passing of the inclosed Resolution:[1] But, such has been the Attention of the Massachusetts Bay to the Safety of all these united States as renders it needless for us to enlarge upon the Necessity of their turning an immediate Attention to the Relief of one in their own Neighbourhood which now bears a large Share in the Calamities of War.

We request that you would lay the Resolution before the General Assembly as an Apology for this Letter. For, supposing them to have before this Time been made fully acquainted with the Circumstances of Rhode Island, we will not doubt but that they are taking such vigorous Measures in Consequence as to supersede all Necessity for the Resolve which furnishes this particular Occasion of our professing ourselves with much Respect, Sir, Your very humble Servants,

Samuel Adams Fra Dana
E Gerry James Lovell

RC (M–Ar). Written by Lovell and signed by Lovell, Adams, Dana, and Gerry.
[1] Earlier this day Congress had directed the delegates from New Hampshire, Massachusetts, and Connecticut to write to their respective states urging them to raise troops for the planned Rhode Island expedition commanded by Gen. John Sullivan. See *JCC*, 11:605; and Henry Laurens to John Sullivan, June 14, 1778.

Henry Laurens to George Johnstone

Dear Sir, York-Town June 14. 1778.[1]

Yesterday I was honoured with your favour of the 10th,[2] and thank you for the transmission of those from my dear and worthy friends Mr. Oswald and Mr. Manning.[3] Had Doctor Ferguson been the bearer of these papers, I should have shewn that Gentleman every degree of respect and attention, that times and circumstances admit of.

It is, Sir, for Great-Britain to determine whether her Commissioners shall return unheard by the Representatives of these United States, or revive a friendship with the Citizens at large, and remain among us as long as they please.

You are undoubtedly acquainted with the only terms upon which Congress can treat for accomplishing this good end; terms from which, although writing in a private character, I may venture to assert, with great assurance, they never will recede, even admitting the continuance of hostile attempts, and that, from the rage of war, the good people of these States shall be driven to commence a treaty westward of yonder Mountains. And permit me to add, Sir, as my humble opinion, the true interest of Great Britain, in the present advance of the Contest, will be found in confirming our Independence.

Congress in no hour have been haughty, but to suppose that their minds are less firm in the present, than they were, when, destitute of all foreign aid, even without expectation of an alliance, when, upon a day of general public fasting and humiliation, in their House of Worship and in the presence of God, they Resolved, "to hold no conference or Treaty with any Commissioners on the part of Great-Britain, unless they shall, as preliminary thereto, either withdraw their Fleets and Armies, or, in positive and express terms, acknowledge the Independence of these States," would be irrational.[4]

At a proper time, Sir, I shall think myself highly honoured, by a personal attention, and by contributing to render every part of these States agreeable to you; but until the basis of mutual confidence shall be established, I believe, Sir, neither former private friendship, nor any other consideration, can influence Congress to consent that even Governor Johnstone, a Gentleman who has been so deservedly esteemed in America, shall see the Country. I have but one voice, and that shall be against it. But let me intreat you, my Dear Sir, do not hence conclude that I am deficient in affection to my old Friends, through whose kindness I have obtained the honour of the present correspondence, or that I am not with very great personal respect and esteem, Sir, Your most obedient and most humble servant,

Henry Laurens

Reprinted from *Pennsylvania Gazette,* June 20, 1778. Addressed: "The Hon. George Johnstone, Esq; Philadelphia." Laurens sent a copy of this letter to Washington on June 18 that is virtually identical to the text printed here. See Laurens to Washington, June 18, 1778.

1 Laurens originally planned to send a private reply to Johnstone's June 10 letter, but because corresponding with the enemy was treasonable under Pennsylvania law and considered impolitic by many delegates, he decided instead to allow William Henry Drayton to arrange for publication of his letter in the *Pennsylvania Gazette.* See Laurens to John Laurens, and Thomas McKean to Ceasar Rodney, June 17, 1778.

2 Johnstone's June 10 letter to Laurens, which was also printed in the June 20 issue of the *Pennsylvania Gazette,* reads as follows.

"I beg to transfer to my friend Dr. Ferguson, the private civilities which my friends Mr. Manning and Mr. Oswald request in my behalf. He is a man of the utmost probity, and of the highest esteem in the Republic of Letters.

"If you should follow the example of Britain in the hour of her insolence, and send us back without a hearing, I shall hope, from private friendship, that I may be permitted to see the country, and the worthy characters she has exhibited to the world, upon making the request in any way you may point out."

3 William Manning's April 11 and Richard Oswald's April 12, 1778, letters to Laurens are in the Laurens Papers, ScHi. Manning, was a London banker and the father-in-law of John Laurens; Oswald, an old acquaintance of Laurens', was a Scottish merchant living in London who later served as one of the British negotiators of the Treaty of Paris. See David D. Wallace, *The Life of Henry Laurens* (New York: G.P. Putnam's Sons, 1915), pp. 50, 126, 464–65.

4 For the April 22, 1778, resolve quoted here by Laurens, see *JCC,* 10:379.

Henry Laurens to John Sullivan

Sir 14 June [1778]

I have been honoured with your several favors of the 26th and 31st May which were duly presented to Congress, the commands which I have received thereon are contained in the inclosed Resolve of the 13th to which I beg leave to refer.[1]

I have sent to the Delegates of the three States mentioned in the Resolve to hasten their dispatches, and have not to add, but assurances of being, With great Regard & Esteem &c.[2]

LB (DNA: PCC, item 13).

1 General Sullivan's May 26 and 31 letters to Laurens, which were read in

Congress on June 8 and 11, described recent British depredations in Rhode Island and the deficiency of arms among Rhode Island troops. See PCC, item 160, fols. 125–30; *JCC*, 11:576, 585; and Sullivan, *Papers* (Hammond), 2:57–59, 62–63. In consequence of these letters Congress resolved on June 13 to request the delegates of Connecticut, Massachusetts, and New Hampshire to urge their states to send reinforcements to Rhode Island. See *JCC*, 11:605.

2 Laurens noted in his private letterbook that this day he also sent Sullivan "on a quarter of a sheet the current news and a newspaper." Laurens Papers, ScHi. This "sheet" has not been found.

Henry Laurens to George Washington

Sir,

York Town 14th June 1778

My last to Your Excellency went by Davis, dated the 11th.

Between one & two oClock yesterday the Packet which Your Excellency sent to Congress accompanied by Your Excellency's favor of the 11th was brought into the House, among other Papers it contained an Address from the British Commissioners to Congress, at that minute Congress were determining on a proper reply to be given to Sir H Clinton's application for a Passport for Doctor Ferguson, I was ordered to read the Address, when I had advanced to the second Page, the House directed me to Seal up all the Papers & adjourned to Monday Morning.

Your Excellency will be pleased to receive within the present Inclosure an Act of Congress of the 9th Inst. for adjusting Rations due to Officers in the Army—& also an Act for Repelling the attempts of hostile Indians & granting 932,743⅓ Dollars for that service.[1]

Congress have ordered a Brevet to Major Mullins to Rank as Lieutt. Colonel the 11th Inst. And a Commission of Lt. Colonel the 13th to Monsr Du Cambray to be annexed to the Corps of Engineers.[2]

I have the honor to be, With the highest Esteem & Respect, Sir, Your Excellency's Most Obedt. servant,

Henry Laurens,
President of Congress.

RC (DLC).

1 See *JCC*, 11:581–82, 587–91.

2 See *JCC*, 11:586, 604–5.

Joseph Reed to Robert Morris

Dear Sir

Mr Nixon's Sunday Afternoon [June 14, 1778].

I think the common Forms of Civility & Politeness require that I should answer Governor Johnstones Letter—but as such Correspondence is of a delicate Nature & liable to Misrepresentation I did not chuse to forward my Letter untill I had submitted it to better Judgment than my own, & have therefore taken the Liberty to leave it for your Perusal, that if there are any improper Sentiments I may revise it.[1] My Boy will call for it in the Morning. I have also left the Governour's Letter as the Complimts. contained made it disagreeable to me to read it entire the other Day.

I am with due Regard, Sir, Your Obed. Hbble Serv.

Jos. Reed

RC (DLC).

1 Reed had enclosed for Morris' "Perusal" his draft of a letter to George Johnstone written in response to Johnstone's April 11, 1778, letter to him. For the text of these two documents, see Reed to Johnstone, June 15, 1778.

The following day Reed also sent a copy of this draft under cover of a similar letter to George Washington, soliciting the general's advice on the propriety of his reply to Johnstone. Reed's letter to Washington has not survived, but for Washington's June 15 reply to Reed, see Washington, *Writings* (Fitzpatrick), 12:59.

Charles Carroll of Carrollton to Charles Carroll, Sr.

Dear Papa, 15th P.M. June 1778.

I have yours of the 10th. It gives me pleasure to hear Molly is well; my love to her & her Mama.

I wrote to you in my last to send Sam off with my horses, so as to be here before the 20th instant imagining Chase would be here before that day; but he writes me he shall not be here before the 23d. I would not have Sam come before the 23d as it will be difficult to procure Stable room for my horses. If Sam should set off from Doohoragen the 23d he will be here time enough; Pray do not forget to send me £100 by Sam.

The Commissioners Ld. Carlile, Willm. Eden, & Govr. Johnstone have written a letter to his Excellency Hen. Laurens Esqr. & the other members of Congress. Had they offered such terms before the Declaration of Independance, they would have restored peace & tranquility to the British Empire, but being short of Independance are *now* inadmissible.

I believe we shall return an answer to morrow; it will be in the spirit of our Resolves of the 23d [*i.e.* 22d] April. They must either withdraw their fleets & armies, or acknowledge our Independance, otherwise we shall not treat with them. This is *our* ultimatum: and a good one upon every principle of justice, Policy & Interest.

The Enemy still hold Pha. and perhaps, notwithstanding appearances to the contrary, they may continue to hold it until they are driven from thence by the superiority of our arms, which will not happen so soon as I could wish.

When do you think of going to the Springs? Let me know this in your next. Wishing you health I remain, yr. affectionate Son,

Ch. Carroll of Carrollton

P.S. The Commissioners' letter will be published in next Saturday York Gazette. I shall send it you by the first opportunity.

RC (MdHi).

Robert Morris to Joseph Reed

Dear Sir At Mr. Nixon's, June 15th 1778

I admit that a Correspondence between People in Public Stations on opposite sides of this unhappy Contest is delicate in its Nature & liable to misrepresentation, therefore I shall carefully remember the propriety of those Sentiments you have offered to Governor Johnstone in the letter you have submitted to my inspection for that purpose.[1]

Persons who think so justly & express themselves so Elegantly as Mr. Reed, have little occasion for other Mens judgement on their performances & I have neither the Vanity to think myself deserving of the Compliment you are pleased to pay, nor presumption to think of amending what you have done. Indeed I am certain the Governor must approve and Your Country applaud Your Sentiments. I am Dear Sir, Your Obedt Hble Servt, Robt Morris

RC (NHi).

1 See Reed to Morris, June 14, 1778.

New Hampshire Delegates to Meshech Weare

Hond. Sir, York Town Pennsylvania June 15th. 1778

Congress having receiv'd advice by Letters from General Sullivan of the late Ravages of the British Troops in his Department, & of his present inability to prevent the like in future should they come out with any considerable force have directed the Delegates of New Hampshire, Massachusetts Bay & Connecticutt to address the Legislatures of their respective States, requesting them forthwith to send forward their Quotas of Troops destined for the defence of the State of Rhode Island.[1]

Tho' We think there is no reason to doubt but that the Quota of our State will be raised and Marched, before this reaches you: Yet, in Obedience to the Orders of Congress, we cannot do less than solicit your Attention to a Matter so important in its Consequences, that if by any means our State should be wanting in that respect, Your immediate Care might supply the Deficiency.

We have only to add our hearty Wishes that this & every other Exertion of the State in defence of every thing valuable may be attended with the best Success. We are with great Esteem, Sir, your Obet very humle Servants, Josiah Bartlett

John Wentworth Junr

RC (MHi). Written by Wentworth and signed by Wentworth and Bartlett.

1 See Massachusetts Delegates to the Massachusetts Council, June 13, 1778, note.

Joseph Reed to George Johnstone

Sir Head Quarters June 13 [*i.e.* 15], 1778

I take the earliest Oppy. to acknowledge your Favour of the 30 April[1] & to thank you for your obliging Care in forwarding the Packets which accompanied it. The Partiality of my Friends in England has greatly overrated my Services & Consequence in the present Dispute;[2] I claim little other Merit beyond that of Zeal for the Interests of my Country & entertaining a very high Veneration for those illustrious Characters who have long tho unsuccessfully patronized her Rights & those of Mankind. America, Sir, has seen & admired your seasonable tho' unavailing Efforts to prevent the Dismemberment of the British Empire & place us on the great & generous Scale of equal Freedom with yourselves.[3] This must be your Consolation as it is your Glory, while the Event affords a most instructive Lesson to other Nations & Senates how to treat in future their Johnstone's & their Barry's, their Chathams & their Camden's. If it is within the Line of human Events to reconcile the People of this Country to a Submission to the Sovereignty of Brittain[4] the Ministry has in this Appointment (really honoured by Your Acceptance) shewn some Degree of Wisdom, as it may rescue them from the Imputation of repeating an insiduous Manucevre to divide, disarm, & enslave us.[5] But you will so soon receive the Sense of Congress on this important Point that any Opinion from me would be equally useless & improper. I will only say that after the unparallel'd Injuries & Insults this Country has received from the Men who now direct the Affairs of Brittain, a Negotiation under their Auspices has much to struggle with. I speak from no Authority but I can easily conceive that America would willingly exchange the Calamities of War for the Blessings of Peace & prove as faithful in Alliance as she has been great in Arms. If therefore the Resolution of Congress should be unfriendly to your present Views, if they should suppose that all Confidence & Affection the only Grounds of Harmony & surest Support of all Government are so erased as to leave no Hope of a happy Reunion, I cannot but flatter myself that Men of Virtue & enlarged Views on both Sides of this great Question will endeavour to close the Scene of Blood on the only Terms now practicable & that Great Brittain will give up her visionary Schemes of Conquest & Empire for the solid Benefits she may yet derive from our Amity & Commerce. I will even hope, Sir, for your Aid in so good a Work. Should the same fatal Influences which blasted your firm salutary Counsils again frustrate your humane & generous Purpose, come to America, the future Asylum of the brave & virtuous from every Quarter of the Globe. She will think herself honoured to receive unto her Bosom so illustrous a Citizen, his Eloquence will not then be spent in vain nor his eminent Worth pass unrewarded.

My Desire to make the earliest Acknowledgment of the Honour you have done me has prevented my troubling you with a few Lines for my Friends in England who are interested in the Welfare of my Family. My Brothers Letter[6] & the Politeness of yours encourages me to take this Liberty which I shall do by some early Oppy. Too many cannot present themselves to shew the very great Respect & Esteem with which I am Sir, Your Sincere Admirer & most Obed. Hbble Servt.

Jos. Reed

FC (DLC). In the hand of Joseph Reed and addressed: "The Honorable George Johnstone Esqr., One of the Commissioners &c. &c. &c." Now located in the Washington Papers, this copy is apparently the final draft of Reed's reply to Johnstone that Washington requested from Reed on June 15. It is virtually identical to the text of the reply to Johnstone that Reed published in a 1779 pamphlet except that therein he rendered the dateline "Camp at Valley-Forge, June 14, 1778." Joseph Reed, *Remarks on Governor Johnstone's Speech in Parliament* . . . (Philadelphia: Francis Bailey, 1779), pp. 13–16. The first draft of this letter, sharper in tone and much longer than the final draft, is in the Reed Papers, NHi. Major variations between the two are set forth in the notes below.

Reed apparently sent copies of a slightly revised version of his first draft to Robert Morris and to Washington for their evaluation. One of these, in a clerical hand and signed by Reed, may be the copy that is in the Sol Feinstone Collection, DLC microfilm. It varies only slightly from Reed's first draft—except for the addition of a single sentence inserted in braces in the excerpt quoted in note 5 below. It is easy to imagine that Reed recopied his original draft (now in NHi), for either Morris or Washington, making slight revisions and adding a sentence in the process, and then employed a clerk to transcribe this copy for the other intended recipient. Morris suggested no revisions, but Washington clearly did, and Reed subsequently produced the text printed here for Washington's second perusal. See Reed to Robert Morris, June 14; Morris to Reed, June 15, 1778; and Washington, *Writings* (Fitzpatrick), 12:59.

Whether this revision or another version was ever sent to Johnstone is open to question. In the postscript of his June 15 letter to President Laurens, Reed obviously had not yet made up his mind on how to respond, deciding at the time to send only "a bare complimentary Letter of Acknowledgment which is not worth troubling you with." And in his 1779 summary of the incident he wrote: "After reading [Johnstone's] letter, I gave it into the hands of General Washington, and two or three other Gentlemen at Head-Quarters, who returned it to me without any remark. In a few days after, I wrote an answer, which I communicated to Mr. Morris, one of the Delegates for Pennsylvania, then at camp, who returned it to me with a general approbation. I afterwards shewed it to General Washington, asking his friendly opinion of it, which he gave, by telling me, he thought some of the complimentary part might be spared. Upon which I abridged it, and having shewn it to the General, he approved it, and I left it at Head-Quarters to be forwarded with other letters. Whether this letter ever reached Governor Johnstone, I do not know, but I rather believe that it failed by some accident." Reed, *Remarks on Governor Johnstone's Speech*, pp. 12–13.

1 Actually Reed was responding to a letter from Johnstone dated April 11, 1778, the original of which is in the Peter Force Collection, DLC. His letter to Reed was one of several he had written to prominent Americans in his attempt to marshall support privately for the overtures being made simultaneously and officially by the Carlisle commissioners. "Your near & worthy relation Mr. Dennis De Berdt," Johnstone had written to Reed, "has made me happy by favoring me with a Letter to you. I had been informed by General Robertson of your great worth & Consequence in the unhappy disputes that have subsisted between Great Britain & her dependants. Your Pen & your Sword have both been used with glory & advantage in Vindicating the Rights of Mankind & of that community of which you was a Part. Such a Conduct as the first & Superior of all Human dutys must ever Command my Warmest Freindship & Veneration.

"In the midst of those affecting Scenes my feeble Voice has not been wanting to stop the Evils in their Progress & to remove on a large and Liberal footing the Causes of all Jealousy That every Subject of the Empire might live Equally free & Secure in the Enjoyments of the blessings of Life Not one Part dependant on the Will of another with opposite Interests But a general Union on Terms of perfect Security & mutual Advantage. During the Contest I am free to Confess my wishes have ever been that America might so far Prevail as to oblige this Country to See their Error & to reflect & reason fairly in the Case of others, Heirs to the Same Privileges with themselves. It has pleased God in his Justice so to dispose of Events that this Kingdom is at length convinced of her folly & her Faults. A Commission under Parliamentary Authority is now Issued for Settling in a Manner Consistent with that Union of Force on which the Safety of both Parties Depend all the differences that have or can Subsist between Great Britain & America Short of a total Seperation of Interests. In this Commission I am an unworthy Associate, tho' no man can feel the desire of cementing in Peace & Freindship every member of what was called the British Empire Stronger than myself. Yet I am sensible it might have fallen to the Lot of many Persons better Qualified to Attain the End Proposed. All I can claim is Ardent Zeal & upright Intentions. And when I reflect that this negotiation must depend much more upon perfect Integrity than refinement of understanding where a Sensible magnanimous People will See their own Interest & carefully Guard their own honour in every Transaction I am more Inclined to hope from the good will I have always born them I am not altogether Unqualified for the Task.

"If it be (as I hope it is) the disposition of Good Men in the Provinces to Prefer freedom in Conjuction with Great Britain to an Union with the ancient Enemy of both, If it is their generous inclination to forget recent Injurys & recall to their remembrance former Benefits I am in hopes we may Yet be greatly Happy. I am Sure the People in America will find in my Brother Commissioners & myself a fair & Chearfull Concurrence in adjusting every Point to their utmost wish not inconsistent as I said before of Interests wch. is the object of our commiss[ion].

"Nothing could Surpass the glory you have acquired in Arms except the generous Magnanimity of meeting on the Terms of Justice & Equality after demonstrating to the World that the fear of Force could have no Influence in that decision.

"The Man who can be instrumental in bringing us all to act once more in Harmony & to unite together the Various Powers which this Contest has drawn forth will deserve more from the King & the People from Patriotism, Humanity, Friendship and all the Tender ties that are reflected by the Quarrel & reconciliation that ever was Yet bestowed on human Kind.

"This Letter from Mr. De Berdt I Shall consider as an Introduction to you, which Line of communication I shall Endeavor by Every means to Improve by Publick Demonstration of respect or Private Freindship as your Answer may enable me."

2 Reads "in this unhappy Contest" in the NHi draft.

3 In the place of this sentence, Reed had written the following passage in the NHi draft: "But with these Sentiments I want your own elegant Pen & forcible Language to express how much I feel my Character enobled, & my Life dignified by the Approbation of a Man the Ornament of his own Country & the most endeared & approved Friend to this. America, Sir, has seen & felt with fervent Gratitude your early disinterested & unremitted Labours to avert the heavy Calamities which your enlightened Mind discerned & pointed out while at a distance; your *seasonable* tho unavailing Efforts to prevent the Dismemberment of the British Empire & place us on the great & generous Scale of equal Freedom with yourselves."

4 Reads "to a Reunion with Brittain" in the NHi draft.

5 At this point in the NHi draft Reed had written the two following long denunciatory paragraphs, which he only partially incorporated into the remainder of this paragraph in the final draft.

"But whatever may be their Intentions the Day of Reconciliation & Dependance is past, & the Sovereignty of Brittain over this Country gone forever. The Voice of weeping Nature, true Policy & unspotted Honour bids us part—the inexorable Rigour with which our humble Petitions were treated, the cruel edicts which stain your parliamentary annals, the savage barbarities, Insults & outrages which have marked your military Proceedings & the merciless Treatment of our Prisoners, have so eradicated every Particle of ancient Affection & Respect, that there does not remain the smallest Point on which to raise the Superstructure of that Peace which is the Object of your Commission. A Series of Events in which he must be an Infidel indeed who does not discern the temper of him who governs all Nations, have so changed the Views and Inclinations of this Country that a Dependence on your Nation which was once our Glory, Happiness & our Pride would now be deemed our greatest Infamy, & deepest Misfortune. Our Engagements with other Nations who have generously assisted & inabled us to rise to our present Pitch of Respect & now on the Eve or most probably actually engaged in a War in which we are principals bind us by the most sacred Ties of Gratitude & Honour to support the Independance we have declared. It is a Principle of universal Extent (a few Paricides & contemptible Neutrals excepted) a Principle we are resolved to fight, bleed & die for & transmit with our expiring Breath to our Children after us. The Ground, Sir, is irrecoverably changed from Taxation to Empire & nothing remains but the hopeless Prospect of Conquest & unconditional Submission or a foederal Union upon rational, fair & independant Ground. That America would willingly exchange the Calamities of War for such a Peace & prove herself as faithful in Alliance as she has been brave in War, I think not to be questioned & that G. Brittain would derive great & essential Benefits from her Amity & Commerce appears to me equally clear. This perhaps may yet be attained under our present Engagements, if such a Disposition on her Part is manifested by an immediate withdraw of her Fleet & Armies; but how long even this Opportunity of stopping the Effusion of human Blood may continue is extremely uncertain, &, if lost by Delay, as those of Reunion have been, may never be retrieved—but the present Hostilities grow into inveterate Hatred & irreconcilable Enmity. {I flatter myself you will advocate this salutary measure from the sentiment that you have so politely and happily expressed that the decisions of a brave and magnanimous people ought not to be influenced by the fear of force.} I should be very undeserving of that Honour of your Attention & Friendship if I flattered you with the smallest Hope of Success in your Commission of reuniting America to the Crown of Great Brittain. I do not therefore animadvert upon the Acts of Parliament upon which your Powers must depend, nor am I curious to know their Extent; I shall only say that there appears no solid Security for those Privileges to which you have so long & ably contended as were justly intitled. All—All is to depend upon the future Fiat of a Parliament governed & directed by a set of Men Authors of all the Calamities we have suffered & whom I am at a Loss to determine whether they are most the Objects of our Hatred or Contempt. Pardon me if I say a Negotiation under such Auspices has much to struggle with. Every succeeding Day furnishes fresh Proofs with what frugal Caution a young & ignorant Country unskilled in the Arts of Treaty & Negotiation should bestow their Confidence: from authentick Documents received since your Arrival we find that the Proclamations of the former Commissioners are acknowledged by themselves to be as calculated to deceive & betray. In their Proclamation of the 30th Novemb. 1776, Pardons were promised to all complying with its Terms without any Exception & yet in their Letter of the same Day & inclosing the same Proclamation to Ld. George Germain there are these remarkable Words 'exceptions from his Majesty's Pardon as well as any Prolongation of the Time within which a Pardon may be obtained will be a Matter of future Consideration according to the Circumstances that may arise.' To the Man of Honor & Probity to whom I am now writing this Fact needs no Comment. And for the Safety & Interests of America it must be known to her remotest Shores. All Confidence, the only Ground of Harmony & sure Support of Government being lost, I cannot but hope Men of Virtue [&] enlarged Views on both Sides of this great Question will endeavour to close the bloody Scene on the only Terms now practicable & that Great Brittain will give up her visionary Schemes of Empire & dependance for the solid Benefits she may yet derive from our Commerce."

6 See Reed to Dennis De Berdt, July 19, 1778.

Joseph Reed to Henry Laurens

Dear Sir Camp near the Valley Forge, June 15. 1778

Your Politeness & Attention during my short Stay at York Town have left such Impressions on my Mind that I cannot but take every Oppy to shew my very sincere Regard & Respect. And as the late Intelligence from England is both interesting & curious I have taken the Liberty to inclose you Extracts from a Letter received from a Relation there formerly Agent for one of the States, & a letter from Governor Johnstone one of the Commissioners lately arrived.[1] If they are not otherwise useful they will for a few Minutes soften & releive that intense Application to Business which adorns the Patriot, while it weakens the Man. To these I have also added a Copy of my Answer to the Governor. The Opinion I have given is so universal on the great Subject of their Commission, that I cannot suppose there is the least Danger that the Reply of Congress will set our Claim upon lower Ground. And as Politeness required an Answer, Sincerity & Candour would not allow me to flatter him. One Part of my Brothers Letter which seems to intimate the Admission of our Independance, if claimed by a new Congress chosen after the present Terms are propounded, appears to me to deserve particular Attention as an insidious Manœvre to distract & divide us. Your good Judgment will lead you to make such Use of it as you think best to guard against the Mischief intended—indeed any Use you please of the whole except printing them which I do not conceive myself altogether at Liberty to do. The Fact alluded to in my Letter & [evidence?] of the base Duplicity of the former Commissioners is proved by their Letter laid before the House of Lords last Session of Parliament & now printed in the parliamentary Register sent me among other Papers by Governor Johnstone. Unless it can receive some Explanation I am not capable of giving it I cannot conceive more palpable Treachery & ineffable Meanness.

I cannot but congratulate you, Sir, on the respectable Appearance of our Army & their Improvement in Discipline & every soldierly Quality—On the Extinction of every Spark of Discontent & Faction against the best of Men & the Regularity with which the several Departments seem now to be conducted. To the latter I ascribe very much of the former, as the Attention & Care of the General being no longer called off from his Command to exercise the Duties of the Staff, his Time & Talents are devoted more directly to the military Duty of his Troops, the happy Consequences of which are more & more conspicious every Day. I have now been here near two Weeks (great Part of the Time waiting for Mr. Dana to complete the Business of the Arrangement of the Army) & can assure you that in the whole Time I have not heard a single Complaint of those Departments which formerly afforded so many, nor indeed of any other. I will not tax your Politeness with an Answer to this Letter, I know the Nature & Extent of your Engagements do not admit the Waste of a Moment, but I shall nevertheless do myself the Honour of communicating any Occurrencies here which are of Importance & not likely to reach you thro the publick Channel.

With every Sentiment of Respect & Esteem I remain, Sir, Your very Obed. Hbble Serv.

Jos. Reed

P.S. As I have not Time to copy the Governours Letter I have inclosed the original which you will be so obliging as to return me under Cover when you have made what Use you please of it. Upon farther Consideration I have thought best to delay an Answer to the Governours Letter least as the great Subject is under the Consideration of Congress I might say too much or too little & have therefore only concluded to send a bare complimentary Letter of Acknowledgment which is not worth troubling you with.

RC (NN).

1 See the preceding entry, note 1. For the "Letter received from a Relation

there, formerly Agent for one of the States"—Reed's brother-in-law Dennis De Berdt—see Reed to De Berdt, July 19, 1778, note 1.

Joseph Reed to Esther Reed

My dear Hetty Mr Henry's June 15. 1778

I received your Favour of the 12th by the Express together with the Papers for which I thank you; tho I am sorry to learn that you do not recover so fast as you expected. I have had Thoughts of sending Home the Phaeton that you may ride out frequently which I fear you cannot do at present, & which I think would do you a great deal of good, but the daily Expectation of finishing our Business & returning myself has hitherto prevented. But why do I say finishing—when we have not begun the other Gentleman not being yet arrived. I hope the next Time you write your Health & Spirits will admit a longer Letter, & let me know what Dennis says of himself as he refers me to his Letters to his Mamma & yourself for Family News. The two Letters which accompanied them I suppose from the Handwriting to have come from our new Relation. By the Time they must have been wrote, I suppose they were settled down solid Man & Wife & going on in the old patriarchal Style begetting Sons & Daughters. This is a Chance Oppy. being left at Moore Hall to find its Way to you & they are not the most careful there; on this Account I do not inclose your Brothers Letter which is very long & contains many Things both of a private & publick Nature which I would not have get out, but I will forward it by the very first Oppy. on which I can depend. If any offers from your Part of the Country I wish you would get him to call on me here. Or if you can get any Person to come on easy Terms, I want the Hessian Mare to sell & have the little old Horse for him to ride back, but he must remember to bring my Saddle & the blanket I formerly wore under it which lays in the Garret as the little Horse's Back is sore. Col. Lowry writes me he will pay you all possible Attention in any little Matters which from his former Kindness I cannot doubt. He writes me that my Horses are doing well but are very troublesome which I did not expect after making such an Alteration in their Condition. I would have Cyrus endeavour to raise them in Flesh & when he goes of Errands lead them together so as to use them to each other but on no Account to tamper with them in the Grass till I return. I have been disappointed in getting Cows from this Part of the Country so that we must either do with what we have or get them where we are. Mrs. Yard has sent me out your Bobbin & a small Bottle of Howe's Acid to make Punch which I will send you by the same Oppy. as your Brothers Letter, but she cannot get out the other Things. I expect the Gentleman from Boston every Day by whom I sent for Linnen &c. As soon as he arrives will forward my dear Girl what he brings. The British Army would certainly have left Philad. if the Commissioners had not arrived as they did & the prevailing Opinion is that they will go yet—at present it seems a dead Calm. The Commissioners have announced their Arrival to Congress in Form but no Answer is yet received tho hourly expected. We flatter ourselves when the Answer comes they will go off & commence Operations in some other Part of the Country. I have such an Acct. from our Friend in Town as makes me hope this will be the Case. She has sent me a Message desiring me not to leave the Neighbourhood & to come in as soon as possible. None of the Vessels are yet returned but they get the Provisions from Hand to Mouth by Boats. Sam cannot be heard of. I fear he is pressed, but you will judge whether Hannah should know it. I think rather not. I am very impatient to see you & the dear Children, their diverting Prattle & Company makes them every Day more dear. I was very near buying a Poney for Joe the other Day but had Resolution enough to get over the Temptation; I do not know whether I should do as well if it fell in my Way again. Kiss them all for me & endeavour to keep up your Spirits. I would not have you a dull, moping, dejected Wife for the World. As we have our Joys & Pleasures, my dear Creature we must not expect them unmixed with some Trouble & Sorrow. It is not the lot of human Nature nor the Portion Providence assigns its Creatures. Let us therefore be resigned & endeavour to be chearful as it conduces to our own Happiness & promotes that of those about us.

I repeat again that I long to see you & shall rejoice to hear from you as often as you find Time & Oppy. & am my dear Love with unabated Affection, most sincerely yours, J Reed

P.S. Since writing the above our Commissy. of Prisoners has come from Germantown & says Mr. Loring assured him they should leave Philad this Week, that he had embark'd such Prisoners as were not to be exchanged & would send out those that where [were], which he has done this Day. Many other Circumstances concur to make this credible. Their Route will be thro the Jersey but what Parts we can only yet conjecture. The Answer from Congress is momently expected. Ld. Carlisle with his Girl has taken Possession of the Front Part of Mr Powel's House much to Mrs. Powels Mortification I dare say. Once more my Love Adieu.

RC (NHi).

Francis Dana's Notes

[June 16? 1778][1]

The great point may be to draw us into a conference.

For this purpose they offer to negotiate upon many matters beyond their powers under the Act of Parliamt.

They guard these extra propositions by asking things they cannot imagine we shall grant.

Our refusal therefore brings the real matters of negotiation within the Act.

But should they accede to those extra propositions, Parliamt. might & wou'd reject them.

The King has, or he has not a right to treat with us beyond the limits of the Act.

If he has not, every proposition intimated as a ground of treaty without the Act is insidious.

If he has, then they may be supposed to be instructed to accede to our claim of independance provided they find peace can be no otherways effected. This they may think necessary if they are informed of the substance of our treaty of Alliance.

Is it not wiser for Britain to acknowledge our Independance now, than to refuse it and thereby expose the few colonies she holds in America to be added to the Union.

If so we ought to conduct as if she was prepared to do it.

The King I think may treat with us by virtue of his prerogative, as Independant States.

For are we not in fact such?

Hath not our Independance been acknowledged by France?

Did she not ground her connection with us upon our having been in full possession of Independance ever since July 1776?

Have we not reason to expect other Nations will follow the example of France?

MS (NN). In the hand of Francis Dana.

1 These undated notes, and a similar set in the hand of Charles Thomson printed below under this same date, contain the substance of debates over Congress' response to the British peace commissioners' June 9 letter, which was debated on June 13, 15, and 16. For a discussion on the circumstances that led to these debates, see Samuel Adams to James Warren, June 13, 1778, note 3.

The committee appointed on June 16 to prepare Congress' response to the commissioners included William Henry Drayton, Richard Henry Lee, Gouverneur Morris, John Witherspoon, and Samuel Adams, in the last of whose collection of personal papers these notes are now located. Dana's notes may have been prepared for a speech he delivered at this time or may simply reflect sentiments he passed on to Adams for the committee's consideration. The fact that Secretary Thomson's notes on the same subject printed below are also located in Adams' papers strongly supports the assumption that Adams made use of both documents in his work on the committee, whose draft letter for the commissioners was reported to Congress the afternoon of June 16 and adopted the following day. For additional information on Congress' response to the commissioners, see the documents of Richard Henry Lee, Charles Thomson, and John Witherspoon printed under this date; *JCC*, 11:605–6, 608–10, 614–15; and Henry Laurens to the Carlisle Commissioners, June 17, 1778.

Richard Henry Lee's Draft Letter to the Carlisle Commissioners

My Lords & Gentlemen [June 16, 1778][1]

I have reced your letter of and laid it before Congress with its inclosures. In answer I am instructed to inform you, that Congress ever ready to stop the effusion of human blood have been induced to hear your letter read thro out[2] and to consider its inclosures notwithstanding the very inadmissible and offensive things that are contained in the former. Tho It is impossible Congress can fail to be affected with the highest resentment at the indignity offered them by the indecent reflections you have thought proper to make upon his most Ch. Majesty the Great & good ⟨*&faithful*⟩ally of these States. The Commission from his Britannic Majesty under which you act, a copy of which you have inclosed, and the Acts of Parliament on which the Commission is founded, being both formed upon the idea of the good people of these States being Subjects of the Crown of Great Britain, and proposing peace upon dependent principles and a return to the domination of a power that hath accumulated every injury and insult on their unoffending States, Congress consider them both as totally inadmissible, and cannot consent to any further communication on such grounds. I am further instructed to inform your Excellency that Congress will be always ready to enter upon the Consideratn. of a Treaty of Peace, when a sincere disposition thereto shall be evidenced on the part ⟨*G.B.*⟩ of his B M by an explicit acknowledgement of the Independence of these States and by withdrawing his Fleets from our Coasts and his Armies from the 13 States.

MS (PPAmP). In the hand of Richard Henry Lee and endorsed by him: "Letter from Congress to the King's commissioners."

1 Lee drafted this letter as a member of a committee appointed on June 16 to prepare a response to the Carlisle commissioners' June 9 peace overture. A comparison of the texts of the Lee draft and the committee draft prepared by Gouverneur Morris indicates that Morris followed the sequence of points presented by Lee and incorporated many of Lee's words and phrases into his own more concise and moderately toned version. Morris' draft, introduced by a preamble in Lee's hand, was reported to Congress on the 16th and approved the following day. See *JCC*, 11:610–11, 614–15; and Henry Laurens to the Carlisle Commissioners, June 17, 1778. For additional information on Congress' response to the British commissioners, see Samuel Adams to James Warren, June 13, note 3; and

the documents of Francis Dana, Charles Thomson, and John Witherspoon printed under this date.

2 At this point in the draft the following passage is set off by diagonal marks: "and have Considered it with a coolness that that having." Both James Ballagh and Edmund Burnett incorporated a part of this passage into their differing versions of Lee's draft, but neither seems to reflect Lee's intent. The appearance of the MS and the sense of the sentence suggest that Lee simply intended to delete these words. See Lee, *Letters* (Ballagh), 1:414–15; and Burnett, *Letters*, 3:296–97.

Richard Henry Lee to Thomas Jefferson

Dear Sir York in Pennsylva. 16 June 1778

I thank you for your favor of the 5th which I received yesterday.[1] It is the only satisfactory account I have received of the proceedings of our Assembly. The enemy have made many insidious attempts upon us lately, not in the military way, they seem tired of that, but in the way of negotiation. Their first, was by industriously circulating the bills of *pacification* as they call them, before they had passed into Acts, in order to prevent our closing with France. These bills received a comment from Congress on the 22d. of April, which no doubt you have seen. The inclosed paper will shew you the second attempt from Lord Howe and Gen. Clinton, with the answer of Congress. The third movement happened very lately, when Clinton desired a passport from Gen. Washington for Dr. Ferguson to come to Congress with a letter from the newly arrived Commissioners Lord Carlyle, Wm. Eden esqr. and Governor Johnston. The General refused the passport until Congress should give leave. The letter from Clinton was transmitted here, but the impatience of the Commissioners did not suffer them to wait for an answer. Thro the medium of the General, leaving their Secretary Dr. Ferguson behind, the packet arrived containing a letter from the Commissioners with a copy of their Commission. Their letter is a combination of fraud, falsehood, insidious offers, and abuse of France, Concluding with a denial of Independence. The sine qua non being withheld, you may judge what will be the fate of the rest. An answer has not yet been sent. In due time you will have both the letter and its answer. I dont know whether to call Governor Johnston an Apostate or not. He has been in opposition to the Ministry and has spoken some speeches in our favor, but I believe he has never been a friend to American Independence. However, there seems no doubt but that he has on this occasion touched Ministerial gold. The others are notorious Ministerialists. It is amazing how the Court of London does mix pride, meanness, cunning, and folly, with Gasconade, and timidity. In short the strangest composition is there formed that ever disgraced and injured Mankind. The King of Prussia has declared in terms explicit, that he would follow France in acknowledging our

Independence and his hobby horse is, to become a maritime power. Yet he seems, by his movements disposed to quarrel with the Emperor about the divisions of the Bavarian dominions, the Elector being dead without Heir of his body, the next Heir who is the Elector Palatine must loose his right between the two great Spoilers. We have been long amused with accounts of the enemy abandoning Philadelphia. I believe they will do so when they can stay no longer, but not until then. They have certainly removed all their heavy Cannon, Baggage &c. And fearing a French war every Moment, they keep in readiness to depart. We did lately shatter extremely a 20 gun ship belonging to the enemy in the North river, and sent her away to York, in no condition for service. I observe by our last delegation, that my enemies have been again at work, however, they shall not gain their point of withdrawing me from the public Councils.[2]

I am dear Sir your affectionate friend and obedient Servant,

Richard Henry Lee

RC (DLC). Jefferson, *Papers* (Boyd), 2:200–201.

[1] Jefferson's June 5 letter to Lee is in Jefferson, *Papers* (Boyd), 2:194.

[2] The Virginia House of Delegates had not included Richard Henry Lee's name on the list of nominees it selected on May 28 to be considered in the annual balloting for delegates to Congress. The senate added his name to the list, but in the house balloting the following day, Lee ranked sixth among the seven delegates appointed. *Journal of the House of Delegates of the Commonwealth of Virginia, 1777–81* (Richmond, 1827), May 1778, pp. 23–27.

Governor Henry expressed his concern over the outcome of this election in his June 18 letter to Lee. "I felt for you on seeing the Order in which the balloting placed the Delegates in Congress," Henry explained. "It is an Effort of that rancorous Malice that has so long followed you thro the arduous Path of Duty in which you have invariably travel'd since America resolved to repel her Oppressors." Lee Papers, PPAmP. In a more accusing tone, Francis Lightfoot Lee offered the following comments in his June 25 letter to his brother. "The junto, by their Lyes & intrigues have so far carried their point, as to throw some little discredit upon us; but have missed their great aim, of removing obstructions to their jobbing schemes. I think you are perfectly right in not gratifying them, by resenting the ill treatment of the Assembly. The Esqr. says, Mr. Harvie, who got to Wmsburg after the election, was much affronted, & made those who had been taken in, by certain gentry, perfectly asshamed of themselves. I suppose they wou'd now willingly return you thanks, to make up with you; tho they will again be taken in by the same wretches." Lee Family Papers, ViU.

Gouverneur Morris to George Clinton

York Town 16th June 1778

I am very sorry to inform your Excellency of the Death of our Friend and my very worthy Colleague Mr. Livingston. He was from the Moment almost of his Arrival here confined to his Room and on Friday last at 4 oClock in the Morning paid the last Debt to Nature.[1] I have before me a Report on the Vermont Business.[2] I do

Philip Livingston

not think it adequate nor can I pretend to say whether it will be adopted. At present we are so plagued by Applications of the most public Nature and among others of the British Commissioners that really the most important Matters slide by. I shall take the earliest Opportunity to bring this Business on and endeavour to procure such Amendments as the Nature of the Case requires. Not having heard any Thing upon the Subject of a former Letter to you as to Money Matters I am left rather in an awkward Situation but shall nevertheless endeavour to obtain from Congress 100,000 Dollars for the State on Account.[3] If it should be disagreeable it can be paid to some of the continental Officers in the Commissary or Qur. Masters Line. We have no News here worth relating.

I am your Excellency's most obt Servt. Gouvr Morris

RC (MHi).

1 Upon being informed of Philip Livingston's death, the delegates had resolved on June 12 that "Congress will, in a body, attend the funeral of Mr. Livingston this evening, at six o'clock, with a crape round the arm, and will continue in mourning for the space for one month." *JCC*, 11:592–93.

2 This report appears in this volume as the first half of the enclosure printed with the New York delegates' July 21 letter to Governor Clinton.

3 Congress agreed on June 22 to advance $100,000 to the New York delegates for the use of their state. *JCC*, 11:627, 630.

Robert Morris to Gouverneur Morris

My Dear Sir Camp at Valley Forge, June 16th. 1778

Prompted by the dictates of Justice I cannot refuse giving you the trouble of a few lines in behalf of a Man of great Merit, that now wishes to attain that rank in our Army, which his usefullness & attachment to the General made him indifferent about on former occasions, when opportunity Offered for pushing his promotion, I mean Capt Gibbs of the Generals Guards.[1] This Gentleman commenced Soldier with the Battle of Lexington and has continued in the army ever since without absenting himself from Duty one Single day since that time; by accepting his present Command he lost the line of promotion in the Troops of his own State & has the Mortification to see many Colonels at this day, that must always have been under his Command, had he continued in that line.

His present Corps consists of 150 Men fine Fellows as you wou'd wish to see (100 of them was out with their Captain & Covered the retreat of the Marquis the other day). These are consequently equal in numbers to three Companies, & indeed to some of our Regiments, where then wou'd be the impropriety of appointing Capt Gibbs Colo. or Lieutenant Colo. Commandant of the Guards & of promoting his Second Mr. Livingston to be Captain therein. The Merit &

past Services of these Gentn entitle them to it, and they have no other chance of promotion, I think they are personally known to you and therefore it is the less necessary to urge the point with a Gentn. of your liberal way of thinking. I came down here about ten days ago expecting to go into Philadelphia immediately, & shou'd certainly have done so, had not the Commissioners arrived at the Critical time they did; since then I have been prevailed on to stay, day after day untill Congress give them their Answer, which, it is expected here, will be such, as will send them off immediately. After that Answer is given I shou'd like to hold an hour or two's Conversation with my Friend, Govr. Johnstone, but have not yet determined on doing so.[2] I think he will be much mortifyed at his disapointed embassy & I cou'd wish to convince him that Great Britain may still be happy & Continue Rich, by forming a Commercial Alliance with us, on the same broad basis that other Nations do; it will be no difficult matter to convince any reasonable Man, that Great Britain wou'd still enjoy under such Treaties the greatest share & most valuable parts of our Trade, but the best & most liberal of the British Subjects feel themselves humbled, in the Idea of quitting their Sovereignty over us, & this with many will preclude all reasoning on the Subject. Whether Govr. Johnstone is of this Number or not, I cannot tell, but we hear he is strongly opposed to our Independance, altho unbounded in offers of every thing else; No offers must tempt us; they ought not to have a hearing of one moment, unless preceeded by an acknowledgement of our Independance, because we can never be a happy People under their Domination. I have frequently ventured to assert here, that Congress will not give up one Iota of their former resolves on this Subject, nor do a thing in the least degree inconsistent with their Public faith, plighted in the ratification of the Treaty with France. I am sure you will make my words good. I think Philadelphia will be evacuated the moment the Commissioners get an Answer from Congress, I shall then go down & will inform you, Whether things are left on such a footing that Congress can be well accomodated there and if they can I hope they will remove accordingly. My time for joining you is near at hand & I had rather it shou'd be in Philada than York Town. I long to take you & Duer by the hand as also some other Worthies your associates and with sincere regard remain Dear Sir, Your most obedient, humble servant,

Robt Morris

P.S. Poor Phil Livingston. I am sorry for the loss of so Honest a Man & hope deserving respect has been shewn to his Memory.

I hope Duer will befriend Capt Gibbs. I shou'd write to him was I sure of his being yet at York.

RC (NNC).

1 A similar letter of recommendation in behalf of Capt. Caleb Gibbs that Morris wrote at Valley Forge this day to Elbridge Gerry is in the Emmet Collection, CSmH. Gibbs was promoted to the rank of major on July 29, 1778. See *JCC*, 11:722, 730.

2 Johnstone had written to Robert Morris in February in a vain effort to stimulate support for a "proposition" he anticipated the North Ministry was about to offer that he hoped would become "a ground of reunion" with the American colonies. For Morris' response to Johnstone's letter, which was read in Congress on April 27, see Henry Laurens to Robert Morris, April 27, 1778, note 1. By coincidence Johnstone was writing another letter to Morris on the same general subject this very day—under the dateline "Philada. June 16th. 1778"—which the latter laid before Congress on July 9 when it was resolved "That all letters received by members of Congress from any of the British commissioners . . . be laid before Congress." *JCC*, 11:678. The copies Charles Thomson made of Johnstone's letters are in PCC, item 78, 13:65–66, 87–88, and have been printed in Wharton, *Diplomatic Correspondence*, 2:487–88, 616–17. The RC of the June 16 letter is in the Peter Force Collection, DLC.

Charles Thomson's Notes

[June 16, 1778]

All agree the terms are inadmissible.[1] Some think the insulting way that the whole letter so far as read is an insult; First as it is grounded on a supposition that we are so devoid of understanding and every sense of honor as to violate the treaties we have just entered into & give ourselves up to the mercy of those, who have demonstrated that they have the will if they had but the power to reduce us to abject slavery and that they would exterminate rather than not subject us.

2. As it accompanies these inadmissible terms with reproaches against that power which steps in to rescue us from destruction; thereby supposing that we have not sense to feel nor spirit to resent abuse offered to our friend.

The question is in what manner to treat this letter.

1. Whether to enter into a train of reasoning & shew that from a regard to safety, & the faith due to treaties Congress cannot listen to terms short of independence, or

2. Leaving the Commissioners to draw that conclusion, to reject it on the footing of the insult contained [*in*] it, or

3. To unite these & comprehend both in the answer

The first is a temporising method & will shew that Congress have not a full confidence in the firmness & persevering spirit of their constituents: For such a train of reasoning cannot be for the purpose of enlightening the understanding or convincing the judgment of the Commissioners but of the people of this continent. What occasion for this if they are convinced of their independence & determined to support it. Besides it will inspirit our enemes as it will convince them Congress have not a full confidence in the establishment of their independance or their resources for supporting it. For who but a simpleton attempts to prove a self evident proposition.

Second. Rejecting the letter on the ground of the insult, which may be considered as double in offering chains to freemen & abusing our frien[ds]; will carry all the force of reasoning on the first ground: It will do more, it will appall our enemies and inspirit the friends of the cause. The Comrs. will thereby see that nothing short of Independance will be listened to & must therefore come to that or break of[f] the conference; and that even admitting independance they must treat our allies with respect. It will carry with it to the comrs a conviction of the confidence Congress have both in their cause & resources, & must therefore force them to a speedier Declaration of their future powers if any they have.

3. Mixing both will only weaken the force of the reasoning on the second ground.

MS (NN). In the hand of Charles Thomson.

1 For a discussion of the circumstances that led Congress to debate the "inadmissible" terms presented by the Carlisle commissioners referred to here, see Samuel Adams to James Warren, June 13, 1778, note 3. It is not known for what specific purpose Thomson prepared this document, but it apparently summarizes the possible congressional responses considered by the delegates in the course of debates held on June 13, 15, and 16. The fact that the manuscript is located in the papers of Samuel Adams, a member of the committee appointed to draft a response to the commissioners, suggests that Thomson prepared it for the committee's use, although delegates other than Adams took the initiative in drafting the reply Congress eventually adopted on June 17. For additional information on the work of this committee, see the notes of Francis Dana and the draft letters to the Carlisle commissioners by Richard Henry Lee and John Witherspoon printed under this date.

John Witherspoon's Draft Letter to the Carlisle Commissioners

[June 16, 1778][1]

I received your Letter & Papers accompanying them which have been laid before Congress and read. By them I am instructed to inform you that they are & invariably have been desirous of Peace as with all the World so more especially with Great Britain. This Desire is not yet extinguished even by the extreme Barbarity with which the present War has been carried on by the Forces of that Nation.

I am particularly desired to mention to you that they are surprised how you could think that throwing out such Reflections as are contained in your Letter against the King of France with whom they are in Alliance would contribute to hasten an Accommodation.

They are sensible of their Obligations to him & firmly resolved to abide by their Engagements.

I am further desired to assure you in the most explicit Terms that Congress are determined to enter into no Treaty unless you have Powers either expressly to acknowledge the Independance of the united States of America or immediately to withdraw the British Forces from every part of these States.

You know best your Instructions & reserved Powers. If therefore you think that after the above Declaration there is Room for any further Discussion Gen. Washington is directed to grant a Passport to Dr Ferguson to come to this Place.

MS (NN). Written by Witherspoon and endorsed by him: "Draught of a Letter to the Commissioners to be given in to the Committee."

[1] Witherspoon drafted this letter as a member of the committee appointed this day to formulate a reply to a June 9 letter from the Carlisle commissioners asking for a meeting with Congress to discuss peace terms. It is unlikely, however, that Witherspoon's draft was ever offered to Congress, for on this day the delegates considered a draft reply to the commissioners written by Gouverneur Morris, one of Witherspoon's colleagues on this committee, that was formally approved the following day. For additional information on the work of the committee, see Samuel Adams to James Warren, June 13, 1778, note 3, and the documents of Francis Dana, Richard Henry Lee, and Charles Thomson printed under this date.

Committee of Commerce to Unknown

Sir,[1]

York-Town 17th June 1778

You are desired to deliver with all possible dispatch to Mr. de Francy or order such quantity of tabacco in hogsheads as you may have in storehouses belonging to the continent, & which he may have occasion for in loading his ship "Le fier Rodrique" taking his receipt therefor.

We are, Sir, your hble servants, per order of the committee,[2]

Signed. Lewis, Chairman

Tr (MH–H). This letter is taken from a Jared Sparks transcription of a document that was written by Jean Théveneau de Francy for his employer Caron de Beaumarchais. The transcript includes the committee letter, a French translation, and an appended note by Francy which has been translated and footnoted below.

[1] In his June 11 letter to Beaumarchais, Francy reported that he would leave York as soon as he had obtained an order of Congress for the commercial agents in Virginia to deliver as much tobacco as possible to him for loading *Le Fier Roderique,* indicating that this remittance would either be credited against the old debt due Beaumarchais or used to pay for the part of the French cargo to be purchased by Congress. And in his July 15 letter to the committee, Francy reminded them that when he met with Francis Lewis on June 18, the day before he left York, Lewis had promised that Virginia agents would be ordered to fit

out vessels to go under convoy with *Le Fier Roderique*. Lewis probably gave this letter to Francy without specifying an addressee and Francy most likely showed it to Carter Braxton, Benjamin Harrison, Jr., and John Norton, as well as other Continental agents he contacted in Virginia. See Beaumarchais, *Correspondance* (Morton and Spinelli), 4:123, 142n.12.

2 The following note appears after the French translation of this letter and ends abruptly at mid-page. "N.B. As this order has been delivered to me after they have been informed of the sale of the cargo of the Fier Rodrique, it is clear that this tobacco has been granted to me in order to be used for the discharge of Congress's debt to you for your other shipments; thus despite the urgent representations of the honest agency of Passy, and the at least not very prudent conduct of Mr. Chevallie, I have succeeded in getting what everyone seems to wish to contest you for. This would be a very good situation to turn to good account in case of new difficulties, but from now on I hope that I will not have great obstacles to overcome considering the contract I have made and besides my claims are supported by Mr. Deane & Carmichael; the only obstacle that I will overcome with great difficulty will be my procuring . . . ." Ellipsis in Tr. For Francy's continuing "difficulties" in completing the transactions Beaumarchais hoped to carry out with Congress, see Henry Laurens to Francy, July 26, 1778, note 1.

William Henry Drayton's Notes for a Speech in Congress

[June 17? 1778][1]

It is with the highest pleasure I think I have occasion to flatter myself that the view we on Saturday took of our foreign affairs, was such a view as may [*have*] enabled this House to distinguish objects at that distance with precision & to form their judgments in prudence & wisdom. Our foreign affairs have long been enveloped in impenetrable darkness: but the rays of light now beam in our political firmament, & reveal the objects to our sight. I trust we will not shut our eyes. We are Sir placed in the watch tower of America. We are stationed on this height, that we may seeing [see] the American affairs, interists in one grand & extensive view. We are placed high in The Imperial car of America that we may guide it with skil, lash on the sluggard, curb in the impetuous, & unharness & discharge the unruly draught. Oh Mr. P[resident] that we were wise, that we would but take notice of the precipice along which we are now driving. Oft Sir have we unknowingly in the night & in the day with our eyes wilfully shut rowled upon the extreem verge of this dreadful height—an invisible hand restrained our passing it. May I be permited to say we have long enough trifled with Providence, trifled with our generous constituents & indulged our private feelings? I will take the liberty to say Sir, it is our indispensable duty so to endeavour to conduct ourselves as may be most likely to conduce to the happiness of the People who seated us here, committing themselves to our impartiality, care & conduct.

Sir, I know not how to account for it, but so it has happened, that it has accidentally general been my lot in every public Assembly or Council in which I have been placed, to move such subjects as draw upon the mover the displeasure of bodies of Men or of individuals. And I have done so, not I trust because actuated by a morose inclination, but because I thought it the duty of my Station. I have not stept into public life, I did not come into Congress to acquire friends but determinately & boldly to discharge the duty of a Citizen. Conscious that it is my duty to speak plainly & act decis[iv]ely I yet feel pain when in doing so any person feels distress or uneasiness. I am sensible sir, the subject I am agitating will unavoidably cause uneasiness in this House. The ties of blood like electrical conductors will convey & communicate the effects of a blow it is my duty to strike. I participate in the feelings which must arise upon this occasion: I lament the cause, I regret the consequence. But Sir, in this place I look upon every Member as connected only with the public, and unconnected with individuals abroad, especially with persons in public office, otherwise freedom of debate must be destroyed, & the public good must yield to private connections. I flatter myself therefore, that nothing I shall say will be construed as ment to give pain to any Mem[ber] I disavow any such unmanly design.

MS (PPL). In the hand of William Henry Drayton.

1 On June 16 Congress had appointed a committee consisting of William Henry Drayton, Samuel Adams, and Richard Henry Lee "to prepare a resolution for preventing any correspondence with the enemy." This action was deemed necessary to counteract the efforts of the Carlisle commissioners to promote support for their mission by distributing private letters in favor of reconciliation from themselves and from various English correspondents to friends and relatives in the United States, both in and out of Congress. Acting with dispatch, the committee submitted a report this day, which was written by Drayton and approved by Congress, calling upon state governments to prevent the delivery of letters from England "addressed to individuals of these United States . . . through the conveyance of the enemy." See *JCC*, 11:608, 616. At the same time, President Laurens reported to Washington, "there was an extraordinary Motion on our floor for calling upon Members to lay before Congress such Letters as they had received from the Commissioners or other persons, meaning persons in Great Britain on Political subjects," which Congress did not approve largely as a result of Laurens' opposition. See Laurens to Washington, June 18, 1778. Although Laurens did not identify the delegate who offered this unsuccessful motion, there is reason to believe that Drayton was the one in question and that he prepared these notes to serve as the basis for a speech in Congress on this issue. To begin with, such a motion would have been a logical extension of Drayton's report on curbing correspondence with the enemy. Furthermore, his admission in these notes that "the subject I am agitating will unavoidably cause uneasiness in this House" and his statement that "I look upon every Member as connected only with the public, and unconnected with individuals abroad," both fit in well with the proposal to require the delegates to submit to Congress all letters they had received from the commissioners and from England dealing with public affairs. Finally, Drayton's mention of "the view we on Saturday took of our foreign affairs" could be a reference to the June 13 debate in Congress on the commission-

ers' letter of June 9, which involved the issue of America's relations with Great Britain and France. Although Congress did not approve Drayton's motion this day, it did pass one to the same effect on July 9. *JCC,* 11:678.

William Henry Drayton to the Carlisle Commissioners

York Town, June 17, 1778

To their Excellencies the Earl of CARLISLE, WILLIAM EDEN, *and* GEORGE JOHNSTONE, *Esqrs. British Commissioners.*

As I have but a few moments that I can, in conscience, appropriate to a correspondence with your Excellencies, I trust this circumstance will, with you, excuse the abrupt manner in which I introduce myself, and my reflections, to your attention.[1]

Your letter of the 9th instant to Congress, your commission, and the acts of the British Parliament upon which they are grounded, are the fashionable subjects of curious enquiry, in how many points of view they are fallacious and incompetent to the object of your *ostensible* negotiation.[2] Although Congress cannot condescend minutely to animadvert upon your propositions, as your Excellencies are empowered to hear individuals, I flatter myself, so anxious is your inclination to restore peace, that you will for a moment honour me with your attention.

In your letter of the 9th instant, Governor Johnstone signed this position, "Notwithstanding the pretended date or present form of the French offers to North-America, yet it is notorious that these were made in consequence of the plans of accommodation previously concerted in Great-Britain, and with a view to prevent our reconciliation, and to prolong this destructive war."

On the 5th of February, in the *House of Commons,* Governor Johnstone also signed this position, "I have had a hint, and have good reason to believe a proposition *will be made* to Parliament in four or five days, by administration, that may be a ground of reunion; I really do not know the particulars, nevertheless, as *I learn some preliminaries have lately gone from France,* I think it cannot be deemed unfriendly to either country, to give you notice of this *intended proposition,* THAT you may in prudence *do nothing hastily* with a foreign power."[3]

The "preliminaries" mentioned by Governor Johnstone, as "lately gone from France," were *at that moment* at sea, with Mr. Simeon Deane, and had been so some weeks; they were to the following purpose: "That his Most Christian Majesty was determined to acknowledge our Independence, and make a treaty with us of Amity and Commerce. That in this treaty, no advantage would be taken of our present situation to obtain terms from us, which otherwise

William Henry Drayton

would not be convenient for us to agree to, his Majesty desiring that the treaty, once made, should be durable, and our amity subsist for ever, which could not be expected, if each nation did not find its interest in the continuance as well as in the commencement of it. It was therefore his intention, that the terms of the treaty should be such, as we might be willing to agree to if our state had been long established, and in the fulness of strength and power, and such as we should approve of when that time should come. That his Majesty was fixed in his determination, not only to acknowledge, but to support our Independence by every means in his power. That in doing this, he might probably be soon engaged in war, with all the expences, risque and damage usually attending it; yet he should not expect any compensation from us on that account, nor pretend that he acted wholly for our sakes, since, besides his real good-will to us and our cause, it was manifestly the interest of France, that the power of England should be diminished by our separation from it. He should, moreover, not so much as insist, that, if he engaged in the war with England on our account, we should not make a separate peace for ourselves, whenever good and advantageous terms were offered to us. The only condition he should require and rely on would be this, *that we, in no peace to be made with England, should give up our Independence, and return to the obedience of that government.*"[4] These preliminaries were, by Mons. Girard, in the name of his most Christian Majesty, announced to the American Commissioners at Paris *on the 16th day of December last.* And in consequence of them, the Treaty of Paris, between America and France, was actually signed *on the 6th of February, 1778.* It is notorious that it was on the 19th day of February that Lord North introduced his propositions to Parliament for a re-union with America.

From this state of facts two points result. First, that the two positions signed by Governor Johnstone militate against each other *in direct* terms. Secondly, that so far were "the French offers" from being "made in consequence of the plans of accommodation concerted in Great-Britain," *that the latter were made in consequence only of the former*; for the French offers were made *on the 16th day of December.* Governor Johnstone (connected with administration) on the 5th of February expressly says, he was then ignorant of any particulars of a plan of accommodation. On the 6th of February the French offers were compleated by a treaty; and it was not *till the 19th of February* that any plan of accommodation was communicated to the British Parliament. Your Excellencies, however, do not scruple, even in your first address to Congress, to assert a position, the contrary to which is known to be the fact. I will not charge you with a designed falsity: The people will use their discretion. At any rate, this conduct on your part warns them to be upon their guard against you.

Having thus vindicated the honour of our good and great ally the King of France, permit me to touch upon your propositions to Congress.

Your Excellencies offer us a seat for our representatives in your Parliament. Happily for us, we are too well acquainted with the *insignificancy* of the Scotch representatives there, to expect that American representatives can, in the same place, possess any importance; or that America can derive any advantage from such a representation.

As an alternative, you propose to send agents to our assemblies. But as we know they would be spies upon us, and *agents to purchase our voices,* we will have no such characters among us.

You propose to concur in measures to discharge the debts of America. By this, as our subjection is implied, so are restrictions of some sort upon our trade; of necessity, so is a *diminution of our ability* to discharge our debts. We know you cannot discharge the debts of your own nation, we therefore cannot expect that you will, or even desire that you should, discharge any part of ours. We are willing and able to discharge our debts, without your concurrence or aid. Your offer therefore wears the appearance of being officious and idle.

You propose to extend every freedom to trade, that our respective interests can require. Do we not know, that you have a natural inclination to monopolize trade? Do we not know, that your and our interest in the point of trade is in direct opposition? It is your interest that our trade should be limited—it is ours, that it should be unlimited—we there differ, *toto cœlo.*

You propose a cessation of hostilities. Withdraw your forces by land, and hostilities there are instantly ended; you need not be anxious for a cessation at sea; on that element we have every thing to fear from you. If you mean fair, why then do you delay to do that which you seem to desire, and which that it be done rests entirely with yourselves?

Such are your principal offers in detail. *Of how little value are they to us!*

But you offer us every thing short of Independence. If you are serious, *of how little value must such a connection with us be to you*! Will your Excellencies condescend, with me, to view Great Britain and America under one Sovereign? The sovereignty in Britain; America possessed of powers of government but short of independence.

America, formed for empire, must naturally arrive at it; having tasted of it she will be ever anxious to possess it again; having by arms acquired a power but short of independence, she will encrease in reputation and ability to become independent, and this will encrease her desire to be so; her former success will possess her with confidence and hope; experience will make her ever suspicious of the intentions of Britain: Hence, being in possession of powers, only short of independent, she will always be prepared to assert her rights, especially having in mind her naked condition at the sudden commencement of the present war. In such a formidable situation, design, accident, suspicion, or the breath of displeasure on either side, must, in a few years, break the cobweb by which you offer to hold her under the dominion of Britain. And is the acquiring dominion to be held by such a tie worth another campaign! Can it be worth the pursuit of a man of *common honesty* and common sense!

But supposing your offers to be, *what they are not,* of sterling value to America: How inadequate are your powers to the purpose of accommodation! The great Lord Abingdon puts this matter in the clearest point of view. In his most elegant protest on this subject, he says, "Although the Commissioners and the Congress be agreed, such agreement is of no effect till confirmed by Parliament; which is giving such advantage to Parliament, by knowing what Congress will do, and is of such disadvantage to Congress, by not knowing what Parliament will confirm, that the very inequality of the conditions will put a stop to accommodation."[5] If America enters into terms with you, see what might be the consequence—Your Excellencies must allow, *that it is our duty to avoid them.*

We have made a solemn treaty with France—the *object* is, the establishment of our Independence. If we treat with you upon the footing of Dependence, we at once break our faith with France, for ever lose all credit with foreign nations, and are, *ipso facto,* cut off even from the hope of foreign succour. In this situation *you will absolutely hold us at mercy*. Your King, Ministers and Parliament may refuse to ratify your engagements, for they have *the power* to do so. Governor Johnstone has long and ably pleaded the cause of America. Is he now come to our shore to invite us to surrender to the justice and mercy of our most unjust and vengeful enemies, who have for a long course of years treated us with the basest deceptions, and calumniated us throughout Europe: Enemies, who have starved to death our countrymen taken prisoners, loading them while alive and in *their power* with every insult. Enemies who gave stretch to their savage allies,[6] to murder our old and unarmed farmers, and their helpless women and children: Enemies who have plundered our country, burned our towns, and armed son against father, servant against master, and brother against brother, in order to subject us: Enemies who have moved even Hell itself to accomplish their purpose of blood, ruin and tyranny: Enemies utterly abandoned to corruption, destitute of public virtue, deaf to the voice of justice, and dead to the feelings of humanity; Can it possibly be expected that such enemies, after the expence of so many millions; the loss of so much of their own blood; the disgraces their arms have sustained;

the insults to which they have been obliged to submit from foreign nations, in their pursuit of our destruction, the impending ruin under which they have been driven by our opposition; I say, can it possibly be expected, that when *such enemies, so provoked,* shall find us lying at their mercy, they will ratify your Excellencies terms but short of Independence, and be content to hold dominion over us by so slender a tie as a cobweb! *Timeo Danaos, et dona ferentes.*[7]

America is independent *de facto et de jure.* She will maintain her station at the expence of her last drop of blood. It is in vain to solicit what your arms, when most powerful, were not able to compel. You are no longer in that situation. America is more competent to the contest than ever she has been. Our resolution is fixed, nor do we fear "the horrors and devastations of war," with which, in the conclusion of your letter, you threaten us. France has acknowledged our Independence; the great powers of Europe smile upon us; we rely upon our own virtue and the favour of Heaven. If we continue firm, we shall continue independent. Farewell.

W.H.D.

MS not found; reprinted from the *Pennsylvania Gazette,* June 20, 1778.

1 This is the first of four newspaper letters William Henry Drayton wrote to the Carlisle commissioners using his initials as a signature. The other three appeared in the *Pennsylvania Packet* on July 18, September 12, and October 29, 1778, and are printed in this edition of *Letters* under the dates July 3, September 4, and October 24, 1778. Although no manuscript drafts of these letters have been found, they are obviously written by a member of Congress and the use of Drayton's initials as a signature point unmistakably to his authorship. It is pertinent to note that Drayton published these letters on his own initiative, for as Josiah Bartlett, who was in Congress throughout the period the letters appeared, observed of the third one: "The letter to the [commissioners] signed W.H.D. was wrote I suppose by Chief Justice Drayton member from So. Carolina as were the former letters under that signature." See Bartlett to Whipple, September 12, 1778.

2 For a discussion of Congress' formal response to the commissioners' June 9 letter, see Samuel Adams to James Warren, June 13, 1778, note 3. Drayton was a member of the committee appointed on June 16 to draft a reply to the commissioners' letter, and the present address probably stems in part from his work on that body. *JCC,* 11:610.

3 Johnstone made this statement in a letter to Robert Morris, dated "House of Commons 5 Feby 1778," read in Congress on April 27. See PCC, item 78, 13:65–66; and Henry Laurens to Robert Morris, April 27, 1778, note 1.

4 Drayton is quoting a statement that Conrad Alexandre Gérard, the French official in charge of negotiating the treaties of alliance and commerce with the United States, made to the commissioners at Paris, "by order of the king." According to the commissioners, Gérard made this statement on December 17, not December 16, 1778, as Drayton asserts in the next sentence. Wharton, *Diplomatic Correspondence,* 2:452–53.

5 See also Henry Laurens to George Washington, June 8, 1778, note 5.

6 Drayton is referring to Gen. John Burgoyne's notorious proclamation of June 20, 1777, threatening supporters of the patriot cause with the horrors of Indian warfare. See Henry Laurens to John Lewis Gervais, August 17, 1777, note 5.

7 "I fear the Greeks, even offering presents." Virgil, *Aeneid* 2.49.

William Henry Drayton to the Printers of the Pennsylvania Gazette

Gentlemen, York Town, June 17th 1778[1]

While I regret that Governor Johnstone has thought it proper to write private letters into these States, upon the subject of his public commission, and highly respect the determination of Congress to prevent a private correspondence with the enemy, I think I render a satisfactory service to the public in laying the following letters before them. The answer was written immediately after the receipt of Governor Johnstone's letter, but was not sent as was intended. However, thinking it too valuable to be lost, I prevailed upon my friend the President to allow it to be published, with the letter which gave occasion to it. I now send them for publication, and am, Gentlemen,

Your most humble servant, W.H. Drayton

MS not found; reprinted from the *Pennsylvania Gazette,* June 20, 1778.

1 Drayton's letter was printed in the *Pennsylvania Gazette* as a preface to George Johnstone's June 10 letter to Henry Laurens and Laurens' June 14 reply, for which see Laurens to Johnstone, June 14, 1778, note 2. Johnstone's and Laurens' letters were published after Congress refused to allow the president to correspond privately with the British commissioner. See Laurens to John Laurens, this date. It is of interest that on June 16 Drayton had been appointed to a committee "to prepare a resolution for preventing any correspondence with the enemy." *JCC,* 11:608.

Henry Laurens to the Carlisle Commissioners

York Town 17th June 1778

I have received the Letter from your Excellencies of the 9th Inst. with the Inclosures and laid them before Congress.[1]

Nothing but an earnest desire to spare the farther effusion of human Blood could have induced them to read a Paper containing expressions so disrespectful[2] to His Most Christian Majesty the good and great Ally of these States, or to consider propositions so derogatory to the honor of an Independent Nation.

The Acts of the British Parliament, the Commission from your Sovereign and your Letter, suppose the People of these States to be subjects of the Crown of Great Britain, and are founded on the Idea of dependence which is utterly inadmissible.

I am further directed to inform your Excellencies that Congress are inclined to[3] Peace, notwithstanding the unjust Claims from which this War originated and the Savage manner in which it hath been conducted; they will therefore be ready to enter upon the consideration of a Treaty of Peace and Commerce, not inconsistent with

Treaties already subsisting, when the King of Great Britain shall demonstrate a sincere disposition for that purpose.

The only solid proof of this disposition will be an explicit acknowledgement of the Independence of these States or the withdrawing his Fleets and Armies.

I have the honor to be, Your Excellencies Most Obedient and humble Servant. Signed by order of the unanimous voice of Congress.

Henry Laurens, President

Tr (PRO: C.O. 5, 180). Addressed: "To their Excellencies The Right Honorable the Earl of Carlisle, William Eden Esquire, George Johnstone Esquire, Commissioners from His Britanic Majesty." Endorsed: "Exd. a true Copy. Adam Ferguson Secretary." This is the copy of Laurens' letter that the commissioners transmitted to England with their July 5 letter to Lord George Germain. Davies, *Documents of the American Revolution*, 15:159. The letter itself is based on a draft prepared by Gouverneur Morris with the following preamble by Richard Henry Lee: "The Committee to whom were referred the Letter & its inclosures from the Commissioners of his Britannic Majesty beg leave to make report—That Mr. President write the following letter to the British Commissioners." PCC, item 23, fols. 43–44.

1 For a discussion of the Carlisle commissioners' June 9 letter to Congress and the provenance of Laurens' reply, see Samuel Adams to James Warren, June 13, 1778, note 3.

2 Reads "terms so opprobrious" in the Gouverneur Morris draft.

3 Reads "desirous of" in the Morris draft.

Henry Laurens to Horatio Gates

Sir

York Town 17 June 1778

Three days ago I had the honor of presenting to Congress your favor of the 10th with several other Papers put into my hands by Colo. Malcomb. These were committed to the Board of War with orders to act upon them without Report & I beleive what appeared to be necessary has been done by the Board from whence Colo. Malcomb intimates he has received his dispatches.[1] I have nothing to trouble you with but the Enclosed Act of Congress for adjusting the value of back Rations due to Officers in the Army,[2] which you will be pleased to communicate to the Officers in your department.

I have the honor to be, With great Respect & Esteem, Sir, Your most obedient, humble Servant,

Henry Laurens, President of Congress

RC (NHi).

1 General Gates' June 10 letter to Laurens, which dealt with "the Distress to which we are upon the point of being reduced to, for want of *provisions, Arms, Men, Money*, &c &c &c," is in PCC, item 154, 1:414–15.

2 See *JCC*, 11:581–82.

Henry Laurens to Horatio Gates

Dear Sir, (Private) York Town 17th June 1778

I troubled you with a few private Lines on the 13th by Crugier.

Congress have not determined their answer to the British Commissioners Address, although I foresee it will be a very short one. When that is finished the whole will probably be published, in the meantime I consider Sir your situation & distance from the Center of intelligence & conclude that the following brief account of the Address will not be unacceptable.

There is rather a repletion in the direction of the Paper leaving no room for cavil on that score.

The Commissioners after the necessary preface observe[1]—"that in the present state of our affairs tho' fraught with subjects of mutual regret all parties may draw some consolation & even auspicious hope from recollecting that cordial reconciliation & affection have in our own & other Empires succeeded to contention & temporary division not less violent than those we now experience.

They wish not to recall subjects now no longer in controversy, observe that the Acts of Parliament which they transmit & refer to, passed with singular Unanimity.

They are willing to consent to a cessation of hostilities by Sea & Land.

To extend every freedom of Trade that our respective Interests can require. [☞ Who is to adjust this point?] To agree that no Military forces shall be kept up in the States without our Consent.

To concur in measures calculated to discharge the debts of America & to raise the Credit & Value of the Paper circulation.

To perpetuate our Union by a reciprocal Deputation in Parliament & in the several General Assemblies.

In short to establish the Power of the Respective Legislatures in each particular *State,* to settle its revenues, its Civil & Military establishment & exercise a perfect freedom of Legislation & internal Government so that the British *States* throughout North America acting with us in Peace & War and as one common Sovereign may have the irrevocable enjoyment of every privelege that is short of a total seperation of Interests or consistent with that Union of force on which the safety of our common Religion & Liberty depends."

The French Court are illiberally charged with insidious practices—this gives much offence. If all the fine things now offered had been tendered some time ago, admitting their solidity, there can be no doubt but that the People of America would joyfully have embraced the proposition—but now what answer can be given but that which was returned to the foolish Virgins—"The Door is shut" more especially when we reflect that there is no solidity—because all is to be transmitted to Parliament for Ratification. "And until such Ratification no such regulation, matter or thing shall have any other force or effect or be carried further into Execution than is hereafter mentioned." Here's a Boy's Card House tumbled down by a Breath.

"If," say Lord Carlisle, William Eden & George Johnstone Esquires, "after the time that may be necessary to consider this communication & transmit your answer the horrors & devastations of War should continue We call God & the World to Witness that the Evils which must follow are not to be imputed to Great Britain"—to whom are the past to be imputed? but are they not now in the very moment of pretended attempts to establish Peace burning, ravaging & murdering?

They seem to mistake our understanding as once they did our Resolution.

Colonel Malcom waits. I must stop short & assure you I am with great Esteem Dear Sir Your obliged & humble servant,

Henry Laurens

RC (NHi).

[1] For the June 9 letter from the Carlisle commissioners to Congress that Laurens quotes here, see Davies, *Documents of the American Revolution,* 15:135–37.

Henry Laurens to John Laurens

My Dear Son, 17th June [1778]

I will endeavor to discharge my debt to your favor of the 14th & 15th both received yesterday.[1]

You will know some time to Morrow the part which Congress will act respecting the late Address from the Commissioners. It is my duty to subscribe not to Comment when a Letter undergoes for two or three days the consideration & correction of a House of 31, but it is very admissible to say the long delay has given me much anxiety.

I wished to have returned Govr. Johnston, Mr. Ozwald & Mr. Mannings answers, but did not think the correspondence Lawful without leave of Congress or *say judged it best to apply for leave,* it was not unanimously granted & I preferred with drawing my petition to a denial, because this might have ruffl'd me. You will Smile with Some contempt when I explain this matter fully. If this refusal would be productive of the expected benefits I should be content, even rejoice it would be a politic measure—in the present case, all the weak & wicked, with whom Govr. Johnstone has corresponded & will correspond, will make him flattering returns. Those Gentlemen who would attempt to open his Eyes & persuade him to undeceive himself will not be heard—honor will command Silence to the latter—the former will laugh at Proclamations. However I will endeavor to Send you the Speeches which were intended to have been Spoken as well as the Letters received from Philadelphia. Possibly the General may spare time to peruse that from Mr. Oswald who, if I do not misconstrue him, only wishes for our Dependence, but does not expect it & hence I conclude the Commissioners are now or soon will be in possession of full powers to acknowledge the sovereignty of these States.

I do not like the history of Doctr. W—— nor the lodging he took nor the present conduct of the person with whom he made his first nights quarters.[2] They are all Suspicious & one or two more—very equivocal Characters.

There must be more in the Doctor's history than you have intimated otherwise he would not have found such ready access to the Table at head Quarters. This consideration suspends a full opinion but watch—watch—every thing in the shape of a Trojan Horse.

I shall be glad to know your Sentiments on the reformation of our Regiments merely for my own information but the business is intirely out of my line & there is a tenacity which is not to be bent by advice, but which does extremely well when it enjoys the Seeming honor of originating. Therefore if applications on this Score shall be found necessary let them be addressed directly to the House or to Some other Member, not the President, however glad he may be to know what is in motion. You shall hear more to morrow from your most affectionate Father.

LB (ScHi).

1 These letters are in Simms, *Laurens Army Correspondence,* pp. 185–91.

2 Dr. Robert Wellford was a military surgeon who had recently resigned from the British army because of his pro-American sympathies and was currently lodging with Gen. Charles Lee. Ibid., p. 186. Contrary to Laurens' suspicions, Wellford's sympathy for the American cause was genuine. See Washington, *Writings* (Fitzpatrick), 37:226.

Henry Laurens to William Livingston

Dear Sir 17 June [1778]

I shrewdly suspect from the politeness of your Excellency's Address of the 8th Instant[1] which I received only last night that you mean to play the old soldier, and to give a new fashioned dunn to poor me; for upon my honor be it so, or not so, I have been labouring several days under self reproach for delinquency in respect to two Letters for which I thought myself indebted to Governor Livingston, private. Public I will not be delinquent or deficient in, errors excepted—so Sir the Beam balances the Mote, and if there has been no error, reciprocal good intentions will appear. I am sure no unjust Stewardship will be found on either side.

The moment I now presume to steal from the Public is devoted to you—to transmit you a Copy of the answer of Congress to the Commissioners. Their Letter and other Anecdotes you shall soon have. You will admire the firmness of this Answer full as much as the composition, it was the work of 31—for a conundrum twice the number of the United States and once the Commissioners.

I have only time to add what always does me honor and gives me pleasure that I Am, With the utmost Esteem & respect, Sir, Your Excellency's Obedient humble servt

LB (ScHi).

[1] Livingston wrote two letters to Laurens on June 8, one private and one official, for which see Livingston, *Papers* (Prince), 2:361–63.

Henry Laurens to George Washington

Sir. York Town 17th June 1778.

On the 14th I had the honor of writing to Your Excellency & sent the dispatches by Messenger Petit.

Yesterday I signed a Commission to William Malcom Esquire to Rank Colonel, by order of Congress,[1] from the 11th March 1776, & if I do not mistake Congress have agreed to confirm your Excellency's intimation relative to Colo. Campbell which rests at the Board of War—or is referred there.[2]

Your Excellency will be pleased to receive within the present Inclosure

1. An Act of Congress of this date approving Your Excellency's conduct in refusing a Passport to Doctor Ferguson.

2. An Act of the same date intended to put a stop to all correspondence between the Inhabitants of these States & the Enemy;[3] Your Excellency will clearly understand the views of Congress & will take the most effectual measures for preventing the evil in Camp. I beg leave to add a Copy of the Letter which Congress has written in Answer to the British Commissioners Address—the Letter will also be inclosed with this. Your Excellency will be pleased to send it forward immediately. I have the honor to be with the highest Esteem & Regard, Sir, Your Excellency's Obedient, humble servant,

Henry Laurens, President of Congress

RC (DLC).

[1] Although there is no mention of this "order" in the journals, William Malcom's commission as colonel, dated June 16, 1778, is in PCC, item 78, 16:391. See also Laurens to William Malcom, June 20, 1778.

[2] For the action subsequently taken by Congress in the case of Col. Richard Campbell, see Laurens to Washington, June 20, 1778.

[3] See also William Henry Drayton's Notes for a Speech, this date.

Thomas McKean to Sarah McKean

My dear Sally, York-Town, June 17th. 1778

Today I received £130, which I waited for, by Colo. George Latimer, and have sent ten thousand dollars to the President of Delaware, which, among other things, had an influence in detaining me here; I have no desire in staying here longer at this time, excepting to know whether the Enemy will evacuate Philadia. or not upon receiving the answer sent to the Commissioners to day; the result of which we shall know on Sunday or Monday next, and therefore if you can spare Sam on Monday or Tuesday, I will return home on Wednesday next, unless something extraordinary should happen. The allowance to me by Delaware will be £3 per day, most of which, if not all, I shall expend; however all I expect is to have my expences born. No other Delegate but myself from Delaware, nor likely to be for some time.

The Commissioners from Great Britain are, Frederick Earl of Carlisle, Richard Viscount Howe, Sir Henry Clinton, Knight of the Bath, William Eden Esquire, one of the Lords for trade & plantations, and George Johnstone, Esquire, Captain of a man of war, commonly called Governor Johnstone. They have sent a copy of their commission from their King to Congress, with a Letter directed to "His Excellency Henry Laurens President & the other members of Congress at York-Town," and call us States (not Colonies or Provinces) throughout. My old correspondent Dennys De Bert Esquire of London has written to me a Letter of recommendation of Governor Johnstone, in very flattering terms, as he desired an intimate acquaintance with a Gentleman of such abilities &c as myself; which Letter the Governor sent with the dispatches from the Commissioners.

The propositions of the Commissioners are—To cease all hostilities by sea and land—to be friendly & have the same privileges in both countries—To support and raise the credit of our paper money, to allow these States to be governed as they now are, or in whatever manner they please, as to their internal policy—To raise & pay their own fleets & armies, and that the King of Great Britain shall not hereafter keep any fleets or armies in any of the British States, without the consent of Congress, or of the respective States—to have a free trade & commerce for the mutual benefit of both Countries, and for this purpose the States to send agents to the British Parliament, who are to have a voice there, and Parliament to send agents to the respective States who are to have a voice there. In fine to any thing short of a total separation, to have the same Sovereign, the same Enemies & the same friends.

To these they have received an answer—"Acknowledge our Independence, or withdraw your fleets & armies, and we will treat with you for peace & commerce &c." This answer was agreed to unanimously, by 31 members, the whole number in York-Town.

I reced. a very affectionate Letter to day from Mr. Borden, all well except Mrs. Borden. No more news.

I am, dear Sally, your most affectionate, Tho M:Kean

RC (PHi).

Thomas McKean to Caesar Rodney

Dear Sir, York Town June 17th. 1778.

Yesterday I was favored by your's of the 11th instant,[1] inclosing a draught in my favor for £90.0.11½, for which I have given a rect. to Geo. Latimer Esquire. He will deliver you the ten thousand dollars, deducting the above sum.

This day you inform me the General Assembly are to meet. I should with pleasure attend them, but am afraid, tho' I should thereby act to the great satisfaction of many, yet some would take it amiss and charge me with deserting my Post, especially at this most critical period.

I have lived to see the day when, instead of "Americans licking the dust from the feet of a British Minister," the tables are turned. The Commissioners are, Frederick Earl of Carlisle, Richd. Viscount Howe, Sir Henry Clinton, Wm. Eden Esquire (one of the Lords for trade & plantations & Brother to the late Governor of Maryland) and Captain George Johnstone, commonly called Governor Johnstone. The last Gentn. sent me a Letter from an old Correspondent in London,[2] warmly recommending him as a Commissioner of peace, and begging that I would receive him among my friends, as he most ardently desired it &c. Several Members of Congress have received such Letters; but no Answers will be given by Individuals, it being treason to correspond with Enemies by the laws of Pennsylvania.[3] The Commissioners have sent us again the three Acts of Parliament, their Commission from their Sovereign, and their Propositions; wch. in brief are, to suspend hostilities by Sea and Land immediately, to join in supporting our Paper money, to agree that we shall govern ourselves in all cases, excepting matters of trade, and for the equal adjustment of that, the British Nation shall have Agents in Congress to have a voice there, and Congress or the several States to appoint Agents in Parliament, who are to have a voice there; and in fine seem willing to any thing but a total seperation; they desire we should have the same King; the same wars and the same peace. In my opinion their propositions cannot be fully supported by the Acts of Parliament. Be that as it may, Congress will again repeat; acknowledge our Independence or withdraw your fleets and armies, and we will enter into treaty with you. This answer will be sent off to day, and as soon as it is received you may expect to hear the Enemy have evacuated Philadia., if that should not be done sooner.

Be upon your guard with regard to Letters from the Enemy; they intend to seduce, corrupt & bribe by every method possible. Keep the whole militia under marching orders, if you have the power. Warn the people to double their vigilance, and not be lulled with these pleasing prospects, lest they meet with some terrible stroke, when they do not expect it.

Present my best compliments to your good Brother Thomas, and tell him I am much instructed and obliged by his strictures on financeering and our paper money, but have not time to write to him. Also let Doctor McCall know, that I have reced. his letter, & wrote to the Commissary General of Prisoners &c. &c. and that Mr. Adams and myself will take every step in our power for the exchange of his son the Captain, and also Mr. Pope.[4]

Remember me with particular attention to Messrs. Read, Killen and the Gentlemen of the Assembly. Confederation is put off 'till Friday, tho' it has been the Order of the day for two weeks. New Jersey is in my situation with regard to Powers but they expect them daily.

I write in great haste, and remain, Dear Sir, with the most perfect regard, Your most obedient humble servant, Thos M:Kean

P.S. Blessed is he that endureth unto the end, for he shall be saved.

RC (PHi).

1 Rodney's June 11 letter to McKean is in Rodney, *Letters* (Ryden), pp. 260–61.

2 That is, Dennis De Berdt.

3 For further information on the delegates' refusal to respond privately to the letters of George Johnstone, see Henry Laurens to Johnstone, June 14, 1778.

4 No letter of McKean to Commissary of Prisoners John Beatty concerning Capts. Mark McCall and Charles Pope has been found.

Henry Laurens to John Laurens

My Dear Son 18 June [1778]

I had intended to write you a Letter yesterday but was obliged to send only a half Letter; such as it is you will accept it and attend to some parts. I foresee it will not be possible now even to write an half. I must content myself with saying that I have sent several Papers to the General which will probably come within your inspection, the Originals from Govr. Johnstone, Mr. Oswald & Mr. Manning you will be so good as to collect and return. I shall have no objection to your reading Mr. Oswalds in which there is some covert meaning and very interresting—to the Marquis de la Fayette—(but I do not wish it to go further)—beg him ten millions of pardons that I do nothing more at this time than transmit several Letters which have just come to my hands for him.

Adieu.

LB (ScHi).

Henry Laurens to William Livingston

Dear Sir, 18th June 1778

I beleive all, I know most of them, meaning the papers accompanying this, are to be published, but the first of important Intelligence is of somewhat more value than even the first fruit of Cucumbers.[1] Therefore I do myself the honor of the present transmission. It would be an affront to hint, the public, I mean Congress, ought not in publication, to be forestalled. I wrote to your Excellency yesterday by Camp & sent Copy of Congress's answer to Lord Carlisle & Company. I wish I had time & good occasions for repeating every day the assurances of being with sincere Respect & Esteem, Your Excelly's obliged & Obedt. Servant &ca.

LB (ScHi).

[1] Laurens sent Governor Livingston a collection of documents pertaining to the Carlisle commissioners that was printed soon after in the June 20 issue of the *Pennsylvania Gazette*.

Henry Laurens to George Washington

Dear sir York Town 18th June 1778.

It has not been in my power with any convenience to make an earlier acknowledgement of Your Excellency's favor of the 11th.

There were Letters in the Commissioners Packet only for Congress & particular Members then present in the House, one for Mr. E. Rutledge unsealed & several also unsealed were brought as being taken from the Express—the utmost caution is necessary in the present conjuncture of our affairs & therefore had any suspicious directions turned up, such should have passed under the Eye of Congress. The Idea of opening other people's Letter's is exceedingly abhorrent to me, but I think Congress have a power over Letters equal at least to that which necessity obliges them sometimes to exercise over persons; but Governor Johnson is too well hackney'd in the ways of Men to trust his deep schemes within our reach.

His private Letter to me, by the bye, is notwithstanding all his good sense, no proof of an infallible judgement, I am sure it is one, of his having mistaken his Man, I take the liberty of transmitting it, together with my intended answer[1] & the Letters from Mr. Oswald & Mr. Manning under this Cover for Your Excellency's perusal. There are some traits in Mr. Oswald's which strongly imply a determination on the part of Great Britain but reserved as the ultimatum, to submit to our Independence, I am much inclined to beleive the Commissioners now are or soon will be vested with powers for that purpose. Mr. Oswald is a Gentleman of solid understanding & quick perception, of a very large Independent fortune much exceeding a quarter of a Million Sterling, often consulted by Administration; for the goodness of his heart I refer you to this particular part of his Character, he is no place Man, but much Esteemed by the first Men of each of the political parties—great reliance may be placed on what he writes or even hints.

Yesterday there was an extraordinary Motion on our floor for calling upon Members to lay before Congress such Letters as they had received from the Commissioners or other persons, meaning persons in Great Britain on Political subjects.[2] I could not forbear offering some objections; it appeared to be a dangerous attempt to stretch the power of Congress. My Letters had been read by many Members & were at the service of every Gentleman who should request a perusal, but I could never consent to have my property taken from me by an Order from my fellow Citizens destitute of authority for the purpose. This circumstance & some remarks which followed have induced me to put Govr. Johnstone's Letter & my intended answer into Mr Draytons hands who is collecting materials for displaying the Governor's good designs & no doubt he will according to his usual tone add pretty severe strictures.[3] Among other Papers I transmit to Your Excellency Copies of the Commissioners Address to Congress & of their Commission. These are to be published by order. If no mistake was made a Copy of the Answer of Congress was sent to Your Excellency yesterday in my Public Letter.

I pray God to support & direct Your Excellency in this Moment of extraordinary tryal & am with the most sincere Esteem & Regard, Dear sir, Your much obliged & Obedient humble servant,

Henry Laurens

RC (DLC).

1 See Laurens to George Johnstone, June 14, 1778.

2 See William Henry Drayton's Notes for a Speech, June 17, 1778.

3 For these "strictures," see William Henry Drayton to the Carlisle Commissioners, June 17, 1778.

James Lovell to Horatio Gates

Dear General

June 18th 1778

I have but few Words to write in answer to your Letter of the 13th received last Evening.[1]

The Express having delivered the Letters under his Charge for Genl. Green to the Genl. himself, and Col. Malcomb having received Instructions from the Board of War, I hope every Thing will speedily be on a good Footing in your Department.

No Peace can take Place in Consequence of any Powers we have seen of the King's Commissioners. Saturday's Paper will contain the whole of what has hitherto passed. I can only say, they do not allow *Independence;* Therefore they might have tarried at Home.

They call on God to witness that *future* Carnage will not be chargeable against Britain, if we refuse to listen to the Terms now offered: So that upon the Appearance of evacuating Philada. you are to expect the Enemy will be restless at York Island; but such Orders are given as will counteract hostile Efforts. I have this Morning recd. a Letter of the 8th from Boston in which I am told "our Reinforcements are now beyond my Expectations. Many good Men are gone & going."

I am much pleased with Col. Malcomb; and I hope you will be greatly relieved by the Service of so good an Officer. And I cannot but intreat that you would continue to count a Post of Danger a Post of the most Honour.

Your Affectionate humb. Serv. James Lovell

RC (NHi).

[1] General Gates' June 13 letter asking Lovell to support Udny Hay's reappointment as deputy quartermaster general in the northern department is in the Gates Papers, NHi.

Marine Committee to the Eastern Navy Board

Gentlemen

June 18th 1778

This will be handed you by Captain Peter Landais whom Congress has appointed to take Command of the new frigate Alliance.[1] We desire you will put that vessel under his care and use your utmost endeavours to have her Speedily fitted and manned for the sea. We have desired Captain Landais to proceed as far as Portsmouth in New Hampshire to give his advice as to the Construction of the 56 Gun ship now building there, he will afterwards return and attend the fitting & manning of the frigate which he is to command, and in which we doubt not you will find him very assidious. You will please to pay him the balance of his wages at the Rate of Sixty

Dollars per Month from the date of his Commission.[2] He hath not been paid any money at this place only what we agreed to allow for his travelling Expences to Boston. Inclosed is a Resolution of this Committee passed in consequence of a Memorial from sundry Captains of French Merchant Ships which you will please to order to be duely executed.[3] We are Gentn, your Hble servants

LB (DNA: PCC Miscellaneous Papers, Marine Committee Letter Book).

1 Although this letter and the committee's letter to Pierre Landais advising him of his appointment to command the *Alliance* are both clearly dated June 18 in the Marine Committee Letter Book, Congress did not actually approve this appointment until June 19. See *JCC*, 11:625.

2 In their letter to Landais the committee informed him that "We have directed the Navy Board to pay you the balance of your wages, and have agreed that the consideration of a gratuity to be made you be deffered until we shall be enabled by consulting with Silas Deane Esqr. to judge with propriety what sum will be adequate to your services." Paullin, *Marine Committee Letters*, 1:259.

3 This committee resolution has not been found, but it was passed in response to "a memorial from Tallemon and others, French captains in the port of Boston, . . . complaining of an affront offered by the captain of the *Warren* frigate to their commandant," which Congress had referred to the Marine Committee on June 16. *JCC*, 11:608.

Marine Committee to John Young

June 18th 1778

Sir

We desire you will repair to Baltimore where we have ordered the Navy Board to hold a Court of Inquiry into the Cause of the loss of the late Continental Brigantine Independence under your Command,[1] and if it shall appear that the same was occasioned by your negligence or Mal Conduct or that of any of the Commissioned officers, that then a Court Martial be held for the trial of the Officer offending agreeable to a Resolution of Congress of the 6th of May last. We have directed the said Board to order Payment of your seamens wages & have agreed that your officers shall be permitted to make a voyage in private service their pay to cease during that time and when they return they are to give us notice that they may be ordered on Public service should there be Occasion for them.

We are sir, Your Hble servants

LB (DNA: PCC Miscellaneous Papers, Marine Committee Letter Book).

1 The committee's letter of this date to the Middle Department Navy Board, requesting an investigation of the loss of the *Independence*, is in Paullin, *Marine Committee Letters*, 1:256–57. Delayed initially by the confusion of the return of both Congress and the navy board to Philadelphia and subsequently by more pressing concerns, the inquiry into the loss of the *Independence* was not completed until October 1779, when Young was exonerated. For Young's activities during this period, see William Bell Clark, *The First Saratoga Being the Saga of*

John Young and His Sloop-of-War (Baton Rouge: Louisiana State University Press, 1953), chaps. 1 and 2.

Samuel Adams to James Warren

My dear sir York Town June 19 –78

I have Time only to write you a few Words by Captn Landais who is appointed by Congress to the Command of the new Ship of War *Alliance*.[1] This Gentleman is esteemed for his Experience & Knowledge in Marine Affairs & will go first to Portsmouth to direct in the Construction of the Ship designd to be built there. I wish you would (with the other Gentlemen of your Board) assist him with a popular as well as able Lieutenant—popular, because as he is a Frenchman, it may be difficult for him to procure a sufficient Number of American Seamen. He is in hopes of geting French Sailors out of the Vessels that are or may be at Boston &c.

I will by the next Post send you a full Account of our late Transactions with the British Peace Makers which conclude with confirming on our Part our former Resolutions.

We have just recd Advice that the Enemy have totally evacuated Philadelphia and we expect every moment to have the News confirmd. Mr. Hancock & Dr Holten are arrivd.[2] The last mentiond deliverd me a Letter from you which I will more fully acknowledge in my next.

Adieu my Friend, S Adams

RC (MHi).

1 See Marine Committee to the Eastern Navy Board, June 18, 1778, note 1.

2 According to the diary of Samuel Holten, he and John Hancock had left Boston on June 3 and arrived at York on the eighteenth. "Being somewhat indisposed & not havg. proper lodgings procured," Holten wrote on June 19, "I did not take my seat in Congress. We are informed by Genl. Washington that the Enemy have left the City of Philadelphia & our people have took possession. The people here are not at all obliging, I want to git from this house." Samuel Holten Diary, MDaAr; and Danvers Historical Society, *Collections* 7 (1919): 59–67.

John Banister to Theodorick and Martha Bland

My dear Sir York June 19th. 1778

I wrote you yesterday[1] that the Commissioners from the Court of G. Britain had received their answer which will put an End to the business of their Mission. Indeed they must have known from our repeated Answers to their General, our Observations on the bills before they had passed into acts, and the Treaty subsisting between America and France, that any Proposals short of Independance would be rejected here. Their Injuries have been so great & so often repeated that they could not expect our return to their domination, & therefore in my Judgement their Views in carrying the Proposals of Treaty so far, were directed to the Reconciling their own People, & to give a colouring to their own Conduct in the Eyes of the Powers of Europe. Whatever may have been their Motives for persevering to Treat on such narrow Ground knowing as they did the Temper of America, the sudden abruption of all hopes of accommodation will immediately bring on some Determinations of considerable Moment respecting the operations of their Army. If they evacuate Philadelphia, and all their Movements & Preparations concur to shew they shortly intend it, their march will be directed to New York & thence up the North River.

Friday Evening the 19th. A letter from the General informs Congress that Capt. M'clean had taken Possession of Philadelphia, after the main Body had gone over to the Jersies, by the way of Coopers Ferry & three thousand had imbarked and proceeded down the River.[2] I hope we shall not expose ourselves to any danger from their Stratagems. I am anxious to know how the Commissioners received our final answer to their inadmissible propositions. These with the answers are inclosed. I wish to be informed how the People in Virginia stand affected as to the rejection of any Treaty or Communication, on the Subject of the late Acts of Parliament bearing the specious Title of Conciliation. If they could be prevailed on to make a vigorous Effort to raise a formidable army capable of resisting the augmenting powers of the Enemy, upon the principle of Self interestedness, & actual venality, as I do not expect it of them from Patriotism, they might the sooner go to the gratification of their Passionate fondness for Wealth, and the extension of that Commerce, the very Idea of which occupys every Faculty of their Souls.

Nothing has occurred since writing the foregoing, respecting the Enemys motions either by Sea or Land & the inclosed Paper contains an exact State of our politicks, so that I have nothing more to add than that I am most truly yr. affect. Friend, John Banister

My dear Mrs Bland[3]

How is it that our correspondence is laid aside? Is it because a Person breathing this thick atmosphere, and inhabiting a Beotian Land, cannot produce a Sentiment that can claim the attention of a Lady of delicacy & Refinement? Perhaps there may be some thing in this Region unfavourable to the Flights of Fancy, & *worse* to the finer feelings of the Heart. The latter I am sensibly alive *to* notwithstanding it is not *here*, that Philantophy & the friendly attachments are often to be met with. Yet even here I have made some Connections that are delightful, and serve to fill up that vacancy which the absence from those I hold in the highest estimation hath occasioned. There is one Lady (Mrs Plater) in our Party. Mr. Plater & some of the first of Congress, who are indeed Men of the World, as well as of the first abilities I have met with Take notice they are not natives of this soil. Beside this particular Society we have a Saturday's Club composed of about fourteen very agreeable Members. Here we sometimes have a few Ladies to drink Tea, on an Island which for its beauty and enchanting situation we have honoured with the Name of Paphos.

I had the Pleasure of seeing at Camp some of your Jersey Acquaintance, Lady Stirling, Lady Kitty, Miss Brown. His Excellency's Lady was at Head Quarters, she is an agreeable, well disposed, excellent Woman.

I had the felicity of being there, when chearfulness & gaiety of Heart enlightened every Countenance—When the Promulgation of our alliance in Europe had brightened every Prospect.

But how are the Ladies in your part of the World? I must return home & pay very assiduous attention to some of them, for I am wearied of my unconnected solitary State.

Kiss my dear Robin in my Name. I hope he is a good Boy & deserves the Endearments & Instruction of his dear Mamma, permit me to assure you that I am with affectionate Regard Dr. Madam, yr. Obedient Servant,

J Banister

RC (PHi).

1 Not found.

2 Washington's letter dated "½ after 11 A.M., June 18, 1778," in which he relayed early intelligence of the British evacuation of Philadelphia and reported Capt. Allen McLane's presence in the city, is in PCC, item 152, 6:115, and Washington, *Writings* (Fitzpatrick), 12:82–83.

3 Martha Dangerfield Bland.

Charles Carroll of Carrollton to Charles Carroll, Sr.

Dear Papa,

19th June 1778

Sam this day delivered me your letter with the £100.10. inclosed. I send him back, and I shall return as soon as Mr. Chase or some other Delegate comes up, for I shall not be able to obtain leave of absence, unless our State be represented, which it would not be if I should go away before the arrival of another member.

By a letter recd. this evening from Gen. Washington we have authentic information of the Enemy's leaving Pha.; they evacuated it early yesterday morning.[1] Capt. M'Clean wrote to the General from the city of which he was in full possession. The General is not fully ascertained of the Enemy's destination: the general opinion is that certain. The General has put 6 brigades in motion towards Jersey & they are going to N. York whether by land, or by Sea was then unthe rest of the army was preparing to follow with all possible expedition.

I desire my love to Molly & the little ones & Mrs. Darnall. I would answer little Poll's letter, but really have my hands too full. Please to present my compliments to your visitants.

Wishing you health and a long enjoyment of it, I am, yr. affectionate Son, Ch. Carroll of Carrollton

P.S. 20th June. I send you by Sam a packet from Joshua Johnson which Mr. Carmichael delivered to me. It contains newspapers, and I presume a letter, which I have not read, or even opened. As the perusal of the London newspapers, altho' of an old date, may afford you some entertainment, I send the packet by Sam. If the Enemy go to N. York, it is my opinion they will acknowledge the Independance of these States in 6 months time, and enter into a treaty of friendship & Commerce with us. I found my opinion on their not having declared war agt. France so late as the 28th April, when the Commissioners left England. Their finances are exhausted, they cannot procure Mercenaries from any Powers in Europe, their own People seem to be averse to the war; in such a juncture & situation of the affairs it would be madness to involve themselves in a war with the whole house of Bourbon, & carry on the present unjust & impolitic war agt. us.

RC (MdHi).

1 One of the earliest reports of the British evacuation of Philadelphia was the following letter written by Robert Morris to Capt. Alexander Clough under the place and date line "Philada. June 18th. 1778." "I have been in this place since one oClock," Morris explained, "and am sorry some of our troops were not here at an earlyer hour as they wou'd probably have Captured many British officers, indeed we are now told that several officers & Refugees are at this moment hid in the City with intent to make their escape this Evening which might be prevented if proper Guards were posted for the purpose. There are also Sundry Public Works, such as the Bridge over Schuylkill, the Public Stables, a Wood Yard with a Considerable quantity of Wood, Forage Yard &c all of which will be destroyed, Plundered & Pilfered by the lower order of Inhabitants, unless Guards are Set over them for preservation. I know that His Excy Genl Washington did not intend that Troops shou'd indiscriminately enter the City, but that a particular Corps destined for this Service shou'd enter it to take care of Public Stores, preserve Peace & good order and for such other purposes as the Commanding Officer shou'd find necessary & proper. The Enemies Retreat has been so sudden, that the Corps intended for this Service have not yet arrived & possibly may not this Night. Under this Idea Colo. Boudinot prevailed on Capt Dandridge & Capt McClean to Enter the City, they have been usefull but their Numbers are not sufficient. I am of opinion Your appearance here with Your whole Force, also Capt McCleans wou'd Answer the valuable ends I have mentioned, of preserving Peace, Preventing Plunder, taking Prisoners &c untill the other Corps arrives and I hope you will find yourself at liberty to comply with the Wishes of the Whigs now in this City, who probably may stand in need of your protection & who are ready to assist & support you in this business. You can if needfull produce this letter to His Excellency Genl Washington & I am confident it will have proper weight with him." Washington Papers, DLC.

Henry Laurens to Horatio Gates

Dear sir,

York Town 19th June 1778

By Colo. Malcolm yesterday I had the honor of writing you a few lines while that active Spirit sat jogging my Elbow for dispatch.[1]

The contents of the several Papers which will accompany this will appear in print some time to morrow,[2] these will probably be two or three days in front, I think Sir you are intitled to some of the first fruits of all important Public intelligence & therefore I had directed the inclosed Copies to be taken for your use.

The correspondence between Govr. Johnstone & my self[3] was not intended for the Public eye but a certain Itch for knowing it both in & out of Doors combined with private considerations respecting my self which you will understand Sir, without explication prevailed on me to send it abroad in the very shape, meaning my answer, in which first impulses had formed it immediately after reading that Gentleman's Address.

I am with great Esteen & Regard, Dear sir, Your obedient & Most humble servant,

Henry Laurens

[*P.S.*] Next Week will produce you curious applications to Members of Congress &c. I have an Instance before me in which a great Man concludes, "lose not the feelings of Christians in the resentment of Men and as you have nobly fought now act more nobly and forgive us."[4] ☞ One part of the Mission is to grant Pardons. Sing tantarara All Mad.[5]

RC (NHi).

1 Laurens' last extant letter to Gates is dated June 17, 1778.

2 Laurens is referring to documents pertaining to the Carlisle commissioners that were published in the *Pennsylvania Gazette* on June 20.

3 See Laurens to George Johnstone, June 14, 1778.

4 The quotation is from a letter to Joseph Reed from his brother-in-law Dennis De Berdt, for which see Reed to De Berdt, July 19, 1778, note 1.

5 Laurens also noted in his presidential letterbook that this day he "Inclosed to [Gates] in my private letter of this date an Act of Congress of the 17th for preventing illicit Correspondence between the Enemy & the Inhabitants of these States." See PCC, item 13, 1:372; and *JCC*, 11:616.

Henry Laurens to the Marquis de Lafayette

Dear Sir

19 June [1778]

I am honored by your favor of the 12.[1] Before this can reach Your Excellency you will have seen the correspondence between those great Personages at Philada. and some in my humble opinion not inferior at York Town. In a leisure hour I shall have the honor of learning your Excellencies sentiments. Govr. Johnstone will know that although I mean and endeavour to be courteous to all Mankind nature has given me understanding enough to distinguish between Freind and Enemies, true politeness and fulsome flattery. If I live to be acquainted personally with that Ciceronian Hero I think I shall notwithstanding all his subtilety and command of Muscles draw a Bluff upon him by recapitulating his present attempts.

Mr. Carmichael had a Letter for your Excellency which I presume he has sent forward. I don't know whether he has any French Papers, but if he has the dates must be old, for he has been long arrived.

Congress have done nothing yet respecting Monsr. Tousard[2] and Colo. Armand,[3] I believe the business lies in the Board of War and will enquire about it. I never heard before of Chevr. De Fayolles or it has escaped my Memory, possibly he may appear under a different appellation which I have observed frequently in the Addresses to French Gentlemen.[4] I delivered the Papers concerning the West Indies to Congress who seemed by expressions to be properly impressed with a sense of your Excellency's Zeal and good will for our Cause, but the late Treaty is a bar to an attempt at this time.[5]

I have the honor to be &c.

LB (ScHi).

1 Lafayette's June 12 letter to Laurens is in Lafayette, *Papers* (Idzerda), 2:74–76.

2 Anne-Louis, chevalier de Tousard, whose promotion from captain to major Lafayette had solicited in several recent letters to Laurens, was made a brevet lieutenant colonel by Congress on October 27, 1778, in consequence of his "Gallantry . . . in the late Action on Rhode Island." See ibid., pp. 61, 71, 76; and *JCC*, 12:1068.

3 For a discussion of Armand-Charles Tuffin, marquis de La Rouerie's plan to raise an independent corps, see Laurens to Lafayette, May 11, 1778, note 4.

4 In reality Laurens had already discussed the case of chevalier de Fayolles in his May 11, 1778, letter to Lafayette.

5 For a discussion of Lafayette's proposed Franco-American expedition against the British West Indies, see Laurens to Lafayette, May 29, 1778, note 3.

Marine Committee to the Eastern Navy Board

Gentlemen June 19th 1778

We have been favoured with yours of the 25th ultimo, 2d & 8th Current which we have considered & as we wrote to you fully by Captain Barry[1] and other late conveyances we shall now only reply to such parts of your Letters as have not been determined on. So soon as will be convenient we wish to be furnished with the Accounts of your transactions. We agree that you shall appoint a Naval Paymaster for your Department and hope you will be able to get some proper person for that purpose. It is an office of much importance and should be filled by a man of integrity and capacity who will keep Regular and fair Books of accounts with all persons belonging to the Vessels of war within your department and pay them their wages as it may become due taking care always to keep a months pay in hand from the seamen until their time of entering is expired. Congress has not yet fixed a Salary for the Paymaster—when they do we presume it will be adequate to the importance of the Office. Before this you will know that we have appointed Captain Barry to the Raleigh & as he is an active good officer, we have strong hopes she will shortly be manned.

Exclusive of the Vessels you have provided to carry dispatches to France, the sloop Providence will also be wanted for that purpose, and we request you will get her ready as soon as in your power. The Committee for foreign affairs will send off their dispatches to go by her in a day or two.[2]

We have only to repeat our former request that you will use your utmost endeavours to get our Vessels fitted for Sea and sent out together as Speedily as possible. We hope the news of the Bostons safe arrival in France may be true and congratulate you on the Enemys having been obliged to evacuate Philadelphia. We are Gentlemen, Your very Hble servants

P.S. We have received a Petition signed by Stephen Hill, Simon Gross, Joseph Adams, Adam Thaxter, Esek Hopkins & John Deamon. Should they not be wanted in their stations on board any of the Continental Vessels, we have agreed that they shall be at liberty to make a voyage in Private service their pay to cease during that time, which you will please to inform them.

LB (DNA: PCC Miscellaneous Papers, Marine Committee Letter Book).
1 See Marine Committee to the Eastern Navy Board, May 30, 1778.
2 See Committee for Foreign Affairs to Benjamin Franklin, June 20, 1778.

Marine Committee to William Smith

Sir

June 19th, 1778

In a letter from the Eastern Navy Board dated the 2nd instant they write to us—"that they have already sent forward to Sinpuxent three schooners which if they arrive safe will take more flour and Iron than is already provided, and shall soon get another which will be sufficient to bring the whole quantity proposed, you will therefore please to order the remainder to be ready." It is the opinion of this committee that if there is not already at Sinepuxent a sufficient quantity of Flour and Iron (which we suppose is the case) to load these Vessels that shall be sent out for that purpose by the Navy

Board of the Eastern Department and arrive & the navigation of the Bay should be open, they should be ordered round to Baltimore and you are desired to send your orders accordingly.[1] We are sir, Your hble servants

LB (DNA: PCC Miscellaneous Papers, Marine Committee Letter Book).

1 For the committee's earlier instructions on this issue see Marine Committee to William Smith, February 24, 1778.

Samuel Adams to James Warren

Dear Sir York Town June 20 –78

In my Letter of yesterday's Date, I promisd to write again by the next Post, and give you a full Account of our Transactions with the British Peace Makers. Cap Landais after the insealing of my Letter obtaind a News Paper which he intends to deliver to you. That will answer the purpose. The President has informd us of an opportunity previous to the Post which I readily embrace. It gave me much Concern to find an omission of your Name in both Houses of Assembly. I indulgd Hopes that it was occasiond by your Time and Attention being so much employd in the Affairs of the Continent, and am sorry that an opportunity was not afforded to you of declining a Seat, if you had thought it necessary, on that occasion. But, my Friend, you must expect and be content to be now and then neglected when the Influence of aspiring but worthless Men shall prevail in an Hour while your own and your Countrys Freinds are unsuspecting and unguarded. Beleive me, you cannot long be unnoticed by your Country, while she remains virtuous and wise; when a People becomes so abandoned (which I trust is far from being the Case of our Country) as to be not worth saving, no wise Patriot, will farther attempt to save them. He will then seek a Place of Retreat where he may enjoy the happy Reflections of his own Mind, and count a private Station the highest Post of Honor. But the Express waits, which obliges me to break off abruptly. Heaven knows best, how to dispose of you and me. Adieu. S A

RC (MHi).

Josiah Bartlett to William Whipple

My Dear Sir, York Town June 20th 1778

I congratulate you on our army's being in possession of Philadelphia. We rec'd the intelligence this morning by express from General Washington;[1] the particulars of which important event and the circumstances and movements of the armies in consequence, I expect you will receive before this reaches you, and I believe we shall soon take leave of this dirty place and remove Congress to some place where we may be better accomodated. I make no doubt you have heard of the arrival of his Britannic Majesty's Commissioners, and of their letters being sent to Congress; I now enclose you a paper which will inform you of all the transactions of Congress relative to that affair which will I hope give full satisfaction to every honest American.

I have the pleasure to inform you that every member of Congress was firm and steady, never to make peace, but, on the principles of absolute Independence. I am sorry that the answer was deferred some days on account of the zeal of some members for sealing the letters up and sending the letters back without reading, in consequence of some harsh expressions against the King of France; however it was overruled as you will see and a more proper method in my opinion taken. What will be their next steps, time only can discover. In the packet to Congress were inclosed a great number of letters to the separate members, Some from Governour Johnstone to such of the members as he was acquanted with, and others from other persons in England who had any acquaintance with them. The enclosed from Robert Trail[2] came directed to you as a Delegate of Congress which was opened and I now enclose it to you.

As to Marine affairs, Congress are very sensible some very essential alterations are necessary and seem determined to attend to it, as soon as the Confederation and some other very important matters are finished. I wish I could inform you that I thought it would soon happen, but the multitude of business that is daily crowding upon us, and the time it sometimes takes to determine on some not very important matters makes me fear it will not take place so soon as I could wish. Besides the want of men in Congress acquainted sufficiently with Marine affairs is another great difficulty and causes that Committee to be filled with some persons like myself, unacquainted with the business they are ordered to superintend.

"I heartily wish (with you) to see the American Navy respectable, and hope it will be put wholly into the hands of men whose private business does not militate with the public";[3] but I cannot be fully of your opinion that it would be for the public service to put an entire stop to privateering, as I think experience has Shewn that privateers have done more towards distressing the trade of our enemies and furnishing these States with necessaries, than continental ships of the same force, and that is in my opinion the greatest advantage we can at present expect from our Navy; for at this early period *we* cannot expect to have a Navy sufficient to cope with the British. However I am quite convinced that it might with proper management be in a much better situation than at present and should be happy to see it soon take place.

The Congress is at this time pretty full. I know not whether you are acquainted with the President, Mr Laurens; I think him a very sensible, judicious man, acquainted with the world and makes an excellent President. Mr Drayton, the Chief Judge of So Carolina is a sensible judicious man, a good speaker, firmly attached to Independance and not given to the chicane common to lawyers. Mr R Morris from New York[4] is an eternal speaker, and for artifice a *Duane* and for brass equal to any body I am acquainted with. Mr. Adams from Virginia is a member; he informs me that he was innoculated with you at Elizabeth Town and desires to be remembered to you. On the whole I think we have a pretty good Congress and if we have nothing more to fear from British arms and policy than from their gold, I think you may make yourself perfectly easy as is your sincere friend & most obt servt,

J B

[*P.S.*] Mr Wentworth desires to be remembered to you.

Tr (DLC).

1 Washington's June 18 letter containing news of Philadelphia's evacuation arrived at York the evening of June 19. See John Banister to Theodorick and Martha Bland, June 19, 1778, note 2.

2 Robert Trail, Whipple's brother-in-law and a former merchant and royal comptroller of the customs in Portsmouth, N.H., was at this time a loyalist refugee on Long Island. See Whipple to Joshua Brackett, March 17, 1776, note 3.

3 Bartlett was quoting from Whipple's June 1 letter to him, which is in Bartlett, *Papers* (Mevers), p. 183.

4 That is, Gouverneur Morris.

Committee for Foreign Affairs to Benjamin Franklin

Sir

York Town June 20th. 1778

By a most unlucky Mistake I did not forward the Resolve of May 5th with the Ratifications of the Treaties sent in that Month in the Packets A.B.C.; but I have sent them in D.E. via Martinique; and now forward them in F.G. via Boston, not allowing myself to wait for the Concurrence of the Committee in a joint Letter.[1]

Our Troops were in the City of Philadelphia the morning of the 18th. The Intentions of the Enemy in evacuating it cannot yet be explained. Our Army is in Motion and will press them. The Gazettes contain every Thing material. By the Arrival of Mr. Sim. Deane May 2d, Capt. Courter May 18th, Mr. Stevenson June 10th, and Messrs. Holker & Carmichael June 18th we have the Favours of yourself and other Friends in Continuance. Commissioners will be particularly nominated to transact our Affairs at Lisbon & the Hague, if those Courts are well disposed towards us.

We are now growing anxious about our worthy Friend Adams.
I am, affectionately, Your most humb Servt.

James Lovell

RC (PPAmP). Written and signed by James Lovell. Endorsed by John Adams: "Mr. Lovel's Letter June 20. inclosing Power to withdraw the 11. & 12 Articles."

[1] For further information on Lovell's failure to transmit this resolve promptly, see Lovell to John Adams, June 8, 1778.

John Hancock to Dorothy Hancock

My Dear Dolly York Town June 20th 1778 Saturday Morng.

I arriv'd at this place the 18th Inst.[1] after a most fatiguing Journey, bad Roads & miserable Entertainment, but thank God I am in tolerable Health. I long much to hear from you & the little John. I hope this will find you well over the hurry of your Week's Company, & that your health is thoroughly Establish'd. This is my fourth Letter, besides many Messages by persons who promis'd me they would Call upon you & inform you of meeting me well on the Road. Do let me know if three Sailors call'd on you with a Message from me, they had been prisoners & were returning, I gave them sixteen Dollars on the Road, & they promis'd to Call. I met Mr. Adams who keeps with my Brother, he will Call.

Mr & Mrs Hillegas are well, desire their Complimts. to you, she wrote you by Mr. Adams. Capt. Landais just going off I have only time to Add my Regards to all Friends, Love to Mr Bant & my Brother, to Mrs. Brackett & all in the Family. I shall write you fully by Mr. Dodd who Sets off for Boston on Monday & shall write Mr. Bant & my Brother. Do beg them to write me & Send me the News Papers. My Dear, I must beseech you to write me often, if you wish my health you will not omit one Oppory., pray do not neglect me in that respect. I will write you particularly by Dodd. I wish you the best of Heaven's Blessings, & am with the most perfect Love, Yours for ever,

John Hancock

York Town 20 June, We have this moment an Accott. that the Enemy have Evacuated Philadelphia & that some of our Troops have march'd in, and taken possession of the City. J H

RC (Sol Feinstone, Washington Crossing, Pa., 1974).

[1] Hancock took his seat in Congress on June 19. *JCC*, 11:621.

Samuel Holten's Diary

June 20 [1778].[1]

I have not taken my seat in Congress for the reasons mentioned yesterday.[2]

I wrote to the Honl. Mr Gill at Boston, Colo. Hutchinson, Revd. Dr. Gordon, Roxbury, & to my wife,[3] the express sits out to morrow.

MS (MDaAr).

1 Although Holten maintained this diary during his entire first term in Congress from June 1778 to July 1780, historians will be disappointed in its contents. "I was careful not to make any remarks upon the public affairs in this diary," he explained in a note appended to the manuscript sometime after August 1780, "for reasons I shall not mention at this time."

2 See Samuel Adams to James Warren, June 19, 1778, note 2.

3 None of these letters has been found.

Henry Laurens to William Barton

Dear Colonel. York Town 20th June 1778

I most sincerely congratulate with all your friends on your late acquisition of Glory & on your present prospect of appearing again with vigor in both fields of engagement.[1]

I interest myself, I cannot help it, in the welfare & happiness of every brave Man, therefore Sir, I request you let me know as soon as you can, under your own hand, the State of your Wound & health in general.

The Gazettes which I here inclose will afford you much information & an hours agreeable amusement.

The Enemy have certainly abandoned Philadelphia but their movements are at present inexplicable. 3000 Troops they say are embarked & gone down the River, the rest encamped between Haddonfield & Cooper's ferry. If this be true & I have it from good authority, it gives scope to much conjecture.

Beleive me Dear Colonel to be, with great Esteem & Regard, Your obedient humble Servant, Henry Laurens, private

[*P.S.*] General Arnold is appointed to Command in the City by General Washington.

RC (NN).

1 William Barton (1748–1831), a lieutenant colonel in charge of a regiment of Rhode Island militia, was wounded while repelling a British raid on Warren, R.I., in May 1778. For the special notice Congress had previously taken of his exploit in capturing Gen. Richard Prescott the previous summer, see John Hancock to William Barton, July 26, 1777; and *DAB*.

Henry Laurens to George Clinton

Sir

20th June [1778]

I had the honor of writing to your Excellency under the 9th and 10th Instant, and of presenting to Congress on the 17th Your Excellency's favor of the 29th May.[1]

The present serves to Cover two Acts of Congress.

1. of the 4th Instant Recommending a suspension or repeal of Acts of Assembly for regulating prices of Goods.[2] This I apprehend applies not to New York.

2. Of the 17th Instant for preventing all Correspondence between the Enemy and private persons Citizens of these United States.[3]

And I take the liberty of adding four of this days Gazettes containing intelligence important and interresting to the public.[4]

Your Excellency will have heard before this can reach your hands of the Enemy's retreat from Philadelphia and probably know more than I do of the motions of the Commander in Chief who decamped from Valley forge the 18th and 19th Instant.

I have the honor to be &c.

LB (DNA: PCC, item 13).

1 Governor Clinton's May 29 letter to Laurens is in PCC, item 67, 2:126, and Clinton, *Papers* (Hastings), 3:373.

2 See *JCC*, 11:569–70.

3 See *JCC*, 11:616. Laurens also enclosed copies of this resolution with brief covering letters that he wrote this day to the chief executive officers of Massachusetts, Connecticut, Virginia, North Carolina, Rhode Island, Maryland, and Pennsylvania, which are in PCC, item 13, 2:1–5; Red Series, R–Ar; Red Books, MdAA; and John F. Reed Collection, King of Prussia, Pa.

4 The *Pennsylvania Gazette* of this date printed a number of documents pertaining to the Carlisle peace commission. See, for example, Laurens to George Johnstone, June 14; William Henry Drayton to the Pennsylvania Gazette, June 17; and Drayton's and Gouverneur Morris' June 17 and June 20, 1778, letters to the Carlisle commissioners. Laurens also sent copies of this issue of the *Gazette* to the chief executive officers of Connecticut, Massachusetts, Pennsylvania, and Virginia with the letters he wrote to them this day cited above. Furthermore, he noted in his private letterbook that on this day he dispatched copies of the paper to Gov. Richard Caswell and Cornelius Harnett of North Carolina, to President Rawlins Lowndes and John Wells of South Carolina, to Samuel Chase of Maryland, and to William Smith and Francis Hopkinson of the Middle Department Navy Board. Laurens Papers, ScHi.

Henry Laurens to William Heath

Sir.

York Town 20th June 1778

Since my last of the 26th Ulto. Your favor of the 25th of that Month came to hand & has been presented to Congress,[1] but I have received no Commands except the Inclosed Act of Congress of the

17th for preventing all correspondence between the Enemy & private persons Citizens of these States.

to which I add three of this days Gazettes containing very Important & Interesting Intelligence.

With respect to the unhappy Culprit under sentence of Death, Mr. Hancock has said nothing since his arrival & Congress take it for granted that the Sentence will be executed on the day which you had assigned.[2]

The Enemy have abandoned Philadelphia, about 3000 tis said embarked & went down the River, the rest were between Haddonfield & Cooper's ferry, movements which carry aspect of stratagem. General Washington Marched with his whole force on the 18th & 19th toward Trenton.

I should acknowledge also the Rect. of your favour of the 1st Inst. & if I mistake not there is another which the Secretary has not given me the date of.[3]

I have the honor to be, With great Esteem & Respect, Sir, Your most obedt. Servt,

Henry Laurens, President of Congress.

[*P.S.*] I recollect the subject of the other Letter to have been on Colo. Armand's inlisting Deserters—it is Committed & not reported.

RC (MHi).

1 General Heath's May 25 letter to Laurens, which dealt mainly with the case of Ensign John Brown and was read in Congress on June 15, is in PCC, item 157, fols. 144–45.

2 The "unhappy Culprit" was Ensign John Brown of the Third Massachusetts Regiment, who had been sentenced to death for engaging in fraudulent recruitment practices and deserting his unit. Brown admitted his guilt but begged for mercy in a May 23 petition to Congress that Heath enclosed with his May 25 letter to Laurens. In that letter Heath also requested Congress to defer action on Brown's case until it had heard from John Hancock, who had promised some friends of Brown that he would intercede with the delegates in behalf of the ensign upon his return to Congress. Despite the fact that Hancock took no apparent interest in Brown's case after returning to Congress and that Laurens instructed Heath to carry out the sentence of the court-martial as scheduled, Brown was saved by the intervention of his friends, who persuaded the Massachusetts Council to order Heath to stay the execution, and by Congress' decision on July 20 to appoint a committee to investigate the ensign's case. After examining the proceedings of Brown's court-martial and considering appeals for clemency from Brown and his wife Mary, the committee recommended to Congress on November 28 that Brown be cashiered rather than executed. Congress debated this recommendation and at length decided on March 9, 1779, to grant Brown a pardon. See *JCC*, 11:704, 12:1174, 1184, 13:296; and PCC, item 157, fols. 129–213 passim.

3 General Heath's June 1 letter to Laurens, which was read in Congress on June 17, is in PCC, item 157, fol. 148. According to the journals, Congress did not read another letter from Heath until June 22. *JCC*, 11:629.

Henry Laurens to William Livingston

Sir 20th June [1778]

Since mine of the 9th and 10th Instant, I have had the honor of receiving and presenting to Congress Your Excellencies favors of the 4th, 11th and 15th Instant.[1]

Commissions for Vessels shall be transmitted to Your Excellency when the Marine Committee shall have made certain amendments judged to be necessary and I can obtain an impression from the Printer.

Your Excellency will be pleased to receive inclosed an Act of Congress of the 17th Instant for cutting off all correspondence between the Enemy and private persons Inhabitants of these States, to which I take the liberty of adding four Copies of this day's Gazette containing very important Intelligence.

I Am with great Regard &c.

LB (DNA: PCC, item 13).

1 Governor Livingston's June 11 letter to Laurens, in which he described his inability to comply with "the many applications for Commissions for privateers and Letters of marque" he was receiving, is in PCC, item 68, fol. 379. His June 4 and 15 letters are not in PCC or the Laurens Papers, ScHi.

Henry Laurens to William Malcom

Sir. York Town 20th June 1778

It is with pleasure I transmit the Inclosed Act of Congress of the 19th for enabling you to hold your Rank in the Army; & your Regiment so long as it shall be kept up[1]—to this I add half a dozen Copies of this days Gazette containing the intelligence of which you had gained but a partial knowledge when you left York.

I am with great Regard, Sir, Your obedient & most humble servant,

Henry Laurens, President of Congress

RC (DNA: PCC, item 78).

1 Col. William Malcom of New York, commander of one of the sixteen additional Continental regiments, was appointed deputy adjutant general in the northern military department by Congress on June 2. *JCC*, 11:560. Shortly before this, Malcom, who was then serving as acting adjutant general of this department at the request of Gov. George Clinton and others, had written to William Duer stating that he would continue in this office only if he could retain his military rank and command. Malcom's May 27 letters was referred on June 6 to the committee of arrangement, which advised Congress to approve the resolve on rank enclosed by Laurens with this letter. See *JCC*, 11:575, 625; and PCC, item 78, 15:347.

Henry Laurens to Caesar Rodney

Sir 20th June [1778]

I had the honor of writing to you the 11th May.[1]

Under this Cover be pleased to receive the following Acts of Congress.

1. 27th, 29th May and 2nd June for Establishment of the Army.
2. 4th June Recommending the suspension or repeal of Laws made in any of the States for regulating prices.
3. 6th June For extending Subsistence Money to Officers of Militia &c.
4. 8 June For laying a general Embargo on provision.
5. 17 June For preventing all correspondence between the Enemy & private Citizens of these States, to which I take the liberty of adding four Copies of this days Gazette much Intelligence of a Public and interresting nature.

Some of the Acts abovementioned should have been long since sent, had they come to my hands in time. I request your Excellency will intimate to me the best method of conveying Letters with public Dispatches to your State, I have frequently apply'd without success for such Information to the honorable Mr. McKean.

I have the honor to be &c.

LB (DNA: PCC, item 13). Addressed: "President Rodney, Delaware." Endorsed: "by Petit either to be conducted by himself or to request the V. Presidt. of Pennsylvania or the Secretary of Council to forward it."

[1] See Laurens to George Clinton, May 11, 1778, note 2.

Henry Laurens to Philip Schuyler

Dear Sir 20th June [1778]

At length I can tell you the Report of the Committee with Charges stated against the Commanding officer in the Northern department & the General Officers who were at Tyconderoga when that Post was abandoned last year is gone to the Commander in Chief.[1] I hope the Secretary will furnish me with Copies tomorrow. Whenever he shall do so one shall be immediately transmitted to you.

Within the present Inclosure you will receive, Sir, six copies of this day's Gazette containing much important and interresting Intelligence. I request you to transmit one or two Copies to my worthy Friend Mr. Duane. When he knows our present circumstances, he will excuse me for not writing by the present conveyance.

The Enemy have at last withdrawn from Philadelphia but their movements have much the aspect of stratagem. 'Tis said 3000 embarked and fell down the Delaware, the rest were Encamped between Haddonfield and Cooper's ferry. General Washington had marched the 18th and 19th towards Trenton. You will learn the progression on each side hereafter at Albany as soon as we shall in York.

General Arnold commands in the City and from the numbers of People who have flocked into it within a few days past I should suppose Whigs out number Tories. When the coast is quite clear, Congress will talk of adjourning from hence, but there will be some struggle against meeting in Philadelphia.[2]

I have the honor to be &c.

LB (ScHi).

[1] For the report in question, which was read in Congress on June 12 and sent to Washington this day, see *JCC*, 11:593–603.

[2] Congress adjourned in York on June 27 and resumed business in Philadelphia on July 7. *JCC*, 11:662, 671–72.

Henry Laurens to John Sullivan

Sir

20th June [1778]

I had the honor of writing to you under the 14th Instant by Mr. Bolden.

The present Cover will convey to you an Act of Congress of the 17th Instant for preventing all Correspondence between the Enemy and private Citizens of these States, to which I add four Gazettes of this date containing much intelligence very important and interesting to the Public.

I do not find by my copy Book any Note, marking the transmission of the Army Arrangement under the 27th and 29th May and 2nd June nor of an Act of Congress of the 6th June for extending subsistence money to Officers of Militia &c. altho' I think it has been made, therefore I shall put under this Inclosure two Copies of each.

The Enemy has certainly abandoned Philadelphia and General Arnold is appointed by the Commander in Chief to command in the City, but from the most authentic accounts we have received Mr Clinton's mode of withdrawing renders his designs extremely suspicious. About 3,000 of his Troops tis said have embarked and have gone down the Delaware, the remainder had encamped some four or five Miles from Coopers ferry in Jersey, if they mean to penetrate to Amboy why this disjunction? General Washington moved with his whole Army the 18th and 19th—a few days more may explain their meaning.

I Am with great Regard &c.

LB (DNA: PCC, item 13).

Henry Laurens to George Washington

Sir. York Town 20th June 1778

Yesterday I had the honor of presenting to Congress Your Excellency's favors of the 18th Inst. A M & P M.[1]

At present I have only in charge to transmit the Report of the Committee appointed to examine the evidence collected & to state charges against the General Officers at Tyconderoga &c which Your Excellency will be pleased to receive inclosed with this.[2]

And I take the liberty of adding twenty Copies of this days Gazette containing the British Commissioners Address to Congress &c &c.

I have the honor to be, With the most respectful attachment, Sir, Your Excellency's Obedient humble servt,

Henry Laurens President of Congress

[*P.S.*] Major Campbel's new Commission is "a Brevet Lt. Colonel, this Rank to have effect only in the Western department not to affect any Officer in the Virginia line nor to entitle him to any other Pay than that of Major the Rank he held previous to this appointment to rank from 20th February 1778."[3]

The bundle of Papers relative to an enquiry came to hand yesterday with Your Excellency's 2d Letter.[4]

RC (DLC).

1 Washington's three June 18 letters to Laurens are in PCC, item 152, 6:109–21, and Washington, *Writings* (Fitzpatrick), 12:81–85.

2 See *JCC*, 11:593–603, 628.

3 At the behest of Gen. Lachlan McIntosh, Washington had urged Congress to grant this brevet to Maj. Richard Campbell of the Thirteenth Virginia Regiment before he left York to join McIntosh "in the Western department." See Washington to Laurens, June 10, 1778, in PCC, item 152, 6:97, and Washington, *Writings* (Fitzpatrick), 12:41. Although there is no record of Campbell's brevet in the journals, Washington's letter of recommendation bears the following endorsement: "(Entered & Examined) Letter from Gen Washington 10 June 1778 read 15—referred to the board of war (Acted upon)." Charles Thomson wrote this endorsement except for the last two words in an unknown hand.

4 Washington sent Congress the records of a court of inquiry into the loss of Forts Clinton and Montgomery in the New York Highlands that had been held in accordance with a congressional resolve of November 28, 1778. *JCC*, 9:975–76, 11:629. Unfortunately these proceedings are not in PCC or the Washington Papers, DLC, but see Washington, *Writings* (Fitzpatrick), 11:69, 94, 100–102, 373, 12:85.

Henry Laurens to Meshech Weare

Honorable Sir. York Town 20th June 1778

I had the honor of writing to you under the 9th & 10th Inst. by William Bolden.[1]

The present serves to Cover an Act of Congress of the 17th for preventing a correspondence between the Enemy & the good people of these States, to which I shall add three Gazettes of the present date containing important articles of Intelligence. Permit me once more Sir to intreat you to intimate the Receipt of my Letters & of the Papers which accompanied them, half an hour on your part will cancel what I hope you will allow me to call a debt of near eight Months standing.

I am with great Respect, Sir, Your most obedient servant,

Henry Laurens, President of Congress.

RC (MHi).

1 The second letter was Laurens' June 10 circular letter to the states.

Richard Henry Lee to John Adams

My dear Sir. York in Pennsylva. 20th June 1778

Our enemies at N. York had contrived to distress us a good deal by a publication that the Boston was taken & carried into England. We were at first greatly concerned for our Friend, until we reflected on the lying genius of our enemies, and the improbability that Heaven would permit such a triumph of Vice over Virtue. Now we are made happy by an account from Boston that you are safely arrived in France. The Treaty with France was soon ratified here, desiring only that the 11th & 12th Articles might be reconsidered and omitted. Three Copies of the ratification have been sent away from hence near a month, and now 3 more are dispatching. The former dispatches would inform you the determination of Congress upon the English Acts of *pacification*, before we knew of our new Alliance, and these will acquaint you with the reception Messrs. the Commissioners from London have met with. The figure they cut is truly ridiculous. If this were all it would be happy for England, but she seems now to be a Setting Star. Two days ago the B. Army abandoned Philadelphia and our Troops are in possession of that City. The enemy are in the Jersies, but whether they mean to push for Amboy, or embark below Billingsport on the Delaware, is yet uncertain. The Jersey Militia are in readiness, & if our Army can cross Delaware in time, the gentry will yet get a parting blow. The friends to the future happiness and glory of America are now urging the Confederation to a close, and I hope it will be signed in a few days.

All but a few Delegates have powers, and those that have not, come from Small States, that will undoubtedly fall in. Our next business is Finance, and this is a momentous point indeed. Every state exclaims, we are overflown with our emissions of Money, yet all seem to be going on in the same beaten Track, and will I fear until invincible Necessity shall force a change. I wish to bring you, and my brother Dr Lee to be well acquainted. Republican Spirits who have so successfully labored for the liberty of their Country, and whose sole object is the security of public happiness, must esteem each other. The Continental Army is now on a much more respectable footing, both for numbers & discipline, and supplies of every kind, than it has been since the War began. It will give me singular pleasure to hear of your happiness at all times.

I am dear Sir most sincerely and affectionately yours,

Richard Henry Lee

[P.S.] Cannot Monsr. Beaumarchais demand against us be fully and fairly explained? There is mistery in this business that demands to be thoroughly developed.[1] Be so kind as to contrive the letters for my brothers safely to them.[2] R.H.L.

RC (MHi).

1 For Lee's earlier comments on Caron de Beaumarchais' commercial "demands" on Congress, see Lee to John Adams, May 13, 1778. On Beaumarchais' accounts, see Committee of Commerce to the Commissioners at Paris, May 16; and Committee of Congress Report, June 10, 1778.

2 No June 1778 letters from Richard Henry Lee to either Arthur or William Lee have been found.

Gouverneur Morris to the Carlisle Commissioners

[June 20, 1778][1]

To the Earl of CARLISLE, *Lord Viscount* HOWE, *Sir* WILLIAM HOWE (*or, in his absence, Sir* HENRY CLINTON), WILLIAM EDEN, *and* GEORGE JOHNSTONE.

Trusty and well-beloved servants of your sacred master, in whom he is well pleased.

As you are sent to America for the express purpose of treating with anybody and anything, you will pardon an address from one who disdains to flatter those whom he loves. Should you therefore deign to read this address, your chaste ears will not be offended with the language of adulation, a language you despise.

I have seen your most elegant and most excellent letter "to his Excellency Henry Laurens, the President, and other Members of the Congress."[2] As that body have thought your propositions unworthy their particular regard, it may be some satisfaction to your curiosity, and tend to appease the offended spirit of negotiation, if one out of the many individuals on this great Continent should speak to you the sentiments of America. Sentiments which your own good sense hath doubtless suggested, and which are repeated only to convince you that, notwithstanding the narrow ground of private information on which we stand in this distant region, still a knowledge of our own rights, and attention to our own interests, and a sacred respect for the dignity of human nature, have given us to understand the true principles which ought, and which therefore shall, sway our conduct.

You begin with the amiable expressions of humanity, the earnest desire of tranquility and peace. A better introduction to Americans could not be devised. For the sake of the latter, we once laid our liberties at the feet of your Prince, and even your armies have not eradicated the former from our bosoms.

You tell us you have powers unprecedented in the annals of your history. And England, unhappy England, will remember with deep contrition, that these powers have been rendered of no avail by a conduct unprecedented in the annals of mankind. Had your royal master condescended to listen to the prayer of millions, he had not thus have sent you. Had moderation swayed what we were proud to call *mother country*, "her full-blown *dignity* would not have broken down under her."

You tell us that "all parties may draw some degree of consolation, and even auspicious hope, from recollection." We wish this most sincerely for the sake of *all parties*. America, even in the moment of subjugation, would have been consoled by conscious virtue, and her hope was and is in the justice of her cause, and the justice of the Almighty. These are sources of hope and of consolation, which neither time nor chance can alter or take away.

You mention "the mutual benefits and consideration of evils, that may naturally contribute to determine our resolutions." As to the former, you know too well that we could derive no benefit from an union with you, nor will I, by deducing the reasons to evince this, cast an insult upon your understandings. As to the latter, it were to be wished you had preserved a line of conduct equal to the delicacy of your feelings. You could not but know that men, who sincerely love freedom, disdain the consideration of all evils necessary to attain it. Had not your own hearts borne testimony to this truth, you might have learnt it from the *annals of your history*. For in those annals instances of this kind at least are not *unprecedented*. But should those instances be insufficient, we pray you to read the unconquered mind of America.

That the acts of Parliament you transmitted were passed *with singular unanimity*, we pretend not to doubt. You will pardon me, gentlemen, for observing, that the reasons of that unanimity are strongly marked in the report of a Committee of Congress, agreed to on the 22d of April last,[3] and referred to in a late letter from Congress to Lord Viscount Howe and Sir Henry Clinton.[4]

You tell us you are willing "to consent to a cessation of hostilities, both by sea and land." It is difficult for rude Americans to determine whether you are serious in this proposition, or whether you mean to jest with their simplicity. Upon a supposition, however, that you have too much magnanimity to divert yourselves on an occasion of such importance to America, and perhaps not very trivial in the eyes of those who sent you, permit me to assure you, on the sacred word of a gentleman, that if you shall transport your troops to England, where before long your Prince will certainly want their assistance, we never shall follow them thither. We are not so romantically fond of fighting, neither have we such regard for the city of London, as to commence a crusade for the possession of that holy land. Thus you may be certain that hostilities will cease by land. It would be doing singular injustice to your national character, to suppose you are desirous of a like cessation by sea. The course of the war, and the very flourishing state of your commerce, notwithstanding our weak efforts to interrupt it, clearly shew that you can exclude us from the sea. *The sea your kingdom.*

You offer "to restore free intercourse, to revive mutual affection, and renew the common benefits of naturalization." Whenever your countrymen shall be taught wisdom by experience, and learn from past misfortunes to pursue their true interests in future we shall readily admit every intercourse which is necessary for the purposes of commerce, and usual between different nations. To revive *mutual* affection is utterly impossible. We freely forgive you, but it is not in nature that you should forgive us. You have injured us too much. We might, on this occasion, give you some late instances of singular barbarity, committed as well by the forces of his Britannic Majesty, as by those of his generous and faithful allies, the Senecas, Onondagas and Tuscaroras. But we will not offend a courtly ear by the recital of those disgusting scenes. Besides this, it might give pain to that humanity which hath, as you observe, prompted your overtures to dwell upon the splendid victories obtained by a licentious soldiery over unarmed men in defenceless villages, their wanton devastations, their deliberate murders, or to inspect those scenes of carnage painted by the wild excesses of savage rage. These amiable traits of national conduct cannot but revive in our bosoms that partial affection we once felt for everything which bore the name of Englishman. As to the common benefits of naturalization, it is a matter we conceive to be of the most sovereign indifference. A few of our wealthy citizens may hereafter visit England and Rome, to see the ruins of those august temples, in which the goddess of Liberty was once adored. These will hardly claim naturalization in either of those places as a *benefit.* On the other hand, such of your subjects as shall be driven by the iron hand of Oppression to seek for refuge among those whom they now persecute, will certainly be admitted to *the benefits of naturalization.* We labour to rear an asylum for mankind, and regret that circumstances will not permit you, Gentlemen, to contribute to a design so very agreeable to your several tempers and dispositions.

But further, your Excellencies say, "we will concur to extend every freedom to trade that our respective interests can require." Unfortunately there is a little difference in these interests, which you might not have found it very easy to reconcile, had the Congress been disposed to risque their heads by listening to terms, which I have the honour to assure you are treated with ineffable contempt by every honest Whig in America. The difference I allude to is, that it is your interest to monopolize our commerce, and it is our interest to trade with all the world. There is indeed a method of cutting this gordian knot which perhaps no statesman is acute enough to untie. By reserving to the Parliament of Great-Britain the right of determining what our respective interests require, they might extend the freedom of trade, or circumscribe it, at their pleasure, for what they might call our *respective interests.* But I trust it would not be to our *mutual satisfaction.* Your "earnest desire to stop the farther effusion of blood, and the calamities of war," will therefore lead you, on maturer reflection, to reprobate a plan teeming with discord, and which, in the space of twenty years, would produce another wild expedition across the Atlantic, and in a few years more some such commission as that "with which his Majesty hath been pleased to honour you."

We cannot but admire the generosity of soul, which prompts you "to agree that no military force shall be kept up in the different States of North-America without the consent of the general Congress or particular Assemblies." The only grateful return we can make for this exemplary condescension is to assure your Excellencies, and, on behalf of my countrymen, I do most solemnly promise and assure you, that no military force shall be kept up in the different States of North-America without the consent of the general Congress, and that of the legislatures of those States. You will therefore cause the forces of your royal master to be removed, for I can venture to assure you that the Congress have not consented, and probably will not consent, that they be kept up.

You have also made the unsolicited offer of concurring "in measures calculated to discharge the debts of America, and to raise the credit and value of the paper circulation." If your Excellencies mean by this to apply for offices in the department of our finance, I am to assure you (which I do with "perfect respect") that it will be necessary to procure very ample recommendations. For as the English have not yet pursued measures to discharge their own debt, and raise the credit and value of their own paper circulation, but, on the contrary, are in a fair way to encrease the one and absolutely destroy the other, you will instantly perceive that financiers from that nation would present themselves with the most aukward grace imaginable.

You propose to us a devise to "perpetuate our union." It might not be amiss previously to establish this union, which may be done by your acceptance of the treaty of peace and commerce tendered to you by Congress.[5] And such treaty, I can venture to say, would continue as long as your ministers could prevail upon themselves not to violate the faith of nations.

You offer, to use your own language, the inaccuracy of which, considering the importance of the subject, is not to be wondered at, or at least may be excused, "in short to establish the powers of the respective legislatures in each particular State, to settle its revenue, its civil and military establishment, and to exercise a perfect freedom of legislation and internal government, so that the British States throughout North-America acting with us, in peace and war, under one common sovereign, may have the irrevokable enjoyment of every privilege that is short of a total separation of interests, or consistent with that union of force on which the safety of our common religion and liberty depends." Let me assure you, gentlemen, that the power of the respective legislatures in each particular State is already most fully established, and on the most solid foundations. It is established on the perfect freedom of legislation and a vigorous administration of internal government. As to the settlement of the revenue, and the civil and military establishment, these are the work of the day, for which the several legislatures are fully competent. I have also the pleasure to congratulate your Excellencies, that the country, for the settlement of whose government, revenue, administration, and the like, you have exposed yourselves to the fatigues and hazards of a disagreeable voyage, and more disagreeable negociation, hath abundant resources wherewith to defend her liberties now, and pour forth the rich stream of revenue hereafter. As the States of North-America mean to possess the *irrevokable* enjoyment of their privileges, it is absolutely necessary for them to decline all connection with a Parliament, who, even in the laws under which you act, reserve in express terms the power of *revoking* every proposition which you may agree to. We have a due sense of the kind offer you make, to grant us a share in your sovereign, but really, gentlemen, we have not the least inclination to accept of it. He may suit you extremely well, but he is not to our taste. You are solicitous to prevent a total separation of interests, and this, after all, seems to be the gist of the business. To make you as easy as possible on this subject, I have to observe, that it may and probably will, in some instances, be our interest to assist you, and then we certainly shall. Where this is not the case, your Excellencies have doubtless too much good sense as well as good nature to require it. We cannot perceive that our liberty does in the least depend upon any union of force with you; for we find that, after you have exercised your force against us for upwards of three years, we are now upon the point of establishing our liberties in direct opposition to it. Neither can we conceive, that, after the experiment you have made, any nation in Europe will embark in so unpromising a scheme as the subjugation of America. It is not necessary that everybody should play the Quixotte. One is enough to entertain a generation at least. Your Excellencies will, I hope, excuse me when I differ from you, as to our having a religion in common with you: the religion of America is the religion of all mankind. Any person may worship in the manner he thinks most agreeable to the Deity; and if he behaves as a good citizen, no one concerns himself as to his faith or adorations, neither have we the least solicitude to exalt any one sect or profession above another.

I am extremely sorry to find in your letter some sentences, which reflect upon the character of his most Christian Majesty. It certainly is not kind, or consistent with the principles of philanthropy you profess, to traduce a gentleman's character without affording him an opportunity of defending himself: and that too a near neighbour, and not long since an intimate brother, who besides hath lately given you the most solid additional proofs of his pacific disposition, and with an unparalleled sincerity, which would do honour to other Princes, declared to your court, unasked, the nature and effect of a treaty he had just entered into with these States.[6] Neither is it quite according to the rules of politeness to use such terms in addressing yourselves to Congress, when you well knew that he was their good and faithful ally. It is indeed true, as you justly observe, that he hath at times been at enmity with his Britannic Majesty, by which we suffered some inconveniences: but these flowed rather from our connection with you than any ill-will towards us: At the same time it is a solemn truth, worthy of your serious attention, that you did not commence the present war, a war in which we have suffered infinitely more than by any former contest, a fierce, a bloody, I am sorry to add, an unprovoked and cruel war. That you did not commence this, I say, because of any connection between us and our present ally; but, on the contrary, as soon as you perceived that the treaty was in agitation, proposed terms of peace to us in consequence of what you have been pleased to denominate an insidious interposition. How then does the account stand between us. America, being at peace with all the world, was formerly drawn into a war with France, in consequence of her union with Great-Britain. At present America, being engaged in a war with Great-Britain, will probably obtain the most honourable terms of peace, in consequence of her friendly connection with France. For the truth of these positions I appeal, gentlemen, to your own knowledge. I know it is very hard for you to part with what you have accustomed yourselves, from your earliest infancy, to call your colonies. I pity your situation, and therefore I excuse the little abberations from truth which your letter contains. At the same time it is possible that you may have been misinformed. For I will not suppose that your letter was intended to delude the people of these States. Such unmanly disingenuous artifices have of late been exerted with so little effect, that prudence, if not probity, would prevent a repetition. To undeceive you, therefore, I take the liberty of assuring your Excellencies, from the very best intelligence, that what you call "the present form of the French offers to North-America," in other words the treaties of alliance and commerce between his most Christian Majesty and these States, were not made in consequence of any plans of accommodation concerted in Great-Britain, nor with a view to prolong this destructive war. If you consider that these treaties were actually concluded before the draught of the bills under which you act was sent for America, and that much time must necessarily have been consumed in adjusting compacts of such intricacy and importance, and further, if you consider the early notification of this treaty by the court of France,[7] and the assurance given that America had reserved a right of admitting even you to a similar treaty, you must be convinced of the truth of my assertions. The fact is, that when the British Minister[8] perceived that we were in treaty with the greatest Prince in Europe, he applied himself immediately to counteract the effect of these negociations. And this leads me with infinite regret to make some observations, which may possibly be by you considered in an offensive point of view.

It seems to me, gentlemen, there is something (excuse the word) *disingenuous* in your procedure. I put the supposition that Congress had acceded to your propositions, and then I ask two questions. Had you full power from your commission to make these propositions? Possibly you did not think it worth while to consider your commission, but we Americans are apt to compare things together, and to reason. The second question I ask is, What security could you give that the British Parliament would ratify your compacts? You can give no such security, and therefore we should, after forfeiting our reputation as a people, after you had filched from us our good name, and perswaded us to give to the common enemy of man the precious jewel of our liberties; after all this, I say, we should have been at the mercy of a Parliament, which, to say no more of it, has not treated us with too great tenderness. It is quite needless to add, that even if that Parliament had ratified the conditions you proposed, still poor America was to lie at the mercy of any future Parliament, or appeal to the sword, which certainly is not the most pleasant business men can be engaged in.

For your use I subjoin the following creed of every good American. I believe that in every kingdom, state, or empire there must be, from the necessity of the thing, one supreme legislative power, with authority to bind every part in all cases, the proper object of human laws. I believe that to be bound by laws, to which he does not consent by himself or by his representative, is the direct definition of a slave. I do therefore believe, that a dependence on Great-Britain, however the same may be limited or qualified, is utterly inconsistent with every idea of liberty, for the defence of which I have solemnly pledged my life and fortune to my countrymen; and this engagement I will sacredly adhere to so long as I shall live. Amen.

Now if you will take the poor advice of one, who is really a friend to England and Englishmen, and who hath even some Scotch blood in his veins, away with your fleets and your armies, acknowledge the independence of America, and as Ambassadors, and not Commissioners, solicit a treaty of peace, amity, commerce and alliance with the rising Stars of this western world. Your nation totters on the brink of a stupendous precipice, and even delay will ruin her.

You have told the Congress, "If, after the time that may be necessary to consider this communication, and transmit your answer, the horrors and devastations of war should continue, we call God and the world to witness that the evils, which must follow, are not to be imputed to Great-Britain." I wish you had spared your protestation. Matters of this kind may appear to you in a trivial light, as meer ornamental flowers of rhetoric, but they are serious things registered in the high chancery of Heaven. Remember the awful abuse of words like these by General Burgoyne, and remember his fate. There is one above us, who will take exemplary vengeance for every insult upon his Majesty. You know that the cause of America is just. You know that she contends for that freedom, to which all men are entitled. That she contends against oppression, rapine, and more than savage barbarity. The blood of the innocent is upon your hands, and all the waters of the ocean will not wash it away. We again make our solemn appeal to the God of Heaven to decide between you and us. And we pray that in the doubtful scale of battle we may be successful, as we have justice on our side, and that the merciful Saviour of the world may forgive our oppressors.

I am, my Lords and Gentlemen, *The friend of human nature, And one who glories in the title of,* An AMERICAN.

MS not found; reprinted from the *Pennsylvania Gazette,* June 20, 1778.

1 This is the first of four pseudonymous newspaper letters that Morris wrote to various members of the Carlisle commission as "An American." The other three appeared in the *Pennsylvania Packet* on July 21, September 19, and Octo-

ber 20, 1778, and are printed in this edition of *Letters* under those dates. Morris revealed his authorship of the first letter in his June 23 letter to John Jay—"The answer to the Commissioners & the annotations signed an American were the product of your friends lucubrations"—and there is a draft of the third in Morris' hand among his papers at NNC.

2 For a discussion of the formulation of Congress' official response to the Carlisle commissioners' June 9 letter, in which Morris played a leading role, see Samuel Adams to James Warren, June 13, 1778, note 3. Morris was a member of the committee appointed on June 16 to draft a reply to the commissioners' letter, and the present address probably stems in part from his work on that body. *JCC*, 11:610.

3 Morris was the author of Congress' April 22, 1778, response to Lord North's earlier conciliatory proposals. See *JCC*, 10:374–80; and Morris to John Jay, May 3, 1778.

4 See William Henry Drayton's Draft Letter to Lord Howe, June 6, 1778.

5 This offer was made in Henry Laurens' June 17 letter to the Carlisle commissioners.

6 For a discussion of the French announcement to Great Britain of the conclusion of the treaty of amity and commerce with the United States, see Henry Laurens to George Clinton, May 11, 1778, note 3.

7 Contrary to Morris' understanding of the situation, the French had not yet informed the British of their treaty of alliance with the United States. Ibid.

8 Lord North.

Joseph Reed to Esther Reed

My dear Hetty Philad. June 20th. 1778

I received your Favour yesterday at this Place which the Enemy evacuated on Thursday. I came into it the same Evening & it exhibited a new & curious Scene, some gloomy Countenances but more joyful ones, few very few Quakers visible even in the Streets, Shops shut up & all in great Anxiety & Suspence. I am now at Mrs. Yards who has been good enough to compleat the Memorandum of the Things we gave her. To which I have added since I came to Town a Qr. Cask of Wine (Lisbon), Some English Cheese, Porter, Plates, Dishes & some Knives & Forks. I directed Queen's Ware but found on Inquiry that China was only a Triffle dearer on which I ordered the latter & bought them with Continental Money only as dear again as with Gold. I have now almost as many Things as will load a Waggon. You will in your next tell me which I shall send or bring up to you. I send you inclosed your Brothers Letter & the Parliamentary Register. The Printer got the News Papers away & has not returned them but I will take Care that he shall. I am very glad to hear that your Brother is so happily settled. Mr. Morris has done all in his Power to get the Affair settled he mentions, but has been used exceedingly ill by his Correspondents there who have refused his Draught tho they have Money in Hand for the Purpose. I hope it will be no real Detriment to your Brother as we shall now have a better Oppy. of doing what is proper. If your Mamma chuses the 10

Guins. you can pay her in Gold which she can do what she pleases with. The Rate of Exchange is too unsettled to put the Matter in any other Line.

I have rode my Horses a great deal of late, shall therefore let them stand a few Days perhaps Tuesday or Wednesday when I hope to have the Pleasure of seeing you at Fleming Town. But as this Letter will go direct to you I shall expect a few Lines before I set out. My Love to Mamma & the Children. My dear Hetty's Affect,

J Reed

[*P.S.*] If my dear Girl would wish me to purchase any Thing more for her she will let me know. There will be Linnen enough. I thought Stockings for you had been in the Mem[orandu]m but found it not so. Would you have any & of what sort?

If this reaches you before Nurse sets out she can take the Hessian Mare & send her from Cornmans to Henry Conrads who will sell her for me. I have spoke to him on the Subject—the Saddle to be left at Cornmans or rather brought to Town & left at Mrs. Fords.

RC (NHi).

Rhode Island Delegates to William Greene

Sir,

York-Town June 20th 1778

Mr. Collins arrived the Day before yesterday, and brought forward Instructions from the Councill of War.[1] By the last Letter from Mr. Ellery and Mr. Marchant, you'l perceive they were not unmindful of, and had not delayed to impress upon Congress the critical Situation of Our State and the late Ravages there committed.[2] There needs no Information or Complaint against the Clothier General. We shall, as soon as we have the least Prospect of Success, urge a further Supply of Monies to Our State, but it cannot immediately be done. We shall also push the Necessity of some armed Vessells for Our Bay; But we are rather fearful of not succeeding in such an Application. A Letter from Genl. Sullivan pointing out the Utillity would however strengthen Our Efforts.[3]

The Enemy evacuated Philadelphia last Thursday Morning; Three Thousand of their Troops were on Board Ship, falling down the River, the Rest were in the Jerseys, nearly opposite the City, their Destination uncertain. Our whole Army were immediately on the March; Genl. Maxwells with about two thousand Men had previously been ordered into the Jerseys. Genl. Arnold was ordered with a small Detachment to take the Command of the City. Congress have given their answer to the British Commissioners. The inclosed News Paper of this Day will give your Excellency the whole Proceedings, which on Our Part we doubt not will be satisfactory to every American Whig. Confederation was this Day taken up by Congress, and we are in Hopes of soon seeing it completed: For this is the Grand Corner Stone. We are with great Respect to the Honorable the Genl. Assembly, Their, and Your Excellencys most obedient and very humble Servants, William Ellery

Hy. Marchant

John Collins

RC (R–Ar). Written by Marchant and signed by Marchant, Collins, and Ellery.

1 The Rhode Island Council of War's June 11 letter to the Rhode Island delegates, which dealt mainly with the state's expenditures on Continental account, is in PCC, item 64, fols. 406–8, and William R. Staples, *Rhode Island in the Continental Congress 1765–1790* (Providence: Providence Press Co., 1870), pp. 185–86. Although Staples dated this letter June 10, the RC is clearly dated the 11th.

2 See Rhode Island Delegates to Greene, June 8, 1778.

3 For the actions Congress subsequently took on the issues discussed in this paragraph, see Rhode Island Delegates to Greene, June 27, 1778.

Oliver Wolcott to Laura Wolcott

My Dear, York Town 20t June 1778

You have I presume recd. several Letters from Me within a month, the Date of my last I do not Remember; Oliver's Letter of the 6t is recd. and I was happy to find by it that the Family was well. I am intirely Satisfied, as to his Acco. of the particular Subject which he mentions. You will probably hear before you shall receive this that the Enemy left Philadelphia the Morning of the 17t.[1] They passed over to the Jersy Side and it is said Went down to Billingsport where they have probably shipped. This last Circumstance is not fully ascertained. It is supposed that the Troops are destined for N York. Genl. Washington has moved after them. Genl. Arnold will as long as it is Necessary Command at Philadelpa.

I Enclose to you the Proceedings of the Commissioners and the Answer of Congress. This Answer as it was most unanimously given, will douptless close the Correspondence unless G Britain will accede to the Terms which it proposes. As the Commissioners are using every means to make some Impression upon the Americans, their Conduct will be carefully Watched, altho I am fully of Opinion that every Art of theirs will be totally ineffectual. No Man except he is a most hardened Tory will hesitate a Moment wheither he shall adhere to the Independency of this Country, An Independency which G Britain must and will finally acknowledge.

Mr. Hosmere I hear is on his Way to Congress. But I do not hear wheither any other Delegate is with him. I expect to Return soon—certain Matters of an Important Nature are now in Consideration which I should be much Satisfied to see determined before I leave Congress.[2] I hope they will be so within about the Course of a Week, after which Congress will undoubtedly adjourn to Philadelphia, thro which I shall probably Return home. I hope I shall See you in about a Month.

By the Blessing of God I injoy Health. May I be thankfull to that God who bestows this and every other Blessing upon me. Put your Trust in the most High whose Providence in the late Event of the Enemys leaving Philadelpha. has been most signal. After having been almost nine months in the Possession of that City, they have now left it, without Compullssion and in Apparent Terror. God will establish us in Peace and safety. My kindest Love to my Children and Freinds. Mr. Thomas Sheldon goes out of this Town this morning but as he does not expect to Return home in less Time than a Forthnight, I shall probably send you this by Mr. Kellogg of Colchester, who will perhaps Return thro Litchfield. I am Affectionately Yours,

Oliver Wolcott

RC (CtHi).

1 That is, June 18.

2 Titus Hosmer took his seat in Congress on June 23, but it was not until July 7 that his colleagues Samuel Huntington and Oliver Wolcott requested leave to return to Connecticut. They apparently left Philadelphia on the 10th, the day after Andrew Adams joined the Connecticut delegation in Congress. See *JCC*, 11:632, 673, 676; and Connecticut Delegates to Jonathan Trumbull, Sr., July 9, 1778.

Oliver Wolcott to George Wyllys

Sir,

York Town 20 June 1778

Before you will receive this you will doubtless be informed that the Enemy evacuated Philadelphia the morning of the 17t. They passed over to the Jersy Side, and it is said they have turned down to Billingsport, where it is supposed they will ship themselves. The Route which the Enemy have taken is not fully ascertained. Their Destination in the first Instance is supposed to be N York. As I well know Sir, you wish to be informed what overtures the British Commissioners have made, and the Determinations of Congress in Regard to them, I do myself therefore the Pleasure to Enclose them to you. As no comments of mine respecting this Transaction can Assist your own Reflections, I shall therefore only observe, that I am in the fullest Manner perswaded that every Veiw of the Enemy to bring about a Pacification short of Acknowledging the Independence of these States will be found totally delusive. And if a Folly of a Very singular Nature did not continually direct the British Councels I should flatter myself that they would admit the Independency of this Country immediately, and Avoid a War which they must otherwise be involved in, which would threaten the Very Existence of the British Nation. The Designs of these overtures might probably be, to Satisfy in some Measure the Opposition to the British Administration, accelerate their Loans, Prevent our Ratifying the Treatys with France, and divide the Americans. In every of these Veiws I trust they will be disappointed as they certainly already are in some of them.

We have no recent Intelligence from Europe. Congress I apprehend will Adjourn to Philadelphia within a Week or ten days. I am Sir with respect, your most Obedient, humble Servant,

Oliver Wolcott

P.S. The Subject of the Confederation is now entered upon and I sincerely hope that it will be soon finished.

RC (CtHi).

Samuel Adams to John Adams

My dear Sir York Town June 21 1778

Although we are exceedingly pressed with publick Business at this Juncture, I cannot omit the opportunity that now offers of writing to you. The general Scituation of Affairs, and the particular Transactions between the British Commissioners and the Congress will be transmited to you by this Conveyance, by the Committee for foreign Affairs. Since I last came to this Place from Boston, several Gentlemen have arrivd here from France viz Mr Simeon Dean, Mr Carmichael, Mr Stevenson, & Mr Holker. Mr Carmichael comes strongly recommend[ed] by Dr Franklin & Mr Silas Dean; but Dr Lee in his Letter gives Reasons why he cannot place a Confidence in him. From a long Correspondence with Dr Lee, I conceive so great an Opinion of his Candor as well as inflexible Integrity & Attachment to our Country, that I cannot entertain a Doubt that he would suffer partial Considerations to operate in his Mind to the Prejudice of any Man. Such a Difference of Sentiments concerning a Gentleman who I imagine must be of some Consequence, could not take Place without at least apparently good grounds; and it may produce such Effects on this Side of the Water as may prove uncomfortable to us if not injurious to our Cause. Would it not then be doing some Service, to exercise your Prudence in endeavoring to investigate the real grounds of it, in doing which possibly some things may open to View of Importance and at present not thought of.[1]

Dr Lee is a Gentleman of a fair and generous Mind. I wish therefore that you would freely converse with him upon this Subject if you think you can do it with Propriety; and let him know that I have lately receivd many Letters from him, which I have duly attended to and would have acknowledgd to him by this Opportunity, if I had Leisure.

By the last Accounts I have had from Braintree your Lady & Family were in Health, though anxiously wishing to hear of your safe Arrival.

I shall write to you as often as I can & shall esteem my self happy in receiving your Favors.

I remain very affectionately, your Friend, S A

RC (MHi).

[1] For further information on Arthur Lee's criticism of William Carmichael, see James Lovell to John Adams, February 10, 1778, note 1. See also Gouverneur Morris to John Jay, August 16, 1778, note 2.

Josiah Bartlett to Mary Bartlett

My Dear

York Town June 21st 1778

I have Reced your letter of the 28th of May and it gives me great pleasure to hear you & the rest of the family are in a comfortable State of health and that Rhoda gains Strength.

I am well & by the favor of Providence I have had my health Ever since I arrived here, hope it will be continued to us all. The weather and air here is Clearer & I believe more wholesome than at Philadelphia.

Last Thursday the 18th Inst. our army took possession of Philadelphia, we had the account of it by Express from Genl. Washington yesterday morning: I Expect you will have the particulars before you Receive this more fully than I can at present inform you.

This Town is not large Enough to accomodate the multitude of people that have constantly Business with Congress. This lays us under great Difficulties and raises the price of Every thing to an Enormous heigth. Beside the Disagreable Manner in which these people Cook their victuals, and the sluttish manner of washing our linnen in Cold water only, which has already almost ruined mine, makes me willing to quit this place, tho I believe it to be a healthy place.

To get rid of these & many other Difficulties and to be nearer the army which is Removed Northward, I Believe Congress will soon Remove to some other place, I Expect to the City of Philadelphia;[1] and by the time this reaches you, it is probable we shall be packing up for that purpose. The Brittish Commissrs. have sent letters with their proposals to Congress and we have given them our answer. All the transactions you will see in the inclosed paper:[2] I think a very short time now, will Determine whither the Enemy will Remove their armies and make peace or whither they will try the fate of another Campain.

Remember my love to all my Children & send Levi word that I am well; I am glad to hear that our mens Business goes on well. The Weather here has been very Seasonable, not over hot, & rather wet than Dry. I want to Know how hay is likely to be with us; how the English Corn is like to be; whither the worms Destroy the Indian Corn; how the flax is like to turn out &c &c. Remember me to David Sanborn and tell him I feel pretty Easy about my farming affairs as long as I know he has the care of it. Remember me to Mr Thurston, Dr Gale, Captn Calef, Mr Thayer &c &c &c.

I have not failed to write to you as often as once a week since I Came to this place and shall Continue to write to you. Your letters Come pretty regularly to me & hope mine will Do the same to you. This letter will go in one to Major Philbrick by an Express sent by the President to Exeter & Sets off this day. I am yours,

J Bartlett

[*P.S.*] Tell Peter if he Behaves well he may Depend on my promise.

RC (NhHi).

1 On June 24 Congress voted to adjourn from York on the 27th and to reconvene at Philadelphia on July 2. *JCC*, 11:641.

2 That is, the *Pennsylvania Gazette* of June 20, 1778.

Committee for Foreign Affairs to William Bingham

Sir York Town 21 June 1778

Your favors to May 10th are come to hand, and lay with different Committees of Congress.[1] Finding that Messrs. Purveyance of Baltimore have sent two Packets for our Commissioners at Paris via Martinique, I think proper at this time to acquaint you that I did not fully expect that course when I asked their care, or I should have written to you by the same opportunities.[2] Fearing now to lose the chance of Communicating some interesting Intelligence to you, if I wait for the meeting of the Committee of Foreign Affairs, I scratch these few lines to accompany the Gazettes, and am affectionately your Friend. Signed James Lovell

FC (DNA: PCC, item 79).

1 Bingham's May 10 letter to the Committee for Foreign Affairs, conveying a "Dominica Gazette" with an account of the French ambassador's presentation of the French treaty with the United States to the British government, is in PCC, item 78, 2:481. His April 24, 1778, letter to the Secret Committee, discussing the

arrival of the sloop *Mesopotamia* with Continental goods and his need to draw bills on the commissioners at Paris, probably arrived at the same time. It is in the Lloyd W. Smith Collection, NjMoHP.

2 See Lovell to John Adams, June 8, 1778, note 1.

Committee for Foreign Affairs to the Commissioners at Paris

In Committee for foreign affairs
York Town in Pennsylva. 21 June 1778

Gentlemen

The British Commissioners have arrived and transmitted their powers and propositions to Congress, which have received the answer you will see in the Pennsylvania Gazette of the 20th instant.

On the 18th of this month Gen. Clinton with the British army (now under his command) abandoned Philadelphia, and the City is in possession of our Troops. The enemy crossed into Jersey, but whether with design to push for So. Amboy, or to embark below Bilingsport on the Delaware is yet uncertain. Gen. Washington has put his Army in motion, and is following the enemy into Jersey. There has arrived here a Mr. Holker from France who has presented a paper to Congress declaring that he comes with a verbal message to Congress from the Minister of France touching our treating with Great Britain & some other particulars which for want of his paper we cannot at present enumerate.[1] The style of his paper is as from the representative of the Court, but he has no authentic voucher of his Mission for the delivery of this verbal message. We desire of you Gentlemen to give us the most exact information in your power concerning the Authenticity of Mr. Holkers mission for this purpose.[2]

We are Gentlemen, with esteem and regard your most obedient and very humble servants,

Richard Henry Lee

Thos. Heyward Junr.

James Lovell

RC (PPAmP). Written by Richard Henry Lee and signed by Lee, Heyward, and Lovell. Endorsed by Arthur Lee: "Count Vergennes Answer respecting Mr. Holker was—that he was astonished that Mr. Holker had no Commission verbal or other from the Ministry; & was only desired to communicate to them his observations on the Country."

1 For the presentation of these papers to Congress on June 18, see Committee of Congress Report, June 27, 1778, note 1.

2 Upon receiving this request, the commissioners began an inquiry into the authority vested in Jean Holker by the French government, in consequence of which they transmitted the following report in their September 17, 1778, letter to President Laurens: "In observance of our instructions to inquire into M. Holker's authority, we waited on his excellency the Count de Vergennes, presented him

with an extract of the letter concerning him, and requested to know what authority M. Holker had. His excellency's answer to us was that he was surprised, for that M. Holker had no verbal commission from the ministry; but that M. de Vergennes, being informed that M. Holker was going to America, desired him to write to him from time to time, the state of things and the temper of the people." See Wharton, *Diplomatic Correspondence*, 2:724; and *JCC*, 11:618–20.

However, even before the commissioners received this request from Congress, their investigation had been rendered moot when on July 23 the French minister to the United States, Conrad Alexandre Gérard, announced to Congress Holker's appointment as "inspector general of trade and manufactures of France, and agent to the royal marine of France in all the ports belonging to the United States," as well as "consul of France in the port of Philadelphia." *JCC*, 11:713. In addition to these official duties, Jean Holker (1745–1822) also served as the mercantile representative of Jacques Donatien Leray de Chaumont, a French merchant who long served as a conduit for French aid to America and as a banker for the American commissioners at Paris. See Kathryn Sullivan, *Maryland and France, 1774–1789* (Philadelphia: University of Pennsylvania Press, 1936), pp. 66–83; and Adams, *Diary* (Butterfield), 2:297n.2, 298n.2.

Despite initial doubts about Holker's credentials, Congress on July 9 directed the Committee of Commerce to contract with Holker for the purchase of hats, blankets, and shoes consigned to him. *JCC*, 11:679.

Henry Laurens to Joseph Reed

Dear Sir 21th June [1778]

I hold myself much indebted for your very obliging Letter of the 15th and for the right of perusing the papers which it contained, a pleasure which I reserve for a very early minute tomorrow Morning. 'Till this moment I had not found time to read yours quite through, and now but slightly, nor can I do more at present than to return very full thanks and a brief reply unless I would lose the opportunity of transmitting this by Colonel Pettit.

The Inclosed Gazette will shew you Sir, the proceedings of Congress respecting the Commissioners, that I also have been honor'd with a Letter from Governor Johnstone introduced by two from my best Friends in England. And that you judged with Congress in with-holding an Answer to the Governor.

Congress seemed by no means disposed to consent that any private Character should correspond with him and I would not hazard a denial. Some strong attempts were made to have all Letters received from Governor Johnstone and from England through him laid before Congress. Many Gentlemen had perused mine and every one who should have asked might have done the same, but I don't relish compulsion unauthorized, to avoid misconstruction therefore I submitted to a solicitation for making his Letter to me and my intended Answer just in the shape in which I had carried it to Congress Public.

Mr. Manning's and Mr Ozwald's Letters are in the hands of Colo.

John Laurens where, if your time will permit, I beg you will run your Eye over them. I think to make the latter a subject in next Gazette, if it reaches me in time, and to add an Answer which I had also written immediately after reading it, but which my Freind cannot now expect to have in any other way.[1] He will, from the tenor of his own Letter know the reply to be intended for him, although both will appear without names.

I have something of another nature to communicate, but am ashamed to keep Col. Petit waiting. I must therefore defer to another opportunity and conclude the present by assuring you that I am, With great regard &c.

LB (ScHi).

1 No text of Laurens' intended reply to Richard Oswald has been found.

Richard Henry Lee to Samuel Purviance, Jr.

Dear Sir, York the 21st June 1778

I have taken the liberty to desire two Boxes the property of Monsr. Loyeauté a French Gentleman now in Virginia to be left in your care by a Waggon that carries them to Baltimore.[1] As Monsr. Loyeauté is a Gentleman of great worth, I wish to serve him by every means in my power and therefore I have directed his Baggage to such safe care as yours. Monsr. Loyeauté will in due time inform you what he would have done with these Boxes. The enemy have at last abandoned Philadelphia, and that City is now in possession of the American Troops. Gen. Washington is gone in quest of the enemy to the Jerseys. I expect Congress will adjourn to Philadelphia 8 or 10 days. My compliments to your Lady, your brother & his Lady. I am dear Sir your most obedient, humble servant,

Richard Henry Lee

RC (ViHi).

1 Anne Philippe de Loyauté had recently resigned as inspector general of Virginia artillery. See Lee to Thomas Jefferson, May 11, 1778, note 3.

Committee for Foreign Affairs to the Eastern Navy Board

Gentlemen York Town June 22. 1778

The bearer Mr Taylor has instructions to proceed to France immediately. This Gentleman having been a long time Confidentially employed by Mr Hancock while President of Congress, we think it proper that the delivery of one of the Packets sent to your care yesterday for our Commissioners in France should be intrusted to him.[1] It is not however meant that you should Suffer any delay in the Sailing of the Vessels in which you intended our dispatches F and G should be forwarded. It is only meant that you should give Mr Taylor the offer of delivering one of them personally at Paris, in preference to other persons mentioned conditionally to you when the Packets were sent. We are Gentlemen &c, Signed,

James Lovell, for the Committee for Foreign Affairs

FC (DNA: PCC, item 79).

[1] Although the committee's June 21 letter to the Eastern Navy Board has not been found, its receipt was acknowledged in the board's July 6 letter to the committee. PCC, item 37, fol. 117.

Samuel Holten's Diary

[June 22, 1778]

22. I took my seat in Congress, and it is a very August Assembly. I wrote to Mr. Hall of Boston & to Miss Holten.[1]

MS (MDaAr).

[1] Not found.

Henry Laurens to John Houstoun

Honorable Sir, 22d June [1778]

I had the honor of writing to you the 9th & 10th Inst.[1] by Messenger Wilkinson through Charles Town & on the 14th Inst. of receiving your Honour's Letter of the 16th April. Congress were so ardently engaged in business respecting the British Commission at Philadelphia at the time your Honor's Letter reached & for a few days after as deprived me of opportunity to present it before the 19th. It was then, with General Howe's Letters & one from the Honorable Mr. Speaker Committed to a Select Committee, from whom no Report is yet come up & possibly in our present crowd of business may not be made.[2] I am persuaded it will not be taken under consideration, for Several days, Congress Seem determined to suffer no other matter to come before them if possible to avoid it until they shall have Ratified Confederation. In these circumstances I have judged it proper to return your Messenger, whose expences are in this place intolerable, & I expect to have an opportunity of writing by Colo. Marbury full as early as I shall receive commands, if it shall happen otherwise an Express Messenger shall be dispatched.

Your Honor will be pleased to receive within the present Inclosure an Act of Congress of the 17th Inst. for preventing all correspondence between the Enemy & private persons of the good people of these States, to which I take the liberty of adding four Copies of the Pennsylvania Gazette of the 20th containing the Commissioners Address to Congress, their Commission, the Answer of Congress &ca &ca & also an hand Bill Supplement, with the Duke of Richmond's remarkable Speech of the 5th March in the House of Lords.[3]

I have this Instant a Letter from General Washington dated 20th in the Evening.[4] He had then advanced within 10 Miles of Coriels ferry. General Lee with Six Brigades was to arrive at the ferry that Evening. The Enemy had advanced as far as Eyres Town & were repairing the Bridge which we had nearly destroyed for retarding their March, a pretty brisk firing had passed between the Enemy & part of Maxwell's Brigade in which a Deserter who had just come in says the former lost several Men.[5]

General Dickinson writes the Jersey Militia had taken up the Alarm & were in good Spirits, the obstructed Roads & Bridges or rather want of Bridges will render the Enemy's passage difficult.[6] General Washingtons whole Army will soon be up with them, between these & the Militia 'tis probable Sir Henry Clinton must run the Gantlet, & I hope will not escape without Several lashes. However this may happen, his whole conduct Still wears the aspect of Stratagem, he had certainly two days to March ahead of our Commander in Chief, he had made no further progress than 15 Miles & General Washington had travelled 40 at least.

I have likewise just received a Letter from Majr. General Gates Peeks Kill 17th June.[7] The Militia & draughts were coming in very fast & he "thanks Heaven for the precious time the Enemy had so foolishly lost." The General adds "I think all preparations for an Indian War will be unnecessary other than those I have already placed in the hands of Brigadier General Stark, I wish this Country to steer clear of that Hornets Nest the Six Nations & their Allies, the Savages from my Country are enough to deal with at one time."

Thus far things in this quarter look well. I hope the prospect in the Sothern States are not more unfavorable.

I am in possession of a Letter written by a Gentleman of Character in London dated 10th April introducing Govr. Johnston & I believe under the Eye of the British Ministry in which among many humiliating concessions these remarkable terms appear.

"Your paper Money shall not only be funded & Secured but if desired we will lend you two or three Million—lose not the feelings of Christians in the resentments of Men, as you have fought Nobly now act more nobly & forgive us"—"and the Door was shut."

People are thronging towards Philadelphia were General Arnold Commands by order of General Washington. When we know the Enemy are in fact going by being gone Congress will turn their faces that way. The several Boards are ordered to hold themselves in readiness.

This day carried us through two or three objections to articles of confederation from Maryland, the third will be decided by a question to morrow Morning without farther debate & without alteration, admitting this, the whole will be ratified in the original form within three days, I am not apprehensive of any long debate except from South Carolina, & her delegates have full power.[8]

I have the honor to be &ca.

LB (DNA: PCC, item 13).

1 See Laurens' letters to Richard Caswell, June 9, note 6; and to the States, June 10, 1778.

2 On June 19 Congress read and referred to a committee consisting of William Henry Drayton, William Duer, and Thomas McKean a letter to Laurens from Georgia Governor Houstoun dated April 16, one from Georgia Assembly Speaker James Whitfield dated May 6, and two from Gen. Robert Howe, commander of the southern military department, dated April 13, 1778. See *JCC*, 11:622; and PCC, item 73, fols. 191–95, 207–14, item 160, fols. 444–55. These letters all dealt with the perilous state of Georgia's defenses and asked Congress to support an expedition against St. Augustine planned by the state, to provide Georgia with $1,000,000 in Continental currency to replace her own depreciated currency, to authorize establishment of an effective cavalry regiment to deter raids from East Florida, and to reimburse General Howe for cannon and stores he had purchased for the state's defense. The only action Congress took on these requests occurred on June 26, when the delegates denied Georgia's application for a loan of $1,000,000, but agreed instead to send her $198,400, the remainder of a $1,000,000 grant made in August 1777. *JCC*, 11:660. Despite Congress' failure to provide more assistance, Georgia launched an expedition against St. Augustine with the cooperation of General Howe that bogged down and had to be called off in July 1778 well short of its objective. See Kenneth Coleman, *The American Revolution in Georgia* (Athens: University of Georgia Press, 1958), pp. 106–8.

3 For the Duke of Richmond's March 5, 1778, speech criticizing Lord North's conciliatory proposals and urging recognition of American independence, see *Parliamentary History*, 19:839–42.

4 Washington's June 20 letter to Laurens is in PCC, item 152, 6:125, and Washington, *Writings* (Fitzpatrick), 12:97–98.

5 The July 3 issue of the *Virginia Gazette* (Purdie) contains portions of two letters written this day by two Virginia delegates that also dealt with the British army's evacuation of Philadelphia and retreat to New Jersey. The first, headed "*Extract of a Letter from a member of Congress, dated* York *town*, June 22," reads as follows:

"I congratulate you upon the late happy turn to our affairs. On the 18th instant, at five in the morning, the enemy totally evacuated Philadelphia, and at eight of the same morning a detachment of our troops took possession. General Arnold now commands in the city, and I expect Congress will remove in a few days."

The second, headed "*Extract of a letter from another member of Congress, of the same date, from* York *town*," states:

"I have the pleasure to inform you, that our army has decamped, and are, in several divisions, on their way to the Jersey side of the river, in order to gall and harrass the enemy on their march through that country. General Lee's division is at Coryells ferry, the main body in the rear, about ten miles. General Maxwell has broke up the roads, and destroyed the bridges, and, at the head of some regulars and the Jersey militia, begins to skirmish with the enemy, who are about fifteen miles from Philadelphia, on their way to Amboy. They quitted the city on Friday last."

Although neither the writers nor the recipients of these letters have been identified, Thomas Adams, John Banister, and Richard Henry Lee were the Virginia delegates in York at this time.

The only known copy of this issue of the *Gazette* is located among the intercepted ship's papers in High Court of Admiralty 32, box 357, no. 35, P.R.O. It has been supplied through the courtesy of the Virginia Colonial Records Project and Dr. Brent Tarter of the Virginia State Library.

6 Laurens is referring to a paraphrase of Gen. Philemon Dickinson's June 19 letter to Washington in Washington's own June 20 letter to Laurens cited above.

7 General Gates' June 17 letter to Laurens was read in Congress on June 23. See *JCC*, 11:632; and PCC, item 154, 1:418–20.

8 The South Carolina delegates offered twenty-one amendments to the Articles of Confederation on June 25, all of which were promptly rejected. *JCC*, 11:652–56.

Maryland Delegates to the Maryland Assembly

Gentlemen, York Monday P.M. 22d June 1778

The Instructions of the House of Delegates of the 18th instant[1] we this morning received in a letter from Mr. Chase, and laid them before Congress; whereupon at our earnest desire, it was resolved to take into immediate consideration the amendments proposed by our State to the Confederation, altho' Congress had previously determined to take up the amendments offered by the several States in the order in which the States are ranged in the Confederacy, beginning first with New Hampshire, and so on.

This evening the 3 amendments offered by Maryland were debated and 11 States out of the 12 present, rejected the amendments to the 4th and 8th Articles, so that our State only voted for them. The fate of the most important amendment is not yet decided, the question being put off by adjournment till tomorrow morning, when it will probably be rejected by a majority of eight States out of twelve.

A Confederation at this critical juncture appears to Congress of such momentous consequence, that I am satisfied a great majority are resolved to reject the amendments from every State, not so much from an opinion that *all* the amendments are improper, as from the conviction, that if *any* should be adopted, no Confederation will take place, at least for some months, perhaps, years; and in that case, many apprehend none will ever be entered into by all of the present united States; the distractions probably consequent on such an event, and the many dangers and evils, which may arise from partial Confederacies (which you may more easily point to yourselves than we can express) have determined some States to accept the present

Confederation altho' founded on principles not altogether consistent, in their opinion, with justice and sound policy. For if any amendments should be adopted, it will then be necessary to send the Confederation back to those States, whose Legislatures have empowered their Delegates to sign and ratify it in its present form; for instance, to New Hampshire, New York, Virginia and North Carolina, the Delegates of which States are positively instructed to ratify the Confederation, as it now stands, and some of them are directed to admit of no alterations, even litterary ones, such as would not affect the true spirit & meaning of any article, but only serve to elucidate that meaning and spirit by removing all ambiguity, and doubt.

In debating our second amendment, vizt to the 8th article, it was admitted on all sides to be the true meaning & intention of that article, that *all* lands, not only those already granted to, or surveyed for any person, but all lands *hereafter* to be granted to, or surveyed for any person, should be subjected to valuation, and considered as a part of the whole wealth of the State in which they lie. It was contended by several members that the meaning of the 8th article is clearly expressed, but confessed by some to be dark and ambiguous, who nevertheless voted against the amendment, for the reasons we have already assigned.

The amendment to the 4th Article was considered by every State, Maryland excepted, as unimportant; the Article not being liable, in the opinion of any other State to the objection made and consequences apprehended by Maryland.[2]

23d P.M.

Our third amendment has just been rejected by a Majority of one State;[3] the division was as follows.

Against the Amendt.	For the Amendment
N. Hampshire	Rhode Island
Massachusets	Jersey
Connecticut	Pennsylvania
N York divided	Delaware
N Carolina absent	Maryland
South Carolina	
Georgia	
Virginia	

Inclosed you have a copy of Gen. Washington's letter received this morning. We are with great respect, Gent, yr. most obdt. huml. Servants,

Geo Plater

Ch. Carroll of Carrollton

P.S. We write in great haste to be in time for the post, you will therefore be pleased to excuse all interlineations, erasures, & blots.

RC (NN). Written by Carroll and signed by Carroll and Plater.

1 The Maryland delegates' June 18 instructions merely reaffirmed that they were to remain bound by the legislature's December 16, 1777, resolutions on the confederation, "and that they do not ratify and confirm the said articles of confederation until congress shall take the said instructions into consideration, and shall enable the said delegates of this state to give a direct and positive answer thereto, and then not without the express authority of the legislature of this state." *Votes and Proceedings of the House of Delegates of the State of Maryland,* June session, 1778, p. 129, DLC(ESR).

2 The delegates had been instructed to endeavor to amend the fourth article on "privileges and immunities" of free citizens in the several states, "by striking out the word 'paupers' and inserting a provision, 'that one state shall not be burthened with the maintenance of poor persons who may remove from another state.'" See ibid., October session, 1777, p. 48; and *JCC,* 9:908.

3 The legislature's instructions on this proposed amendment, which concerned the subject of western lands and ultimately delayed ratification of the Articles of Confederation until 1781, read as follows: "That this state esteem it essentially necessary for rendering the union lasting, that the United States in congress assembled should have full power to ascertain and fix the western limits of those states that claim to the Mississippi or South Sea. That this state consider themselves justly entitled to a right in common with the other members of this union, to that extensive tract of country which lies to the westward of the frontier of the United States, the property of which was not vested in or granted to individuals at the commencement of the present war. . . . And that [the delegates to congress from this state] use their utmost endeavours to obtain, that an article to this effect be made part of the confederation." *Votes and Proceedings of the House of Delegates of the State of Maryland,* October session, 1777, p. 48, DLC(ESR).

Board of War to the Massachusetts Council

Sir War-Office York Town June 23d. 1778.

Congress having been pleased to commit to this board the care of the cloathing arrived & which shall arrive at the eastward, we are under the necessity of requesting the favour of your honourable board to nominate a person of judgment, care & activity, & who, you think, will faithfully execute the trust, to take the immediate charge of such cloathing, and dispose of the same pursuant to the resolve of Congress & our instructions which will be presented to you herewith.[1]

Unfortunately the business has been (from various causes) too long neglected: we hope therefore you will excuse our urging that a proper person be appointed to execute the same without any delay. We shall also thank your honourable board if they will add to our instructions, an injunction on the person appointed, to use all possible diligence in the business committed to his care.

We are, very respectfully, your most obedt. servants. By order of the Board. Wm. Duer, Del. State of New York

RC (M–Ar). In a clerical hand and signed by William Duer. Addressed: "The president of the Council of Masstts. Bay."

1 Congress' order to the Board of War, which was intended to expedite the delivery of imported clothing to Washington's troops, was dated May 28. See *JCC*, 11:547–49; and Washington, *Writings* (Fitzpatrick), 12:445, 453.

Charles Carroll of Carrollton to Charles Carroll, Sr.

Dear Papa, 23d June 1778.

I shall leave Congress next Saturday, perhaps sooner. On that day, I believe, Congress will adjourn to Pha. We are now on ratifying the Confederation: it will be ratified by all the States except Maryd. and no amendments will be admitted to the present Confederation, so it will stand as it is now printed.

By a letter from Gen. Washington of the 20th we learn that the Enemy had got as far as Eyres town 3 miles below Mount holly on their way to Amboy as it is presumed. Maxwell's corps has had Some skirmishing with them. They were repairing a bridge. 6 Brigades under Gen. Lee were at Corryel's ferry, the main army was then (4 o'clock P.M. 20th June) at ten miles distance from Corryel's ferry.

I hope Sam has got safe home. I sent him off last Saturday. I long to be at home. My love to Molly, & her Mama. I wish you health and am, yr. affectionate Son, Ch Carroll of Carrollton

RC (MdHi).

John Hancock to Dorothy Hancock

My Dearest Dolly: York Town, June 23rd, 1778

Mr. Taylor having agreeably to his wish been Charg'd with some Dispatches for our Commissioners in France, sets off for Boston immediately, & to Sail from thence as Soon as the Packett is ready, by him I embrace the oppor'y of writing you, altho' I wrote you Two Letters the Day before yesterday,[1] & this is my Seventh Letter, & not one word have I heard from you since your departure from Boston. I am as well as the peculiar scituation of this place will admit, but I can by no means in Justice to myself continue long under such disagreeable Circumstances, I mean in point of Living, the mode is so very different from what I have been always accustom'd to, that to continue it long would prejudice my health exceedingly. This moment the Post arriv'd, and to my very great Surprise & Disappointment not a single line from Boston; I am not much dispos'd to Resent, but it feels exceedingly hard to be slighted and neglect'd by those from whom I have a degree of Right to expect different Conduct; I would have hir'd any one to have sent a few Lines just to let me know the State of your health, but I must Endeavor not to be so Anxious & be as easy as some others seem to be. I will expect no letters nor write any, & then there will be no Disappointment; So much for that. To be serious, I shall write no more till I hear from you, this is agreeable to my former promise. It really is not kind, when you must be sensible that I must have been very anxious about you & the little one. Devote a little time to write me, it will please me much to hear of you, I am sure you are dispos'd to oblige me, & I pray I may not be disappointed in my opinion of your Disposition.

I hope this will meet you tolerably Recover'd from your late Confinement, I wish to hear of your being below Stairs & able to take the care of our Dear little one. I am much concern'd about your improving the fine Season in Riding. I am sorry I did not take hir'd horses & leave you mine, but I beg you spare no Cost in Riding for the Establishment and Continuance of your health, hire horses whenever you are dispos'd to Ride, be as frugal & prudent in other matters as is consistent with our Scituation; I wish to know every Occurrence since my departure, pray be particular as to your health in your Letters & give me an exact state of little John. Does Mrs. Brackett intend continuing with you? I beg she may at least untill my Return. My love to her, pray her to take great care of the little fellow. As soon as the City of Philada is cleansed, I judge Congress will remove thither, & as soon as we have got over the important Business now before Congress I shall solicit leave to Return home, as it will not be necessary for so many of our Members to be here, but of this more hereafter.

As I have wrote so many Letters & see no Returns, & as I am called to attend Congress, I must Refer you to Mr. Taylor for every particular relative to our Scituation.

My regards to Mr. & Mrs. Bant, my Brother & Sister, & indeed to all Friends as if nam'd. Remember me to Sprigs and Harry, & all in the Family.

Do let me have frequent Letters, you will oblige me much. My best wishes ever attend you for the highest Felicity, & I am with the utmost Affection and Love. Yours for ever,

John Hancock.

MS not found; reprinted from Henry C. Walsh, "Three Letters from Hancock to 'Dorothy Q.'" *New England Magazine* 12 (1892): 537.

1 Although these two letters have not been found, the following extract of Hancock's June 22 letter to Dorothy was printed in *Dodd, Mead & Co. Catalog* no. 61 (Nov. 1901), item 175, p. 40.

"My Dear Dolly: I wrote you two Letters of yesterday's Date by Dodd who set off early this morning, & hope will get safe to you; to which & all my former Letters I pray your Answers, as you recollect our Agreement you will not hereafter expect more from me than to Answer the Number I Receive from you; however, as the frequent hearing of you and from you will afford me very great pleasure & satisfaction I am confident you will Indulge me as often as possible. Nothing has Occurr'd since I wrote you yesterday. I really think my journey has been serviceable to my Health, which I hope will continue to Recruit, tho' the exceeding heat of the Weather & the different mode of Living is much against me. . . .

"I shall write you as often as I can & Expect at least the same kind Conduct from you. Pray remem'r me to your Sister Mrs. Boyle, Mr. Bank, my Brother & all Friends as if nam'd. My Love to Mrs. Brackett, beg her to take care of little John & of you. I wish this may meet you in the perfect Enjoyment of health, if you are as happy as I wish you, you are happy Indeed. I must go to Congress as the hour is come, & can only add, that I long much to hear from you, & will be with you as soon as I possibly can. May a kind providence Bless & protect you.

"I am with the sincerest Love, Yours for ever, John Hancock."

Samuel Holten's Diary

[June 23, 1778]

23. Attended in Congress, and the chief of the day was taken up in Disputing on the Articles of confederation.[1]

MS (MDaAr).

[1] Congress spent considerable time on June 22 and 23 debating and rejecting amendments to the articles offered by Maryland, Massachusetts, Rhode Island, and Connecticut. *JCC*, 11:629–40. For a discussion of the amendments offered by the states, see George D. Harmon, "The Proposed Amendments to the Articles of Confederation," *South Atlantic Quarterly* 24 (1925): 298–315, 411–36.

Henry Laurens to John Lewis Gervais

Dear Sir

23d June [1778]

By Captain Cochran I troubled you with a few lines the 3d Inst. You are guarded as usual against being troubled with many at present. I cannot even acknowledge receipt of such of your favors as have since come to hand. Sitting from 10 oclock to ½ past 1, and from 3 to ½ past 6 leaves Very little interval for executing with propriety the great burthen of Public Business, none for friendly addresses with that decency which I would ever wish to preserve. My Secretaries I really believe submit to work much harder than the common tone merely out of Respect or perhaps Pity to me.

Our Friend the President will shew you all I have written or transmitted to him, there are some extraordinaries contained in the collection. The Chief Justice watchful and indefatigeable as usual, will make up every dificiency of intelligence in my transmissions and you will learn the whole. Within the present Inclosure you will find about twenty Pennsylvania Gazettes and as many supplements. Distribute them for me among my Friends—Mr. Manigault, the late

President,[1] Mr. Wells, Mr. Galphin, Mr. Williamson, Colo. Kershaw, Colo. Thomson, Mr. Ball, Mr. Zahn, Mr. Brisbane, &c. &c. &c. Give one set if you please to Mr. Loveday.

God bless you all. I congratulate with you, my Countrymen and Friends, on the present fair prospect. Let us with grateful Hearts thank God, be watchful and persevere ardently in our duty not trusting to appearances nor exulting in success. This Life is chequered and three days hence may possibly bring Clouds and Storms over our heads. The Enemy is full of cruelty, subtility and mad with revengeful designs.

Until Peace shall be actually proclaimed it will be our Wisdom to know that we are in the depth of War and to Act becomingly.

I have sent Mr. Oswalds and Mr. Mannings Letters to General Washington and Colo. Laurens; when they are returned you shall see them.

My Love and Compliments and humble respects to all my Friends.

A very valuable French Ship just arrived on public Account at Portsmouth, New Hampshire with Military Stores, Cloathing &c. &c.

Col. Armand tells me prizes are brought into Boston every day—The town full of Goods—And Mr Burgoyne's Saratoga Men the foreigners including Officers coming into us in great numbers and many British too. I recommend General Roberdeaus Letter to you.

My Dear Friend Adieu.[2]

LB (ScHi).

1 John Rutledge.

2 Laurens wrote another letter to Gervais this day in which he asked him to initiate legal action against John McNutt, who had refused to pay Laurens a debt of £410, and requested information about the clothing needs of his slaves "in order that I may if necessary write immediately to France." Laurens Papers, ScHi.

Henry Laurens to Rawlins Lowndes

Dear Sir

23 June [1778]

My last private to Your Excellency is dated 13th Instant. I sent it to Governor Caswell for conveyance, as I did on the 20th one of the Pennsylva. Gazettes giving it a possible chance of reaching your Excellency earlier than this.[1]

The Enemy are now certainly out of Philadelphia, but their movements still wear the aspect of stratagem, they had certainly two days start of General Washington, & according to his advice of the 20th he had marched 40 miles or very near it, Sir Henry Clinton only 15. That Letter will be inclosed for your Excellency's information. I request Sir if you cause it to be published order the title to be a Letter from Camp and no name and the same or a similar restriction respecting General Gates' Letter which will also be enclosed.[2]

Admitting the Enemy to be in earnest meaning to penetrate the Jerseys, our affairs at present may be said to be promising. The roads in their way are much encumbered, Bridges broke up &c, surrounded by numerous hosts all in high spirits and thousands in the highest degree of resentment for great injuries received—their Officers and Men all in the dumps, and desertion determin'd upon by the latter in General and executed as often as opportunity offers.

Congress had granted 932,743⅓ Dollars for defraying the expence of an Indian War, which was at that time judged to be inevitable.[3] General Gates now gives us better hopes.

Rhode Island is still possessed by the Enemy and lately reinforced by some 4 or 500 Troops. General Pigot perseveres in ravaging the Country as often and as much as he can. He lately intimated by Letter to General Sullivan that as by the American Laws all Males from 16 to 60 are obliged to bear Arms he should capture as many such as he could, or all of such, which he might capture, should be considered as exchangeable for British Soldiers.[4] In pursuance of this Idea he is attempting to add Glory to his name by stealing Boys and reserving the right of ageing them to himself—this shews, to say the mildest, great distress on their part, from the detention of Mr Burgoyne's Men.

I troubled your Excellency some time ago with a request to obtain certain Evidence from Captain Senff and I hope soon to receive it in confirmation of what has lately been declared by other foreign Officers respecting the Colours which ought to have been surrendred at Saratoga, and which General Burgoyne like an honest candid Man declared had been left in Canada.[5] A copy of this declaration will be found Inclosed and may, with Captain Senf's in general Terms and even with Comments, leaving out names for the present, be published.

Genl. Washington had sent on the Answer from Congress to the Commissioners who had left the City, and there the Subject rests.[6] You will observe Sir, in the Pennsylvania Gazette a Letter from Govr. Johnstone to myself, and my intended answer, made public by the great anxiety of many People to be informed, and indeed by an attempt of a Member of Congress to obtain an order that all Letters from Govr. Johnstone should be laid before the House. This appeared to me to be unjust and inefficatious. Congress have no power to compel & if the unwarrantable Order had passed, it would have produced Letters only from their Freinds who were not inclined to make them secret.

Your Excellency will find within the present Inclosure Copy of a Letter from Govr. Johnstone to a friend of mine in Camp[7] together with Copy of one from a Gentleman in London to my Friend—over these I have all power except printing—even this, I expect in a few days, in the mean time it will serve for information to your Excellency and other Friends & fellow Citizens at home.

Colo. Malcom lately informed me that having heard one of the Enemy's ships lay near ——— in North River he caused an 18 & 24 Pounder to be dragged down in the night with 51 shot, when the flood tide had made strong he opened his little masked Battery of Bushes and at the distance of 500 to 700 yards pierced her 47 times—when he had only 1 shot remaining a breeze of Wind favouring, the Swift, I think she is called, of 16 Guns cut her Cable and towed off, he took up the Cable and anchor and returned without loss. The Crew of the Ship, the Colonel, says passed their time in great confusion but fired not a shot in return.

We are now to the exclusion of all other business closely engaged on Confederation, if I judge right, Ratification of the original Act will be obtained in the course of this week. Were the various amendments to be fully discussed and alterations made I should not live to see Ratification.

When we have evidence of the Enemy's being fairly gone, Congress will turn their faces toward Philadelphia. General Washington has appointed General Arnold to command there, and 'tis probable the City is now under Whig principles again. People are flocking that way from all Quarters, some shamefully to the neglect of the most important duties.

I doubt much whether I shall have time to write to any other Freinds in Charlestown, although I must trouble your Excellency with Packets of Newspapers for a few. I add to the papers abovementioned the Duke of Richmonds very remarkable Speech of the 5th March—if your Excellency shall not have seen a copy earlier this will afford half an hours agreeable entertainment. In the first event your Excellency will be pleased to accept my meaning, and do me the Honor to believe me with great Esteem and Respect, Sir &c.[8]

LB (ScHi).

1 See Laurens to George Clinton, June 20, 1778, note 4.

2 Washington's June 20 letter to Laurens, dealing with the British army's withdrawal across New Jersey, is in Washington, *Writings* (Fitzpatrick), 12:97–98. Gates' June 15 letter to Laurens, explaining why it was unnecessary for him to carry out a June 11 resolve directing him to wage war on such tribes of the Six Nations as were hostile to the United States, is in PCC, item 154, 1:418–20.

3 See *JCC*, 11:589–91.

4 See Gen. Robert Pigot's widely publicized June 3 letter to Gen. John Sullivan in Sullivan, *Papers* (Hammond), 2:69–70.

5 See Laurens to Lowndes, May 17, 1778, note 12.

6 See Laurens to the Carlisle Commissioners, June 17, 1778.

7 John Laurens.

8 Laurens also wrote a brief covering letter to Lowndes this day transmitting four issues of the June 20 *Pennsylvania Gazette* and a copy of Congress' June 17 resolve on corresponding with the enemy. PCC, item 13, 2:8.

Henry Laurens to George Walton

Dear Sir 23d June [1778]

If I had not long since lamented you as one numbered among the dead and been but lately undeceived you would have often heard from me, indeed upon the first Intelligence of that mistake I destroyed a Letter I had written to you which lay sealed on my table. Doubting whether the Correspondence would have been within order until I should learn which side of the question you had taken.[1]

The subject will not admit of congratulation neither for you have gained nothing, you are but where you were.

But The Intelligence which I have transmitted to Governor Houston and that which you will find within the present Inclosure furnish Sufficient matter for one days joy but let us still be watchful and persevere as becomes wise men until danger shall be wholly removed. Excuse this haste and expect to hear by Colonel Marbury or an earlier Express more fully. I heard a mischievous droll fellow say the other day that Georgia was misrepresented.

Your Friend Arnold Commands in the City.

I Am Dear Sir &c.

LB (ScHi).

1 Laurens was evidently responding to letters from Walton of April 26 and June 3, transcripts of which are in the Laurens Papers, ScHi, in which Walton explained that he was unable to attend Congress because he needed to attend to more pressing public business in Georgia. Laurens' reference to Walton's reported demise is obviously facetious.

Richard Henry Lee to Thomas Jefferson

My dear Sir York the 23d June 1778

The inclosed Gazette will shew you the progress, and perhaps the end for some time, of our negotiation with the British Commissioners. They, with their whole Army have abandoned Philadelphia, and our Troops are in possession of that City. The enemy are pushing thro Jersey for South Amboy, and in their front is Gen. Maxwell with a brigade of Continentals and the Jersey Militia. They have impeded the enemies progress by breaking up the roads and bridges; and we have just been told that Maxwell has attacked and gained an advantage over part of their army. Gen. Washington with 13,000 men is in hot pursuit of the enemy. He was about crossing Delaware the day before yesterday. If our Army can come up with them before they embark, we may have a second edition of Burgoyne. Governor Johnsone tries every art to gain admission among us. He abuses his

Masters, flatters America, and is willing to yield us every thing if we will be perfidious to our Ally and again submit to the domination of his King & Parliament. This Man possesses in abundance Scottish cunning and Scottish impudence. But it is too late in the day. The Sunshine of liberty and independence prevails over the dark arts of Tyranny and its Tools.

We hope in 6 or 8 days to ratify the Confederation (all but two or 3 small States, at the head of which is Maryland and all of whom I have no doubt will soon fall in) without amendments—after which Congress will adjourn to Philadelphia. I am dear Sir affectionately yours,

Richard Henry Lee

RC (DLC). Jefferson, *Papers* (Boyd), 2:201–2.

Gouverneur Morris to George Clinton

Sir, York Town 23d June 1778.

On the Application of the Delegates of the State of New York Congress have given a Draft on their Treasury for the Sum of 100,-000 Dollars.[1] This we have properly indorsed and my worthy Colleague Mr. Duer (who by the bye I assure you hath in various Instances rendered the most essential Services not only to the State which sent him but to the united States of which Congress are fully sensible) will transact this Business and as soon as the Treasury is so much in cash as to advance a considerable Part of the Money will return to the State. I am sorry to add that I fear the Public will [*be*] deprived of the Use of his Zeal and Abilities.

I have the Pleasure to perceive that a Spirit of Justice reigns throughout Congress inclining them to do every Thing necessary to quiet the unhappy Disturbances in the North Eastern Part of our State.[2] It is impracticable to force this Business on nor indeed can I as one Member answer it to myself to postpone the great Business of Confederation we are now engaged in even for a Moment. I enclose you the Public Prints from whence you will perceive that Matters of no small Importance occupied our late Deliberations. It is my earnest Hope that our Determinations may be agreable to those whom I have the Honor to represent. The very important Business of regulating the civil Departments of our Army and the numerous Train of et cæteras which go to the Composition of that more important Business of Finance will I hope be prosecuted with unremitted Attention upon our Arrival at Philadelphia. God knows when the great Business of this Continent will be compleated or rather arranged. Untill it is in some good Train I shall think it my Duty to exert the little share of Abilities which Providence hath entrusted to me for the Use of my Country. My Wishes as a private Man to be in the State of New York in this most critical Conjuncture you Sir can readily conceive. My private Wishes however have no Right to interfere with my public Character.

I have the Honor to be, most respectfully, your Excellency's most obedient and most humble Servant, Gouv Morris

RC (NN).

1 See *JCC*, 11:627, 630.

2 Congress was less willing to assist New York in her dispute with Vermont than Morris supposed. See New York Delegates to Clinton, July 21, 1778.

Gouverneur Morris to John Jay

Dear Jay, York Town 23 June 1778

I enclose you the papers. They are important & from my friendship you have a right to expect comment from me; but my friend, I am every moment employed. I am hurried & it gives me pain that a set of little whiffling incidents should deprive me of one out of the few real consolations the world affords. The answer to the Commissioners & the annotations signed an American were the product of your friends lucubrations.[1] When their insolent letter was read in Congress, I opposed going on with it, & laboured hard to send it back with contempt.[2] In this my view was to oblige them to garble it of the offensive Matter & send it back, thereby striking conviction to the souls even of Tories that G.B. is reduced to implore a peace from America. I know not where Robert is.[3] If with or near you my letter is in common. I hope to write you both before I go to Philadelphia—if not I certainly shall shortly after. Remember me to all friends. Adieu, Adieu.

Yours sincerely, Gouv Morris

Tr (MH–H).

1 See the letters to the Carlisle commissioners from Henry Laurens, June 17, and from Morris, June 20, 1778.

2 See Samuel Adams to James Warren, June 13, 1778, note 3.

3 Robert R. Livingston.

Samuel Holten's Diary

[June 24–25 1778]

24. Attend'd in Congress, dined with the President, & Congress did not sit in the afternoon.[1]

25. Attended in Congress. Towards night I walked out with a number of Gentlemen of Congress about a mile, to a farm house. The people was kind, we eat Charies & drank whiskey.

MS (MDaAr).

[1] After previous experiments with sessions twice daily, Congress had resolved on May 30, 1778, "That for the space of one month, commencing on Monday next, Congress meet at ten o'clock and sit till one, and on the same day, except on Wednesdays and Saturdays, meet at three and adjourn at six o'Clock P.M." June 24 was a Wednesday. See *JCC*, 11:558, 640–42.

Richard Henry Lee to George Washington

Dear Sir

York the 24th of June 1778

I should long since have answered your favor of the 25th of May had it been worth while for any thing I had to communicate,[1] to interrupt your attention from the important affairs with which you are surrounded. It is indeed more from motives of complaisance than any thing else that I now write. But I cannot help congratulating you Sir on the enemies abandoning Philadelphia, because, let their motives be what they may, this step evidently proves their prospect of conquest here is vanished. I fancy Gen Clintons future operations depend much upon the Chapter of Accidents. A French war being avoided, efforts will continue to be exerted for sometime against us, but a foreign war must of necessity carry this Army to secure the now defenceless Islands of G.B. in the W.I. A war with France, in the better days of England, would instantly have followed the Message of Marquis de Noailles,[2] but the mean & wicked determination to enslave America, removes all thoughts of every thing but the accomplishment of their favorite object. The British Kings message to his Parliament, altho it shews mortified pride, and strong sense of insult, yet it clearly marks indicision, and doubt about the propriety of resenting the affront. We see by a publication of the enemy in the Newport paper that there is a great probability of Spain having acknowledged the Independence of these States, & joined in our Alliance. The Ambassadors of Spain & of G.B. were on the point of returning each to his respective Country. Of this event taking place, I had no doubt, so soon as the plate fleet should have reached old Spain. Should G.B. be engaged in war with the Bourbon family it [*will*] furnish us an opportunity of pushing the former quite off this Northern Continent, which will secure to us peace for a Century, instead of war in 7 years which the British possession of Canada, N. Sco. & the Floridas will inevitably produce. You have no doubt heard Sir that our last Assembly have voted 2000 Infantry to join the Army & a sum of money to foward Gen. Nelsons Cavalry.[3] The latter may soon be expected at Head Quarters. I am with sincere esteem dear Sir your most affct. & obedient servant,

R.H. Lee

FC (PPAmP). Endorsed by Lee: "Copy of a letter to Gen. Washington 1778."

1 For Washington's May 25 letter to Lee, see Washington, *Writings* (Fitzpatrick), 11:450–52.

2 For Noailles' "Message" to George III, see Henry Laurens to George Clinton, May 11, 1778, note 3.

3 For the acts passed during the May 1778 session of the Virginia Assembly for raising 2,000 infantry volunteers and a regiment of cavalry, see William W. Hening, *Statutes at Large; Being a Collection of all the Laws of Virginia* (Richmond: J. & G. Cochran, 1821), 9:445–53. In his May 25 letter to Lee, Washington had been critical of Virginia's recruiting deficiencies.

Marine Committee to John Wereat

Sir June 24th 1778

We have received your favour of the 18th May advising the Capturing of three of the enemies Vessels by the Gallies under the Command of Oliver Bowen esqr.[1] and approve of your intention to purchase the said Vessels for account of the united States which we expect you have executed and that they are employed in assisting of the Continental Troops upon the expedition to the southward. We expect shortly to have from you an account of your proceedings in that business.[2] We enclose herewith a set of Rules & Regulations for the Navy and a Resolve of Congress of the 30th of October 1776 for your government. A new set of Rules & Regulations for the Navy are now forming; when they are finished we shall send you Coppies thereof.[3] In the mean time We are with much regard, Sir, your very Hble servants

LB (DNA: PCC Miscellaneous Papers, Marine Committee Letter Book).

1 HM schooner *Hinchinbrook*, sloop *Rebecca*, and a prize brig were captured on April 19 off Fort Frederica, Ga., by a force composed of Continental battalions commanded by Col. Samuel Elbert and the Georgia state galleys *Washington, Lee*, and *Bulloch* under the command of Georgia Commodore Oliver Bowen. For Col. Elbert's account of the capture, see Charles C. Jones, Jr., *History of Georgia*, 2 vols. (Boston: Houghton, Mifflin and Co., 1883; reprint ed., 1965), 2:288–303.

The Marine Committee also wrote a brief letter to Capt. Bowen on June 24, acknowledging receipt of his letters of April 6 and 7 and May 17, 1778 (none of which have been found), and praising the efforts of the Georgia navy. "We highly esteem your prudence in the conduct of the squadron under your command and applaud the activity & Spirit of your officers and Men on a late Occasion in Capturing the enemies Vessels on the Coast of Georgia which we request you will Signify to them in the name of this Committee." Paullin, *Marine Committee Letters*, 1:264.

2 For the controversy that developed between Continental agent John Wereat and Continental Army Cols. Samuel Elbert and John White over the sale of the prize vessels, see Marine Committe to Wereat, August 1, 1778, note.

3 On the revision of naval regulations, see Marine Committee to the Eastern Navy Board, April 6, 1778, note 10.

Henry Laurens to George Clinton

Sir, York Town 25th June 1778

I beg leave to refer Your Excellency to my last of the 20th by Dodd.

Inclosed Your Excellency will be pleased to receive a Copy of an information relative to the Colours of the Army late General Burgoyne's which ought to have been surrendred at the Convention of Saratoga.[1]

General Heath is directed by Congress to continue his endeavors for obtaining further evidence & if possible the remains of the Standards.[2]

I have the honor to be With great Esteem & Respect Sir Your Excellency's Most Obedient serv't,

Henry Laurens, President of Congress.

Reprinted from Clinton, *Papers* (Hastings), 3:489.

1 The enclosed "information" was a statement by three Germans captured at Saratoga that was transmitted to Congress by Gen. William Heath on June 6 in order to counteract reports that "since the Convention of Saratoga . . . the Colours of the several British & foreign Regiments were either sent to Canada or burnt." PCC, item 157, fol. 152. For the original German text of this statement, also dated June 6, and a contemporary translation, see ibid., fols. 156–57. A somewhat defective English text is in Clinton, *Papers* (Hastings), 3:489–90.

2 See Laurens to William Heath, June 26, 1778.

Henry Laurens to Horatio Gates

Sir York Town 25 June 1778

In a private Letter of the 19th I had the honor of transmitting you an Act of Congress of the 17th. This will serve as a Cover to an Act of the 23d authorizing you to dismiss supernumerary Staff Officers within the district under your Command.[1]

We know nothing here relative to the Armies in Jersey that you will not have heard before this can reach you. I have the honor to be, With great Esteem & Regard, Sir, Your obedient & humble servant, Henry Laurens, President of Congress.

RC (NHi).

1 See *JCC*, 11:633. Congress approved this "Act" after reading a June 13 letter to Gates from Gen. John Stark, advising Gates of the need to dismiss supernumerary staff officers in Albany, and Gates' June 17 reply, promising to lay this matter before Congress, both of which came enclosed with Gates' June 17 letter to Laurens. PCC, item 154, 1:418–20, 431–34.

Henry Laurens to John Holt

Sir, 25th June [1778]

Some time ago I paid into the hands of Mr. John Browne Clerk to the Honble Robt. Morris Esquire Three Hundred Dollars which Sum by our friend Mr. Duane's direction were to be paid on your account to Mr. Morris, these were two days ago repaid to me by Mr. Browne under an intimation that your [debt?] had been discharged, I think he said, Mr. Lewis or Mr. Lewis Morris.[1] Be that as it may, Three hundred Dollars your property now rest in my hands subject to your Order, which shall be faithfully complied with by Sir yours &ca.

LB (ScHi). Addressed: "John Holt Poughkeepsie."

[1] For further information regarding delegate efforts to assist New York printer John Holt, whose equipment had been destroyed by the British, see Laurens' letters to James Duane, December 24, 1777, and April 7, 1778.

Henry Laurens to George Washington

Sir. York Town 25th June 1778

On the 23d I had the honor of presenting Your Excellency's Letter of the 20th & last Evening of receiving one of the 22d which shall be presented this Morning.[1]

Congress have been so attentive to Confederation some five or six days past, as to admit of scarcely another consideration—& have now Resolved to adjourn to Philadelphia on the 27th.[2] I therefore judge it best to return the bearer with this acknowledgement.

My Prayers & Cordial wishes attend Your Excellency—& I remain, Sir, Your Excellency's Obedient & Most humble servant.

Henry Laurens, President of Congress

RC (DLC photostat).

[1] Washington's June 22 letter to Laurens, dealing with his pursuit of the British through New Jersey, is in PCC, item 152, 6:135, and Washington, *Writings* (Fitzpatrick), 12:108–9.

[2] Congress approved this resolve on June 24. *JCC*, 11:641.

Samuel Holten's Diary

[June 26, 1778]

26. Attended in Congress, and it is the hotest day I ever knew. Went & drank with the Presidt. & drank tea with the Secretary.

MS (MDaAr).

Henry Laurens to William Heath

Sir

York Town 26th June 1778

I had the honor of writing to you by Messenger Dodd the 20th Inst.

The testimony of the foreign Officers relative to Colours said to have been concealed by General Burgoyne's orders I have transmitted to Governor Clinton[1] & Congress request you in the most effectual manner & by all proper means, unalarming to the present Commanding Officer of the British Prisoners, to obtain further accounts of any violation of the Convention of Saratoga & particularly if possible to obtain the very Colours[2]—admitting they are carried off by General Burgoyne or destroyed before he left you a search would prove fruitless & wear an ill aspect, but getting the Colours in hand will carry proof undeniable.

Colo. Armand has obtained an Act of Congress in favor of his measures which he will lay before you.[3]

Inclosed will be found two Acts of Congress of the 24th, One for accepting Colo. Wm. Lee's resignation & the other for accepting the resignation of Major Swasey.[4]

I have a Letter of the 24th from General Arnold Commandant in Philadelphia.[5] "The Main Body of the Army were last Night at the Black Horse seven miles beyond Mount Holly, their movements are but 7 or 8 Miles per day. Our Army was at Prince Town & in advance last Night moving on towards the Enemy with design of improving any favorable opportunity of attacking them. Near 400 Deserters from the Enemy have arrived at this place.

The Rear of their Fleet was yesterday at Reedy Island, two Divisions are gone down the River to Sea."[6]

I have the honor to be, With great Regard, Sir, Your obedient humble servant, Henry Laurens, President of Congress.[7]

RC (MHi).

1 See Laurens to George Clinton, June 25, 1778.

2 There is no mention of this "request" in the journals.

3 See *JCC*, 11:642–44; and Laurens to Lafayette, May 11, 1778, note 4.

4 See Laurens to Washington, April 8, 1778, note 3.

5 Arnold's letter is in PCC, item 162, fols. 114–16.

6 George Plater also wrote a letter this day to Gov. Thomas Johnson of Maryland, which consisted essentially of nothing more than a somewhat longer quotation from General Arnold's letter. Red Books, MdAA.

7 This day Laurens also wrote a brief covering letter to the Board of Treasury transmitting "a State of Money paid by me to Express Messengers in the public Service." PCC, item 13, 2:12. After briefly considering the matter, the board advised Congress to issue a warrant for $3,000 to Laurens so that he could pay express messengers, which Congress agreed to do this day. *JCC*, 11:660–61.

Committee of Congress Report

[June 27, 1778][1]

The Committee to whom were referred the Letter and Papers from Mr Holker beg Leave to report.

That they have considered the said Letter and Papers and conferred thereon with Mr. Holker.

That it appears to your Committee that the said Mr Holker hath no Commission or Credentials from the Court of France neither doth he desire to be received in a public Character or intrusted with any Confidential Matters untill he shall have Authority from the said Court.[2]

That it will be proper for Congress to take Measures either by Bills of Exchange or otherwise for the Payment of the Sum of four hundred thousand Livres mentioned in the said Papers to the owners of the Privateers Hancock and Boston of which he saith 50,000 have been advanced by a certain Mr Williams to the Commissrs. of these States at Paris and must be repaid to him.

Wherefore they submit the following Resolution.

That the Executive Power of the State of Massachusets be requested to make Enquiry and transmit to Congress the Names of the Owners of the Privateers Hancock and the Boston[3] and their respective Shares in the said Ships, & That a Copy of the Letter received by Mr. Holker and his laid before the House be transmitted to the said Executive Power for the Purpose of directing their Enquiry.

MS (DNA: PCC, item 96). In the hand of Gouverneur Morris.

1 On June 18 Congress had appointed a committee, consisting of Thomas McKean, Gouverneur Morris, and John Witherspoon, to consider certain papers on Jean Holker, including Holker's June 16 letter to Henry Laurens, his June 16 summary of verbal instructions he allegedly received from the French court, and Jacques Leray de Chaumont's February 28, 1778, letter to Holker authorizing him to pay 400,000 livres to the owners of two American privateers. Transcripts of these documents are in PCC, item 96, fols. 1–10. The committee's report was read on June 27, but the motion to adopt the report was rejected. See *JCC*, 11:618–20, 661. For an indication of the reasons for congressional disapproval, and information on the eventual payment of the French gratuity, see Titus Hosmer to Thomas Mumford, this date.

2 For the question of Holker's authority, see Committee for Foreign Affairs to the Commissioners at Paris, June 21, 1778, note 2.

3 Henry Laurens inserted "the Boston" in place of "Adams."

Samuel Holten's Diary

June 27 [1778]

Attended in Congress in the forenoon and they adjourned to the City of Philada. to meet on Thursday next 10 o'Clock.[1]
N.B. The weather is very hot.

MS (MDaAr).

1 Although Congress planned to reconvene in Philadelphia on Thursday, July 2, a quorum was not available to resume the conduct of business until Tuesday, July 7. *JCC*, 11:671–72.

Information on the activities of a few of the delegates during the week they traveled to Philadelphia is available in the diaries of Holten, William Ellery, and Josiah Bartlett, whose entries for the period are quoted here as follows:

"28. Sabbath Day. Travd. from York Town. Crossed the Susquehanna 20 miles lower than where I did before. Dined at a good Inn but have a small room to lodge in this night. N.B. & the bugs drove us out.

"29. Travd. 12 miles before brakfast, brakfasted on whartelbary—Still out doors, then Travd. 7 miles, dined at a good Inn, then Travd. 15 miles to Newart in one of the lower Counties in Delaware State.

"30. Travd. from Newart to Wilmanton 11 miles, had Brakfast & dined; we passed thro' part of the State of Maryland, & Wilmanton is a principal Town in the State of Delaware; The building are chiefly Bricke & very commodious; We then Travd. to Chester where we are likely to be well Accomodated.

"July 1. Travd. to the City of Philadelphia 15 miles before brakfast. Dined at a public house; Then took Lodgings at the Wido Robbinson's, in Chestnut Street." Samuel Holten Diary, MDaAr.

"Sat out from Yorktown June 28th, 1778, for Philadelphia in my way to Dighton, in Company, with the Honble Houston, Gerry, Dana, Delegates of Massachusetts Bay. Dined at Major Finnies about 15 miles from Yorktown, very well. From thence to McCall's Ferry on Susquahanna is about 9 miles. We took this route because the road was better than through Lancaster, and because we expected the Inns on that Road, as Congress had adjourned, and were on their way to Philadelphia, were crowded.

"Lodged at McLaughan's, about 2½ Miles from the Ferry. The house is very indifferent; but the housekeeping was very good. He is a staunch Irish true blue Presbyterian. There is a large Parish of that Denomination of Christians in this Quarter, and a very decent Meeting-house, and they are all warm Whigs.

"June 29th. From thence to Warneck's where we breakfasted is 12 miles; the weather was extreme hot, and we drank our Coffee under the shady trees near the house. Were very civilly treated. From Warneck's to Richie's is 7 miles. Here we dined and were entertained very agreeably. Mr. Richie's wife's sister who kept the house in the absence of her Sister, hath an Austrian Lip so much like one I had seen before.

"30th. From thence to Newark where we lodged at . . . is 13 miles. Here is good entertainment for Man and horses. To Wilmington is 12 miles. Here at Brinton's we breakfasted and dined elegantly; the Weather very hot. Sat off at 5 o'clock. From thence to Carlin's in Chester, is 13 miles. Here we found good Cyder, good lodging and good housekeeping. To Philadelphia is 15 miles, where I put up at my good friend's William Redwood. From Derby to Schuylkill, the Fencing was destroyed and the fields lay entirely open; but as the stock had been removed by the owners or taken by the enemy, the grass was luxuriant. As I passed the Schuylkill, the naked Chimnies of destroyed houses on my left expressed in emphatick language the barbarity of the British Officers and Soldiery. The City however was in a much better state than I expected to have found it. At Chester heard the glorious news of the defeat of Genl Clinton at Monmouth." William Ellery Diary, *PMHB* 11 (1887): 476–77.

"July 2nd 1778. Set out from York Town for Philadelphia, rode to Susquehannah 11½ miles, Crossed, Dined at Boyds, then 11 miles to Lancaster wid. Rankin to Lodge. [July] 3d, rainy, rode 7 miles to Willsons to breakfast then 10 miles to Hopkins the Bunch of Grapes, then 10 miles to the Sign of the Waggon to Lodge, very rainy. [July] 4th, rode 6 miles to the Ship tavern to Breakfast then 13 miles to the Paoli then 15 miles to the Sign of the Black horse then 6 miles to Philadelphia." Josiah Bartlett Diary, Nh.

Titus Hosmer to Thomas Mumford

Dear sir York Town June 26th [*i.e.* 27]. 1778[1]

Immediately upon my arrival here, which was last Monday, I made it my first Care to attend to the Business you had charged me with.

Mr. Holkers Advertisement in the enclosed News papers will direct you where to apply for your Money;[2] he had laid his Credentials before Congress & requested them to take measures for ascertaining the Owners of the privateers and other persons interested in the prizes & their several proportions of Interest in Order to his drawing on France in their favour, a Comittee reported a Resolve[3] referring it to the Executive Powers of Massachusetts Bay to enquire after & Certify who were Owners &c, Congress upon Consideration did not adopt the Resolve, because it was a Matter that did not concern the public Interest, & might open a Door to endless applications.

Congress is adjourned to Philadelphia to meet there next Thursday, whither it is probable Mr. Holker will likewise transfer himself; it will be proper to be furnished with clear & Authentic Evidence who are Owners & proprietors of this Donation, whoever applies to him, & with full powers to act for those they represent.

The News papers contain most of the news that can be sent you from Congress, I can only add that the Articles of Confederation are settled and will probably be ratified at Philadelphia next Saturday (the anniversary of our Independance) by such Delegates who are impowered to ratify them, which are all except New Jersey, Maryland, Georgia & the Delaware Counties, and it is hoped and expected that all or some of them will by that Time receive their Powers for that purpose.

The Armies are in New Jersey, the British proceeds slowly, seems embarrassed & is lessened fast by numerous Desertions, Mr. Peters of the Board of war, who came in from Philadelphia this Evening reports that by their Accounts there upwards of one Thousand have deserted since they left Philadelphia, Genl. Washingtons Army is at and near Princeton, I cannot tell you precisely where the Enemy Are, we may expect great Events to take place in a few Days, may they be fortunate & happy for the united states.

I expect the Connecticut News from You, you will please to direct to me at Philadelphia for which Place I shall leave this on Monday next. Please to make my Compliments acceptable to your Good Lady & Family, & believe me to be, with the highest Esteem, Your Friend & humble servant, Titus Hosmer

RC (Robert J. Sudderth, Jr., Lookout Mountain, Tenn., 1973).

1 References in the text to specific proceedings of Congress indicate that this letter could not have been written before June 27, for it was on that day that Congress considered the report of the committee on Jean Holker's papers, agreed to adjourn to Philadelphia, and postponed signing the Articles of Confederation. *JCC*, 11:661–62.

2 Holker's "Advertisement" has not been found, but a paraphrased extract of Jacques Leray de Chaumont's February 28 letter to Holker is printed in the June 20, 1778, issue of the *Pennsylvania Gazette*. Chaumont had announced that the king of France had ordered a gratuity to be paid to the owners of two American privateers equal to the value of two prizes they had sent to Nantes in August 1777 but which had been returned to their British owners because of their false entry as Dutch vessels. Chaumont's letter to Holker, which authorized him to pay 400,000 livres to the American privateer owners, had been carried to the United States by Simeon Deane, along with the February 18 letter from the commissioners at Paris notifying Congress of the gratuity. Wharton, *Diplomatic Correspondence*, 1:503. For further information on this subject, see Simeon Deane's letters to Holker of May 16 and 30, and Holker's June 19, 1778, letter to Chaumont in the Jean Holker Papers, DLC.

It was not until October 1778 that Holker paid the authorized agents of the American owners in Boston. The October 17 order of the Massachusetts Council, recognizing Joseph Foster as agent for the owners of the privateer brigantine *General Mercer*, Capt. James Babson, called the *Hancock* while in France, and John Grennell and Adam Babcock as owners and agents for the other owners of the *Fanny*, Capt. John Kendrick, called the *Boston* while in France; and the October 28 notice of the agents, acknowledging receipt of 400,000 livres from Holker, are printed in the November 9, 1778, issue of the *Independent Ledger, and the American Advertiser*.

Thomas Mumford is listed as one of seven owners of the Connecticut privateer brigantine *Fanny* in a December 17, 1776, memorial to the Massachusetts Council, which sought exemption from the embargo and permission to sail from Dartmouth, Mass. Morgan, *Naval Documents*, 7:503.

3 See Committee of Congress Report, this date.

Henry Laurens to William Greene

Sir

York Town 27th June 1778

I beg leave to refer to my late address to Your Excellency under the 20th Inst. by Messenger Dodd.[1]

Your Excellency will be pleased to receive under the present Cover an Act of Congress of the 25th for the better defending & protecting the State of Rhode Island &c against the attempts of the Enemy. Also an Act of the 25th for Issuing three Warrants in favor of that State, for 250000 Dollars together with the three Warrants therein specified.[2]

I have the honor to be, With great Respect, Sir, Your Excellency's humble servant, Henry Laurens, President of Congress.

RC (R–Ar).

1 See Laurens to George Clinton, June 20, 1778, note 3.

2 See *JCC*, 11:645–47, 659; and Rhode Island Delegates to Greene, this date. Congress actually approved the issuance of these warrants to Rhode Island on June 26.

Henry Laurens to Patrick Henry

Sir, 27th June 1778

My last to your Excellency is of the 20th Inst. by Captn. Cottineau.[1]

Yesterday I had the honor of presenting to Congress two Letters from your Excellency both dated the 18th.[2] I apprehend within a few hours of that date your Excellency received my Letter of the 13th which contains a full answer from Congress respecting the purchases of goods the Cargo of Monsr. Beaumarchais Ship, Major Lee had charge of that dispatch & promised the necessary care.

The bearer of this will deliver a packet directed from the Committee of foreign Correspondence to your Excellency,[3] another packet directed by my hand contains Letters of importance to the United States from Don Juan de Miralles which I request you Sir, to Send in company with those from the Committee.[4] I also take the liberty of requesting your Excellency to forward the inclosed Letter to the President of South Carolina by the earliest opportunity.[5]

This days Gazette which will be also inclosed will give the Current Intelligence at York Town[6] except that desertions from the Enemy far exceed the Number intimated in Majr. General Arnold's Letters from Philadelphia, I have such accounts as leave no room to doubt Sir Henry Clinton's having lost upwards of 1000 Men Since he crossed Delaware.

No reply from the Commissioners. I have the honor to be &ca.

LB (DNA: PCC, item 13).

1 See Laurens to George Clinton, June 20, 1778, note 3.

2 Governor Henry's June 18 letters to Laurens are in PCC, item 71, 1:153–57. The longer of the two is also in Henry, *Patrick Henry*, 3:177–78.

3 In his July 4 reply to Laurens, Henry acknowledged receipt of "several packets for the Ambassadors of the United States at Paris" and promised to forward them to France as soon as possible. Ibid, p. 178. One of the items in question was

undoubtedly the Committee for Foreign Affairs' June 21 letter to the commissioners at Paris.

4 Among these letters was Miralles' June 22, 1778, dispatch to Diego José Navarro, governor general of Cuba, which is in Papeles Procedentes de Cuba, Legajo 1281, Archivo General de Indias, Seville. In this report, his first since his arrival at York on June 9, Miralles related his activities since leaving Baltimore, explained the "contradictory opinions as to what the British army will decide to do," and summarized what had transpired between Congress and the British peace commissioners from the documents that had been printed in the *Pennsylvania Gazette*. For Miralles' mission to America, see Francis Lewis to John Langdon, June 12, 1778, note 1.

5 See Laurens to Rawlins Lowndes, this date.

6 Laurens noted in his presidential letterbook that this day he also sent "several" copies of this issue of the *Pennsylvania Gazette* to Gov. Richard Caswell of North Carolina. PCC, item 13, 2:16.

Henry Laurens to Rawlins Lowndes

Dear Sir, 27th June [1778]

Congress will adjourn this Morning to Philadelphia. I have many things to day & to hear in a short space of time. Your Excellency will therefore account for brevity.

The inclosed Gazette of this date will give the current Intelligence but I may venture to add that the number of Deserters from the Enemy since they crossed Delaware amounts to near three times that mentioned in Major General Arnold's advice of the 24th.

I expect every hour an account of an attack by General Washington & the Jersey Militia on Sir Henry Clinton whose present situation must be felt by him as extremely unpleasant.

This instant a person who left Philadelphia on the 26th avers that in the Morning of that day Platoon firing on the Jersey side for two hours had been distinctly heard.

After spending 4½ hours in Congress I am just going to Philadelphia without Ratifying Confederation which would have been done by all the authorized Delegates about 9 or 10 States but there appeared such a number of interlineations & mistakes in the Secretary's Engrossed Copy as rendered it necessary to delay this great work. Saturday 4 July is now the order of the house.[1]

I remain with the utmost respect &ca.[2]

LB (ScHi).

1 In fact Congress did not resume consideration of the Articles of Confederation until July 9. *JCC*, 11:677.

2 A summary of this letter was printed in the July 23, 1778, issue of the *South Carolina and American General Gazette* under the heading "Extract of a Letter from York-Town, dated June 27, 1778."

Henry Laurens to John Sullivan

Dear Sir, 27th May [*i.e.* June] [1778]

Permit me to refer to my last under the 20th Inst. by Messenger Dodd.

My present duty is to forward the Inclosed Act of Congress of the 25th for putting two Thousand Stand of Arms into your hands for the better defence of Rhode Island & Providence Plantations &ca.[1]

This Days Gazette which I take the liberty of adding will inform you of the Current Intelligence.

Congress will adjourn this Morning to Philadelphia, & I shall begin my journey in the afternoon, it is not necessary therefore to tell you that I have many things to do in a short space of time.

I have the honor to be

LB (DNA: PCC, item 13).

1 See *JCC*, 11:646; and Rhode Island Delegates to William Greene, this date. Laurens noted in his presidential letterbook that this day he also sent "an Act of Congress of 25th for the defence of Rhode Island & Providence Plantations & a Gazette of this date" to General Washington. See PCC, item 13, 2:15; and *JCC*, 11:645–47.

Robert Morris to John Brown

Dear Sir Manheim June 27th 1778

I wrote you yesterday[1] & must now trouble you again, to request you will send to Mr. Jona. Hudson Mercht in Baltimore the Sum of £1243.17.6 Curry on my Acct. and the further Sum of £1681.14/ Curry being the amot of that draft you recd from Young Mr Sellers to enable you to send him these Sums & perhaps some others to another Quarter, I shall inclose herein a draft on [. . .] which will be paid on Monday next.

Mr Braxton in a letter dated the 1st Inst. which I find here, says he has transmitted the Commercial Committee his Accts and desired them to pay the balance thereof to me. He dont mention the Sum, but you will see the Acct. You may apply to the Committee for it and give them a receipt on my behalf or if they choose it I will send one & you'l inform me the Sum. I have just heard that Congress have adjourned to Philadelphia, if that be true, your stay will be short at York, therefore I will not trouble you with more business than is mentioned above. You will find herein a draft of Jos. Shippen Esqr. on Mr. Wm Smith who is the bearer of this letter in your favour for Eight thousand Dollars on my Acct. Be pleased to go with him to Mr. Helligass & receive this Money. Send the Sums I have mentioned to Mr Hudson & at your leisure send my Acct Current. I beg of you to present my Compliments to Mr Irwin, tell him I both wrote & Spoke to Colo Boudinot about Mr Robison and he promised to get his discharge which I hope has been done.

I dont know whether I shall go over to York or not before my return to Philada. but if I do not, you will leave my Salt &c in Mr. Irwins care & bring his receipt for it. Tell him I will hereafter write him [about] that & Wine & Spirit. My Compts also to Mr Donaldson. I beg his particular care of my five pipes of Wine in his Store respecting which I will write to him hereafter. I send by Mr Smith some Public letters, please to see [. . .] & let me hear from you for I am Dr sir, Your Obedt hble servt. Robt Morris

P.S. Please to forward the sundry Letters that will be delivered you herewith soon as possible. Give my Compts to Bob, tell him I have been in Philada. & that I intend to see him before I return thither again. R M

RC (PHi). Addressed: "To Mr. John Brown, York town."

1 Morris' June 26 letter to Brown—reporting his return to Manheim "yesterday after these three Weeks absence, one of which I passed in Philadelphia," speculating on the effects of the British occupation of Philadelphia, and directing Brown to remit "Eighteen hundred pounds Virginia Curry . . . [to] Messrs. Hooe & Harrison's Merchts in Alexandria"—is in the Dreer Collection, PHi.

Rhode Island Delegates to William Greene

Sir, York Town June 27th 1778

Your Excellencys Letter of the 13th Instant came to Hand, as also one other of the 11th Instant from the Councill of War. Your Excellencys Letter addressed to Congress was also recd.[1] We observe a Mistake made by the Councill; In their Instructions to Us of the 4th of June[2] They say the State had advanced to the Dep. Clothr. seventy Thousand Pounds; In their Letter of the 11th Instant They say They have advanced to that Department untill Their Accounts amount to forty six Thousand, nine hundred and forty six pounds. Such material Mistakes are apt to lead us into Errors and Inconsistancy with Congress. In the last Letter from the Councill of War, They mention a Letter from Mr. Mease, which they say they enclose; but it was omitted.

However we have from our first Knowledge of the late Attempts of the Enemy upon Our State, reflected upon the Subject with Seriousness, and pressed for Relief of every kind; and upon the Receipt of the Letters from Your Excellency & the Councill of War, we have again applied with Ardour and unremitted Zeal; and have obtained Warrants for 250,000 Dollars which the President will enclose to the State; also Orders for supplying the Military Chest there with 300,000

Dollars; also an Order for 2000 stand of Arms, which Order will be forwarded by the Board of War to Genl. Sullivan. Also a Resolution for building three Gallies on certain Conditions.[3] Also an Order to Genl. Washington, to send the Rhode Island Battallion now in Camp to Our State, if it can be done consistantly with the genl. Interest.[4] We place no great Expectations from that Resolution, unless the Campaign should soon end successfully on Our Part in the Jerseys, And which by the Blessing of God we have great Hopes of. The Papers and Capt. Talbot will inform You of the State of Affairs there.

We hope, if at Length Our Sister States come forward, that our long depressed State will in Consequence of these Resolutions be again put upon Ground that shall enable Her to make a powerfull and successfull Opposition to the Attacks of Our Enemies; And that by making the wisest Application of the Monies, and holding Our Hands with Resolution from continental Advances in Future, unless by immediate & express Request of Congress, that our State Financies may get into a better Situation, and in a regular Course of Reduction.

The Matter respecting Cloathing advanced to Our Officers at 4/ Ster for 1/ is laid before a Committee; We shall give You the earliest Intelligence of the Result.[5] We are in hopes the State and the Dep. Clothr. will be justified, altho' it is said the Advance was not quite large enough. The Propriety of the Advances to Officers of State Battallions are also doubted. We shall carefully attend to it, And are most respectfully, Your Excellencys most obedt and humble Servants,

William Ellery
Hy Marchant

P.S. Mr. Collins is gone to Philadelphia. Congress this Day will adjourn there.

RC (R–Ar). Written by Marchant and signed by Marchant and Ellery. Addressed: "His Excely, Govr. Greene or Council of War, Providence."

1 Governor Greene's June 13 letter to President Laurens, dealing with Rhode Island's "extreme weak and defenceless condition," is in PCC, item 64, fols. 410–11, and William R. Staples, *Rhode Island in the Continental Congress, 1765–1790* (Providence: Providence Press Co., 1870), p. 187. For the letters to the Rhode Island delegates from Greene and the Rhode Island Council of War, see Staples, *Rhode Island in the Continental Congress*, pp. 185–86.

2 Not found.

3 See *JCC*, 11:646. In regard to this resolve Henry Laurens wrote the following letter this day to the Eastern Navy Board: "Within the present Inclosure be pleased to receive an Act of Congress of the 25th for building, Equipping & manning three large Gallies for the defence of Providence, Warren & Taunton Rivers & for purchasing in Lieu of the Gallies proper Vessells for that purpose." Navy Board Papers, RNHi.

4 For the resolves on the defense of Rhode Island listed here, which were approved by Congress on June 25 and 26, see *JCC*, 11:645–47, 659–60.

[5] Not until October 13, 1778, did Congress approve the arrangements made by Rhode Island authorities to procure clothing for the state's Continental officers. See *JCC*, 11:642, 12:880, 1006–7.

Josiah Bartlett to Mary Bartlett

My Dear York Town June 28th 1778

Yesterday Congress adjourned from this place to meet in Philadelphia on Thursday the 2nd of July next. The President & many of the Members are gone, and by tomorrow noon Scarcely any English person will be left in this Town, as the original Setlers here are German & talk that Language. I Expect to Set out in a few Days so that the next letter you Receive from me will likely be Dated in Philadelphia, I have not had any letter from you Since yours Dated the 28th of May; hope you have Recd mine regularly as I have wrote you almost Every week, my last was the 21st Inst Enclosed in one to major Philbrick and went by Express. I am in health & have been as well since I have been here as I am Commonly or rather better, I hope the air of Philadelphia will suit me as well, Tho I had rather not have moved there Quite so soon, till the City had been more thoroughly Cleansed. Charles Chace is well. Mr Wentworth is not well which will hinder me from going to Philadelphia for some Days at least otherways I should set off to morrow morning.[1]

The Enemy left the City the 18th and the last account we have of them, they were not half the way to Amboy & our army very near them, so that it seems probable a Battle will soon take place between the two armies. God Grant it may prove Decisive in favor of America. As the armies are about 100 miles nearer you than I am, it is probable before you Receive this you will have later accounts from them than I can send you, many of the German Troops have Deserted from the Enemy Since they left Philadelphia.

We happened to have sight of the Ecclipse of the Sun last Wednesday; it was so Cloudy all Monday & Tuesday & Wednesday till about 8 of the Clock in the morning that the Sun did not once appear, afterwards the Clouds broke so that we had a pritty good Sight of it. It was much the largest Ecclipse I Ever Saw, it was all covered Except a very Small rim at the Nortwest, smaller than the bright part of the moon when she first appears after the change. The weather here now is very hot & have been so for 3 Days past.

June 29th. I am sorry to inform you Mr Wentworth is very sick with a fever & a Billious vomiting and Purging, and has been confined for above a week. He is *not* willing his friends should be informed of his Sickness which is I fear attended with great Danger.

Remember me to all friends and particularly, Remember my Love to all my Children and my sincere affection to your self; yours,

Josiah Bartlett

RC (NhHi).

1 Bartlett remained in York until July 2, when John Wentworth's health appeared to improve. But illness kept Wentworth in York until early August, and although he then went to Philadelphia, he apparently did not attend Congress before leaving for New Hampshire on August 21, 1778. See Bartlett's letters to Mary Bartlett, July 6, to Meshech Weare, July 20 and September 8, and to William Whipple, August 18, 1778.

Gouverneur Morris' Proposals on Fiscal and Administrative Reform

To the Congress. [June–July? 1778][1]

In the present Situation of our Affairs it must be evident to every Observer that America must be victorious if she can prosecute the War since it is impracticable for Great Britain to pursue it much longer. Now America can prosecute the War so long as she can keep an Army in the Field, but to keep an Army it is necessary to have Men to clothe, arm, Feed & pay them. To all these Purposes Money is the great Thing needful. A Paper Circulation may depreciate to such a Degree as no longer to answer the Purposes of Money. And this hath been the Case in a great Measure from the Want of Attention, Management and Method. To look thro the Causes of our Misfortunes may lead to the Cure. The Want of Men arises from sundry Sources. 1st. the short Enlistments at the Commencement of the War. 2ly. the Advance in the Price of Labor & Commodities. 3dly. the enormous Bounties given by several of the States. 4thly. the great Sums paid for Substitutes in the frequent Calls of the Militia. 5thly. from the Want of Discipline by which Means Soldiers not only desert in great Numbers but no Attention being paid to their Manner of Living by their Officers they loose their Cloaths become sickly & finally die or are rendered unfit for Service. 6thly. from the Want of Cloathing, Blankets and the like & lastly from the Defects of the Hospitals by which many die & the Sufferings of those who survive prevent ReEnlistments.

The Money also hath depreciated from several Causes as 1st. From the very Nature of it it was a Matter of very great Doubt among many whether it would not finally sink in the Hands of the Possessor hence the Aspect of our Affairs hath a manifest Influence upon its Credit. 2ly. From the many different Kinds of Paper Money Counterfeits became easy and therefore Men were less inclined to receive it. 3dly. The great Wages given to our Soldiery, The frequent

Gouverneur Morris

Calls of Militia and after that every other Cause which hath caused great Emissions tends by the Quantity of the Money to lower it's Value. 4thly. The great Prices given for Commodities the natural Produce of the Country by the Servants of the Public from the Want of due Arrangement in the several Departments. 5thly. The Want of Oeconomy & Frauds in those Departments. 6thly. All those Laws which were framed to regulate Prices from that of Gold & Silver down to every other Article the necessary Consequence of which was to exclude such things or at least the greater Part of them from Commerce and therefore to raise the Price of the Remainder from the Scarcity, from the Plenty of Paper Money & from the Risque of breaking the Law. 7thly. From the Depreciation once begun arose a Depreciation consequent upon it distinct from other Causes since from thence the Possessors of Commodities would ask more than what would otherwise have been the Market Price foreseeing that tho' that Price might be the just Value at the Time of Sale it must soon become less, others also from this Depreciation would be led to engross and moneyed Men continually receiving their Debts in nominal Money of decreasing Value would be led to *realize* (or purchase any thing not perishable such as Land, Gold, Silver, Iron & the like) all which was taken out of the Circle of Commerce. 8thly. No Taxes having been laid and the Authority of the Governments in many Instances shaken it became doubtful with many whether even any Attempt would be made to redeem any Part of it and therefore, 9thly. When the Continent offerd to loan their own Money there being no visible Funds to pay the Interest Men were disinclined to trust them.

In order to restore the Value of Money it becomes necessary to lessen the Quantity & Kinds to provide Ways and Means to procure Funds for carrying on the War and to use Oeconomy in the Expenditures.

(1) To lessen the Quantity & Kinds of Money I would propose that every State should instantly by Law cry down their own Emissions and redeem them with Continental Loan Office Certificates and be duly charged by the Continent with the Interest of such Certificates.

(2) If Credit can be procured in Europe (of which more presently) to absorp a considerable Quantity of the Paper by selling Bills of Exchange.

(3) To gain a Credit to our Funds in Order to procure Loans and here

1st. The Payment of the Bills drawn for the Interest of the Debt will have a considerable Influence but it is necessary to extend that Influence into foreign Countries & gain Credit there, for which Purpose I propose

2ly. That the States should each pass an Act restricting their several Limits within a certain Line to be drawn for that Purpose and declaring that the Residue shall appertain to the Congress of the united States in Consequence of which Cession the States which really Part with Territory to receive a Compensation by the Abatement of some Part of their future Quota of the Continental Debt. From this Land I would set off a well sized State for our own Soldiers, for Deserters from the Enemy and for such Gratuities as Congress or their public Ministers may chuse to make from a proper Distribution of which Land the Men of great Influence in Europe may be brought to favor our Cause. The Remainder should be divided into other large Districts by Natural Boundaries and be called by separate Name which should denominate our Funds and supposing these names to be A,B & C any Man in Europe who put into the Fund A should be entitled at any Time to so much Land in that Country as could be purchased there at that Time for his Debt by which Means we should be able to give Security for the Principal of our Debt which no Nation in Europe can do.

3dly. It should be an Additional Article in the Confederation that an Acknowledgement of 2½ per Cent should be paid on the Value of all Commodities imported into America from any Port not within one of the united States and that this Acknowledgement and also every other Duty for the Regulation of Trade or otherwise laid should be paid to the Continent as a sinking Fund for the Principle & Interest of Debts by them contracted during the War. This Acknowlegement alone would produce from the American Commerce in 1772 £125.000 Stg. equal to 1,250,000 Dollars of our present Money at least and if we add 250,000 for what would arise from other necessary Duties over and above the Cost of collecting the Whole this would make 1,500,000 Dollars which would be the Interest of a Debt of 25,000,000 Dollars at six per Cent. The Post Office also properly regulated would in Time produce a very considerable Remedy without Burthening the Community it being rightly observed that this is the most agreable Tax ever invented. But as these would yield little or nothing at present I would propose

4thly. that a Capitation Tax of one Dollar upon every Inhabitant be paid as a sinking Fund at present and that this be faithfully and honestly applied notwithstanding any Exigency to pay the Interest & Part of the Principle or where the Interest is payable in Europe there the Principle of the public Debts at the same time taking Care that the Debt of highest Interest be paid first.

(4) In Order to raise the Value of the Money which is always a saving to the public it will be proper.

1st. To take off all Restrictions upon the Sale of every Commodity Gold and Silver not expected.

2dly. As soon as a State of the public Debts can be made out after adopting the other Plans proposed to publish such State and thereby undeceive the Public who think it much greater than it really is.

3dly. To devise a proper Mode of calling all those to Account who have received any public Monies and provide Checks in the further Issues of which more hereafter.

(5) In providing Money for the public Exigencies I would observe that from January to January Congress should Vote a particular Sum, for Instance 20,000,000 Dollars of which 10,000,000 should be raised by the several States by Tax and the Remainder on Loan in America and as at present 27 Livres Tournois are equal to 15 Dollars supposing Exchange to fall so low as that a Dollar shall be worth two Livres then a Credit of 20,000,000 Livres Tournois will enable us to buy up a Sum of Paper Money equal to the whole Tax by which Means the Cash will be in the public Coffers in Advance and the Credit of the Money at Home just as high as we chuse to make it for by this Means the public will not be indebted to its own Subjects one Shilling more after borrowing 10,000,000 Dollars than before, and the circulating Medium will be 10,000,000 less and as the foreign Debt is to be paid in Produce whenever the Money is made valuable the Produce will become cheap & the Debt consequently small, for Instance, 5 Livres as above will purchase 2½ Dollars which in the State of New York will purchase one Bushel of Wheat but the Money being made valuable as above the Wheat may be bought for one such Dollar, that is for the same Money two Bushels and an half of Wheat may be purchased which in France will sell for twenty Livres Wherefore 5 Livres borrowed and invested in Paper now will pay twenty Livres hereafter or in other Words the Debt is lessened ¾ tho By pursuing the above Plan with Judgment it will be very easy to regulate the Value of our Money which ought not be very high for the following Reasons. 1st. The Pay of our Soldiery is now fixed at 6½ Dollars per Mo. which at par Exchange is 1/Stg. per Day but at present about 4d½ or less If Exchange be lowered to 2½ Livres for 1 Dollar in Paper the Pay of the Soldiery will be 6d per Day. 2dly. The Money being below Par thus much, that is 2½ instead of 5, We shall by paying our Interest in France give in Effect 12 per Cent which will finally bring all our Money into our own Coffers so as that our Subjects will eventually be our Chief Creditors the Good Reasons for which in sinking the Debt are obvious. 3dly. It will enable us to regulate our Contracts for Supplies to the Army as we please of which more hereafter. Many other Reasons will shew themselves in the Course of time.

These Means being pursued to get Money and render it valuable the next Consideration is to be cautious in the Expenditures without which it is impossible to provide Funds even could we mortgage the Mines of Potosi. (1) The Treasurey Board, the Navy Board, and the Commercial Board, I am unacquainted with but I must confess that I wish to see all this Business executed by Commission[er]s.

1. The Treasury Board should consist of three Parts, the Treasurer,

Auditor & Comptroller. The Auditor should be a Gentleman of Great Industry, Accuracy & Integrity & have in his Office at least six Gentlemen each of them a good Accomptant & faithful which six should form two Chambers, one of Dues the other of Claims. The former should adjust all Accompts brought into the Treasury for Payment, the other All Accompts unsettled where it is supposed that the Public Money lies in the Hands of Individuals. These Accompts being Adjusted should be laid before the Auditor (who should be impowered by the several States to call Persons to accompt by particular Process) and he should examine them & mark them thus Audited for the Sum of this Day of 177 , and sign it, He and the several Chambers under him always taking Care that exhorbitant Prices are not allowed if charged. Copies of these Accounts should be kept in his Office marked filed & Entries made in his Books of the Sums audited and on what Accounts and make Monthly Returns of such Entries made to Congress, then the Accounts with the Vouchers referred to should be handed over to the Comptroller whose Business it should be to examine them anew and see from whom and to whom the Sums audited are payable & pass the same and make proper Minutes thereof in his Books and draw Bills on the Treasurer comformable to the Manner in which such Accompts are passed (to which the treasury Seal is to be put) and make monthly Returns to Congress of the Accompts by him passed. The treasurer is simply to receive and pay Money taking Care that he pay it only to those duly authorized to receive it, to keep the Check Accompt of the Loan Office & the like and ought also to render monthly Accompts to Congress.

The Navy Board or Board of Admiralty ought as I conceive to be submitted to five Intelligent Sea Officers well acquainted with maritime Affairs and otherwise qualified as Men of Business. Untill our naval Affairs are a little more reduced to System it must require Great Knowlege in Sea Affairs upon a large Scale to qualify a Man for a Seat at that Board. Nor shall we find for many Years Persons duly qualified to act in it from having made such things the Object of their Attention as a Branch of political Science. These Persons should from Time to Time make Report as should the Board of War, the treasury Board & the like to an Executive of which more hereafter.

The Commercial Board should consist of the five most intelligent Merchants to be met with. At present it will be their Duty to attend simply to the Commercial Concerns of the Continent but such a Board ought to exist for the Purpose of continually collecting, comparing & examining the Commerce of the Several States, the Course of Exchange &ca &ca by the Help of which they would be enabled to give Information from Time to Time what Laws, Treaties & Regulations would be proper and beneficial, what Number of Seamen could be had in Emergencies & the like.

The Board of War being at present in Commission I shall say Nothing upon that Chapter only that Men of Experience, of Business & acquainted with the Resources of America should be always upon that Board which for many Years Yet to come will have infinite Concerns to attend to. For whether we have Peace or not I state it as certain that we must have some Soldiers & many Magazines of Artillery, Field Equipage, Ammunition & military Stores &ca.

I will here take an Opportunity to observe upon what must strike the Observation of every Gentleman acquainted with our public Affairs. It is that a Body such as the Congress is inadequate to the Purposes of Execution. They want that Celerity & Decission upon which depend the Fate of Great Affairs. Other Reasons not less cogent might be adduced Wherefore it might be proper especially during the War to have either a Committee of three or a single officer such as Chief of the States Who should superintend the Executive Business, receive the Reports of the several Boards of the Secretary for foreign Affairs and the like and prepare the whole in the Form of Memorials for the House where there Authority is necessary & where it is not there to perform the necessary Acts.[2]

(2) The Next Thing which demands a most serious Attention is to involve all the military Affairs of the Continent into one Department which would prevent a Variety of Abuses by which the public is injured in many Respects but particularly by the Destruction of Vast Sums of Money. Thus there are at present a Commissary's Department, a Quarter Masters Department & an Hospital Department to the Northward and no army besides the several Departments clash in Purchases double, treble or quadruple the Number of Persons are employed in procuring the same Articles and the like not to mention the absolute sineCures &ca but the Detail is infinite.

(3) As to the several Staff Departments of the Army viz the Quarter Master's, Commissaries & Hospital in their order.

1. The Quarter Masters Department is open to such an Endless Train of Frauds from the very Nature of the thing that it is impossible to devise any adequate Checks. A thing which hath never as I can learn been done by any Army. The only Way to keep it within any Bounds is by examining the Accounts frequently, the Vouchers accurately, taking Care that the Purchases and Expenditures agree & that Losses, Casualties & the like be properly ascertained, after all the Head of the Department is most to be depended on if he is vigilant, industrious & honest he may do much towards preventing Frauds. Further a constant Return should be required of his Deputies, their Pay & Appointments &ca. where they are &ca. This Detail should be monthly. I would observe particularly that the Article of Forage alone is ruinous without accurate Managemt. Wherefore

there should always be in the Army a Forage Yard and Rations of Forage delivd. with Accuracy as also at the several Magazines and Receipts taken without which the Expenditures should not be allowed. At present any of the Depy. Qur. Mrs. may purchase on the Contl. Acct. & sell on his own Acct. without being detected.

2. The Commissaries Department upon which but too much is to be said. Generally I will venture to affirm that every Step is capitally defective. Let me be indulged in a small Detail. *A* who is a Commissary of Purchases buys 100 Cattle whose Average Weight is in Beef 400, Hide & Tallow 100, in the whole 50,000 wt. for these he gives Certificates at 25 per Ct. Advance upon the Market Price supposing that to be 1/ then his Certificates are at the Rate of 1/3 and to color it the Cattle estimated and marked accordingly to weigh on an Average 600. 50,000 wt. @ 1/ is £2,500 to which add 1/4 or £625, the Price Charged is £3,125, the Difference he pockets by purchasing the Certificates at a Discount by the Intervention of a third Person. These Cattle are driven at the Public Expense during all Seasons favorable or unfavorable to the Camp. When they get there they consume Forage for which the Army is always in great Distress, grow lean, some of them die, some when killed returned unfit for Use, some sent out of Camp into the Country to be fattened, of the Beef, some putrifies almost all the Tallow is lost, a great Part of the Hides lost, many of them much damaged, the Heads are thrown away, the Entrails & Filth serve to generate putrid Diseases, the Horns are lost, the Feet from which Oil to curry all the Hides might be extracted are also thrown into the general Mass of Corruption, finally the Beef itself in the Hot Weather renders the troops liable to Diseases of a bilious Kind. I say Nothing of the purchases of Spirits, of Vinegar, of Bread, of Pease &ca. &ca.

The Remedy I would here propose is 1st. To contract within particular Districts of Country with Individuals for the Cattle of that District as thus to be delivered at some Place on the Banks of the Rivers Susquehannah, Delaware or Hudsons (where it is to be presumed the Enemy could not penetrate) at a certain Time from so many thousand to so many thousand Wt. of Beef, the Beef to be weighed as thus, the four Quarters, the Hide & the rough Tallow at so much per Pound. At these Places should be the public works necessary and Magazines of Salt, Nitre, Allum, Pot or Pearl Ashes, Barrills &ca. &ca. The Cattle should be here killed the Beef cut into Mess Pieces of 4lb. each and 50 Pieces put in a Barrill with a proper Proportion of Salt, Nitre (or Pot Ashes) & Allum to preserve it. The Hides taken proper Care of. The Tallow made into Candles & Soap. The oil extracted from the Feet. The Tripe taken Care of and the Heads made into portable Soap. It is worthy of Observation that those who contract with the Crown in Ireland clear nothing but the Horns & Hoofs by their Bargain. It may be said that the Transportation of Provisions would be by this Means rendered too expensive to which I answer that the Transportation should be by Water as much as possible and if there be 40 Miles Land Carriage for the Provision of 20,000 Men it will require daily twenty good Teams being eighty Horses whereas the same Men would require 40 large Oxen per Day and with 5 Days Provision before Hand there would be a constant Demand of Forage for 400 large Cattle instead of eighty Horses.

As to Purchases of Flour they may I am confident be better made by Contract than at present as may the Baking Business for which the Contract should be that the Quarter Master provide ovens & Fuel and that the Contractor deliver so many Pounds of Bread as he shall receive of Flour.

Spirits & Whiskey ought by a Resolution to be fixed at a certain Standard in the Delivery to Soldiers for otherwise great Frauds may happen of which more hereafter.

Vinegar which I will venture to say is absolutely necessary to an Army should be procured by Contract in very large Quantities at different Places by which Transportation would be saved and the Article itself if not used one Year be infinitely better the next. So much for the Purchases but in the Issues a still more terrible Scene opens upon us, to trace which let us suppose a Regt. to consist of 500 Rations daily & take the year @ 350 Days, & examine the Perquisites, private & public Frauds.

1st. Perquisites.

500 Rat. Salt Prov. 50 Days is 130 Blls. in each of which is ¼ of a Bushel of coarse Salt @ 40 Dlls per B.	1300 Dlls.
20 Rat. daily on an Average to the Sick in the whole 10,000 @ ⅕ of a Dollar	2000
Perquisites.	3300

Private Frauds.

500 Gills of Rum or Whisky for abt. 250 Days, 125,000 from which deduct ⅓ (sometimes more) and add Water leaves 40,000 say 32,000 or 1000 Galls @ 4d per Gall is	4,000
For Rat. not delivered, scant Weight & Measure &ca &ca say 20 Rat. for 350 Days, 9000 @⅕	1,400
Private Frauds.	5,400

Public Frauds.

500 Rat. fresh Beef @ 1¼ for 300 Days & usual Allowances for Wastage is abt. 200,000 from which the Real Weight killed viz 240,000 deduct ⅙ for false Returns of Wt. by issuing Comy. of Brig. is 40,000 @ ⅛	5,000

Absent on Detachments, With Leave, Deserters &ca. always

some wherefore suppose the whole Regt. abt. 10 Days in the Year during which time they draw Provisions elsewhere is 5000 @ 1/5 1,000

For setling back Rations they give (due Bills) wherefore the whole Quantum being issued & due Bills given to such as do not draw the whole say 20 Daily for 250 Days. 5,000 @ 1/5 1,000

Public Frauds. 7,000

The Account then stands thus

Perquisites	3,300
Priv. Frauds	5,400
Public do.	7,000
	15,700. Peculation on 500 daily, or 157 on 5

Suppose 100,000 Rat. daily issued is three Million Dollars. If to this be added the Frauds in purchasing, Losses from Mismanagemt. &ca. which may be fairly stated at two Millions more this will be five Millions, or 50 Dollars on each Ration supposing them worth 1/3 each to the Public then for a Year it is 120. Now if as the Case is at least 3 Rat. be delivered out on the Continent for every soldier actually in Service then each Soldier must be estimated at 360 Dollars per Annum to feed him from which is peculated & wasted in different Ways to the Amount of 150 Dollars, on the whole it will appear that at least 5 times as much is paid as is necessary. But to remedy this.

1. I observe that for this Purpose as well as many others, it is absolutely necessary to procure Muster Masters and Adjutant Generals well acquainted with their Business and possessing Industry and strict Integrity. These Officers are the great Checks of an Army particularly the former who should at every Muster make Return to the Genl. & to the Board of War noting in the same all Differences between the Musters and the Returns.

2. The Officers of every Rank except Genl Officers should be confined to the drawing of but one Ration which if not drawn should not be paid for and a Subsistence Money equal to their present Rations should be allowed in Lieu of what they are now entitled to Under this Head also we may comprehend another Abuse & the Remedy. No Officer should be allowed to keep a Soldier as his Servant but should be allowed the Sum of 8 Dollars per Mo. to pay & subsist his own Servant.

3. No Ration should be allowed to the sick but the same ought to be specifically drawn for by the Surgeon who in his sick Return should also return the Provisions drawn for to the End that the Orders if improper may be corrected by his Superiors and such Orders should be copied by the Clerk of the flying Hospital weekly & transmitted to the Commissary General. From this Regulation also the

frequent Absence of Surgeons from their Regts. would be prevented a thing much to be lamented at present.

4. No Rations should be drawn unless for those present fit for Duty and where officers on Command & Detachments not joined &ca. draw Provisions either of Commys. or Inhabitants, they should be charged with the same and obliged to pay therefor unless within a Month Copies of their Receipts are by them filed with the Commissary Genl. or his Deputy or Agent, this being the only Means of checking the Waste occasioned by Detachments.

5. The present Pernicious Practice of serving out Rations to Artificers in Places where they can find Subsistence should be stopped since among many other Evils which arise from it the Infinity of Commissaries is by no Means the least.

6. The Quarter Masters in drawing Provisions should be obliged to make duplicate Returns of their respective Regts. & of the No. of Rations drawn and duplicate Receipts of the specific Articles & one Copy of each should be filed with the Adjutant Genl. who should weekly annex to the same a Copy of the Weekly Return of such respective Regt. & send the same to the Comy. Genl. who should be allowed proper Clerks of the Check to examine and check the same.

7. When any Spirits shall be delivered out below the Standard the Qur. Master should be obliged to make up in Quantity the Defect of Quality.

3dly. of the Hospital Department I will venture to affirm generally that it is replete with Abuses of the greatest Consequence.

1st. In the very great Number of Persons employd in it which partly arises from the Number of Departments into which it is divided.

2ly. In the Ignorance of many of its Members owing to the Promotion of improper Persons to higher office originally than they had Right to expect &

3ly. In the Want of Method and Arrangement throughout or rather in the pernicious Systems adapted.

As this Business is not that to which I am most adequate, so on the other Hand I will venture to say that from Inquiry & Attention I have put myself in a Situation not to be quite ignorant of it. By the last Returns prior to which a great Number were discharged it appears there were in Pay of the Cont. 1 Director Genl., 3 Deputy Directors Gen., 2 Assistant Deputy Directors Genl., 3 Phisicians Genl., 3 Surgeons General, 3 Phisicians & Surgeons Genl., 3 Apothecaries General, 30 senior Surgeons, 36 Junior Surgeons, 56 Surgeons Mates and seven Apothecaries Mates over and above all the Regimental Surgeons & Mates & over and above what may be in the Southern Departt. Here it is worthy of Remark that from 1st Jany. to the 1st May all the Sick of our Army were Attended by 1 Senr. & 2 Junr. Surgeons as also 3000 Patients innoculated. To remedy the

Evils in this Business, I would propose to institute a Medical Board to consist of a chief Director Genl., Inspector Genl. & chief Phisician & Surgeon. These three should examine all medical Men Candidates for Office & give Certificates according to their talents. Moreover the Chief Director should mark out the several Places for erecting Hospitals, who should attend at them and the like. The Inspector Genl. should visit & examine the Hospitals from Time to Time & the Conduct of those whose Business it might be to take Care of them & the like, and the Chief Phisician & Surgeon should receive regular transcripts of the Diseases & Wounds with the Prescriptions & Operations & examine the same. Under these Gentlemen should be one Purveyor and three Assistants, one Commissary & such Deputies as Occasion might require, 4 Surgeons & Phisicians, 8 Senior Surgeons, 16 Junior Surgeons & 32 Mates, 1 Apothecary, 2 Assistants & as many Mates as Circumstances might require. These with occasional Detachments from the Regtl. Surgeons in Times of great Sickness would be amply sufficient for an Army of fifty thousand Men if one-fifth were constantly in Hospital besides Accidents. By this also Men of Science might be got into the Service, a thing which would save the Lives of many brave Soldiers.[3]

4. The Cloathier Genls Department will require considerable Attention but for this Purpose it will be proper to appoint a special Committee to examine into this Matter & report some Method of putting Cloathing into the Hands of the Regt. Paymasters with the Prices to be charged the troops.

Finally as to every Department.

It should be an unalterable Decree that whenever any Person in the public Service either in the Quarter Masters, Commissaries or Medical Departments shall be guilty of trading or of following any other private occupation such Person should be discharged & forfeit all the Pay & Appointments of his Office.

And to all this let it be added that exact Discipline in an Army is essential to Oeconomy & without it no possible Arrangments can be effectual.

G.M.

MS (NNC). In the hand of Gouverneur Morris. A 12-page transcript of the last two-thirds of this document, in the hand of James Custer, is in the William Gilmore Simms Collection of Laurens Papers, item 30, deposited at MHi.

1 There are few clues in this draft address to Congress for establishing precisely when Morris penned it. "The present Situation of our Affairs" to which he refers in his opening statement, for example, must remain a matter of conjecture. In the most thorough analysis of the document yet undertaken by a student of Morris' congressional career, Mary-Jo Kline concluded simply that it was composed during the period June-August 1778. Morris' reference in it to medical department returns of May 1 indicates that it could not have been composed before those reached Congress, which might have been several weeks after May 1. And he probably completed it before the end of July, when he was appointed to a committee on the treasury that submitted a report drafted by him which contained several features and details adumbrated in the present document.

The use he intended to make of this proposed address also remains something of a mystery. Kline believes that Morris intended to present it as an address to Congress, but that he eventually decided not to. The document reveals Morris' remarkable knowledge of fiscal and administrative details, matters that were germane to the formulation of congressional policy, but it teems with so many facts and includes such sweeping recommendations that the delegates would certainly have been unable to respond constructively to it had he presented it as a whole.

The document records the ferment of Morris' mind and the remarkable energy that characterized his service in Congress. Young, able, confident, and possessed of an extremely facile pen, he was a member of nearly a third of the congressional committees appointed in 1778 and the author of a large percentage of the reports generated by those committees. As a member of the committee at camp during the winter of 1778, he had acquired detailed knowledge of numerous problems related to the army's distress, and his admiration of Washington made him a passionate supporter of the various reforms proposed for "arranging" the army that occupied Congress into the spring and summer, including the half-pay plan that monopolized the delegates' attention in April and May. Something of an optimist by nature, he was also generally confident that America could resist British conquest. Thus when news arrived at York that a Franco-American alliance had been negotiated at Paris in February and that the North ministry was prepared to launch a new peace initiative, he apparently concluded that Britain would not long be able to prosecute the war and that America would be victorious if she could but maintain her army in the field and stave off fiscal collapse. In such a mood, Morris focused his thoughts on the reforms that would yet be required and took up his pen to set forth a comprehensive plan for Congress' consideration.

Although his plan was probably never presented in this form, several of the features contained in it did find expression in proposals Morris subsequently laid before Congress during the summer and autumn of 1778. Read in this light and viewed in the context of the conditions faced by Congress and the army at this time, Morris' proposals offer many insights into the complex issues confronted by the delegates during this difficult period.

For an analysis of Morris' congressional activities in 1778, several of which directly pertained to issues developed in this document, see Mary-Jo Kline, *Gouverneur Morris and the New Nation, 1775–1778* (New York: Arno Press, 1978), pp. 109–26. See also *JCC*, 11:731, 779–86, 843, 12:929–33, 956–63; Committee at Camp to President Laurens, February 5, 6, 11, 12–25, 14, 24, and March 2, 3; and Morris to Robert R. Livingston, August 17, 1778, notes 2 and 3.

2 Morris' interest in the creation of an executive committee is also expressed in the following undated draft resolve, which is in his hand, located in the Gouverneur Morris Papers, NNC. No evidence has been found, however, to indicate that he ever submitted the motion to Congress.

"Whereas Experience hath shewn that the Congress of the United States cannot go through the Variety of Business which necessarily comes before them And, Whereas in Cases which require speedy executive Acts Great Delays do at Times arise to the public Detriment, Resolved that an executive Committee be appointed to consist of   Members which Committee shall do the Business of the executive Department being always accountable for their Conduct to Congress, That the said Committee shall receive the Reports of the Board of War and lay such of them before Congress as require their legislative Authority."

3 These recommendations for improving the administration of the Continental hospitals were expanded by Morris in the following proposed resolutions, which he may have drafted in connection with his official work on the Medical Committee. Although he had been a member of that committee since April 18, 1778, it seems probable that Morris penned this undated document, which is also in his hand and located in the Gouverneur Morris Papers, NNC, some time after writ-

ing the preceding remarks on abuses in the hospital department. It is possible that this was the unidentified motion "respecting the medical department" offered in Congress on November 4, 1778, but no evidence has been found to confirm this conjecture, and it contains no specific information that can be used to determine when Morris wrote it. See *JCC*, 10:366, 12:1101.

"Whereas it hath been found by Experience that the Rules and Regulations adopted for the Hospitals, Surgeons & other, the medical Departments within these united States are materially defective and great Evils have thence arisen to the public Service and much Expence unnecessarily accrued for Prevention thereof in future and to the End that the Officers and Soldiers who may fall sick or be wounded in the Defence of their Country may be attended and treated with the utmost Care, Tenderness and Humanity which Circumstances & Situation will admit of, It is Resolved as follows to wit.

"Resolved that there be one Director of the Hospitals, one Chief Phisician & Surgeon and one Inspector of the Hospitals & Surgeons of the united States appointed by Congress that they do each of them receive the Sum of Dollars per Month Pay, Dollars per Month Subsistence, Dollars per Month for their Horses and also their reasonable travelling Charges in the Public Service.

"Resolved that the said three Officers or any two of them do form a Board for the Superintendance of all the medical Affairs of these States and that they be allowed for an Office, Pens, Paper &ca the Sum of Dollars per Month and for a Clerk the Sum of Dollars per Month. That the Duty of the said Board be to examine all Candidates for any medical Office and to grant to them Certificates of their Qualifications directed to the Board of War the which Certificates shall at the Request of such Candidates be filed in the said Office there to be of Record in Case Vacancies shall offer, and where no such Recommendations be and a Vacancy shall happen when the said Board cannot in due Season be convened then any one of the said Board with the Assistance of two or more of the Phisicians and Surgeons hereafter mentioned shall be impowered to examine and grant such Certificates as aforesaid, the which Certificates shall be in the Form following. "Medical Board at——the Day of 177 Present &ca. To the Board of War A B of the in the County of in the State of having been carefully examined appears to be well qualified for the Office of whereof as in Duty bound we certify you"—And the same shall be signed by such of the said Board as shall approve of the Candidate Provided that without a Majority no Certificate shall be granted. That the said Board shall meet at least once in every three Months & from Time to Time issue their Orders to the Purveyor what to provide and where to distribute the several Articles and Things by him purchased. And also shall from Time to Time make such Rules & Regulations for the Hospitals, hospital or regimental Surgeons, Apothecaries & Commissaries of the Hospital as they shall deem expedient for the public Service the which Rules and Regulations are hereby declared to be of full Force and Effect Provided always that the same shall be regularly transmitted to the Board of War and also to the Commander in Chief or of a separate Army. That the said Board whether at their regular Meetings to be by them appointed or at any special Meeting to be called by the Director for particular Purposes shall have a general Controuling Power, Superintendance & Direction not only of all Officers in the several Hospitals but also of all Regimental Surgeons & Surgeon's Mates & be impowered to remove any Phisician or Surgeon or Surgeons Mate from his Office for Neglect of Duty, Mal Conduct or Incapacity. And also that they or either of them or (if the Service shall require it and neither of them be present) one of the sd. Phisicians & Surgeons shall be and they hereby are impowered to call any of the Regimental Surgeons or Mates to do Duty in the Hospitals on special Occasions and to assign the Care of the Sick of any such Regiments to such other regimental Surgeon as shall be expedient. And also on

Complaint made and Evidence of great Neglect, Insufficiency or Mal Conduct to the Detriment of the Public Service or of his own personal Knowl[ed]ge to suspend any Officer either of the Hospital or a Regimental Surgeon or Mate untill the Determination thereon of the Board certifying unto them such Suspension with the Cause thereof & the Evidence, which Officer so suspended shall be immediately incapable of drawing any Pay or Subsistence untill by the said Board he shall be reinstated in his Office.

"Resolved that it shall be the Duty of the Director to determine and direct by and with the Advice and Consent of the Commander in Chief or of any seperate Army the Situation & Number of Hospitals and also that it shall be his Duty to direct how many and which of the Medical Officers hereafter mentioned shall attend at such Hospitals respectively And shall be impowered to appoint & remove from Time to Time or cause to be removed and appointed such inferior Officers as may be necessary at the several Hospitals. That he shall receive weekly Returns from the several superior medical officers at the Different Hospitals, Posts and Places and shall transmit General Monthly Returns to the Commander in Chief and to the Board of War. And shall direct the Distribution of such Medicines and Stores as may from Time to Time be purchased or in Possession of the proper Officers unto and among the several Hospitals and Posts. That he shall from Time to Time visit such of the Hospitals as may by him be visited consistently with his other Duties and shall certify their State and Condition to the Board of War and to the Commander in Chief by contingent Returns from Time to Time as such Visitations shall happen to be made.

"Resolved that it shall be the Duty of the Chief Physician and Surgeon from Time to Time to regulate the Practice of Physic and Surgery in the Army & Hospitals of these States for which Purpose and also to prevent unnecessary and dangerous Innovations regular weekly Returns shall be made to him from every Hospital of the sick and wounded their Diseases and the Prescriptions, Operations and general Mode of Treatment as well as to Diet as Medicine to check which Returns the Prescription Books shall be delivered to him once in every six Months. That the said Chief Phisician and Surgeon shall be impowered from Time to Time to order the Purveyor to purchase and the Apothecary to dispense such additional Medicines, Stores, Instruments and Dressings as he may from Time to Time deem necessary & proper. And further to make such Temporary Appointments to be afterwards approved of as Circumstances may require.

"Resolved that it shall be the Duty of the Inspector constantly to visit the Hospitals, examine into all the Detail, see Whether the several Officers do their Duty whether the Hospitals are kept clean and good Order preserved in them and Whether a proper Attention is paid to the sick, wounded and convalescent Patients Upon all which he shall make special Reports to the Director to be by him laid before the Board."

John Hancock to Dorothy Hancock

My Dear, Philadelphia July 1st. 1778

The Inclos'd was design'd to have been forwarded by Mr. Fessenden, but his ill health prevented. I therefore forward it by the Post, and must very earnestly request your serious Attention to its Contents; I will only Add that I am made exceedingly unhappy by not having any kind of Intelligence from you & the Family, I did not expect this Conduct after my Repeated Solicitations on this head. I had many things to propose respecting my Domestick concerns, but as I am kept so ignorant of the present State of them, I must Submit to suffer them to go on without my Interference. How happy should I have felt to have Experienc'd a different conduct. Absence from you is of itself sufficiently disagreeable, without any Aggravating Circumstances. I will however hope that some Friend will give me the pleasure of hearing from my Family, it would be as refreshing to me as Cool Water to a Thirsty Soul.

I Congratulate you & all my Friends on the happy & glorious Issue of the Engagement on Sunday last. The Two Armies Engag'd in the Jersies, we forc'd them from the Field & Encamp'd on the Ground, The Loss on either Side not yet known, theirs much more than ours, they have lost some Field Officers, among their Slain is Col Monckton, brother to General Monckton; as soon as particulars come you shall know them. I inclose Copy of a few Lines Rec'd from General Washington.[1] Col. Walter Steward, whom you know, is wounded & several other of our Officers whose names I do not Recollect; a Captain in Col Jackson's Regimt. it is said is mortally wounded, but I cannot learn his name. Jackson's Regiment was order'd from hence to harrass the Rear of the Enemy. This will be a dear Remove to General Clinton's Army, it is the universal opinion that should Clinton reach New York, his army will be lessen'd 4000 in effective men; Desertion has taken very deep Root. This Battle has so discompos'd, & Ruin'd Clinton's Army, that it is hardly possible they should be able to effect any Operations this year; in short the Game is over with them. Do Congratulate all my Friends, give them the Substance of this Scrawl, I write in great haste, being much Engag'd in the Business I came from York Town upon.

Remember me to every Friend, I will write them as soon as I get settled, have not got Lodgings, have some thoughts of Taking Mr. Williams's house, if I should, & I find I must Tarry here, I shall take the Liberty of Sending for you, but have come to no Determination. The Confederation will soon be Ratified, & a new Congress will bring on the Conclusion of my Plan.

May the best of Heaven's Blessings ever attend you, My Dear, & believe me with the Strongest Affection, Yours forever

John Hancock

[*P.S.*] Do Employ some person just to let me know if all my Letters have Reach'd you.

RC (DLC). Addressed: "To Mrs. Hancock At her House near the Common, Boston. Mr. Hastings is Requested to Send this Letter as soon as possible after its arrival."

1 General Washington's brief letter of June 29 reporting the battle of Monmouth on June 28 is in Washington, *Writings* (Fitzpatrick), 12:128–29.

Samuel Holten's Diary

[July 2–3, 1778]

July 2. Attended in Congress, & Congress adjourned to 10 oClock tomorrow morning.[1]

3. Attended in Congress, & Congress adjourned to 10 o'Clock to morrow morning; This has been a very rainey day; no News material.

MS (MDaAr).

[1] Failing to secure a quorum until July 7, Secretary Thomson recorded the following statement in the journals when he resumed his minutes that day: "According to adjournment, the president and a number of members met at the State House in Philadelphia on Thursday the 2d, and adjourned from day to day, to the present." *JCC*, 11:671.

Samuel Adams to Samuel P. Savage

My dear Sir Philade July 3d 1778

Yesterday I arrivd in this City and to day I have the Pleasure of receiving your Letters of the 10th & 18th of June, the last of which inclosd the News Papers of that Day. I observe a Paragraph under the Head of Paris the 15th of April, mentioning the Arrival of Mr Adams a few days before. I hope it is true; but I wonder that no Notice was taken of it in a Letter from Portsmouth of the 22d of the same Month, which mentions the sailing of the Commissioners from St Helens on the 21st and this was taken from a London Paper of the 25th ten days after the announcing of his Arrival in Paris.[1] Capt Courter brought us nothing new from France. You have commonly had News from Europe earlier than we, though not so authentically. Your Papers give us brilliant Accounts from that Quarter. "Spain has this day avowd her Acknowledgement and Support of the Independence of America"—"It is expected that Holland will be the next Power to recognize the Independence of America" &c &c. These Things we expected to hear of before this Time. They are the Effects of Instructions given to the Agents of Congress so long ago as while they were at Baltimore in Decr. 76,[2] and at a Time when the Enemy were striding through the Jerseys. Our Affairs were then at a low Ebb indeed; but *Nil desperandum* was the Motto of the *true* Patriots of America. Heaven has since done great Things for us, for which, I fear, we are not so thankful as we ought to be. Our Army has gaind considerable Advantages over the Enemy since they left this City. The Particulars are not yet come to Hand. You will doubtless have them before I shall be able to inform you of them. I now begin to promise my self the Pleasure of seeing the Liberties of our Country establishd on a solid Foundation. It will then be my most earnest Wish to be releasd from all publick Cares, and sit down with my Family and a little Circle of *faithful* Friends in the Cottage of Obscurity. There we will give Thanks to the God of Heaven for the great Things he has done for America, and fervently pray that she may be virtuous, without which she cannot long enjoy the Blessings of Freedom.

I am greatly concernd for my dear native Town, lest after having stood foremost in the Cause of Religion & Liberty she should lose her Glory. We may say *inter Nos*, Her Principles & Manners have had great Influence in securing the Liberties of America. But has she not exchangd her manly Virtue, for Levity & Luxury and a Train of ridiculous Vices which will speedily sink her in Contempt. I am affraid the Cry of too many is, *Quærenda Pecunia primum est!*—"Get Money, Money still, And then let Virtue follow if she will!" The inordinate Love of Gain, will make a shameful Alteration in the Character of those who have heretofore sacrificed every Enjoyment to the Love of their Country. He is the best Patriot who Stems the Torrent of Vice, because that is the most destructive Enemy of his Country. Adieu my Friend. S A

[*P.S.*] My Friendly Regards to Mrs Savage, Mr Scollay &c &c.

The inclosd Letters from General Washington have been receivd & publishd since writing the foregoing.[3]

RC (MHi).

[1] The news of John Adams' arrival at Paris, which was taken from a captured London newspaper, had been reprinted in the June 18 *Independent Chronicle* at Boston.

[2] See these *Letters*, 5:629–35, 695–97.

[3] Adams is referring to General Washington's letters to President Laurens describing the battle of Monmouth, which were printed in the July 6 supplement of the *Pennsylvania Packet*. See Henry Laurens to Washington, July 7, 1778, note 1.

James Lovell to Abigail Adams

Dear Madam July 3d. 1778

I have this Afternoon received your Favour of June 12th and at the same Time a Gazette from Boston, of later Date, in which I find a pleasing Entry in Regard to Mr. Adams's Arrival in France. It is so likely to be true from the blundering Manner of it that I venture to congratulate you upon it.

Mr. Thaxter is not yet arrived here,[1] but is expected hourly. He will heartily participate in the Joy of your Family.

Disgrace pursues the Army of our Enemies in their Passage from this City. The particulars are not yet come to Hand of the Battle at

Montmouth; but we know it has been very fatal to the best of the British Troops. I shall communicate the partial Account this Day to Mr. Adams, and acquaint him with the Health of his dearest Friend and her little ones.

Nothing can exceed the Filthiness of the Houses which have been occupied by the Enemy here; but, externally, the central Part of the City does not appear much abused. The northern Liberties as they were called are gone intirely, and Southwark has been much injured. The Schuylkill appears from five miles Distance; so totally have the Woods and Orchards been destroyed.

I think you need not apprehend a Visit from the shattered Army now at Sandy Hook. The Desertion which prevails must shortly ruin it. When the foreign Troops were sent for to support the broken Grenadiers and Light Infantry of the British Divisions, it was answered that *many* of the *Officers* were willing to obey but *none* of the *Soldiers*.

I am continually Yr. affectionate humble Servant,

James Lovell

RC (MHi). Adams, *Family Correspondence* (Butterfield), 3:55.

1 That is, Philadelphia.

Samuel Chase to Thomas Johnson

Dear Sir Philada. July 4th. 1778

I Received your favor by Capt. Jarrold, with one from Mr. Wallace. I have with pleasure rendered him every Service in my Power. He goes off this Morning with the Certificate of Mr Deane, Mr Carmichael, and the Depositions of the prize Master & Mr. George Digges, which sufficiently prove the Pass granted by our Commissioners.

Your Letter by Mr. Randall was delivered. We advised him not to purchase any Quantity of Rum, as all articles especially West India are falling. We will attend to the Shirting. I do not believe our Army will want Cloathing this Year. It appears by the Returns of the Cloathier General, that We now have sufficient for 22,000 Men.

I was yesterday favoured with your Letter of last Fryday. No Application has been made to Congress for Leave to export to Burmuda, nor do I believe it will be granted. The Virginia Delegates discredit the assertion that their State has granted Leave.[1]

We have no News from Europe, except that the King of Prussia and the Emperor are going to War with each 250,000 fine Troops. No Intelligence from Rhode Island.

I wish You Health & Happiness and am, Dear Sir, Your Affectionate, obedt. Servt. Saml. Chase

RC (MdAA).

[1] Although there is no evidence in the journals or PCC that Congress at this time received a request for or considered granting exemptions to the embargo adopted on June 8, 1778, charges that Maryland was permitting the export of embargoed products from Baltimore were aired in Congress in September. In October Congress reaffirmed its determination to maintain the embargo in force (extending it from November 15 "till the last day of January, 1779"), as it did again in November in response to a petition asking an exemption permitting the export of grain to Bermuda. See *JCC*, 12:903, 976–79, 1165–66; and *Md. Archives*, 21:195–97, 199, 202, 205–6.

Samuel Holten's Diary

[July 4, 1778]

4. It being the Anniversary of the Independence of America, the Congress dined together at the city Tavern & a number of the Council of this State, several Genl. officers & other Gentn. of Distinction, & while we were dining there was an Agreeable band of Musick, & we had a very elegant diner.[1]

MS (MDaAr).

[1] Although a quorum of delegates had not yet gathered in Philadelphia, an informal congressional decision on the subject of the celebration of independence day was communicated to the public by means of the following notice printed in the July 4 issue of John Dunlap's *Pennsylvania Packet*. "Friday, 3d July, 1778. Notice is given to the inhabitants of Philadelphia that the Honorable Congress does not expect they will illuminate their houses to-morrow evening. Lewis Nicola, T[own] M[ajor]."

This effort to conserve candles is a reminder of the austere conditions Philadelphians faced during the period immediately following the British evacuation of their city. But those conditions by no means prevented a spirited celebration of the fourth of July, as the following vivid description by William Ellery, written sometime after his return to Rhode Island three weeks later, attests.

"The glorious fourth of July, I celebrated in the City Tavern with Brother Delegates of Congress and a number of other Gentlemen, amounting in the whole to about 80—the anniversary of Independency. The entertainment was elegant and well conducted. There were four Tables spread, two of them extended the whole length of the Room, the other two crossed them at right angles. At the end of the Room opposite the upper Table, was erected an Orchestra. At the head of the upper table and at the President's right hand stood a large baked Pudding, in the centre of which was planted a Staff on which was displayed a crimson Flag, in the midst of which was this emblematic device: An eye, denoting Providence, a Label in which was inscribed an appeal to heaven; a man with a drawn sword in one hand, and in the other the Declaration of Independency, and at his feet a scroll inscribed 'The declaratory acts.' As soon as the Dinner began, the Musick consisting of Clarinets, Haut-boys, French horns, Violins and Bass Viols, opened and continued making proper pauses until it was finished. Then the Toasts followed each by a discharge of Fieldpieces, were drank, and so the afternoon ended. In the evening there was a cold collation and a brilliant exhibition of Fireworks. The Street was crowded with People during this exhibition. In the afternoon a strumpet, I suppose, with a head-dress in imitation of those worn by the Tory Ladies while the British Army held the City, was paraded thro' the

Streets attended by a crowd of the vulgar. What a strange vicissitude in human affairs! These, but a few years since, colonies of Britain, are now free, sovereign and independent States, and now celebrate the anniversary of their Independence in the very city where but a day or two before Genl Howe exhibited his ridiculous Champhaitre!" Henrietta C. Ellery, ed., "Diary of the Hon. William Ellery, of Rhode Island, June 28–July 23, 1778," *PMHB* 11 (1887): 477–78.

And the following account of this celebration by Congress of the fourth was printed in the July 6 supplement to the *Pennsylvania Packet.*

"Saturday the fourth of July, the glorious Anniversary of the INDEPENDENCE OF AMERICA was celebrated by the Honorable the Congress with a grand festival at the City Tavern in this metropolis. The principal civil and military officers and strangers in town were present at it by invitation. After dinner the following Toasts were given by the Honorable the President of Congress:

"1. The United States of America.
2. The Protector of the Rights of Mankind.
3. The Friendly European Powers
4. The happy era of the Independence of America.
5. The Commander in Chief of the American Forces.
6. The American Arms by land and sea.
7. The Glorious 19th of April, 1775.
8. The Glorious 26th of December, 1776.
9. The Glorious 16th of October, 1777.
10. The 28th of June, twice Glorious, 1776–1778.
11. May the Arts and Sciences flourish in America.
12. May the People continue Free forever.
13. May the Union of the American States be perpetual."

William Henry Drayton to William Alexander

My Lord. Philadelphia July 5. 1778

While I present my thanks for your favour of the 30 ultimo, I snatch the opportunity to present my personal thanks for your distinguished services on the 28th,[1] services glorious to yourself, & truly important to the United States. The Hero Stirling has done much, very much to raise the resources of the States to Sterling value.

Your Lordships name & actions are in every mouth & ear: they will give employment to the pen of the historian. My Lord, you have far advanced in the road of Fame: it is a dangerous defile: you have my most affectionate wishes, that you may pass it with glory & safety.

I need not tell your Lordship, how happy you make me by honouring me with your correspondence. As I flatter myself you will continue it, I beg leave to tell you how you may make it more agreeable to me. It will be made so, by being more particular respecting your own proceedings. I am My Lord with the greatest respect, Your Lordships most obliged & humble Sert. Wm. Hy. Drayton

RC (NN).

[1] A reference to Alexander's conduct of the artillery at the battle of Monmouth.

William Henry Drayton to George Washington

Sir. Philadelphia July 5. 1778.

While I am sensible that I hazard your Excellency's censure of my discretion; yet, I cannot resist the impulse I feel, to pay you my little tribute of thanks for the important Victory of Monmouth; and to express, how much I feel myself tenderly & anxiously interested in every thing respecting your safety and glory. Your Excellency's invariable conduct, naturally exposes you to such intrusions; and I rely upon it, that your good nature will pardon this.

Personally almost unknown to you as I am, yet Sir, this obstacle is too weak to prevent a gratification on my part, which gives me the highest pleasure. Some how or other, Nature has composed me of materials, which are apt to force the bounds of common decorum, when my affections and gratitude are excited.

That your Excellency's life may long be preserved in your glorious and disinterested defence of your country; & in the enjoyment of the fruits of your labours and victories, is my most fervent prayer: being Sir, Your Excellency's most obligd & most humble sert.

Wm. Hy. Drayton

RC (MH–H).

Richard Henry Lee to Francis Lightfoot Lee

My dear Brother, Philadelphia 5th July 1778

I wrote you four days ago by Mr. Armstead who promised to send the letter[1] to Mount Airy by his Servant from Fredericksburg. Since that we have had a more accurate account of the battle in the Jersies from Gen. Washington. The number of the enemies dead buried by our people was 252, and several graves besides on the field in which they had buried their dead during the Action. Upon the whole, the battle was fairly won by our Army, & the best troops of Britain beaten in an open field. The whole loss of the enemy in killed, wounded, & deserters is at least 3000 since they left this City. The American Army is now at Brunswick and will presently proceed to the North river. Gen. Conway came here the other day, and having been informed of some disrespectful words spoken of him by Gen. Cadwallader, the former challenged the latter and they met on the Common yesterday morn. They threw up for the first fire & Cadwallader won it. At the distance of 12 paces he fired and Shot Conway thro the side of the face, on which he fell & was carried off the field. He is supposed not to be in danger unless an unforeseen inflamation should produce it. We had a magnificent celebration of the anniversary of Independence yesterday, when handsome fireworks were displayed. The Whigs of the City dressed up a Woman of the Town with the Monstrous head dress of the Tory Ladies and escorted her thro the Town with a great concourse of people. Her head was elegantly & expensively dressed. I suppose about three feet high and of proportionable width, with a profusion of curls &c. &c. &c. The figure was droll and occasioned much mirth. It has lessened some heads already, and will probably bring the rest within the bounds of reason, for they are monstrous indeed. The Tory wife of Dr. Smith, has christened this figure Continella, or the Dutchess of Independence, and prayed for a pin from her head by way of relic. The Tory women are very much mortified notwithstanding this. As we have left York, and Dunlap publishes a Gazette here, I have entered your name with him instead of Hall & Sellers, & I shall pay him for your years papers. I have directed him to send me your paper weekly, whilst I stay, that I may inclose it to you. We have heard nothing from the English Commissioners since our answer from York, and I suppose they conclude us less liable to be amused since the late drubbing we have given their Army. I this day went round the enemies lines. They pass from Delaware to Schuylkill so as to include Govr. Hamiltons House about 200 yards within the line, and consist of very strong redoubts at a quarter of a mile distant from each other, and the spaces between guarded by very thick Abbatis made of Apple Trees fast staked down, and the ends of the twigs sharpened. All the houses, except Bush Hill, for a considerable distance without & within the lines are burnt down. My love to Mrs. Lee and kind remembrance to all friends in Richmond. I am most affectionately yours, Richard Henry Lee

RC (ViHi).
1 Not found.

Josiah Bartlett to Mary Bartlett

My Dear Philadelphia July the 6th 1778

In my last of the 28th June from York Town I informed you of the Removal of the Congress to this place & that I Should tarry there a Short time on account of Mr Wentworths Sickness: on Thursday the 2nd Inst Mr Wentworth being better, I left him & his waiter there, & arrived at this place on Saturday Evening. Yesterday I Recd yours of the 4th & of the 13th of June, and am very Sorry to be informed that Rhoda is not so well as She was for some time before. However I hope & trust She is better again, and in due time will Recover her former health & strength if it is for the best & consistent with the will of the great Ruler of all Events. If she should

Remain in a poor State of health, I would have you use your discretion about taking the advice of Dr. Rowe or Ordway & any other you may think proper; But you know my opinion, that proper Exercise, air & Diet & to keep the mind as Easy & Contented as possible in Such Disorders, is of much more Service that a multiplicity of Medicines, Tho some I make no Doubt will be useful.

I have not time to write you any news at present as I am looking out for a place to board at & find Great Difficulty in procuring a place, I write this in a tavern where I put up at present, I will try to Enclose you the latest news paper, which will inform you of the news here. Give my Respects to Mr Thurston & tell him I will Endeavor to answer his letter next post.[1] I have not had time to view the City & Know what Destruction is made by the Enemy, will inform more next post.

I can now inform you & my Children that there will be no Difficulty in Deviding our prize money in the Lottery as Every one of the Tickets in our family are *Blanks*. The Nine that I took to Sell are all Blanks Except one I sold to Mr Peterson & one I sold to Mr Griffing, they have each a 20 Dollar prize. I Enclose you the list, a Cross is made at the End of the Blanks & the figure 20 at the End of the prizes. Tell Polly & Lois I Recd their letter and am Glad they Remember me. Yours &c J. Bartlett

P.S. I had like to have forgot to tell you I am in good health. Charles Chace is well; Mr. Wentworth had a fever for about 10 or 12 Days with a Billious vomiting & purging, much like Mr Thurstons last fall, but began to mend on Tuesday & was much more Comfortable when I left him, hope he will be here in a week or ten Days from this time.

I Expected to have Sent this off this morning but the post not Seting off till to morrow I have time to write a little more.

Genl Washingtons account of the Battle in the Jersies I have inclosed, The Enemy are getting aboard their Ships by the last account and it is the Common opinion that the whole of them will Soon quit the United States.

2, of the Clock afternoon, the post has just arrived & Brought me your Letter of the 20th June which has made my mind Easier about Rhoda, hope She will continue to mend. I Dont think of any thing proper for me to advise her to use more than I formerly mentioned to you, The Tincture of antimony in Small Doses may likely be Serviceable, however you & Dr Gale will be able to Judge by the opperation. I hope hereafter our letters will Pass to & from Each other Quicker & more certainly than before as this place is 60 miles at least nearer to you than York Town.

I hope Sally is well as hers was only a Great Cold. I am Glad to hear there is a good prospect of the fruits of the Ground; About ten

Days preceeding last Thursday was as Severely hot, at York Town as was Ever Known so Early in the year: Thursday & Friday we had Severe Thunder & Setled to a Steady rain which Cooled the Air finely. My old Landlady where I formerly Boarded, is full of Lodgers, but I have now a prospect of being pretty well accomodated in a few Days with pretty good Lodgings. Remember me to all my Children & to all friends and accept My Sincere Love to your self,

Josiah Bartlett

RC (NhHi).

[1] Bartlett wrote to Benjamin Thurston on July 8, according to Thurston's August 28 letter to Bartlett, but Bartlett's letter has not been found. Bartlett, *Papers* (Mevers), p. 217.

Titus Hosmer to Richard Law

Dear Sir [July 6? 1778][1]

After a most tedious Journey thro Heat and Wet, having been sick five Days by the way, I reached York Town just soon enough to accompany Congress to this place, four Days more of travelling in the hottest Season I ever felt brought me to Philadelphia, where I am at present settled in Lodgings with Mr Sherman at his old Landladys Mrs. Cheeseman & have almost cooled down the fervor which the Extreme heat on the last Stage of my Journey had kindled in my Blood.

Congress before they left York Town had gone thro and considered all the Objections & Amendments proposed by the different states respecting the Articles of Confederation, and upon the whole, to deal impartially, rejected them all and determined to adhere to the Articles as they were settled, Nine States will ratify them as they stand, the remaining four have yet neglected to Instruct & Impower their Delegates to ratify, but it is expected they will soon do it.

Enclosed are printed Copies of General Washingtons Letters giving an Account of the movements of the Army in New Jersey & of the Battle of the 28th Ulto.

The Genl. says five or Six Hundred Deserters is the least Number that have come into his Army, besides these, there are upwards of five Hundred which came directly to this City & here took passes for such places as they chose to retire to, and many more, it is said, are gone directly into the Country, without going to the Army or coming here, a number of which I saw myself at Lancaster. There is a Letter in Town from Lord Sterling in which he gives it as his Opinion that the Enemys Army is lessened Three Thousand by Desertion, skirmishes and in the late Battle since they left this City.

The Tories here tell us that General Clinton is directly to leave the Continent and draw off his Myrmidons, that he has positive Orders to do it, that some are to go to the West Indies, some to England, a little Time will discover the Truth of this Story.

Adieu. If you have any News in Connecticut, or if you have not a Letter will be very acceptable to your obedt. huml Servant,

Titus Hosmer

RC (NjP). Endorsed: "Titus Hosmer Esqr, Letter from Congress, No date Recd in 1778."

1 This letter was written no earlier than July 6 and no later than July 9. In it Hosmer mentioned enclosing "printed Copies of General Washingtons' Letters" dealing with the battle of Monmouth, which were printed in a *Pennsylvania Packet* supplement on July 6, and he indicated that the ratification of the Articles of Confederation by certain states—an event that occurred on July 9—had not yet taken place. *JCC*, 11:677.

Titus Hosmer to Thomas Mumford

Dear Sir

Philadelphia July 6. 1778.

I wrote You at York but had no Opportunity to send my Letter forward till the present,[1] the enclosed printed Letters give so full an Account of the late battle and success in New Jersey I could not deny myself the pleasure of transmitting it to you, at the same Time I can assure you the Account they give of the Enemies loss is modest and much within bounds, the Numbers they carried away & disposed of in the Time of the Action which begun with a Cannonade & skirmishing at Eleven in the forenoon and lasted in the different Attacks untill just dark, they had leisure & opportunity to do, I am assured by a Gentleman of Character on the spot that the numbers buried from the Ground where Genl. Wayne attacked was upwards of Two Hundred & Forty, that is nearly all, what fell in other parts were taken away & buried or sunk in the morass, it was a glorious for the Arms of the United states, an untoward Accident probably prevented the total Ruin of Genl Clinton but as that will be the Subject of a public Enquiry I will at present say no more about it.[2]

I congratulate you most cordially on this Auspicious Opening of the Campaign, may it close with equal Glory and success, one Circumstance should not be omitted, that the Victory is under God to be ascribed to the personal Address, Bravery & presence of Mind of our admired Genl. & Commander in Chief, but General Lees present Situation forbids a further Explanation of the matter at present, in a few Days you will have the whole.

Accept my best Wishes for Yourself, Mrs. Mumford, Your Son (who I hope will be soon at Liberty) & your amiable Daughter, and believe me, your affectionate Friend,

Titus Hosmer

Charles Lee

RC (Robert J. Sudderth, Jr., Lookout Mountain, Tenn., 1973).

1 See Hosmer to Mumford, June 27, 1778.

2 This reluctance to discuss Gen. Charles Lee's controversial conduct during the battle of Monmouth is also found in the surviving extract of a letter written by John Banister this day. "A few days ago," Banister explained to Theodorick Bland, Jr., "I wrote you an account of all the public concerns then appearing of moment. But the inclosed will inform you of an action, which has displayed the military abilities of our general, in the highest point of view. Its consequences on the affairs of America will necessarily be great. General Lee is under great suspicions of misconduct, and bad intentions, but being under arrest, and his trial now going on, I forbear to mention what is related by officers, who were in the battle, and were eye-witnesses of his retreat at the head of 5000 of the best troops in the American army.

"The English army is supposed (not without foundation) to have been lessened in number, from its departure out of this place until this affair happened, between two and three thousand. Their best troops were engaged with our army after the select five thousand had been taken out, and in fair battle were defeated, ours keeping possession of, and sleeping on the field." Theodorick Bland, *Bland Papers*, ed. Charles Campbell, 2 vols. (Petersburg, Va.: Edmund & Julian C. Ruffin, 1840), 1:96.

On July 1 Washington had ordered a court-martial to try General Lee on charges of "disobedience of orders, in not attacking the enemy on the 28th of June . . ., misbehaviour before the enemy on the same day, by making an unnecessary, disorderly, and shameful retreat . . ., [*and*] disrespect to the commander in chief in two letters." Although Lee hoped for speedy vindication, the court did not give its verdict until August 12—finding Lee guilty as charged and sentencing him to be suspended from command for one year—and it was not until December 5 that Congress ordered this sentence to be executed. See *JCC*, 11:824–26; 12:1184–85, 1188, 1195; and Washington, *Writings* (Fitzpatrick), 12:132–33, 147. For discussion of Lee's court-martial and the charges against him, see John R. Alden, *General Charles Lee Traitor or Patriot?* (Baton Rouge: Louisiana State University Press, 1951), pp. 220–58; and Freeman, *Washington*, 5:57–60, 89–90.

Henry Laurens to John Laurens

My Dear son, Philadelphia 6th July 1778

I have before me your acceptable favors of the 30th Ulto. & 2d Inst.[1]—these afford subjects for the exercise of a grateful heart. I thank God for the deliverance of our great & good Commander in Chief & of our Army, from the Snare which had been set for them, for the escape of you my Dear fellow Citizen from the danger to which your duty had necessarily exposed you—& while I bless God for the providential interposition in our favor, I congratulate with my Country Men on the partial Victory gained over our Enemies on the 28th June at Monmouth.

Repair your particular loss immediately by purchasing one of the very best Horses you can meet with & more than one or two if needful, draw on me for the Amount or tell me how I may remit a sufficient Sum.

The term Snare shews the present sentiments of my mind, that my former jealousies respecting the conversation with an old friend at the lines, the reception & lodging Doctr W.[2] were not groundless—these circumstances will naturally recur to your own—but antecedently to either of these, a conversation at York Town, téte a téte which, if the Gentleman had ever been sincere, discovered a change, together with some ungracious hints applied to an Officer whom you & I love, had alarmed me.[3] You will admit too that there were grounds for my suspicions of Sir H.C.'s[4] sincerity in his pretences to leave Philadelphia, at least you will grant the justness of my observation that the whole of that Officers conduct in this City carried the face of Stratagem. Had these not subsisted, a concerted Plan by which our Army was to have been disgraced, perhaps ruined, he would not have subjected himself to the fatigue & hazards of loss by various means, in a Land March, or if necessity had obliged him to undertake it, his Army would have been far enough out of the reach of Ours. Whatever is is best. I now hold my self as much indebted to the Man I suspected, as I am to Judas—whose example in all cases ought to be followed by Men of his disposition.

Certainly for my Country's sake I rejoice at the late happy event, certainly for your sake, but I have a feeling of joy respecting your General which, uncommon as such impressions are on my mind, stronger for an Individual than for a general good, for an Individual stranger than for one so very nearly bound to my heart, seems to overbound all other joy. There are rational grounds for this apparent excess which shall be explained to your conviction & satisfaction whenever I am so happy as to take you into my Arms.

I thank you very much my Dear son for the minute Account of the transactions at Monmouth. Such intelligence enables me to make acceptable transmissions to my friends at home, & without such I should be very barren, for notwithstanding the advantages which I might avail myself of, by the first possession of public Letters from all Quarters, yet the executive parts of my Office & the constant interruptions which I am subject to from visitors, seldom leave me time enough to peruse Letters attentively before I present them to Congress, where they are parceled out to different Boards & Committees & are seen no more by me.

My good friend the Chief Justice has written to you again[5] & I am sure you will make him proper returns—but enter nous, I must tell you that I expect to hold my first place in your correspondence. He has written long circumstantial Circular Letters, to which I had contributed not only all the materials in my power but assisted him also by the Loan of my Secretary which consequently increased my own labour. My Idea was that these Addresses were to have been signed by all the Delegates from So. Carolina or at least that I might upon principles of Justice claim the honor of adding my signature to his,

& so I intimated to him. He jocularly replied, he should not labour for A B & C—& has continued to send forward his dispatches without admitting L. to a fair Coparceny or favouring him with an explanation. L. is not possessed by an appropriating Spirit, he is always happy in fair mutual communications with his friends, but when it becomes necessary he knows how to take care of himself without breaking the line of harmony. His friends in Carolina expect from him ample Accounts of all public affairs & he knows it would vex them to see him forestalled or eclipsed. The Chief Justice is collecting materials for History,[6] every Gentleman will chearfully cast in his Mite for the benefit of Posterity, none more heartily than myself, all I covet is the quiet enjoyment of my own. I often hint to my friend that he loses the enjoyment of Riches in avidity for gain. You know, moderation, & submission to events, have been the lines of my walk.

You will learn from other hands that General Conway received on the anniversary of Independence a Pistol Ball on one side of his Nose which passed to the back part of the Neck where it was extracted by a very light scission. How this came to pass & the condition in which he Lies, the subject is not for me to dwell on.

How can you expect me on the Banks of Rariton, not even the pleasure of riding there with you, the highest but one this World has in Store for me, can tempt me to abandon or neglect my Post, your example instructs your Father, I submit to the painful Separation with chearfulness.

I must now although I have not said half I wish to say take leave of you, & address a few respectful Lines to your General, to the Marquis & to Baron Stuben but before I conclude it will be proper to assure you I shall pay every mark of respect to those worthy heroes enumerated in your Letter when opportunity presents. I now live in a House & in a stile somewhat better than those which I had patiently humbled myself in, from the 28th September to the 27th June at York Town—somewhat below the rank of my Overseers, I have now a Bed for a friend, & Board for half a dozen or more every day. Come see for a fortnight how I live, & let me tell you, you will feel it whether you come or do not come.

Adieu My Dear Son. Persevere in your Duty, God will bless you & make your Father happy. Henry Laurens

[*P.S.*] Your General transmits his dispatches by a common Messenger. I Love & reverence him.

If there shall happen any remarkable circumstances in the Trial of General Lee which are not set forth in the general proceedings of the Court Martial to be transmitted to Congress I request you note them to me.

Doctor Read, a young Gentleman from Georgia, with whom you

were formerly acquainted goes to Camp with a view of improving his knowledge in Surgery by attending in the Hospitals. If you can facilitate his attempts I am persuaded you will.

RC (MHi: William Gilmore Simms Collection deposit, 1973). LB (ScHi). RC damaged; missing words supplied from LB.

1 John Laurens' June 30 and July 2 letters to his father, in which he sharply criticized Gen. Charles Lee's behavior at the battle of Monmouth and urged that he "be tried for misconduct," are in Simms, *Laurens Army Correspondence*, pp. 193–203.

2 Dr. Robert Wellford, a recent defector from the British army and an acquaintance of Gen. Charles Lee whose loyalty to the United States Laurens regarded as suspect. See Laurens to John Laurens, June 17, 1778, note 2.

3 Laurens is referring to an otherwise undocumented conversation he had with Gen. Charles Lee at York shortly after the general's release from British captivity early in April 1778, in which Lee had apparently made some unflattering remarks about Washington. See John R. Alden, *General Charles Lee: Traitor or Patriot?* (Baton Rouge: Louisiana State University Press, 1951), pp. 190–91.

4 Sir Henry Clinton.

5 No letters from William Henry Drayton to John Laurens have been found, except for one of September 7, 1778.

6 Although William Henry Drayton's untimely death in 1779 prevented completion of his intended history of the American Revolution, the notes and documents he compiled for this purpose formed the basis for a work on the subject by his oldest son, John Drayton, entitled *Memoirs of the American Revolution, from its Commencement to the Year 1776 . . .*, 2 vols. (Charleston, S.C.: A.E. Miller, 1821).

Elias Boudinot to Hannah Boudinot

My dearest Love Philadelphia July 7th. 1778

Thro' the goodness of God, I arrived here, after a very disagreeable tedious ride, on Sunday Morning. Yesterday took my seat in Congress,[1] and am unexpectedly and happily lodged at Mr. Thomas Franklins a very agreeable family and one of the most pleasant Houses in the City. I found your two Letters here, which you wrote at Princeton, for which am much obliged, as I am by every thing that suggests my share in the affection of the dearest of Women. My Scene of Labour is opening rather larger than I could wish, but usefulness in Life & a blessed Prospect of Happiness in Death ought to be our continual desire.

How much are we indebted to our gracious Protector for his amazing interposition in our favour on the fields of Monmouth; altho' I suppose you are filled with every Circumstance of that important Day, by this Time, yet I enclose the Letter of our great & worthy General, whose Modesty in the diction is only exceeded by his Bravery in the Execution of the Plan of that great Days work.

My kind Love to the Family, Neighbours & friends. Kiss my dear

Susan. My Stomach still continues disordered, and I am afraid I must have recourse to a Puke.

Am my dearest Wife with a most sincere Affection & Esteem, Your loving, Boudinot

RC (NjP).

1 Since Congress did not achieve a quorum after its return to Philadelphia until this day, the journals record that Boudinot first attended Congress on the seventh. *JCC*, 11:672.

Henry Laurens to George Washington

Dear Sir. Philadelphia 7th July 1778.

I have had the honor of presenting to as many Members of Congress as have been convened in this City since the adjournment from York, Your Excellency's several favors of the 28th & 30th June & 1st Inst: & at their special Instance have caused them to be printed for the information of the Public.[1]

I arrived here on Thursday last, but hitherto have not collected a sufficient number of States to form a Congress, consequently I have received no Commands.[2] Your Excellency will therefore be pleased to accept this as the address of an Individual intended to assure you Sir of my hearty congratulations with my Country Men on the success of the American Arms under Your Excellency's immediate Command in the late Battle of Monmouth & more particularly of my own happiness in the additional Glory atchieved by Your Excellency in retrieving the honor of these States in the Moment of an alarming dilemma.

It is not my design to attempt encomiums upon Your Excellency. I am as unequal to the task as the Act is unnecessary, Love & respect for Your Excellency is impressed on the Heart of every grateful American, & your Name will be revered by posterity. Our acknowledgements are especially due to Heaven for the preservation of Your Excellency's person necessarily exposed for the Salvation of America to the most imminent danger in the late Action; that the same hand may at all times guide & Sheild Your Excellency is the fervent wish of, Dear sir, Your much obliged & faithful humble servant, Henry Laurens

RC (DLC).

1 Washington's June 28, June 29 (not 30), and July 1 letters to Laurens, which dealt with the battle of Monmouth, are in PCC, item 152, 6:139–41, 143, 147–56, and Washington, *Writings* (Fitzpatrick), 12:127–29, 139–46. These Laurens sent to the printer of the *Pennsylvania Packet*, who published them in a July 6 "Supplement" to the July 4 issue along with the following prefatory note:

"Mr. Dunlap, Be pleased to print the following Letters from his Excellency

General Washington, together with the return of the killed, wounded &c. for the information of the good people of these United States. I am, Sir, your most humble servant, Henry Laurens, President of Congress."

2 Laurens must have written this letter early in the morning on the seventh as the journals reveal that later in the day Congress resumed business with ten states in attendance. *JCC*, 11:672–73.

John Mathews to Thomas Bee

Dear Sir Philadelphia July 7th. 1778

I inclose you an account of the action of the 28th June, a day that I imagine will be remembered by Clinton all his life. It is very remarkable that we have never fought a battle but what some of our General Officers have behaved ill, & thro' whose means, it has been principally owing why we have not been so successful, as the bravery of our troops have intitled us to be. Had Lee's conduct been such, as we had reason to expect from him, in this action, in all probability we should have gained a Compleat victory. The body he commanded was the cream of the army, selected for that Service. When the General came up & found him retreating he was very much provoked indeed, & when he asked Lee his reasons for doing so, he replyed: the service he was sent upon, was impracticable to be performed, & that Genl. Washington knew that he had given it as his opinion in the Council that it was so. The General ordered him to retire to the rear & with all the intrepidity, & coolness, that he so eminently possesses put himself at the head of the troops, led them back again, and conquered. The troops he had to contend against were the Granadiers, light infantry, & Cavalry of the British army, but both our Officers & Men were determined to Conquer, & nothing could stand against them, when led on, by their Great & illustrious Commander. Some of the Deserters who have come in since the action, say, that it is allowed by their Officers, they have never yet been so shamefully beaten, not that the loss of Men, have been so great, but that their choicest troops were defeated. It is said that the foreign troops peremptorily refused to fight. There was not one of the General's family, except himself, but what was either wounded, or had their horses shot.

We are thrown into a good deal of confusion with regard to the Confederation. Before we left York Town, Congress proceeded to the consideration of the amendments offered by the different States to the confederation, every one of which have been rejected. It was then ordered to be ingroced, to be ready for ratification when we came to Philadelphia. Now that it is so, Mr. Laurens, Mr. Drayton, & Mr. Hutson say they will not sign it, because they do not think themselves authorized by our instructions to do so, unless the other twelve States will agree to sign it likewise. Maryland has refused to ratify. Mr. Heyward & myself are of a different Opinion, & think we are Authorised, notwithstanding One or even two States were to refuse, nor do I apprehend that inconsistency will arise in the Confederation, from the Defection of one or two States, which these three Gentlemen seem to imagine.[1] However they mean, I believe, to write their sentiments on the subject, either to the Presidt. or to you, to be laid before the Assembly.[2] I do not think it necessary for Heyward & myself to write on the subject, in our public Characters, as we think we are authorised to sign it, but as three are necessary to a final Ratification we must wait for your decision. This I am clear in, from what I have seen, & known, since I have been in Congress, that if we are to have no Confederation untill the Legislatures of the thirteen States agree to one, that we shall never have one, & if we have not one, we shall be literally a rope of sand, & I shall tremble for the consequences that will follow, at the end of this War. France I have good reason to think would never have entered into the Treaties, she has done with us, had she known we were not Confederated, & when the present misunderstanding comes to be spread abroad, I am afraid it will give such an Alarm that those powers, who have lately shewn so good a Disposition to an Alliance with us, will immediately fall back, & stand aloof, untill they can see on what footing our jaring interests are to stand. But suppose they were ever so well inclined who are they to enter into an Alliance with? It can't be with the *United* States. Nor can I conceive they will ever do it with such a body as Congress at present is, bound together by no other Law, than that of the bare necessity of the present situation of our affairs, & lyabel to fall to pieces, from the Ambition or caprice of one or two States, but the Alarm will operate still more strongly still when it is known, that we have attempted to confederate & can't. All Europe for some time past, have looked upon us, as in a State of Confederacy. But the greatest danger in my Opinion yet remains. Is not the Sovereign will & pleasure of Congress at this time the law of this Continent? Some men may deny it, & will, but a late Act of theirs (I mean the case of the Embargo) proves it beyond a doubt.[3] If they can do this, they can do anything else. Are they bound by any Law? Have they any line marked out for their Rule of conduct? No they have not. And it's my sincere belief that some men wish it to continue so. As an individual I have very strong objections to the Confederation, exclusive of what were pointed out by our State,[4] but still, I would rather have this, than none. I think it is beyond a doubt that in the course of the next six months, Great Britain would have offered us our own terms, for peace she must have. But when they come to know that we have begun to split, Why it's just the very thing they have all along been endeavouring to effect. Divide & Conquer, has been their favourite maxim. This will to be sure encourage her to risque another Campaign, it will certainly be their best policy to try the experiment, & they will hardly let so favourable an opportunity slip, without doing something. I have wrote to you for leave to come home in December;[5] for God's sake procure it for me, & I'll be dam'd if ever you catch me here again. Those who have dispositions for Jangling, & are fond of displaying their Rhetorical abilities, let them come. I never was so sick of any thing in my life. This is all under the rose tho', for notwithstanding it's only my private sentiments of things, yet I would not wish to impress on the mind of any one, the least disrespect of Congress. I should be obliged to you for the particulars, respecting the application now made with regard to the Confederation, when decided upon by you.

The enemy are now almost all over on Staten Island. Our army are moving slowly up the No. river. I am, Dr. Sir, with the most sincere regard, your most Obed. servt. J Mathews

RC (ScC). Although Burnett, *Letters*, 3:322, identified former South Carolina president John Rutledge as the recipient of this letter, it is endorsed by Thomas Bee: "1778 John Mathews from Congress July 1st [i.e. 7th] 1778."

1 Henry Laurens, William Henry Drayton, and Richard Hutson seem to have strained the meaning of the South Carolina Assembly's February 4, 1778, instruction on the Articles of Confederation, which merely stated "That the delegates of the State in the Continental Congress, or any three of them, be, and they are hereby authorized, on the part of this State, to agree to and ratify the Articles of Confederation between the United States of America." *JCC*, 11:670. Mathews' and Thomas Heyward's "Opinion" on this point soon prevailed within the South Carolina delegation, and accordingly on July 9 the South Carolina delegates agreed to ratify the Articles of Confederation. *JCC*, 11:677.

2 Bee was speaker of the South Carolina House of Representatives.

3 For the embargo on certain provisions that Congress had approved on June 8, see *JCC*, 11:578–79.

4 On June 25 the South Carolina delegates had offered twenty-one amendments to the Articles of Confederation, all of which were rejected. *JCC*, 11:652–56.

5 Not found.

Thomas McKean to William Atlee

Dear Sir, Philadelphia July 7th. 1778.

On Thursday last Congress met at the State-House, when 13 cannon were discharged on Market street wharff; and on Saturday the Anniversary of Independance was celebrated at the New Tavern, where there was an elegant entertainment, & a fine band of musick. The firing of a vast number of cannon proved that there was no want of powder.

My time has been taken up principally in taking the surrender of the persons proclaimed, and writing recognizances of bail. Not one has been yet committed, nor has any evidence appeared except the general charge in the proclamation, notwithstanding I sit daily in the Court-house from 9 to 11 oclock, and sometimes to 12, having James Young and John Ord Esquires, two of the Justices of the peace here, as assistants to inform me of the abilities of the persons who offer themselves as sureties, and to hear accusers, if any should offer. The Inhabitants appear to be either afraid of one another, or the Whigs cannot yet believe that their friends have the government of the city.[1]

The General Assembly are called by the Council to meet here on the 4th day of August next, in which month we shall be obliged to hold courts of Oyer &c. for Philadelphia, Bucks and Chester. The Supream court must be held on the 24th September being the usual time, and after that we shall find it necessary to go into the other Counties.

Generals Conway and Cadwalader fought a duel on Saturday on the common, as tis said, when the former was shot in the cheek bone and fell the first fire. The wound is said not to be dangerous, and I know nothing of it but by common report, and therefore have not sent for Mr. Cadwalader, especially as it might be attributed by uncharitable persons to resentment rather than justice, as, I have heard, he has made use of very unseemly expressions respecting the Government, and acted in such a manner as savours too much of weaknes and vanity.

Enclosed herewith I send you the Pennsylvania Packet which give an account of the battle of the 28th last near Monmouth Court-House in the Jerseys. General Lee's sentence is not yet known. The Army did well, but had some officers done their duty, it would have terminated in a compleat victory.

Just now I am favoured with your letter of the 3d instant, and for the reasons you assign think it would be for the public good to admit the Chalfants to bail; at all events no public injury can arise from it. James Fitzpatrick is likely to do so much mischief, that I have not a doubt if these young men apprehend him they would get a pardon.

Near forty of the principal persons named in the proclamations of Council have rendered themselves to me, and are to take their trials in the city. We are likely to have business enough in our Stations.

Please to present my compliments to Mrs. Atlee. Adieu, Dear Sir, Your most obedient servant Thos M:Kean

RC (DLC).

[1] For further information on Justice McKean's controversial handling of the hearings and trials for people accused of traitorous or disloyal activities during the British occupation of Philadelphia, see John M. Coleman, *Thomas McKean, Forgotten Leader of the Revolution* (Rockaway, N.J.: American Faculty Press, 1975), pp. 229–31; and Gail S. Rowe, *Thomas McKean: The Shaping of an American Republicanism* (Boulder: Colorado Associated University Press, 1978), pp. 112–20.

Elias Boudinot to Alexander Hamilton

My dear Sir Philadelphia July 8 1778

I had concluded your Laurels had produced a forgetfulness of your old friend, but am now rejoicing in my disappointment having your obliging & very entertaining favour of the 5th Inst. just handed me.[1] With the utmost sincerity I congratulate you & my Country on the kind Interposition of Heaven in our favour on the 28 Ultmo. It seems as if on every Occasion we are to be convinced that our political Salvation is to be as through the fire. I scarcely know whether I am more distressed that any Person engaged in the Cause of America & to whom she *has entrusted her Safety* could be capable of betraying her Interest in the critical moment of decision, or more really gratifyed & pleased that the supreme disposer of human Events is continually baffling not only the formidable & open force of our Enemies, but also the more dangerous & secret Efforts of false or lukewarm Friends. The General I allways revered & loved ever since I knew him, but in this Instance he has rose superior to himself. Every Lip dwells on his Praise for even his pretended Friends (for none dare to acknowledge themselves his Enemies) are obliged to croak it forth. The share that his family (for whom I retain a real friendship) has in the Honors of the day has afforded me real Pleasure, and among the rest none more than that of your Lordship.

The Congress have not made a House 'till yesterday. I am afraid I shall have my Hands full here, and I am not greatly elated at the Prospect.

We have undoubted Intelligence of the sailing of a French Fleet for this Country, under the Command of Vice Admiral Count de Estang consisting of 12 Ships of the Line, 6 frigates & two xebeques. I have reason to believe the French Ambassador is on Board; an English fleet lay at St. Helena ready to follow them, consisting of Eleven Ships—1 of 90— 9 of 74— and one of 64 Guns.[2]

I am sorry to inform you that there is also intelligence of the Settlement of Wyoming being cut off by Coll Buttler with about 1000 Indians Tories & British Troops.[3] It is supposed that Carlisle will soon be the frontier of this State as the Inhabitants are flying in from all Quarters. About 200 Inhabitants were Scalped.

I must beg the favour of your presenting my most respectfull Compliments of Congratulations to his Excellency and the family, especially my worthy friend Harrison.

I am Dr Sir &c

FC (PHi). Hamilton, *Papers* (Syrett), 1:515–16.

[1] Alexander Hamilton's July 5 letter to Boudinot, which contained a detailed account of the battle of Monmouth that was highly critical of Gen. Charles Lee, is in Hamilton, *Papers* (Syrett), 1:510–14.

[2] Congress received part of this "Intelligence" this day when it read a June 30 letter from Gen. William Heath to President Laurens and an enclosed May 18 letter from John Adams and Benjamin Franklin "to the governor or any counsellor or senator or member of any house of representatives in any of the thirteen United States of America." See PCC, item 157, fols. 165–66; and Wharton, *Diplomatic Correspondence*, 2:589. As a result, Congress immediately ordered publication of the letter from Adams and Franklin and began to make preparations for the reception of the French fleet. *JCC*, 11:675–76.

[3] This day Congress read a letter from Col. Zebulon Butler to the Board of War, dated "Westmoreland 3d July A D 1778," describing the devastating raid on the Wyoming Valley by a mixed force of loyalists and Indians commanded by Maj. John Butler. PCC, item 78, 2:501. Since many of the Indians involved in this raid were Senecas, Congress immediately directed the Board of War to send for some "Seneca chiefs" who had recently been in Philadelphia seeking the release of one of their warriors, but after the Senecas understandably refused to return, board members sought to excuse the failure of their mission by telling Congress they "did not think themselves authorized to use force in the case." See *JCC*, 11:675, 697; and Washington, *Writings* (Fitzpatrick), 12:98–99. For an account of Butler's raid, see Barbara Graymont, *The Iroquois in the American Revolution* (Syracuse: Syracuse University Press, 1972), pp. 167–74.

Samuel Holten's Diary

[July 8, 1778][1]

8. Congress receivd. a packet from France giving an Acct. of a French Fleet comg. here. I dined with General Arnold; very hot.

MS (MDaAr).

[1] In his preceding entry Holten noted that on July 7 he "Attended in Congress until half past 2 o'Clock."

Henry Laurens to Israel Putnam

Sir

Philadelphia 8th July [1778]

On the 5th Instant I had the honor of receiving your favor of the 30th Ulto. by the hand of Major Putnam, but have not had opportunity for presenting it to Congress.[1] Until yesterday a sufficient number of States had not been convened to form a house for business, and the accumulation of Papers between our adjournment from York and meeting in this City has prepared more work than we shall be able to accomplish in two or three days.

A Report I know came to my hands from General McDougall respecting the loss of Fort Montgomery &c. on North River, which Congress directed me to send to the Board of War; that Board has not yet settled in an Office, nor unpacked their Papers, therefore the Report is not accessible, as soon as it shall be so, I will procure a Copy and transmit it to you, together with such directions as I shall receive from Congress.[2] To detain Major Putnam in these circumstances I think would be improper: I have for this reason recommended his return, and I beg Sir, you will accept this assurance that I will not delay the necessary applications on your Business, and that I am with the highest Esteem & Regard &c. Sir &c.

LB (DNA: PCC, item 13). Addressed: "Major General Putnam, Hartford in Connecticut."

1 General Israel Putnam's June 30 letter to Laurens is in PCC, item 159, fols. 135–36. In it Putnam asked to be apprised of the result of the investigation of a court of inquiry into the loss of Forts Clinton and Montgomery, which had been captured by the British in October 1777 while he was in command of the Highlands. Laurens must have written the present letter before the delegates met this day because according to the journals the reading of Putnam's letter was Congress' first order of business on the eighth. *JCC*, 11:673.

2 After considering the report of the court of inquiry on the loss of Forts Clinton and Montgomery, Congress resolved on August 17 that "those posts were lost, not from any fault, misconduct, or negligence, of the commanding officers, but solely through the want of an adequate force under their command to maintain and defend them." *JCC*, 11:743, 803–4. Gen. Alexander McDougall, Putnam's successor as commander of the Highlands, was one of the officers whom Washington had appointed to conduct this inquiry.

Henry Laurens to George Washington

Sir Philadelphia 8th July 1778

I beg leave to refer to a private Letter of yesterday by Gray, in which I acknowledged the receipt of Your Excellency's Letters to Congress of the 28th & 29th Ulto. & lst Inst. I should have added the 21st Ulto. which came to hand the 2d Inst.[1]

With some difficulty a Congress was collected yesterday, Your Excellency's Letters were immediately taken under consideration & the House unanimously Resolved a Vote of thanks for Your Excellency's approved conduct from the time when the Army left Valley forge Camp to the conclusion of the Battle of Monmouth a Certified Copy of which I have the honor & particular happiness of transmitting within the present Cover.[2]

I have likewise the pleasure of conveying an Act of the same date for thanking the Gallant Officers & Men under Your Excellency's Command who by their conduct & valor distinguished themselves in that Battle.[3]

I have the honor to be, With the highest Esteem & Regard, Sir, Your Excellency's Most obedient & Most humble servant,

Henry Laurens, President of Congress.

RC (DLC).

1 Washington's June 21 letter to Laurens is in PCC, item 152, 6:127–28, and Washington, *Writings* (Fitzpatrick), 12:98–99.

[2] See *JCC*, 11:673.
[3] Ibid.

Samuel Adams to Elizabeth Adams

My Dear Betsy Philada July 9 1778

Mr McLean the Bearer of this Letter arrivd in this City yesterday, and tells me he saw you on the Day he left Boston, and that you were then in Health. He now returns in so great Haste as to afford me Time only to let you know that I still enjoy that inestimable Blessing. I now write at the Table in Congress, having just put my Hand to the Confederation with my Colleagues & the Delegates of seven other States. North Carolina and Georgia whose Members are absent have acceded to the Confederation.[1] Mr H—— has just obtaind the Leave of Absence and is going home on Account of his ill State of Health & the Circumstances of his Family. He tells me his Wife is dangerously ill.[2]

Adieu my dear, S A

RC (NN).

[1] See *JCC*, 11:677, and Henry Laurens to Certain States, July 10, 1778.

[2] Congress granted John Hancock a leave of absence on this date. *JCC*, 11:677. It is doubtful that Adams' explanation of the reasons for Hancock's return home, which took place less than a month after he arrived in Pennsylvania, is an accurate one. In his July 1, 1778, letter to his wife, Hancock wrote that his plans for remaining in Philadelphia hinged on the ratification of the confederation, when "a new Congress will bring on the Conclusion of my Plan," but he did not explain the nature of his plan and his surviving letters to her for this brief period suggest that he was simply unwilling to settle into the drudgery of representing his state now that he was no longer president of Congress. For an examination of Hancock's abbreviated stay in Congress at this time, see William Fowler, *The Baron of Beacon Hill; a Biography of John Hancock* (Boston: Houghton Mifflin Co., 1980), pp. 230–32.

On July 11 Hancock was appointed to the official welcoming committee for the newly arrived French ambassador, Conrad Alexandre Gérard, and thus he did not leave Philadelphia until July 15. *JCC*, 11:685; and James Lovell to Samuel P. Savage, July 14, 1778.

Elias Boudinot to Hannah Boudinot

My dearest Love, Philadelphia July 9 1778

It is so hot that I cannot sleep, so I must spend a few Minutes in letting you hear from me. This City is enough to kill a Horse, and if I had not been highly favoured in obtaining most excellent Lodgings, I should have been overcome with the Heat. We have recd. advice to day from France of a fleet being on our Coast consisting of

12 French Ships of the Line, Six Frigates and two Xebeques, all under the Command of the Admiral Count de Estang, with an Ambassador &c &c. An English fleet has followed them, so that we daily expect to hear of some bloody work. The Indians have struck on this Frontier and entirely cut off the Wyoming Settlement. It is said 200 Inhabitants were scalped. May a holy God deliver us from this barberous Enemy.

Enclosed you have the publication of the Day.[1] My Love to all as if mentioned. Kiss my Susan and excuse this Scrawl and believe me with cool reflection & Sincerity, Your most affectionate,

Boudinot

[*P.S.*] Shoes three Pounds a pair—Linnen 30 to 50/ per yard—wine £600 per Pipe.

RC (NjP).

1 This day's issue of the *Pennsylvania Packet* contained, among other items, William Henry Drayton's June 17 letter to the Carlisle commissioners and John Adams' and Benjamin Franklin's May 18 letter to various American officials containing news of d'Estaing's fleet.

Connecticut Delegates to Jonathan Trumbull, Sr.

Sir

Philadelphia July 9th. 1778

We have now the Pleasure to inform You that the Articles of Confederation are ratified by nine States, to wit the four New England States, New York, Pennsilvania, Virginia, North & South Carolina, and the Ingrossed Copy with a proper form of Ratification is signed by the Delegates of said States except those of North Carolina which were not present. The remaining four states are called upon to impower their Delegates to ratify. Georgia it is supposed will not hesitate; Maryland, Delaware & New Jersey had their Objections, but it is hoped and expected they will not prevail to prevent their uniting with the confederated States in ratifying the Articles.

There were many Amendments proposed from the States, but none were adopted; it seemed to be the Opinion of Congress that an immediate Confederation was of greater Moment to the Interest of the States, than any present Alteration of the Articles to accomodate the Opinion of particular States on the Amendments proposed.

Yesterday an Express arrived from Boston with Dispatches from France, which advise that the Count D'Etaing an Admiral of France sailed from Toulon with a Squadron of French Men of War consisting of twelve sail of the Line, Six Frigates and three Chebecs bound for Delaware or Chesapeak Bays on board of which is Monsieur Girard, Minister plenipotentiary from the Court of France to the united states. That this fleet sailed from Toulon the 15th April last, and that an English Fleet of Eleven Ships, one of ninety Guns, nine of Seventy four & One of Sixty four sailed from St. Hellens the Twenty fourth of April, and that Seventeen Sail of the Line, which were to be joined in a few days by eight more, lay in the road of Brest ready to put to sea to watch the motions of the English fleet.

We are this day[1] advised by Mr. Blair McClanighan of this City a Gentleman of Character, just returned here from Maryland that the Fleet under the Count D'Etaing, mentioned above arrived off Chincioteage in Maryland two or three days ago, & proceeded directly for Sandy Hook, that it consisted of a Ninety Gun Ship, two Eighty and nine Seventy fours & Sixty fours, Six Frigates & three Chebecs, that they had four Thousand Land forces on board, this Information he had from a Gentleman, who piloted the Fleet in & was landed at Chinciotegue, who likewise informed that the Admiral told him that War was declared against England at Paris the 19th Day of May, and that this Fleet was destined to shut up Genl. Clinton in Philadelphia, but will now attempt to pound him in New York. We beg leave to Congratulate your Excellency upon this important Event.[2]

Genl. Wolcott & Mr. Huntington left us this morning[3] & will be able to inform your Excellency of the State of the Armies in New Jersey, & New York better than it is in our power, and of many particulars which we have not time to write.

We are &c

FC (CtY). In the hand of Titus Hosmer.

1 The remainder of this letter was doubtless written on July 10. Samuel Holten's diary and letters of Henry Laurens to the comte d'Estaing and to Washington of July 10 state that Blair McClenachan's report of the arrival of the French fleet was received on that day; and Hosmer repeated the information contained in this paragraph in his July 10 letter to Richard Law.

2 At this point a formal closing was deleted and the following paragraph was added.

3 Samuel Huntington and Oliver Wolcott had been granted leave on July 7. They had delayed their departure until their colleague Andrew Adams had taken his seat on July 9 and they had been able to join Adams, Hosmer, and Roger Sherman in signing the Articles of Confederation on behalf of Connecticut on that day. See *JCC*, 11:673, 676–77, 19:222. Huntington's account with Connecticut, which claimed "Service at Congress from the 30th of January to the 18th of July inclusive . . . 170 days at 18s," undoubtedly included his travel time. Gratz Collection, PHi.

Samuel Holten's Diary

July 9th, [1778]

Attended in Congress, the Articles of confederation was signed by all the States that had receivd instructions for that purpose, being 8 States.

MS (MDaAr).

Henry Laurens to Richard Caswell

Sir 9th July [1778]

By Captain Cottineau I had the honor of writing to Your Excellency from York the 20th Ulto.[1]

Inclosed herein Your Excellency will receive Copy of a Letter from the Commissioners at Paris, which I had the honor of receiving and presenting to Congress yesterday.[2] The English fleet mentioned in that Letter is supposed were equipped for intercepting a French squadron intended for some part of North America, probably Chesapeak bay. Your Excellency is therefore requested to pursue the most effectual measures to apprize the Commander of the French squadron Le Compte d'Estaing of any English ships of War which may come into any of the Harbours or Inlets of the state of North Carolina, their force, number and station, and to accommodate the squadron or any of the ships of our Ally the King of France with proper Pilots, if required.[3]

Monsr. Girard in the Character of Plenipotentiary from the Court of Versailles to these states is expected in the French fleet, which consists of twelve sail of the Line, six Frigates &c.

I shall add printed Papers containing much public intelligence, to which I beg leave to refer.

A private Letter from Genl. Washington's Army of the 7th informs me[4] "the Army was then in motion from Brunswick for North River. The Enimy had passed the Breach between Sandy Hook and the Main, and had taken up their Bridge after them, they were embarking with the greatest expedition, had left a number of Waggons behind them, and cut the throats of many horses, three signal Guns had been fired from the fleet on the 5th and the whole were under sail the 6th in the Morning—uncertain whither bound—Colonel Morgan had taken about 30 Prisoners and received about 100 Deserters."

English Papers of the middle of April shew the Debates in both Houses of Parliament to have been on a motion for acknowledging

American Independence,[5] and the whole Nation in great distraction.

I have the honor to be &c.

LB (DNA: PCC, item 13).

[1] See Laurens to George Clinton, June 20, 1778, note 3.

[2] See Elias Boudinot to Alexander Hamilton, July 8, 1778, note 2.

[3] See *JCC*, 11:675–76.

[4] What follows is an accurate paraphrase of John Laurens' July 7 letter to his father. Simms, *Laurens Army Correspondence*, pp. 204–5.

[5] For the debate in parliament on Thomas Powys' April 10 motion that the Carlisle commissioners "be authorised to declare the Americans absolutely and for ever independent," see *Parliamentary History*, 19:1080–88.

Henry Laurens to William Heath

Sir, Philadelphia 9th July 1778

I beg leave to refer you to my last of the 26th Ulto. by the hand of Colo. Armand.

Your favors of the 19th & 30th June have been duly presented to Congress & the Inclosed Act of the 7th Inst. will shew you that your conduct respecting Major General Philips has received the approbation of the House. Your correspondence with that Officer is published by order, as you will see in the paper which will accompany this.[1]

That part of your Letter of the 19th relative to Gold which you have received for supplies to the Troops of the Convention is committed to the Treasury, that Board is not yet fixed in an Office in this City, & therefore a Report cannot be expected for some days, the moment I receive Commands, I shall put them in motion towards you,[2] in the mean time I have only to repeat what I have often said with equal truth & pleasure that I am with great Esteem & Respect, sir, Your obedient & humble servant,

Henry Laurens, President of Congress

RC (MHi).

[1] General Heath's June 19 letter to Laurens and accompanying enclosures, which are in PCC, item 157, fols. 283–304, dealt with the case of Lt. Richard Browne, a member of the Convention Army at Boston who had been shot to death by an American sentry on June 17 "for not stoping when repeatedly challenged as he was riding out of the lines with two Women." The day after this incident Heath informed Gen. William Phillips, the ranking officer of the Convention Army, that Browne's death would be thoroughly investigated, but Phillips infuriated Heath by replying that Browne had been murdered and by ridiculing the notion that the British could expect justice from "rebels." In retaliation, Heath ordered Phillips' movements to be confined strictly and demanded that he sign a new parole promising to remain on his good behavior. When Phillips refused to accept this parole, arguing that it violated the Saratoga Conven-

tion, Heath had referred the matter to Congress, which on July 7 expressed its approval of his treatment of the British general. *JCC*, 11:672.

In regard to Heath's June 30 letter to Laurens, which forwarded to Congress some recently received dispatches from France, see Elias Boudinot to Alexander Hamilton, July 8, 1778, note 2.

2 No report by the Board of Treasury has been found on Heath's inquiry about whether he should send Congress the gold that would be left over after he paid for supplies for the Convention Army.

Henry Laurens to Patrick Henry

Sir 9th July [1778]

My last to your Excellency was dated at York 27th Ulto. and conveyed by the hand of Major Talbot.

Within the present cover Your Excellency will receive a printed Copy of a Letter from the Commissioners at Paris of the 18th May, the original I had the honor of receiving and presenting Yesterday to Congress.

Congress have directed me to request Your Excellency to take the most effectual Measures in case of the arrival of a British squadron in the bay of Chesapeak for intimating to any French fleet which may appear on the coast the number, force and station of the Enemy, and for supplying with good Pilots any French ship or fleet, whose Commander may be disposed to come within the bay.[1] Monsr. Girard, Plenipotentiary from the Court of Versailles to these United States is expected hourly, having embarked in the fleet which sailed from France the middle of April.[2]

I am with very great Regard &c.

LB (DNA: PCC, item 13).

1 See *JCC*, 11:675–76.

2 Laurens wrote virtually the same letter this day to Gov. Thomas Johnson of Maryland. Red Books, MdAA.

James Lovell to Abigail Adams

Dear Madam July 9th. 1778

I heartily congratulate you upon the indubitable Proofs of our Friends[1] Arrival in France. You might imagine that the Congress had received some important Intelligence in the large Packets sent lately from Boston, if I did not acquaint you that they were chiefly for Monsr. Girard who is not yet arrived. A French Fleet having sailed for America, an English One being ready to follow, and a second French One to pursue that, if there is to be a War between the two Nations, it will probably commence in our Seas.

The Indians & Tories have cut off Wyoming; and They must be eradicated Root and Branch as soon as ever we get a little Relaxation from War on the Sea Coasts.

I am not inattentive to Mr. Adams's Boxes which shall be forwarded by the first Opportunity. I presume I shall now get that which contained his Papers left under the Care of the Rev. Mr. Sprout.[2]

With every friendly Attachment, I am, Dear Madam, your humble Servt.,

James Lovell

RC (MHi).

[1] That is, John Adams.

[2] For the recovery of papers and personal articles which John Adams had left at York and at James Sproat's house in Philadelphia, see Adams, *Family Correspondence* (Butterfield), 3:121, 198.

Titus Hosmer to Richard Law

Dear Sir, Philadelphia July 10th 1778

An Express arrived Yesterday from Boston with Dispatches brought in there by a vessell on a short passage from France. By these we learn that Admiral the Count D'Etaing sailed from Toulon the 15th of April last with a Fleet of twelve Ships of the Line, Six Frigates and three Chebecs, bound for Delaware or Chesapeak Bay. That an English Fleet of Eleven Sail of the Line sailed from St Hellens the 24th of April to intercept the French Squadron, and that seventeen Sail of the Line lay in the Road of Brest ready to put to Sea and pursue the English Fleet.

This Day Mr Blair McClanighan of this City a Gentleman of Character returned here from Maryland & informs that the Count D'Etaings Squadron arrived off Chinicoteague in Maryland Three days ago, & immediately bore away for Sandy Hook. He had his Intelligence from a Gentleman who piloted the squadron in to Chinicoteague, and was landed there, who further told him that war was declared against England at Paris the 19th day of May, that Monsieur Gerard Minister Plenipotentiary from the Court of France to the united states is on board the Fleet, and may be daily expected in this City, that Four Thousand land Forces are on board the Fleet, that their Object when they left France was to shut up General Clinton in Philadelphia, the English Ministry prevented this by ordering the precipitate Retreat we have lately seen executed, that they will now attempt to block up the port of New York, & favour an attack upon the Main body of the Enemy there from our Land Army.

The enclosed Newspaper will give you some Intelligence which perhaps you may not have seen, and I must add one piece of Information which you will not find any where else, the old Coat & Breeches, which you left here, have made their Escape from the British Army and are safe at Mrs Cheesemans. Would you have them sent to you?

The Confederation has at length got thro' Congress. A Multitude of Amendments, Alterations and Additions were proposed from Different States, which have taken up much Time to Consider. After long Debates, all are rejected. It seems to be the Opinion of Congress that a speedy Confederation was of more Importance than to endeavour further to accommodate the Articles to the Opinion & Views of particular States. It was ratified in form by nine states yesterday, the Delegates of the remaining four, to wit, New Jersey, Delaware, Maryland & Georgia, are expected soon to have powers sent them, when it will be compleated.

I have only to add my Compliments to Mrs Law, & my best wishes for your Happiness.

I am Dr Sir, with great Respect, your most obed & most humble servt, Titus Hosmer

Tr (CtHi).

Titus Hosmer to Thomas Mumford

Dear sir Philadelphia July 10th 1778

Tho I wrote you so lately[1] I cannot forbear availing myself of this Opportunity to give you the Important News we have just received.

An Express arrived from France via Boston yesterday[2] with Dispatches for Congress. By these we learn that Admiral Count D'Etaing sailed from Toulon the 15th of April last with a squadron of Twelve sail of the Line, Six Frigates & three Chebecs bound for Delaware or Chesapeak Bay, that an English Squadron of Eleven Sail of the Line left St. Hellens the 24th of April in pursuit of them, and that 17 Sail of the Line lay in the road of Brest ready to put to Sea and Intercept the English Squadron.

Yesterday we had Intelligence from Maryland that Count D'Etaing's Squadron arrived off Chinicoteague in that State three Days ago, & immediately took pilots on board & bore away for Sandy Hook, that he had four Thousand Land Troops on board, who are to act in Conjunction with our Army, while the fleet blocks up the Port and Intercepts Supplies. Our further Advice is that War was declared at Paris against England the 19th day of May (but of this I have yet some scruples)—That Monsr. Girard is on board the Count D'Etaings fleet, he comes in Character of Minister & plenipotentiary from the Court of France to the united States, and is accompanied by our old Friend Mr. Silas Dean, they may be expected every Day in this City.

Thus you see a Grand scene is opening which, if we have Wisdom to Act our part Well, will probably terminate in the compleat Establishment of our Independence, Liberty & Happiness. I hope the Inhabitants of Connecticut, if called & needed, will exert themselves by one Vigorous push to drive this Consuming Army of Locusts from our Coasts, this Once done there is reason to hope the war will only Thunder on our Coast, and that we may be free from these Bloody, cruel, Inhuman Inmates in our Quarters.

The Articles of Confederation were ratified in Form Yesterday by the Delegates of nine states. The remaining four, Viz. New Jersey, Delaware, Maryland & Georgia, are waiting for their full powers which are soon expected when that very Important Business will be compleated.

My Heart bleeds for Wyoming. The Tories and Indians under Colo. Butler, the British Superintendant of Indian Affairs fell upon it the Third Instant, and have ravaged it with more than Indian Cruelty & Barbarity. Our Accounts are yet indistinct, we have Reason to fear the whole settlemt. is desolated. We hope soon, if any of the miserable Inhabitants have escaped the Carnage, to have a more full & particular Account.[3]

July 11. Mr. Dean is expected here this night. We had Letters from him to Day & from Count D'Etaing.[4] The fleet have taken the Rose Frigate, an Eighteen Gun Ship & chased the Roebuck on Shore, five or six Mercht. Ships are said to be in this River coming up here. The Express is going out, accept the cordial Wishes for your Happiness of dear sir, your affectionate,

Titus Hosmer

RC (Robert J. Sudderth, Jr., Lookout Mountain, Tenn., 1973).

1 See Hosmer to Mumford, July 6, 1778.

2 The Boston express arrived on July 8: The "Intelligence from Maryland" mentioned below was received on the morning of the 10th.

3 For further information on John Butler's raid, see Elias Boudinot to Alexander Hamilton, July 8, 1778, note 3.

4 Comte d'Estaing's July 8 letter to President Laurens, announcing the arrival of the French fleet, and Silas Deane's July 10 letter to Laurens, requesting that pilots be sent to meet d'Estaing at Sandy Hook, were read in Congress on July 11. *JCC*, 11:683–84. Comte d'Estaing's letter with translation is in PCC, item 164, fols. 542–49; a transcript of Deane's letter is in PCC, item 103, fols. 109–10. Both letters are in Wharton, *Diplomatic Correspondence*, 2:640–43.

Henry Laurens to Certain States

Sir 10th July [1778][1]

Congress intent upon the present and future security of these United States has never ceased to consider a Confederacy as the great principle of Union, which can alone establish the Liberty of America and exclude for ever the hopes of its Enemies.

Influenced by motives so powerful, and duly weighing the difficulties, which oppose the expectation of any plan being formed that can exactly meet the wishes and obtain the approbation of so many States, differing essentially in various points, Congress have, after mature deliberation agreed to adopt without amendments the Confederation transmitted to the several States for their approbation. The States of New Hampshire, Massachusetts Bay, Rhode Island & Providence Plantations, Connecticut, New York, Pennsylvania, Virga., North Carolina and South Carolina have ratified the same & it remains only for your State with those of and to conclude the Glorious Compact, which, by uniting the wealth, strength and Councils of the whole, may bid defiance to external violence[2] and internal dissention, whilst it secures the Public Credit both at home and abroad. Congress is willing to hope that the Patriotism and good sense of your State will be influenced by motives so important, and they request Sir,[3] that you will be pleased to lay this Letter before the Legislature of in order that if they judge it proper, their Delegates may be instructed to ratify the Confederation with all convenient dispatch, trusting to future deliberation[4] to make such alterations and amendments as experience may shew to be expedient and just. I have the Honor to be &c.

P.S. to Georgia (only).[5] It cannot be doubted that Georgia so distantly situated will consider that new Delegates are to be appointed to meet in Congress under articles of Confederation on the 1st Monday in Novr. & give suitable dispatch to this important business.

LB (DNA: PCC, item 13). Addressed to the governors of New Jersey, Maryland, and Georgia and the president of Delaware. Endorsed: "the Blanks filled with the Names of the States Mutatis Mutandis." MS (DNA: PCC, item 47). In the hand of Richard Henry Lee, with amendments by Laurens. Addressed: "To the Speaker of the House of Representatives of New Jersey &c Mutatis Mutandis." Endorsed: "Draught of a letter to sundry states urging a Ratification of Confederation." Significant variations between the LB and the Lee draft are noted below.

1 On July 9, after eight states had ratified the Articles of Confederation, Congress appointed a committee consisting of Richard Henry Lee, Francis Dana, and Gouverneur Morris to draft a circular letter to the three states whose legislatures had not yet ratified the articles—New Jersey, Delaware, and Maryland—"desiring that such states will, with all convenient despatch, authorize their delegates to ratify the confederation in the Congress of the United States." The following day the committee submitted to Congress a draft letter in the hand of Lee,

which, after being "read and amended," was approved for transmittal by President Laurens. Laurens also sent this letter to the governor of Georgia, because although that state's legislature had authorized her delegates in February to ratify the confederation, Congress did not receive official confirmation of this until Edward Telfair arrived in Philadelphia on July 13. See *JCC*, 11:670, 678, 680–81; Samuel Adams to Elizabeth Adams, July 9; and Josiah Bartlett to John Langdon, July 13, 1778.

2 Laurens added this word to Lee's draft in place of two others that are lined out and illegible.

3 The following florid conclusion is lined out in Lee's draft: "that your Delegates in Congress may be authorized to ratify the Confederation with all convenient dispatch, trusting to future deliberation and to timidless embassadors for a more perfect accommodation of opinions."

4 Laurens added the remainder of this sentence to Lee's draft.

5 There is no postscript in Lee's draft.

Henry Laurens to the Comte d'Estaing

Sir 10th July [1778]

Congress received Intelligence this Morning of the arrival on this Coast of a fleet of Men of War under Your Excellencies command.[1]

The Packet which I have the honor of transmitting you herewith reached my hands on the 8th Instant, together with the Inclosed intelligence of an English squadron lying near Portsmouth on the 18th of May, supposed to have been intended to annoy your Excellencies progress towards this shore. To the force of that squadron Your Excellency will be pleased to add the Inclosed enumeration of the English ships of War supposed to be in the harbour of New York,[2] which is the most accurate we have been able to collect.

If it shall be your Excellency's design to act offensively against the British Marine, it may conduce to success that the Commander in Chief of the forces of these United States should cooperate in the measures intended to be pursued on your part. I beg leave therefore to inform you, Sir, that His Excellency General Washington with the Army under his command is at this time between Morris town in New Jersey and the North river which forms part of the waters which encircle New York. If your Excellency should be pleased to open a Communication with General Washington, your dispatches will be quickly conveyed to him by means of the Inclosed Warrant to be sent on shore with your Excellency's Packets.[3]

To the several Papers already said to be inclosed with this, I add three which will lay before your Excellency the proceedings and determinations of Congress consecutive upon the various attempts of the British Parliament and Administration for effecting a Reconciliation between Great Britain and the United States of America;[4] as Your Excellency cannot have seen these papers on the other side the Atlantic, a perusal of them will afford some amusement at the same time that you will learn from the contents the firmness of the good People of this Country.

I have the Honor to assure you, Sir, if it shall be necessary after referring to the papers last mentioned that Congress will be ready to render you every service in their power for facilitating your Excellency's operations against our common Enemy.

I have the Honor to be, With the highest Esteem and Regard, Sir, Your Excellency's Most Obedient & Most Humble Servt.

LB (DNA: PCC, item 13). Laurens noted in his presidential letterbook that he sent the original of this letter to d'Estaing by Anthony Dougherty and a duplicate by Charles Freeman.

1 Samuel Holten noted in his diary for this date: "Attended in Congress, a man came to this city this day & informs that a France Fleet is of[f] Maryland." MDaAr. The man in question was Blair McClenachan.

2 Not found, but see also Laurens to Washington, this date.

3 For a discussion of the checkered history of cooperation between the United States and d'Estaing's expeditionary force in 1778, see William C. Stinchcombe, *The American Revolution and the French Alliance* (Syracuse: Syracuse University Press, 1969), chap. 4.

4 See *JCC*, 10:374–80, 11:574–75, 615.

Henry Laurens to Henry Fisher

Sir 10th July [1778]

The Bearer hereof will deliver a Packet directed to His Excellency Count d'Estaing, Vice Admiral and Commander of a squadron of French ships of War. If it be practicable to send the Packet on board the fleet from Lewistown I request you in the name of Congress to do it without loss of time and the expences which may arise from this service shall be paid upon sight of your Account.

If the Admiral shall have passed to the Northward of the Capes, and be out of reach from your station; be pleased to return the Packet by this bearer to, Sir, Your Obedient & Most Humble Servt.[1]

LB (DNA: PCC, item 13). Addressed: "Henry Fisher Esquire, Lewistown." Sent "by Anthony Dougherty at half past 10 at night."

1 This day Laurens also wrote the following letter to Richard Westcott "at the Forks of little Egg Harbour":

"The Bearer hereof will also deliver to you a Packet directed to His Excellency Count d'Estaing, Commander of a French fleet of ships of War which were a few days ago at Chincoteague, and said to be bound for Delaware or Sandy Hook. If the fleet shall be accessible I request you in the name of Congress to send the Packet at all expence to the Admiral, otherwise be pleased to return it by the same hand which will deliver it to you." PCC, item 13, 2:26. Sent "by Charles Freeman at ½ past 10 at night."

Henry Laurens to Horatio Gates

Sir,

Philadelphia 10 July 1778

The derangement of the affairs of Congress in consequence of their removal from York Town, rendered it impracticable to present Your favors of the 23d Ulto. & 2d Instant & the sundry Papers which accompanied them at an earlier day than the 8th Instant.[1] The whole were then committed to the Board of War & I have received no particular commands. I therefore judge it best to order the bearer hereof to return without further expence & dangling.

No Intelligence that I can give you from the Army under His Excellency General Washington would be new to you. I shall therefore only offer you two printed News Papers parts of which may be so, & add Copy of a Letter from the worthy Govr. Johnstone to Robert Morris Esqr. which was laid before Congress yesterday & which with many other of his attempts to bribe by Gold or flattery will soon stare him in the face & display to the World the purity of his intentions.[2]

I add another Paper intimating an English fleet prepared for intercepting or annoying a French Squadron of 12 Sail of the Line, 6 or 9 Frigates & 3 Xebecs which sailed from Toulon the 15th April probably bound to Chesepeak or Delaware. I have a Packet for the Admiral Count d'Estaing & many for Monsr. Girard who is coming out in the Character of Plenipotentiary to these States.

I am with the highest Esteem & Respect, Sir, Your obedient & very humble servant. Henry Laurens, Presidt. of Cong.

RC (NHi).

1 General Gates' June 23 and July 2 letters to Laurens, in which he alternately described his preparations for an expedition against the Cayugas and the Senecas as called for by a congressional resolution of June 11 and suggested that the British evacuation of Philadelphia made this campaign unnecessary, are in PCC, item 154, 1:443–48, 2:3–4. A June 28 letter from Gates to Laurens on the same subject, which Congress also read on July 8, is in PCC, item 154, 2:453–54. Laurens' endorsements on the letters of June 23—"read at the State Ho. Philada 2 July, to Members"—and July 2—"Received at Noon in the Meeting House Arch Street 6 July"—suggest that the delegates did not entirely neglect official business in Philadelphia before a quorum was achieved on July 7.

2 See Robert Morris to Gouverneur Morris, June 16, note 2; and William Henry Drayton to the Carlisle Commissioners, July 18, 1778, note 8.

Henry Laurens to John Houstoun and Rawlins Lowndes

Sir,

10th July 1778

My last to your Excellency is dated 23d June, it went forward in the hands of Messenger Richardson.[1]

The present is intended to convey a printed Copy of a letter from the American Commissioners at Paris dated 18th May, intimating the preparation of an English squadron at the Isle of Wight, supposed to be designed for intercepting or annoying a fleet of French ships, consisting of twelve of the line, six or nine Frigates three Xebecks &c said to have sailed from Toulon the 15th of April bound to America, and probably to some port within these States, it being certain that Monsr. Girard is on board one of the ships in the Character of Plenipotentiary to Congress, for whom I have already received many dispatches from his Court. I have also a Packet for Count d'Estaing the Admiral of that Fleet.

I am directed by Congress to request Your Excellency to give such Orders as will be most effectual for affording aid to our Ally should any part of his squadron abovementioned put into any of the Ports or Harbours of South Carolina or appear on the Coast.[2] I have the honor to be &c.

LB (DNA: PCC, item 13).

1 Immediately above this paragraph Laurens wrote: "first paragraph to Governor Houston. 'My last trouble is dated with the present & relates to the Articles of the Confederation'—the remainder as below X changing So Carolina for Georgia the last Line." The "X" referred to by Laurens appears at the beginning of the second paragraph of this letter in his presidential letterbook.

2 See *JCC*, 11:675–76.

Henry Laurens to the Marquis de Lafayette

Dear Marquis 10th July [1778]

I have many of Your Excellency's favors to reply to which I shall do very soon, in the mean time none of your Commands shall remain unnoticed. I have delivered Your Excellencies Letters in favor of Marquis de Vienne and Monsr. Touzard to Congress, whence the Letters were transferred for consideration and report to the Board of War.[1]

I congratulate with your Excellency on the partial victory over the Enemy on the 28th Ulto. at Monmouth; to intimate why it had not been more brilliant might in this moment seem inviduous. I regret, however, that Your Excellency had not continued in the Command of the Van and every body appears to be of my opinion.

A large Mail arrived a few days ago in Congress from France, I found it to contain many Packets for Monsr. Gerard but not one for my noble friend Marquis de la Fayette, this deficiency will probably be made up by the arrival of Monsr. le Compte d'Estaing and Monsr. Gerard, a circumstance on which I have the honor of offering my congratulations. 'Tis highly probable you will have heard of it before this can reach you, we must now expect some important event. If the Brest fleet have restrained that of the Enemy which was lying at St. Helens the middle of May, the English ships of War on this Coast will be in a piteous plight, but if that squadron shall speedily join these, the Tables may be reversed to our disadvantage. I will not indulge a fear of this kind. A few days more will produce some grand stroke.

One of the Gentlemen in the American Commission at Paris sent me the few French Papers which I present to Your Excellency under this cover and I can only repeat that I continue with the highest Esteem and Regard, Sir, Your Excellency's &c.

[*P.S.*] We are told from on board the French squadron that War was to be declared against England by France and Spain 19th May.[2]

LB (ScHi).

[1] In one of his two June 23 letters to Laurens, Lafayette urged Congress to accept the services of Louis-Pierre, marquis de Vienne, a major of dragoons in the French army. On July 15, after reading an undated petition from Vienne asking permission to raise "a body of Two hundred and Eight Dragoons," Congress approved a motion to grant him "the brevet commission of a colonel, without army pay annexed to the said rank," though not before first rejecting a proposed amendment to make him a lieutenant colonel instead. See *JCC*, 11:692–94; PCC, item 42, 8:29–30; and "Lafayette-Laurens Letters," *SCHGM*, 9:67. For the action Congress later took in the case of the chevalier de Tousard, see Laurens to Lafayette, June 19, 1778, note 2.

[2] See also Richard Henry Lee to Francis Lightfoot Lee, July 12, 1778.

Henry Laurens to George Washington

Sir, Philadelphia 10th July 1778.

I had the honor of writing to Your Excellency by Major Putnam the 8th Inst.

Congress while sitting before Noon received intelligence of the following import.

Mr. Blair McLenahan said he had seen a Capt. Selby or Selwin off Chincoteague who had fallen in with the French Fleet Eastward of Bermuda. The Admiral had taken him on board & injoin'd him to Pilot the fleet to this Coast, the fleet arrived near Chincoteague in the Evening of the 5th Inst. There they found the Ship Lydia of 26 Guns from New York on a Cruise—she was sunk by a French Frigate of 36 Guns. On Monday Capt. Selby was sent on Shoar in order to procure Pilots; he engaged six to go on board the French fleet upon Wednesday. The Fleet consisted of the Admiral Count d'Estaing of 90 Guns—2 Ships of 80—8 of 74—1 of 64—4 of 36, & said to have 12,000 Men. They had taken a Ship of 18 Guns from Providence before they had made the Land.

War was to be declared against England by France & Spain on the

19th May. They had originally intended for Delaware but hearing that the Enemy were gone to New York they required Pilots to conduct them to Sandy Hook, they had then six Months provision on board.

Your Excellency will perceive by the inclosed Printed Paper that a Fleet had been prepared at Portsmouth in order to intercept or annoy this Fleet of which 'tis possible the Count d'Estaing may be ignorant as he sailed from Toulon the 13th April.[1] 'Tis possible also that a Check may have been put upon that by a Fleet from Brest. Be that as it may, Count d'Estaing should be apprized of this important circumstance & also of the strength of the British Marine power in New York, which from the best accounts we have been able to collect is made up of the following Ships.

Boyne	70 Guns.	Experiment	50.	Phœnix	44.
Eagle	64.	Preston	50.	& many Frigates	
St. Alban	64.	Renown	50.		
Ardent	64.	Chatham	50.		
Sommerset	64.	Isis	50.		
Trident	64.	Vigilant formerly	64.		
Centurion	50.	Roebuck	44.		

I shall endeavor to reach Count d'Estaing with the necessary advices on the Coast of New Jersey or off the Capes of Delaware. Your Excellency will, if he shall have proceeded nearer Sandy Hook endeavor to meet him with a Letter where it may reach him, & you will also concert measures for improving the force under Your Excellency's immediate Command & that under the direction of Major General Gates, in the present critical conjuncture.

Your Excellency will also if you have a more exact Account of the British Fleet at New York make proper corrections upon the list above enumerated.

I have the honor to be, With the highest Esteem & Respect, Sir, Your Excellency's Most obedient & most humble servant,

Henry Laurens, President of Congress

[*P.S.*] It is almost unnecessary to intimate to Your Excellency the propriety of opening & keeping up a correspondence with the Admiral Count d'Estaing.

RC (DLC).

1 For the May 18 letter from John Adams and Benjamin Franklin to which Laurens is referring, see Wharton, *Diplomatic Correspondence*, 2:589.

Robert Morris to Jonathan Hudson

Sir

Philada. July 10th. 1778

I wrote you a few days since & have since supplyed Mr. Blake with £2226.15.0 this Cury on Your Acct. with which he is gone down to Egg Harbour in expectation of buying a Bermuda Sloop respecting which he will doubtless inform you particularly. I find since my return here, a prospect of having my time & attention much engaged for a few Months in Public business, consequently that I shall not be able to mind my private affairs as they shou'd be. I have therefore entered into a Concern with Mr. Peter Whiteside who will henceforward Correspond with you relative to Speculations, purchases, Sales &c &c under the Firm of Peter Whiteside & Company. This Concern & Jona. Hudson & Compy may be of great material advantage to each other by Constant Correspondence, joint Concerns & frequent intelligence of prices &c. You may place entire Confidence in them as they will in your concern & by this means I shall be personally released from the Correspondence except when particular Circumstances may render it necessary. I have advised Mr. Whiteside to write you immediately to Commence a purchase of Tobacco on the joint Accts. of these two Concerns to be sent to him here for Sale as soon as possible. It will be a good Speculation and I beg you will attend to the order.[1] I am Sir, Your obedt hble servt.

Robt. Morris.

RC (PHarH). Addressed: "Mr. Jonathan Hudson, Mercht., Baltimore."

1 A mutilated letter that Morris wrote to Hudson on July 13 discussing similar affairs is in the Franklin D. Roosevelt Naval History Collection, NHpR. In it he explained that "I am not very fond of your plan for purchasing up Rum &c to the Southward unless it can be bought very reasonably, because that Article is lyable to great changes and I think it probable that the French Fleet will send in large supplies in Prizes," and cautioned Hudson not "to pursue with eagerness the purchase of Goods until we see what may be the Issue of the Count d'Estaings attack on the Ships at New York, for if he succeeds there he will take ample supplies of every kind which will reduce prices immediately." He also reported that he expected tobacco prices "will keep up," and that because Carter Braxton was planning a trip to Philadelphia he would soon be able to discuss "complaints" against him and have an opportunity to see "all these things settled properly."

Joseph Reed to Charles Lee

Dear Sir

Fleming Town July [10?] 1778[1]

I did not receive your Letter of the 3d Inst. till yesterday & then it came accompanied with the News Paper from Trenton containing your Note to the Printer respecting the Publication in his preceding Paper.[2] I cannot but feel myself exceedingly hurt by the Manner in which you have treated this Matter while you supposed me the Author of the whole Publication. The Terms of your Letter to say nothing of the Publication seem to me to be such a Deviation not only from the Line of Frindship but even of Civility which I might have expected from you as can only be excused by the Embarassments & Anxiety of your Situation. But while I truly regret the Occasion I cannot discern the Prudence or Wisdom of diminishing the Number of your Frinds at such a Time—& especially those who have Seats in Congress where alone you can expect to have those "enormous Injuries" redress'd of which you complain. The Additions & Corrections I made to the Acct. received from Gov. Livingston by the Printer were made in such Haste that I did not pay so much Attention to the Performance as I have since done; but now upon a careful Perusal ⟨*I find my Opinion confirmed by that of every Gentleman & I have spoke to several that*⟩ I am totally at a loss to discover where there is the least disrespectful Mention of you or a Fact related from which a censorious Enemy could have extracted an unfavourable Idea of your Conduct. I am very sure so far as my Pen was concerned nothing of that kind was intended, but the reverse. Tho not a Soldier by Profession I have seen enough of Armies to caution me against forming hasty Judgments of Men or Actions from mere Report. Tho I heard much therefor on that Day I suspended my Opinion & if you will again read the Paper with Attention which I cannot think you yet have done I am sure you will see a favourable Construction put on every Part of your Conduct. When compared with the official Account since published by Congress it must appear even to yourself to contain Matters of Praise & Approbation. It says that you did attack & drove the Enemy for some Time & at last only retired toward the main Army on Account of the Enemy's great Superiority of Force. It made your Numbers short I believe of the Reality but therefore more favourable to your Conduct. What does the Acct. sanctified by publick Authority say, that you brot 5000 instead of 1500 Men, that you retreated without making any Opposition except by a small Party under Col. Butler which was successful & in short that your Conduct was Matter of Surprize & Mortification to the Commander in Chief. It is admirable to every person I have conversed with first & will be so to the whole world. In what Circumstance the first Publication was unfavourable to you & secondly, Why you should attempt to destroy the Veracity of That Account & thereby fully establish the Credit of one which so much wound your Feelings so sensibly. Upon the whole tho I cannot admit that the Epithet you have applied to it as invidious, dishonest & false are by any Means proper & as you have only made a general Charge without pointing out wherein it is false & dishonest I cannot tell how much of this unhandsome Language I am to take to myself or whether any. But this I can & shall say that the Additions & Alterations I made were strictly true & founded chiefly upon my own Observation & you will excuse me for differing entirely with you in supposing I could possibly know nothing of the principal Part of the Action as that I believe will be allowed to have been after I met you [. . .] from which Time till the Close of the Affair I was either with the General at his Desire or reconnoitering in Front but chiefly the former where all Intelligence came & from whence the Movements were directed. I am at a loss to know what Individuals you mean whom you censure as directing & giving Opinions without Authority. If you had any Reference to Gen. Cadwallader & myself I shall not hesitate to say the Charge is unwarrantable as we gave no Directions nor did we on any Occasion offer an Opinion but when requested by the Commander in Chief. As Gentlemen of the Country we had a Right to attend the Army as Volunteers & as Frinds to the General to Attend him at his Desire without being liable to Censure for either. That I entertained a very high opinion of your talents & Abilities in common with my Countrymen & that they were displayed much to the Advantage of this Country & your own Honour during our Retreat from Kingsbridge to Peeks Kiln in 1776 are sentiments which I have on every Occasion expressed & that in the Affair of Fort Washington Genl W. manifested an Indecision of Mind which if unamended would shade the brighter Parts of his Character are Facts equally true: but I can easily conceive that more Experience & happier Arrangements may have given him greater Confidence in his Troops as well as in his own Judgment. From long Acquaintance & ⟨*close Observation I think him to* [. . .] *clearly of Opinion*⟩

FC (NHi).

[1] Reed wrote this letter the day after he received a copy of the July 8 issue of Isaac Collins' *New-Jersey Gazette,* "the News Paper from Trenton containing your Note to the Printer" mentioned by Reed in the first sentence below. Reed had moved his family to Flemington, N.J., twenty miles north of Trenton, in April, and had joined them there for a brief stay after the battle of Monmouth before he returned to Philadelphia, where he resumed his seat in Congress on July 15. See Roche, *Joseph Reed,* pp. 128–30; and *JCC,* 11:688.

[2] The July 1 issue of the *New-Jersey Gazette* contained a lengthy report on the battle of Monmouth which Lee assumed Reed had written and which he denounced as "a most invidious, dishonest, and false relation" in a letter to the printer that Collins published in the *Gazette's* July 8 issue. For a discussion of Lee's response to this report and his relations with Reed and various delegates to Congress at this time, see John R. Alden, *General Charles Lee, Traitor or Patriot?* (Baton Rouge: Louisiana State University Press, 1951), pp. 243–49.

Josiah Bartlett to Meshech Weare

Hond. Sir Philadelphia July 11th 1778

This is Just to inform you that a French Squadron of 12 ships of the Line & 4 frigates under the Command of vice admiral Count De Estang is arrived off the Capes of Delaware & finding the Brittish Fleet & army had Escaped from this City Sailed last Thursday Morning for New York, with orders to Cooperate with us for the Destruction of the Brittish fleet & army in America. They have taken the Rose Frigate, Sunk a 30 Gun Ship, taken several prizes & run aground & taken the Roebuck in the Capes of Delaware. Monsier Girard Ambassador & Plenipotintiary from the Court of France Came in the fleet, has sent to Congress to notify his arrival and He is expected in this City tomorrow, Mr. Deane is with him. An Officer from the admiral is now here to procure fresh Provisions (for which they will pay the Hard money). There are so many Landmen & marines on Board that they Can land four Thousand Troops on occasion. In order if Possible to put an End to the Brittish Fleet & army before the arrival of Succors the Congress have authorised Genl. Washington to call on any or all the States he may think proper from New Jersey to New Hampshire Inclusive for the assistance of militia & voluntiers. If he should Call on our State I hope they will Exert themselves to the utmost & at once put a final End to the Power & hopes of our Enemies in America.[1]

Mr Wentworth had a fever at York Town, was pretty bad. I tarried with him 4 days after the Congress adjourned, left him better Thursday the 2nd Instant, have not heard from him since. Hope he will be here the begining of the week.

I am Sir with great Respect, your most obedient Servant,

Josiah Bartlett

[*P.S.*] I would not have you consider this as a publick letter as I write in the greatest haste as tis 10 at night & the Express Setting off cannot correct much less copy it.[2] J.B.

RC (MHi).

1 See *JCC*, 11:683–85; and Henry Laurens to Washington, this date.

2 This day Bartlett also wrote the following brief note to his wife: "I have time only Just to inform you that I am in health, for news must refer you to Mr. Thurstons letter [*not found*] which I Send open that you may See it. Have Recd 3 letters from you Since I Came here, wrote you answers by the post the 7th Instant to which I Refer you." Watt Collection, NhHi.

Samuel Holten's Diary

[July 11, 1778]

11. This day was the first time that I took any part in the debates in Congress.[1] We have certain Accts. of the Arrival of a France Fleet of[f] the Delaware, 12 ships of the line & 4 Frigats.

MS (MDaAr).

[1] No other information has been found to determine the nature of Holten's participation.

Henry Laurens to George Washington

Sir, Philadelphia 11th July 1778.

I beg leave to refer Your Excellency to the contents of a Letter which I had the honor of writing to you last Evening by Barry.

The present Cover will convey to Your Excellency two Acts of Congress of this date

1. Empowering Your Excellency to call in the Aid of such Militia as shall appear to be necessary from the four Eastern States, from New York & New Jersey for carrying on operations in concert with Count d'Estaing.

2. Intimating the desire of Congress that Your Excellency Co-operate with Vice Admiral Count d'Estaing in the Execution of such offensive operations against the Enemy as shall appear to be necessary.[1]

Congress have directed me to propose for Your Excellencys consideration an attack by Vice Admiral Count d'Estaing upon the British Ships of War & Transports in the harbor of Rhode Island, by which possession of a safe Port may be gained & the retreat of the British forces on that Island be cut off, as an alternative to a hazardous or ineligible attempt upon the British Squadron within Sandy Hook.

I have the honor to be, With the highest Esteem & Respect, Sir, Your Excellency's Most obedient & most humble servant.

Henry Laurens, President of Congress.

[*P.S.*] Sometime ago I informed Your Excellency that Congress had adopted the Stile of "North America" to these States—this day that Resolution was reconsidered & reduced to the former mode of "America."[2]

Congress Resolved on the 9th Instant that the Committee appointed to arrange the Army do repair without delay to Head Quarters for that purpose as Your Excellency will perceive by the Inclosed Certified Order.[3]

RC (DLC).

1 See *JCC*, 11:684.

2 See *JCC*, 11:683; and Laurens to Horatio Gates, May 19, 1778, note 1.

3 See *JCC*, 11:676.

Henry Marchant to William Greene

Sir, Philadelphia July 11. 1778

GLORIOUS NEWS. I have but a few Moments before the Express goes off, to inform You—That a French Fleet is arrived on this Coast commanded by the Count De.Stang, 1 Ship of 90 Guns, 4 Do. of 80 Do., 2 of 74 and 5 of 64 and four Frigates. Congress this Day recd. a Letter from the adml. dated Delaware Bay. The French Ambassador Monsr. Gerard & Mr. Deane in a Frigate are now coming up the River. The adml. also forwarded Us a Letter directed to Congress from the King of France & signed by His Majesty addressing us in the most respectful and tender Manner.[1] The French Fleet have sailed for, and before this are at Sandy Hook, to attack the British Fleet. Genl. Washington is pushing forward in order to cooperate with the Admiral.

Another British Fleet is however hourly expected—So that it's possible How's Fleet may refuse to give Battle, & should the other British Fleet come on the Coast, The Count De. Stang may put into Newport Harbour. Congress have hinted this to Genl. Washington to be improved upon, so that Measures may be taken to call in a Force sufficient to opperate agt. the British Forces on the Island, but this upon a Supposition that the Count De.Stang should think proper to push for Newport Harbour. I give you a hint of this, That Genl. Sullivan and the Force he has may be preparing for such a possible Event, and that our Millitia may be called upon, not merely as in Course of Duty, but as Volunteers, upon so glorious an Occasion to stand ready to step forward if called upon which I have not a Doubt they will to a Man, to rid Themselves at once by an easy Effort under the Blessing of Heaven, of the vilest Banditty that were ever suffered to curse the Earth. I have the Honor to be your most humble Servt. Hy. Marchant

P.S. The Rose Frigate formerly commanded by Wallace was taken by One of the French Frigates upon Their arrival off Chesepeak Bay. The Roebuck of 44 guns at the Mouth of Delaware was drove on the Maryland Shore. Her Crew cut her Masts & fled a Shore where they must fall into Our Hands, & the Ship as she is one of the finest in the British Navy will be a fine Acquisition. The Frigate coming up the River, has two Prizes with her, They sunk a British Privateer of 26 Guns, just as they made Land. H.M.

You'l Excuse a Scrawl for the Love of the Matter.

RC (R–Ar).

1 Louis XVI's March 23 letter to Congress, announcing Conrad Alexandre Gérard's appointment as minister plenipotentiary to the United States, is in PCC, item 111, fols. 4–5, and Wharton, *Diplomatic Correspondence*, 2:521.

Marine Committee to the Eastern Navy Board

Gentlemen Philada July 11th 1778

Your Several Letters lately received have not been considered because of the obstructions created by a removal of Congress from York Town to this place where as yet the committee have not been able to get themselves properly fixed for business. The sense entertained of the increasing importance of your Department will secure a close attention to it from this Committee and every care shall be taken to furnish you with the money requisite for the proper Accomplishment of the ends proposed by your appointment. The immediate design of this Letter is to inform you of the arrival on the Coast near the Capes of Delaware of a French squadron consisting of 12 ships of the Line and four frigates under the command of the Count D Estaing Vice Admiral of France who is proceeding immediately to Newyork there to act in conjunction with the Army of the united states for destroying the fleet & army of the common enemy in that Harbour. Congress being determined to give every possible aid to the execution of so salutary a purpose has directed us to order all the Continental frigates and armed Vessels within your Department to be immediately made ready for Sea and dispatched one after another as soon as each can be prepared, to join the Squadron of France and to act in such manner as the Count D Estaing shall judge most proper for distressing and destroying the enemys force upon the Coast of North America.[1] Congress trust to the bravery and good disposition of the American seamen that they will on this great occasion step forth with alacrity and exert themselves in supporting our freinds who have come so far to assist us to vanquish an enemy too long triumphant upon the Sea. The expence attending this business no doubt will be considerable, altho we are well assured your Œconomical wisdom will lead you to abridge it as far as may be possible. We shall without delay forward you as large A Sum of Money as can now be spared, and in the mean time desire you will on the credit of the States push the business forward with all possible vigor.[2]

We are to observe to you that the French fleet is more than fully manned, so that some small aid in way of seamen may be expected, and we mention this that you may not wait for the most compleat manning of every Vessel altho we wish you to procure as many Seamen as you can consistant with the great object we have in view viz a speedy junction of our force with that of France.[3]

We are Gentlemen, Your very hble servts

LB (DNA: PCC Miscellaneous Papers, Marine Committee Letter Book).

1 See *JCC*, 11:685.

2 On July 16 Congress granted the Marine Committee $524,000 for the use of the Eastern Navy Board. See *JCC*, 11:696; and Marine Committee to the Eastern Navy Board, July 24, 1778.

3 As chairman of the Marine Committee, Richard Henry Lee wrote the following letter to Gov. Patrick Henry this date:

"A French Fleet of 12 Sail of the Line and 4 frigates being on the Coast near the Capes of Delaware under command of Count D'Estaing vice Admiral of France which is proceeding to New York in order to co-operate with the American Army in destroying the Sea and Land force of our enemy in that Harbor and it being understood here that some of the French Ships now in Virginia were desirous of joining the Admiral when he came here; the Marine Committee request of you Sir, that you will be pleased to give immediate Notice to Such French Vessels. that they may if they choose proceed to assist in the Accomplishment of the great work meditated against the common enemy." Paullin, *Marine Committee Letters*, 1:264–65.

Henry Laurens to Certain States

Sir or Honorable sir, 12th July [1778]

The present circumstances of public affairs afford me barely time for referring you to the inclosed Act of Congress of yesterdays date, empowering General Washington to call on the state of New Hampshire and other States therein enumerated for such Militia as he shall think requisite for co-operating with Count d'Estaing commander of the French Fleet arrived on this Coast against the Enemy, and earnestly recommending to each State the forwarding with the utmost dispatch such force as shall be called for by the Commander in Chief.[1]

I expect Monsr. Girard in the character of Plenipotentiary from the Court of Versailles in Philadelphia early this Morning, a novelty in these infant States which cannot but occasion some uncommon and extraordinary movements, among those whose proper business it is to pay due attention to the first European Ambassador to Congress.

I have the Honor to be &c.

LB (DNA: PCC, item 13). Addressed to the governors of Rhode Island, Connecticut, New York, and New Jersey and the presidents of New Hampshire and Massachusetts.

1 See *JCC*, 11:684. Laurens made the following notation about this "Act" in his

presidential letterbook: "Memorandum—The abovementioned Act of Congress having been sent to me from the Secretarys' Office unsigned by the Secretary; I have certified each in my own name." PCC, item 13, 2:29.

Henry Laurens to William Heath

Dear sir,

Philadelphia 12 July 1778

I have barely time to intimate in this private, that Your last correspondence with Major General Philips met the approbation of Congress as the former had done.[1]

Vice Admiral Count d'Estaing with a formidable French fleet of 1 Ship of 110 Guns called 90—2 of 80—8 of 74—1 of 64, 4 of 36 & said to have 12000 Men on board were at the Capes of Delaware two days ago & are now probably at Sandy Hook.

On the Voyage hither this fleet took a privateer of 26 guns from New York cruising on the Virginia Coast, a Ship from New Providence bound to London & Recaptured a French Snow laden with dry Goods. These two are now coming up the River.

They have also driven on Shoar & destroyed a British Ship supposed to be the Roebuck.

Mr. Girard Plenipotentiary from the Court of Versailles will be here some time to day, he arrived at Chester in a French Frigate last Evening, Mr. Silas Deane accompanies him.

Having no public Commands you will do me the honor to accept this as the private Offering of, Dear sir Your most obedt. & most humble servt,

Henry Laurens

RC (MHi).

[1] See Laurens to Heath, July 9, 1778, note 1.

Richard Henry Lee to Francis Lightfoot Lee

My dear brother,

Philadelphia 12 July 1778

I had prepared a letter for you three days ago intending to have sent it to Chantilly by a Mr. Muse, but he slipt me without calling for my letter. Since that the Count D'Estaing, with a French Squadron under his command, has arrived in Delaware Bay, and last Thursday morning he proceeded to N. York with determination to loose no time in attacking the English in that Harbour. On the 19th of May he declared war against G. Britain on board his fleet then at Sea, and since that he takes every English Vessel that he meets with. The strength of this fleet is one 90, one 80, Six 74, Three 64 & one 50 with 4 frigates and between 10 & 12,000 men on board.

In this fleet came the French Ambassador Monsr. Gerard who is expected in Town every hour Carriages being sent to Chester for him. Silas Deane is also arrived in this fleet, and I expect that he & Carmichael will soon begin to intrigue. We have received a very polite Address from the Count D'Estaing inclosing us a copy of his powers from the King of France which are plenipotentiary to treat with Congress. The King styles us his most dear friends and great Allies. The Count says that nothing but the necessity of immediately executing the duties of his Office as Commander of the Fleet would have permitted him to delay paying his respects to Men famous thro Europe for their wisdom and firmness. We have been very busy in Marine Committee this morning, altho 'tis Sunday, directing fresh provisions and Water to be sent to this fleet.[1] Gen. Washington is directed to Cooperate with Count D'Estaing in offensive operations against the common enemy. We may expect good events from this if Keppel with his 11 sail of the Line do not interrupt us too soon. He was in St. Helens the 19th of May bound to N. America. But we expect he will be narrowly watched by the Brest fleet which consisted of 25 Sail of the Line ready for Sea. Thus the Ball begins to open, and the guilty Sons of G. Britain upon the eve of making severe retribution for the heavy crimes both in the east and the west.

The Ambassador is arrived, and during the course of dinner I have had an opportunity of conversing largely with him.[2] I find that the King of France considers the King of Englands message upon Marquis Noailes communication of our Alliance as anouncing hostility and determines to act accordingly. With effective hostility indeed, but witht. a formal declaration of war in Europe, for this he says, we must wait until Spain is ready. The flota was not arrived on the 10th April. Monsr. Gerard seems rather above 50 years of age, is as grave as a Frenchman can be, and he is a wise well bred Gentleman. We are told that many of the first Nobility of France solicited his mission in vain.

I am much grieved to hear that my honored friend Colo. Tayloe grows worse. Is it impracticable for him to visit the Springs? The Indian irruptions I expect will be presently quieted by the Army under Mc.Intosh going to Fort Detroit, and the expedition into the Seneca Country. These must wall and keep every Indian at home.

My love to Mrs. Lee and respects to all friends. Most affectionately yours, Richard Henry Lee

P.S. The post this day brings me no letters from the N. Neck except from my friend Mr. Page.[3] I have none from Susquehannah or Potomac. From Boston we learn of a quick arrival that brings account Lord Chatham died on the 1st of May, he was forming a party against the Independence of America, which he has lately thunder'd against in Parliament and was opposed by the Duke of Richmond with great spirit & force of reason.[4] Stocks fallen greatly, and the

Kingdom in much confusion—40 frigates recalled from N. America. But Count D'Estaing wont let them get out of the Harbor of N. York. [It is?] true that Capt. Jones has carried a 20 gun Ship of the Tyrants into Brest with 3 other prizes. He had a severe conflict with the Ship of War & killed the Captain & first Lieutenant, killed & wounded 42 men, lost 8. He landed at Whitehaven & fired the shipping in the Harbour, and did them other damage, where he also spiked 30 or 40 pieces of Cannon.[5] R.H. Lee

RC (ViU).

[1] See Marine Committee to the Comte d'Estaing, this date.

[2] Lee had been appointed on July 11 to the committee to receive Gérard. *JCC*, 11:685.

[3] Probably Mann Page's June 23 letter, in which he expressed the hope that Congress would not deal with the Carlisle commissioners. Lee Papers, PPAmP.

[4] Lord Chatham died on May 11, 1778, but he had fallen ill in Parliament on April 7 while debating a motion of the Duke of Richmond that advised the king to withdraw British forces from the United States. See *Parliamentary History*, 19:1012–31.

[5] For John Paul Jones' account of his raid on Whitehaven, England, and his capture of the HMS *Drake*, see Gerard W. Gawalt, ed. and trans., *John Paul Jones' Memoir of the American Revolution* (Washington: Library of Congress, 1979), pp. 17–21. See also Samuel Eliot Morison, *John Paul Jones* (Boston: Little, Brown and Company, 1959), pp. 138–42, 156–62.

Marine Committee to the Comte d'Estaing

Sir Philadelphia July 16th [i.e. 12?] 1778

The marine Committee of Congress have received information that the Squadron under your Excellencies command has occasion for a supply of water and fresh provisions, and they have taken proper measures to furnish both with all possible expedition. The frigate Chimere, and the two Vessels with her, will be dispatched immediately with as much water as we can find Casks for; the enemy lately here having destroyed every thing of this kind that they could discover. The same vessels will bring your Excellency some hundred barrels of bread and flour, with a small supply of fresh provisions. A Commissary has orders quickly to collect near Shrewsbury and the Hook 50 Bullocks, 700 Sheep, with a quantity of vegitables and a number of poultry; and he will wait on your Excellency to know your pleasure concerning the particular place on the water where he must bring them to be shipped.

The same Commissary has general orders to furnish your Excellency [with] such further supplies as you may please to direct.

The accidents of wind and weather may possibly prevent the Chimere from arriving with water so soon as it shall be wanted, and therefore I am to inform your Excellency that in Little Egg harbor or Thoms river, neither of them far from the Hook, fresh water [may] be conveniently obtained. The Pilots on board the Fleet will conduct Vessels sent for the purpose to either of these places.

Your Excellency may be assured that Congress is disposed to supply your Excellency, and the Squadron under your command, with every thing in their power that may conduce to the accomplishment of the valuable ends you have in view against the common enemy.

I have the honor to be, with the highest respect, your Excellencies most obedient and most humble servant,

Richard Henry Lee,
Chairman of the Marine Committee

RC (Archives Nationales: Archives de la Marine, B4:146. Written and signed by Richard Henry Lee.

[1] Although Lee dated the RC of this letter "July 16th," it is dated "July 12th" in the Marine Committee letterbook, where it is followed by Lee's July 17 letter to d'Estaing, which begins "I had the honor of writing to your Excellency on the 12th instant about the means of procuring fresh Water and the measures taken by the Marine Committee of Congress to furnish fresh provisions for the squadron under your Excellencies Command." Furthermore, on July 12 Lee reported to his brother: "We have been very busy in Marine Committee this morning, altho 'tis Sunday, directing fresh provisions and Water to be sent to this fleet." Considering this flurry of Sunday activity, and the urgency of provisioning the fleet, it seems unlikely that Lee waited four days before sending off this letter to d'Estaing. It is more likely that he inadvertently misdated the RC. PCC Miscellaneous Papers, Marine Committee Letter Book, fols. 163–64; and Richard Henry Lee to Francis Lightfoot Lee, July 12, 1778.

Josiah Bartlett to John Langdon

Dear Sir Philadelphia July 13th 1778

I this day rec'd your favor of the 20th ulto.[1] The account of the money you rec'd of the Marine Committee I procured and was enclosed in Mr Wentworth's letter to you of the 20th ult[2] which I hope you have rec'd. Your letter to the Marine Committee of the 20th ulto came by today's post and will be considered as soon as opportunity permits: the removal of Congress to this City has greatly retarded business. We have not yet procured proper offices for our several Boards and Committees—hope in a few days we shall be better accomodated and attend with more alacrity to business. The Congress meets in the College Hall, as the State House was left by the enemy in a most filthy and sordid situation, as were many of the public and private buildings in the City. Some of the genteel houses were used for stables and holes cut in the parlor floors and their dung shovelled into the cellars. The country Northward of the City for several miles is one common waste, the houses burnt, the fruit trees and others cut down and carried off, fences carried away,

College Hall

gardens and orchards destroyed—Mr Dickenson's and Mr Morris' fine seats all demolished—in short I could hardly find the great roads that used to pass that way. The enemy built a strong abattee with the fruit and other trees from the Delaware to Skuylkill and at about 40 or 50 rods distance along the abattue a quadrangular fort for cannon and a number of redoubts for small arms; the same on the several eminences along the Skuylkill against the City.

Mr Wentworth was taken Sick the 21st ulto, with a fever and a bilious vomiting and purging which lasted him near ten days and hindered me from leaving York Town till the 2d inst. when I left him better—have not heard from him since—hope to see him here in a few days.

The confederation was Signed last week by the delegates of the New England States, New York, Pennsylvania, Virginia and South Carolina; North Carolina have sent their ratification of it, but had no delegates in Congress to sign it. This day a delegate is arrived from Georgia[3] who says he is authorised to sign it in behalf of that State. New Jersey, Delaware and Maryland have objected to it and not authorized their delegates as yet to sign it. Congress have wrote to them and I have reason to think they will accede to it.

In forming a plan of Govt. for our State, I hope particular care will be taken to form a proper Executive Body to see the Laws carried into execution; our present plan is more deficient in that, than in any thing else. When I came to Congress the President asked me if our Govr. had rec'd any letters from him for eight months past, and seemed very uneasy that he had rec'd no answers to his letters; I excused the matter as well as I could—but really Sir, is it to be expected that our very worthy president (who by the way is only paid by the day as other members, a small sum not sufficient to half maintain himself) should be at the trouble to receive, file, copy and answer from time to time all such public letters without any compensation; to do it properly he ought to be allowed a Clerk for the purpose and receive something handsome for his own time. No State in the Union is without some such executive officer or body and I am persuaded no State can long exist with any tolerable degree of order and dignity without it. Some supreme executive power must be somewhere lodged separate from the Legislature, no matter by what name it is called, whether Governor, President of the Council, or Executive Council; but such a power there must be to act, when the Legislature is separate and cannot act, otherwise there is at such times a partial dissolution of the Govt. Beside the impropriety and danger many States think there is in the Leglislative and Executive being lodged in the same body. Such a sort of Executive as the Governor of Connecticut is possessed of, I should think would answer the purpose very well.

The occasion of my writing the above is owing to a paragraph of a letter I received from Major Philbrick wherein he informs me the Convention voted that the Supreme Executive should not be wholly separate from the Leglisative.

As to news here I beg leave to refer you to my letter of this date to General Whipple[4] and request you to inform him of such parts of this as you may think worth communicating.

I am with respect your friend & humble servt,

Josiah Bartlett

[*P.S.*] Pray did Mr Paine, Woodward and the others on Connecticut River join you in Convention? How did they like what was done? Will they join in forming a plan of Govt. &c. &c.[5]

Tr (DLC).

1 Langdon's June 20 letter is in Bartlett, *Papers* (Mevers), pp. 188–89.

2 Not found.

3 That is, Edward Telfair. See *JCC*, 11:685.

4 Not found.

5 Elisha Payne and Bezaleel Woodward were leaders of the effort to join 16 New Hampshire towns east of the Connecticut River to Vermont. They did not attend the constitutional convention then meeting in Concord, N.H. E.P. Walton, ed., *Records of the Governor and Council of the State of Vermont*, 7 vols. (Montpelier: J. and J. M. Poland, 1873), 1:275–78; and *N.H. State Papers*, 9:833–37.

Samuel Holten's Diary

[July 13, 1778]

13. Yesterday Monsieur Gerard the French Ambassador Arrived here, and I waited on him this day & welcomed him to these united states of America.

MS (MDaAr).

Henry Laurens to Patrick Henry

Sir

13th July [1778]

I had the honor of writing to your Excellency by Jones the 9th Inst. The inclosed Act of Congress of this date requests Your Excellency will spare for the use of the Army all the Vinegar purchased by Virginia in the Cargo of the Ship Rodorique.[1]

If success shall attend this application I presume payment and directions for transportation will immediately follow.

I am with the highest Esteem &c.

LB (DNA: PCC, item 13).

1 See *JCC*, 11:686.

Nathaniel Scudder to John Hart

My Dear Sir, Freehold July 13th. 1778

I do myself the Honor to address you upon an affair to me of the most serious and alarming Importance. The Honorable Council and Assembly of this State have not thought proper to invest their Delegates with Power to ratify and sign the Confederation; and it is obvious that unless every of the thirteen States shall acceed to it, we remain an unconfederated People. These States have actually entered into a Treaty with the Court of Versailles as a Confederated People and Monsieur Girard their ambassador Plenipotentiary to Congress is now on our Coast with a powerfull Fleet of Ships, which have taken Pilots on Board for Delaware. He probably may be landed by this Time, and will at all Events be in Philadelphia in a few Days. How must he be astonished & confounded? and what may be the fatal Consequences to America, when he discovers (which he will immediately do) that we are ipso facto unconfederated, and consequently, what our Enemies have called us, "a Rope of Sand"?

Will he not have just Cause to resent the Deception? and may not insidious Britain, knowing the same, take Advantage of our Disunion? For my own Part I am of Opinion She will never desist from her nefarious Designs, nor ever consider her Attempts upon our Liberties fruitless and vain, untill she knows the golden knot is actually tied. I left Congress last Wednesday Evening. The Affair of Confederation was to be taken up next Day. The Magna Charta of America was amply engrossed and prepared for signing. Ten States had actually authorised their Delegates to ratify; a Delegate from an eleventh (vizt. Georgia) declared he was so fully possessed of the Sense of his Constituents, that he should not hesitate to subscribe it.[1] New-Jersey and Maryland only stood out.[2] Mr. Chase, one of the Delegates from that State, told me the Day I left Philadelphia, that he imagined the Determination of Maryland would depend much upon *that* of New-Jersey, and thought if our State should acceed, theirs would also—he therefore concluded to go immediately down and try what could be done. I at the same Time assured him I would write you on the Subject on my Return. I ought to inform you, Sir, that the Objections stated by New-Jersey were read and considered by Congress, and after being entered at large on their Minutes, a Question was taken, whether Congress at that Time judged it expedient to take up the said Objections so as to admit any Emendations in the Plan of Confederation, or not? and it passed in the Negative.[3] In Consequence of which they remain both upon the Journal and Files to be taken up and considered at any future Time when they may be called for.

I expect my Colleagues will soon address you on this Subject. I left Doctr. Witherspoon, Doctr. Elmer & Mr. Boudinot at Philadelphia, whither I expect to return in a few Days.

I should have been much more uneasy, when I was last at Princeton, and should have taken more Pains to convince the Members of the Necessity of granting the Powers of Ratification to their Delegates, had I not been encouraged to expect, that the Legislature would not rise without doing it; at the same Time supposing the Reason, why they were witheld at that Juncture, to be, that their Objections might have the greater Weight with Congress. Indeed I all along expected Doctr. Witherspoon would have brought on such Powers with him, especially as I hoped the Honorable Houses would be clearly of Opinion, that it were better to confederate under all the Disadvantages they apprehended, than that the general Union should be broken or even greatly endangered.

I know not Whether I ought to say any Thing respecting the Objections themselves; some of them are perhaps not very essential. The Obtaining an Admission of several of them would doubtless be of great local Advantage to this State; but every State must expect to be Subjected to considerable local Disadvantages in a general Confederation. Indeed upon the whole I am fully [*of*] Opinion, that no Plan can or will ever be adopted more equal, or less generally injurious to the confederating States than the present. I also declare it as my Opinion that if the general Business of Emendation were to be fairly taken up in Congress to morrow, several Alterations would be made exceedingly disadvantageous to the smaller circumscribed States, and which perhaps might more than counterbalance the obtaining what we apply for. As to the grand and capital Objection respecting the Lands &c.[4] I will only observe, that in Case we never obtain an original Quota of them, we shall only loose a Share in the prime Sales of them, which will probably be very low, while we shall inevitably reap a permanent and encreasing Benefit from the rapid & enormous growth of the larger States; for surely in Proportion to their Extent and Population their Quota of the public Expence & Debt will be encreased, while ours will be proportionably diminished. What avails it therefore to us, whether five Pounds of our national Debt be paid by the Accession of a Subject to this State, or whether our Quota be really lessined five Pounds by the Settlement of a Person in the State of Virginia at the Distance of a thousand Miles from the Atlantic? For my own Part I think we shall have greatly the Advantage of these enormous unwieldy Governments; nor do I judge it unlikely they will soon find it necessary to sue for the curtailing their own extravagant Jurisdiction.

In the Settlement of our Soldiery & the foreign Deserters at the Expiration of the War, we shall incur considerable Disadvantage; however as the larger States will doubtless rejoice to have their Frontiers immediately enlarged, and will vie with each other in

Courting so great an Accession of Inhabitants, there will probably be no greater Expence than barely that of locating the Lands, our Quota of which cannot be any very considerable Sum.

I congratulate you on the signal Success of our Arms in this Neighbourhood on the 28th of June. Great Plunder and Devastation have been committed among my Friends in this Quarter, but through the distinguishing Goodness of Providence my Family & Property escaped, & that almost in a miraculous Manner.

I wish you to take the above Representation into your serious Consideration, and, if with me you shall judge it a Matter of sufficient Importance, that the Legislature may be as speedily as possible convened to deliberate and determine thereon.[5]

I am Dear Sir with great Esteem Your most Obedt. Hble Servt.

Nath. Scudder

RC (Nj). Addressed: "Honorable John Hart Esqr., Speaker of the Assembly of the State of New Jersey."

1 Edward Langworthy was the Georgia delegate in question, though it is not clear when he made this remark.

2 Delaware had also not yet authorized her delegates to ratify the Articles of Confederation. *JCC*, 11:677.

3 For New Jersey's objections to the Articles of Confederation and Congress' June 25 decision not to consider them, see *JCC*, 11:648–51.

4 New Jersey insisted that the Articles of Confederation should vest Congress with authority over crown lands to facilitate the payment of the expenses of the war "and for other such public and general purposes." See *JCC*, 11:650.

5 On November 20, 1778, the New Jersey legislature authorized the state's delegates to ratify the Articles of Confederation, which they accordingly did six days later. See *JCC*, 11:1161–64.

Samuel Adams to James Warren

My dear sir Philade July 14 1778

I am to acknowledge the Receipt of your favors of the 26th & 28th of June.[1] I have long been apprehensive, *you* know, that false Ideas of Politeness would injure the Minds of our Countrymen and prove destructive to Morals and Liberty. But I own, I did not expect that the most ridiculous Folley would have taken so early and large a Stride as it appears to have done in the Instance you mention.[2] It cannot in my opinion be supported by any Principles of Truth & Propriety and discovers a Degree of Servility shocking to sober Humanity. And yet a Conduct so void of common Sense will find Advocates among many who never had and never can have a Spark of that Republican Feeling which you have always possessd. These People are formd to be Asses & Slaves; Let them remain so. But surely they ought not to be advanced to Places of Influence, to spread by their Examples, the Principles of Servility and Slavery among the People. I will take an Opportunity when I am at Leisure to answer your Letter of the 26, which I have communicated to my Friend Colo Lee.[3] Yesterday I made a short Visit to Monsr. Gerard. If I can form any Judgmt of him, his Manners would suit our Country. But I expect to be better acquainted with him soon. Mr H—— has asked & obtained Leave of Absence & is going home! Adieu.

S A.

RC (MHi).

1 Warren's letters of June 26 and 28 are in *Warren-Adams Letters,* 2:24–29.

2 In his June 28 letter Warren had complained about the fraternization of Americans with captured British officers of the Convention Army in Massachusetts. Ibid., p. 28.

3 In his June 26 letter, Warren had reported his efforts in the Massachusetts legislature to reward Arthur Lee and had voiced dissatisfaction with the Marine Committee's refusal to delegate the power for appointing ship captains to the regional navy boards. Ibid., pp. 24–27. See also Adams to Warren, July 20, 1778, note 7.

Josiah Bartlett to Mary Bartlett

My Dear Philadelphia July the 14th 1778

I had not the pleasure of Receiving any letter from you by yesterdays Post, Shall Expect one by the next. It give pleasure to hear from my family more Especially to hear they are well. By the favor of Heaven I have had my health as well since I came from Home as I had it for sometime & I think rather better than usual. Hope it will be Continued if for the best. God grant you & the Rest of my family may Enjoy an Equal Share of Health of Body & peace & contentment of mind.

We have had some Exceeding Hot weather here, it is now a little Cooler. We are troubled with one of the Plagues of Egypt which the Enemy left here when they Evacuated this place, I mean Swarms of flies. They are much lessened Since cleansing the place of the Filth & Dung &c &c Tho they are still very troublesome. I wrote you the 6th Inst. soon after I came here & a Line with Mr Thurston the 11th by Express which I hope will Come Safe to your hand. On Sunday about two o'Clock Mr Girard the French Ambassador made a Publick Entry into the City from Chester 15 miles Down the River where the Ships Stopt for want of wind to bring them up. He was attended by three members of Congress who were ordered to Conduct him to Lodgings here. 13 Cannon were fired when He Dismounted at his Lodgings. I was introduced to him the same Day at the Presidents Lodgings about an hour after his arrival where he Came to pay his Respects to our President. He is a pretty Large Man not very fat about 50 years old as I guess, Speaks English tollerably well for a Frenchman, was Richly but Decently Dressed, Behaved with Ease & Dignity without any of the foppish airs of your low bred French men. He has the Sole power of ordering the Count de Estaing the French admiral with his Squadron as he pleases.

The names of the French Line of Battle Ships in the Squadron are, the Languedock 90 Guns, Tonant 80, Caesar 74, Zele 74, Hector 74, Protector 74, Marselles 74, Guerrier 74, Fantesque 64, Province, 64, Valliant 64, Sagittaire 50 Guns.

RC (NhHi).

Elias Boudinot to Hannah Boudinot

My dearest Love Philadelphia July 14th. 1778

I am distressed to account for your total Silence, not having recieved a Line from Home since my departure: my [fears] are raised in proportion to my Anxiety for your welfare and Comfort. I have wrote you several Letters lately, by different Opportunities. Yesterday I had the Honor to dine with La Sieur Gerard Minister plenipotentiary to his most Christian Majesty. He is about 50 Years of Age, appears to be a Modest, Grave, decent, cheerfull Man—highly pleased with our Country and the Struggles we have made for Liberty. A Committee of Congress were appointed to wait on him at Chester.[1] On their Arrival a Barge with 12 Oarsmen dressed in Scarlet trimmed with Silver, were ready to recieve them. When the Barge was half way to the Ship, she lay on her Oars and fifteen Guns were fired. When they came to the Ship her Sides were Manned & our Committee were recieved on the Deck by the Marines with posted Arms. At the Gang way they met the Plenipotentiary &c &c and were conducted into the great Cabbin, where the Compliments of Congratulation being given they returned to the Shore in the same Manner and with the same Ceremony, accompanied by the Sieur Gerard, Mr Deane &c &c. Here were four Coaches with four Horses our Committee had prepared, in which they returned to this City, when they were saluted with 15 Guns. We have had an Acct. yesterday, that one of our Armed Ships called the Ranger of 18 Guns & 123 Men, being on the Coast of Ireland, the Drake a frigate of 20 Guns & 158 Men was sent out to take her, but after an Engagement of 65 Minutes, she struck to the Ranger, Capt. Jones—having lost the Capt., Lieut. & 42 Men. Capt. Jones lost the Cap of his Marines and about 8 Men. After this the Ranger sailed into Whitehaven, burned all the Ships in the Harbour, and spiked up about 30 Cannon in the fort & came off. [During?] his Passage he took 5 Prizes besides the Drake. Whitehaven is on the Coast of England in the Irish Channel.

I am very happily situated here, considering my absence from a beloved Wife. Am under great Obligations to Mrs. Franklin for her kind attention. I shall soon be quite settled when I hope to have some leisure, to write you fully. We are preparing for a publick Reception of the Sieur Gerard when he will have a publick Audience. I will let you know the Ettiquette used on this Occasion. I know it will tend to divert your lonely moments, altho' I confess I should prefer another mode, was it in my Power.

My most affectionate Love to Susan—remember me to all as if named—And believe me to be with very peculiar Esteem, My dearest Love, Your highly [. . .] Husband, Boudinot

RC (NN).

1 See *JCC*, 11:685. For Gérard's arrival in America, and his July 15 report to the French foreign minister Vergennes on his trip to Philadelphia, see John J. Meng, "Philadelphia Welcomes America's First Foreign Representative," *Records of the American Catholic Historical Society* 45 (March 1934): 51–67.

James Lovell to Samuel P. Savage

Sir, July 14th. 1778

Yesterday came to hand the Letters which you were so obliging as to inclose to me the 2d Instant. I thank you for your Care and congratulate you upon the fair Prospect of ruining the Plans of our Enemies if not of also destroying many of themselves by the Cooperation of General Washingtons Army with the Fleet under Count D'Estang wch. is before this Time at Sandy Hook. The Count is plenipotentiary as to military Operations. Should he find it best to visit Rh Island first I hope you can find Voluntiers enough to cooperate instantly with him. A small spirited Number would be sufficient for the Purpose. Every armed Vessel which you have in port should be ready for Business. First Moments are precious. The Enemy must not have Time to recover from the Surprize which this unexpected Activity of France will occasion. Several of their Vessels have been taken by this Fleet of our Allies.

Mr. Hancock setts off Tomorrow and will give you many particulars which I now omit.

Your obliged, humble Servant, James Lovell

RC (MHi).

James Lovell to William Whipple

Dear Sir, July 14th. 1778.

Your Satyrveimic favor of the 30 of June came yesterday to hand. I enviously thank you for it; for you write like a man happy by the side of a charming woman, and whom nothing can vex. I will now only say you *ought* to be here at this period as a balance to the days of vexation you have formerly known in the service of your country in this rotten hearted State. Though our own Navy has dwindled Sadly, we now hold up our heads upon the strength of our allies by sea. The Count d'Estang is plenipotentiary for co-operation with General Washington and has proceeded immediately to Sandy Hook. The Languedoc is a very swift sailor, and though called a 90, has upwards of 100 carriage guns and 1200 men. The enemy have many ships, but their fifties half manned will not be able to stand an engagement with double manned 74's & 64's of the French. Mr. Hancock sets out for *Town* to morrow and will probably gain Some intelligence in his rout which being published in the Gazettes at his arrival will reach you and discover interesting events of the joint operations of France and America.

Nine States have Signed the Confederation and there is no doubt but Georgia, Delaware and Jersey will soon sign. Maryland will take airs and plague us, but upon our determination to confederate anew, 12 will do as She has always done before—come in without grace.

J. P. Jones has behaved to your liking—his conduct alone will make England keep her ships at home. *My* love to *your* friends,

J.L.

Tr (DLC).

Henry Marchant to John Carter

Sir,[1] Philadelphia July 14th. 1778.

Your agreable Favour of the 2d Instant, I recd. yesterday. As Congress was designed by its Institution to be a true Representation of the Minds of its Constituents; So that Body finds itself happy when Acts and Resolutions of material Consequence, merit the Universal Approbation.

The Scene brightens, grows more and more interesting, and calls for new and fresh Exertions of Senatorial Wisdom. We advance into the Circle and Standing of mighty Nations—Adepts in all the Pollicy of Peace and War. May Heaven protect Our Youth and prove the Friend, Protector and Councellor of America!

I shall inclose you the Paper of this Day; which will render many Observations useless.[2] I had the Honor last Sabbath of welcoming in Person the Plenipotentiary of France to these United States. Grand and important is the Year 1778. We behold with Wonder and Astonishment a Leap of at least a Century. Sturdy indeed and wonderfully Successfull thro' Divine Assistance, have been the efforts of the well sinewed American Confederacy.

As I was present at, so I never was Witness to a more elevating and unspeakably joyous Interview than that between the Plenipotentiary of His most Christian Majesty, and the President of Congress in the Name and Behalf of the thirteen United States of America. It was reciprocally easy, graceful, Endearing and Noble. May it presage a happy Issue to the American Struggle and a growing and undecaying Glory that shall diffuse its grateful Influences thro' the World.

You inform me the Enemy are mowing the Islands (for us I hope). I expect They will soon leave Rhode Island. They must gather in their Forces—and I hope They will find enough to do beyond Our Coasts.

I should be surprised indeed to find The Towns in our State at present not in a Situation to be taxed, thrown out of a Representation. Can there be a Man that apprehends the Doctrine of Taxation & Representation used agt. Great Britain, to be in Point. Who are the greatest Sufferers, those who pay Taxes, or those whom the Enemy have deprived for the Present of any Ability to pay any? Who may be presumed to be most attached to Our Cause—or can it be supposed that with Their Estates they have lost the Powers of Wisdom to advise in Councill, or Hands to fight in the Field? Tenderness to Tories uniformly Enemies to Our Existance, and Listening Ears to the Female Prophetess, are dangerous Symptoms.

I am greatly pleased that Genl. Sullivan's Exertions gains him Confidence and Honor with our State. Should the British Troops continue there still—And the French Fleet by & by enter our Harbour—I hope the Genl. will signalize himself, and will have a noble Train of *Volunteer* Spirits following his Example and supporting his Measures.

I have in my Turn Sir to acknowledge Your Politeness, for a Long Time while in another publick office in the State, and during the Time I have had the Honor of a Seat in Congress, in favouring me with your interesting Paper. As I know you would choose to be informed, that so abuses may be rectified if possible, The Post before the last, of yesterday, & the Post before that brought me no Paper; which from the regular manner in which you have pleased to supply me, I attribute to some Abuses in the Post-Offices.

I have given you a long galloping Letter, but as I have not often Time enough to oblige You to submit to so great a mispenditure of Time in reading, You'l excuse it.

My compts. to Mrs. Carter and all enquiring Friends. I am Your Friend & Servt.
Hy Marchant

RC (R–Ar).

[1] John Carter (1745–1814) was the printer of the *Providence Gazette*. *DAB*.

[2] This day's issue of the *Pennsylvania Packet* contained an account of Gérard's arrival in Philadelphia.

Henry Marchant to William Greene

Sir, Philadelphia, July 14th, 1778.

As I shall enclose to your Excellency the newspaper of this day, I have no occasion to add, but that I had the honor of being present the last Sabbath at the most interesting interview that ever took place in America, or perhaps in the world, between Monsieur Gerard, the Plenipotentiary of France, and the President of Congress, on the part of the Sovereign, Independent United States of America.

This interview was most cordial, generous and noble. In my turn, I had the honor of personally congratulating his Excellency upon his safe arrival, and giving him a hearty welcome to the United States of America.

I am in daily expectation of hearing that Rhode Island is evacuated. Most respectfully I am, Your Excellency's most obedient and humble servant,
H. J. Marchant.

MS not found; reprinted from "Revolutionary Correspondence from 1775 to 1782," *Collections of the Rhode Island Historical Society* 6 (1867): 215.

Samuel Adams to James Warren

My dear sir, Philade July 15 1778

Mr H.[1] informs me that he will certainly set off for Boston immediately after Dinner, and being now in Congress I have Time only to write you a short Letter.

The Sieur Gerard will soon have an Audience in Congress, in the Stile of "Minister Plenipotentiary of his most Christian Majesty the King of France." Would you think that one so little of the Man of the World as I am should be joynd in a Committee to settle Ceremonials. It is however of some Importance that we agree upon Forms that are adapted to the true *republican* Principles; for this Instance may be recurrd to as a Precedent in Futurity.

The Articles of Confederation were signd last Week by seven States. North Carolina has sent a full Ratification of it, so the Members of that State will sign when they arrive which is expected in a few Days. Congress has written a Letter to the States of Georgia, Maryland, Delaware & Jersey pressing them to authorize their Delegates to joyn in this most necessary Transaction.[2] I believe there will [*be*] no Difficulty except with Maryland, & she will finally accede. The Articles have undergone no Alterations.

The French Minister arrivd in this City on Lords Day, and the day following, last Monday, the Delegates of Massachusetts Bay paid him their Compliments in Town. I know not that those of any other State have observd this Ceremony. It appeard to us highly proper. We were receivd with Politeness and heard some handsome Things said of the State we have the Honor to represent.

The Minister plenipotentiary deliverd to Congress a Letter from his Sovereign expressd in the strongest Terms of Affection & Friendship.

I can at present add no more than to inform you, that your Nephew, the son of my old Friend James Otis Esq, came into this City a few Days ago with the Intention of purchasing some Necessaries, but being destitute of Cash his Friends were under a Necessity of supplying him with the Sum of twenty pounds Lawful Money for the Repayment of which I have taken his written Request to his Grandfather, agreably to his own Proposal. I have indorsd the order and inclosd it in this Letter. I know not whether this will altogether meet with Approbation. I was the rather inclind to interrest my self for this young Gentleman, because I have been satisfactorily informd that he has behavd well in his military Character. I gave my best Advice respecting his *Morals*. When you receive the Money you will please to repay to Mr. Hancock fourteen Dollars and thirteen & two thirds to Mr Dana, (both which Gentlemen will be at Boston shortly) and the Remainder to Mrs A., upon Notice of which I will account with two other Gentlemen concernd, Mr Holten & Col Pickering.[3]

I remain Your very affectionate, S A

[*P.S.*] Mr Dana desires his particular Respects to you.

RC (MHi).

1 That is, John Hancock.

2 See Henry Laurens to Certain States, July 10, 1778.

3 The younger James Otis was also the subject of a special entry in the diary of Samuel Holten: "July 14, 1778. I let the Hon. Samuel Adams, Esqr. have £4, of which he is to pay unto James Otis (a minr) being my part of what the Delegates of our State have agreed to advance to sd minr., and Mr. Adams is to write to his friends and procure the money, & acct with me for the same." MDaAr.

Henry Laurens to John Lewis Gervais

Dear Sir 15th July [1778]

I confirm and beg leave to refer to the preceding duplicate of a letter which I had the honor of writing to you the 23d June by way of Maryland.

I could now if circumstances permitted fill two or three pages with important Intelligence and nothing would give me more pleasure than devoting an hour or two to your service or amusement, but I am limited. I was not allowed to write a single line to any body by Mr. Archibald Brown who left me the 9th Instant, and I believe waited on the road a day in expectation of Letters from me. At present I must be brief and refer you for particulars where you can find them in papers which will be wrapped up with this, and to our friend Mr. Lowndes, to whom I shall send other papers and write a little more copiously. You will learn also almost every thing from the Chief Justices communications, he devotes all his leisure minutes to collecting and transmitting news, and I help him upon all occasions with materials. He is a perfect Miser in gathering but very liberal in diffusing and by his means Carolina will be fully informed, the great end will therefore be answered and I must avail myself of the advantage of so good a Colleague. If I have any objection to his conduct 'tis that he will not frame public Letters to be subscribed by all the Delegates which ought to be done, but here he is a Miser again, why should I write, says he, for A.B.C. From one and another you must therefore expect to collect all that is fit and necessary to offer.

You will have such free access to the Papers in the hands of His Excellency as will save you the trouble of reading here, what passes away like a shadow, news only begets appetite for more and never satisfies. When you are told that Monsr. or Le Sr. Gerard is arrived, you will be anxious to learn the reception he has met, and the important concerns he is charged with—That Monsr. le Count d'Estaing had passed Barnagat and had anchored off Sandy Hook, there will be a chasm, and a painful one too on your mind until you hear whether he has Burgoyned the British Fleet and Army at New York or caught a Tartar.

Informing you that I have transmitted orders to General Washington to co-operate with the French Vice Admiral to dispose of the Army under General Gates at North River, and to call in the aid of the Militia from the six northern and eastern States[1]—the wonder will be, whether General Pigot surrendered his garrison at Rhode Island, or made his escape, or maintained his ground? When I tell you that hitherto Congress have only talked of a Table but seem to evade all Measures for covering one, either with an House or Viands,[2] that I am forced every day to entertain Delegates, Strangers and sometimes Minister plenipo. you will naturally ask, will Mount Tacitus, Mepkin &c support the expence? I can assure you their produce must be uncommonly ample if they answer in the affirmative. If my diurnal Account amounted at York Town to near fifty Dollars, what will be the sum in Philadelphia, I hope not much more. Be that as it may, I must bear it until the Celebration of All Saints—the first time I ever wished for the arrival of a Saints day since I left school; then by the Grace of God I mean to break up.[3]

You will see that Your friend Colo. Laurens has again been in the way of danger and honor, besides having his horse fall under him by a deadly shot he has received a slight contusion from a spent ball which he has not mentioned. I learnt it from Colonel Boudinot.

When General Lee's tryal is ended, you shall be informed of certain particulars which had excited my jealousy of my old friend antecedent to the march from Valley Forge—he has written two Pieces and caused them to be published in the Jersey Gazette relative to the Battle of Monmouth. I have not read them, but have been informed they contain no proofs of his discretion.[4]

I intend to draw on Mr. Nutt for eight hundred and ten Pounds Sterling,[5] which will produce me here at least ten thousand two hundred and sixty dollars, perhaps five hundred and forty more. I am offer'd 475 Currency for 1 Sterling, and am taught to expect five for one. You will take this under consideration in lodging the attachment, if he pays my Bill the expence of the attachment will of course be mine, e contra, the precaution will be found to have been necessary.[6]

LB (ScHi).

1 See Laurens to Washington, July 10, 1778.

2 For further information on this point, see Laurens to Rawlins Lowndes, May 17, 1778, note 9.

3 All Saints Day, which falls on November 1, would mark the first anniversary of Laurens' election as president of Congress.

4 See Joseph Reed to Charles Lee, July 10, 1778.

5 See Laurens to John Nutt, July 21, 1778.

6 For the continuation of this letter, see Laurens to Gervais, July 18, 1778.

Henry Laurens to Rawlins Lowndes

Dear Sir 15th July [1778]

I had the Honor of addressing your Excellency the 27th Ulto. through the hands of Governor Henry via Williamsburg. On that day I left York Town and arrived here the 30th—from various impediments I could not collect a sufficient number of States to form a Congress earlier than the 7th Instant; one was the offensiveness of the air in and around the State House, which the Enemy had made an Hospital and left it in a condition disgraceful to the Character of civility. Particularly they had opened a large square pit near the House, a receptacle for filth, into which they had also cast dead horses and the bodies of Men who by the mercy of death had escaped from their further cruelties. I cannot proceed to a new subject before I add a curse on their savage practices.

Congress in consequence of this disappointment have been shuffling from Meeting House to College Hall the last seven days & have not performed half the business which might and ought to have been done, in a more commodious situation.

The several Papers which your Excellency will receive within the present cover, No. 1 to No. 15 will contain much Intelligence of our Public Affairs, and more minutely than my time will allow me to repeat in a Letter, wherefore Sir, I beg leave to refer to these and to request you will communicate to Mr. Wells all that your Excellency shall judge proper for publication, he is very good in sending me his Gazettes and other Intelligence and my duties will not always permit me to make exact and direct returns.

On Sunday last the Committee appointed for the purpose received Monsr. Gerard at Chester, and under a respectible Cavalcade conducted him to temporary Apartments at General Arnold's, where the Committee, a few other Members of Congress including myself dined with him. On Monday he dined with me, walk'd an hour in the Evening and yesterday Morning Monsr. Girard breakfasted with me and explained his Mission for the information of Congress. He intimated to me his powers for appearing in the Character of Minister Plenipotentiary, or more simply a Resident; "that which he should assume awaited the determination of Congress respecting the public Character of their Minister or Ministers at the Court of Versailles, who without full powers would in many instances find themselves incapable of accomplishing essential services to these States."

He marked the distinction of Ambassador, a character in which he did not appear, and put into my hands Copy of the Kings' sign Manual appointing him Minister Plenipo: another by which he is appointed Consul General in the several United States with powers to depute and several other Papers,[1] Copies of some of these Your Excellency will find among the numbers abovementioned. No. [ ] respecting Prizes which may be made by American Vessels of War is another mark of the good will of our illustrious Ally and ought to be published immediately.[2] These Papers I laid before Congress and reported all the necessary articles of conversation with Monsr. Girard. A Committee of three are appointed for considering & reporting upon the subject and upon a proper mode for receiving Monsr. Girard in form.[3]

The Court of France probably could not have discovered a Man in Europe so equal to the task assigned the Minister Plenipotentiary as is Monsr. Girard—a Man of Politeness, Good Breeding and affability without troublesome ceremony. Of good sense and quick perceptions without shew or ostentation, and well read in the History of Man. Very seldom, Sir, do I suffer myself to pronounce an opinion of any Man upon so short and slight an acquaintance; even the present Case, although I have seen many marks which induce me to believe well of this Gentlemans candour and integrity of Heart, I proceed in my judgment not a step beyond visibility, and keep as I hold we ought all to keep upon every Stranger in high Character, all the necessary Guards awake. One article of Conversation with Sier Gerard I ought not to omit, I think it important, and that it will please Your Excellency. With a view of learning what reception at home those French Gentlemen had met, who had returned some eight or nine Months ago murmuring and dissatisfied; I took occasion to intimate some concern at the disappointment which many of them had suffered, and in honor of Congress added brief Accounts of what had been granted to numbers of French Officers now in our Army, that it had been impossible to gratify the wishes of every one for grade, that in general such as had been Commissioned by Congress had performed good service, and done honor to their Nation, that some of these Gentlemen from their bravery and propriety of conduct were held in the highest esteem &c. &c. Mr. Gerard replied, The Court had seen with pain so many French men applying for permission to resort to the American Army, very few of whom had received encouragement, the Court were sensible that crouds of Foreigners applying for Commissions would tend to embarrass Congress, that since his arrival in Philadelphia there had been many applications made to him for recommendations, every one of which he had refused to listen to, and that I might rest satisfied Congress would never be troubled with Petitions under his auspices.

Mr. Silas Deane is returned to Congress in pursuance of an Order in the last Winter, the dissentions among our croud of Commissioners at Paris are become notorious and I was going to add scandalous, particulars have been imparted to me in several Letters, but I have hitherto sealed my lips, and I hope Congress will, by a judicious seperation, supercede the Call for investigation and avert the impending evil of keeping jarring minds in one employ.

Mr. Deane has delivered me an handsome testimonial in his favor from Monsr. Vergennes, one of the Ministers at the Court of Versailles, signed by the Kings order and accompanied with his Majestys' Picture in a Gold Box, superbly surrounded by two rows of Diamonds.[4] Le Sier Gerard speaks of and entertains him with distinguishing respect. Doctor Franklin has also written to me, expressing an high sense of Mr. Deane's merits[5]—those who differ in opinion with the Doctor, say all these recommendations are mere etiquette and partiality. I shall form no conclusion until I learn much more than has hitherto come to my knowledge. I believe they are all good Men, but I know there are in some of them vile tempers, which alloy their general goodness.

Inclosed herein your Excellency will find a Bill dated 4th June 1778 by the Marquis de la Fayette on Messrs. John Crips and Comp. for seven thousand dollars, and a Promisary Note by Archibald Browne Esqr. 7th July for £1726.5.–Carolina Currency, sums which I supplied those Gentlemen respectively as a good means of removing so much out of the public treasury here into our own, and shall with the concurrence of my Colleagues remit all that remains after ascertaining a sum necessary to be reserved for the use of the Delegates, unless Your Excellency and the Privy Council shall otherwise direct.

I had relied on my Colleague the Chief Justice for the frame of a general Address from the Delegates from our State to Your Excellency, accounting for our proceedings respecting Confederation, but am disappointed, I believe he has written fully on the subject in his private Letters to Your Excellency,[6] to his Advices therefore I beg leave at present to refer, but I shall urge the propriety and necessity for laying before the Legislature from whom we derived our authority, a proper report of our conduct.

I foresee I shall be obliged to detain this Messenger a day or two, in which time articles of Intelligence will accumulate, whatever happens worthy Your Excellencys notice shall be transmitted in the Packet which shall be kept open to the last moment. I have taken the liberty to refer the late President[7] and Mr. Gervais as well as Mr. Wells to Your Excellency for news, in my present circumstances 'tis barely possible for me to keep pace with my public duties, my own private concerns receive not the smallest attention from me.

Your Excellency's favors of the 28th May and 17th June lie before me,[8] and I had intended to pay the respect due to them by this Messenger, but 'tis now impossible. I therefore intreat your indulgence, Sir, until the next—and that you will be assured I Am with very great Esteem and Respect, Sir, Your Excellency's &c.

LB (ScHi).

1 The March 28 documents authorizing Gérard to act as minister plenipotentiary and consul general are in *JCC*, 11:753–54, and Wharton, *Diplomatic Correspondence*, 2:522.

2 This day Congress ordered publication of part of a July 14 letter from Gérard to Laurens stating that American vessels could retain custody of any British ships they captured while operating with d'Estaing's squadron. See *JCC*, 11:691; and Wharton, *Diplomatic Correspondence*, 2:645–46.

3 See *JCC*, 11:688, 696–701, 703, 707–8, 753–57.

4 Vergennes' "testimonial" on Deane's behalf is in Wharton, *Diplomatic Correspondence*, 2:519–20.

[5] See Franklin's March 31 letter to Laurens in Franklin, *Writings* (Smyth), 7:128.

[6] No letters from William Henry Drayton to President Lowndes have been found.

[7] John Rutledge.

[8] There are transcripts of these letters in the Laurens Papers, ScHi. Although both letters were private, on July 11 Laurens had read to Congress extracts of the June 17 letter "respecting the cloathier's department in South Carolina, and . . . some practices relative to loan office certificates," which were then referred to appropriate committees for action. See *JCC*, 11:682.

John Penn to Richard Caswell

Dear Sir, Philada July 15th 1778.

Colo. Williams never gave me the certificate of our appointment untill a few days ago when we parted, he chusing to be inoculated for the small pox at Alexandria. I was then hurried & did not examine it, not having the least reason to doubt but that the powers given to the Delegates were the same as usual, however on producing the Commission it was so worded as to make it absolutely necessary that all the Members should be present to give us a right to vote. As it may be a long time before Mr. Harnet arrives or Colo. Williams gets over the Smallpox I have thought it my duty to write to you by express, requesting that your Excellency would be pleased to mention whether one Gentn. by the design of the Genl. Assembly cannot vote, if so you will be pleased to send a Commission for that purpose; but if no alteration can be made pray inform Mr. Harnet that it is absolutely necessary for him to repair to Philada. without delay. I find my self in a disagreeable situation wch. is the reason of my application to you, I was told that the Assembly expected that the Delegates were upon the same terms as formerly.[1]

Mr. Gerrard a French Minister is here. He is to reside in America. War is declared by France against England—a large Fleet from that Nation arrived at Sandy hook several days ago & are gone to New York to take possession of the British Fleet there, we expect to hear of an action every hour.

General Washing has crossed the No. River, & General Gates is in the neighbourhood of King's bridge with a considerable body. Our force will be upwards of 20,000. The French have 3 or 4000 men more than they want to man their ships who may be disposed of as Genl. Washington thinks proper, so that most Gentn. are of opinion we shall soon be in possession of New York, in short our affairs seem to be in as good away as we could wish.

Mr. Deane is in Town, he is highly recommended by the King of France. I beg your Excellency will let me hear from you as soon as possible. I had almost forgot to tell you that Genl. Lee is under an arrest, what the sentence will be is not known, however he has made it a quarrel with Genl Washington & of course you know he must fail. I shall write you by every opportunity. I am with due respect, Your Excellency's most obt. hble Servt. John Penn

P.S. Some matters of very great Importance will soon come on, it is the wish of the Southern States that No. Carolina should vote as I am confident it was not the design of the General Assembly to alter our old mode of one Delegate's representing the State, I hope your Excellency will send a Commn. for that purpose, however the Clerks may have expressed the resolution of the Assembly, or we shall have nothing to do or say this year.

Inclosed is a news paper. J.P.

RC (NcU).

[1] The somewhat ambiguously worded May 22, 1778, credentials of the North Carolina delegates are in *JCC*, 11:695. In response to Penn's plea for clarification of them, Governor Caswell wrote to him on August 13 and enclosed a new commission raising the number of North Carolina delegates from three to five and authorizing any two of them to cast the state's vote in Congress. *N.C. State Records*, 13:207–8, 467–68. Long before these documents reached Philadelphia, however, Penn began to cast North Carolina's vote after Congress decided, on July 24, that "any one of the delegates of North Carolina is empowered, when only one is present, to give the vote of that state." *JCC*, 11:715, 718.

Jonathan Bayard Smith to Caesar Rodney

Sir Philadelphia July 15th. 1778

I am informed that a party of the militia of your State has destroyed all my buildings on Bombayhook; & it is said to have been done by your orders on an idea of its being necessary for the public service.[1] In this case I would not presume to suppose you judged wrong, & my uniform opinion has been that private interests must give way to the public necessities. But as I have also been informed that it was a voluntary sacrifice on the mere inconsideration of the persons who made it; & some suggestions have been intimated that personal & interested motives had some influence with the party, I beg the favor of your Excellency to indulge me with information of the orders under which the militia acted, if they had any. The loss of the buildings, of the current rents, & of considerable arrearages which must take place is considerable, & not merited by a person who has sacrificed already so much of his interest, & his whole time for several years to the service of his country.

I beg your Excellencys pardon for giving you this trouble; and shall only add that if you, or the government of your state have directed the measure, I shall have the fullest confidence in its having been proper & necessary.

With very great Respect, I am, your excellencys most humble servant,

Jona. B Smith

RC (PHi).

1 President Rodney's August 11 letter explaining that Continental, not Delaware, troops had been responsible for the destruction of Smith's property at Bombay Hook, Newcastle County, Del., is in Rodney, *Letters* (Ryden), pp. 278–79.

William Henry Drayton's Draft Address to Conrad Alexandre Gérard

[July 16–30, 1778][1]

Fully sensible of the blessings which are likely to flow from the treaties between France & these United States, it is with true pleasure Congress view those engagements at once demonstrating his wisdom & magnanimity & commanding the Reverence of all Nations. His beneficent attention to the rights & Happiness of Mankind has gained to him the veneration of the virtuous Citizens of America & intitle him to gratitude of their latest posterity. It is the hope & opinion of Congress that the Confidence His Majesty reposes in the firmness of these States will receive additional strength from every day's experience of their conduct.

Had the Independence & Repose of America depended solely on the King your Master, there is no doubt, but that both had been long since established. That lust of domination which has drawn so much blood, must ever be detested.[2] By deception, fire & sword these States were driven to assume a station among the Nations of the Earth to which they were intitled by laws human & divine.[3] They could not but virtuously endeavour to sustain a war brought upon them from afar: a war arising from a lust of domination ever to be deplored: a war prosecuted by the enemy with a degree of outrage & cruelty, as disgraceful to their arms & counsels, as unprecedented among civilized Nations. Maturely reflecting upon the ruinous consequences of a passive conduct America met the attack aimed at every thing her People held valuable & dear, when she scarce had arms to oppose the shock:[4] the unexpected conflict reduced her to the last extremity, but relying upon the justice of her cause she had no apprehension for the event. During the progress of the war the Divine interpositions in her favour became manifest; & in no instance more conspicuous than in moving the heart of your Sovereign in favour of our exertions. He has the glory of being the first Prince in Europe who declared himself a friend & ally to the oppressed United States alone struggling in defence of rights not confined to them but extended to all mankind. That same lust of domination which originated the war yet prolonges & extends its calamities. America wishes to sheathe the sword & stop the further effusion of blood. The King of G. B. pretends to have sent commissioners to restore peace;[5] but such a peace as would benefit these United States is not in their hearts—at least they have not acceded to any condition preparitory to that end, which Congress has proposed. Hence it is with pity & concern Congress view the necessity of continuing the war & they are determined by every means in their power to fulfill those eventual engagements formed between France & these United States which from the hostile measures & designes of the common enemy have compleatly acquired positive & permanent force & operation.

The arrival of the Naval force so wisely sent by His Most Christian Majesty to cooperate with the arms of these States under God promise the speedy establishment of that Peace which is the object of the Alliance between the two Nations. The common enemy deaf to the voice of reason, are to be roused to a sense of justice only by the din of Arms. We trust that our combined efforts will secure the Independence of N. America in a peace promoting the true interests of France, America, Europe & Mankind. Nor do we doubt but that those who administer the powers of government within these United States will in all things labour to confirm & cement that Union with the Subjects of France, the beneficial Effects of which have been already so sensibly felt.

Informed of your past conduct in the affairs of these States, it is with the most cordial pleasure Congress receive you Sir, as His M. C. M. Minister Plenipotentiary, & they are perfectly satisfied that you will endeavour to obey your instructions in such a manner as will intitle you to the confidence & friendship of the Representatives of the United States of America.

MS (PPL). In the hand of William Henry Drayton.

1 The provenance of this document is obscure. On July 16 Gérard submitted to Congress a copy of the speech he intended "to deliver at his public audience," which was referred to a committee consisting of Richard Henry Lee, Gouverneur Morris, and John Witherspoon. This committee, on July 25, reported a draft reply to Gérard's speech, but their effort was found inadequate and Congress instead referred the matter to a second committee consisting of Joseph Reed, Francis Dana, and Witherspoon. The following day, July 30, Congress approved "a new draught" submitted by this committee, which was used by President Laurens on August 6 during Gérard's public reception in Congress. See *JCC*, 11:695, 722, 726, 730, 733, 753–57.

William Henry Drayton's draft reply to Gérard is a longer version of the one President Laurens used on August 6—and therein lies the mystery. For Drayton was not a member of either of the committees appointed to draft a reply to the French envoy, and there is no evidence in other surviving papers of the delegates that he took part in this process. Yet a careful comparison of Drayton's draft reply with the one approved by Congress clearly shows that the latter borrows heavily from the former. In the absence of positive evidence, one can only conjecure that either President Laurens, a fellow South Carolinian, or a member of one of the aforementioned committees solicited Drayton's ideas on a proper response to Gérard. In any event, it seems that Drayton prepared this manuscript sometime between the appointment of the first drafting committee on July 16 and the approval of the second draft on July 30.

2 Drayton originally wrote "That lust of domination which has drawn so much blood, & prolonged & aggravated the miseries of mankind is to be lamented deplored: we" and then altered it to read as above.

3 After this sentence Drayton first wrote and then deleted: "The blood that has been shed lies upon the heads of those who."

4 At this point Drayton first wrote and then deleted: "and but relying on the justice of her cause, altho' reduced to the last extremity she never relaxed in her exertions in defence of her rights."

5 At this point Drayton first wrote and then deleted: "they have applied to Congress upon this subject."

Samuel Holten's Diary

July 16 [1778]

Attended in Congress; I was invited to dine at the city Tavern with Monsr. Gerard, but declined on account of my health.[1]

MS (MDaAr).

1 Holten had also commented on his health in his diary entry for the 15th. "Attended in Congress, am some better as to my health. I sent a Packet of Letters by Mr Hancock to Mrs. Holten."

Gouverneur Morris' Notes on George Johnstone's Letter to Francis Dana

[July 16, 1778][1]

Dear Sir, Private. Philadelphia June 10th 1778.

It gives me great pleasure to find your name among the list of Congress, because I am persuaded from personal knowledge of me and my family and connections you can entertain no jealousy that I would engage in the execution of any commission that was inamicable to the rights and privileges of America or the general libertys of mankind. While on the other hand your character must be so well known that no man will suspect you will yield any point that is contrary to the real interest of your country and therefore it will be presumed we will loose no opportunity from false punctilio of meeting to discuss our differences fairly, and that if we do agree, it will be on the most liberal, and therefore the most lasting terms of union. There are three facts I wish to assure you of. First that Doctor Franklin on the 29th of March last in discussing the several articles we wish to make the basis of our treaty was perfectly satisfied they were beneficial to North America and such as he should accept.

Second that this treaty with France was not the first treaty that France had *exacted* and with which Mr. Simeon Dean had put to sea, but granted and acceded to after the sentiments of the people of Great Britain had fully changed, after the friends to America had gained their points for reconciliation, and solely with a view to disappoint the good effects of our endeavors. You will be pleased to hear the pamphlet wrote by Mr. Pulteney[2] was a great means of opening the minds of the people of England to the real state of the question between us, and that it has run through 13 editions. The third fact is that Spain unasked, had sent a formal message disapproving of the conduct of France. These I will engage to prove to your satisfaction. I beg to recommend to your personal civilities my friend Doctr. Ferguson. He is a man of the greatest genius and virtue and has always been a steady friend to America. Private.[3]

. . . .

If you follow the example of Britain in the hour of her pride, insolence, and madness and refuse to hear us, I still expect, since I am here, to have the privilege of coming among you and seeing the country, as there are many men whose virtues I admire above Greek or Roman Names that I should be glad to tell my children about. I am with esteem & affection, Dear Sir, your friend and servant,

Geo. Johnstone.

The Substance of the above Letter is truly diverting. Let it be remembered that it is to a Member of Congress and informs him of what? Why that Doctor Franklin on the twenty ninth of March, approved the Propositions of which Govr. Johnstone was the Bearer. At the Moment of receiving this Letter the Gentleman to whom it was directed had before him the Treaties executed with France & signed by Doctor Franklin. One of two Things must be the Case either Govr. Johnstone believes what he says or he does not; if the latter he is a Knave if the former a Dupe. The next piece of Information is that France *exacted* as he is pleased to express himself another Treaty which had been sent to Sea by Simeon Deane. Unfortunately again Mr. Simeon Deane was on the Spot to meet the false Allegation. But the third glowing glaring Stroke of Intelligence is the Conduct of Spain. Govr. Johnstone will learn in a very few Weeks what will be the Conduct of his most Catholic Majesty. And I venture to pledge myself that it will be found as different from his Representation as Light from Darkness.

MS (DLC). Although Morris' appended notes are in his own hand, this text of George Johnstone's letter to Francis Dana is a transcript in a clerical hand. For Dana's copy of this extract of Johnstone's letter, see William Henry Drayton to the Carlisle Commissioners, July 18, 1778, note 5.

1 On this day Francis Dana submitted to Congress the following extract—"as far as relates to public matters"—of a June 10 letter he had received from George

Johnstone, an action prompted by Congress' July 9 order requiring the delegates to lay before it all letters addressed to them by "any of the British commissioners or their agents, or from any subject of the king of Great Britain, of a public nature." See *JCC*, 11:678, 694. Although Morris' notes were obviously intended to serve as the basis for a newspaper essay on Johnstone's letter, he probably decided not to expand them for publication because of William Henry Drayton's comprehensive refutation of Johnstone's allegations in his July 18 letter to the Carlisle commissioners.

2 See William Johnstone-Pulteney, *Thoughts on the Present State of Affairs with America, and the Means for Conciliation* (London: J. Dodsley and T. Cadell, 1778). Johnstone-Pulteney was a member of the House of Commons and the brother of George Johnstone. Gerrit P. Judd, IV, *Members of Parliament, 1734–1832* (New Haven: Yale University Press, 1955), p. 243.

3 This word was inserted in the extract to indicate the omission of an indeterminate part of Johnstone's letter pertaining to private affairs.

Henry Laurens to William Livingston

Sir

17th July [1778]

Your Excellency's Letter of the 25th Ulto. reached me in this City.[1] Here many impediments prevented the forming Congress earlier than the 7th Instant. On the 8th I had the honor of presenting that Letter and the pleasure of perceiving an high degree of indignation kindling in the minds of Members as I advanced in unfolding the villianous attempts of the Enemy against Your Excellencys' Person. This indignation was discernable even in Gentlemens countenances, but more strongly marked in expressions suitable to the occasion which broke forth from many quarters of the House. The Letter was committed, but our attention almost ever since that period has been drawn to the businesses which Your Excellency well knows, naturally arise from the arrival of a Minister Plenipotentiary in the City where Congress sit—And the fleet of an Ally on the Coast which Congress wished to have cleared of Enemies—from these considerations Your Excellency will not be surprized that a report has not yet come up from the Committee.

A Gentleman who says he is of Jersey, has pressed me closely for a Commission and instructions for a private ship of War equipped by him in that State. In order to put the business in the best course I have in a seperate Packet folded four Commissions, Instructions and Bonds and directed the Packet to Your Excellency. From you, Sir, this Gentleman may, if it shall be proper, obtain a Commission and Instructions upon executing a Bond in due form. I should, if I were hastily to gratify his importunity, act blindfold.

I Am, With the highest Esteem & Regard

LB (DNA: PCC, item 13).

1 Governor Livingston's June 25 letter to Laurens is not in PCC or the

Laurens Papers, ScHi. Although this letter was referred to a committee on July 8, there is no evidence in the journals that Congress took further action on it. *JCC*, 11:674.

Henry Laurens to George Washington

Sir. Philadelphia 17th July 1778.

Your Excellency's favor of the 14th Inst. which came to hand pretty late last Evening I shall have the honor of presenting to Congress this Morning.[1]

At present I have no other Commands on me, but to transmit the Inclosed Act of Congress of the 15th Inst. for receiving & subsisting Prisoners of War which may be taken by the Squadron under the Command of Vice Admiral Count d'Estaing, to which I beg leave to refer.[2] And remain, With the most sincere Regard & Respect, sir, Your Excellency's Most obedient & most humble servant,

Henry Laurens, President of Congress.

RC (DLC).

[1] Washington's July 14 letter to Laurens, dealing with his plans for cooperating with the comte d'Estaing, is in PCC, item 152, 6:167–68, and Washington, *Writings* (Fitzpatrick), 12:180–81.

[2] See *JCC*, 11:690–91.

Marine Committee to the Comte d'Estaing

Sir July 17th 1778

I had the honor of writing to your Excellency on the 12th instant about the means of procuring fresh water and the measures taken by the Marine Committee of Congress to furnish fresh provisions for the squadron under your Excellencies Command. The Casks that could be obtained here since the late ravage of the enemy are delivered to the Chimere, and the three Vessels with her. They will bring the Squadron a present supply of water and I am informed that in future this article can be obtained easily and near to Sandy Hook as I formerly wrote your Excellency. The Chimere brings likewise Bread, flour, fresh meat, and vegitables for the fleet, which we hope may answer present purposes; until the larger quantity shall be carried thro the Jersey and taken on board the Squadron at such places as your Excellency shall appoint for the Commissary to deliver them at.[1] I am desired by the Marine Committee to request your Excelly will be pleased to accept from them a small present of live Stock and vegitables in testimony of the high respect the Committee entertain for your Excellencies character.

I must beg leave Once more to repeat the Assurances already made, that the Marine Committee will at all times have pleasure in directing such further Provisions for the Squadron as you shall think proper to desire.

I have the honor to be with great respect your Excellencies Most obedient & Most Hble servant,

Richard Henry Lee
Chairman of the Mar. Comee.

LB (DNA: PCC Miscellaneous Papers, Marine Committee Letter Book).

1 The following list of provisions, in the hand of secretary John Brown and signed by Richard Henry Lee, is dated "Marine Committee July 16, 1778."

"A List of Provisions to be furnished by the Commissary for the use of the French Squadron under the Command of Vice Admiral D'Estaing

	Hundreds Avoirdupois Wt
Bread	11,000
Salt Pork	1,771
Hogs heads & feet	332
Salt Fish	221
Cheese	221
Peas, Beans, Caravances	1,960
Rice	185
Mustard seed	6
Beer 6110 Casks of	480 Pints or 60 Galls. ea
Vinegar 60 Do	Do

"The Third part of these Provisions, Particularly of the Biscuit must be immediately provided taking proper measures to procure the remainder Successively at the Time the Commander of Squadron may Appoint. All the above articles Are to be procured Specifically if possible. If any of them cannot be obtained, the deficiency is to be made good by adding to those that can observing always that vinegar is indispensible. If the Commissary should find that some of the Articles of Provisions are much dearer in Proportion to the rest, he will diminish the quantity of such articles, and add to the Others. Richard Henry Lee, Chairman M. C." Slack Collection, OMC.

This list is probably based on Gérard's "memorandum of the provisions which will hereafter be necessary" that Congress referred to the Marine Committee on the 16th. *JCC*, 11:695–96.

William Henry Drayton to the Carlisle Commissioners

Philadelphia, July 18, 1778

To their Excellencies the Earl of CARLISLE, *Sir* HENRY CLINTON, *and* WILLIAM EDEN, *and* GEORGE JOHNSTONE, *Esquires, British Commissioners.*

Your letter to Congress of the 11th instant, induces me again to request your Excellencies attention to the reflections of an individual.[1]

If I can penetrate the sentiments of Congress, I may assure you that your reply was unexpected; for it was with reason imagined you would have understood their answer of the 17th of June:[2] That was a full and plain return to your letter of the ninth; and it was taken as a natural consequence, that the correspondence between the Congress and your Excellencies was then *ipso facto* suspended, until you, being fully authorized to do so, had acceded to one or other of the explicit preliminaries they proposed. It appears your Excellencies discernment has been misconceived—I am sorry for it.

You say, Congress propose to you, as matter of choice, one or other of two alternatives, as preliminaries necessary even to the beginning of a negociation for peace; one, "an *explicit acknowledgment of the Independence* of these States;" and you add, "you are not inclined to dispute with Congress about the meaning of words." Why then do you construe that *explicit* alternative as applicable to an *inexplicit dependence* upon Britain? By your construction, our ideas of language are totally different. We cannot conceive that a state of *independence* can possibly admit of an state of *dependence*: If you called the night, day, we should as clearly understand you. I beg your Excellencies will allow me to throw out another reflection upon this abstruse subject.

"You are not inclined to dispute with Congress about the meaning of words; but so far as by the independence of these states Congress mean the entire privilege of the people of North America to dispose of their property, and to govern themselves without any reference to Great Britain, beyond what is necessary to preserve that union of force, in which our mutual safety and advantage consist;" so far their independence, you say, is fully acknowledged in your letter of the 10th of June, you forget, it is dated the ninth, adding you "are willing to enlarge that independence."

In the first place, I would ask your Excellencies, whether you mean to include the people of the two Floridas, Nova-Scotia and Canada, under your terms, "the people of North America." I believe you do not; but we mean to raise them to the rank of independent freemen. Again, you say, you have offered us such an *independence*, as is calculated but to preserve the union of the force of America and Britain in the hand of the latter, and you now offer "to enlarge that independence." If you are serious and mean something, you must mean the independence we mean, which is, to preserve the force of America *independent* of Great-Britain, not in union with Great Britain and in her hand. There can be no intermediate degree of independence between that which is *but* calculated to preserve the union of the force of America and Britain, and the degree we demand. If you enlarge that degree, which is but sufficient to preserve that union, the union cannot be preserved, and the independence of consequence becomes compleat: We ask nothing more; we will accept nothing less. If you understand the term independence as we do, why are you not explicit? If you do not, why do you delay to draw the line between the independence you offered and the enlarged independence you offer? You ought to do this; we are plain men, and cannot divide that, which from the nature of it we think indivisible.

As to the other alternative of withdrawing your fleets and armies, you openly and at once refuse "to begin with this measure." Here we understand each other clearly, and this point is settled at once. This proceeding on your part is conspicuous, because it is singular; and as it deserves, so it receives my commendation. Your reasons, in support of your decision, are of no consequence to Congress: I believe they neither asked, expected or wished for them. It was their business to demand; their reasons remained with themselves; it was your business to grant or refuse. It was known you would not grant the demand if you could possible avoid it; and it was not doubted but that your ingenuity would furnish you with reasons for your refusal. However, as Congress have nothing to do with the principles of your conduct, I will dismiss them without any further observation upon them.

"In making your declarations, you do not wait for the decision of any military events;" but "shall abide by the declarations you now make in every possible situation of your affairs." I admire the magnanimity of your sentiments; they are worthy an old Roman, or modern American; you will be pleased to pardon me if I add, they are not *a la mode d'Anglaise*; and also, not to be offended at this phrase of expression: For as all America is intent upon learning the elegant language of our ally of France, in order to improve our friendly correspondence, so such phrases naturally slip from our tongues and pens. The air of America seems to have produced a sudden effect upon your Excellencies; indeed, all animals feel the effect of a change of climate. The rulers in England, as they are in a very different climate from that which you now enjoy, so they are in a habit of thinking and acting very different from yours. They regulate their demands, refusals and concessions, according to the "situation of their affairs;" you declare you will not. As this is a striking contrast, perhaps it may be disputed; and as I know your Excellencies are able disputants at the point of the tongue, pen and sword, I think it is but prudent to place the subject out of all dispute; I shall endeavour to do this, by drawing it up in the following manner: In the years 1774 and 1775, when America was destitute of arms, your King and Ministers were deaf to her supplications for redress of grievances.

In the years 1776 and 1777, when America had but a raw soldiery, and scarce the appearance of a regular army, your king and Parliament having 45,865 and 48,616 effective regular forces, amply supplied in every respect, besides 22,337 seamen assaulting these United States on all sides, your rulers breathed nothing but unconditional submission on our part. On the ninth of March, Lord Camden declared in your House of Lords, that this high tone continued so late as the 16th day of February last, and that it was suddenly altered on the 17th, when your rulers resolved, to use his Lordships expression, "to bend their knees before America." The alteration of the *situation of their affairs,* was the occasion of this sudden change. At this point of time, by the returns from America, it appeared that the British army had by death, desertion and otherwise, lost 19,581 men; that 5336 men had been taken prisoners, that the sick amounted to 4639; and that the navy had lost 4314 seamen.[3] Capital as these losses were, yet the men in power breathed unconditional submission, till finding that a treaty between France and America had been signed on the 6th of February, and feeling the mortal blow to their tyranny, on the 17th of February Lord North and his coadjutors, goaded by the situation of their affairs, bent their knees before America, upon the bills which your Excellencies presented to Congress in the form of acts of Parliament. It is thus plain to a demonstration, that your rulers are deaf, demand or concede, according to the situation of their affairs; and notwithstanding your heroics, you must concede, for you are but instruments in their hands. On the 28th of June last, you sunk beneath the arm of America;[4] France now confines your haughty flag to the port of New-York, and threatens you with destruction.

But you would have the treaties entered into by Congress communicated to you, both for your own consideration and that of the constituents of Congress, who you say are to judge between them and you. Your Excellencies are then inclined to appeal from Congress to their constituents? How little are you acquainted with the disposition of the people of America! Sir Henry Clinton has seen a similar appeal by Lord and General Howe in their proclamation dated the 19th of September, 1776; our affairs were then in the most ruinous situation; and are you yet to learn that the appeal was rejected! Can you gravely expect that your appeal will now be sustained, now that our affairs are not only *en bon train,* but that we have every moral assurance of decisive victory, and success! Are we not masters of the field, which we never before have been? Are we not in pursuit of your forces? Has not your grand army retired to Islands for safety? Are you not at war with the House of Bourbon? Does not the House of Bourbon prosecute the war in conjunction with the United States? The fleet of France at this moment holds you blocked up at New York, and daily seizes your ships in sight of your flags displayed in vain parade. Your inferior army is full reduced by draughts to the defense of your capital in Europe; a proof that you will receive no more land reinforcement. You are upon the brink of perdition, and yet you pretend to hold dominion over us, and to reason us into an *independent dependence*—a jargon of words—a very chaos of ideas.

Your Excellencies have been so long in the school of deception, and seem so fond of the art, that for want of other subjects to practice upon, you are resolved to deceive yourselves. If this contributes to mitigate the uneasiness of your present situation, continue to enjoy the artifice a little longer, I cannot but pity your distress.

You think yourselves intitled to *a full communication of the powers by which Congress conceive themselves authorized to make treaties with foreign powers,* and you add, you do not find *promulgated* any act or resolution of the Assemblies of particular States, conferring this power on them. Whatever you may think upon this point, I believe I may venture to assure you, Congress do not *conceive* themselves answerable to you on the subject. They know their own powers, they know they are answerable to their constituents for the due exercise of them. However, I will endeavour to satisfy you substantially in this point, and to do it the more agreeably, I will state a fact and use your own stile of argument.

On the sixth of May, Congress announced to the United States, that they had ratified treaties of alliance and commerce with France: This is the 18th of July, and have your Excellencies heard that any one of the United States has *"promulgated"* any censure upon Congress for such ratification? As, because you do not find *promulgated* any act or resolution of the Assemblies of particular States conferring this power on them, you infer, they have no such power: is it not more reasonable, that as two months and an half have passed since Congress announced their act to their constituents, and you do not find *promulgated* any act or resolution of the Assemblies of particular States censuring Congress for this exercise of power, therefore *you ought to infer,* that the constituents of Congress think they did not exceed their authority? Politicians should never say more at any time than is necessary. You produce a negative argument, and an answer in the same manner is quite sufficient. Having thus far touched the subject of your Excellencies letter, I take the liberty of addressing myself in particular to his Excellency Governor Johnstone, and that in presence of his colleagues. I have no ambition to have a *tête a tête* with the Governor.

A letter has been laid before Congress, signed Geo. Johnstone, dated Philadelphia, June 10, 1778, directed to the Honorable Francis Dana, Esq;[5] and among other things the writer says, "there are three facts I wish to assure you of."

First, "That Doctor Franklin on the 29th of March last, in discussing the several articles we wish to make the basis of our treaty, was perfectly satisfied they were beneficial to North America, and such as she should expect." Decisively to destroy this position, I have only to state two or three points.

The Honorable Silas Deane has informed me, that a secret negociator from Britain did arrive at Passy, immediately preceding the 29th of March last, and applied to Doctor Franklin. That he himself left Paris the first of April, in order to embark at Toulon for America. That at Toulon he received a letter from Doctor Franklin, dated the 7th of April. Mr. Deane put the letter into my hand, and with his permission I extracted the following paragraph. "The negociator is gone back apparently much chagrined at his little success. I have promised him faithfully, that since his propositions *could not be accepted* they should be buried in oblivion."[6] With every American I have no doubt but this testimony by Doctor Franklin, will greatly outweigh the testimony given by Governor Johnstone and his negociator, who has divulged the propositions he desired the Doctor to bury in oblivion. But there was design in this conduct—it is so obvious that I need not point it out.

Second, "That this treaty with France was not the first that France had exacted, and with which Mr. Simeon Deane had put to sea, but granted and acceded to after the sentiments of the people of Great Britain had fully changed," meaning with regard to the measures to be pursued with America, conciliation instead of coercion.

Upon this second article I must observe, that the Honorable Silas Deane, to whom I read it, and who was at the Court of France during the whole time of any negociation there for a treaty between France and America, assures me that France never "*exacted*" any terms from America but those contained in the treaties of the sixth of February, and that Mr. Simeon Deane had never put to sea with any other treaties. That it is true he had put to sea preceding this period, but only charged with the declaration of the Court of France, delivered by Monsieur Girard on the 16th of December to the American Commissioners, of whom Mr. Deane was one, and with letters from the Commissioners informing Congress, that the treaty would be formed agreeable to that declaration, a declaration which I have already stated in my letter to your Excellencies, of the 17th of June, at York-Town. And thus from the express authority of the Honorable Mr. Deane, Governor Johnstone stands fully confuted.

As for the third fact "that Spain unasked had sent a formal message disapproving of the conduct of France," I have only to say, that as I cannot offer evidence against it, for argument I will admit the fact may be so; and what then? Will governor Johnstone pretend to say, Spain now disapproves the conduct of France? It is known to the world that France and Spain are in the most perfect confidence together. France is now at war with Great Britain. Governor Johnstone *now* knows this fact, and I assure myself that he does not doubt that Spain is either at this moment also at war with Great Britain, or very shortly will be. A few weeks will ascertain this matter, and demonstrate that the Governor is content to catch at a straw. When his Excellency wrote this letter on the 10th of June, he had then to learn, that the Count D'Estaing had sailed from Toulon; and that the Spanish plate fleet had arrived at Cadiz.

I now call upon Governor Johnstone relative to a more serious subject. His personal honour is interested: The following particulars are not unworthy his notice.

A letter signed by him, dated Philadelphia, June 16th, 1778, and directed to the Honourable Robert Morris, contains the following paragraph:

"I believe the men who have conducted the affairs of America uncapable of being influenced by improper motives. But in all such transactions there is risque; and I think whoever ventures should be secured, at the same time that honour and emolument should naturally follow the fortune of those who have steered the vessel in the storm, and brought her safely to port. I think Washington and the President have a right to every favour that grateful nations can bestow, if they could once more unite our interest and spare the miseries and devastations of war."[7] Than this I cannot conceive a more genteel bidding for secret services. The offer by common implication reaches every Member of Congress; every man entrusted with public authority for the maintainance of the independence of America. The attempt is horrid! Has not Governor Johnstone for years past declaimed against bribery, corruption, undue influence! Then he was anti-ministerial—now he feels the effects of ministerial favour. But if this does not shew the Governor in a clear point of view, let him be seen through another medium: The Honourable General Reed inclosed to me the following particulars signed with his name: "On Sunday the 21st June, a few days after the evacuation of the city of Philadelphia by the British troops, the subscriber received a written message from a married lady of character, having connections with the British army: expressing a desire to see him on business which could not be commited to writing. Attending the lady agreeable to her appointment, in the evening, after some previous conversation respecting her particular connections, the business and characters of the British Commissioners, and particularly of Governor Johnstone, were the subjects of general conversation, which becoming more confined, the lady enlarged upon the great talents and amiable qualities of that gentleman, and added, that in several conversations with her he had expressed the most favourable sentiments of the subscriber, and it was particularly wished to engage his interest to promote the object of their commission, viz. a reunion between the two countries if consistent with the subscriber's principles and judgment; and in such case, it could not be deemed unbecoming or improper in government to take a favourable notice of such conduct, and that in this instance the subscriber might have 10,000£. Sterling, and any office in the colonies in his Majesty's gift.

To which, finding an answer was expected, he replied, he was not worth purchasing, but such as he was the King of Great Britain was not rich enough to do it. Here the conversation ended. JOS. REED."[8]

It is needless for me to make any reflections upon such particulars. I bid your Excellencies farewell. W.H.D.

MS not found; reprinted from the *Pennsylvania Packet, and Daily Advertiser,* July 21, 1778.

1 The RC of the Carlisle commissioners' July 11 letter "To His Excellency Henry Laurens The President and other The Members of Congress" is in the Peter Force Collection, DLC, and bears the following endorsement by Charles Thomson: "Letter from Carlisle, H Clinton, Wm Eden, Geo. Johnstone. New York 11 July 1778. Read 18." Congress resolved this day not to answer the commissioners' letter because they failed to accept either of the congressional preconditions for peace negotiations—recognition of American independence or withdrawal of the British army and navy from the United States—and then ordered this resolve and the commissioners' letter to be published. As a result, both appeared in the July 21 issue of the *Pennsylvania Packet,* together with Drayton's open letter to the commissioners of this date. For a discussion of Drayton's series of newspaper letters to the Carlisle commissioners, of which the present letter is a part, see Drayton to the Carlisle Commissioners, June 17, 1778, note 1. See also Gouverneur Morris' Proposed Resolves, this date.

2 See Henry Laurens to the Carlisle Commissioners, June 17, 1778.

3 Drayton derived his statistics on British military and naval forces in America from a lengthy motion that was offered in the House of Lords by the Duke of Richmond on April 11. *Parliamentary History,* 19:1012–21. For Lord Camden's March 6 remarks on Lord North's conciliatory bills, see ibid., pp. 860–65.

4 A reference to the battle of Monmouth.

5 On July 16 Francis Dana had submitted to Congress a letter written to him on June 10 by George Johnstone and Congress had directed that an extract of it be lodged in Secretary Thomson's office. *JCC,* 11:694. This extract, in Dana's hand, is in the Peter Force Collection, DLC, and bears the following endorsement by Thomson: "a true copy compared with the original. Examined in Congress July 16 1778. Chas. Thomson secy." See also Gouverneur Morris' Notes on George Johnstone's Letter to Francis Dana, July 16, 1778.

6 In a section of his December 21, 1778, memorial to Congress that first became available in 1928, Silas Deane offered a fuller account than Drayton of British efforts to enlist Benjamin Franklin's support for Anglo-American peace negotiations:

"Within a Day or two of the Commissioners being presented at Court, which was on the 19th of March, 1778, Doctor Franklin informed me of the arrival of an Agent from the british Ministry, with proposals, which were to be made secretly to him. Doctor Franklin after waiting on him shewed me a Copy of them which he afterwards gave me to bring to America. The Fleet from Toulon then ready for sailing, and his Excellency Monsr Gerard, & myself on the point of setting out from Paris, Doctor Franklin waved giving him a positive Answer, until we should be well on our Journey. On the 7th of April, he wrote me as per Letter of that Date, that having engaged that the proposals should not be communicated, as he had positively rejected them—he desired me instantly to destroy them without either copying or communicating them to any one. I complied instantly on the Receipt of his Letter, with his request. On my arrival in America, I was informed that the british Commissioners had declared that those Propositions had been shewn privately to Doctor Franklin at Paris, & that he approved of them. To contradict this Assertion, I have produced Doctor Franklin's Letter,

& related the Circumstances of that Transaction in as few words as possible." Charles M. Andrews, ed., "A Note on the Franklin-Deane Mission to France." *Yale University Library Gazette* 2 (1928): 59–60.

The relevant section on this issue in Franklin's April 7 letter to Deane reads: "The Negociator is gone back apparently much chagrin'd at his little Success. I have promised him faithfully that since his Propositions could not be accepted they should be buried in Oblivion. I therefore desire earnestly that you would put that paper immediately in the Fire on receipt of this, without taking or suffering to be taken any Copy of it, or communicating its Contents." Ibid., pp. 65–66.

Although neither source identifies the British "Negociator" who approached Franklin, Samuel F. Bemis has plausibly conjectured that the person in question was Paul Wentworth, a British agent who before the conclusion of the Franco-American alliance had been employed to sound out Franklin and Deane as to the prospects for a settlement between Great Britain and the United States. Samuel F. Bemis, *The Diplomacy of the American Revolution* (New York: D. Appleton-Century Co., 1935), pp. 58–60, 68n.21.

7 See Robert Morris to Gouverneur Morris, June 16, 1778, note 2.

8 A text of this statement in Joseph Reed's hand is in the Pierre Eugene Du Simitière Papers, PPL. For a discussion of George Johnstone's effort to bribe Reed through the agency of Elizabeth Graeme Ferguson, a Philadelphia loyalist, see Roche, *Joseph Reed*, pp. 137–41. Mrs. Ferguson was the wife of Hugh Ferguson, a former commissary of prisoners for Gen. William Howe, and the sister-in-law of Adam Ferguson, the Carlisle commission's secretary. Ibid., p. 138.

Samuel Holten's Diary

[July 18, 1778]

18. Congress received a letter from the Comrs. of the King of Great Britain, but it was couched in such terms, no Answer is to be given.

MS (MDaAr).

Henry Laurens to John Lewis Gervais

[July 18, 1778]

18th. My Letter has been kept open, and the Messenger detained in hopes of procuring one Morning or Evening for filling a page or two of News to you, but all such expectations are vain. I must therefore, again refer you to my Friend; to his Excellency as first Magistrate without attention to my respect for the Man, he is justly entitled to the first fruits of intelligence—you will there learn all I could say in a dozen sheets.

Your friend Colonel Laurens is detached upon a very honorable Embassy by his General to Count d'Estaing,[1] his knowledge of the French tongue in some measure qualifies him for the errand and I trust he will not be found deficient in other necessary qualifications, making reasonable considerations for his Youth, when I learn particulars from him, you shall be informed. 'Tis highly probable, Count d'Estaing's squadron will capture many English Vessels while lying at Sandy Hook, but I have doubts concerning their getting within; the large Men of War draw 25 to 27 feet water—if they fail at that place, I think Rhode Island must be their next object, there they must succeed.

My best Compliments, Love and Respects to Mrs. Gervais, Mr. and Mrs. Manigault &c. &c. &c. My Dear friend, Adieu

LB (ScHi). A continuation of Laurens to Gervais, July 15, 1778.

1 John Laurens had recently been chosen by Washington to establish liaison with the comte d'Estaing. See Washington, *Writings* (Fitzpatrick), 12:175, 179–80, 186, 206, 208–10.

Henry Laurens to John Houstoun

Dear Sir 18th July [1778]

I had the honor of addressing you under the 10th and the same date in public letters which this will accompany. The subjects contained in those are now obsolete, nevertheless I do not think it proper to suppress them. Georgia has at present only one Delegate in Congress who alone cannot on her part ratify confederation.[1] I am very unhappy from having received no further commands from Congress respecting poor little Georgia; in hopes of such I had detained the Bearer three days, but the arrival of a French squadron and a Minister Plenipotentiary has accumulated the labours of Congress insomuch that many necessary considerations for the benefit of particular States unavoidably lie dormant. The First hour of leisure I will give Mr. Telfair all the aid in my power to bring his state on the tapis.

Count d'Estaing is exceedingly chargrined at the impracticability of attacking the English ships of War, who lie in his sight within Sandy Hook—his large ships draw too much water for the Bar and keep him without where prizes are daily dropping into his net, and not a few very valuable. I presume he has already lessened the number of British Seamen 500. If he proceeds to Rhode Island he will probably recover that place, capture the Garrison said to be upwards of 3000, make prizes of some ships, and secure a good Harbour.

I shall have the honor of writing to you again in a few days, at present must content myself with subscribing Dr. Sir, With great Regard and Esteem, Your Obedient Humble Servt.

P. S. I send you a few News papers.

LB (ScHi).

1 Edward Telfair, who had taken his seat in Congress on July 13, was the only Georgia delegate in attendance at this time. *JCC*, 11:685. On July 24 Telfair and John Walton, who had arrived in Congress the day before, ratified the Articles of Confederation on behalf of Georgia. *JCC*, 11:712, 716.

Henry Laurens to the Marquis de Lafayette

Sir

18th July [1778]

I have with pleasure executed an Order of Congress by signing and delivering a Brevet to the Marquis de Vienne to rank Colonel in the Army of the United States of America.[1] My pleasure as an individual would not have been less if my name had been ordered to a full Commission. Such an one I make no doubt will be readily granted if the Marquis de Vienne shall think it more valuable than the present, when he shall be returning to his Native Clime. Your Excellency cannot conceive the embarrasment which is often occasioned to Congress by granting Commissions to foreign Gentlemen to the prejudice of rank to many of our own home born Officers who have served the public with honor from the very commencement of the War.

The Board of War have not yet reported on the application in favour of Monsr. Touzard, possibly there may be policy and good will towards that Gentleman concealed in the delay—requests do not so well succeed, when crouded together.[2] Be this as it may for I know not how it be, when Gentlemen recommend an A or B a Foreign Gentleman of great merit to receive a Commission far above any which he had formerly enjoyed it is natural, and Your Excellencys Candour will admit that it is also just, for other Gentlemen to produce in contrast the merits of American Officers in the Army who are and must be content to wait for grade until they shall be entitled to advancement in due course.

When it is urged that French Gentlemen have come a long Voyage and at great expence to serve the United States the reply without observing that the Act was voluntary is that many of our American Officers have abandoned their Homes, all their domestic happiness, the education of their Children, the improvement of their fortunes &c. &c. and in the course of three years hard duty have advanced gradation to the heighth of Captain or Major and have the mortification of being commanded by Gentlemen who had held Lieutenancies in their Native Country, and who were promoted here after one battle to Lieutenant Colonels, Colonels, and in some instances As it is said to higher ranks—such opposition my dear Marquis, is not to be answered by an ingenious mind. Your Excellency must not think me from these observations less devoted to your service upon every occasion in which your own impartiality and wise discernment shall be pleased to command.

The Marquis de Vienne is so polite as to afford me the present opportunity of Paying my respects to your Excellency and at the same time of acknowledging the receipt of your Excellencys favor of the 15th Instant.[3] Conscious of being greatly in arrears, I am grieved that I cannot go back to several Letters which your Excellency has lately honored me with, and which require such notice as my present circumstances will not allow me to go into. Surely I shall be Blessed with one day in the course of next week which may be applyd to a serious review of the Marquis de la Fayette's Letters, I will embrace the first leisure hour for this purpose. I know I am immensely in debt, I do not want candour to acknowledge, and I trust Your Excellency will find that I am not deficient in honesty to pay to the utmost of my abilities. At present indulge me Dear Sir, in confining myself to that which lies immediately before me.

I have the satisfaction to assure Your Excellency that from the first moment we were apprized of the arrival of Count d'Estaings squadron on this coast, Congress have vigorously pursued every measure for facilitating and effectuating the Vice Admirals operations against the Enemy. We were not unmindful of the great utility of Advice Boats—but alass! such are not to be built in so short a time as we can write the name, and you well know Sir, the Enemy while they had possession of this river stretched an unsparing firebrand over all our navigation which they could reach and could not carry off, consequently they have left us very little, and none of the sorts which you allude to. I have great hopes that Count d'Estaing will find means for supplying himself with necessary Vessels for contingent services upon the Coast and within the Harbour of New York. In the mean time Congress will in every respect contribute to his success and the mutual honor and benefit of the Alliance.

But here comes Marquis Vienne and indeed has been waiting half an hour in the Audience Room, theres for you Dear Marquis. I am not quite so squeezed up as at York Town where Miss Katy and your Humble Servant lay within very narrow bounds and without the smallest breach of decorum. Yes Sir, I have now what Mr. Burgoyne could not obtain in America, a little Elbow room. How happy should I be to be honored with the Company of the Marquis de la Fayette at the consumption of a great Turtle tomorrow in addition to Monsr. Girard &c. &c.—but I flatter myself the time will soon come, when without impeachment of honor or danger to the State Your Excellency may sit quietly under the Roof of Your Excellencys much obliged &c.

[*P.S.*] And longer under your own.

LB (ScHi).

1 See *JCC*, 11:692–94; and Laurens to Lafayette, July 10, 1778, note 1.

2 See Laurens to Lafayette, June 19, 1778, note 2.

3 Laurens is undoubtedly referring to Lafayette's July 14 letter, for which see "Lafayette-Laurens Letters," *SCHGM* 9 (1908): 61.

Henry Laurens to William Livingston

Dear Sir 18th July [1778]

I take particular pleasure in laying before Your Excellency a second production from the Bed of British Commissioners which Your Excellency will find within Copy of a Letter addressed to Congress dated New York 11th Instant and signed by four of that honorable group of Itinerants.

Upon a very cursory view of the performance I pronounced it exceedingly childish and a little insolent. The opinion of Congress will be seen in a transcript of their Act upon this occasion, which will be also inclosed. I think I can guess what Your Excellency's opinion will be. You see Sir, it is to be published, and therefore it is wholly at Your Excellency's disposal.[1]

When Congress were on the point of adjourning, Your Excellencys' Letter of the 17th was brought in to me, and I immediately presented it to the House, but I received no order, therefore I speak to it only private. Your Excellency's opinion respecting common Lands will have my simple voice, provided we agree in the necessary preliminary Lines.[2]

The Inclosed Courier de L'Europe[3] was sent to my Lodge, intended as I have learned for Doctor Witherspoon who had promised to say Grace for me at Dinner today, but went suddenly out of town. I have a right to convey it to the Dr. through the best Channel, this will Answer two good purposes.

Believe me Sir, I continue with the most perfect Esteem and Regard, Your Excellencys' &c.

LB (ScHi).

1 See William Henry Drayton to the Carlisle Commissioners, this date, note 1.

2 In his July 17 letter to Laurens, Governor Livingston promised that he would submit to the New Jersey legislature Laurens' July 10 circular letter urging prompt ratification of the Articles of Confederation, and added "but I sincerely hope that this State will never ratify it, till Congress is explicit in doing us that Justice respecting the common Lands, which I think no man of common Sense, or the least acquainted with human Nature would trust to the *future deliberations* of any Body of Men (I speak it with the highest respect for that assembly which I verily believe to be the most illustrious upon earth) a considerable part of which must necessarily be gainers by a contrary determination." PCC, item 68, fols. 391–93. See also Nathaniel Scudder to John Hart, July 13, 1778.

3 *Courier de l'Europe*, a French language newspaper which Samuel Swinton had been publishing in London since June 1776.

Henry Laurens to John Rutledge

Dear Sir 18th July [1778]

The Respect and Esteem I bear for you will not allow me to suffer a good opportunity to pass without some demonstration. I had intended by the present to have filled a sheet of Intelligence addressed immediately to yourself. I am in possession of sufficient matter, but time, precious time, has flown from me and left but a moment to intimate that I have particularly requested His Excellency the President to communicate to you the whole of my transmissions to him. The arrival of a French squadron and a French Minister Plenipotentiary have added much to the labours of Congress in general, and not a little to those of one who had been before sufficiently loaded. You will readily under these circumstances excuse, Dear Sir, Your Obliged and Respectful Humble Servant.

LB (ScHi).

Henry Laurens to George Washington

Dear Sir. Philadelphia 18 July 1778

Yesterday I had the honor of writing to Your Excellency a public Letter by James Martin, & also of presenting to Congress Your Excellency's favor of the 14th which the House received with satisfaction.

Permit me Sir, to recommend to Your Excellency's protection two Packets from the Sieur Gerard to Count d'Estaing, which will accompany this, I have assured Monsr. Gerard that it is altogether unnecessary to urge Your Excellency to give these dispatches the quickest safe passage to the Vice Admiral.

Prizes are finding the way into Delaware, one laden with Rum, Limes &c. intended for the Enemy's refreshment embraced one of our Wharves the Evening before last & I learn a Rich Ship is on her way up.

I have this moment Received a second Letter from the British Commissioners. If I dared to venture an opinion from a very cursory reading of the performance, it would be that this is more puerile than any thing I have seen from the other side, since the commencement of our present dispute, with a little dash of insolence, as unnecessary as it will be unavailing. If the Marquis de Vienne will indulge me till I return from Congress Your Excellency will find a Copy of that Letter within this. At present as he is on the Wing I must send to obtain his permission & in order to be quite ready in case he shall refuse to wait, conclude this with respected assurances of being, with the highest Esteem & Respect, Dear sir, Your Excellency's Obliged & Obedient, humble servant,

Henry Laurens, Private.

[*P.S.*] Returned from Congress 3 oClock—A Resolve relative to the Commissioners Letter that it ought not to be answered &c. with the Letter will appear in Print.

RC (DLC).

Henry Laurens to John Wells

Dear Sir 18th July [1778]

Although I have detained this Bearer in hopes to have written to many of my friends in South Carolina, and to yourself in particular a full Letter of News, I must send him away without gratifying my own desires.

I thank you for your late favors, and will soon take a more respectful notice of them. I have enquired but cannot learn where Mr. Rittenhouse is to be found, as I was writing this a Gentleman informs me he is returned to Philadelphia. Depend upon it I will apply to him immediately for an Ephemeris—another opportunity will offer to me about seven days hence.

I have sent abundance of Intelligence to his Excellency President Lowndes, and particularly requesting him to give you access to the whole. Hence you will be as well supply'd as if the whole had been sent directly to yourself; and within the present cover you will receive a few printed Papers, with which be content for the present and expect more by every Post which now seems to go and come with tolerable vigor.

I remain with great Regard, Sir, Your Obedient &c.

LB (ScHi).

Gouverneur Morris' Proposed Resolves

[July 18? 1778]

A Remonstrance &ca &ca being read Congress took the same into Consideration and thereupon

Resolved that on the 4th Day of July 1776 The Colonies of New Hampshire &ca &ca being duly represented by their Delegates in Congress did declare themselves to be sovereign, free and independent States—That being in full Possession of the Independence so declared these united States by their Commissioners at Paris thereunto duly authorized did on the [6th] Day of February 1778 enter into Treaties of Commerce and Alliance with his most Christian Majesty thereby further asserting and being admitted to their Station among Sovereign Powers—And therefore that the said united States are entitled to and in possession of all the Dignities and Privileges which appertain to such Powers by the Laws of Nature and Nations.

Resolved that it is the indispensible Duty of Congress to claim and maintain the Dignities and Privileges aforesaid in their fullest Latitude & Comprehension.

Resolved that no Person can ⟨*have Authority or*⟩ be authorized or admitted to treat with or make Propositions to any Prince or State on Behalf of the King or Kingdom of Great Britain unless by Powers derived from the said King in the Manner and Form customary and acknowledged among Nations.

Resolved that neither[2] of the Commissioners abovementioned appears to be duly impowered either as an Ambassador, Minister Plenipotentiary Resident or otherwise to represent the King of Great Britain to these united States.[3] Wherefore

Resolved that Congress can by no Means hold any Treaty with or answer any Propositions which may be made by the said Commissioners or either of them.

MS (ScHi). In the hand of Gouverneur Morris and endorsed by Henry Laurens: "Mr. Morris's Motion for ansr to Commissrs."

1 Although the provenance of these resolves cannot be established with certainty, it is probable that Morris wrote them in response to the Carlisle commissioners' July 11 letter, which Congress read this day and refused to answer. See *JCC*, 11:701–2; and William Henry Drayton to the Carlisle Commissioners, this date, note 1. In any event, they bear directly upon a request in that letter for "a full Communication of the Powers by which you [Congress] conceive yourselves Authorized to make Treaties with Foreign Nations"—an issue the commissioners did not raise in any of their other letters or manifestos to Congress. Peter Force Collection, DLC. The resolves' location among President Laurens' private papers may indicate that Morris submitted them to Congress this day but that the delegates chose to ignore them because they had no desire to explain their treaty making authority to the commissioners, deciding instead that a summary refusal to answer their letter was the best course to follow. Despite the fact that the brief entry on this issue in the journals gives the impression that Congress decided not to reply to the July 11 letter almost immediately after reading it, the delegates may in fact have discussed this matter at length before reaching a decision. Secretary Thomson commonly omitted recording motions in the official record that failed of adoption.

2 Morris must have meant none because all of the communications from the Carlisle commission to Congress were signed by at least three commissioners.

3 This statement is a bit puzzling. George III's commission to the Carlisle commissioners, dated April 13 and read in Congress on June 16, 1778, specifically authorized them to act in his behalf, though it did add that any settlement reached with the United States had to be ratified by Parliament. See *JCC*, 11:605–6, 610. The text of the royal commission that was actually sent to Congress is in the Peter Force Collection, DLC.

Joseph Reed to Dennis De Berdt

Dear Dennis Philad. July 19, 1778

The Inspection which this Letter may probably undergo will restrain me from answering fully yours received by Gov. Johnstone.[1] The Sentiments it contain'd are in my Opinion not unworthy your Character as a Friend to America or a Patriot of Brittain, but as the Passions of Men on both Sides the Atlantick are highly fermented, I have only made such Use of it as a prudential Regard to all Circumstances would require. The Object of it both at the Time of writing & ever since has been unattainable. America will endure the Extremity of human Woe before she will ever submit to the Sovereignty of that Power which has so oppressed, insulted & distress'd her. My Opinion is with my Countrymen fully upon this Point & therefore I cannot give the Commissioners the smallest Encouragement. To a Heart so open, candid, & generous as yours I do not wonder that the Professions of great Men apply with greater Efficacy than they ought. The Voice of Peace is soothing to a humane Mind, but a Peace which does not at least promise permanent Tranquillity by being founded on mutual Interest or reciprocal Affection has nothing which can attract the Wishes of a wise Man. We may possibly forgive you the Injuries we have received but it is not in your Power to forgive us. You must be sensible that you have given us Cause of such lasting Enmity that you neither can nor ought to trust us. But I am entering upon a Subject which I had determined to avoid. As I have not nor shall see Governor Johnstone in his publick Character I shall only say that his Attachment to our Cause had very much endeared to this Country & I should feel a real Concern if he should be found to be one in the long List of Apostates from Virtue & publick Honour which have blackned the English History for 50 Years past. If any Thing could sanctify the insidious Manuœvre the Agency in it of such Characters would do it, but we are got far beyond the Influence of private Characters. Measures not Men are attended to & if the whole Knot of illustrious Characters who have so ably contended for our Rights & those of Mankind had landed on this Shore with the same Terms they would have met with the same inauspicious Reception. I had answered very shortly Govr. Johnstones Letter before some Transactions were disclosed which give too much Reason to suspect he has deviated from that Line of Integrity which adorns a publick Character. The Touch of Corruption has been tried under his Auspices, & to the eternal Honour of my Country as well as Reproach to the Seducer without the least Success. You know the Correspondence I held with Ld. Dartmouth before these unhappy Contests & with what honest Sincerity I warn'd him of the Consequences of those fatal Measures. I have not lost all Affection for England nor Feeling for my Friends in it. I would therefore urge them by every Motion dear to the human Heart to lose no Time in closing the Scene of Blood on the only practicable Terms of a fœderal Union. A thousand Circumstances concur to give you a great Share of our Trade, our Remittances in my Opinion will be better than formerly & we are not so fond of War as to continue it one Moment beyond the severest Necessity. You have made a sufficient Sacrifice of human Blood & Treasure on the Altar of false Dignity—the farther you proceed the more disgraceful will be your Fall—for nothing short of Omnipotence can now check the rising Glory of this Western World. Your truest Policy is therefore to call Home your Fleets & Armies, acknowledge our Independance & as you have been such unfortunate Gamesters Try now for a saving Game of your Islands in the West Indies & your Debts in this Country.

Now as to private Affairs—your Situation as to Mr. Thompson has given me much Concern. From the Situation of the two Countries it was impossible to make your Remittances, & our not being possessed of the Deeds is an insuperable Bar to our drawing the least Benefit from the Purchase.[2] In the Year 1775 I remember I desired you to forward them to Barbados but I have never heard that it was done. I wish you had taken the Advantage of the Oppy. by Govr. Johnstone as he sent me all your Packets with great Politeness unopened. I must now repeat my Request that you would either by conveying Duplicates to France to be forwarded hither or by some other Oppy. enable us to relieve you from your Embarassment. In the mean Time you may rely upon it that every possible Step will be pursued for this Purpose. The Dutch will undoubtedly preserve a Neutrality, perhaps you could get them conveyed to some Dutch Island or to St. Croix where the Name of Willing & Morris is well known & much respected.

I have now intirly taken Leave of the Army having had another Escape on the 28th June in the Battle of Monmouth when my Horse was again shot under me, & have taken my Seat in Congress of which I have been a Member now more than a Year. I have also been strongly sollicited to accept of the Government of this State to which I can be unanimously appointed, but now the Liberties of my Country are secured & its Independance established my Ambition & present Intentions are to remain a private Citizen & attend to the Advancement of my Family & Fortune both which have been neglected while I attended to the publick Interests. I wrote you so fully the State of my Family in my last[3] that I need say no more than that they are well & remain in their Country Situation till the Fall. Your Mother & Sister were made very happy by yours & Mrs. D B's. Letters & could they have availed themselves of this Oppy. would have said every Thing tender & affectionate to you both. The Intrest we take in your Happiness must naturally excite the most pleasing Sensations to see you thus possessed of one of the finest Means of it—for after all it is

The cordial Drop which Heaven in our Cup has thrown
To make the nauseous Draught of Life go down.

The great Events which have happened in this Country within a few Weeks will I hope e'er long open a surer & more frequent Channel of Correspondence, which I doubt not you will improve as I need not say that we wish to hear from you as frequently as possible. In Consequence of your Letter I have received from Mr. Miller 4800 Dolls. Continental Money which he reckons at 4/6 Stirlg. making in that Case £1080 Stg. but as that is not the current Exchange I have only given him a Receipt for so many Continental Dollars. In the Uncertainty of the Payment of British Debts & a general Opinion that at most they are only Debts of Honour I did not chuse to return the Money but rather to leave it to future Settlement, for it is certain that it would take 19,200 Dollars to purchase £1080 Stg. At all Events by this Mode you cannot lose your whole Debt & if a better Mode takes Place with others I will endeavour to avail myself of it—if not you must submit. I shall put it into our Funds in your Name & keep the Certificates by me subject to your Order.

I am much grieved at the Account you give me of my Brother John. Aware of his Failings I put him into a Line of Duty & Expence which I supposed he had sufficient Capacity for, but as he has no Fortune & is only a half Brother I do not mean to subject myself to a fruitless Expence in attempting to raise what I fear is naturally groveling & low. I shall therefore be glad you would if possible fall upon such Measures for preventing any farther Expence as you think most effectual & not suffer him to contract Debts unauthorized upon the Presumption of my Payment on Acct. of his Connection. I have educated him & done all in my Power to enable him to provide for himself, all at a considerable Expence & with very little Prospects of his Advancement in the World. My own Family now has its Demands upon me which I must comply with.

You desire me to pay your Mamma 10 Guineas which I will do as soon as I can procure them, but they are now in this Country as Medals in yours—not to be procured but at a great Expence of our Paper as you may judge by the Rate of Exchange. As she does not therefore stand in any immediate Want of any Thing & every Day appreciates our Paper in which my Money lays I will do it whenever she requires it.

As this is an unexpected Oppy. I have wrote in great Haste & in many Places I fear scarcely legibly which in such Case you will excuse.

Every kind Wish & most affectionate Regard attend you & Dr. Mrs. DBerdt from Yours most sincerely, JR

P.S. The Messenger waiting a little longer I take up my Pen again to advise you to lose no Time in making such Arrangement of your Affairs as will enable you to profit from the future Trade to this Country it will be very great & very lucrative. The first Step will be to establish as far as Circumstances will permit a Connection in the several trading Cities in Europe especially in France, Spain, Holland & Portugal which will give you Weight & Credit here. And if availing yourself of whatever Knowledge you could procure of the pacifick Intentions of your Court & leading to a Settlement of the Dispute you could send out a parcel of Goods chiefly Woollens, hard Ware & Manchester Manufacturies & to arrive as early as possible directed to my Order it might produce you something very handsome. If you have any Doubts I will take equal Risque with you—for tho my Profession has not been of much Service to me lately—my Fortune has not been impaired by the War but otherwise from Circumstances not within the Compsass or Propriety of a Letter.[4]

RC (PHi). Endorsed: "Joseph Reed, Philada. July 19th, Received Sept. 15."

1 Reed was responding to his brother-in-law's letter to him of April 10, 1778, for which see Reed's letters to Esther Reed of June 11 and July 21, 1778. De Berdt's letter to Reed has been printed in William B. Reed, *Life and Correspondence of Joseph Reed*, 2 vols. (Philadelphia: Lindsay and Blakiston, 1847), 1:372–77.

2 A reference to Reed's purchase—through De Berdt's efforts and in partnership with Robert Morris and Thomas Willing in 1774—of a claim to a neglected title to a 10,000-acre tract of land held by the heirs of a Major Robert Thompson, whose grant rested upon a 1686 conveyance from William Penn. Reed and De Berdt were also shareholders in the West Jersey Society, formed in 1692 by a group of London investors who acquired extensive tracts in East and West Jersey and Pennsylvania, whose claims the two men pursued intermittently from 1772 until Reed's death in 1784. For an account of much of this activity, derived from the recently discovered records of the society located in the Treasury Solicitor Papers of the P.R.O., see Frederick R. Black, "The West Jersey Society, 1768–1784," *PMHB* 97 (July 1973): 388–406.

3 Not found.

4 Reed's closing line is obscured by a fold in the manuscript.

Samuel Adams to James Warren

My dear sir Philada. July 20 1778[1]

Last Saturday a Letter was brought into Congress from the British Commissioners. You have it in the inclosd News Paper with a short Resolution upon it.[2] This shuts the Door and it will remain shut till they will be pleasd to open it again. Governor Johnston has acted so base a Part as to hint the offer of Bribes to the President and every other Member of Congress, as well as the General, as you will see in the printed Letter to Mr. R. Morris. By this he has in my Opinion forfeited the Character of an honest Man and exposed himself to the just Comtempt of the World.[3] I hope some Strictures will be made in the News Papers on this, as well as the disrespectful and even insolent Language in the Commissioners Letters, not so proper to be noticed by Congress. I have lately been well assured that a Bribe of ten thousand Guineas has been offerd to a Gentleman of Station & Character here. He refusd it, as you might well suppose, with proper Resentment, telling the *Lady* who negociated this dirty Business, that the British King was not rich enough to purchase him.[4]

Mr D,[5] of whom I may hereafter have much to say to you, is arrivd with the Sieur Gerard. I have long ago made up my Opinion of the American Commissioner, & have not yet alterd it. That of the French Minister is a sensible prudent Man, not wanting in political Finesse, and therefore not to be listend to, too implicitly. The French Squadron lies off Sandy Hook. I have inclosd the Names & Rates of the Ships that compose it; together with those of the British Ships in the Harbour of N York as deliverd to the Marine Committee by a Prisoner lately escaped from thence. Their Force bears no Proportion to each other. I am told that this is a favorite Expedition of Count D Estaing himself, proposd by him[6] to the French Court, and that his Reputation depends upon the Issue of it. What Foundation there is for this, I do not know. From the Character of this Admiral, I make no Doubt he will fully answer the reasonable Expectations of the King his Master and of America. Mr. Ds political and *commercial* Friends, some of whom I suppose are in Boston, are disposd to give him great Eclat, on Account of the Aid afforded us in sending this Squadron. His Interest is represented as having been very forceable in procuring it, and the News Papers mention the Tokens of great Respect shown to him by the King & his Ministers at Versailes. The Truth, as I conceived it is, The total Overthrow of Burgoyns Army was an Event which it was thought, would produce Overtures from Britain, and France was apprehensive of our listening to Terms and compromising Matters. Hence it was, more than from any other Cause or the Interest of any Individual, that a Treaty was facilitated and agreed to; and to secure us in their Alliance and support us in our Independence was, I suppose, their Intent in sending this Squadron as well as the Purpose of Mr Gerards Mission.[7]

I have not yet answerd your Letter of the 26th of June. I declind it until I could assure you that the Sum you wishd for, for the Use of your Department, was granted.[8] I now have the Pleasure of acquainting you, that it is done and the Money will be orderd on as soon as it arrives here from York Town, which is every hour expected.[9] I am in Pain about the Ship in your Harbour. Her Owners neglect to put her into Repair, and I fear, some of her officers for Want of Skill and Experience will be at a Loss what to do with her if she should meet with a Storm. What a Pity it is that an honest old Pilot, who used to steer successfully through Rocks and Quicksands has lately been dischargd from Service! And that he should suffer this hard Usage, only because unknown to him, One who was a hearty well wisher to the Voyage, and was anxious that Capacity and Merit should always govern Promotions, had ventured to declare him the fittest Man to take the Command, when it was thought a Commander would be wanted. Vanity and Avarice, which create an insatiable Desire of Places and Preferment, without Ability or Intention to fulfill the Duties of them, if gratified, would effect the Ruin of a Country. It would be the Glory of the American Republick, to find Men having no ruling passion but the Love of our Country, and ready to render her the most arduous Services, with the Hope of no other Reward in this Life, but the Esteem of their Virtuous Fellow Citizens. But this, some tell us, is to wish for more than it is in the Power of human Nature to give.

I find Mr Dana an excellent Member of Congress. He is a thorough Republican, and an able Supporter of our great Cause. I am satisfied it would be for the great Benefit of our Country if you and he were to form an intimate Connection with each other. This I am the more desirous of, because I have no Idea of your being long secluded from the publick Councils. He will go home shortly.

Adieu My Friend. S A.

P.S. I shall take it as an Act of Kindness if you will call on Mrs A & let her know I am well—not having Leisure to write to her by this Post.

RC (MHi). FC (NN).

1 The FC of this letter, whose form Adams altered considerably when he redrafted it to send to Warren, was dated simply "July 1778" in Adams, *Writings* (Cushing), 4:45–48.

2 For the documents printed in the July 21 issue of the *Pennsylvania Packet*, see William Henry Drayton to the Carlisle Commissioners, July 18, 1778.

3 See Robert Morris to Gouverneur Morris, June 16, 1778, note 2.

4 On the attempted bribe of Joseph Reed by George Johnstone, see William Henry Drayton to the Carlisle Commissioners, July 18, 1778, note 8.

5 That is, Silas Deane.

6 Adams had added "& not Mr. D" in the FC.

7 In the FC Adams had added: "We are informed that Eleven Sail of Merchantmen & a Frigate have fallen into his Hands."

8 On July 16 Congress had ordered that $524,000 be sent to the Eastern Navy Board. *JCC*, 11: 696.

9 At this point in the FC Adams wrote, "The Marine Committee have agreed that the Navy Board shall appoint Commanders for Vessels of War under Twenty Guns," for which see Adams to Warren, July 14, 1778, note 3. See also Marine Committee to the Eastern Navy Board, July 24, 1778, note 4.

Josiah Bartlett to Mary Bartlett

My Dear Philadelphia July 20th 1778

Last week I had not the pleasure to Receive any letter from you, but as many things might occur to prevent it, I was not very uneasy about it, fully Expecting to Receive one by this Days post, but to my great mortifycation, the Eastern Post is arrived & I have no account of the Situation of my family, and what gives me the more uneasiness is, that in the last letter but one I have Recd, you informed me that Rhoda was worse & some others of the family unwell. I well know, that, at the Distance I am, my fears & apprehensions about you, will Do you no Service, and that we must Leave our affairs to the Government of the *Great Supreme Disposer* of all Events; Humbly Hoping that *He* will order all things so as shall be for the Best; Yet, Some how or other, my fears & anxiety is Such that I shall not be able to get rid of them, till I hear from you, which I have no reason to Expect till the arrival of the Post next Monday. This will seem a long week to me, and hope I shall then hear from you let your Situation be what it will, And in the mean time will Hope, it is owing to the miscarriage of your Letters, and not to the bad State of my family that I have not heard from you the two last weeks. I have the pleasure to inform you that I am well, and as our publick affairs wear a good aspect, I should be as Happy as my Distance from my family would permit me to be, Did I know you & my family were well and under no Special misfortunes.

Pray write me as offten as you can & inform me of your welfare. Mr. Wentworth who I left Sick at York Town is not arrived here, nor have I heard from him Since I left him. Charles Chace is well.

As to news nothing material has turned up Since I wrote you last week, Shall inclose you some newspapers for your perusal.

Remember my Sincere Love & affection to all my Children and Believe me to be, affectionately yours,

Josiah Bartlett

RC (NhHi).

Josiah Bartlett to Meshech Weare

Hond. Sir Philadelphia July 20th 1778

I have Received your favor of the 3d Inst. This Day with the order of the Committee of Safety to Mr Wentworth & my Self to apply to Congress for Two Hundred Thousand Dollars in behalf of our State, And will take the Earliest oppertunity to lay the Same before Congress.[1]

The Enormous Sums of money it takes to Supply the army & navy at the present advanced price of things, and the great Desire of Congress to avoid as much as possible the Emission of more bills of Credit, will I fear retard the Business, and perhaps lessen the Sum granted, But I shall use my best Endeavors that the Requisition may be Complied with.

The former commissions and instructions for armed vessels being Judged very Defective, The Congress some time ago appointed a Committee to make a new Draft & lay it before the Congress for their approbation, but by reason of the multiplicity of Business, it has not yet been Done; as soon as any are printed, I will Endeavor to send some forward to our State.[2]

I am sorry to inform you, that Mr Wentworth is not yet arrived here from York Town; He was taken Sick about the 20th of June with a fever & a Bilious vomiting & purging, Remained bad about ten Days, and occasioned my tarrying with him till the 2nd Inst. when I left him better, and was in hopes to have seen him here before this time, But I was Just now informed by Secratary Tompson's Lady who left York Town last Wednesday, That a few Days after I left him, He had a Relapse, but was again better before she left the place.

The Confederation is agreed to by all the States, Except New Jersey, Delaware & Maryland, and I have Signed it in Behalf of our State, but as the Power to Ratify was Given to the *Delegates* in Congress, I have some Doubt (as have some others) whether my Signing it is a Sufficient Ratification notwithstanding our appointment authorises us severally to Represent the State in Congress, and if Mr Wentworth should not be able to Come here soon & sign it, I Earnestly Request the State to give some order about it.

As I am informed that the Legislature of our State is to meet the Begining of next month, I Desire their attention to the appointment of Delegates to meet in the new Congress that is to be Convened the first Monday in November, agreable to the Confederation: and I would Beg leave to Remind them, that after that time no State Can be Represented by less than two Delegates at a time in Congress, so that if two Delegates only are Sent, and Sickness or any other misfortune should prevent the attendance of one of them in Congress (as has unhapily been the case most of the time since my arrival) the State will have no vote.

Your answer to several letters sent by the President of Congress to our State has been Receivd & read, and I am glad to be informed by you that in future all such letters will Receive an answer as soon as may be after their Receipt.[3]

I am Sensible Sir, that the present Plan for the Government of our State is in nothing more defective than in the want of a proper Executive power whose Duty it should be to Receive & answer all letters sent to the State, and see its good Laws Carried into Execution: Ours is the only State in the union (I Believe) who are destitute of such a power and I sincerely hope our Convention will take proper care of that very necessary & important article in their Plan for the future Government of the State.

I am with greatest Esteem & Respect, your most obedient Servant,

Josiah Bartlett

RC (MHi). FC (PHC).

1 President Weare's July 3 letter to the New Hampshire delegates, directing them to obtain $200,000 from Congress, is printed in Bartlett, *Papers* (Mevers), p. 193. Not until October 5, 1778, did Congress advance this sum to New Hampshire. *JCC*, 12:981–82.

2 Congress had instructed the Marine Committee on March 5 "to revise the commission and instructions" for privateers. *JCC*, 10:255.

3 Weare's July 4, 1778, letter to President Laurens, which acknowledged his obligation to communicate more frequently, is in PCC, item 64, fols. 33–34.

Josiah Bartlett to William Whipple

My Dear Sir, Philadelphia July 20th 1778

Since I wrote you last week nothing very material has happened. Mons Girard has informed Congress that the King his master, has left it to Congress to receive *him* as Minister Plenipotentiary or as a simple resident; that he had two commissions and would produce that which would be most agreeable; that it was expected our Ministers at their Court would be entrusted with the same commission we should choose to receive Mr Girard in; signifying at the same time, that it was the wish of the French Court he should be received as Minister Plenipotentiary, as it would be doing more honor to these States, and would be entrusted with greater powers, which would be a great advantage at the distance the two States were from each other and he likewise requested a public audience as soon as convenient. The Congress have agreed to receive him as Minister Plenipotentiary but the adjusting the ceremonial has taken some time and is not yet agreed on, nor the day appointed. Beside he will be rec'd in the State House which was left by the enemy in a most filthy situation and the inside torn much to pieces and is now cleansing and repairing for the purpose.

Mons Girard is appointed Consul General for the United States, with power to appoint others under him at the several respective ports. The conduct of the French Court at this time, the several letters from the French King to Congress and the behavior of Mons Girard seems to indicate a greater degree of sincerity in that Nation than my prejudices formerly allowed them. In short I believe they design to attach us firmly and fully to their interest hereafter.

Last Saturday we rec'd another letter from the British Commissioners dated at New York the 11th inst: they seem much dissatisfied with our answer to their former letter, dispute our authority to make treaties, demand to know the nature of the treaties we have entered into, intimate that we are not the representatives of the people and threaten to submit to the people at large to judge between the Congress and them. The Congress resolved that as the Commissioners had not complied with the terms we had laid down in our answer to their last, no answer ought to be given to this and ordered it to be published. If it comes out before the post goes out, I will try to send it for your perusal. Sundry letters rec'd by private members from the Commissioners are ordered to be printed, which will I think convince the world (if it is not already convinced) of the meaness and depravity of the Commissioners. They have not only in a polite manner in some of their letters hinted at bribes to be given to bring their purposes to pass, but have actually (by means of a woman in this City) offered ten thousand guineas to one of the members of Congress and any office he should choose, for his assistance in carrying their plan of reconciliation into effect. Probably similar offers have been made other persons who may not yet have informed of it.

As the Commissioners are now to apply to the people at large, since they find they have nothing to hope for from Congress, probably the leading men in the different States may have an offer of some of their gold; So you had best prepare yourself for the attack.

The French fleet have taken a number of British vessels and are sending the prisoners by land to this city and the French Minister has requested Congress to provide for them which cost he will pay.

I am Sir, your friend and humble servant,

Josiah Bartlett

Tr (DLC).

Board of War Lease

Philadelphia July 20, 1778.

It is agreed this day between Messrs. Wm. Duer, Timothy Pickering, and Richard Peters, members of the Board of War empowered by a Resolution of Congress[1] to engage a House for Monsr. Gerard the French Minister, on the one part, and Mr. John Dickinson on the other part, in the following Manner—Mr. Dickinson leases his House & Lott on the North side of Chestnutt street and adjoining Sixth Street, to Messrs. Duer, Pickering and Peters for one year from the Date, paying to him five hundred pounds, for the Rent, and they engage that the Premises shall be put to no other use, than for the Residence of the Said French Minister. And as the House has been damaged by being used as a Hospital in the Service of the United States, the Said Members engage that the House shall be perfectly cleaned and repaired without any expence to Mr Dickinson, or any deduction to be made from the Rent above mentioned, on account of such cleaning and repairing, or of any addition which the said Members may think proper to make for the convenience of the person residing there.

Wm. Duer.

Tim. Pickering

Richard Peters

Test. Geo. Morgan

MS (PHi). In a clerical hand and signed by Duer, Peters, and Pickering. Endorsed by John Dickinson: "Lease to Messrs Duer, Pickering & Peters for Congress.

"Settled with the Sieur Conrad Alexander Gerard Minister of France for this Year's Rent—recd. 4 Bills of Exchange for one hundred pounds Sterling payable in Paris.

"NB. I have conveyed one Half of this House & Lott to my Brother—& We have this Day 27th July 1779 let the same from this Day to the said Minister for another Year at the Rent of Three hundred pounds Sterling."

1 See *JCC*, 11:685. For additional information on steps taken by the board to assist in preparing a residence for Gérard, see also PCC, item 147, 2:215–20.

Samuel Holten's Diary

[July 20, 1778]

20. Attended in Congress, wrote to Mr. Hall of Boston;[1] & recd. an Acct. that the France Adml. is sending a number of Prisoners here.

MS (MDaAr).

1 Holten's letter to Joseph Hall has not been found. In a separate note in this diary, Holten listed the men who "have asked me to Correspond with them from York Town," and then tabulated in the margin the number of letters he wrote to each while he was in Congress. The tabulation is rendered here by the number in brackets. The last name on the page and the tabulation for the correspondents at the bottom of the list cannot be determined because the manuscript is damaged; and the number of letters written to Batchelder, Huntington, and Hall have had to be estimated for the same reason.

"The Revd Dr. Wm. Gordon of Roxbury [7]
The Revd. Mr. Wadsworth, Danvers [9]
Honl. Tho. Cushing, Boston [9]
Moses Gill, Boston [4]
Joseph Palmer, Braintree [13]
Josiah Batchelder Junr. Esqr., Beverly [11?]
Colo. Israel Huntington, Danvers [12?]

Capt. George Williams, Salem
Capt. Wm. Shillaber, Danvers.
Amos Putnam Esqr., Danvers.
Joseph Hall of Boston [6?]
Nathl. Appleton, Boston."

Richard Henry Lee to Thomas Jefferson

Dear Sir Philadelphia July 20th 1778

The condition of our affairs is much changed since last I had the pleasure of writing to you, as by the favor of his Most Christian Majesty we now are become Masters of the Sea, on our own Coast at least. Ten days ago arrived in the Delaware a French Squadron commanded by Count D'Esteing consisting of 12 sail of the Line and 4 frigates, having of Seamen and land Troops 11,000 Men on board. There is one Ship of 90 guns, one of 80, 6 of 74, three of 64 and 4 frigates. Having missed the English here, they have proceeded to N. York in quest of them, and are now before that Harbour, the depth of water being unfortunately insufficient to admit such large Ships. The English, whose fleet is inferior, are well contented to remain within the Narrows, and suffer Monsr. the Count to intercept every Vessel coming to N. York. He has already taken 15 Sail. But the French Admiral being an Officer of great activity and spirit, he seems not content with this small work, and therefore I believe he will go immediately to R. Island where he can easily destroy the Ships, and with the assistance of our force there, make prisoners of 2000 British Troops on that Island. With this Squadron came Le Sieur Gerard Minister Plenepotentiary from his most Christian Majesty. He is a sensible well bred Man, and perfectly well acquaint- with the politics of Europe. From him I learn that the Court of France consider the Message of the King of England to his Parliament and their answer, upon the Count Noailles notification of our Alliance, as a denunciation of War on the part of G. Britain, and that they mean to Act accordingly, without an express declaration, leaving this last to England. We are busied now in settling the Ceremonials for the reception of foreign Ministers of every denomination. And I assure you it is a work of no small difficulty. When this is finished, Monsr. Gerard will have his audience in Congress—I suppose this week.[1] Gen. Washington has crossed the N. River, and will cooperate with the Admiral in Measures to be concerted against the Common enemy. The B. Commissioners have sent us a second letter, very silly, and equally insolent. The preleminaries insisted on by Congress (an acknowledgement of Independence or a withdrawing of their fleets and Armies) not having been either of them complied with, this letter is to receive no answer. We have detected and fully exposed Govr. Johnstone, who under the plausible guise of friendship and Virtue, has endeavored to bribe Members of Congress—The whole body indeed as well as individual Members. The confederation is ratified by 10 States,[2] there remains only Jersey, Delaware and Maryland; but I suppose their obstinacy will e'er long submit to their interest, and a perfect coalition take place. I am, much hurried, tho with great esteem, dear Sir your most obedient Servt,

Richard Henry L[ee]

RC (DLC). Jefferson, *Papers* (Boyd), 2:204–5.

1 Lee had been appointed to a committee on July 14 that was charged with reporting on "the time and manner of the public reception of Mons. Gérard." After considering the committee report on the 16th, 17th, and 18th, Congress approved the protocol for receiving a minister plenipotentiary on the 20th but postponed consideration of codes and rules for receiving officials of other diplomatic ranks. Gérard was received in Congress on August 6. See *JCC*, 11:688, 696–701, 703, 707–8, 753–57.

2 Delegates from North Carolina and Georgia ratified the Confederation on July 21 and 24, respectively. *JCC*, 11:709, 716.

Henry Marchant to William Greene

Sir,

Philadelphia July 20th 1778.

I this Day recd. yours of the 10th Instant. I am glad to find the *Warrants* came safe to Hand, and that thereby aided by the other Resolutions obtained of Congress, the aspect of publick Affairs in Our State is much altered for the better. My most unremitted Endeavours shall be continually exerted for the Relief of the State I have the Honor to represent. The Request relating to the Depy. Clothier has been committed. I have hitherto been unable to procure a Report, but I am in Hopes it will be favourable throughout.[1] I am glad to hear the Spirit for Taxation continues, it ought to encrease at least in Proportion as Prices rise. For till Prices fall, it is evident there is too much money out, and therefore, that Taxes should encrease.

The French Fleet have taken off the Hook, ten or twelve Sail of Ships, four from Cork, & others from the West Indies, with valuable Cargoes and also a Frigate of 32 Guns their Convoy.

I expect the French Fleet will soon sail for Rhode Island, and I am in daily Expectation of hearing that Rhode Island is evacuated. I enclose your Excellency the Paper of the Day and am most respectfully your Excellencys most obedient and very humble Servt.

Hy. Marchant

RC (R–Ar).

1 See Rhode Island Delegates to Greene, June 27, 1778, note 5.

Henry Marchant to His Children

Dear Children, Philadelphia July 20th 1778

I recd. your endearing Letter of the 7th of July this Day and you can't conceive what a heartfelt Satisfaction it gave me; go on my dear Children and strive to excell in all useful Knowledge, especially such as relates to God and that other World, where we are all to go. To them that behave well in this World, the next will be a World of Happiness indeed—but to such as do ill here, it will be a world of everlasting Torment. God grant that when we have all left this World, we may not be parted from each other in the World to come; but that all, Father and Mother, Brother and Sisters, may meet together, never to part again, but live a whole Eternity with God and Christ—with Abraham, Isaac & Jacob, and all other good Men & Women and Children who have gone there before us. Remember that God hates a Lye, and every thing that is dishonest—and that you must always be chearful and willing to do your Duty to God and Man, and to your Parents and to love one another and all good People, and that you must try to perswade naughty Children to behave better and to quit all their wicked words and ways, if they would ever expect to be happy.

I was pleased to see Billys Mark, He will in good Time I hope learn to write his Name. I wish Miss Sally & Betsy may begin to learn him his Letters, and how to spell. Betsy I think minds her Hand—and I think considering the Length of the Letter Miss Sally needed no Appology. I have shewn the Letter with great Pleasure and it is much admired. There was but two or three Words misspelt, and one or two Errors in Grammar, and which I am sure Miss Sally could correct herself if She had had Time to look it over again. For Instance She spelt the word *School—Skool*. Miss Sally has been very industrious to have read the Books She mentions twice over. I rejoice that She does not forget her Bible—her Catechism & Prayers. I am glad to find Mr. Pemberton has been with and that he kindly advises you. I will agree with him, that You may not make a Task of your Grammar. Indeed my dear Child I know you love your Book so well, that I think it needless you should task yourself with any Book. I think a good and edifying Book will never be a Task to Miss Sally, I hope it will not with Miss Betsy. A little Exercise in Cyphering now and then I think is very well. I am also pleased that You take such Notice of the Business of the Farm, and that you are able to give me so good an Account of it.

Your Curiosity is excited to know the Meaning of the Tow upon some of the Trees. I got some small Twigs from Trees of another Sort of Apples and Pears and cut off a Limb and stuck the small Twiggs into it, to grow, and wrapt the Tow & Clay round to keep the Rain out. Mr. Webster will explain it to you further if you ask him.

Are you like to have a good many Pears, Peaches, and Apples? have you any Currants? And how have You been for Strawberries, huccleberries and Blackberries? I hope I shall continue to receive Letters from You. We have a Gentleman from France called a Plenipotentiary, that is, having full Powers and Authority from the King of France to join with us, his advice and to assist us against Our Enemies—And the King of France has also sent us a great many large Ships, to assist in taking the British Ships & People, and to drive them away from this good Land which Heaven gave to Our Fore-Fathers, and to us their Children, and which the King of England and his wicked People have been endeavouring to take from Us—And I hope by the Blessing of God that We shall by & by have Peace thro' all this Country, and that you may live to grow up and enjoy it with Thankfulness to God, and never forget what great Things the Lord hath done for You. Was it not for this Hope my Dear Children, I could never consent to leave you & your good Mamma so long year after year. Hoping we may soon meet & praise God for his great Goodness to Us all, I remain Your affectionate Father,

Henry Marchant

RC (RHi). Addressed: "Miss Sally, Miss Betsy, and Mr. [Billy] Marchant."

Samuel Holten's Diary

[July 21, 1778]

21. Colo. Partridge from our Court paid me a visit & informed me he was charged with several Public matters from said Court to Congress.[1]

I wrote to Miss Holten by Post.[2]

MS (MDaAr).

1 George Partridge, who previously had come to Congress in November 1776 to defend Massachusetts' recruitment practices, was now supporting the state's requests for money and for the allocation of clothing to Massachusetts troops. These requests had been submitted in a June 23 letter from President Jeremiah Powell to Henry Laurens, which is in PCC, item 65, 1:320. On August 5 Congress allotted $300,000 to Massachusetts; and in response to the clothing request, on August 8 ordered the Board of War to "take such measures and give such orders thereon as they judge proper." *JCC*, 11:709, 750, 767.

2 Not found.

Henry Laurens to John Nutt

Dear Sir[1] Philadelphia 21st July 1778

As I have not had the pleasure of a line from you since I left London in October 1774, I know nothing more of my Account than appears in the state which you delivered to me while I was with you, except that the Ship Heart of Oak had been sold and one fourth part of the Amount passed to my Credit. The former balance ¼ of the ships value together with growing Interest according to my computation will Amount upward of £850 Sterling.

You cannot have forgot the motives which induced me to leave a balance in your hands for a considerable time before I left England as well as at the time of my departure. You had repeatedly intimated to me that the use of the Money would be a convenience to you and you know I had another friend who would have been equally glad to have had the little deposit lodged in his hands, but delicacy towards you forbad my drawing it out of yours. The same consideration for you has restrained me from securing myself and giving your honor or Credit the smallest wound by means which have been often practised on both sides the water. I reflected that the use of such means being extreamly expensive in these times would also give a deep wound to your Purse.

The time is come when I find it convenient to myself to draw for a part of the sum which I suppose stands to my Credit in your Books. I have therefore under the present date passed a Bill on you payable at thirty days sight to the Order of Sarah Yard for eight hundred & ten pounds to which you will give due honor, and pay the whole,[2] if the balance due to me extends so far or so much of it as my said balance will reach, and send the remainder of the whole as you shall judge proper to determine to my friend William Manning Esquire, who I am sure will find means for shewing my Draft compleat honor, but I dare not indulge a thought so injurious to your Character as a Man of Honor and gratitude as that you will send the bills out of your own house, even admitting it shall appear I have overdrawn a few Pounds. The time is not very far distant when a free correspondence will be opened between your kingdom and these Confederated United States. In the mean time let our whole conduct distinguish between private mutual faith and honor, and the necessary unavoidable Acts of authorized public seizures and hostilities. I have been tenacious on my part in all my proceedings during this little War to avoid every Act which might prove a Bar to a revival of those happy friendships in Great Britain which I had long enjoyed. Under a persuasion of your having been actuated by the same principles, I freely and respectfully subscribe, Dear Sir, Your Most Obedient and Most Humble Servt.

LB (ScHi).

1 John Nutt was a London merchant with whom Laurens had had commercial dealings for over twenty years. Henry Laurens, *The Papers of Henry Laurens*, ed. Philip M. Hamer et al. (Columbia: University of South Carolina Press, 1968–), 2:47, 52–53.

2 Laurens entered a copy of this "Bill" just above the text of the present letter in his private letterbook.

Gouverneur Morris to the Earl of Carlisle

To the EARL of CARLISLE.

My Lord, [July 21, 1778]

As you, in conjunction with your brother Commissioners, have thought proper to make one more fruitless negociatory essay, permit me, through your lordship, once more to address the brotherhood. It is certainly to be lamented that gentlemen so accomplished should be so unfortunate. Particularly, my Lord, it is to be regretted that you should be raised up as the topstone to a pyramid of blunders.

On behalf of America I have to intreat that you will pardon their Congress for any want of politeness in not answering your letter.[1] You may remember, that in their last letter they stated certain terms as preliminaries to a negociation.[2] And I am sure your lordship's candor will do them the justice to acknowledge that they are not apt to tread back the steps they have taken. In addition to this it so happens that they are at present very indifferent whether or not your King and Parliament acknowledge their independency; and still more indifferent as to withdrawing his fleets and armies.

You mistake the matter exceedingly when you suppose that any person in America wishes to prolong the calamities of war. No, my lord, we have had enough of them in all conscience. But the fault lies on you or your master, or some of the people he has about him. Congress when Sir William Howe landed on Staten-Island, met him with their Declaration of Independence. They adhered to it in the most perilous circumstances. They put their lives upon the issue; nay their honor. Now in the name of common sense how can you suppose they will relinquish this object in the present moment?

I am fully of your lordship's opinion, when you decline any dispute with Congress, about the meaning of the term Independence. They would have infinite advantage over you logically, but what is worse, they are politically in capacity to put upon the term just what construction they please: Nay, my lord, eventually Great-Britian must acknowledge just such an independence as Congress think proper; they are now in the full possession and enjoyment of it. How idle in you to talk of insuring or enlarging what is out of your power and cannot be encreased.

You give two reasons for not withdrawing your fleets and armies.

The first is, that you keep them here by way of precaution against your ancient enemies. Really, my Lord, I was at a loss for some time to comprehend the force of this reasoning, or how a body of men in this country and a large fleet could protect you against an invasion from France. And I am even now perhaps mistaken, when I suppose your sea and land forces have been kept here to draw the attention of your enemies to this quarter, and leave their coast exposed, that so you may have an opportunity of invading France. If this was the object, it hath had the desired effect. Your armies are doubtless assembled in readiness for the descent, which, considering the unprovided state of that country, cannot but prove successful; and therefore I congratulate your lordship on the fair prospect you enjoy of seeing your Sovereign make his triumphant entry through the gates of Paris.

Your second reason for staying here is to protect the Tories. Pray, my lord, ease your mind upon that subject. Let them take care of themselves. The little ones may be pardoned whenever they apply. The great ones have joined you from conscientious or from interested motives. The first in having done what they thought right will find sufficient comfort. The last deserve none. I offer you this consolation, my lord, because we both know that you cannot protect the tories, and because there is every reason to believe that you cannot protect yourselves.

You have, it seems, determined your judgment by what you conceive to be the interest of your country, and you propose to abide by your declarations in every possible situation. I rather imagine that you are determined by your instructions; but if otherwise, surely, my lord, you are not to learn that circumstances may materially alter the interest of your country and your conceptions of it. The decision of some military events which you did not wait for, would put you in a situation to speak to Congress in much more decent terms than those contained in your last letter.

But you want to know, my lord, what treaties we have entered into. In pity to your nerves Congress have kept this knowledge. It will make the boldest among you tremble. As we are not about to negociate at present, there is no need of the communication. However, to satisfy your curiosity as far as an individual can, I pray you to recollect, that the Marquis de Noailles told you his Court, when they formed an alliance with America, had taken eventual measures.[3] You cannot but know that a French fleet is now hovering on the coast near you—draw your own conclusions, my lord.

It is a most diverting circumstance to hear you ask Congress what power they have to treat, after offering to enter into treaty with them, and being refused. But I shall be glad to know by what authority you call on them for this discovery. The Count de Vergennes had a right to it, but the Earl of Carlisle certainly has not. Let me add, my lord, that in making the request there is a degree of asperity not suited to your situation. When you were in the arms of victory we pardoned an insolence which had become habitual to your nation. We shall revere it if preserved when you are reduced to the lowest pitch of wretchedness. But in the present moment, when you certainly cannot terrify, and have not suffered so as to deserve pity, such language is quite improper. And it forces from me certain facts which I am sorry to mention, as they shew your masters to be wicked beyond all example.

When they found that an alliance was actually on the carpet between his Most Christian Majesty and these States, they offered to cede a part of the East-Indies, to give equal privileges in the African trade, and to divide the fisheries, provided they might be at liberty to ravage America. And when that would not do, they told the French Ministry that it was absurd to treat with Congress; that they were faithless; nay, that the bargain was actually struck for the purchase of America, and money, to the amount of half a million, sent over to pay the price. These, my lord, are facts—facts which will hang up to eternal infamy the names of your rulers.[4] The French, my lord, laughed at the meanness and falshood of these declarations. But they suffered themselves to appear to be deceived. They permitted you to flounder on in the ocean of your follies and your crimes. You and your brethren, I find, are directed to play the same game here; to call our allies faithless; to tell an hundred incoherent fictions about our treaties, the substance of which you confess yourselves at this moment ignorant of. And what is the very complication of absurdity, you pretend to tell Congress the manner in which the negociations were carried on, when Mr. Deane, the principal negociator, on their part, is on the spot to give information. For shame. For shame. It is for these reasons that Congress treat you with such utter contempt.

There is but one way left to sink you still lower, and, thank God you have found it out. You are about to publish! Oh my lord! my lord! you are indeed in a mighty pitiful condition. You have tried fleets and armies, and proclamations, and now you threaten us with news-papers.[5] Go on, exhaust all your artillery, But know, that those who have withstood your flattery and refused your bribes, despise your menaces—Farewell. When you come with better principles, and on a better errand, we shall be glad to meet you: Till that moment, I am your Lordship's most obedient And most humble servant,

An American.[6]

MS not found; reprinted from the *Pennsylvania Packet and Daily Advertiser*, July 21, 1778.

[1] Morris is referring to the Carlisle commissioners' July 11 letter to Congress, for which see William Henry Drayton to the Carlisle Commissioners, July 18, 1778, note 1.

2 See Henry Laurens to the Carlisle Commissioners, June 17, 1778—a letter Morris himself drafted.

3 See Henry Laurens to George Clinton, May 11, 1778, note 3.

4 Sometime near the end of 1777, according to a statement made by the French foreign minister Vergennes to the Spanish ambassador in Paris, count d'Aranda, Great Britain offered to grant France, if French ports were closed to American shipping, Cape Breton, Nova Scotia, and a liberal share of the Newfoundland fisheries. Edward S. Corwin, *French Policy and the American Alliance of 1778* (Princeton: Princeton University Press, 1916), p. 6n.11. This seems to have been the only basis for Morris' otherwise unsubstantiated description of British overtures to France prior to the conclusion of the French alliance with the United States. For a brief account of other British efforts to prevent French assistance to the United States, see Samuel F. Bemis, *The Diplomacy of the American Revolution* (New York: D. Appleton-Century Co., 1935), p. 20n.11.

5 "As we have Communicated our Powers to you," the Carlisle commissioners had written to Congress on July 11, "and mean to proceed without reserve in this business we will not suppose that any objection can arise on your part to our Communicating to the Public so much of your Correspondence as may be necessary to explain our own proceedings." Peter Force Collection, DLC.

6 For a discussion of the newspaper letters Morris wrote to the Carlisle commissioners using the pseudonym "An American," see Morris to the Carlisle Commissioners, June 20, 1778, note 1.

New York Delegates to George Clinton

Sir, Philadelphia 21st July 1778.

Just before we left York Town (in Conjunction with our Colleague Mr. Lewis) we moved for, and obtained from the Congress, an advance of 100,000 Dollars for the Use of the State, and for which they are to be accountable.[1] The Reasons were as follows: We found, by various Intelligence laid before Congress, that the Savages were about making an Irruption upon our Frontiers, & from the probable Evacuation of Philadelphia, it was not unlikely that the British General would again pursue his favorite Object of Hudson's River. In this Situation of Affairs, it appeared to us that money might be wanting in our Treasury, which we had Reason to believe was not very full; and, further, we were informed that our militia remained unpaid for Services formerly done, and, therefore, might not turn out with their usual Alacrity. These Things were laid before Congress, and they, (surprized at the moderation of a Demand which we venture to say from any other State in similar Circumstances would have been at least three Times as great), instantly made the Grant: The adjournment to Philadelphia, the Change of political Circumstances by the Battle of Monmouth, and arrival of the French Squadron (on both of which Incidents we heartily congratulate your Excellency) and the want of a safe Opportunity, have delayed the sending forward of the money.

We have further to observe to your Excellency, that the Complaints of our Fellow Citizens who are unpaid by Commissaries, Quarter Masters and the like, have been laid before Congress; but unfortunately the Complaint is universal, &, therefore, it is objected that a general Remedy is necessary. In this Situation, we have it in View, to obtain a Recommendation to the State to liquidate and adjust those accounts, in like manner as their own accounts are liquidated and adjusted, and this money may be of Use in discharging them. Besides this, it is to be further observed that the Continent are very considerably indebted to our State, and the accounts will be settled with greater Ease full than empty handed. Mr. Duer would have gone forwards long ago, but Mr. Lewis was under the Necessity of going to Baltimore to bring up his Family, and the State would have been unrepresented if Mr. Duer had left this Place. We hope that the arrival of Genl. Schuyler or of Mr. Lewis will soon put it in his Power to return to the State.[2] We do ourselves the Honor to enclose to your Excellency, a Report brought in but never yet read upon our Vermont affairs.[3] We think it short of what is necessary, and shall, therefore, urge Congress to such amendments as may render it more equal to the Purposes proposed to be answered by it. It is possible, Sir, that our Constituents may be led to believe, that there hath been a Remissness in their Delegates in not urging this Business with a Degree of Rapidity which in their Opinion would have ill answered the wise Purposes of the application. Your last Letter on this Subject is now before us,[4] and we shall do ourselves the Honor to present it, as soon as the matters necessary to the audience of the French Minister shall be adjusted, which is not yet done, so dilatory are the Proceedings of our Body. The Presenting your Excellency's Letter, will afford a proper Opportunity to call for and urge the Report; the amendments to which will be, if within our Power such as are stated on the enclosed Paper. We are with greatest Respect Your Excellency's most obd't & humble Serv'ts.

Wm. Duer,
Gouv'r Morris,

ENCLOSURE

(Copy)

The Committee to whom was referred the letter from Gov'r Clinton, of the 7th of April, A. D. 1778, with the Proclamation enclosed, take leave to report the following resolutions, viz:[5]

Resolved, that the independent government attempted to be established by the people styling themselves the inhabitants of Vermont cannot derive any countenance or authority from the Congress of the thirteen United States of America.

Resolved, that no number or body of people within any part of the United States can be justified in attempting to form & establish any new independent State within any part of these United States, without the consent of the State or States in which they are & were included at the time the Congress were at first elected & convened for the Safety & defence of these United States, & the approbation of Congress.[6]

And it is recommended, in the Strongest terms, to the people aforementioned, & all other the good people of these United States & any particular State interested or claiming to be interested in the premises, to refrain from all acts of violence & coercive measures, as they regard the peace & welfare of these States.

The Committee who brought in this report were: Mr. Huntington, of Connecticut, Mr. J. B. Smith, of Pennsylvania, & Mr. Francis Lightfoot Lee, of Virginia.

Amendments intended to be proposed to the Report:

Resolved, that no man or body of men can of right on any territory within North America form or establish any State, (other than those which were called the British Colonies, Provinces, or Plantations in North America,) without the Special consent of that State within which such territory shall lie, & the approbation of Congress.

Resolved, that Congress do highly reprobate all attempts to set up, form, or establish any new State or government, as tending to break the Union of the States they represent, to produce civil wars, & to destroy the peace, freedom, & happiness of America.

Resolved, that Congress have not given & will not give any countenance or authority to the discontented subjects of the State of New York, Styling themselves the inhabitants of Vermont, but do disapprove of their proceedings.

Resolved, that it be most earnestly recommended to the persons aforesaid, forthwith to submit peaceably & quietly to the jurisdiction, government, & authority of the said State of New York, & that they represent unto the said government any grievances they may labor under.

Resolved, that the State of New York be requested to forbear, for the present, all coercive measures to compel the submission of their discontented subjects, & also, on a proper representation, to redress the grievances they labor under, if any there be.[7]

Reprinted from Clinton, *Papers* (Hastings), 3:567–70. Enclosure: ibid., pp. 569–70. According to an editorial note the enclosure is a "copy . . . in the handwriting of George W. Clinton." Ibid., p. 569n. A draft of the body of this letter, unsigned but in the hand of Gouverneur Morris, is in the James Duane Papers, NHi. The same collection also contains a draft in the hand of Samuel Huntington of the first four paragraphs of the enclosure.

1 See *JCC*, 11:627, 630.

2 Although Francis Lewis returned to Congress later in July, William Duer continued to serve as a delegate until November 1778. But Philip Schuyler—whose March 25, 1778, election as an "additional Delegate" was not noted by Burnett—did not attend Congress until 1779. Burnett, *Letters*, 3:lvi–lvii. An important reason for General Schuyler's delay was that he was yet awaiting the outcome of the

inquiry into his role in the loss of Fort Ticonderoga in 1777, the effect of which was discussed by James Duane in an August 22, 1778, letter to John Jay. See Jay, *Papers* (Morris), 1:492–93.

[3] There is no evidence in the journals of when this report was submitted to Congress.

[4] Governor Clinton's July 8 letter to the New York delegates on the "late extraordinary Proceedings of the Government of the pretended State of Vermont in ordering Drafts to be made in that Quarter for filling up the Continental Regiment, commanded by Col. Warner," is in Clinton, *Papers* (Hastings), 3:532. For a letter of the same date from Clinton to President Laurens on the same issue see ibid., pp. 533–35.

[5] For a discussion of the committee that had been appointed on April 20 to consider Governor Clinton's April 7 letter to President Laurens and his enclosed proclamation on the vexing issue of New York's claim to govern Vermont, see Henry Laurens to George Clinton, April 20, 1778, note 2.

[6] Immediately after this paragraph in the text of the committee report written by chairman Samuel Huntington, the following paragraph is lined out.

"Resolved that a Copy of these Resolutions be forthwith Transmitted to the people Stiling themselves Inhabitants of Vermont & that they be directed to lay before Congress the Causes & reasons of their proceedings in attempting to Establish a new Government to this end that Such proceedings may be had thereon as to Right & Justice Shall be found to appertain."

[7] For a series of resolves on the Vermont issue that the New York delegates offered to Congress on May 22, 1779, which represent an amalgam of the resolutions of the committee that considered Governor Clinton's April 7 letter and the amendments to them proposed by the New York delegates, see *JCC*, 14:631–33.

John Penn to Richard Caswell

Dear Sir, Philadelphia July 21st. 1778

I wrote to you the 15th Inst. by an express informing you, that by the Commission Col. Williams obtained it would require the three Delegates to be present before the State could have a Vote, and then indeed we must be all of one Opinion. As there are several Gentlemen here that represent the State they belong to singly, and as I proposed to our Assembly that they would choose four Delegates confining two to be here at a time, which was not done, the Members saying they would proceed the old way, I am induced to wish that your Excellency would send a Commission giving all or either of us a right to vote until November, when I think the confederation directs two.[1] I mention this again lest some accident should happen to the Express.

Monsr. Gerard the French Minister is here, he is a very polite well bred man, Mr Deane says he has been our first friend in France. The French Fleet cannot get nearer to New York than Sandy Hook, on account of their size, they have lately taken thither Transports loaded with provisions going to Lord Howe. We had a curious letter from the Commissioners lately, calling upon us to know by what authority we presume to make treaties with the King of France, or any other foreign power, declaring we had no authority delegated to us for that purpose by the Assembly's of the different States, before or since the supposed confederation; the answer was short, "that the British Fleet and Army not being sent away, nor the Independence of America acknowledged, no answer be given."[2] Enclosed is a News paper. I hope Sir you will forward a Commission by the first Opportunity as desired unless you find some express resolution to the Contrary, of the Assembly. Indeed I am perfectly satisfied from what I heard when at New Bern, that no alteration was intended. I feel myself in an awkward situation not having a right to vote, matters of importance will soon be debated.

I have the honor to be with due respect your Excellencys most Ob. Servt. J. Penn

Tr (Nc–Ar).

1 See Penn to Caswell, July 15, 1778, note.

2 See *JCC*, 11:701–2.

Joseph Reed to Esther Reed

My dear Hetty Philad. July 21 [1778]

I send you inclosed all the News Papers published since I wrote you last by Capt. Mercers Harry. You will in the last Paper find Govr. Johnstones Letter to me published by Order of Congress. I had some Difficulty to prevent the Extracts from your Brothers Letter published in the same Paper.[1] You will perhaps wonder at this as supposing it contains nothing disadvantageous to him, but I assure you a very different Idea was entertained of it in Congress & I only got it withdrawn on the Plea of personal Favour. I hope my Disclosure of Govr. Johnstones Transactions will not injure your Brother in England as he cannot be in any Degree affected by it, & I could not but think it a point of publick Duty.[2] Least the Mention of your Brothers Name in Govr. Johnstones Letter may prejudice him here I shall publish such Parts of his Letter to me as will do him Service here without Prejudice in England.

We have no authentick Acct. of the Proceedings of the French Fleet at New York farther than that they cannot get into the Harbour for Want of Water. They take Prizes hourly of Vessels arriving from every Part of the World & a great Number of Prisoners are now on the Way to this City.

Mrs. Yard not remaining in Town,[3] after much Deliberation upon all Circumstances I have concluded to go into Mr. Cox's House which is now in my Possession with what necessary Furniture Mrs. Yard spares me—to get Numa to keep a sort of Batchelor Table for me. My Reasons are that in the 1st Place it is very difficult to get good Lodgings even at 30 Dollars per Week, the few Boarding Houses being extremely crowded. I pay Rent for this House if unocupied & as a Number of Persons are continually calling on Business of various Kinds I must have some Persons to give Answers. You when you come or any of the Family in the mean Time will have a House to come to. In short tho it may be somewhat more expensive it will be attended with Conveniences. Mr. Pettit is soon expected in Town who will also want such a Home.

Numa had done nothing with your Memorandum but I have since taken it in Hand—tho Prices are yet very extravagant but for your Comfort they are falling.

I wish to have my Books got down as Oppy. offer & for that Purpose would have you write to Mr. Forman that whenever he sends empty Waggons towds Trenton he would direct them to call upon you when you can occasionally forward the Books & such Articles as you do not want to Trenton where the Shallops can take them up.

I am in some Expectation of going to Camp to finish the Business which the moving of the Army interupted. If so I shall see you pretty soon. If not I fancy the Month will come round, but whether present or absent I am my dear Hetty's faithful & affect.

J. Reed

P.S. I wonder Mr. Lowry does not come down. It is absolutely necessary & that the Things at Quaker Town be got down as soon as possible. He knows what I mean. I have an Oppy. of getting you a tolerable Assortment of Queens Ware—if you chuse it & will send me a List of Particulars will endeavour to please you. Let me hear from you frequently. Kiss the Children for me. I shall not forget them.[4]

RC (NHi).

[1] For the efforts made by Congress on July 9 and 16 to examine all correspondence "of a public nature" recently received by delegates from British subjects, see *JCC*, 11:678, 694; Gouverneur Morris' Notes on George Johnstone's Letter to Francis Dana, July 16; and Joseph Reed to Dennis De Berdt, July 19, 1778, note 1.

[2] For Reed's "Disclosure of Govr. Johnstones Transactions," see William Henry Drayton to the Carlisle Commissioners, July 18, 1778, note 8.

[3] Reed had written the following brief letter to Sarah Yard on July 19. "Mr. Reed begs the favor of Mrs. Yard to take up any letters of a private nature she may find for him in New York, and if she meets with any difficulty in that or any part of her own business, Mr. Reed will presume so much upon the politeness of Gov. Johnstone as to request his favor to her as Mr. R.'s friend. Should she wait on Gov. Johnstone in this, or any other occasion, Mr R. begs her to present him respectfully to that gentleman, and acquaint him that Mr R. received his letter and did himself the honour of answering it from General Washington's head-quarters, at the Valley Forge the latter end of last month. Mr. R. wishes her a good journey, and a safe return with all possible success in her business." Reed Papers, NHi.

[4] Reed wrote to Esther again the following day, but reported only the following public news. "Our News besides what you have in the Paper herewith is that

the Count d'estaing is yet at the Narrows taking British Vessels every Day—that Genl. Washington was as far down as The White Plains & that Gen. Clinton had moved out of New York to Kingsbridge with his whole Force. We had a Report of two English Frigates cruizing between our Capes but they prove to be French Prizes." Reed Papers, NHi.

Andrew Adams to Oliver Wolcott

Sir Philadelphia 22d July 1778

The Arival of the French fleet added to the Battle of Monmouth seams to put our affairs upon a respectable Footing and Difuses a general Joy among the friendly Inhabitants of this City. However I must freely own I dont feel myself so compleatly flushd. upon this Occation as many do: I cant say but it may be attended with the happy Consiquences expected, but when I view the Matter upon a larger Scale sundry Questions suggest themselves for our Consideration. I was fully of Oppinion that the War was drawing to a speedy issue. I lookd. upon the present Campaign as the last & that we had before us every prospect of Success, and our Independe as fixd. Upon this View of the Case I would quere whither the arival of this Fleet will not be a Means of lenghtening out the War, and also lay us under an Obligation of affording France an armd. force in Case they Need it which as the Case may be circumstanced as to time, place &c may be very disagreable to our Northern people. Besides would it not be much to our Advantage had we settled the present Controversy in our favour without a foreign Aid.

Under such Ideas I have never been fond of the assistance of any foreign power. However I am no adept in Politicks, nor do I pretend to determine those Questions either Way. I only hint some things that have ever been upon my Mind & leave the Decission to abler Politians or future Time. Should be glad of your Sentiments upon those Matters.

The Seiur Gerard with Mr. Dean arived in this City (if I mistake not) the 12th instant;[1] he has not as yet been admitted to an Audience. The Cerimonials for that purpose are fixd. and that will now be done, in a very few Days. He is not to be recd. as Ambasador but as Minister Plenipontentiary.

Have just recd. Intelligence that there are three English Ships of force now lying in Delaware Bay, for other News must beg Leave to refer you to yesterdays paper which I have inclosed in a Letter to Miss Adams[2] designd. to have inclosed one to you but was disappointed.

Hope you had an agreable Journey home as the Weather was much more favourable than I expected.

I am Sir with great Esteam & Regard, Your very Obedt. hum Servt.

Andw Adams.

RC (CtHi).

[1] In a letter dated Philadelphia, July 19, 1778, and directed to an unknown correspondent, Adams' colleague Titus Hosmer also reported the recent arrival of Gérard and Silas Deane, but only the following brief extract of it has been found. "I am plunged in the Ocean of Congress, it is a maze, a Labyrinth of which I have not yet got hold of the Clue; some Business is done in Congress some in Committees, and Boards, I am labouring to explore these different powers, & provinces . . . our Friend Mr. Dean is here, with a Minister from France to Congress, he has the most decisive proofs of the Friendship of the King & Court of France . . . he is well received here by a considerable Number of Gentlemen who within are full of Envy, Malice, and all uncharitableness towards him." *The Collector* 61 (June 1948), p. 135, item M1098.

[2] Not found.

Elias Boudinot to Hannah Boudinot

My very dearest Love, Philadelphia July 22d 1778

I wrote you an hour ago in great Haste,[1] since which our door keeper has brought me your kind & obliging favour of the 18th Inst. which is the first Syllable I have recd. from Home for 23 long days. I have wrote you at least 8 or 10 Letters in that time,[2] and one particularly by Mr. Handcock who promissed me faithfully to deliver it as he passed, and yet find by your Letter that he neglected it, which was very unkind indeed. Ee'r this reaches you, you will certainly be informed of the ill state of my Health, and I hope also of my being on the recovery. The fever is entirely broke and nothing but the dull weather keeps me from going out. Mrs. Franklin has nursed me with as much Tenderness as if I had been her own Child and indeed I have ever occasion of gratitude & Praise to gracious God who has so continually provided for me in every changing Scene. I hope you are not in earnest when you talk of being low spirited. You know the fatal Effects of such a disposition and there can be no reason for it, as when we are filling up our days labour, it is but of little Consequence what part of our Master's Vineyard we are in, if placed there by him, in the Evening if faithfull we shall receive our Penny. I have enclosed you several News Papers, which I hope from time to time come safe to hand.

I am not quite satisfied with my Prospects here, they do not quite answer my Expectations, and I am afraid that I am only wasting Time, but perhaps, my Ideas of Things may hereafter alter. If honor or publick Applause was my Object, it may be that I might be gratified.

My kind Love to my dear Susan and Family—Sister, Neighbours &c &c.

I am with every tender & affectionate Sentiment of Love & Esteem, My dearest Wife, Your faithfull, Boudinot

July 24th. I have been abroad to day, and am bravely.

RC (NjP).
1 Not found.
2 Of these only three have been found—those of July 7, 9 and 14, 1778.

Committee of Congress to William Heath

Sir Philadelphia July 22. 1778

Your letter of the eighth instant to Congress with its inclosed papers relative to the case of Ensign Brown was referred to us by Congress as a Committee to report thereupon.[1] To do this with propriety, we applied to the Board of War for the proceedings of the Court Martial upon Ensign Brown, a return of which we expected to have found there. But as no such return has been received at the Board of War, we request that you will be so good as to transmit to us, a copy of the proceedings at large by the first opportunity. We are Sir, Your most humble Serts. Roger Sherman

Hy. Marchant

Wm. Hy. Drayton

RC (MHi).
1 See *JCC*, 11:704; and Henry Laurens to Heath, June 20, 1778, note 2.

Henry Laurens to Denis Nicolas Cottineau

Sir 22nd July 1778

I was honored with your favor of the 30th Ulto. three days ago.

Congress are not disposed to grant Marine Commissions for Vessels in distant States unless descriptions more special than those you left are laid before them; in order therefore to avoid as much as possible any disappointment to you and to promote the general Interest of the Allied Powers of France and these United States I shall transmit by this conveyance to His Excellency Governor Caswell a number of Commissions, Instructions and Bonds, from whence you may obtain so many as he shall judge proper.

From the conversation at York Town when you were going to Camp I had expected you would have received it at your return and that some Plan for your proceeding on a voyage in joint concern would have been reduced to writing, but as you did not even touch upon the subject, I concluded you had determined your Affairs to go in some other Channel, and now a concern in the extent you mark, would not be convenient to me even if I were as much disposed as I was at York, because I had the very day before your Letter reached me agreed to draw for a considerable part of the Money I had lodged in England.[1] Besides I cannot venture to risque the good opinion of my friends by an attempt to persuade them into an Association where so large a sum as £6000 Sterling is required on their part, without having a Plan of particulars for their consideration. Hence Sir, you will after one moments reflection perceive how impossible it is for me to return a more direct answer—and will govern your future determinations accordingly.

We have received no certain account of a Declaration of War, but beyond all dispute hostilities are mutual between France and England, and captures made upon every occasion. Already the Count d'Estaing has taken a great number of British ships, and some he has destroyed, among them it is said five armed Vessels, and I know he is exceedingly chagrined, because he cannot get into Sandy Hook with his large ships. His intention was to have tried the powers of the English squadron under the command of Lord Howe at New York—failing in this place the Admiral is gone to Rhode Island, where he may play a smaller Game than he had aspired to—but will render much service to the common cause.

You perceive Sir, from this intelligence, which is the best I can give, that you are at liberty to enrich yourself from the spoils of the Enemy—an Enemy who a very little time ago panted for our destruction and had avowed their designs to accomplish it.

Accept my wishes for your prosperity, and believe me to be with great Regard, Sir, your Obedient Servant.

LB (ScHi). Addressed: "Captain Cottineau, North Carolina."

1 See Laurens to John Nutt, July 21, 1778.

Jonathan Elmer to Ebenezer Elmer

Dear Brother Philada. 23d July 1778

A few days ago I recieved a Letter from you informing me of your promotion to Surgeon of Col. Shrieve's Regiment. I am not at all surprized at the attempts to supplant you in that Birth. The numerous greedy appendants of the Army who are incessantly fawning upon the heads of every department and soliciting for every post that happens to become vacant, render immediate application & a resolute claim of right necessary in order to obtain that which is justly due to an honest and meritorious man. I hope you will use your endeavours to discharge the duties of your present Station faithfully, &

to the general satisfaction of the particular Corps to which you belong.

The complaints of the Officers of the Army which you mention I acknowledge are in general but too well founded. But when you reflect upon the rapid progress of our political affairs, the multiplicity of business Congress have had to transact, & the many difficulties they have had to surmount; I am convinced you will readily percieve that Congress is often unjustly complained of. The depreciation of our paper Currency is irremediable at present, as it arises in a great measure from the superabundency of it in circulation. But as our affairs now begin to wear a smiling aspect, & as we are beginning to sink our bills of credit by Taxes, the value of our money will indubitably soon begin to appreciate. This in my opinion ought to afford some satisfaction to those who are at present sufferers in the service of their Country.

You inform me that your present situation renders it necessary for you to have a Horse. The price will undoubtedly be extravagant. I hope however you will have the good luck to get one that will answer your purpose on reasonable terms.

I have very little reason to believe that any new regulations respecting the medical department in the Army will take place this Campaign, Congress having too much business on hand of a more general & important nature to attend to that matter.

I remain (in haste), Yours &c, Jonathn. Elmer

RC (NjHi).

Henry Laurens to Richard Caswell

Sir, Philadelphia 23d July 1778[1]

As I have nothing public in charge for your Excellency I must request you Sir to indulge me in this private for the cover of six Marine Commissions, Instructions & Bonds, and of a letter to Capt Cottineau. The Captain applied to me in York Town for a Commission for his own ship, and for one or two which he said he intended to equip and to form a little squadron. Congress are not inclined to grant Commissions for vessels in distant States, unless special descriptions are previously laid before them. Your Excellency will be capable of judging of the propriety of Capt Cottineau's pretensions, and will act as you shall think for the benefit of the public. At this critical moment 'tis highly probable demands will be made on your Excellency for all that remains after Capt Cottineau shall be supplied.

I am told no less than twelve prizes lately taken are advertised for sale on Tuesday next at Egg Harbour. Vice Admiral Count d'Estaing has captured a much greater number at Sandy Hook, some of them armed vessels, and some very valuable, but we have not learned particulars. The Admiral finding his large ships of too great a draught of water for the Bar of the Hook after lying several days in view of the British Squadron within, sailed as we are informed for Rhode Island where he must be content to play a smaller game than that which he originally had in view. If General Pigot and his Garrison shall be compelled to surrender, the thing will not be very inconsiderable.

I take the liberty of enclosing to your Excellency two of the latest news papers.

I am anxious that Congress should resolve to hold no conference with men who have dared to tempt them with bribes of Gold, and I trust that through the endeavours of some diligent Patriots in the House, those men will be compelled to return, the bearers of their own impeachment, will be held up to the severe resentments of their much injured Countrymen, and their names transmitted to posterity in characters which will render their memory infamous.

I have the honor to be with great esteem & respect, Sir, your Excellency's Obedient Servant. Henry Laurens.

Tr (Nc–Ar).

1 The LB of this letter in the Laurens Papers, ScHi, is clearly dated "22nd July."

Gouverneur Morris to John Jay

Dear Jay, Philadelphia 23d July 1778.

I received yours of the 4th[1] some Days ago but I was in so unsettled a Situation that I could not answer it. At present I must be short for I have Company waiting. I have no Apprehension that these Money Matters can affect *me*. I have not taken nor would I on any Consideration have taken the Agency of Business. Duer I trust will do what is right. Your Caution however is useful and proper and I thank you for it. On no Occasion do I wish to give Room for the Exercise of Slanderous Tongues much less where money Matters are in Question for they are indeed delicate very delicate.

As to the Malevolence of Individuals It is what I have to expect. It is by no Means a Matter of Surprize that I should be hated by some Men but I will have my revenge. By laboring in the public Service so as to gain the Applause of those whose Applause is worth gaining I will punish them severely. You will see another American to another Letter of the Commissioners.[2] I mention this to convince you I am not quite idle.

The Letter you refer to was one enclosing me a Libel against myself. I think I have answered it but am not sure as I was then in a moving state. My servant being sick also hath prevented me in some Degree from the Worship of the Regularities. Let me hear from you often. My Love to all Friends. Remember me to Lewis & when you see him Richard who by this Time has no small Reason to lament his non Acceptance of a certain Office.[3] Adieu. Believe me with sincerity, your Friend,

Gouvr Morris

[*P.S.*] I hear by Accident of the Arrival of your Brother.[4] I congratulate you on it. Again Adieu.

RC (NNC).

1 Since Jay's July 4 letter to Morris has not been found, it is difficult to explain some of Morris' allusions in the present letter.

2 See Gouverneur Morris to the earl of Carlisle, July 21, 1778.

3 Lewis and Richard Morris were Gouverneur's half-brothers. Richard had turned down appointments as judge of the New York Admiralty Court in 1776 and as clerk as the New York Supreme Court in 1777. Jay, *Papers* (Morris), 1:420–21.

4 Sir James Jay.

Gouverneur Morris to the New York Assembly

Sir [July 23, 1778]

In Conjunction with my Colleagues Duer & Lewis I lately obtained from Congress an Advance of 100,000 Dollars.[1] Mr. Duer has received the Money and will forward it by the first safe Opportunity. If I might at this Distance advise I would give my Opinion that A Law should be passed directing the Treasurer and auditor to pay all Demands by the Subjects of the State against the Continent untill such Day and under such Restrictions as might be most proper on a Consideration of all Circumstances. Then the Continent being made Debtor in our general Accounts with all Monies advanced for them & receiving Credit for the Sums they have advanced & for our Quota of Taxes a Ballance might be struck & if against us paid. By these Means a very considerable Sum would either remain in the Treasury to sink our Emissions or at least be in the Hands of our People to pay future Taxes & furnish themselves with the foreign Articles necessary for them and which Nothing but that can obtain. After all this should there be still which I rather wish than Expect a considerable Sum in the Treasury it might perhaps be properly lent to the Continent. I hope that the Restoration of our Territory at both Ends of the State will enable us soon to put our particular Finances upon the most respectable Footing.

I am sorry to hear from several Gentlemen that the Recommendation of Congress to pardon the disaffected under certain Limitations[2] hath given Uneasiness to Persons in the State of New York.

And I almost wish to know whether they are among those who were steady in Times of great Doubt & Distress because I have observed that such Men from a natural Fortitude of soul are much more inclined to Mercy than those who are under a Necessity of manifesting an extraordinary Zeal. But be this as it may the Lenity & active Spirit of the State I represent were too generally felt and acknowledged by the Members of Congress to suppose they meant a particular Relation to that State. Neither would it be proper to suppose they had any particular Views. I will only mention Facts. When this Recommendation came out it rendered the Troops which they call new Levies worse than useless to the Enemy as another Manœuvre of a similar Kind had the Germans. The British Officers candidly acknowledged the Wisdom and that they felt the Force of the Policy. The State of Pensilvania did not. They issued a Proclamation in the Light and Nature of a Proscription against hundreds some of them the meanest of their Citizens.[3] The Greater Part staid in the City and I daily have the Mortification to meet capital leading Tories not only in the Street but I have seen them in Company. Not a Man hath been and I will venture to say Not a Man will be condemned. How a New Yorker feels on this Occasion I leave you to judge. At the same Time I do myself the Justice to declare that as a Man I freely forgive every of them every Thing which personally they may have meant against me. But as a Statesman I think Great Examples necessary to deter the small Fry who on almost all Occasions ought to have much pardoned to their Ignorance, to their Prejudices, to their Situations, to their Dependences, their Connections and the thousand things which combine to lead such Men into Evil. Adieu. Believe me, sincerely yours

FC (NNC). In Morris' hand and endorsed by him: "Letter of 23d July to the Speaker of N York Assembly." Walter Livingston was speaker of the New York Assembly at this time.

1 See *JCC*, 11:627, 630.

2 For Congress' April 23, 1778, resolve on this issue, see *JCC*, 10:381–82.

3 Morris is referring to the Pennsylvania Council's May 8, 1778, proclamation on the attainder of certain Pennsylvania loyalists. *Pa. Council Minutes*, 11:483–85.

Samuel Holten's Diary

[July 24–25, 1778]

24.[1] I dined with the President, & went & viewed the Hospital & workhouse & City Goal. They are very Elegant & great Buildings.

July 25. Two months this day since I left home. Congress set late & I dined between 4 & 5 oClock, Colo. Partridge spent the afternoon with us.

MS (MDaAr).

1 Holten had noted in his preceding diary entry that he had changed his residence on July 23. "Thursday evening I removed from the Wido. Robisons, to board at the house of Miss Dalley & Clarke in 2d Street. I dined & drank tea at Doctr. Shippens, Directr. Genl. of the continental Hospital."

Henry Laurens to John Burnet

Sir 24th July [1778]

I received much satisfaction by learning from Mr. Zahn that you continued at Mount Tacitus. I hope I shall find you there or in some other of my Plantations where you shall think you may be most serviceable. My return to my own Country hardly depends upon my will; my interests and my inclination call loudly for it, but already I have received several applications requesting me not to leave Congress so early as the first of November, which day I had lately named. I will not finally determine until I shall have seen our public affairs two Months further advanced, in the mean time if leisure can be found at Mount Tacitus I desire about five thousand square feet of Cypress may be provided and shingles sufficient to cover an House of about 50 feet square; there must also be a large quantity of boards and plank for inside work, and also flooring boards of the best Pine. I mean to build a log House such as I have seen and lived in, at York Town, where they are neat, wholsome, durable and built at a very moderate expence. Mr. Zahn will speak to you on this subject and you will be governed in your proceedings by his advice and direction.

Except one visit of the Gout last Winter I have enjoy'd my usual good health ever since I left Carolina. That stroke of the Gout was extreamly severe, confined me a month and kept me lame near three months. You must have heard from time to time all public occurrences in this part of America up to the middle of the present Month, what follows and the newspapers which you will find inclosed with this will give you a pretty full Account of the present state of Affairs.

The French fleet which lately arrived on this Coast is now lying off Sandy Hook, unfortunately there is not water enough on the Bar for their large ships, otherwise the whole English squadron at New York would fall into their hands, these are at present block'd up, and the French fleet have taken a great number of Prizes some of them armed ships, and some with gold and silver and valuable Cargoes.

General Washington has now an army upwards of 20,000 Men—all in high spirits and I hope we shall soon learn of his having accomplished some important Act. Every one whose opinion I have heard, say, if general Lee had done his part at the battle of Monmouth, Sir Henry Clinton would have been reduced to circumstances little, if any thing, better than those which Burgoyne experienced last year. The General's trial before a Court Martial is not yet ended.

While I was at York Town I lived in a stile much below that of my Overseers. All the room I had for my Office and lodging, was not near so large as the Hall at Mount Tacitus, more than once I have been obliged to dine upon bread and cheese and a glass of Grog—here I fare much better, but in both places I have found hard work enough and at so enormous an expence as would astonish you to hear of—but thank God there begins to be a ground for hoping we shall obtain an honorable Peace before another year expires—this however is not to be relied on, we ought therefore to persevere in every endeavour to oppose and repel the Enemy.

The cruelties of the English, exercised upon our People who were their Prisoners is not to be parallel'd in History of Civilized Nations—nor indeed are they exceeded by the practices of the barbarous Indian Allies of our Enemies.

The Indians have scalped and butcher'd and burnt many of our inhabitants—these means were cruel and severe but death soon ended all pain. The English have starved our People, suffer'd them to lose their limbs by frost and to linger out a miserable life for many days and weeks, have refused to let us cloath and feed them—they have compelled our friends to drink unwholsome water when good water was in plenty wasting before their Eyes, they have smother'd them in Prison Ships, killing every night five, six, and more, have kick'd, beat and abused, have loaded Officers with Irons and a thousand other savage Acts they have been guilty of—sometimes murdered the Masters of families, burned all the houses, goods and provisions and left poor helpless Women and infant Children exposed to the rigor of frost, snow and rain without food or covering. A volume might be filled with Accounts of their barbarities—in several instances of which even General Howe and General Clinton have been directly concern'd. But thank God their hands are now bound up, they are confined within their Lines at New York—from whence deserters come into our Camp 6, 8, 10 of a day, lately a Cornet of Horse and a Captain of their new Troops deserted and came over to General Washington. If time permitted I would give you further information, but I have many other Letters to write by this conveyance. I must therefore close this, assuring you I continue Your friend And Humble Servt.

[*P.S.*] With respect to yr. wages, whatever Mr. Zahn does shall meet my approbation.

LB (ScHi).

Henry Laurens to Patrick Henry

Sir 24th July [1778]

I have to acknowledge the receipt of Your Excellency's several favors of the 4th, 8th and 16th Instant, which have been in due course presented to Congress, but hitherto I have received no commands in return.[1] Supposing Your Excellencys' Messenger, who will be the bearer of this may have been employed for the special purpose of bringing your favor of the 20th[2] and that expences are consequently increasing every day; I have judged it best to dispatch him without further delay. I have Men here employed as Messengers in constant pay, one of these shall conduct to your Excellency such Resolves as Congress shall form on the last mentioned Letter immediately after the Act shall be sent to me. That Letter had been committed to the Board of War on Monday last, a Report was made yesterday, and after some Debate re-committed. If I dare judge of opinions not yet delivered Congress will coincide with your Excellency's respecting the intended expedition against Detroit, and the further raising troops of horse.[3]

The Intelligence from your Sea coast must have been founded on the little Actions between some of Count d'Estaing's squadron and the Lydia Privateer of New York of 26 Guns and the Mermaid Frigate.[4] The Lydia was destroyed—the Mermaid driven on the shoals on the Coast of Maryland where the sequel of her history is probably known: we have not learned it yet.

Count d'Estaing lay many days at Anchor near Sandy Hook mortified by looking at Admiral Gambiers' squadron within, and perfectly safe from his assaults. The Large French ships draw too much water for the Bar, many British Vessels were taken by the French fleet while lying at the Hook, five of them armed, two said to be British Frigates, but we have received no Account of particulars. The Count must by this day have arrived at Rhode Island where he must be content with playing a small game, not very small if he has the good fortune to Burgoyne General Pigot and his Garrison. I entertain some hopes that Congress will Resolve to hold no Conference with Men who have attempted to corrupt them by bribes, and to divide the good People of these States, that those Men will be made the bearers of their own Impeachment, exposed to the resentments of their injured Countrymen and their fame transmitted to Posterity in Characters which will render their memory infamous. I have the prosecution of this measure very much at heart. I take the liberty of inclosing this days newspaper, and remain with great Respect & Esteem, Sir, Your Excellency's Obedient Humble Servt.

LB (DNA: PCC, item 13).

1 Governor Henry's July 4, 8, and 16 letters to Laurens are in PCC, item 71,

1:161–68, 179–81, and Henry, *Patrick Henry*, 3:178–83, 185–86. Laurens is in error when he states that he had not yet received any "commands" from Congress in regard to these letters, for on July 13, after reading the letter of the fourth, Congress had ordered him to ask the governor "to spare, for the use of the army of the United States, all the vinegar composing part of the cargo of the ship *Roderique*, purchased by the State of Virginia." See *JCC*, 11:686; and Laurens to Henry, July 13, 1778.

2 Laurens means Governor Henry's July 10 letter, which was referred to the Board of War on July 20, together with Henry's letter of the eighth. See PCC, item 71, 1:169; and *JCC*, 11:704, 710. There is no July 20 letter from Henry to Laurens in PCC or Henry, *Patrick Henry*.

3 In response to the points Governor Henry made in his July 8 and 10 letters to Laurens, Congress approved a report by the Board of War on July 25 calling for the suspension of an expedition against Detroit, which the delegates had ordered on July 11, and stating that in consequence the governor could dispense with the "reinforcement of infantry and cavalry for the main army" recently approved by the Virginia Assembly. *JCC*, 11:720–22. See also Laurens to David Espy and Others, May 17, 1778, note.

4 Governor Henry had described this "Intelligence" in the July 16 letter cited above.

Henry Laurens to Jonathan Trumbull, Sr.

Sir 24th July [1778]

In the recess of Congress I am called upon by His Excellency Le Sr. Gerard, Minister Plenipotentiary from his Most Christian Majesty to the United States of America in order to obtain from Connecticut such aids as His Excellency Count d'Estaing, Vice Admiral of France, commander of a squadron of ships of War of his Most Christian Majesty may stand in need of, admitting Count d'Estaing shall proceed from Sandy Hook to Rhode Island.

I have therefore taken the Liberty in the name of Congress to address your Honor requesting you to afford all the assistance in your power to Count d'Estaing upon His Excellency's requisition for the general service of the French fleet, and for facilitating the Vice Admiral's intended operations, particularly that a sufficient number of skilful Pilots may be held in constant readiness for conducting the fleet if necessary into New London.[1]

From a reflection His Excellency General Washington has undoubtedly written to you on this subject as well as from a certain persuasion that your Honor will upon every occasion chearfully and vigorously contribute to promote the service of his Most Christian Majesty our good Ally, in which the safety and welfare of these States is strongly interwoven, I have intimated to Monsr. Girard the present application will scarcely be necessary. Be this as it may 'tis with great pleasure I embrace the opportunity of assuring your Honor of the continued good wishes, Esteem and Respect with which I have the Honor to be, Sir, Your Most Obedient &c.

LB (DNA: PCC, item 13). Addressed: "The Honorable Jonathan Trumbull Esqr., Connecticut." Endorsed: "Delivered Monsr. Girard by M[oses] Y[oung]."
1 There is no mention of this matter in the journals.

Marine Committee to the Eastern Navy Board

Gentlemen July 24th 1778

We have received your sundry Letters of the 12th, 24th & 29th ultimo and of the 4th, 7th & 8th Current to which we shall now reply in their order. To yours of the 12th ultimo. Our letter to you of the 11th instant will convey our Instructions for every possible endeavour being exerted in preparing for Sea the continental Vessels of war in your department and for sending them out one after another to join the squadron of France under the command of vice Admiral the Count D Estaing; therefore we hope before this will reach, that you will have despatched the Warren and that others will shortly follow. We enclose herewith a Set of Signals received from the French Admiral, copys of which you will deliver to our Commanders enjoining great secrecy and in case of necessity that they destroy them.[1] We approve of your having purchased A Schooner for bringing round the flour and Iron from Sinepuxent. In a Letter from William Smith Esqr our Agent in Maryland of the 18th instant is the following Paragraph. "I am sorry to inform you there is the greatest reason to believe Captain Whippy of the Schooner Loyalty is Captured by the enemy in his outward bound passage from Sinepuxent—he had on board upwards of 900 Barrels flour and a quantity of barr Iron, and I am informed he was so imprudent as to go to sea when three of the enemies Cruizers were in sight—they were seen in chase of him, and as he is so dull a sailor, there is very small hopes of his having escaped.[2] The Swan, Captain Stiles, arrived from Boston at Sinepuxent about the 23d ultimo, her Cargo of flour and Iron was all ready and doubt not she is despatched before this." Should the Schooner be taken it will be a disapointment and we think Captain Whippys conduct will be highly reprehensible. To yours of the 24th ultimo. The estimate of Monies wanted in your Department hath been laid before Congress who have granted the full amount.[3] We therefore send you five hundred & Twenty four thousand by the Bearer according to his Receipt enclosed—this large sum we hope will be fully adequate to all your wants, and enable you to prosecute with vigour the business of your Department, we have no doubt but that you will render the expenditure thereof as beneficial to the public as possible.

To yours of the 29th ultimo. We are much pleased to hear of Captain Summers Success and the arrival of his Prizes. To prevent delay and inconvenience hereafter as was the Case with regard to the

Brigantine Resistance being without a Commander, we empower you to appoint to any Vessel under 20 Guns any Captain that may be unemployed in your department.[4]

We shall lay before Congress the Sentences of the Courts Martial relative to Captains Manly and McNeill.[5] The Account you give of the Hamdens Stores has determined us to Countermand the orders we formerly gave to build a hull Accomodated to them, therefore we desire you may drop that plan. When a proper opportunity shall present and you may think Mr. Pecks Talents in the construction of Ships will be useful to the Public, you will please to give us notice. We shall overlook Captain Waters mistake and consider his appointment the first opporty.[6] We enclose herewith an order of the Board of War to their Agents in the Eastern States to furnish you with Blankets, Duck, Oznabrigs, Coarse Linnen, Stockings and Coarse Cloths, lead, Copper &c. which they may have in their possession, and you may want for fitting out the ships of war in your Department. As most of these articles are essentially necessary for the Army and will be much wanted in the Winter we request you will be sparing of them as possible.

To yours of the 4th instant. We inclose herein a Resolve of Congress of the 15th November 1776 respecting the Bounty allowed for Men and Guns taken from the enemy at sea. It is the opinion of this Committee that Men of War and Privateers are the only Vessels that comes within the meaning of this Resolve, therefore on all Vessels coming within this discription the Bounty is to be paid but none other. We have ordered the Navy Board here to make a return of the British Seamen that are Prisoners within their district, when they do we shall attend to your proposal of Exchanging them for ours at Halifax and will write you. For the present we desire you will engage Pilots for our Ships of War on the best terms you can. We wish to know your reasons for having Pilots established in the Navy—we apprehend they are founded on some local custom with you with which we are unacquainted. You will also inform us what pay and share of Prize Money should be allowed to Pilots. We never have allowed any Commission to any of our Captains for disbursing Money, and would by no means have that Custom introduced. As we do not think proper that the Public should be concerned with individuals in Vessels of War we cannot accept of Mr. Ginons proposals.

To yours of the 7th instant. We do not approve of going into the custom of allowing travelling expences to the officers of the Navy, but on account of the particular circumstances attending Lieutenant Leeds of the Brig Resistance we make him a gratuity of the amount of his account viz £56.17.9 which you will please to pay.

To yours of the 8th instant. As you think the ship Queen of France will do for a Cruizing Ship we desire she may be equipped accordingly and the Command of her given to Captain Joseph

Olney. The One half of the sea Books you mention you will please to send forward to this place.

It is our desire that you have the accounts of the building, fitting &c of the Hancock & Boston frigates compleatly settled and examined and sent forward to us. It is also our desire that you keep seperate and distinct accounts of all Vessels ordered to be built within your Department, and that you regularly furnish this Committee with the Cost of each when fitted for the Sea; and that afterwards you keep seperate and distinct accounts of the Disbursements of each Vessel and furnish us with them in that manner. You will direct the Commanders that sail by your Orders to inform this Committee of all occurrences that may happen on their Voyages.

You will please to hold a Court of Inquiry on Captain Johnstons conduct relative to the loss of the Continental Brig Lexington of which he was Commander.[7] Mr. Bradford the Agent at Boston hath lately remitted to us a bill drawn by Otis & Andrews on the Clothier General James Mease Esqr. at this place for 29,651⅓ Dollars being for Prize Goods which they purchased of him. We desire you will inform Mr. Bradford, that he is to charge this Bill to your Board and not to the Marine Committee, as he and all other Agents in your department are to settle their transactions with you. We shall shortly transmit you the Money for the above Bill.

We are Gentlemen, Your Hble servants

P.S. We send this Letter by Post being anxious to communicate the contents—the 524000 dollars shall be sent off immediately after it.

LB (DNA: PCC Miscellaneous Papers, Marine Committee Letter Book).

1 Congress had referred these signals, which had been received from Ambassador Gérard, to the Marine Committee on July 15. *JCC*, 11:691.

2 On July 20 James Warren informed his navy board colleague William Vernon that the schooner *Loyalty* was "drove on Shore on the Vineyard with a load of Flour" and offered hope that the vessel and cargo could be saved. "Papers of William Vernon and the Navy Board," *Publications of the Rhode Island Historical Society* 8 (January 1901): 253.

3 Congress had granted the Marine Committee $524,000 for the use of the Eastern Navy Board on July 16. *JCC*, 11:696.

4 See Samuel Adams to James Warren, July 20, 1778, note 9.

5 On July 29 Congress read and referred to the Marine Committee Hector McNeill's July 25 petition requesting Congress to revise the court-martial proceedings that had ordered his dismissal from the Continental Navy. This petition and one from McNeill to the Marine Committee dated October 3, 1778, are in PCC, item 42, 5:73–84. Although the Marine Committee recommended in January 1779 that the sentence against McNeill not be executed, Congress never countermanded McNeill's dismissal. The proceedings of the June court-martial exonerating John Manley were laid before Congress on August 5. *JCC*, 11:727, 749, 13:69–70. For additional information on McNeill and Manley, see Marine Committee to the Eastern Navy Board, October 26, 1777, note 2; and Samuel Adams to James Warren, July 27, 1778, notes 1 and 2.

6 On Daniel Waters' refusal to command the *Resistance*, see these *Letters*, 9:778n.2.

[7] Henry Johnson, who arrived with the French fleet, had applied to Congress on July 13 regarding an inquiry into his conduct. *JCC*, 11:687. On the loss of the *Lexington* in September 1777, see William J. Morgan, *Captains to the Northward*, pp. 109–10.

Joseph Reed to George Bryan

Sir
Saturday Morning [July 25, 1778]

At the Hour you was pleased to appoint yesterday to attend your Board I was pre-engaged on the Committee of the Frontier Business which on the breaking up of Congress I mentioned to a Member of Council who promised to make it known so as to save the Council the Trouble of Meeting. As there is seldom more than one Member from this State in Congress I could wish that a future Appointment may be out of Congress Hours as this was.[1] And I will endeavour to attend it punctually. I am very respectfully, Sir, Your most Obed. & very Hbble Servt,

Jos. Reed

RC (NHi). Addressed: "The Honorable George Bryan Esqr., Vice Presidt. &c." Endorsed: "1778 July 25th from Honble Joseph Reed."

[1] The demands on Reed's time had increased on July 15 when he was named to the Pennsylvania Executive Council in a special election held to fill the vacancy created by the death of the former president, Thomas Wharton, Jr. According to the council's minutes he managed to attend its proceedings at least four times during the period July 21–25 despite his explanation on the 21st that he would be obliged to neglect his work on the council because of the press of his congressional assignments. This letter provides proof that Reed did indeed experience difficulties in meeting the obligations of his two offices, but his situation changed a few days later when it was discovered that under the Pennsylvania constitution his election to the council was invalid, because no delegate to Congress could be chosen to that office. See *Pa. Council Minutes*, 11:535–40; and Roche, *Joseph Reed*, p. 147.

Reed's prominence in Philadelphia affairs is also attested to by the fact that his name headed the list of 185 citizens who signed an antiloyalist declaration published in the July 25 issue of the *Pennsylvania Packet*. The subscribers to this declaration asserted their determination to combat the efforts of "sundry persons, notoriously disaffected . . . [who] have endeavoured to suppress all evidence and discovery of the oppression of the friends of America, and other misdoings before and during the enemy's possession of this city, by intimidating and discouraging the good people of this state from appearing against them."

Elias Boudinot to Hannah Boudinot

My dearest Love
Philadelphia July 26t 1778

I have just been made exceedingly happy by the Reciept of your Packett of the 15 Inst. enclosing Mr. Pintards &c. I have wrote you 8 or 10 lately but this is only the second I have recd. I know not of any mode of assuring you of the importance of a Letter from your Valuable Pen, but by referring you to your own feelings on the like occasion. To recieve a Letter from any Friend is agreeable, but to be honored with a sweet endearing Letter from a dearly beloved Wife—the Wife of your Youth and the Partner of all your Joys, & Hopes & fears, is Indulgence, Gratification and next to Possession itself. I must beg that you will not let a Post pass without a Line, if it is but to say that you are well. Mr. P. informs me that he has sent me a Hat, if so pray forward it to me by some very safe Hand—send it to Princeton and it can easily be sent on from there. How kind is our gracious God in protecting my Dear Family amidst the surrounding Evills, that others have been liable to. Poor Mr. MacWhorter, I pity him greatly altho' he has reason to rejoyce in the goodness of a merciful God in the midst of Judgment.[1] But indeed I scarcely live a Day, without some striking fresh call to praise our God for his Goodness and to say that his Mercy endureth forever. I have lately experienced it in removing my disorder in so speedy a Manner. Could We but live answerably to such mercies it would increase our Happiness to the summit of Earthly felicity. I have nothing new to tell you only that the French fleet is gone to attack Rhode Island by sea, while 5000 Men under Genl. Sullivan attack by Land. God grant them success & take the Glory to himself.

I dare not think too much of my beloved Wife & dear Family, as I know it is apt to have too great an Effect on my determinations—to say I begin to hanker after the leeks & onions of Egypt is but to give the mere Shadow of the real feelings of my too anxious Heart—I often am in evening—but enough I must impose Silence on my Heart & Pen. Suffice it to say, that neither Love, Esteem, Friendship nor any of the tender, delicate & finer feelings of a Heart alass too, too sensible towards the Object of its affections, are no ways lessened or impaired by a disagreeable & unwilling Absence from the delightfull Subject of them.

I have wrote you to endeavour to store the Sugars with you, or send them on to me hence, as you find it convenient—the first will be best.

If the Teams belong to Mr. Messereau, you must let them have money to bear their Expences taking their reciepts. If they go back to Boston, they must take some Load back.

Let my Dr Susan know how much I am obliged by her Letter. It deserves an Answer as soon as I have leisure. I am pleased to see that she is improving.

Love & a Kiss to her. Remember me to the Family, Sister & all Friends as if named.

I am my Dearest Love with the greatest Sincerity & Esteem, Your truly Affect. & loving Husband, Boudinot

RC (NjP).

1 The wife of Rev. Alexander McWhorter, pastor of the Presbyterian church in Newark, N.J., had recently been seriously injured when struck by lightning. William B. Sprague, *Annals of the American Pulpit; or Commemorative Notices of Distinguished American Clergymen* . . . , 9 vols. (New York: Robert Carter & Brothers, 1857–68), 3:209–10.

Henry Laurens to Théveneau de Francy

Dear Sir 26th July [1778]

I thank you for your favor of the 15th,[1] particularly for those Polite and kind marks of your friendship for me which you are pleased to express, and shall endeavour to merit the continuance of your Esteem.

The favorable Events which you allude to make a proper impression upon my mind. I view them as Harbingers to an honorable Peace, and the Universal acknowledgment of American Independence, but a Man who has paid some attention for fifty years to the continual fluctuation of Human Affairs, feels not those raptures from the appearances of good Fortune which had been wont to seize his Heart between the Stages of 20 and 40—perhaps a moderate degree of anxiety for permanizing present advantages may appear to younger Men an alloy of Happiness. I feel as if led by it into the true Sphere.

Many days have past over since I heard any thing from the Fleet or from His Excellency General Washington. Count d'Estaing has been making Prizes in great numbers and of great value in sight of the Enemys squadron safely anchor'd behind Sandy Hook extreamly chagrined at finding his own Ships drew too much Water to admit his coming nearer to them. The Newspaper which I shall here inclose will further inform you. I can add nothing on this head but that Mr. Gerard and myself conjecture the Admiral is gone to Rhode Island. The choice of le Sieur Gerard for the Minister Plenipotentiary displays the Wisdom of His Most Christian Majesty's Councils. I will venture to say in one word France does not contain a Man better fitted for the People among whom he is to reside, with whom he is to Negociate, than is this Gentleman, nor have I a lower opinion of the Competency of Monsr. Girards' Abilities for Negociating nor of his Integrity.

The Letter which you sent to the Commercial Committee was deliver'd to me by that Board and immediately presented to Congress.[2] The House order'd it to be returned to the Committee, and that they should after full consideration make a special Report. This happened yesterday Morning, Congress did not rise 'till near four o'clock P.M., this is Sunday, consequently the Report cannot be made before tomorrow, but considering the business which we have to transact with Mr. Girard I rather think nothing will be done in your Affair before Wednesday; to prevent anxiety therefore to yourself and perhaps some expence I submit to your Servant's importunity to return and you may be assured of hearing from me by a special Messenger without the loss of one minutes time after I shall have received the commands of Congress. And if I form a right judgment from the sentiments of particular Members you will be convinced that Congress have in view nothing short or that you can in our present Circumstances require in favor of Monsr. Beaumarchais, and in fulfilment of the Contract lately entered into.[3] Some Gentlemen who were at my House last Evening discovered much displeasure at the Orders which you say have been given for consigning public Cargoes to Mr. Ross. I will not trouble you with my own opinions or conjectures, it would be altogether improper to do so since you are acquainted with my sentiments and more especially as your complaints are now before the proper Tribunal and will very soon receive an Answer, I trust a satisfactory answer.[4]

I am glad you have made no purchases on my account. I have found it necessary to go into very large expences since my return to Philadelphia for such Articles as I had requested you to procure, and the extravagant prices demanded for every species forbid laying in double stocks—but I would except the article of Claret which you say is good, therefore, if it can be purchased at a price not exceeding 30 or 32 dollars per dozen bottles, & you find a good opportunity for transporting it soon I request you to send me four of five boxes, containing as I compute 20 dozen little more or less. I have now an house almost as elegant as that in which I have enjoyed the company of my friends at York Town. I shall be happy to see Mr. Francy and to pass an opinion on his Claret.

Within the present Cover you will find two Letters for yourself which are all that have come to my hands in your absence—one for Versailles from Baron de Kalb, two for Martinique and one for the Cape transmitted to me by Marquis de la Fayette, for all these I request you to procure safe and speedy passages.

Your Dispatches for Baron Steuben and Captain Landy shall be sent forward this Morning.

I have the Honor to be, With great Respect &c.

LB (ScHi). Addressed: "Mr. De Francy, Williamsburg."

1 Francy's July 15 letter to Laurens, in which he enclosed a copy of his letter of the same date to the Committee of Commerce and urged Laurens to have it read before Congress, is in the Laurens Papers, ScHi.

2 Texts of Francy's July 15 letter to the Committee of Commerce are in the Laurens Papers, ScHi, and Beaumarchais, *Correspondance* (Morton and Spinelli), 4:142n.12. In this letter Francy, who was Beaumarchais' agent in America, urged the committee to use the cargoes of a number of ships that had been recently laden with tobacco in Virginia to discharge part of "the debt owed by the 13

united states to the house of Roderiqu Hortales and comp. otherwise Mr. Beaumarchais." After reading a report on this letter by the Committee of Commerce, which noted that the cargoes of all but one of these vessels had already been designated to pay for debts contracted by John Ross, an American agent in Nantes, Congress agreed on August 1 to consign the cargo of the remaining vessel to Roderique Hortalez & Co. and to authorize the American commissioners in Paris to pay this firm, "as they judge proper," the balance left over from the sale of the other cargoes after the settlement of Ross' accounts. See *JCC*, 11:716, 738–40; the letters of John Banister and Robert Morris to Francy of July 28; and Committee of Commerce to Francy, August 3, 1778.

3 See *JCC*, 10:315–21; Committee on the Claims of Roderique Hortalez & Co. Report, March 5; Robert Morris' Proposed Report on the Claims of Roderique Hortalez & Co., March 12; and Committee of Commerce to the Commissioners at Paris, May 16, 1778.

4 According to a statement by Francy in the July 15 letter to Laurens cited above, Laurens agreed with his contention that the United States was under an obligation to pay Beaumarchais for the military supplies he had provided them: "I remember with a very great pleasure that from the first time I Spoke to your Excellency, you was Convinced of Mr. de Beaumarchais' right in claiming the munitions & goods Sent by the house of Roderique Hortalez & Co; but it has not been a So easy matter to Convince every Gentleman of Congress."

In a July 31 report to Beaumarchais on recent efforts to secure a settlement of his claims, Francy explained that they also had an ally in the person of William Carmichael, a point made explicit by Carmichael himself in a September 3 letter to Beaumarchais on the injustice and ingratitude of his countrymen in failing to discharge their debts to him. Beaumarchais, *Correspondance* (Morton and Spinelli), 4:173–75, 224–25.

Henry Laurens to Patrick Henry

Sir

26th July [1778]

I beg leave to refer Your Excellency to my last Letter under the 24th by the returning Messenger.

Inclosed with this Your Excellency will receive an Act of Congress of the 25th consisting of divers Resolutions founded on a Report from the Board of War to whom Your Excellencys' Letters of the 8th and 10th Instant were referr'd; either the Board of War have misquoted these dates or the Secretarys' return led me into an error in reciting them in my last.[1]

This Act contains so full an Answer to Your Excellency's Letters on the intended Expedition against Detroit, and the raising a Reinforcement of Infantry and Cavalry in Virginia as leaves me nothing to add, except an explanation which I am directed to make on the 5th Resolve. It is meant and intended by Congress by the inexpedience of the march and services of those Troops that an immediate abatement of expence shall be made.

Nothing from His Excellency General Washington or from Count d'Estaing since my last.

I have the Honor to be, With great Respect & Esteem &c.

LB (DNA: PCC, item 13). Addressed: "Governor Henry, Virginia, by James Dobbin Monsr. Francys Messenger."

1 See *JCC*, 11:720–22. Virginia's response to these resolves is the subject of Governor Henry's August 7 letter to the Virginia delegates, which is in Henry, *Patrick Henry*, 3:190.

Henry Laurens to John Laurens

26th July [1778]

My Dear Son

Members of Congress and Citizens in general are under uncommon anxiety to hear from His Excellency the Commander in Chief—and to learn something further than we know of the present position of Count d'Estaing's fleet. You know very well how I feel, we are not new acquaintance—improve the present moment; events will be produced in due course. This maxim smooths much the path through Life.

Doctor Scudder is not a Free Mason, you have had many escapes, but I submit it to your wisdom and Philosophy whether it be necessary to tempt the fates or to brave them, and to your friendship whether a person so dear and so much beloved is not entitled for the sake of his Connections to ordinary protection. I shall never be surprised until I hear you have in one instance attended to the preservation of your Life by means which the bravest Man on Earth would not blush to adopt.

From Charlestown I learn they had lately captured Bachop a second time, and with him or in company with him in another Privateer which had long infested our Coast the very infamous Osbourne.[1] General Howe had advanced on his march towards East Florida as far as the Bank of St. Johns, the Season of the Year will not allow me to entertain very sanguine hopes of his success although the Enterprizing, never failing Colonel Williamson with 1000 of his own trusty Men were with him. I had intended to have written you a full sheet but the patience of Le Chevalier Failly who has been waiting above two hours in the Parlour must be near expiring. I have been all that time producing this scrap, six words at a time between interruptions.

P.S. I send in the Packet with this, four Letters for yourself and sundry for Head Quarters and the Camp. I am sorry nothing lies on me for paying my Respects to the General. I have no public commands and will not be so unkind as to take up a moment of his time with Ceremony—but I love and pray for him. There is a Letter in the Packet for his Excellency the General from Don Juan De Miralis who appears to be *a worthy old Castilian*. I have much of his company.

LB (ScHi).

[1] Laurens had received news of these events in a July 6 letter from President Rawlins Lowndes of South Carolina, a transcript of which is in the Laurens Papers, ScHi.

Samuel Adams to James Warren

My dear Sir Philada. July 27 1778

Capt Manly has obliged me with your favor of the 5th.[1] He and McNeil are here with different Views. The one to obtain another Ship, and the other to get the Sentence of a Court Martial reversd. Perhaps both may be disappointed. I have receivd a Number of Letters by both. To yours I shall pay a particular Regard, because I am well satisfied you never suffer Prejudices to divert your Attention from the great Object—the publick good. "Manly is a blunt, honest and *I believe* brave Officer." I observe your caution, and am pleasd with it; for I think it is a fresh Proof of your Integrity. Manlys Bravery is an Article of your *Belief*. His Bluntness & Honesty are Matters of Certainty. I have not yet lookd into the Papers; but I recollect to have heard, when they were read, the Want of *Experience* imputed to him, and some thing that had the Appearance of blaming him for not giving any Signals for the Direction of the Ships under his Command. This it must be ownd, strongly implys a Want of *Discretion.* Does the Character of a blunt & honest officer intitle him to the Command of a capital Ship if he is deficient in Point of Experience & Discretion? Especially if he has had the Misfortune of losing one already. "McNeils Address is insinuating—His Assurance great—He will tell you fine Storys" &c. I should think he had taken his lessons out of Hutchinsons political Book, if I had not Reason to believe that he used to despise him most heartily. When I advert to a Letter from another of my Friends, I find him "open & sincere" "His Temper naturally warm, which he has sometimes indulgd in speaking his Mind freely of Persons in office." This you know has always been deemd an unpardonable Sin, and I am affraid it always will be. To be sure it always will be so deemd by that Kind of Men *in office,* who meet with none to hinder them from persisting in the most egregious and expensive Blunders, but the *open, sincere* & *warm* Friends of the Country. We all know, says my Correspondent, his Zeal & Sufferings for our glorious Cause." Such a Character, I must confess, commands my Friendship; but it has no Consideration in the present Appeal. Has he had a fair Trial? I pay a proper regard to the Decisions of Courts Martial, and shall not give my Voice for altering them, but when Error, Partiality or Injustice shall appear plainly to my own Satisfaction.[2]

Our Navy Officers must not expect to pick & chuse for themselves.

They ought to be content with such Appointments as are given to them. Indeed Appointments should be made with more Judgment than I think they can be by any Set of Men at three or four hundred Miles Distance. For this Reason I movd that they not be made by the Navy Board, which obtaind in a certain Degree, as you will see by a Letter from the Marine Committee.[3] Had this been the Case before, Olney would have remaind in the Resistance, and Bush must have waited for another. If the Queen of France is a better Vessel, it will turn out not to the Disadvantage of Olney. While we have more Captains in Commission than we have ships to give them, there must be Disappointments, Envys, and Suspicions (oftentimes unreasonable) of each other. This is the Make of Man and we may as well think of stopping the Tide as altering it. "The Appointment of Cap Landais affords an ample Subject for the observations of Speculatists, & the Resentment of Navy officers." I think he is, as you observe, an ingenious & well behavd Man; and if he is an able & experiencd officer, as we are assured he is by those who ought to give us the best Information, it is a Pity that two very good Lieutenants should leave the ship & the service on that Account. I hope others may be found to fill their places. "It is an opinion that I was Landais chief Patron." This is a mistaken Opinion. You discover yourself on this occasion, as you are disposd to do at all Times, Partial in my Favor. If I was in any Degree instrumental in the Promotion of Landais, it was because I really thought him a considerable Acquisition & that he would be eminently useful to our Navy. And I am apt to believe it would have been thought a judicious Appointment, if there had not been a fanciful Predilection in favor of another. Even the Name of the Ship may have given Disgust to some Men.[4] I hope when Manly is provided with such a Ship as will please him, the Difficulties or obstructions in the Way of getting the Alliance manned will be removed. I am sure your Exertions will not be wanting to forward the Service.

July 29. Yesterday I sent you a fresh News paper by the Post which I intended as an Apology for not writing to you. I kept this Letter open, knowing that Mr Dod the Express was to set off soon, and designing to say a few things in Addition to what I just hinted to you in my last. But I must defer it till another opportunity. I shall be obligd to you if you will give my Respects to Mr Storey & tell him that his Petition with a Number of others was put into the Hands of Mr Lovel when Mr H[ancock] left this City. We will take the first oppty to present it, and endeavor to get his Wishes answerd.[5] Adieu my Friend.

RC (MHi). In Adams' hand, though not signed.

1 Warren's July 5 letter to Adams, in which he discussed the qualifications of

several Continental Navy captains, particularly those of John Manley and Hector McNeill, is in *Warren-Adams Letters*, 2:30–31.

2 Manley's July 27 letter to Congress asking for a new command was referred to the Marine Committee on July 28, but Congress took no further action on the request and Manley eventually turned to privateering. *JCC*, 11:724; and William J. Morgan, *Captains to the Northward: The New England Captains in the Continental Navy* (Barre, Mass.: Barre Publishing Co., 1959), p. 147. For McNeill's petition requesting that the sentence dismissing him from the service be set aside, see Marine Committee to the Eastern Navy Board, July 24, 1778, note 5.

3 See Marine Committee to the Eastern Navy Board, July 24, and Adams to Warren, July 20, 1778.

4 On the appointment of Pierre Landais to command the *Alliance*, see Adams to Warren, June 1 and 19; and Marine Committee to the Eastern Navy Board, June 18, 1778.

5 The petition of William Story, clerk of the Eastern Navy Board, asking for a raise in salary was read in Congress on July 31. On August 4 Congress accepted the Marine Committee's report that no raise in salary be made but that Story be given $500 for "extra services and expenses." *JCC*, 11:735, 747.

Josiah Bartlett to Mary Bartlett

My Dear Philadelphia July 27th 1778

I have Just Received your letter of the 10th Inst. which has greatly Relieved my mind from the uneasiness I felt in not hearing a word from you Since yours of the 20th of last month, and am still much at a loss what should be the reason of my not receiving any letter from you the two last posts, as I Recd. letters from Exeter & Portsmouth by both of them, nor Do I Know what letters you have Recd. from me, as you have not informed me. Wish you would be more particular what letters you Receive; I am thankful to hear Rhoda is better, & the rest of the family well. May the *Supreme Ruler* Continue your health and make us truly thankful for all his favors.

I am Glad to hear there is a Good prospect of a plentiful harvest; Here haying & English harvest has been over sometime. The weather, the latter part of June & forepart of this month, was Exceeding Hot, it has since been more Comfortable & Continues so at this time.

The French Fleet is gone to Rhode Island & I Expect you will hear of their opperations sooner than I shall, as you are much nearer. There has nothing very remarkable happened here since I wrote you last, shall inclose some papers for your perusal. I am by the favor of Providence in good health, so is Charles Chace, Mr. Wentworth had an Ill turn after I left him at York Town & is not arrived here yet. I shall Endeavor to write to you every week & hope our letters will not be obstructed as they have been. Remember me to all Enquiring friends. Give my sincere Regards to Mr Thayer & inform him I Recd his letter of the 9th Inst. and will write to him as soon as I have Leisure & any thing worth Communicating to him.[1] Let him see the newspapers if he Desire it. Yours &c,

Josiah Bartlett

RC (NhHi).

1 Rev. Elihu Thayer's July 9 letter to Bartlett is in the Bartlett Papers Microfilm, NhHi. No letters from Bartlett to Thayer for 1778 have been found.

Josiah Bartlett to William Whipple

My Dear Sir, Philadelphia July 27th 1778.

Your's of the 12th instant is just rec'd and am glad to hear that our conduct to the British Commissioners has given general satisfaction.[1] By their last letter they seem to threaten us with an appeal to the people at large; I hope and believe they will gain no great advantage by that measure.

I am fully sensible of the force of your arguments against privateering and if some proper methods were taken to restrain it to proper bounds, I make no doubt the public would be much benefitted by such restrictions; but (for want of a competent knowledge of those affairs I make no doubt) I am not quite satisfied that a total prohibition would be serviceable. The Congress have some time since determined as soon as possible to take up the Marine affairs and make some very essential alterations in it and also the affair of our money which seems to be going to confusion by the enormous rise of every thing, but when it will be done *God knows*. The almost innumerable letters and business that daily crowd upon Congress for want of regular Boards, properly appointed and filled, and the time it takes in such large Assemblies, to transact business, keeps us forever behind-hand in our affairs and I am sorry to say that sometimes matters of very small importance waste a good deal of precious time, by the long and repeated speeches and chicanery of gentlemen who will not wholly throw off the lawyer even in Congress.

Till we get into better regulations as to our Marine Affairs, I am persuaded no class of men are so much wanted in Congress as men acquainted with that business, for though Navy Boards are established, yet there is a constant appeal to the Marine Committee of Congress, who I am sure are at this time inadequate to the business. I hope our State will have wisdom enough to appoint you to relieve me here in the fall and that you will have virtue enough still to forego your own private interest for the public good and will accept of their appointment and without flattery. I really think you would be very serviceable to the public here, especially in the Marine Department. If I knew you would not attend Congress I should be glad you might be appointed one of the Navy Board at Boston, for I am sure that Board does not attend sufficiently to the business.

Mons. Girard has not yet had the ceremony of an audience but believe it will take place some day this week; the ceremonials are agreed on by Congress and the House clearly cleansed and fitted up. The *Minister* seems urgent to have it as soon as may be.

The French fleet are gone to Rhode Island and you will hear of their operations sooner than we. The Admiral seems very desirous of doing something to effect and was greatly mortified when he found there was not water sufficient for his large ships to go up to New York. I have nothing to write you in the new's way—have sent you a paper or two by which you will see what is stirring here.

Please to inform Col Langdon I rec'd a letter for Mr Wentworth, which by the superscription I believe came from him and shall keep it till Mr. Wentworth arrives here which I hope will be the latter end of this & beginning of next week.

Remember me to Col Langdon, Mr King, Mr Gain's, Col Wentworth and all friends and believe me to be your sincere friend,

J. Bartlett

[*P.S.*] As this is erased, blotted and huddled together in a shameful manner please to destroy it as soon as read for I have not time to write it over.

Tr (DLC).

1 Whipple's July 12 letter is in Bartlett, *Papers* (Mevers), pp. 195–97.

Richard Henry Lee to Francis Lightfoot Lee

My dear Brother, Phila. July 27th 1778

Your letter of the 12th came only to hand this day by Post, amazing delay, but I have spoken to the Post Master on this business until I am tired. It astonishes me that neither you or my other friends receive my letters, altho I write so many. To you I have not missed above one post since we parted & then I wrote by Mr. Armstead. I trust that before this gets to hand you will have received my letters in which I have given you a full account of the transactions in the Jersies, of the arrival & progress of the French Squadron, & of the coming of a Plenipotentiary from the Court of France to Congress. The Squadron is gone to Rhode Island to make a sweep there as the large Ships of this fleet cannot find water enough to enter the Harbour of N. York wherein the English Ships keep themselves close. I understand that measures will be taken to prevent egress from York or succours getting in. It is this day confidently reported that 27 sail of the provision fleet from Cork have fallen into the hands of Count

D'Estaing, this is not yet certain, but we know such a fleet has been long & daily expected. We understand the enemy are greatly distressed for provisions in N. York, particularly of the bread kind. Gen. Washington has sent 2 Brigades to join 3000 Men under Gen. Sullivan to assist in the business of Rh. Island. Where you are nothing better can be done than to inform the people and prevent their being imposed on. The change in affairs has occasioned Congress to desire that both supplies of Infantry & Cavalry from Virga. voted by last Assembly may be not sent forward & the Expedition agst Detroit is changed to a Chastisement of the offending Indian Tribes to the West & Northwest.[1] I will attend as you desire to the payment of Hillsymer [Hiltzheimer] & will keep the rest of yr. money for your further orders. There has been no time yet to procure an order for settlement of Accounts either here or abroad, but I hope it will be done soon. Mr. D——r[2] is deep in the {plot}[3] for supporting {Deane} & the {party} so that he remains {here} tho leave of absence has been long asked & granted.[4] I am realy tired with the folly & the wickedness of Mankind, and wish most earnestly to be retired absolutely. Mr. Holker has been, since the arrival of the Plenipotentiary, appointed by him Agent for the Marine of France in these States, but more of this hereafter. I will send yr. bark if a good oppertunity offers & I thank you for your offer to use what I want, but I am pretty well supplied.

My love to Mrs. Lee & regards to all friends. Much hurried. Yours sincerely. Richard Henry Lee

[*P.S.*] Let me know how Colo. Tayloe does, I am greatly concerned for him.

RC (ViU).

1 See Henry Laurens to Patrick Henry, July 24, 1778, note 3.

2 William Duer.

3 Words in braces, here and below, are written in cipher in the RC. For an explanation of the cipher used by the Lee brothers, see Richard Henry Lee to Arthur Lee, May 12, 1778, note 2.

4 In his July 12 letter to his brother, Francis Lightfoot Lee had inquired whether William Duer was still at Congress. He also offered the following comments, partially in cipher. Words in braces were supplied above the cipher by Richard Henry Lee.

"The {Message} which two of the {Consort} are playing at {Congress} is so barefaced; that I am surprised any {Member} of that {body} shou'd be so {blind} as to be {imposed on} by it. As you know them to be in {Trade} with {Deane}; & engaged in the {Scheme} to {ruin} those who are likely to {detect} their {villany}; if the {message} should relate to either of these {Objects} the {plot} will be very plain, & they I hope, & their {Principal}, meet the {fate} they {deserve}. I think you have enough of hieroglyphics.

"Suppose Mr. H——r [Holker] was asked if any American & which of them is concerned with him in commerce to this Country. I fancy he must either make a discovery, or subject himself to be proved a Liar." Lee Family Papers, ViU.

James Lovell to William Whipple

Dear Sir,

Philadelphia July 27th 1778

Your favor of the 13th came this day to hand. I will not go into an examination of Dr & Cr in correspondence, but I give you warning that I am about turning bankrupt. I find it to be totally impossible to do my duty to the public and at the same time pursue as I have done the fulfilment of private epistolary devoirs. New scenes of parade and interruption attend the multiplied foreign business. A multitude of circumstances connected with the books of our Committee[1] are now to be eclaircised by those who have most attended to those books for months past. Mutual jealousies having prevailed, as you know, the time is come for mutual explanations. This makes work for me in particular, as having been uniformly connected with *foreign applications* and much also with foreign correspondence.

I cannot find Gazettes for all my friends, and therefore must refer you to the Boston Papers or to Dunlap's which is doubtless sent to your printer weekly. General! Read[2] will probably be at the head of this Govt which will thence acquire strength and permanence. Maryland, Delaware and Jersey have not yet signed the confederation. Count d'Estaing is gone for Rhode Island not finding water enough at the Narrows of New York. I hope Sullivan will do credit to himself and New Hampshire by cooperating with the Count.

The Minister Plenipotentiary from France will have his public audience in a day or two of which more hereafter from your's affectionately,

J.L.

28th. With the Mumps or something of the kind I am out of the way of Gazettes, this morning at my lodgings, but am told there is nothing material in print.

Tr (DLC).

1 That is, the Committee for Foreign Affairs.

2 Joseph Reed.

Joseph Reed to Jeremiah Wadsworth

Dear Sir

Philada. July 27th. 1778

I perswade myself you will excuse the Freedom I take on this Occasion as it arises solely from the Interest I take in the Reputation of your Office & the Share I had in getting you into it. In a late Application for Money laid before Congress there were some Expressions of Discontent which seemed to give Offence to some of our Members who think a great deal of & feel a great deal for the Dignity of Congress.[1] As you have accepted the Office there appears to me not only a Propriety in the Thing itself, but that it is your Interest to stand as fair as possible with them. You will have Accounts to settle with them in future; Allowances perhaps to ask & possibly future Favours to request. The Effect of condescending Language even upon the Minds of wise Men is wonderful & has done more for some Men in certain Places than all their real Merit.

Congress seems so perfectly satisfied with your Conduct that there is not the least Murmur from any Quarter, and as great & decisive Events have happened since which will certainly realize & substantiate your Acquirements I cannot but believe you must consider the Department in a more desirable point of View than when you first accepted it.

I am with much Esteem, D Sir, Your Friend & Obed. Hbble Servt.

Jos. Reed

RC (PHi). Addressed: "Jeremiah Wadsworth Esqr., Commissary Genl. of the Continental Army."

1 No "Application" from Wadsworth fitting this description has been found in the PCC.

John Banister to Théveneau de Francy

28 July 1778

I have very carefully examined everything that was reported about your case (according to your letter to the committee and the one that you privately wrote to me).[1] I have thus taken note of only the articles of your contract on which your complaint rests, and I have presented it to Congress, which not wishing to decide without having the report of the committee, transmits to us your letter and my observations. I hope that this report will be made in two days. Congress is busy at this moment with matters so serious that it is impossible to interrupt them, but understand that I will seize the first moment to resolve your case. I know how important it is to you not to delay for one moment the ship you say will be ready to set sail.

I am well informed about every obligation that America has to Mr. de B[eaumarchais] not only through the particulars that you have given me, but also through a private conversation that I have had with Mr. Deane on this subject and my opinion is that Congress cannot make too great an effort to recognize the outstanding services that he has rendered us and to promptly pay off the debt that it owes him.

The ships which you mention in your letter to the committee were consigned 15 and 18 months ago; as they were entrusted to Mr. Ross, who accordingly made advances to Congress, it is not possible to change their consignment, but our report will be that the first ships that are dispatched must be directed to Mr. Beaumarchais, and if the Virginia, which you say is to be sent to our agents and is loaded with 355 hogsheads of tobacco, is in condition to set sail, we will direct that it must be delivered to Mr. de B[eaumarchais].[2]

I have just formed a trade partnership with Mr. Deane and a few other delegates, who are prepared to raise as much capital as we shall have need of and who besides have a great deal of influence in their own state. We wish to have join us a powerful firm in France, which according to what Mr. Deane tells us will have such an interest in becoming acquainted with us that there is no doubt it will accept without hesitation the proposition that he will make to it. I will go myself to France next November, but I want to see you before, having many things to tell you on the subject.[3]

Tr (MH–H). This extract of John Banister's July 28 letter to Francy is taken from a nine-page document, written in French, that was transcribed for Jared Sparks. The original manuscript was undoubtedly written by Francy as a report to his employer Caron de Beaumarchais. It bears the heading "Extrait de plusieurs lettres de differents membres du congress" and consists of two letters from Henry Laurens to Francy of July 26 and 28, 1778, and single letters of July 28 from John Banister and from Robert Morris. The two letters from President Laurens are also available in his letterbooks at ScHi and have been printed in this volume from that source. The letters from Banister and Morris printed under this date are our translations of Sparks' transcript of Francy's report. Francy's notes to and parenthetical comments on these two letters have also been translated and footnoted to the documents where they appear in the "Extrait."

Francy's extract of Banister's letter bears the following heading: "du 28 Juillet par la poste, du Col. Bannister membre du comite de commerce."

1 For Francy's "case," see Henry Laurens to Francy, July 26, 1778, note 1.

2 The following note appears in parentheses at this point in the document. "Not doubting that the order of Congress was consistent with the committee report, as regards this vessel, I requested that Mr. Duval go to the James River where he is, in order to visit it. His report is that the vessel cannot be ready to sail before 2 or 3 months at the soonest having to unload all its cargo and be repaired. If however it is worth the trouble I will be observant in case they dispatch it that it not be sent to others and I will take the greatest care to make inquiries about expeditions that are to be made." For "the committee report, as regards this vessel" (the *Virginia*), see *JCC*, 11:740.

3 The following note appears in parentheses at the end of this document. "This Col Bannister is a very valuable and honest man whom I have always had great reason to praise in all my transactions. If I knew your intentions for the future I would perhaps be able to interest you in this partnership, but I throw that out as you are in a great commercial transaction, the results of a great political concern, I do not know if you wish to begin others or form any concerted action for the furthering of your transactions. I will hand over some letters to Col. Bannister in order to bid him to consult you before any other."

For another reference to a partnership formed by Banister with Silas Deane and five or six delegates—which was apparently designed to conduct trade with L'Orient—see Francy's July 22, 1778, letter to Beaumarchais in Beaumarchais, *Correspondance* (Morton and Spinelli), 4:154. For Francy's correspondence with Beaumarchais at this time focusing on the transactions he was arranging at Philadelphia and Williamsburg in consequence of the contract he had negotiated with the Committee of Commerce on April 16, 1778, see ibid., pp. 131–224.

Henry Laurens to Théveneau de Francy

Dear Sir 28th July [1778]

As your Servant affected to be in a very great hurry to return, I had prepared Letters for him on Sunday Morning which I should have been glad to have been exempted from, but he contrived matters so as not to begin his journey 'till very late Yesterday. Soon after he was gone, the two Letters which you will receive under this cover came to hand from Mr. Gardner from Portsmouth.[1]

The Commercial Committee have not yet reported, nor do I expect they will before Thursday.[2] Do not be uneasy Sir, I am persuaded Congress will act upon the whole with justice & propriety in your case, the task of accounting for impediments is too painful for me and it is not necessary. The Newspaper inclosed will give you the current Intelligence. Believe me to be, With great Respect &c.[3]

LB (ScHi).

1 On July 27 Laurens had written a brief letter to William Gardner of Portsmouth, N.H., thanking him for forwarding letters from France to Francy. PCC, item 13, 2:35. Although this was a private letter, it was entered by mistake in Laurens' presidential letterbook.

2 See Laurens to Francy, July 26, 1778, note 1.

3 Francy's report to Beaumarchais on his dealings with Congress at this time contains the following brief July 28 letter from Laurens on the same subject, which he had apparently written earlier this day.

"I am writing you two lines in order to set your mind at ease and to give you notice that the committee report has not yet been done as I had anticipated in my last letter of the 26th. You know how much I am an enemy of tardiness, thus do not fear any from me, but I can respond to everyone as soon as this report is done, which I hope will be Thursday, and as soon as the Congress will have determined something I will inform you of the matter." Sparks Collection, MH-H.

Henry Laurens to William Smith

Dear Sir 28th July [1778]

I had the pleasure of writing to you a public Letter, in which was intimated, that agreeable to your request Congress had accepted your resignation of your seat at the Navy Board.[1]

It is time that I should cancel the Account which I stand indebted to you, for this purpose you will find inclosed one hundred and seventy seven dollars, which you will be pleased to pass to my Credit.

General Washington joined by General Gates is now with a very respectible Army at White Plains. Count d'Estaing finding it impracticable to enter with his large ships Sandy Hook, sailed the 21st Instant for Rhode Island. His Excellency the Commander in Chief has made large Detachments to reinforce General Sullivan, who will soon have upwards of five thousand Men. In the mean time it is said the object in view, General Pigott and his Garrison, are withdrawn and safely arrived at New York.[2] Be it so, we shall know where to find them. The Evacuation of Philada. and Rhode Island, the Battle of Monmouth, and the arrival of a French fleet will operate more powerfully to ends of Peace upon the minds of our Enemies than Governor Johnstone's profer'd Gold wrought upon Congress.

The Indians Westward and Northward are exceedingly troublesome. We are beginning to be very serious with them.

I have been told of a new, neat, light English carriage for sale at Baltimore in the hands of a Mr. Hopkins or Hopkinson, and I am in great want of one—Bringhurst of Germantown who had built one for me having refused to deliver it at the price agreed for without any better reason than that of a higher offer in these times from somebody else. I request you Sir to do me the favour to enquire for this carriage, inform me of particulars of the fashion, colour, lining &c &c and the Gentlemans lowest price in a Bill of Exchange, or in paper Dollars.

Have you received a further supply of good Wines and Brandy and at what prices? be so kind as to inform me, which will oblige, Dear Sir, Your Respectful & Obed. Servt.

LB (ScHi). Addressed: "William Smith Esqr., Baltimore."

1 Laurens had written a brief letter to Smith on July 24 transmitting a copy of Congress' July 22 resolve accepting his resignation from the Middle Department Navy Board. PCC, item 13, 2:34; and *JCC*, 11:710. Smith's July 17 letter of resignation is in PCC, item 78, 20:225–27.

2 This report about the British evacuation of Rhode Island was false.

Robert Morris to Théveneau de Francy

[July 28, 1778]

I have received your private letter and the one that you wrote to the committee:[1] both dated the 15 instant. Allow me to tell you that the style is a little too ardent, the complaints that you make regarding the orders that I gave for the consignment of two vessels to Mr. Ross are not founded, because these orders were given not only before the existence of your contract, but even before your arrival on the continent. The Congress owes a great deal to this same Mr. Ross who some time ago received notice that these vessels which you mention were dispatched to him, as soon as the bay was free and their destination cannot be changed, but have faith that we are all very prepared to carry out the obligations that we have made with you so as to pay back what the Republic owes to Mr. de B[eaumarchais], and as for me to prove to you how much I am disposed towards it I have proposed to the committee to send the vessel the Virginia loaded with 355 hogsheads of tobacco. Our report on this subject has not yet been made to Congress,[2] but I do not doubt that it will not consent to change the consignment of this ship which was not directed to the agents in order to pay back someone his notes and as the one that you claim is one of the oldest ones, it is just that they busy themselves to discharge it. The conversations that I have had on this subject with Mr. Deane confirm my opinion that we have great obligations to M. de B and that we must not avoid any occasion to show our recognition of it.[3]

Tr (MH–H). For the provenance of this document, see John Banister to Francy, this date.

1 For Francy's July 15 letter to the Committee of Commerce, see Henry Laurens to Francy, July 26, 1778, note 1.

2 For the Committee of Commerce's August 1 report on the consignment of tobacco to defray the expense of transactions negotiated with Beaumarchais, see *JCC*, 11:716, 738–40.

3 The following note appears in parentheses at the end of the document. "This response is very seemly in view of the complaints that I made to the Commerce Committee concerning its conduct; that makes manifest to me indeed that everything that I have told you in my letter B is at least in great part true."

At the end of this parenthetical note, Francy continued his report to Beaumarchais as follows:

"N.B. Three other members of Congress to whom I wrote on the same subject say roughly the above, just as a fourth, the secretary of the Commerce Committee.

"A letter from Carmichael of the 27th of July says that he has made the best use possible of what I have written him on the same subject, that he had a few of the still uncertain members of Congress read it and that he has taken the opportunity to tell everyone what you have done for America and what ingratitude followed on the part of the representatives of the French nation &c, they assured him as the letters herewith joined say that the Congress was very ready to acknowledge the services that you have rendered. I sounded out Mr. Gerard regarding his point of view on the subject. He replies that he seems to him to be your friend at least in appearance, and that he has some orders to speed up the conclusion of your case, that he wrote on the subject in great detail in two letters that I have not received. Since the messenger will arrive once again before the departure of Le Fier Rodrique I will attach to this copy anything that he brings me which may interest you.

"A second letter from Carmichael dated the 29th July says: 'Finally I have the pleasure to assure you that the Congress seems generally very ready to render justice to Mr. De B. that is properly due to him and it is indeed time for it. I have seized the occasion of your letter to publicly request the opinion of Mr. Gerard on the case of Mr. De B. and he speaks with much ardor and interest in his favor. Some people have been quite confused at thus hearing praises sung to this worthy friend of America and since then a few have changed their tone. I have been astonished in some private conversations with different members of Congress to learn what infamous calumnies have been spread against him and these reports were not contradicted by the agents' letters. It is not astonishing that you have had so vigorous prejudice to fight upon your arrival; you may be assured that all the services that he rendered are recognized but there is no way to make a suitable return to good will. The Commerce Committee is now preparing for him a letter in which they explain the reasons for their silence until this moment and promise to be very exact henceforth as much in their correspondence as in their accounts. (You will do well to wait this letter before beginning the new supply.) I have insinuated to a few members of Congress that Mr. Girard had orders to hurry the settlement of your accounts, that it was much better to yield in good grace than to allow oneself to be told, and I believe I can assure you that it is their intention.

"My affairs and those of Mr. Deane will be handled next Thursday.' &c."

Rhode Island Delegates to William Greene

Sir, Philadelphia July 28th 1778.

We are to inform your Excellency officially (of what we however expect before this you are better informed of) That, The French Fleet were to sail the 21st Instant for Rhode Island—And that Genl. Washington has detached a considerable Body of Troops from the main Army to reinforce Genl. Sullivan in order to make a Desent upon Rhode Island.[1] It is expected on this Occasion that a most vigorous Exertion will be made by Our State. We know in this the Publick will not be disappointed. We doubt not all possible Respect will be paid to Admiral Count D'Estaing. The Fleet will want to be watered, and some Supplies of fresh Provisions, Vegitables &c. We wish all possible Success to this Expedition and are with great Respect to the Honorable the Genl. Assembly, Your Excellencys most obedient & very humble Servts. Hy Marchant

John Collins

RC (R–Ar). Written by Marchant and signed by Marchant and Collins.

[1] Washington had notified Congress of these developments in a July 22 letter to President Laurens that was read in Congress on the 27th. See *JCC*, 11:722; and Washington, *Writings* (Fitzpatrick), 12:209–14.

Marine Committee to John Wereat

Sir July 29th 1778

Inclosed is a list of Timber wanted for repairing Two of our Continental Frigates which were partly burn'd by the Enemy while at this place.[1] It is our request that on receipt hereof, you immediately provide a Suitable Vessel, put on board of her the Timber Specified in Said List and despatch her for this Port, ordering the Captain to use all expedition in the Voyage.

As there is a considerable quantity of Timber belonging to the Public in your State and under your care, which will be wanted at this place for the use of our Navy, we now direct that you take speedy measures for sending it round here. In procuring Vessels for that purpose we have no doubt but you will be as attentive to the Interests of the States as possible. We are, Sir, Your Hble Servants.

400 middle Foothooks 400 upper Do 400 Top Timbers 400 half Timbers 10 Haws. Ps. [20?] counter Timbers	To repair two Frigates one of 36 the other 28 Guns

LB (DNA: PCC Miscellaneous Papers, Marine Committee Letter Book).

1 The frigates *Effingham* and *Washington* had been burned during the enemy's May 1778 raid up the Delaware. Gardner W. Allen, *Naval History of the American Revolution*, 2 vols. (Boston: Houghton, Mifflin Co., 1913), 1:310–11.

Massachusetts Delegates to Henry Fisher

Sir Philadelphia July 29. 1778

Mr. Pelatiah Webster of this Place, having in the fall of the Year 1776 by Desire of the Gentlemen who represented in Congress the State of Massachusetts Bay, made Sale of a quantity of Flower belonging to that State, which had been shipped for Boston & confined in the Delaware by the Enemy has applyed to Us for the Settlement of his Account, & informs Us, that a considerable Part of the Cargo of the Snow Champion was sold by You, the Effects of which are still in your Hands, We therefore request You to transmit to Us the Sales & Ballance arising theron that We may make a final Adjustment of the Accounts as soon as may be.

We are Sir &c.

Samuel Adams	J Lovell	Members
E Gerry	F Dana	of Congress
	Saml Holten	from Mass Bay

(Copy)

Tr (MH-H). In the hand of Elbridge Gerry. Addressed: "Major Henry Fisher at Lewis Town."

Henry Laurens to William Heath

Sir. Philadelphia 30th July 1778.

Since my last of the 9th Inst. I have been honoured with your several favors of the 6th, 8th, & 9th, which I duly presented to Congress.[1] The first was committed to the Board of Treasury where

I believe proper attention has been given to the demand for Money. That of the 8th Committed to the Honble Mr. Sherman & others from whom you will by the present Messenger receive a Letter respecting John Brown's Case to which I beg leave to refer you.[2]

You will see by the Inclosed Act of the 15th July that Congress had no intention of interposing authority in his favor,[3] & had I had any other subject for a Letter, the applications to which he is indebted for the present respite would have come too late.

Congress are disposed to hear every thing that can be offered on his behalf & therefore the intended effect of this Act is suspended.

Your last quoted Letter is committed to the Board of War & remains unreported.

I have nothing new except the inclosed Advertiser of this date.[4] Be assured I continue with great Esteem & Respect sir, Your obedient & hum st. Henry Laurens, Presidt. of Cong.

RC (MHi).

[1] General Heath's July 8 and 9 letters to Laurens are in PCC, item 157, fols. 170–75. His July 6 letter is not in PCC, nor is it mentioned in the journals.

[2] See Committee of Congress to Heath, July 22, 1778.

[3] See *JCC*, 11:690.

[4] Laurens also wrote two brief letters this day to Paymaster General William Palfrey and to Jonathan Trumbull, Jr., transmitting to each a copy of a July 29 resolve accepting Trumbull's resignation as paymaster for the northern military department. See PCC, item 13, 2:36; Lloyd W. Smith Collection, NjMoHP; and *JCC*, 11:726–27.

Henry Laurens to George Washington

Sir, Philadelphia 30th July 1778

I have had the honor since my last under the Inst.[1] of presenting Your Excellency's Letter of 22d to Congress,[2] whence it was committed to the Board of War & I received no order except to Issue a Commission for Capt. Caleb Gibbes to rank Major in the service of the United States. I shall transmit the Act of Congress upon that occasion to Major Gibbs, & under the present Cover Your Excellency will receive the Commission.[3]

The 15th Instant I signed & delivered by order a Brevet to the Marquis de Vienne Certifying his Rank, Colonel in the Army.[4] Another Brevet is ordered for Monsr. Noirmont Lanuville to Rank Major from the date of his appointment as Aid de Camp to Gen Conway 28th Jany. 1778—and another the 29th Inst. to Monsr. Francis Joseph Smith to rank Ensign.[5]

I have the honor to be, with the highest Esteem & Regard, Sir, your Excellency's Most Obedient & humble servant,

Henry Laurens, President of Congress.

RC (DLC).

1 Laurens had last written to Washington on July 18.

2 Washington's July 22 letter to Laurens is in PCC, item 152, 6:183–90, and Washington, *Writings* (Fitzpatrick), 12:209–14.

3 See *JCC*, 11:730. Laurens notified Gibbs of his promotion in a brief letter he wrote to him this day. PCC, item 13, 2:36–37.

4 See *JCC*, 11:692–94.

5 See *JCC*, 11:728–30.

Henry Laurens to Alexander Wright

Dear Sir 30th July [1778]

I have been honor'd with your favor of the 11th Inst. and beg you'l accept my thanks for the two Letters from my youngest Son. You are not pleas'd to intimate any thing respecting your now present circumstances. I know your delicacy and therefore without an application I am prompted by my friendship and Regard to request you will let me know by the earliest opportunity if by any means I can contribute to your happiness.

At present I think it necessary to transmit a Certificate which you will find here inclosed. It has at least the quality of Innocence and may possibly be of use. I request you Sir to intimate to Captain Pond that he will find me disposed to render him every service which I may with propriety in our respective circumstances and that I shall be glad to hear from him.

If on your return to South Carolina you shall take this City in your way I beg you will do me the favor to call first at my house in Chesnut Street, nearly opposite the State House and that you will there think yourself at home and look for no other lodgings. I believe you will meet as good Bed and Board as at any Inn in Philadelphia and no where a more hearty welcome.

I am with great Regard, Your Affectionate Humble Servt.

ENCLOSURE

I Certify that Alexander Wright Esqr. Citizen of the State of South Carolina obtained Permission in writing to leave that State and to proceed from thence to Europe on his own private concerns when I was Vice President of that State. That he had always acted with propriety and was held to be a friend to the liberties of the United States of America.

That Mr. Wright is a Man of Probity and Honor and possess'd of a large landed Estate in So. Carolina.

Philadelphia 30th July 1778

LB (ScHi). Addressed: "Alexander Wright Esqr., Norwich, committed to the particular care of Ladd."

Marine Committee to John Beatty

Sir July 30th 1778

Your letter of yesterdays date hath been received and laid before Congress. You will find herein a Copy of a Resolve[1] passed in consequence thereof which for the present will answer all the questions you have proposed except what relates to the French Seamen—on that head we expect you will receive Instructions from the French Minister through Colo. Boudinot. We think it necessary to explain that you are not to consider the means to be furnished the seamen for going on to Boston as meaning the advance of Money, that being to be done at Boston, but you will give Orders to the proper Continental officers to supply them on the way with Provisions.

We are Sir, Your Hble servants

LB (DNA: PCC Miscellaneous Papers, Marine Committee Letter Book).

1 For this resolve directing Commissary General of Prisoners Beatty to engage as many of the recently exchanged American seamen as he could to serve on Continental vessels at Boston, see *JCC,* 11:730–31. Although his "letter of yesterdays date" has not been found, Beatty's July 24 request for hard money to pay off prisoners' debts, requisite to exchange, had been read in Congress on July 28 and tabled. See *JCC,* 11:725; and PCC, item 78, 3:13–20.

Joseph Reed to Timothy Matlack

Dear Sir Market Street, July 30. 1778.

I have observed a Publication in Dunlaps Papers of this Day, obliquely censuring The Executive Council for a supposed Failure of publick Duty. As I conceive myself in some Degree involved in the Censure I propose to publish something by Way of Answer in Saturdays Paper; in which I shall do Justice to the Attention & Vigilance of Council who in my firm Opinion have acted wisely on this Occasion.[1]

I am Sir, Your Obed. & very Hbble Servt. Jos. Reed

P.S. I have taken the Liberty to trouble you on this Subject as having an Oppy. to satisfy the hona. Members of the Board that any Attack upon them will not pass unanswered.

RC (NHi).

1 The July 30 issue of John Dunlap's *Pennsylvania Packet* contained a letter signed only "C—— S——" censuring the Pennsylvania Council for failing to investigate a report that "Governor Johnstone, *one of the British Commissioners has made an offer of ten thousand guineas to General Joseph Reed a Member of Congress for this State, for the purpose of procuring his services in assisting the British Commissioners in the execution of the powers they derive from the King*

and Parliament of Great Britain." For Reed's "Answer in Saturdays Paper," see Joseph Reed to the Printer of the Pennsylvania Packet, July 31, 1778.

Matlack was secretary to the Pennsylvania Council.

Roger Sherman to Jonathan Trumbull, Jr.

Dear Sir Philadelphia July 30th. 1778

I received your letter of the 25th Instant directed to the Connecticut Delegates. I heartily Condole with you on the News of the death of Your Brother, Congress have Accepted Your resignation.[1]

I should with great pleasure have recommended Mr Pierce to have filled the vacancy had it not appeared by your Letter to Congress that by the junction of the two Armies the office was become unnecessary, but I did mention him in Congress as a person well qualified for Such an appointment, and whose continuance (for Some time at least) might be necessary to close the Accounts, he being perfectly Acquainted with the business. It was Supposed that if the money was delivered over to Col. Palfry he could do what was necessary without any Special appointment by Congress.

A Treasurer of loans has lately been appointed, whose business is to Sign loan office Certificates & Bills of Exchange, & Send them to the loan officers in the Several States; and, to receive all Bills of Credit called in to be Sunk &c with a Salary of 2000 dollars per annum.[2] I nominated you for that office but your Friends in general were of opinion that you would be wanted for a more important one that of a Commissioner of the Treasury Board. There is a report for putting that Board into Commission and if it Shall be accepted as have no doubt but that it will either three or five persons will be necessary for that business. I Suppose the Salary will be the Same as the Commissioners of the Board of War, which is 2500 dollars per annum. I wish to know if such an appointment would be acceptable to you.[3] That I suppose will be a permanent Office. We have no later accounts from Europe than You have had in the public papers, the Operations of war you have earlier intelligence of than we. Our public affairs at present Seem to be in a favourable Situation—except that of the currency which demands immediate attention and I think measures may be devised to put it on a better footing. I think our enemies can have but little prospect of Success in Subduing us, and I believe they wish for peace on almost any terms. The conduct of the British Commissioners, especially of Govr. Johnston has been Scandalously mean in endeavouring to Bribe members of Congress, though I know of no instances but those published in the news papers. I hope & believe that by the Interposition of Divine

Providence in our favour, all their counsels against us will be turned into foolishness.

I am with Esteem & Regard, your humble Servant,

Roger Sherman

RC (CtHi).

[1] Jonathan Trumbull, Jr.'s July 25 letter to Henry Laurens, in which he requested permission to resign as paymaster general of the northern department and reported the death of Joseph Trumbull, late commissary general, is in PCC, item 78, 22:583–84. Congress had accepted Trumbull's resignation on July 29. *JCC*, 11:726–27. See also Henry Laurens to William Heath, July 30, 1778, note 4.

[2] Francis Hopkinson was elected treasurer of loans on July 27. *JCC*, 11:724.

[3] On the subsequent reorganization of the treasury and Trumbull's election as comptroller, see Oliver Wolcott to Jonathan Trumbull, Jr., May 18, 1778, note 3.

John Banister to Theodorick Bland, Jr.

Dear Sir, Philadelphia, July 31st, 1778.

I take the Liberty of recommending to your attention & Civilities, the Bearer, Mr. Vial, a Frenchman who came to America on commercial views, but has been unfortunate in being captured, & losing thereby his whole adventures in Goods.

Having made his Escape from New York, he is going to Virginia, on a visit to some of his Countrymen there, at present, & proposing to reside in our Country untill his Connections shall send him in a Cargo. I wish you to render his Time agreeable to him, if he should visit our Neighbourhood.

When I have the happiness of returning home, I shall make it my care to render this Gentleman every Service; as I am by no means of opinion, that the having experienced in *Some Strangers*, a Turn to deception, should deter me or you, from affording Consolation to the distressed, where there is a probability that the object of such civility possesses a considerable share of Merit. There is besides in this Man, an appearance of Candour, & I wish to indulge my feelings in his favour. From experience of the Gentleman's Sentiments & Consistency of Character, you will be capable of judging, whether it may be advantageous to enter into commercial views with him.

I write this in Congress, & must be brief. The English army of our Enemies is now in a very fair way, to experience the utmost distress, & perhaps may in the End meet a similar Fate, to that of Burgoyne. The French fleet, on one side, have blocked up the Port, while our army numerous, & extremely provided with every thing necessary, is on the White Plains, Its numbers greatly augmented by a junction of the Troops, under Command of General Gates, with the Grand army. The Count D'Estaing (it is probable) may get Possession of the Provision fleet, expected from Cork. You will have seen in a Paper, I enclosed you the other day, an account of Captain Paul Jones's exploit against White-Haven, & giving them a small specimen of that Conflagration & distress, we have so often experienced from our Enemies, in a much higher degree. The action was however intrepid & bold.[1] I shall write by the Post on Tuesday next, & once more before I set out for Virginia, about the 1st of September, unless something extraordinary shou'd occur.

I am my dear Sir, with the greatest Regard, Your Friend, &c. &c.

John Banister

Tr (NcD). Addressed: "Col. Theodorick Bland junr. of the 1st Regimt. of L Horse at Farmingdell, Virginia."

1 Accounts of John Paul Jones' April raid on Whitehaven, England, appeared in the July 14 and July 30 issues of the *Pennsylvania Packet*. See also Richard Henry Lee to Francis Lightfoot Lee, July 12, 1778, note 5.

Henry Laurens to Richard Marven and Samuel Shaw

Gentlemen 31st July [1778]

Inclosed with this you will receive an Act of Congress of the 30th Inst. for defraying the reasonable expences of defending the suit against you by Captain Eseck Hopkins, together with attested copies of the Records of Congress respecting his appointment and dismission to and from a Command in the Continental Navy.[1]

I am Gentlemen, Your Most Obedient, Humble Servant

P.S. Inclosed is a duplicate of the Act of Congress of the 30th which if necessary you will deliver to the Inferiour Court.

LB (DNA: PCC, item 13). Addressed: "Richd. Marven & Saml. Shaw, late Officers, directed to the particular care of Govr. Greene."

1 On January 13, 1778, eleven days after his summary dismissal from Continental service, Esek Hopkins brought suit for criminal libel in the Rhode Island Inferior Court of Common Pleas against 11 naval officers whose complaints to Congress had been instrumental in his removal as commander in chief of the Continental Navy. As the time for the trial approached, Richard Marven and Samuel Shaw, the only two defendants who were in the jurisdiction of the court after Hopkins filed suit, sent a petition to Congress, dated July 8, in which they asked for assistance in defending themselves. In response, Congress agreed on July 30 to assume the cost of their legal expenses and to provide them with congressional records pertaining to Hopkins' naval career. Congress' intervention on behalf of Marven and Shaw played a part in subsequently persuading a jury to find them innocent of Hopkins' charges. See *JCC*, 11:713, 732–33; PCC, item 42, 5:98–100; and Edward Field, *Esek Hopkins, Commander-in-Chief of the Continental Navy during the American Revolution* (Providence: The Preston & Rounds Co., 1898), pp. 219–36. See also Thomas Jefferson's Notes on the Inquiry into Esek Hopkins' Conduct, August 12, 1776; Marine Committee Examination of John Grannis, March 25, 1777; and Henry Laurens to Esek Hopkins, January 2, 1778.

Henry Laurens to George Washington

31st July [1778]

I Am this minute favor'd with Your Excellency's very obliging Letter of the 24th.[1]

The British Commissioners, for, in the Act of one, there is good ground for charging the whole, having by various means attempted to bribe Congress and thereby offer'd the highest possible affront to the Representatives of a virtuous Independent People, are in my humble opinion rendered wholly unworthy of the further regard of Congress in their Ambassadorial character.

Viewing them in this light I have been from the first reading of their last Address[2] under that kind of anxiety which had possessed my Mind when there was some cause for apprehending that General Burgoyne and his Troops would have slipt thro' our fingers into New York or Philadelphia, an anxiety to which I am a stranger, except in such momentous concerns.

I have for several days past urged my friends to move Congress for a Resolve that they will hold no conference with *such Men,* assigning reasons in ample, decent terms—to transmit the Act by a flag to the Commissioners, and make them the bearers of their own indictment; they will not dare to withhold the Resolve of Congress from their Court. Thence it will soon descend to the Public at large and expose themselves and their Prompters to the just resentment of a deluded and much injured Nation, whose deplorable circumstances I must confess deeply affects my heart. These Commissioners will be also held up in scorn at every Court in Europe, and finally be transmitted to Posterity in Characters which will mark their Memory with Infamy.[3]

An immediate display of the intended bargain and sale will discourage the impudent, polemic Writers on American Affairs in London, or invalidate their bold assertions and give force to the declarations of Congress.

If we leave the story to be related after Governor Johnstone's departure from this Continent, he will confidently deny the fact and how few in the World will be thenceforward well informed? Attack him Letters in hand upon the spot, his guilt will be fix'd from his own confession, for he cannot deny.

I am not commonly tenacious of my own Ideas, but in the present, as in the former case, I feel as if I clearly perceived many good effects which will be produced by a proper Act on our part. Justice is due to our own Characters, to the present age of America and future Generations will with much satisfaction dwell in history upon the transactions of Congress with these corrupt insidious Emissaries.

If a predilection to my fellow Citizens when standing in competition with strangers, of no more than equal merit, be criminal I must own myself not free from guilt.

From habit I am disposed to give countenance to strangers, and I have beside endeavoured, for obvious reasons, to be civil to such French Gentlemen as have called upon me, hence my conduct had been mistaken and I discover'd at a certain time that my friends had expressed doubts whether my courtesy had not been carried to excess. I had the happiness soon to convince them that good manners and plain dealing were not incompatible. Upon this occasion I intreat Your Excellency will excuse the freedom which I take of sending with this extracts of Letters written by me in answer to applications from foreign Gentlemen for employment and promotion in the Army;[4] the same sentiments have always governed my replies in private oral importunities. I have carefully avoided amusing or flattering any of them.

I have often regretted the hesitation and indecision of our Representatives, on some occasions, and perhaps as often, their precipitancy on others respecting foreign Officers—as a free Citizen I hold myself warranted to speak with decent freedom of the conduct of those whom I have appointed my Attornies, respectful animadversion tends to produce reformation.

From the fluctuations which I allude to have sprung, to speak in the mildest terms, many inconveniencies. Your Excellency's experience may call them Evils. The dilemma to which we are now reduced in the case of the elder Lanuville is one instance; if encouragements tantamount to promises are of any weight this Gentleman must receive a Brevet to rank Brigadier General the middle of next Month.[5] At his first arrival he presented a Memorial in which was set forth the vast expence which had attended his voyage & journey to York Town.[6] He solicited the grade above mentioned or an immediate negative; intimating that in the latter case he would return to his own Country. A direct Answer was not return'd, he was amused from time to time: an increase of expence and the plea of flattering hopes strengthened his claim. At length he was put into a state of probation. Certificates which he produced of his abilities and assiduities in the character of "*Inspector of the Northern Army*" were expressed in terms somewhat higher than merely favorable.[7] I eyed the Paper signed by General Parsons with some degree of jealousy as I read it, but it did not become me to paraphrase, and it passed unnoticed by every body else. On this ground I have said, he must obtain the Brevet in a few days; you would smile Sir if I were to repeat the principle upon which the delay is founded. This Gentleman is now gone with an intention to act as a Volunteer in the suite of Marquis de la Fayette, and I understand him, he means soon to return to France.

The younger de Lanuville your Excellency is informed has obtained a Brevet to rank Major—what title had he to this promotion?[8] Were I to draw the Gentleman into comparison with Major Gibbs and many other worthy Officers, I should answer, none. But he has only a Brevet. Your excellency is appriz'd of the restrictions on that kind of Commission by an Act of Congress of the 30th of April[9] and I trust the good sense of my Countrymen will lead them to reflect and distinguish properly, and to make some allowances.

Your Excellency will discover in one or more of the extracts the strong desire of French Gentlemen for printed Commissions. I dont know what peculiar advantage they might have had in view but in opposition to them and even to some attempts here, I have always confin'd myself to the mode of a simple Certificate in pursuance of the Resolve of Congress referr'd to in each case.

In the first conversation I had the honor of holding with Monsr. Girard with a view of learning what reception those French Gentlemen had met, who had return'd some 8 or 9 months ago, murmuring and dissatisfied to France; I took occasion to signify my concern for the disappointment which some of them had suffer'd, and in honor of Congress made brief recitals of Commissions granted to many French Officers now in the Army, observing that it had been impossible to gratify the wishes of every one for promotion. Mr. Girard reply'd His Court had seen with pain so many Frenchmen applying for permission to resort to the American Army, and that very few had receiv'd encouragements; the Court were sensible that crowds of foreigners pressing for Commissions would tend to embarrass Congress, that since his arrival at Philada. he had been solicited in many instances for recommendations, every one of which he had refused to listen to and added I might rest satisfied, Congress would never be troubled with Petitions under his auspices. In this sensible declaration methinks I discern sound Policy, be that as it may it will in some measure relieve Congress. I most earnestly wish our noble friend the Marquis could be persuaded to adopt the determination of Monsr. Girard.

Very soon after I shall have the pleasure of conversing with Baron Stüben, his pursuits in the journey to Court will be known to me.[10] I shall be equally explicit on my part and your Excellency shall be as candidly informed, if it shall appear to be necessary.

On Thursday the sixth of August Congress will receive Monsr. Girard in his public character. Your Excellency will find within the copies of the intended Address of the Minister and Answer of the Representatives of the thirteen United States of America.[11] Speaking as a Citizen I cannot forbear disclosing to you Sir, that there is a reluctance in my Mind to acknowledgments of obligation or of generosity where benefits have been, to say the least, reciprocal—this opinion has not been formed since I read the Address and Answer, as I am warranted to say from the Extract of a Letter to Monsr. Du Portail.

After hours of disputation shall be exausted the point will remain moot.

Among other Papers I take the liberty of inclosing copy of a curious performance of a Mr. Maduit which is believed to be genuine.[12] If he is not delirious at the present time, his friends must conclude that he was raving from 1774 to the commencement of the present Year, time employed by him in dinning the Coffee houses with his cries against the Inhabitants of these States and against their Claims, down with America! I will not further presume on Your Excellency's moments but to repeat that I continue with the most sincere and respectful attachment and the highest Esteem, Sir, Your Excellency's &c.

LB (ScHi).

1 Washington's July 24 letter to Laurens, in which he discussed the issue of foreign officers in general as well as the cases of the chevalier de La Neuville, Noirmont de La Neuville, and baron von Steuben in particular, is in Washington, *Writings* (Fitzpatrick), 12:222–26.

2 See William Henry Drayton to the Carlisle Commissioners, July 18, 1778, note 1.

3 On August 11 Congress rejected a motion that it conduct no further negotiations with the Carlisle commissioners, but approved one declaring that it would be "incompatible with the honor of Congress" to have any further dealings with Governor Johnstone because of his "direct attempts to corrupt and bribe the Congress of the United States of America." *JCC*, 11:770–74.

4 These "extracts of Letters" have not been found.

5 Although on July 29 Congress had postponed consideration of a report by the Board of War recommending that the chevalier de La Neuville "have the Rank of a Brigadier General by Brevet in the American Army," it eventually agreed on October 14, 1778, to grant him a brevet commission for this rank, "to be dated 14 August 1778." *JCC*, 11:728, 12:1011. The chevalier had been serving since May 1778 as inspector of the army in the northern military department. *JCC*, 10:498–500.

6 This "Memorial" is not in PCC.

7 Certificates by Gens. Samuel H. Parsons and Horatio Gates attesting to the excellence of the chevalier de La Neuville's performance as inspector of the northern army, dated June 21 and July 24 respectively, are in PCC, item 41, 5:328.

8 See *JCC*, 11:729; and Laurens to Washington, July 30, 1778.

9 According to a resolve passed by Congress on April 30, 1778, "no commissioned officer in the army of the United States" who received a brevet commission "shall be entitled . . . to any higher rank in the regiment, troop, or company to which he belongs, than he before held therein." *JCC*, 10:410.

10 As a result of Congress' failure to define his duties as inspector general to his satisfaction, baron von Steuben had come to Philadelphia intending to resign this office and seek a field command instead. After satisfying himself that Congress planned to redefine his duties, however, and after realizing the depth of the opposition to his assumption of a field command, Steuben decided to continue to serve as inspector general. John M. Palmer, *General von Steuben* (New Haven: Yale University Press, 1937), chap. 27. See also Laurens to Steuben, September 17, 1778.

[11] See *JCC*, 11:754–57.

[12] Laurens is undoubtedly referring to a handbill advocating British recognition of American independence that was written by Israel Mauduit and published in London in March 1778. See Paul L. Ford, *A Hand Bill Advocating American Independence, Inspired by the English Ministry, and Written and Published at London in March 1778* (Brooklyn: Historical Printing Club, 1890), passim. See also Richard Henry Lee to Thomas Jefferson, October 5, 1778, note 2.

Joseph Reed to the Printer of the Pennsylvania Packet

Mr. Printer, Philadelphia, July 31, 1778.

The confidence we ought to repose in public authority, and the respect due to it, should prevent our forming hasty judgments, or passing unguarded censures upon its measures. A writer in yesterday's paper influenced, I have no doubt, by very laudable motives, thinks the Executive Council inexcusably negligent, in passing silently over a late attempt to corrupt a Delegate of their State.[1] Justice to those vigilant and upright Magistrates requires it to be known, that they have deliberated upon it with attention and decided with wisdom. No person conversant with law can suppose the attempt direct treason by any statute or act of Assembly, now in force; and would any lover of his country, or friend to mankind, wish to see the doctrine of constructive treason, that engine of tyranny and iniquity, introduced into governments founded in freedom, and reforming the best systems in Europe? I hope not. Besides, Mr. Printer, a very slight attention to the transaction will shew, with what guarded nicety it was managed; how cloathed with circumstances of fairness, and made dependent only on its being reconcileable to principles of conscience and virtue. Every one will have his private opinion of the intent, but a court of justice must judge of the whole—can presume nothing, and must make a strict construction of penal laws. Hence we see how difficult it is even in Britain, that hot bed of venality and corruption, to detect and punish offences of this nature, notwithstanding the many salutary laws for that purpose. Ineffectual exertions of power weaken and disgrace government—the wise Magistrate will ever avoid them, nor aim his blow without at least a moral certainty of hitting his mark. Upon these principles, and others equally weighty, the Council resolved to leave Governor Johnstone to the infamy attending detected baseness, and both he and his instruments the consciousness of having well deserved it—A line of conduct which they did not adopt with due consideration, and which I am bold to say is justified by many respectable opinions in this city.

A Signer of the Association.

MS not found; reprinted from John Dunlap's *The Pennsylvania Packet, or the General Advertiser,* August 1, 1778.

1 For the censure directed at the Pennsylvania Council that was printed in the July 30 issue of Dunlap's *Pennsylvania Packet* and to which Reed is here responding, see Reed to Timothy Matlack, July 30, 1778, note.

Marine Committee to John Wereat

Sir August 1, 1778

We have to acknowledge your favour of the 1st of June last which with its enclosures were laid before Congress, in consequence whereof a resolve was passed Copy of which we now enclose.[1] This Resolve we have sent to the Governor and Council of your State and have informed them that you would produce Copies of the papers which occasioned it, which we request you will do.

We wrote you the 24th of June last, and sent you a book containing extracts from the Journals of Congress relative to the Capture and Condemnation of Prizes together with the Rules and Regulations of the Navy. In that Book page 12. is a resolve which relates solely to prizes made by the people or detachments from the Army without the Agency of Continental Vessels, and therefore not to effect Captures made by Continental Vessels having Accidently Continental Troops on board, but Prizes made by Continental Vessels altho they may have accidentally Continental Troops on board are to be governed by the General Regulations made respecting Prizes taken by Continental Vessels.

We are much pleased with your Zeal and attention to the public Interest, which you have testified in many instances and are with great regard Sir, Your very Hble serts

LB (DNA:PCC Miscellaneous Papers, Marine Committee Letter Book).

1 In his June 1 letter to the Marine Committee, Wereat, Continental agent in Georgia, complained that Cols. Samuel Elbert and John White had obstructed the sale of the *Hinchinbrook* and two other libeled prize vessels by requesting that their proceeds be delivered to Elbert, the Continental officer responsible for the capture, rather than to himself. On July 29 Congress ordered the Marine Committee to refer Wereat's complaint to the governor of Georgia so that this conduct could be investigated. *JCC,* 11:727. For the Marine Committee's July 31 letter to the governor and council of Georgia requesting the execution of the "enclosed resolve," see Paullin, *Marine Committee Letters,* 1:277. Although no report on such an inquiry was ever made to Congress, the papers enclosed with Wereat's July 23 letter (which are in PCC, item 78, 23:517–34) further document the prize proceedings that culminated in a July 10 decree by the assistant justices of Liberty County, Ga., declaring the *Hinchinbrook* to be United States property and ordering Wereat to pay $10,000 to the captors.

On August 20 Wereat's appeal of the Georgia decision, arguing that Congress should not be forced to purchase a vessel against its will, was referred to the Committee on Appeals. Although the committee never rendered a formal decision in this case, Congress apparently never took action on a September 1781 committee report recommending that Wereat "prosecute said appeal to final judgment," thus letting the July 1778 Georgia court ruling stand. *JCC*, 11:818, 21:981–82. Few details about the *Hinchinbrook's* disposition are known, but for two additional documents containing pertinent information on the episode, see PCC, item 41, 6:247–50, item 136, 4:647; and *JCC*, 20:767–68. See also Henry Laurens to John Laurens, May 31, note 2; and Marine Committee to Wereat, June 24, 1778, note 1.

Gouverneur Morris to George Washington

Dear General

Philadelphia 2 Augt. 1778.

I was in your Debt. It is my Fate always to be so with my Friends. But beleive me my Heart owes Nothing. Let me add that you can do me no Favor so great as to comply with your Wishes except an Opportunity to serve the Public which indeed is your highest Wish as you have evidenced fully to all the World & particularly to your Friends. I feel the full Force of your Reasoning.[1] The Faith of Congress is in some Measure plighted to Mr. De la Neuville but it is not their Intent that his Brevet shall give Command. I will take care to get this expressed by a particular Resolution.[2] The Baron has a Claim from his Merit to be noticed but I never will consent to grant what I am told he requests & I think Congress will not. At least they wont if I can help it. I this Instant was informed of the Opportunity for Camp which goes immediately. Let me however congratulate you on the Affair at Monmouth. On the *whole* Affair. It might have been better it is said. I think not for you have even from Your Enemies the Honor of that Day. You have Enemies. It is happy for you that you have. A Man of Sentiment has not so much Honor as the Vulgar suppose in risquing Life & Fortune for the Service of his Country. He does not Value them as highly as the Vulgar do. Would he give the highest evidence let him sacrifice his Feelings. In the History of last Winter Posterity will do you Justice. Adieu.

Beleive me sincerely yours, Gouv Morris

RC (DLC)

1 Morris was responding to a letter of July 24 from Washington, which dealt in general with "the appointment of so many foreigners to offices of high rank and trust in our service" and in particular with the cases of baron von Steuben and the chevalier de La Neuville. Washington, *Writings* (Fitzpatrick), 12: 226–28.

2 Although Congress delayed until October 14, 1778, before adopting the board of war's recommendation that the chevalier de La Neuville be commissioned a brigadier general by brevet, its resolution was silent on the issue of command. The date of rank was August 14, 1778. See *JCC*, 11:728, 12:1010.

Josiah Bartlett to Mary Bartlett

My Dear Philadelphia August 3d. 1778

Altho, I have not the pleasure of Receiving letters from you as often as formerly I shall Continue to write to you Every week and hope this will find you & the rest of my family well as I am at this time. The last letter I have Recd from you was Dated the 10th of July & the last before that, the 20th of June, whither you have Sent others & they have miscarried, or whither you have not an oppertunity to send them I Cant say, but should be glad to hear from you as often as you can conveniently.

The weather here has for some Days past been very Disagreably hot & muggy. We have now while I am writing this, a very Smart Thunder Shower. Hope it will Cool and Clear the air. Charles Chace is just taken Sick of a Dysentery & Something of a fever. Whither he will be bad is uncertain but I hope he will not. He seems at present pretty bad for the time. Mr. Wentworth is not yet arrived here from York Town where I formerly wrote you I left him Sick, nor have I heard from him for a week past, he was geting better when I last heard from him. It is something uncomfortable to be here so long without a Colleague, as it obliges me to attend Congress Constantly and have not so much time for Relaxation as would be for my health. However I have as yet Enjoyed my health very well by the favor of Providence and hope I shall Continue so to Do.

I wish you would inform me what letters you Receive from me, that I may Know whither any of them miscarry.

I have no important news to inform you of. Suppose you will hear of the Success of the Rhode Island Business before you Receive this, as it is within about 90 miles of you.

The French Fleet is gone there.

Please to inform me how my farming business goes on, whither there is like to be good Crops &c.

Monsr. Girard the French Ambassador is to be admitted to an audience of Congress next Thursday. I have had frequent oppertunity of seeing & Conversing with him & have Dined with him several times. He talks pretty good English for a foreigner, and seems heartily Desirous to Humble the Haughty pride & Insolence of Brittain. There is a Spaniard of Character here and a Prussian,[1] Each of them sent here as it is thought by their Respective Sovereigns Tho at present they Do not appear in their Public Characters as ambassadors, yet Keep up a Correspondence with their Courts.

Remember my love to all my Children. Does Levi Continue learning Latin or has he begun to Study French.

Remember me to all friends. I am yours &c.

Josiah Bartlett

RC (NhHi).

1 The "Spaniard of Character" was undoubtedly Juan de Miralles. The "Prussian" was probably baron de Knobelauch, who had volunteered to serve the American cause and to sell Prussian military supplies to the United States. See Henry Laurens to George Washington, August 13, 1778, note 5; and *JCC*, 11:725, 764, 778–79.

Committee of Commerce to Théveneau de Francy

Sir Commercial Committee, Philadelphia 3d August 1778

Your Letter of the 15th Ulto. was laid before Congress together with the Committees Report thereon,[1] Congress having taken the same under consideration, made the following Resolves viz.

Ordered, That the Cargo's of the Snow Speedwell; of the Brigs Braxton, Governor Johnston, and Morris, now ready to sail from America for France, be consigned to the Commissioners of Congress at Paris, who are directed to settle the Accounts of Mr. John Ross with Congress and to pay him the Balance thereof, out of the Proceeds of said Cargoe, and the residue, if any, to the house of Hortalez and Company as they judge proper.

Ordered, That the ship Virginia now lying laden with a Cargo of Tobacco on public Account in Virginia be consigned to Messrs. Roderique Hortalez and Company.[2]

It is the request of the Commercial Committee that the aforesaid Vessels sail under Convoy to the Armed Ship Fier Roderique.

I am directed to inform you that the four first mentioned Vessels were destined to the Address of Mr. John Ross previous to your arrival at York Town, in order to enable him to make good some contracts he had entered into on the Public Account; the Commissioners are now directed to adjust his Accounts, pay him the Balance that may be due, and the remainder will I suppose pass to your House.

I have the honor to be, Sir, Your Most Obedient Humble Servt.

Per Order Francis Lewis, Chairman

Tr (ScHi). In the hand of Moses Young.

1 On Francy's July 15 letter and the committee's August 1 report, see Henry Laurens to Francy, July 26, 1778, notes 1 and 2.

2 This August 1 resolution of Congress was also sent to Francy this day by President Laurens, who explained in his brief covering letter that "this Act was sent to me by the Secretary late yesterday, otherwise it should have been sooner dispatched." See PCC, item 13, 2:39; and *JCC*, 11:738–40.

Henry Marchant to William Greene

Sir, Philadelphia August 3d. 1778

Finding that all Persons who had the Disposal of Continental Lottery Tickets in the several States were required by a certain Day to make Return of all Tickets they had on hand & unsold to a Majestrate, to be by him sealed up & forwarded to the Contl. Treasury Board—and finding no such Returns from Our State, I am affraid the Resolution has not been properly attended to, and that Damage may accrue thereby to some Gentlemen of Our State. I take the Liberty to enclose to Your Excellency Copies of those Resolutions which relate to that Subject, & by Your Excellency to make some Enquiry into the Matter, that if there has been any Neglect it may be mended as much as possible.[1]

By this Day I expect the French Fleet under Count D. Staing in Conjunction with the America Troops have made an Attack upon Rhode Island.

Heaven prosper the Enterprize. Genl. Sullivan has now an Opportunity of procuring unfading Laurels for his Brow—indeed I hope the Brow of every Soldier will be encircled with Crowns of Honor. My Countrymen of Rhode Island step forth—and maintain that Rank you so worthily hold amongst the American brave Sons of Freedom. Every Moment swells with important Events. One glorious Effort—and this fall by the Blessing of God settles the United States in Safety and Honor, and brings a Harvest of lasting Blessings to Posterity.

But Amidst all let me say a Word as to Œconomy. We have scarce to fear, but from the inordinate Extravagance of the Times, a lawless Thirst for Riches, and a Spirit of monopolising and speculation—big with more Evils than all the Armies Europe could afford. A most strict attention must be paid to Our Finances. I hope Our State will make a very wise Application of the large Sums of Money lately recd. by Her.

I hope We shall be careful to advance as little as possible on Contl. Account. Every Sum advanced hazards some Loss upon a Settlement. Let us call in as much Money as possible And of Our Treasury Notes. I have but Time to add, I am &c.

Hy Marchant

RC (R–Ar).

1 For Congress' January 6, May 2, June 3 and 4, 1778, resolves on the Continental lottery, see *JCC*, 10:24–25, 11:415–16, 564, 568.

John Banister to Theodorick Bland, Jr.

My dear Sir

Philadelphia August 4th. 1778

The Report you allude to,[1] at the first perusal, struck me to the Soul. That there should be permitted in human Societies, *Characters* of so deep a Cast of depravity to roam at large blasting the Reputations of those above them in station & Merit is to me unaccountable. That in the spre[ading of such?] Calumnies there should [not] be found a Person to vindicate the [. . .] and drag to light the diabolical Writer who could take Pleasure in robbing an Innocent Man of his good Name, is Stranger Still. Certainly my Friends shd have taken some little Pains to expose to the World Malice of this nefarious, this infernal Cast. Is it *fitting* that one who has f[or a] Series of years Sacrificed his time and in many Instances his Property [. . .], be traduced and vilified & that no Friend shd. start up to vindicate his injured Fame.

I shall not wonder if it is reported that I murdered the Man, tho I was in this City & he in the remote parts of Virginia.

Can Vice be carried to a more Damning height than it is in our Country once the Seat of innocence & Industry.

I am happy however that the Man met [wi]th so [ju]st a Punishment & doubt [not b]ut he is gone to fast in fire till his Slanderous Soul shall become purified.

May all such Miscreants who would baulk the fair Fame of their fellow Creatures meet a like Fate. Human Iniquity can go no higher & therefore I hope not to be thought uncharitable. As to the Remedy my dear Sir, where shall I find it? To traverse a Country in quest of [the] Propagator [of] a [. . .] less Slander [. . .] & infamous man would leave the Ma[tter] as it is. The author must be Base to the [. . .], among Gentlemen it cannot gain credit. If it is possible trace out the Traducer & then I shall be under no difficulty how to conduct myself.

I wish some Person could be employed to Sift this matter out, but he must be a Man of Prudence & Judgement. It will not long be in the Power of any Villain's Prejudices to operate against me; having formed a valuable [. . . I shall?] soon repair thither to take [care] of the business incident to it, being resolved n[ever] more to intermeddle in publick Concerns; I hope no Person will touch my Reputation unjustly. When I shall have withdrawn myself from any conspicuous point of View Envy & Malice will cease. Your letter shall be delivered to the President,[2] when I go to Congress, & immediately after breakfast I will go & enquire the Lady my Friend Mrs. Bland has directed the Cotton to. Adieu. May the Malice of the World never reach you, your daies be peaceable [&] your [. . .] happy. Yr. Friend,

J. Banister

RC (ViHi).

1 The nature of this "Report," which obviously was a recent attack on Banister that greatly distressed him, has not been discovered.

2 Col. Theodorick Bland's July 18 letter to Congress "respecting rank," which was read in Congress on August 4 and referred to the Board of War, is in PCC, item 78, 3:21–24. See also *JCC*, 11:744–45.

Josiah Bartlett to Meshech Weare

Hond. Sir   Philadelphia August 4th 1778

Your favor of the 18th July is Just Recd[1] and must beg leave to Refer you to a letter I wrote (previous to the Receipt of yours) to Colo Nicholas Gilman[2] Giving him an account of what is Done in Consequence of the application for money for the use of our State. Money Cannot be Sent from this place at present nor will it be Easy to procure an order for money till the Difficulties I mention in my letter to him is Cleared up by Letters from our State as is therein mentioned. Afterwards Drafts on the Loan Office or on our own Treasury as part of the Money to be raised for Continental use as has been Done on the Treasurer of Connecticut & Massachusetts Bay if Such Drafts would answer please to inform me.

I am Sorry to hear that the condesending measures used by the State to the Inhabitants of Some part of the County of Grafton has not been attended with any Salutary Effect. The Hampshire Grants by Receiving & Countenancing them, have fell into the Snare laid for them by New York, to prevent the State of New Hampshire from interesting themselves in favor of said Grants. Some transactions of Vermont in Banishing some of their Inhabitants has been loudly Complained of by the State of New York and the men Stopt from being Sent to the Enemy according to the order of Vermont. This & some other Complaints will be likely to bring those affairs before Congress who must finally Settle those Disputes as soon as our other affairs give a little opportunity.[3]

I have nothing material to Communicate to you. The French minister is to Receive audience of Congress on Thursday next. The Success of the affairs from Rhode Island will be likely heard before the Recept of this.

Mr. Wentworth is not arrived from York Town nor have I heard from him for some time. I hope the State will take Care at their next session to appoint Delegates to Relieve us in the fall.

In haste I am Sir, with great Respect your Most obedient Servant,

Josiah Bartlett

[*P.S.*] Please to Consider this as a private letter as it is wrote in a hurry.

RC (MHi).

[1] Meshech Weare's July 18 letter to Bartlett repeating an earlier request for a $200,000 grant from Congress for New Hampshire is in Bartlett, *Papers* (Mevers), p. 200. See also Bartlett to Weare, July 20, 1778, note 1.

[2] Not found.

[3] In his July 18 letter Weare had reported the secession of 16 Grafton County towns from New Hampshire. After three years of unsuccessfully seeking increased representation in the New Hampshire Assembly, these towns on the eastern bank of the Connecticut River had voted at a convention in Hanover to unite with Vermont. The Vermont Assembly, after consulting with the Vermont town governments, had voted on June 11 to accept the New Hampshire towns, further complicating efforts to settle Vermont's status. Subsequently, in response to the widespread condemnation of Vermont's action encountered by its agent Ethan Allen in Philadelphia in September, the rebel assembly rescinded its annexation of the New Hampshire towns. But the movement for union with Vermont remained strong along the Connecticut River, and in 1781 the New Hampshire towns made another attempt at union with Vermont on condition that Congress approve. When Congress again opposed the proposal, the Vermont legislature in 1782 finally decided to ignore this unification movement and accepted the Connecticut River as the state's eastern border with New Hampshire. See E.P. Walton, ed., *Records of the Governor and Council of Vermont,* 7 vols. (Montpelier, Vt.: J. & J. M. Poland, 1873–80), 1:405–41; Everett S. Stackpole, *History of New Hampshire,* 4 vols. (New York: American Historical Society, 1916), 2:151–223; Bartlett, *Papers* (Mevers), pp. 200, 211–12; and Bartlett to Weare, September 26, 1778.

Henry Laurens to Rawlins Lowndes

Sir

4th Augt. [1778]

The last I had the honor of writing to Your Excellency is under the 10th July and sent forward by Messenger Sharp, on the 25th I had the honor of receiving and presenting to Congress Your Excellency's favor of the 6th of the same Month,[1] this was referred to the Medical Committee, who have not yet reported, and as no commands have been since laid on me relative to South Carolina, I have only to repeat assurances that I remain, With very great Respect &c.

P.S. I shall add to this twelve Commissions with Instructions and Bonds for private ships of War. The Bonds when duely executed Your Excellency will be pleased to transmit to Congress.

LB (DNA: PCC, item 13).

[1] See *JCC,* 11:716. A transcript of a July 6 letter from President Lowndes to Laurens is in the Laurens Papers, ScHi, but as it contains nothing to suggest that it would have been referred to the Medical Committee, it seems probable that Laurens is referring to another letter of that date written by Lowndes.

James Lovell to William Whipple

4th August 1778.

Dear Sir,

In a confusion of papers I cannot make a particular acknowledgement of your favors according to their dates. I only remember that a *modest* strain of *scolding* was under the seal of some of them; as though I could have idle moments on my hand without improving them in an epistolary way with one I much esteem at Portsmouth. To prevent such things in future, know, that living together at the State House in the old style of Mrs. Ross' at Baltimore my hours are less my own than they used to be, as company naturally turns into Sedition Hall, as the Quakers used to term it, when the Massachusetts delegation formerly were here with Mrs. Yard.

There is nothing material passing this morning except a confirmed account that a vessel from Liverpool, large, was ashore at the Capes and completely unloaded by Militia though a British armed vessel was firing upon them all the time.

Thursday next the *Minister Plenipotentiary* of France to the Congress of the United States of America will have a public audience for the first time.

My love to your own and brother's family. Your affectionate hble Servt.

J.L.

[*P.S.*] I enclose you a fate of certain tickets whether your's or some other person's, time and the usual practice in such cases must discover. But of this more hereafter.

Tr (DLC).

Samuel Holten's Diary

[August 5, 1778]

5. Congress Sit from 9 'till almost 3 & from 5 'till almost 10 o'Clock;[1] I am much indisposed.

MS (MDaAr).

1 The previous day Holten recorded in his diary that he had "attended in Congress 'till after 4 o'Clock."

Henry Laurens to Benedict Arnold

5th August [1778]

I had the honor this morning of presenting to Congress your Letter of the present date, and in obedience to the order of the house I now inform you "that it is the intention of Congress that Colonel

Benjamin Flower should be securely kept in a convenient room under a sufficient guard."[1]

I am with great Respect & Esteem, Sir, Your Obedient & Most Humble Servt.

LB (DNA: PCC, item 13). Addressed: "General Arnold, Head Quarters Philada., dd. by M. Young."

[1] Arnold's August 5 letter to Laurens, requesting clarification of an August 3 order directing that Commissary of Military Stores Benjamin Flower "be arrested and safely kept until the further order of Congress," is in PCC, item 162, fol. 136. Congress had issued this order as a result of allegations by Flower's deputy, Cornelius Sweers, that together they had conspired to defraud the public by purchasing arms "at a moderate price, then charging an advanced price, and sharing the profits equally between us." Although Congress had initially directed the Board of War to carry out this order, the board had balked at doing so, pointing out in an August 4 letter from Timothy Pickering to Laurens that it had the utmost confidence in Flower's integrity and arguing that Sweers' testimony should be regarded with suspicion because he himself was under investigation for fraud. As a result, the delegates instructed Arnold to arrest Flower and made preparations to summon board members before Congress in order to explain their refusal to obey a direct congressional order—a fate they avoided by submitting a timely letter of apology that Congress accepted on August 8 as "sufficient atonement" for Pickering's letter. See *JCC*, 11:698, 737, 741–43, 747–48, 761–64; and PCC, item 78, 18:193, 20:235–47, item 147, 2:163–66.

In the event, the Board of War's confidence in Flower was justified, for on August 24 Congress decided after investigation that there was no substance to Sweers' accusations against him and therefore directed the Board of Treasury to employ a lawyer to prosecute Sweers for "divers forgeries and frauds against the public in his official transactions." See *JCC*, 11:751, 791, 831–34; and PCC, item 78, 9:171, 20:249–63.

Henry Laurens to Rawlins Lowndes

Dear Sir 5th August [1778]

The date of my last private Address which went by Messenger Sharp is the 15th July.

I have now in view Your Excellency's several favors of the 28th May, 17th June and 6th July.[1]

Nothing has been done in the arrangement since the return of Congress to Philada. and it appears to me that nothing will be done while the Army continues migrative. I am very sensible Your Excellency will in the mean time have experienced much inconvenience and trouble from the demands of our local Continental Officers for Commissions. The terms in which our Carolinian Regiments were originally established, as far as I know, are singular and entitle the officers to claim all the benefits which were held up to them; and I am persuaded Congress will not contend the point when fully and clearly explained, but every attempt to this end has been overrul'd by the repeated reply "we cannot interfere in or consider these matters until the Army Arrangement is finished." From this consideration, and from that of the peculiar circumstances of the troops in our State, I am also persuaded that Congress will not censure the Executive, should they advise Your Excellency to grant so many Commissions as shall appear to be absolutely necessary. I am farther confirmed in this opinion from the silence of the house when they were informed that Your Excellency had granted from necessity a few Commissions subsequent to the Act of the 31st Decr.[2] And therefore I shall inclose with this 20 signed Commissions, submitting these and my private sentiments to your Excellency's final determination referring at the same time to the Act above mention'd compared with the circumstances of our Regiments.

The testimony from Captain Senff is extreamly wanted;[3] from the late humiliations of Great Britain I shall not be surpris'd to see by one of the first Packets a ratification of the Convention of Saratoga, immediately after which, the remaining troops will be hurried away; and from the repeated breaches of faith in the Ministers and officers of that Nation I shall be as little surprized to hear that those troops had immediately landed in New York or Charlestown; admitting the practicability and their opinion of the utility of such an Act.

I am much affected by the relation of my fellow Citizens conduct in opposition to your Excellency's Proclamation of the 13th of June.[4] The Act of Congress upon which that Proclamation was founded was well intended, but it passed after much contention and proves to be the most unpleasing to the states in general of any determination of Congress within my experience. There is a distinction made by Tories between moral private honor and Political honor in the practice of which Men of the first Character have been detected and driven to a necessity for explaining in order to preserve some Character which has rendered every Man coming within the description suspicious in the highest degree. It would be tedious and probably unnecessary at this date to adduce particular proofs in the conduct of General Sir William Howe, Sir H. Clinton, Sir Wm. [*i.e.*, George] Johnstone, Governor Franklin and twenty etcetera. Nevertheless nobody here thinks your Excellency was faulty in pursuing the Recommendation of Congress in terms of the Proclamation, and by advice of the Privy Council.

I was well aware the embargo would press heavily on our State, and upon that occasion I desired to deliver my sentiments to Congress from the Chair. Your Excellency may rest assured I shall watch the earliest opportunity for recommending to Congress a revocation of the Act. In the mean time it may merit our attention whether other states pay that implicit obedience to *such* an Act of Congress as we do in South Carolina and our future submission with or without Remonstrance may be warranted by the discoveries which shall be made.

The General Gazette of the 4th Augt. will shew Your Excellency what respect has been paid to the Resolve of Congress by this State. I am determin'd to introduce Vice President Bryan's Proclamation into the house;[5] Your Excellency shall be duly and as speedily as possible inform'd of the reception which my application shall meet with. My Countrymen will Act accordingly. I must do them the justice to say, they have hitherto acted with as much uprightness and fidelity in the common cause of the Union as any State of the thirteen. I will say nothing that shall appear to be invidious, altho' I have feelings against the expressing of which I can scarcely resist.

My Ideas relative to the views of the Court of Madrid were exploded at the time of reading the Treaties with France. I endeavoured to impress them upon the mind of my Colleague the Chief Justice, and now the Eyes of many Gentlemen begin to be opened.

Part of Your Excellency's Letter from the words *"I am extreamly happy"* to the words *"I mean to the public"* I presented to Congress: 'twas extreamly approv'd of, and committed, instead of saying to the grave, I will only intimate that no Report has been made thereon.[6]

Your Excellency *"would be very unwilling to change situations with me"* undoubtedly, and for very obvious reasons. Nevertheless I have a thousand times wished most anxiously, and do at this instant ardently wish that you were here a Representation from South Carolina either with or without me. Yourself, Sir, and a few more whom I could name, without meaning to disparage the present Delegates or any individual of them, are extreamly wanted in General Congress. This remark excites very serious reflections in my mind, important perhaps beyond your Excellencys apprehensions, but I feel a necessity for reserving a disclosure to a future opportunity. Happy shall I be to see such amendments in Public Measures as will render disclosure unnecessary—I esteem the capture of Bachop and Osborne a fortunate stroke in favor of all the States. Georgia and South Carolina receive the most immediate benefit.[7]

LB (ScHi).

1 Transcripts of these letters are in the Laurens Papers, ScHi.

2 On December 31, 1777, Congress had decided to ask all state governments "to suspend filling up any vacancies in their respective regiments" because of the disproportionate ratio of officers to men in the Continental Army. *JCC*, 9:1073.

3 Laurens wanted to obtain information on British violations of the Saratoga Convention from Capt. John Christian Senf, a former member of General Burgoyne's army, in order to justify Congress' continued refusal to allow the Convention Army to return to England. See Laurens to Lowndes, May 17, 1778, note 12.

4 For an account of popular opposition in South Carolina to President Lowndes' June 13 proclamation offering amnesty to loyalists, which was issued in accordance with an April 23, 1778, resolve of Congress, see Carl J. Vipperman,

The Rise of Rawlins Lowndes, 1721–1800 (Columbia: University of South Carolina Press, 1978), pp. 211–13.

5 Vice President George Bryan's August 3 proclamation, which laid an embargo on the exportation of provisions "for Thirty days . . . & no longer," contravened Congress' June 8 embargo, which forbade the exportation of these commodities until November 15, 1778. See *JCC*, 11:578–79; and *Pa. Council Minutes*, 11:545. There is no evidence in the journals that Congress ever considered Bryan's proclamation.

6 This particular section of President Lowndes' June 17 letter to Laurens described the confusion caused by the system under which Continental and state officials competed to procure clothing and supplies for Continental troops and suggested that the procurement of these items be assigned strictly to state appointees. See also *JCC*, 11:681–82.

7 In his July 6 letter to Laurens, Lowndes had discussed the recent capture of Capts. Peter Bachop and George Osborne off the Carolina coast.

For the continuation of this letter, see Laurens to Lowndes, August 7, 1778.

Marine Committee to the Eastern Navy Board

Gentlemen August 5th 1778

Since our last of the 24th ultimo, we have received yours of the 17th and 22d. to which we shall now reply.

As we shall often want small Vessels for Packets we desire you will order three Schooners to be built of about 50 or 60 Tons burthen and let swift Sailing be the Object—Mr. Peck may be employed to exercise his Talents in constructing One of them. We are glad to hear of the arrival of the Schooner Loyallty as you will perceive by our last we had reason to fear she had fallen into the hands of the enemy. We hope the Schooner Swan, Captain Stiles, will arrive safe.

We enclose herein a Resolve of Congress passed yesterday directing a Compensation of 500 Dollars to be made to Mr. Storey the Clk of your Board for his extra services and expences since his appointment which you will please to pay him. You will also find another resolve of Congress allowing you 365 dollars each for travelling expences in visiting the different parts of your department for the year past which we hope will be deem'd sufficient.[1]

We are very sorry to hear of the misfortune that had befallen the Schooner Ranger—we have no doubt but you will duely attend to have such things as have been saved from her applied to the public Account.

The Prices you are obliged to give for Cordage, are indeed very extravagant, but at this time we cannot remedy that evil as the Ships that are now built must be fitted out. It will be an object with us when we order other Ships to be built to provide their materials on the best terms. We hope the Warren has gone to Sea and that the Raleigh will shortly follow her. We wrote by yesterdays post to the Governor and Council of Massachusets to aid you in Manning the ships at Boston,[2] which we expect they will do, and that you will thereby be enabled to send out the Vessels very Shortly.

We have directed the Paymaster of this department to send you a State of Lieutenant Morans Account. Mr. Trevet was at York Town when Congress were there, but went off without making any application.

We have already sent you by Mr. Dodd 200,000 Dollars, and wish we could now send you the remainder of the Warrant granted by Congress for your department.[3] The Treasury hath not yet got money sufficient for that purpose, but in a few days we expect to get the balance which shall be immediately sent forward together with the Money for Mr. Bradfords Bill.

We are with regard Gentlemen, Your Hble Servants

P.S. You will in future send forward the proceedings at large of all Courts Martial—at present those relative to Captains Manly and McNeill are wanted; please to Send by the first opportunity.[4]

LB (DNA: PCC Miscellaneous Papers, Marine Committee Letter Book).

1 See *JCC*, 11:747.

2 In this August 4 letter the committee requested the Massachusetts Council to "aid the Navy Board with the powers of Government in Manning the Continental ships of war that are at Boston, which have been ordered out to join the French Fleet under the command of Vice Admiral the Count D'Estaing." Paullin, *Marine Committee Letters*, 1:278. The RC of this letter, which was signed by chairman Richard Henry Lee, is in Revolutionary Letters, M-Ar.

3 On this July 16 warrant, see Marine Committee to the Eastern Navy Board, July 24, 1778, note 3.

4 See Marine Committee to the Eastern Navy Board, July 24, 1778, note 5.

Committee of Congress to the Pennsylvania Council

Aug. 6th, 1778.

Messrs Richard H. Lee and Samuel Adams, a Committee of Congress, present their respectfull Compts to the Hon. the Vice President & Council of the State of Pennsylvania, and beg the favor of them to order a sufficient number of Peace Officers to prevent any Interruption of the Minister of France, in his Passage to and from the Congress Chamber, this day.[1]

MS not found; reprinted from *Pa. Archives*, 1st ser. 6:677.

1 On this day Congress held an elaborate reception for Conrad Alexandre Gérard at the State House in Philadelphia. Congress' account of the proceedings was published in the *Pennsylvania Packet*, August 11, 1778. For translations of Gérard's reports to the comte de Vergennes on the day's events, see Gérard, *Dispatches* (Baisnée and Meng), 57:92–96.

Conrad Alexandre Gérard

Samuel Holten's Diary

[August 6–7, 1778]

6. Monsieur Gerard Minisr. Plenipotentiary from his most Christian Majesty had a public audience with Congress, & dined with them, the proceedings was conducted with great decorum; The entertainment was grand & elegant, the band of musick was very agreeable.

7. Monsieur Gerard made a visit, in the edge of the evening (about an hour) to the Delegates of the Massa. Bay agreeable to the public ceremonies agreed on by Congress for a Minisr. Plenipotentiary, my colleagues being absent upon his first coming in, I had the Honor of his company alone.

MS (MDaAr).

Henry Laurens to Benedict Arnold

Sir 7th August [1778]

Congress are much interrupted in the course of business in their Sessions at the State House by the beating of Drums & noise of the Soldiery at the Guard House. Will you be so obliging as to give the necessary order for preventing in future the inconvenience complained of.

I have the honor to be with great Esteem & Regard &ca.

LB (DNA: PCC, item 13).

Henry Laurens to John Lewis Gervais

My Dear Friend 7th August [1778]

I am compel'd as usual to refer you for news to His Excellency the President, and to Newspapers which will accompany this.

Since my last of the 15th Ulto. I have received your obliging favors of the 2nd and 6th of that Month.[1]

I am well satisfied with your determination respecting Monsr. Jaussaud; I have a long Letter from Mr. Delagayè but tis French, and I have not yet read it.

Your Packet to Colonel Laurens is gone after him, perhaps it may overtake him at Rhode Island[2] where he is sent by his General, with private orders and Messages to General Sullivan and probably to Count d'Estaing. I am glad he is found useful and to be trusted with important charges.

I tell you my dear friend, our situation which you say "is certainly much more promising" is not what you believe it to be; don't start when I say it is deplorable. I am sorry for Pompey and Tom. You judge right with respect to Cuffy and March. Mr. Bayley & all the rest of my affairs are under your direction and controul. Whatever you have done, or shall do respecting those affairs will meet my thanks. If you have paid Mr. Blundell, a dead loss of the sum will be sustained.

Dispose of Lewis Roux as you shall judge most for his advantage, consistently with his inclinations and also with his circumstances. I cannot expect to see him before the middle of December.

The Act of Congress in favor of Tories reformed was well intended but has produced no good effects,[3] indeed from experience I am now of opinion that the most honest men amongst them do not hold themselves bound by any promises made to the most honest Men among those whom they stile Rebels; the latter, therefore, are guilty of falling in the extreme when they trust them. You know, Sir, I had formerly more charity for my neighbours & for Mankind in general. It is but of late that I have learn'd of the distinction establish'd by our Enemies between moral and political honor, however, I do not say there is not one of the persons call'd Tories whom I would not rely upon. There are certainly exceptions. Captain James Willings' expedition will end as I prognosticated in the beginning of it. These States will incur a heavy debt, loss of lives, and receive no kind of benefit from it. It was the project of a private Member without the knowledge of Congress—a Member who has done and does what he pleases.[4]

The name of new hope is very applicable to a Plantation whose buildings and improvements have been burned and destroy'd.

Bachop certainly promis'd me he would never bear Arms against America, provided he was allow'd to return to St. Augustine on his Parole, but I presume he has been regularly exchanged—even in that case from repeated declarations which he made to me he is very criminal for cruising upon our Coast—pray has he repaid the money I advanced him?

Your President is not unpopular in Congress. I am sorry he is so, as you say at home. A sound conscience shields the Mind against all attacks of tongues and Pens.[5]

I am rejoyc'd to learn of Mrs. Gervais's perfect recovery. I salute her and the children with my best Respects—I grieve for your friend the elder Mr. Trapier.

Well but Sir! surely such full tables as I perceive mask'd in your Letter of the 6th of July is not a proof of unpopularity.

If Monsr. Galvan is looking for promotion, he takes the wrong road.[6]

You will be inform'd by His Excellency the President my Ideas about the Embargo—this was also a well calculated and well design'd Act of Congress, but abuses are creeping in.[7] I shall be as attentive as possible, and upon the earliest discovery ring an Alarm. I beg you will present my best Compliments to Mr. and Mrs. Manigault. I hope to find time for writing to my worthy old friend next week. Remember me also to every other friend, and be assured I remain, with the highest esteem and affection Dear Sir &c.

P.S. Have you sold my last years' Indigo? and for how much. If you have not purchas'd the Negroes woolen cloathing yet, delay a Month or so, or until I write again on the subject.

Mr. Drayton two days ago told me a story which almost surpris'd me, that General Gadsden has again endeavour'd to injure me, by a groundless charge or insinuation, that I had presented the Letter, intimating the resignation of his Commission, either improperly in the manner, or at an improper time. All his suspicions have been equally unjust, but it has not always been in my power to prove it, as I shall do in the present case. His resignation was tendered to Congress the 2nd of October by Mr. Hancock. I was order'd in the Chair the 1st of November. It is true I said nothing upon the occasion; neither did any Member in the house, except those who said, "accept it," "accept it," I was not one of them. I should have been very cautious had it been put to a vote, even of giving my voice against it. 'Tis probable I should have withdrawn upon such an occasion—the risk of offending would have been equal on either side. When Mr. Gadsden was in the service I now am in, he knows, I endeavoured to assist and serve him & God knows I never attempted to undervalue or depreciate him—if he had had any foundation for censuring me, he should have communicated his complaints directly to myself or have reserv'd them to be communicated at my return, instead of such generous procedure, he has, according to his custom, stabb'd me in conversations and private letters. It was by mere accident I learn'd his discourteous, injurious, attempts, from Mr. Drayton, and this, as I said above, but two days ago.[8] I wish you would read every word of this to General Gadsden; it will keep up a consistency in all my conduct towards that Gentleman.[9]

LB (ScHi).

1 Gervais' July 2 and 6 letters to Laurens are in the Laurens Papers, ScHi.

2 "Providence" is written above "Rhode Island" in the LB.

3 See also Laurens to Rawlins Lowndes, August 5, 1778, note 4.

4 Robert Morris, whose former business partner Thomas Willing was Capt. James Willing's brother, was the "private Member" mentioned by Laurens. See John Caughey, "Willing's Expedition Down the Mississippi, 1778," *Louisiana Historical Quarterly* 15 (1932): 5–36; and Robert V. Haynes, "James Willing and the Planters of Natchez: The American Revolution Comes to the Southwest," *Journal of Mississippi History* 37 (1975): 1–40.

5 For an analysis of the causes of President Rawlins Lowndes' unpopularity in

South Carolina at this time, see Carl J. Vipperman, *The Rise of Rawlins Lowndes, 1721–1800* (Columbia: University of South Carolina Press, 1978), pp. 205–13.

6 For additional information on William Galvan, see Laurens to John Laurens, August 29, 1778.

7 In the letters to Laurens cited above, Gervais had explained that Congress' June 8 embargo on the export of certain provisions was highly unpopular in South Carolina because it had caused a sharp decline in the price of rice. See also *JCC*, 7:578–79; and Laurens to Rawlins Lowndes, August 5, 1778.

8 Congress had accepted Christopher Gadsden's resignation from the Continental Army on October 2, 1777, after reading an August 28 letter from Gen. Robert Howe, the commander of the southern military department, explaining that Gadsden was resigning because of a jurisdictional conflict with him. Drayton, who had supported Gadsden in the South Carolina Assembly during his dispute with Howe, raised the issue of Gadsden's resignation at this time after receiving a July 4 letter from Gadsden rebutting Howe's account of the events leading up to his decision to resign and criticizing the "conduct of the then Carolina Delegates" when Congress accepted his resignation. See *JCC*, 8:757; and Christopher Gadsden, *The Writings of Christopher Gadsden*, ed. Richard Walsh (Columbia: University of South Carolina Press, 1966), pp. 134–44. Interestingly enough, Gadsden did not single out Laurens directly or by implication in his letter to Drayton, a transcript of which, endorsed "Copy of a Letter from General Gadsden to his Friend in Congress," is in the Laurens Papers, ScHi.

9 Although Burnett, *Letters*, 3:361, prints the foregoing paragraph as a postscript to Laurens' August 5–7 letter to Rawlins Lowndes, it is actually part of the present letter, as the following statement by Laurens in his September 6 letter to Gervais clearly indicates: "I expect to hear from you such Answer as General Gadsden should have given." Laurens also returned to this subject in his September 10 letter to Gervais.

Burnett was misled into assigning this paragraph to the letter to Lowndes as a result of a clerical error by Laurens' secretary Moses Young. Young entered part of the letter to Lowndes on pp. 241–45 of the letterbook, part on p. 240, and the rest on pp. 249–51, entering the letter to Gervais on pp. 247–48 and 252–53. In the process of copying the latter, however, Young stopped with the complimentary close on p. 252 and then prepared to transcribe another letter, first inserting two lines across the page wherein to write the name and address of the recipient. At this point he realized he had forgotten to copy the postscript of the letter to Gervais and therefore wrote the first paragraph of it between these lines and the second underneath them. Burnett erroneously assumed that the line separating the first and the second paragraphs on p. 252 meant that the second was a continuation of Laurens' letter to Lowndes, which ended on p. 251, a mistake made also by the transcriber of the copy of the letter to Lowndes that is in unit 16 of the microfilm edition of the Laurens Papers, ScHi.

Henry Laurens to Rawlins Lowndes

[August 7, 1778]

It is now the 7th of August: what is written above is the product of four or five attempts in Minutes stolen from the hard service of the last three days. The Messenger has been and is detained for my Letters only, I must therefore hasten to conclude.

We have heard nothing late from General Washington or from

Count d'Estaing. The Newspaper intimates the landing of 4000 British Troops from New York at Rhode Island, this is probably a mistake.

General Putnam from the Army informs me that Deserters were daily coming in, generally ten per day. A Green coat Captain and a British Cornet of Horse among them.

We do not yet know the result of General Lee's tryal.

I have been many days under that kind of anxiety which I felt during our debates on motion for detaining Lieut General Burgoyne and his Convention troops. I then feared he would slip through our fingers into this City—now from an unaccountable delay on our part I dread losing the proper time for treating the British Commissioners according to their deserving. In the Acts and attempts of Governor Johnstone I charge the whole with having offered the highest possible affront to a virtuous, Independent Nation by attempting to bribe their Representatives in Congress. I have therefore much at heart a desire that Congress should resolve to hold no conference with such Men, to assign their reasons in ample decent language, and to transmit the Act by a flag to the Commissioners in New York, and make them the bearers of their own disgrace.[1] They will not dare to suppress the Resolve, they must lay it before their Court, it will soon descend to the public at large, and expose themselves and their Prompters to the resentments of a deluded and much injur'd People, whose deplorable circumstances I must confess affects me. The Commissioners and the group of Politicians who have led on the British Nation to ruin will be held up and scorned at every Court in Europe, & their names will be branded with infamy in history.

If we leave this business to be transacted at our leisure, Governor Johnstone may in the mean time return to Great Britain, there he will confidently deny the fact and charge Congress with a calculated forgery. I am for attacking him immediately, Letters in hand, his guilt will be fix'd, for he cannot now deny.

I am not commonly tenacious of my own opinions, but in the present case I feel as if I clearly foresaw many good effects resulting from a proper Act on our part, I am therefore, day by day urging my Colleague Drayton to force a Resolve for this purpose, which he has had in his pocket more than a fortnight.[2]

The Captain Hawker, formerly the Instrument for Mr. Collector Moore at Charlestown lately Commander of the British frigate Mermaid is now in Goal with his Officers and Crew under the law of retaliation. I have lost or mislaid a Note which he sent to me a few days ago, but from my Answer which Your Excellency will find among other Papers the purport may be gathered—he has address'd to Congress in a Memorial[3] signed by himself and his Officers praying[4] for enlargement on parole—this has found able advocates and as strong an opposition, Mr. Drayton is firm against it.[5]

This instant we hear two articles of intelligence of some importance—a Gentleman from New York says, a fire had happen'd in that City which had consumed upwards of 200 houses, among which were some store houses full of Kings' stores, and that five store ships with their lading were also burnt.

That Admiral Byron with four British Men of War and supposed Cork fleet were on the coast, the Admiral had sent a frigate before him, this frigate or her barge had been up to the city, Sir Henry Clinton had confer'd with the Commander, and that a thousand hogsheads of Water were immediately filled and ship'd.

We shall soon learn particulars of these crude accounts—I believe neither of them are groundless, and begin to have some fears I may properly say, rather strengthened than beginning that the British fleet will be an overmatch for that of our Ally's in this Quarter—there is also a rumour that we have taken Rhode Island out of the hands of the Enemy; this I regard only as report.

A discovery having been made of frauds in the Accounts of the Deputy Commissary General of Military Stores, he was arrested and committed to Goal; there, he made some confessions and charg'd the Commissary General, hitherto a Gentleman of very fair character, as a tempter and accomplice. Congress had directed the Board of War to arrest and safely keep him also—the Board proceeded not with proper vigor and wrote such a letter to the house as is deemd a disobedience of Orders and an high insult. The adjusting this troublesome affair will much retard business of the greatest importance—it has already cost us two days, stagnated correspondence with the Board, and is not ended.

I will trespass no longer upon Your Excellencys' time but to repeat, that I am with very great Respect and Regard, Sir, Your Excellencys' Obedt. Servt.

P.S. While I was signing to the preceding Page, Monsr. Girard very politely transmitted to me the Treaty of Alliance general & defensive between the King of France and the "Laudable Helvetique Body" or Swiss Cantons concluded the 28th May 1777 sign'd by the King on one part, and by Deputies from the thirteen Cantons and seven free States in Alliance with them, on the other. This was sworn to or finally ratified the 25th of August following; until this event France had not acknowledged the Independence of the Helvetic Body but in all their former correspondencies had treated with them as parts of the German Empire—an annecdote known to very few in Europe or America.

I view this, an Act preparatory to acknowledging the Independence of America, although I will not hazard my conjecture with the Minister.

With this Treaty Mr. Girard sent me a ponderous and beautiful silver Medal struck upon the above occasion. On one face the Kings head encircled Ludovicus XVI Franc. et Nar. Rex.—on the other—Fœdus Cum Helvetiis Restauratum Et Stabilitum, MDCCLXXVII, and ornamented by a Garland or wreath of Olive Branches.

The States are Zurich, Berne, Lucerne, Ury, Schwitz, Underwald le haut, Underwald le bas, Zug, Glaris Evangelique, Glaris Catholique, Basle, Fribourg, Soleure, Schaffouse, Appenzell, Abbé de Saint-Gall, Ville de Saint-Gall, Vallais, Mulhause, Bienne.

I have also just learn'd that upon the appearance of the French fleet near Rhode Island the Enemy set fire to the King Fisher Man of War and two of their Gallies and abandoned them. The vessels were totally consumed—some of their regiments which had been stationed on Connecticut side also retired into the Garrison at Rhode Island, where they are now about 5000 strong—we now know where they are. When the Marquis de la Fayette shall have joined General Sullivan, an immediate attack will be made—we may expect to hear somewhat important in a few days.

I sincerely condole with Your Excellency and Mrs. Lowndes. Your experience Sir, will point out the true way of softening and reconciling every stroke of Providence.[6]

Papers inclosed to Mr. Lowndes—
Copies of Letters from G.W. 14th, 17th, and 22nd July[7]
Mr. Maduits Paper[8]
Account of forces in England and Scotland
The Answer to Captain Hawker
Report of Treasury, sums advanc'd to staff officers
Mr Girard's Address to Congress
The President's Answer
His Most Christian Majesty's Letter to Congress[9]
Twenty Army Commissions

The damage by fire at New York is ascertained to be confined to 120 houses including Stores, a great quantity of Wine, and a very large quantity of King's stores destroy'd—only two Vessels burnt which happen'd to be aground.

The Account of the Arrival of Byron's fleet is groundless.[10]

LB (ScHi). A continuation of Laurens to Lowndes, August 5, 1778.

1 See *JCC*, 11:770-74.

2 See William Henry Drayton's Notes for a Speech in Congress, August 11, 1778.

3 Laurens wrote "Letter to the President" above "Memorial" in the LB, without indicating which he used in the now missing RC.

4 Laurens inserted an asterisk at this point in the LB to key the following marginal note: "He does not pray, but after asserting his humanity to American

Prisoners and referring to Governor Johnstone's Letter, says he shall acknowledge an enlargement on parole an indulgence." The letter from "Governor Johnstone" was actually a letter to the Board of War from Gov. Thomas Johnson of Maryland that is not in PCC.

5 The August 2 letter to Laurens from Capt. James Hawker and five of his subordinates, in which they requested to be released on parole from the "Common Goal" in Philadelphia, was read in Congress on August 3 and debated on the fourth, at which time the delegates decided to postpone consideration of it. After satisfying themselves that Hawker had in fact treated his prisoners humanely, however, the delegates agreed on August 26 to direct the Marine Committee to parole him, though not his subordinates. See *JCC*, 11:743, 747, 840; and PCC, item 78, 9:313–14.

6 President Lowndes had mentioned the recent deaths of two of his children in his June 17 letter to Laurens. Laurens Papers, ScHi.

7 Washington's letters of these dates to Laurens and the comte d'Estaing dealt with his efforts to cooperate with the French fleet. Washington, *Writings* (Fitzpatrick), 12:173–74, 185–87, 209–14.

8 See Laurens to Washington, July 31, 1778, note 12.

9 For texts of the preceding three documents listed by Laurens, see *JCC*, 11:753–57.

10 In his August 11 letter to Lowndes, Laurens indicated that he did not finish the present letter until August 10, but what portion of it he added after the seventh has not been determined.

Henry Laurens to John Wells

7th August [1778]

I hope to send your Ephemeris two days hence by Capt. Paine. Please to apply to His Excellency the President and request him to communicate to you from my dispatches all such Articles as His Excellency shall think proper to be published, not meaning to bar a communication by any other paper which may be coming abroad earlier than Yours. This is all fair with respect to the Printer and due to the Public.

I am &c.

LB (ScHi).

Henry Laurens to Christopher Zahn

Dear Sir 7th August [1778]

I am indebted for your very obliging favor of the 13th of June, which I had intended to answer in all its parts with that respectfulness and attention which is due to it, but that is now impossible. I have not many minutes allowed for writing this. Permit me then briefly to say your Ideas and mine with respect to slavery appear to me, from your expressions, to accord.

We shall, I hope, talk this matter over before Christmass to our mutual satisfaction. In the mean time, let it suffice to repeat my thanks for all you have done for me.

Inclosed with this you will receive the latest Newspapers, and also a letter to Mr. Burnet[1] which you'l be pleased to peruse, and then seal and deliver it.

Count d'Estaing's arrival at Rhode Island, obliged the Enemy to burn the King Fisher Man of War and two of their Gallies, and to call in all their out Posts—they are now about 5000 strong in Garrison on the Island, these will soon be attacked by General Sullivan, aided by the French fleet and about 3000 French Troops. The Army of the Allies will then amount to about 8000 commanded by some of our very best officers. We must with patience wait the event.

General Washington closely hems Sir Henry Clinton within his lines upon New York Island, except such of them as come off as deserters; these are seldom less than 8 or 10 a day.

I have hopes we shall be in a state of Peace, in a few months. Neither the French nor English had declared War the 28th of May, although hostilities are committed by each party against the other as effectually as if War was actually declared.

The general voice of England from the latest Accounts appear to be for declaring these States Independent—and those from Men who had hurried the People of that much deluded Nation into ruinous measures are paving the way for reconciling the minds of the Public to an event which one year ago they affected to treat with scorn.

Adieu, Good Sir, I wish you health and all happiness and am with great Respect, Your Most Obedt. Servant.

P.S. Please to let Mr. Burnet have the perusal of the Newspapers.

LB (ScHi).

[1] See Laurens to John Burnet, July 24, 1778.

Elias Boudinot to Hannah Boudinot

My dearest Love, Princeton August 8th 1778

Can you imagine my disappointment on arriving here this Evening after a very hot & disagreeable ride, and finding that I must be deprived of what I had foolishly set my Heart on. However I am now perfectly satisfied, as I would rather have taken two such rides than that you should have exposed your Health. I had agreed to come this Jaunt with Mr. Ch. Justice Drayton—but he gave up the Scheme on Friday Evening, and lest you should have your ride for nought, I set off & came alone. The Sieur Gerard Minister plenipotentiary had engaged me to attend him to the Valley Forge, and politely put it off till Tuesday that I might see you this Evening.

I have many Thanks to address to you as well as many additional Obligations for the several Letters recd this Day by Mr Skinner & Mr Webb—How shall I repay you—it can only be by loving you with a still more ardent affection if possible. On Thursday we gave the Sieur Girard his Publick Audience. The Ceremony as follows. Our President was Seated in a Mahogany armed Chair on a Platform raisd about two feet with a large Table coverd with Green Cloth & the Secretary along side of him.

The Members were all seated round within the Bar, and a large Armed Chair in the middle opposite to the President for the Plenipo. At twelve oClock—our State Coach & Six waited on the Minister at his Quarters. He was proceeded by his own Chariott & two with his Secretaries. The Minister was attended by two Members who introduced him thro' the Crowd & seated him in the Chair. He then sent to the President (by his Secretary) the Letter from the King of France to Congress, which was opened & read aloud first in French & then in English. It was then anounced to the House by the waiting Member, that the Stranger introduced was the Minister Plenipotentiary from his most Christian Majesty, upon which the Minister arose & bowed to the President & then to the House, and the House rising returned the Compliment. The Minister then addressed the Congress, and was answered by the President—On which the Bowing again took Place and the whole Concluded.[1] A publick Dinner succeeded at which was a Band of Musick and the firing of Cannon. The whole was plain, grand & decent. The Minister was much pleased as well as the Audience.

Enclosed is a return for some Land which I wish Elisha to go & see & let me know the Value of it—any surveyor there can inform him where it lies.

You do not tell me how Mrs. Caldwell is, pray let me know it. My love to them all, I wrote to Mr. Caldwell lately.[2] The Cloathier says he will try to get him Cash whenever he comes.

It is past Midnight & I am tired so cannot be particular, only you may dispose of some of the old Money, Pennsylvania if possible. Love to my dear Susan & all Friends. Am with great Love & Affection, Your faithfull, Boudinot

RC (NjP).

1 For Gérard's speech to Congress and President Laurens' reply, see JCC, 11:753–57.

2 Not found.

Samuel Holten's Diary

[August 8, 1778]

8. Attendd. in Congress, & at 5 oClock P.M. met a joint Come. of Congress & the Executive Council of this State in search after British property in this City.[1]

MS (MDaAr).

1 A committee consisting of four delegates—Holten, William Duer, John Harvie, and William Henry Drayton—and four members of the Pennsylvania Council had been appointed to determine ownership of property left behind during the British evacuation of Philadelphia. The committee met sporadically for six months to little effect, because, as the council had warned on July 25, most of the property at issue had already been sold before the committee was appointed. See *JCC*, 11:571, 713–14, 792–93, 12:892, 904; and *Pa. Council Minutes*, 11:540. Holten subsequently noted in his diary that he attended meetings of the committee on August 10, 12, September 9 and 16.

For one of the more troublesome issues encountered by the committee, which illustrates how and why its work became so protracted, see *Pa. Archives*, 1st ser. 6:703–4, 724–25, 740–41, 754.

Henry Laurens to John Beatty

8th August [1778]

Inclosed with this you'l please to receive two Acts of Congress that which will be first mentioned I apprehended had been forwarded many days ago.

1. . . . of 15th July for securing and subsisting Prisoners of War captured by the squadron of His Most Christian Majesty, under the command of Count d'Estaing.[1]

2. . . . of 4th August for taking proper care of sick prisoners receiv'd in Exchange from the Enemy.[2]

3. . . . 30th July for engaging Seamen received in Exchange from the Enemy to serve on board public Vessels of War at Boston.[3]

I Am with great Regard, Sir, Your most Obedt. Servant

LB (DNA: PCC, item 13). Addressed: "Major John Beaty Esqr., Commissary of Prisoners."

1 See *JCC*, 11:690–91.

2 See *JCC*, 11:746–47.

3 See *JCC*, 11:730–31. Laurens also transmitted a text of this resolve to the Eastern Navy Board with a brief covering letter he wrote this day. PCC, item 13, 2:41.

Henry Laurens to William Heath

Sir, Philadelphia, 8th August 1778.

Since my last of the 29th Ulto. I have not received any of your favors nor any command from Congress respecting your Sphere except the Inclosed Act of yesterday for defraying the expence of the late abortive expedition against Rhode Island out of the Public Treasury.[1]

We have nothing New in this quarter. I have the honor to be, With great Esteem & Respect, Sir, Your most obedient humble servant, Henry Laurens, President of Congress

[*P.S.*] The sequel of your late correspondence with Maj. Gen Philips —transmitted in a private Letter will oblige me very much.[2]

RC (MHi).

[1] Laurens is referring to the unsuccessful expedition against the British in Rhode Island during the fall of 1777. See *JCC*, 11:758–61.

[2] See Laurens to Heath, July 9, 1778, note 1.

Henry Laurens to Meshech Weare

Honorable Sir, Philadelphia. 8th August 1778

Since my last of the 12th July I have been honourd with your favors of the 4th & 17th of that Month & am much obliged by the particular recitals of such Letters as Your Honor had received from me.[1]

Within this Inclosure be pleased to receive Sir an Act of Congress of yesterday Resolving that the expence attending the late abortive expedition against Rhode Island shall be a Public charge.[2]

I have the honor to be, With great regard & respect, Honorable Sir, Your most obedient, humble servant,

Henry Laurens, President of Congress.

RC (MHi).

[1] President Weare's July 4 letter to Laurens is in PCC, item 64, fols. 33–34; his July 17 letter has not been found. Laurens had long been offended by Weare's failure to acknowledge receipt of his letters.

[2] See *JCC*, 11:758–61. Laurens also transmitted copies of this resolve with brief covering letters that he wrote this day to Govs. William Greene of Rhode Island and Jonathan Trumbull, Sr., of Connecticut. Red Series, R–Ar; and PCC, item 13, 2:42–43.

James Lovell to John Lamb

Sir Augst. 8th 1778.

Mr. Hancock having left Philada. before the arrival of your Letter of July 6th, which was delivered to me from the Post Office the 4th Instant, I have sent you the Resolve passed on the 30th of April relative to the officer concerning whom you wrote to Mr. H——.[1]

I apprehend this is what the General Orders refer to. You will let me know whether it is in my Way to do you any other Pleasure than by inclosing your Letter to Mr. H—— having already mentioned to him that I should do so. Your humb Servt. James Lovell

RC (NHi).

1 John Lamb (1735–1800), colonel of the Second Continental Artillery and a former New York wine merchant, had written to John Hancock complaining that Gen. Horatio Gates had appointed Maj. Ebenezer Stevens—Lamb's junior in rank—as commander of the artillery in the northern and middle departments, superseding Lamb. Lovell enclosed an April 30, 1778, resolve that merely promoted Major Stevens to the rank of lieutenant colonel by brevet. *JCC*, 10:410. For a fuller explanation of the dispute, the satisfactory settlement for Lamb, and relevant correspondence, see Isaac Q. Leake, *Memoir of the Life and Times of John Lamb* (Albany: Joel Munsell, 1857), pp. 199–210.

Samuel Adams to James Warren

My dear sir Philada. Augt 9. 78

As Mr Dana purposes to set off early tomorrow Morning I am unwilling to omit writing a Letter to you to be delivered by him.[1] I part with him with great Reluctance, because I esteem him a very valuable Member of Congress. It is a Consolation to me that he has a Seat in the General Assembly, where I am satisfied he will be greatly instrumental in promoting the Reputation and true Interest of our Country. I sincerely regret that you have not a Seat there; nevertheless I hope you will not withdraw your Influence, which though not a Member, you may employ for the publick good. There are yet remaining some of the old Patriots who have long struggled with you against the publick Enemies. You will derive to yourself great Delight by a Recapitulation of past Scenes, in a Circle of such Friends, and by joyning with them in further Efforts, you may make your self still more serviceble to our great Cause. I know you are engagd in an important Continental Department and your Hands are full of Business; but I hope you will find time to continue and further to cultivate an Intimacy with the leading Men of that State in the Government of which, I will venture to say, you must again have a great Share.

Adieu my Friend. SA

RC (MHi).

1 Francis Dana apparently did not leave Philadelphia until after August 11, when he is recorded in the journals as voting in Congress. *JCC*, 11:774.

Josiah Bartlett to Mary Bartlett

My Dear Philadelphia August 9th 1778

This will go by Express inclosed in a letter to Colo. Langdon,[1] just to let you Know I am well: Charles Chace has had a very bad turn of the Camp Distemper; I am in hopes he is rather better, as he Could not be taken Care of where I board & the Gentlemen who board here were not willing he Should Remain Sick in the House, I have procured a place for him at a Distant part of the Town where he is taken good Care of, and I visit him Morning & Evening, his fever Continues but his Bloody flux is abated. I hope & believe he will Recover.

Mr. Wentworth is arrived here, but in so bad a State of health that he Does not attend Congress. If he Does not get better Soon I Suppose he will Set out for Home.[2] Last Thursday the minister Plenipotentiary of France had his Public audience of Congress: The Speches made by him & the answer of Congress, with the King of France's Letter of Credentials to Congress will be printed tomorrow[3] and I will try to Send them by the Post on Tuesday.

The next news of importance is Expected from Rhode Island and I Suppose you will hear what is Done there before you Receive this letter. We have nothing very material here at present. I am &c,

Josiah Bartlett

[*P.S.*] Remember my Love to all my Children.

RC (NhHi).

1 Not found.

2 In a brief August 11 letter to Mary, Bartlett added little to this assessment of the condition of Charles Chace and John Wentworth. "I have not Recd. any letters from Newhampshire by yesterdays post. Charles Chace Remains Sick," he explained, "his fever Continues. The Dysentery is abated. He begins now to have some hopes he shall see Kingstown again. Mr Wentworth is here but not able to attend Congress; by the favor of Providence I am well notwithstanding the unwholesome, Disagreable, Sultry weather we have here at this Season. Watt Collection, NhHi.

3 These documents were published in the *Pennsylvania Packet*, August 10, 1778.

Henry Laurens to William Malcom

Sir 9th Augt. [1778]

I had the honor of receiving your dispatches of the 1st Instant by the present bearer.[1] I duly presented them to Congress, but the house has been so very much engag'd with other business of great importance as to prevent your Letter and the Papers which accompanied it from coming under consideration. Mr.   the bearer intimates to me that he is not a common Messenger, therefore I judge it best to submit to his importunity to return—when I receive any Commands from Congress respecting your department, you shall be immediately advised. I beg, Sir, you will be so good as to send by express the Letters which accompany this to Connecticut, Rhode Island and Boston.

I have the Honor to be wth. great Regard Sir Your Obedt. Humble Servt.

LB (DNA: PCC, item 13). Addressed: "Colonel Willm. Malcom, West Point, by Edwd. Bryne."

1 Col. William Malcom's August 1 letter to Laurens, describing a number of deficiencies in the garrison at West Point and asking for the appointment of a garrison chaplain, is in PCC, item 78, 15:365–71. Enclosed with it were various returns relating to the manning and fortification of that post. Ibid., fols. 372–73. According to Laurens' and Secretary Thomson's endorsements on Malcom's letter—which was "Recd. & presentd. 7th. Ord[ere]d to lie"—Congress did not read it until November 2, 1778, at which time the delegates did nothing more than approve his request for the appointment of a chaplain. *JCC*, 12:1091. Malcom had been appointed commander at West Point by Washington on July 21. Washington, *Writings* (Fitzpatrick), 12:196–97.

Andrew Adams to Oliver Wolcott

Sir Philadelphia 10th August 1778

I have the pleasure to inclose this Day's paper to which I beg Leave to refer you for what News we have here. You will see the Minister has recd. his Audience and those eventual Engagements containd. in the Treaty of Alliance have now been declared by both parties to have become possitive.

This is the Day assignd. to strike a blow at Rhodeisland. Should it succeed the Event would be important but I was this Morning informd. by Mr. Barns. Dean who arived in Town last Night that Lord Howe saild. from the Hook for Rhodeisland last Thursday; that he was superior to the Count D'Estaing in point of Number tho inferior in other respects. This acct. he had from Genl Maxwell as he came along. I understood from him that the Enemy had recd.

some Reinforcements of Ships tho other very late Accts. we have had from persons who have been in New York say that no Reinforcements have arrived, how the truth is remains uncertain. That you will know before this reaches you. Cornelious Sweers who is now in Goal has since you left this City wrote a Leter to the president in which he confesses some part of the Charge against him. He says that he has altered some Accts &c: that he purchased a Number of Arms and returnd. them into the Stores at a greater price than he gave and that Col. Flowers was equally concerned with him in this and every fraud he may have been guilty off in that Department: he refers to some papers which he says will tend to evince the Matter (those papers I have not seen). In Consiquence of this Col. Flowers is now under an arrest by Order of Congress. How it will appear upon examination I cant pretend to say. A Comtee. is appointed to take Sweers's Examination upon Oath in the Matter: a Measure this I dont very well approve off; for should Col. Flowers be acquited perhaps Sweers may avail himself by haveing given his Deposition. This was objected but it was carried notwithstanding.[1]

Nothing is yet done in Regard to our Currency. The Report from the Treasury Board upon that Subject yet lies on the Table. A special Comtee. have been appointed upon the Matter of Arrainging the Treasury who are ready to report.[2] The want of that Report has been assignd. as a Reason for Delaying the other matter. I hope in Consience it will be soon taken up as I think every other Matter is comparatively [but tithing][3] Mint, Annis &c until that is done. The Cloather Generals' Department is in a most wretched Situation: as are our Commercial Affairs and indeed some others by the best Intelligence I can obtain. But of these things I need not inform you.

Mr. Sherman is appointed immediately to repair to the Army for the purpose (with others) of compleating the arraingmt. This will make it necessary for Mr. Elsworth to Come forward.

Please to make my Compliments acceptable to Mrs. Wolcot &c. I am with sincerest Esteam and Regard your Obedt huml Servt.

Andw Adams

RC (CtHi).

1 For further information on the disposition of the charges against Benjamin Flower and Cornelius Sweers, see Henry Laurens to Benedict Arnold, August 5, 1778, note.

2 For the work of reorganizing the treasury office, which resulted in allocating various functions to separate offices of comptroller, auditor, treasurer, and two chambers of accounts on September 26, see Wolcott to Jonathan Trumbull, Jr., May 18, 1778, note 3.

3 Although the manuscript is marred at this point, Adams was doubtless paraphrasing Jesus' condemnation of the Pharisees for tithing "mint, and anise, and cummin," while omitting "the weightier matters of the law," recorded in Matthew 23:23.

Samuel Chase to Edward Lloyd

[August 10, 1778]

Congress this day received Letters from Count Destaing of the 4 Inst. and from General Sullivan of the 5th—the three passages into New Port are block'd up—on the appearce. of two french Ships between Camarunt[1] Island and the main, the Enemy burnt the Kings Fisher of 20 guns and two gallies stationd there, the Enemy have 6 or 7 Frigates & a large Indiaman and 70 or 80 Transports in the Harbour, and about 5400 Men in different Redoubts about the town of Newport. General Sullivan leads 2000 Continental Troops and 3000 Militia; part of the Marquiss de la Fayette's division had arrived and about 2000 more militia were hourly expected. The French Troops & Marines about 3000 and the whole squadron were to Cooperate, and this is the day appointed for the attack. General Green is to command, yesterday Week a fire broke out said by Accident in New York & burnt 40 dwelling houses & a great number of Stores & dwellings.

Tr (Archives du ministère des affaires étrangères: Correspondance politique, États-Unis, vol. 4). Endorsed: "Extract of a Letter from Mr Chace at Congress to Coll Lloyd, sent by post to him dated 10 August and transmitted by his Excellency T. Johnson Esqr. at Anapolis to Mr Joshua Johnson at Nantes by the Ship Porpus, Cap Martin, arrived at Nantes." Reproduced as document no. 1935 in Benjamin Franklin Stevens, comp., *B.F. Stevens's Facsimiles of Manuscripts in European Archives Relating to America, 1773–1783*, 2107 facsim. in 24 portfolios (London: Photographed and printed by Malby & Sons, 1889–95); and enclosed in Joshua Johnson's October 1, 1778, letter to Vergennes, Stevens' no. 1968.

1 Probably the transcriber's misreading of the word "Conanicut," which appears in several contemporary accounts.

Samuel Holten's Diary

[August 10, 1778]

10. Attendd. in Congress, & met the joint Come. at 4 o'Clock, Sit 'till night.[1]

MS (MDaAr).

1 That is, the joint committee of Congress and the Pennsylvania Council on British property in Philadelphia. See Holten's Diary, August 8, 1778, note.

Henry Laurens to Thomas Nelson

Sir 10th Augt. [1778]

I have the honor of presenting to you within the present inclosure a Resolve of Congress of the 8th Instant recommending for reasons intimated in that Act the return of the Volunteer cavalry lately from Virginia under Your command, and, expressing the thanks of Congress to yourself Sir, and to the rest of the Officers and Gentlemen of that Corps for their brave, generous, and patriotic efforts.[1]

I feel a very sensible pleasure, Sir, in the discharge of this public duty, and a peculiar satisfaction in the opportunity of subscribing to a Gentleman of your distinguished Character in these States. The high Respect and Esteem with which I have the honor of being, Sir, Your Most Obedient & Most Hbl. Servant

LB (DNA: PCC, item 13). Addressed: "General Nelson, Philadelphia, by M[oses] Y[oung]."

[1] Congress decided that as a result of the British withdrawal to New York there was no need for Nelson's volunteer cavalry corps to join Washington's army. *JCC*, 11:766. The "Resolve . . . of the 8th Instant" and an August 11 letter of thanks from Nelson were printed by order of Congress in the August 15 issue of the *Pennsylvania Packet*. *JCC*, 11:777.

Henry Laurens to Baron Steuben

Dear Baron. Chestnut Street, 10 Augt. 1778.

You have done me the honor of intimating more than once your sentiments respecting certain necessary attentions to a River defence. Will you be so good my Dear Baron, when you can spare half an hour for this purpose to communicate your Ideas, including if you please your advice, in writing to Your much obliged & Obedient humble Servant,[1]

Henry Laurens.
Not written as President of Congress.

[*P.S.*] Can you without inconvenience stop at my House one minute to morrow Morning on your way to that of the Minister Plenipotentiary?

RC (NHi).

[1] Instead of formulating a detailed plan for the defense of the Delaware, as Laurens requested, Steuben, who was in Philadelphia at this time, wrote the president a brief letter on August 27 urging him to submit this important issue to Congress. Laurens Papers, ScHi.

Richard Henry Lee to Thomas Jefferson

Dear Sir,

Philadelphia 10th Augt. 1778

I agree entirely with you concerning the importance of the confederation, and have never failed to press it. Ten States have ratified—Jersey, Delaware, and Maryland have not, and one of them, Maryland, has adjourned until November, so that the new Congress under the Confederation cannot meet this year at the time proposed by the Confederacy. The inclosed paper contains all the news we have, except that it is well reported that Lord Howe being reenforced by 4 Ships of the Line sailed from N. York on Thursday last with his whole force to Attack the French Squadron now at Rhode Island. Howe has a greater number of Ships, but Count D'Esteing has heavier Metal. The attack by Sea and Land was to be made this day on the enemy at R. Island, where they have 5500 men strongly posted and 3 or 4 frigates. Our force will be about 14000 men besides the Squadron. Success seems certain if Ld. Howe does not get up in time to prevent it. The Count D'Esteing is an Officer of approved merit, and his Ships very strong in every respect, so that I think he will check the British insolence on the Sea as we have already done on the land. No war in Europe on the 10th of June, nor do I believe G. Britain means to resent the proceedings of France. It seems to be a contest between the two Nations which shall be last in declaring War. Some advantages to accrue from Treaties is the cause of this. To us it matters little, since we so powerfully experience the aid of France. For it is certain this Squadron is to Act with and for us so long as the enemy by continuing here renders it necessary. There is great probability that the Emperor of Germany and the King of Prussia will fall out about the Bavarian dominions. Theirs will be a battle of Giants, each party having 300,000 men, the best disciplined Troops in the world. France, I fancy, has taken measures to avoid engaging in this quarrel, that her whole force may be employed against England.

The design against Detroit is abandoned for the present, and a force will be sent into the Indian Country to chastise their late insolences.[1] I heartily wish that the wisdom of our Country may be early next Session employed to regulate our finance, restore public credit, determine about our back lands, and if possible get rid of our public Commerce. If it succeeds with us, I believe it will be the first instance that has ever happened of the kind. But many there are of injury derived from such Trade. Whilst necessity impelled, it was unavoidable, but now that private Commerce will furnish abundance of all things, I incline to think our interest will consist in withdrawing from governmental Trade. Remember me to Mr. Mazzie. I am yours dear Sir very sincerely, Richard Henry Lee[2]

RC (DLC).

1 See Henry Laurens to Patrick Henry, July 24, 1778, note 3.

2 On August 17 Lee also wrote a brief letter to "Reverend Bartholemew Booth, To the care of Richard Potts Esquire at Frederick Town in Maryland," inquiring on what terms Booth would consent to undertake the education of his two nephews, recently placed in his charge because of the death of his brother Thomas Lee. Gift Collection, MdAA.

James Lovell to William Whipple

Dear Sir August 10th 1778.

Your favor of July 24th is now before me, but the banter of it is not rightly founded, for the superscription told where I was on the 6th of July as plainly as you may know by the present where I am; and I assure you I am not now under the fatigue of a frolic, though by the enclosed Advertiser you may see we have been at it again.

Our letters from the Count d'Estaing and General Sullivan are quite encouraging; but a report prevails that Lord Howe being reinforced is in pursuit of the French Squadron. I hope however that the latter will be well in the harbor of Newport before the former reaches the Island. I do not wish to have any engagement without a considerable superiority on the side of our Allies.

The encouragement which is given by the Count d'Estaing to Privateers, I should think was sufficient to make them ply in the track of his fleet. You did not appear, by your letter, to know what he had declared, which is, that prizes taken in sight of his squadron shall belong entirely to the captors.[1] I am quite chagrined that we have not a force of ships ready to join the Count immediately—4 or 5 days are of immense importance, nay the fate of Rhode Island may depend upon 24 hour's preparation on our part. The French fleet begins to grow sickly, to want the refreshment of an encampment for a few weeks. I notice your remarks upon the Navy Board but you know times and seasons are to be watched here and I do not find that your ideas would thrive at this period, if I was to strive to cultivate them. I will not miss any right occasion I assure you. Mr D has had no formal conversation with C——ss[2] but I expect something of the kind soon—but it is a difficult matter to communicate any thing to you on that head without being minute and exposing myself to disagreeable chances of the fate of my letters. The French have not a proper naval force in the West Indies to enable the General of Martinique to begin operations in that quarter agreeable to instructions sent to him from Europe. I suppose you would choose to reduce Halifax before you undertake the English West India Islands.

Good night, Dear Sir, J.L.

Tr (DLC).

[1] See *JCC,* 11:691.

[2] Lovell's reference to Silas Deane's "connection" with Congress was in anticipation of the hearing that actually began on August 15. *JCC,* 11:799.

Roger Sherman to Jonathan Trumbull, Sr.

Sir Philadelphia Augst. 10th. 1778.

I hope Your Excellency will not impute my omitting to write so long a time to neglect of duty—the true reason was I have had nothing important to write. We have no late account from foreign parts, nor has anything remarkable occurred here. Congress has been employed about the ordinary affairs of the Continent. The Minister Plenipotentiary from the Court of France had a public audience last Thursday—the manner of it is contained in the enclosed paper. The operations of War being at the Eastward Your Excellency has earlier intelligence of them than we have here—our affairs wear a prosperous aspect except the currency—I expected it would have been attended to by Congress long before now—but a multiplicity of other affairs have prevented it. I am appointed one of a Committee to repair (to?)[1] the Camp, and assist in the new arrangement of the army.[2]

The Indians and more barbarous Tories have desolated our Settlements at Westmoreland. Congress sent two Regiments of Continental troops with some Militia to repel the enemy. The account given in a Poughkeepsie paper is said to be much beyond the truth. Expect to go the Army this week, and from thence intend to go home before I return to this place.

I heartily condole with Your Excellency (on?) the death of your Son the late Commissary General. His great public services deserve a grateful remembrance.[3]

I am with great Esteem, Your Excellency's Obedient humble Servant.

Roger Sherman.

Tr (DLC).

[1] Thus in Tr.

[2] Sherman and John Banister were added to the Committee of Arrangement this day. *JCC,* 11:769.

[3] Joseph Trumbull, former commissary general of the Continental Army, had died on July 23 after a long illness. *DAB.*

Andrew Adams to Jonathan Trumbull, Sr.

Sir, (private) Philadelphia 11th. Augt 1778

The unexpected Death of the late amiable and I think much injured Commissary Genl. (on which I do most sincerely condole your

Excellency) renders it at present impracticable to have any thing done on the Subject of his Accounts; tis my Oppinion something would have been done notwithstand[ing] a late Resolution of Congress:[1] some Gentlemen I know felt that Matter most Sensably: and I beleave Congress themselves (that is a Majority) would have been willing to reconsider that Matter.

I see no prospect of haveing any thing done in favr. of Col. Derricks. Mr Hancock on whom he seamd. to have some dependance left Congress soon after my arival.[2] I had therefore no Oppertunity of consulting him upon the Subject but the Objections appear to me at present insurmountable, tis said he went voluntarily out of the Line into the Staff; that the Conduct of that Department was such as not only to Occation great Uneasiness but even endanger the Existance of the Army in Consiquence of which a Court of Inquiry has been ordered by Congress, and tho no particular Objection is made to him: yet the Inquiry extends not only to Genl. Miflin but to the whole Department: it would be altogether improper to advance any Gentlemen from thence while the Inquiry is pending. And besides we have at present many supernumerary Officers in the Line; and a Comtee. Of Arraingment appointed to reduce the Number so that it becomes impossible to introduce any new Officers without turning out some of our own against whom there is not the least Objection: I am very sorry for the particular Situation of Col Derricks: but I know of no other Way at present for his Employ in the Army unless he can be again introduced into the Staff By an Application to Genl. Green who is at the head of the Quartermaster's Department. The Commissary Genl. of Military Stores & his first Deputy are now under an Arrest by Order of Congress for fraud and Mal-Conduct in the Execution of that Office. The Deputy has confest a part of the Charge and accuses Colo. Flowers the Comisy. Genl. of being concerned with him. The Clothier Genls. Department is in a most wretched Situation as is also some other Branches of our Affairs: many things are conducted very different from what I could wish: which it is improper to mention in a Letter. The Deplorable Situation of our Currency I have expected would come under Consideration ever since I have been here, but as yet Nothing has been done. I think every Regulation in vain so long as that is neglected. There is a prospect of its being taken up soon: but I hardly know what to depend upon as to the Course of Business.

We have no News more than what is containd in the papers or comes from the Eastward.

I am with highest Esteam your Excellencys most Obedt. & very huml Servt. Andw Adams.

RC (Ct).

1 Adams is undoubtedly referring to Congress' May 19, 1778, resolve "that Mr.

Joseph Trumbull, late commissary general, be informed of the disposition of Congress not to grant money to such persons as, having been officers of the United States, are now out of office, until they shall have accounted for the public money which shall have been previously advanced to them respectively." *JCC*, 11:509. Trumbull's accounts remained unsettled for more that four years.

2 For an earlier request by Jacob Gerhard Diriks for advancement in the Continental Army, see Henry Laurens to Washington, May 9, 1778, note. Although the precise nature of Trumbull's interest in Diriks at this time is not known, the latter was one of the subjects of Trumbull's October 16, 1778, letter to President Laurens. In that communication Trumbull endorsed a plan of Gosuinus Erkelens for obtaining an American loan in the Netherlands of £2 million, a plan in which Diriks, who was identified as a cousin of baron Joan Derk van der Capellen, would serve as Erkelens' personal emissary. Congress subsequently decided to reject Erkelens' offer, but Diriks was nevertheless granted permission to return to the Netherlands and simultaneously promoted to the rank of lieutenant colonel by brevet. See *JCC*, 11:507, 509, 12:1106, 1246–47; Trumbull to Laurens, October 16, and Erkelens to Laurens, October 18, 1778, in PCC, item 66, fols. 422–29. For evidence that Diriks subsequently played a part in the efforts of his friend C. W. F. Dumas, Congress' agent in Amsterdam, to secure a Dutch loan for the United States, see Trumbull, *Papers* (MHS Colls.), 2:468–71. For discussion of his pro-American activities—including an explanation of his decision to change his family name Dircks to Diriks when he volunteered for a Continental commission—see Jan Willem Schulte Nordholt, *The Dutch Republic and American Independence*, trans. H. H. Rowen (Chapel Hill: University of North Carolina Press, 1982), pp. 27, 29, 33.

Samuel Adams to Samuel P. Savage

My dear Friend   Philade, Augt 11 –78

I had yesterday the pleasure of receiving your Favor by the Post covering the News Papers and a Letter as you emphatically express it "from one of my closest Friends," for all which I thank you most heartily.

You ask me what occasiond the very sudden Return of Mr H. I answer in his own Words to me "His own want of Health & the dangerous Illness of his Lady"—You say he arrivd quite unexpected—You must surely be mistaken, for he publickly said he had Leave of Absense from his Constituents. You add, various are the Conjectures of the true Cause. It is the Lot of a great Man, to have every Movement he makes critically scannd, and oftentimes the strangest Constructions are put upon those Parts of his Conduct which are the most easily explaind. You have so many Twistings in your Typography, and my Eyes are grown so dim with Age, that I cannot well discern whether you inform me that his Friends say the *Air* or the *Airs* of Philadelphia *doth* not suit him,[1] tho I must conclude the former from your usual Correctness in grammar, for there would be an evident false Concord in admitting the Latter. Pray let me know whether the News papers did not do him Injustice in announcing that he made his Entrance into Boston upon Sunday. I should think so, because a well bred Man will carefully avoid counter acting the *vulgar Prejudices* & injuring the Feelings of the People where he may happen to be.

I congratulate you on the present happy Appearance of our publick Affairs & heartily joyn with you in praying that Heaven may still prosper them.

I shall take it as a favor if you will deliver the inclosd Manuscript without suffering a Copy to be taken, to Mrs. A. I told her I should send it to her as being not an unfit Subject of female Inspection & Criticism. I am, your affectionate, A

RC (MHi).

1 In his July 29 letter to Adams, Savage had made the following inquiry concerning John Hancock: "Pray my Friend what occasioned the very sudden Return of Mr. H. He arrivd quite unexpected. Various are the Conjectures for the true Cause; his Friends say the Airs of Philadelphia doth not sute him." Samuel Adams Papers, NN.

Samuel Adams to Peter Thacher

My Dear Sir[1] Philad Augt 11 –78

I am quite ashamd that I have not yet acknowledgd the two letters which I have had the Pleasure of receiving from you since I left Boston; you will excuse me when I tell you, I have many Letters, which are daily accumulating, unanswerd, and very little Leisure. This by the Way, must convince you how unfit a Person I am even if I were otherwise qualified, to undertake the important Task you require of me in your last.[2] While I am giving you the true Reason of my Silence, I hope it will not prevent your writing to me by every opportunity. Herein you will lay me under great obligations.

By the late Publications, you have seen, and doubtless have made your own Comments on the epistolary Correspondence between the British Commissioners & Congress. The short Resolution on their last Letter, has put an end to it. Last Week the Minister from France had an Audience in Congress. The Manner of conducting this Ceremony, together with a Letter from his most Christian Majesty and the Speeches of the Minister and the President are publishd in the inclosd News Paper. I have had several opportunitys of seeing him at his own House, and a few days ago, he made a Visit to the Delegates of the Massachusetts who live together. He is easy and polite in his Manners and converses freely without much Ceremony.[3]

Nothing can equal the barefaced Falshood of the Quakers & Tories in this City, unless perhaps their Folly, in giving out that M. Gerard does not come in the Character of a publick Minister, but only to obtain Pay for the Stores we have receivd from that Country. These Quakers are in general a sly artful People, not altogether destitute, as I conceive, of worldly Views in their religious Profession. They carefully educate their Children in their own contracted Opinions and Manners, and I dare say they have in their Heads as perfect a System of Uniformity of Worship in their Way, and are busily employd about spiritual Domination as ever Laud himself was, but having upon professed Principle renouncd the Use of the carnal Weapon, they cannot consistently practice the too common Method made Use of in former times, of dragooning Men into sound Beliefe. One might submit to their own inward Feelings, whether they do not now & then secretly wish for fire from Heaven in support of their Cause, in order to bring them upon a footing with those whose *Consciences dictate* the kindling fires on Earth for the pious Purpose of convincing Gainsayers, and who keep the Sword in their Hands to enforce it. He who in the Spirit of the Apostle professes to wish Peace to all those who love the Lord Jesus Christ in Sincerity, must discover an unmortified Pride & a Want of Christian Charity to destroy the peace of others who profess to have that sincere Affection to the Common Master, because they differ from him in Matters of mere opinion—But the Post is just going. I must therefore conclude with assuring you that I am affectionately, Yours,

FC (NN). In the hand of Samuel Adams.

1 Peter Thacher (1752–1802), a Malden, Mass., minister, who had delivered several fiery patriotic sermons on public occasions and later served as a delegate to the 1780 Massachusetts constitutional convention. "Memoirs of Rev. Dr. Thacher," Massachusetts Historical Society, *Collections*, 1st ser. vol. 8 (1802): 277–84.

2 Thacher's "last" letter to Adams has not been found; only his May 19 letter to Adams is in the Samuel Adams Papers, NN.

3 At this point Adams wrote and then crossed out the following sentences: "Under an Apprehension that our connection with France might lead us to partake in her wars, which might be grounded on Views of Ambition and Conquest, I took occasion to hint to him that the sole object of America was independence. He frankly said that whenever Great Britain should acknowledge our Independence, there would be an End of Dispute between her and us, and it would not be the Inclination as it was not the Interest of France to continue the War."

The "apprehension" Adams voiced here was also shared by Richard Henry Lee, who preserved among his papers the following notes on Gérard's response to this issue. Lee doubtless wrote these at about this same time, after availing himself of an opportunity for questioning the French Minister on possible consequences of the Franco-American treaties. The notes appear on the verso of a sheet on which Lee had outlined the thirteen articles of the treaty of alliance.

"That the Treaty of Alliance has not effect until War or rupture, which are made Synonimous. Therefore no Guarantee, nor obligation to carry on the war. The former more desirable than the latter ineligible. Because the Object of War clearly pointed out in 2d. 3d. & 8 Articles, which being obtained, the war in reason ceases.

"All words of Monsr. Gerard." Lee Family Papers, ViU.

John Banister to St. George Tucker

Dear Tucker Philadelphia August 11th. 1778

Your letter upon the planetary System was ingenious, and possessed *eminently* what is not generally reckoned a Perfection *on writing, Obscurity*. Yet so much was I interested in the Subject that the Obscure became clear, & all was unfolded to my mental eye. It is a strange Planet whose Influence some People live under. It attracts but is not attracted. I wish in your deep Researches & persevereing attention you could find out a Remedy for this Phenomenon.

You are versed in the doctrine of mutual attraction, but in the instance here alluded to I am & I fear must remain a Stranger to this vivifying Principle. I wish on a certain occasion a certain Luminary could add to the splendor that I know will brighten the Banks of the old Appomattox. I am determined to be there. How much are you to be envied! In a fair way to possess the very object your Soul holds the most dear. Can any Prospect of the future more elevate the Mind? I do not expect to see you under the etherial Seale of spirits this Seven years. Tomorrow I go to Camp, at the White Plains, on business delegated by Congress.[1] This will be a pleasing Jaunt after a long confinement in this hot Place; And yet I really do not dislike Philadelphia. There is such a variety of Company especially of the fair "Sex" that it is with all its inconveniences supportable. It may be indured, But I long more than ever Swiss did to revisit my native Land; and rejoin my amiable Connections. What astonishing Events have crouded together in our favour within a few Weeks.

In the Spring every department of the Army was distressed, our Success doubtful, the Enemy near us with a powerful & well appointed Army.

Our's small, naked, unprovided, in no good expectation that things would be better. The alliance with France not expected, the Continental Money Daily Sinking in value from a bad opinion generally entertained of the Event, and other Causes naturally producing that Effect.

The Army liable to attack & yet incapable of Motion for the want of Waggons, Horses, &c. and thro a total derangement in the Q. Masters Department. In this extremity this Office was filled by a new appointment, & the business entrusted to other Hands.

The Army which had been in iminent danger several times of starving was now by the appointment of a new Commissary put into a way of being supplied. These measures Taken the Month of April elapsed, & May ushered in the joyful account of the treaty of alliance with France.

This gave Life & animation to every thing. The Army recruited.

Supplies became certain instead of being precarious. Discipline began to prevail, & the Month of May had not expired before the attack of our Army in its Camp would have been madness, tho but a few Weeks before such an attempt might have been made with a full assurance of Success. But Providence saved us here again. I think we should be grateful, for I am clear in his interposition. How do you like the doctrine my Friend?

The next favourable Event was the Enemy's determination to evacuate this City. The good Effect of this Resolution expanded itself 'thro all Order of Men & Produced an amazing change in the Minds of the wavering & undetermined.

To this succeeded our Victory at Monmouth, & then the arrival of the Fleet under the command of the Count D'Estaing.

This force is now employed against Rhode Island in conjunction with a formidable Body of Land Forces. If this attempt proves Successful I think the Remainder of the Conflict will be easy to us. Mr. Bolling waits for this. Adieu therefore yr. affect.

J Banister

[*P.S.*] If you see my fair[2] remember to tell her softly that I wish her every happiness.

RC (ViW).

[1] Although Banister states that he expected to set out for Washington's headquarters on August 12, having been appointed to the Committee of Arrangement on the 10th, he probably did not leave Philadelphia until the weekend, for he is recorded in the journals as having cast his vote on a number of issues on Saturday, August 15. *JCC*, 11:769, 794–800.

[2] Probably Anne Blair, regarding whom see Banister to Tucker, April 23, 1778, note 1.

Samuel Chase to Thomas Johnson

Dear Sir. Philada. Augst. 11. 1778.

Your Letter to Congress was delivered, and is referred to the Marine Committee.[1] It will be difficult & a Work of Time to procure the different Resolves of Congress relative to Captures. I have seen only one of the Marine Board, The only Instance he knows of is, that Capt. Hawker says he struck to the united States. As to the Jurisdiction, it unquestionably belongs to our Court of admiralty.[2] I am almost sure the Effects are a prize to the Individuals. There is a Resolve on this Subject, bound in a Pamphlet, which is at my House. Jerry can give it to you. I will attend to the other Parts of your Letter. For News I beg Leave to refer You to my Letter of yesterday to Colo. Lloyd.

I much obliged by your kind & friendly Enquiry after my Health. I have been very unwell, but am not quite recovered. I wish you every Happiness & am, Your Friend, S Chase

RC (MdAA).

1 The Maryland Council's August 5 letters to Congress and to the Maryland delegates concerning Richard Harrison's sale of the Maryland sloop *Molly* to Congress' agent in Martinique, William Bingham, which the state protested as an unauthorized sale, are in *Md. Archives*, 21:176–77. The letter to Congress was referred to the Marine Committee on August 10. *JCC*, 11:768–69. See also George Plater to Thomas Johnson, August 18, 1778.

2 A reference to the capture of H.M. Frigate *Mermaid* when it ran aground on the Maryland coast after an encounter with the comte d'Estaing's fleet. Maryland apparently retained jurisdiction in this case. For references to the disposition of Capt. James Hawker and his crew as prisoners of war, see *JCC*, 11:743, 747, 840, 12:889, 916, 964, 1114; and *Md. Archives*, 21:162, 172, 176, 178.

William Henry Drayton's Notes for a Speech in Congress

[August 11, 1778][1]

I yesterday had the honor to make an important motion which I had during many days waited for an opportunity of introducing. To my mortification it was postponed—& I regard the decision as fatal to it. Thus am I reduced to the necessity of hurrying forward another motion which I prepared as a consequence of the first. The importance of the subject & rapid progress of time will not allow me to delay it: in my humble opinion, the subject has already been too long passed over in silence. I beg leave to read the motion & having done so, I will make a very few observations to shew that propriety which in my humble opinion will have already appeared self evident.

Sir, it cannot be doubted but that Gover. Johnstone in the particulars of his conduct stated in the motion, has made a plain, direct & base attempt to corrupt this honourable body—to induce us to betray that inestimable charge which the Free & virtuous Citizens of America have hardened with their blood & committed to our care. Nor can it be doubted but that Congress do most sensibly feel the attack upon their integrity. Their honor calls upon them to resent it. I trust it is their inclination to do so, & in the most pointed manner. Censure Governor Johnstones conduct in the strongest terms—hold him up to present age & the latest posterity as an object of universal detestation—cut off all communication with a person who has dared to seduce you; a Virgin so attacked must do this or she will be thought to hesitate, & in danger of being lost—cut off also all communication with a company of Men, who act in concert, who come

New York August 26th 1778—

George Johnstone One of the Commissioners appointed by His Majesty to carry into Execution the gracious Purposes of his Majesty and his Parliament for quieting the disorders now Subsisting in North America and for maintaining the People of these Provinces in the clear and perfect enjoyment of their Liberties and Rights having seen a declaration of the American Congress signed by Henry Laurens their President dated 11th of August to which for certain assumed reasons therein specified is Subjoined the following Resolution.—

"That it is incompatible with the Honor of Congress to hold any manner of Correspondence or intercourse with the said George Johnstone Esquire especially to Negotiate with him upon Affairs in which the cause of Liberty and Virtue is interested."—

The said George Johnstone for himself says That he is far from considering the said Resolution of the Congress as offensive to him That he rather receives it as a

mark

George Johnstone's Declaration

from the same school of venality—who come to transact the same business—and among whom is one who vainly has stepped forth & attempted to corrupt you in order to procure their common object. Your injured honor, your interest demand such a conduct on your part—your constituents require it—the world expect it.

As to the point of honor I have said enough. With regard to the point of interest, I say the avowed purpose of sending out these Commissioners was to unite your enemies—to divide your friends. You have now a fair opportunity to turn the tables upon those who would destroy you—cut off all communication with the Commissioners because of their recent conduct, & you cover your enemies with infamy, divide them & unite your friends. Demonstrate to the People of Britain by a light as the meridian glare, that their affairs are conducted by Men dead to a sense of virtue, & that they plundered for the purpose of corruption. By such a light let our own people determine what conduct they ought to pursue. You have long experienced their judgment—you know you can rely upon it.

MS (PPL). In the hand of William Henry Drayton.

1 Internal evidence clearly indicates that Drayton delivered these remarks in Congress in support of a motion, which the delegates approved this day in the form of a lengthy "Declaration," stating that Congress deemed it incompatible with its honor to have any further dealings with Gov. George Johnstone because of his efforts to bribe and corrupt certain delegates. See *JCC*, 11:770–73. Moreover, Henry Laurens noted on August 7 that Drayton had had "a Resolve for this purpose . . . in his pocket more than a fortnight"; and nine days later he testified that the "Declaration" on Johnstone was "the Paper Mr. Drayton has kept so long in his Pocket and which I had so often solicited should be brought forward." See Laurens to Rawlins Lowndes, August 7 and 16, 1778. The "important motion" that "was postponed" on the 10th may have been a proposal that Congress refuse to treat with any member of the Carlisle commission in consequence of Johnstone's devious tactics, a course of action which, as these men unmistakably reveal, Drayton strongly favored. If this conjecture is correct, then perhaps Drayton was the delegate who offered the motion for banning further congressional negotiations with any of the British commissioners that Congress rejected this day after having first approved his "Declaration" concerning Johnstone. See *JCC*, 11:773–74. Since Congress had been aware at least as early as July 9 of Johnstone's objectionable efforts to entice the support of certain delegates, it is not clear why Drayton waited so long to introduce his motion to censure the British commissioner.

Titus Hosmer to Oliver Ellsworth

Dear sir Philadelphia Augt 11. 1778

I have your agreable favour of the 19th Ulto., & will write you a long Answer as soon as leisure will admit, but have Time now only to make you one Request—it is this that you would join us and take your Seat in Congress as soon as You can.

Mr. Sherman leaves us next day after tomorrow to go to the Army, & Home, I fear he will be detained two Months. Mr. Adams proposes to go home the middle of Next Month when I shall be alone. I write by desire of both those Gentlemen and wish your Answer & that it may be favourable to my wishes for I cannot be contented to be left here alone.[1]

Believe me, tho in Haste, your Affectionate Friend & humble servant,

Titus Hosmer

RC (CtY).

[1] Ellsworth assumed his seat in Congress on October 8. *JCC*, 12:988.

Titus Hosmer to Jonathan Trumbull, Sr.

Sir

Philadelphia Augst. 11th. 1778

Since my arrival at Congress nothing of a public nature has presented to furnish the subject of a letter that your Excellency would not be apprized of by the public papers more fully & at large than you could in a private letter. The removal of Congress from Yorktown, & the reception of the French Minister have engrossed a great part of our time, the remainder has been spent principally in the common routine of business, which arises daily, and the very necessary to be done, could not deserve Your Excellency's attention in the recital. The extreme heat of the season which threw me into a slight fever on the road confined me several days & having kept me in a feverish habit ever since, hath obliged me to be cautious of writing, or applying to any business or exercise tending to increase it.

Congress are very industrious, yet many affairs of great importance are crowded out & postponed by an inevitable attention to events & business constantly arising; & although I have nothing of consequence to inform you of which they have done I have many things I can mention which they have not done—they have not taken into consideration the state of our paper currency—nor devised any means to stop the headlong current of depreciation. They have not settled their accts. with the Army—the Commissary Genls., the Quarter Master Genls., the Clothier Genl., the Commercial Committee, or any other large Department. They have not settled any mode by & in which they can call their great servants authoritatively to account for the expenditure of public monies—they have not constituted and empowered a Board of Treasury—nor a Marine Board—though each seems to be generally allowed to be necessary to release the attendance of members of Congress, & give them leisure to attend to more general & necessary business which can be done only in Congress or by its Members. All these matters are in prospect and are to be attended to as soon, and as fast as other business will admit; yet I fear much time will elapse before they are brought to a conclusion. I beg leave to condole with Your Excellency in the loss you have sustained in your amiable son, the late Commissary General. I am sensible your own mind must have suggested every argument and consolation which reason or religion can furnish yet permitt me to express my tender concern, and wish you may be supported under so severe a trial, and that your important loss, may be compensated by spiritual blessings.

I have made it my business since I was here to endeavour to sap the foundation, and overturn that Resolution which forbids issuing money to any person out of office, until his accounts are settled, which appears to me in many cases very unreasonable and had good hopes soon to accomplish it, with the assistance of sundry gentlemen of more experience and weight than I could prevent to, but am now at a loss how to apply it to the advantage of the late Commissary General's accounts, if effected, or what method will be adopted for their settlement; but shall be always happy to contribute all in my power to procure justice to be done to the family and heirs of one, for whom I had so great an esteem and friendship; whom I always believed to possess strict integrity, & to have served his Country with honor and fidelity and great success.

Will Your Excellency be pleased to remember me to Col. Williams and Mr Wales, to whom I intended to have wrote by this post, but the time will fail me and to the other Gentlemen of your Council and permit me to subscribe myself, Your Excellency's most respectful most obedient and most hble Servant, Titus Hosmer

Tr (DLC).

Henry Laurens to Rawlins Lowndes

Dear Sir 11th August [1778]

I had the honor of writing to your Excellency under the 5th and 7th by a Messenger from Don Juan de Mirallis, who had very politely permitted me to detain him as long as I should think proper —my public engagements the week last past had rendered it impossible for me to devote much time to private affairs, my letter was therefore performed piecemeal and not finish'd till the 10th.

My present Address will be deliver'd by Captain Pyne, late of the Comet State vessel of War, or, by lieutenant Martin of our regiment, these Gentlemen will in company begin their journey for South Carolina some time today. They arrived here from imprisonment by the Enemy, and were destitute of Money and apparel; they apply'd to me for aid, and with the concurrence of all my present Colleagues, I supply'd out of the fund belonging to South

Carolina, Captain Pyne 1000 Dollars, Lieutenant Martin 940 Dollars, for which sums your Excellency will find his several acknowledgements within this cover.

In my last letter I suggested some apprehensions of receiving shortly a ratification of the Convention of Saratoga. Last night a paper pretended to be a Ratification signed by four of the British Commissioners and usher'd by a Letter of the 7th from Mr. Ferguson their Secretary was sent to me by General Maxwell, the General had received it as he writes by a Flag which had come by an indirect and prohibited road.[1] The whole affair it is to be presumed, is calculated for insulting Congress by a retort on their late resolution that "no Answer be given to the Commissioners letter of the 11th" published by Charles Thomson, Secretary of Congress.[2] In this view it appears trifling with serious matters, admitting their character to come within that description—and in what other light can it be viewed—the Commissioners knew that Congress had resolved that the embarkation of the troops of the Convention should be suspended "till a distinct and explicit Ratification of the Convention of Saratoga shall be properly notified by the Court of Great Britain to Congress." And those gentlemen have ground for believing that Congress will not hastily depart from important Resolutions. Possibly they may now pretend that their powers from their Court are tantamount—admitting this they ought to have been "distinct and explicit."

What the determination of Congress will be after I shall have presented this paper is uncertain, in the mean time my fears are, that the motion and Resolve which I have so anxiously wish'd will not be effected, or, not with that grace and perspicuity which would have been produced by a deliberate consideration antecedally to the receipt of this outrer illegitimate Remonstrance & requisite. Yesterday I again repeated to the Chief Justice, "you will by this unaccountable procrastination slip an opportunity of doing justice and honor to your Country."

Among other papers which will accompany this Your Excellency Will receive Copy of the Remonstrance and the Secretary's letter; these Papers contain nothing like a distinct explicit Ratification properly notified by the Court of Great Britain to Congress, and therefore I estimate the correspondence and the mode, a calculated Insult; and were I to direct, probably it is best I should not, I wou'd immediately return the whole, accompanied by a few proper lines from Charles Thomson to Adam Ferguson—Nothing has happen'd during the present Contest so embarrassing to the Court of Great Britain as the Resolve of Congress on the suspension.[3] A conformity with the terms will amount to an acknowledgment of our capacity to treat as a Nation—any thing below this will be to retain her claim upon us as Subjects in Rebellion, with whom faith is not to be held but for the benefit of the Sovereign, as in the exchange of Prisoners; and even in that communication there have been many attempts on the part of our Enemy to exercise arbitrary and cruel impositions. Your Excellency will recollect a recent instance which occasioned the seperation of Commissioners at Germantown who had met for establishing a Cartel.[4]

If the Court shall, from necessity, find her interest in ratifying the Convention in the terms prescribed by Congress, it will then be for us to consider the Articles and to enquire whether the whole have been strictly comply'd with by the contracting powers, and thus, according to strict justice and sound Policy, which are inseperable the work will be to begin.

Admitting these Ideas to be just 'tis not to be doubted, that the Court of Great Britain perceives the dilemma to which she is reduced by a few deeply designing words of her Marionnette, Lieutenant General Burgoyne, who has acknowledged in Parliament that he penned every syllable of his infamous Proclamation and, at the same time declared he had no intention to carry the severe threats contained in it, into execution[5]—she must consequently view the troops of Saratoga as prisoners of War, unless she will engage in a tacit concession of our Independence, and for which, she will be in the judgement of all her European Neighbours—no wonder therefore, that in her entangled situation her Ministers are persevering in practices of ambi-dexterity—and as little that I continue anxiously wishing for the attestations of Captain Senff.[6]

LB (ScHi).

1 Gen. William Maxwell's August 8 letter to Laurens is in PCC, item 57, fol. 328. Enclosed with it were an August 7 remonstrance from the Carlisle commissioners and a covering letter of the same date from Adam Ferguson, the commissioners' secretary. Ibid., fols. 321–26. In this remonstrance, which was read in Congress on August 12, the commissioners offered to ratify the Saratoga Convention and demanded in consequence that the Convention Army be allowed to return to England. Although the delegates initially ignored this unwelcome demarche, they were prompted by criticism of their policy on this issue in an August 26 "Declaration" by George Johnstone to reaffirm on September 4 that they would not agree to the release of these troops unless the Saratoga Convention was explicitly ratified by "the court of Great Britain." *JCC*, 11:776, 12:876–78, 880–83. See also Laurens to William Heath, December 27, 1777, note 1.

2 See *JCC*, 11:701–2.

3 See *JCC*, 10:29–35.

4 Laurens is referring to Washington's unsuccessful effort in the spring of 1778 to negotiate a prisoner cartel with Gen. William Howe. See Laurens to James Duane, April 20, 1778, note 3.

5 For Gen. John Burgoyne's May 26 speech to the House of Commons, in the course of which he justified his June 20, 1777, proclamation threatening Americans with Indian warfare, see *Parliamentary History*, 19:1176–96.

6 For the continuation of this letter, see Laurens to Lowndes, August 16, 1778.

Henry Marchant to the Rhode Island Assembly

Gentn: Philadelphia Augt. 11th. 1778.

Last Thursday, Congress gave publick Audience to Monsr. Gerard, the Minister Plenipotentiary of France. It was an Important Day. An Important Transaction; and I hope replete with lasting Advantages to the United States in General, and much so to the State of Rhode Island in particular. By this Day, perhaps at this Moment, We are reaping the Blessings arising, from a Treaty with so powerful an ally. I think the Connection brought about by the Hand of Heaven, and that therefore, it promises to be as lasting as it is mutually beneficial, generous and noble. The particulars of the Proceedings of the Day, Your Honors, will have in the enclosed News Papers.

Congress have at length come to a Resolution upon a Report of their Committee, that the Expenses of the Expedition agt. Rhode Island last Fall shall be born by the United States.[1] The Report was recd. & agreed to without Argument and without the least Division. Nothing could ever have stired such a Question, but for a Letter from Genl. Heath, wrote I conceive in Consequence of some Dispute he had had with Genl. Spencer, In which Letter he is pleased to say *he* never knew how the Expedition came to be formed, nor from whence it originated.[2] I have the Honor to inclose your Honors the Report & the Resolution of Congress.[3] With ardent Wishes for the growing Honor & Glory of the State, and Success to the present Expedition for the Recovery of its Capital, and that this War may be soon closed with Honor & Reputation to Our Arms, and the Establishment of Our Liberty, Peace and Independence. I beg Leave to subscribe myself, Your Honors, most obedient, and very humble Servt.

Hy. Marchant

RC (R–Ar).

[1] See *JCC*, 11:758–61.

[2] Marchant is referring to Gen. William Heath's November 24, 1777, letter to the Board of Treasury, which had been referred on December 15 to a committee appointed "to enquire into the rise of the expedition against Rhode Island." See PCC, item 157, fol. 29; and *JCC*, 9:1027. The committee report that Congress approved on August 7 mistakenly gave the date of Heath's letter as "November 27, 1777." *JCC*, 11:758.

[3] Marchant actually had to wait until August 17 to transmit a copy of this report. See Marchant to the Rhode Island Assembly, August 17, 1778.

John Penn to William Woodford

Dear Sir Phila. Augt. 11th. 1778

I am sorry that you have forgot me, you are where Intelligence is Interesting, do my good Friend write me now & then what you are about, what are the charges agt. Genl. Lee & how goes on his trial? What are you all doing? From our last letters from Europe it appears that the King of Prussia is determined to have Bavaria, havg. marched his Plenipotentiaries to take possession, 180,000 choice men well officered, will reason most Powerfully, indeed Russia & the Port will find business for each other, Spain & Portugal are with France, Holland on no side. What can Britain expect if she persists—tho' from some late publications it seems that the Court are preparing the People to approve of our Independence, which I cannot help expecting will be acknowledged by England before they declare war against France. Inclosed are two letters. Colo. Banister will be with you soon on the Committee about regulating the Army. I am, Dear Sir, Your obt Servt. J Penn

RC (NN).

John Williams to Robert Burton

My Dr Sir[1] Philadelphia 11th Augt 1778.

As I have but very few Minutes to Spare before the post Sets out I Just Mean to Inform you that I am here well where I arived the 3d Instant perfectly Recovered of the Smallpox which I had lightly. I also Inclose you a paper which conveys all the Intelegence worth Notice in this part of the world Except one other Act which came to Congress after those contained in the paper of this date Informing that the Enemy had on the arival of Count D'Estaing with the French fleet of Rhode Island & on our Landing some Men Evacuated two of their fortifications, spiked up their Cannon & Repaired to an Elivated spot on the Island where it is Supposed they will make their Main Stand.[2] I hope by the next post shall be able to give some Intilegence worth Notice as Matters of the utmost Importance to the Continent are Now in agitation. I suppose the conduct of Genl. Lee at the Battle of Monmouth 28th ult is a Matter of great Spiculation. Nothing Respectg. his Tryall by the Court Martial has yet Transpired as the Tryal is Not yet over nor won't be some time. I wait with Impatience to Receive a letter from you Informing the Situation of My family &c. Which hope you will find some Means to Contrive. I have Not time to Say any thing Relitive to my Domistick affairs—should any thing go amis Shall Rely on yr. good offices to

Right it. Present My affectionate Compliments to Aggy & the little Boys—I suppose before this little John is pretty well Master of the house. I am Dr Sir with Real Esteem yr. affectionate Hble Sert,

Jno. Williams

P.S. I have to apolligize for taking your great Coat from yr. Brother's, and the best I can make is that I could not do without it. I hope the freedom will be Excused. Am yours &c. JW

RC (NcU). Addressed: "To Colo. Robert Burton, Granville County, North Carolina."

1 Robert Burton (1747–1825), a North Carolina planter and member of the North Carolina Council, 1783–84, served as a delegate to Congress in 1787. *Bio. Dir. Cong.*

2 The delegates received this news about developments in Rhode Island from Gen. John Sullivan's August 1 letter to President Laurens, which was read in Congress on the 10th. See *JCC*, 11:768–69; PCC, item 152, 6:223–26; and Sullivan, *Papers* (Hammond), 2:165–67.

Samuel Holten's Diary

[August 12, 1778]

12. A very cool day, attendd. in Congress 'till ½ after 3 o'Clock, met the joint Committee. Went & paid a visit to Monsr. Gerard but he was not at home, left my name on a Card.

MS (MDaAr).

Marine Committee to John Beatty

Sir August 12th, 1778

You are hereby directed forthwith to send into New York an equal Number of British Seamen Prisoners of War to the United States, to those of American seamen lately Sent out from thence by Admiral Gambier,[1] or that may hereafter be sent out agreeably to the tenor of our proposition, which was to return an equal number of Prisoners of the same rank and condition—making a distinction betwixt men and Boys, Sick and well.

Mr. Barney 2nd Lieutenant of the Continental frigate Virginia and Lieutenant Pownal of Marines of the Said Frigate having come from New York, It is our desire that you send in Exchange for them the Second Lieutenant of the British frigate Mermaid and the first Lieutenant of Marines belonging to said frigate who are in captivity at this place.

You will please to observe that British seamen taken by the

French and now Prisoners within these States are not to be exchanged by you.[2]

We are Sir, Your Hble servants

LB (DNA: PCC Miscellaneous Papers, Marine Committee Letter Book). Addressed: "John Beatty Esqr., Comy Genl. of Prisoners."

[1] See *JCC*, 11:730–31.

[2] See *JCC*, 11:690–91.

Marine Committee to John Bradford

Sir August 12th. 1778.

We have received your favour of the 30th Ultimo advising the arrival of the Prize Brig Nancy with 2070 quintals of Fish taken by the Continental Brigt. General Gates which is a pleasing Account and we hope to hear Shortly of the other Prizes arriving from Captain Skimmer. As the Continental portion of the above Cargo of Fish will be wanted for the use of the Army and the French Fleet, we desire it may not be sold but that you will deliver to the Commissary General of Purchases or his Order any quantity thereof he may require taking receipts for the Same.[1]

We are Sir, Your Hble servants.

LB (DNA: PCC Miscellaneous Papers, Marine Committee Letter Book).

[1] This day Richard Henry Lee, writing as chairman of the Marine Committee, sent a brief letter to Jeremiah Wadsworth, the commissary general of purchases, advising him of the committee's instructions to Bradford, a Continental agent in Boston. Jeremiah Wadsworth Papers, CtHi; and Paullin, *Marine Committee Letters*, 1:283–84.

Marine Committee to the Comte d'Estaing

Sir August 12th. 1778

The Marine Committee of Congress have heard with concern that the Squadron under your Excellency's command was on the 4th instant Supplied with no more than 20 days provisions, but you may be assured Sir, that accident and concurrence of Circumstances, not a want of Zeal and Industry to supply you has hitherto delayed the arrival of Provisions.[1] The enclosed paper[2] will shew your excellency what orders have been issued from the Marine Committee on this Subject, with the Measures taken and taking to comply with these Orders. The movement of the Squadron and the Number of the enemies Cruizers, between this place, the great resource of Provisions especially of the Bread kind, rendering a long Land carriage necessary have chiefly produced this delay. In future we hope you will receive a more regular Supply, except it be of Salt provisions which the want of Salt, the great consumption of the army, and the season of the year, renders scarce and dificult to be obtained.[3] To your wisdom must be left the propriety of Spareing the Salted provisions as much as possible, and useing fresh whilst you remain in a Country capable of furnishing the latter in abundance, but for the reasons above given not well provided with the former at present. A considerable quantity of bread, flour, live Stock, vegetables and water have been put on board the frigate Chimere and the Transports with her, but these I apprehend have not reached the Squadron. The Commissary General has fixed directions to Supply your Excellency from time to time with such quantities of Provisions as you shall call for.[4] I have the honor to be with sentiments of the highest respect and esteem, Sir, Your Excellencies Most obedient Hble servant,

Richard Henry Lee,
Chn of the Marine Committee

LB (DNA: PCC Miscellaneous Papers, Marine Committee Letter Book).

1 This concern had led the committee on August 10 to make the following inquiry of John Chaloner, the deputy commissary general of purchases: "It is the desire of the Marine Committee that you will lay before them tomorrow morning at Congress a written account how far you have executed their orders respecting furnishing the French Fleet under the Count D Estaing with Provisions &c, and what measures are pursuing for carrying them into full execution." This brief letter, written by the committee's secretary John Brown, is in the Roosevelt Naval History Collection, NHpR.

2 Not found.

3 This day Richard Henry Lee wrote nearly identical letters on behalf of the Marine Committee to the governors and councils of Connecticut and New York, requesting them to "assist the Commissary General with the Powers of Government in procuring as much Salt Provisions as can be had within your State, the same being indispensibly necessary for supplying the French Fleet under the command of the Count D Estaing." Peter Force Collection, DLC; and George Clinton Papers, WHi.

4 See Marine Committee to d'Estaing, July 12, 1778.

Marine Committee to the Eastern Navy Board

Gentlemen August 12th 1778

We are favoured with yours of the 29th Ulto. And now desire you will send to us an Account of the value of the Provisions which you have spared to the Commissarys for the use of General Sullivans Army in Order that the same may be duely settled.

We beg you will enquire for Mr. Galletheiu a French Gentleman lately gone from this place to Boston and inform him that it is our desire that you Accomodate him with a free Passage to France in the first Continental Vessel that may be going that way.

The Treasurer has given us assurance that he will be able to pay the balance of the Warrant for the use of your department in a few days which shall be immediately sent forward.

We have only to repeat our great desire to have the Continental Vessels at Sea, which no doubt you are using your endeavours to accomplish.

We are Gentlemen, Your very Hble servants

LB (DNA: PCC Miscellaneous Papers, Marine Committee Letter Book).

Robert Morris to the Maryland Delegates

Gentn Philada. August 12th. 1778

In Consequence of a Contract my late House made sometime past with your State, they gave Sundry Orders for the Importation of Muskets & Powder from which they have been enabled to fullfill their engagement, but in Consequence of those multiplied orders they have both Powder & muskets still lying in the West India Islands, and having just recd from thence one small parcell of 155 Muskets, which were originally intended for your State, I conclude to make you the first offer of them at the Current price or at the Valuation that shall be put on them by two or three honest impartial Men, judges of their quality & Value. As I only make this offer in Compliment to your State a refusal of it will be no disapointment & you are entirely at liberty to accept or reject it.[1]

I am very truely Gentn. Your Obedt Servt. R Morris

RC (MdAA).

[1] The Maryland Council's August 27 response to Morris, declining his offer of the muskets described above, is in *Md. Archives*, 21:191.

Joseph Reed to James Potter?

Dear General[1] Philad. Aug. 12. 1778.

I this Morning received your Favour of the 1st Instt. No one I assure you could take a more sincere Part in the Distresses & Apprehensions to which you have been exposed than I did, & I feel no common Pleasure in hearing that the actual Stroke of Desolation & Blood did not reach your Family & Habitation. Every Exertion within the Reach of my small Abilities & Influence was made to forward Relief, tho for my own Part from the Nature of an Indian Irruption I expected little more than to discover to our Friends on the Frontiers that we felt most sensibly for them & were anxious to return some Part of those friendly Offices which in the Hour of our Distress they had rendered us. Offices which I trust will not be forgotten or neglected by the real Whigs in the interiour Country. I am sure I never shall. I must say that our Abilities did not equal our Wishes. The Continental Army has so exhausted all our military Stores, & we have had so little Time to recruit them that when we made the necessary Inquiries we found we could neither arm nor equip Men in Time to give any effectual Assistance by personal Service. The city which you know was formerly our Magazine was as you may suppose utterly destitute & from the Dispersion of our Artificers the Repairs could not be made on the broken Arms of which we had some in Store: Under all these Circumstances we did the best we could in calling off Broadheads Troops then on March to Fort Pitt, recalling Col. Hartley then on March to the Grand Army—ordering such of Pulasky's Horse as could be had to go up to countenance & encourage the unhappy Fugitives. And I must do the Gentlemen in Authority here the Justice to say that both in their importunate Applications to Congress & their own Exertions they discovered all that Anxiety & Concern which so unhappy a Circumstance must create in a feeling Mind. We got Congress to consent to Col Hartleys remaining on the Frontier till the Harvest could be got in & the Minds of the People quieted. But we are all clearly of Opinion with you that a defensive System against Indians is vain & ineffectual. That the War must be carried into their own Country & nothing short of severe Chastisement for their Perfidy & Cruelty will give Security to our Frontiers. Under this Idea two Expeditions are now actually on Foot, one against the Wiandots & others under the Protection of Detroit & the other against the Senecas & Cayugas, from Albany & Mohawk River. Our Colonel Butler with a Pennsylva. Regiment is upon the latter with Troops from New York & some friendly Indians—both Expeditions are in great forwardness & I trust will afford you more real Security than 20 Regiments posted on the Frontiers. These Expeditions were on foot before the late Irruption & the Route fixed or I should have thought a Passage to the Senecas & Cayugas more favourable from the Waters of the Susquehannah. As you have had great Opportunities of knowledge in these Subjects I shall be much obliged to you to give me your Sentiments upon them as Time & Oppy. admit and you may depend upon my making such Use of them as I hope will conduce to the Happiness & Honour of the State as well as the safety & Comfort of the worthy Inhabitants of the back Counties in whose Behalf from the Spirit & Zeal which they have discovered in the common Cause I feel myself deeply interested. Write freely I beseech you & tell us in what Way we can render you most Service, I trust you will not find us backward or ungrateful.

I am much obliged to you, my dear Sir, for the favourable Sentiments you express of me. The Approbation & Esteem of Gentlemen whose Courage & Integrity have stood the Proof of Danger & Adversity does more Honour than the time serving Adulation of a whole Nation of timid skulking Neutrals or half converted Tories, I hope I shall act so as to deserve it. The County of Philadelphia did me the Honour to chuse me to fill up the late Presidents Chair in Council but being then a Delegate in Congress the Election was not valid. I hope some Person of more Experience, Ability & Fortune may be found before another Election, as my Attention to the publick has so drawn off my Regard to my private Affairs that they suffer exceedingly: & the Opportunities of making proper Provision for my Family are so great that I cannot neglect them without doing Injustice to those whom I am bound by every Tie of Duty & Tenderness to consider.

I suppose it is hardly in your Power to leave Home at this Juncture, otherwise I should express a strong Wish to see you as soon as possible upon several Accounts. It is an important Crisis in this State & true Whigs should attend to it.

My best Wishes attend you & if I can be of Service to you in any Shape, command freely my dear General, Your sincere Friend & Hbble Servt.

Jos. Reed

RC (PHi).

1 Apparently Brig. Gen. James Potter, who since his resumption of command over the Pennsylvania militia in May 1778 had been serving on the state's frontiers in response to pleas from Pennsylvanians for protection against the Indians. Although little of his correspondence survives, two letters he had recently written to the Pennsylvania Council from Penn's Valley and Sunbury, Pa., covering several of the topics discussed here by Reed, are in *Pa. Archives*, 1st ser. 6:665–66, 729.

Elias Boudinot to Hannah Boudinot

My dearest Love, Philadelphia Augt 13 1778

Being again confined by a return of my fever & Ague, attended with (I believe) the Rheumatism in my Breast, I have a little leisure to converse with the dear object of my warmest Affections & Esteem, altho' I do not write without Pain. I am applying the Bark in such Quantities that I hope to be out again tomorrow, God willing.

I left our Friends at Princeton well, altho' your Brother, the two Girls & one of the Servants had been very unwell, your Brother rather dangerous. Oh! how was I mortified at a disappointment my Judgment approved of, and perhaps would not have been pleased had you ventured your Health in pursuit of so trifling an Object. If my Health should not be restored in a few days, I shall not be easy without visiting my beloved Cottage, where all my Earthly Treasure is almost buried. Perhaps if I could forget it more than I do, it would add to my present Pleasure. I know that the things of this

Life, are generally unsatisfactory & illusory and the Enjoyment disappoints us at the best, but notwithstanding as I verily believe that thro' the indulgent Mercy & Kindness of a holy God, as little of that disappointment has fell to my share, as to any one Person in the World, I cannot conquer my desire of risquing the Event—I have tried almost every Station in Life, and if you judge from the common Sentiments of Mankind, you might imagine that I am now in the highest, being actually in my Representative Capacity, on a par with the greatest Monarchs of the Earth—but if you could see my Heart, you would discover less exultation there, than when I considered myself, the humble Peasant of Baskenridge, in the enjoyment of domestic Happiness with a beloved family (perhaps as high as human Nature will allow) as unenvied as undisturbed. I can say my present Situation has greatly humbled me, and I am truly convinced that all the envied Greatness & dignity of Offices & Titles is Sound & nothing else.

My desire is to be usefull, and as my gracious God has in his all wise Providence been pleased to favour me beyond the common Lott of the Children of Men, and that not only in the best of Women for my Companion thro' Life, but in a beloved Daughter, Family, Friends and every other earthly blessing, with the means & hopes of eternal Life, so I would endeavour at the Risque of every earthly comfort & Enjoyment, to do his will under every circumstance of Life. This my dearest & best beloved, is my consolation & only satisfactory reason, for the loss of your inestimable Company, and those sweet & delicate Enjoyments of a domestic nature, which cannot be replaced by all the Grandeur, Parade & Noise that this world affords. My ambition is satisfied, and when it pleases him whose I am, and ever wish to be, a return to my original obscurity will be acknowledged with gratitude & Praise. I am but of little Consequence here, and can add but a trifle on the great Scale of publick Movement. I wish to retire & shall take the first favourable Oppertunity. I have nothing new to tell you, except what is contained in the enclosed. I have had a visit from the French Minister & have dined & breakfasted with him. If well enough I go to morrow with him to the Valley Forge.

My kind Love to all Friends—Kiss my Susan & remember me to the Family. Am with all the ardor of the sincerest Affection & Esteem, Your grateful, Boudinot

[*P.S.*] Mrs. Franklin remembers Love &c

RC (NjP).

Samuel Holten's Diary

[August 13, 1778]

13. The following Gentlemen dined with the Delegates of Massa. Bay, at their invitation (vizt) Monsr. Gerard Minisr. Plenipotentiary from his most Christian Majesty, his Nephew, and Secrey.[1] The President of Congress, Honl. Silas Dane Esqr., Honl. R. H. Lee Esqr., Honl. Genl. Read, Genl. Putnam, Genl. Arnold, Baron Stuben & his aid; We dined at 4 o'Clock, and had a grand elegant diner, & I think it was conducted with good decorum, we drank coffee before we rose from Table.

MS (MDaAr).

1 Pierre Prothais Meyer was the nephew and chief secretary of Gérard. After Gérard's 1779 return to France, Meyer served as a secretary to Ambassador La Luzerne and as a political adviser to the comte de Rochambeau before returning to France in December 1780. For further information on Meyer's activities, see John J. Meng, "Secretary of Legation Meyer," *Records of the American Catholic Historical Society of Philadelphia* 46 (March 1935): 22–48.

Henry Laurens to the Eastern Navy Board

13th August [1778]

I had the honor of presenting to Congress the 10th Inst. your favor of the 28th Ulto. whence it was committed to the Marine Committee.[1] My present business is to transmit with this, twenty four Commissions for Vessels of War, together with proper instructions & bonds.[2]

I am with great Respect, Gentlemen &c.

LB (DNA: PCC, item 13). Addressed: "The Honorable The Commissioners of the Navy Board, Eastn. Dept., by Messenger from Monsieur Girard."

1 The Eastern Navy Board's July 28 letter to the Committee for Foreign Affairs, reporting that it had sent to France "the remaining packages you Intrusted to our care" but had not yet had an opportunity to forward the "Letters for Martinico," is in PCC, item 37, fol. 119. See also Committee for Foreign Affairs to the Eastern Navy Board, June 22, 1778.

2 Laurens also transmitted "Thirteen Commissions for Vessels of War with Instructions & Bonds" with a brief covering letter he wrote this day to Gov. William Greene of Rhode Island. Red Series, R-Ar.

Henry Laurens to John Laurens

13th Augt. [1778]

Your favors of the 7th to General Washington & myself[1] have given much information and equal satisfaction in public and to private friends.

You will do me a great favor by continuing your Narrative of the proceedings against Rhode Island. I have nothing new to offer you except the paper of this date. My Compliments to General Sullivan & Colonel Barton—also to Genl. Greene if he is with you—dont forget to present me respectfully to the Marquis & to all who are in my Acquaintance. Don Juan de Mirallis is an honorable Spaniard strongly recommended to Congress & to yr. Genl. by the Govr. of Havanna. He wants nothing but leave to spend his Money & look on.

I am &c.

LB (ScHi).

1 Laurens is actually referring to John Laurens' August 4 letters to him and to Washington, which were forwarded to Philadelphia with Washington's August 7 letter to the president. *JCC*, 11:768. A transcript of John's letter to his father is in the Laurens Papers, ScHi; transcripts of his letter to Washington are also in that collection as well as PCC, item 152, 6:223–39. Both letters deal with the younger Laurens' experiences in Rhode Island as Washington's liaison to the comte d'Estaing.

Henry Laurens to George Washington

Sir

13th August [1778]

Since my last of the 30th July[1] I have had the honor of presenting to Congress Your Excellency's several favors of the 3d, 4th and 7th Inst.[2]

The transcript from the journal of Congress dated the 10th Inst. and here inclosed will shew Your Excellency how those of the 3d and 4th were dispos'd of.[3]

I likewise inclose with this, an Act of Congress dated the 10th, and three dated the 12th Inst. together with the declaration of the last mention'd date.

1. . . . for adding two Members to the Committee of Arrangement[4]
2. . . . for permitting Colonel Knobelock to act as a Volunteer in the Army, and for allowing him 125 Dollars per Month[5]
3. . . . for allowing a compensation for horses kill'd in battle.[6]
4. . . . a Declaration That Congress hold it incompatible with their honor in any manner to correspond or have intercourse with George Johnstone Esquire one of the British Commissioners.[7]

5. . . . An Act of Congress of the 12th for sending the said Declaration to the Commissioners by a Flag.

Congress request Your Excellency will give directions for carrying this immediately into execution.

Yesterday I presented to Congress a letter from Mr. Ferguson, Secretary to the Commissioners of the 7th Inst. and the Paper referred to in that letter.[8] Copies of these I take the liberty of transmitting herewith, merely for Your Excellency's information. I have the honor to be, With the highest Esteem and Regard.

LB (DNA: PCC, item 13). Addressed: "General Washington, White Plains, by a Messenger from Monsieur Gerard."

1 The last letter Laurens wrote to Washington was actually a private letter dated July 31, 1778.

2 Washington's August 3–4 and August 7 letters to Laurens are in PCC, item 152, 6:199–206, 211, and Washington, *Writings* (Fitzpatrick), 12:273–79, 291.

3 Congress had referred to the Board of War such parts of Washington's August 3–4 letter as dealt with the artillery corps and the enlistment of draftees and to a specially appointed committee such parts as related to the deficiencies of Clothier General James Mease. *JCC*, 11:767–68.

4 Congress added John Banister and Roger Sherman to the Committee of Arrangement after reading Washington's request, in his August 3–4 letter to Laurens, that this committee "immediately repair to Camp." *JCC*, 11:769.

5 Congress decided to allow baron de Knobelauch, "a Nobleman of an ancient Family in the Electorate of Brandenburg" who had had thirty years service in the Prussian, Russian, and Danish armies, to serve as a volunteer in the Continental Army after reading a July 27 letter from the baron in which he expressed the wish to serve the American cause in any way Congress deemed fit. See *JCC*, 11:725, 764, 778–79; and PCC, item 78, 13:459–61. In addition to his letter, Knobelauch also submitted to Congress a proposal by the Prussian consul at Nantes, dated November 22, 1777, offering to sell Prussian frigates and military supplies to the United States. Congress referred this proposal to the Board of War and the Marine Committee on August 12, but neither body took any action on it. See *JCC*, 11:778; and Knobelauch to Congress, August 6, 1779, PCC, item 78, 13:527–29.

6 See *JCC*, 11:777–78.

7 This "Declaration" was approved by Congress on August 11. *JCC*, 11:770–74.

8 See Laurens to Rawlins Lowndes, August 11, 1778, note 1.

Samuel Chase to Thomas Johnson

Dear Sir, Philada. Fryday Morning [August 14, 1778][1]

We have this Moment a Letter from Gen. Sullivan's—dated Providence Augst. 6. 1778—giving an Account that some of the Enemies Frigates had sailed & anchored between Dyans Island & Bristol Ferry, upon which Count D Estaing ordered two of his Ships to attack them, on the 5th, that on their approach the Enemy set fire to & abandoned their Vessels without making any Defence or appearance of Resistance—& adds I am this Moment informed that four frigates & one Tender were destroyed—he further adds, the Militia are exceedingly tardy, but is considerably reinforced by the Militia of Connecticut, nor do I expect much from them, those of N Hampshire, & Massachusetts, I am informed, are on their March, & have Reason to expect them by Saturday next.

Gen. Maxwell writes from Elizabeth Town—7 Augst. 1778, 9 oclock A.M. "Early yesday Morning Lord Howe sailed out of the Hook with his whole fleet of [. . .] Vessells. They were out of Sight in afternoon & were supposed to be gone for Rhode Island. No Troops or Trans[ports] supposed to be with them"—No Br. fleet arrived yet as he can tell of.

I have not been able to get further Information respecting the Mermaid than the inclosed will give you.[2] I in[tend] to mention the Matter to Congress, but believe it would be adviseable for [you] to maintain the Jurisdiction of our Court of Admiralty. Be pleased to excuse this Scribble & the paper. [I] write this in Congress, to take the opportunity by Colo. Richardson to give you the Intelligence received & to inclose the two papers.

Your Friend. S Chase

[*P.S.*] It is reported here, that a Brig was load in Baltimore, & cleared for France. ⟨*but*⟩ went to N York, that the owners went to that City by Land.

RC (MdAA).

1 Gen. John Sullivan's August 6 letter cited by Chase below was read in Congress this day. *JCC*, 11:787.

2 Chase enclosed a brief August 14 letter that he had received from Marine Committee secretary John Brown reporting the committee's plans for disposing of the stores from the recently captured British frigate, *Mermaid*. Red Books, 10:60, MdAA.

Samuel Holten's Diary

Augt. 14, [1778]

Congress sit late, we dined at four. I walked out with Mr. Gerry, & visited the Gentlemen from Connecticut, & the Revd. Mr. Duffel our Chaplain. It has been a cool rainy day.

MS (MDaAr).

Elias Boudinot to William A. Atlee

Dear Sir

Philadelphia August [15, 1778][1]

Having been confined for some time past with a disagreeable fever, have been prevented [the plea]sure of answering your favour of the 18th Ultimo. [It will?] give me great Satisfaction to be able at any time to [favor?] you with Intelligence that may in the least gratify your C[uriosity] or afford Entertainment for your leisure Moments.

At present we are all anxiously looking as the [. . .] of old used to do, for good to come from the East. You [. . .] know that Genl. Sullivan with 7000 Men and [. . .] of an Attack on Rhode Island from [the land?] while Count de Estaing was to do the same with [his?] fleet from the Water. We were informed on Monday that every Thing was ready for the Commencement [of opera]tions as on that Day.[2] The fleet consists of [. . .] Line and two frigates, with some little assistance [from about?] 3 or 4000 land forces & Marines. The East River [. . .] up and the Islands in the Harbour evacuated. This Morning an Express arrived with an Account that [they] evacuated the North part of the Island on the approach [. . .] and they landed without Loss, but just at this [time a fleet] of 27 Sail of Vessels appeared off the Harbour [thought?] to be the Cork fleet; on which the Count with his [fleet] made Sail & gave them Chase, and they pushed for it as [. . .] as possible. Thus Matters stood on Monday last 11 oClock. I had forgot to mention that Lord Howe put to Sea on Thursday, was a week from the Hook, returned on Saturday and lay there [. . .]day Night.

Genl Washington lays near the Enemy above [. . .] Head Quarters at White Plains.

I must beg the favour of your settling the [. . .] in that you may have agt. me till the 23d June, [. . .] to settle all my late department and pay off [. . . .][3]

I had great Hopes of seeing Lancaster again [and went]? as far as Potts grove on my Way, but turned [back on hearing?] that the Congress was moving to this City.

My most respectfull Compliments to Mrs. A[tlee &] family, to whom I wish every good Thing.

I am with great Esteem Dr Sir, Your most obedt Hb Ser,

Elias Boudinot

P.S. I broke open this in order to congratulate you on your Brothers Exchange,[4] which is perfected & he is now a free Man—Remember me to him and wish him Joy.

RC (DLC). The margin of the RC is damaged; numerous conjectured readings and omissions are indicated in brackets.

1 Boudinot's description of military and naval operations in Rhode Island suggests that he wrote this letter in light of Gen. John Sullivan's August 10 letter to President Laurens, which was read in Congress this day. See *JCC*, 11:801; PCC, item 160, fols. 139–40; and Sullivan, *Papers* (Hammond), 2:191–92.

2 On Monday, August 10, Congress had read an August 1 letter concerning this matter from Gen. John Sullivan to President Laurens. See *JCC*, 11:769; and Sullivan, *Papers* (Hammond), 2:165–67.

3 Boudinot is referring to Atlee's claims on him in his previous capacity as commissary general of prisoners, the position Boudinot held before he entered Congress in July 1778.

4 Samuel J. Atlee (1739–86), who had been captured during the battle of Long Island in August 1776. He was elected a delegate to Congress in November 1778, assumed his seat the last week of December, and continued to represent Pennsylvania in that body the following four years. *Bio. Dir. Cong.*

Elias Boudinot to William Peartree Smith

My Dear Sir,[1] Philadelphia Aug 15 1778

Your two several very Friendly & obliging Favours of the 23d July & 9 Inst came safe to hand,[2] the last I recd at Princeton, since which have been again confined with a Return of my Fever, but I hope to get out as soon as the present rainy Season passes over.

I am so confined to Business here, that a Letter from a Friend is truly valuable as it is a very agreeable relaxation to the Mind at the same Time that it affords a Satisfaction that is hard to express. We are on the tenter Hooks of anxious Expectation for news from Rhode Island. Our Hopes are raised to a high pitch as we have certain Intelligence that Lord Howe had not sailed from the Hook on Sunday last, so that the Count de Estaing cannot be interrupted in the least. From the best Accounts we have from England & especially from a publication sent us by a Friend, who informs that it was made under the immediate patronage of Lord North, I conclude that England will acknowledge our Independency & settle this unhappy dispute in many Months.[3]

I have conferred with Belcher, fully on the Subject mentioned in your Letter, and if nothing better turns up in a very short time for him, will endeavour to accomplish what you propose as I think it highly reasonable.[4]

The office I wrote you about is filled up,[5] and altho' another equally advantageous might be had, yet as it would require your personal & constant attendance in this City, I think it will not answer for the reasons you mention—and I am clear that there is a Berth in our own State awaiting you that you will fill with credit & reputation, and be of eminent publick Service while you may at the same time enjoy all your domestic Comfort at Eliz. Town in which you know I am personally & greatly interested.

The Express that arrived from the Commissioners, brought nothing but a requisition for permission to send Transports for the Convention Troops, &c &c

Being really & truly interested in your welfare I am distressed for the many Losses that you have met with in these unhappy Times, and the only consolation you can have, is that it is a general evill and in a good Cause, but when these misfortunes happen from other means & are some measure arguing from our own faults and do not answer so valuable purposes they are the more distressing; it is upon this account that I condole so much more with you in the apprehension of your present Danger in the threatened Loss of your heavy Baggage, especially as it is your all of this kind of property.[6] I think you are in a great measure to blame, as you must know by Experience that Sheets tho' with the addition of Locks & Keys, have been generally found a very insufficient Barrior agt. a regular & secret attack. It becomes you without delay to swear the Peace agt every suspected Person, and even if necessary to get an additional Class or two of the Militia to keep a Town watch especially as the Enemy are so near as to afford the necessary assistance particularly by way of a retrograde manoeuver. Whenever you think it for the publick advantage, I can move Congress to pass some spirited resolutions agt. attempts of this nature, if not to make it high Treason, even to the Corruption of Blood any former Resolution notwithstanding.

It will give me great Pleasure to forward your Letters to Belcher, and beg you will allways enclose them to me, as By this means I shall hope to hear oftener from you.

You must excuse my Scrawl as I write in Pain, my Breast being greatly affected. My kindest Love to Dr Mrs. Smith & kiss Katy, And believe me to be with great Affection, Dr Sir, Yours sincerely

FC (NjP). In the hand of Elias Boudinot.

1 William Peartree Smith (1723–1811), a graduate of Yale and a trustee of the College of New Jersey, who was about to become the father-in-law of Boudinot's younger brother Elisha. Franklin B. Dexter, *Biographical Sketches of Graduates of Yale College*, 6 vols. (New York: Henry Holt and Co., 1885–1919), 1:719–20.

2 Smith's July 23 letter to Boudinot is in J.J. Boudinot, *The Life, Public Services, Addresses, and Letters of Elias Boudinot,* 2 vols. (Boston: Houghton, Mifflin and Co., 1896) 1:167–71.

3 See Henry Laurens to George Washington, July 31, 1778, note 12.

4 In the July 23 letter cited above, Smith had asked Boudinot to obtain the post of deputy secretary of Congress for his son, Belcher Smith, who was serving as a clerk to Secretary Thomson.

5 No earlier letter from Boudinot to Smith has been found since Boudinot's entrance into Congress.

6 Boudinot is responding in kind to Smith's facetious description in the July 23 letter previously cited of the courtship of his daughter Catherine by Elisha Boudinot.

Samuel Holten's Diary

[August 15, 1778]

15. An express arrived in five days from New-Port & informed that our army was on the Island & that 29 sail of vessels was off the har-

bour, & Count d'Estaign's fleet had sailed in quest of them. We had heavy showers in the morng.

MS (MDaAr).

Henry Laurens to Thomas Mifflin

Sir 15th August [1778]

By permission of Congress I inform you that no Orders are given in consequence of your Letters of the 10th and 12th.[1] I am thus particular because I wish you to believe Sir, that had I received any order, the duty I owe to the House, as well as the respect I bear to you would have prompted an immediate intimation.

I have the honor to be, Sir, Your Most Obedt. Hbl. Servt.

[*P.S.*] 5 o'clock the minute I am releas'd from Congress

LB (DNA: PCC, item 13). Addressed: "Major General Mifflin, Chestnut Street."

1 Gen. Thomas Mifflin's August 10 and 11—not August 12—letters to Laurens, insisting that Congress appoint a committee to investigate his conduct as quartermaster general and that it settle his quartermaster accounts as soon as possible, are in PCC, item 161, 1:41–44. Laurens wrote the present letter in reply to one of this date from Mifflin demanding to know why his two earlier letters had elicited no response from Congress. Mifflin had all four of these letters printed in the August 20 issue of the *Pennsylvania Packet*, together with an August 17 letter he wrote to Laurens denouncing Congress' failure to conduct the investigation he had requested and announcing his resignation from the Continental Army. Although the RC of Mifflin's second letter to Laurens is clearly dated August 11, the text that appeared in the *Packet* was dated August 12. See also Laurens to Washington, June 11, 1778, note.

Richard Henry Lee's Notes on Silas Deane's Testimony

[August 15–21? 1778][1]

This a general resolution.
Letters shewn & insinuations made.
Did you or the Committee desire a settlement of Accounts?
Mr. D. to settle his accotts with Commissioners.
He was frequently called on to settle.
Gave a list of partial expenditures—Ves[se]l in Hol[lan]d—Arms.
Mr. D. left his papers.
Was he to leave his Vouchers—with an enemy.
Said one Getn. shd. be Comr. at France and every other place.
Redescribe the Test of truth.

Approve of the Treaty & now Criminate the Minister for a part of it.
Did not lend his confidence.
Worm out answers to his own Condemna[tio]n.
Gentn. wanted to entrap me—my papers absent.

MS (ViU). In the hand of Richard Henry Lee.

1 Although a month elapsed after his arrival in America before Congress invited him to testify on the "general state" of foreign affairs and on Congress' "commercial transactions in Europe," Silas Deane finally appeared in Congress on August 15, 17, and 21 to give an account of his conduct in France since 1776. Opposed by many delegates and intruded at an inconvenient time, the Deane hearings immediately provoked dissension within Congress and opened an era of sustained factional conflict previously unknown. Although the purpose of these notes can only be conjectured, they appear to have been made by Lee during the course of one of Deane's three August appearances before Congress. They are written on the verso of a brief "Memorandum of sums received & paid out on account of the United States from January 1777 to April 1778" which Lee endorsed "Mr. Deanes Account of the expenditure of the pub. money, Aug. 1778"; and they are concerned with a number of topics that were probably discussed in the course of Deane's testimony. See *JCC*, 11:787, 799, 802, 813, 826; Richard Henry Lee to Arthur Lee, September 16, note 3; and Gouverneur Morris' Proposed Resolve on William Carmichael, September 18, 1778. For a discussion of the scope of the factional conflict in Congress that was occasioned by Deane's return to America at this time, see Jack N. Rakove, *The Beginnings of National Politics: An Interpretive History of the Continental Congress* (New York: Alfred A. Knopf, 1979), pp. 246–74. And for an assessment of Deane's public career in the context of his conduct of family and business affairs before the war, which concluded that his activities and responses during the Deane-Lee controversy "were prefigured and influenced, if not determined, by the events of his earlier life," see Kalman Goldstein, "Silas Deane: Preparation for Rascality," *Historian* 43 (November 1980): 75–97.

Titus Hosmer to Oliver Ellsworth

Dear Sir[1] Philadelphia Augt. 16th. 1778.

You are pleased to say on the Subject of our Paper Credit "What is like to be done, or can be in this Emergency you know a Thousand Times better than I." Admitting this to be just, I find you know a Thousand Times less than Nothing about it for I assure I know just Nothing, and am therefore qualified to keep the secret & will tell you Nothing about it: one word more, I think by what I can discover that I know just as well what will be or can be done as Congress in General which constitutes the true Reason why Nothing is yet done upon the Subject—we are soon to consider it, and if I can come at any knowledge I will most chearfully tell You, but there are gigantick Difficulties on every Hand, and I can only wish they may be surmounted.

As I hope you are determined and preparing to come here as soon as possible will you give me leave to introduce you to Congress, & attempt to give you an imperfect Idea of the Course of Business in Congress and in the several Subdivisions of Congress. We meet at nine & continue sitting till two in the Afternoon, after prayers the States are called, nine are a quorum to proceed on Business, the public Letters are first read & disposed off, next reports from the Treasury & then reports from the Board of War, these Matters by a standing Order must be gone thro' before any other Business can be moved, for the rest points are started, debated, & determined in nearly the same Manner as in our Assembly, saving that much Time is spent, too much I think in all Conscience in debating points of Order, they are referred to the House, and the Decision does not seem to depend on any fixed or known Rules, but the present Opinion of what is decent & proper in the Case before us, which gives much the same, indeed a greater Latitude than in debating points of Common Law in our Courts.

Besides the General Business which is originated & discussed in Congress, the House is subdivided into standing Comittes or Boards each of which is to pay their Attention to some one Capital Branch, give Orders in the Executive part, and report to Congress where its Aid is wanted to regulate and enforce. These are as follows

1. A Board of Treasury, this should consist of one member from a State, five are a Quorum, they Superintend the finances, consider in the first Instance all Applications for Money, & report what is to be advanced, regulate the Striking of Bills, give their Opinion when Emissions are Necessary, & prepare draughts of Resolves for that purpose, consult of & propose Ways and means for raising Money, propose regulations to prevent Counterfeiting, Depreciation of, or to Appreciate the Currency, they examine Claims, adjust Accounts & in general do every thing in this Branch, they are assisted by an Auditor General & Commissioner of Claims—the Auditor keeps Accounts & the Commis[sioners] examine the particular Articles, correct over-charges, reject improper ones & state Ballances, all sums to be granted in Advance, on Account or for Ballances due are reported to Congress, granted by them, & drawn for by Warrant under the Hand of the president.

2. A board of War, formerly consisting of Members of Congress, now of Commissioners chosen at large, assisted by some Members, the Objects of their Duty is particularly enumerated in the Resolve for Constituting & impowering them which I trust you have Seen. It extends to the superintending the Departments of the Commissary Genl., Quartermaster Genl., Clothier Genl., Adjutant General, Commissary General of Ordnance & Military stores, planning Expeditions & in short every thing almost that relates to the Army or Military Operations.

3. Marine Comittee, this board considers of Rules and Regula-

tions for well governing the Navy, the number of Ships & other Vessells to be built, superintends & directs the Building & employing them, examines into all mismanagement of Officers, directs Enquiries & Trials, furnishing transports & in short exercises the Office of Lord high Admiral with more extensive Powers than any British one ever had, & are only checked by the Necessity of obtaining the sanction of Congress to their rules and regulations which however in general is given of Course, as far Gentlemen have ability or Leisure to canvass their Measures, this observation may indeed be extended to all the other Committees General as well as the Marine Committee.

4. A Commercial Committee, all the Commercial Business of Congress is under their Direction, & is you will find a very extensive & perplexed branch of Business.

5. A Committee of Foreign Affairs, they Correspond with our Ministers at foreign Courts, with Agents in Europe and with all such Gentlemen of Character in foreign parts as are disposed to give us Intelligence, they prepare Instructions for Ministers & propose proper Courts or States to send embassys to.

6. The Committee of Foreign Applications, they are Gentlemen acquainted with the French or other European Languages, and receive Applications from foreign Officers, proposals, Schemes, & projects from a Shoal of Europeans who wish to fish for Wealth or Honour in our troubled Waters.

7. A Medical Committee, who superintend the Medical Department in the Army, & are consulted by & direct the Director General.

These Committees proceed in general upon the present State of Information & decide upon the Circumstances of each particular Case without any general or established Rules, at least if they have such Rules I have not been able to find them—some of them are Temporary & will end with the War, others are in their nature permanent, these last it is an object with Congress, when they can find Time, to put into Commission, & critically to limit, define & regulate their Jurisdiction.

I hope to hear by the next post that You will comply with my request in my last & set out for Congress, in which Case I shall take the Liberty to delineate, or give you a rough Sketch of the Characters of the Gentlemen you will find. I do not mean their moral nor political, but their Congress Characters.

I am Dear Sir, with great Respect, your most obedient & most humble servant. Titus Hosmer

RC (PHi).

1 Although the recipient of this letter is not identified, this is undoubtedly the "long Answer" Hosmer had promised in his August 11 letter to Ellsworth. Before concluding the present letter Hosmer repeated his "hope . . . that you will comply with my request in my last & set out for Congress," a request contained in that same August 11 letter.

Henry Laurens to Rawlins Lowndes

[August 16, 1778]

I am now at the 16th. Mr. Martin has been detained by bad weather and sickness.

Your Excellency will read in the Penna. Packet of the 13th a declaration of Congress of the 11th—this is the Paper Mr. Drayton had kept so long in his Pocket and which I had so often solicited should be brought forward.[1] I now regret that some previous corrections had not been apply'd to it and that the house was hurried in its passage without such amendments as at first view your Excellency will see it stood in need of—be this as it may, it contains matters of fact, and such as it is, the Commissioners may criticize words and Phrases but the whole group will not be able to explain away our meaning, nor do I believe that even a Man of Governor Johnstone's command of features will have Art enough smoothly to laugh off his feelings whenever this Act of Abnegation shall be brought on the Carpet in his presence on either side of the Water. I put it in motion the 13th and it is probable the Governor has receiv'd his first shock this Morning. He has been severely lampoon'd in New York as will be seen in another paper to be inclosed with this.[2] The Declaration and other unavoidable business fill'd up the Session of the 11th and barr'd the delivery of the Remonstrance and Requisition before the 12th, it was then committed to a special Committee, a compliment which, in my humble opinion it did not merit.[3]

LB (ScHi). A continuation of Laurens to Lowndes, August 11, 1778.

[1] For Congress' August 11 declaration that it would be dishonorable to deal with Gov. George Johnstone after his efforts to corrupt several delegates, see *JCC*, 11:770–74; and William Henry Drayton's Notes for a Speech in Congress, August 11, 1778.

[2] Laurens is referring to the following updated squib, a copy of which, in the hand of Secretary Thomson, is in the Charles Thomson Papers, DLC:

"To be sold at private sale

"The British rights in America consisting of amongst other articles *The thirteen provinces* now in rebellion, which *Britain in the hour of her insolence* attempted to subdue, the reversion of the government of Quebec, Nova Scotia, Newfoundland, East and West Florida, the territory of the Hudson's bay company; a respectable body of his majesty's troops and a considerable part of the royal navy together with all the loyal subjects of America.

"The British West Indies will be included in the sale if agreeable to the purchaser—Apply to George Johnson esqr. who is desirous of concluding a private bargain. The condition of sale to be seen in the hands of Henry Laurens esqr. prest. of Congress.

"P.S. To make it easy to purchasers a seat in Congress will be taken in part payment the rest in continental Money. N.B. Discount will be allowed for all the loyalists which have been murdered since the 10th April 1773. The British Army & navy, all printers & news writers, all mobs and disorderly persons are forbid to obstruct the sale."

At the foot of his copy of this satirical piece Thomson noted: "The above is a genuine copy of an Advertisement lately printed & pasted up in Newyork at all the public places in the city." This document was printed in the August 13 issue of the *Pennsylvania Packet*.

3. For the continuation of this letter, see Laurens to Lowndes, August 18, 1778.

Henry Laurens to William Shippen, Jr.

Sir 16th Augt. [1778]

Please to receive within the present Cover an Act of Congress of the 14th Inst. for repealing an Act of the 9th of June last, for regulating Hospitals in the Eastern department;[1] which is transmitted for the government of your conduct in that respect.

I have the honor to be, With great Regard &c.

LB (DNA: PCC, item 13). Addressed: "Dr. Wm. Shippen, Dir. Genl. at Head Quarters, White Plains."

1 Congress' August 14 resolve withdrew its previous authorization to the deputy director general of hospitals in the eastern department, Dr. Isaac Foster, "to superintend the medical affairs of that department" in the absence of Director General Shippen and directed Shippen to investigate medical conditions in that department. See *JCC*, 11:582, 787–88. Laurens also transmitted a copy of this resolve with a brief covering letter he wrote this day to Dr. Foster. PCC, item 13, 2:47. The passage of this resolve was prompted by the reading of an August 1 letter to the Connecticut delegates from Samuel Huntington, written in Norwich, Conn., while he was on leave from Congress, the relevant parts of which read as follows:

"Since my return home as also on the way at Danbury I thot proper to make inquiry concerning the State of the Hospitals especially at Danbury & am Informed by persons of veracity who have the best means of knowledge of many Evils & abuses in that department which ought to be remedied.

"In particular that the number Employd in one Office or other as Doctors & Surgeons &c are double to what is Necessary—that the Apothecary general is very often Intoxicated with Liquor, That the Representation made in Congress when the Last Resolution passd appointing Docr. Foster Superintending Officer in the Eastern Department was directly the reverse of the truth, the truth was I am most Credibly Informed that he (Docr Foster) was determined to build a very Expensive Hospital at Danbury but was prevented by Doctors Cutler & Turner while it was in their power to prevent it.

"I am fully perswaded that some further regulations & attention is due for the Medical department, that one half the expense is totally unnecessary and hope it may Claim the attention of Congress." PCC, item 78, 11:310–11.

Henry Laurens to John Sullivan

Dear General Philadelphia 16th August 1778.

I have lately been honored with your several favors of the 27th July, 1st & 10th Inst.[1] which I presumed were all intended as Public, & therefore duly presented each to Congress—I have received no commands from the House; nevertheless I think an intimation of the receipt of your Letters will be acceptable. You will be so kind as to take it in this private address.

When you can find half an hours leisure, you will much oblige me by a general or detail Account as time may permit of the proceedings of the Allied Fleet & Armies at or near Rhode Island, although I must confess I have now some apprehensions that the late seperation was the period of our hopes of subduing the Enemy in that Quarter until quite new measures shall be taken. I wish my fears that the Count de' Estaing is decoyed, may prove groundless—the Enemy's seeming flight gives this alarm. Were they in earnest to fly they might have taken, with much less danger, the start from Sandy Hook—but we must with patience wait events. If you are so good as to communicate Intelligence of public transactions for my private use I intreat you Sir, to mark each Cover (Private). This will enable me to make acceptable offerings to my friends in the State I come from & on my part, besides the obligation which I shall feel, I will endeavor to make suitable retaliation. At present I have nothing to transmit but the last News Papers & to inform you that the British Commissioners have attempted to open a correspondence with Congress by means of a Remonstrance & requisition, demanding the Prisoners of the Convention of Saratoga & offering to Ratify that agreement on the part of Great Britain.[2] I will not say which is the most glaring in this Act their Insolence or their folly. I can see however they have with all their supposed Cunning ensnared themselves & exposed their Court to further contempt—they must either be possessed of powers "distinctly & explicitly" to Ratify & "properly notify to Congress" or they have no such powers. If they have, their weakness & folly will appear in withholding or neglecting to declare it—if they have not their Insolence will be seen in the attempt to negotiate without authority & I may repeat, their "folly" in supposing they could amuse Congress by a stroke of Newmarket Jockeyship. Upon the whole these Wiseacres have inadvertently given their Seal to the Act of Congress of the 8th of January.[3]

I wish you all success & happiness & am with very great Regard & Esteem Dear sir, Your obedient & very humble servt,

Henry Laurens
private

RC (NhHi).

1 General Sullivan's August 1 and 10 letters to Laurens are in PCC, item 160, fols. 135–37, 139–41, and Sullivan, *Papers* (Hammond), 2:165–67, 191–92.

2 See Laurens to Rawlins Lowndes, August 11, 1778, note 1.

3 That is, the resolution suspending the Saratoga Convention. *JCC*, 10:29–35.

Henry Laurens to George Washington

Sir 16th August [1778]

I had the honor of writing to Your Excellency the 13th by a Messenger from Monsr. Girard, since which Your Excellency's several favors of the 9th, 11th, and 13th, together with the several papers refer'd to have reached me.[1] The latter I receiv'd Yesterday at half past four P.M. in Congress, and immediately presented that and General Sullivan's of the 10th to the House.

By the Messenger above mention'd I forwarded a Packet from the Secretary of Congress directed to Major General St. Clair, and I shall transmit another directed to Your Excellency by the present conveyance, these I am informed contain all the documents relative to the charge against the General.[2] They had been long out of my custody.

Your Excellency will find inclosed with this duplicates of the Acts of Congress of the 26th and 30th of November and 27th of December 1776, for raising the regiment of Artillery in Virginia and appointing Colonel Harrison to the command, and for raising three Battalions of Continental Artillery.[3]

Also an Act of Congress of the 13th Inst. for correcting abuses and granting passes to persons to go into New York.[4]

Your Excellency's Letter of the 11th I received late last Evening, it shall be laid before Congress with Colonel Palfrey's tomorrow morning and I trust the application of that Gentleman will be immediately attended to.[5]

I have the honor to be, With the utmost Respect & Esteem &c.

LB (DNA: PCC, item 13).

1 Washington's August 11 and 13 letters to Laurens are in PCC, item 152, 6:243, 247, and Washington, *Writings* (Fitzpatrick), 12:313, 320–21. A draft of his August 9 letter is in the Washington Papers, DLC, and Washington, *Papers* (Fitzpatrick), 12:303–4.

2 Washington had requested these "documents" so that he could proceed with the court-martial that was supposed to determine Gen. Arthur St. Clair's responsibility for the loss of Ticonderoga and Mount Independence in the summer of 1777. See Washington, *Writings* (Fitzpatrick), 12:321; and John Hancock to Arthur St. Clair and Philip Schuyler, August 5, 1777, note.

3 See *JCC*, 6:981, 995, 1045. Washington had requested copies of these resolves to help settle some disputes over rank among Continental artillery officers. Washington, *Writings* (Fitzpatrick), 12:321. For the resolution of these disputes by a board of officers he subsequently appointed, see ibid., pp. 458–59. See also Committee of Arrangement to Laurens, September 7, 1778.

4 This resolution stated that only Congress or Washington could issue passes to persons going into New York and directed Gen. Benedict Arnold to recall such of these passes as he had issued and had not been used. *JCC*, 11:779.

5 Laurens also wrote the following letter this day to Paymaster General William Palfrey: "Last night your favor of the 11th by the hands of Mr. Witherspoone reach'd mine. It shall be presented to Congress tomorrow, and I trust the young gentleman will be soon dispatch'd with a supply of money for the general

Military Chest." PCC, item 13, 2:48–49. The August 11 letter from Palfrey to Washington to which Laurens refers is not in PCC or the Washington Papers, DLC, but Washington's covering letter of the same date reveals that it dealt with Palfrey's urgent need for funds. Washington, *Writings* (Fitzpatrick), 12:313. On the other hand, an August 12 letter from Palfrey to Washington, which dealt with the same issue and which was read in Congress on the 17th, is in PCC, item 165, 2:486–89. Not until October 16, 1778, did Congress respond to Palfrey's pleas by agreeing to provide $1,000,000 "for the use of his department." *JCC*, 11:802, 12:1014.

Henry Laurens to Meshech Weare

Honorable Sir, Philadelphia 16th Aug. 1778.

I had the honor of addressing you the 8th Inst by a Messenger to Rhode Island.

This will be accompanied by twelve signed Commissions & Instructions for private Vessels of War & a like number of Bonds. The latter when duly executed your Honor, will be pleased to transmit[1] to Congress.

I have sent these at the request of Colo. Bartlett.

I remain, Honorable sir, With very great Respect, Your obedient & humble Servt, Henry Laurens, President of Congress.

RC (MHi). LB (DNA: PCC, item 13).

[1] Preceding two words supplied from LB.

Gouverneur Morris to John Jay

Dear Jay, Philadelphia 16th Augt. 1778

We are at Length fairly setting about our Finances and our foreign Affairs. For the latter particularly I much wish you were here. Many Persons whom you know are very liberal of Illiberality. Your Friend Deane who hath rendered the most essential Services stands as one accused. The Storm increases and I think some one of the tall Trees must be torn up by the Roots.

I have not heard from you in a long Time. I did expect a letter by your Brother James but was disappointed. I am informed that he brought letters from you to Nobody here. How happened that? Apropos I will give you a little History.

Just before his Arrival, I saw a Letter from Arthur Lee speaking of him most disrespectfully. I was informed and induced to believe that he was come to Congress charged with Lee's Information & to promote his Designs. The Length of my Acquaintance with him required Nothing. But it was my Duty to take Care that your Brother did not render himself ridiculous. I felt more than I can tell at the

Idea of a Connection between him and some Persons also I am confident you do from your Soul despise and abhor. In Consequence I waited of him. I told him candidly that I suspected him to be charged with Matter which was to militate much in favor of Mr. Lee, That Mr. Lee had in a Letter which would then shortly become public traduced him. I had forgot to tell you that the Letter was to Mr. Carmichael who (being accused before Congress by Mr. Lee) shewed it in his own Defence to a Committee of which I was a Member. And I stated the Ridicule which far from being instrumental in forwarding the Views of a Man who had said of him that he was a Vilain.

He was as you may well suppose much obliged by this Instance of my Friendship and so far all was Right. So far I had saved him out of bad Hands. As the Devil would have it I was appointed one Member of a Committee to superintend an Entertainment given by the Congress to Monsr. Girard. Unfortunately the line which by the general sense of the Members of Congress had been drawn for Invitations excluded him. He was offended. He made Inquiries into the Reasons. You may readily imagine what some Folks would say on the Occasion. He inquired of me in a Stile which really put it out of my Power to give him satisfactory Answers. It is a Pity for his own sake that he appeared to feel the Omission. To you the Reasons need not be assigned. I fear he is now in the Possession of those Gentlemen. I would dilate upon the Consequences but the idea is painful to me and cannot be pleasant to you. I have only to add on this Chapter that I will save him if I can even from himself. The Mischief is he is now in such Dudgeon that any Advances from me would produce the direct contrary Effect from what they ought. Adieu my Friend. Remember me to our Friends. To your Wife particularly. Write to me oftener. In all cases believe me, most sincerely yours,

Gouvr. Morris

RC (NNC).

1 Sir James Jay, John's older brother, had recently returned to America after a sixteen-year stay in England in the course of which he had been knighted by the king for his fundraising efforts on behalf of Kings College. *DAB*. The letter from Arthur Lee to William Carmichael criticizing Sir James, to which Morris refers, is not in PCC or the microfilm edition of the Lee Family Papers.

2 In an April 14, 1778, letter to the Committee for Foreign Affairs, as well as in other letters to certain delegates, Arthur Lee charged that William Carmichael had propagated reports of dissension among the American commissioners at Paris, that he had intercepted Lee's mail, and that his political beliefs were suspect. See Wharton, *Diplomatic Correspondence*, 2:550–52; and James Lovell to Richard Henry Lee, December 18, 1777, and to John Adams, February 10, 1778. Carmichael, who had recently returned to America after serving as a sort of unofficial secretary to the American commissioners, replied to these charges in an August 6 letter to a committee of Congress that is not mentioned in the journals or located in PCC but is printed in *Papers in Relation to the Case of Silas Deane,* ed. Edward D. Ingraham (Philadelphia: Printed for the Seventy-Six Society, 1855), pp.

137–40. Although the recipient of Carmichael's letter is not designated in this source, internal evidence suggests that it was written to the committee considering certain dispatches from the commissioners, which had been appointed on June 19 and of which Morris was a member. *JCC*, 11:622.

3 See *JCC*, 11:688.

Joseph Reed to Esther Reed

My dear Hetty Philad. Augt. 16 1778, Sunday

As I expected to have spent this Day with you I feel no small Disappointment in being obligd to substitute Pen & Ink in Place of the more substantial Pleasure of a personal Interview—but the Weather has turnd out so bad & some Events have happened in Congress that would have deprived me of the Satisfaction of meeting you if the Weather & other Circumstances had been favourable. I was for a Week confined to the House & suffered more Pain than I ever did in the same Time. You may judge how desirable your Company would have been to me under such Circumstances, tho I had no Reason to complain of Solitude. I am now perfectly well & mean to take such Precautions as I hope will secure me against a Return of this troublesome Complaint. About 8 Days ago the Committee of Arrangement was ordered to proceed to Camp, at that Time I was confined & immediately afterwards The Business of Congress led to Inquiry into the Conduct of our Commissioners abroad when mutual Recrimination brought out the Charge made by Dr. Lee against Mr. Langdon & myself as holding a treacherous Correspondence with the British Ministry. It seems Dr. Lee transmitted it to Paris to be forwarded to America somehow concealed in the blank Leaves of "Enticks Dictionary." The Gentlemen at Paris on examining it fearing it would have fatal Effects on our Characters kept it back—after a little Time Mr. Lee having joined them as a Fellow Commissioner & soon falling out with them he endeavoured to get the Dictionary from them which was refused, & last Spring it was sent over to Mr. R. Morris who seeing only a Dictionary & no Explanation could not tell what to make of it but laid it by & it being at Manheim we have not yet seen the Contents. The Story having now taken Wind & a strong Party formed in Congress against the Lee Connection they are resolved to avail themselves of this indiscreet & imprudent Measure to turn him out of Employ if they can—or at least that it shall be a make Weight in the Scale.[1] For my own Part, my Opinion of Dr. Lee is not altered by the Transaction. I shall vote just in the same Manner as I should have done if another Person had been the Object of this Charge & am really sorry that the Talent he unquestionably possesses should be useless to himself & dangerous to others for Want of a little Portion of Candour & common ordinary Sense to mingle with them. And at all Events we ought to be thankful that while Rocks & Precipices were all round me, Providence has so ordered Matters that I have not only not fallen but possess a greater Share of publick Confidence than I ever did. But every Event of this kind lessens my Attachment to publick Life & enhances the Pleasures of domestick. There no Doubt nor Suspicions enter—your Love & Tenderness & the Prattle of our dear little ones affords Pleasures without any Alloy of Scruple or distrust & I look forward with infinite Pleasure to the Time when I can enjoy them with less Interuption.

I hope Cyrus will have a good Place—he sent to desire he might see me & I sent him Word to come & stay here while he staid in Town which I expected he would have done as his Master seemed pleased with it but he did not come. When I came to Town I found at Mrs. Yards a Boy belonging to Mrs. Badger hired to Mrs. Yard. I got her to engage him for me which she did—but when I came to speak to his Mistress I found she wanted to sell, not to hire him—As Cyrus was now gone I was therefore obliged to purchase him several Persons offering to take him at her Price but the Boy had set his Heart upon living with Genl. Reed. I have accordingly got him & hope you will like him—He has been brought up to House Work & his Mistress assures me he is healthy, good tempered, sober & honest. Mrs. Yard also spoke well of him. I shall get him up to you as soon as possible as Idleness of which he has enough here will do him no Good. I shall endeavour to purchase the Calico for you as the Returns from New York are uncertain. I send you by this Oppy. a Cask containing 4 Pieces of Linnen, a Piece of Cambrick—the Ticking & Table Cloths—A Pine Apple & a few Limes. The latter I have kept waiting an Oppy. till they are almost spoilt, but my dear Girl in this Care must take the Will for the Deed. You must spare one of the Pieces of Linnen at least to Mrs. Pettit & I have given Polly also some Expectations of Assistance—Perhaps your Mamma may also by this Time have her Wants. I have now been moved above a Week & am so much pleased with the House that I flatter myself you will be happier in it than in any we have had in this Country. The Rooms are large & commodious—Kitchen convenient & Yard &c. very pleasant, in short it is what I think you will like. I have got one of the parlours painted & the other now looks so shabby that I have serious Thoughts of getting that done also—tho the Walls being to be done will make it cost four Times as much as the other, & That was dear enough of all Conscience. Among other Conveniences there is a Spire & a Smoak House—nor do we find the Kitchen smoak as Hannah represented.

Monday Morn. I endeavoured to change your Stockings but the Man had no Cotton ones that would fit you—He has thread but as the cold Season was coming on I would not get them without your particular Directions.

As I have concluded to send Tom to you by this Oppy. he will deliver you a Bundle of News Papers which contain all our publick Affairs, except what we had last Saturday from Rhode Island viz: That Genl Sullivan & the Count de Estaing having settled a joint Attack on the 9th Inst. while the Troops were actually landing & a Part of them had taken Possession of some Works which the Enemy had abandoned a Fleet of 29 Sail appeared in View which since proves to be Ld. Howe upon which The French Troops which had been landed were immediately taken on board & the Count stood out to Sea after them—the British Fleet then tack'd about & when the Accounts came away the Count was in full Chase. Genl. Sullivan upon this Event relinquished his Design for the present. Ld. Chatham is actually dead. £4000 per Ann. is settled on his Family by Act of Parliamt. & his Corpse has laid in publick State at Westminster Hall.

I should have wrote you last Week if any Oppy. had offered—this long letter will I hope make up my Deficiency. I have sent to Burlington for the Things provided Bowers can get a suitable Person to come down with them. I have made out extremely well as to House keeping; Numa pleases me much but I am not so enamored with her as not to wish to change her for my own little House keeper as soon as I can. About this Time next Month or the 1st October at farthest you must come. The Town was not very healthy before this series of Cloudly, rainy, sultry Weather especially for Children & I suppose it must be much worse now. I am glad you have got a school for ours. They will be much happier & less troublesome to you. If an Oppy. offers I think you had better sell one of the Cows. You will judge which but I believe it must be the speckled as Steins Cow will be a good Winter Cow & the other a summer one. I believe she will fetch £20 at least.

Kiss The Children for me, remember me to Mamma & Polly who I suppose is with you & believe me, my dear Hetty, Your faithful & affect.

J Reed

P.S. I expect to be with you on Wednesday Night at farthest on my Way to Camp.

I have sent Joe's Hat among other Things. Parish has had it in Hand. If it will not do now you must send a Measure taken a different Way—the string should go round his Head not across it.

I have pack'd up a few Bottles of Pork in the Box as I remember you seemed pleased with my having bought some.[2]

RC (NHi).

1 Arthur Lee's June 3, 1776, letter to the Committee of Secret Correspondence referred to here was written on the blank leaves of a copy of John Entick's *New*

Spelling Dictionary, two pages of which survive in PCC, item 83, 1:21–24, where they are located with a copy of the entire letter transcribed by James Lovell. To his transcript of the letter Lovell added the following endorsement which contains much of the information now available concerning the circumstances of its delivery to Congress. "Comtee of Secret Correspondence date June 3d. and taken from the Original in the Cover of a Dictionary wch was delivered to the Secretary of Congress by Mr. Robt. Morris on the 4th of Sepr 1778 and delivered to the Comtee of foreign Affairs Decr. 7th following. Attest James Lovell. with Feb. 13. 13. 14, March 19, Apr. 15. 1776." One of the surviving leaves of Lee's letter also contains another Lovell endorsement: "1778 Sepr. 4 Recd. in Congress from Mr. Morris Decr. 7 delivered to the Com'tee of foreign affairs. Attest James Lovell." The best printed text of Lee's letter is in Force, *Am. Archives*, 4th ser. 6:685, although it is also available in Wharton, *Diplomatic Correspondence*, 2:95.

An account of Lee's letter similar to that related here by Reed is in Samuel Adams to James Warren, December 9, 1778. Silas Deane's comments on the episode can be found in the "Narrative" that he read before Congress in December 1778. *New-York Historical Society Collections* 21 (1888): 154–56.

For the use Lee made of Entick's *Dictionary* in his cipher correspondence with his brothers Francis Lightfoot and Richard Henry Lee, see Richard Henry Lee to Arthur Lee, May 12, 1778, note 2.

2 This day Reed also wrote the following brief letter to Lt. Col. William Bradford, deputy commissary general of musters. "If it is consistent with your Orders & Judgment, I should be obliged to you to permit Capt Harrison to stay in Town this Day unconfined as I have some Business to transact in which he is necessary." Chamberlain Collection, MB. Although Harrison's identity is difficult to establish, he was apparently New Jersey loyalist Charles Harrison, who had been confined in Pennsylvania since December 1776. *JCC*, 8:427, 472–73.

South Carolina Delegate to Unknown

[August 16, 1778][1]

By a letter from General Sullivan, dated Portsmouth, Rhode-Island, August 10, we are informed, that on the morning of the 9th, the enemy abandoned all their works on the north end of the island, in consequence of the French fleet coming up the river; and immediately thereupon General Sullivan pushed over all his troops, and took possession of the enemy's works. On the same day a fleet of 29 sail, 8 or 10 of which appeared to him to be of force, were discovered standing in to Newport under English colours. Count d'Estaign kept his station, there being but little or no wind; but the next morning, the 10th, he got underweigh, with a fine breeze, and gave chace; and at 11 o'clock, General Sullivan writes, he had the pleasure to see the British fleet fly before him. The Count left three frigates in the east passage. General Sullivan adds, that General Hancock, our late amiable and worthy President, had joined him from Boston, at the head of a number of volunteers. The French Fleet, in passing up the river of Newport, silenced two batteries of the enemy.

MS not found; reprinted from the *South Carolina and American General Gazette*, September 10, 1778, where it is headed: "Extract of a Letter from a Member of Congress, August 16."

1 Although the author and recipient of this extract have not been identified, William Henry Drayton, Thomas Heyward, Henry Laurens, and John Mathews were the South Carolina delegates in Philadelphia at this time.

Andrew Adams to Samuel Lyman

Dr. Sir Philadelphia: 17th August 1778

I have this Day the happiness of receiving your Favr. of the 14th ulto. trust you have before this recd. a Line from me.[1]

I have as you observed taken a Seat in Congress, and mixd among the great States-Men of America, among whose shining Talents you may well imagine my feable Genious is lost in obscurity. Dont think this remark fishing for a Compliment, I barr every thing of that kind: you speak of gratifying my Curiosity & Ambition: as to the former it is both gratifyed and disapointed, in regard to the latter I can with utmost Sincerity say I have none in this way.

I am happy to hear that Mrs. Adams keeps up her Spirits in my Absence. I fealt much on her Account; my own health I think is quite restored. You Reason perfectly Just in my Oppinion in regard to our Currency: so far as I can Judge there is not the least Idea in Congress to let the Money die: as to one particular Member we had some Conversation about I beleave Nothing is further from his thoughts, he is extreamly urgent to have something effectual done to appretiate the Currency; this indeed seams to be the full determination of Congress & accordingly three Days in each Week (except some necessary Business such as attending to the publick Letter &c) are now set apart to attend to our Finances: this subject is very extensive and will take up much time. The Money in my Oppinion can & must be appretiated. Tis of Infinite Importance, but this must not be done suddenly, as that would greatly injure the poor & Virtuous part of the Community and throw a prodigious advantage into the hands of the present Money holders, a great part of whom are some of the greatest Rascals that ever disgraced humanity & deserve infinitly greater punishment than is in the power of any state to inflict.

All the News we have here comes from the eastward which you know before it reaches us: I dont know that I can better gratify your Curiosity at present than by giving a general account of the Proceedings of Congress: according to order we should meet at Nine and adjourn at two: but in fact we Meet about ten & sit till three, four and five before we adjourn: this you will say is very inconvenient but leaves us much leasure; but you will consider that much of the

Business is transacted by special Committees in the Recess of Congress: besides these there is a Marine Board, a Navy Board, a Treasury Board, a Commercial Board & Comtee. of foreign Affairs who have no other time to do their Business but in the Recess of Congress: these Boards are at present almost wholly composed of Members of Congress: some of them meet at six in the Morning & sit till eight constantly every day. Others meet at five in the afternoon or immediately after they Dine & sit till Night and sometimes till late: I beleave there are but very few Members but what are employed in some of these Ways, so that those who do their Duty have not much Leasure to spare. The Debates in the House are simular to those in the British House of Commons: there are here as in most other Assemblys some very Sensable Speakers, & some very loud Talkers: you may make one exception & then conceive a House composed of very able sensable Gentlemen: but belonging to different States, whose Laws, Mannors, Genious of Inhabitants and indeed almost every thing else very different.

Many things have occurrd. since I left home such as the arival of a French fleet, the Minister Plenipotentiary & his publick Audience &c which have now become obsolete, a particular Account of which I have from time to time given to Miss Adams either by Letters or the Publick papers sent to her, which immagin you have seen: as also the Conduct of the British Commissioners & Resolves of Congress thereon—some of which have mentiond in my former Letter to you.

I have now Just returnd. from a Visit to the French Minister which every Member of Congress is obliged to receive and give for a formal Mannor, he appears to be very sensable & a Man of Business. Mr. Dean has Just began to give us a full Acot. of all Matters relative to his Business &c &c &c this you would esteam entertaining, more I may not say at present upon this head.

I am Sr. with great Esteam your real Friend & very humble Servt.

Andw Adams

RC (MH–H). Addressed: "Saml Lyman Esqr., Goshen, Connecticut."

1 No earlier letters from Adams to Lyman have been found.

Andrew Adams to Reynold Marvin

Sir[1] Philadelphia 17th August 1778

I can give you no new Ideas from Congress. The proceedings and Debates here are very simular to those in the British House of Commons: should I tell you that some are fond to be thought a Barre, or a Burk I might be thought reprehensable but should I compare any to a Wilkes I might Deserve Censure.

I have not yet attempted to make any formal publick Speach in Congress, nor do I design it, (I can give you my Reasons at a proper Time) many Times I sit with almost infinite impatience but have hitherto kept in; nor has Mr. Hosmer yet spoke in publick; I know not his Reasons but imagin I could guess them; I beleave he will do it soon. I cant say but I should do the same if my Return was not at hand.

The State of our Currency is Just come under Consideration: two Days in each Week is now chiefly set apart for that & our Treasury Matters and Finances. This is so Difuse and important a Subject that it will doubtless take up a long Time: several other Departments loudly call for the Attention of Congress, but they are so crouded with Business of almost every kind, and git along with it so slow, that Nothing can be immediately expected, but what cant be dispensed with.

All our news now comes from the Eastward. We have very frequent Accounts from Rhode Island and are anxious for the Event of that Expedition, which must be a Matter of high Importance.

Genl Sullivan writes to Congress that his Supplys from Connecticut are very inconsiderable [& he] intimates that he has no great Expectations from there [. . .] if we consider our Quota of Continental Troops which [I am] told is more than full upon the present Establishment, Matrosses &c stationd. upon the Sea Coasts, two Battalions [. . .] men and two more raised by percentory drafts from the Militia &ca. the prodigious Number of Men employed in the various [. . .] of the privateering Business; we might perhaps assign [many?] good Reasons why large Numbers more should not be [taken?] from Connecticut: without assigning another Reason [. . .] perhaps has its weight with many good Soldiers (vizt) The [. . .] they have heretofore met with in the State of Rhode Island [. . .] Regard to the high prices demanded of them for Necessaries [. . . .] But I am sorry after all to have such a Clause in the Genlls Letter without the true Reason, being assignd. which I beleave Govr. Trumbull will do: I intend to write him upon the Subject. Remember me suitably to Mrs. Marvin &c.

I am with Respect Your Obedt. Serv.

Andw Adams

RC (CtLHi).

1 Reynold Marvin (1726–1802), a lawyer of Litchfield, Conn., was formerly king's attorney for Litchfield County. Franklin B. Dexter, *Biographical Sketches of the Graduates of Yale College*, 6 vols. (New York: Henry Holt and Co., 1885–1919), 2:168–69.

Elias Boudinot to Hannah Boudinot

My dearest Love, *16.* Philadelphia August 17th 1778

I had been diverting myself with a revisal of all your very kind & affectionate favours with which I have been honored since my residence here. Great is the Enjoyment & Satisfaction my fond Heart feels on the recapitulation of those tender & endearing Sentiments & Expressions that fall with so good a Grace from the Pen of my lovely Wife. I have been just made happy by the rect of your additional favour of the 12t Inst. which is just like yourself, and filled me with those gratefull, pleasing Sensations that humanize the otherwise ferverous Mind of Man.

Will my dearest Love accept my warmest acknowledgments of her goodness, and supply my want of capacity, by suggesting to herself every thing tender & loving from her beloved Husband.

I have not the least doubt of the propriety of your not meeting me at Princeton, altho' I cannot say but I felt a little disappointed having raised my Expectation rather too high.

I wrote you twice or three Times since the 30 July which is the last you acknowledge the rect. of—for the future pray Number all your Letters, as I shall do, by which means you will know if any Miscarry.

We have advice that Lord Howe's fleet went to Rhode Island—arrived there this day a Week—that Count de Estaing immediately went out to attack them. They fled & he pursued. On Tuesday afternoon they were left at Sea just drawing in line of Battle. They have burned five of their frigates at Rhode Island and it is said a number of Transports. Genl Sullivan has landed on the North part the Island and is only waiting for the return of the French Squadron.

I have been much afflicted with the pain in my Breast, but not as formerly. I was greatly threatened with a Swelling under my Arm, but I believe it will go off & with it the Pain in my Breast. The soreness wears away fast.

Your Letters by the Post come the safest of any. I found my Sulkey without Harness, & broke in the Shafts. The workman asks me only £50—to repair it.

I will make another assignation with you as soon as I am clear that I shall not have liberty to pay you a Visit before Fall—do not be out of the way, in Case I should succeed. If my Health does not mend I shall certainly take liberty myself.

Kiss my Susan, I am sorry she has not got my Letter however I'll try to supply its place.

Love to sister & all Friends, Family &c.

Am with all that Love, esteem & Sincerety that you could wish, or desire, My dearest Wife, Your most Aff, E Boudinot

RC (NjP).

1 Boudinot's continued poor health brought his brief first term at Congress (July 6–ca. August 20, 1778) to an end soon after he wrote this letter. As he explained in a December 5, 1778, letter to Gen. Alexander McDougall: "I had not taken my Seat in Congress above Six Weeks, when I was seized with a Nervous fever that has confined me now about three Months. This with some other Reasons, has induced me to resign that important Post." Huntington MSS, CSmH.

Samuel Holten's Diary

[August 17, 1778]

17. Monday I received a letter by the post from Joseph Hall Junr. of Boston a minor. Congress sit late, hearing Mr. Dean.[1] Rainy & very hot.

MS (MDaAr).

1 Holten's comment that "Congress sit late, hearing Mr. Dean" probably means that the Deane hearing forced Congress to sit late, not that the hearing itself actually continued to a late hour. According to the journals, Deane was heard in the morning, but before he completed his testimony he was asked to withdraw, and Congress then proceeded to several other items of business. See *JCC*, 11:801–6.

Holten also made the following entries in his diary for August 18 and 19.

"18. I wrote to Capt. Batchelder & Mr. Hall, & also wrote a letter to Mrs. Holton (No. 13). Congress sit late—a very hot day.

"19. Dined at Mr. R. Morris's about 2½ miles out of the city. Very hot & Showry. I hear there is a Ball at the City Tavern this evening. I am sorry for it."

Henry Laurens' Proposed Resolve

[August 17–21? 1778][1]

Mr. Deane having observed on Saturday last (when it was suggested by a Member that he should appear before the house on a future day to answer to such questions as might be proposed) "That as letters had been privately shewn, and insinuations made tending to reflect upon his conduct in the public Character he sustained, and as questions asked of him may be calculated to draw forth Answers, which may be so construed as to support Charges against him, he prays to know if there be any such Charges now before the House, and if so, that he may have them stated to him, previous to his answering questions."

Resolved

That Mr. Deane be inform'd, that as Congress cannot draw a line between those questions which tend to throw light upon their foreign Affairs, and Commercial transactions in Europe, and those which may be calculated to support Charges and Insinuations, of which they have no Knowledge, and which he declares to have been thrown out against his public Character, they expect he will Answer such questions in general as may be propos'd to him: but should he be of opinion, that any of the questions propos'd have a tendency to support such charges and insinuations as may have come to his knowledge, he be at liberty to decline Answering such questions till the further Order of the House, assigning his reasons for so doing.

MS (Laurens Papers, ScHi). In the hand of Moses Young.

[1] Although the nature and date of this document can only be conjectured, it seems probable that Henry Laurens drafted it when Silas Deane initially appeared before Congress in August 1778 to report on his conduct in Europe. The substance of Congress' proceedings at that time is not known, but the journals indicate that Deane attended Congress on Saturday August 15 and on August 17 and 21 the following week. As Deane did not appear in Congress again until Tuesday and Wednesday December 22–23, it seems clear that the opening reference in this document to an observation Deane made "on Saturday last" could have been made only on August 15.

For information on Deane's arrival in America and the dissension generated among the delegates by suggestions that he be given a hearing before Congress, see Richard Henry Lee's Notes on Silas Deane's Testimony, August 15–21? 1778, note.

Henry Laurens to George Bryan

Sir, Philadelphia 17th August 1778

I have the honor of inclosing you under this Cover an Act of Congress of the 14th Inst. requesting the supreme executive power of this State to adopt measures for insuring a strict observance of the present Embargo on Provisions.[1]

I am with great Respect & Esteem, Honorable Sir, Your most obedt. humble servt.

Henry Laurens, President of Congress.

RC (Privately owned, 1975).

[1] See *JCC*, 11:788. Congress adopted this resolve to prevent food supplies from reaching the British in New York. Laurens also transmitted a similar resolve of this date with a brief covering letter he wrote this day to New Jersey Gov. William Livingston. See PCC, item 13, 2:49; and *JCC*, 11:788.

Henry Marchant to the Rhode Island Assembly

Gentn, Philadelphia Augt. 17th. 1778

In my last to the Honorable the Genl. Assembly, I mentioned that I had inclosed a Report and a Resolution of Congress thereon, that the Expence of the Expedition last Fall agt. Rhode Island should be born by the United States—but I could not, as I expected I should have done, get the Report and Resolution from the Secretarys Office timely for the Post:—I therefore now enclose Them, with several News Papers of the Week.

Our Last Letter from Genl. Sullivan of the 10th Instant, informing Us that he had landed with his whole Force upon Rhode Island & taken Possession of the Enemies Works upon the North End of the Island which they had abandoned—That an English Fleet had appeared off, & that Count D'Staing had sailed after them, fills our Minds with much Anxiety. However, hoping that this will rather invigorate and cause a redoubled Exertion—We remain in great Hopes of Success. We have had a long Series of very heavy Rains & Easterly Weather—This has brought one of Ld. Hows Galleys upon the Jersey Shore. They say that on Tuesday while closely pursued by the French Fleet She parted from the British Fleet & put away for New York having sprung a Leak, but gives us no further Particulars. Last Evening we had advice that four or five Ships were at Cape Henlopen firing for Pilots as was supposed, Whether those Ships are of either the two Fleets is uncertain—it is rather apprehended that both Fleets must have got scattered, if the Storm was as hard at Sea as it was here on Tuesday & almost the whole Week. As the Event is greatly interesting, relying upon the same kind Providence which hath hitherto so signally appeared for Us I remain in Hope of soon having an Account which shall do Honor to the American Arms, and call up afresh the most grateful Acknowledgement of the Divine Interposition on Our Behalf.

I am Your Honors, most obedient, & very humble Servt.

Hy Marchant

RC (R–Ar).

Gouverneur Morris to Robert R. Livingston

My dear Friend. Philadelphia 17th Augt. 1778

You complain of my Silence. Forgive me. My Heart never did you wrong. It is incapable of it. You wish you had Intelligence to communicate, interesting Intelligence. You have for you can tell me of those I love.

I will not apologize for Silence by Business. On every Principle I owe a little of that Time and Health of which I sacrifice so much to the ungrateful to those who deserve it so well by their favorable Opinion.

I did really believe Captain Bedlow's Business was compleated.[1] I was told so. I will make Enquiry (mark I received your Letter in Congress at three this Afternoon) and endeavor to get him righted. Your Reasoning on the Occasion is just. I have to observe however that I never yet put it in the Power of Congress to refuse an Application for one of my Friends. I trust that whenever I am called to account for my public Conduct whatever may have been my Want of Ability it will never be said that I have preferred private Connections to the general Weal. I shall have the Satisfaction to feel that I have spent Time, Health and Money and risqued Life and Reputation freely and disinterestedly. Whether usefully or not it is for others to determine.

A Variety of those little Incidents which postpone great Affairs especially in a Body so constituted as the Congress together with a Want of that Providence and Arrangement of Business which I have labored to inculcate and establish ever since I have been here have produced the Evil you complain of in your Loan Offices. It is now in a Train for speedy Redress.[2]

The Vermont Business doth indeed press and daily with additional Weight. Let our Situation be considered. The Attention of *the Members of* Congress to this Affair must be intreated not forced. At present three Days in the Week are set apart for the Treasury and Finances, two more for the Consideration of foreign Affairs, add to this that Congress is also an executive Body. I do not mean to apologize. I know I shall be charged by my Enemies. Let not my Friends pretend to excuse. If the State have not a Confidence that their Delegates are willing and able to serve them it is Time they were recalled. Justice will shall be done to us. I am sorry to add that the unavoidable Delays render it almost Injustice.

You tell me that I must be with you at the opening of the Session but you do not let me know when the Session is. Let me paint my Situation. I am on a Committee to arrange the Treasury & Finances. I am of the medical Committee and have to prepare the Arrangements of that Department. I have the same Thing to go thro with Relation to the Commissary's, Quarter Master's & Clothier General's Departments.[3] I am to prepare a Manifesto on the Cruelties of the British.[4] I have drawn and expect to draw almost if not all the Publications of Congress of any Importance. These are leading Things but the every Day Minutia are infinite. From Sunday Morning to Saturday Night I have no Exercise unless to walk from where I now sit about fifty Yards to Congress and to return. My Constitution sinks under this and the Heat of this pestiferous Climate. Duer talks daily of going hence. We have nobody else here so that if I quit the State will be unrepresented.[5] Can I come to you? If there be a Practicability of it with any Kind of Consistency I will take half a dozen Shirts and ride Post to meet you. Oh that a Heart so disposed as mine is to social Delights should be worn and torn to Pieces with public Anxieties.

I am distressed infinitely distressed at the Idea that a full, entire, perfect Cordiality should not take Place among those I love. Whenever ye are together my Spirit shall be with ye. And let me intreat that you will not wrong my Friendship by the smallest Dispute with each other. Remember our joint Labors in the public Cause. We have labored jointly upon the purest best Principles, for Heaven's Sake let not the Effects be lost by Divisions which will give to those who have personal Views an Opportunity of effecting the Ruin of our State. I cannot dwell on this Subject. I would that you could both of you see my Heart and feel how much I should suffer at the least coldness between you.

I shall make every Inquiry about the Gentleman you mention that you could wish. If I understand your Letter I am led to hope that the Result of it may be as favorable as possible. Whatever it be you shall know candidly & truly.

Return most Cordially the Greetings you sent me. I do most earnestly wish to see my Claremont Friends. To lounge, to idle, to dissipate the Moments and the Clouds, to live, to smile, to be happy. May you and all of you be so supremely.

Adieu. I am with Sincerity, your Friend, Gouv Morris

P.S. This goes by my Friend Colo. Bannister of Virginia to Camp, see him if you can.

RC (NHi).

1 Livingston's July 27 letter explaining the hardships experienced by the family of deputy paymaster William Bedlow, to which Morris is here responding, is in the Robert R. Livingston Papers, NHi. On August 26 Congress approved a $35 per month raise in pay for Captain Bedlow. *JCC*, 11:839.

2 Morris is undoubtedly referring to his plan for the reorganization of the Board of Treasury, which also dealt with Continental loan offices. It was submitted to Congress on August 13. *JCC*, 11:779–86.

3 Morris made some interesting comments on the way he transacted committee business in a letter he wrote years later to a correspondent who had requested permission to consult his papers for the revolutionary era: "I have no notes or memorandums of what passed during the war. I led then the most laborious life, which can be imagined. This you will readily suppose to have been the case, when I was engaged with my departed friend, Robert Morris, in the office of finance. But what you will not so readily suppose is, that I was still more harassed while a member of Congress. Not to mention the attendance from eleven to four in the House, which was common to all, and the appointment to special committees, of which I had a full share, I was at the same time chairman, and of course did the business, of three standing committees, viz. on the commissary's, quartermaster's, and medical departments. You must not imagine, that the members of these committees took any charge or burden of the affairs. Necessity, preserving the democratical forms, assumed the monarchical substance of business. The chairman received and answered all letters and other applications, took every step which he deemed essential, prepared reports, gave orders, and the like, and merely took the members of a committee into a chamber, and for the form's sake made the needful communications, and received their approbation, which was given of course. I was moreover obliged to labor occasionally in my profession, as my wages were insufficient for my support. I would not trouble you with this abstract of my situation, if it did not appear necessary to show you why I kept no notes of my services, and why I am perhaps the most ignorant man alive of what concerns them." Jared Sparks, *The Life of Gouverneur Morris*, 3 vols. (Boston:

Gray & Bowen, 1832), 1:217–18. Although Sparks gives neither the date nor the recipient of this letter, it is clear from the fragmentary text of it in Morris' private letterbook, 1804–1814, Gouverneur Morris Papers, DLC, that it was written about December 1809.

4 Morris had been appointed on January 21, 1778, to a committee charged with the task of preparing "a manifesto on the injurious treatment our prisoners and faithful citizens receive from the enemy." *JCC*, 10:81–82. Although Morris' interest in this subject may have been reawakened by the August 7 remonstrance of the Carlisle commissioners, which charged that Congress' failure to honor the Saratoga Convention represented a blow to the "means . . . devised by mankind to mitigate the horrors of war," the delegates did not approve a manifesto on British cruelties until October 30, 1778. See *JCC*, 12:1080–82; and PCC, item 57, fols. 325–26. Internal evidence suggests that Morris drafted this manifesto, but in the absence of the original manuscript its authorship can only be conjectured.

5 Francis Lewis was also representing New York in Congress at this time.

Josiah Bartlett to John Langdon

My Dear Sir, Philadelphia August 18th 1778.

Your favor of the 2d inst[1] is come to hand and I have communicated to the Commercial Committee what you wrote me concerning the French Ship *Duchess of Grammont* and find they have rec'd your letter to them on that Subject. I have urged their immediately taking up the matter and sending you directions as soon as possible.[2] I am sorry to say our Treasury, Marine & Commercial Affairs are in a very bad Situation owing to their being conducted by members of Congress who can spare but little of their time to transact them, and are so constantly changing that before they get acquainted with the business they leave Congress and new members totally ignorant of the past transactions are appointed in their stead. This gives me great uneasiness and I wish I could see any prospect of a speedy remedy, but the multiplicity of business that is daily crowding on Congress and the time it takes to transact matters in so large an Assembly filled with lawyers and other gentlemen who love to talk as much as they, will not allow me to hope that our affairs will be very soon properly arranged.

As to your loading vessels with provisions in Maryland &c, while the Embargo lasts you are sensible it cannot be done without an Order of the Congress for that special purpose which I fear will be hard to procure at present unless the French squadron shall be so successful as to block up the enemy's ships of war and prevent the danger of it's falling into their hands.[3] August 18—Mr Wentworth has signed the confederation[4] and is still here but in such a state as not to be of any service to himself or the public and I fear there is but little hope of his getting well while he tarries here. I believe it would be for the best (if he could be persuaded to think so) for him to set out immediately for home and another delegate for our State to come forward as soon as possible. I hope you have appointed delegates to relieve us early in November when the confederation takes place, as I shall be unwilling to tarry any longer if I should be able to stay so long; please to take particular care that others may be sent forward seasonable.

All the talk here is about Rhode Island and the French fleet, of which you know more than I, so shall say nothing about it, wish it may prove fortunate.[5]

I am Sir, your friend and humble servant,

Josiah Bartlett

Tr (DLC).

1 Langdon's letter of "the 2d inst" to Bartlett is printed under an August 1 date in Bartlett, *Papers* (Mevers), pp. 203–4.

2 On October 6, 1778, Congress authorized the Committee of Commerce to pay Langdon $16,686 2/3 "for the purpose of lading the French ship *Dutchess de Gramont*, and other contingent charges." *JCC*, 12:986.

3 Congress had imposed a general embargo on provisions on June 8, but the issue of grain importation became more critical in New England as demands to support the Convention Army, the Continental Army in Rhode Island, and then the French fleet began to outstrip the poor 1778 wheat harvest. To alleviate the shortage in the eastern states, Congress on September 2 urged Pennsylvania and states to the southward to grant embargo exemptions to ships carrying official authorization from the New England governments. See *JCC*, 12:861; Henry Laurens to William Smith, September 12; and Samuel Chase to Thomas Johnson, September 29, 1778, note 1.

4 Bartlett had signed the Articles of Confederation on behalf of New Hampshire, but, in his July 20 letter to Meshech Weare, he had questioned the validity of his sole signature.

5 Bartlett also wrote a brief letter to his wife Mary this day which contained only the following news, also on the subject of Rhode Island, of a public nature. "We have Recd no account from that place since Gen. Sullivans letter of the 10th Inst giving an account of his being landed on the Island and the french Fleet leaving him to Engage the British Fleet." Bartlett, *Papers* (Mevers), p. 207.

Josiah Bartlett to William Whipple

Dear Sir, Philadelphia August 18th 1778.

Your favor of the 2d inst. I rec'd yesterday[1] and perceive you intend for Rhode Island and I suppose you are now in the vicinity of that place. Rhode Island and the French and English fleets at present engross all the conversation here. I wish we may have a pleasing account from them—as for foreign intelligence we have none later than the 3d of June which has been published in the newspapers. The faces in Philadelphia were much altered but the Whigs are returning fast, so that it begins to look more natural. Our old landlady is the same as usual and remains in the same house when the true Sons of America went off at the approach of General Howe and left her house. She was soon after supplied with British officers for boarders, and as soon as they left her, her house was filled up again with Whigs, so that when I came here I could not be supplied with lodgings at her house.

The majority of the Quakers remain the same dark, hidden, designing hypocrites as formerly—however as the laws of this State are very strict against all persons who do not take the Oath of allegiance to the State and abjuration of the King of England, not allowing of their buying or selling, receiving debts and in short nearly outlawing them, the Quakers many and I believe most of them are coming in with a sanctified phiz and taking the oath of affirmation, for if you touch their worldly interest you touch their conscience and their best beloved deity.

While affairs remain as they are at present I believe it will be difficult to obtain from Congress a permission to load vessels with provisions for New Hampshire, least they should supply the enemy instead of the inhabitants of New Hampshire. I am very sorry to hear bread is so scarce with you and am persuaded it is not owing to the natural scarcity but to other causes among which the fluctuating state of our money is the principal. The Congress are this day to take up that matter and try to provide a remedy. But the affair is so embarassed, I have but little faith, and fear we shall not be able to effect much, during the war such amazing sums being necessary for the supply of the Army and Navy.

Mr Wentworth is in town but does not attend public business.

Mr Deane has been called in before Congress to give an account of our affairs in Europe and of his conduct there—this has taken up some time and is not yet finished.

The letter to Judge Brackett was handed to me while sitting in Congress by one of the members, it seems to me by Mr Hudson of South Carolina,[2] who is now at Boston, but I am not certain. When I took it I asked I recollect from whence it came and the member said it was handed to him and could give me no account about it.

I am your affectionate friend, Josiah Bartlett

Tr (DLC).

1 William Whipple's August 2 letter to Bartlett is in the Emmet Collection, NN, and Bartlett Papers, NhHi microfilm.

2 Richard Hutson.

William Duer to George Clinton

Dear Sir, Phila'a Aug't 18th 1778.

I have had for some Time past a Considerable Sum of the Public money in my Hands, which the Delegates of the State of New York obtain'd from Congress on the Principle as stated to your Excellency in a Late Letter from Mr. Morris and myself.[1]

When I first received it, my Determination was to proceed to the State of New York within a few Days—but the Foreign affairs becoming interesting from the arrival of the French Minister; and the Necessity of getting a Decision of Congress upon the Conduct of the State of Vermont,[2] and their late Proscription growing every day more Urgent—I have been induced to stay since Mr. Lewis arrival from Baltimore—in hopes of finishing a Business which in my Judgment strikes at our very Existence as a State. I have endeavoured in vain to get several trusty Persons to take the Charge of this money in order to deliver it to you for the Purpose of its being paid into the Treasury of our State—but one or two out of that Number, who might with some Inconvenience to themselves have carried at least Part of it did not chuse to run the Risque. I have endeavor'd to prevail on Mr. Dennig to become the Bearer of it but on finding disagreable to him have been obliged to desist from my Request. As I have pass'd a Receipt in my own Name of this money, I am not willing to hazard it with a Person at my own Risque, Unless I should find a very trustworthy Character, who will consent to take the Trouble. I have, therefore, to request that your Excellency will be pleas'd to direct some Person, who may be depended upon, and who may be coming to Philadelphia, to call upon me for the money; and in case I should not be there to call on his Return to New York at Baskinridge in New Jersey, where I purpose staying some Days on my Return on a Visit to Lord Stirling's Family.[3] Mr. Dennig being in a hurry to Set out, I am obliged to conclude myself with great Respect, & Esteem Your Excellency's Obed't H'ble serv't,

Wm. Duer.

Reprinted from Clinton, *Papers* (Hastings), 3:660–61.

1 See New York Delegates to Clinton, July 21, 1778.

2 Ibid.

3 Duer married Gen. William Alexander's daughter Catherine in 1779. *DAB*.

Henry Laurens to Rawlins Lowndes

[August 18, 1778]

It is now the 18th. Captain Pyne and Captain Martin having declared themselves quite ready I would not attempt to detain them. They began their journey this Morning. I understand they are to halt at Baltimore a day and an half on business of their own—there I hope to overtake them, otherwise this will go by the common Post and not arrive so early as I could wish.

Mr. Deane late one of our Commissioners at the Court of Versailles, has already been two Mornings engaged before Congress reporting from Notes and Memory his own transactions seperately as well as conjunctly with his Colleagues and the state of our Affairs at different periods at that and other Courts in Europe, how many Mornings more the whole Narrative will consume is extreamly uncertain; hitherto he has been very little impeded by questions, when these Commence the progress will be slow—above two hours were employed some days ago in debate upon a motion that Mr. Deane should report to Congress in writing and the motion lost[1]—very much loss of time I foresee will be the consequence; in this debate I clearly discovered that my fellow labourers had as absolutely taken sides as it can be supposed Gentlemen are capable of in a *pure unbias'd* Assembly. Were I to say as ever Attornies had taken at a Bar I might be charged in the modern term with aberation, nevertheless I have taken the liberty to recommend the fillet and scales of Justice to one of my worthy Colleagues[2] who appears strongly attached to one of the parties, no doubt from conviction that that side is right adding the reply which I had made to Mr. D. after he had related to me in private conversation his state of the case. "Your Account Sir, appears to have been very candidly deliver'd, but I dare not flatter you with promises; when I shall have heard the other side I will give my voice as reason and conscience shall dictate." Mr. Deane thank'd me. I remark'd further to my Colleague that nothing short of a written and correct narrative ought to have been accepted by Congress—that if Mr. Deane had acted, which I made no doubt he had, with that accuracy and perspicuity which is the duty of a Gentleman in the Great trust of a Plenipotentiary, nothing could be easier than to render a detail in writing.

As it was incumbent on Mr. Deane to transmit from time to time to Congress advices of all his proceedings, discoveries and observations, and as I could not entertain so degrading a sentiment as a belief of the contrary would involve, very little more than a fair transcript of his letters and journals would be necessary for satisfying the fullest inquiry—without assuming to myself any superiour knowledge I cannot help regretting that the Chair was a bar to the delivery of that opinion in public which arrived too late in friendly conversation after the question had been determined by a majority of nine of thirteen States, thirty two Members present.

Gentlemen had reasoned upon the immense labour of reducing to writing occurences, in three whole years, that the work would procrastinate the business several months, that all that would be deliver'd in writing might in less time and with equal accuracy be related viva voce; those who had not been much accustomed to business, and who lament the waste of time in almost all our proceedings were captivated—but the most curious objection, considering it was started by Mr. Deanes friends, was, that should a narrative in writing be demanded, that Gentleman might avail himself of the advantage of representing glossing &c. &c. as he pleas'd—every unbias'd Man now, after reflection sees that the mode we have adopted will extend debates and often lead disputes into warm contests, wandering from the point.

Whose memory will retain all that has been and shall be related on different days at distance times? Whose notes will quadrate with those of a friend on the other side of the question? Who will acknowledge the accuracy, and precision of the memory or minutes of his opponent? Will you Call on Mr. Deane to recollect what he had said and to decide?—here is a field without limits for Oratory and wrangle, and finally for mutual dissatisfaction.[3]

I have troubled Your Excellency thus minutely, because the subject is not minute, it is of the highest importance to our Union. I have been long of opinion and have intimated my sentiments to my friends—that there have been errors on both sides among our Commissioners—Errors, probably not of the heart, and therefore I had wished that a veil had been judiciously drawn, and a wise seperation made of Gentlemen whose tempers when mixed in joint Commission excluded all harmony.

Already we have made this unhappy discovery that our funds abroad are exhausted, our resources dried up, our credit lost in the West Indies; our Bills of Exchange which are pledg'd for the Interest of loans will go forward at the utmost hazard of dishonor—my sentiments on foreign debt conducted in the manner and by the Men it has been, were declared without reserve to my friends in Charlestown some twelve Months ago, and from the present gloomy prospect it was, that I lately intimated to one of them that our Affairs were in a deplorable state, more so my Dear Sir, than you can form an Idea of, & more so than I ought just now to express—the value of our Current paper Money, is to be determined by the price of articles given in Exchange—this comparison will sink it low indeed—add to all this the injudicious behaviour of people in general, who flatter themselves with persuations that our troubles are at end and who act accordingly—the cunning ones striving to depreciate the value of our Money in order to get as much of it as by all means they can obtain—the simple by an almost total neglect of measures essentially necessary to be continued and pursued by a Nation in our circumstances. Immediately after we had repossessed this City, General Washington in the spirit of a watchful and wise Commander in Chief, sent General Duportail with a letter to Congress[4] recommending the immediate securing the River against Assaults from the Enemy, and for that purpose gave the General, who is principal Engineer ample instructions. We have been here upwards of seven weeks, I have repeatedly urged Congress to hear the instructions read, yet to this moment no step is taken—we are in danger of being routed again whenever two or three English ships of War shall be ordered up this River, and should Count d'Estaing be over power'd or block'd up at Rhode Island, Congress will again be shamefully exiled, possibly in the absence of our Army, captured and all our prisoners retaken—all these things Your Excellency and the state I have the honor of representing should know with proper reservations—there are a thousand other things you are entitled to be informed of, which time and political propriety forbid in the present moment. Therefore I shall leave the subject after one sentence more—I remember to have read or heard some where of a Chief Justice's recommending to a Grand Jury to present the King—permit me to ask my Countrymen if it would be a greater outrage, to present their Attornies (I am in earnest Sir,) for neglect of duty—why are not public Accounts adjusted? Why are not the proceedings of the Confederal Attornies published? I have by strife this day obtain'd a continuation in two volumes including 31st December 1776 which I sent to Your Excellency by this conveyance—half, even quarter diligence would have reached to 1st August 1778 in boards, and to the 19th where I am now in sheets—for the correctness of these which I now transmit I will not be answerable, I know not how they are compiled nor if by any body corrected at the Press.

Major General Mifflin has taken one step on the line of presentment, and although, with submission to his better judgment I think his ground unfirm, yet it may hereafter prove to have been an happy Omen—the first Commandment is the basis of true religion.[5]

Concerning the present Embargo, Congress have recommended to this State and New Jersey to take Measures for ensuring a strict observance, and for preventing infractions by evil minded Men on this extensive unguarded Coast and upon the numerous Creeks Bays and Inlets[6]—the Commercial Committee have recommended to their Agent in Charlestown[7] to dispatch two Vessels with Rice from that Port. I wont affront Your Excellency by intimating that this is no authority—the motive for the Order is good, to save a faithful Confederal Agent at Hispaniola[8] from absolute ruin by paying protested Bills drawn on our Account, but who brought the unhappy Gentleman into this dilemma? I will not say a faithless Secret Committee, but I have no doubt of proving the fact when I get home. Thank God this is the 19th August and that I have strength enough to write on without dinner at 6 o'clock P.M.—a report from the Committee recommending a relaxation of the Embargo in the particular case abovementioned was offer'd two days ago and remains unconsidered[9]—break one link, the gap will be thirteen wide—maugre any and all particular considerations.

20th August. When I had written Yesterday as above, Muckinfuss came in and honored me with your Excellency's favor of the 29th July[10] which I shall endeavour to pay my respects to, before I lay down the Pen. In the mean time a few scraps of intelligence shall precede.

Count d'Estaing from a happy prospect of immediate Conquest at Rhode Island, has in my opinion been decoy'd, what may be the consequence respecting himself is uncertain, but Your Excellency will learn from General Sullivan's last letter of the 14th that our insulated Army were in danger of a Coup de Burgoyne.[11] Who but my friend General Sullivan would have thought that Lord Howe came within ken of the French fleet merely for the benefit of running away from it? Sandy Hook would have been a much more advantageous starting Post. The French ships are extreamly foul, the bottoms of the English Squadron quite clean, these may take or leave; even the immagination of gaining time for the arrival of a Reinforcement was good, the hope encouraged the risque, but I can hardly think Lord Howe as well as he knows the Count's impetus for fight, could have expected such sudden success to his stratagem. The storm which General Sullivan suffered in will have made a great indisposition of both fleets, and they may have since met by single Combatants—the story of a number of ships of War and others in this River and this bay is not yet explained to us—this draws forth another complaint, upon a conference with Monsr. Girard I pressed, weeks since for a regular daily Courier to and from the Capes and Lewistown either by land or water or both. The expence being for an essential service ought to have been no objection, nor indeed has that Article been the obstacle—mere inattention has kept us in ignorance three days, of vessels of War being in the River.

Three hours of this Morning passed in debate whether Governor Franklin should be given in Exchange for Governor McKinly the previous question by aye and nay—an Oration by S.C. Esquire[12] on the improvement of time with the life and characters of Elizabeth and Mary Qu. of Scots—the comparative beauty of black eyes and blue eyes—adjourned.[13] Seldom a question upon a Million of Dollars, seldom an unquestionable demand for an hundred.

The Confederation is now signed by Delegates from ten States as Your Excellency will see in a paper inclosed—Delaware and New Jersey will probably be instructed when their respective Assemblies meet, Maryland 'tis said will not come in without she receives a dower of Land, New York is not bound unless the whole confederate—the decimal is therefore equal to, a 0.

General Lee's tryal ended a week ago. The sentence of the Court Martial is on the road, and ought to have been a secret until Congress had approved or disapproved, but I have been pretty well informed he is acquitted from the charges for disobedience of Orders and shameful retreat, and censured only for insolent letters to the Commander in Chief[14]—the British Officers in New York, who were good judges of fact have passed quite a different Verdict. Governor

McKinly assures me upon his honor, they aver he might have taken the whole party before whom he retreated. That his retreat astonished them and led some of them to suspect stratagem—that animadverting on his term "Check"—Sir Wm. Erskine the best Soldier they have, replied, "Lee may call it a check if he pleases, but, by —— I call it a very handsome flogging, Gentlemen may be convinced now the Americans can and will fight."

By a return lately reported from the Board of War, it appears we have ample stores of Cannon, Powder, Balls, Lead &c. &c. and are not deficient in Muskets—and a Member of that Board promises a report in a few days which will demonstrate cloathing of all species for upwards of 40,000 Men—and yet however strange, near half our little Army have long been and are half naked.

A Schedule to be subjoined or inclosed will shew your Excellency what papers are intended to accompany this & to which please to be referred.

And now in order to give Your Excellency some prospect of relief from a tedious Epistle, I turn to Your Excellency's favour above quoted.

The sequel of the Expedition towards Augustine does not strike disappointment upon my Mind.[15] I will say no more upon the subject at present.

Your Excellency will have received Commissions, both Marine and Army and I will endeavour to transmit more of each by Muckinfuss' return, all Commissions signed by the late President and dated on and after 1st November 1777 ought undoubtedly to be exchanged, the objections against them are good.

The Commission granted by Governor Caswell to Colonel Carroll appears to me a bad precedent,[16] nor will it I apprehend be regarded as a Confederal; were Commissions to be granted by the Executive power of each State, and regular immediate notice given to Congress of name rank and date, it would answer all the ends of the present mode and save trouble, but the law and practice being otherwise, I should suppose the instance in question will be deemed invalid. I can perceive much regulation is wanted in this branch, there is ground for believing that a great, very great number of Officers are receiving pay and Rations who have never been in a field of battle, who are scatter'd over the face of the Country on various pretences and many employ'd in their private occasions, who will also by means of Certificates and good swearing entitle themselves to half pay after the war. This circumstance leads into deep reflection upon the total derangement of every important department in the Union.

The Enemy do not exchange Seamen for any but Seamen of equal rank, and they treat all our Seamen whom they capture with a rigor and barbarity unheard of before the present contest, hence we have begun to retaliate, but our returns of severity bear no kind of proportion—I would not advise to exchange Bachop and Osborne for any persons but Seamen of equal Rank—there is no Cartel established—I have already intimated the interruption—but the Commissaries on each side proceed in exchanging Officer for Officer, Soldier for Soldier, Citizen for Citizen—regarding Rank, the Marine Exchange has been govern'd nearly by like principles, but capriciously and arbitrarily executed on the part of the Enemy—after having by every species of cruelty exercised on our Seamen in order to compel them to enter into their service, under which thousands have died languishing miserable deaths, they have exchanged the emaciated survivors, for healthy well fed fellows, compassion for fellow Citizens on our part has induced us to submit to the injustice and inequality of the Exchange.

I shall make enquiry of the Bills of Exchange vended by Mills and communicate to Your Excellency according to discoveries.

The conduct of the Committee under which Mr. Dorsius acted is misterious. I can say nothing of his own, but from them we can obtain no Accounts—upwards of twelve Months since Accounts of their proceedings were order'd by Congress have elapsed—about ten since Mr. Robert Morris desir'd to take the books into his own custody in order to settle them in a six Months leave of absence which he said he had obtained from his State,[17] and eight Months he threatened to send them back to Congress, which they by no means forbid, yet to this hour we are without books and remain in total ignorance of the expenditure of 2½ Million of Dollars except that we know a very large sum has been shamefully squandered by a brother of Mr. Morris, supported by him after being fully informed of the infamous practices of his brother by the Commissioners at Paris.[18] This, my dear Sir, is another circumstance leading the Minds of Men who have devoted their time and their fortunes to the public service into deep and melancholly reflections.

I have always held a favourable opinion of Mr. Dorsius, nevertheless I would have no further exchanges of Money or Accounts take place between our treasury and him or his Successor whom as an individual I have likewise a good opinion, without an express order or recommendation from Congress. Meaning hereby to deliver only my own opinion in answer to Your Excellency's enquiry. If the waste in the stream makes your heart ache Sir, the prodigality and profusion at the fountain would break it, and yet I believe it will be necessary to draw you there.

My Colleague Mr. Heyward informs me of his determination to return to South Carolina in a day or two, Mr. Hudson is in Boston, Mr. Matthews sick—I shall do myself the honor of addressing Your Excellency again by the conveyance of Mr. Heyward, and also of Muckinfuss—in the mean time as I am now at the 21st I have an opportunity of adding the sentence of the Court Martial on General

Lee and a copy of a letter from General Sullivan,[19] to which I beg leave to refer, and possibly I may get in tomorrows' Packet—I shall send this to Maryland hoping to overtake Captain Pyne and Martin, whose business at Baltimore they said would detain them till Sunday Noon the 23d.

I have the honor to be &c.

P.S. Your Excellency will do me great honor by communicating such parts as you shall think relative to the late Prest. to Mr. Gervais and to permit Mr. Wells to extract such parts of the papers inclosed for publication.

Schedule of Papers inclosed Mr. Lowndes.

1. General Lee's letter to the Commander in Chief & Answer 30th June
2. General Sullivan's Letter to the President, dated Providence 1st Aug.
3. Colonel Lauren's Journal dated Providence 4th Augt.
4. Captains Pine and Martins Receipts for 1940 Dollars.
5. Adam Ferguson's Letter to the President 7th Augt.
6. General Sullivan's Letter to Genl. Washington 13th Augt.
7. J. Morris to Governeur Morris Esqr. 14th Augt.
8. General Sullivan's Letter to the President 17th. Augt.
9. List of Members who have signed the Confederation.
10. New York Lampoon upon Govr. Johnston.
11. Sentence of the General Court Martial on General Lee.

LB (ScHi). A continuation of Laurens to Lowndes, August 16, 1778.

1 Congress had defeated this motion on August 15 by a vote of nine states to four. *JCC*, 11:799–801.

2 William Henry Drayton.

3 Laurens' encounter with Deane and his increasing involvement in the deepening controversy over charges that Deane mishandled public funds during his mission to France have been analyzed at length by Laura Page Frech, "The Career of Henry Laurens in the Continental Congress, 1777–79" (Ph. D. diss., University of North Carolina, Chapel Hill, 1972), pp. 334–60.

4 Laurens is probably referring to Washington's June 30 instructions to General Du Portail on the defense of "[Philadelphia,] the River Delaware and their environs." Washington, *Writings* (Fitzpatrick), 12:134–35.

5 See Laurens to Thomas Mifflin, August 15, 1778.

6 See *JCC*, 11:788.

7 Abraham Livingston. See also *JCC*, 11:815–16.

8 Stephen Ceronio. *JCC*, 11:810.

9 Laurens seems to be referring to an August 19 report by the chairman of the Commerical Committee, Francis Lewis, recommending that cargoes of rice used by Congress or state governments to make remittances "for the payment of arms, ammunition, or other Military Supplies" be exempted from Congress' June 8 provisions embargo. See *JCC*, 11:815–16; and PCC, item 31, fol. 185. Although there is no mention of this report in the journals, it is endorsed by Laurens: "Report Commercial Committee on Embargo." In any event, there is no evidence

in the journals that the Commercial Committee submitted a report on the embargo to Congress on August 17.

10 A transcript of President Lowndes' July 29 letter to Laurens is in the Laurens Papers, ScHi.

11 Gen. John Sullivan's August 14 letter to Laurens, describing the precarious situation of his army in Rhode Island, is in PCC, item 160, fols. 149–50, and Sullivan, *Papers* (Hammond), 2:212–14.

12 Samuel Chase.

13 Although Congress did not approve the exchange of John McKinly, the former president of Delaware, for William Franklin, the last royal governor of New Jersey, on August 20, it did so on September 14. *JCC*, 11:816–18, 12:909–13. McKinly, who had been in British captivity since September 1777, had proposed his exchange for Franklin in an August 20 letter to Laurens while he was in Philadelphia on a month's parole granted by Sir Henry Clinton. Congress' subsequent decision to approve this exchange was prompted by a September 11 letter from McKinly to Laurens, pointing out that his parole would expire on the 16th and he would be obliged to return to British captivity if the delegates did not act quickly. PCC, item 70, fols. 655, 663; and *Del. Archives*, 3:1416–17. See also Thomas McKean's Charges against William Thompson, November 19, 1778.

14 In fact Gen. Charles Lee was found guilty of all three charges. John R. Alden, *General Charles Lee: Traitor or Patriot?* (Baton Rouge: Louisiana State University Press, 1951), chap. 15.

15 In the July 29 letter to Laurens cited above, President Lowndes dealt with the aftermath of an unsuccessful expedition against St. Augustine that had been undertaken by the government of Georgia in conjunction with Gen. Robert Howe, an undertaking Laurens had long opposed.

16 "I have lately seen a Commission," Lowndes wrote to Laurens on July 29, "Issued by Govr. Caswell of No. Carolina to a Colonel Carrol a French Gentleman to Command a Regiment on Continental establishment"—an action Lowndes heartily approved as a rightful exercise of state sovereignty.

17 Lowndes informed Laurens on July 29 that he had rejected a demand by John Dorsius, a Continental agent in Charleston, that South Carolina reimburse him "for supplying some French Gentlemen on their Journey to Congress with Cash &ca.," citing Dorsius' failure to repay a large loan the state government had previously advanced him for Continental ends. Robert Morris was still trying to settle the accounts of the old Secret Committee, which had been replaced in July 1777 by the Committee of Commerce—a task in which he had been engaged for about a year. See *JCC*, 8:423–24, 12:878–79, 1216–17; and Robert Morris to William Whipple, September 4, 1777.

18 For an account of Thomas Morris' misconduct as a Continental agent in France, see Robert Morris to Laurens, December 26, 1777.

19 A transcript of Gen. John Sullivan's August 17 letter to Washington, which was read in Congress on the 21st, is in PCC, item 160, fols. 153–54. Laurens incorrectly described himself as the recipient of this letter in the list of documents he appended to the present letter.

George Plater to Thomas Johnson

Sir, Philadelphia Aug. 18th 1778

Your last Favor is now before us, & we shall pay all due Attention to the Contents.[1] The Consideration of your last relative to the Vessel sold by Mr. Harrison is before the marine Committee, but it does not appear that Mr. Bingham purchased her for the Continent, perhaps for his own private Use. The Appearance of a Fleet off Rhode Island drew the Attention of Count DEstaing from that Object, just at the Time an Attack was preparing to be made—this will consequently retard the Operations there for some Time.

I am with due respect, Yr Excellency's most obt. Servt.

Geo. Plater

RC (MdAA).

1 The Maryland Council's August 14 letter to the state's delegates, concerning Richard Harrison's sale of the *Molly* to William Bingham and Maryland's difficulties in obtaining bills of exchange in the West Indies, is in *Md. Archives,* 21:186. See also Samuel Chase to Thomas Johnson, August 11, 1778, note 1.

Henry Laurens to Hannah Sweers

Madam 19th Augt. [1778]

Your present distressful state so affectingly described in your Letter of Yesterday's date, receives all that is in my power to offer in alleviation, very sincere compassion.[1]

Colo. Sweers' unhappy Affair is now under the consideration of a Committee, of which Mr. Drayton or Mr. Marchant is Chairman,[2] possibly an application to them, or an address to Congress might obtain some relaxation of the unhappy Gentleman's confinement upon a true representation of his bad health.

I am, Madam &c.

LB (ScHi).

1 Hannah Sweers was the wife of Cornelius Sweers, a deputy commissary of military stores who was being confined in a Philadelphia jail pending an investigation of charges that he was guilty of fraud. Although Mrs. Sweers' August 18 letter to Laurens has not been found, her August 21 letter seeking the release of her husband from prison because of his poor health is in PCC, item 78, 20:255–57. Congress read this letter on August 22 and then tabled it. *JCC,* 11:827. See also Laurens to Benedict Arnold, August 5, 1778, note 1.

2 Joseph Reed was chairman of the committee conducting this inquiry. *JCC,* 11:737–38.

Samuel Holten's Diary

Augt. 20 [1778]

Congress Sit late. I walked out with Mr. Gerry. A number of the members of Congress Spent the evening with us. The weather very hot.

MS (MDaAr).

Henry Laurens to John Bailey

Sir

20th August [1778]

I had the honor on the 17th Inst. of laying before Congress your favor of the 11th. Inclosed herein please to receive an Act of the 18th for appointing the Reverend Mr. David Avery to be Chaplain to the Brigade, late Brigadier Learned's.[1]

I am with great Esteem &c.

LB (DNA: PCC, item 13). Addressed: "Colonel John Bailey, Colo. comdt. of the late Genl. Learned's Brigade, White Plains."

[1] See *JCC*, 11:810. Col. Bailey's August 11 letter of recommendation on behalf of the Rev. Avery is in PCC, item 78, 3:103. This day Congress also appointed chaplains for brigades commanded by Gens. James Clinton, John Nixon, George Weedon, and Col. Thomas Clark. Laurens notified Clinton and Nixon of these appointments in brief letters he wrote to them this day; and on August 23 he wrote brief letters to the Revs. Adam Boyd and John Hurt, informing them of their appointments as chaplains to Clark's and Weedon's brigades respectively. PCC, item 13, 2:50, 52.

Henry Laurens to George Washington

Sir

20th Augt. [1778]

My last to Your Excellency went by Dunn dated the 13th since which I have had the honor of receiving and presenting to Congress Your Excellency's second of the 13th and one of the 16th Inst.[1] I have at present nothing to trouble Your Excellency with but an Act of Congress of the 17th for exonerating the Commanding Officers on Hudson's river from any censure for the loss of the Posts in the Highlands.[2]

I have the Honor to be, With great Esteem and Respect &c.

LB (DNA: PCC, item 13).

[1] Washington's letters are in PCC, 152, 6:247, 263–64, and Washington, *Writings* (Fitzpatrick), 12:320–21, 330–31. Among the enclosures Washington transmitted with his August 16 letter to Laurens were the proceedings of Gen. Charles Lee's court-martial. *JCC*, 11:824–25.

[2] See *JCC*, 11:803–4.

Henry Laurens to George Washington

Sir

20th Augt. [1778]

I had the honor of writing to Your Excellency this Morning by Burwell and late the present Evening of receiving Your Excellency's dispatches by Captain Riley.[1] These shall be presented to Congress tomorrow. Inclosed with this will be found a Report of a Committee on Your Excellency's letter, relative to Baron Steuben, which Congress request Your Excellency will take under consideration, and return it as speedily as the case will admit of, together with Your Excellency's opinion on the several parts, and any amendments or additions which shall appear to be necessary.[2]

I am with great Respect &c.

P.S. Baron Arndt has obtain'd from Congress leave of absence for twelve months.[3]

LB (DNA: PCC, item 13). Addressed: "General Washington, White Plains, by Colo. Boudinot." This address confirms the surmise in Burnett, *Letters*, 3:1v, that Elias Boudinot left Congress this day.

1 Washington's August 19 letter to Laurens is in PCC, item 152, 6:269, and Washington, *Writings* (Fitzpatrick), 12:337. With it Washington enclosed a copy of an August 17 letter he had received from Gen. John Sullivan describing the military situation in Rhode Island. PCC, item 160, fols. 153–54.

2 On August 1 Congress had referred to a committee made up of Joseph Reed, Elias Boudinot, and Samuel Chase a July 26 letter from Washington to Laurens describing baron von Steuben's wish to resign as inspector general and assume a field command. Soon realizing that the opposition to his assumption of a field command was too great for him to overcome, however, Steuben elected to continue to serve as inspector general and in consequence he submitted to this committee certain proposals for delineating more fully than before the duties of this office. The Committee thereupon drew up and submitted to Congress on August 20 a plan for "a well regulated Inspectorship for the Army of the United States," which the delegates read and ordered to be sent to Washington for his observations. Washington sharply criticized this plan for concentrating too much power in the hands of the inspector general, and therefore on September 15 Congress referred his observations as well as the plan itself to the Committee of Arrangement, with instructions to draw up a new plan for regulating the inspectorship. Accordingly, the committee devised a new plan that took into account Washington's criticisms of the original one and was approved by Congress on February 18, 1779. See *JCC*, 11:737, 819–23, 12:914, 13:196–97; and Washington, *Writings* (Fitzpatrick), 12:233–35, 436–44.

3 See *JCC*, 11:808–9. Baron d'Arendt had requested leave to return to France in order to recuperate from wounds he had recently received in battle. See Arendt to Laurens, August 18, 1778, PCC, item 78, 7:197.

Marine Committee to John Greene

August 20th. 1778

Sir

The Brigantine Retaliation being at present in the Service of the United States and under your command; on being ready you are immediately to join the French Frigate Chimere and proceed with her down the Delaware in search of the enemies Ships said to be on the River or this Bay. If you fail meeting with the enemies Ships in the River or the Bay, you are after parting with the Frigate Chimere at the Capes of Delaware, to continue to cruze of[f] the said Capes for the time stipulated with your Crew, not exceeding ten leagues from Cape Henlopen.

Should you be fortunate to take prizes, you must send them to the most convenient port in the United States, and the Cruize being ended you are to return with your Brigantine to Philadelphia and make report of your Cruize to this Committee together with the Journals of the same. You will use your endeavours to prevail with the directors of the Brig Convention belonging to this State to order the said Brigantine to make the Cruize aforesaid in company with you. On going down the Bay you will proceed ahead of the Frigate Chimere if desired so to do by the captain of that frigate in order to reconnoitre the enemy, and receive on board your Brig the Pilot of the Chimere should the Captain request it.

Wishing you Success we are sir, Your Hble servants

LB (DNA: PCC Miscellaneous Papers, Marine Committee Letter Book).

Josiah Bartlett to Mary Bartlett

My dear Philada. August 21st 1778

This letter will be forwarded & perhaps handed to you by Mr. Wentworth my Colleague who is to set out tomorrow morning for Home on account of his bad State of Health. I hope it will find you & the rest of my family in health and that my affairs are well Carried on so that you meet with no uncommon Difficulties on that account.

As to my Self I have been & Continue to be in a pretty good State of health. Charles Chace is got about but in a poor State. I have given him leave to ride out into the Country 15 or 20 miles & tarry 2 or 3 weeks for his health which will I hope Recruit him. He is to Set out tomorrow. The weather here is very Disagreably wet & muggy which has occasioned Dysenteries & Diarrheas to be very Common but not very mortal as I am told by some Physicians of my acquaintance. I hope in a few weeks the weather will be Cooler & more healthy.

Your letter of the 17th of last month is the last I have Recd from you. I have nothing new to write to you at present. Expect to have some interesting news from Rhode Island & the French fleet soon. Give my Respects to all friends.

[*P.S.*] Mr. Wentworth sets [*out*] to Day. Hope another Delegate will be sent forward immediately.

RC (NhHi). In Bartlett's hand, with the signature clipped.

Samuel Holten's Diary

[August 21, 1778]

21. By a letter from Genl. Sullivan datd 17th Instt. we understand that he was almost ready to attack the enemy at Rode Island. Congress sit late. The weather is very hot.

MS (MDaAr).

Henry Laurens to William Livingston

Dear Sir 21st Augt. [1778]

I was honor'd with Your Excellency's very obliging favor of the 3d Instant on the 12th,[1] not a day has since passed without an earnest desire in my Mind to pay my respects to it, but other employment obliged me day by day, to say, "tomorrow."

We have nothing new from Spain, I mean new to me, Gentlemen not only smiled, but laughed at my Ideas, expressed while we were reading the Treaties with France, that the Spaniard had his Eye upon the Floridas and Providence, in order to secure the straights of the Gulph. My conjecture was founded on seeing the bawble of Bermuda thrown in to us, and not a word said of Bahama[2]—I have lately received strong confirmation of my suspicions—the Post of St. Marks having been withdrawn by the English, a Spanish Guard I suppose from Pansacola succeeded them, these had a conference lately with our friendly Creek Indians, and in the course of their Talks intimated to the Savages that Spain would soon be repossess'd of that Post and adjacent Country. A venerable Don[3] who lately din'd with me let the Cat a little further out—speaking of the late abortive expedition against St. Augustine, a Gentleman[4] observ'd in French that East Florida would be a great acquisition to South Carolina and Georgia, my good friend Don Juan, either unwarily or supposing I did not understand, replied with much gravity, "and also for Spain." I drank a glass of Ale with the Don.[5]

This I really mean Sir, as a secret, and if we keep it so, the discovery may be apply'd to good purposes when we come to treat in earnest.

I am afraid our present Commissioners are not appriz'd of the immense value to our whole Union of St. Augustine and Bahama, and that too many of us here, view the possession in a light of partial benefit.

If the lampoon of New York hurt Governor Johnstone,[6] W.H. D's. declaration[7] will not be received as an healing plaistir; this thing by the bye, was sadly hurried up; I had been for a fortnight anxiously soliciting my friend out of doors to introduce an Act or Resolve to the same effect, but thro' delay, we were necessitated to accept of a stiff performance without time for proper amendments.

Your Excellency may not have seen the late Remonstrance and requisition of Governor Johnstone and his Colleagues.[8] I shall inclose with this a Copy of that, and of Mr. Adam Ferguson's Letter which usher'd the Paper, calculated as I presume to retort upon Congress for the late publication signed Charles Thomson.[9] It is impossible they can conceive that Congress will admit their Commission for quieting disturbances, founded on a special Act of Parliament as sufficient authority for making a "distinct and explicit Ratification of the Convention of Saratoga"—or, that it contains "a proper notification by the Court of Great Britain to Congress."

Congress have committed their paper, an honor which in my humble opinion it is not entitled to.

The Act of the 8th of January[10] has exceedingly embarrassed the wise Men in the East, a conformity with the terms will Amount to an acknowledgement of our capacity to treat as a Nation, any thing below will imply a continued claim upon us as Subjects in rebellion, to which we will not subscribe, since the Court perceive the dilemma to which she is reduced by a few cunningly designed words dropt from the pen of her marionnette Lieutenant General John Burgoyne Esquire, who has acknowledged in Parliament that he, solely, penned his infamous Proclamation, and in the same moment declared, he had no intention to carry his threats into execution—and it is not to be wondered that in such circumstances they instruct their present minions to try the effect of a little ambi-dexterity.

Your Excellency must know more than I do of the affairs of the fleets and Armies, late of Rhode Island and New York. My last accounts were very unpleasant.

Colonel Boudinot will inform you Sir, the sentence of the Court Martial on General Lee, I presume Congress when they have approved or disapproved will order the tryal to be publish'd.[11]

I Am, With high Esteem &c.

P.S. I have been long out of humour with the too comprehensive term "Continental," and have a strong inclination to coin "Confœderal." If Your Excellency has no objection, it shall pass.

LB (ScHi).

1 Governor Livingston's August 3 letter to Laurens is in Livingston, *Papers* (Prince), 2:406–7.

2 See the fifth and sixth articles of the treaty of alliance with France in *JCC*, 11:450.

3 Don Juan de Miralles.

4 The marquis de Brétigney.

5 Miralles gave a somewhat different account of his dinner conversation with President Laurens on the subject of the marquis de Brétigney's plan for the re-

duction of St. Augustine in a report he wrote for the Minister of the Indies in Madrid: "On the 16th of this month I was invited to dine in the home of the President of Congress, and the Marquis de Brétigny was there. After dinner he spoke to the President about his plan. I was seated beside the President, and took the opportunity to whisper in his ear that the conquest of San Agustín should be undertaken in agreement with our August and Benevolent Sovereign. The President agreed, remarking that the conversation was merely a pastime while we drank a bottle of wine. Nevertheless, the Marquis de Brétigny told me on the 19th that he had presented the plan in French to the Congress, and I am sure it has been sent to the interpreter to be translated." See Miralles to José de Gálvez, August 20, 1778, Papeles Procedentes de Cuba, Legajo 1290, Archivo General de Indias, Seville (Aileen Moore Topping translation, DLC). For Brétigney's plan, see Laurens to John Houstoun, August 27, 1778, note 2.

6 See Laurens to Rawlins Lowndes, August 16, 1778, note 2.

7 A reference to Congress' August 11 declaration that it would have no further dealings with George Johnstone. *JCC*, 11: 770–74.

8 See Laurens to Rawlins Lowndes, August 11, 1778, note 1.

9 The "late publication" was Congress' July 18 resolve that it would not reply to the Carlisle commissioners' letter of July 11. *JCC*, 11:701–2.

10 A reference to Congress' suspension of the Saratoga Convention on January 8, 1778. *JCC*, 10:29–35.

11 See Titus Hosmer to Thomas Mumford, July 6, 1778, note 2.

Marine Committee to Richard Peters

Sir August 21. 1778.

As Colonel Pickerings letter to this Committee of the 19th instant Stated the Military Stores at Baltimore to be so small as to render it unnecessary to appoint a Commissary to take charge of them, it was concluded that these Stores were not wanted on this quarter; and therefore altho an immediate call for them in the Marine way did not exist, the Committee upon consideration of probable want, did determine that the stores should be sent to Portsmouth where a Continental agent already appointed might take charge of them. But your letter of this day representing that the Stores may be wanted here, the Committee have reversed their order of yesterday, and the Stores are now at the disposal of your board.[1] I have the honor to be Sir, Your very Hble servant, R. H. Lee Chairman

LB (DNA: PCC Miscellaneous Papers, Marine Committee Letter Book).

1 The aforementioned letters of Board of War members Peters and Timothy Pickering are not in PCC.

New York Delegates to George Clinton

Sir In Congress Philadelphia 21st Aug't 1778

Just now a Letter was read from the Governor of Virginia to Congress in which his Excellancy (in polite Language) informs

Congress that having in vain endeavoured to get their accounts adjusted and the United States being indebted to it, the State of Virginia have determined not to pay any Proportion of their Quota untill the accounts are settled.[1] We think it our Duty to inform your Excellency of this Circumstance. Whether the State we have the Honor to represent will imitate this Example it is in their wisdom to determine. Many States have received such astonishingly large advances from the Continent that we have no Conception how they can have been expended on the continental account and, therefore, are led to believe that considerable Sums are due from some Individual, to the United States while on the other Hand it is certain that the Union is considerably indebted to others. Whatever may be the future Determinations of wiser Persons in Congress certain it is that on any Principle Injustice will be done unless all these different accounts be finally closed in a short Time. We do not presume to censure or commend the Conduct of any Sister State much less to hold up any Example to be pursued or avoided, having as we have the fullest Confidence in the Wisdom of our Legislature and that they will upon an intimate Knowledge of their own Circumstances pursue the Line of Conduct which shall be dictated by wisdom, Justice and that patriotic attention to the American Cause by which they have hitherto been distinguished among the several States which compose the Confederacy.

We have the Honor to be with deep Respect Your Excellency's most obedient & humble Servant,

F. Lewis,
Gouv'r Morris.

P.S. Mr. Duer is now on Business at the Board of War[2] wherefore he hath not an Opportunity of seeing this Letter.

Reprinted from Clinton, *Papers* (Hastings), 3:676–77.

[1] This day the Board of Treasury laid before Congress letters from Govs. Patrick Henry of Virginia and Thomas Johnson of Maryland written in response to a July 24 circular letter to the states from the board urging them "to make Monthly Returns to this Board of the Sums of Money paid into their Hands, for the purpose of supplying the Continental Treasury, conformable to the Resolution of Congress of the 22nd Day of November last." *JCC*, 11:826. In reply, Henry stated that Virginia would not pay a Continental requisition for $240,000 because Congress' debt to his state already exceeded that amount, and Johnson declared that Maryland could pay only $50,000 of a requisition on her for $130,000. PCC, item 136, 2:481, 485–86. According to a brief note by President Laurens, Congress this day ordered both of these letters "to lie for information of the Members." Ibid., fol. 479.

[2] See James Lovell to Horatio Gates, November 3, 1778, note 6.

Henry Laurens to John Lewis Gervais

My dear friend. 22 August [1778]

You shall hear from me by Muckinfuss, at present let me refer you for News and Newspapers directed to you, to our friend the President—who I know will use my opinion upon the various subjects which I have touched—with his wonted discretion and wisdom.

I had not heard of Colo. Laurens from the 4th Instant till the advice from Mr. Morris, therefore had concluded he had been with Count d'Estaing in order to tempt his fortune on Sea.

Sullivan's letter looks very like a Burgoynade.[1] I wish happier consequences respecting us may attend.

Adièu.

LB (ScHi).

[1] Laurens is referring to Gen. John Sullivan's August 17 letter to Washington in which he boasted that he was on the verge of a great victory over the British in Rhode Island. PCC, item 160, fols. 153–54. Congress had read this letter on August 21. *JCC*, 11:825.

Henry Laurens to James Pyne

Sir 22nd Augt. [1778]

I hope this with six Packets which I take the liberty of troubling yourself and Mr Martin with will overtake you at Baltimore, altho' I hope you have not tarried a moment for these.

My dispatches to His Excellency the President of South Carolina contain Intelligence, which will give general pleasure in that State, I wish therefore to forward it with all possible dispatch, of which you will properly consider, and lose no time unnecessarily on the Road.

General Sullivan in a Letter of the 17th gives us great hopes that he would reduce the Enemy to terms of Capitulation in a few days. I wish you and Mr. Martin a good Journey.

And Am &c.

LB (ScHi). Addressed: "Captain James Pyne, Baltimore."

Henry Laurens to John Beatty

Dear Sir 23 Augt. [1778]

You will oblige me very much and inable Me to accomodate our friends by procuring and sending to me as early as convenience will admit of an Almanack or other Pocket book containing the latest

Army and Navy lists of the kingdom of Great Britain, the best approved Charts of North America, and two dozen neat silver Table Spoons. The Amount of which shall be paid to your Order on demand in Gold or a Bill of Exchange which will be considered in the price.

I Am, With great Regard &c.

P.S. Be so good as to send the inclosed letter[1] forward by the first conveyance.

This moment I have the honor of yours of the 20th Instant and thank you Sir for your politeness. Sending me New York papers as early and as constantly as possible will be very obliging, and I will with pleasure repay any expence, and endeavour to retaliate the favor. Inclos'd will be a letter from F. Raveneau a Marine prisoner in New York, permit me to recommend him to your attention—not meaning to ask a partial favor nor to give you unnecessary trouble.

LB (ScHi). Addressed: "Colonel Jno Beatty, Com. Genl. of Prisoners, Princetown."

[1] See Laurens' August 21 letter to William Livingston.

Henry Laurens to James Graham

Sir[1]

23d August [1778]

This moment your favor of the 10th together with letters for Mr Johnston and Mr. Houston were delivered to me. These shall go forward in the course of the present week.

Were it as inoffensive Sir, without further enquiry to grant a free passage to yourself, I would with great pleasure remove the difficulties you complain of, and add every means in my power for the happy prosecution of your wishes, but your application is met by a question which you have not enabled me to determine; Is the Gentleman a Citizen of any of these States?

If Sir, you are a Subject of His Britannic Majesty, the moment you pass the line of usurpation, you will consider yourself and be considered as in an Enemy's Country, liable to penalties common in such cases, unless you are guarded by a special licence from the Representatives of the good People of the Union. All therefore that I can at present contribute towards your relief, is to lay your Letter before Congress—and you shall be presently advised of the result.

I write now, because I have an immediate opportunity and because as I perceive your Letter has been long on the road I would not hold you in more than unavoidable suspense.

I have the honor to be &c.

P.S. Having since writing the above intimated to Mr. Telfair the receipt and contents of your letter, that Gentleman observd there were circumstances in your favor which he should urge to Congress.[2]

LB (ScHi). Addressed: "Jas. Graham Esqr. at the house of Richd. Yates Esqr., New York."

1 James Graham (d. 1786), a native of Scotland, was a former Georgia planter whose loyalty to the crown had led him to return to Britain as support for independence grew in Georgia. His brother, John, was the last royal lieutenant governor of Georgia. See *DAB*, s.v. "Graham, John."

2 On August 24 Congress simply referred Graham's August 10 letter to the Georgia and South Carolina delegates. The letter itself is not in PCC.

Henry Laurens to John Laurens

My Dear Son 23 Augt. [1778]

I writ to you the 13th. Have not had the pleasure of hearing from you since yours of the 7th.[1]

Variety of Reports occupy the attention of all Classes in Philadelphia. Count d'Estaing has beat Lord Howe—Lord Howe has been beaten by a hurricane—Lord Howe has drove Count d'Estaing—the British Isis engaged and had nearly taken Languedoc—the Renown flog'd the Languedoc &c. &c. &c.—all these; and many supplmentary particulars you know are in my regard, flying Clouds. I patiently wait for more solid Intelligence, and flatter myself with hopes of receiving such from your hand in due time.

If General Sullivan falls short of his views of the 17th his Letter will be christened a Burgoynade and be deposited with the Proclamation of the 23d July 1777. My Compliments to the General and assure him of my better thoughts. I persuade myself of the honor of congratulating with him upon his giving Mr. Prescott a *coup* de Burgoyne. Inclosed with this you will find three foreign Letters, which from the dates of my own I believe will convey to you nothing new.

I am &c.

LB (ScHi).

1 See Laurens to John Laurens, August 13, 1778, note.

Henry Laurens to Lachlan McIntosh

Dear General 23 Augt. [1778]

I receiv'd the inclos'd letters two or three days ago from South Carolina.

The last intelligence from Rhode Island is seven days old. General Sullivan writes, that on the 18th he should make an assault on the

Enemy, begirt within their lines nearest to Newport town, that he hoped to necessitate General Prescott to come out and fight on very disadvantageous terms, or to Capitulate. General Sullivan had of all sorts 9000 rank and file, his right wing commanded by General Greene, his left by Marquis de la Fayette, Lieutenant Colonel Laurens commanded the advanced Party. The Enemy's strength about 6500 including all their Seamen collected from 6 frigates, 2 gallies, and a great number of transports &c. which Count d'Estaing had oblig'd them to burn and sink.

Count d'Estaing had been drawn out to Sea the 10th Instant upon the appearance of Lord Howe's Squadron close in with the Island, he fled upon the Count's making sail and there was every appearance of stratagem for diverting our Allies from the siege of the Island, for gaining time in expectation of a Reinforcement under Admiral Byron and drawing us into an equal fight—on the 11th it happened a very violent storm of Wind continued to the 13th which had almost ruined our insulated Army—General Sullivan's prospect was then cover'd by gloom, he apprehended the Enemy would take an advantage of his distress; and he had only to trust to his Bayonets, and as he express'd himself, "to conquer or die." From Mr. Prescotts silence at so critical a time, I conjecture he is by no means as strong as 6500, or that he dare not trust his Men out of the lines and from under his Eye. The desertions from him of scores of Men almost every night, warrants the latter opinion.

How our floating friends and Enemies fared in that storm, or what is become of them, we know not with precision, a Letter from a French Gentleman in the Camp to Monsr. Girard reports that Count d'Estaing had taken one capital English ship and six frigates, or small armed Vessels.

A deserter from New York examin'd by me last night, and he is a very sensible Man, says, the Eagle had been driven on shore back of Long Island, that Lord Howe had saved his person and return'd in a Frigate, that three or four more English ships of the Line were likewise driven on shore and left, but whether the storm of wind or Count d'Estaings cannon had been author of these disasters he could not aver—upon the whole, it is reasonable to conclude the Enemy's fleet is scatter'd and much hurt—that, of our friends we wait to learn the fate of, probably tomorrow will inform us, and I also expect to know tomorrow whether General Sullivan has succeeded according to his sanguine expectations, or has met with a Burgoynade.

General Washington's Army remained at White Plains hemming in Sir Henry Clinton and ordering rations for deserters who are continually coming in. I conjecture Sir Henry has not lost less than 400, since General Washington established his Encampment.

Two Hessian Lieutenants lately deserted from New York, the brother of one of them is Aid de Camp to General Knyphausen, I expect him every hour. I receiv'd an indirect message from him last night—Deluded, wretched old England! Inclosed you will receive Copy of the sentence of the General Court Martial on General Lee. Observe I send this only for yourself. I have added a Note or two on the paper. I have been assur'd by a Gentleman on whose words I rely that he has often heard the British Officers express their astonishment at the retreat of my old friend, and repeatedly say the party before whom he retired expected nothing less than being every Man Captured. Sir Wm Erskine, particularly animadverting General Lee's phrase of an "handsome check," said "Lee may call it what he pleases but by —— I call it a handsome flogging. We had not receiv'd such an one in America." My dear General I wish you all happiness; and am with great Regard, Your friend and Most Obedt. Servant.

[*P.S.*] Whenever you write to me, carefully separate private from Public. I beg Sir, you will deliver the Inclos'd to Monsr. de Cambray, and communicate the News. I would have written by this bearer but he would not wait, had I attempted to write to both, I should have lost the opportunity.

LB (ScHi). Addressed: "General Lachlan Mackintosh, Commandant, Fort Pitt."

Henry Laurens to the Chevalier de La Neuville

23d Augt. [1778]

Sir

Your Servant called on me twice at the times you had directed him, and I have since been twice reminded by Notes from yourself of the expected Brevet for Rank of Brigadier General—I have as often addressed Mr. Duer on the subject and as often received promises from him that he would make the necessary report to Congress, but the multiplicity and hurry of business in which that Gentleman is engaged has hitherto kept it back.[1]

As soon as the Report shall be made and a Resolve formed thereon, you may be assured Sir, of being properly inform'd in the course of my duty.

I have the honor to be &c.[2]

LB (DNA: PCC, item 13). Addressed: "Monsr. de Laneuville, White Plains."

1 See Laurens to Washington, July 31, 1778, note 5.

2 This day Laurens also wrote the following letter to baron de Kalb:

"I had the honor of receiving yesterday, and presenting to Congress your favors both of the 18th Inst., the other respecting the Vicomte Du Muroy &c. is committed. When a Report and Resolve are matured you shall be immediately informed." PCC, item 13, 2:52–53.

The August 17 and 18 letters of Kalb, to which Laurens meant to refer, are in PCC, item 164, fols. 318–22. Congress never approved Kalb's request to appoint Mauroy a major general in the Continental Army.

Henry Laurens to George Washington

Sir 23d Augt. [1778]

I beg leave to refer Your Excellency to my last letter of the 20th. The Morning following I had the honor of presenting to Congress Your Excellency's favor of the 19th, together with the proceedings of the general Court Martial appointed for the tryal of Major General Lee, the consideration of which is made an Order for the 26th.[1]

I have the honor to be &c.

LB (DNA: PCC, item 13). Endorsed: "Not sent." No evidence has been found to explain why Laurens decided not to send this apparently innocuous letter to Washington.

[1] See also Titus Hosmer to Thomas Mumford, July 6, 1778, note 2.

Josiah Bartlett to Mary Bartlett

My Dear Philadelphia August 24th 1778

This Day your two letters of the 24th & the 31st of July were brought me by the Eastern Post, and am very happy to hear you were all well & that Rhoda in particular had in a great Measure Recovered her health; I am glad to hear of rains being Sent, after the Sharp Drought you mention, Hope they will be Continued so as to Revive the Languishing fruits of the Ground Especially the Indian Corn, a Scarcity of which would be very Distressing in Newhampshire, Tho but of little consequence here. I am sorry to hear there is like to be a Scarcity of Cider, as I sensibly feel the want of it here, where there is always a Scarcity or rather where they never use much of it, and what is made is very inferior to the New England Cider; If I am not likely to make any I hope you will purchase a few barrels if you Can Conveniently at the proper time of making, as I should be glad of a little (after so long fasting from it) when I return home.

I wrote you last Friday by Mr. Wentworth, who Set out that Day for his own Home for the Recovery of his health. He was not able to attend business here and his health grew rather worse than better. Charles Chace is better but so poorly that I have sent him out of the City into the Country ten or a Dozen miles for 2 or 3 weeks for the Recovery of his health, so that I am here at present without Colleague or waiter but in a pretty good State of health, hope it will Continue, as I have used Every precaution I thought would Contribute to my health. The weather was very wet, with a Disagreable muggy heat for near a fortnight, but is now Cleared up Cool & pleasant & much more agreable. The very irregular Manner in which I Receive your letters, sometimes 2 or 3 at once & then missing 2 or 3 weeks without receiving any, Makes me Suspect that the Post has left off riding to Exeter as usual. Does my letters Come to you in the same irregular manner.

I have no news of importance to write you. Rhode Island & the French Fleet are the great objects from which we Expect the first news of Consequence.

As I have no great news to write you, I will fill my letter with Smaller matters. This State have made a law for Confiscating all the Estates real & personal of those Inhabitants who Joined the Enemy, and are Seizing & Selling them for the use of the State, and no person is allowed to sell or buy or recover any Debt, make a will or transact any business, who Does not take an oath of allegiance to the State & an abjuration of the King of England before a Certain Day.[1] Monsr. Gerard the French ambassador has given all the Members of Congress an invitation to Dine with him to morrow being the Birth Day of his most Christian Majesty the French King. The ambassador has paid visits in form to all the Delegates; he began with Newhampshire and paid me the first visit about ten Days ago.

Board & Every thing here is very Dear, I give 20 Dollars per week for my own Board, that is only my victuals and Lodging; my Drink & washing I pay for Besides, horse-keeping in proportion, wine 16 Dollars per Gallon &c &c &c. Now for fashions; when the Congress first moved into the City, they found the Tory Ladies who tarried with the Regulars, wearing the most Enormous High head Dresses after the manner of the Mistresses & Wh——s of the Brittish officers; and at the anniversary of Independance they appeared in public Dressed in that way, and to mortify them, some Gentleman purchased the most Extravagant high head Dress that Could be got and Dressed an old Negro wench with it, she appeared likewise in public, and was paraded about the City by the mob. She made a most shocking appearance, to the no Small Mortification of the Tories and Diversion of the other Citizens. The head Dresses are now shortning & I hope the Ladies heads will soon be of a proper size & in proportion to the other parts of their Bodies.

The little bobed Hats for the men are growing fast out of fashion, the mode now is large round brims & cocked Nearly 3 Square, no hats are now made in any other mode here, So much for fashions, for the Satisfaction of my Children. Remember my love to them and to all Enquiring friends. Yours, Josiah Bartlett

RC (NhHi).

1 Although the Pennsylvania act confiscating the property of people attainted by the assembly or convicted of treason was passed on March 6, 1778, its operational impact remained insignificant until after the British evacuation of Philadelphia exposed many loyalists to the state judicial system. See Thomas McKean to William Atlee, July 7, 1778, note.

Marine Committee to John Barry

Sir August 24th. 1778

Immediately upon receipt of these our orders you will commence on a Cruize in Company with the Continental Brigt. Ressistance, Captain Bourke, between Cape Henlopen and Occracock on the Coast of North Carolina, with a view to take certain armed Vessels fitted out by the Goodriches,[1] or any other of the enemies Vessels that may be infesting that Coast.

As both the Raleigh and Resistance may soon be wanted to answer the purpose of Convoy, you are to manage your Cruize assd. as that you may be ready to receive the future orders of this Committee. For this purpose you are once a week to put into Cheseapeake Bay and call at the Town of Hampton, where you will find such orders lodged and you are to continue to cruize and call at Hampton in this manner until you receive our Instructions. We are Sir, Your Hble servants

P.S. You will communicate to Captain Burke these our Orders, and as Senior officer will give such Instructions for the Cruize as may be necessary.[2] We have written to the Governor of Virginia to furnish you at Hampton with such provisions or Supplies as you and captain Bourke may want.[3] We expect that Governor will appoint some person at Hampton to supply you—let us know by every opportunity the progress of your Cruize.

LB (DNA: PCC Miscellaneous Papers, Marine Committee Letter Book). Addressed: "Captain John Barry of the Frigate Raleigh."

1 See also Cornelius Harnett to Richard Caswell, September 15, 1778, note 2.

2 This day the Marine Committee also wrote the following letter to Capt. William Burke:

"We have given orders to Captain John Barry of the Frigate Raleigh for a Cruize on the Coast in which he is to be accompanied by the Brig Resistance under your command. Captain Barry will communicate to you a Copy of our orders and as Senior officer will give you such further Instructions as may be necessary which you are to obey." Paullin, *Marine Committee Letters*, 1:288.

3 The Marine Committee's letter to Patrick Henry has not been found.

South Carolina Delegate to Unknown

[August 24, 1778]

There is abundant reason to suppose that an engagement has happened at sea between the French squadron and Lord Howe's fleet. Reports are strong that the latter has got a drubbing, and there is reason to believe it from the superiority of the French, and the great ability and spirit of Count d'Estaign. General Sullivan's last letter placed him under regular approaches, within 200 paces of the enemy's works round the town of Newport, and gave us reason to expect a speedy and favourable issue. We expect soon to receive authentick accounts of these two great events.

By our last accounts from England, a very extensive commotion had taken place in Ireland, so that the former is obliged to send all the troops they can spare to the latter.

MS not found; reprinted from the *South Carolina and American General Gazette*, September 24, 1778, where it is headed: "Extract of a Letter from a Member of Congress, August 24."

Samuel Holten's Diary

[August 25–26, 1778]

25. Tuesday. Congress dined with the French Minisr. at his invitation & about 40 other Gentlemen. The Diner was grand & Elegant, & the band of musick was very agreeable. I wrote to Colo. Hutchinson & Mrs Holten (No. 14).[1] The weather is exceeding hot.

26. Wednesday. The weather is very hot, met a Committee at 5 o'Clock, & then took a walk with the Honl. Mr. Adams.

MS (MDaAr).

[1] Not found.

Henry Laurens to William Smith

Dear Sir 25th. Augt. [1778]

The receipt of your favor of the 22nd recalled to my attention that of the 5th which through constant application to Public business had not received the respect due to it.

I have this Morning dispatch'd Mr. Custer a Young Man out of my own house to view the Post Coach at the Head of Elk. If he approves of it and has an opportunity he will write to you from thence, in order to prevent the disposal or removal of it until I shall have corresponded through your favor with Mr. Hudson on the great point, the price.

I am inform'd he purchas'd with the Carriage, Harness for four horses, and that there were too cushions, the whole for £250 Currency. His demand therefore, after deducting one set of Harness and one Cushion is enormous.

The Idea that every thing is cheap enough for the present will ruin me unless he takes care to lay a proper restraint. You would be astonish'd if I were to tell you the daily Amount of my expence. I nevertheless, my Dear Sir, thank you for the purchase of the Wine, and within this Cover remit a reimbursement in 134 dollars.

It is said a ship from Bourdeaux is in the Delaware. I am persuaded when it is known in the West Indies the River is open we shall have Vessels dropping in with all kinds of goods, hence I am induced to lay the restraint intimated above for a few days.

Dunlap's Packet will give you the current News of Philadelphia—Let me assure you not one word relative to the French and English Fleets deserves higher regard than as mere report—the most authentic Account respecting them I received from a very sensible Man of the rank of Commissary who lately came in from the Enemy at New York. He says that on the 18th Inst. it was whisper'd among the British and Foreign Officers that Lord Howe's Squadron had receiv'd very great injuries; the Eagle and 3 or 4 other ships of the line were driven on shore on the back of Long Island, but whether by the French fleet or by the storm, he could not positively tell, but believe the latter, except the ragged and distressed state of the Isis and that one frigate dismasted had got into New York all is conjecture. I expect this Evening or tomorrow Morning to receive regular Advices.

You will find within, Copy of General Sullivan's late letter, by no means let this be publish'd. I sent it for your amusement and information. My hopes of success at Rhode Island without the further aid of Count d'Estaing are exceedingly faint—'tis probable however there will be much blood spilt. I not only dislike the vaunting of his Burgoynade Proclamation but another material circumstance which need not at present be intimated.

This instant I have a Letter from the General of the 19th inclosed in one of the 21st from His Excellency the Commander in Chief.[1] The 19th General Sullivan had advanced his Batteries within Musket shot of the Enemy's Redoubts, and intended to open upon them the next Morning—they had kept an incessant fire on him two days without injuring a single Man—Count d'Estaing not return'd.

General Washington writes, "By advices from an Officer of Rank and intelligence I am informed that 16 ships entred the Hook on the 17th, one having a flag, and that on that and the preceding day a heavy Cannonade was heard at Sea."[2] 'Tis nine o'clock. I must repair to duty. Believe me to be, With very great Esteem and Regard &c.

LB (ScHi).

[1] Gen. John Sullivan's August 19 letter to Laurens is in PCC, item 160, fol. 156, and Sullivan, *Papers* (Hammond), 2:236–37. Washington's brief August 21 forwarding letter to the president is in PCC, item 152, 6:273–74.

[2] Closing quotation mark editorially supplied. This quotation comes from the August 21 letter from Washington to Laurens cited above, which is not printed in Fitzpatrick's edition of his writings.

Henry Marchant to William Greene

Sir: Philadelphia, August 25, 1778.

I have the honor of yours of the 13th inst.[1] We have been favored with letters from Gen. Sullivan of the 17th, and affairs were then in a hopeful train. We are in momentary expectation of advices important. Heaven grant they may be of favorable success. The treasury was a little uneasy at finding that our State money had not been received upon the warrant which issued in their favor. I have wrote Mr. Clark upon it,[2] and have not time now to add, but that I wish the State money now in the Loan Office may be redeemed at all events. It may assist us in future applications. I enclose the papers of the week, and am, Your Excellency's most obedient and humble servant,

Henry Marchant

MS not found; reprinted from William R. Staples, *Rhode Island in the Continental Congress, 1765–1790* (Providence: Providence Press Co., 1870), p. 198.

[1] Governor Greene's August 13 letter to Marchant, describing recent military developments in Rhode Island, is in Staples, *Rhode Island in the Continental Congress*, pp. 194–95.

[2] Marchant's letter to Joseph Clark, the Continental loan officer in Rhode Island, has not been found.

New York Delegates to George Clinton

Sir, Philadelphia 25th. August 1778.

We do ourselves the Honor to enclose to your Excellency a Letter delivered to us this Morning.[1] Whether any Redress can be given to the Petitioner it is certainly impossible for us now to determine. You will permit us however to observe that the Instance is by no Means singular. If by the Blessing of divine Providence the City of New York should this Campaign fall into our Hands It is in your Excellency's Wisdom to determine whether any Measures should be taken to secure for the Use of the true Owners the numerous Slaves which have been seduced by the Enemy.

With deep Respect, We have the Honor to be, Your Excellency's most obedient and most humble Servants,

F. Lewis
Wm. Duer[2]
Gouv Morris

RC (ViU). Written by Gouverneur Morris and signed by Morris, Duer, and Lewis.

1 Margaret Childe's August 18 letter to the New York delegates, requesting their assistance in obtaining the return of her slave Milford Smith, who had left Philadelphia with the British army and was now in New York, is in Clinton, *Papers* (Hastings), 3:662–64. Although Clinton informed the delegates on September 7 that he would do his best to help Mrs. Childe, that is the last reference to this subject in the printed edition of the governor's papers. Ibid., p. 743.

2 Although the paucity of surviving contemporary manuscript materials makes it difficult to document Duer's activities as a delegate to Congress, a contract in the papers of the French agent of the Royal Marine dating from this period indicates that Duer found opportunities to pursue his mercantile career while in Philadelphia. This "Contract for Masts &ca," which Duer and Silas Deane signed on August 29, 1778, specifying that they would supply the French navy with "Twenty Ship Loads of Masts, Spars, Plank & ship timber within the space of Eight Years from the date hereof, or three Cargoes annually during the said Term, as shall be approved of by the Minister of the Marine of France," is in the Jean Holker Papers, DLC.

George Plater to Thomas Johnson

Sir Philadelphia Aug. 25th 1778

In Consequence of your Letter respecting the Bills of Exchange[1] we applied to Mr. Morris, who recommended us to Mr. Holker Agent for the Marine of France, & from him I expect to get them at the Exchange you mention—when done shall transmit them without Delay. The Commission shall likewise be forwarded. I have desired Mr. Morris to make out his Account against the State, which he has promised to do. We are in hourly Expectation of something important from R. Island.

I have the Honor to be—Yr. Excellency's most ob. Servt.

Geo. Plater

RC (MdAA).

1 See George Plater to Thomas Johnson, August 18, 1778, note.

Henry Laurens to William Maxwell

Sir 26th Aug. [1778]

Mr. Thomson Secretary of Congress, shewed me a Note Yesterday in which you enquired of him whether he had any dispatches for Head Quarters; this message I apprehend arose from Your having receiv'd no Answer from me to your favor of the 8th which had accompanied a Packet from the British Commissioners.[1] I beg you will be assured Sir, my silence has not been the effect of disregard ⟨*the practice of Congress is to receive public Letters from the President, and to make such order or no order as the house shall think proper. The President when there is an Order carries it into Execution, but he has the letter no longer in his custody. It is filed in the Secretary's Office.*⟩

⟨*Upon Your letter there was an Order made, but directed to his Excellency General Washington which I transmitted immediately, and should have paid the same attention to General Maxwell.*⟩

Your Letter, Dear General together with the Commissioners Paper which is of a very extraordinary nature were referred to a special Committee who have not reported. Be assured of hearing from me immediately after I shall have received any Order from Congress. In the mean time accept this as a private Correspondence intended to signify the respect and regard with which I have the honor to be &c.

LB (ScHi). Addressed: "Brigadier General Maxwell, Elizabeth Town, New Jersey."

[1] See also Laurens to Rawlins Lowndes, August 11, 1778, note 1.

John Mathews to Thomas Bee

My Dear Sir, Philadelphia Augt. 26th. 1778

The time to which I am confined, deprives me of the very singular pleasure I always feel in communicating in the fulest manner my sentiments, to a person for whom I entertain so high an Esteem, & will only admit of my acknowledging the receipt of your very exceptable & most agreeable favor of the 18th July which I received this morning, & hearing Mr. McLean was to set off in an hour, I thought it would be some satisfaction to you to know your letter was come to hand.

Nothing very material has happened since Heyward left us. We had a letter from Sullivan yesterday dated 19th. He says he has two Batteries erected within musket shot, & one half Musket shot, from the Enemies principal works, he shall continue untill he has compleated the whole of his works before he fires a shot, & then he is to play the Devil with them in a very little time. He says They keep up an incessant heavy fire upon him but hitherto had done him no harm, not even kill'd a Man, in short he speaks as confidently of success as if he was already in possession of New Port, I shan't believe him a bit the sooner for it. It was but four days before that he wrote Congress the Damndest jumping, whining letter, that ever old Woman did. We have not yet heard a Syllable of Count De Estaing that can be depended on. I am in hopes by McInfuss, to give you a more satisfactory acco. of these matters.

You can't conceive the Joy, the sight of your well know hand afforded me, it was indeed inexpressable, for Mr. Hall mentioned to me, some time ago, the dangerous situation you were then in, & never having heard anything of you since my anxiety was great indeed. This state of uncertainty has prevented me writing to you. But now that I am assured of your recovery, you may expect to have your time again broke in upon, as it has hitherto been by the obligation that I know your politeness will lay you under, of perusing my scribbling. Such as it is, be Assured it comes from one who feels no small share of felicity, in being admitted to subscribe himself your most sincere Friend & Obdt. Serv. Jno. Mathews

RC (ScC).

Joseph Reed to Esther Reed

My dear Hetty Camp at White Plains Aug 26, 1778

We did not reach This Place before Sunday Evening owing to The Heat of The Weather & some other Circumstances which usually attend the Travelling of Ladies, however upon the whole it has not been unpleasant. The Weather since we have been here has been if possible more disagreeable than before & we feel it more sensibly, as our Quarters are hot & very dirty. I think I never met with such a Combination of Smells & every one offensive. This Army seems at present to be stationary & indeed both main Armies appear to be looking at Rhode Island where there is hourly Expectation of something important. The French Fleet have returned, but very much shattered by the late Storm which has handled both Squadrons pretty severily. Two French Men of War are dismasted & one missing. We have Papers from New York from which we can gather that some of the British Fleet are returned but from Rivington's Silence there is great Reason to think they have suffered very much. I have very great Doubt of the Rhode Island Business—Sulivans Evil Genius I fear will follow him, & some Circumstances daily transpire which countenance my Apprehensions. I shall forward the Business here with all possible Expedition that I may return to Philad. where I am much wanted & where my Interest evidently calls me. I shall have the Pleasure of seeing you on The Way & staying with you as long as I can. In the mean Time I must bid my dear Girl Adieu & assure her that I am with unalterable Affection, most Sincerel[illegible] J Reed[1]

RC (NHi).

1 Reed wrote to his wife again on the 28th, but had little public news to report "except that there are strong Appearances of a Movement on the Part of the Enemy—but their Destination is a profound Secret—if I was to hazard a Conjecture it would be that they will proceed to Newport & from thence either attempt something on the Eastern Colonies or leave the Continent altogether. Time must determine which." Reed Papers, NHi.

Committee of Arrangement to Henry Laurens

Sir, Hd. Qrs. White Plains August 27th. 1778[1]

An opinion is prevalent in the Army that the officers of it have no authority to enlist the drafted Levies for three years or during the continance of the War, on a supposition that Congress do not incline to have such enlistments made. Whence this opinion may be derived is uncertain but it would be surely wise to clear up a doubt which in its consequences may prove so injurious to the keeping up a respectable Army.

A great spirit for enlisting has taken place among the Soldiery who are brought into the Army as drafts for a short *Term*, on a supposition that the war will speedily be determined.

This event being at best *uncertain* & may be rendered more so in a few days, we beg leave to suggest to Congress the expediency of authorizing the enlistment of all Soldiers in the Army for *short periods*, during the term of three years or the continuance of the War. We wish an immediate adoption of this measure, that all possible advantage may be derived from the present temper of the Army.

We are most respectfully, Sir, Your most Obt. Servants,

Jos. Reed
John Banister

[*P.S.*] We beg the opinion of Congress on this business may be transmitted as soon as possible to the General or Committee, as it seems of the utmost Consequence.

RC (DNA: PCC, item 78). Written by Banister and signed by Banister and Reed.

1 The Committee of Arrangement, consisting at this time of John Banister, Joseph Reed, and Roger Sherman, probably left Philadelphia about August 17 and joined the Continental Army at White Plains on August 23. It was the successor of the Committee at Camp that had worked with Washington at Valley Forge to reform the army the preceding winter, and it had its origin in Congress' June 4 resolution empowering "Joseph Reed and Francis Dana, Esqs, or either of them" to proceed to headquarters to assist the commander in chief in "arranging" the army in accordance with a series of recently adopted resolutions dispatched to him that day. But other duties, Congress' return to Philadelphia, and several major movements of the army following the British evacuation of Philadelphia delayed plans for immediate implementation of the "arrangements" envisioned in those resolutions, despite Washington's repeated requests for com-

mittee assistance. See Committee at Camp to Henry Laurens, February 5, note 1; Henry Laurens to Washington, June 4, 1778, note 2; Washington, *Writings* (Fitzpatrick), 12:36, 163, 274; and *JCC*, 11:570, 676, 769.

The establishment embodied in Congress' May 27 resolutions reforming the army, which Washington published in his general orders for June 7, 1778, resulted in the reduction and reorganization of many regiments and increased the list of superseded officers whose complaints taxed the commander in chief's patience. "The present unsettled state of the Army," he had explained to Congress on August 3, "is productive of so much dissatisfaction and confusion and of such a variety of disputes, that almost the whole of my time is now employed in finding temporary and inadequate expedients to quiet the minds of the Officers and keep business on a tolerable sort of footing." Thus Congress on the 10th added Banister and Sherman to the committee and empowered "the Commander in Chief, with the advice and assistance of the said committee or any two or more of them . . . to proceed in arranging the army according to the resolutions of Congress." The present letter is one of more than a dozen surviving documents emanating from the committee during August and September that illustrate some of the steps taken to assist Washington in quieting discontent in the army.

2 For Congress' response to this letter, see Henry Laurens to the Committee of Arrangement, August 31, 1778, note 1.

Cornelius Harnett to Thomas Burke

Dear Sir: Philadelphia 27th August 1778.

Upon my arrival here, I met with the Enclosed Letter. Congress seems to go on in the Old way, sometimes disputing upon trifles, & neglecting the greater matters of the Law.

The Expedition against Rhode Island seemed to be in train for Success. *Your* friend Genl. Sullivan[1] having landed without Opposition with between 3 & 4000 Regulars, & a Body of Militia from the N England States, & the French Squadron under the Count De Estaing having made an Attack upon the Enemy's Fortifications & had in a very short time Silenced two of their Batteries, but were Surprised at the Appearance of a British fleet off the Harbour, which Obliged the French Admiral to put to sea the next Morning in Order to Engage the Enemy; this, Lord Howe endeavoured to avoid by flight, & the French fleet were seen in pursuit of him at 11 O'Clock —no certain Intelligence had been since received of the event of this Manieuvre. Genl Sullivan however Marched up Near the Enemy, who had evacuated all their Out Posts & retired within their lines near the Town. Our Genl. had under Cover of a fog, erected a Battery within 250 yards of the Enemy's works, & intended to begin a Cannonade as soon as the fog Cleared away. Indeed the General seems to promise himself success at all events and is by his Letter to Congress, in high Spirits. He has heretofore been unlucky; who knows but Fortune, who is a fickle Jade, may favour him at last. I hope she will.

Inclosed are the last papers, to them I refer you for what little news is Stirring.

When the Assembly meets I beg you will endeavour to get their Account of expenditures for Continental Services Sent: in which Ought to be included, the expence of the Armament to quell the Insurrection, the Expedition against the Indians, the Militia sent to Virginia, & those raised on several Other Occasions. I am firmly of Opinion these matters ought to be made a Continental Charge, as *you know* such Charges are made, & allowed to the Other States daily. I hope you, Mr. Hooper, Maclain, &c., will exert yourselves on this Occasion. Coll Hogan is arrived with near 600 Men, & as soon as they are furnished with money &c will proceed immediately to White Plains, where Genl. Washington with the Main Army are Encamped, ready to Act as Circumstances may require. Genl. Lee's Tryal is ended and the Sentence of the Court Martial is in these words—"The Court do Sentence Major Genl. Lee to be suspended from any Command in The Armies of the United States of North America for the Term of Twelve months." Signed—Sterling, Major General & President. The Whole proceedings of the Court Martial are now before Congress, but nothing, as yet done in it. They are only Ordered to be Printed.[2] Our friends are all well & desire their Complmts to you—be pleased to present mine to Mrs. Burke. I am with great truth, Dr Sir, Your real friend & Obt. Servt.

Cornl. Harnett

[*P.S.*] I left with you a Letter directed to John Purviance who was at Baltimore. He has not received it. Can you reccollect by whom it was sent? It contained some money for Lottery Tickets.

RC (NcU).

1 Harnett's facetious reference to Burke's "friend" John Sullivan is an echo of the bitter controversy that had grown out of Burke's criticism of the general's performance at the battle of Brandywine. See Burke to Sullivan, October 12, 1777.

2 On August 21 Congress had ordered the printing of 100 copies of Gen. Charles Lee's court-martial for the use of the delegates. *JCC*, 11:826.

Cornelius Harnett to Richard Caswell

Sir Philadelphia August 27th. 1778

I embrace the first opportunity since my arrival to throw a few lines to your Excellency which I am obliged to do without method or correction. Col. Hogan is just arrived with 500 odd men, and will I believe proceed immediately to Head Quarters at White Plains. I take the liberty to inclose some of the last papers. Our affairs at Rhode Island seem to wear a promising aspect. You will find that the French Admiral the Count de Estaing after beginning an attack upon the Enemy's Fortifications, had silenced two of their Batteries—when an English Fleet appeared off the Harbor in the Evening which obliged the Count to proceed to Sea the next morning to engage them, and was seen at 11 o'clock in pursuit, & the Enemy flying before them, Genl. Sullivan who commands our Army on the Island seems to be in high Spirits, the Enemy having evacuated all their out Posts, and retired within their lines near the Town of New Port. Our Army under cover of a fog, had erected a Battery within 250 yards of their lines, and seem to intend to force them, we are in Anxious expectation of the Event as our General seems confident of success. The Enemy having no prospect to retreat, having been obliged by the approach of the French Fleet to burn Five of their Frigates and two Gallies, and had by the last accounts received but one Frigate left at Newport which upon the return of the French Fleet must be also destroyed or fall into their hands.

Genl. Washington with the main army remains still at White Plains, waiting I suppose the event of the expedition against Rhode Island. I also enclose the sentence of the Court-Martial which sat on the trial of General Lee.

I must now beg leave to call your Excellency's attention to some matters which particularly concern the state which I have the Honor to represent.

I cannot find as yet that Congress have reduced the number of supernumerary Officers in the several Battalions of the different states in the manner they have done to our Officers, if so, the states have not been equally dealt by.

Our Troops of Light-Horse have been shamefully neglected, having been long in want of accoutrements, while other new raised Corps have been completely Accoutred.

No General Officer from our State has been as yet appointed, altho' the General Assembly recommended two Gentlemen to be nominated by their Delegates which was done in the most pressing manner in December last.[1]

The requisition of the state for 500,000 dollars for Bounty pay &c of the men raised to complete the 6th Regiment as the Quota of our State, agreeable to the new arrangement has been refused by Congress without assigning any reason as I find on their Journal, only a very short resolve to send 100,000 Dollars in lieu of 500,000 required, and that resolve enclosed to your Excellency without a letter from the President mentioning the notices which induced the measure.[2]

I am informed it has been asserted in Congress in the absence of our Members, that the state of No. Carolina had received from the Continental Treasury more than their proportion of money, and until their account against the United States should be properly liquidated, no farther sums should be advanced. This will convince you

Sir, of the absolute necessity of sending on the accounts and vouchers, not only those relative to the supplies to the Continental Troops, but also those relative to the Insurrection, The Indian Expedition, the militia sent to Virginia and those called out on several other occasions. As I find all the other States are endeavouring to do the same, I am very well convinced that No. Carolina is largely in advance to the Continent, much more I expect, than will pay the state requisition, which if I remember right was 250,000 dollars. I have been exceedingly hurt when called upon to produce the demand our State has against the United States, and must repeat to your Excellency my earnest desire that you will be pleased to send on the accounts and vouchers stated by Gentlemen well acquainted with accounts as every matter of this sort will be very strictly scrutinised by Commissioners of Claims appointed for that purpose.

I wish we could have been represented in Congress, at the time the requisition for 500,000 dollars was made.[3] I flatter myself the State would not have been affronted in so gross a manner, I stayed at York Town until the very last day to which I was appointed, being resolved to travel home at my own expense, rather than leave the State unrepresented. If I had an opportunity of attending the General Assembly, I would propose that 6 Delegates for Our State should be annually appointed and that three of them should attend 6 months, and the other three the remaining 6 months, and there to continue until they were relieved by others of the new appointment, and no delegate to be paid for a longer time, than his traveling to, attendance on, and returning home. By this means the state would be at very little expense (annually) more than they are at present, and be continually represented. I need not mention to you, Sir, the necessity of having your state constantly represented in Congress; you are too well acquainted with public assemblies to doubt of such necessity. Had either of my associates or *even myself* been present, the credit of the State of No. Carolina would not have been so wantonly sported with. Myself and my Colleagues intend as soon as we can find an opening to introduce this subject. For my own part, I can't be easy, until Congress explain to the state, the reasons of their conduct. They have been so taken up since my arrival with business of very great importance to the public; that we have not had it in our power as yet to bring this matter on, but are determined to do it, as soon as possible. I could have wished that Congress had appointed a Deputy pay Master General in our State, and had taken care to have supplied a Military Chest with money necessary for the pay & subsistence of their Troops, this measure has taken place in almost every One of the other States. I assure you, altho' I sincerely wish the accounts & vouchers may be speedily sent on, I shudder at the difficulty I expect to meet with, in the passing them in such a manner, as may give satisfaction to the state; I shall contribute all in my power toward accomplishing these purposes.

The bearer of this is Col. Marbury of Georgia who has promised me to call on your Excellency in his way home, this Gentleman comes well recommended to me by Genl. Howe, & I beg leave to mention him to you, as a Gent. of Merit.

I have the honor to be with great respect your Excellency's Most Ob. humbl. servt. Corns. Harnett

Tr (Nc–Ar).

1 See Harnett to Jethro Sumner, April 1, 1778, note 1.

2 See *JCC*, 11:530, 550–51; and Henry Laurens to Caswell, May 26, 1778, note.

3 North Carolina had been unrepresented in Congress between April 29 and July 15, 1778. The delegates had read Governor Caswell's request for $500,000 on May 25 and acted upon it four days later. Ibid.

Henry Laurens to John Houstoun

Dear Sir 27th Augt. [1778]

I should not have remained so long in arrear for your Excellency's obliging Letter of the 9th June,[1] had I not flatter'd myself with hopes that long before this day the circumstances of Georgia would have been introduced as a subject demanding the consideration of Congress—but it has happen'd otherwise. To account for the probable reasons would be extremely unpleasant, and perhaps at this time equally improper; nevertheless, 'tis my duty Sir, as a fellow Citizen to suggest to you in that, as well as in the character of Supreme Magistrate of a State that in my humble opinion we cannot fairly ascribe the dormancy of this and of very many other momentous concerns, to want of leisure.

I see with grief the return of our troops from East Florida without that success which Your Excellency had hoped for, this unhappy circumstance will add to the distresses of Georgia and increase her cries for relief.

While St. Augustine remains in possession of the Enemy, Georgia will be unhappy, and her existence as a free and Independent State rendred very doubtful. South Carolina too will be continually galled by Rovers and Cruizers from that Pestiferous nest—another Expedition must therefore be undertaken at a season of the Year which will not out vie the bullets and bayonets of the Enemy in the destruction of our Men.

I have before me a Plan for reducing East Florida which I will have the honor of communicating to Your Excellency very soon;[2] in the mean time I am constrained to say that unless the several States will keep their representation in Congress fill'd by Men of competent abilities, unshaken integrity, and unremitting diligence, a *Plan* which I very much fear is laid for the subduction of our Confederal Independence will, by the operations of mask'd Enemies be completely executed, so far I mean as relates to all the Sea Coast and possibly to the present Generation. Were I to unfold to you Sir, scenes of venality, peculation and fraud which I have discovered, the disclosure would astonish you, nor would you Sir be less astonished, were I by a detail which the occasion would require, prove to you, that he must be a pitiful rogue indeed, who, when detected, or suspected, meets not with powerful advocates among those, who in the present corrupt time, ought to exert all their powers in defence and support of these friend-plundered, much injured, and I was almost going to say, sinking States. Dont' apprehend Sir, that I colour too highly or that any part of these intimations are the effect of rash judgment or despondency. I am warranted to say, they are not; my opinion, my sentiments, are supported every day by declaration of Individuals; the difficulty lies in bringing Men collectively to attack with vigour a proper object. I have said so much to you Sir, as Governor of a State, not intended for public conversation, which sound policy forbids; and at the same time commands deep thinking in every Man appointed a Guardian of the fortunes and honor of these Orphan States.

Colonel McClean who will do me the honor to bear this Address to Your Excellency is well acquainted with the present state of our Arms. Copies of two Letters from General Sullivan, which will accompany this, will shew that of his particular and important department as it stood 8 days ago—every hour I expect further intelligence, had he been successful and as expeditiously so, as his sanguine hopes had mark'd out I should have received the important tidings the day before yesterday.

Not a word that has been said or printed respecting Count d'Estaing's and Lord Howe's fleets, merits confidence, an engagement, and a smart one too, there has undoubtedly been, but who was victorious and what losses each party sustained are unknown in this City—this fact only, that the British fleet had greatly suffer'd and had carried in no prizes four days ago, is ascertained; and from the following paragraph in General Washington's letter of the 21st there is ground to hope that many of Lord Howe's original shew of ships at Rhode Island have been detained by his rival or lost in the late storm. "By advices from an Officer of Rank and intelligence who is stationed in view of the Sea I am inform'd that 16 ships enter'd the Hook on the 17th, one having a flag, and that on *that* and the preceding day a heavy cannonade was heard at Sea."[3] This days Packet may afford Your Excellency more intelligence. I will trouble you Sir, no further at present, but to repeat that I am with very great Regard and Esteem etc.[4]

LB (ScHi).

1 This letter is in the Laurens Papers, ScHi.

2 The marquis de Brétigney's plan for the reduction of St. Augustine is in PCC, item 78, 3:31–46. It was enclosed in an August 18 letter from Brétigney to Laurens which is not in PCC, but a translation of it is in the Laurens Papers, ScHi. Brétigney was a lieutenant colonel in the bodyguard of the king's brother, the comte d'Artois, who had recently escaped from prison in St. Augustine after having been captured by a British frigate off South Carolina while on his way to America to volunteer for service in the Continental Army. The committee to which his proposal was referred on August 26 never issued a report, and the plan for an expedition against East Florida that Congress approved on November 2, 1778, was based upon proposals by the South Carolina Assembly and Gen. Robert Howe, the commander of the southern military department. See *JCC*, 11:808, 837, 12:940, 1091, 1095, 1116–21; Lasseray, *Les Français sous les treize étoiles*, 1:135–38; and Laurens to Richard Caswell, November 14, 1778, note 2.

3 Quotation marks editorially supplied. See also Laurens to William Smith, August 25, 1778, note 2.

4 During the conquest of Georgia, the British obtained the RC of Laurens' letter to Governor Houstoun and published it in the May 5, 1779, issue of the *New York Royal Gazette*. For the controversy that the President's caustic comments in this letter subsequently caused in Congress, see Lauren's Notes for a Speech in Congress, May 15, 1779. The text printed in the *Royal Gazette* differs in no significant way from the LB printed here. In the *Royal Gazette* the complimentary close continues: "Sir, your excellency's obedient and humble servant, Henry Laurens (Private)."

Committee of Arrangement to George Clinton

Sir Head Quarters, White Plains, Augt. 28. 1778

The Committee of Congress for the Arrangment of the Army, had flattered themselves that they should meet with little or no Difficulty in the New York Line; but find themselves mistaken, & under a Necessity of requesting Information & Advice from you on this Head.

Col. Gansevorts Regimt. not being on the Ground, we have no Materials, nor the requisite Assistance to arrange it, but we are informed it has been arranged agreeable to the Establishmt. by the Authority of the State, or Col. Gansevort acting under such Authority: If so, we should be glad to be favoured with a Report of it, that we might make the Arrangement as complete as possible: and that we might have an Oppy. to provide for any worthy supernumerary Officers. We presume in this Case, Col. Gansevort would make a Return of his Proceedings to you or if he has not done so, we hope it may not be altogether out of Your Power to procure it.

We also find Disputes of Rank subsisting both as to the Rank of the Regiment, & the Officers. Col. Dubois claims of all under Van Schaick in both Points: but we have had a Rank Roll as settled by the Authority of the State contrary to his Claims: we wish you to explain it, as his Commission bearing Date the 25 June 1776 will apparently give him Rank over Messrs. Cortlandt, Livingston & Gansevort.

We also beg Leave to acquaint you, that there will be several Vacancies in the Regiments which the commanding Officers propose to give no Recommendations for: but as it is not only a Point of Propriety, & Policy—but conformable to a Resolve of Congress that the States should fill up all Vacancies except in Cases of ordinary Succession, we have not received any of these Recommendations: But it may be worthy of Consideration, whether the Authority of the States might not intrust their General Officers to recommend Persons for the Subaltern Commissions.

As we are very anxious to return to our Duty in Congress, we shall be much obliged by an early Answer, & of a Communication of such Papers as you think may facilitate the Discharge of our present Duty.[1]

We are with due Respect, Sir, Your most Obed. Hbble Servts.

Jos. Reed.

John Banister.

RC (CtY). Written by Reed and signed by Reed and Banister.

1 For Governor Clinton's August 29 response to this letter explaining that he had already sent the information requested to New York delegate Gouverneur Morris, a member of the Committee at Camp, the predecessor of the Committee of Arrangement, see Clinton, *Papers*, (Hastings), 3:704–5.

Samuel Holten's Diary

[August 28, 1778][1]

28. Friday. The news from Rode Island not aggreeable Count d Estaign Ships being so damaged by the late storm he is going to Boston to repair. I expect the expedition will fail. I wrote to Miss Holten by Mr. Jones (No. 15.).

MS (MDaAr).

1 Holten's preceding diary entry reads: "Aug 27. The consul of France [Jean Holker] & 10 other Gentlemen of distinction dined with us (by invitation), we had a grand elegant diner. Very hot."

2 Not found.

Henry Laurens to Peter Colt

28th Augt. [1778]

Sir

On Monday last I had the honor of presenting to Congress your favor of the 15th.[1]

A duplicate Loan Office Certificate dated 16th July 1778 for One hundred thousand Dollars, payable at the Loan-Office in the State of Connecticut to William Buchannan Esqr. was ordered to be transmitted agreeable to your request,[2] and you will find within such duplicate—when the original shall come to your hand be pleas'd to return it or this, if you shall have made use of the other.

I am, With great Respect &c.

LB (DNA: PCC, item 13). Addressed: "Peter Colt Esquire, Dep. Com. Genl. of Purchases, Hartford in Connecticut."

[1] Peter Colt's August 15 letter to Laurens is in PCC, item 78, 5:193.

[2] See *JCC*, 11:835.

Henry Laurens to William Heath

Sir,

Philadelphia 28th Augt. 1778

I have not had occasion to trouble you since the 8th Inst. nor have I since received any addition to your former favours. The present is intended only as a Cover to an Act of Congress of the 26th for settling Rations when it shall be necessary by commutation of species,[1] and to assure you that I remain with great Esteem & Regard, Sir, Your obedient & most humble servant,

Henry Laurens, President of Congress.

RC (MHi).

[1] For this resolve, which was designed to give the commander in chief and departmental commanders greater flexibility in administering regulations on army rations, see *JCC*, 11:838.

Henry Laurens to John Paterson

Sir

28 August [1778]

I had Yesterday the honor of receiving and presenting to Congress Your favor of the 11th Inst. in consequence of which the Reverend Mr. Enos Hitchcock was appointed Chaplain to the Massachusetts Brigade under your Command, and within this Cover you will find an Act of Congress for that purpose which you'l be pleas'd to deliver to the Chaplain with my good wishes.[1]

I have the honor to be &c.

LB (DNA: PCC, item 13). Addressed: "Brigadier General Patterson, Commander of the Massachusetts Brigade, White Plains."

[1] See *JCC*, 11:840. General Paterson's August 11 letter of recommendation on behalf of the Rev. Hitchcock is in PCC, item 78, 18:201.

Henry Laurens to John Sullivan

Sir, Philadelphia, 28th August 1778.

I have had the honor of presenting to Congress in due course your several favors of the 1st, 10th, 19th, & 21st,[1] together with Copies of three or four Letters which you had written to His Excellency the Commander in Chief since your landing on Rhode Island;[2] Congress are sensible of your diligence, Spirit & good conduct & entertain strong assurances of the completion of the enterprize you are engaged in, to your own Glory & the honour & Interest of the United States of America.

I have nothing in charge but to transmit an Act of Congress of the 26th which will be found within this Cover for settling Rations by commutation of species when circumstances shall require it.

I am with the utmost Regard & Esteem, Sir, Your most obedient servt. Henry Laurens, President of Congress.

RC (RHi).

1 General Sullivan's August 1, 10 and 19 letters to Laurens are in Sullivan, *Papers* (Hammond), 2:165–67, 191–92, 236–37. The letter of August 21 was actually a letter from Washington to Laurens transmitting Sullivan's letter of the 19th. *JCC*, 11:836.

2 Sullivan's August 10, 13, 17, and 19 letters to Washington are in PCC, item 160, fols. 143–48, 153–54, 160.

Henry Laurens to John Sullivan

Sir 4 o'clock P.M. 28th Augt. 1778

The Letter of the present date which will accompany this was written this Morning and waiting for the Messenger when I attended Congress, while I was there, a Letter from General Washington of the 25th was brought and usher'd a Copy of Yours to His Excellency of the 23d—General Greene's sensible and spirited Remonstrance to Count d'Estaing; the Count's Letter of the 21st to you—the Protest of Officers at Camp before Newport of the same date, and your questions to the General Officers and Commandants of Brigades;[1] these papers having been read and considered, the House adopted two Resolutions, 1st for requesting Baron Stüben to repair to your Head Quarters in order to contribute his advice and assistance, and 2ndly for preventing the publication of the Protest.[2]

I flatter myself with hopes that before the Act, in which these Resolves are included, and which will be here inclos'd shall have reach'd you, a glorious Conquest or a safe and honorable retreat will have been effected.

I have the honor to be &c.

LB (DNA: PCC, item 13). Addressed: "Major General Sullivan, Rhode Island, by Baron Stüben."

1 Washington's August 25 letter to Laurens is in PCC, item 152, 6:285–86, and Washington, *Writings* (Fitzpatrick), 12:358–59. The enclosed documents listed by Laurens are in PCC, item 152, 6:289–311. Since these papers dealt with the controversy caused by the comte d'Estaing's decision to break off operations in Rhode Island and proceed to Boston, Congress decided to keep them private to minimize damage to the French alliance. For a full account of this episode, see Charles P. Whittemore, *A General of the Revolution: John Sullivan of New Hampshire* (New York: Columbia University Press, 1961), chap. 7.

2 See *JCC*, 11:848–49.

Henry Laurens to George Washington

Sir 28 Augt. [1778]

Since my last of the 20th I have had the honor of receiving Your Excellency's several favors of the 16th, 19th, 21st, 21st, and 24th and of presenting them together with the several papers which accompanied them to Congress in due course.

The proceedings of the General Court Martial for the trial of Major General Lee had been made an Order of the day for Wednesday the 26th, Congress then ordered the whole to be printed. The work is large, and I do not expect it from the Press before the 5th of September.

At present I have only in charge to transmit to Your Excellency an Act of the 26th for settling Rations when needful, by commutation of Species.[1]

I have the honor to be &c.[2]

LB (DNA: PCC, item 13).

1 See *JCC*, 11:838. Laurens also transmitted a copy of this resolve with a brief covering letter he wrote on August 30 to Charles Stewart, the commissary general of issues at White Plains. American Manuscripts, MH–H.

2 Laurens also wrote a brief letter this day to Capt. James Knox of the Eighth Virginia Regiment at White Plains, transmitting an August 27 resolve "for permitting you to withdraw your Petition dated Whitemarsh Camp 19th November 1777." See PCC, item 13, 2:54; and *JCC*, 11:842–43.

Henry Laurens to George Washington

Dear Sir 28th Augt. [1778]

I am indebted for Your Excellency's favors of the 20th and 25th,[1] the former receiv'd three days since, and the latter while I was in Congress this Morning; this takes my immediate attention. I feel convinc'd that had Your Excellency named a sum in Gold and apply'd for it to Congress, an order for the Amount would have pass'd without hesitation—but from circumstances which I have more than a few times observed to attend Motions made from private Letters by Gentlemen of Merit and influence transcending far, any that I presume to claim I feared on your Account Sir, to hazard a question in the present case. There is a jealousy in the Minds of Men as unaccountable and unreasonable, as it is unnecessary to add a word more upon the subject; to contribute, however, towards forwarding Your Excellency's labours for public good, and from a melancholly conviction of the policy and necessity for constantly prosecuting the measures for which Gold in the present critical moment is wanted, I have pack'd up a few pieces the particulars noted below, which had been lying by me altogether useless and which do not comprehend my whole stock; these may possibly be of immediate service and I may be reimburs'd when Congress shall order a supply, which I am persuaded will be in the instant of Your Excellency's demand; be this as it may I intreat your Excellency will permit me to insist upon the receipt and application of this mite. I do not presume to offer it to General Washington but as a loan to our Country who will repay me amply even by permitting my endeavours to serve her.

I do not remember that ever an application was made by the Camp Committee of Congress. I am more inclined to believe those Gentlemen relied on each other and that neither of them attempted the business, but I may be mistaken. I shall without waiting for a dispatch from your Excellency to Congress which I would wish to receive seperately from all other business, and with permission to deliver or return it as occasion may require, consult a few friends on the point, and if they approve the Measure prevail on one of them to move under a proper introduction for 2 or 300 Guineas to be remitted to your Excellency for public service.[2] If more hundreds are necessary your Excellency will be pleas'd to signify it, and even thousands.

I return your Excellency my hearty thanks for the kind intimation respecting my Son, or as I now hold him, my worthy fellow Citizen, Lieut. Colonel Laurens, which came the more acceptably as full three weeks had elapsed since the date of his last Letter.

I am, With the most sincere Esteem & Regard, Sir, your Excellency's much Obliged Humble Servant

Two double & six single Joannes
Two Doubloons
Two Pistoles
Eleven Guineas
}[3] Contain'd in a Packet to be deliver'd by Messenger Jones

P.S. Baron Steuben was much surpris'd at the Act of Congress requesting him to repair to Rhode Island, and seems to be very apprehensive the measure will be displeasing at Head Quarters. I had been directed during the sitting of Congress to communicate the Intelligence receiv'd from General Sullivan to Monsr. Girard, and to confer with that Gentleman. I found at my return the Resolves on the Table.[4]

LB (ScHi).

[1] Washington's private letters to Laurens of August 20 and 25, in the latter of which he observed that his efforts to gather intelligence would be greatly facilitated if Congress provided him with specie to pay his informants, are in Washington, *Writings* (Fitzpatrick), 12:339–41, 356.

[2] Washington returned the gold Laurens sent him after Congress agreed on August 29 to provide the commander in chief with 500 guineas "for the public service." See *JCC*, 11:851; Washington, *Writings* (Fitzpatrick), 12:397–98, 400; and Laurens to Washington, August 30, 1778.

[3] At this point in the LB the word "Returned" was written vertically.

[4] Laurens also dealt with these resolves in a third letter he wrote to Washington this day as follows:

"I beg leave to refer your Excellency to a letter written this Morning, and which this will accompany, and also to an Act of Congress of the present date for obtaining the advice and assistance of Baron Stüben in the Army under the command of Major General Sullivan, and for preventing the publication of the Protest of the officers of that Army against Count d'Estaing's abandoning Rhode Island." PCC, item 13, 2:57.

James Lovell to William Whipple

Dear Sir, Philadelphia August 28th 1778

Your favor of August 3d was rec'd by me time enough to have been acknowledged last post-day, but verily I expected to have been able by a short delay, to send you a verification of my hopes expressed in a former letter, but not in your judgment well grounded. It is with chagrin I now own you a prophet in matters respecting French Marine.

Mr. John Langdon will inform you fully of affairs at Newport upon which my chagrin is founded. I will never bet upon Sullivan's luck while I live—Heaven will blast such vanity.[1]

I enclose you the paper of yesterday though it contains nothing material; and I remain under every cloud as well as in the Sunshine, your affectionate, humble servant, J. L.

Tr (DLC).

[1] Contrary to Lovell's assumption that Whipple was still in New Hampshire, Whipple was at this time serving as the commanding general of the New Hampshire militia in Rhode Island. Sullivan, *Papers* (Hammond), 2:249–50.

Marine Committee to John Barry

Sir August 28th. 1778.

Agreeable to what we wrote you the 24th instant which Letter you will receive at Rhode Island, this will meet you at Hampton in Virginia where we hope you will get safe and you are duely to observe the following Orders.

So soon as you shall receive information from Colonel Jeremiah Wadsworth Commissary General of Purchases, who will be in Virginia, that he hath any number of Vessels not less than Six, loaded and ready for the Sea, you are to proceed and take such Vessels under your Convoy and conduct them to the places of destination pointed out by the said Commissary, which having done you and Captain Burke of the Resistance are to return to your Cruizing station directed by our Letter of the 24th instant and you are again to call in at Hampton once a week and on receiving information from the Commissary General that he hath other Vessels ready for your convoy you are to proceed with them as he shall direct.

We wish you much Success & are sir, Your very Hble servants

LB (DNA: PCC Miscellaneous Papers, Marine Committee Letter Book).

Gouverneur Morris to Robert R. Livingston

Dear Livingston Philadelphia 28th Augt. 1778

I enclose you a Resolution passed Yesterday or the Day before on Colo. Bedloes I would say Captn. Bedloes Business.[1] I shall esteem it a Favor if you will write me without the Colorings of Friendship or Pity exactly his Character, Particularly in Accounting and the like. Suppose at the same time that it were a Question to put Officers in the Treasury, marine or Commercial Departments and under this Idea converse with our common Friend and our Governor and let me know Names & Characters. I think I shall serve the public by nominating to Employments Men who can produce so flattering a Testimonial as that must be which you thence shall sanction. Duer who ought to have been gone hence long since will I believe soon go. What will become of your Representation I know not. I think I cannot much longer attend. The Depreciation here rapidly increasing hath arrived to such a Pitch that I am confident my Expences are between 15 & 20 Dollars per Day. Where is Duane? Above all where is Schuyler? In Times like the present I dare not cannot quit my Post tho to continue at it is big with Ruin. Should I leave the State unrepresented I shall be censured by all. If the Representation is defective in Abilities, our true Interests will receive an irreparable

Injury. This Continent now suffers from the Want of a Representation from New York in the Winter of 1776 & 1777. Should our State again neglect this most essential Point we shall from that Moment loose the Confidence of five States which It gives me Pleasure to say we now fully possess. I might have said six perhaps seven. For Heaven's Sake contrive if possible to have in the Delegation Men of Abilities & Industry and who possess such Property that they can afford to sacrifice a few thousands to the general Cause. For sacrifice they must unless the Expenditures of the Delegation be placed on a more respectable Footing by far than they are at present or they will content themselves to live in a Style which will deprive them of all Weight & Influence. My warmest sincerest Love awaits you, your Family & all our Friends. We have here no News of any Quality. I can however with Pleasure inform you that we make Approaches towards regulating our Finances tho slowly. This is an object which I shall not loose Sight of. I ardently wish to see it placed on a proper Basis. I know the Thing to be practicable but to accomplish the End in View it is necessary that those who preside should be liberal & wise, and that they should steadily pursue a well digested System. I see Interests to reconcile, Passions to assuage and Men to be found. After all Time alone can render any Measures effectual. We may indeed patch up our sinking Credit by Expedients but a life of Expedients is a Life I abhor. After every Expedient hath been used the Business will be only more complex. After exhibiting every Quack Remedy the Patient will [*be*] more exhausted the Case more desperate. Adieu. Vive Vale. Yours sincerely, Gouv Morris

RC (NHi).

1 See Morris to Livingston, August 17, 1778, note 1.

Robert Morris to Monsieur Bertier

Sir Philada. Augt. 28th. 1778

Your Letter of 16th March last has come safe to hand & I am obliged to Messr. Deucher Riedy & Co. of Nantes for their Introduction of this Correspondance.[1] In Answer to the Questions you ask I must now tell you that the best Method of extracting Merchandise from France is by Vessells bound from thence direct to this Country, formerly we made use of the French & Dutch Islands in the West Indies & first carried the Goods thither in Vessells belonging to those Countries, but as I expect France & Great Britain must be at open War before you receive this Letter it is useless to send Goods to the French West India Islands as that would only expose them to double freight & Insurance with charges in the Islands & not as formerly lessen the Risque of Captures. The Goods you mention are all Saleable here & much wanted; formerly we were entirely supply'd with those articles from England & our Intercourse with them having been so long stopped, Supplys from other Countrys are yet very inconsiderable & our own People too much employed in War & Agriculture to Manufacture. You may readily judge what must be our Wants therefore you have nothing to do but send hither soon as you can any Quantities of the Articles mentioned in your Letter. We raise Considerable Quantities of Hemp & Flax ourselves, but do not manufacture Sufficient of Cordage, Sail Cloth or Linnen & these Articles are always in good Demand, Lace is chiefly used by the Ladies, some Quantities will sell well but they must not be too large, Muslins sell well, as will also Hardware, Paints, Woollen Stuffs & Cloths but you will take care that every thing is of a good Quality, proportioned to its cost. Wines that come here should be of a good Body & round, not sweet, dry Wines being most used. Hardware is much wanted but should be good & that from England is preferred to any other. Shoud you send any Goods put them on board Small fast Sailing Vessells, if you can meet with such & your Returns may be made in Tobacco, Rice, Indigo, Wheat, Flour, Tar, Pitch, Turpentine, Skins, Furrs &c! Should you adventure you may depend on my Zeal & Attention in your Service as I am, Sir, Your Obed. hble Servt.[2] Robt. Morris.

Copy

RC (MWA). In the hand of John Swanwick and signed by Morris. Addressed: "Monsr. J. Bertier, Negt. & Changeur du Roi a Nancy en Loraine."

[1] Little has been discovered about Morris' commercial relations with Bertier, although various endorsements and notations on this letter indicate that it was received on November 23, 1778, after being forwarded on the 17th from Bordeaux by Samuel & John H. Delap. Bertier apparently replied to it on June 10, 1780.

[2] Morris had also written the following brief letter to his business associate Jonathan Hudson at Baltimore on August 18. "I have your favour of the 17th. Sorry I am to hear of such rapid rise in the price of Tobacco, if it gets to 20 Dollrs per hundd. will it not be best to sell ours, consider of this & we will come to some determination when we meet." PPRF.

Andrew Adams to Horatio Gates

Sir Philadelphia 29th August 1778

I do myself the honor to write you tho I have not the happiness of your Acquaintance: On Acct particularly of Major Bigelows being so long detaind at Congress, as the Reasons of his Delay in my Oppinion really Plead an Excuse: at least I wish to show my full Disapprobation of the Measure. On Major Bigelow presenting yours & Genl Parsons Letter to Congress & makeing known his Business: I perceived an Opposition against granting the Money proposed and of such a Nature as not to be agreable to me.[1] The first attact seamd. to be levelld. agt. the State of Connecticut in general and at Govr. Trumbull and Genl Parsons in particular: But this being so fully obviated by one of my worthy Colleagues: that it subsided: The Matter was committed and a Report brought in stating a Number of facts and proposeing sundry Resolves: one of which was designd as a Censure upon you. This appeard. to some Gentlemen so illfounded and unjust that they were lead to examine into the facts stated. I have not the Report before me & can not pretend to be very exact: but it was said that you had no Right to order the purchase by Major Bigelow as there was a Clothier with the Army (vizt) Major Measom: that the Resolution of Congress under which you acted directed the Clothier Genl. to send a Deputy or assistant to the Army on the North River & that in the Mean Time the Commanding Officer take such Orders &c: (The words of the Resolve I pretend not to repeat). The Argument was that as you had a Clothier with you, your Power in that respect ceasd. & This lead some Gentlemen to examin into Mr. Measom & Col. Hews's[2] appointments as it was represented that Mr. Measom succeed Col. Hews: and for my own part I considered them only in the lights of Issuing Commissary. The Report however was in favour of granting the Money notwithstand you had no power to appoint Major Bigelow. This Matter was fully discussd. and it was urged that the Resolve negating your power and expressing a Censure on you should not pass: as there appeard no kind of Necessity for such a Step and it rather appeard. like seeking an occasion agt you. 2dly that it was unconstitutional to censure any Gentleman much less a high Officer in his publick Conduct unheard. 3dly that the proposed resolve was ill founded &c. Many other Arguments were made off and on the whole the matter passd. in the Negative and the Money was ordered &c.

I am sorry to Observe that in the whole progress of this Affair it appeard. to me that every Obsticle was thrown in the way by one Gentleman from a State which is under the highest Obligation to you. The Gentleman I refer to Major Bigelow well knows.[3] I ask your Pardon for the Freedom I have used. I write in Confidence. I should not have giveing you this but was assured by Major Bigelow you would accept it well: In this I Claim no Credit as it was the Cause of Truth & Justice alone which Influenced him who has the Honor to be with the highest Esteam, Your Obedt. humbe Servt.[4]

Andw Adams

RC (NHi).

1 Acting in response to letters from Generals Gates of July 22 and Samuel H. Parsons of July 21 urging payment for clothing supplies purchased by Maj. John Bigelow, Congress approved payment for the goods despite misgivings about Gates' authority to appoint Bigelow.

A censure of Gates in the committee report—that he "was not warranted by the Resolution of Congress of the 4th of March last, to make an Appointment of any

Person to procure Cloathing for the Troops in that Quarter"—was voted down in Congress. See *JCC*, 11:722–23, 844–47; and PCC, item 78, 3:169–70; item 154, 2:11–14.

2 Peter Hughes.

3 Probably a reference to William Duer of New York, who was appointed with William Henry Drayton, John Harvie, and Joseph Reed to the committee to consider Gates' and Parsons' letters cited above. *JCC*, 11:722–23.

4 Gates' September 23 reply to Adams, which is at NIC, is available in the Gates Papers microfilm edition, DLC.

Andrew Adams to Oliver Wolcott

Sir, Philadelphia 29th August 1778

I have the pleasure of acknowledging the Rect. of your favour of the 14th Instant by Mr. Sheldon: and am happy to find you have none of those fears which my Timidity & want of Experience as well as Want of knowledge in Politicks suggested.[1]

Had Great Britain acknowledged our Independence (which I am convinced she must and will do) before actual Hostilities had been commenced between her and France I conceive we should have had no occation of Consulting France in making peace with Britain: which perhaps we must now do as both France and we have acknowledged those eventual Ingagements contained in the Treaty have become positive: in this View not the Alliance itself so much as the arival of their Fleet in Consequence of which those acknowledgments between us have been made is what gave me some Apprehensions. For should a simular Treaty take place between us and Spain (which perhaps may already be the Case) and should France think of posessing the West India Islands: and Spain the two Floridas, (which in my Oppinion is not altogether chimerical) and then both unite in the Idea of totally extirpating England, A Quere would arise whether they would not expect our Assistance; Besides the Inconvenience of their posessing those places. However I confess this is looking forward some ways: I fully agree with you that we are not blindly to trust the Justice: much less the Generosity of any Nation unconnected with their Interest.

An Instance on which to ground our Caution I think we have before us is the french fleet leaveing R. Island in the Midst of an Expedition Jointly undertaken and going to Boston in order to refit when they might as well refitted there and at the same time Co-operated with our forces: & also in Carrying off their Land as well sea forces. However this Matter requires some further Explanation; I feal anxious for the Event of that Expedition: and am in hourly expectation of further Intilligence: We receive constant Official Accounts by Expresses.

Our main Army it seams are lying Still to watch the Motions of

Genl Clinton. I Quere wither the Appearance of investing if not an Actual Attact upon Newyork should not have taken place before now. I have seen the Duke of Richmond's proposed Address and am fully of your Oppinion upon that Subject. Our foreign Intelligence gives us Reason to expect that a Treaty of Neutrality and Commerce with Holland will soon take place; and continues to assure us of the favorable Regards of most of the great Powers of Europe. Three Days in each Week are set apart for considering the Subject of our finances: and a lengthy complex plan for organizing a New board of Treasury has been laid before Congress. Genl. Mackentosh now at Fort Pitt is to be reinforced with 1500 Men from Virginia in Order to make an Attact upon the Nearest Settlements of the hostile Tribes of indians.

A flood of small Business from every Quarter continues to crowd out the great important Matters.

The great Neglect in Congress I think unpardonable. I can more properly express (orally) than write my Sentiments upon some particular Members.

I have the honor to be with great, Respect your Obedt. huml Servt.

Andw Adams

RC (CtHi).

1 Wolcott's letter is misdated August 14, 1776, in George C. Thomas, *Autograph Letters and Autographs of the Signers of the Declaration of Independence* (Philadelphia, 1908), unpaged. In it he had sought to reassure Adams about the benefits of the alliance with France.

Committee of Arrangement to Samuel H. Parsons

Sir

Head Quarters Aug. 29 1778

Your Command during last winter being at a distance from the Committee of Arrangements prevented their making an Application to you for a Return of your Officers in order to fix them in their proper Line of Rank.

As you are possessed of the Plan adopted for the new Establishment we would now acquaint you as we then did the other Brigadiers that it was intended to dismiss such Officers from the Service as could be spared without Prejudice to the Publick & should there be any worthy Men who cannot be employed consistent with our Plan, you will recommend them to Congress that they may be properly noticed.[1]

It is expected that this Return will be made in concert with such Field Officers as may be present & we cannot doubt from your Attachment to the publick Interests that both yourself & the Gentlemen whom you may Consult will make such Report as to enable us to distinguish the most deserving Officers & retain them in the Service. We would wish that as little Time as possible may be lost in making us this Return directed to the Committee of Arrangement at Head Quarters & are Sir, Your Obed. Hbble Servs.

Roger Sherman }
Jos. Reed } Committee of Congress

RC (OClWHi). Written by Reed and signed by Reed and Sherman.

1 No response from Brigadier General Parsons of the Connecticut Line has been found in PCC.

Connecticut Delegates to Jonathan Trumbull, Sr.

Sir Philadelphia 29th Augst. 1778.

The desire we have of preserving every appearance of attention in our correspondence with your Excellency induces us to embrace this opportunity to write by Major Bigelow, though nothing very material hath come to our knowledge worthy to be communicated.

The finances of the States are at present the principle subject of the deliberations of Congress. Tuesday, Thursday and Saturday of every week are set apart for this purpose; but little progress is yet made.

A plan for organizing a Board of Treasury is laid before Congress, and is to be taken into consideration this day. It is long and complex, time will not allow us to attempt giving you an abstract of it.[1] The Army on the North river is lying still to watch the motions of Sir Henry Clinton in New York. The Rhode Island expedition seems only fruitful of events—these operations must be better known to Your Excellency than to Us.

Various accounts give us reason to fear an extensive confederacy to fall upon our frontiers is forming under the auspices of Col. Butler, and other British incendiaries, among the Indian nations & unless prevented by some speedy and vigorous movements on our part, may open a scene of ravage and desolation on our borders, more distressing than any this war, calamitous as it has been hath prevented. The Senecas, Otawawas, Wiandawts, and Mingoes (if we are not mistaken) are the principal of the hostile tribes, and threaten to fall upon the Indian nations who will not join. Genl. McIntosh is at Fort Pitt, where he is to be joined by 1500 men from Virginia and to fall upon the settlements of such of the hostile Indians as are nearest to him—carrying the war into their settlements, is thought the best expedient to break their confederacy, and induce them to give over their hostile designs. Our European Intelligence gives us reason to expect that a Treaty of neutrality and commerce with Holland will soon be concluded—and continues to assure us of the favorable regards of most of the great powers of Europe.

We have nothing further worthy of Your Excellency's notice; a flood of small business daily pours in from every part of the Continent, & pushes aside the great & important concerns of the States, which we can only lament as an evil at present inevitable, and worthy to be remedied if any remedy can be found for it.

Permit us to add our cordial wishes that your Excellency's important services may be continued and that you may live to see the fruits of your Labour, in the establishment of liberty peace & happiness in these States & to assure you that we are with the greatest respect, your Excellency's most obedient, and very humble Servant,

Titus Hosmer.

Andrew Adams.

Tr (DLC).

1 For information on the reorganization of the treasury, see Oliver Wolcott to Jonathan Trumbull, Jr., May 18, 1778, note 3.

Henry Laurens to John Laurens

29th Augt. [1778]

I had the pleasure of addressing you last Sunday & of hearing since by a kind intimation from your General that you were then well; but I have not receiv'd a line from you later than the 7th.

I should not have troubled you just now had not an odd circumstance of this Morning rendered it in some degree necessary.

A Monsr. Galvan lately a Lieutenant in the second South Carolina Regt. call'd on me and requested with very little Ceremony introductory Letters in his favor to His Excellency the Commander in Chief, and to Major General Sullivan. I had heard from Mr. J. Rutledge that Galvan had resign'd his Commission upon Colonel Motts refusing him a furlough for making a Campaign and seeking promotion in the Army now at White Plains—with great candour and I am sure no less politeness and civility I lamented to the Gentleman that he had committed so great an error, assuring him that I could give him no hopes of promotion, and producing many instances in order to convince him that he was spending his Money and time in a fruitless pursuit—he would then be content he said to act as a Volunteer, but press'd for Letters to the Generals, from which I attempted to excuse myself by remarking that I had receiv'd repeated informations of the inutility and even troublesomeness of supernumerary Gentleman Volunteers in the Army, that therefore I could not consistently with my own honor and with that respect which is due to General Washington add the slightest weight to his present burthen.

Mr. Galvan continuing to importune I prevail'd upon myself to say there was one Gentleman in the Army with whom I might take liberties. I had a Son who I understood was in good Credit there, to him I would give a recommendatory letter, the Gentleman reply'd he should be glad of an acquaintance with my Son, but he knew he had no Command in the Army and then demonstrated that he had as little command of good manners by abruptly retiring. Mr. Silas Deane sat impatiently during this dialogue, fearing that I should have acquiesc'd in Mr. Galvans intreaties: immediately therefore after he had turned his back, Mr. Deane informed me of some very naughty tricks this young French Adventurer had play'd in Paris, which he discover'd from my Conversation I was ignorant of. You will therefore be on your guard—Galvan speaks perfect English, is well read and can behave like a Gentleman in all exterior deportment when he is not chagrined by disappointment.[1]

When I was at York town I sent Letters which I had receiv'd thro' Governor Johnstone from my friends Mr. Oswald and Mr. Manning either to Your General or to yourself for perusal. I request you, my dear Son, return them as soon as you can.

I need not tell you that I have written in great haste and under many interruptions nor that I shall be glad to receive a two and twenty days Epistle from you.

I pray God to protect you.

LB (ScHi).

1 William Galvan's military service in America is briefly described in a petition that his brother Francis Galvan de Bernoux submitted to Congress in 1784. PCC, item 42, 3:264–67.

Henry Laurens to George Washington

Dear Sir, Philadelphia 29th Augt. 1778

I did myself the honor of writing to Your Excellency Yesterday by Jones to which I beg leave to refer.

This Morning upon enquiry I was confirmed in my belief that the former Camp Committee had made no application to Congress for Gold or Silver to be deposited in Your Excellency's hands for public uses, wherefore I suggested to two or three Members the necessity & utility of establishing such a fund & prevailed upon one of the Gentlemen to move the House for that purpose; the motion was accepted & without a pause the sum of 500 Guineas voted,[1] these I shall presently receive and if possible convey them to Your Excellency under the protection of Capt. Josiah Stoddard of the Light Dragoons.

I have just received new addresses to Congress from the British Commissioners at New York—Gov. Johnstone in graceless & almost scurrilous terms without exonerating himself from the charges alleged against him submits to the decree of Interdiction lately pronounced by Congress—Nor do the Gentlemen late his Coadjutors so highly resent the Proceedings on our part as to refuse to treat without the support of the Governor's name.[2]

Your Excellency will judge best from their respective performances on the present occasion, Copies of which shall accompany this Letter.

I take the liberty of inclosing with the present dispatches a Letter directed to Lieutt. Colo. Laurens under a flying Seal & of requesting Your Excellency to peruse a Paragraph contained in it, which speaks of a Monsr. Galvan.

Monsr. Girard is exceedingly affected by the late determinations on the Water near Rhode Island & has communicated his sentiments to me with great candour.[3] Good accounts from General Sullivan will do more towards recovering him from a slight intermittent which really seized that Gentleman immediately after he had received Monsr. Chouin's Letter, than four ounces of Bark—indeed I never saw people in general more anxious than my acquaintances are under the present suspence—within the next two hours I make no doubt there will be fifty inquiries for news within this door.

I remain with the utmost Regard, Dear Sir, Your Excellency's Obliged & Hum servt, Henry Laurens

private

RC (DLC).

1 This money was intended to finance Washington's efforts to gather military intelligence. See *JCC*, 11:851; Washington, *Writings* (Fitzpatrick), 12:356; and Laurens' second letter to Washington of August 28, 1778.

2 Adam Ferguson's August 26 letter to Laurens and two enclosed declarations of that date by George Johnstone and by the earl of Carlisle, Sir Henry Clinton, and William Eden—all three endorsed by Secretary Thomson as read in Congress on August 31—are in the Peter Force Collection, DLC. Both declarations sought to divert attention from congressional charges of bribery and corruption by Johnstone, the first by announcing Johnstone's intention to return to England and criticizing Congress' refusal to allow the Convention Army to leave America and the second by denouncing the French alliance. Although at first Congress did nothing more than read these documents on August 31, Johnstone's jibes about the Convention Army were probably partially responsible for the delegates' decision on September 4 to reaffirm their suspension of the Saratoga Convention. *JCC*, 11:855, 12:880–83. See also William Henry Drayton to the Carlisle Commissioners, September 4; and Gouverneur Morris to the Earl of Carlisle, September 19, 1778.

3 For Ambassador Gérard's August 29, 1778, report to the comte de Vergennes on the French fleet's abrupt departure from Rhode Island waters, see Meng, *Gérard Despatches*, pp. 236–39.

Richard Henry Lee to William Maxwell

Sir, Philadelphia August 29th. 1778

I was yesterday favored with your letter of the 25th instant, for which be pleased to accept my thanks. I do recollect that when my brother practised physick in Virginia about ten or eleven years ago, I then heared him sometimes mention a Doctor Berkenhout who had written a pharmacopea which he esteemed, and that he had an acquaintance with and regard for the Doctor.[1] Beyond this my knowledge of Doctor Berkenhout or his concerns extends not; having never had a word concerning him from my brother since that time, nor did I ever see the Doctor that I remember.

I have laid your letter before Congress,[2] and their sense seems to be, that you use your discretion in cases similar to that of Doctor Berkenhout, governing yourself by the nature of the circumstances.

I have the honor to be, with regard, Sir, your most obedient and very humble servt, Richard Henry Lee

FC (ViU). In the hand of Richard Henry Lee.

1 Brig. Gen. William Maxwell (ca. 1733–96) of the New Jersey Line, was at this time stationed at Elizabethtown, N.J., guarding the coast opposite Staten Island, where on August 24 Dr. John Berkenhout appeared under a British flag of truce and applied for a pass to proceed to Philadelphia. Although suspicious of Berkenhout, for news of his trip to America had already been published in American newspapers and many Americans correctly surmised that his visit was more than coincidentally related to the mission of the Carlisle commissioners, Maxwell had granted the doctor a pass largely on the strength of his acquaintance of several years with Arthur Lee. Reaching Philadelphia on the 27th and introducing himself to Richard Henry Lee, Berkenhout was permitted to move about unmolested for a few days, but the Executive Council of Pennsylvania ordered his arrest on September 3. Whereupon he wrote a letter to Congress appealing for his release and thereby forced the delegates to inquire closely into the purpose of his journey and possible connections with the British government.

Those connections were real enough, for Berkenhout was, as described by one historian who made a careful study of the journal he kept during his American venture, "one of the propaganda agents selected to assist in the work of the [Carlisle] commission." That selection clearly rested upon Berkenhout's acquaintance with Arthur Lee, which dated from their student days at Edinburgh in the 1760s and which provided the excuse for his introduction to Richard Henry. Although the North Ministry originally expected that he and Mr. and Mrs. John Temple with whom he traveled would accompany the Carlisle commissioners to America, Berkenhout and the Temples sailed several weeks later and did not reach New York until early August, long after prospects for the success of their mission had faded and notice of their "private embassy to the Congress" had been printed in American newspapers. Just two weeks after Pennsylvania authorities placed him under arrest he was escorted back to Staten Island, having totally failed in his aspiration to serve as an intermediary in the opening of serious peace negotiations between Britain and America.

For discussion of Berkenhout's mission, see Howard Peckham, "Dr. Berkenhout's Journal, 1778," *PMHB* 65 (January 1941): 79–92; and Carl Van Doren, *Secret History of the American Revolution* (New York: Viking Press, 1941), pp.

106–11. For his arrest and Congress' response to this case, see Henry Laurens to William Maxwell, September 5, 1778.

[2] There is no mention of Maxwell's letter in the journals and it is not in PCC.

Richard Henry Lee to Unknown

Dear General, Phila. Augt. 29th. 1778.

I am to entreat your pardon for not having sent you the inclosed letter before now, and I think I shall obtain my request when you know the reasons that have caused the detention. This letter arrived before we left York, and before my brother returned to Virginia from Congress. Among many other foreign letters, this by mistake was carried to Virginia by my brother,[1] and not until lately returned. I hope however that no ill consequence will have arisen from its not reaching you sooner.

It grieves me that our flattering prospects at Rhode Island are so changed. This change of affairs will probably sustain the hopes of our enemies, and induce them to disturb our tranquility much longer than otherwise they would have done. I do not see how a war between France and G. Britain can now be avoided. Yet you may discover by Admiral Keppels letter about the taking of the two french frigates, that he considers his Ministry as acting with fear and trembling about things that may involve the necessity of rupture. I cannot help wishing that they may get heartily at it, because I think that during the progress of such a contest, we may find means of most effectually securing our independency.

The Dutch, according to custom, are for neutrality and commerce, and commerce with these States. How the latter can be prosecuted without destroying the other, time will discover. But it would seem that G. Britain must, upon her own principles oppose such commerce; whilst the Dutch I presume will not acquiesce with the capture of the Ships coming here.

I wish you happiness and success being very sincerely dear Sir your most obedient and very humble servant.

Richard Henry Lee

RC (MH–H).

[1] Francis Lightfoot Lee.

James Lovell to Horatio Gates

Dear General, Augst. 29th. 1778, Philadelphia

After having committed an unpardonable Sin by the Triumph at Saratoga your Knowledge of the World must have led you to equip yourself instantly with a Coat of Mail against Envy. You had not far to look. It is always hanging in the Wardrobe in the Man of Integrity. There are, however, always some even [*in*] this bad World, who take Pleasure in giving Merit its just Rights, and who will strenously defend the Character and Fame of Heroes.

Major Bigelows Delay in this Place was founded on the Conquest of Burgoyne, poor Major Bigelow, how has he suffered for the Sins of another!![1] You are also sometimes in Hair breadth Escapes by the honest ill directed Zeal of your Friends. What could you do at Rh Island on the 3d & 4th[2] of Sepr. 1778 but meet with Chagrin? Who would there be under you that would not undermine your Fame? Sullivan, Green & Fayette *might* devote themselves to support it. In the Name of America! what Plan is to be persued? Is Ld. Howe at Liberty go & come as he pleases? Is not his Fleet essential to the Safety of Clinton? May he cover N—— Yk—and Rh Island, alternately, as he pleases?

Notwithstanding the most unpromising State of Things at this Moment let us nurse the new born Alliance. Stiffle the Sentiments of the *Protest* however just they are in themselves, they should not be spoken at Noon Day without the most absolute & fatal Necessity. The Printers should be warned at the Eastward. And however chagrined we may be now, Perseverance or the Blunders of the Enemy will produce a favorable Turn. A good Cause under the Direction *united* honest & brave Men will prosper. *Disunion* alone opens that Door of Fear. Hurried as you are I must expect some of your Conjectures upon the late Turn of our Affairs at Newport. We have no Intelligence from our Friends abroad, nearly so late as what you may get from N. York.

I am most affectionately, Your humb Servt. James Lovell

RC (NHi).

1 See Andrew Adams to Gates, this date.

2 The approximate date, Lovell apparently assumed, that Gates might have reached Newport from his headquarters in the New York Highlands if he rather than Baron Steuben had been directed by Congress to go to Rhode Island to aid Gen. John Sullivan. See *JCC*, 11:849.

Charles Thomson to Benedict Arnold

Sir, Aug 29 1778

I return enclosed the letter from Mr Lamb with the resolutions respecting col Harrison's regimt. of artillery.[1] It does not appear that the regiment was raised with a view to any particular service. When genl Lee was going to the Southward to command there a compy of Artillery at his request was ordered to be raised in Virginia, afterwards another was added. When the regiment was determined on these two companies were to compose part of the regiment. I wish the information I give may settle the matter to the satisfaction of all concerned and particularly of Col Lamb of whom I entertain a high Opinion.

I am sr, Your humble Servt, Cha Thomson

RC (NHi).

1 Perhaps Congress' resolutions of November 26, 30, and December 27, 1776, pertaining to raising a regiment of artillery in Virginia that President Laurens had recently sent to Washington. See Henry Laurens to Washington, August 16, 1778, note 3. For Col. John Lamb's seniority dispute with the various colonels of the Continental artillery, see James Lovell to John Lamb, August 8; and Committee of Arrangement to Washington, September 10, 1778.

Committee of Arrangement to George Washington

Dear Sir Head Quarters, Sunday at 12 o'Clock [August 30, 1778]

It is submitted by the Committee to your Excellency's Judgement, whether it would not be better to direct an adjournment of the Court Martial, which is composed of the principal Part of the Genl. officers, for a few daies untill the Arrangement of the Army shall be completed, as all Information, & subject matter for the Committee to proceed upon is derived from these officers.[1]

The Committee also request your Excellency to order the attendance of Generals Poor, Patterson & Nixon, Tomorrow. They were Part of yesterday at a loss for Information, & have in Consequence thereof troubled you with the above Requests, hoping that no inconvenience may be derived from postponing the business of the Court martial, & great good result from a permanent Settlement of the Army. I am with every Sentiment of Attachment & Regard yr. Excellency's respectful & obedient Servant.

By desire of the Committee, John Banister

RC (DNA: RG 93). Written and signed by John Banister. Endorsed: "30 Augt. 1778 from Committee of Arrangement."

1 Washington's general orders for August 23 had directed that a general court-martial (consisting of Generals Benjamin Lincoln, James Clinton, Peter Muhlenberg, John Nixon, and Anthony Wayne and eight colonels) be convened the following day to hear testimony regarding Maj. Gen. Arthur St. Clair's role in the evacuation of Ticonderoga and Mount Independence in 1777. Washington, *Writings* (Fitzpatrick), 12:352, 354. For Washington's orders on the adjournment and reconvening of this court-martial, see ibid., pp. 406, 495.

Henry Laurens to the Committee of Arrangement

Dear Sir 30th Augt. [1778]

You will find within the present inclosure the several Papers undermention'd which Congress have order'd me to transmit to the Committee of Arrangement at Camp, and for which purpose you are troubled with this Address.

1. . . . Extract of a Letter from Brigadier Moutrie dated Charlestown 20th July 1778 to the President of Congress.[1]
2. . . . An Act of Congress of the 29th for referring to the Committee of Arrangement the Memorial of Captain Stoddard and other Officers of the 2nd Regt. of Light Dragoons
3. . . . The Memorial
4. . . . Report of the Board of War on the said Memorial
5. . . . An Estimate of Expences for equipping an Officer of the Cavalry. And also six other Papers respecting this Article.[2]

I beg Sir you will do me the honor to present my Compliments to all the Gentlemen of the Committee.

And believe me to be, With very great Esteem & Regard

LB (DNA: PCC, item 13). Addressed: "The Honorable Joseph Reed Esquire for the Committee of Arrangement at Camp, White Plains, by Captain Josiah Stoddard."

1 Gen. William Moultrie's July 20 letter to Laurens, dealing with various personnel and supply problems in the southern military department, is in PCC, item 158, 2:161–62. What part of it was sent to the Committee of Arrangement has not been ascertained.

2 Of the papers listed above pertaining to the case of Capt. Josiah Stoddard and the officers of the Second Regiment of Light Dragoons, only the "Act of Congress of the 29th," directing the Committee of Arrangement to ascertain Washington's opinion on compensation to be allowed cavalry officers "for the extra expences they are at in equipping themselves," has been found. *JCC*, 11:851–52. An August 20 letter from Stoddard to Laurens, written in Philadelphia and requesting that Congress increase cavalry allowances, is in PCC, item 78, 20:283. For an October 27, 1778, resolve granting additional compensation to officers of the light dragoons, which was based upon a report of the Committee of Arrangement, see *JCC*, 12:1066–67.

Henry Laurens to George Washington

Sir 30th Augt. [1778]

I had the honor of addressing Your Excellency twice on the 28th Instant by Jones, in that which was written last, I ought more explicitly to have acknowledged the receipt and presentment to Congress of Your Excellencys favor of the 25th and of Copies of the several Papers from General Sullivan's Camp.

Congress Yesterday ordered the public Treasurer to pay into my hands five hundred Guineas to be transmitted to Your Excellency to be expended at your discretion Sir, for public service. These I have put under a firm cover and committed the safe conveyance and delivery of the Package to the bearer of this, Captain Josiah Stoddard of the 2nd Regt. of Light Dragoons.

Captain Stoddard has been long soliciting Congress on behalf of himself and twelve other Memorialists of the same Regiment for a compensation equivalent to their extra expence in equipping themselves for the service in which they are engaged. The Memorial was committed and a Report made which together with divers concomitant Papers are referred to the present Committee of Arrangement at Camp who are desired by an Act of Yesterdays' date, to make necessary enquiries of Your Excellency respecting the application of Captain Stoddard, I shall therefore for Your Excellencys' information inclose with this a Copy of the abovemention'd Act.

I have the honor to be &c.

LB (DNA: PCC, item 13).

John Mathews to Thomas Bee

My Dear Sir, Philadelphia Augt. 30th. 1778.

I wrote to you a few days ago by Mr. McLean of Georgia, in which I promised to answer yours of 11 July, more fully by McKinfus, who tells me he shall go tomorrow morning.

It is true I did oppose the Embargo act, as I shall uniformly do, every act of Congress, where I perceive an attempt to step over that constitutional line which has been chaulked out to them, even independent of the Confederation, for if they can exceed their powers in one instance, they may claim an equal right to do it in any & which was the case in this affair for the favourers of the measure claimed a right to do it, because they had done it before & surely said they if we had a right to do it once, we have a right to do it again. This proves to what dangerous lengths Precedents may be carryed, for which reason, I think every, the least attempt in Congress to go beyond the bounds of their Constitution should be immediately checked. Never suffer the plea of necessity to justify the Act, for a specious pretext can never be wanted, by artful men, to cover even the most arbitary measure, under the guise of necessity & if such a doctrine is once admitted, what is to hinder them, from at last totally subverting the Liberties of America. Examples of this nature are within the knowledge of every Man of reading, & because the people of America have a very high Opinion of & a very extensive confidence in the present Congress (I mean previous to our being Confederated) I would for that very reason be doubly watchful of their Conduct, as the precedents they now make will hereafter be excercised by a set of men less virtuous, to the worst purposes. I'll assure you I don't remember any thing that has come within my knowledge since the beginning of these troubles, that has given me more uneasiness, than the *eager disposition* that appeared in Congress to have that Embargo carryed into execution, they even suspended taking up the Confederation, untill this measure could be carryed, which I think was taking a very uncandid, & unjustifyable advantage of the unlimited powers they *conceived* to be prior to the ratification of the Confederation, lodged in their hands, but which was, notwithstanding, in my humble opinion, a very gross mistake, for I must ever deny they had at any time this power, for if this is conceded to them, then they have indisputably a right to legislate for the whole whenever they see fit, & which acts of legislation must be binding, whether approved by the States or not, the contrary position, I have always understood to be the true one. If they ever had this right or if it had been deemed eligible, they ought to have had it. Why was it not made an Article in the Confederation? That this right was never given up to Congress, is already proven, by the Acts of the different legislatures, & which speak their sense of the matter, for you find them lodging the power of laying Embargos, in their Executive branc[h]es for a certain limited time. This evidently is productive of a confused clashing of the Acts of Congress, with those of the different States. The same Arguments that may be made use of for the propriety of lodging this power with Congress may be adduced for giving them several other important powers they at present have not. For God's sake let's stop where we are, & take a breath a little. Let anyone attentively examine, what the powers of Congress are, when they have done this, I cannot perswade myself they will be for giving more, in my poor opinion they are already enormous. That single one of borrowing & making what money they please, & I may truely say without controul, is sufficient for, & I am affraid in the end will, be our destruction. I know my sentiments on this point, are rather singular, however, I also know your candour therefore I speak freely. This a most extensive field for Argument, & will admit of a great deal being said on it, but I am sure I must already have tired your patience, therefore shall make but one observation more. There are two reasons assigned by the Proclamation for laying this embargo. The first is, the better to feed our own army. Now let us consider from whence the resources for this purpose are drawn. The four New England States raise very little more meat provisions than is necessary for their own consumption together with that of the convention troops, and Sulivans army, what they have to spare, they are glad to exchange for bread from hence. The Distressed situation of New York & Jersey enables them to raise a bare sufficiency for themselves. Then it is Pensylvania, Maryland,

Virginia, & No. Carolina that must produce these supplies, for it is most evident that So. Carolina & Georgia contribute nothing, or next to nothing, towards it, as their chief provisions are such, that the army do not, nor will not, if they had it in even so great abundance consume scarcely any part of it, but if they were ever so fond of it, the almost insurmountable difficulty of getting it to them, would render it an object not worthy of the least attention, As to the other reason, vizt. to distress the enemy it is in itself so glaring an absurdity, that cannot require an argument to prove it. Here are the interests of two States, compleatly sacrificed to answer us one valuable purpose—does this shew the propriety of this power being lodged with Congress?

I would be glad to know, by what authority our President carryed the Act of Congress fully into execution, when by our Constitution, he can only lay an Embargo for thirty days?[1] The Devil's in these Mighty men, I think. Under the rose. All the news I have at present to inform you of, is, the return of Count De Estaings fleet to Rode Island prodigously shattered in the late Violent storm, the Lanquedoc of 90, & one 74 Gun ships are intirely dismasted, & otherwise much damaged, one 74 still missing. We don't learn that there has been any action between them & the British fleet. The French fleet are obliged to proceed to Boston to get refitted. This I am apprehensive, will produce a necessity for our quitting the Seige of Rode Island, as in case of a failure of [. . .] success. The Insular situation [. . .] would be subject to [. . .] being cut off by two or three [of th]eir frigates. The chance of succeding [. . .] is, in my opinion, against us.

The Delegates of So. Carolina give an entertainment to the French Minister on the 2d Septr. at the expence of the State, which we hope will be approved of. Hutson is not yet return'd from Boston. I shall rely on the House granting me leave to return home, agreeable to my request & propose setting off, about the 20th November. I am Dr. Bee, with the most sincere regard, Yr. most Obedt. Servt. Jno. Mathews

RC (ScC).

1 In view of Mathews' criticism of President Rawlins Lowndes on this issue, it is pertinent to note that in October 1778 the South Carolina legislature authorized Lowndes to embargo provisions "at his discretion." See Carl J. Vipperman, *The Rise of Rawlins Lowndes, 1721–1800* (Columbia: University of South Carolina Press, 1978), p. 216.

Andrew Adams to Samuel Lyman

Dr. Sir, Philadelphia 31st August 1778

Your kind favour of the 19th instt. has just come to hand: that of the 14th ulto. was recd. on the 17th instant & has been answer'd which hope you have recd. before now; that has anticipated the Substance of your last Letter and contains all the Intelligence of Consequence I have in my power to communicate. Our foreign Intelligence gives us Reason to expect a Treaty of Neutrality and Commerce with Holland will soon take place and continues to assure us of the favorable Regards of most of the great European Powers. But it is a principle with me never to Trust to the Justice much less to the Generosity of any Nation any further than their Interest is connected therewith.

In regard to our Currency every one Admits, that it is a Subject of the highest Importance, and though three Days in each Week are set apart for the Consideration of our Finances, yet our Slow Way of Doing Business, added to the ferago of small Matters constantly crauding upon our hands gives me no great Assurance that this Matter will be soon Accomplishd. However Congress have it much at heart and I make no Doubt that something effectual will be done as soon as possible. In regard to your ingenious proposal, the Subject is delicate as you observe. But there are other Difficulties than those you mention for we have not a sufficient Quantity of hard Money on hand for the purpose and no way to obtain it but by Establishing a fund in some foreign Nation and this will be very difficult if not impracticable at present—or at least so soon as to produce an immediate Effect. Perhaps Holland is the most probable place for that purpose and whether the Treaty will be such as to produce that Effect is yet uncertain: if not it must perhaps be done through the Intervention of France But suppose we had a fund already establishd., would it not be much better for us to draw Bills of Exchange and sell them for our continental Bills than to bring the hard Money here and sell it for that purpose. It would at least save the Insurance which is very high besides it would not seem to Carry this Appearance of so direct a Discount: and perhaps a Fund might more easily be establishd. abroad in Case the Money was to be laid out there where they could answer many if not most of our Orders in the Way of their Trade than it could be done if the Money was to be brought directly to America; But Sir you will consider these hints meerly as my own private Thoughts upon the Subject. The Matter has not been mentiond. in Congress nor have I heard it discussd in private Conversation. I have had thoughts of suggesting some such Ideas: when that Matter comes upon the Carpet: But as I am neither Merchant, Politician nor Financier, I have no very raised Expectations from any plans of my own, whenever I venture to suggest anything in this great Councel I do it with Diffidence But I find you have lead me further into the Matter of Finances than I intended: however I can chearfully submit my thoughts to your Candour & that of your Freinds: And Am with sincerest Esteam & Regard, Your very Obedt. humbl. Servt. Andw Adams

[*P.S.*] Desire your Brother &c &c kindly to accept my Compliments. I wish to hear of the progress of one particular Affair that you and I have some times conversd. about when alone: you will easily know to what I refer.

RC (PHi).

Josiah Bartlett to Mary Bartlett

My Dear Philadelphia August 31st 1778

The Eastern post this day brou't me two of your letters, one Dated the 7th and the other the 14th of this month, and I have the satisfaction to hear you & the rest of my family were well at those times. I hope this will find you all so; tell Rhoda I have Recd. her letter and am particularly glad to hear she has recovered her health after her long indisposition. I am glad David Sanborn had finished haying So Early as the 7th inst. before the great rains Set in, as the hay will be much the better, I make no Doubt he has Conducted my farming Business very well and feel Quite Easy on that account, I Seem to be a little mortified however to hear I am like to be Deprived of Cider on my return home having fasted from it ever Since I left New England. However if I find you all well, I shall be very happy notwithstanding; Mr Wentworth I informd you in my last, Set out for home the 21st Inst. I hope he will be with you as he returns home & Deliver a letter I Sent you by him.

Charles Chace set out with him to ride into the country & tarry some time for his health. I have not heard from him Since, I shall keep the letter Directed to him till I see him which I Expect will be in a few days; I have wrote to our State to Desire them to Send Delegates here to Relieve me by the last of October when I intend to set out for home. I shall be unwilling to tarry here after the last of October or first of November as it will be bad Jorneying after that time. I hope I Shall not be Disappointed, please to put major Philbrick in mind to send Delegates forward Seasonably. As your letters are often 3 or 4 weeks coming to me, I Believe it will not be worth your while to write after the 10th or 15th of October as it is probable I may not tarry to Receive them. I have hitherto been remarkably favored with health, hope it will Continue. As to news I have none at present that will be new to you. The misfortune that happened to the french fleet by the Storm, will I fear Defeat our Designs on Rhode Island, if nothing worse happen from it, we must Expect bad fortune Sometimes as well as good, but hope it will all turn Right in the end. This month has been a wet Disagreable month here and Seems likely to Continue so. Give my Regard to all Enquiring friends, Yours Josiah Bartlett

RC (NhHi).

Samuel Holten's Diary

[August 31, 1778]

31. Monday. The Revd. Mr. Dufell, Mr. Hopkinson, & 4 Gentlemen of Congress dined with us. Congress sit late, we dined at four. I drank tea at Mr. Hopkinsons.

MS (MDaAr).

Titus Hosmer to Jonathan Trumbull, Sr.

Sir Philadelphia Augst. 31st. 1778

We were this day honored with your favor of the 25th Inst.[1] Mr. Sherman is at present with the Army on a Committee to arrange the affairs in the Battalions and reduce them to the form prescribed in a plan lately adopted by Congress, which I presume your Excellency has had laid before you.

Mr. Adams and myself joined in a letter to your Excellency which went by Maj. Bigelow on Saturday last, since which nothing hath happened to make a public letter necessary.

I lament with you Sir the sickness and death of your Son—and the distress and melancholy it hath occasioned to you; your family and his near connections and friends, and am pleased to find Col. Dyer hath undertaken his accounts and business: when he arrives as Mr Ellsworth is to relieve Mr Adams, it will naturally fall to me to give place to him; I shall do it with pleasure, as I have informed him by this post.[2]

I wish I could with truth, assure Your Excellency that in my view, our affairs are in a happy train, and that Congress has adopted wise and effectual measures to restore our wounded public credit, and to establish the United States, their liberty, union, and happiness upon a solid and permanent foundation. I dare not do it, while my heart is overwhelmed with the most melancholy presages: the idleness and captiousness of some gentlemen, maugre the wishes and endeavours of an honest and industrious majority in my apprehension threaten the worst consequences. The Southern States are fixed against holding Congress more than once a day, our hours are fixed from nine in the forenoon to two in the afternoon. If these were punctually attended it would be perhaps as much as could be spared from Committees, other business which must be done out of Congress hours—nine States make a Congress—some States have Delegates so very negligent, so much immersed in the pursuit of pleasure or business, that it is very rare we can make a Congress before near 11 o'clock and this evil seems incapable of a remedy as Congress hath no means to compel gentlemens attendance; and those who occasion the delay are callous to admonition and reproof which have often been tried in vain. When we are assembled several gentlemen have such a knack at starting questions of order—raising debates upon critical, captious, and trifling amendments, protracting them by long speeches, by postponing, calling for the previous question, and other arts, that it is almost impossible to get an important question decided at one sitting, and if it is put over to another day, the field is open to be gone over again—precious time is lost, and the public business left undone. I am sorry to add that the opposition between the States and the old prejudices of North against South; and South against North seem to be reviving; and are industriously heightened by some who I fear would be but too well pleased to see our union blasted and our independence broken and destroyed. I wish what I have wrote may not seem too much like complaining of Congress; but besides that, I am sure it is a just picture of our present situation, when I look back & see how little has been done since I came here, and consider how much there was to do and the vast importance that it should be done without loss of time, I feel myself under an obligation to account for my own conduct among others, and can think of no better way to do it than by telling the truth; which I do the more freely, because I can appeal to every gentleman in Congress whether any blame lies upon Connecticut; whether she hath ever been an hour unrepresented, or whether any time hath been lost by the remissness, or captiousness, or long-windedness of her Delegates; besides that while hopes of a speedy reform prevailed I thought prudent to be silent; now those hopes have vanished, I thought it best and my duty to state our real, though unhappy situation to Your Excellency, that we might have the benefit of your wisdom and advice in concerting proper measures to retrieve us from the unhappy lethargy (shall I call it phrenzy) into which we have fallen.

Major Adams hath seen what I have wrote above as far as it respects Congress, and their mode of doing business, and permits me to fortify my narration with his concurrent testimony. I have not taken the liberty to hint anything of the above to any friends, except to Col Dyer, in a letter of this date, as I hope yet some measures may be fallen upon to remedy the evil, and it may not be so proper to throw out any thing that may become public to lessen Congress in the general estimation, at a time when the British Commissioners are preparing to appeal from them to the people at large and would be pleased to lay hold of any thing which might affect their character in the minds of their constitutents in hopes to derive an advantage from it. I have only to add my wishes and prayers for the preservation of Your Excellency's important life, and the continuance of your usefulness, and to subscribe my self with the greatest respect, Sir, Your most obedient and most hble Servant,

Titus Hosmer

Tr (DLC).

1 Trumbull's August 25 letter to the Connecticut delegates informing them that Eliphalet Dyer would return to Congress to settle Joseph Trumbull's accounts is in Trumbull, *Papers* (MHS Colls.), 2:256–57. For further information on the settlement of these accounts, see Andrew Adams to Jonathan Trumbull, Sr., August 11, 1778, note 1.

2 Hosmer's letter to Dyer has not been found.

Henry Laurens to John Beatty

Sir 31st Augt. [1778]

You will receive under the present Cover an Act of Congress of the 28th for not exchanging John Connelly without special orders and for other purposes therein mention'd, and also duplicate of an Act of Congress of the 30th Decr. 1777 which is therein referr'd to.[1]

I have the honor to be &c.

P.S. Permit me to recommend 3 Letters which will accompany this from Capt. Willm. Nicholls late Commander of the Eagle Packet, if you can facilitate his Exchange it will be an Act of Kindness to a worthy Man whose gratitude will never forget it and you will also oblige me.

H. L.

LB (DNA: PCC, item 13). Addressed: "Colo. John Beatty Esquire, Com. Genl. of Prisoners, Princetown."

1 On August 28, after reading an August 25 memorial from John Connolly requesting permission to be freed from jail in Philadelphia so that he could go to New York to negotiate his exchange, Congress unanimously denied Connolly's request. See *JCC*, 11:848; and PCC, item 42, 2:52–53. The enclosed resolve of December 30, 1777, directed that Americans captured while in British service "be delivered up to the respective states to which they belong, to be dealt with agreeable to the laws thereof." *JCC*, 9:1069. For further information on Connolly's offenses, consult volume 2 of these *Letters*. See also Committee of Congress to John Connolly, November 5? 1778.

Henry Laurens to George Bryan

Honorable Sir 31st August [1778]

Agreeably to the request of the Council signified in Your Honors Letter of the 28th Inst. but this moment brought to me, I herewith transmit 24 Marine Commissions, with Instructions and blank bonds; the bonds when duely executed to be returned to Congress—three bonds are deficient on the late grant of twelve Commissions.

I have the honor to be &c.

LB (DNA: PCC, item 13). Addressed: "Vice President Bryan, Vice President of the Commonwealth of Pennsylvania, Philada."

Henry Laurens to the Committee of Arrangement

31 Augt. [1778]

I had the honor this Morning of receiving and presenting to Congress your favor of the 27th Instant. I am directed in return, to transmit the inclos'd Act of the present date for engaging in the Confederal service for three Years or during the War such of the drafts of the Militia as are at present incorporated in the Battalions of the respective States.[1]

If upon tryal it shall be found that 20 Dollars bounty is insufficient to induce Men to enlist be pleased to consult His Excellency the Commander in Chief and to intimate to Congress such additional consideration as in your opinion will be necessary.

I have the honor to be &c.[2]

LB (DNA: PCC, item 13). Addressed: "The Honorable Jos. Read & Jno. Bannister Esqrs. for the Committee of Arrangement, White Plains."

1 See *JCC*, 11:853–54.

2 Laurens also wrote the following brief letter to the Committee of Arrangement on September 5:

"I had the honor of writing to you the 31st Inst.

"Under this Cover you will receive an Act of Congress of the 3d Instant for arranging the Regiment of Artillery Commanded by Colonel Proctor." PCC, item 13, 2:64.

For the "Act" referred to by Laurens, see *JCC*, 12:865–66.

Henry Laurens to George Washington

Sir 31st Augt. [1778]

Yesterday I had the honor of writing to Your Excellency by Captain Josiah Stoddard who was so obliging as to take upon him the safe conduct of 500 Guineas to be lodged in Your Excellency's hands for public service.

Be pleas'd Sir to receive here inclosed an Act of Congress of the present date for engaging in Confederal Service for three Years or during the War such of the drafts of the Militia as are at present incorporated in the Battalions of the respective States.

If twenty dollars bounty shall be found insufficient to accomplish the purpose intended by the Act Your Excellency will be pleas'd to signify to Congress what sum will in Your Excellency's opinion be necessary.

I have the honor to be &c.

LB (DNA: PCC, item 13).

Gouverneur Morris to George Washington

Dear General. Congress 31 August 1778.

I wrote you a Letter long since which went backwards & whether it hath ever Yet got so far forwards as to reach you I am utterly incapacitated even to guess, trusting however that you have got or will get it I shall not from Memory repeat what if there at all is at best but faintly traced.

At present I trouble you on the Subject of recruiting your Army which is at this Moment in Debate before the House. It hath been proposed to give ten Dollars in Specie and ten Square Dollars to Recruits which I have offered and it is determined in the Negative.[1] I will not fatigue you with the Reasons opperating on my Mind, they derived not inconsiderably from the probable Consequences of the Measure even upon the Army. Among others I fear to inflame the Rapacity of Soldiers with the Love by the Possession of a Metal of which we have such a plentiful Lack. However let me have your Sentiments for I can promise you a Mind open to Conviction if you differ in Opinion desirous of Information in all Cases and willing to urge your good Reasons should the Matter be again opened.

I can send you no News and therefore I shall only repeat what you knew before that I am, most sincerely yours,

Gouv Morris

[*P.S.*] My compliments to Bannister, to Genl. Reed, to all Friends.

RC (DLC).

1 See *JCC*, 11:854n.1.

John Penn to William Woodford

Dear Sir [August 1778][1]

I send you a copy of the Resolve you desired. General Weedon was not well pleased with the determination of Congress, indeed he was quite the reverse as I have been informed.

If he is not employed soon, I do not expect he will, as no Gentn. can think of permitting any officer to return to the line, a little before the end of the war to entitle him to receive half pay.

It never was intended by Congress that General Weedon should have any other rank than what was given him in March, should he be employed again. I shall take pleasure in obliging you in any thing I can, you will therefore inclose me your letters & I will forward them & also send those directed to you by express, for this purpose I shall direct the Postmaster to send me your letters. I have nothing by way of news to give you, and shall be glad to hear from you as often as you can conveniently. I am very respectfully, Dear Sir, Your obt. Servt.

J. Penn

RC (DLC).

[1] On August 18, after reading a memorial from Brig. Gen. George Weedon stating that he could no longer serve in the Continental Army unless the delegates reversed a March 19, 1778, resolve granting Brig. Gen. William Woodford precedence over him in the Virginia line, Congress resolved that Weedon be allowed to retire and retain his current rank, pending his return to active service. See *JCC*, 11:807; and Weedon to Congress, August 14, 1778, PCC, item 159, fols. 388–90. Penn's inclusion of a copy of this resolve on the verso of this undated letter suggests that he wrote it sometime near the end of August to Weedon's rival Woodford, with whom he had previously corresponded on this issue. For further information on the dispute between these two officers, see Penn to Woodford, November 19, 1777; Committee at Camp Minutes of Proceedings, February 16–20, note 3; Committee at Camp Statement, March 2, note 1; and Francis Lightfoot Lee to Weedon, March 31, 1778, note.

Samuel Adams to James Warren

My dear Friend Philada Sept 1. 1778

After having been disappointed several Weeks I am at length favord with your very acceptable Letter of the 18th of August by Yesterdays Post.[1] You formerly hinted to me your Apprehension that I might think your Letters came to me too frequently. I could not suppose you then in earnest; but your Silence, from the 17 of July to the 18th of August, which you own to be *many Days*, is a very serious Comment, and obliges me in a formal Manner to assure you that you cannot gratify me more than by writing to me often.

My Enemies in Boston are exceedingly mistaken if they think I have condescended to become a Party Man in their unimportant

Disputes about Manly & McNeil; neither of whom, in my opinion, derived much Honor from the Decisions of the late Courts Martial. I wonder that Manly should attribute his Disappointment to me. At my Request he called to see me. I found him to be one of those Men who stand in Need of Advice, and gave him the best I could. I told him what Questions I thought would be put to him, that he might be prepared to answer them. In short I said every thing to him as a Friend which was proper for me to say. Perhaps I was too candid to be thought a Friend. I intended to have been present at the Committee[2] but was unavoidably hindered. He left the City without calling on me a second time. McNeil is still here—He has called on me twice or thrice. I know not in what Part of the City he lives. His Friends and his Enemies may be assured that I shall give my Voice upon the Subject Matter of his Petition according to my best Skill & Judgment. In this I am sure to be justified by those to whose good opinion alone I pay the least Regard, the candid & impartial.

I heartily despise the small Dealers in Politicks who are propagating idle Stories to injure me. *Little Insects will be for ever playing round the glimmering Light of a farthing Candle.* It is out of the power of those Men to disturb the Peace of my Mind. You took too much Pains, my dear Friend, to stop their Clamor, when you read a Paragraph of my Letter, which was designd for your Perusal & not theirs.[3] I am however much obligd to you for your kind Intention.

Your Letter informs me Mr ——[4] is gone on the Expedition to Rhode Island. This is also announcd in the Boston News Papers; which, to do them Justice I must observe, never fail to notice the important Movements of a great Man. I am very anxious to know the Event of this Expedition—But I am called off & must leave you abruptly. Adieu I must write you again very soon.

[*P.S.*] Be so good as to let Mrs A know that I am in good health.

RC (MHi). In Adams' hand, though not signed.

1 Warren's August 18 letter to Adams is in the *Warren-Adams Letters*, 2:41–43.

2 That is, the Marine Committee.

3 Adams is apparently referring to a paragraph in his July 27 letter to Warren in which he discussed the cases of John Manley and Hector McNeill.

4 John Hancock, who was a major general in the Massachusetts militia.

Samuel Holten's Diary

Sepr. 1. [1778]

Congress sit late. By invitation the Delegates from Massa. dined with Mr. Duer, Mr. Dean & Genl. Arnold at their lodgings. Sent 2 letters dated yesterday one to General Palmer & the other to Mr Websters.[1]

MS (MDaAr).
[1] Not found.

Titus Hosmer to Oliver Ellsworth

Dear Sir Philadelphia Septr. 1. 1778

I am favoured with your Letter of the 24th ulto. in which you have encouraged me to hope you will be here by the first of October. I hope nothing will divert your Resolution. I fear but one thing. Colo. Dyer we learn is coming here to transact some matters relating the Estate of the late Commissary General & whilst he continues here will resume his Seat in Congress, but besides its being uncertain how long he will continue, my State of Health renders it absolutely necessary that I take a ride this fall; the Heat, which has been long and Intense has kept me upon the verge of a fever ever since I came here, some times for days together was so great as actually to raise a fever in spite of all my Efforts to prevent it tho I used the same preventives & lived upon the same Regimen I would in an incipient fever, it is now cooler, my feverish tendency is abated, but my Strength is gone at the same time, and I have no prospect of its being restored but by riding, & retiring into the Country. I mention this to shew you that a recess is indispensible for me before winter, when Colo. Dyer comes on I shall retire, & when his Business is done I will return & relieve him if my Commission continues,[1] & you must if you please relieve Major Adams, who is now earnestly pressed to his return by his Aged Father who is sick & wants to see him before his Death which he thinks not very distant.

We have nothing of News worth imparting. It is nine Days since we heard any thing from the Island, please to make my Compliments to your Spouse, and believe me very affectionately, your Friend, & humble Servant, Titus Hosmer

RC (MeHi).
[1] Despite this assertion, Hosmer obtained leave from Congress on September 10 (three months before Dyer returned to Philadelphia) and probably departed for Connecticut the following day. Dyer, delayed by illness, did not resume his seat in Congress until December 15, 1778. See *JCC*, 12:898, 1219; and Jonathan Trumbull, Sr., to Henry Laurens, October 6, 1778, PCC, item 66, fols. 414–17.

Henry Laurens to Conrad Alexandre Gérard

My Dear Sir 1 Septr. [1778]

You need not to have apolgiz'd for the hints which you have so politely and kindly transmitted to me this Morning.[1] I feel myself happy that I cannot with respect to my own sentiments, add, necessarily.

At the receipt of the Commissioners first Address the Act of Congress of the 22d of April instantly drew my attention.[2] My opinion and my advice was to have returned them all their Papers together with a Copy of that Act accompanied by a few necessary and proper lines from our Secretary intimating that Congress not being subjects to their Master were willing for the present to impute their conduct to pure mistake or something in these terms. I trust we shall *still* recover our ground.

Believe me to be, With the highest Esteem & Regard, Dear Sir, Your Obliged Humble Servt.

LB (ScHi). Addressed: "Monsieur Gerard, Minister of France, Philada., by M[oses] Y[oung].

1 These "hints" consisted of Gérard's proposals for a public congressional response to the August 26 declaration of the British peace commissioners, which called upon Congress to release Gen. John Burgoyne's army under the terms of the Saratoga Convention. See Gérard to Vergennes, this date, Meng, *Gérard Despatches*, pp. 248–52. On September 4 Congress merely reaffirmed its previous decision not to carry out the Convention until it had been ratified by the "court of Great Britain"—a far less elaborate response to the British commissioners than the one suggested by the French minister. *JCC*, 12:882–83. See also William Henry Drayton to the Carlisle Commissioners, September 4, 1778, note 1.

2 For Congress' response to the Carlisle Commissioners' "first Address," see Laurens to the Carlisle Commissioners, June 17, 1778. The "Act of . . . the 22d April" was Congress' initial response to Lord North's conciliatory bills. *JCC*, 10:374–80.

Henry Laurens to William Livingston

Dear Sir 1st September [1778]

Your very obliging favor of the 21st reach'd me the 25th and has been ever since lying in my view, a scroll of the same date which I had the honor of writing will have inform'd Your Excellency that I was not dead. I have not leisure for attending to a business which we ought to be least concern'd about.[1]

More of my time than usual had indeed been engag'd in eating and drinking in that interval of silence which is so kindly pointed to in Your Excellency's Letter, and as I make it a rule never to neglect my Duty a faithful discharge had incroached largely upon hours which are generally passed on the Pillow, this excluded much of my satisfaction in private correspondence, but the honey Moon is over. We have slack'd into an easy trot again, and Mr. Gerard is an excellent sensible, sociable Neighbour, and conducts his visits without that formality which is an interruption to a drudging President. I presented a day or two ago Governor Livingston's Compliments to him, he longs to see you, and I Sir shall think my Paper correspondence realiz'd by the honor of Your Excellency's company. Upon my honor Sir I have many things to say which ought to be said and which I would attempt to say as properly as loudly were I not exactly in the station I am.

I do assure You Sir, our circumstances are truly deplorable. I would touch gently on profligacy of time and treasure upon connivals or collusion, folly or tyranny, especially when I meant to impute any or all of these to a person whose bottom of heart was good or where the innocent might suffer for the errors of the mistaken, as soft a term as I can think of, but 'tis high time to pursue Measures for the protection of those innocents who are kept in an implicit belief that all is solid gold because of the much glistering—a worm in one night destroy'd the Mansion of Jonah.

Mr. Deane late one of our Commissioners has been near two Months with us. We know too much, and yet I almost fear we know nothing of our affairs in Europe, I do not mean hence to impute blame to Mr. Deane, he has complain'd heavily to me in private of inattention on our part xxxxxxxxxxxxxxxx serious matters entrenous.

Three hours my Dear Sir have I been writing not studying one second, what I should write, these two pages, perpetual influx of Personages of all sorts this Morning as if People had determin'd I should never write to Governor Livingston again, the finger now points to 9 I must fly to be in the way of my duty altho' experience has taught me I shall have squandered an hour and an half when I enter upon it.

For Your Excellency's amusement, entertainment and information I shall send with this Copies of a set of curious Papers which I have just receiv'd from Messrs. le Commissioners[2] who as the Merchants express have discarded one Partner and opened a house under a new firm—in the language of an old fellow I say, *had my advice been followed, at York town*, we should have preserv'd our dignity, given satisfaction to our Constituents, and have been free from the impertinent attacks of these People. Mr. Johnstone's Declaration in particular cannot escape in New Jersey the correction it deserves, when the proper time shall come, of which due notice shall be given, it ought to be bated every where.

I go now to see whether we can with good grace recover the ground on which we stood on the late fast day 22nd of April.

Adieu Dear Sir, I Am with much affection And Respect &c. Your Excellency's Obliged Humble Servt.

LB (ScHi).

1 Governor Livingston's August 21 letter to Laurens, in which he called for public funding of a "History of the present War, & the rise & Progress of the Contest which occasioned it," is in Livingston, *Papers* (Prince), 2:416–17.

2 See Laurens to Washington, August 29, 1778, note 2.

James Lovell to Abigail Adams

Philada. Sepr. 1st. 1778

Yesterday the Letters of Portia of June 24th. and Augst. 19th. came to my hand together, by Post. The wishes expressed in the *latter*[1] have made all the Impressions of the most pleasing Commands, and shall be strictly attended to upon the first possible Occasion of fulfilling them; which must, I think, be soon, tho the Embargo is not *yet* taken off.

As to the *former*, I will not now make it the Baisis of a Declamation against Flattery. I will only tell the sudden Effect which it produced, upon the quick glancing of my Eye over it. Did it add to my former great *Respect* for the Writer of it? No, Portia, not at the *first* Reading; but it forced from me, almost audibly, in a grave Assembly where I broke the Seal, "gin ye were mine ain Thing how dearly I would *love* thee"! Excuse me, Ramsay,[2] if I now misspell you; I am sure my Feelings did Justice to your Sentiment! A second Reading restored me to *Decorum*, and I recognized my *Age*, tho I did not find any sudden Aids from *Philosophy*; nor do I now think that one *single* Plunge into the Waters of Lethe would quite prevent all after Recollection of the pleasing Impulse which I felt on this Occasion.

I will not, at this Moment, suffer my Ideas to deviate so widely from the Track they have been in as to go into the Trenches and covered Ways at Newport. I will still make them attend to *your* American Republican, who can, as readily as Vertumnus, throw aside an *"awkward"* Cloak, in the Presence of a Pomona. You will think less of what he *can* do than of what he really *will*. You may contemplate *Judge* Adams at the *Louvre*; while he will render you Justice with Interest, by contemplating the Mistress of his Happiness, *a Portia*.

Though I have just avoided a certain Part of your Letter, yet, perhaps, in the Shade of Evening a Raven or a Screech Owl may send Voices to my Ears which will attune my Nerves for a Dirge upon blasted Hopes and abortive Victory.

But,—I almost forget that the Post is to convey this memorandum of my constant affectionate Wishes for your Happiness.

James Lovell

RC (MHi).

[1] For Abigail's letters to Lovell, see Adams, *Family Correspondence* (Butterfield), 3:76, 84n.1.

[2] The Scottish poet Allan Ramsay. For this quotation and the reference below to Vertumnus and Pomona, see ibid., p. 84 nn.2–3.

Marine Committee to the Eastern Navy Board

Gentlemen

September 1st. 1778

We are favoured with yours of the 18th Ultimo and are now to direct that you will distribute from time to time the One half of the Sea Books amongst such of the Continental officers as may be in want thereof. On the 28th Ultimo we transmitted to you by William Jones an Express 324,000 Dollars which we hope will be safely delivered, and are Gentlemen, Your Hble servants

LB (DNA: PCC Miscellaneous Papers, Marine Committee Letter Book).

Gouverneur Morris to George Clinton

Sir,

In Congress 1st Sep'r 1778.

A Debate just now in the House relative to some Cannon the Property of the United States, which lately arrived in a Southern Port,[1] calls my Attention to a matter which I had the Honor of mentioning shortly before I left the State either to the Assembly or the Council of Safety of which I was a member. Your Excellency is not to be informed that the Cannon of the State of New York as well those in the City as those which were at the Posts of Ticonderoga and Crown Point were frankly and generously submitted to the Use of the United States. A Day of Reckoning must arrive and I hope the State will be prepared with an accurate Account (among other things) of the military Stores which they have furnished to the Continent. I know well there will be great Difficulty in collecting the necessary Documents on this Occasion and, therefore, it is the more worthy of the early Attention of your Excellency and of the Legislature. You will excuse, Sir, my mentioning to you a matter perhaps not strictly within my Line upon a Principle which I beg you to believe, that I cannot on any Occasion omit attending to matters which respect the Interests of those I have the Honor to represent. I am most respectfully Your Excellency's obedient & humble Servant,

Gouv. Morris.

Reprinted from Clinton, *Papers* (Hastings), 3:713.

1 This "Debate" was over a proposal by the Board of War to purchase some cannon that had recently arrived in North Carolina from Spain in order to strengthen the defenses of Philadelphia. See *JCC*, 11:835, 858; and Board of War to Congress, August 21 and 29, 1778, PCC, item 147, 2:200, 243–44. After referring this issue to a committee, Congress decided on September 29 that these cannon should be sold to Virginia and North Carolina. *JCC*, 12:961–62, 968.

Roger Sherman to Andrew Adams

White Plains Sepr. 1. 1778

Sir

I dont think I shall be able to return to Philadelphia So Soon as the 10th of this month, the Business of arranging will take longer time than I expected. If you Set out for home at that time please to write to me by the Post, perhaps I Shall not take a waiter with me if you determine to come away before I arrive there.[1] The General received a Letter to day from Genl. Sullivan giving an Account of An Action on Rhode Island in which our forces repulsed the enemy & kept the Field—with some Considerable loss on both side but was not then Able to Ascertain the numbers.[2] Count D.Estaign with his Fleet are gone to Boston to refit with intent to return as soon as possible. I hear that Some of our people have incautiously censured the Conduct of the Commander of the French Fleet which have given Some disgust. I think every thing of that kind ought to be carefully avoided. I have no doubt of the good disposition of Count D.Estaing to do every thing in his power to render the Expedition Successful & to promote the Common Cause. The damage by the Storm that disabled part of his Fleet could not be foreseen or provided against. When you write please to Inform me what has been done in Congress Since I left it, especially concerning the currency & Treasury matters. I am Sir, Your humble Servant, Roger Sherman

RC (CtY).

1 Adams did not leave Congress until October 3—after Sherman returned to Philadelphia from army headquarters. See Sherman to Jonathan Trumbull, Sr., October 6, 1778.

2 For Gen. John Sullivan's August 29 letter to Washington, which was read in Congress on September 4, see PCC, item 160, fol. 166; Sullivan, *Papers* (Hammond), 2:275–76; and *JCC*, 12:880.

Samuel Holten's Diary

[September 2, 1778]

2. By invitation, I dined at the City Tavern, with the Delegates from South Carolina. Congress & a number of other Gentlemen dind. with us.

MS (MDaAr).

Gouverneur Morris to George Clinton

Sir,

Philadelphia 2d Sep'r 1778

The rapid Depreciation of the Continental money as it greatly occupies the attention of Congress, so it calls aloud for the united Efforts and wisdom of every State of every Individual. Taxation is the only Remedy and it is by no means a meer metaphor to say that Expedients, however they may for a Time palliate, only encrease the Evil considered with a View to the radical Cure. Need I to you, Sir, or to those who I have the Honor to represent and whose political Character for wisdom & Firmness I am most happy to say stands high, Need I observe, that if by Funding our Paper the immense circulating medium could be so reduced that the Bills were brought on a Par with Specie, the Debt tho nominally the same, would in Fact be much greater because the Produce of the Country being low, it would require so much more of it to pay the same Sum. Early in this Controversy, the War carried on in Canada, brought a very great Sum of money into our State. At that time I wished to adopt Taxation which would even at that Hour have been productive in a great Degree. It was not adopted. Money it is said and justly is like water always seeking a Level; heap it up and it will run from you; take it out and it will run to you. The amazing Price of the Produce of our State at Present demands serious attention. If the Farmer is taxed a Bushel of Wheat now, he is taxed (as I am told) four Dollars; by and bye if taxed a Bushel of Wheat he will be taxed only one Dollar. I will not draw any Consequence but add that if a considerable Sum is taken now it will releive the State greatly hereafter.

I am most respectfully Your Excellency's most obedient & humble Servant,

Gouv. Morris.

Reprinted from Clinton, *Papers* (Hastings), 3:724–25.

Joseph Reed to George Bryan

Sir Camp at White Plains, Sept. 2d. 1778

I was this Morning honoured with your Favour of the 21st August. I beg you to present me respectfully to the Honbl. Council & return them my Thanks for this Mark of their Attention. I shall endeavour to render every Service my Abilities will admit & when they are deficient I hope my Zeal will in some Degree compensate for it.[1]

I shall endeavour to obey your Commands with respect to the Officers of the Pennsylvania Line in Continental Service as soon as the Arrangement is completed & shall also call upon the Adjutant Genl. for a Report of the Strength of those Regiments. From what I have already seen I have the Satisfaction to assure you that several States who figure much higher in Quota have not their proportionate Number in the Field in the same Degree.

I am with the greatest Respect & Regard Sir, Your Obed & very Hbble. Serv. Verte, Jos. Reed

P.S. Since the Account from Genl. Sullivan of his retreating from New Port & the Attack of the Enemy upon him the 29th in which they were repulsed with considerable Loss, we have had no Intelligence from that Quarter. The Count d Estaing has got to Boston & the Necessity of his going into Port is now more evident than at first it appeared. However the Retirement of [. . .] Fleet from before Newport has drawn such Expressions & Orders from Gen. Sullivan as have given the admiral & his Officers & the other French Gentlemen so much Offence that it is much to be doubted whether they can again act in Concert with any Prospect of Advantage. As to our Situation here it is at present a very composed one—frequent Skirmishes happen between our light Parties & theirs without any Thing of Consequence flowing from them. The Army makes a much more respectable Appearance in Point of Cloaths, Discipline & Zeal for Service than I ever knew it. Our Intelligence from New York is very dark & uncertain. Ld. Howe is certainly sailed again & there has been a Reinforcement to Rhode Island but how large we do not know, nor can the remaining Force at New York be precisely Ascertained.

RC (NHi).

1 The Pennsylvania Council's August 21 letter appointing Reed assistant to the state's attorney general to help prosecute "the important trials of traitors, which will employ the Supreme Court during the next winter," is in *Pa. Archives*, 1st ser. 6:712.

Samuel Adams to James Bowdoin

Dear Sir, Philadelphia, Septr 3, 1778.

A few days ago I receivd a letter from your son in law Mr Temple dated New York, August 23d, requesting me by the first opportunity to inform you of his & Mrs Temple's arrival there, & that, for particular reasons he should be exceedingly happy if your affairs would permit you to meet them at Philadelphia, or as near it as might be convenient to you. He requested this of me, because excepting that letter & another to Mr President Laurens,[1] he had not written a line since his arrival at N. Y., & he had still weighty reasons for declining it. He also desired me to cause it to be made as convenient as might be (at his expence) for Mrs Temple & her little boy, who had not been well since their arrival, to get to Philadelphia. His baggage which is both heavy & bulkey, he intended to get transported in a Flag, if any should be suffered to pass, to Boston, or some port as near it as might be, & hoped to see me soon in this city. His letter to the President was read in Congress. It was short and contained little more than to sollicit leave to come to Philada to pay his respects to Congress. This was refus'd upon the idea that he might be a secret emissary from the British Court. I think it is best for him that his request is not granted; for the jealousy of the people at large would, I believe, render his residence here very uncomfortable. A certain Doctor Burkenhout, who came from London in the same packett with Mr T——, is now in prison in this city, committed by the authority of this State, under the same suspicion.[2] I took occasion to inform Congress from my own knowledge of Mr Temple, that although he had been formerly an officer of the Crown of Great Britain, and in the Customs, yet he had constantly given great offence to his brother Commissioners & other friends of that government, particularly Bernard & Hutchinson, by his attachment to those who espoused the liberties of America; that he went to England seven years ago, where, I understood, he had since lived the greater part of the time, entirely out of favor at Court & in private life; and that I had reason to think his connexions in Boston had long expected his return to spend his days there. Congress afterwards orderd the Secretary to inform Mr Temple, that if it was his intention to reside in any one of the United States, the same should be signified by him to the State in which he intends to reside, & the approbation of that State obtaind before a passport could be granted to him. Thus the matter stands in all its particulars, a view of which I thought it proper you should be acquainted with. I wish Mr Temple had turned his attention first to Boston. It is probable he will now do it, and that you will soon receive a letter from him.

I am with the greatest sincerity, Your affectionate friend, and humble servant, S. Adams.

MS not found; reprinted from *Bowdoin-Temple Papers, Massachusetts Historical Society Collections,* 6th ser. 9:423–25.

1 John Temple's August 23 letter to President Laurens is in PCC, item 78, 22:589.

2 John Temple (1731–98), a native of Boston and former surveyor general of the North American customs in Massachusetts, had returned to America with the avowed intention of resettling in his native state. Despite newspaper accounts that he and Dr. John Berkenhout were coming to America to aid the Carlisle commissioners, Temple said that his American sympathies were the cause of his precarious situation. He claimed he had been dismissed from his British customs position in 1774 as a result of his aid to Benjamin Franklin in obtaining the notorious Hutchinson-Oliver-Whately correspondence in 1772, and that subsequently the British government had prevented him from returning to America with Franklin.

In reality Temple was returning as a secret emissary to seek support for the Carlisle Commission among his old friends and relatives in New England, and Samuel Adams was one of his prime objectives. An April 1778 memorandum in the British Secret Service papers of William Eden indicates that Temple received £2000 and a baronetcy, with the promise of a £2000 yearly pension if the Carlisle Commissioners "now going out to America shall approve his conduct in that country."

Although Congress did not know the particulars of this mission, they were immediately suspicious of both Temple and Berkenhout, the latter of whom was jailed soon after his arrival in Philadelphia. On September 1 Congress refused Temple's request to travel to Philadelphia and, apparently at the urging of Adams, directed him to send his residency application to the state in which he wished to reside. See *JCC,* 11:858–60; Richard Henry Lee to William Maxwell, August 29; and Henry Laurens to William Maxwell, September 5, 1778.

After this rebuff, Temple went to Boston, where he attempted to keep his credibility intact by offering to serve American interests in England. Trading on his past services and family connections, he even obtained formal recommendations from the Massachusetts Council and several revolutionary leaders such as Meshech Weare, Jonathan Trumbull, Sr., James Warren, and William Livingston. Thus armed, he set off for Philadelphia, where he arrived on December 1 and immediately approached both Adams and Henry Laurens, renewing speculation that he had indeed come to America to arrange secret negotiations. *Bowdoin-Temple Papers, Massachusetts Historical Society Collections,* 6th ser., 9:425–36, 445–47, 455–69; Lewis Einstein, *Divided Loyalties: Americans in England during the War of Independence* (Boston: Houghton Mifflin Co., 1933), chap. 3; Meng, *Gérard Despatches,* pp. 251–53, 406–7, 409–11, 420, 432, 444; and *JCC,* 12:1186, 1201.

Among those who suspected from the outset that Temple was in fact a secret British agent was the French minister, Gérard, who explained his views in a September 1 report to the French foreign minister, the comte de Vergennes. "I have made it clear," Gérard stated, "that he can be only a secret emissary substituted for the underhand dealings of Mr. Johnstone, or a sort of hanger-on that they propose to attach to me, a spy to dog my foot-steps. I have demonstrated that if he was charged with some particular commission, even a secret one, the rule to be followed in war-time would require that he make his overtures on that head before setting foot on the territory of the United States. I am so impressed, Monseigneur, with the importance and the delicacy of anything which tends to establish the slightest thread of communication and of correspondence with Great Britain that I have no fear lest these details seem unimportant to you. I shall be easy in my mind only when Congress shall have resolved no longer to receive any agents from that Power, at least until they shall be provided with letters of credence in diplomatic form." Gérard, *Despatches* (Baisnée and Meng), 58:151; and Meng, *Gérard Despatches*, pp. 248–52.

For the delegates' reaction to Temple's visit to Philadelphia in December, see Adams' letters to Elizabeth Adams, December 13, to Bowdoin, December 19, and to John Winthrop, December 21, 1778.

Samuel Holten's Diary

[September 3–4, 1778]

Sepr. 3. Thursday. Congress Resolved to meet twice a day for 2 months.[1] A cool day & evening.

4. Congress received a letter from General Sullivan informing of a Battle at Rhode Island & our army took possession of the ground.

MS (MDaAr).

[1] That is, Congress resolved to meet twice daily "till the first of November next . . . Wednesdays and Saturdays excepted." For the difficulty Congress experienced in reaching agreement on the hours the delegates should attempt to observe the following two months, see *JCC*, 12:870–76.

George Plater to Thomas Johnson

Sir, Philadelphia Septr. 3d. 1778.

I have the Honor herewith to forward to your Excellency the Bills of Exchange, drawn, I hope, in the Manner you directed, & indorsed by Mr. Robert Morris, which I thought best. The Commissions shall be sent as soon as a new Form is made out, which is now under the Consideration of the marine Committee. I have the Honor to be, Yr Excellency's most obt., & very hble Servt. Geo. Plater

P.S. Mr. Morris desires (& we promised it shall be done) that you pay Mr. Stephen Steward eight thousand Pounds Cur—— & we will endeavor to get the other four thousand from Congress, which is the Amount of the Bills.

RC (MdAA).

John Witherspoon to Unknown

Dear Sir, Philadelphia, Sept. 3, 1778

Your very acceptable letter of the 21st of March, I received about the middle of June, and would have answered it long ago, if there had been any encouraging prospect of conveying it safely. As to writing you a short letter that must have gone open through the enemy's posts, I did not think it worth while. I have, however, now come to a resolution of writing you pretty fully, and trying to convey it by France or Holland; and if it should fall into their hands, and never get to your's, there will be no other loss than my time in writing; for as to any other consequences, either to the public or to myself, I have not the least apprehension.

Your letter came to me sealed, and apparently never opened, in a packet from the British commissioners, which arrived at York-town while the Congress was sitting; and consequently it, as well as one from Mr F——, was delivered to me in presence of the whole members. As the same packet, besides the public message, contained some private letters addressed to particular members, some of them from Governor Johnstone, one of the commissioners, a proposal was made by a member, who read publicly one received by himself, that every gentleman who had received private letters from any person with the enemy, should deliver them to Congress, that they might be read.[1] This would have been attended with no difficulty as to me; except some family affairs in Mr. F——'s letter very improper to be publicly read, and some expressions in his letter a little offensive speaking of Congress. However, it was not done at that time; and afterwards, in a diet at many days distance, every member who had received any such letters, was called upon to read from them what related to public affairs, which was done.[2]

I am and have been greatly concerned, as you seem to be, for the contest between Great Britain and America; and certainly, from my own interest, have by far the greatest reason of the two; and as I suppose, it will be agreeable to you, shall make a few observations. 1. Upon the public cause; and, 2. On my own conduct, which I understand from many different quarters, to be highly blamed in my native country.

As to the public cause, I look upon the separation of America from Britain to be the visible intention of Providence; and believe, that in the issue it will be to the benefit of this country, without any injury to the other—perhaps to the advantage of both. It seems to me the intention of Providence for many reasons, which I cannot now enumerate, but in a particular manner for the following—that I cannot recollect any instance in history, in which a person or people have so totally and uniformly mistaken the means for attaining their own ends, as the king and parliament of Britain have in this contest. I do seriously and positively affirm to you, my dear Sir, that it is my opinion, that Congress itself, if they had been to direct the measures of the British ministry, could not, or would not, have directed them to measures so effectual to forward and establish the independence of America, as those which they chose of their own accord. They have had a mistaken opinion of the state of things in America, from the beginning to this hour, and have founded their whole conduct upon their mistakes. They supposed sometimes, that the people of America, in general, were seditious and factious—desirous of a separation from Great Britain, and that their conduct on occasion of the stamp-act was the effect of this disposition. Nothing could be more untrue. I am a witness that the people of this country had an esteem of, and attachment to the people of Great Britain, exceedingly strong. They were proud of them, and of their own descent from them. British fashions, British goods, and even British persons, were in the highest esteem. A person educated in the old counties had a degree of rank and credit from that circumstance, independent of every other. I think they were even partial in this respect. I believe, had I myself been born and educated in America, I should have met with a degree of acceptance and success in my station, far inferior to what actually happened. When an American spoke of going to England, he always called it going home; and wherever you are in this country, you meet with almost nothing but counties, townships, and houses, called by English names. I live at Princeton in Middlesex county; and on the opposite side of the street is Somerset county, and indeed, I believe all the counties in New Jersey, are called by English names.

From this I desire that you may infer, that the opposition made to the claims of parliament, arose from a deep and universal conviction in the people, that they were inconsistent with their own security and peace. In this I am satisfied that they judged right; for had the claim set up been acquiesced in, the provincial assemblies would have become contemptible and useless, and the whole colonies no better than a parcel of tributary states, which, placed at so great a distance, would have been, from error, ignorance, and self-interest, loaded in the most insupportable manner.

Another mistake, into which the ministry and parliament of England fell, was, that this was a deep-laid scheme of a few artful and designing men, who stirred up the multitude for their own ends; that the sentiments in favour of America, were by no means general; but that the artful leaders imposed upon them. This I have seen asserted from the beginning to the end of the quarrel; and to complete the absurdity, the very commissioners now here from Britain, continue to reason in the same manner—impeach the Congress with ambitious and designing views, and seem disposed to appeal to the people. Alas! they know nothing of the matter. The Congress is a changeable body: members are going from it, and coming to it every month, nay, every week. . . .[3]

MS not found; reprinted from John Witherspoon, *The Works of John Witherspoon . . .*, 9 vols. (Edinburgh: J. Ogle, 1815), 9:166–70.

[1] See William Henry Drayton's Notes for a Speech in Congress, June 17, 1778.

[2] On July 16, according to the journals, Witherspoon had "laid before Congress

sundry letters he received from his friends in Scotland, and the same containing nothing important of a public nature, were returned." *JCC*, 11:694.

3 Thus in Tr.

John Banister to Thomas Adams

Dear Sir, Camp at White Plains. September 4th, 1778.

Above you have the most circumstantial account of the attack upon Rhode Island and of the safe Retreat Gen. Sullivan has made with every thing belonging to the army down to a spade. This is a Journal of Major Gibbs's.[1] I hope no Construction may be put upon the Departure of the Count D'Estaing that may tend to weaken the Alliance, or weaken that amity & Concord which if continued will be productive of such happy Consequences to both Nations. In the Warmth of Gen. Sullivan's Zeal he has in his Orders of the 29th ult. censured with great Imprudence the Count's sailing for Boston. I shall be with you next Week & shall set out in a few daies for Virga. I hope there will be a Representation without me.[2]

I am dear Sir yr. obed. Servant, J Banister

[*P.S.*] My best Regards to Harvey & other Friends in Congress.

RC (ViHi).

1 Banister penned this letter at the end of a four-page "Journal" covering the period August 5–30, 1778, written by Maj. Caleb Gibbs at Providence. Gibbs' "Journal of the late Expedition against Rhode Island" was also enclosed by Joseph Reed, Banister's colleague on the Committee of Arrangement, in a brief letter that he wrote this day from "Head Quarters, White Plains," and apparently directed to George Bryan, vice president of the Pennsylvania Executive Council. Both Reed's letter, which is in the Gratz Collection, PHi, and Gibbs' account have been printed in *Pa. Archives*, 1st ser. 6:733–36.

2 Although Adams had obtained leave on August 28, Virginia was represented in Congress at this time by Cyrus Griffin, John Harvie, and Richard Henry Lee.

Committee of Arrangement to Robert Wilson

Sir Head Quarters at White Plains Sept 4. 1778.

Being appointed one of a Committee of Congress to inquire into the Deficiencies & Defaults of the late Qr. Master Generals Department, I recollect your having mentioned to me some Circumstances which fell within your Knowledge, or of which you had good Information which might be of Use to us in this Inquiry. I therefore now think myself bound in Duty to call upon you for such Information on this Subject as your Opportunities have enabled you to give us. You may depend upon it, I shall make no Use of it that will be prejudicial to you, & I hope you will think it your Duty to assist us in the Inquiry, & neither this false Delicacy or Timidity suppress any Knowledge tending to serve the publick.[1] I am with due Regard, Sir, Your Obed. Hbble Serv. Jos. Reed

P.S. Direct to me under Cover to Mr. Freeman or send it to Mrs. Reed at Fleming Town.

RC (NCooHi). Written and signed by Joseph Reed. Addressed. "To Robert Wilson Esqr., Hacket's Town."

[1] No record of Deputy Commissary General of Purchases Wilson's reply to the committee has been found.

William Henry Drayton to the Carlisle Commissioners

September 4, 1778

To the Earl of CARLISLE, *Sir* HENRY CLINTON, *Knight of the Bath, and* WILLIAM EDEN, *Esquire.*[1]

Your Excellencies must be sensible, that it does not comport with the measures of Congress to make any observations upon your declaration of the 26th of August.[2] But as it was evidently calculated for the people, I make no doubt you will be glad to know what effect it is likely to produce; and that your Excellencies may form some opinion, I take the liberty to shew you, in what light it is considered by an individual: *Valeat quantum valere potest.*[3] I do not flatter myself that my observations upon your applications to Congress are very agreeable to you: However, I am in no degree discouraged from writing a third letter to your Excellencies.

It seems the declaration of Congress on the 11th of August,[4] drew forth yours of the 26th. The storm of military war has lost its violence; on your part it has spent itself; you now assail us with words.

You are pleased "solemnly to declare," that you had not any knowledge, either directly or indirectly, of the letters and conversation alluded to in the declaration of Congress, until you saw them made public in the newspapers. This declaration related to your colleague, George Johnstone, Esq; nor did it charge your Excellencies with a *privity* to, or participation in his very exceptionable conduct. *Unaccused,* you have thought proper to endeavour to exculpate yourselves; a circumstance which strongly brings to my recollection a rule which Charles the First recommended to his favourite Stafford, as one that may serve for a statesman, courtier or lover—"never to make a defence or apology before you are accused." Without doubt, your Excellencies will not be at a loss to comprehend the meaning of the Royal hint.

That you would *publicly* have *assented* to the construction

Congress gave to Governor Johnstone's conduct, or that you would *intimate* a belief that any person was authorized to hold the conversation stated to have been held with Mr. Read, "to engage his interest to promote the object of your commission," was not expected. Neither was it imagined, that there was any obligation upon you to vindicate Mr. Johnstone's "abilities and integrity." The first we never doubted, till we saw his declaration of the 26th of August; the last he himself has not even attempted to vindicate; and I mark this as an instance of his prudence: It is laudable to point out merit wherever it is distinquished. On the other hand, it is also proper to observe the public shades of a public character: The Governor appears to have lost that calmness and circumspection necessary in the profession of a statesman. The declaration of Congress has precipitated him into abuse, mistake and contradiction. He censures Congress for *bowing* to a French Ambassador! Did his Britannic Majesty *never bow* to a French Ambassador? The Governor thinks "many individuals" of Congress "now entertain different sentiments" from those in the declaration of Congress: He is certainly mistaken, for I have heard every individual Member declare, he considered him as no longer an enemy to corruption. As to his contradiction of himself, I need only contrast these two ideas in his declaration— "The said George Johnstone for himself says, that he is far from considering the said resolution of Congress as *offensive* to him, that he rather receives it as a mark of distinction:" However, "he reserves to himself the liberty of publishing, if he shall judge proper, a justification of his conduct against the *aspersions* thrown on *his character*." This *unoffended*, yet *aspersed* gentleman, who considers a resolution which *asperses his character, "as a mark of distinction,"* draughted his declaration *ad populum*, and with them I will leave it, that I may proceed to shew a proper respect to your Excellencies performance.

Why do you tell the world, you "were authorized to *restore* peace, *to preserve* the value *and promote* the credit of the paper circulation, *to give* satisfaction and security for ever on the subject of military establishments, and *to extend* every freedom to trade?" Your Excellencies sent to the Congress copies of the instruments by which you were, and by which only you are authorized. They were published, and the world have not yet forgot, that they only allow you *to treat*, not *to determine* upon any of those particulars. Nay, you are expressly prohibited, and it is declared your proceedings on those points shall not be of any validity unless ratified by the British Parliament. Need I hint, that every word you deliver is accurately weighed, and critically examined; and that consequential ideas naturally follow?

And do you really think you have "offered everything that is, or can be proposed by the French alliance?" I am apt to suspect that your Excellencies are inclined to pleasantry. Pardon me if I introduce a serious idea: I will be short; nay, I will use but a single word. INDEPENDENCE! This is proposed by the alliance with France: This is not to be found in your offers.

As you are astonished at one circumstance, I may be permitted to express a little surprize at another, it is at your assertion that France "has *ever* shewn itself an ememy to *all* civil and religious liberty." I cannot suppose you are unread in the histories of France, of Germany, and of the Low Countries, especially for the eighty years preceding the peace of Westphalia; and it is painful even to remark, that there is an alternative. The civil and religious liberties of Germany and of the Seven United Provinces *found* in the power of France *a friend* and a guarantee; and the same power is *now a friend* and a guarantee to the civil and religious liberty of America. On the other hand, the power of England *has been,* and *now is an enemy* to civil and religious liberty. Witness your penal laws against Roman Catholics, and the rejected petitions of Dissenters. Witness the reigns of Charles the Second and his successor. Witness the present reign in Britain; the stamp act, the Quebec bill, the cotemporary and subsequent outrages of laws and arms, respecting America. Your Excellencies ought to have looked at home, before you ventured to cast your eyes and censures abroad.

It is a favourite point with you, and you *constantly press* to have it established, that the offers of France "were made only in consequence of the plan of accommodation previously concerted in Great Britain." And to prove this, you aver, first, "that public intimation of the conciliatory propositions on the part of Great Britain was given to the British Parliament, and consequently to the whole world, in the month of November last." Secondly, "that the preliminaries of a French treaty, did not bear earlier date than the 16th of December." We will examine the subject. The terms in which the first point is couched, give an idea, that the intimation was pointed and public, descriptive of the propositions, and that they were important in their nature. I wish your Excellencies had condescended to give us *the terms* in which the intimation was expressed, and the authority expressing them: Because from these lights, we might have seen, whether the propositions were, or if you please, the intimation was, of *sufficient* weight to affect, change and give a *ton* to the measures of the court of France. The evidence was in your hands, you have not thought proper to lay it before us, and no doubt you have *reasons* for the suppression. However, as my object is truth, I will endeavour to supply the evidence that you have withheld.

The late sessions of the British Parliament began on the 20th day of November last. On the 21st, your House of Lords presented their address to your sovereign in answer to his speech. In that they say, "we cannot but applaud your Majesty's unwearied vigilance and wisdom in recommending to us, to prepare at all events, for such further operations as the contingences of the war, and the obstinacy of the rebels may render expedient." "We thankfully receive your Majesty's *declaration of perserverance* in the measures now pursuing, for the re-establishment of a just and constitutional subordination through the several parts of your Majesty's dominions." On the 22d of November your House of Commons also presented their address in answer to the speech; nor does this address contain any thing repugnant to the other; nor can it be denied, that these addresses are always mere echoes to the speech, and that the three *flow from the Ministers*. Thus, at one view, we have the public and joint sense of the Ministers, King, Lords and Commons of Great Britain. It is sufficient here to observe, that sense was a "perseverance" in military coercion—not a change to "conciliatory propositions."

This "public intimation" "given to the British Parliament, and consequently to the whole world in November last," of the public measures to be pursued, perhaps may not be *that* public intimation, to which your Excellencies allude? Well, I am not tired in my research after truth, I will make another attempt. I hope your Excellencies will patiently attend, while I endeavour to discover the *intimation* you mean; and whether it was in its nature such, as *ipso facto* made a mere nullity of the *declaration* from the throne, couched by the Ministers, and approved by the Houses of Parliament.

On the 17th of February last, Lord North made a decisive speech in the House of Commons. This states what he said in November relative to terms that might be offered to America; and it is probable this may be the public intimation to which your Excellencies allude. This speech strikes my attention, because it not only states what Lord North said on the 20th of November, but it demonstrates his conduct and the reasons for it, from that time to the 17th of February.

It was on this memorable day that Lord North declared himself in the following manner. "At the opening of the present sessions, on the first day during the debate upon the address to his Majesty, I told the House, that in my opinion terms might be made with the Colonies short of unconditional submission, and that the time of making them was the moment of victory." Here Lord North himself gives evidence of what he had said, and it must be deemed absolutely sufficient. Thus it undeniably appears, that on the 20th day of November Lord North, speaking upon another subject, *en passant*, threw out a mere speculative "proposition," the truth of which was self evident: Terms *might* be made in the moment of victory. His Lordship did not intimate, that he *would* offer terms, nay, that he *intended* to do so. And is this mere speculative proposition "the *con-*

ciliatory propositions on the part of Great Britain," to which you so anxiously point! Already it appears lighter than a *straw*; you *catch* at it, but it is not capable of supporting you. Place this in one scale—the public *persevering declaration* of the Ministers and the King on the same day, approved by the Houses of Parliament on the two following days, in the other scale—suspend the balance—Of what weight is your public intimation?—*vox et prœteria nihil.*[5] Was it possible such a public intimation affected the counsels of France, and changed their very nature! It is too extravagant to be supposed. But let us attend to the speech.

"The time of making them was the moment of victory. I said this, thinking that the victory gained by Sir William Howe, was more decisive than it really was; and ignorant of the disaster which had fallen on General Burgoyne's army."

It appears then, terms *might* be offered in the moment of victory, and that on the 20th day of November Lord North thought the moment *then* existed. The question is, what use did he make of that moment? Did he intimate that he *would* offer generous terms of conciliation? No! Even terms short of unconditional submission? No! He only threw out a mere speculative idea, the truth of which no man could deny: But in this fancied moment of victory, *under his auspices*, the speech from the throne made a "declaration," and the houses of Parliament applauded the "declaration of *perseverance* in the measures then pursuing," to coerce America to an unconditional submission: And large supplies in men and money were immediately voted. It is true his Lordship very ingeniously intimated, *en passant*, when on another subject, in what manner the moment of victory might be used, but at the same time he took care, that the Ministry *should demonstrate*, and the whole legislature should declare, in what manner they were *resolved to use it*—to redouble the blows upon the party supposed to be then staggering under a late victory.

Lord North continued, "When the news of that melancholy event arrived, I was struck that the time of proposing terms was past; and that the first point to be done was the raising of new levies and a new force." The *point* with me at present is, to acertain a moment in which his Lordship thought "the time of proposing terms was past."

It is notorious, that on the fourth of December Lord George Germaine was obliged, for the first time, to inform the House of Commons, (who were stunned at it) that he had received private accounts of that event, which I may call a glorious one: And I will therefore lay it down, that on that day Lord North was of opinion, "the time of proposing terms was past." Thus we find, that from the first day of the sessions in November to the fourth of December, a *perseverance* in coercive measures, new levies, and a new force, were the declared objects of the British Government. Do not your Excellencies think it reasonable to conclude, that his Lordship continued in the same sentiments and measures for ten or twelve days? The contrary is not to be supposed. This allowance, then, brings us to the 16th of December, the day when the offers of France were formally made to the American Commissioners in Paris: A point of time when every public intimation that could be given of a perseverance in measures of coercion on the part of Great-Britain, actually and clearly existed.

You are pleased to say "the propositions to be made were occasionally a subject of discussion in Parliament during the whole interval between the 20th of January and the 17th of February; during which interval, and not before, France being informed of the liberal and extensive nature of the intended offers, thought it expedient to new model and enlarge her proposals."

From hence these conclusions result: That on the 20th of January the propositions were *yet "to be made*:" That previous to that day they were *not made, nor discussed, nor* the liberal and extensive nature of them *known* to France. Yet we have found that the offers of France were made on the 16th of December preceeding! But, say you, "the concessions then made by France on the one hand were so *unsatisfactory*, and the conditions required by America on the other so exceptionable, that the Commissioners of Congress did not think proper to proceed, until they should be specially authorised." We will candidly consider every thing you offer.

About the end of the year 1776 Congress made out the terms of the treaties they were desirous of forming with France; and also instructions to their Commissioners, materially to relax, if necessary, in many important points from those terms: And the Commissioners received these terms and instructions long before they had occasion to make use of them.

On the 16th of December last, when your conciliatory proposition, according to your own shewing, were neither made nor discussed, and consequently their "liberal and extensive nature" *not known* to France, Monsieur Girard, by order of his Most Christian Majesty, thus declared himself to our Commissioners. "That his Most Christian Majesty was determined to acknowledge our independence, and make a treaty with us of amity and commerce. That in this treaty *no advantage* would be taken of our present situation, to obtain terms from us which otherwise would not be convenient for us to agree to, his Majesty desiring that the treaty once made would be durable, and our amity subsist forever, which could not be expected if each nation did not end its interest in the *continuance* as well as in the *commencement* of it.

Having thus from the records stated the authorities of the Commissioners on the one hand, and "the concessions" as you are pleased to term them, "then made by France" on the other; allow me to ask whether these terms by France on the 16th of December last, could possibly be deemed "*unsatisfactory*"? And whether it is possible to suppose that the Commissioners, having early in the year 1777 received instructions, by which they were "specially authorized," in case of necessity, to agree to *unequal* terms, "did not think proper to proceed" to agree to the terms of France on the 16th of December following, which were perfectly *equal*? The facts are, they had no occasion to wait for any special authority—they did not wait—the treaties *were* absolutely made upon the *satisfactory* principles declared on the 16th of December. What then becomes of your assertion, that in the interval between the 20th of January and the 17th of February, *eleven days after the treaties were actually signed,* "France being informed of the liberal and extensive nature of the intended offers, thought it expedient to new model and enlarge her proposals."

I cannot avoid presenting to your attention another point of evidence against your favorite position, "that public intimation of the conciliatory propositions on the part of Great Britain was given to the British Parliament, and consequently to the whole world, in the month of November last." And the point is this—On the 5th of February last Governor Johnstone, *in the House of Commons,* wrote a letter to a gentleman in Pennsylvania,[6] and I have seen the original, in which is this paragraph. "I have had a *hint,* and have good reason to believe a proposition will be made to Parliament in four or five days by Administration that may be a ground of re-union: I really *do not know* the particulars; nevertheless, as I learn some preliminaries have lately gone from France, I think it cannot be deemed unfriendly to either country to give you notice of this *intended* proposition, *that you may* in prudence do nothing hastily with a foreign power."

Hence your Excellencies must admit, that your public intimation of the conciliatory propositions on the part of Great Britain, given to the British Parliament and consequently to the whole world, in November, was not so *public* an intimation as to strike the attention even of Governor Johnstone a member of that Parliament, and then present. And that it was not till the 5th of February, the day before the signing the treaty of Paris, that he had even a *hint* and good reason to believe, that a conciliatory proposition was to be made to America—a period when he even *had not* any knowledge of the particulars of it. The time of his receiving the hint is to be absolutely presumed from the place in which the letter was wrote and the date it bore: and I will just add, it is violently to be presumed, the proposition to be made, was to answer the same end for which the letter was expressly wrote—"that we might in prudence do nothing hastily with a foreign power."

Incontrovertible as these dates, facts and arguments stand, I will not press their combined force upon your Excellencies: Your sensibility is too great, and your feelings are too much awake, not to be sufficiently affected without my doing so. I am not an ungenerous adversary, and to demonstrate this, I will for a moment admit your assertion, "that public intimation of the conciliatory propositions on the part of Great Britain, was given to the British Parliament in the month of November last." And the nature of them now becomes a matter of important enquiry.

Lord North has told us the propositions were only "short of unconditional submission:" The terms you offer are only *short of independence*; and your Excellencies are sensible there is a vast difference between the two points: Will you excuse me if I ask the cause of it? You hesitate; I will therefore endeavour to resolve the question.

The British Administration, at the adjournment of the Parliament for the Christmas holidays, were moving heaven and earth for "the raising of new levies and a new force" "struck that the time of proposing terms was past." The Parliament met against on the 20th of January; the Administration was then "struck that the time of proposing terms was" returned; for France had offered her terms on the 16th of December preceeding. Conciliatory propositions were now *occasionally*, for the first time, discussed in Parliament, though *not even then made*. Well, the treaty of Paris was signed on the 6th of February; the time for proposing the British terms now pressed: on the 17th of the same month, Lord North "formally stated" them; and as soon as possible afterwards, you on the part of Great Britain offered terms only short of independence, and immediately after, on the 11 of July, you offered "to enlarge" those terms. In a word, the Courts of France and Great Britain were sat down to a game of chess. On the 10th of November the game was to be carried on by Great Britain on this principal—"*perseverance* in coercive measures:" By France the principle was a *decisive stroke*. Britain declared her principle—France did not. Upon these principles France made the first move: She moved *equal terms*, on the 16th of December. Before Britain could have advice of this, she was engaged at the Christmas feast; but that being ended on the 20th of January, knowing the step France had made, she was "struck" she must abandon her principle of *perseverance*, and she immediately moved, *the discussion* of conciliatory propositions. France upon her principle of a *decisive stroke*, on the 6th of February moved, *the treaty of Paris*. Britain soon heard of this, and on the 17th of the same month, she moved, *the formal state* of conciliatory propositions. The game of chess can be as easily played when the players are at a distance, as when they are present; the whole difference in the two cases, consists in the space of time necessary for playing the game. Already France seems to have reduced Britain to *a state of consideration*, whether she must give up the game as too desparate to be recovered. From this plain figure, it is demonstrated, that the motions of France caused the vast difference between terms but short of unconditional submission, and terms only short of Independence.

Governor Johnstone in his declaration of the 26th of August, is pleased to reproach Congress for allying with France "after all their just claims are gratified." Your Excellencies ordered the transmission of this reproach: You are thereby parties in making it: And therefore, I am justified in taking some notice of it to you.

In consequence of the offers you have made, you say, all our just claims are gratified. You then admit, that when you began the war, we had just claims. You must admit, that notwithstanding our most humble petition in behalf of our just claims, you refused to grant those claims. You must also admit, that for three years you have by force of arms, and all the horrors of war, endeavoured to reduce us to unconditional submission, notwithstanding we had just claims. Upon those points then there is no mistake or doubt; nor can there be any upon these. The just claims of America ought to have been granted when they were stated, and you were desired to give redress. You denied us common justice, by refusing to grant redress upon those just claims. You enormously added to that injustice, by letting loose upon us all the calamities of war, to oblige us to abandon those our just claims. And we have now a just claim to receive satisfaction for all the damage which we, through your injustice, have received, in supporting our just claims. Your injustice has ruined thousands of our families. You have unjustly burned our towns and ravaged our country. Fathers, mothers, brothers, and friends, mourn the loss of their children, brothers and friends, by your injustice slain in the field of battle, scalped in their peaceable dwellings, murdered in your horrible prisons. America, by your injustice has lost thousands of her best citizens, and has been obliged to expend millions of her treasure. Nor is the loss her youth have sustained by your injustice, the loss of those important years for the improvement of their understandings, which they can never regain, the least loss she has sustained. Look at this short list of damages, and say, whether you have *even offered* to gratify America in all her just claims! Say, is it in the nature of things possible for you to gratify America in all her just claims! There was a time when you might easily have done so: You threw it away; you must be "struck that the time of proposing terms is past," never to return.

Your Excellencies wish to move our gratitude: You speak of your conciliatory propositions as "the *generous* measures of Great-Britain:" Your Excellencies are rather unfortunate in the means you use to touch the passions. Louis the Sixteenth, the PROTECTOR of the rights of mankind, has some title to speak of the generous measures of France—generous, because just and noble. He magnanimously declared, that in forming a treaty with us, he did "not pretend that he acted wholly for our sakes, since besides his real good will to us and to our cause, it was manifestly the interest of France, that the power of England should be diminished by our separation from it." But, can Britain say, her offers proceed from "real good will to us and to our cause?" Can she say, she wished "to promote and establish the liberties, peace, opulence, increase, security and permanent happiness of the inhabitants of this continent?" No! Her whole system of government since the year 1763, has operated—her laws have been enacted—her arms have been used for the very contrary purposes. Her Ministers and Parliaments have long oppressed in order to plunder us. When we were unarmed, she ungenerously drew her sword upon us. She treated our most humble petition for "peace, liberty and safety," with silent contempt. Her Minister, Lord North, declared he was fighting for substantial revenue—he would lay America prostrate and drag her to his feet. In the ideal "moment of victory," her Ministers and Legislature declared they would redouble their blows upon America supposed to be staggering under a late victory. Her veterans unjustly burned our towns, ravaged our country, and slaughtered our citizens. She let loose her Indian allies to massacre the unarmed, the aged, the sick, the infant, the matron, wife and virgin. Her Generals and Admirals in *cold blood,* in their prisons and prison ships, murdered our countrymen by suffocation, filth, hunger and nakedness; refusing to them the food and raiment provided for their necessities by public authority and private affection; with gold and food tempting these virtuous citizens, in the agonies of misery and despair, to dip their hands in the blood of their country! Behold "the generous measures of Great-Britain!" Your Excellencies have unwarily touched a string, that already trembles throughout America—a subject that rouses the indignation, and calls forth the vengeance of the people! America has experienced too much to be surprized at any thing; she therefore cannot be surprized at your decorating your offers with the title, "the generous measures of Great-Britain." Generous measures proceed from magnanimity, not cruelty—from choice, not necessity. Already have I met your assertions with Lord North's speech; allow me once more to have recourse to it. His Lordship proceeded,

"The resistance of America is greater, and the war has lasted longer than was at first apprehended. In the present situation of affairs, only three propositions can be made:

"1. To strengthen our force, and continue the war upon the present plan.

"2. To recal it from America. And

"3. To offer terms of conciliation to her.

"The first proposition is attended with too great an expence of men and money. The second is to subscribe to the Independence of

America. The third is that which appears to me to be the best and wisest."

Your Excellencies will be so good as to glance your eyes over the first and last propositions, and be sensible, that prior to the 17th of February last, conciliation was not the "present plan." And if you look upon his Lordship's reflections upon the three propositions, you *must remain convinced*, that he closed with the last proposition from necessity, not choice—he closed with it because he could no longer prosecute the first. Tell me now, in what consists the *boasted generosity* of the present measures of Great-Britain?

And have your Excellencies so unfavourable an opinion of the understandings of the Americans, as to think you can induce them, by your reasonings and negociations, to yield that Independence which they declared after the most *mature reflection*—which they have purchased with their *hearts blood*, and at every risk! Are you so much in the dark with respect to their inclinations and determination, as to have an idea, that if you proved to them, as clear as the meridian sun, that the offers of France were only the consequence of your conciliatory propositions, that therefore they would renounce their glorious independence! Is it possible you have forgot, that on the 22d of April last, when Congress were utterly ignorant that a treaty had been signed by their Commissioners, nay, that a treaty with France even had been, was then, or was expected to be in agitation, that on that very 22d of April Congress absolutely refused your conciliatory acts of Parliament! Are you now for the first time to be assured, that the people throughout the United States, with one voice, applauded and rejoiced in that "*decisive*" refusal! It was not "on the ground of the treaties" with France, that Congress took "the decisive part," of which you so much complain; nor was this decisive part taken as you suppose it was, "without previously consulting the Assemblies of their different" States. The Members of Congress individually knew the sense of their respective Assemblies, before they came to Congress. The present Members of Congress were sent by their several Assemblies, *at every hazard to maintain* the Independence of America. I solemnly assure you upon this great point. Should a Member of Congress be so imprudent as but to move to accept your propositions, he must prepare to make *attonement with his head*, or fly to you for refuge. Congress have no power of themselves: Their power arises from the support of the people. So long as they possess this support, they hold the reins of government; the moment they lose it, that moment they cease to direct the affairs of the continent. As long, therefore, as you see them at the head of the American Empire, be convinced they are supported and obeyed by the people, in every measure tending to the establishment of their Independence. Deceive not yourselves by continuing to nourish the vain idea, that Congress have "*assumed* the decisive part which they have taken."

Your Excellencies have it in your power to make a faithful representation of the utter improbability of your acquiring, in any degree, the subjection of America by your arms, or your negociations; to save your country by making such a representation; and thereby preserving your names from infamy, render them respectably immortal. That such may be your conduct and reward, is the wish of

W.H.D.[7]

MS not found; reprinted from the *Pennsylvania Packet, and Daily Advertiser*, September 12, 1778.

1 It should be noted that Gérard, the French minister in Philadelphia, claimed that he collaborated with Drayton in writing this letter. However, since it is written in Drayton's style, Gérard probably did no more that supply background information on French diplomacy and history. In any event, Gérard assisted Drayton because he hoped that the publication of this letter would frustrate British efforts to undermine American confidence in the French alliance. See Gérard to Vergennes, September 10, 1778, in Meng, *Gérard Despatches*, p. 267. See also Henry Laurens to Gérard, September 1, 1778.

2 This "declaration," signed by Carlisle, Clinton, and Eden and endorsed by Secretary Thomson as read in Congress on August 31, is in the Peter Force Collection, DLC.

3 "Let it pass for what it is worth."

4 For Congress' August 11 denunciation of George Johnstone's efforts to corrupt certain delegates, see *JCC*, 11:770–74.

5 "A voice and nothing more."

6 For the "gentleman" in question, Robert Morris, see Henry Laurens to Robert Morris, April 27, 1778, note 1.

7 For a discussion of the newspaper letters Drayton wrote to the British peace commissioners using his initials as a signature, see William Henry Drayton to the Carlisle Commissioners, June 17, 1778, note 1.

Henry Laurens to John Beatty

Sir 4th Septr. [1778]

I had the honor of writing to you the 31st Ulto. by Messenger Ross.

This will be conducted by Josiah Tatnell Esqr. a Gentleman late of the State of Georgia decended from an Ancient and very respectable family in South Carolina, and himself no less respected in both those States, his political determinations, excepted.

Mr. Tatnal was lately made Prisoner of War by the Count d'Estaing's Squadron; the Honorable the Minister Plenipotentiary of France has permitted him by a writing of his hand subscribed and seal'd to go into New York in order to work his discharge by the releasement from thence of a Subject of His Most Christian Majesty in Exchange—this Paper and also a Copy of his parole Mr. Tatnal will produce for your inspection. Congress have directed me to give this Gentleman a Pass through Jersey, which he will also shew you, and as Mrs. Tatnal with a little family are under his charge I request you Sir, to do me the favor of facilitating their passage.

Congress have also permitted Captain William Nicholls late Commander of the British Packet Eagle to go into New York for the like purpose of effecting a proper Exchange which you will prescribe and determine upon, and will also take Captain Nicholls' Parole and restrict the term for his absence in failure of his attempt, in which I would wish you to be very pointed, because from my particular application this indulgence has been obtain'd.

Your Predecessor in Office the Honorable Mr. Boudinot will say much in favor of Captain Nicholls' conduct during his parole confinement within this State. I have known the Captain some five or six years, and have from thence a regard for him.

I am with great Esteem & Respect Sir Your Obedient & Most Humble Servt.

ENCLOSURES

By Permission of Congress assembled at Phila. 3d. Septr. 1778 Josiah Tatnal Esqr. late of the State of Georgia a Prisoner of His Most Christian Majesty is to pass thro' New Jersey in terms of written subscrib'd and Seal'd Act of Egress granted to him by the Honorable the Minister Plenipotentiary of France residing at this City.

Captain Nicholl's Pass.

By permission of Congress sitting in Assembly at Philadelphia 3d of September 1778, Captain William Nicholls late of the British Packet Eagle now a Prisoner of War in this State is to pass unmolested from Philadelphia by the direct Road to Princetown in New Jersey or to any place within that State in which Colo. John Beatty, Commissary General of Prisoners holds his Residence and Office.

LB (DNA: PCC, item 13). Addressed: "Col. John Beaty, Com. Genl. of Prisoners, Princetown, by Mr. Tatnal."

1 Beatty reported to Laurens on September 11 that he had allowed Tatnall and his family and Captain Nichols to proceed to New York. PCC, item 78, 3:181–82.

Richard Henry Lee to George Bryan

Sir, Philadelphia Septr. 4 1778

Mr. President Laurens having this day informed Congress that your honorable board desired he would write to Gen. Maxwell concerning Doctor Birkenhout, it was desired by Congress that I should furnish you with the Generals letter to me upon the subject, which I have now the honor of doing.[1]

I must do Dr. Birkenhout the justice to say, that when I informed him General Maxwell had written me that he, the Doctor, said he had "intelligence of much import for Congress" he replied it was a mistake, and that he attributed it to the General being at the time engaged in business with many people, and to his having said his business was to see a Member of Congress, meaning myself. He has further, in conversation told me, that his plan in coming to America was to find a proper place to fix himself and his family in a country of freedom, and where he might advantageously practise physick which is his profession. For this he assigned many reasons that appeared to me very forcible ones.

Be pleased Sir to return me the letter of Gen. Maxwell when you have done with it.

I am, with due regard, Sir your most obedient and very humble servt. Richard Henry Lee

RC (DLC).

1 There is no mention in the minutes of the Pennsylvania Council of a decision to request information on John Berkenhout from President Laurens, or in the journals of Congress of a decision to ask Lee to send Maxwell's letter to Vice President Bryan. But for information on Berkenhout's case and references to the Pennsylvania Council's determinations concerning the doctor, see Richard Henry Lee to William Maxwell, August 29; Henry Laurens to William Maxwell, September 5, 1778; and *Pa. Council Minutes*, 11:567, 569–70, 576.

James Smith to Eleanor Smith

Congress Chamber, September the fourth, 1778.

This morning I sent a bundle of newspapers and a half finished letter[1] by Mr. Hahn. Yesterday I dined with the president at his own house, he lives elegantly and keeps house himself, we had an elegant dinner and very good claret and Madeira. No further accounts from Rhode Island that can be depended on, but one letter mentions they expect the French fleet from Boston again, and if so they will not quit the Island. If any thing certain arrives before this letter is sealed, I will mention it in a postscript. But for this unlucky storm that scattered the fleets of France and England we had the best ground to hope that Rhode Island would have been recovered, and that would have put an end to the war in all human probability, but if Heaven determines otherwise, we must submit; I am tired of the city heartily, it is very expensive living and not very agreeable; since I left the Indian Queen, I have paid for my room and bed, and breakfast and supper, six pounds per week, and four pounds per week more, for my dinner at another house without any drink.

Yesterday, congress agreed to meet twice a day, so that we break up at one, and meet at three o'clock.[2] I told Mr. Shee my lodging was too dear, and I did not like to lodge at one house and dine at another half a mile off. He agreed to board me at twenty dollars per week including dinner, which is fifty shillings less than I had paid. I breakfasted with Mr. Wilson and Ross at Mrs. House's, she said her price was twenty dollars a week, which I will accept of, unless I can lodge at captain M'Collough's or Mr. Nichols', for being now able to dine at the usual time, I can get board in many places where I could not while we dined at four o'clock.

I am laying my account upon returning about the tenth of next month, to be able to attend Carlisle and York courts.

Beef and mutton are half a crown, veal three shillings, and all kinds of goods as dear as ever.

I put fifteen hundred pounds in the loan office, and have got about ninety pounds fees, and a promise of a hundred pound fee more, these are the first fees I ever got in Philadelphia; my fees here must clear my teeth, and my pay in congress go to you my dear, and the children. I believe if you would consent to come here and live, I could get into pretty good business in the law way, but it is a hazard, and two thousand a year would, as times go, be not more than enough to live in any tolerable style here. York and Carlisle are sure for business though fees are not so high as here.

Mrs. Stevenson sent me a forty dollar fee, to turn her husband out of her house, and general Thompson assures me, she will sign her claim to the widows' house on any separate paper, but not where he signed.

Poor Mrs. Shugart with Mr. Armor called on me to assist in getting a pass from congress, for leave for her to go to New York to try if she can get her husband home, I much doubt her success, but got her the pass.[3] Our prisoners there whose friends cannot send them hard money suffer greatly. I tried to get Tommy Armor a good post in the army, but missed it; had he spoken or written to me in time, I believe it might have been had for him.

I dined at major Nichols' one day and Kitty seems very clever, and is visited by good sort of people.

You, my dear, have been fatigued to death with the plantation affairs; I can only pity but not help you. Did you hear from Betsey's; is Peggy any thing more talkative? She sent a good letter, tell her to write me another.

I went to Mr. Hillegass (where I go often,) with Mrs. Nichols to deliver the letters. I have not time to finish, but you will have nonsense enough.

Your loving husband, whilst, James Smith.[4]

MS not found; reprinted from John Sanderson, *Biography of the Signers to the Declaration of Independence*, 9 vols. (Philadelphia: R.W. Pomeroy, 1820–27), 7:231–33.

1 Not found.

2 See *JCC*, 12:876.

3 Lt. Zacharius Shugart of Col. Michael Swope's Pennsylvania Battalion of the Flying Camp was taken prisoner at Ft. Washington on November 16, 1776, and was not exchanged until December 31, 1780. Heitman, *Historical Register*, p. 366.

4 Sanderson quoted part of a postscript Smith added to this letter "dated fifth September, 1778," reporting that "an account has arrived that there was a battle at Rhode Island, in which the English were worsted."

Andrew Adams to Jonathan Trumbull, Sr.

Sir Philadelphia 5th Septr. 1778.

I wrote your Excellency some time past respecting the matter of Col.   &c,[1] since which we have been honored with your favor of the 25th Ulto, and cant but again lament your distresses occasioned by the sickness and death of the late Commy. General and the melancholy of your mind in consequence of that event. I sincerely pray that under your present heavy and grievious affliction you may be comforted with the consolations of God—which are neither few nor small, & that while you are deprived of such tender connections, and dear enjoyments in life, you may at the same time, rejoice in the *God* of your Salvation.

I am very glad to hear Col. Dyer is coming on, not only on account of the late Commissary's affairs, but also of the public, and shall be happy to resign my Seat in Congress to his superior abilities and experience, and especially at such a time as the present when every effort of the greatest abilities is necessary to be exerted in behalf of the suffering public, for the manner of our conducting or rather delaying business in Congress gives me the most sensible uneasiness. I should think it my duty to give your Excellency a particular account of our proceedings had not Mr Hosmer done me the honour of presenting me his letter of the 31st Ulto. which had my full approbation, and which states that matter with such justice as to supercede the necessity of any observations from me upon the disagreable subject; other than most sincerely to lament the disagreable truth it contains. It is a most unwelcome consideration & what fills my mind with the deepest anxiety & concern, that the conduct of any of the members of Congress should be such, as to create in my mind strong suspicions of their moral and political virtue. But these things lead me more and more to remove my confidence from man, and to comfort myself with that consideration, that none of the wicked machinations of the deceitful and vile shall ever be able to defeat the kind instructions of the *Deity*.

Yesterday we began to meet twice a day, which is to continue till the 1st of Novr.—A measure this—extremely disagreable to many members; but it has long been urged by the New England States.

We have just received Intelligence by General Sullivan's letter of a battle fought at the North end of Rhode-Island, in which our people kept the field, and that considerable numbers fell on both sides, we have no particulars as yet: nothing of consequence has concurred since Mr Hosmer wrote, have only to add my sincere wishes that you[r] extensive usefulness might be long continued—and that you might live to see the fruits of your arduous labours in the independence freedom and happiness of your Country, and be finally admitted to the glorious rewards of the Righteous.

I am with esteem, sincerity and regard Your Excellency's, most obedient & very hble Servant, Andw Adams.

Tr (DLC).

[1] That is, Jacob Gerhard Diriks. See Andrew Adams to Trumbull, August 11, 1778, note 2.

Henry Laurens to the Auditors of Army Accounts

Gentlemen 5th Septr. [1778]

Inclosed with this you will receive an Act of Congress of the 3d Instant for admitting Oaths and other Evidence in particular cases in proof of back Rations.

For regulating the Salaries of Brigade Chaplains, for allowing subsistence to each Auditor in the Army and for augmenting the pay of their Clerks.

I likewise inclose an Act of the same date for appointing James Johnston Esqr. an Auditor.[1]

I am, With great Respect &c.

LB (DNA: PCC, item 13). Addressed: "The Auditors of Accounts at the Main Army, White Plains."

[1] For the resolves listed here by Laurens, all of which were passed by Congress on September 3, see *JCC*, 12:863–64. Laurens also transmitted copies of the first and second of these resolves with a brief covering letter he wrote this day to Paymaster General William Palfrey. PCC, item 13, 2:64.

Henry Laurens to Richard Caswell

Sir 5th September [1778]

I have had no Commands from Congress respecting North Carolina since my last date of the 9th July, until the present to transmit to Your Excellency two undermention'd Acts, nor have I been honored with any of Your Excellencys' favors.

An Act of the 2nd Inst. for permitting the Exportation of vegetable Provisions to the Eastern States.[1]

An Act of this date for issuing four hundred thousand Dollars for compleating the Continental Battalions of North Carolina.[2] Which Acts will be found under Cover with this.

I have the honor to be &c.

LB (DNA: PCC, item 13).

1 See *JCC*, 12:861. Laurens also transmitted copies of this resolve with brief covering letters he wrote this day to the governors of Rhode Island, Connecticut, New Jersey, and Virginia, the presidents of Massachusetts and Delaware, and the vice president of Pennsylvania, and on the following day to the governor of Georgia. See PCC, item 13, 2:67–68, 70; Red Series, R–Ar; Continental Congress Papers, Vi; Revolutionary Letters, M–Ar; and Lloyd Smith Collection, NjMoHP.

2 See *JCC*, 12:883.

Henry Laurens to William Heath

Sir. Philadelphia 5th Septem 1778.

I had the honour of writing to you the 28th Ulto. by Messenger Jones, & of presenting to Congress on the 1st Inst. your several favors of the 20th July, 1st & 11st Inst. which had reached me the preceeding evening.[1]

That of the 1st August was committed to the Treasury & no order made on the other two. Wherefore it only remains to repeat, which I do with great truth & respect that, I am Sir, Your most obedt. & most hum servant, Henry Laurens, President of Congress

RC (MHi). The text of this letter in Laurens' presidential letterbook is dated September 6. PCC, item 13, 2:69.

1 General Heath's July 20 and August 11 letters to Laurens are in PCC, item 157, fols. 178–81, 190–91. In the first letter Heath asked if a unit under his command that had captured a British brigantine off the coast of New Jersey during the Trenton campaign was entitled to a share of this prize. Instead of enlightening Heath on this point, however, Congress simply tabled the letter. *JCC*, 11:858. In the second letter the general merely described recent military developments in Rhode Island. A file copy of Heath's August 1 letter to Laurens, which dealt with the need to raise the pay of the general's secretaty, Jotham Loring, and which was referred to the Board of Treasury, is in the Heath Papers, MHi.

Henry Laurens to Thomas Johnson

Sir. Philadelphia 5th Sept. 1778

I have not troubled Your Excellency since the 10th July,[1] since which I have had the honor of receiving & presenting to Congress

Your Excellency's favor of the 5th Ulto. Committed to the Marine board & I presume the subject matters contained in it have been duely attended to.[2]

I have at present no other Commands from Congress respecting Maryland but to transmit an Act of the 2d Inst. for permitting the exportation of Vegetable Provisions for the consumpt[ion] of the Eastern States which will be found within.[3]

I have the honor to be Sir, Your Excellency's Obedient & most humble servant, Henry Laurens, President of Congress

[*P.S.*] Your Excellency will receive with this 12 blank Commissions, Instructions & Bonds for Ships of War.

RC (MdAA).

1 See Laurens to Certain States, July 10, 1778.

2 See Samuel Chase to Thomas Johnson, August 11, 1778, note 1.

3 See *JCC*, 12:861.

Henry Laurens to William Maxwell

Sir 5th Septr. [1778]

I had the honor of paying my respects to you the 26th Ulto. in a private Address, this is intended also as a private, having received no Commands from Congress respecting your late Letter.

The Executive Council of this State lately ordered Doctor Berkenhout who came from within the Enemy's Lines at New York thro' your Head Quarters into this City where he had remained some days without explaining himself or the nature of his errand to the Vice President of the State, the President of Congress, or to any Magistrate, to be apprehended and committed to Goal, where he now lies, under suspicion of being a Spy—from the contents of a Paper found in his custody it appears he had a design of offering himself to Congress as a private Negociator for terms of peace consistent with Independence between these United States and Great Britain, and 'tis certain that upon his journey hither, he, in conversation with a Gentleman in Jersey assum'd the Character of Agent or Commissioner from the Court of Great Britain to Congress.[1]

In a letter to Congress written since he has been in confinement, in terms which appear to be extremely equivocal he claims no public Character, says, "he came hither under the sanction of a Pass from an American General," complains of the hardship of being imprisoned "in a Country which he had been taught to revere as the asylum of liberty" and "requests to be permitted to return from whence he came."[2]

Congress have declined interfering in this business, but I am particularly requested by a Gentleman of the Council to inquire of You,

Sir, what were Dr. Berkenhout's pretensions of business or Character when he apply'd to you for a pass and under what authority or permission he gained access to you.

I have also to request you to inform me if you can possibly learn how many ships of the Line which lately went out of the Hook under the command of Lord Howe in order to divert our attack Count d'Estaing returned after the storm into New York—a very sensible Man a deserter from the Enemy, assures me, the Eagle and 3 or 4 more capital ships were driven on shore on Long Island and totally lost, that Lord Howe returned in a frigate which bore his Flag, and hitherto I have seen no other names in the New York Papers of his Lordships squadron but the Isis, Renown, and Prescott, which gives an air of truth to the deserters narrative. This is an interresting subject, if you will make the necessary enquiry and communicate the result together with every particular information you can collect of the state of the British Fleet you will thereby render a favor which will oblige me very much, and of which I will embrace all opportunities for making proper acknowledgments.[3]

I have the honor to be, With great Respect &c.[4]

LB (ScHi).

1 After arriving in Philadelphia on August 27, whither he had been sent by the North ministry and the earl of Carlisle to engender support for the British peace commissioners, Dr. John Berkenhout met with Richard Henry Lee, Nathaniel Scudder, Samuel Adams, and "several other members of Congress." Although Lee subsequently claimed that he only spoke to Berkenhout about the doctor's professed wish to settle in America, Berkenhout maintained that he had conversed with Lee and other delegates on such subjects as "The cause of their declaration of independance—Their treaty with France—Reasons why Britain ought immediately to make peace with America—State of the American Army—Cause of their success—Governor Johnstones private letters; his political opinions and conduct &c." Unfortunately, since Lee had every motive to depreciate his contacts with Berkenhout after it became clear that the doctor was a British agent, and since Berkenhout may have magnified his with the delegates to impress his English superiors, it is difficult to determine which account is closer to the truth. In any case, Berkenhout's mission came to an abrupt end on September 3 when he was arrested by the Pennsylvania Council after the appearance of a letter in the *Pennsylvania Packet* recalling previous stories in the paper that described the doctor as a British agent. Although Berkenhout sought in vain to have Congress intervene in his behalf, he was eventually released from jail in the middle of September and allowed to return to New York when the Pennsylvania authorities failed to find incriminating evidence against him. See Howard Peckham, ed., "Dr. Berkenhout's Journal, 1778," *PMHB* 65 (1941): 86–88; Lee, *Letters* (Ballagh), 1:457–60, 466–67, 2:25–26; and Richard Henry Lee to William Maxwell, August 29, 1778, note 1. Berkenhout's relationship with Richard Henry Lee and his brother Arthur soon became inextricably entangled in the Deane-Lee affair. See Samuel Adams to James Warren, October 11 and 14, 1778.

2 Berkenhout's September 4 letter to Congress is in the Laurens Papers, ScHi. Laurens wrote a brief reply to it this day, stating: "I presented your Letter to Congress this Morning—it was order'd to lie on the table, the house declining the consideration of a subject which is already and properly before the Executive Power of this State." PCC, item 13, 2:65.

[3] The following day Laurens wrote a brief letter to General Maxwell, instructing him to grant passports to William Telfair and John Burguin, "late inhabitants within these States," so that they could travel from New York to Philadelphia. PCC, item 13, 2:69.

[4] The following "Memo." appears at the foot of this letter. "Sent the Secretary's Letter to Wm. [John] Temple Esqr. under cover to Genl. Maxwell." Secretary Thomson's letter to John Temple has not been found but for an explanation of its provenance, see Samuel Adams to James Bowdoin, September 3, 1778.

Henry Laurens to George Washington

Sir

5th September [1778]

My last was dated the 31st Ult. forwarded by Messenger Jones,[1] since which I have had the honor of receiving and presenting to Congress Your Excellency's dispatches, one of that date and one of the 3d Instant, the first is committed to the Board of War & remains there.[2]

This will be accompanied by two Acts of Congress of the 3d Instant.[3]

1. . . . An Act for raising a Corps of troops by the name of the German Volunteers—for granting the Pay and Subsistence of a Lieutenant to Lieutenant Charles Juliat a Volunteer in the Infantry of General Pulaski's Legion—for appointing Monsr. Girard to the Rank of a Lieutenant of Dragoons by Brevet to serve at his own expence—for laying aside the intended Expedition against the Seneca and other Indians, and for authorizing Your Excellency to pursue proper measures for defending the frontiers against the incursions of those Indians.[4]
2. . . . An Act for guarding this City by 300 Militia in place of the Confederal Troops who are to join the Main Army.[5]

I have the honor to be &c.

LB (DNA: PCC, item 13).

[1] At this point in the LB Laurens first wrote "Yesterday I had the honor of receiving and presenting to Congress Your Excellencys' favor of the same date together with Copy of General Sullivans referr'd to" and then altered it to read as above.

[2] Washington's August 31 letter to Laurens is in PCC, item 152, 6:313–16, and Washington, *Writings* (Fitzpatrick), 12:375–78. No September 3 letter from Washington to Laurens has been found. However, Laurens was probably referring to a September 1 letter from Washington, which forwarded a copy of an August 29 letter from Gen. John Sullivan to the commander in chief and was read in Congress on the fourth. See PCC, item 152, 6:321; and *JCC*, 12:880. Sullivan's letter, which described his success in fending off a British attack on his retreating army, is in Sullivan, *Papers* (Hammond), 2:275–76.

[3] At this point in the LB Laurens first wrote and then deleted: "Which are all the Commands at present lying on me. Your Ex."

[4] For these resolves, see *JCC*, 12:866–68.

[5] See *JCC*, 12:865.

Henry Laurens to Meshech Weare

Honorable Sir 5th Septr. [1778]

My last was dated the 16th Ulto. by Messenger Dunn forwarded through General Washington's Camp.

On the 22nd Instant and not earlier I had the honor of receiving and presenting to Congress your favor of the 25th July.[1] I observe that Letters by the Post are always very long on their passage, and have detected in several instances miscarriages to and fro several towns beyond where Congress sat before a proper delivery was made. This will inclose an Act of Congress of the 2nd Inst. for supplying the Eastern States with vegetable provisions under certain restrictions.[2]

I have the honor to be &c.

LB (DNA: PCC, item 13).

1 President Weare's July 25 letter to Laurens, in which he promised to comply with a July 11 resolve "Impowering General Washington to call for such Militia as he shall think Requisite to Cooperate with Count d'Estaing," is in PCC, item 64, fol. 37. According to the journals and Secretary Thomson's endorsement, this letter was read in Congress on August 24. *JCC*, 11:835.

2 See *JCC*, 12:861.

Richard Henry Lee to Adam Stephen

My dear Sir, Philadelphia September 5. 1778

I am much obliged to you for your favor of the 26 August, and for the satisfaction you are pleased to express at knowing that I was in good health. My health is indeed not bad at this time, but I am quite worn down with so long and constant attention to public business. I suppose you will have heared before this reaches you, that a violent Storm saved Lord Howe and the British fleet from the vengeance of Count D'Estaing. This ill timed tempest shattered and dispersed both fleets so that a very partial fighting took place between a few single Ships. The F. Admiral lost all his Masts before he fired a gun, they were carried away by the Storm. He returned to Rhode Island in that condition with a 74 that had lost her foremast & Bowsprit. The rest of his fleet safe, except the Caesar of 74 guns that has since arrived at Boston, where the whole fleet went immediately to refit, after touching at R. Island only. In this situation of things Gen. Sullivan was to consider, whether to retreat, or continue to press the Seige of Newport and risk the arrival of succors from York. A Council of War determined upon the former. The consequence was as you will see in the paper inclosed. I should suppose that Gen. Sullivan will find no great difficulty in effecting his retreat whilst the enemy continue sore from their late drubbing. It appears by the last accounts from England, that Adml. Keppel had taken two French frigates in the Channel, which he seems to have done with fear and trembling, for he apologises for his conduct. Whether the Duke des Chartres, who commands a superior fleet in the harbor of Brest will admit his apology, time must discover. I like much your ideas about the best manner of proceeding to the westward, and will in due season avail myself of your plan.

Remember me, if you please, with affectionate respect to Greenway Court, and do not forget my other friends in your parts.

I am, with sincere regard, dear Sir your real friend and most obedient servant.

Richard Henry Lee

P.S. Tell Colo. Martin that I forwarded his letters to Alderman Lee, but I am uncertain when they will reach him, or where they will find him. He is either at the Imperial Court, or at that of Berlin.

R.H. Lee

7th. Septr. Since writing the above we have had an Express from Gen. Sullivan with a more particular account of his action on R Island, by which it appears that our loss was very small, 23 killed only, no Officer of consequence killed or wounded, and his retreat to the Main effected without any loss whatever, except the few men in the battle. Gen. Clinton with a reenforcement of 5000 men arrived on the Island thro the Sound a few hours after our Army crossed the Water.

Six ships of 74 guns each have lately arrived at N. York from England, and joined with the Ships formerly here are sailed Eastward in quest of Count D'Estaing. He is safe in Boston Harbour, and we have no doubt but that these Ships from G. B. will [*be*] quickly followed by a superior force from France.

Since the R. Island expedition began, the thing stands thus—Lost by the enemy 5 frigates, 2 sloops of War, 3 Gallies, a large number of Transports, and their Army, 6000 on R. Island have got a severe drubbing—On our side 23 Men killed, 211 Wounded & missing. We brought off near 70 Prisoners with some Officers. The account of the enemies dead not returned, but said to be very considerable.

RC (NbO). Addressed: "General Stephen, in Berkeley County, Virginia."

Henry Laurens to the Eastern Navy Board

Gentlemen

6th Septr. [1778]

I had the honor of writing to you the 13th Ulto. by Messenger from the Minister Plenipotentiary, and then transmitted twenty four Commissions with the necessary concomitant Papers, the sole purpose of my present Address is to intimate that I now add fifteen setts to the former, these will be found within the present Cover, you will be pleased Gentlemen, in due time to acknowledge the receipt of the whole.

I am, With very great Respect &c.

LB (DNA: PCC, item 13). Addressed: "The Commissioners of the Navy Board for the Eastern District, Boston."

Henry Laurens to John Lewis Gervais

My Dear Friend 6th September [1778]

My last was dated the 22nd Ulto. conveyed by Captain Pyne, since which I have received none of your favors. I must again beg leave to refer you to our worthy friend the President for news in General. I have sent him a Budget—much of it ought to be confined within the knowledge of a few friends for the present.

Within the present cover I give you several of Dunlaps' Packets, Copy of a Letter from Your friend John Laurens of 1st September, and of one relative to him from General Washington.[1] I know you will be glad to see these; if you think proper to publish the first in order to do justice to some characters of whom he writes don't *publish* his name. I am sure he is as averse as I am to that sort of Newspaper Parade.

I was in great hopes to have sent you General Lees' trial at length, but 'tis not out of Press.

You will read what I have written to His Excellency the President respecting the Embargo and the Article of Rice an intimation intended for public good,[2] to yourself, I say if you are disposed to purchase 4000 Barrels of very good Rice at the Current price as speedily as possible after you receive this I shall be glad to hold a moiety of the concern, you will be the best judge of quality, goodness of Barrels and convenience of Storage, I shall therefore not trouble you on these Points, nor do I mean to impose myself on you as a Partner unless it shall be quite agreeable to yourself and that you can pay for one half the purchase out of my own funds.

My next shall mark my sentiments respecting the shipping or otherwise disposing of the Rice.

A swift sailing Sloop or Schooner to run into Delaware with 2 or 300 Barrels immediately if you have general permission will probably make a good Voyage provided the freight is not too extravagant. I judge it will sell here at 40/ or perhaps 6 dollars per 112 w[eight] if the Vessel be light, you may dispose of as much rough Rice as will fill the hollows in stowage of the Cask—but note 'tis not impossible that British Men of War may again appear in the Bay, and that there is no great hope of a back freight—these circumstances you will duly consider.

I shall also in my next talk seriously to you concerning my return. 'Tis high time, and yet when I reflect—Mr. Heyward gone, Mr. Hudson absent, Mr. Mathews going, I feel a sensible pain at the prospect of leaving our State again almost unrepresented, but if my Countrymen are totally inattentive to their dearest Interests, the continuance of my feeble efforts to serve them will be in vain with respect to them, although it may work the ruin of my Estate.

I expect to hear from you such Answer as General Gadsden shall have given.[3]

My respectful Compliments to Mr. and Mrs. Manigault, Mrs. Gervais and all Friends. I continue with great Regard and Esteem, Dear Sir, Your Affectionate Hbl. Servant

LB (ScHi).

[1] Laurens is referring to a private letter Washington wrote to him on September 4 quoting Gen. Nathanael Greene in praise of John Laurens' bravery during the Rhode Island campaign. Washington, *Writings* (Fitzpatrick), 12:397–98.

[2] See the next entry.

[3] See Laurens to Gervais, August 7, 1778, note 8.

Henry Laurens to Rawlins Lowndes

Dear Sir

6th September [1778]

Mr Heyward left us so suddenly about the 10th Ulto. it was impossible for me to pay my respects to Your Excellency by him. I writ the 11th continued to the 21st and my Packet overtook Captain Pyne the 23rd at Baltimore which I hope will supply that defect.

In that Dispatch I omitted to send Copy of the Decree of the Committee of Appeals on the case of the Brigantine Success, because indeed I could not procure it in time from the Register.[1] It will now be found under cover with this among diverse other papers which will accompany it, as will appear by an inclos'd Schedule of the whole.

I am much dissatisfied with this determination and have doubts concerning the respect which will be paid to the Decree in Charlestown. Certainly a very formal and solemn Verdict given there is intended to be set aside by the judgment of a Court far inferiour to that of our Admiralty in every view—besides the 280 Dollars to be paid in obedience to his judgment for the Costs and charges of Captain Arthur the law charges which I must pay here will Amount I am inform'd to seven hundred Dollars and upwards.

I have lately been call'd upon by three Persons who had made their escape or been exchang'd from imprisonment at New York, and who had been captur'd on Voyages from Charlestown whither they were desirous of returning, but could not proceed without assistance of Money. I have supply'd each of them, viz.

Lieut. Richard Wells of the Comet	200 Dolls.
Captain Joseph Price of the Active	109
Captain George Leacey of the General Gadsden	350

Their several Receipts will be found within. I trust our State will suffer no loss from such unavoidable advance of Money to her distressed Citizens, and in any case that I shall not incur censure—indeed in every instance except that of Lacey I have had the concurrence and approbation of my Colleagues.

The sundry Papers alluded to above, together with the printed Papers which I shall add, will give Your Excellency almost a clear knowledge of our public intelligence to this day, and therefore I will not be troublesome with repetitions.

Bad as General Sullivan's Case appears to be, and the appearance is bad indeed, I do with grief assure Your Excellency the state of our Treasury and finances, of our Loan Office Certificates, our foreign Debts—our waste of time & neglect of the most important concerns, are infinitely more alarming—were I to indulge suspicions too well warranted from appearances, and the daily intimations which are given to me from different quarters, I should be provoked to say there are Berkenhout's and Temple's, and more dangerous Engines than either in the vitals of our Union.

At this very instant the arrival of Major Lewis Morris Aid de Camp to General Sullivan is announc'd—I must attend him.

Major Morris has deliver'd me Letters from General Washington, General Sullivan &c. which will soon spread that joy which I myself feel, throughout an anxious City.[2] I will add to the pile of Papers a Copy of the Generals Letter—the general anxiety was not without cause. The Major's words in a whisper to me were "I do assure you Sir, we are indebted to that good Man General Washington for our escape, he gave us notice and press'd again our Retreat." The day following 5000 Men landed from New York at Newport—Sir Henry Clinton said to be at the head of them—when General Sullivan had determin'd to retreat he cover'd his design by a stratagem which compleatly deceiv'd the Enemy and happily effected his purpose. The Enemy were then at least equal in number Man for Man with himself—the retreat of Major General Hancock and his Volunteers and of the Militia &c who had followed his example had nearly ruined our cause, or to say the least reduced America to extreme distress—we have cause to be thankful for an almost unparalle'd escape.

Major Morris informs me there are now upward of 10,000 British and foreign troops on Rhode Island and a fleet of British Men of War riding in parade in Boston Bay, this will probably however, end in parade furnishing Mr Rivington with small means for long vaunting Paragraphs.

Will your Excellency pardon me in my present haste for making this private letter a vehicle for conveying an Act of Congress of the 2nd Inst. for relaxing the general Embargo in so far as to procure a supply of Vegetable Provisions for the necessary consumpt of the Eastern States.[3] I find the Embargo in this State is in existence and to run about fourteen days longer, Peccadillo evasions excepted, whether it will be renew'd is a question, probably it may be under the present relaxation which will answer every purpose to the 15th November.

I am desired by the Honorable the Minister Plenipotentiary to encourage the exportation of Rice to the French West India Islands, & to Count d'Estaing's fleet, and I am persuaded small Cargoes will meet with good sales in this City—which I intimate for the general benefit of my Countrymen that each may have timely notice and an option to adventure when the term of the present restriction shall expire. I am persuaded it will not be renewed this Year.[4]

I have the honor to be, With the highest Esteem & Regard[5]

Schedule of Papers sent Mr. Lowndes

No. 1. The Marquis de Bretigney's Memorial and Plan
2. General Sullivan's Letter to the Commander in Chief 21st Augt.
3. Dr. Berkenhout's Letter to Congress 4th Septr.
4. Dr. Berkenhout's unfinish'd Letter intended to R. H. Lee
5. Dr. Berkenhout's Letter to the Printer
6. Mr. Temple's Letter to the President 23d August
7. Colonel Lauren's Letter to the President 22nd August
8. Declaration of the British Commissioners 26th August
9. Requisition by the British Commissioners 26th August
10. Governor Johnstone's Declaration 26th August
11. Dr. Ferguson's Letter accompanying the Declaration 26th Augt.
12. Resolves of Congress on the Declaration &c. 4th Sepr.
13. Lieut. Richard Well's Receipt for 200 Dollars, 24th August
14. Captain Joseph Price's Receipt for 109 Dollars 29th August
15. Capt. Geo. Leacey's Receipt for 350 Dollars 5th Septr.
16. List of British Men of War arriv'd at Sandy Hook the 28th of August with remarks on Lord Howe's Squadron & upon the reported loss of Admiral Byron
17. Decree of the Committee of Appeals at Phila. 7th Augt.
18. An Act of Congress of the 2nd September
19. General Sullivan's Letter to the President 31st August

20. Return of the kill'd, wounded and missing in the Action on Rhode Island 29th August

LB (ScHi).

1 This committee decree, dated August 7, 1778, and signed by Elias Boudinot, Francis Dana, and Joseph Reed, is in case no. 24, RG 267, DNA. In reversing the judgment of the South Carolina Admiralty Court in this case, the committee declared "that the Brigantine or Vessel called the Success with her Tackle, Apparel and Furniture, and all and singular the Goods, Wares and Merchandizes laden and found on board the said Brigantine at the Time of her Capture as mentioned in the Bill of the said Edward Weyman be restored and redelivered unto George Arthur the Claimant in the said Cause And We do further adjudge and decree that the said Edward Weyman pay unto the said George Arthur two hundred and eighty Dollars for his Costs and Charges by him expended in sustaining and supporting his said Appeal." See also Laurens to John Lewis Gervais, October 18, 1777, note 4.

2 John Sullivan's August 31 and Washington's September 4 letters to Laurens, both of which dealt with Sullivan's safe retreat in Rhode Island, are in PCC, item 152, 6:337–38, item 160, fols. 170–77; Washington, *Writings* (Fitzpatrick), 12:398; and Sullivan, *Papers* (Hammond), 2:280–86. Congress read these letters on September 7 and two days later voted to thank Sullivan and his men for "their fortitude and bravery." *JCC*, 12:884–85, 894.

3 See *JCC*, 12:861.

4 A slightly altered version of this paragraph was printed in the *South Carolina and American General Gazette* under the heading "Extract of a Letter from a Member of Congress, dated August 6."

5 This day Laurens also wrote a brief personal letter to Charles Cotesworth Pinckney, enclosing "a Schedule of Sundry articles which Mrs. Morton late housekeeper to Mr. Middleton put into my hands as your property." Laurens Papers, ScHi.

Henry Laurens to John Rutledge

My Dear Sir. 6 September [1778]

I had the honor a few days ago of receiving your favor of the 18 July by Mr. Galvan;[1] this Gentleman called on me for Letters of introduction to General Washington & General Sullivan, which I declined giving & Stated the reasons for my refusal in terms equally civil & candid, he discovered much chagrin at the disappointment & retired in a manner which discovered he was angry.

Mr. Silas Deane happened to be present, & immediately after the young Gentleman had turned his back intimated to me that he had sat with impatience during the Dialogue, fearing I should have acquiesed in Mr. Galvan's importunity, that he knew this Gentleman's conduct at Paris, adding a detail of several particulars; the most important to our State is—that Monsr. Beaumarchais & Monsr. Montieu hold South Carolina Debtor for Amount of the Warlike Stores imported there by Monsr. Galvan.

I congratulate with your Excellency on the escape of our Army from the danger to which it had been exposed upon Rhode Island. His Excellency the President will shew you Sir, particulars of this affair & all the papers of intelligence which I shall Send to him by Muckinfuss.

I am happy in assuring you that Colo. John Laurens has not in any instance dishonored your recommendation. Thank God he is well & generally esteemed a Man of as much virtue as personal bravery; I ought not to Say less to a Gentleman who has been pleased to patronize a fellow Citizen so nearly allied to me.

A Sensible shrewd Gentleman of a very considerable class of people called Tory applied to me lately & engaged me in a private & Interesting conversation of a public nature, he requested at parting another opportunity of Speaking to me. I conjecture these people know more than I minutely do of the designs & necessities of the British Court & that they are paving the way, by means of an Emissary, for making their peace.

I have the honor to be &ca.

LB (ScHi).

1 See Laurens to John Laurens, August 29, 1778.

Richard Henry Lee to Arthur Lee

My dear Brother, Philadelphia Septr. 6. 1778

Having written you very lately[1] from hence it would have been unnecessary to write so soon again if some military events had not taken place that you may be desirous to know. The Count D'Estaing has no doubt informed his Court of his Manœuvres with the British fleet commanded by Lord Howe. We have here no accurate knowledge of this affair, but what we do know is as follows, that the Count, in conjunction with Gen. Sullivan who commanded the Continental Army, was beseiging about 6000 English & foreign Troops that had retired within Lines round the Town of Newport on Rhode Island, when Ld. Howe appeared in the offing. This suspended operations on the Island as the Count immediately reshipped his Troops and went out to fight the British fleet, which, tho consisting of many Vessels, was inferior in number of guns & weight of metal to the Counts fleet. The British fled & were pursued the first day, on the next day a furious Storm arose which saved Ld. Howes fleet by dispersing both fleets. The Count lost all his Masts before he fired a Gun, and a ship of 74 lost her foremast and Bowsprit. A partial fighting between single ships took place but nothing of consequence happened in this way. The Count returned to R. Island missing the Cæsar of 74 Guns and he carried in prizes the Senegal Sloop of war & a Bomb Ketch. We hear the Cæsar has since arrived at Boston. The French Admiral determined to go to Boston (and refit his Squadron) which he did immediately. By this time Gen. Sullivan had approached within Musket Shot of the enemies Lines. The departure of the fleet, exposing our Army to the arrival of Succors from N. York quickly thro the Sound, and Ships also to cut off our retreat, determined a Council of War to raise the seige of Newport and return to the Main. The enemy, upon our retreat came out, and a battle ensued, the consequence of which was victory on our Side as you will see by the inclosed Gazette. The Army was not off the Island when the last Express came away, but no doubt they would soon as possible return to the Continent. We hear that Succors were on their way from N. York thro the Sound for R. Island. Gen. Clintons Army is still shut up in N. York by the American Army which lays just above Kingsbridge at White Plains. Congress has not yet taken up the consideration of foreign affairs, but they soon will, I expect in a few days, when I will write you more fully. We are very anxious here to know that Spain has acceeded to our Alliance, and it would be very pleasing that Holland had determined to open Trade with us. We impatiently expect to hear from Europe—I refer You to my last in which I request, with regard to Ludwell that you may either keep him with you, or send him to me, as your judgment and most perfect convenience shall direct, remembering that I have a large family, and that I wish to do them equal justice—That I am very willing to assist Ludwells genius & application as far as I am able to render him useful to himself and beneficial to his Country. Send our brother Alderman this intelligence with my love, Farewell,

Richard Henry Lee

[*P.S.*] My love to my dear Ludwell. We do not know whether the British fleet has ever returned to N. York in the whole—Reports are various—Some say they are all returned—Others that they have met with great loss.

RC (ViU).

1 Richard Henry's most recent letter to Arthur that has been found is dated May 27, 1778. Other letters that Lee wrote at about this time which do not survive include one of September 6 to Washington and one of the seventh to Edmund Pendleton. For an indication of the substance of these, which is reflected in the responses of his correspondents, see Washington, *Writings* (Fitzpatrick), 12:484–85; and Edmund Pendleton, *The Letters and Papers of Edmund Pendleton, 1734–1803*, ed. David J. Mays, 2 vols. (Charlottesville: University Press of Virginia, 1967), 1:269–70.

2 Arthur Lee's conduct as American commissioner to Spain as well as his diplomatic and personal activities in France and Prussia are sensitively analyzed in Louis W. Potts, *Arthur Lee: A Virtuous Revolutionary* (Baton Rouge: Louisiana State University Press, 1981), chaps. 5–7.

Henry Marchant to William Greene

Dear Sir, Philadelphia Septr 6th. 1778

I recd. yours of the 20th of August, and I now enclose your Excellency a Letter from the Treasury Board enclosing the Resolution at Length, directing the Manner of sealing up the Tickets under Seal of the State—& the Certificates of the Numbers unsold to be forwarded.[1] Govr. Cooke has sent me one. But You'l perceive others are also to be sent. Your Excellency will now have no Difficulty in forwarding the Tickets.

I am sorry to find that for want of the Aid justly expected from our Sister States (New-Hampshire excepted) We were obliged to exert so uncommon a Force from Our small State. But I somewhat console myself upon such Occasions with the Consideration of the Honor we procure to Ourselves, as well as a Consciousness of having well discharged Our Duty to Ourselves & Posterity. And however this Expedition is not likely to prove so successful as we had much Reason to perceive it might, Yet no Dishonor I think as yet at least, can be reflected on the American Arms. Our Conduct will raise our Characters abroad as well as at Home, even under Disappointments. For to conduct well, & bravely under unforseen Events & Misfortune is great Heroism. I hope also that Phylosophy & good Temper will be exercised under any Misfortunes; and that we may in some good Measure suppress Observations upon the Conduct of others, which may do us no good, but may do harm. Besides, Candor will teach Us, allways to put the most favourable Constructions upon the Conduct & Opinion of others—and we may sometimes doubt at least whether or no we are not mistaken Ourselves. Your Excellency I presume will perceive my Meaning. Whether all Things considered it was a Right Measure in the French Fleets going out after the English Fleet, And whether the going out the second Time was advisable, are Points not the most easily to be Determined—it is political however that We should be delicate upon the Point, if we would not gratify Our Enemies—The Tories especially. This is certain, that no Man could possibly express more uneasiness on that Occasion than the F——h M——r[2] And whether the C——ts[3] Conduct was the most prudent or not. The goodness of his Intentions cannot be doubted of. The Friendship of his Royal Master most assuredly cannot. And we may depend upon a Vigour of Conduct that will shew His Royal Resolution to make good his Ground And to anticipate Our Wishes & Expectations in Him.

It is said that a Person has come out of N. York a Native of Virginia who was a Passenger in Ad'l Byrons Fleet, & declares that on the Passage he was an Eye Witness to the Loss of the Admiral and two other Ships. They all foundered in a terrible Gale of Wind. We hear of the Arrival of but 6 or 7 of that Fleet. We presume upon no slight grounds that a French Fleet is after them—And we yet Trust that we shall see Our Worthy Ally superior in Our Seas to the British Fleet, within a few Days or Weeks. This however it may not be proper to publish.

I should be glad to know the Real Loss of the Enemy in their Shipping at Rhode Island—Whether Their Transports were so sunk as to be destroyed—Whether their Hay &c at Connecticut was destroyed. Our last account from Genl. Sullivan was after the Battle of the 29th but he was not particular as to our Loss, or the Enemies. But we presume it was great on both Sides. We are very anxious to hear that he got off safe, before the Reinforcements got to the Enemy which sailed more than a Week ago. My Respects to your Lady & Family. Most respectfully I am Yr. Excellency's most obedt. and very humble Servt. Hy Marchant

RC (R-Ar).

1 Governor Greene's August 20 letter to Marchant is in William R. Staples, *Rhode Island in the Continental Congress 1765–1790* (Providence: Providence Press Co., 1870), pp. 196–98. The Board of Treasury's letter to Greene has not been found.

2 That is, the French minister, Conrad Alexandre Gérard.

3 Comte d'Estaing.

Gouverneur Morris to George Clinton

Sir, Philadelphia 6' Sep'r 1778.

By Doctor Jones who will deliver this to your Excellency, I do myself the Honor to enclose a short memorandum of the Sums advanced from the Continental Treasury to the several States of the Union. I shall make no Comments. The Paper contains Information and, therefore, I have sent it to your Excellency's Prudence.

Doctor Jones hath informed me that a Law lately passed bears very hard upon many Individuals of the State of N. York, who being willing to become faithful Subjects are nevertheless incapable from what they call conscientious Principles to take an Oath prescribed in it.[1] This Information is corroborated from other Quarters. What the Law or Oath are I know not, nor will I pretend even to suppose that against either there is well-grounded Cause of Complaint. Seriously, I have too good an Opinion of our Legislature to believe they would wantonly sport with the Feelings of mankind. But, Sir, I cannot help mentioning, that in my Opinion it is not good Policy to banish useful Citizens, and that it is better to bend the Spirit of Legislation at Times even to the Prejudices of the People, than to scatter the Riches and Strength of the State among Strangers—what is worse among Enemies. Excuse me, Sir, If I am too free. I am of no Party but that of my Country and as I always have, so I trust I always shall, consult her Interests according to that measure of abilities which it hath pleased Heaven to dispense to me.

I have the Honor to be with deep Respect Your Excellency's most obedient & humble Servant, Gouv. Morris.

ENCLOSURE

New Hampshire	679,000	Maryland	607,000
Massachusetts	1,150,000	Virginia	370,000
Rhode Island	1,392,000	North Carolina	700,000
Connecticut	676,000	South Carolina	930,000
New York	485,000	Georgia	1,036,000
New Jersey	546,000		11,002,000
Pensilvania	2,182,000		
Delaware	49,000		

MS not found; reprinted from Clinton, *Papers* (Hastings), 3:740–41.

1 Morris is referring to an act passed by the New York legislature on June 30 that required all who had hitherto remained neutral to take an oath acknowledging New York "to be of right a free and independent State" or else be banished behind British lines. See Larry R. Gerlach, ed., *The American Revolution; New York as a Test Case* (Belmont, Cal.: Wadsworth Publishing Co., 1972), pp. 113–15. See also Morris to Peter Van Schaack, September 8, 1778.

Gouverneur Morris to Robert R. Livingston

Dr. Livingston Philadelphia 6th Sepr. 1778.

This will be transmitted to you if not delivered to you by my Friend Jones. I have made every Enquiry relative to Doctor Tillotson which was within my Line of Ability.[1] I have asked every of the Representatives from the State of Maryland. I am sorry to add that I can learn Nothing. I then asked negatively and find that he is of Maryland but *not* of any distinguished Family *not* of great and Distinguished Abilities and the like. I enquired his Professional Knowledge and I learn that he is *not* eminent in that Line. To all this I must add of my own that I think I have met him in my Walks thro Life tho at which of the Stages or odd Corners I know not that he appeared to me neither above or below the common Mass of Men Brilliant in Nothing and yet of that Kind of Being calculated to take Care of his own Menage, cure the Fever and Ague, superintend his Farm and kiss his Wife and his Children and the like. After all quis quis Artifer suæ Fortunæ.[2] I may not have met with those who know this young Gentleman or I may have met with those who envy him or I may be much mistaken in him. Should you wish any further Inquisition let me know and I will persist in endeavoring to discover such Particulars may still lie behind. Remember me to all & believe me yours, Gouvr Morris

RC (NHi). Addressed: "honle. Robert R. Livingston Esqr., Chancellor of the State of N York, Poughkeepsie."

1 Chancellor Livingston was evidently interested in the background and social standing of Dr. Thomas Tillotson, who married his sister Margaret in 1779. See George Dangerfield, *Chancellor Robert R. Livingston of New York, 1746–1813* (New York: Harcourt, Brace and Co., 1960), genealogical chart facing p. 516.

2 That is, "who is the master of his own fate." Cf. "faber est suae quisque fortunae," Appius Claudius Caecus, *Oxford Classical Dictionary*, (Oxford: Clarendon Press, 1949), p. 198.

Joseph Reed to Esther Reed

My dear Hetty Camp White Plains, Sept. 6, 1778.

I have wrote you twice since I have been here which I hope you have received tho the Conveyance was uncertain. I have nothing new to make a Letter necessary or even agreeable but that I know it gives you Pleasure to hear from me & therefore I take Pleasure in Writing. Notwithstanding the hot Weather & other Circumstances I have enjoyed a very good Share of Health & am now happy in the Thoughts of seeing you at least by this Day Week as I propose to set out for Home on Thursday Morning. We shall not have quite compleated our Business but so little will remain to do more than Clerkship that I think it not very necessary to stay. My Colleagues are neither of them Men of Business, so that if I should leave them the whole Business stands still—that is they are not sufficiently acquainted with military Business as to render me the Service they otherwise would. I am the more induced to hasten my Departure, as the Assembly of Pennsylva. have appointed me Assistt. to the Atty. Genl. with an Allowance of £2000 per Ann.—an Appointment which for various Reasons I believe will please you & is therefore very acceptable to me. I have wrote to the Council accepting the Appointmt. & thanking them for it.[1] As to News a few Days have wrought a great Change—Sullivan has been obliged to give up his Interprize on Rhode Island & was happy to get off with little Loss. Ld Howe has got a Reinforcement of Ships & is once more Master of the Coast. He has now block'd up the French Fleet at Boston. If you see Mr Lowry soon you may inform him that I think these Circumstances will change the Views I had when I wrote him last.[2] The Evacuation of New York appears now to be a more questionable Event than when I wrote you the other Day. By Advice from thence yesterday it seems they are impatiently waiting for the August Mail which they expect will announce a French War or The Independence of America. The latter seems to be their Wish.

Mr Pettit has very good Health, but has a very great Weight of Business upon him—Mr. Cox being at Philad. & Gen. Greene at Rhode Island.

Adieu my dearest Love. Remember me to the Children, your Mamma & Polly & believe me to be ever, Your Afft, J Reed

RC (NHi).

[1] See Reed to George Bryan, September 2, 1778.

[2] Not found.

Committee of Arrangement to Henry Laurens

Sir Camp at White Plains, Sept. 7th. 1778

Your Committee beg Leave to sollicit your Attention to the Situation of your Cavalry while destitute of a general Officer. Each Regiment having its own Colonel, & he only attending to the Concerns of his particular Regiment, a general Confusion & Neglect must take Place, for Want of an Authority which can extend its Influence to the whole & correct their Abuses, & that Profusion of Expenses, which hitherto has been incurr'd by this Corps. Nor do we conceive it possible for the publick to derive the same Service from them in their present State, that it would do if under the general Direction of an active, & intelligent Officer. The present Colonels, tho' Men of Merit, are upon such Terms with each other, that it is probable the Appointment of either would occasion the Loss of the other three; there may also be other Reasons to determine another Choice, & we can think of no Person so proper, or so likely to be acceptable to the present Officers, as General Cadwallader. At least it is the Wish of the Committee that the Experiment may be made—the other Gentleman recommended by the General having turn'd his Views to civil Life, & wholly declining this Service now. If the Committee are so happy as to meet the Opinion of Congress, with Respect to Gen. Cadwalladers Appointment, they beg Leave to suggest the Expediency of immediately making the Choice, & leaving it to him to accept, or refuse; as they have Reason to fear a previous Consultation will be more likely to defeat, than advance their Views.[1]

The Cloathing of the Army is also an Object of very great Importance—in the present State of Suspence with Respect to that Department, we fear vigorous Measures are not taken either by the States, or the Officer of the Department; & that when the Season advances your Army will find itself suffering as it has been done formerly. If the Committee appointed on that Service, have made a Report, we hope Congress will not delay the Consideration of it, as the Consequences will be extremely prejudicial to the Service. It is an Opinion universally prevalent here that the several States would effect this Business with great Œconomy, & more Satisfaction to the Army.

We are to acknowledge your several Favours of the 30th & 31st Augt.: the former inclosing the Papers respecting the Cavalry, upon which we have not yet come to any Resolution but shall in a few Days report to Congress the Allowance to be made them.

As to any additional Encouragement beyond the usual Bounty of Twenty Dollars given to the new Recruits his Excelly. has intimated his Opinion, that it will be best to keep it out of Sight at present & has communicated his Sentimts. to Congress to this Effect.[2] In which we concur.

I have the Honour to be with the greatest Respect & Regard, Sir Your most Obed. Hbble Servt. Jos. Reed, Chairman

RC (DNA: PCC, item 33). Written and signed by Joseph Reed.

1 Congress named John Cadwalader brigadier general and commander of the Continental Cavalry on September 10, but he declined the appointment. *JCC*, 12:897, 941.

2 For Washington's views on this subject, see Washington, *Writings* (Fitzpatrick), 12:402–4.

Committee of Arrangement to George Washington

Head Quarters, Sept. 7th, 1778.

The Committee observe that the Board have not determined one Point of Importance in the Arrangement viz.

What Rank in the Line shall now be given to Officers of the Staff who have had rank annexed to their Offices by a Resolve of Congress as Paymasters &c and whether when such Rank is given it implys a Right to command according to that Rank in the Line of Succession in the Army of the United States.[1]

Jos. Reed, Chairman of the Committee

RC (DLC). Written and signed by Joseph Reed.

1 Beneath this letter the following "opinion of the board of Genl Officers," signed by Horatio Gates, Baron de Kalb, Alexander McDougall, Samuel Parsons, William Smallwood, Henry Knox, Enoch Poor, John Paterson, and William Woodford, was appended. "That the Adjutants, Paymasters & Quarter Masters taken from the line, be again admitted into it in the rank they would have been entitl'd to had they continued in the line. And such Adjutants, Paymasters & Quarter Masters, not taken from the line may be admissable into the Line, in such Subaltern Ranks as by a sign'd certificate from the field officers of their respective Corps shall be deem'd competent." And at the foot of the manuscript Reed then added the following committee statement. "The Rules above laid down for the Determination of Rank between Officers of difft. States are to govern between Officers of the same State, unless when a Rule has been laid down by the State or Rank already settled. In which Case it is the Intention of the Committee not to interfere."

William Henry Drayton to John Laurens

Dr. Sir. Phil. Sep. 7. 1778

I most affectionately congratulate you upon the glory you have gained in the late action on Rhode Island, & upon your having continued safe in the midst of so many balls & dangers. Your post was in the most important, most honourable & most perilous quarter. We had received a copy of Gen. Sullivans letter to Gen. Washington. Your Father had received a letter from the Marquis la Fayette.[1] Three days passed & not a word from or of you after the action. A report prevailed that you had fallen. And it had weight from the above circumstances. However, yesterday Major. Morris arrived with the desired account & relieved us from our anxiety:[2] & I felt particularly happy on the occasion, as well upon your Father's as your account.

A Man who is ever vigilant to discharge his duty to his country, is pleased to have objects pointed out. Give me leave to point one. The public is fully convinced that in you they possess a most valuable officer, & upon this point great hopes are established. It is your duty then in action to take some care of such an officer, & not unnecessarily expose those hopes to a blasting shower of balls.

We have had but little information with respect to the operations of the French fleet during their expedition against Lord Howe. Gen. Sullivan *forgot* to inclose a copy of D'Estaing's letter to him *immediately* upon his return to Rhode Island. We have no account of the names of the Officers who signed the Protest. Nor of the answer of the Gen. Officers to General Sullivans 3 propositions to them immediately upon the departure of the French Fleet for Boston.[3] Nor of the precise time when the Fleet sailed for & arrived at Boston. These you know are of importance to me. The stationary nature of the Camp at White Plains may enable you to inform me on these points & on those relative to Monmouth.

I am my dear Sir, Your most obedient humble Ser,

Wm. Hy. Drayton

RC (NN).

1 Drayton is referring to Lafayette's private August 25 letter to Henry Laurens and Gen. John Sullivan's official August 29 letter to Washington, which reached Philadelphia on September 3 and 4 respectively. See *JCC*, 12:880; "Lafayette-Laurens Letters," *SCHGM* 9 (1908):64–66; and Sullivan, *Papers* (Hammond), 2:275–76.

2 Washington's September 4 letter to Henry Laurens praising John's bravery and reporting that he was well, is in Washington, *Writings* (Fitzpatrick), 12:397–98.

3 See Henry Laurens' second letter to John Sullivan of August 28, 1778, note 1.

Samuel Holten's Diary

[September 7, 1778]

7. Congress sit late; We received intelligence from Genl. Sullivan respecting the battle & retreat from Rhode Island, I think Genl. Sullivan conducted as well as could be expectd.[1]

MS (MDaAr).

1 Gen. John Sullivan's August 31 letter "giving an account of his retreat to the main the preceding Evening, without any loss of men or stores" was read in Congress this day and referred to the Committee of Intelligence. *JCC*, 12:884–85.

Henry Laurens to Charles Lee

Sir 7th September [1778]

Immediately upon receipt of your favor of the 4th Inst. I presented it to Congress, and offered the Letter which it had inclosed—the house after some deliberation ordered the Letter to be returned as you will be further informed by an Act of this date, which with the said Letter will be found within the present inclosure.[1]

I have the honor to be &c.

LB (DNA: PCC, item 13). Addressed: "Major General Lee, Camp at White Plains."

1 General Lee's September 4 letter to Laurens, in which he asked Congress to consider an enclosed account of his behavior at the battle of Monmouth that had just been written by one of his aides, Maj. John Clark, is in PCC, item 158, 1:117–18. Laurens' endorsement on the general's letter indicates that Congress returned Clark's account to Lee unopened and unread—no doubt because of reluctance on the part of the delegates to consider evidence that had not been submitted to Lee's court-martial. See also *JCC*, 12:887.

Robert Morris to John Imlay

Sir[1] Philada. Septr. 7th. 1778

Cap Rath. Cook who lately commanded a Brigt called the Industry formerly belonging to some of my Friends abroad, was taken by the British; Retaken, & brought into the Jerseys, where upon Tryal, she was Condemned one half to the Recaptors & the other half to the former Owners as appears by your Honors Decree dated the 16th July last. Cap Cook informes me that the Vessell was Sold at Public Vendue the 29 July agreable to the Decree & also part of her Cargo of Salt, the remainder of the Salt he thinks has been Sold at private Sale at higher prices than that Sold at Public Sale. He complains that the Marshall has never furnished him the Accts & has delayed settling with him altho often applyed to for that purpose, & that he has been detained waiting for said Settlement since the Month of July, at a very heavy expence which amounts to a denyal of Justice. At his request I wrote to the Marshall Mr Stotler Eight days ago on this Subject but he has not thought proper to give an answer. Capt Cook has empowered me to Act on behalf of his Owners, *my Friends & Correspondants* and I am bound to see justice done them. This application to You I consider as the Second Step towards obtaining it having before applyed to the Marshall & from my knowledge of your private Character I am sure you will not suffer any irregularities under Your Authority, therefore I hope to be favoured with a line on this Subject.

I must also beg leave to trouble Your Honour on another, which is just opened to me by the Receipt of the enclosed letters. I beg of you to peruse them and if any Steps be necessary in the Law to procure Messrs Penet & Co their property, you'l oblige me much by putting those papers into the hands of some Gent. of the Law that Practices in your Court (as I am entirely ignorant who has practice in the Jerseys) desire him to do the needfull & I will pay for his Services. I observe the Brigt. Govr. Henry is advertized for Sale, very soon I hope it may be necessary to stop that proceeding unless the Decree has ordered due restitution to her former owners. I hope my Good Sir You will excuse me for giving you this Trouble and in return I shall be happy to comply with any of your Commands being very respectfully, Sir, Your Obedt hbl servant, Robt Morris

RC (NjMoHP).

1 John Imlay (1719–92), a merchant of Bordentown, N.J., was for several years judge of the New Jersey Court of Admiralty.

John Penn to Richard Caswell

Dear Sir, Philadelphia Sept. 7th. 1778.

When I was at Newbern last and was informed that several Gentlemen of the Assembly proposed to ask more money for the purpose of raising Troops for the Grand Army, I was against it; and gave my advice that application should be made to Congress for whatever money was necessary for public use—giving them as a reason, that I thought it more for the interest of No. Carolina to be indebted to the United States, than the reverse that all the other States were occasionally supplied with money, and I was authorised to say (to the Treasury Board) that they would have money by the 10th of May; besides what money was made in our State was confined there. I also knew that our[1] governor or State when I left Congress was treated with more respect than your Excellency and those you presided over. I therefore had no doubt but that you would have received whatever money was necessary for marching the Troops without delay. Judge then Sir, of my surprise and Chagrin when I found by your letter, which I got a few days ago, in what manner your application was treated.[2] I own I most sensibly felt the indignity offered the State, I belonged to, by the little respect that was paid to her first magistrate, and loudly complained of it in Congress. The Members seemed much concerned and resolved to grant us the sum you wrote for, indeed they appeared willing to do every thing that tends to our interest.[3]

We shall send off the money as soon as we can, which will I expect be in a short time. Congress are obliged to meet twice a day, business still increases, in short unless persons are appointed not members to do some part of it, we must all be ruined. A few days ago we were in high expectations of taking all the British Troops on Rhode Island, now rejoicing that our army was able to get away without being taken. The Newspapers will inform you the reason. We have no late intelligence from Europe. If the Assembly did not discharge the Soldiers it is the wish of Congress that they may be kept in Carolina, under proper officers until, your Excellency can hear from them. The express is setting off sent by the President which obliges me to stop. I should be happy to receive any intelligence that you may think proper to give me and with my Colleagues to do every thing in my power for the benefit of No. Carolina. I hope you will excuse the manner in which this appears from the hurry I am in.

I have the honor to be with great respect, your Excellency's Most Ob. huml. Servt. J. Penn

Tr (Nc–Ar). *N.C. State Records*, 13:214–15.

1 Reads "no" in *N.C. State Records* text, which is undoubtedly what Penn wrote in the now missing RC.

2 Governor Caswell's August 13 letter to Penn, complaining that Congress had provided him with only a fifth of the "sum wanted for raising & marching the men voted to complete our Continental Battalions," is in *N.C. State Records*, 13:207–8. See also Henry Laurens to Caswell, May 26, 1778, note.

3 Congress had agreed on September 5 to grant $400,000 to North Carolina to enable the state "to complete their continental battalions." *JCC*, 12:883.

Samuel Adams to Hannah Adams

My Dear Daughter Philadelphia Sept 8th 1778

Your very dutiful and obliging Letter of the 28th of August came to my Hand yesterday and brought me the afflicting News of your Mothers Illness. When you tell me "the Doctor thinks she is on the mending Hand," and "he hopes she will be cleverly in a Day or two," I am apt to conclude her Disorder had not much abated when you wrote. I know "she is exceedingly loth to give me the least Pain," and therefore I suspect she has dictated to you to make the best of it to me. "She begs of me not to make myself very anxious for her." This is a Request which it is impossible for me to comply with. I shall be very uneasy till I hear again from you. I pray God she may recover her Health and long continue a rich Blessing to you and me. I am satisfied "you do all that lies in your Power for so excellent a Mother." You are under great Obligations to her, and I am sure you are of a grateful Disposition. I hope her Life will be spared and that you will have the opportunity of presenting to her my warmest Respects. I rejoyce to hear that your late Disorder was so gentle and that you have got over it. I commend you my dear, to the Care and Protection of the Almighty. That He may reward your filial Piety is the ardent Prayer of, Your very affectionate Father,

RC (NN). Adams, *Writings* (Cushing), 4:56–57. RC damaged, missing words supplied from Tr.

Samuel Adams to John Bradford

My Dear Sir Philada Sept 8th 1778

I have lately had the pleasure of receiving two Letters from you, one by Capt Manly and the other by yesterdays Post.[1] The latter makes mention of some Notice you had receivd "from a warm Friend to you & me" that "Cap. McNiel was making Misrepresentations at Philada to your Disadvantage." I have a particular reason for my Curiosity in wishing to know who this Friend is. If I had that Knowledge I might perhaps see grounds of Suspicion that the Design was far different from that of giving you a friendly Hint. I assure you I have heard Nothing here to your Disadvantage. If Capt McNiel is the Person I am to understand to be your Enemy, I will tell you that he has called on me not more than twice or thrice, since he arrivd here, and that he has not mentiond your Name to me nor any thing relating to your Department, nor indeed any thing that would tend to bring you to my Thoughts. I know not in what Part of the City he lives. I suppose he is preparing to meet the Marine Committee to whom his Petition is referrd. When it may be proper for me to give my opinion, I intend to do it, with Freedom & Impartiality; not feeling my self interrested in the Party Disputes which I perceive there are in Boston between two Men, neither of whom in my opinion has derivd much Honor from the Decisions of the Courts Martial respecting them. If I shall hear any thing said to your Prejudice here, you may depend on my letting you know it; being determind if possible to prevent your suffering an Injury which one of your Friends at least thinks he has in being stabbd in the dark. I intend to write you more fully of these matters at another Time. At present I can only add a Request that you wod be so kind as to deliver the inclosd letter to my Daughter and forward the other which is from my Servant to his Friend in Milton. My dear Mrs A, I am informd is very unwell.

I am with the most friendly Regard to your Family, very affectionately, yours, S.A.

FC (NN).

1 The second of these letters, dated "Boston 26th August 1778," in which Bradford expressed concern that he had been accused by Capt. Hector McNeill with having charged "too high a Rate" for supplies provided to sloops outfitted at Continental expense, is in the John Bradford Letterbooks, 2:155–56, DLC.

Josiah Bartlett to Mary Bartlett

My Dear Philadelphia Septr 8th 1778

I have Receivd yours of the 21st of August and have only Just time before the post goes out to inform you I am in a Comfortable State of health Tho I find I want more Exercise of body and less of mind, Hope I shall be able to hold out till the first of November when I Design to Set out for Newhampshire: Charles Chace is returned from the Country much better in health. We had two or 3 Days here the begining of this month pretty Cold for the Season, I fear you had a hard frost about that time in Newhampshire.

The chief news here is from Rhode Island and the French & English Fleets but as it will not be news to you I shall write nothing about it.

The Brittish Commissioners at New York have Sent to Demand General Burgoines men and Offer to Ratify the Convention of Saratoga but as it Does not appear the King of England has Ratified it, they will not be allowed to go back at present.

Remember my Love to all my family. I thank Polly & Lois the Line they sent me. I am yours, J. Bartlett

RC (Mr. and Mrs. Rodney M. Wilson, Kingston, N.H., 1975).

Josiah Bartlett to Meshech Weare

Hond Sir Philadelphia Septr 8th 1778

I have Received your favors of the 8th & 19th ulto[1] and must inform you that I can see no prospect at present of my being able to procure money to be advanced & Sent to our State by Conngress and for the reasons I mentioned to you & to Colo Nicholas Gilman in my letters of the 3d & 4th of last month;[2] when I Receive answers to those letters I Shall Conduct my self in that matter according to your Directions; The Delegates of Massachusetts Bay took an order on their own Treasury for 300,000 Dollars to be advanced to them out of the money they were to raise for the use of the Continent, but as I was Doubtful whither a Similar order on our Treasury would answer your end, I Did not move for it, as I make no Doubt you will make use of the money raised by taxes in our State if necessary for the public Service.

I have Communicated to Several of the N.E. Delegates what Relates to some of the Towns of our State Joining themselves to the State of Vermont (as they are pleased to Call themselves). My present opinion is, that it will be best to lay the matter before Congress for their Direction, but I shall Consider more of it, & take further advice before I proceed. Those Delegates to whom I have Communicated the affair, Seem Surprised at the ungenerous and impolitic Conduct of Vermont, and I have reason to Believe they will find few or none in Congress that will Justify their Conduct or Espouse their Cause.

I have Reced a Copy of the appointment of Delegates to attend Congress the first of November next, and I must beg leave inform you that I can by no means attend Congress after the last of October next. By reason of Mr Wentworth's Sickness I have not Recd the least assistance from him, and am obliged to attend So Closely to public business without any interval of Relaxation, that it will be necessary for my Constitution of body & mind to be relieved then, if I am able to hold out till that time. I hope Sir you will give Mr Whipple & Frost notice & that they will be here Seasonable as the State will not be represented after that time till they arrive.

Mr Wentworth left this place the 21st ulto. and is by this time I hope nearly arrived home.[3]

I am Sir with great Respect your most obedient Servant,

Josiah Bartlett

RC (Nh–Ar).

1 Weare's August 8 and 19 letters to Bartlett are in Bartlett, *Papers* (Mevers), pp. 205–7, 210–11.

2 Bartlett's letter to Nicholas Gilman has not been found.

3 John Wentworth apparently reached home on September 11, according to the accounts he submitted to the New Hampshire government, in which he listed expenses of £638.2.11, including £198 "To my Time as a Delegate for said State to Congress from the third Day of May to the 11th Day of September being 132 days at 30s." Gratz Collection, PHi.

Committee of Commerce to Thomas Johnson

Sir Committee of Commerce, Philadelphia 8th Septem. 1778

The inclosed Papers was transmitted to this Committee by Colo Aylett Dy Commissary of Purchases wherein he complains of undue practices committed by the Marshall &c of the Admiralty Court for the State of Maryland.[1]

If the Allegations therein set forth are true I hope your Excellency will devise such steps to be taken in the premises so that justice may be done to the parties.

I have the honor to be, Your Excellencys Most Obedt hble servant, by Order, Fra Lewis Chairman

RC (MdAA). In a clerical hand and signed by Francis Lewis.

1 William Aylett's August 13 letter to the Committee of Commerce is in the Red Books, MdAA. *Calendar of Maryland State Papers: The Red Books*, 3 vols. (Annapolis: Hall of Records Commission, 1950–55), 2:260–61.

Committee of Congress Observations on a Proposed West Indian Expedition

Philadelphia, 7ber 8. 1778[1]

It is proposed by Major Gen. Arnold to a Committee of Congress appointed to confer with him in consequence of a resolution of the 7 7ber to undertake an expedition against Barbadoes, and, in returning from that Island to take possession of Bermudas in the name of the United States. The force proposed to be employed is 5 or 6 frigates and (if to be procured from our Allies) one or two line of battleships including two companies of artillery, together with a troop of horse. The expedition to be fitted out from Boston, and to sail about the 1st of February next.

The objects of the expedition are

1. To lay Bridgetown, and the Island under a contribution of money and plate.
2. To secure the merchant men which arrive from Britain with goods and to lade them for America with merchandize, and produce found at Bridgetown.
3. To secure the cannon, musquets and military stores on the Island of which there is a considerable quantity.
4. To engage in the marine service of the united states about 5 or 6 hundred black and Mulatto Slaves who are employed as mariners in coasting vessels, by giving to them the pay and priviledges of American Seamen, and assuring them of the[ir] freedom after the war, or three years Service.
5. To take and hold possession of on the return homeward of the Is-

lands of Bermudas from which a swarm of privateers may be fitted out to cruise upon the enemies West India commerce, and where inhabitants who are now our friends must from necessity become formidable enemies to our commerce if this measure is not adopted.

6. To raise the reputation of American Arms, to alarm and distress the enemy, and thereby hasten their acknowledgment of our independance.

7. To serve the interest of our Allies by giving up to them the right of conquest to the Island if they shall think proper to send a sufficient and timely force to keep possession of it.

In order to form a judgment of the practibility of the plan proposed, and of the means necessary to carry the same into execution, it will be proper to take into consideration the situation and strength of both Islands.

Barbadoes

Barbadoes is situated in latitude 13 N. Long. 60 W. is about 30 leagues S.E. from Martinico about 24 leagues east of St. Vincent and 103 leagues S.E. by S. from Antigua. It is 25 or 30 miles long and about 12 broad. It contains about 10000 white inhabitants and about 50 or 60000 slaves. The Capital sea Port is Bridgetown situate on the southwest of the Islands upon the side of Carlisle Bay where there is a good harbour for ships of any size, and in which almost all the ships which bring Supplies to the Island and carry produce home in. To defend the habour there is a fort on Needham's point mounting betwixt 30 or forty pieces of heavy cannon; no embrasures towards the land side where it is only defensible against small arms. There is another battery on the north side of the bay in which there is about 25 or 30 pieces of heavy cannon. This battery is open and accessible in the rear. There are no other posts or forts of any consequence so as to prevent taking possession of the town, which may be immediately occupied and the harbour opened as soon as the above fort and battery are taken possession of. This may without difficulty be done by landing a body of men and some heavy artillery at Austin's bay about 8 miles from the fort and making a breach in the rear, should they on summons refuse to surrender, which considering their weakness is not probable. There is seldom more than two frigates in Carlisle bay and sometimes a 40 gun or line of battle ship. There is no regular force on the Island and only about 2500 militia, 200 of which are horse and who are by no means formidable. Should the enemy obtain intelligence of the invasion of the Island, it would be at Least 12 days before any reinforcement could be sent either from Antigua or Dominica, where the principal force of the English is stationed, and before that time every object of the expedition will be effected. But to render the success of this Enterprise still more certain, it might be proper that an expedition should at the same time be undertaken by our allies either against of the Islands of Antigua, Dominica, or St. Christophers, in order to prevent the enemy from sending reinforcements to the succour of Barbadoes.

The objects of this expedition being effected, which it is presumed may be done about the middle of March, it is proposed that the fleet should immediately proceed for the Islands of Bermudas.

N.B. Here followed the Observations of the Committee on the situation, strength and importance of Bermudas, but it being no wise connected with the present object of our Allies, I have omitted inserting here. W. D.

A True copy from the papers of the Committee appointed to confer with Major Gen. Arnold on the[2] Wm. Duer.

Tr (Archives du ministère des affaires etrangères: Correspondance politique, États-Unis supplement, vol. 1).

1 This document consists of part of a committee report on Gen. Benedict Arnold's proposed joint Franco-American expedition against Barbados and Bermuda that William Duer submitted to Gérard, who sent it on to Paris. Arnold first broached this plan to Samuel Adams and Richard Henry Lee of the Marine Committee, who both approved it, and then wrote to President Laurens on September 7 urging Congress to consider it. Arnold's letter is in the Samuel Adams Papers, NN, and bears the following endorsement by Charles Thomson: "Letter from Major General Arnold 7 Sept 1778. Read, Referred to Mr R. H. Lee, Mr S. Adams, Mr R. Morris, Mr Duer, Mr. Chase." After this committee had examined Arnold's proposal, Congress appointed another committee on September 10 to confer with Gérard on "the future operations" of the comte d'Estaing's fleet, whose support Arnold was relying on. The membership of the second committee was identical with that of the first, save for the substitution of William Henry Drayton for Samuel Chase, though two days later Chase was added to the second committee and Drayton to the first. The second committee met with Gérard on September 12 and found him unenthusiastic about a West Indian expedition which would intrude the United States into the primary theater of Anglo-French operations in America. Thus it is not surprising that Arnold's proposed expedition was never undertaken or that there is no evidence in the journals that either committee ever submitted a report to Congress.

The document printed here was transcribed immediately beneath the following September 7 resolution of Congress.

"A Letter of this day from Gen. Arnold was read.

"Resolved that the said letter be referred to a Committee of five and that they be directed to confer with Major Gen. Arnold, and in case they approve the plan, that they be empowered to take the most effectual measures and give the necessary orders for carry[ing] the same into execution, provided the plan thought prudent by the Commander in chief."

The entire document was enclosed by Gérard in his September 12 dispatch to French foreign minister Vergennes. See Meng, *Gérard Despatches*, pp. 282–84, 289–91; and *JCC*, 12:885–86, 897, 905.

2 Thus in Tr.

Gouverneur Morris to Peter Van Schaack

Dear Sir:[1] Philadelphia, 8th September, 1778.

I received your favor of the 24th of last month just now, and I write an answer which may or may not reach you. I am much obliged by the sentiments you profess for me, and I hope to deserve them from you, from all, from enemies and from friends. I always have regretted, and I trust I shall, that you did not take part with us in the cause, which, let the success of it be what it may, I cannot but consider as the just cause of all mankind. I am particularly afflicted, that you should be now obliged to relinquish your country, for opinions which are unfavorable to her rights. If I am rightly informed, your situation is by no means singular; a circumstance which, I believe, is far from alleviating your feelings, and which most sincerely affects mine.

What may be the law you allude to, I know not; and therefore shall not be so hardy as to arraign its policy or humanity:[2] should it be contrary to the principles of the former, the infancy of the state must apologize for the defects of its legislature; should it revolt against the latter, while we lament the consequence, let us pardon something to the cause. Being men, we are all subject to human frailty. We are not therefore to be surprised, that some sparks of resentment shed their baleful light on the conduct of human affairs. I fear that the very best will, in the years of cool reflection, pay melancholy tribute of repentance to the hours of contention. Adversity is the great school of moderation. If any of my countrymen are come thence unlearned, I will not blame, though I cannot commend; and let me entreat you not to tell tales of them to high-judging Job, or pray him that he will teach them to feel what wretches feel.

It was always my opinion, that matters of conscience and faith, whether political or religious, are as much out of the province, as they are beyond the ken of human legislatures. In the question of punishment for acts, it hath been my constant axiom, that the object is example, and therefore the thing only justifiable from the necessity, and from the effect. I implore the Omnipotent on all occasions to direct my conduct by this great, and I trust just principle. Could the American contest have been decided without blood, I should have been happy. While the appeal lay to reason, I reasoned; when it was made to the sword, I thought it my duty to join in the great issue. While reconciliation appeared practicable, I labored for reconciliation. When the breach was so widened that no hope remained of cure, I solemnly pledged my faith to support the independence of my country, which had then become essential to her liberties. In the hours of distress, I was secured from fear by the *mens sibi conscia recti*, and the dawnings of prosperity have not inflated me, because I have seen too much of the instability of human affairs, to confide in appearances.

As I am determined not to share in gains which arise from public distress, I will continue in public life till the establishment of the liberties of America. It shall be my object to narrow as much as possible the circle of private woe. I would to God, that every tear could be wiped away from every eye. But so long as there are men, so long it will and must happen that they will minister to the miseries of each other. It is a delightful object in history, to see order, and peace, and happiness result from confusion, and war and distress. It is a pleasing hope in life. It is your misfortune to be one out of the many who have suffered. In your philosophy, in yourself, in the consciousness of acting as you think right, you are to seek consolation, while you shape your old course in a country new.

Whatever may be the fate of the great controversy, and whatever may be your individual lot, I pray you to believe there are very few who will more rejoice in ——[3]

MS not found; reprinted from Henry C. Van Schaack, *The Life of Peter Van Schaack, LL.D., Embracing Selections from his Correspondence and other Writings during the American Revolution and his Exile in England* (New York: D. Appleton & Co., 1842), pp. 130–32.

1 Peter Van Schaack, a New York lawyer and close friend of Morris and other prominent revolutionary leaders, was about to leave America for England, when he spent seven years in exile because of his refusal to take an oath of allegiance to the government of the State of New York. See these *Letters*, 1:137.

2 See Morris to George Clinton, September 6, 1778, note.

3 Thus in Tr.

Robert Morris to James Duane

My Dear Sir Philada. Septr. 8th. 1778

When I look at the date of your last Friendly & affectionate letter, I cannot help reproach myself for having so long delayed to acknowledge the Receipt of it, and indeed my immagination is obliged to trace back the busy Scenes that have employed my Mind since the Month of April (in which this letter arrived) before I can find the shadow of excuse for this seeming Neglect. I say *seeming* for be assured I shall never incur the charge of *real* Neglect of the Man I love & esteem so much & so justly as I do Mr Duane. Many important Scenes have occurred since we parted, often have I wished for opportunities of Consulting *you* on whose judgement & Friendship I cou'd safely rest myself. Duer in many instances supplied your place and a Worthy honest fellow he is, that Man deserves the Esteem & Confidence of his Constituents in the highest degree, for his only fault is an over zeal & anxiety in their affairs. They have an able advocate in my Namesake[1] & really the Representation in Congress from N. York does honour to the State. You called on me to give my feeble Voice in support of your representation of the Indian affairs & in bringing forward the Tryal of General Schuyler and had I attended Congress, I certainly shou'd have promoted the points you wished all in my power because I did then as I do now think them just & reasonable, the first have not produced all the evils you expected especially to N York & the latter is I hope brought about by this time. I make no doubt our Friend Genl. Schuyler will be acquitted with honour & I shall rejoice very sincerely with you whenever it happens.

I did not join Congress seriously untill since they came down here, now & then I paid them a visit of a few days in York Town during the Winter & Spring. Notwithstanding this a great part of my time was employed in Public business for People were perpetually coming after me about it. The recess I obtained from my State was of real service to my own affairs & enabled me to arrange & bring them again into some order. I find also that this recess has caused the strongest desire to take place in my mind to get back into my private Station again.

Ambition had no share in bringing me forward into Public life nor has it any Charms to keep me there. The time I have spent in it has been the severest Tax of my life and really I think those who have had so much, shou'd now be relieved & let some fresh hands take the Helm. These notions prompt me to get out of Congress at the next appointment of Delegates, but my Namesake swears I shall not depart. Philadelphia my Good Friend is vastly changed, the avowed Tories are I think more inveterately so than ever, our Circle's of Friends & acquaintance are all broke up and it is with difficulty we cou'd patch up a little Social Club at Dick Peters's Spring during the hot weather, in short our greatest Society is now in the Company of Strangers. Shou'd the British evacuate New York you will experience this & many other changes that I cannot spare time to tell you of. The Hills, poor Hills alas have changed, a Melancholly cast of Countenance covers the Face of Nature & the Works of Art exhibit Such Melancholly pictures in their present Views that Hospitality can no more cherrish nor Festivity exhilerate the chearfull guest but I hope to see the day when the Scene again shall change & all be bright & gay.

The Alliance with France certainly Secures our Independance & has procured us temporary advantages but I wish these may be properly followed up and the most made of them, our Money is at present the only stumbling block. I wish you was here to assist on that Subject, it is as Intricate as important & we really want lights & help. God Bless you my Good Friend. I hope Mrs. Duane has recovered her health & that you & yours may always enjoy that first of blessings. I am most truely yr. affectionate, R. Morris.

P.S. I send this by a Monsr. Hütner who has in view to make some enquiries into the Fur Trade & to make some Speculation thereon. If you can give or Procure him any information on that Subject you will oblige me & Serve the interest of Monsr. LeRay du Chaumont a Gentn who has rendered the United States great & Important Services in France. RM.

RC (NHi).

1 Gouverneur Morris.

Robert Morris to John Jay

Dear Sir Philada. Septr. 8th. 1778

Our Friend Governeur Morris shew'd me a letter from you to him this day in which you make kind mention of me and you may be sure I was much pleased thereat,[1] observing that you expected to have heard from me in reply to your last letter. I cannot help thinking there has been a miscarriage in the case, for the last letter I have received from you is dated at Fish Kill 4th June & the entire purport is to tell me that Capt Stewarts Family live at New-Town on Long Island with a Mr. Vanderbilt. Whether you expected that I shou'd in consequence of this notice have sent forward their Money I don't know, as it is neither express'd nor Implyed in that letter, and as I thought the place mentioned was in the Enemies possession it never occured to me to take further trouble about the matter, but waited to hear when you cou'd convey the Money to those it is intended for, and I shall be glad to get rid of it by sending it to you or paying to the Delegates whenever you will tell me to do so. I perceive my Namesake gives you the *doings* of the Day and I need not trouble you with them, I think our Friend D.[2] has much Public merit, has been Ill used, but will rise Superiour to his Enemies.

Shou'd the bearer Monsr Hütner fall under your Notice I shoud be glad if it suited to pay him some little attention because he is sent out by a Monsr Le Ray du Chaumont a Gentn. these States are much indebted to for many Acts of Friendship to D. & uncommon exertions to serve us. Monsr Hütner seeks after Furrs & Fur Trade, any information you can give or procure him on that Subject will be very acceptable.[3] I am Dear Sir, Your Obliged and Obedt. humble servant, Robt Morris

RC (NNC).

1 Jay's August 29 letter to Gouverneur Morris is in Jay, *Papers* (Morris), 1:496–97.

2 Doubtless Silas Deane.
3 This day Morris also wrote a similar brief letter to Gen. Philip Schuyler recommending Mons. Hütner. Schuyler Papers, NN.

Robert Morris to Anthony Wayne

Dear Sir Philada. Septr. 8th. 1778

I have long delayed a reply to your letter on the Subject of Cloathing in hopes of giving you a very satisfactory one, but I have found insurmountable difficulties to the accomplishment of what you wish, at least for the present Moment. The Cloathiers departmt. is shortly to undergo a new arrangement and as there is plenty of Cloathing on the Continent I expect and hope that when that department is properly organized, not only your Brigade but the whole Army may be perfectly satisfyed in this particular. The Cloathier Genl promised me a Return of the Issues from his Office to the Pensylva. Troops but has not given it to me. I applyed to the Members of the Council & Assembly & they desire me to wait Genl. Reids return from Camp, it being expected that he will bring a full & clear State of the Condition of our Troops and I doubt not you will make him Sensible of this necessity there is to comply with Your Requisitions, I beg to trouble you with my Compliments to him, tell him to make haste back for he is wanted here.

I was exceedingly gratifyed at seeing such honourable mention made of your Name in the Genls. letter after the Battle of Monmouth[1] and as a Pennsylvanian I seem to share in the glories her Soldiers acquire, as a Friend & acquaintance you have my most ardent Wishes that future Victories may Plant those Laurels on your Brows, [. . .] am sure your Bravery & Good Sense will always secure your claim to. You may depend on it as a certainty, that it will always afford me particular satisfaction to be instrumental in promoting such measures as tend[2]

RC (PHi).
1 General Washington's July 1 letter to Congress describing the action at Monmouth and extolling the conduct of Gen. Wayne's detachment is in Washington, *Writings* (Fitzpatrick), 12:139–46.
2 The remainder of this letter with Morris' signature has been clipped from the manuscript.

North Carolina Delegates to Richard Caswell

Sir, Philadelphia Sept. 8th. 1778.

Upon our application to Congress to have a reconsideration of your Excellency's letter relative to the 500,000 dollars, to be sent for the use of the Continental Troops in our State, We have procured a Warrant on the Treasury for the remaining 400,000 which we shall send on, with the utmost expedition, as soon as we can receive it from the Treasury.[1] We have our hopes that the General Assembly have neither disbanded the Troops or emitted more paper currency. We wish it may come, in time, to answer your Excellency's intention to satisfy the Troops. The President has enclosed the resolve of Congress on this business, and we are with great respect, Your Excellency's most Ob. hume. Servts.

John Penn
Corns. Harnett
Jno. Williams

Tr (Nc–Ar).
[1] See *JCC*, 12:883.

Committee of Arrangement Resolutions

[September 9, 1778][1]

The Committee of Arrangement after mature Consideration of the many disputes of rank, subsisting in the Army of the United States have agreed to the following resolutions founded upon a report made by a board of General Officers of the whole line (vizt.):

1st. That the relative rank in the Continental Line of the Army between all Colonels and Inferior Officers of different States, between like Officers of Infantry and those of horse and Artillery appointed under the Authority of Congress by Virtue of a resolution of the 16th. of September 1776, or by Virtue of any subsequent Resolution, prior to the 1st. of January 1777, shall be deemed to have their Commissions dated on the day last mentioned, and their relative rank with respect to each other in the Continental line of the Army shall be determined from their rank prior to the 16th. of September 1776.

This rule shall not be considered to affect the rank of the Line within any State or within the Corps of Artillery, Horse, or among the Sixteen Additional Battalions where the rank hath been or shall be settled; but as there is a difficulty in settling the rank of the Line of Artillery by reason of the peculiar Circumstances attending some Appointments in that Corps, it is recommended that the general rule now to be established for the great line of the Army should be the rule to determine the relative rank within the particular line of Artillery so far as their rank remains unsettled.

2ndly. That in determining rank between Officers of different States previous to the 16th. of September 1776, preference should be given in the first instance to Continental Commissions, and to State

Commissions of those Corps which have been incorporated into the Continental Army, the latter being considered as Continental from the time of their entering the Continental service: That in the second instance Preference shall be given to Commissions in the New Levies and Flying Camp. That in the third Place Commissions in Militia be considered where they have served in the Continental Army for the space of one Month at least.

3rd. That all Colonels and Inferior Officers appointed to vacancies since the 5th. of January 1777, shall take rank from their Right in Succession to such Vacancies.

4th. That in all Cases where the rank between two Officers of different States is equal, or between an Officer of State Troops and one of Cavalry, Artillery or the Additional Battalions, their Seniority is to be determined by Lot.

5th. That a resignation entirely precludes any Claim of benefit from former rank, under a new appointment.

6th. Adjutants, Pay Masters and Quarter Masters taken from the line shall be again admitted into it in the rank they would have been entitled to had they continued in the Line, and such Adjutants, Pay Masters and Quarter Masters not taken from the Line may be admitted into the line in such Subaltern Ranks as by a signed Certificate from the Field Officers of their respective Corps they shall be deemed competent to.

7th. The rules above laid down for the determination of rank between Officers of different States are to govern between Officers of the same State unless where a rule has been laid down by the State or rank already settled, in which Case it is not the Intention of the Committee to interfere.

Signed in behalf of the Committee of Arrangment.

Jos. Reed, Chairman.

Reprinted from Washington, *Writings* (Fitzpatrick), 12:413–15. Two copies of these resolutions, misdated 1779, are in PCC, item 152, 8:1–4, 9–12.

1 These resolutions were published in Washington's general orders for September 9, 1778.

Samuel Holten's Diary

[September 9–10, 1778]

9. Congress Sit but half the day; In the evening I met a Number of Gentlemen of Congress upon Business at the City Tavern.

10. Thursday. A fine clear air. Genl. Miflin, Colo. Lee, Mr. Vandike & Mr. Smith dind with us. Congress sit late.

MS (MDaAr).

Henry Laurens to Silas Deane

Dear Sir 9th Septr. [1778]

I had the honor of presenting to Congress your Note of Yesterday and have only to say, the House came to no determination thereon.[1]

I Am with great Regard &c.

LB (DNA: PCC, item 13).

1 Deane's brief letter to Laurens of September 8, asking the delegates to "inform me if they desire my further attendance," was read in Congress on the eighth and tabled. See PCC, item 103, fols. 111–12; and *JCC*, 12:891.

Committee of Arrangement to George Washington

Sir Head Qr. 10 April [September] 1778.

Before a proper Arrangement can take place in the Line of Artillery, it is the opinion of the Committee that a dispute Subsisting between Cols Harrison, Lamb & Crane, respectively, should be settled; they therefore request the Subject of this difference may be referred to a board of Officers, of some other Corps, as soon as it may be convenient.[1] We are with the highest Respect your Excellency's Most Obed. Servants,

Jos. Reed, Chairman of the Committee

P.S. The Committee also request that the Board will at the same Time determine the Seniority of the Regimts.[2]

RC (DLC). Written by John Banister, with signature and postscript by Joseph Reed.

1 For the arrangement of the Continental Artillery, which a board of general officers determined on September 15 in keeping with "the rules of settling rank as published in General Orders of the 9th instant (with the Approbation of the honorable Committee of Congress for arranging the Army)," see Washington's general orders of that date in Washington, *Writings* (Fitzpatrick), 12:458–59.

2 The first casualty of the arrangement of the artillery settled upon at this time was Ebenezer Stevens, who as the junior lieutenant colonel of artillery (holding a commission by brevet) was immediately deprived of a battalion command he had long held. Accordingly a special certificate was issued to him, dated September 14 and signed by John Banister, Roger Sherman, and Washington, recommending "that he be entitled to the first vacancy that may fall in the Line," a recommendation that was implemented on November 24, 1778, when Congress adopted a series of proposals contained in the final report of the Committee of Arrangement. See PCC, item 59, 2:75–80; Washington, *Writings* (Fitzpatrick), 12:457; and *JCC*, 12:1158.

Henry Laurens to the Comte d'Estaing

Sir

Philadelphia 10th September 1778

I have the honor to inform your Excellency that your Letters to me of the 8th July and 26th August have been laid before Congress.[1]

The Trust reposed in your Excellency by His Most Christian Majesty in your present Command is so high an evidence of your Excellency's proved Abilities, Zeal and Bravery as to secure your Reputation against those injuries which the ill success of the best laid Plans sometimes brings upon less established Characters.

I am to assure you, Sir, that Congress, not admitting a doubt of your Excellency's attachment to the joint interests of your Sovereign and of these United States have readily concluded that your Excellency has been influenced in all your aims for the general good, since your Excellency's arrival in America by a strict attention to your Orders, and to the peculiar state of your Squadron under the varying circumstances of time and Place.

The People of America must indeed regret the failure of the late expedition against Rhode Island, but certainly they will not omit to do just Credit to the Martial zeal of their Naval Allies, which, in pursuit of an hostile fleet was overborne by the power of a sudden and severe Tempest. From such an unfavorable casualty they will look forward in hope of Events more consonant to the wise intentions of His Most Christian Majesty, the Glory of his Fleets, and the security & interest of the United States.

You may be confident, Sir, that every possible aid will be afforded to your Excellency for the repair of your Ships. The most immediate and active Measures were taken to furnish your squadron with all the supplies which Congress was at first informed were wanted. The true cause why you did not earlier receive them was the difference between that facility with which Ships move from one place to another, and the embarrassments of distant land carriage. The Plan for furnishing Your Excellency's Squadron at Sandy Hook was rendered abortive by its removal to Rhode Island; and the Provisions ordered for this latter Place, were afterwards to be transported by land to Boston.

The public officers are now diligently employed in forwarding to that Capital such supplies as Congress have been informed will suffice for the Squadron thirty days, and if more is required to be sent thither, Congress will continue in the exertion of every practicable means to comply with your Excellency's future requisitions: but it is to be wished that the delay and expence of so long a land carriage in victualling the Squadron could be prevented by its change of Harbour as speedily as possible to Chesapeak Bay or that of Delaware.

I have the honor to be, With the highest Esteem & the most profound Respect, Sir, Your Excellency's Most Obedient and Most Humble Servant, Henry Laurens, President of Congress

RC (Archives Nationale: Archives de la Marine, B4:146). In the hand of Moses Young and signed by Laurens. Addressed: "His Excellency Count d'Estaing, Lieutt. General of the Armies of His Most Christian Majesty, Vice Admiral of His Fleets, And Knight of His Orders, Boston."

1 D'Estaing's July 8 letter to Laurens, which had been read in Congress on July 12, is in Wharton, *Diplomatic Correspondence*, 2:640–42. The comte's August 26 letter to the president, in which he dealt in general with his actions since arriving in America and in particular with his reasons for breaking off operations in Rhode Island and sailing to Boston, is in PCC, item 164, fols. 555–72. Congress read the second letter on September 9 and appointed a committee to draft a reply. The committee submitted a draft letter the following day that was "read and agreed to" and ordered to be "signed and forwarded by the President to the Count d'Estaing." See *JCC*, 12:892, 897. The committee draft has not been found.

Henry Laurens to John Lewis Gervais

My Dear Friend 10th September [1778]

I had the honor of writing to you the 6th Instant by Muckinfuss to which I beg leave to refer, the opinion which I then intimated refering the Article of Rice, I now confirm, more on your Account than mine; I am altogether indifferent respecting a Concern in any purchase you may think proper to make, except the wish ever uppermost in my mind to promote your Interest. I do not apprehend you will be a loser, should you venture to lay up even ten thousand Barrels, a small Cargo at Egg Harbour or Sinnepuxent will be in a fair way for Count d'Estaing's fleet and for further Orders. I shall persevere in offering my opinion by every opportunity.

Within the present inclosure you will receive two Newspapers—also a Copy of Count d'Estaings late letter to Congress and the Answer to it, which shew, that all at present is harmony, altho' I may truly say, and say it with some concern, there is a cursed, unreasonable, impolitic jealousy resting in some Minds. What this observation alludes to will afford Annecdote when I shall have the happiness of seeing you at Ansonburgh—you will shew these Copies to His Excellency the President, then be so good as to deposit them among my own Papers.

Mr. Timothy Matlack of this City has been so polite and generous as to put into my hands a long Letter which he receiv'd from Mr. Gadsden,[1] and if I understand him right he has hitherto shewn it to no other Person, altho' the Author has intimated that it should be shewn to any body or every body but me; It is highly probable you have seen or learned the Contents of that Letter. As Mr. Gadsden has, in this new instance without the least grounds, most injuriously and unjustly treated me, first, by what he has written, and aggravated in the second place by his manner of wounding an innocent Man in a secret manner, and at a time when such a stroke in the dark must be most affecting; and as he must feel conviction of his error, I expect from him an immediate and ample acknowledgment to each of the Persons to whom he has written, and to as many as possible to whom he has related such Articles contained in that Letter as respect my Character; even this will fall far short of that justice which a vindictive Mind would demand, and which a generous Heart would, without prompting, express immediately upon discovery of so great a fault. I am willing once more to sacrafice at the Shrine of Peace all that I might further with strict propriety exact from him.

You will, I am persuaded Sir, do me the honor to read all the preceding Page to Mr. Gadsden; be so friendly as to transmit me that Gentleman's Answer, which I hope you will obtain in a few plain, explicit Words.

Mr. Drayton, I find, has a Copy of that Letter, it was from thence he gave me the information which I formerly spoke of,[2] but I had not known he was possess'd of the letter until I mentioned to him this of Mr. Matlack's. Mr. Drayton expresses himself upon the occasion with much sorrow and concern on my Account. He is also vested with full powers "to make what use he pleases of it, *either in Congress or out*, but by all means to shew it to Heyward, Mathews and Hudson, and his old particular friends in Congress."[3] Here it was calculated to ruin me among People with whom I live in the strictest harmony, and from whom I have the honor of receiving daily marks of friendship and respect. I should have felt the blow, without knowing the hand from whose Art or power it had been struck—but Alas poor Man! he mistakes his friends as egregiously as he does his Enemies. I do not, my Dear Sir, restrict you from reading the whole of this to Mr. Gadsden if you think proper, but I could wish whatever may be the Event of this Circumstance it may not be talk'd of abroad. I have written in great haste. The dictates of a Heart, honest, feeling, and disposed upon every occasion to pursue such Measures as may produce good effects public & private. My Compliments to each friend ennumerated in my former Addresses, and to all, if any, whom I may have inadvertently omitted.

God Bless you, and keep you in health and Peace. H.L.

LB (ScHi).

1 Christopher Gadsden's letter to Timothy Matlack is not in Christopher Gadsden, *The Writings of Christopher Gadsden, 1746–1805*, ed. Richard Walsh (Columbia: University of South Carolina Press, 1966).

2 See Laurens to Gervais, August 7, 1778.

3 Laurens is quoting here from Gadsden's July 4 letter to William Henry Drayton, for which see ibid., note 8.

Henry Laurens to Rawlins Lowndes

10th Septr. [1778]

I had the honor of writing to Your Excellency on the 6th which I sent after Muckinfuss whom I had engaged to wait eight and forty hours—business had crouded in upon me for the preceding week in such quantity and numbers as to render it impossible for me to write while he remained in the City—my Colleague Mr. Drayton had detained him five days. I have therefore paid Muckinfuss for the whole, 70 Dollars, which I charge to our State; had we sent a special Express which our variety of Intelligence seemed to call for, the expence would have been ten times as much.

By mere accident I have learned of an opportunity for Charlestown, and have half an hour allowed me to write.

General Sullivan writes the 3d Inst. that a perfect harmony subsisted between the Count d'Estaing and himself,[1] this points at certain Circumstances which had happened upon the Count's determination to go into Boston, the knowledge of which Congress had engaged to keep within doors, therefore I have not spoke of them to Your Excellency or any other friend and I think myself not yet releas'd.

The General adds that the British fleet in Boston Bay consists of 8 ships of the line, 10 frigates, one Sloop and a Schooner. They cannot lie there long without coming to blows with the French Squadron whose re-equipment is proceeding with great celerity and whose Admiral is brimfull of desire for Action.

We are too ignorant of the State of our Enemy's forces in this neighbourhood both on land and water. I am endeavouring since I perceive the public neglected to collect the fullest intelligence for their benefit.

General Washington the 4th of September says "the designs of the Enemy as to their future movements remain yet entirely unfolded; but the expectation of their leaving the Continent is daily decreasing." The reasons which his Excellency assigns for the ground of this opinion appear to me as good premises for a quite contrary conclusion. Mr. Gerard concurs in my sentiments, therefore I am not very presumptous in saying, that important point remains doubtful; in the mean time I am grieved by knowing from General Washington in the same Letter that our Army are again likely to suffer exceedingly for want of Cloaths and Blankets, yet we have been amused for Months past with Reports of Cloathing enough in the public Stores for forty thousand Men.

The management of Provision is equally improvident. In a word, Sir, every complaint which I have lately made to Your Excellency of the deplorable state of our Affairs gathers strength from every days melancholly experience—if Congress continues inert, the States will soon be alarmed by informations which will throw the whole into convulsions. I have written in the utmost haste, and under many interruptions and hear the person who is to conduct my Letter calls, and will not be detain'd.

I shall inclose certain Resolves of Congress approving the late conduct at Rhode Island,[2] and two of Dunlap's Advertizers. The Resolves may be published. I intimated to the House a Resolve of November last for enquiring into the causes of miscarriage of every Expedition &c. as a bar to hasty approbation and thanks but my sentiments were lost.[3] I have not time to expatiate on a subject which seems to require attention.

On the 5th Inst. a Member of Congress Mr. R. Morris declared in the house in a formal Address to the Chair that the Embargo was not regarded in Maryland, that flour was daily exported thence under, or under the Idea of, Tobacco. The Delegates of Maryland were present. No Contradiction was intimated. No doubts of the fact suggested, and the matter passed over without notice. This is a simple relation of a fact which duty to my country has prompted.[4]

I have the honor to be &c.

P.S. I have prevail'd on this Messenger to wait a few hours for the benefit of my Colleagues, if any thing important shall come to light in the meantime, Your Excellency will be troubled with an additional Postscript.

LB (ScHi).

1 Laurens is referring to Gen. John Sullivan's September 3 letter to Washington, which the commander in chief transmitted to Congress with his September 4 letter to Laurens. See *JCC*, 12:889; PCC, item 152, 6:325–31, item 169, 5:13–14; Washington, *Writings* (Fitzpatrick), 12:399–403; and Sullivan, *Papers* (Hammond), 2:299–301.

2 See *JCC*, 12:894.

3 This remark indicates that Laurens may have been the author of the motion calling upon Congress to reconsider its September 9 resolve approving General Sullivan's retreat from Rhode Island, which was defeated that day by a vote of ten states to two, with only New York and South Carolina voting in the affirmative. See *JCC*, 12:895. The "Resolve of November last" refers to a resolve Congress adopted on November 28, 1777, requiring an investigation of any unsuccessful "expedition which may be undertaken either by sea or land, by order, or at the expence of the United States." *JCC*, 9:976. Immediately after defeating the aforementioned motion to reconsider, Congress turned aside a motion to direct Washington to conduct an inquiry "into the causes of the failure of the late expedition against Rhode Island, agreeably to the resolution of Congress of November 28, 1777." *JCC*, 12:895–96.

4 See also Laurens to William Smith, September 12, 1778.

Henry Laurens to George Washington

Sir 10th Septr. [1778]

Since my last of the 5th by Burwell, I have had the honor of receiving and presenting to Congress Your Excellency's favors of the 4th and Inst.[1] together with Copy of Major General Sullivan's Letter of the 31st Ulto. and other Papers referred to.

Your Excellency will be pleased to receive under the present Cover the following Acts of Congress.

1. . . . of the 4th Inst. for allowing 3 Dollars per day for the expences of Officers ordered to a distance from Camp upon extra Services.
2. . . . of the 8th for augmenting the Continental Bounty to Recruits enlisting for 3 Years or during the War.
3. . . . for expressing the sense of Congress respecting the late Retreat from Rhode Island, and the Action there the 29th Ulto.[2]

I have the honor to be, With the highest Respect & Esteem &c.

LB (DNA: PCC, item 13).

[1] The letter from Washington whose date escaped Laurens was that of September 7. See *JCC*, 12:896; PCC, item 152, 6:341; and Washington, *Writings* (Fitzpatrick), 12:409–10.

[2] For the resolves listed here by Laurens, see *JCC*, 12:878, 889–90, 894.

Robert Morris to William Lee

Sir Philada. Septr. 10th 1778

Your several favours of the 14th & 28th Feby & 23d March came duely to my hands.[1] I was sorry to observe some parts of the Correspondance between Mr Ross & you relative to my Brothers papers, but surely as he possessed my orders he ought to have been present at the delivery of them by the Kings officers at Nantes, when those of a private Nature shoud have been delivered to him.

To prevent further altercation which I dislike exceedingly, I obtained an order of Congress for the delivery of the whole of those papers to my order and send a duplicate thereof by this Conveyance.[2] I have the honor to remain, Sir, Your Obedt hble Servt.

Robt Morris

RC (ViHi). Endorsed by Arthur Lee: "There was no Order enclosd."

[1] No letters of these dates from Lee to Morris have been found, but several letters of February 4, 13, and 28 and March 23, 1778, discussing his activities concerning the papers of Morris' late brother Thomas are in William Lee, *Letters of William Lee*, ed. Worthington C. Ford, 3 vols. (Brooklyn, N.Y.: Historical Printing Club, 1891), 2:353–62, 370–87, 402–11.

[2] For Congress' September 4 resolve ordering that "the commissioners or com-

missioner, who shall be possessed of the said books and papers when this order arrives, deliver the same, both public and private, to the said Robert Morris, or to his order," see *JCC*, 12:879.

Committee of Arrangement to Theodorick Bland, Jr.

Dear Sir Head Quarters September 11th. 1778

The Committee of Arrangement request you would transmit to Head Quarters either to the Commander in Chief or them an exact Return of your Regiment, or if possible an arrangment of it pursuant to the new Regulation of Congress; specifying in the Return the particular State from which each Recruit was raised. If any disputes subsist among the Captains or Subalterns they are to be settled by a Board to be appointed for that purpose, & if any such prevail among the Field Officers you will please to make a State[men]t & Report thereof to this Committee, & as no Claims not represented before the Committee make their Report can be admitted without an application to Congress they wish the utmost dispatch. With a return of the officers Names Send the dates of their Commissions. I am in Behalf of the Committee your mo. obed Servant, J. Banister.

[*P.S.*] Inclosed is a Copy of the new Arrangment, prescribed by Congress, for your direction.

RC (PHC). Written and signed by John Banister. Addressed: "Col. Theok. Bland or in his absence to the Commanding Officer of his Regimt. of Horse."

Samuel Adams to James Warren

My dear Sir Philade. Sept. 12. 1778

Your obliging Letter of the 25 of August came duly to my Hand.[1] As you again mention Captn. Manly I will speak of him to you with Candor. I never saw him but once, viz. the last spring in Boston, till he came to this City. I had preconceivd an opinion of his Bravery, in speaking of which you tell me "no Caution ought to be used," though I have never yet been pointed to a single Instance. I confess his Appearance in Boston did not strike me most agreably. He was in the midst of a Crowd who were shouting his Entrance into Boston, and like some of his Superiors, he seemd to be intoxicated with popular Applause. I had some other Apprehensions, but I give you my most charitable Thoughts. I retaind however an Opinion of him; for I concluded, that *Huzza for the brave Manly*, might be sufficient to induce him to lay a Pop Gun Schooner alongside the Eagle if good Fortune should throw her in his Way. You think his Judgment and Abilities would not be equal to others in the Direction of more Ships than one. Here lies a Difficulty; for let us consider the Rank he holds in our little Navy, and judge how soon the Time may, perhaps *must* come when he may have the Command of more Ships, if you give him the Command of one. Having said this to you and to no one else though I have frequently heard the same thing mentiond by others, I am sure *you* will not conclude that I am here deeply engagd in a Party against him. Some, I know have formd or pretended to form such a Conclusion, not from a real Regard to the Merits of Manly, the Honor of our Navy or the great Cause we are engagd in, but to serve a different and very inferior Purpose than either. Such Men, you know, I hold in ineffable Contempt.

I am glad that Landais rises in your Esteem—that the other Captains are convincd that he is Master of his Business, which with his agreable Manners & Disposition forces Conviction of the Judiciousness of his Appointment, I fancy now, that I shall soon be dischargd the shameful Imputation of being "his chiefe Patron here." I have a particular Reason to urge that every Exertion may be made to get his and every other Ship manned.

Last Evening a Letter from Governor Trumbull was read in Committee, strongly recommending a Captain for the Ship at Norwich, who, added to great Qualifications, can readily get Men for her.[2] I mentiond Manly as having the Character of a brave and very popular Officer, and read those Parts in your Letter to me that related to Him; But I am convincd he woud not impute his being overlookd to any other Cause, than the Desire of the Court Martial, which acquitted him with *Honor*.

The Rhode Island Expedition is at length finishd. Our Cause is not dishonord though we have not succeeded to our Wishes. Congress have approvd of the Retrial, thanked General Sullivan & his brave Troops and applauded the patriotick Exertions of New England. Major General Hancock was unluckily at Boston and missed the Laurels. In my opinion it would be in a great Degree impolitick at this Juncture to suffer an Odium to be cast on the Count D'Estaing. If there should be a Disposition to do it, I am perswaded Men of Discretion & Influence will check it. The Tories will try their utmost to discredit our new Alliance. And he who not long ago expressed his Opinion, that "A Connection with France would serve America," will not fail to promote a Jealousy if he can thereby establish his Popularity.[3] Such Men should be critically watchd on this Occasion.

Adieu my Friend. S A

RC (MHi).

1 Warren's August 25 letter to Adams is in the *Warren-Adams Letters*, 2:43–44.

[2] Trumbull's August 27 letter recommending Seth Harding to command the frigate *Confederacy*, which was under construction at Norwich, is in PCC, item 66, 1:410–12. For Congress' appointment of Harding to this command, see Marine Committee to Jonathan Trumbull, Sr., September 25, 1778.

[3] Notwithstanding Adams' concern that resentment over d'Estaing's precipitate withdrawal from Rhode Island might be used by the unscrupulous for political advantage, John Hancock, the object of Adams' immediate suspicions, joined in Massachusetts' conspicuous public pro-French displays, praising the French and entertaining d'Estaing's fleet during its brief stay at Boston. This official show of solidarity nevertheless failed to extinguish vestiges of the traditional anti-French sentiment that was more typical of the region, which found expression in a series of clashes that occurred between French and American sailors at Boston during September and October 1778. For discussion of Anglo-French relations at this critical juncture, see William C. Stinchcombe, *The American Revolution and the French Alliance* (Syracuse: Syracuse University Press, 1969), pp. 53–61.

Josiah Bartlett to Mary Bartlett

My Dear

Philadelphia Septr 12th 1778

This will be Sent by Express to Boston and I have only just to inform you that I am in a Comfortable State of Health; Charles Chace is got well; and I hope to Set out for home the first of November. The Congress are very much Engaged in Business So that we are obliged to Set twice a Day Besides being on Committees Morning or Evening which is very tedious but while I tarry shall Endeavor to Stick Closely to the Business.

I have nothing new to write you; we are very uncertain what are the Designs of the Enemy. Some think they are going off to leave us, others think they will make a trial on New England. A Short time will Determine their Designs.

The inclosed paper will Shew you the letters that have been Sent by the Brittish Comissioners to Congress.[1] You will please to lay up Carefully the news papers I Send you as it is probable I Shall hereafter Desire to read some of them.

I hope you & the rest of my family are well and that I Shall have the pleasure to find you all So in about two months from this time.

I have wrote to Genl Whipple to Desire him to come forward Seasonably. Give my Regards to all friends. If David Sanborn's time is out before I Return I hope he will tarry till the fall Business is quite Compleated.

I am yours

Josiah Bartlett

RC (NhHi).

[1] That is, the *Pennsylvania Packet*, September 12, 1778.

Josiah Bartlett to William Whipple

Dear Sir, Philadelphia Sept 12th 1778.

By the last post I had the pleasure to receive a copy of the Vote of the General Court appointing you a delegate to Congress[1] and I hope that no private considerations of any nature will prevent your acceptance and that you will have as great a hand in making peace and confirming our Independence as you had in carrying on the War and declaring our total separation from Britain; as it is very probable negotiations for peace will be carried on the ensuing winter, I Sincerely wish you may be present in Congress when they are under consideration. I could wish you and your colleague would be here the latter end of next month that I might have a day or two with you before I set out for home, which I shall do the 1st of November, as I can by no means tarry over the winter and every day after that time will make the journey more and more disagreeable and my tarrying longer will be of no service, as being alone, I cannot represent the State after that time. I shall therefore think myself at liberty and that it will be best for me to return at that time whether you are arrived here or not.

Please as soon as you receive this to send me an answer that you have accepted and that you will be here by the latter end of next month.

The enclosed paper will inform you what the British Commissioners have been Sending to Congress and that we have not thought proper to make them any other answer than the Resolve concerning releasing the convention prisoners. The letter to them signed W.H.D. was wrote I suppose by Chief Justice Drayton member from So. Carolina as were the former letters under that Signature.[2] We are at a loss to guess at the future designs of the enemy. Some think they are about to leave these States others that they will make an attack on New England in order if they are strong enough by sea to destroy the French fleet—whatever their designs are I think a few days will discover.

I am much chagrined at the disappointment in the Rhode Island Expedition and I dare say you were equally so, especially if you was on the Island as I suspect you was by your last letter to me in which you informed me you designed to set out in a day or two if your health permitted. I am with respect your friend and Servt.

Josiah Bartlett

Tr (DLC).

1 Whipple, Bartlett, George Frost, and John Wentworth had been appointed delegates to Congress by the New Hampshire assembly on August 14 and 18. *N. H. State Papers*, 8:789–90, 792.

2 For William Henry Drayton's public letters to the Carlisle Commissioners that were printed in the *Pennsylvania Packet*, see Drayton to the Carlisle Commissioners, June 17, 1778, note 1, and September 4, 1778.

Committee of Arrangement to Samuel B. Webb

Sir Head Quarters. September 12th. 1778

The Committee of Arrangement wish to be furnished with the Means of properly adjusting your Regiment, in Conformity to the Plan lately adopted by Congress, and therefore request you to make a Return of your Officers to the Commander in Chief, as they shou'd stand in point of the Rank & Seniority, Specifying at the same time the dates of their Commissions. We are respectfully, Sir your Mo. obed. Servants.[1]

Roger Sherman

John Banister

[*P.S.*] A Return of the Strength of the Regiment is also requested.

RC (NN). Written by Banister and signed by Banister and Sherman. Addressed: "Col. Webb or the Commanding Officer of his Regiment at Providence." Because Webb had been a prisoner of war since December 1777, this letter probably went to Lt. Col. William Smith Livingston, the ranking officer of Webb's Additional Continental Regiment.

1 This day the committee also sent a similar request to Col. Henry Jackson, commander of the Additional Continental Regiment that was incorporated into the Massachusetts line in 1780. This letter was also written by Banister and signed by Sherman and Banister, but because the latter's signature was clipped from the manuscript it has been identified simply as a letter from Sherman. Emmet Collection, NN.

Committee on Appeals Decree

September 12th. 1778.

Wingate Newman &c. App[ell]ees vs. Andrew Caldwell App[ellan]t } Appeal from the Court of Admiralty of the State of Pennsylvania[1]

We the Commissioners appointed by the honorable Congress to hear, try and determine all Appeals from the Courts of Admiralty of the several American States having heard and fully considered as well all and singular the Matters and Things set forth and contained in the Record or Minutes of the proceedings of the Court aforesaid in the above Cause as the Arguments of the Advocates of the respective parties in the above Appeal do thereupon adjudge and decree that the Judgment or Sentence of the Court aforesaid be in all it's parts revoked, reversed and annulled. And We do further decree and adjudge that the above named Wingate Newman pay unto the above named Andrew Caldwell two hundred and eighty Dollars for his Costs and Charges by him expended in sustaining and supporting his said Appeal.

Jno Harvie
John Henry.
Jas. Smith

MS (DNA: RG 267, case no. 23). In a clerical hand, and signed by Harvie, Henry, and Smith.

1 Andrew Caldwell, a Philadelphia shipowner and a member of the Pennsylvania Navy Board, had appealed this case to Congress after the Pennsylvania Court of Admiralty had awarded ship and cargo to its captor, Wingate Newman, a Philadelphia privateer captain. Congress had received this appeal on September 8, 1777, and referred it to the Committee on Appeals, which rendered this reversal decree on September 15, 1778. See *JCC*, 8:723; and Morgan, *Naval Documents*, 6:1111, 7:405, 1306, 8:102.

The Committee on Appeals had evolved from an ad hoc system of committees appointed in 1776 to hear appeals from state admiralty courts based on Congress' Continental authority over matters such as admiralty law. The first standing committee of five members had been appointed on January 30, 1777, "to hear and determine upon appeals brought against sentences passed on libels in the courts of Admiralty in the respective states."

The Committee on Appeals subsequently heard at least 42 appeals before February 1780 when it was replaced by a Court of Appeals in Cases of Capture, a judicial body created to shift a burden from members of Congress and to regularize the appeals process in a formal court of judicature rather than a legislative committee. The need for a formal court was soon dramatically demonstrated when the appeals process virtually collapsed in the face of Pennsylvania's refusal ro recognize the committee's authority in the case of the sloop *Active*, which is discussed in the Committee of Appeals decree of December 15, 1778, printed below. See *JCC*, 7:75; and Henry J. Bourguignon, *The First Federal Court: The Federal Appellate Prize Court of the American Revolution, 1775–1787*, Memoirs of the American Philosophical Society 122 (1977): 89–90.

Samuel Holten's Diary

[September 12, 1778]

12. Saturday. Congress sit but half the day.[1] The Delegates from Mass. dined with the minister of France & a number of other members of Congress, the diner was grand & elegant, & in the french taste. A heavy shower at evening.

MS (MDaAr).

1 Holten's preceding diary entry reads: "Sepr. 11th. Congress sit late. The weather is much cooler. Nothing material turnd. up this day."

Henry Laurens to John Cadwalader

Sir. Philadelphia, 12th Septr 1778.

His Excellency General Washington having recommended to Congress the appointment of a General of Horse, the House took that subject under consideration the 10th Inst. when you were unanimously elected Brigadier & Commander of the Cavalry in the service of the United States.[1]

From the general voice abovementioned you will perceive Sir, the earnest desire of the House that you will accept a Commission & enter as early as your convenience will admit of upon the duties of the Office & I flatter my self with hopes of congratulating you in a few days upon this occasion.

I have the honor to be, with particular Esteem & Regard, Sir, Your Obedient & Most humble Servant,

Henry Laurens, President of Congress.

RC (PHi). Addressed: "The Honorable John Cadwalader Esquire, Brigadier General & Commander of the Cavalry in the service of the United States of America, Kent County, Maryland."

1 See *JCC*, 12:897. Both Washington and the Committee of Arrangement had recommended that General Cadwalader be appointed to this office. See Washington, *Writings* (Fitzpatrick), 12:276; and Committee of Arrangement to Laurens, September 7, 1778. However, in a September 19 letter that the delegates read three days later, Cadwalader notified Congress that he was unwilling to accept this appointment "as the war appears, to me, to be near the close"; and not until November 14, 1778, did Congress direct Washington to name a new commander of cavalry. See PCC, item 78, 5:221; and *JCC*, 12:941, 1158.

Henry Laurens to Thomas Johnson

Sir. Philadelphia 12 Septr 1778.

I had the honor of writing to Your Excellency the 5th Inst. by Millet.

This will convey to Your Excellency an Act of Congress earnestly recommending to the Government of Maryland to take measures for preventing infractions upon the Embargo.[1]

I have the honor to be, With great Esteem, & Respect, Sir, Your Excellency's Obedient & most humble servant.

Henry Laurens, President of Congress

RC (MdAA).

1 See *JCC*, 12:903.

Henry Laurens to William Smith

Dear Sir 12th Septr. [1778]

I have been twelve days indebted for your favor of the 5th.

The Carriage which I so much troubled you about proved to be extremely dirty, damaged, and unfit for my use.

The fellows who brought up my Wine tax'd me eight Bottles.

It has been acknowledged that a Member of Congress did give the Information respecting exportation of flour to the Eastern States, intending it only for the private information of your Governor and Council but that you my good friend opened the Letter and let the contents pass under the Eye of several Merchants and others, pray, between you and I, how stands this Mystery?[1]

General Sullivan, you see, made a safe Retreat and Congress have applauded him, this applause would have been in my humble opinion of no less value had it been founded on an inquiry in terms of our Resolution of November last[2]—it is known to very few, and I do not mean to depreciate General Sullivan's merit when I assure you the Union is indebted to that good Man General Washington for the escape of that part of our Army.

The Newspaper under Cover with this will shew you W.H.D. versus British Commissioners,[3] and from a Copy of General Heath's Letter of the 2nd Inst. you will see Lord Howe is determined at great hazards to attempt a further interview with Count d'Estaing.[4] What if Clinton with his 10,000 should from Rhode Island penetrate to Boston and the Troops of the Convention struggle to join him? Such an attempt would give us some trouble, and might end the War in their ruin—four or five days will produce great and probably bloody accounts. I write in haste & for your information, don't publish me.

I Am with great regard &c.

LB (ScHi).

1 Samuel Chase was the "Member of Congress" who accused Smith of opening his letter to the governor and council of Maryland and divulging the news that on August 24 Congress had directed Commissary General Wadsworth to purchase 20,000 barrels of flour in Pennsylvania, Delaware, Maryland, and Virginia for shipment to New England despite a congressional ban on exporting provisions. Smith, a Baltimore merchant and former delegate to Congress, indignantly denied the charge in his September 15 response to Laurens. "I am astonished that any Gentleman," Smith explained, "should insinuate or assert, That I ever oppened any letter Addressed to the Governor & Councill, on the subject refered to, or even on any other. The only letter which I have seen, was a letter from Mr. S. Chase directed to Col. Lloyd of this state, brought from Philadelphia by a Mr. Charles Harris of this Town, who said he had Mr. Chases directions to permit any Gentlemen, on his way to open & read. It was oppend in my presence, A Number of other Gentlemen by. I am not certain whether I broke the seal, or some other person. Its Contents was published in the Philadelphia & Maryland Gazettes, which to the best of my remmembrance contained little more, than a

letter from a Mr. Fisher at Lewes & something respecting the movements of the French fleet And of some ships of war having appeared in Delaware Bay. I do most solemnly declare, that, I never saw or heard of any letter to the Governor or Councill or Any member of Councill, giving information, respecting exportation of flour to the eastern states, Nor did I at the time I gave you the intimation, ever hear any Gentleman Named as suspected, nor did I believe it *at that time*.

"If such a declaration, so injurious to my character has been made in a public manner, I must beg, My Dear Sir that you will read or permit Mr. Secry to read this letter in Congress. Otherwise if the declaration has been made in private to your Honor I would only request youll shew the Gent. My letter & if he will be kind enough to write me on the Subject, I will give him all the satisfaction in my power. For I do declare I do not even yet know with certainty to whom I am indebted for this groundless slander." Laurens Papers, William Gilmore Simms Collection deposit, MHi.

In reply, Laurens wrote a letter to Smith on October 4, 1778, that has not been found except for an extract quoted by Charles Carroll of Carrollton in a public letter to Chase printed in the *Maryland Gazette* in 1781. "You appeared to me to have been abused, and yet I was not so clear in the fact, as to authorise me to write names. In conversation with Mr. Forbes, he informed me lately who said you had opened the letter, and circulated the contents; this gentleman is now going to Baltimore, and will be so polite as to take charge of my letter, to him therefore, I beg leave to refer you. Believe me Sir, from the first moment I heard the intimation alluded to, I treated it not only with discredit, but indignation, and expressed my feelings in the very instant to a particular friend. I know, said I, Mr. Smith's honor and his discretion are never so unguarded, as this imputation seems to imply."

"I am authorised to say," Carroll continued, "that Mr. Forbes made no scruple to declare, at Mr. Smith's table, that Mr. Chase was the member of congress who said Mr. Smith had opened his letter to the governor and council and betrayed the secret intended only for their information."

Although Chase's letter to the governor and council has not been found, and much of the information on the episode derives from documents relating to the investigation of his misconduct in 1781–82, it seems clear that Chase's accusation against Smith was designed to divert attention from himself. Congress received warning of the threat to American troops at Rhode Island posed by New England's flour shortage in a July 23 letter from Commissary Wadsworth that was referred to committee on July 31. Soon thereafter Chase advised John Dorsey, a business partner in Baltimore, to start purchasing flour, and after the August 24 resolve was passed he urged Dorsey to increase his purchases. Eventually Dorsey bought 7,000 bushels of wheat and 400 barrels of flour and sold them to the Continental Army for a handsome profit in October 1778.

News of Chase's transgression, which posed a grave threat to the maintenance of Continental leadership, quickly spread beyond the halls of Congress and had significant political repercussions. Alexander Hamilton vigorously criticized Chase's behavior in three pseudonymous letters published in the *New-York Journal* in October and November 1778. The Maryland legislature left Chase out of the new slate of delegates it selected in November 1778, and in its instructions to the delegates issued the following month it pointedly warned against "combining with the monopolizers and engrossers of the necessaries of life," asserting the duty of delegates "to be watchful each one over the conduct of the other" to expose such dishonorable practices. And in a final burst of anticommercial sentiment in 1779, it adopted an "Act to restrict the delegates of this state in Congress from engaging in any trade, either foreign or domestic."

The issue was not laid to rest until January 1782 when the Maryland Assembly declared Chase not guilty "of a breach of his duty, as a member of Congress, by revealing a secret resolve of that assembly," but it is clear that this outcome was achieved only because the formal charge was very narrowly focused and the details of Chase's 1778 activities could not be reconstructed by his opponents after the passage of over three years. For discussion of this episode, as well as the political ramifications of it in 1779 and 1781 when Chase attempted to divert attention from his own misdeeds by charging that there were "traitors in the Senate" of Maryland, see Daniel of St. Thomas Jenifer to Charles Carroll, Sr., May 24, 1779; Ronald Hoffman, *A Spirit of Dissension: Economics, Politics, and the Revolution in Maryland* (Baltimore: Johns Hopkins University Press, 1973), pp. 244–50, 263–67; and James Haw et al., *Stormy Patriot: The Life of Samuel Chase* (Baltimore: Maryland Historical Society, 1980), pp. 104–9.

For documentation of details discussed here, see *JCC*, 11:734, 793–97, 831; Jeremiah Wadsworth to Ephraim Blaine, July 23, and to Henry Laurens, August 24, September 6 and 29, 1778, PCC, item 78, 23:513, 537, 561–62, 569–70; Charles Carroll of Carrollton to Samuel Chase, July 16, 1781, *Maryland Gazette*, August 23, 1781; Chase to Carroll, September 24, 1781, ibid., September 27, 1781; John Cadwalader, *To the Public* (Annapolis? 1782), pp. 4–13, 22–24; Hamilton, *Papers* (Syrett), 1:562–63, 567–70, 580–82; and Maryland, *Votes and Proceedings*, House of Delegates, October 1778, p. 58, Senate, July 1779, pp. 55–59, House of Delegates, November 1781, p. 67, DLC(ESR).

2 See Laurens to Rawlins Lowndes, September 10, 1778, note 3.

3 See William Henry Drayton to the Carlisle Commissioners, September 4, 1778.

4 Gen. William Heath's September 2 letter to Laurens, reporting the arrival of British ships outside Boston harbor, is in PCC, item 157, fols. 194–95.

Henry Laurens to George Washington

Sir 12th Septr. [1778]

This will be accompanied by a Letter of the 9th, since which I have had the honor of presenting to Congress Your Excellency's favor of the 7th which the house were pleased to commit to the Board of War.

My present duty is to transmit to Your Excellency the undermentioned Acts of Congress which will be found within the present inclosure.

1. An Act of the 11th Septr. for removing if necessary the Troops of the Convention of Saratoga—for obtaining Passports for American Vessels to transport Provision and fuel for the said troops—for establishing Magazines of Provision the Eastern States—for removing the Cavalry now with the Main Army if their service can be dispensed with, to places where they can be best subsisted, and for reducing the number of Horses kept by Officers in the Army.
2. Duplicate of the Act of the 13th of January last refer'd to in the Act above mention'd.[1]

I have the honor to be &c.

P.S. Since writing the above I have been directed to transmit an Act of Congress of the 4th Inst. Resolving that no Ratification of the

Convention of Saratoga not equivalent to the terms prescribed in the Act of the 8 January last can be accepted which Act will be found inclosed with this & Your Excellency is requested to transmit it to the British Commissioners at New York.[2] And this Instant the Secretary has brot. me an Act of the present date for regulating the purchase of forage & other purposes therein mentioned which will be also inclosed.[3] By an unanimous ballot in Congress on the 10th Inst. General John Cadwalader was appointed Brigadier & Commander of the Cavalry in the service of the United States & on the 9th a Brevet to rank Lieutt. Colo. granted to Maj Lewis Morris.[4]

LB (DNA: PCC, item 13).

1 All of these resolves were passed in response to a report by a committee appointed on September 8 to consider letters from Washington, Deputy Commissary of Purchases Ephraim Blaine, and Deputy Quartermaster General Henry Hollingsworth dealing with the emergency created by a severe shortage of wheat in several states. See *JCC*, 12:889, 898, 901–3; Blaine to Congress, August 31, PCC, item 59, 3:195–96; Hollingsworth to the Board of War, September 4, PCC, item 78, 11:321; and Washington to Laurens, September 4, 1778, Washington, *Writings* (Fitzpatrick), 12:399–403.

2 See *JCC*, 12:880–83.

3 This "Act" was also passed in response to a report by the committee mentioned above in note 1. See *JCC*, 12:906. Laurens noted in his presidential letterbook that on September 13 his secretary, Moses Young, delivered copies of this resolve to subordinates of Quartermaster General Nathanael Greene and Commissary General of Purchases Jeremiah Wadsworth. PCC, item 13, 2:82. At the same time Young also gave Greene's subordinate a copy of a September 11 resolve on "the propriety of reducing the stationary teams of the Army." Ibid.; and *JCC*, 12:903.

4 See *JCC*, 12:894, 897. This day Laurens also wrote a brief letter to Nathaniel Falconer, transmitting "an Act of Congress of this date for appointing you a Superintendent of the Presses for striking Bills of Exchange &c. &c." PCC, item 13, 2:77; and *JCC*, 12:905.

James Lovell to Abigail Adams

Sepr. 12th. 1778

I have the Mortification of being obliged to tell the amiable Portia that the Council of Pensylvania will not grant a partial Exportation of Flour from their State while the general Embargo lasts: So that I cannot *soon* have the Pleasure of executing the Commission which that lovely Woman has entrusted to me. The State of Massachusetts [Bay?] will have the Direction of a Quantity out of which the distressed Inhabitants may get a Pittance. I shall join Portia in my Attentions to my dear Mrs. Lovell upon the first free Exportation from hence.[1]

With affectionate Esteem, J L

RC (MHi). Adams, *Family Correspondence* (Butterfield), 3:89–90.

1 Acting in response to a motion of Elbridge Gerry, Congress had recommended on September 2 that Pennsylvania and the states to the southward allow the exportation of provisions in ships properly authorized by any of the New England state governments. *JCC,* 12:861.

Henry Marchant to the Rhode Island Assembly

Gentn. Philadelphia Sepr. 12th. 78

While I lament the Failure of the hoped for Success against Rhode Island, and submit to the Will of Heaven, and resolve all into the Wisdom of His Providence, and which I doubt not we shall soon have a full Conviction of, however disagreeable the present Check may be to our eager Pursuit, I have however the Pleasure and Happiness to congratulate You and Our Countrymen, that Our Honor is not tarnished. In the Course of a Retreat, made necessary by circumstances out of the Power of Mortals to prevent or foresee—a Victory was obtained by the Continentals and Militia of New-England, and a safe and honorable Retreat effected. And in that Expedition the Exertions of the State of Rhode Island and Providence Plantations, the Spirit of its brave Officers, Troops and Volunteers, has gained them high Honor & Reputation and a very advanced Standing amongst the United States. Upon this Occasion as well as many others, which the Patriotism, Valour and Spirit of thy State I have the Honor to represent has furnished me with, I have not been wanting in my Exertions to place them in that Point of Light which Justice demanded. 'Tis true, however, such distinguished Merit and display of Spirit and Fortitude had no call for an Advocate. They stood confessed.

I must however observe, that Major Genl. Sullivan has done great Justice to the Honor of the State, and has not failed to exert himself in obtaining the Attention of Congress to his Merits, and to Her Relief, from the Burthens she has so long & with so much Magnanimity sustained.

By a Resolution passed this Day, & which will be forwarded to him by the President, Genl. Sullivan is impowerd with the Advice of the Legislature or Councill of War for the State of Rhode Island &c to call upon all the New England States for such Numbers of Militia as he shall think necessary upon great Emergencies.[1]

This is to be understood exclusive of the Standing proportions.

I enclose Your Excellency and Honors the two last Papers. I hope I need not assure you, How much I am Your most devoted and faithful Servant, Hy. Marchant

RC (R–Ar).

1 Congress approved this "Resolution" in response to a September 2 letter from

Gen. John Sullivan to President Laurens asking the delegates to authorize formation of a militia reserve in neighboring states that he could draw upon for help at Rhode Island. See *JCC*, 12:907; and Sullivan, *Papers* (Hammond), 2:295.

Henry Marchant to John Sullivan

Sir,

Philadelphia Sepr. 12th. 1778

I have to congratulate you upon the acknowledged generalship which You displayed in the late Expedition against Rhode Island. Not to you Sir, or the brave Troops under your Command is to be attributed the failing in the full Success which Appearances at first gave Us rational Expectations of. I resolve that, into those Accidents, or rather Counsells of Divine Providence, which are often for good & wise Purposes hid from human Investigation, and so resolving, I wish we may humbly submit, Thankful that it Pleased Heaven in the midst of some Disappointments to crown Our Arms with Laurells of Honour.

I did myself the Honour of bringing into Congress such Resolutions upon that Occasion as I thought were due from the Publick, to Your Zeal, Bravery and good Conduct, and that Display of fortitude and Spirit which annimated the Officers and Troops.[1] Those Resolutions with some small alterations were passed, they are contained in the Papers inclosed.

I shall not fail to inform the State I have the Honor to represent, of the Justice you have done to their great Exertions; and the Interest You take in procuring them some Relief from their uncommon Burthens.

I assure You Sir, I felt myself interested in whatever affects either Your Honor or Happiness, And it shall ever be my Study to promote both, while you are thus eminently continuing to merit them. And I doubt not You will find Your Reward in a grateful Country. Be pleased Sir to present my Respects to such of the worthy Sharers of those Publick Honors, as You may find I have the Honor to be acquainted with, and assure Them I have the Honor to be theirs, & Your very humble Servt.

Hy Marchant

RC (MHi). This letter is incorrectly dated September 17 in Sullivan, *Papers* (Hammond), 2:349–50.

[1] See the September 9 resolutions on the recent unsuccessful Rhode Island expedition in *JCC*, 12:894.

Henry Laurens to John Beatty

Sir Philadelphia 13th. Septr. 1778.

I had the honor of writing the 23d August an Address to you private, and the 4th Instant another, public, to which I beg leave to refer.

This you will be pleased to receive as of the former Class, a Lady who has much importuned me to contribute my endeavours to effect the Exchange of her Husband a Prisoner in New York, has prevailed so far as to draw a promise from me to transmit a Letter which she lately received from the unhappy Captive, in order that you may know his name, and pay that degree of attention to him which is consistent with due preference. I shall inclose with the Letter an Advertiser of Yesterday as a very small compensation for the present trouble.

I am with great Regard &c.

LB (ScHi).

Henry Laurens to William Heath

Sir Philadelphia 13th. Septr. 1778.

I writ to you the 6th Inst. by Messenger Brown & have since been honored with, & duly presented to Congress your several favors of the 29th & 30th August & 2d Inst.[1] At present I have only to transmit an Act of Congress of the 11th which will be found inclosed with this, for removing the Troops of the Convention of Saratoga & for demanding Passports for American Vessels for the transportation of Provision & fuel for the future subsistence of those Troops.[2]

I apprehend Congress conclude that you will continue in force your order respecting Major General[3] untill he shall have made such concessions as shall be satisfactory to your own honor as Commanding Officer of a department in the service of the United States.

I have the honor to be with particular Respect & Esteem, Sir, Your obedient & most humble servant,

Henry Laurens, President of Congress

RC (MHi). LB (DNA: PCC item 13).

1 General Heath's September 2 letter to Laurens is in PCC, item 157, fols. 194–95. File copies of his August 29 and 30 letters are in the Heath Papers, MHi. For the actions Congress took in response to these letters, see *JCC*, 12:888–89.

2 See *JCC*, 12:901–2.

3 For Heath's relations with British Maj. Gen. William Phillips, whose name appears in Laurens' presidential letterbook but was inadvertently dropped in this RC, see Laurens to Heath, July 9, 1778, note 1.

Henry Laurens to the Marquis de Lafayette

Sir 13th Septr. [1778]

I am sensible of a particular degree of pleasure in executing the Order of Congress signified in their Act of the 9th Inst. which will be inclosed with this, expressing the sentiments of the Representatives of the United States of America, of Your high Merit on the late Expedition against Rhode Island.[1]

You will do Congress justice Sir, in receiving the present acknowledgement as a tribute of the Respect and Gratitude of a free People.

I have the honor to be &c.

LB (DNA: PCC, item 13).

[1] See *JCC,* 12:894.

Henry Laurens to John Laurens

My Dear Son 13th Septr. [1778]

I had last Evening entertained hopes of paying my Respects to you this Morning in full and proper terms, but after near nine hours drudging at this form, I find myself necessitated to submit to a bare acknowledgement of your favors of the 1st and 2nd Inst. You know, much more satisfactorily than I can express just now, the joy which the former must have afforded me. I congratulate with you on your safety, on your increased honor, on your enlarged Circle of honorable friends. You well know how to make the wisest use of these great gifts of Providence, and I think I feel your Heart swell with grateful thanks to God Almighty.

I earnestly wish to hear from you again, and I long to embrace you, consider my time for residence in this Country will expire the first of November. If I retire without seeing you, what a lump will be dragged from hence to Charlestown, and what a heavy hearted Creature shall I exhibit to our friends there.

Do you never think of your Brother? You know I postponed determinations respecting him upon an opinion of your own. I want much to see you on that important account.

I pray God continue to you his protection.

LB (ScHi).

Henry Laurens to the Massachusetts Council

Honorable Sir. Philadelphia 13th Sep. 1778

I had the honor of addressing you the 5th Inst.[1] by Messenger Brown since which I have not been favored with any Letter from you.

Within the present Inclosure will be found four Acts of Congress under recited.

1. . . . An Act of the 8th Inst. for making up Clothing for the Army from materials in the Eastern States.[2]
2. . . . An Act of the 9th expressing the high sense of Congress, of the patriotic exertions of the Eastern States on the late expedition against Rhode Island.
3. . . . An Act of the 11th for removing, if it shall be necessary, The Troops of the Convention of Saratoga & for demanding Passports for American Vessels for transporting Provision & Fuel for said Troops.
4. . . . An Act of the 12th for reinforcing the Troops under the Command of Majr General Sullivan in Cases of great emergency.[3]

I have the honor to be, With great Respect Honorable Sir Your obedient & most humble servant,

Henry Laurens, President of Congress.

RC (M-Ar). Addressed: "The Honorable Jeremiah Powell Esquire, President of Council, Massachuset's Bay."

1 See Laurens to Richard Caswell, September 5, 1778, note 1.

2 Laurens also transmitted a copy of this resolve with a brief covering letter he wrote this day to Gov. George Clinton of New York. PCC, item 13, 2:82. Congress passed this resolve after reading a September 4 letter from Washington pointing out that his troops were "in great want" of blankets and clothing. See *JCC*, 12:891; and Washington, *Writings* (Fitzpatrick), 12:402-3.

3 Laurens also transmitted copies of all but the third of these resolves with brief covering letters he wrote this day to President Meshech Weare of New Hampshire and Govs. William Greene of Rhode Island and Jonathan Trumbull of Connecticut. See Meshech Weare Papers, MHi; Red Series, R-Ar; and PCC, item 13, 2:79.

Henry Laurens to William Maxwell

Sir 13th Septem. [1778]

I had the honor of addressing you the 13th[1] Instant since which I have received none of your favors.

I now write at the special request of the Honorable the Minister Plenipotentiary of France, and from my own feelings of the necessity of knowing the present state of the British fleet at New York, and if possible the number and strength of the whole Naval Power of

Great Britain on this Continent from New York to Hallifax. I intreat you, Sir, attempt a proper enquiry and inform me as speedily as possible, what ever expence may attend the essay, shall be reimbursed with thanks.

I have the honor to be &c.

[*P.S.*] This will be accompanied by an Advertiser of Yesterday. A private Gentleman a friend of yours, has requested me to add two more with his Wishes that they may get speedily into New York.

LB (ScHi). Addressed: "Brigadier General Maxwell, Elizabeth Town, New Jersey."

[1] Laurens apparently meant his September 6 letter to Maxwell, for which see Laurens to Maxwell, September 5, 1778, note 3.

Henry Laurens to Baron Steuben

My Dear Sir Philadelphia 13th Septem 1778

With this you will receive the Paper left at my House & an Advertiser of Yesterday. Tomorrow Morning shall be devoted to a more particular address in acknowledgement of your several favors lately received. I am now entered upon the ninth hour of drudgery at this Table abating about 30 Minutes conversation with Mons Ternant & for 150 Interruptions. This is the Rest of my sabbath. Be assured My Dear Baron I will not be inattentive to any one of your Commands & that you shall be soon informed how much & how respectfully, I am, Your friend Your obedient humble Servant,

Henry Laurens

RC (NHi).

Henry Laurens to John Sullivan

Sir 13th September [1778]

The last I had the honor of writing to you was under the 28th of August, since which your several favors of the 31st Ulto. the 1st and 2nd Inst. have been duly presented to Congress.

Permit me Sir, to congratulate with you on the Action of the 29th and the honorable Retreat which you afterward so judiciously and happily effected. These circumstances will be always combined with your Glory, in conversation and in History.

I have the honor of transmitting with this an Act of Congress of the 9th which speaks the sense of the Representatives of the United States of America respecting your own Conduct and that of the brave Officers and Troops under your Command, to which I beg leave to refer.

You will also find Inclosed an Act of the 12th for augmenting your force in cases of great emergency.

I have the honor to be &c.

LB (DNA: PCC, item 13).

Samuel Adams to Samuel P. Savage

My dear sir, Philad. Sept 14 1778

I received your favor of the 3d with the News Paper inclosed. I note well the Contents. Our Boston Papers never fail to mark all the Movements of Great Men, and to give Honor where Honor is due. The *Spirited Exertions* of our Major Generals to be sure ought to be properly noticed, Some of them have the good Fortune to be never out of the Way of making a Figure, while others are wisely following the unpopular Steps of Fabius or Count Daun. The Marquis, every one acknowledges, made surprising Dispatch in going to Boston and returning to Rhode Island; but he was sadly mortified in not being present in the Action on that Island. He did all that Man could do. Impossibilities are not to be expected. But he arrivd in Season to take a distinguished Share in the well timed & well conducted Retreat. In *Him* we indeed see an Instance of a young Nobleman "of Rank & Fortune foregoing the Pleasures and Enjoyment of domestick Life and voluntarily exposing himself to the Hardships & Hazzards of a Camp", not in *his own* but a foreign Country, "in the glorious Cause of Freedom." His Example must be "animating" to our young American Heroes; and who would not covet to be *coupled* with him? Congress have requested the President to write to him & in their Name acknowledge his Zeal and spirited Services on this Occasion, by which he has given a fresh Proof of his warm Attachment to our Common Cause.

I am sorry to hear that there is a Disposition in some Persons in Boston to cast an Odium on the French Admiral for leaving Rhode Island. In my opinion it is at this Juncture impolitick in the Extreme. Even if his Conduct shd be thought blameworthy, Prudence, I think, dictates Silence to us. Men of Discretion and Influence will surely by all Means check such a Disposition. The Tories will try their utmost to discredit our new Alliance. You know how much depends upon our culvitating mutual Confidence. It is not in the Power of undisguisd Tories to hurt our Cause. The Injudicious, though honest, Whigs may and too often do injure it. Those whose chief Aim is to establish a Popularity in order that they may obtain Emoluments of Places or the Breath of Applause, will think they can serve *themselves* by declaiming on this Subject or prompting others to do it; and they will not fail doing it though they essentially wound their Country. If there be any of my virtuous & *publick* Spirited fellow Citizens, who pay any Regard to my Opinions, I wish they would particularly regard what I have said to you on this Occasion.

I have written in Haste & must break off abruptly.

Adieu.

S A

[*P.S.*] Pray let Mrs A know that I am well and am disappointed in not hearing from her by the last post.

RC (MHi).

Samuel Holten's Diary

[September 14–15, 1778]

14. Monday. Congress Sit till after 8 in the Eveng. Colo. Foster dined with us, he came from Glocester in Masa. & brot me a letter from Sister Suckey.

15. Tuesday. Dr. Weatherspoon, Genl. Reed & Colo. Harnet dined with us. The weather much cooler. I wrote to the Revd. Dr. Gordon & Miss Holten (No. 17).[1]

MS (MDaAr).

[1] Not found.

Marine Committee to the Deputy Quartermaster at Albany

Sir

September 14th 1778

The French Squadron under the command of vice Admiral the Count D Estaing now in the harbour of Boston being in want of Provisions, we have this day given Orders to the Deputy Commissary of Purchases at Albany immediately to purchase three thousand Barrels Flour and to deliver the Same to you which we desire you will take the most speedy and effectual measures to have transported to Boston and there delivered to the Count D Estaing for the use of his fleet.[1] You will take proper receipts on the delivery of the flour which with an Account of All Charges Attending the transportation transmit in due time to this Committee. We have wrote to General Schuyler requesting him to give you his Opinion touching the quickest and best manner of conveying this Flour, and to use his influence in assisting you.[2] Relying upon your activity in the Speedy execution of this business, We are sir, Your Hble servants[3]

LB (DNA: PCC Miscellaneous Papers, Marine Committee Letter Book).

1 The Marine Committee's letter of this date to the deputy commissary at Albany is in Paullin, *Marine Committee Letters,* 2:7. This day the committee also wrote a similar letter to the Albany Committee. Ibid., pp. 6–7.

2 For the Marine Committee's letter of this date to General Schuyler, see ibid., p. 6.

3 After learning from the deputy quartermaster and deputy commissary at Albany that they could not ship flour to Boston in time to reach d'Estaing, John Brown, the Marine Committee's secretary, notified Commissary General Jeremiah Wadsworth on September 29 "that 1500 Barrels flour more than what has already been ordered, should be sent from the Magazine nearest to Boston for the use of the French Fleet." Ibid., p. 11.

Marine Committee to Eastern Navy Board

Gentlemen September 14th 1778.

We are favoured with yours of the 26th August in answer to which we highly approve of your supplying the French fleet with what they may want, and recommend your giving them every assistance in your power, you will please to take proper receipts for every thing you furnish them with, and keep distinct and clear Accounts of the cost and charges attending this business which in due time you will transmit to this Committee in order that they may be settled with the Marine Agent of France at this place.

We desire you will order the Commanders of the Frigates Raleigh, Warren, (should she be returned) or the Deane and the Brigt. Resistance to proceed on a Cruize in Company between Cape Henlopen and Occracock on the Coast of North Carolina with a veiw to take certain armed Vessels fitted out by the Goodriches, or any other of the Enemys Vessels that may be infesting that coast. That as the Raleigh, Warren or Deane and the Brig Resistance may soon be wanted to answer the purpose of Convoy, they are so to manage their Cruize as that they may be ready to receive the future orders of this Committee and for this purpose they are once a Week to put into Cheseapeake Bay and call at the Town of Hampton where they will find such Orders lodged, and they are to continue to Cruize and call at Hampton in this manner until they receive their Instructions.

If you think the Vessels ordered to be built for Packets will answer best to be rigged as Brigantines you have our consent so to do.

We are also favoured with yours of the first instant and desire you will apply to General Heath to order the commissarys to return the Provisions you lent General Sullivan of the like kind and quality. We are glad to hear of the arrival of the Brigantine General Gates with her Prizes, but regret very much the loss of her late gallant commander captain Skimmer. You will please to appoint another commander and fit her out on a Cruize as soon as possible.

We enclose an Order from the Board of War for 100 Muskets and Baynets for the use of the Alliance.

The Officers of the Navy since the 10th of October, 1776 rank according to the dates of their Commissions, we shall in our next transmit you a List of them and are Gentlemen,

Your very Hble servants

P.S. We approve of the purchase you have made of the Cannon Iron and other Articles taken out of the British frigates burned at Newport.

LB (DNA: PCC Miscellaneous Papers, Marine Committee Letter Book).

Marine Committee to Jeremiah Wadsworth

Sir

September 14th 1778

As the dificultys attending sending flour by water from Virginia to Boston woud be so very great, It is our desire that the Orders you have had for that purpose may not be executed but instead thereof the following order. We desire you will purchase without delay 18000 Barrels flour in Virginia or if necessary in Maryland for the use of the French Squadron and collect the same quickly as possible, and Store it at such place in Virginia as the Governor and Council of that State Shall advise will best answer the purpose of speedy delivery to the Squadron when it is called for, and avoid at the same time danger from the enemy and interruption from the frost.[1]

We are sir, Your very Hble servants

P.S. This new order of 18,000 Barrels of Flour is to be considered as over and above all former Orders, that you have received from Congress or the Marine Committee, and it requires to be purchased and collected in Virginia with all possible despatch, as it may be soon called for by the French Admiral. It should be so placed as to be taken off with the greatest facility by the fleet, yet care should be taken against surprize from the enemy and delay from the frost. The enemy being now masters of the Sea between the Capes of Virginia and Boston, perhaps you may see it convenient not to send out flour yet by water for the Army. Lord Howe with a powerful Squadron is hovering between Rhode Island and Boston Bay.

LB (DNA: PCC Miscellaneous Papers, Marine Committee Letter Book).

[1] This day the Marine Committee also wrote a letter to the deputy commissary at Boston, requesting him to forward certain food supplies to the comte d'Estaing. Paullin, *Marine Committee Letters*, 2:4–5.

Robert Morris to John Bradford

Dear Sir Philada. Septr. 14th. 1778

Having received several of your favours during the time that I was moving about from Manheim to Camp, from thence hither, & from hence to Manheim & back, which hindered me from answering them regularly, I have them now Spread before me & find their dates are the 13th, 21st & 25th May, 23d & 30th July, 13th & 26th August. Such of the Contents as now require reply shall be annswd. & the rest passed over in Silence. The first of these letters advises the unloading of the Henrietta; the damage of some goods and the pains you had taken to recover them, which was very obliging & Merits thanks. The freight of the Three Friends I got Settled with the Commercial Committee & Remitted the same to Mr Williams.

Your second letter advises the unloading of the Three Friends & enclosed Mr. Richd Browns draft on me in your favour which is at your Credit. Your favour of the 25th May mentions the circumstances of the Brigt. Fame by which it appears the former Owners were excluded from any benefit of Recapture & we must be content thanking you for your trouble in the inquiry. You Congratulate me on my return to this City in yours of the 30 July & add many obliging wishes for which I am not ungratefull; nor unmindfull of your hint to endeavour at making up by Trade the losses I sustained by the destructive hands of the Enemy & in this View I have lately extended my Concerns considerably. I note by your letter of 13th August, that you had sold Mr Ross's Salt at 30/ per bushl. paya. in Jany, this last part of the bargain I think a bad one, because the Trade is chiefly carried on now a days with ready Money, on Acct of the depreciation, however we must be Content. You'l please to furnish me with Acct Sales thereof soon as you can conveniently. You have omitted to Send me a Receipt for the Muskets out of the Three Friends delivered to the Order of the Board of War and it will be a necessary Voucher to my Accounts. By your favour of the 26 August I am in hopes the Henrietta sailed the next day and that she went clear of the British Fleet. I wish you had mentioned the Captain's Name as I do not know it.

It will afford me great pleasure to hear of your Sons returning safe home from Rhode Island & sorry I am that he had not an opportunity of rejoicing in the Success of his exertions in that expedition, but it was not practicable to carry the place after the departure of the French Fleet & there seems a necessity for the Count D'Estaings doing as he did, so that we must rest content and look forward to other events that may be more fortunate.

I have not seen Capt. M. nor heard any thing of the reports you mention, this you may depend, that if any such come to my ears I shall not be backward in your justification.

Thank you for the Account of the engagement between the French 74 & English 64 Gun Ship, the former seems to have suffered a heavy loss in Men but I am glad she proved & maintained her superiority.

We are taking public measures to Supply the French fleet with Provisions and I hope they will be successful. I have been well employed in Committees on this & other business since joining Congress, so that altho I got myself clear of the Standing Boards it makes little difference as nearly the whole of my time is taken from me & I never shall be master of it untill I get quite clear of Public business, which I do most Ardently long for. Pray give my best respects to my Worthy Friend Mr Hancock & tell him I hope he will come back by the end of next month & be ready to fill that Chair he before filled with so much Reputation & then my respect for it will again be as perfect as ever it was. We have a report that the British Fleet after shewing themselves off Your Light House, have departed again, I dont think they have received Reinforcements and without them, they cannot block up the Count D'Estaing. I hope you will exert yrself to get the latter ready for Sea, & that he will immediately come this way to be Supplyed with Provisions.[1] I am Dr Sir, Your Obedt hble Servt. Robt Morris.

P.S. the 15th. I have now recd your favour of 3d Septr. & sorry the Henrietta was not gone before the British Fleet appeared. I fear now she will not get to Virginia. Something must be done for poor Capt. Skimmers Family.[2]

RC (MHi).

1 Morris' private transactions were also the subject of the following letter, which he sent to his associate Jonathan Hudson at Baltimore on September 15.

"I thank you kindly for calling on Mr Holland," Morris explained, "& the information you gave me respecting his Island. Mr White is gone that way & will have some conversation about it, but I doubt if I shall make the purchase as it will not be in my power to manage it properly at least I fear so. I observe your new purchase of a Sloop and wish her Success. Tobo will certainly answer at Surrenham as well as at St. Eustatia or Curracoa because it can be reshipped to Holland on equal terms. I am still of opinion that well bought goods will answer I mean imported Articles but I pray you not to Speculate in Provisions.

"Mr Geo. Irwin of York Town will deliver You this letter, he tells me that my salt under his care was delivered to Mr Kahain of that place by Your order, this was not right as you know I meant to keep mine, therefore you must replace my quantity & of Salt equal in quality & at York Town which you will certainly think right or else Credit me for the Cost of it as you please." Willing-Morris-Swanwick Co. Records, PHarH.

2 For Congress' decision to provide $400 annually for the support of the widow and eleven children left by Capt. John Skimmer, the commander of the *General Gates* who had recently been killed in an engagement with the *Montague*, see *JCC*, 12:909, 946.

Cornelius Harnett to Richard Caswell

Sir, Philadelphia Sept 15th. 1778

The Delegates of the State wrote you a few days ago, that they had at last obtained a grant of the remaining 400,000 dollars to complete your draft for 500,000.[1] This was an object which on my arrival I had much at heart, to accomplish; fearing the General Assembly might have been induced to have disbanded the new raised Troops for want of money, or emitted Procl. money for the purpose of paying them off—neither of which was I hope done. Had our state been represented in Congress at the time of Mr Blounts' arrival, I am well convinced the money would have been sent. I am happy to find Mr. Burke and Mr. Hill are appointed for a year, by that means I hope the state will not again meet with such usage.

Should your Excellency think proper to instruct your Delegates on matters relative to the state, especially such as may not occur to us; I should be happy. I find when Governors recommend any measure to the Delegates of their States, it generally has greater weight with Congress than when propositions are made by them, without any letter or instructions for such purpose.

As soon as the 400,000 dollars can be procured from the Treasurer I shall in conjunction with my Colleagues send it forward by some safe conveyance, in the most expeditious manner. I must take the liberty once more to press your Excellency to forward as speedily as possible the States account & vouchers. I am daily told that No. Carolina has received more money from the Continental Treasury in proportion, than any other state in the union. In vain do I tell them that we never had a Military Chest established in our State, or a Pay Master; that the expense of drawing out a considerable part of our Militia to quell a very dangerous Insurrection in the very heart of our Country; another very expensive Expedition against the Cherokees; the raising, paying, clothing and subsisting Ten Continental Battalions, for a considerable space of time, has been defrayed out of the Treasury of our State. To this they only answer why don't you produce your accounts? I wish this may be done, as I am confident the Continental Treasury must be largely indebted to us. I hope the gentlemen who are or may be appointed to state these demands, may be careful to procure every necessary voucher for the charges made against the Continent, which must be sent on with the Accounts. If your Excellency should in future think it necessary to establish a Military Chest, Pay Master, Commissary &c. you will be pleased to mention it to your Delegates. Perhaps it may be necessary, more especially should another requisition for men be made this winter against the Spring which may happen—should the Enemy be determined on another Campaign this is the opinion of some.

By the Newspapers enclosed you will find Genl Sullivan on the

29th August gave the Enemy a severe check on Rhode Island before his retreat. This enabled him to cross to the main with all his baggage & stores without molestation. The French Fleet are in Boston harbor and Lord Howe with a Superior Fleet having been lately joined by 6 or 8 sail of the line, being a part of Admr. Byrons Squadron, are cruising off that place. We are told another fleet is hourly expected to reinforce the Count De Estaing. I wish they may not be intercepted by Lord Howe, before a junction is formed with the Count.

If I can persuade Mr Burke or Mr Hill to relieve me, my intention is to return home before the winter sets in too severe. I am with great respect, Your Excellency's most Ob. huml. Servt.

Cornl. Harnett

P.S. A very great noise has been made in Congress by the Virginia Delegates relative to a Cap Harper driven into Curretuck by Goutrage. And an attempt is now making to recommend to the state to make restitution to Virginia, this matter has been pushed much by the Virginia Delegates, and altho' they have been assisted by the Gentlemen from New York &c. they have hitherto failed in their attempt. I hope your Excellency will enquire into the matter, and see that the persons who took the vessel out of the Inlet be brought to punishment. The Bill of Costs of the Court of his Excellency's Admiralty is exorbitant. *More of this in my next.*[2]

Genl. Sullivan acquaints Congress that by Accounts received by Deserters, but which is more to be depended on Accounts from persons on Rhode Island, The Enemy had 1061 killed & wounded in the late Action, 321 of which were killed and mortally wounded on the field. This seems to account for the Enemy's suffering our Armv to make good their retreat, with all their Stores and baggage, without molestation—tho' equal in Numbers before the Action.

Tr (Nc–Ar).

1 See North Carolina Delegates to Caswell, September 8, 1778.

2 Harnett is referring to the case of the *Liberty,* a schooner owned by John Harper of Virginia, among others. The case began with the capture of the *Liberty* off the coast of North Carolina on June 8, 1778, by a British privateer commanded by one of the Goodriches, a family of Virginia loyalists. After the *Liberty's* captain, Middleton Belt, deliberately ran her aground the following day, she was abandoned by her captors and boarded by a party of North Carolina militiamen led by Capt. Caleb Ansell, who then repelled an attempt by Goodrich to retake her. The militiamen claimed the *Liberty* as a lawful prize, whereas Captain Belt insisted that she had not been in British custody when they boarded her. A North Carolina admiralty court found in favor of the militiamen, ruling that they were entitled to one-eighth the value of the ship and her cargo, and stymied Captain Belt's effort to appeal the decision to Congress. Then after the court adjourned, the *Liberty* and her cargo were stolen by an unidentified group of North Carolinians, apparently in connivance with a detachment of Captain Ansell's militia.

Frustrated by events in North Carolina, John Harper sought Congress' intervention in his behalf. Thus he prepared a memorial to Congress setting forth the facts in the case, which was read on August 26 and referred to a committee consisting of Samuel Chase, James Smith, and William Duer. Congress considered the committee's report on September 11 and 12, but took no action until October 31, 1778, at which time it approved committee recommendations that Harper be allowed to appeal the North Carolina court's decision to Congress and that North Carolina apprehend and try those responsible for the theft of his ship and cargo. The committee also recommended that Congress ask the North Carolina Assembly to investigate this affair and make restitution to Harper if the facts warranted it, but it is uncertain whether Congress approved this. Harper did not appeal the *Liberty* case to Congress, and he was unsuccessful in obtaining redress from North Carolina. See *JCC*, 11:837–38, 12:904, 907, 1087–90; *N.C. State Records*, 13:734n; and Joseph Harper to Charles Thomson, July 12, 1785, and Charles Thomson to Joseph Harper, July 19, 1785, PCC, item 18A, fol. 111, item 78, 12:415.

John Harvie to Thomas Jefferson

Dear Sir Septr the 15th. 1778.

I should have done myself the pleasure of Answering your letter of July the 19th[1] several weeks ago, if I had not wished to have made a through enquiry after the workmen you want to Employ previous to my writeing to you on that Subject. Ben Randolph professes an Inclination to Accomodate you with an House joiner and tells me that he has been Constant in his researches after one since I informed him that his recommendation to me of a proper Character in that way would be rendering me an Agreable Service to you, but from his and other Accounts of the Scarcity of Skillful hands now following this Branch of Business and the Exorbitant prices prevalent in this City and its Vicinity, I would by no means advise you to depend on one from this Quarter. I cant hear of a Stone Cutter of any kind, the prisoner that I hoped to have Engaged for you who was a Master of this Trade being in Common with a Number of others moved from where I formerly heard of him to some other place of Confinement that I am not able [*to*] discover. It is possible that a number of the Convention prisoners may be sent to Virginia this Fall or Winter. If so probably some Tradesmen of the Professions you want may be found amongst them and procur'd. Whilst I stay here I shall still Continue to look out for the person you want and shall never Consider a triffling Enquiry in this Way a trouble even for a Stranger and much less so for a man to whom I acknowledge myself in many Instances most Sensibly and highly Oblidged.

Haveing sent the papers Regularly to my wife since I have been here I expect their Contents have been Usually Desiminated through the Neighborhood wherefore I Conjecture a Circumstantial Account of the Action on the 28th Ultimo at Newport with the timely Regular and well Conducted Retreat of General Sullivan from Rode Island has either Struck your Eye or Ear. A Letter received last Evening from that General makes the Enemys loss in Kill'd and wounded in the Action (above) amount to upwards of One thousand men. The Hurry and Bustle of the Enemy in New York Indicates a Movement some where. General Washington Conjectures to the Eastward and therefore designs very soon to break up his Camp at White Plains, posting his Army on Ground more Advantageous for covering our Works on the North River and Counteracting their measures in the New England States. A Marauding Division of the Enemys Light Infantry and Dragoons have made a Descent from Newport on the Massachusets, Burnt many Valuable Houses in their Route and destroyed a Magazine of Considerable Consequence at Bedford in that State.

It is reported by pretty good Authority that ten 74 Gun Ships of Byrons Squadron has lately join'd Admiral Howe which Combined fleet now Hover about Boston Harbour. Upon the Appearance of this formadable force the Count D'Estaigne Stationd his Ships except those which are Damaged in Nantucket Road and Erected Batteries on George Island which Command the Entrance and Afford a Cross fire to the Ships which will render it extremely difficult, if possible, for a fleet greatly Superior in force to Enter. However I acknowledge I rather Consider the Count at present in a perilous Situation, but hope that the Brest fleets Arrival will again make him Out Number the Enemy.

I have Spoken at least a Dozen times to Dunlap relative to his account against the Albemarle Subscribers for his paper. He has not yet render'd it in. I will certainly Settle it before I leave this City. I intended to have been at the October General Court Early in the Session, but there is such a Strange Remissness in our Delegates if I leave Congress now, our State will be unrepresented at a time two when Business of the Utmost Consequence to us particularly is in Agitation. I must therefore Sacrifice My own private Interests to a publick Duty. The Moment F Lee or Mr. Smith arrive I quit this place I hope for ever.[2] Adieu, Jno. Harvie

[*P.S.*] I have sent Mrs. Harvie the two last papers.

RC (DLC).

[1] Not found.

[2] The Virginia delegates attending Congress with Harvie at this time were Cyrus Griffin and Richard Henry Lee. John Banister, a member of the Committee of Arrangement, which had left in mid-August to confer with Washington at White Plains, was probably on his return to Philadelphia at this time, for he was back in Congress the 22nd. He apparently left Congress almost at once, obtaining leave to return home on September 24. But since Meriwether Smith assumed his seat on September 28 and Francis Lightfoot Lee arrived on November 9, the Virginia delegation had no difficulty in maintaining their required quorum of three for the remainder of the year. *JCC*, 12:943–45, 948, 963, 1112.

Harvie's dates of attendance cannot be determined precisely, however, from the documents that are available. In his accounts with the Virginia treasurer sworn to May 28, 1779, he claimed compensation for "attendance in Congress from 1st Septr. 1777 till . . . the 10th Apl. 1778," and "from 1st June 1778 till the . . . 25th Octo'r." Continental Congress Papers, Vi. But it is clear from the journals that he did not take his seat originally until October 15, 1777, or for his second term until July 13, 1778. Clearly Harvie claimed expenses for considerable travel time in both instances. His departure in the spring of 1778 is also not clear, but because there is no record of his presence in Congress after March 18, it can be assumed that he returned to Virginia shortly after he cast the vote that is recorded in the journals on that date. He probably left Congress permanently on October 16, the day his last roll call vote is recorded, although he claimed travel time through the 25th. He is mentioned in surviving documents bearing dates of October 17 and 19, but these merely indicate that he had left papers pertaining to congressional business with fellow delegate Cyrus Griffin, who submitted them to the appropriate officials on those dates. *JCC*, 9:804, 10:267, 11:685, 12:1017, 1019, 1023n, 1025n.

Henry Laurens to John Lewis Gervais

My Dear Sir 15th September [1778]

I had the pleasure of writing to you the 10th Instant by Mr. Frisch, a chance opportunity, this will go by such another—a Mr. Whitney, his short notice, and the extreme long sittings of Congress afford me very few minutes for paying my respects to private friends.

Inclosed with this you will find a Character of Joshua Brown, said to be imprisoned in Ninety six Goal, I intreat you Sir, interest yourself as speedily as possible in this Mans case, and if it may be done without offence to the laws of the Land obtain his enlargement and supply him on my Account with such Money as may be needful to help his return to Philadelphia. I need say no more on this occasion, you will take every necessary step for relieving a Man from suffering, if it has been brought on him from mistake of his Person, Principles or Conduct.

The Subscribers to this Paper are all Quakers. There have been several little Addresses from these People to me which indicate a desire to be reconciled to the present ruling Powers—and one of a very extraordinary extent to Mr Gerard which the Minister detailed to me last night strengthens my belief—I have promised one of the principal Persons of the Society a meeting for conferring on subjects which we have barely sketch'd, I am to point the time, but when shall I have leisure?

There are now strong Prognostics of an evacuation of New York by the Enemy, none stronger in my Mind than the advance which these friends are making. They have always been in the Secrets of the opposite Party, having Emmisaries in each, and I am persuaded their Religious Principles will lead them to abide with the strongest, provided they may do so in Peace and free from persecution. The

Policy of America will be to retain them after Independence is established in the enjoyment of all their ancient priviledges.

The Newspapers which you will receive under this cover together with Extracts of Letters from General Washington, General Heath, General Sullivan and Colonel Laurens will inform you the present Intelligence. I have not time to comment—Lord Howe's leaving Boston Bay and appearing off Rhode Island is the only inexplicable Manouvre—a few days will clear up doubts.

I have long predicted what has happened at Bedford,[1] and I dread such a stroke every hour in this River, the Enemy's great policy is to ruin our navigation, and here have we been sitting near three Months, and nothing done to prevent four frigates from destroying every ship and other Vessel accumulated at the Wharves of this City and laying the Town in ashes or under contribution of Money or Members of Congress.

Be so good as to communicate the inclosed intelligence to His Excellency the President, the late President, and other friends and all of it that is proper to the Public.

My thoughts are to return to my own Country early in November, but I am staggered when Mr. Matthews tells me that he must absolutely go home in that Month—the remaining Representation will not be competent, for if one happens to be sick or absent, you will have no Vote.

Mr. Whitney calls and presses to be discharged. Present me as usual to all friends, and believe me to be, With the utmost Regard &c.

[*P.S.*] Mr. F. Kinlock lately from New York brought me a Message from Mr. R. Williams whom he left 5 days ago in that City—Mr. Williams, and several other late Inhabitants of So. Carolina and Georgia were attempting a Voyage to Charlestown under a Flag of Truce, tis probable therefore you will soon see them.

LB (ScHi).

1 On the previous day Congress had read an August 10 letter from Gen. John Sullivan to Washington describing a devastating British raid on New Bedford, Mass. See *JCC*, 12:913; and Sullivan, *Papers* (Hammond), 2:328–29.

Henry Laurens to Rawlins Lowndes

Dear Sir 15th September [1778]

I had the honor of addressing Your Excellency on the 10th Instant by Mr. Frisch, on that or the next day Congress framed a Resolve earnestly recommending to the Government of Maryland to take Measures for preventing infractions on the general Embargo, but yesterday we received repeated Intelligence of illicit exportation of

Provisions from that State; it appears to be an indubitable truth, that refraining on our part from Exportation of Provision would be a more sure means of driving the Enemy from our Coast, than all our troops. If we export freely the Enemy will be supported and our Army starved.

Colonel Gervais will do me the honor to communicate to your Excellency the contents of Intelligence which I have transmitted to him; I will not therefore be further troublesome but to repeat that I am, With the highest Respect &c.

LB (ScHi).

Henry Laurens to William Read

Dear Sir[1] 15th Septr. [1778]

I don't know where your favor of the 5th[2] has been detained, but it reached me no earlier than the present morning and unluckily half an hour too late for a conveyance to South Carolina of the letter to your Brother.[3]

Your returning health is a subject for congratulation. I hope the present temperate weather will confirm it in strength and vigor. When you have occasion for Money, draw on me without apology, and your Bills shall be honored, or, if it suits you better, I will transmit the sum necessary, by such hand as you shall direct.

The latest News from Charlestown is unpleasant, the shipping in the Harbour had suffered greatly in the late tempest which seems to have taken its course from the Gulph of Florida along Shore to Newfoundland, the Column was wide, since we find many Vessels were destroy'd by it an hundred leagues from the Coast—In Charlestown 'tis said about 20 Vessels were lost or had suffered great damage in the harbor—but this I apprehend will be trifling when compared with the loss of the Planters Crops of Indigo and Rice, of which I have not yet received accounts.

I have not receiv'd or seen a Letter for you since our departure, an Express Messenger from Charlestown has been some days due to me, I expect every day his appearance; depend upon it, Sir, if he imposts any dispatches for you, they shall be immediately forwarded, and now that I know where to address, you may expect to receive from me the Carolina Gazettes when such come to my hands. I am with great Regard &c.

LB (ScHi). Addressed: "Doctor William Read, General Hospital, Princetown, by Isaac Titsworth to be deliver'd Mr. Humphreys."

1 William Read (1754–1845) had been raised in Savannah, but most of his adult life was identified with South Carolina. His medical education had been in-

terrupted by the Revolution, and after studying under Benjamin Rush at the College of Philadelphia he had volunteered his medical services to the Continental Army shortly before the Battle of Monmouth. He subsequently became a deputy surgeon general, serving in the middle department until 1780 and in the southern department during the later campaigns. See Walter B. Edgar et al., eds., *Biographical Directory of the South Carolina House of Representatives* (Columbia: University of South Carolina Press, 1974–), 3:599–600.

2 Read's September 5 letter to Laurens is in the Laurens Papers, ScHi.

3 Jacob Read, whose letters of April 5 and July 16, 1778, to Laurens contain considerable information on William's career at this time. Laurens Papers, ScHi.

Francis Lewis to Thomas Johnson

Sir

Phila 15th Septmr. 1778

I wrote you a letter by the last Post covering one I received from Colo. Ayllet D.C.G. at Williamsburg with several affidavits inclosed relative to some transactions in the Court of Admiralty at Baltimore;[1] being then pressed in point of time, I am induced to believe that a Bill drawn by Messrs. Maxwell & Loyell of Suffolk Virginia on the Marine Committee in favor of Holt was inadvertently put up with the other inclosures, if so you'l favor me in returng it.

Various complaints have been lately made to Congress, purporting that some Traders at Baltimore are engrossing the flour & other provision, and shipping off the same in direct violation of the Embargo, which if not immediately remedy'd will tend to ruin our Armies & the Fleet of our Allies.

By the last advises from Boston, the British Fleet under Ld Howe, with part of Byron's Squadron appeared off that Harbour. By transient accounts received from New York it is conjectured that the British Troops are going to quit that City.

I have the honor to be Sir Your very Humble Servant,

Fra. Lewis

RC (MdAA).

1 See Committee of Commerce to Thomas Johnson, September 8, 1778.

William Henry Drayton to Henry Laurens

Dr. Sir.

Sep. 16. 1778

I cannot but frankly confess myself hurt at the manner & substance of your expressions to me, when I was in conversation with Mr. Adams upon the adjournment of Congress today: I should not have been hurt at either had you thought proper to have used them in private.[1]

As it is your right to make any representation on my conduct, that you may think proper to be made, it is not possible for me to be hurt at your exercise of it; especially as I know, any such representation could proceed only from your sense of your duty to the public, & that if you make it, you will think it proper to furnish me with a copy of it. In a word the intention of this note is only to desire, that to the many marks of your friendship which I have received & feel, you will be so obliging as to add this: That when you differ in opinion with me, & think my conduct deserving of your disapprobation, you will reserve the subject for a private hour. You know I always communicate to you, my ideas & intended conduct, & that I always receive your advice with defference & as marks of your regard. Being Dr. Sir, Your most obedt. & most humble Servt.

Wm. Hy. Drayton

RC (NN).

1 The "expressions" by Laurens that moved Drayton to write this letter remain unknown. For Laurens' prompt apology, see his letter of this date to Drayton. The frequently strained relationship between Drayton and Laurens during their service in Congress is analyzed in William M. Dabney, "Drayton and Laurens in the Continental Congress," *South Carolina Historical Magazine* 60 (1959): 74–82.

Samuel Holten's Diary

[September 16, 1778]

16. Wednesday. Congress Sit but half the day. I met a number of Gentlemen of Congress at evening at the City Tavern, on business.

MS (MDaAr).

Henry Laurens to William Henry Drayton

Dear Sir, [September 16? 1778][1]

I am not asham'd, & particularly to you to acknowledge a fault. The declaration you allude to was improper, on my p[art] as well in the m[anner] of address as in point of time. Chafed by the daily waste of the most precious moments of these Orphan States, I was into the bargain hurried into expressions which a designing Man would have avoided. Upon this confession I am sure you will forgive me & that you will not entertain a thought so injurious to me, as that I would make a representation in which your Name should appear without your privity. I have no Idea of making any which can glance the least dishonor on you as I shall explain when I have the honor of meeting you next which I wish may be in the course of the present day, but further pardon me for saying with equal candor that I lament your being engaged as you are, if I am in an error believe me all that I have said to you on the subject at different times has arisen from a very sincere regard for your Character in an extensive view. ⟨*I am not afraid to say to a Gentleman of your candor & good sense that you do not appear competent to the particular point.*⟩

FC (ScHi).

[1] This undated, unaddressed manuscript is doubtless Laurens' draft of his reply to William Henry Drayton's letter to him of this date, although it is possible that Laurens actually wrote it a day or two later.

Henry Laurens to George Washington

Sir 16th Septr. [1778]

I had the honor of addressing Your Excellency under the 12th Inst. by Dodd, and have in the mean time receiv'd & presented to Congress Your Excellency's favors of the 11th and 12th.[1] In answer to the latter, I am directed to intimate, "That Congress highly approve of laying up Magazines of forage and Provisions at such places as Your Excellency shall judge proper for prosecuting an Expedition into Canada in the Winter, if the motions of the Enemy shall render the measure expedient."[2] And Your Excellency is "desired to make every preparation of Cloathing, Snow Shoes, and other articles for this purpose which you shall deem necessary."

I have the honor to be &c.

LB (DNA: PCC, item 13).

[1] Laurens must be referring to the two official letters that Washington wrote to him on September 12 and that Congress read on the 14th and the 15th. See *JCC*, 12:913–14; PCC, item 152, 6:351–58; and Washington, *Writings* (Fitzpatrick), 12:434–38. There is no September 11 letter from Washington to Laurens in PCC or the Washington Papers, DLC.

[2] Congress approved this resolve this day after first having read and referred to the French minister Gérard a "plan for invading Canada," which had been enclosed with one of the September 12 letters from Washington cited above. See *JCC*, 12:914, 919.

Richard Henry Lee to Arthur Lee

My dear Brother, Philadela. 16th Septr. 1778

This will be delivered you by the Baron Arand who has served some time in our Army, and who now returns to France, with leave, on account of his health.[1] Your two letters of July the 3d. & March 2d. came to my hands two days ago. Where the latter has so long been, I do not know. I shall observe the caution contained in the former, and give Loudon[2] the same. I do not know that we have erred in this way upon any occasions of consequence. I must here repeat my former advice, not to use the book cypher you have hitherto done, unless where you have reason to suppose the Bearer of the letter will deliver it himself. It may be good against his curiosity, but not against that of many others who by Carmichaels treachery have got possession of the key to this mode of corresponding. You were not mistaken in the union you supposed would be formed here between Carmichael & {Deane}.[3] They go hand in hand & are closely allied in forming {faction}—Nor have they been unsuccessful in their wicked labors—But I trust, not in a manner to avail them much, or to {injure} you. The {scheme} is not yet completely opened, but before we part with {Deane}, we shall endeavor to get as much truth out, as will save the public from injury. I wish we had all the evidence on your side—But Mr. Stephenson is alone here,[4] and we must call for his evidence to fix Carmichaels charges against {Deane} when the former was at Nantes. The necessity of immediately appointing a {plenipotentiary} for our {ally} has occasioned a vote for the {Doctor},[5] and his credentials & instructions will soon be sent. In a few days the other {Courts} will be determined on—{You} and our {brother}[6] I think will not be {shaken}, but I assure you that envy, selfishness, and {Deane's} arts have created a strange spirit among many, and will require on your parts great wisdom and much {caution} in all your {conduct} and {correspondence}. The {Doctor} is as I always thought him, I am not in the least disappointed or informed by any thing {immoral}[7] that I hear of him. We do not know he has {written} any thing against {you} but I strongly {suspect} it from the conduct of some Men. However, virtue will prevail over vice in the end if tolerable prudence support the former. The {Doctor} is {old} and must soon be {called} to {account} for his {misdeeds}; therefore {bear} with him, if possible. In order to provide for {Deane} I suppose, it has been proposed to have a {consul} {general} in France, but this I think will never prevail. {One} in each {port} of consequence, and appointed by {Congress} the public good demands, and this will probably be done.

But {Deane's} pride nor avarice will let him in here. I wish our brother may succeed in either of his missions—I fear he will in neither until these Courts have taken decided parts with regard to their contemplated war. The arrival of Byrons Squadron has given the enemy superiority at Sea over our friends, but we hope it will not long continue so. The Count is at present refitting safely in Boston from his damage in the Storm where he will soon be ready. The English fleet has been off that harbor but are now off Rhode Island. The movements in New York denote an intention soon to abandon that place, I suppose to strengthen Canada, Hallifax & the West Indies. Our accounts are now very good that the enemy lost between 12 & 1500 killed & wounded in the late battle where they were defeated on Rhode Island. I pray you my dear brother not to keep Ludwell[8] a moment longer than it is convenient for you. A well grounded knowledge of eloquence, Civil & natural law will fit him for pursuing in Virginia the study of the laws of Engd. & his own Country. Besides, the justice I owe my other children will not allow very great partiality in expence on any one or two. Yet I would not withhold what may be necessary for good foundations. But my income is chiefly paper money, and that you know will not reimburse you in Europe or serve my Sons there. Can you contrive the contents of this letter to William, I know not whether to address him at Vienna or Berlin. The Bark you kindly sent me has been of great service to me, but I shall want more next year, therefore pray send me some, if possible, directly to Virginia. I shall be glad of any valuable new publications whether in France or England.

Not being forewarned at the time, and it being so long since Sim. Deane's arrival that I cannot recollect all the letters you sent me a list of—I did receive several by him, but I do not remember those for Owen or Pringle. I believe the rest came.

I sincerely wish you health, happiness & success. Adieu,

Richard Henry Lee

[*P.S.*] My best love to my boys, brother & sister. Remember me affectionately to Mr. Adams

RC (ViU).

1 Baron d'Arendt's August 21, 1778, letter to Richard Henry announcing his plan to return to France is in the Lee Family Papers, ViU. See also *JCC*, 11:808–9.

2 Francis Lightfoot Lee.

3 Words in braces here and below are in cipher in the RC. For discussion of the cipher used by the Lees, see Richard Henry Lee to Arthur Lee, May 12, 1778, note 2.

The "union you supposed would be formed here between Carmichael & Deane" was about to become a matter of concern to the Lees, for this day Congress resumed consideration of Silas Deane's request for clarification of his status and concluded by directing him to attend Congress on the 18th "to answer such questions as the house may propose to him, for the better understanding of the state and progress of public affairs during his mission in France." *JCC*, 12:908, 920, 927. But before Deane was permitted to appear, debate on his request was apparently reopened the morning of the 18th (Secretary Thomson's journal entry on this point has been lined out), and subsequently Congress was diverted by a report, submitted by Richard Henry Lee the same afternoon, that William Carmichael had knowledge of instances of Deane's "misapplication of public monies &c." Thereupon attention shifted to Carmichael's relations with Deane in France and allegations against Deane made by Arthur Lee growing out of reports he had received from two American merchants in France, John Lloyd of South Carolina and William Stevenson of Maryland. "I am confident in my opinion," Lloyd had reported in a January 24, 1778, letter to Lee, "that Mr. Carmichael is at present positively determined to expose upon his arrival in America, Mr. Deane's conduct as a Commissioner, in the fullest extent," a view repeated in a February 1 letter to Lee from Stevenson. The circumstances that frustrated the Lees at this time, however, was simply that Carmichael had patched up his relationship with Deane but had had a falling out with Arthur Lee before he had left France and was now reluctant to offer information against the former, although he had once so freely admitted to Lloyd and Stevenson that he was prepared to. The originals of their letters to Arthur Lee are located in the Lee Papers, MH–H; but the fact that copies of these and other related Lloyd and Stevenson letters can be found in the Laurens Papers, ScHi, Lee Papers, ViU, and Peter Force Collection, DLC, suggests that considerable significance was attached to their intelligence and that several delegates obtained access to it.

For the examination of Carmichael before Congress and the steps taken to compel his testimony, see Gouverneur Morris' Proposed Resolve on William Carmichael, September 18; and Charles Thomson's Notes on William Carmichael's Examination, September 28, 1778. For information on Carmichael, and an extended analysis of Richard Henry Lee's role in the entire Deane-Arthur Lee affair, see Floyd B. Streeter, "The Diplomatic Career of William Carmichael," *Maryland Historical Magazine* 8 (June 1913): 120–27; and Paul C. Bowers, "Richard Henry Lee and the Continental Congress, 1774–1779," (Ph.D. diss., Duke University, 1965), pp. 280–341.

4 William Stevenson, whose arrival in America in June had been reported by James Lovell in the Committee for Foreign Affairs' June 20, 1778, letter to Benjamin Franklin.

5 Benjamin Franklin.

6 William Lee.

7 Whether "immoral" or "immoderate" was intended must be conjectured.

8 Richard Henry's son Ludwell, whose education in France was being supervised by Arthur.

John Witherspoon to William Churchill Houston

Dr Sir Philadelphia Septr 16. 1778

Receive inclosed an Extract of the Minutes of Congress relating to the Representation from New Jersey.[1] We have not copied the Representation itself as You must have it—I believe there is not another State which has its Sense in its own Words on the Records of Congress the rest having generally had only Instructions to their Members. I have no News. It begins to be believed that the Enemy are to leave New York & it is thought to be with a view of going to the Westindies. The Arrival of the August Packet alone will make that definitively certain. My Complements to Mrs. Houston.

I am, Dr Sir you most obedt, humble Servant,

Jno Witherspoon

RC (PHC).

1 For Congress' rejection on June 25 of a representation from the New Jersey legislature proposing amendments to the Articles of Confederation, see *JCC*, 11:648–51. Houston was in Princeton attending a session of the New Jersey As-

sembly that had just received President Laurens' July 10 circular letter urging prompt ratification of the Articles. New Jersey Assembly Proceedings, September 14, 1778, DLC(ESR).

Jonathan Elmer to the New Jersey Council and Assembly

Gentlemn. Philada. 17th Septr. 1778

Sensible of the important trust reposed in me & the honour you have done me in appointing me one of your Delegates in Congress for two years past, I esteem it my duty to embrace every opportunity of returning you my sincere thanks therefor.

A willingness to comply with your requisition & an earnest desire to serve my Country as far as my slender abilities would enable me, were the sole motives that induced me to accept of the appointment. How far I have answered your expectations in executing the trust I willingly submit to your candour to determine. Permit me however to assure you that the public Interest & the good of my Country, particularly of the State which I have had the honour of representing, have constantly been the objects of my attention. I hope the integrity of my conduct at least, will meet with your approbation.

As the circumstances of my family & private affairs render it impracticable for me to attend Congress any longer I take this opportunity of acquainting the honourable Council & Assembly therewith & of soliciting leave to resign.[1]

I have the honour to be, Gentlemen, Your very Humble Servant,

Jonathn. Elmer

RC (PHC).

[1] The New Jersey Assembly read Elmer's letter on October 1 and referred it to a joint conference of the assembly and council, but there is no other reference to it in the journals of either house for 1778. New Jersey Assembly Proceedings, October 1, 1778, DLC(ESR).

Henry Laurens to John Laurens

My Dear Son 17th September [1778]

My last was under the 13th Instant, I am now to thank you for your several favors of the 10th, 12th and 12th Inst. Continue your intelligent correspondence by every opportunity I intreat you, and be as ample as circumstances will possibly admit of.

I shall upon every occasion pay particular attention to those brave Officers whose names you have specified. It mortifies me exceedingly to see a Gentleman of Mr. Ternant's merit held in suspense without ability on my part to afford him any aid—I can do no more than to ask him to a Dinner and entertain him civily.

Can you, my Dear Son, appologize for asking me to supply you with common necessaries? You know nothing affords me more pleasure than acting the part of your Friend.

The first proper person going to Camp shall be the Bearer of Money, and probably a Piece of Linnen. I presume you may get it converted into shirts with as much accuracy & expedition at Camp, as any where else.

If I had been where you were treated with so much hospitality I should have been invited to accept the same sort of kindness, although the Person knows I hold him extremely cheap because I have detected him in some mean, and even in some dishonest Acts,[1] therefore I am sorry it has happened that you are laid under any obligations, especially as I am told you are more indebted to the Creditors of the Person than to himself. This is a disagreeable subject, but you know I hate Imposters, and I believe there never was a greater—but dont misunderstand me, I never passed an angry word with the Man in my Life; my present sentiments are not new, they are grounded in observation and conviction.

Your friend F. Kinloch will probably salute you in Camp this day sinnight, another friend of yours R. Berresford is in New York.[2] I hope to obtain permission for his coming here in a few days, this indeed should have been done four days ago, but Mr. Kinloch had omitted till last evening to deliver me a message from Mr. Berresford.

Mr. Robert Williams, his son, and many other Carolina and Georgia Gentlemen are also in New York, among them Mr. J. Hopton—the Chief Justice assures me this young Gentlemen and my old friend R.W. will meet the people in Charlestown full of resentment against them.

Mr. H. Peronneau and his brother in law Mr Cooper are both at New Providence waiting, no doubt, for the moving of the Waters. How very kind Great Britain has been to her Votaries. How very unkind these devotees, to themselves and their families.

Sir E.L. Mr. Kinloch informs me is wretched, and he will relate to you the melancholly Catastrophe of the unfortunate M.B.

I again recommend to your serious Consideration the near approach of the 1st of November. I do not say that I shall leave Philadelphia immediately after its arrival, nor can I promise not to leave it on the 2nd. I have a duty to you, to your Brother, to your sisters, and some to myself which call loudly on me. My Country is like all other collective Bodies, extremely easy when they can get a Man to serve them diligently and faithfully, be the consequence to himself what it may, even Ruin.

God Bless, and keep you in health and safety.

P.S. Inclosed you will find 2 Letters from England, and a Newspaper.

LB (ScHi).

1 The letter from John Laurens mentioning this "person" has not been found, and he is not identified in the younger Laurens' September 24 reply to this letter. Simms, *Laurens Army Correspondence*, pp. 225–29.

2 See Laurens to Richard Beresford, September 19, 1778.

Henry Laurens to Baron Steuben

Dear Sir Philadelphia 17th September 1778

Notwithstanding my promise which was really grounded on determination to pay my respects to you the 14th this is the first moment I have been able to redeem for that purpose since my last of the 13th.

I think it fortunate to yourself that you did not proceed to Rhode Island, it would have been on every account a disagreeable embassy.[1]

The Commander in Chief having returned to Congress the report of the Committee on the Inspectorate with His Excellency's remarks & observations the whole is recommitted & will probably be soon reported on, but the House is so overcharged with business as renders it impossible even to guess at a time when it will be taken under consideration & concluded.[2]

My Man James having been sick for several days & no other person in my house knowing where to find your Servants, I can only hope that Mr. Peters & Mr. Melcher have done the needful, nevertheless I shall request Major Young while I am at Congress this Morning to make special enquiries & if there shall remain any room for my interposition, it will be immediately applied & you shall be further informed.

Nothing, I am extremely sorry to say it, is yet reported respecting Mr. Ternant. I am grieved to see this meritorious Officer kept in suspence.[3]

Be assured Dear Baron my inclinations are warm for rendering you every service in my Power, that I will embrace every opportunity of confirming this assurance, proving that I am with great truth, Dear Sir, Your most obedient, & Most humble Servant,

Henry Laurens.

RC (NHi).

1 Although Congress had requested Steuben on August 28 to join General Sullivan in Rhode Island, Washington had instructed him to disregard this request

and remain at his post as inspector general of the army. See *JCC,* 11:849; and John M. Palmer, *General von Steuben* (New Haven: Yale University Press, 1937), p. 197.

2 See Laurens' second letter to Washington of August 20, 1778, note 2.

3 On September 11 Congress had read a letter of the fifth from Steuben to Laurens recommending the appointment of Jean Baptiste Ternant as "Inspector of the Light Troops" with the rank of lieutenant colonel. As a result, Congress appointed Ternant a lieutenant colonel on September 25 and ordered him to serve as inspector of Continental troops in Georgia and South Carolina. See *JCC,* 12:904, 952; and PCC, item 164, fols. 146–48.

Medical Committee to Jonathan Potts

Sir Philadelphia 17th Sepr. 1778.

It appearing by the Returns that there are more Medicines on Hand in your Department than are necessary for the public Use, And it appearing also that by the Removal of the Army to the Eastern Department the Medicines and Stores of that Department are insufficient for the Troops and Sick here, You are therefore desired to furnish to the Orders of the Director General such Medicines and Stores as he may think proper for the Use of that Department, And also to consult with him and dispose of by public Sale or otherwise for the greatest public advantage such of the Medicines now in your Possession as may not be necessary for the Armies & Hospitals of the United States.[1]

I am Sir, Your humble Servant

Gouvr. Morris of the Medical Committee

RC (PHi). Written and signed by Gouverneur Morris. Addressed: "To Doctor Jonathan Potts, Deputy Director Genl., Middle Department."

1 Potts had written to the Medical Committee on September 3 to ask whether he should comply with a request for medical supplies from William Shippen, Jr., the director general of hospitals. PCC, item 143, fol. 63.

Henry Laurens to George Bryan

Sir 18th September [1778]

Mr. Jackson of Jamaica captured on his voyage from that Island bound for New York, where he was going to reside for the benefit of his health, and now a Prisoner of this State on Parole is desirous of going to South Carolina. I request you Sir, to enlarge his bounds and permit him to pass to that State. I will take proper means for holding him under such restrictions as that he shall be forthcoming if this State shall hereafter judge it necessary to demand his appearance.

Mr. Richard Beresford, a young Gentleman Native of South Carolina is now in New York and wishes to be permitted to pass to his own Country where he has a large Estate and where he means to become a Citizen. I pray you Sir, grant him a Permit to come to Philadelphia on his way to Carolina. I shall write to Governor Livingston in order to obtain from His Excellency permission for Mr. Beresford to pass thro' New Jersey.[1]

I have the honor to be &c.

LB (ScHi). Addressed: "The Honble George Bryan Esquire Vice President of Pennsylvania, Phila., by M[oses] Y[oung].

[1] Although no reply by Bryan to this letter has been found, he must have approved Laurens' request because on September 19 Laurens wrote to Richard Beresford and assured him that he could safely come to Philadelphia.

James Lovell to Horatio Gates

Dear Sir Sepr. 18th. 1778

Your Favor of the 11th brought by Col. Hazen was a Confirmation of my former good Opinion of our late Alliance. As I always make the best of every Misshap, I think we ought to conclude that the Events at Newport will prevent too much of our Independence being attributed to the Arrival of the allied Fleet on our Coasts.

It is reported here that War is declared in the West Indies by the French. The Print of Tomorrow will have the Accounts, if it is authentic. I own I wish we could have settled our Quarrel with Britain without a general War. Our Ally seems to see an Advantage in the Declaration, and therefore, for the present, I repose myself on the *old* Skill of France in such matters.

I have catched part of a Story that offends me much relative to some late Transactions between you and a former Officer of yours.[1] I will not, outright, condemn your Condescention, because I do not know critically all Circumstances. I readily conceive that you view [latent?] Springs as giving Dignity to the Tool. I am uneasy with you; and I am astonished that among your large Number of Pupils, many are not found to crush intended Insults, that might in its Consequences prove most fatal to the Public.

There must be a great Change of Men in a certain Assembly before you can fail of many Friends there; or, as much less probable Circumstance, you yourself must be reversed in Character.

I suppose you feel confirmed in your Winter's Opinion that New England would have the main Struggle of this Campaign. But, the Period for much Business is too far over. The Enemy are themselves greatly at a Loss what Orders they shall receive from Europe; and appear to me to be putting themselves into Posture for going off, which can easily be changed if the Will of the Ministry dictates it to them.

I will depend upon Col. Hazen to tell you what the Prints do not except so far as to my being Dear Sir, Your affectionate Friend & humb Sert, James Lovell

RC (NHi).

1 Lovell is probably referring to Gates' second duel with his former aide, Gen. James Wilkinson, on September 4 at Harrison, N.Y., which grew out of a confrontation between the two at the court-martial trial of Gen. Arthur St. Clair. After Wilkinson had fired three times and missed, while Gates did not defend himself, Gates sought to end their dispute with an exchange of written testimonials, but the effort failed to move Wilkinson and almost led to a third duel. For further information, see Paul David Nelson, *General Horatio Gates* (Baton Rouge: Louisiana State University Press, 1976), pp. 195–97.

Gouverneur Morris' Amendment to John Witherspoon's Motion

[September 18, 1778][1]

Amendment.[2]

Congress being informed by a Letter of Arthur Lee Esqr. Commissioner of the United States at the Court of Madrid & one of the Comm'rs of the said States at the Court of Versailles dated at Paris the 4 Day of April[3] last that the Papers left in France by the Honle. Silas Deane Esqr. late one of said Comm'rs at the Court of Versailles were not sufficient for the Purpose of setling the Accounts of public Monies received and expended in Europe. And being further informed by the said Silas Deane that the time between the Receipt of the Letter to recall him and his Embarkation was so short as to render it impossible to adjust the said Accounts which were from their Nature both various and extensive Wherefore he had left his Papers and Vouchers in the Hands of a Friend in France lest by Accidents of the Sea or Enemy they might have been destroyed. Resolved that the sd. Silas Deane be directed to lay before Congress the most accurate Accounts which the Materials now in his Possession will admit of, of all monies by him received or expended on Acct. of the united States of America.

MS (ScHi). In the hand of Gouverneur Morris, with insertions by Henry Laurens. Endorsed by Laurens: "Mr. G. Morris's Amendment (Mr. Duer's withdrawn 18 Sept) on Dr. Witherspoon's Motion respectg Mr D's accounts.

"Debated A.M. 18th adjrd.

"P.M. call'd for, interrupted by report on Carmichl & Mr Lee's information Ent'd Jour'l."

1 As President Laurens' endorsement indicates, this manuscript consists of an amendment that Gouverneur Morris offered this day to a motion originally intro-

duced by John Witherspoon on September 16, calling upon Silas Deane to appear before Congress to testify on "the state and progress of public affairs during his mission in France." *JCC*, 12:920–21. For the action taken by Richard Henry Lee on the afternoon of the 18th that diverted congressional attention from Witherspoon's motion and Morris' amendment, see the following document. The amendment Laurens mentions as having been withdrawn by William Duer has not been identified.

2 Inserted by Henry Laurens.

3 Arthur Lee's April 4, 1778, letter to the Committee for Foreign Affairs, in which he indirectly criticized both Deane and Benjamin Franklin for lax handling of public funds, is in Wharton, *Diplomatic Correspondence*, 2:536–37.

Gouverneur Morris' Proposed Resolve

[September 18? 1778][1]

A Paper was delivered from the honorable Richard Henry Lee Esqr. in the Words following viz. (insert it)[2] thereupon Resolved that William Carmichael Esqr. be directed to attend at the Bar of the House on Monday next to be examined on Oath touching the Charges ⟨*contained in the said Paper*⟩ exhibited against the honorable Silas Deane Esqr. for Mis Application of the Public Money for Misconduct in his public and private ⟨*Conduct*⟩ Character and for pursuing ⟨*an improper*⟩ a reprehensible System and Measures in his public Character—contained in the ⟨*Information exhibited by the Honble R. H. Lee to Congress*⟩ said Paper.[3]

MS (ScHi). In the hand of Gouverneur Morris.

1 Internal evidence and the fact that this manuscript is now part of President Laurens' private papers suggest that Morris offered this resolve in Congress on the 18th shortly after the delegates had read Richard Henry Lee's "Paper" dealing with William Carmichael's allegations against Silas Deane.

2 This "Paper" is printed in *JCC*, 12:927–28. The original is in the Peter Force Collection, DLC, and bears the following endorsement by Secretary Thomson: "Information given to the house by R. H. Lee Sept 18 1778." For Lee's interest in Carmichael's testimony, see Richard Henry Lee to Arthur Lee, September 16, 1778, note 3.

3 Although there is no mention of Morris' proposed resolve in the journals, on September 22 Congress approved a more moderate set of resolves that he drafted summoning William Carmichael to appear before the delegates to testify on the conduct of Silas Deane and the dissensions among the American commissioners in Paris. *JCC*, 12:941–42. See also Charles Thomson's Notes on William Carmichael's Examination, September 28, September 30, and October 5, 1778.

Robert Morris to John Hancock

My Dear Sir Philada. Septr. 18th. 1778

I heard with great Satisfaction of your joining, as a Volunteer, the army at Rhode Island and was sanguine in my hopes & expectations that Mars wou'd have been propitious and sent you home crowned with Laurels. The brave & virtuous know how to deserve Success, and altho they cannot command it when they please, yet the appointed hour will come when Merit must have its reward. It may be wise not to enquire into the causes that operated the failure of that expedition, but look forward & try to get rid of these troublesome Enemies, that teaze & harrass us from one end of the Continent to the other. I hope they will not dare, to undertake an Expedition against Boston, or if they do, my firm perswasion is that they will smart severely for it, but the situation of the British affairs in general is such, that I cannot help thinking they must quit the United States very soon, in order to take care of those territories they have some title to. I shall not venture to write You on any Political matters because I hope it will not be long before I see you here again in time to fill that Seat again which you so well grace. This will be delivered You by my Friend John Holker Esqr whom you are already acquainted with, but unless you have an intimacy you know not half his Virtues. I have had an opportunity of seeing & knowing a great deal of him and am convinced he is a Man of the *right sort* as such I recommend him and at the same time I must go a little further with you on his behalf, he goes to Boston to assist Count D'Estaing & may probably have occasion for very considerable Sums of Money. I must beg of You therefore if it becomes necessary to assist in accomodating him, I shall pay whatever bills he draws on me and if the Sums wanted are very large Congress will no doubt make him the needfull payments or advances towards the discharge of the Public debts in France, indeed they will be glad to make payment in this way and consequently you will see that yourself & Friends cannot Run any Risque in accomodating Mr Holker.[1]

I beg my Compliments to Mrs. Hancock in which Mrs. Morris joins & with the Warmest Wishes for your Felicity I remain, My Dear Sir, Your affectionate Friend & Obed Hble Servt,

Robt Morris

RC (CSmH). Addressed: "The Honble Major Genl. Jno Hancock Esqr, Boston."

1 Morris also wrote Jean Holker, "Agent to the Royal Marines of France," the following brief letter on September 19. "I find it impracticable to get in the accots. against the prizes in time to perfect the accounts as the officers employed by the Marine Committee have not Collected all the Petty charges, therefore you must accept the accot. Sales in their present form without all the charges thereon being ascertain'd, but I shall continue my applications untill they are obtained and then transmit you the Accounts compleated." Holker Papers, DLC.

Cornelius Harnett to Thomas Burke

Dear Sir Philadelphia 19 Sepr 1778

Your agreeable favour of the 22d August only came to my hands last night. Believe me when I assure you that I have heart-felt Satisfaction in finding Our Genl. Assembly have shewn a proper resentment at the unpresedented [trea]tment you met with at York Town.[1] They could not have given you a more Convincing proof of their Approbation of your Conduct in Congress; than by appointing [you] again in the very face of their ridiculous resolves, [to] represent them in that Body.

I have Consulted my Associates in regard to the time of returning home. Mr. Penn *seems* Content to remain, & Mr. Williams & myself have concluded to stay until the 1st December & to return immediately on your & Mr. [Hill's] Arrival. The appointment of Mr. Hill with yourself has given me great pleasure.

Our Assembly have been wise in determining [tha]t three of their Delegates shall always be present in Congress.[2] I only wish they had appointed Six, which would have made it more Convenient for the Gentlemen to Attend.

I send News Papers. As to the business of Congress, [it] goes on in the Old way, doing more in three hours at one [. . .], than they do at another in three days.

Nothing Interresting has happened at Head Quarters, The preparations making at New York seem to indicate the Enemys intention of removing from that City. Perhaps it may only be a feint.

You will be pleased to present my res[pectful] Compliments to Mrs. Burke & be assured that I am Dr Sir, Your affect. friend & Obedt [Sert.] Cornl Harnett

[*P.S.*] Mr. Allison was not so Obliging as to call upon me, or even to let me know where he lodged.

RC (NcU).

1 For a discussion of the North Carolina Assembly's approval of Thomas Burke's temporary withdrawal from Congress in April 1778, see Burke's Proposed Statement to Congress, April 13, 1778, note 1.

2 Although the North Carolina Assembly had resolved on August 12 that the state should be represented by three delegates in Congress, it also specified that any two of them could cast the state's vote in that body. See *N.C. State Records,* 13:467–68; and John Penn to Richard Caswell, July 15, 1778, note.

Henry Laurens to Richard Beresford

Dear Sir[1] 19th September [1778]

Mr. Kinloch but a few days ago informed me he had left you in New York, desirous of passing thence to this City.

I shall immediately lodge Letters in the hands of Brigadier General Maxwell and His Excellency Governor Livingston which will secure you against Arrest or Insult in the Journey thro' New Jersey[2]—when you cross Delaware and arrive in Philadelphia, do me the honor to call here, the North East corner of Chesnut and sixth Streets, where you will meet the further attention, of, Dear Sir, Your Obedient, and Most Humble Servant.

LB (ScHi). Addressed: "Richard Beresford, a Gentleman lately from London, New York."

[1] Richard Beresford (1755–1803), a South Carolina lawyer who had studied at the Middle Temple in London, served as a delegate to Congress, 1783–84. *Bio. Dir. Cong.*

[2] Not found.

Henry Laurens to John Laurens

My Dear Son 19th Septr. [1778]

My last was dated the 17th, this is intended to introduce to your acquaintance Monsr. Holker, or, in English, John Holker Esquire, a Man of Sense, and in all his deportment a Gentleman—he has lived in a reputable stile at the Court of France, and is treated here by Monsr. Girard with respectful attention. I need not say any thing more to secure to him your Civilities during his stay at Camp.

I pray God Bless and protect you.

LB (ScHi).

Henry Marchant to Robert Treat Paine

Dear Sir, Philadelphia Sepr. 19th. 1778

It is long since I had the Pleasure of your Favour of the 2d. of June. I had thought of pleading some Excuses for my Delay, but upon the whole, it is the shortest Way at least, to plead guilty and throw myself upon the Mercy of the Court.

I find there has been some Difference in Opinion upon the Resolution of Congress you refer to. The most prevailing I believe has been against Your Construction of it. Upon the present Instance however, I should readily concur in giving up the Contl. share to

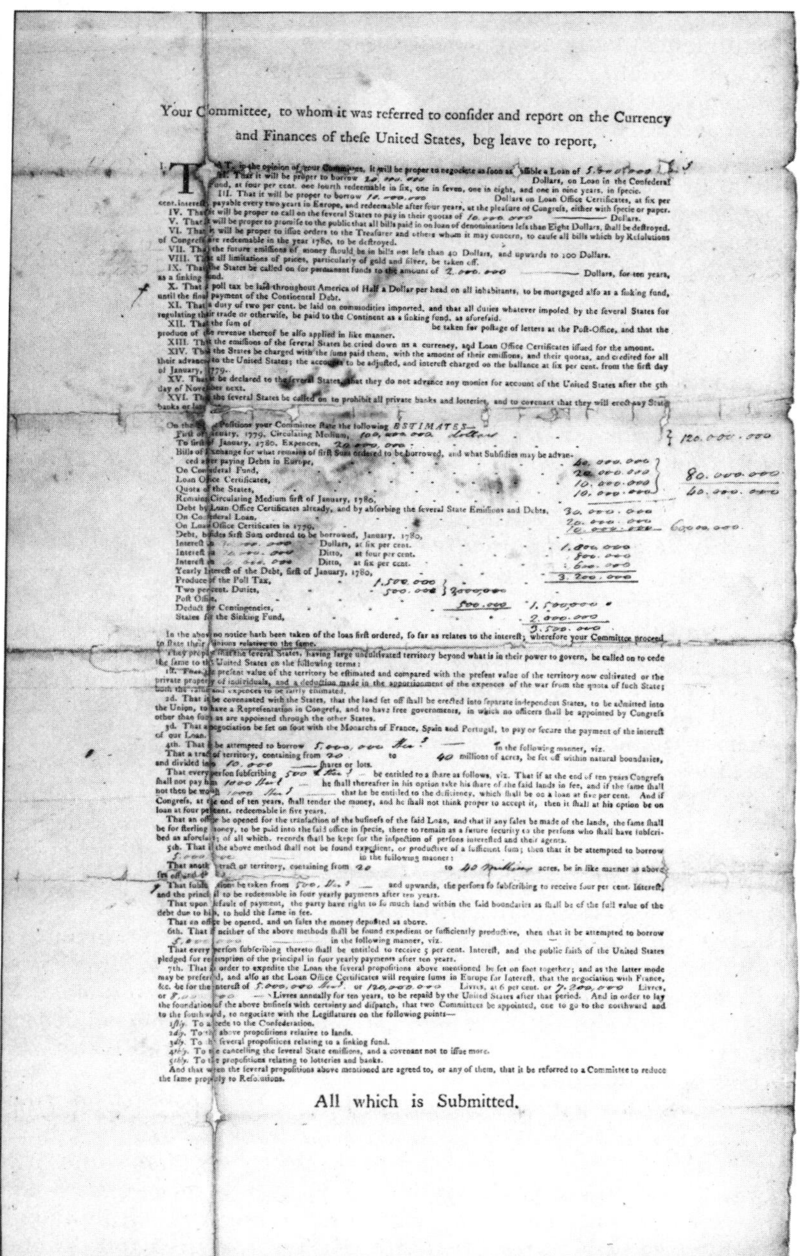

Your Committee, to whom it was referred to consider and report on the Currency and Finances of these United States, beg leave to report,

I. That, in the opinion of your Committee, it will be proper to negociate as soon as possible a Loan of 5.000.000 [illegible]

II. That it will be proper to borrow 20.000.000 Dollars, on Loan in the Confederal Fund, at four per cent. one fourth redeemable in six, one in seven, one in eight, and one in nine years, in specie.

III. That it will be proper to borrow 10.000.000 Dollars on Loan Office Certificates, at six per cent. interest, payable every two years in Europe, and redeemable after four years, at the pleasure of Congress, either with specie or paper.

IV. That it will be proper to call on the several States to pay in their quotas of 10.000.000 Dollars.

V. That it will be proper to promise to the public that all bills paid in on loan of denominations less than Eight Dollars, shall be destroyed.

VI. That it will be proper to issue orders to the Treasurer and others whom it may concern, to cause all bills which by Resolutions of Congress are redeemable in the year 1780, to be destroyed.

VII. That the future emissions of money should be in bills not less than 40 Dollars, and upwards to 100 Dollars.

VIII. That all limitations of prices, particularly of gold and silver, be taken off.

IX. That the States be called on for permanent funds to the amount of 2.000.000 Dollars, for ten years, as a sinking fund.

X. That a poll tax be laid throughout America of Half a Dollar per head on all inhabitants, to be mortgaged also as a sinking fund, until the final payment of the Continental Debt.

XI. That a duty of two per cent. be laid on commodities imported, and that all duties whatever imposed by the several States for regulating their trade or otherwise, be paid to the Continent as a sinking fund, as aforesaid.

XII. That the sum of be taken for postage of letters at the Post-Office, and that the produce of the revenue thereof be also applied in like manner.

XIII. That the emissions of the several States be cried down as a currency, and Loan Office Certificates issued for the amount.

XIV. That the States be charged with the sums paid them, with the amount of their emissions, and their quotas, and credited for all their advances to the United States; the accounts to be adjusted, and interest charged on the ballance at six per cent. from the first day of January, 1779.

XV. That it be declared to the several States, that they do not advance any monies for account of the United States after the 5th day of November next.

XVI. That the several States be called on to prohibit all private banks and lotteries, and to covenant that they will erect any State banks or [illegible]

On the [illegible] Positions your Committee state the following ESTIMATES—

First of January, 1779, Circulating Medium, 100.000.000 dollars			} 120.000.000
To first of January, 1780, Expences, 20.000.000			
Bills of Exchange for what remains of first Sum ordered to be borrowed, and what Subsidies may be advanced after paying Debts in Europe,	40.000.000		
On Confederal Fund,	20.000.000		80.000.000
Loan Office Certificates,	10.000.000		
Quota of the States,	10.000.000		
Remaining Circulating Medium first of January, 1780,			40.000.000
Debt by Loan Office Certificates already, and by absorbing the several State Emissions and Debts,	30.000.000		
On Confederal Loan,	20.000.000		
On Loan Office Certificates in 1779,	10.000.000		60.000.000
Debt, besides first Sum ordered to be borrowed, January, 1780,			
Interest on 30.000.000 Dollars, at six per cent.	1.800.000		
Interest on 20.000.000 Ditto, at four per cent.	800.000		
Interest on 10.000.000 Ditto, at six per cent.	600.000		
Yearly Interest of the Debt, first of January, 1780,	3.200.000		
Produce of the Poll Tax, 1.500.000 } 2000,000			
Two per cent. Duties, 500.000			
Post Office,			
Deduct for Contingencies, 500.000	1.500,000		
States for the Sinking Fund,	2.000.000		
	3.500.000		

In the above no notice hath been taken of the loan first ordered, so far as relates to the interest; wherefore your Committee proceed to state their opinions relative to the same.

They propose that the several States, having large uncultivated territory beyond what is in their power to govern, be called on to cede the same to the United States on the following terms:

1st. That the present value of the territory be estimated and compared with the present value of the territory now cultivated or the private property of individuals, and a deduction made in the apportionment of the expences of the war from the quota of such State; both the value and expences to be fairly estimated.

2d. That it be covenanted with the States, that the land set off shall be erected into separate independent States, to be admitted into the Union, to have a Representation in Congress, and to have free governments, in which no officers shall be appointed by Congress other than such as are appointed through the other States.

3d. That a negociation be set on foot with the Monarchs of France, Spain and Portugal, to pay or secure the payment of the interest of our Loan.

4th. That it be attempted to borrow 5.000,000 Ster.[illegible] in the following manner, viz.

That a tract of territory, containing from 20 to 40 millions of acres, be set off within natural boundaries, and divided into 10.000 shares or lots.

That every person subscribing 500 Ster.[illegible] be entitled to a share as follows, viz. That if at the end of ten years Congress shall not pay him 1000 Sterl — he shall thereafter in his option take his share of the said lands in fee, and if the same shall not then be worth 1000 Sterl — that he be entitled to the deficiency, which shall be on a loan at five per cent. And if Congress, at the end of ten years, shall tender the money, and he shall not think proper to accept it, then it shall at his option be on loan at four per cent. redeemable in five years.

That an office be opened for the transaction of the business of the said Loan, and that if any sales be made of the lands, the same shall be for sterling money, to be paid into the said office in specie, there to remain as a future security to the persons who shall have subscribed as aforesaid; of all which, records shall be kept for the inspection of persons interested and their agents.

5th. That if the above method shall not be found expedient, or productive of a sufficient sum; then that it be attempted to borrow 5.000.000 in the following manner:

That another tract or territory, containing from 20 to 40 Millions acres, be in like manner as above set off and [illegible]

That subscriptions be taken from 500. Ster.[illegible] and upwards, the persons so subscribing to receive four per cent. Interest, and the principal to be redeemable in four yearly payments after ten years.

That upon default of payment, the party have right to so much land within the said boundaries as shall be of the full value of the debt due to him, to hold the same in fee.

That an office be opened, and on sales the money deposited as above.

6th. That if neither of the above methods shall be found expedient or sufficiently productive, then that it be attempted to borrow 5.000.000 in the following manner, viz.

That every person subscribing thereto shall be entitled to receive 5 per cent. Interest, and the public faith of the United States pledged for redemption of the principal in four yearly payments after ten years.

7th. That in order to expedite the Loan the several propositions above mentioned be set on foot together; and as the latter mode may be preferred, and also as the Loan Office Certificates will require sums in Europe for Interest, that the negociation with France, &c. be for the interest of 5.000,000 Sterl. or 120,000.000 Livres, at 6 per cent. or 7.200,000 Livres, or 8.[illegible] Livres annually for ten years, to be repaid by the United States after that period. And in order to lay the foundation of the above business with certainty and dispatch, that two Committees be appointed, one to go to the northward and to the southward, to negociate with the Legislatures on the following points—

1stly. To accede to the Confederation.

2dly. To the above propositions relative to lands.

3dly. To the several propositions relating to a sinking fund.

4thly. To the cancelling the several State emissions, and a covenant not to issue more.

5thly. To the propositions relating to lotteries and banks.

And that when the several propositions above mentioned are agreed to, or any of them, that it be referred to a Committee to reduce the same properly to Resolutions.

All which is Submitted.

Finance Report, September 19, 1778

the Merits of the Captors; I cannot presume however what will be the Sentiments of the Court, or of Congress. Not knowing whether the Resolution of Congress respecting the allowance to be made the Court appointed to inquire into the Causes of the failure of the Expedition against Rhode Island was ever transmitted to you, I enclose it to you[1]—By which it appears we are referred to the Dep Paymaster Genl. in the Eastern Department. I mean to exhibit my Account for my Services only, noting that I have already recd. my Expences. And I mean to charge the same per Day as was allowed me by the State at that Time as a Delegate in Congress, viz five Dollars. I have also sent a like Copy to Mr. Ellsworth. He is expected here in a few Days. Nor are we without Hopes of seeing You this Fall.

Before this I dare say you have heard of the Fate of Stateing Bills, or Regulations of Prices. They all fell to the Ground—Thus you may see the Weight & Influence of Monopolizers & Extortioners. The Necessity of such Acts I early foresaw, and also the present Consequences from the non-complyance with Them. But some great State Pollliticians will spin their Thread till it breaks. Had those Acts been carried into Execution—Millions would have saved—The Credit of the Money mainly supported, at least as far as further Emissions have tended to sink it.

I entirely agree with you Sir, that we have had & still have more to fear from the Decay of publick & private Virtue, than from the Arms of Britain, With any possible Aids she might procure. This is an Evil that not only Congress, but every Legislature, ought immediately with Might & Main to pay their Attention to.

America would have had Peace before this Day had she deserved it; and I wish to God she was as ready for the Blessing, as Heaven is to grant it. It is to Miracles we are to ascribe Our present Situation—But appearances which strike with Wonder and astonishment all Europe, are scarcely noticed by two many amongst ourselves. They Expect that Congress and Washington, have some magick Wand, to raise, feed & cloath Armies with.

However that be, tis certain, that Thousands of vile Extortioners and devilish monopolizers rise up with more magick Acts & Spells to counteract every Attempt to give Strength and Vigour to our Arms and Accomplish the Blessings of Peace, Liberty and Independence. To such Men as those, Tories are virtuous Men, and Britons & Hessians less unnatural.

I lament Sir the Failure of the Expedition agt. Rhode Island. I rejoice however that the Arms of America far from being sullied, have reaped Glory & Honor in the Attempt. I resolve the Misfortune into the just Providence of God. Again I say Heaven knows we were not under proper Habits and Temper of Mind to receive the fulfillment of the Blessings, which yet I trust are reserved for this Land. I hope Time & Reflection will put the most candid construction upon the

Conduct of the Count De Staing. We may not Doubt of His Honor & Integrity—much less of the strongest Assurances we have of the Friendship of his Royal Master. I have not Room to add, unless I tire you with a new Sheet. I am Dear Sir, your Friend & Servant,

Hy. Marchant

RC (MHi).

[1] Marchant and Paine were among the five commissioners appointed by Congress on December 11, 1777, to investigate the failure of a proposed Rhode Island expedition in September 1777. *JCC,* 9:1018–20. For Congress' March 27, 1778, resolve on their compensation, see *JCC,* 10:290.

Gouverneur Morris to the Earl of Carlisle

[September 19, 1778]

To his Excellency the Earl of CARLISLE.

MY LORD,

THROUGH the medium of a news-paper, I see a declaration and requisition, signed by yourself and your brethren Clinton and Eden, together with an apologetic Epistle from Governor Johnstone.[1] As these papers are transmitted by *your* Secretary, and reflect light upon each other, your Lordship will excuse a few animadversions on them addressed to *you.* My intention is, to undeceive you in some matters you seem to have mistaken, and to state the true ground on which you stand with respect to America.[2] This I attempt from a sincere desire of peace; considering it as a blessing, the loss of which can never be compensated by the splendors of victory.

Your first error, a leading one, which hath tinged the complexion of all your national acts since the early commencement of the controversy, is a supposition that Congress do not speak the sense of the people of America. Of all the people they do *not,* but of a considerable majority they certainly *do.* Considerable for the numbers, property, principles, temper and character of those who compose it.

The number, according to my best estimation, is at least two-thirds of the whole; and the remaining third are of very little political consideration. They consist of a few who adhere to you from principle, a few more from interest, and a very few (now) from fear, as Indians worship the Devil. The remainder are attached to *no* side, unless indeed they could discover with absolute certainty which is the *strongest* side, being, as they term it *moderate men.* Add to this, that your American friends, from their religious notions and other circumstances, are generally averse to war.

The majority are further considerable from their property. It is by no means a figurative expression to say that the land of America is against you. This may seem extraordinary after what you have heard, especially if you have had the *honor* of a conversation with some of those traders who have lately, taken it into their heads to call themselves the *Gentlemen* of America. But if your Lordship will condescend to enquire for the ten greatest landholders of the state of New-York on the whig side of the question, you will find that no forty tories throughout the whole Continent have an equal property; considered as to the extent, the fertility, or the value in coin.

The principles of your opponents are republican, some indeed aristocratic; the greater part democratic, but all opposed to Kings, from a thorough conviction by reason, by history, and above both by experience, that nine times in ten they are the scourges of mankind.[3]

The temper of this majority is not only vigilant and irascible, but much roused and exasperated. Exasperated by the injustice, the treachery, the cruelty of Great-Britain. Respect, my Lord, for your feelings forbids that odious detail which justifies these charges.[4] Should you doubt, ask Sir Henry. Ask the officers in your regiments and on board your ships. Let them paint the violations, the burnings, the massacres, the starvings they have been witness to. And if this evidence is insufficient, invocable the manes of those wretches who died at Philadelphia in the paroxisms of madness and despair, from reflecting on the horrors they themselves had executed.[5]

Lastly, the character of those who compose the majority in America is of no small importance. Many of them are the most respectable members of the community; others again are distinguished by superior talents; and a great number are of that aspiring cast who look on high, and will neither be thrown out in pursuit of their favourite objects, nor dropped into insignificancy. To these things, I add the perseverance of the lower class in a cause which they think, with me, is just and righteous. At the Valley-Forge I was an eye witness to the sufferings of our soldiery: Many of them lay literally on the earth naked without fire and without food. It is to their honor that they did not mutiny; that they did not desert; that they did not even complain. The sentiment expressed by these brave citizens was, "We know every measure is taken to relieve our wants, and if we are distressed, it is because distress is unavoidable." Of such a majority, my Lord, the sense is spoken by Congress. To convince you of it, look at their publications; see how frequently, how fully, how directly they appeal to the people. Can you lay your finger on any falsehood sanctioned by their authority? Have they ever descended to meanness or artifice to cajole or to deceive their constituents or even their enemies? I know that your Gazetteers have charged all these things upon them; but, my Lord, I can hardly suppose that you was sent hither to read or to write news-papers.[6]

A second error which hath affected your national conduct, is an opinion that Congress lead the people. The direct contrary is so much a fact, that the business of Congress is, in a great measure, to discover the sentiment of the people and clothe it in words. Whenever any step is to be taken, they ask, what is the opinion of the people? For should they go beyond the ground on which they are supported by popular favour, that instant their power is at an end. To prove this further, I ask if the people have ever refused obedience to the matters proposed by Congress? Have the accumulated distresses of the present war, distresses almost beyond example, prevailed on them to desert their Congress? Nay, have all your efforts impaired the credit of our continental money, resting, as it did, merely on the public opinion and confidence in Congress?

An error of another kind appears in the papers now before me. From them it is manifest that you really misinterpret the language, and mistake the meaning of Congress. You seem to suppose, that when they declared it *incompatible with their honor to hold intercourse with George Johnstone, especially to negociate with him upon affairs in which the cause of liberty and virtue is interested,* they indirectly receded from their determination to have nothing to say to any of you till you sent away your fleets and armies, or acknowledged the Independence of America.[7] It is a maxim, my Lord, that a positive act cannot be repealed by implication. The plain language of the resolution, therefore, is this, "Perhaps the British Commissioners may have collateral matters to urge, such as the exchange of prisoners, &c. If he who hath insolently tendered bribes to us should join in any application of this sort,[8] we cannot listen to it. Let us therefore give our enemies a timely notice, that they may square their conduct accordingly. Let us not leave them the shadow of a reason to charge us with any disingenuous procedure."

From the best information, I take on me to assure your Lordship, that not the remotest idea was entertained of departing from their resolutions. The candour which dictated this last determination, is entitled to a very different language from what it hath met with. But since the conduct of Congress is stigmatized with the charge of duplicity, it may not be improper to shew the entire consistency of that Body, notwithstanding the many changes it hath undergone of the individuals. This will corroborate my former position, that they are simply the mouth of a people steadily attached to, and determined to support their rights and liberties.

The declaration of Independence will form a principal part of the present question. But, though much hath been, and much more may be speculated on the right of a people to become independent, it will perhaps ultimately turn on their power. You yourselves tender to Congress every thing they may ask short of a total separation of interests: Therefore, you offer to confine the union simply to the person of the Prince. Supposing it accepted, then without enquiring whether Americans might afterwards choose a King for themselves, clearly the English might, or else as clearly their now King is an usurper. If the people of Britain should exercise this right, then America continuing under her old King, would be independent. But a contract which one party can break, and the other cannot, is void; and therefore America could of right break the bargain as well as Great Britain; and therefore either party might at pleasure be independent of the other. And if America could of right declare herself independent after the agreement, certainly she could before. But further; from your own shewing, we are not subjects of the Parliament: If subjects therefore, we are subjects of the King. Again, it is agreed that if we do not like a King, we can send him away and take another in his stead, for our fathers did so before us. Therefore, as the greater contains within it the lesser, so we could do just one half of the proposition, viz. get rid of one King without getting another; and this is precisely what we have done. Take it lastly as a question of force, and then we fight to determine the moot point of which side are rebels. So much for the right to Independence.

In the commencement of this controversy, Congress prayed to be placed in the situation of sixty-three. This was practicable at that time, for nothing more was necessary than on your part to repeal the impolitic acts you had passed. You refused; they pressed it earnestly. For tho' the situation of sixty three was not very eligible, yet, as the event of war was uncertain, and the costs and the miseries but too certain, it was prudent and right to urge this request. Still you refused and appealed to the sword, and prosecuted and persecuted us to obtain what you now acknowledge you had no right to ask. Thus then were we plunged into a war against our inclinations, and of consequence could not be bound by any offer made with a view to avoid it. Besides, the situation of sixty three was no longer attainable: For, though the paper acts of your Parliament could have been repealed, yet the bloody acts of your soldiery could not. You could not pour back into the veins of our citizens the blood you had wantonly spilt. Previous to the year sixty three, points which should always have remained in oblivion, had never been started. But the question of supremacy once made in the rude language of arms, a decided line of authority and subjection became necessary to a future union. Desirous of avoiding the further calamities of war, we intreated you to pursue the measures necessary for reconciliation. This you refused, pertinaciously adhering to your first postulatum of *unconditional submission,* and with a view to the great object of *solid revenue.* You therefore urged the war, and applied to every little Prince in Europe for troops: We deprecated it, and did not even seek an alliance with any foreign power, knowing well that such alliance would close the door of reconciliation forever with all the bars of national faith and honor.

The situation of America was at length such by your obstinacy, that the evils Congress laboured to avoid were to become certain. At the same time it was a decided fact, that the interests of England and of America were directly opposed to each other. It was your interest to restrict our commerce, and it was our interest to extend it: It was your interest to take our money, and it was our interest to keep it. In a word, it was your interest to tyrannize, and it was our interest to be free. We therefore could not trust you, and you would not trust us. The King and his Ministers no body would trust. So that a re-union became every day more problematical.

The great fleets and armies you had employed, and the pains you had taken to deprive us of all military stores, obliged us to seek foreign aid, and it was clear that no Prince would assist us while we acknowledged ourselves to be rebels. Thus it was certain that we should experience the horrors of war, notwithstanding we had offered a part of our rights to avoid them. It was highly probable that without help we should be conquered. The object of reconciliation was distant and precarious at best, and by no means worth the blood and treasure necessary to attain it; and therefore, the people of America, through their Congress, declared themselves free and independent, as the only mode left to obtain their great end of peace, liberty and safety.

The war continued, and success seemed to be yours. Swoln with the hopes of conquest, you disclaimed every thing which looked like concession. At length the fate of the brave unfortunate Burgoyne recalled you to your senses: You sent to Congress the draft of your conciliatory bills. They, at that time, knew nothing of what their Commissioners had done in Europe. They saw, however, that your concessions proceeded from weakness, and were dictated by necessity. They knew your insincerity, and therefore wisely determined to have nothing to say to you till you acknowledged our independence, or withdrew your forces. Between this period and your Lordship's arrival, Congress received a copy of the treaties with his Most Christian Majesty. In answer to your letters therefore, they informed you, that after you had complied with the alternative just now mentioned, they would consent to a treaty with your Prince, not inconsistent with those already entered into. At length a war hath broken out between your sovereign and France, which, if I am rightly informed, will again alter the situation of affairs as far as they relate to negociation. From this detail your Lordship will perceive that the most perfect consistency hath been maintained on our part. We have acted from a conviction of your force and your violence, of your weakness and your insincerity.[9]

I come now to a matter of some delicacy, which I shall nevertheless, treat with freedom, and hope your Lordship's pardon for the unpolished terms of a republican. In your declaration you state a series of facts (as you call your assertions) to shew the insincerity of France. My Lord, you are deceived, or you mean to deceive; for the assertions you make are not founded in truth. Not only so, but you grossly mistake our disposition; for were every thing you say admitted, it would not produce the effect you wish for. You say, it is well known to the whole Continent of America, that public intimation of the conciliatory propositions was given in November last—Permit me to undeceive your Lordship. The direct contrary of what you say is perfectly well known to the people of America; and further, they know your Ministers breathed nothing but conquest and war at that period. You say, it is equally well known that the preliminaries of a French treaty, sent by Mr. Simeon Deane, did not bear date earlier than the sixteenth of December. The people of America do not enquire into such trifling circumstances. It is very immaterial to us when Mr. Simeon Deane went to sea, or why he put back, or when he came out again: If these things had been of consequence, we know that[10] Congress would have published them. One thing, however, is very clear to *me,* that you know not when those preliminaries, as you call them, were dated, nor indeed any thing about them. Let me ask one question: Are you certain, my Lord, that when Mr. Simeon Deane first sailed he had any papers whatever with him? You suppose that difficulties arose in the negotiation with France, for want of power in the American Commissioners. No such thing, my Lord; they had powers as ample as they could wish. Our Congress know better than to send their servants on a fool's errand. Perhaps your Lordship may find it convenient to recommend their example by the old adage of *fas est et ab hoste doceri.*[11] You roundly assert, that the conciliatory propositions were a subject of discussion in all the debates upon the state of the nation from the twentieth of January. Those your Lordship will revise, and correct that sentence, before the next edition of your declaration. A reputation for veracity may be of service to you at some time or other. You assert also, that no treaties were sent from France before the eight of March: Your Lordship's intelligence is not to be depended on. From better evidence I assure you, that dispatches containing the treaties were sent by the way of Corunna much earlier. The gentleman who brought them left Paris immediately on conclusion of the treaty, which by the bye is not antidated.

I have said above, that the affair of Saratoga determined your conduct; I mean, my Lord, that it opened the scene of American politics at St. James's, at Versailles, through-out all Europe. You have laboured to prove that France did not act from motives of Generosity but of interest. You have failed; but I will admit the conclusion, though I deny the premises; and then I add, that if she had consulted any thing besides her interest, America would by no means have been pleased with the alliance. The generosity of statesmen, my Lord, is but another name for caprice, and we wish no connection with the capricious. It is the interest of France to be allied to America; it is the interest of America to be allied to France. The rulers of the two nations see their interest and pursue it. What more can be desired? Did you expect, when you told the Congress a long story about reviving free intercourse and mutual affection, with other the airy forms, ideal nothings, to which you had given a local habitation and a name; did you suppose them such coxcombs as to pay the least attention[12] unless, at the same time, you could convince them it was their interest? No, you did not. Your conduct shews you did not. Unfortunately you applied to the private interest of the Members, instead of the general interests of their constituents. We wish to be at peace with all the world, and therefore we will make peace with you *when you are properly authorized to speak,* and have proper terms to offer. In the mean time, if you like fighting better, why we will fight with you.

My Lord, you are come hither for the very modest purpose of persuading a free and independent nation to surrender their rights and privileges: You are confessedly incompetent to the business of subduing them and are therefore to proceed by what you call reasoning. Now, as public addresses are not always the most clear and intelligible compositions, in order to simplify the matter, I will suppose you in conference with such an honest farmer as myself: You ask me *to become a subject of the King of Great Britain;* and what shall I get by that? *Security of your person and property.* My person and property are secure already. *He will make laws for you and govern you.* I had much rather make laws for myself and govern myself. *But he will regulate your trade.* Pray what is that? *Why he will tell you where your ships* SHALL *go, and where they shall* NOT *go, and what they* SHALL *carry, and what they shall* NOT *carry.* But I had rather our merchants should send their ships where and with what cargoes they please; I fancy they know as much of trade as your King, and how to get the best prices and the cheapest goods. *Aye, aye, but this is for the sake of a union of force, and for the interests of the whole British empire.* My good friend, the force of America is already united, and I have nothing to do with the British empire. *Yes, you have; for unless you comply with these terms, the King of England will conquer you.* I do not think he is able. *He will try however; and therefore, if you do not instantly submit your person and property to his disposal, you are answerable to Heaven for all the miseries of the war he shall carry on for that purpose.* I do not believe a syllable of the matter. I wish your King would mind his own affairs, and not trouble other people. But if he will send armies hither to fight, we must e'en fight. And so I wish your Lordship a good morning. I am, my Lord, with the most profound veneration, Your Lordships most obedient, and most humble servant,

AN AMERICAN[13]

Reprinted from the *Pennsylvania Packet, and Daily Advertiser,* September 19, 1778. FC (NNC). In the hand of Gouverneur Morris. Significant variations between the draft and the printed text are noted below.

1 Morris is referring to the August 26 declarations by George Johnstone and by the earl of Carlisle, Sir Henry Clinton, and William Eden, for which see Henry Laurens to George Washington, August 29, 1778, note 2.

2 At this point in the draft Morris first wrote and then deleted: "and according to the narrow Compass of my slender Abilities and Information to point out the means of restoring Peace and Harmony to the British Empire. These Endeavours flow from a sincere Desire of Peace. It is a Blessing at all Times & the Loss of it is not to be compensated by the Splendors of Victory. To the Weak it is necessary, to the strong useful and highly estimable to the humane."

3 At this point Morris first wrote and then deleted: "and that for one Trajan or Lewis the sixteenth there are twenty Neroes and Georges."

4 Morris first wrote and then deleted: "against a Country which from the philosophic Mildness of your Brother Eden I believe it pains him to be Member of."

5 At the end of this sentence in the newspaper text, there is an asterisk to which the following printer's note is keyed: "For the use of persons at a distance, it may be necessary to state the facts above alluded to. Some of the British, who had been concerned in butchering a few Americans they had surprized, became melancholy, and afterwards mad. One of them died exclaiming here we are; which was the watch-word on that cruel occasion."

6 Morris first wrote "Open your Eyes, be candid, it is of Importance to those you represent" and then altered it to read as above.

7 Morris first wrote and then deleted: "And further that they said by Implication they were willing to negotiate about such Affairs with the Rest of the Commissioners if he would be put out of the Way."

8 Morris first wrote "and especially to negotiate on any such Affairs in which eventually the Cause of Liberty and Virtue is concerned" and then replaced it with the ending printed above.

9 Morris first wrote and then deleted: "It may be of Use to you to resolve these Things in your Mind & thence to learn that Respect for your Enemies which is always of Advantage to a Negotiator."

10 In the draft the rest of this sentence originally read: "our Servants the Congress would have published them for they know the Citizens of America have a Right to judge for themselves."

11 "It is permissible to learn from an enemy."

12 At this point in the draft Morris originally wrote: "We know it is our Interest to be at Peace with you and that it is your Interest to be at Peace with us."

13 For a discussion of the series of newspaper letters that Morris wrote to the British peace commissioners using the pseudonym "An American," see Morris to the Carlisle Commissioners, June 20, 1778, note 1.

Josiah Bartlett to Mary Bartlett

My Dear Philadelphia Septr 20th 1778

Since my last I Received yours of the 28th of August and have the pleasure to hear you were all in pretty good health and that my farming Business goes on well. I thank you for informing me about it & what Crops there is like to be of the Several fruits of the Ground. I have wrote to Mr Whipple & Folsom[1] & Requested them to be here by the first of Novembr & have informed them and the President of the State, that I Cannot tarry after the first of Novembr, hope they will be here seasonably that I may Return before the Cold weather will render the travelling Difficult. Mr Wentworth has got home I hope before this time. Charles Chace is well, and I am Comfortable tho lately something troubled with my usual Headack. Remember my Love to all my Children and inform Miriam I have Receivd her letter of the 28th ulto. and that I Dont Expect to come home Early Enough to Innoculate her this fall, So that She must Content her Self to wait till Spring if She Depends on my Doing it.

News here is very uncertain, one Story is told to Day & another to-morrow, Deserters are almost Daily Coming from New York but their accounts Differ, what is Generally believed, is that the Enemy are about to leave New York but for what other place is uncertain.

By accounts from the west Indies (which is believed) we are informed that war was proclaimed by france against England the 8th of July in Europe, & the 15th of August in the west Indies.

Septr 22nd. I have Recd yours of the 3d Instant with one inclosed to Mr Wentworth which I Shall Send back to him. I wrote you in my last to Engage David Sanborn till my Return if you think it for the best. By the leave of Providence I Shall Set out for home the Begining of November, & Soonner I Cannot; hope to be at Home by the 20th of that month. Tell Peter from me, if he Behaves well I will Remember & fulfill my promise to him, if he misbehaves himself he Knows what he is to Depend upon. I Believe I have mentioned in one of my letters that it will not be worth your while to write to me after about the middle of October as it is not probable I Shall tarry here long Enough to Receve them. I want much to be at home & See you & my family & take Care of my affairs, but the time is hastning along and will Soon bring us (by Divine permission) to the wished for period, when I Shall Return to my own house & I hope find you all well. I am yours

Josiah Bartlett

[*P.S.*] Please to inform Mr Thurston & Major Philbrick that I have Recd a letter from Each of them[2] but have not time at present to write to them nor any thing material to Communicate to them.

RC (NhHi).

1 See Bartlett to William Whipple, September 12, 1778. Bartlett's letter to Nathaniel Folsom has not been found.

2 These letters—from Samuel Philbrick, August 26, and Benjamin Thurston, August 28, 1778—are in Bartlett, *Papers* (Mevers), pp. 214–18.

Henry Laurens to Ebenezer Hancock

Sir 20th Septr. [1778]

I do not find that I have troubled you with a Letter since the 28 January last,[1] nor does it appear by the Secretary's list that Congress have received any from you since that date.

The present Cover will convey to you an Act of Congress of the 17th Instant for remitting to Mr. Stelle, Deputy Paymaster at Rhode Island five hundred thousand Dollars and for making you accountable for that sum.

There will accompany the abovementioned Act another of the same date for obliging Commanding Officers of Regiments, Regimental Paymasters, and Officers commanding Companies to account for Monies drawn for and received and not applied, agreeable to the Resolves of Congress the 6th February 1778.[2]

I am With great Respect &c.

LB (DNA: PCC, item 13). Addressed: "Ebenezer Hancock Esquire Dep. Paymr. Genl. Eastern District, Boston."

1 Laurens' last letter to Hancock was actually written on January 21, 1778. See these *Letters,* 8:637n.2.

2 For the two "Acts" enclosed by Laurens, see *JCC,* 12:924–25. Laurens also transmitted copies of the second of these with brief covering letters that he wrote on September 22 to Paymaster General William Palfrey and to the auditors of accounts for Washington's army and for the eastern military department. PCC, item 13, 2:84–85.

Henry Laurens to George Washington

Sir 20th September [1778]

I write to Your Excellency the 16th by Titsworth. The present is to inclose an Act of Congress of the 17th for marching Pulaski's Legion to Trenton, there to receive Your Excellency's Orders.[1]

I have the honor to be &c.

LB (DNA: PCC, item 13).

1 See *JCC,* 12:922. Congress was prompted to pass this resolve by a September 12 letter from Washington asking that "all the Confederal troops" at Philadelphia be sent to join him and by a September 17 letter from Casimir Pulaski complaining of the lack of an assignment for his legion, which was stationed near that city. See Washington, *Writings* (Fitzpatrick), 12:437; and PCC, item 164, fols. 13–14.

Samuel Adams to Unknown

My Dear Sir, Philada Sept 21, 1778

I beg you not to impute my omitting hitherto to acknowledge your Favor of the 4th of July to Negligence.[1] I have frequently thought of its Contents; and although I was not able to obtain what you wishd for, I think you will not doubt my Sincerity when I assure you that whenever it shall be in my Power to render you substantial Service I shall do it with the utmost Cheerfulness. It is the Opinion of Gentlemen here that the Appointment of Auctioneers to make Sale of such Prize goods as fall to the share of the Continent should be made by the Authority of the particular States where such Goods may be forfeited.

Your Letter was delivered to me by Capt Manly. I am informed by some of my Boston Friends that he speaks of me with a Degree of Bitterness, supposing that I prevented his having another Ship. This gives me not the least Disquietude. He may have been taught to believe it, by Persons who care but little for him and less for the Honor of our Navy or the great Cause we are contending for. Neither he nor his Friends could be at a Loss for the true Cause of his Disappointment, if they would advert to the Judgment of the Court Martial which acquitted him *with Honor*. What a strange Inconsistency was there in that Court, in recommending Cap Manly for another Ship, and at the same Time holding up so great a Deficiency in his Conduct as the neglecting to prepare Signals for a Fleet under his Direction, and in general his Want of Experience. This was said by many; and it ought to be satisfactory to Cap Manly, that though I clearly saw the Justice of the Remark, I was silent. In this, it is possible, I was not altogether blameless. I have never felt my self disposed to take a Side in the Disputes which I understand have run high between Partizans of Manly & McNiel. I think Neither of them can derive much Honor from the Decisions of their respective Courts Martial. I wish for the Credit of our Country that both had behavd more to the Satisfaction of the Publick. One of them is still here. I suppose he is preparing to meet the Committee to whom his Petition is referrd. When it may be proper for me to speak my Mind his Friends & his Enemies may be assured I shall do it with Candor & Freedom. In doing this I expect to be justified, by sensible & honest Men. If I stand fair with them, *you well know*, how unsolicitous I am whether others are pleasd or not.

There is another Matter of greater Consequence which I wish to mention to you. I am informd there are Persons in Boston disposd to make a popular Clamor against the french Admiral for leaving Rhode Island. I cannot help remonstrating to my Friends against it as in a great Degree impolitick. Even if it should be thought he had taken a wrong step, it is our Wisdom at this Juncture to forbear criminating him. The Tories will try their utmost to discredit our new Alliance. They cannot succeed but by making injudicious Whigs their Instruments. There are two things from which I am more apprehensive than I am from the joynt Efforts of all our Enemies, viz the intemperate and misplacd Zeal of our honest Friends, and an insatiable Desire in others who are called Friends to establish a Popularity in order to obtain the Splendor or Emoluments of Places, or that Vanity of Vanities the Breath of Applause.

Adieu my Friend,

FC (NN). In the hand of Samuel Adams.

1 There is no July 4, 1778, letter to Samuel Adams in the Samuel Adams Papers, NN, in the absence of which it has not been possible to identify Adams' correspondent.

Josiah Bartlett to John Langdon

Dear Sir Philadelphia Septr 21st 1778.

Your favor of the 5th inst is now before me. We have had all the particulars of the Rhode Island expedition transmitted to us by General Sullivan and have rec'd a letter or rather a folio book from Count d'Estaing in justification of his conduct.[1] I make no doubt he acted what he thought for the best and had it not been for the unlucky storm which it was impossible for him to foresee, it is very probable that it might have been for the best; nor do I think him so much to blame for going to Boston with his shattered fleet when he knew Admiral Byron's fleet might be hourly expected which joined to Lord Howe's fleet and all the troops at New York ready to be sent immediately to assist them might endanger the total destruction of the whole French Squadron. I hope great care will be taken not to throw too much blame on the French, and raise a misunderstanding between us and them in this early period of the Alliance, than which nothing could give our enemies greater pleasure. The Rhode Island expedition though not successful, yet brought no disgrace on our arms, nor have the enemy any great cause of boasting.

Our commercial, marine and treasury affairs are in a very bad Situation and will never be otherwise while they are managed by Committees of Congress who are many of them unacquainted with the business and are continually changing and by that time they begin to be acquainted with the business they quit, others come in who know nothing that has been done; thus we go on from time to time to the great loss of the public. But you will ask why don't you put those affairs in other hands to be conducted who may give their whole time to the business. There are several reasons—first we have not time to make the proper arrangements and form proper Systems for conducting the business; above Six weeks ago we ordered that Tuesdays, Thursdays and Saturdays in every week should be set apart for arranging the Treasury Board and for the affairs of Finances and nothing is yet completed;[2] so much business is daily crowding on Congress, and so much time taken up in doing business in so large a body of men a great number of whom are lawyers and who think proper to make a long speech or two on every question however trifling &c &c &c &c that I fear it will be a long time before proper systems will be formed and when that is done I fear we shall be as much put to it, to find *proper men* to fill those important departments who will lay by, all their own business and attend wholly to the public for years together and perhaps for life; they ought to be men of the first character for probity, integrity and attention to business, but such men can always find employment in a more private life, more to their ease and advantage.

Generals Whipple and Folsom I am informed are appointed to represent our State after the first of November. I hope they will be here by the last of October as I shall be glad to see them before I set out for home.

By accounts from the West Indies (which is credited here) we are told that France declared War against Britain the 8th of July and that it was proclaimed in Martinico the 15th of August.

I am Sir your friend and most obedient Servant,

Josiah Bartlett

Tr (DLC).

[1] See *JCC*, 12:884, 892; and Henry Laurens to the comte d'Estaing, September 10, 1778.

[2] After weeks of wrestling with the issue of fiscal reform, Congress finally adopted a plan to reorganize the treasury on September 26. *JCC*, 12:956–61.

Samuel Holten's Diary

[September 21, 1778]

21. Monday. Congress sit late, I dined at Mr Stephen Collins's with the Delegates of our State & Genl. Arnold, Misrs. Deane, Marchant & Colo. Bartlett.

MS (MDaAr).

Samuel Adams to James Warren

My Dear Sir Philadelphia Sept 22 –78

The Bearer of this Letter Ebenezer Hazard Esq is a sensible Gentleman of good Character, and has had a liberal Education at the College in Princetown. He has a few years past been at Pains to obtain Copies of publick Records and Manuscripts relating to America. These with such others as he may be able to avail himself of he intends to publish, in hopes that some other gentleman finding Materials thus collected may be induced to furnish the Publick with the History of the United States. Congress has countenanced his laudable Undertaking.[1] As I am sure you are ready to afford Assistance to a Person disposd to serve Mankind in this or any other Way, (and I can assure you he is true Republican Whigg) I have taken the Liberty to recommend him to your patronage. Might he not be permitted to have Access to the Records of our State–Are there not some valuable Manuscripts in the Hands of private Gentlemen in the County of Plymouth or in the Records of that County or Town? The Papers which were carefully collected by the late Revd & curious Mr Prince were left to the Hon Mr Gill. It might *perhaps* serve Mr Hazards Purpose to be introducd to that Gentleman. But I forget that you have your Hands full of publick Business. Excuse me my Friend. Adieu. Your affectionate,

S Adams

RC (MHi).

1 In a July 11 letter to President Laurens, Deputy Postmaster Ebenezer Hazard had solicited Congress' "Patronage and Assistance for a COLLECTION OF AMERICAN STATE PAPERS." "The Design of it," Hazard explained, "is to furnish Materials for a good History of the UNITED STATES, which may now be very well done; for so rapid has been our political Progress that we can easily recur to the first Step taken upon the Continent, and clearly point out our different Advances from Persecution to comparative Liberty, and from thence to independent Empire. In this Particular we have the Advantage of every Nation upon Earth, and Gratitude to Heaven and to our virtuous Fathers, Justice to ourselves, and a becomining Regard to Posterity strongly urge us to an Improvement of it, before Time and Accident deprive us of the Means. The Undertaking will appear, at first View, to be too great for an unassisted Individual; and Experience has convinced me that although several Years incessant Application has produced an important Collection, yet, so numerous are the Materials, and so much dispersed, that a whole Life would be insufficient to compleat it in the Way in which I have been hitherto obliged to proceed. I now propose to visit each State for that Purpose, and must request of Congress a Certificate of their Approbation of my Design, should they approve of it, and a Recommendation to the several Governors and Presidents to grant me free Access to the Records of their respective States, and Permission to extract from them such Parts as may fall within the Limits of my Plan." Peter Force Collection, DLC.

Congress referred Hazard's letter on July 11 to a committee consisting of Richard Henry Lee, William Duer, and Samuel Adams, who recommended in a report drafted by Lee that Congress appropriate $1,000 to help defray his expenses, explaining that "Mr. Hazard's undertaking is laudable, and deserves the public patronage and encouragement, as being productive of public utility." The committee also urged "the several states in this union, to assist Mr. Hazard, and give facility to his labors in making a collection of the various State papers relative to the origin and progress of the several European settlements in North America; and such as relate to the rise and progress of the present war with Great Britain: that, for this purpose, he be admitted to an inspection of public records, and be furnished, without expence, with copies of such papers as he may judge will conduce to the valuable end he hath in view." This report, which was submitted on July 20, was adopted by Congress the same day. See *JCC*, 11:682, 705–6; and PCC, item 19, 3:75–76, item 36, 4:227–28.

Adams' letter to Warren paved the way for Hazard to spend several weeks during the winters of 1779–81 copying most of the official records in New Hampshire and Massachusetts, including those of the New England Confederation in Plymouth. Over the course of the next several years, Hazard copied documents whenever and wherever he could find the time from his government duties and later as clerk of the Insurance Company of North America.

Hazard finally published the first volume of *Historical Collections of State Papers and Other Authentic Documents, intended as Materials for an History of the United States of America* in 1792, but sales were disappointing and after publication of a second volume in 1794 the project was dropped. A considerable quantity of the transcripts, newspaper clippings, and manuscripts that he accumulated are now part of the Peter Force Collection, DLC. For further information on Hazard's historical collecting and editing career, see Fred Shelley, "Ebenezer Hazard: America's First Historical Editor," *William and Mary Quarterly*, 3d ser. 12 (January 1955): 44–73; and Ralph E. Blodgett, "Ebenezer Hazard: The Post Office, the Insurance Company of North America, and the Editing of Historical Documents" (Ph.D. diss., University of Colorado, 1971).

John Mathews to Thomas Bee

Dear Sir Philadelphia Septr. 22d. 1778.

I Received your favour of the 19 July a few days ago & imbrace this opportunity by Capt. Arthur of answering it.

The conduct of the Court of Spain, I must confess appears to me very ambiguous. We have certain accounts of their flota's being safe arrived some time ago, we have got a list of their marine force, which is powerful & when united with that of France, will be by far too formidable to apprehend any danger from the British, in short they are in all respects, at this time as well prepared for a rupture, as that nation for some ages past ever has been, but still we have no open and positive declaration in our favour on their part. To be sure state policy is a Machine—the main springs of which are extreamly difficult to be develop'd & which of them are at this time, so far out of order, as to induce in them so long a suspension of the fair promises they have made, is to me (& I believe to C——s) altogether impenetrable. They can have nothing to do, in the dispute between Germany & Prussia. Why Germany and Prussia have not as yet acknowledged our Independency is obvious.

You'll have heard 'ere this reaches you, of Clinton's late expedition to Bedford. These exhibitions of bonfires every now & then, I suppose he thinks will so captivate the hearts of the Americans, as soon to bring them to consent to a peace upon his own terms. A peace I would make with them to be sure, because it will be our present interest to have peace, for many cogent reasons. But I would see the whole nation at hell, before I would have any thing more to do with them, than barely to make peace. I would sooner enter into a treaty of Alliance with the Devil than I would with the King of Great Britain or any of his damn'd Crew. Whenever I am induced to forgive them for their last march through the Jerseys, it must be when, I am no longer capable of reflection. Such a pack of Hell hounds, I believe was never before let loose upon a distressed, innocent country. The theme is too painful to be dwel't upon.

Our Army are moving higher up the North river in order to oppose the penetration of the British army that way, should they attempt it. A part of the army under Gates is filing off towards the eastward. These movements are making to be in readiness to oppose the enemy in which ever quarter they may next bend their ravaging course. That they have some new expedition in contemplation, we have good reason to believe, as there are strong marks of their intention, soon to quit New York. The account here, of their destination is, that six regiments are to go to the West Indies, the remainder to Hallifax & Cannada. I believe it is more conjecture, than certainty. I fancy the arrival of their August packet from England will determine their next plan of operations.

By a Vessel arrived at Baltimore from Nantz a few days ago, there is an account, that the french fleet, had drove the British fleet into Portsmouth, & had compleatly block'd them up. This may be true, but there is one thing that appears misterious to me, which is, that Byrons squadron, should be permitted to sail for America, & no reinforcements sent to Count De Estaing, for they must be well apprised, that Howe's squadron, when joined by Byrons, must be far Superior to De Estaing, & in all probability without a timely reinforcement, he must fall a sacrifice. Happily for him this can not now be his fate, as he is so well secured in Boston harbour, but had Byrons squadron joined Howe, before De Estaing had had time to effect this security, his fate might have been the very reverse of what it now is. When I reflect on these great matters, I draw this consolation, that I find we are not the only blundering Polititians in the world.

Oh! my Worthy friend, never was Child more sick of a school, than I am, of this same business, I am sent here upon. I have frequently heard heavy complaints in our Assembly of the tedious progress of business, but I will venture to say, you do more business in one day than we do, in three. To be a Witness of this, & no prospect of amendment, when there is business of such magnitude before us, every day's delay to the completion of which gives an almost fatal stab to the Interests of this Great Continent, I can assure you without exaggeration, frets me in such a manner, as frequently to deprive me of that indifferent share of health which I should otherwise enjoy. As far as my poor abilities extend I will never flinch from any duty that I may be called upon by my country to undertake but at the same time, I could wish to be placed in some station, where I could render some service. I fully intended when I came into Congress, to have accustomed my self to deliver my sentiments upon every important Question, but I have found the thirst for Chattering so extremely prevalent, that it absolutely disgusts me, & frequently seals my lips, least my conscience should upbraid me with the commission of that very Sin against our righteous cause that I see daily committed by others, Vizt. the loss of so much precious, irretrievable time, & I am affraid the day will shortly arrive when some men, will be made sensible, that all the future services they can render their Country can never compensate for the invaluable moments, nay hours, days, & months they have trifled away, in idle debate. For my own part I seldom speak, except it is a subject in which the State I belong to, is particularly interested, for I most commonly find some member or other, speak my sentiments, then when is the necessity of a repetition? I thank God, I am not Coxcomb enough to conceive, that my cloathing the same sentiments, in a different garb, can have greater influence over the minds of men, than the picture that has already been exhibited by my Neighbour. If any thing has been left unsaid by others, that has struck my mind, & which I think material why I throw it out in as few words as possible. If every member would observe this line of conduct, the business of the Great Public may be done, but whilst every member is so tenacious, & so cursedly conceited of his own rhetoric, it never can. I am affraid, my Dr Sir, you will think your old acquaintance, has of late grown very ambitious, thus to presume to lay down a rule for the Government of so Wise & August a body as this one of whom I have been speaking, & that Egotisms, of all things, are most peculiarly disgusting. I submit it all to your candour, & will most chearfully abide by your decision.

It is now a month ago since I moved the enclosed resolution,[1] but it has been postponed from time to time, & as I See the disposition of the house is decidedly not to comply with it I bear it with patience. I have done my duty.

I wait with anxious expectation for your answer to my request for leave to return home. I hope you will be kind enough to forward it to me, as soon as possible.

There are some parts of this letter that your good sense will point out to you as not proper to be communicated, except to a very few, to you, I write with unreservedness, well knowing you will make allowances for my weaknesses, when others may think me an errant disclaimer & a conceited Coxcomb.

I am My Dear Bee with the most sincere Esteem, Yr. Obed. Servt.

Jno. Mathews

RC (ScC).

1 This resolution has not been identified. Although Burnett, *Letters*, 3:421n.3, conjectured that Mathews was referring to an August 19 Committee of Commerce proposal for a partial exemption of rice from the embargo on provisions, this seems unlikely because Mathews was not a member of that committee and the proposal itself is not in his hand. See *JCC*, 11:815–16; and PCC, item 31, fol. 185.

Gouverneur Morris to Robert R. Livingston

Dear Livingston Philadelphia 22d Sepr. 1778.

You have given me very excellent Reasons why I should be at Poughkeepsie.[1] Jay hath given me a very good Reason why I should not. I am no longer a Member of your Legislature.[2] You say that I have my *Soulagements* & I thank you for your Wish. I have experienced much Pain during my short Life from being said to be happier than I was.

Duer means to send his Resignation. Who will be chosen I know not. I think I shall because it will answer the small Politicks of some Men better to keep me here than to let me be at Home. On the other Hand it is possible my good Star may prevail to take me from this here and place me in a better, I mean among my Friends. For certainly I was formed for the Sweets of private Life (i.e.) if Nature had any Thing in View at the Time.

I return to Politicks. We want as a proper Melange to our present Arrangement an intriguing industrious Body a Duane. If Schuyler and Duane should spend the Winter here with me I am convinced the most beneficial Effects would flow from it. Schuyler I believe would be made President and certainly the best President Congress ever had.[3] His Wife Would be worth the Gold of Ophir Yea the purest Gold. She would out intrigue Adams. Lewis I suppose will be left here and who the other is to be I know not. If there is any Man of the lower Order whom you can trust, A Dewit [DeWitt] for Instance, I think it would be advisable to be open mouthed and loud for him. Such a Man would be of infinite Service if appointed by US.

I repose myself entirely with you and Jay. You shall act for me. Let me tell you that your Tempers are so very different that you will make the best Friends in the World. You are too lazy he is too proud. He is too hasty you too inattentive to the public Affairs. Shall I go on. No. With all the Faults both of you have I have as many as both of you together. You both pardon me therefore you must pardon each other. And do you hear. None of your Stomaching. Tell the Women they must all love me for I love them all. And tell yourself and make yourself believe it too that I am, most sincerely & sacredly, Your Friend, Gouv Morris

RC (NHi).

1 Livingston's September 10 letter urging Morris' attendance at the New York Assembly convening at Poughkeepsie, to which Morris is here responding, is in the Robert R. Livingston Papers, NHi.

2 See John Jay's September 13 letter to Morris in Jay, *Papers* (Morris), 1:497–98.

3 Although Gen. Philip Schuyler did not return to Congress in the winter of 1778–79, the New York delegates remained interested in placing him in the president's chair. For the effort made to secure his election to this Post in December when President Laurens suddenly resigned, see James Duane to George Clinton, December 10, 1778.

John Williams to Robert Burton

Dear Sir Philadelphia 22d. Septr 1778

For News consult the Inclosed paper & if you find None there I have None to communicate that is Not Stail unless I should again Spake of things in Embryo as I did of the Rhode Island Expedition which promised so Certain Cuccess that I thought proper to Mention it tho from a Variety of unforeseen Accidents it fell threw. I Received your favour of the 15th of August last for which I was greatly obliged to you. Our Assembly being called in July last was what I fully Expected as soon as I heard that congress had Not complied with Governor Caswills Requisition of 500000 Dollars and that they would proceed to strike Money for paying of the new Raised levies, I as Much Expected which Occationed with me a very considerable Imbarressment but with the approbation of My Coliegues lade the Matter again before congress who had I believe no Substantial Reason for not granting it at first but that North Carolina hapned at that time to be unrepresented in congress—but upon Reconsideration granted the other 400000 Dollars which in short time will be Sent on to North Carolina.

I Suppose there will be an Expedition carried on this Winter against the two Floradies & that North Carolina will be called upon to furnish Men.[1] I doubt Not but that those of the New Raised Troops of Carolina Not Sent forward to head quarters will be Solicited, I am Not so Clear that them Troops under their former Inlistment can be compelled to go to Floradi, I shall oppose their going there but by their own Consent, as it was Not the Design for which they were Raised tho' if they choose to go all will be well.

I am very well pleased that the assembly have at length condesended to Inhance the Number of Delegates to Congress & I am no less please[d] of the Gentlemen Elected. Depend upon it that Doctor Burk has & will again be a very usefull Man at this place & I Shall be happy in Seeing him here & wish it could be made his Interest to give his constant attendance in congress which will be quite the contrary for I assure you Sir tho' the allowance of the assembly of North Carolina to their Delegates is as Genteel as any in the union yet to Such a hight of Extravagance has Every thing got here, that the greatest Acconomist will not be able to do More than Make his Salery bear his Expences, if that. The late appointment has [. . .] My plan & put it Out of My power to Return before My place is Supplied by one of the Gentlemen last Chosen to whom I have wrote desiring them to [come] here if possable by the first of Debr. [so] that I may Certainly get home by Christm[as].

Should [. . .][2] a little Cash, shall be obliged to you to furnish her what she May want which Shall be Replaced on My Return. Remember My love to Magg & the little Boys. My Respectfull Compliments to all Enquiring friends, & Am Dr Sir, your friend & Hbble Servt, Jno. Williams

RC (NcU). Addressed: "Colo. Robert Burton, Granville County, North Carolina."

1 Williams was undoubtedly reflecting upon the probable consequences of the action taken by Congress on September 21 to strengthen Georgia against "the frequent inroads and depredations of the Floridians and Indians." *JCC*, 12:937–39.

2 Two lines damaged, approximately thirteen words missing.

Committee of Congress to the Board of War

Gent. Sept. 23d. 1778

The Committee have recd. the Papers respectg. Count Pulaskis Corps—but do not find the Direction of the Board of War given last Winter to inlist Prisoners, a Copy of which was given by Count Mumford to Mr. Atlee Commiss. of Prisoners at Lancaster.[1] You will please to send us a Copy of that & any other Instructions which may have been given him. By Direction of the Commte.

J. Reed. Chairman

RC (MHi). Written and signed by Joseph Reed.

1 Almost from the moment Pulaski was authorized to raise an independent corps in March 1778, Congress' February 26 prohibition against enlisting prisoners into the Continental Army had been under attack, and the status of that prohibition as applied to Pulaski's corps remained ambiguous during most of the year. Although Congress resolved on March 28 to exempt Pulaski from the prohibition, the delegates struck out the exemption just two days later, apparently out of fear that enlisting prisoners would complicate prisoner exchange negotiations with the British. Nevertheless, Pulaski's officers proceeded to enlist prisoners despite Congress' opposition, in part because they received encouragement from the

Board of War to do so. Although the board had been called to task for this breach of congressional policy early in June, Pulaski's enlistment of prisoners came under renewed attack during efforts to complete the final arrangement of the army when a motion was offered on September 21 that would have purged all prisoners of war from Pulaski's corps. When an effort to postpone consideration of the motion failed, it was simply referred to a committee consisting of Joseph Reed, James Lovell, and John Witherspoon for further study. Thus Reed penned the present letter to determine what recruiting instructions Pulaski had actually received from the board, and the committee eventually delivered a report reaffirming the ban on recruiting prisoners and recommending that his corps be purged of troops enlisted in violation of that ban.

Despite the appearance that this report had finally laid the issue to rest, consideration of the committee's recommendations was postponed in order to consult Washington again on the subject. Although he had long opposed recruiting prisoners of war, the commander in chief subsequently recommended that in this instance past recruiting violations be ignored to avoid offending Pulaski and weakening his corps, and as a consequence Congress never resumed consideration of the committee's report. See *JCC*, 12:939–40, 965–66; Henry Laurens to Washington, March 30, note 1; Henry Laurens to William Atlee, May 29, note 2; Thomas McKean to William Atlee, June 5, note; and Committee of Arrangement to Washington, September 30, 1778.

Henry Laurens to John Lewis Gervais

My Dear Sir 23d September [1778]

Let me upon this occasion refer you to His Excellency the President for Intelligence, and for the security of my property in case of another visit from Sir Peter Parker to your friendship—should the menaces of Governor Johnstone be attempted you will be exceedingly distressed; the earlier removals begin, the more likely to save something.

Your Letters by Sharp are just come to hand but 'tis impossible for me even to read them 'till tomorrow.

I shall write again about the 25th.

I pray God protect you all.

LB (ScHi).

Henry Laurens to Rawlins Lowndes

Dear Sir 23d September [1778]

Mr. Richard Beresford arrived at a late hour last night from New York and immediately called on me and delivered a verbal Message from Robert Williams Esquire.[1]

Mr. Williams had been frequently in conversation with Governor Johnstone, at the last interview which happened on or about the

17th he discover'd, as he presumed, the design of the Enemy to detach part of their Squadron together with 10,000 Troops immediately after the Hurricane Season to South Carolina to land at Charlestown or at Port Royal, or both. Governor Johnstone intimated the Conquest would be easily made, and the acquisition extremely beneficial by annexing South Carolina and Georgia to Florida, he particularly enquired who were the leading Men in South Carolina and other minutia which I have communicated to my Colleagues and to Major Butler and whose advices will supply my deficiencies.[2]

Mr. Williams intreats me to avoid naming him as my informant, hence Mr. Beresford did not enter upon his disclosure until he had with great form shut the Parlour door.

The Idea of secret, in this case, is truly ridiculous. Mr Williams, Mr Hopton, Mr. Graham[3] and some others are going to Charlestown with a Flag of Truce.

I asked Mr Beresford upon what principle Sir Henry Clinton had permitted these Gentlemen to go over to the Rebels, he replied with a smile, "a mark of extraordinary favor, certainly."

The announced enterprize is the most likely to succeed so far as to create a favorable diversion of any I can think of at this juncture of circumstances. It is the favorite Plan of General Grant and 'tis not improbable Sir Henry will be glad of an opportunity to recover the honor he left in the Sands of Long Island.

Is it likely that Governor Johnstone would have communicated a design of such importance to Mr. Williams? How shall I account for Mr. Williams' betraying to me the confidence reposed in him. These are questions I have answered to my own satisfaction—and submit them to your Excellency. Mr. Williams is exceedingly cautious. I have received two Messages but no writing from him.

All that Governor Johnstone has said to Mr. Williams may have been calculated for amusement—at the same time his Flag may cover two or more Engineers in Frocks and Trowsers and other dangerous instruments in disguise. Your Excellency will be governed by your own judgment and the best advice respecting the admission of either the Vessel or any individual contained in it higher than five fathom hole or Cumings Point and admitting her arrival, whether she ought not to be detained, and the Officers and all their people belonging to her secured out of Charlestown.

I have written fully on this subject to His Excellency General Washington, and will have the honor of writing more fully than the present to your Excellency in two or three days.

I have ordered this Messenger Wilkinson to ride night and day, and hope he will be in Charlestown on the 8th of October and be returned as expeditiously as possible.

I have the honor to be, With the highest Esteem and Regard.

P.S. This instant I have received repeated intelligence by escaped Prisoners from New York that the Enemy have abandoned Rhode Island, but I rely not upon such Reports.

LB (ScHi).

1 See also South Carolina Delegates to Robert Williams, September 24, 1778.

2 For the steps Congress took on September 25 to counter these reported British plans, see *JCC*, 12:949–50.

3 See also Laurens to James Graham, August 23, 1778.

Henry Laurens to George Washington

Dear Sir Philadelphia 23d September 1778

Mr. Richard Beresford, a Native of South Carolina a Young Gentleman of family, fortune and good Character who left New York on the 20th Instant called on me at a late hour last Night and delivered a verbal Message from Robert Williams Esquire another Native of that State, a very sensible Man, long a Practitioner in the Law, a respectable Character in general but not well affected to the Independence of the United States, more than cooly attached to his own private Interests, and I believe held by the British Ministry to be a fast, *prudent* friend to their Government.

In the last Conversation Mr. Williams held with Governor Johnstone at New York, he discovered, as he presumed, the design of the Enemy to detach part of their Squadron, together with 10,000 Troops immediately after the Hurricane Season to South Carolina to land either at or near Charlestown, or at Beaufort Port Royal about 70 Miles from Charlestown, or at both—the conquest, Governor Johnstone apprehended would be easily made, and the acquisition extremely beneficial by annexing South Carolina and Georgia to the Floridas. Mr. Williams requests me to avoid as much as possible intimating from whom I have derived my intelligence, hence Mr. Beresford with great form shut the Parlour door before he would enter upon the disclosure—the Idea that I could conceal his name was a little ridiculous—this Gentleman with a Mr. Hopton, not so good a general Character as his own, and several other disaffected Persons are to embark in a few days under a flag for Charlestown.

The enterprize is the most likely to succeed so far as to create a favorable diversion of any I can think of at this juncture of time and circumstances—it is a favorite Plan of General Grants nor is it improb[ab]le that Sir Henry Clinton will be anxious to recover the honor he lost upon the sands of Long Island.

Is it likely that Govornor Johnstone would have communicated a design of such importance to Mr. Williams? it is possible he might for valuable considerations, and also to Mr. Hopton—how shall I account for Mr. Williams' betraying to me a confidence reposed in him—he is a wiley Man—does not give a word in writing—may have in view ultimately to secure his own Estate—for his attachment to the Enemy if their attempts prosper—for the faithful and timely notice given to his Countrymen should they from thence defeat the meditated Attack—this, he may think will also secure to himself and his present Companions admission into Charlestown, which otherwise would be extremely doubtfull.

I asked Mr. Beresford upon what principle, Sir H. Clinton permitted Mr. Williams and the rest to proceed to Charlestown, he replied with a smile, "a mark of extraordinary favor certainly."

All that Governor Johnstone has said to Mr. Williams may have been calculated for amusement, or, merely for obtaining a safe re-entrance upon his Estate to a friend of British Government.

Upon the whole my Idea is to give immediate notice to South Carolina, preperations will be made for guarding against the effects of the menace—necessary steps will be taken for stopping the flag-ship far below the town, and after a proper detention for returning her and her whole Cargo to the Ocean; if a stroke is really intended she may contain skilful Engineers in Frocks & Trowsers and many other dangerous instruments in disguise—if the Vessel shall be ahead of my Intelligence and shall not have left the Port when that arrives, means may be devised for detaining her according to Circumstances—upon her return to New York or, meeting the Fleet, the mode of operation may be decided—the Voyage and return will be completed within October—the next will be the best Month for carrying the project into execution.

I therefore admit the possibility of the design, and will recommend to my Countrymen to act as they ought if there was no ground for doubt.

Your Excellency may possibly derive some advantage by a comparison of this with other Accounts from New York. I have from this reflection and from considering that all public important Intelligence is due to Your Excellency made the present communication without delay.

I request Your Excellency to order forward the several letters for Boston &c. & believe me to be with the most sincere & respectful attachment, Dear Sir, Your Excellency's Much Obliged & obedient humble servant,

Henry Laurens

[*P.S.*] This Instant an escaped Prisoner from New York informs me of the Enemy's having abandoned Rhode Island. The acquisition of Provision of Rice &c &c for the support of the British W India Islands which may be made in the Months of November & December—in So Carolina & Georgia with perhaps 10000 Negroes—& also the destruction of all our Navigation are no inferior objects.

RC (DLC). In the hand of Moses Young, with signature and postscript by Laurens.

South Carolina Delegates to Robert Williams

Dear Sir[1] 24 Septr 1778

We thank you for the Intelligence by Mr. B——.[2] He had a quick journey and communicated your Message the moment of his arrival.

Fortunately we have there and in the neighbourhood so many Regulars and so many good Militia who always are held ready to join our own as will meet them with grace either in force or detachments—but we will not boast, let them try again—the Account is now $\frac{1}{6}$th of the distance on the way to C.T.[3]

One article we anxiously wish to know, the number of ships of the line destined for the service, we mean ships of 50—they know better than to risque larger—it will be in our favor at this Season even to attempt 50's—the time when the Enterprize is to commence is another important article you omitted—the services you have rendered your Country on this occasion will be properly acknowledged.

We understand by your two Messages that you are in such good Cr[edi]t with the heads there as to leave no room to fear the miscarriage of this—pray tell us when you expect to sail.

A Letter directed to the President under Cover to Brigadier Maxwell will come very safe.

FC (DLC). In the hand of Moses Young, with the last paragraph by Henry Laurens. Endorsed by Laurens: "Delegates of So Carolina to R Williams Esquire."

1 Robert Williams (ca. 1733–1808), a prominent Charleston attorney who had once served in the South Carolina Assembly, was a loyalist waiting in New York City for an opportunity to return to South Carolina after a year's stay in England. Williams arrived back in South Carolina in 1779 and pledged his loyalty to the new state government, but he reaffirmed his allegiance to the crown after the British conquest of Charleston in 1780 and returned to England after the war was over. Walter B. Edgar and N. Louise Bailey, eds., *Biographical Directory of the South Carolina House of Representatives* (Columbia: University of South Carolina Press, 1977), 2:717–18.

2 Richard Beresford.

3 Charleston.

Samuel Holten's Diary

[September 25, 1778]

25. Friday, I dined with the President, Congress Resolved to Send 3,000 troops into the States of South Carolina & Georgia.[1]

MS (MDaAr).

1 This day Congress resolved to send 3,000 men from North Carolina and 1,000 men from Virginia to aid South Carolina and Georgia. *JCC*, 12:949–50. Holten's brief diary entries for the preceding two days record little more than that on Wednesday "Congress sit 'till two o'Clock" and that on Thursday "Congress sit late, nothing material turned up this day."

Marine Committee to Jonathan Trumbull, Sr.

Marine Committee
Sir Philadelphia, Septr. 25th. 1778.

The Marine Committee have been honored with Your Excellency's letters of the 2nd April & 5th of May last. The regard due to your recommendations induced the Committee to move in Congress the appointment of Captn. Seth Harding for the command of the Continental Ship of War building at Norwich in Connecticut—And I have the pleasure to acquaint you that he had the unanimous vote accordingly.[1] The Ship is named The Confederacy.

I am with the most cordial esteem and respect, Your Excellency's most obedient & very humble Servant.

Richard Henry Lee. Chairman

Tr (DLC).

1 See *JCC*, 12:949, 951. Congress doubtless adopted this recommendation this day in response to Harding's September 24 letter to President Laurens urging quick congressional action on his proposed appointment. PCC, item 78, 11:333. See also Samuel Adams to James Warren, September 12, 1778.

Andrew Adams to Jonathan Trumbull, Sr.

Sir Philadelphia 26th Septr. 1778.

Your favor of the 31st Ulto with its enclosures has been duly received and laid before Congress.[1] In obedience to Your Excellency's orders, I have done myself the honor to use my little influence in favor of Capt. Harding. He has been waiting some time on this business but was last evening unanimously elected to the command of the Ship Confederacy now building at Norwich, Notwithstanding considerable opposition was made against it by individuals, the ostensible reason, for which was the number of Continental Officers now out of employ. But the reasons assigned by your Excellency were so strong as to prevail with all the States against the opposition made by individuals. I hope and trust every exertion will be made by Capt Harding & that nothing will prevent the Ship being manned and got to Sea immediately—as I now look upon the honor of the State concerned in some measure in this matter. We have reason from appearances to expect the enemy are about to leave the Northern part of the Continent. The evacuation of New York &c is soon expected, and 'tis apprehended that there is some probability of their making a visit to South Carolina—under this idea cautionary measures have been taken by Congress, which perhaps may eventually have a more extensive operation—but of this hereafter.

We have had no foreign intelligence of consequence since my last. The state of our finances is in a most wretched situation, and nothing as yet has been done decisively by Congress upon that important subject. A Report of a Committee upon that head is to come under consideration this day which I hope may produce something effectual tho' in my opinion the Report (which is very lengthy and complex) is exceptionable. As the State has for some time past depended singly upon my feeble abilities for their representation I strongly wish the arrival of some of my Colleagues.

I have the honor to be with great esteem Your Excellency's obedient Servant, Andw Adams

Tr (DLC).

[1] Governor Trumbull's August 31 letter to the Connecticut delegates is in Trumbull, *Papers* (MHS Colls.) 7th ser. 2:263–64.

Josiah Bartlett to Meshech Weare

Hond Sir Philadelphia Septr 26th 1778

Soon after I Recd your letter of 19 Augt with the Inclosures Relative to a number of Towns on the Eastern Side Connecticut River Joining themselves to & being Recd by the Nominal State of Vermont[1] I Communicated the Matter to the New England Delegates & to Some others all of whom Seemed much surprized at their Conduct. After Some time for Consideration they Advised me to lay the Letter & papers before Congress and Request their advice in the matter which I accordingly Did and had the satisfaction to find that Every person who Spoke on the Subject Severely Condemned the Conduct of the Revolted Towns & of Vermont; What was proper to be done was all the Difficulty. After Some little time Spent as it appeared to be a matter of Consequence the Congress Resolved that on Friday the 18th Inst.; the Congress would go into a Committee of the whole House to take into Consideration the said letter & papers.

The Delegates of New York moved that Sundry letters & papers from their state, which had been presented and some others that they had further to lay before Congress Relative to the Conduct of Said Vermont might be taken into Consideration at the same time and tho it was opposed by some members as a Distinct & seperate matter it was nevertheless agreed to. On the 18th matters of a very pressing nature laying before Congress the affair was ordered to be postponed. On the 19th Colo Ethan Allen Came to this City from Said Vermont and understanding in what Situation the affair was and that their Conduct with Regard to the Said Towns was universally Condemned,[2] He earnestly Requested me not to press Congress to take up the matter till he had an oppertunity to Return to Vermont & lay the matter before their Assembly who are to meet the 9th of October and he Says he is perswaded they will Resind their vote for Receiving those Towns and Disclaim any pretensions to the East Side of Connecticut River. He informs me the vote was past by a Small majority[3] soon after his Return home from his Long Captivity and that agreable to a promise he made me when I See him in the Jersies as I went to Congress and he was returning home he had opposed the Measure and that if Vermont Does not Rescind the vote, He with a very Considerable Number who he is Sure will Join him will petition Congress against it and that he will himself present the petition to Congress and will use Every other means in his power to procure New Hampshire Redress against So unjust and impolitic a measure. He has also promised that he will immediately write to you & inform you what the Assembly Shall Do in the matter whither they Rescind it or not, and will also write to our Delegates here or Come himself in Case their assembly Does not Renounce their Connection with those Towns. According to his Desire and the Desire of a number of the Delegates here, who think it much best to have it Settled in that way at this Critical time, I have agreed not [*to*] move for it being taken up by Congress till I hear further from him or Receive further orders from our State.

If Vermont Should Renounce any Connections with those Towns, I Could wish our State would Continue Still to use Every proper Condescending & Lenient measure to unite them firmly with us, as those Broils in the States are very injurious to the Common Cause and Keep up the Spirits of our Enemies, who get intelligence of everything of that Kind.

One of the New York Delegates has informed me that they have wrote to their State advising them Either to send a Committee to our Assembly, or to Request our State to appoint a Committee to meet with one from theirs, to Consult & agree on measures to be Jointly taken by the two States relative Vermont. But as the Claim of New York to the whole of Vermont, in my opinion, is not better founded than is the Claim of New Hampshire to the same, and as the Decision of the Question to whom it properly belongs, will probably at this time be attended with very important Consequences and as our present Dispute Concerning the Towns of the East Side of the River is of a very Different Nature from the other, and will probably Soon be Setled to our Satisfaction, I humbly beg leave to Submit it to your Consideration whither it will be advisable for our State to be hasty in Entring into any agreement with New York on the Subject at least till you know what the Conduct of Vermont will be relative to those Towns.

I believe it is the Desire of the major part of the members of Congress (if possible) to keep off the final Decision of the old Dispute Concerning the New Hampshire Grants to Some future time when it may be Setled without any Danger to the Common Cause.

I have the honor to be with great Respect your most obednt Humble Servt, J.B.

P.S. As I Cannot Represent the State in Congress after the first of November and can by no means tarry over the winter I shall Consider myself at liberty to Set out for home the beginning of the month of Novr. whither other Delegates have arrived or not. J.B.

FC (VtHi). In the hand of Josiah Bartlett.

1 Weare's August 19 letter with its enclosures was presented to Congress on September 16. *JCC*, 12:916–17. For further information on the brief union of the New Hampshire towns with Vermont, see Bartlett to Weare, August 4, 1778.

2 Bartlett first wrote and then crossed out: "condemned by every member of Congress."

3 Bartlett first wrote and then crossed out: "and that he opposed it."

Cornelius Harnett to Richard Caswell

Dear Sir Philadelphia 26th Sept. 1778.

I take the liberty to enclose your Excellency the accot. as it stands in the Treasury Books against Our State. Your Excellency will be pleased to observe that a Warrant has been procured for 400,000 Dollars the balance of your draft for 500,000 for the use of the new raised Levies, as soon as the money is received it shall be sent forward with all convenient despatch.

Congress did yesterday come to a resolution of sending 1000 Men from Virginia, and 3000 from North Carolina, to March immediately to So. Carolina as the people of the State apprehend that Genl. Clinton, (should he leave New York, which we have reason to believe) may take Charles Town in his way, to endeavour to retrieve his lost honor in that Quarter.[1] The movements of the Enemy at New York & Rhode Island seems to indicate an Evacuation of those places. Their destination is not known—but as we have reason to believe there is a declaration of War between France & England, and that the Spaniards will very soon take part in it—Congress are led to believe the British Troops in America must proceed to England, and perhaps a part of the West Indies.

By the resolve of Congress, enclosed to your Excellency by the President, you will Find, it is the desire of So. Carolina that you should take the command of the No. Carolina Troops, with the rank and pay of a Major General in continental Service.[2] I am informed the new Levies are let out on furlough, until next March; could those men be collected and Sent forward to So. Carolina it might save a good deal of expense in calling out the Militia. The President of Congress will mention to your Excellency some other matters relative to this movement, which I am not at present at Liberty to communicate, indeed they are not yet fully determined upon. You may be assured that a Supply of money will be sent on immediately to defray the expense of our Troops not to be drawn out exclusive of the 400,000 dollars mentioned above. I should be sorry to hear of any more Troops received or Militia embodied in our State unless provision is first made by Congress for their bounty and pay and subsistence &c by sending money forward for that purpose. I am necessitated once more to remind your Excellency, to endeavour by all means to send on the accounts & vouchers of our State against the Continent. Surely we must be largely in advance, not having since the beginning of the War a Military Chest established in our State, had such an establishment taken place in Ours, as in other States, the charge against No. Carolina would have been trifling indeed.

The So. Carolina and Georgia Delegates are so incensed against Genl. Rob. Howe that he is directed immediately to join Genl. Washington at Head Quarters. And Genl. Lincoln is to command in the Southern department. This Gentleman is a valuable and experienced Officer, he is ordered immediately to repair to Charlestown.[3]

I have not had the pleasure of a line from your Excellency, since my return to Congress. I hope I have not given you offence, I am sure I have not intentionally. I mentioned in my last that it was the wish of myself and Colleagues, that your Excellency would give us instruction on any matter to be brought before Congress relative to our State. We find it the practise of the Governors or Assemblies of the other States; requests there made, are seldom if ever refused. The affair of the Virginia vessel secured from the Enemy by our Militia at Currituck, has made a great noise in Congress; as she was taken away by persons supposed (by the Virginians) to be some of our people.[4] I hope Your Excellency has taken care to have this matter inquired into, and the parties brought to punishment—if any proof appears against them. It has been with great difficulty that your Delegates could prevent a recommendation to the State to make restitution. The affair is postponed at present, whether it will again be taken up I know not. I have the honor to be with great regard, Your Excellencys Mo. Ob. Huml. Servt.

Corns. Harnett

Tr (Nc-Ar).

1 See *JCC*, 12:949–50; and Henry Laurens to Rawlins Lowndes and to Washington, September 23, 1778.

2 See *JCC*, 12:950.

3 Although Gen. Robert Howe had long been unpopular with certain South Carolina delegates because of his feud with Christopher Gadsden, and had offended some Georgia delegates by his reluctance to cooperate with their state's expeditions against East Florida, Harnett later claimed that the delegates from these states were finally prompted to ask for Howe's removal from the southern military department by their disgust over the "little ridiculous matter he has been concerned in in So. Carolina with regard to a female." See Harnett to Caswell, November 24, 1778.

4 See Harnett to Caswell, September 15, 1778, note 2.

Henry Laurens to Richard Caswell

Sir Philadelphia 26th September 1778

I had the honor of addressing Your Excellency under the 5th Instant, since which I have received none of Your Excellencys favors.

This will convey an Act of Congress of the 25th for the immediate defence of South Carolina and Georgia to which I beg leave to refer.

The apprehension which gave rise to this Act, springs from a private verbal Message sent to me by Robert Williams Esquire a Native of South Carolina, a Practitioner of the Law, a Man of good understanding, and of a very respectable general Character, possessor of a large Estate in that Country, but more attached to his private Interests, than zealous for the establishment of our Independence and held to be a friend and favorite of the Ministers of Great Britain. This Gentleman's communication which I received three days ago imported that he had on or about the 19th Instant, learned from Governor Johnstone that an attack by an Army of ten thousand troops, and a sufficient number of Ships of the Line was intended upon South Carolina at Charlestown and Beaufort-Port-Royal, or both; that Governor Johnstone obtained permission for him and several other unstaunch Carolinians to proceed to Charlestown under a flag of Truce. Mr. Williams anxiously pressed a very ridiculous request "that I would not give him up as the Author of this important discovery"—which strongly implies a degree of treachery and no less a degree of artifice.

Is it likely that Governor Johnstone would have informed Mr. Williams the Plans intended by the Commanders of the British Land and Sea forces? It is possible he may have intrusted him with the secret for valuable considerations, the flag Vessel may contain skilful Engineers in the habit of Mariners, and she may Return with such intelligence as may greatly facilitate the meditated execution—how shall we account for Mr. Williams' breach of confidence? only by supposing that in any event he means to secure his own Estate, and wishes to meet a more hospitable reception in Charlestown than his fears had indicated without this harbinger.

The recovery of South Carolina and Georgia is a project of the first magnitude to Great Britain in her present circumstances—it is consistent too with the declared intentions of her Minister from the commencement of the present War, "that those Provinces should be the dernier resort"—the subduing those States in the approaching November, unless in the mean time an ample aid shall be supplied by their Northern neighbours, will certainly be no difficult work—the expected plunder of an abundance of Provisions Merchandize many thousands of Negroes, great quantities of Cannon and warlike stores, Horned Cattle, Sheep, Hogs, and Horses, an immense value of Indigo and upwards of 200 Sail of Ships & other Vessels appears to be a sufficient temptation to the Enterprize.

I have lately examined upward of 30 Diserters from Byron's fleet and many other persons from New York, all of whom concur in opinion that an abandonment of that City and Port is intended but none pretend to know whither the forces are to be transported; the most intelligent Person among these Informants intimated that the Enemy had contrived to circulate whispers of their designs so contradictory in terms as to leave the truth undiscoverable. He had been much on board the Eagle Man of War, and although he professed his ignorance in general, he had collected so much from various conversations as had induced him to believe the Enemy intended a complete evacuation of New York and Rhode Island; that Hallifax would be strengthened by one part of the Troops the West India Islands by a second part, and the remainder cross the Atlantic for reinforcing Great Britain and Ireland.

A sensible Correspondent in General Washington's Camp gives me as his opinion, that the destruction of Count d'Estaings' Squadron will not be left unessay'd.[1] If Your Excellency will have patience to hear my private sentiments, I will add that Sir Henry Clinton is taking every necessary step for a sudden removal when he shall receive Orders from Whitehall expected about this time by the August Packet, and there is no place more inviting than South Carolina, an attempt therefore upon that State is most to be dreaded, especially as the Expedition may be made consistently with a voyage to the West Indies, consumes but little time, and success be the means of securing a twelve Months food for the most populous of all the Islands, and for many political considerations which will in a moment strike Your Excellencys Mind.

General Washingtons' Camp was on the 19th Instant at West Point. We know nothing of transactions at Rhode Island except the return of Sir Henry Clinton to New York from thence and from thence the successful descent of General Gray upon Bedford and Marthas Vineyard.

It is said that about 50 empty transports came out of Sandy Hook and steered southerly in view of Egg Harbor four days ago, and that the Enemy have landed about 5000 Troops at Hackinsack: these I regard only as Reports.

This instant came in two Seamen who left New York the 21st. They say the Isis to which one belonged has lost upward of 50 Seamen by desertion. The other from the Conqueror reports near 100 Deserters from that Ship, both confirm the Accounts of intended evacuation—the Packet was not arrived—all the Men of War have lost Men in proportion, as these fellows aver. They add that the fleet in general were extremely sickly, provisions extremely dear and scarce—and repeat the landing at Hackinsack, and that the troops as well as Seamen were inclined to desert.

I have the honor to be, With the highest Esteem & Regard, Sir, Your Excellency's Most obedient & humble servant,[2]

Henry Laurens,
President of Congress

RC (CtY). In the hand of Moses Young and signed by Laurens.

[1] See John Laurens' September 15 letter to his father in Simms, *Laurens Army Correspondence*, pp. 222–24.

[2] Laurens wrote a nearly identical letter this day to Gov. Patrick Henry. PCC, item 13, 2:88–91.

Henry Laurens to John Houstoun

Sir 26th September [1778]

I had the honor of writing to Your Excellency the 6th Inst. by Muckinfuss thro Charlestown.[1]

Within the present Cover will be an Act of Congress of Yesterdays date for the defence of South Carolina and Georgia for appointing Major General Lincoln to the Command in the Southern Department and for other purposes therein mentioned.

This Act is founded on a presumption that the Enemy intend to make an immediate attack upon the two Southern States, an intimation to this effect having been transmitted to me by Robert Williams Esquire, late of Charlestown. This Gentleman, Mr. John Hopton, and several other return'd Americans are now, or will soon be on their passage to Charlestown in a Vessel bearing a flag of Truce. It is possible that Vessel will find it necessary to put into Tybee and highly probable she will contain Engineers and other Spies in disguise, who after having made their observations will return and make their Report to the Commander in Chief of the British forces either at New York or on the Coast of Carolina.

Your Excellency will judge the propriety of suffering any one person to land from a Vessel coming upon so questionable an errand, or of permitting her suddenly to depart again should she be arrived and remain in Port when this reaches you.

I have examined many Deserters and escaped Captives lately from New York. These vary in their several accounts of the destination of the British forces in that Port, some of them say their grand object is the destruction of Count d'Estaing's fleet, consequently an immediate and forcible attack upon Boston by Land and Sea; others, that the whole are destined to the West Indies—one, a very sensible Man, intimated the impossibility of determining where they are bound, "they give out said he three places, Boston, Philadelphia, and the West Indies, but from my observation I think part of them are going to Hallifax, part to the West Indies, and the remainder to England or Ireland." Hence Your Excellency will see that all agree in opinion that the abandonment of New York is determined. South Carolina and Georgia are grand objects in the Plan of the British Ministry, and were from the commencement of the present War held as a dernier resort, it behoves the inhabitants therefore of those States to exert their utmost abilities in the present critical conjuncture—my private sentiment is that the Commander in Chief and the British Commissioners are waiting for orders from Whitehall.

I have the honor to be &c.

LB (DNA: PCC, item 13). Addressed: "Governor Houston, Georgia."

[1] See Laurens to Richard Caswell, September 5, 1778, note 1.

Henry Laurens to Rawlins Lowndes

Sir 26th Septr. [1778]

Since the date of my last the 4th August,[1] I have received no Commands from Congress respecting the State of South Carolina, except an Act of Yesterday which will accompany this, for reinforcing South Carolina and Georgia by four thousand troops exclusive of Officers. For taking into the Pay of the United States such of the Militia of South Carolina and Georgia as may be called forth on the present emergency, meaning the necessary defence against an attack supposed to be intended by the Enemy upon those States.

For directing Major General Howe to repair immediately to General Washington's Head Quarters.

For appointing Major General Lincoln to the Command in the

Southern department—and Governor Caswell to the rank and Pay of Major General in the Army upon terms therein set forth, meaning if he shall march with the Troops from North Carolina to the aid of South Carolina and Georgia.

I have the honor to be &c.

LB (DNA: PCC, item 13).

[1] Since then Laurens had also written six private letters to President Lowndes, the earliest on August 5 and the latest on September 23.

Henry Laurens to Jonathan Trumbull, Sr.

Honorable Sir 26th September [1778]

I beg leave to refer to my last of the 13th Instant by Mr. Dodd.[1]

Yesterday Congress took under consideration a Report from the Marine Committee, and thereupon Resolved that the new frigate at Norwich be called the Confederacy, and that Seth Harding Esquire be appointed to the Command of the said frigate, the vote for Captain Harding was unanimous. I declared it accordingly, but I perceive the Secretary has omitted to insert it in the Act of Congress which your Honor will find within this Cover. Captain Harding is a Man of more dispatch than vanity, and will not wait the necessary time which an amendment will require, I commend him.

I Am with the most sincere esteem & Regard, Honorable Sir &c.

LB (DNA: PCC, item 13). Addressed: "Governor Trumbull, Connecticut, by Captain Harding."

[1] See Laurens to the Massachusetts Council, September 13, 1778, note 3.

Marine Committee to Luke Mathewman

Sir September 26th 1778

You are to proceed with all the despatch that wind and weather will permit to the Island of Martinico and deliver the letters for the Marquise De Bouillé to him with your own hands.[1]

The Letter No 1 you are to deliver to the Captain of the first french or spanish Vessel that you may meet with at Sea. The Letters for Mr. Bingham Agent for the United States in Martinico[2] you will deliver safely to him, and you are to follow his directions touching the manner in which the schooner under your command is to be employed until the season arrives in the Spring when you may safely venture to return to Philadelphia. You will avoid unnecessarily Speaking with vessels at Sea, least you fall into the hands of an enemy; and you are to put your despatches all into a Bag with a proper weight therein effectually to Sink the Letters if unavoidable danger of being taken should threaten you. Wishing you a good Voyage and a safe return, I am Sir, Your hble servant

P.S. Should you have a short passage to Martinico and think you can return here before the winter becomes severe we would have you loose no time but return immediately.

LB (DNA: PCC Miscellaneous Papers, Marine Committee Letter Book). Addressed: "Lieutenant Luke Mathewman, commanding the Contl. Schr. Phœnix."

1 The letters that Lieutenant Mathewman was to deliver to the marquis de Bouillé, the French governor of the Antilles, consisted of dispatches from Gérard and the Spanish agent Don Juan de Miralles. See Meng, *Gérard Despatches*, pp. 306–7, 311–12.

2 These letters to William Bingham have not been identified.

Henry Laurens to George Clinton

Sir 27th Septr. [1778]

On the 21st I had the honor of receiving and presenting to Congress Your Excellency's favor of the 9th Instant, and in answer I herewith transmit an Act of Congress of the 21st, duplicate of the Act of the 17th and Copies of the Sundry Papers which Your Excellency desired to be furnished with,[1] in these I trust there will be found no deficiency, and I intreat Sir, you will be assured the late omission, of which you have justly complained was not the effect of inattention on my part.

All our Public Offices, which have hitherto been conducted as well, I presume, as circumstances in an infant State would admit of, now call for inspection and improvement, and none more than the Secretary's Office, from whence alone, according to the present mode, I derive subject for every public Letter. The Act of the 21st signifies the entire approbation by Congress of Your Excellency's conduct as Commander of the Forts on Hudsons River, which I repeat with great pleasure in obedience to the Order of Congress, and from that sincere respect and esteem for your Excellency's Character with which I have the honor to be, Sir, Your Excellency's Most Obedt. & Most Humble Servant.

LB (DNA: PCC, item 13).

1 Governor Clinton's September 9 letter to Laurens is in PCC, item 67, 2:134–36. In it he complained that an August 17 resolve of Congress absolving Gen. Israel Putnam and his subordinates of blame for the autumn 1777 loss of certain posts in the Highlands implied criticism of his own conduct in that affair and asked for copies of the records relating to the inquiry so that he could dispel the unfavorable impression of him. Consequently Congress agreed on September 21 to provide Clinton with the records in question and at the same time ordered

Laurens to inform the governor that the delegates were "well satisfied with the propriety of his conduct as commander of the forts on Hudson's river." *JCC*, 11:803–4, 12:936.

Henry Laurens to George Washington

Sir 27th Septr. [1778]

I had the honor of writing to Your Excellency the 20th Instant by Colonel Hazen.

This will be accompanied by an Act of Congress of the 25th Inst. for the immediate defence of South Carolina and Georgia, to which I beg leave to refer.

Congress have appointed Mr. John Ternant Lieutenant Colonel in the service of the United States, and Inspector of the Troops in South Carolina and Georgia and ordered that he be allowed the Pay and subsistence of a Lieutenant Colonel from the 26th March last.[1]

I have the honor to be &c.

LB (DNA: PCC, item 13).

[1] See *JCC*, 12:952; and Laurens to Steuben, September 17, 1778, note 3.

Gouverneur Morris to George Clinton

Sir, Phila. 27th Sep'r 1778.

I write this short note to your Excellency to suggest the Hint of sending a Committee to confer with the Legislature of New Hampshire on the Affairs of Vermont. You are not to learn that these new States men have debauched some of the Western Townships of New Hampshire. The temper of Congress in this Business from what passed lately, seems to be if possible to keep matters quiet untill the Enemy leave us, when the Forces of the whole Continent may be turned to reduce them if refractory to the Resolutions of that Body. Application was made for a Commission of Colo. to Ethan Allen which I opposed. When he was redeemed I moved a Brevet Rank for him which was granted, and he would certainly have had the Commission if I had not learnt that he hath lately interfered in Opposition to the authority of the State of New York.[1]

I am with Respect Your Excellency's most obedient & humble Servant,

Gouv. Morris

[*P.S.*] As Mr. Duer intends soon for the State I have not written at large. Should he delay I shall be more full and more particular on our private Affairs. I mean those of the State as distinct from the

Continent. I have the Pleasure to tell you that at Length with infinite Pains and many Disappointments we have got an arrangement for our Treasury which promises the best Consequences.[2] We are now to be employed in Finance. A proper System is before Congress. But will they adopt it?

Reprinted from Clinton, *Papers* (Hastings), 3:100.

[1] See *JCC,* 11:505–6, 12:947.

[2] For this "arrangement," see *JCC*, 12:956–61.

Josiah Bartlett to Mary Bartlett

My Dear Philadelphia Septembr 28th 1778

Major Gardner of Portsmouth Came here last Saturday and informs me the He Called at my House as he came along & that you & the family were well the 14th of this month. I have nothing material in the news way to inform you of, and can only Repeat the old Story, that I am in a comfortable State of health & Remember my Love to you and the Children, Charles Chace is well. The weather here is very pleasant & agreable neither too cold & too hot at this time; it has been very Sickly & a Considerable Dying time in this City for a month or Six weeks past, but is now more Healthy as the weather Grows Cooler, Dr Rush who took Care of Charles Chace when he was sick, has been at the point [of] Death, but is geting better, and I believe the sick are Generally [get]ting better.

September 29th. Yours of the 10th inst. Recd yesterday afternoon am glad to hear Mr Wentworth was arrived & better in health.

Yesterday afternoon an Express arrived from Baltimore with Letters from our agent at Martinico a french Island in the west Indies who tells us war was proclaimed there the 16th of August against England, and that Spain had Declared openly for France.[1] The vessel left the Dutch Island of Statia the 13th of this month; and informs that the french had taken the English Island of Dominica the 7th of the Month, and that the Inhabitants of the English west India Islands were in the greatest Consternation & flying to the Dutch & other neutral Islands with their Effects &c &c &c but if my letters are as long geting to you as formerly you will hear the news before you Receive this. In haste, I am yours, Josiah Bartlett

RC (NhHi).

[1] See next entry, note.

Committee for Foreign Affairs to William Bingham

Sir Philadelphia Septr 28. 1778

Your Several favors up to the 28th July came duly to our hands, and, having been communicated to Congress, were received as agreable proofs of your regular Correspondence.[1] The papers which you enclose are with the Marine Committee, who will doubtless take occasion soon to report upon the Contents. This will be conveyed to you in a small Schooner which perhaps is not fit for a Winters return to this Coast, you will determine in conjunction with the Captain whether to send her back immediately, or to make the best use of her for the public in your Neighbourhood, till a proper Month for her return. She is confided thus to your discretion.

No absolute judgement can at this instant be formed of the intended movements of the Enemy. A course of Dunlaps papers will convey to you a general insight into the posture of our Military affairs. It is not probable that any considerable decision in the field will take place this fall; and the Councils in Britain appear to be for relinquishing the mad project of subjugating us by Arms.

It was to give conveyance to the Letters of the French Minister that the bearer, was at this Season dispatched for Martinique; so that you will get further information of our affairs through the Genl. with whose confidence you are so much honored. You will herewith receive the 2d Volume of the journals of Congress but lately published, and, as it was uncertain whether you had ever received the first, that also is sent. The Index, at least, will be new to you and Serviceable. We are Sir &c,

Signed { Richard H Lee
James Lovell

Tr (DNA: PCC, item 79).

[1] Only Bingham's July 6 letter to the committee is in PCC. See item 78, 2:503. Bingham's August 26 letter to the committee, which was read in Congress on September 29, apparently arrived after this letter was written. *JCC*, 12:965.

Marine Committee to John Barry

Sir September 28th 1778

We have received your favour of the 8th instant from Boston and are sorry to hear that so many of the Guns on board the Raleigh had burst in proving but we hope they will be Speedily replaced and that you will Shortly receive this letter at Hampton agreeable to our former Instructions which you acknowledge having received.[1]

As you represent the Raleigh to be exceedingly foul and on that account very unfit to cruize upon the Coast, we have concluded that you had best proceed with her to Portsmouth in Virginia where there is a Continental Ship Yard and on applying to our Agents there, Messrs. Maxwell & Loyal & to Mr. David Stoddart the Master Builder in the yard they will furnish you with conveniencies and lend you assistance to have her Bottom cleaned. You will advise us of the time that you think that business will be compleated, and should you not receive fresh Orders from us, you will proceed to cruize upon the Coast, and call in at Hampton once a fortnight for our Orders until you receive them. Should the frigate Deane and any other Vessel be in company with you, you will order them to cruize while you are carreening. We wish you Success & are Sir, Your very hble servants

P.S. Since writing the foregoing Instructions we have had information that the british frigate Persius of 32 Guns is cruizing singly on the Coast of South Carolina. This intelligence has determined us to give you orders to extend your Cruizing along the Coast provided the Deane or any other vessel is in company with you, therefore if you have a Concert as soon as you have got your Ship cleaned in Virginia, we desire you will proceed to the Southward in Search of the Persius and use your best endeavours to take, burn, sink or destroy the said frigate or any other of the enemies vessels that you may fall in with. Should you be so fortunate as to take the Persius, carry her into Charles Town and there have her fitted and manned and take her to Cruize in company with you.

LB (DNA: PCC Miscellaneous Papers, Marine Committee Letter Book).

1 See Marine Committee to Barry, August 24, 1778.

Marine Committee to Eastern Navy Board

Gentlemen September 28th. 1778

We have received your favour of the 8th instant and intirely approve of your proceedings mentioned therein. We are now to inform you that Congress have named the new frigate Building at Norwich in Connecticut the Confederacy and have appointed Captain Seth Harding of that State to command her.

That Gentleman hath given us very strong assurances that he will be able to man her in a very short time; and we now request that your exertions may be used to have her fitted for the Sea as speedily as possible. We are Gentn, Your very Hble servants

LB (DNA: PCC Miscellaneous Papers, Marine Committee Letter Book).

Charles Thomson's Notes on William Carmichael's Examination

Septr. 28, 1778.[1]

Mr. Carmichael having before taking the Oath[2] intimated that as he might be embarrassed by the Novelty of his Situation he wished to have The Questions propounded to him in Writing and that his Answers might be received in Writing that he might answer with that Clearness and Precision which he would wish.

Ordered, That Mr. Carmichael be informed that the Questions will be propounded to him by the Chair and that he is to Answer Viva voce but that if he should find himself embarrassed Time will be given him in the House for Recollection.[3]

Mr. Carmichael called in and sworn.

Q. At what time did you become acquainted wth Mr. Deane?

A. In the month July or Aug. 1776.

Q. Did Mr. D Acquaint you with the nature of his mission to France, And at wt. time?

[*A.*] I was introduced to Mr. D by Mr. Rogers of Maryland who informed him I was zealously attachd to the int. of Am., & some time after Mr. Deane acquainted me with the nature of his Mission.

[*Q.*] How long after being introduced to Mr. D., were you acquainted with the Nature of his Mission?

[*A.*] I cannot recollect precisely.

[*Q.*] Did you assist Mr. D in his public business?

[*A.*] On knowing the nature of his mission I Offered to Assist Mr. D in any way in my power while I was in France.

[*Q.*] Did Mr. D accept your offer?

[*A.*] He did.

[*Q.*] In what respect did you assist Mr. Deane?

A. In various respects; I assisted him copying letters, & in conversations.

Q. During the time you assisted Mr. D. were you acquainted with the rect. & expenditure of public monies wch. passed through his hand?

A. I knew Mr. D. recd. money & made purchases & contracts on the public Account but as I never wished to charge Myself or make myself responsible where I cod. have no merit, I did not pay sufficient Attention to answer with precision.

Q. Do you know whether Mr. Deane misapplied the public Money or converted any of it to his own use?

A. My answer to the former qu. will shew that I am not an adequate judge of the application of public money & can't answer with precision. At the same time wd. entreat that the House wd. not put an interpretation on my silence to the prejudice of any person whatever.

Q. From the knowledge you had of Mr. Deane's transactions, do you recollect any instance which you apprehended to be a misapplication of the public Money?

A. I beg to know whether I am to answer from my knowledge or suppositions or opinions in my own mind.

Ordered That Mr. C. withdraw.

On the question whether the last be a proper Question the yeas and nays being required by Mr. Marchant

New Hampshire	Mr. Bartlet	Ay	Ay
Massachusetts	Mr. S. Adams	Ay	
	Mr. Gerry	Ay	Ay
	Mr. Holton	Ay	
Rhodeisland	Mr. Marchant	Ay	Ay
Connecticut	Mr. A. Adams	Ay	Ay
New York	Mr. Lewis	Ay	
	Mr. G. Morris	Ay	Ay
Pensylvania	Mr. R. Morris	Ay	
	Mr. Clingan	Ay	Ay
Maryland	Mr. Chase	No	
	Mr. Plater	No	
	Mr. Stone	No	No
	Mr. Forbes	No	
	Mr. Henry	No	
Virginia	Mr. Harvie	No	
	Mr. R. H. Lee	Ay	
	Mr. M. Smith	Ay	Ay
	Mr. Griffin	Ay	
N. Carolina	Mr. Penn	Ay	
	Mr. Harnet	No	No
	Mr. Williams	No	
S Carolina	Mr. Laurens	Ay	
	Mr. Drayton	Ay	Ay
	Mr. Matthews	No	
Georgia	Mr. Walton	Ay	
	Mr. Telfair	Ay	Ay
	Mr. Langworthy	No	

So it was resolved in the affirmative.

Ordered That Mr. Carmichael attend at the [bar] on Wednesday next at ten oclock to be farther examined.[4]

MS (DNA: PCC, item 54). In the hand of Charles Thomson.

1 For Congress' decision to call William Carmichael to testify this day on Silas Deane's conduct of public business in France, see *JCC*, 12:927–28, 941–42. See also

Richard Henry Lee to Arthur Lee, September 16, note 3; and Gouverneur Morris' Proposed Resolve, September 18, 1778.

2 In addition to Thomson's notes on Carmichael's examination, at least two other sets are known to have been made. A slightly abridged version in the hand of Gouverneur Morris is in the collection of Morris' papers at NNC. A slightly fuller version, made by or for Henry Laurens, was obtained by Edward D. Ingraham from Laurens' heirs about 1854 and published by the Seventy-Six Society. The following passage appears at this point in this printed version of Laurens' notes, which apparently have not survived: "to give true answers, to speak the truth, the whole truth, and nothing but the truth, touching such questions as shall be asked." *Papers in Relation to the Case of Silas Deane*, ed. Edward D. Ingraham (Philadelphia: Printed for the Seventy-Six Society, 1855), pp. 141–49.

3 Except for three words—"in the House"—inserted by Henry Laurens near the end of the second paragraph, these two introductory paragraphs, which are on a separate sheet filed with Thomson's notes, are in the hand of Gouverneur Morris. Morris also wrote at the top of the page, in pencil, the following variant of the second paragraph: "That Mr. Carmichael be informed that the Questions to be answered will be propounded to him by the House and that he answer viva voce but if on any Question he should find himself embarrassed he will Have ⟨*full*⟩ Time allowed him for Recollection."

4 For the continuation of these notes, see Charles Thomson's Notes on William Carmichael's Examination, September 30, 1778.

Josiah Bartlett to William Whipple

Dear Sir, Philadelphia 29th Sept. 1778.

Your favor of the 13th inst. by Major Gardner came to hand last Saturday and find you seem to be hesitating about coming forward to your duty here; however as I have a better opinion of your patriotism than to suppose you will desert the ship till she is safe in the harbor notwithstanding any disagreable feelings on account of former unrewarded services, I expect you will be on your journey here before this reaches New Hampshire or immediately after, so I shall not write to you after this while I tarry here.[1] By a letter from Mr Bingham dated Martinico the 16th of August[2] who says that a packet had just arrived from France, that a war was declared against England in Martinico that day that Spain had declared openly in favor of France &c. Letters from Statia of about the 10th inst, beside the news mentioned in the enclosed paper under Philadelphia head, say that the inhabitants of St Kitts and other islands were flying with their effects to the neutral islands.

I am in haste Sir your friend &c, Josiah Bartlett

Tr (DLC).

1 Whipple did not return to Congress until November 5, 1778. See *JCC*, 12:1102.

2 That is, August 26. See Committee for Foreign Affairs to William Bingham, September 28, 1778, note.

Samuel Chase to Thomas Johnson

Dear Sir, Philada. 29 Septr. 1778, 12 o'Clock

Immediately on the Receipt of your Letter of the 17th,[1] to the Delegates of Maryland, I communicated the Contents to Congress, and laid two Resolutions on the Table, one for a Permission for such Persons as you approvd to export to the Eastern States, and another to extend the Embargo. The first seemed to meet with the general Approbation of the House. The second was approved by some and doubted by others. The two Resolves were referred to the Consideration of a special Committee.[2]

I waited on the Post Master. I am in Hopes there will [*be*] no Cause for Complaint in future. The Post is not yet come in.

His most Christian Majesty's *Letter* of War to the Commandant at Guadaloupe will not be disagreeable to you. The Enemy landed about 5000 Troops at Paulus Hook, & marched towards Hackinsack—their Business is to procure Forage.

I wish [*you*] & yours Health & Happiness and am, Dear Sir, Yr. Affectionate and Obedient Servant, Saml. Chase

RC (PHi).

1 The Maryland Council's September 17 letter to the state's delegates is in *Md. Archives*, 21:206–7. The council was seeking to broaden Congress' September 2 exemption to the embargo so that vessels of Maryland registry, as well as those "recommended by the executive powers" of "the eastern states," would be permitted to clear Maryland ports with provisions for those states. See *JCC*, 12:861.

The council also wrote a letter to President Laurens on September 17, protesting Congress' September 11 resolution singling out Maryland for failure to prevent evasions of the embargo, which was laid before Congress on September 24. See *JCC*, 12:903, 947; *Md. Archives*, 21:205–6; and PCC, item 70, fols. 277–80.

2 There is no record in the journals of any action taken by Congress on these Maryland proposals.

Henry Marchant to William Greene

Dear Sir, Philadelphia Sept. 29th. 1778.

Yours of the 18th Instant came to Hand Yesterday.[1] My last Letter to you will afford you proper Directions as to the Lottery Tickets &c. You can be in no Doubt of sending Them by Mr. Ellery & Collins. I expect they will set out the beginning of Novr. But you had better see them early, and deliver the Tickets, lest they should be left. I enclose Your Excellency the Papers of the Week—and a Pamphlet wrote by one of the People called Friends[2]—An able Hand and one of the most unexceptionable Characters in that Society. Great Pains were taken to suppress the Publication. They beset the author on all Hands, & he was prevailed upon to suffer them to pay the printer for the whole Impression & Stifle it. But several happen'd to get out of the Printers Hands before the Business was completed and Another Printer has put it forth. You'l be pleased to present it to the Honble. the Genl. Assembly.

I am theirs & Your Excellency's most obedient & very humble Servt.

Hy. Marchant

RC (R–Ar).

1 This letter is dated September 17 in William R. Staples, *Rhode Island in the Continental Congress, 1765–1790* (Providence: Providence Press Co., 1870), pp. 200–201.

2 See Isaac Grey, *A Serious Address to such of the People Called Quakers, on the Continent of North-America, as profess Scruples Relative to the Present Government* . . . (Philadelphia: Robert Bell, 1778), Evans, *Am. Bibliography*, no. 15843. This pamphlet was first advertised for sale in the September 26 issue of the *Pennsylvania Packet.*

Robert Morris to Jean Holker

Dear Sir

Philada. Septr. 29th. 1778.

I hope this will find you Safe and Sound in Boston after an agreable journey. As you will probably have many things to claim your attention in Boston, I mean to trouble you as little as possible and Shall therefore avoid writing to you, unless when matters of business require it.[1] This is now the case—Major Franks having informed me that the Schooner Dolphin of Virginia lately commanded by Capt. Josh Peck and belonging to my friend Mr. S. Bealle of Williamsburg is now with the Count D'Estaing. She was taken by the Roebucks Tender a Brigt & Retaken by your fleet when lying off Sandy Hook. She was laden with 70 hogsheads of Tobacco, which was taken out as Mr. Franks tells me and distributed amongst the Fleet, and the Vessell being a fast Sailor and having Guns was detained for a Tender to the Fleet. I imagine that the former Owners of this Vessell have a good claim to her and paying Such Salvage as the Recaptors may be intittled to by the marine ordinances of France provided for Such cases, for this Schooner had been but a Short time in possession of the British When retaken and had not been in port to be Condemn'd. Mr. Bealle has wrote me Several Very pressing letters to put in his Claim and he can make all the Needfull Proofs of his property, &c. I am however a good deal at a loss as to the proper mode of proceeding and must rely on you to do in the Premises whatever is right and I beg you will advise me as Soon as you can of your proceedings and of what may be necessary for Mr. Bealle to do in the matter. Col. Langdon has Sent a young Gentleman here who proposes paying me the ballance due me and in that case you will not have any money to receive from him on my Accot. I have not Sold any bills Since you left this altho' Some enquiries have been made after them; *but that business may perhaps as well remain untill you return as you are not here to draw the bills if agreed for.* I congratulate you on the good news from Dominica and hope Soon to hear of Some more important Strokes in the West Indias. Mrs. M joins me in best compliments & Wishes, Being Dear Sir, your affectionate Friend & obedt. hble sert. S[igned]. R.M.

Tr (DLC).

1 Morris wrote to Holker again on October 6, 8, 19, 20, and 27, November 3 and 10, and December 1 during the latter's trip to Boston at this time, but because Morris quit attending Congress about the middle of October 1778, only two of these letters appear below. See Morris to Holker, October 6 and 19, 1778. Two sets of transcripts of Morris' letters to Holker during this period are in the Holker Papers, DLC. These were apparently transcribed in this form in 1780 when Holker was pursuing a claim against Congress for supplies furnished on Continental account that depended heavily upon testimony derived from Morris dating from 1778–79. Among the papers related to this case that Holker preserved are several documents which shed considerable light on his relations with Congress after his arrival in America in June 1778 and a lengthy "Statement" concerning that claim written by Morris in 1780. For an analysis of Morris' private commercial activities during the latter half of 1778, including a discussion of "the Morris-Holker relationship," see Clarence L. Ver Steeg, *Robert Morris, Revolutionary Financier* (1954; reprint ed., New York: Octagon Books, 1972), pp. 28–36.

North Carolina Delegates to Richard Caswell

Sir, Philadelphia Sept 29th. 1778

We are sorry to inform your Excellency, that we have not been able to send forward the money granted for the use of North Carolina. The very great demands on the Treasury previous to our Grant, has been the cause, however we are assured that it will be ready in a day or two at farthest.

Congress have been alarmed that our Enemies were about evacuating Rhode Island and New York—& that another attempt would be made on Charles Town by them. To prevent their getting possession of that place so important to our Neighbours, it has been recommended to Virginia and North Carolina, to send some of their Militia to assist in the defence of So. Carolina. The high opinion entertained of your Excellency here, and the very great desire the Delegates of that state had, that you would accept the Command, was the reason of the resolve relative to you, but in this you will no doubt consider the interest of No. Carolina and the propriety of being absent from your Government. Genl. Howe is directed to repair to Head Quarters, and Genl. Lincoln goes to South Carolina.

We are informed that the French are busily employed, in taking possession of the British Islands, this if true will furnish Genl. Clinton some other employment, than ravaging these States. Enclosed is a news paper by which you will see the manner in which this intelligence is obtained, we can only observe that it is believed here.[1] We should have written by the express that was sent by the President, but he went away without our knowing it. We have the honor to be with great respect, Your Excellency's Mo. Ob. huml. Servts.

John Penn
Cornl. Harnett
Jno. Williams

P.S. France has certainly declared war against Great Britian.

Tr (Nc–Ar).

[1] This day's *Pennsylvania Packet* contained a June 28 letter from Louis XVI to the commandant of Guadeloupe calling for retaliation against the British in the West Indies and an account from Martinique via Maryland of the French capture of Dominica.

Joseph Reed to Baron Steuben

My dear Baron Philad. Sept. 29, 1778

Your Business[1] has very unhappily been turn'd over by Congress upon the Committee of Arrangement of whom one is in New England, an other set off for Virginia tomorrow & I am so immersed in Business as to make it extremely difficult to devote that Time to it which its Importance demands & which my very Sincere Respect for you exceedingly urges me to do. But you may depend upon it as soon as Mr Sherman arrives from the Eastward I shall most chearfully set apart some of my Time for the Purpose.

Believe me to be my dear Sir, Your most Obed & very Hbbl Serv.

Jos. Reed

RC (Mr. Sol Feinstone, Washington Crossing, Pa., 1979).

[1] For the background of this "Business," see Henry Laurens' second letter to Washington of August 20, 1778, note 2.

John Williams to Robert Burton

Dear Sir Philadelphia 29th Sept. 1778.

For the news current I refer you to the paper of the day Inclosed, the report of a French War & their having taken Dominica on the 7th Instant Came to Town yesterday Evening, and tho' not officially to Congress yet it came in such a way as gained Credit and was printed as you see, after which came an official account to Congress this morning confirming the account, the several reports from New York for some time past all point to an Evacuation of that City, which I Incline to think they will do soon, whether they will go to Boston the West Indes or to Charles Town South Carolina is very uncertain, it has been [secretly sus]pected they would make a Decent on or the latter, assistance has been requested by the Gentlemen of South Carolina for men to prevent their taking possession of Charles Town, Virg. & No. Carolina are advised by Congress to send assistance; from N. Carolina 3000 men to be Immediately Marched to Charles Town, tho' I am convinced now that the Enemy will not go to South Carolina, I suppose their assistance will be wanting in the West Indes to prevent the french taking possession of their Islands about which they are now busily Imploid, should their men be sent to South Carolina it is probable they may be Imploid this Winter in an Expedition agt the Islands or in opposing the Indians who are we are told making inroads into Georgia, I suppose they will hardly think of carrying to the Southward any more of our late raised levies than Choose to go, as I believe they could not be compelled having been raised for the Express purpose of filling up the continental Batallions in the grand army; we this day Received Information of the Enemy having 5000 men in the Jerseys, near Havensack, the Malitia are conveening to oppose them under the Command of General Maxwell, if they continue there I suppose part of General Washington's army will Immedeately join Gen'l Maxwell—tho' it is thought the Enemy will soon retire being only foraging, or Manoeuvering before their departure. Our assembly you tell me have struck 850000 pounds so much will be in circulation when the former Emissions are called in besides the circulating continental currency the quantity of which was not small when I left home, Immediately after 100000 dollars was sent from Congress and now 400000 dollars the remainder of the 500000 required by the state & heretofore withheld, then several sums of Money with what will necessarily flow in from raising troops purchasing comodities &c &c we shall have a great redundancy of money & I fear a great depretiation, and tho' congress are Endeavoring to regulate her Treasury, finances & loan offices in such a manner as it is hoped will tend to appretiate the paper currency yet this will take some time, this hint is perhaps useless, as I suppose you have seen what would happen from a variety of causes obvious to men of speculation, some time, I doubt whether it will be in my power to procure you a farmer to come to North Carolina at any price which you would choose to give, all kind of labour has rose to such a hight here that men can't be got, when I have time to ride into the Country shall make further trial, I received your favor of the 15th of August, am happy to know all were then well, I hope they continue so, if Doctor Burk & Wm. Hill comes, as I hope they will some time in November at farthest, I shall Immedeately set out for North Carolina, I assure you I am already perfectly wearied of this place, if it should so happen that Mrs. Williams should want money on any occation before I return please furnish her with what she wants which shall be replaced on my return—I spoke to you before I left home to buy Mrs. Williams a negro girl if one should fall in your way which you thought would suit her, I wish you may have been lucky Enough to have met with one if you have not please attend to that object, I have little more to add my race will come on shortly. Capt. Mitchell & yourself will conduct it as you think best. I am happy to hear that notwithstanding the storm in August last that we are like to make corn, many of my friends will I doubt take umbrage at my not writing to them, I assure you that our confinement will by no means admit of it without neglecting our business. We set at 9 of oclock adjourn at one—set again at 3 and continue till dark & some times to 8 or 9 Of Clock. Remember my love to Magg and the little boys. I suppose John has pretty well forgot me by this time. My compliments in the Most respectful Manner to all friends & am D'r Sir your friend &c. &c. John Williams

Tr (NcU).

Samuel Adams to William Cooper

My Dear Sir Philade Sept 30 1778

I have the pleasure of committing this Letter to the Care of your youngest Son who having been unfortunately taken in the Brig Resistance, was sufferd to come to this City to be exchangd for the Purser of the British Ship Mermaid, who is now in N York on his Parole. This Exchange I effected without Delay; and procured from the Navy Board here an Advance of fifty Dollars, for which he is to account with the Eastern Navy Board in the Settlement of his Wages. I apprehended this Sum would not be sufficient to discharge the Expence of his Board in this very expensive place & carry him through his Journey & therefore I advancd him forty Dollars more, taking his Draft upon you which you will please to repay to Mrs Adams in Boston.[1]

I introducd your Son to your old Friend the President who receivd him with great Courtesy. Upon my hinting to the President that if he had publick Letters to send to Boston, this young Gentleman would take good Care of them, and it would be the Means of providing him with an Horse for his Journey, he very politely told me he should be glad to serve him in that Way, He as well as Monsr Girard having Letters which m[igh]t be as well sent by him as by any other Person. I assure you it is not Flattery to tell you that I am exceedingly pleasd with your Son. His modest Assurance is very engaging. If his Life is spared and his Morals well fixed, I think he will make an excellent Citizen. That the Children of N England may rise and serve God & their Country in the Room of their Fathers is the most ardent Prayer of, Your cordial Friend,

FC (NN). In the hand of Samuel Adams.

1 For Adams' September 28 letter to his wife, in which he expressed great pleasure at recently learning of her "Recovery from a dangerous Disorder," see Adams, *Writings* (Cushing), 4:65–66.

Committee of Arrangement to George Washington

Sir Philada. September 30. 1778

When the Committee of Arrangement had the Honour of conferring with you on the Affairs of the Army it appeared to them that it was your Excellys. Opinion that no Prisoners or Deserters should be inlisted, & farther that such as had been inlisted should not join the Army: The Treachery of Armand's Corps about that Time having too fatally demonstrated how little Dependance could be placed on such Characters. In Consequence of which the Committee whose Sentiments perfectly corresponded with what they supposed to be yours wrote to Congress representing the Necessity of putting an immediate Stop to such Inlistments & also of purging such Corps as were proceeding to join the Army under your Excellency's Command. In this Representation they did not expressly point out the Count Pulaski's Corps, but as it comprehends a considerable Number of those exceptionable Characters we fully intended to include it in the Reform we then recommended.

This Letter the Committee forwarded to Congress about 2 Weeks after their Arrival at Camp,[1] having first shewn it to your Excelly. & received your Approbation of its Contents. Upon their Return to This City they found nothing had been done with Pulaski's Corps but our Letter had inadvertently been referr'd to the Board of War who also mistaking the Nature of the Reference had wrote to your Excelly. for your farther Opinion on this Subject. This Letter your Excelly. has answered[2] so as to leave it doubtful whether for some Reasons not express'd you do not mean that Count Pulaski's Corps should go forward as it is, one half of which at least is composed of Deserters & Prisoners, & We are inclined to think that upon a strict Scrutiny there will be found a much greater Proportion. If this is the Case we presume your Excelly. has altered your Opinion, at least with Respect to this Corps, either upon farther Consideration or upon some particular Circumstances not attended to when we had the Honour of convening with you on this Subject. Your Excelly.

will see by this State that the Committee find themselves in an awkward Situation as having represented the Necessity of a Measure founded upon your Opinion—in which some Gentlemen who favour the Employment of Prisoners & Deserters think we were not sufficiently warranted. And of Course the proposed Scrutiny of this Corps has been delayed & will in all Probability finally fail, unless some farther Advice is received from your Excelly. on this Head.

We must observe that in all Probability if the Corps should be purged there will remain sufficient to compose the original Establishment of 68 Horse & 200 Foot—As the Count has extended his Number far beyond it—by adding what he calls supernumerary Troops & Companies.

The Committee are sensible of the Value of your Excellys. Time but as the Determination of this Matter will probably lead to the Settlement of other Corps of like Character, & they are attended with a very heavy Expence, we trust you will not think a few Moments unusefully employed on the Subject.[3]

With the most respectful Sentiments & very sincere Regard, We are, Your Excellys. most Obed., Hbbl Servts.

Jos. Reed, Chairman[4]

RC (DLC). Written and signed by Joseph Reed.

1 Undoubtedly the letter from the Committee of Arrangement that was read in Congress on September 7 and referred to the Board of War. *JCC*, 12:887.

2 For Washington's September 19 response to the Board of War's September 9 inquiry on this point, see Washington, *Writings* (Fitzpatrick), 12:470.

3 For Washington's October 6 reply to Reed, see ibid., 13:41–43.

4 Although Reed was here undoubtedly representing himself as a spokesman for the Committee of Arrangement, his letter was actually occasioned by his appointment to the special committee appointed on September 21 that had on the 29th delivered a report recommending the purging of prisoners of war recruited into Pulaski's corps. Because Congress postponed consideration of that report, however, Reed apparently believed that no action would be taken on his recommendation until he obtained a clarification of Washington's present view of the matter. As the commander in chief replied that he now thought it advisable to exempt Pulaski from Congress' ban on recruiting prisoners, no action was ever taken on the report.

Charles Thomson's Notes on William Carmichael's Examination

Wednesday [September 30, 1778.]

The last question proposed.[1]

Although I think the house by their determination has put me into a Very delicate and to me disagreeable Situation, as I am desirous of giving the house every information, I am ready to answer the question, provided the question relates to apprehensions that may have arisen on w[ha]t I conceived to be fact at the time.

A. I do.

Q. What were the instances?

A. The instance I allude to particularly was the equipping a vessel of war where I apprehended the public money had been appropriated to private uses.

Q. What vessel was it you allude to?

A. It was a vessel intended to be equipped in the Mediterranean partly at the expence of the public, and partly of individuals.

Q. The name of the Capt and of the vessel?

A. The name of the capt intended to be employed was Bell. As there were vessels bought which were afterwards obliged to be given up there was no name given any of them that I recollect.

Q. From w[ha]t circumstances do you apprehend that there was a misap[plication?]

A. From this circumstance that Mr. D. having recd. Money from M. Beaumarchais, which I conceived to be public Money did appropriate it to private uses, that is in the purchase of those vessels as far as regarded individuals.

Q. Why did you suppose that to be public Money?

A. Because M. Beaumarchais, having as I apprehended advanced before to the public to a large amount, I thought it was likewise on the public credit he advanced this sum.

Q. Are you clear there were more vessels than one bought in the Mediter[ranean?]

A. There was but one intended to be bought but the person employed bought two as I understood.

Q. Who Compelled the giving up of the vessels?

A. I understood the State of Genoa had interposed and compelled the purchaser to restore them to the orig[inal] proprietors.

Q. What were the names of private persons that were to have been concerned ⟨*in the purchase of*⟩ the public in those vessels?

A. I do not recollect all the private names.

[*Q.*] Do you recollect any?

A. I understood M. Beaumarchais was to have been concerned.

Q. Do you recollect any other?

A. I understood that Mr. Thomas Morris was to have been concerned for others, but who those others were I cannot possitively say.

Q. Was Mr. Deane to have been concerned in his private Capacity?

A. I do not know that he was.

[*Q.*] Did you understand or were you informed that Mr. D. was to have been concerned in his private capacity?

A. I did not receive such information as to induce me to believe he was concerned.

[*Q.*] If you did not believe that Mr. D. was concerned in his private capacity in those vessels what did you mean when you said that you apprehended the public money was applied to private purposes in that instance?

[*A.*] I meant that I thought Mr. D. had applied the public Money to supply the deficiencies of the money that others were to have[2] advanced but did not towards the purpose of fitting out these vessels.

[*Q.*] On what grounds did you think that Mr. D. meant to supply those deficiencies?

[*A.*] From conversations with diverse persons & other occurrences at that period.

The question being read, On what grounds etc., and the answer thereto, Mr. C. gave this explanation.

The idea I meant to convey to the house was this—I apprehended Mr. Deane had applied the money which I conceived to be public to a private use. I judge that I had my information of Mr. Dean's rect. of the money from Mr. Beaumarcha[i]s, Mr. Deane himself and others. But that this information was merely of the fact that he received it, not whether it was public or private money which he had received and so applied.[3]

[*Q.*] What persons?

A. I apprehend Mr. D. and M. Beaumarchais were two of the persons that informed me at that time.

[*Q.*] Were the other Commissioners or either of them acquainted with this transaction?

[*A.*] I apprehend Dr. Franklin was acquainted with the fitting out these vessels. I cannot charge my memory whether Mr. A. Lee was then at Paris or not.

[*Q.*] Are you sure that Mr. D. and M. B. were two of the persons with whom you had the conversations you before mentioned?

⟨*The house having agreed that I should answer from my apprehensions I have answered so, not that I am certain as to the fact. I know from conversations with M. B. that he advanced sums of Money. I knew from Mr. D. that he had rcd. sums and from these & other circumstances I apprehended there was to be a misapplication of public money, but I am not certain.*⟩

[*A.*] I apprehend from the nature of the transaction it must have been these persons but I cannot be sure.

[*Q.*] Had you reason to believe from conversations with other persons or other occurrences that Mr. Deane applied the public money to supply the deficienc[i]es of those who were to have advanced but did not towards the purpose of fitting out those vessels in the Mediterranean?

[*A.*] I cannot at present absolutely recollect, but probably there might have been other occurrences at the time which I do not now recollect that induced me to apprehend an application of the money to supply of those deficiencies.

[*Q*.] Do you know whether the particular sum you allude to was charged by M. Beaumarchais to the united States?

[*A*.] Since my arrival in this country I have understood from M. de Francy the Agent of M. Beaumarchais that this particular sum was lent by M. B. to Mr. Deane on his private Account. M. Francy is in this country and he can give more full information.[4]

[*Q*.] Did you know or believe that Mr. D. applied the public money to the paymt. of such parts of those vessels as were to have been the property of the public?

[*A*.] I do not know, I believe that Mr. D. wd. have applyed the public money to that purpose but cannot say that he did.

Ordered to withdraw.

To have notice at what hour to attend on friday after noon.[5]

MS (DNA: PCC, item 54). In the hand of Charles Thomson.

1 See Charles Thomson's Notes on William Carmichael's Examination, September 28, 1778.

2 Thomson wrote the preceding five words above the line over the words "ought to," which he failed to line out in the MS but which have been deleted here.

3 Thomson wrote these last two paragraphs on the verso of his preceding sheet of notes but left no notation to indicate the point of their insertion. In the printed version of Henry Laurens' notes on Carmichael's examination, however, they appear at this point, and their content clearly indicates that they properly belong here. For the Laurens notes, see Charles Thomson's Notes on William Carmichael's Examination, September 28, 1778, note 2.

4 In the printed version of Laurens' notes the following four paragraphs appear that are not found in Thomson's notes.

"*Q*. By Mr. Adams. Whether from conversation with other persons or from other occurrences, he had reason to believe Mr. Deane had advanced or was to have advanced moneys to make up these deficiencies?

"*A*. I cannot at present absolutely charge my recollection with what I had reason to believe at that time—probably there might have been other occurrences which may have induced me to apprehend a misapplication of the money upon that occasion.

"*Q*. By Mr. Duer. Do you know that the particular sum you allude to was charged by M. Beaumarchais to the United States?

"*A*. Since my arrival in this country, by conversation with the agent of M. Beaumarchais, I have reason to believe the particular sum was charged by M. Beaumarchais to Mr. Deane's private account. M. Francis is now in the country and can answer the question."

5 For the continuation of these notes, see Charles Thomson's Notes on William Carmichael's Examination, October 5, 1778.

INDEX

In this index descriptive subentries are arranged chronologically and in ascending order of the initial page reference. They may be preceded, however, by the subentry "identified" and by document subentries arranged alphabetically—diary entries, letters, notes, resolutions, and speeches. An ornament (☆) separates the subentry "identified" and document subentries from descriptive subentries. Inclusive page references are supplied for descriptive subentries; for a document, only the page on which it begins is given. Eighteenth-century printed works are indexed both by author and by short title. Other printed works are indexed when they have been cited to document a substantive point discussed in the notes, but not when cited merely as the location of a document mentioned. Delegates who attended Congress during the period covered by this volume appear in **boldface type.**

Advisory Committee

Library of Congress American Revolution Bicentennial Program

John R. Alden
James B. Duke Professor of History Emeritus, Duke University

Julian P. Boyd*
Editor of The Papers of Thomas Jefferson, *Princeton University*

Lyman H. Butterfield*
Editor in Chief Emeritus of The Adams Papers, *Massachusetts Historical Society*

Jack P. Greene
Andrew W. Mellon Professor in the Humanities, The Johns Hopkins University

Merrill Jensen*
Editor of The Documentary History of the Ratification of the Constitution, *University of Wisconsin*

Cecelia M. Kenyon
Charles N. Clark Professor of Government, Smith College

Aubrey C. Land
University Research Professor, University of Georgia

Edmund S. Morgan
Sterling Professor of History, Yale University

Richard B. Morris
Gouverneur Morris Professor of History Emeritus, Columbia University

George C. Rogers, Jr.
Caroline McKissick Dial Professor of American History, University of South Carolina

*Deceased.

☆U.S. GOVERNMENT PRINTING OFFICE : 1983 O - 385-620 : QL 2

Valley
TUSCARORA
MOUNTAINS
Hugh's Mill
Jordan's Mill
Schuylkill
UNTAINS
Wilderness
Swatoro Cr.
Kaufman's Cr.
THE BLUE
Bern
Fort Henry
Tulpehocken
Nassau
Sails Hill
Surman's Cr.
Rehrers
Bethel
Little Swatawro
one of the Best Gaps in Crossing the Mount.ns
JONES'S
Charming Forge
Dutch Calvinist Church
Dutch Luther Church
MIDDLE TOWN
TULPEHOCKEN TOWN
Monday Cr.
Great Swatawro Cr.
Quitipahilla Cr.
Moravian Meeting
Conrad Weiser
NEWMANS TOWN
READING
LEBANON
FLYING HILLS
Sinking Spring
Cumry
Pextang
HEIDELBERG
Galbreath
Cornwall Forge
Elizabeth's Forge
ADAMS TOWN
MIDDLE TOWN
Olds Forge
REEMS TOWN
Brecknock
LANCASTER
Derry
Warwick
EPHRATA
Cocolico
Muddy Cr.
Caernarvon
B. Hughes
MANHEIM
COUNTY
Quaker Meet
Donegal
Bayles
Rapho
LENTS
Bears Mill
Earle
Great Conestogo Cr.
WELSH MOUNTAINS
Ewings Mill
Hempfield
Chickisalunga Cr.
Chickies Rock
the three Tuns
Manchester
Hallam
Wrights Ferry
LANCASTER
Lampeter
Leacock
Salisbury
Calvinist Meeting
Manor Township
the Red Lyon
Presbyterian Meeting
Mill Creek
Pequea Cr.
Strasburg
Conestogo
Saw Mill
Sadsbury Meeting
YORK
Reeds Ferry
Otter Cr.
Lead Mine
Bart
Martick
Collerain
Hunters
York
Fallowfield West
Chesnut Level
the White Horse
Drummore
Codorus
Octoraro Creek
Presbyterian Meet
Oxford
Chanceford
Falls
Presbyterian Meeting
Nelson's Ferry
Londonderry
Morrisons Saw Mill
Peters Cr.
Little Britain
Shrewsbury
Dennys Mill
Muddy Creek
Nottingham
West and East
Little Muddy Cr.
Fawn
Peach-Bottom
Run in 1739
Powder Cr.
Deer
SUSQUEHANNA
NOTTINGHAM